Lecture Notes in Comput 8

Commenced Publication in 1973
Founding and Former Series Editors:
Gerhard Goos, Juris Hartmanis, and Jan van Leeuwen

Lecture Notes in Computer Science 4218

Susanne Graf   Wenhui Zhang (Eds.)

Automated Technology for Verification and Analysis

4th International Symposium, ATVA 2006
Beijing, China, October 23-26, 2006
Proceedings

Springer

Volume Editors

Susanne Graf
VERIMAG
Centre Equation - 2, Avenue de Vignate
F-38610 Gieres, France
E-mail: Susanne.Graf@imag.fr

Wenhui Zhang
Chinese Academy of Sciences
Institute of Software
P.O. Box 8718, Beijing, China
E-mail: zwh@ios.ac.cn

Library of Congress Control Number: 2006934115

CR Subject Classification (1998): B.1.2, B.5.2, B.6, B.7.2, C.2, C.3, D.2, D.3, F.3

LNCS Sublibrary: SL 2 – Programming and Software Engineering

ISSN 0302-9743
ISBN-10 3-540-47237-1 Springer Berlin Heidelberg New York
ISBN-13 978-3-540-47237-7 Springer Berlin Heidelberg New York

Springer is a part of Springer Science+Business Media

springer.com

Printed in Germany

Typesetting: Camera-ready by author, data conversion by Scientific Publishing Services, Chennai, India
Printed on acid-free paper SPIN: 11901914 06/3142 5 4 3 2 1 0

Preface

The Automated Technology for Verification and Analysis (ATVA) international symposium series was initiated in 2003, responding to a growing interest in formal verification spurred by the booming IT industry, particularly hardware design and manufacturing in East Asia. Its purpose is to promote research on automated verification and analysis in the region by providing a forum for interaction between the regional and the international research/industrial communities of the field. ATVA 2006, the fourth of the ATVA series, was held in Beijing, China, October 23-26, 2006. The main topics of the symposium include theories useful for providing designers with automated support for obtaining correct software or hardware systems, as well as the implementation of such theories in tools or their application.

This year, we received a record number of papers: a total of 137 submissions from 27 countries. Each submission was assigned to three Program Committee members, who could request help from subreviewers, for rigorous and fair evaluation. The final deliberation by the Program Committee was conducted through Springer's Online Conference Service for a duration of about 10 days after nearly all review reports had been collected. In the end, 35 papers were selected for inclusion in the program.

ATVA 2006 had three keynote speeches given respectively by Thomas Ball, Jin Yang, and Mihalis Yannakakis. The main symposium was preceded by a tutorial day, consisting of three two-hour lectures given by the keynote speakers.

ATVA 2006 was supported by the National Natural Science Foundation of China and the Institute of Software of the Chinese Academy of Sciences. Their generous sponsorships are gratefully acknowledged. We would like to thank the Program Committee members and their subreviewers for their hard work in evaluating the submissions and selecting the program. We thank the keynote speakers for their extra effort in delivering the tutorials. We thank the Steering Committee for their advice, particularly Farn Wang, who also served as program chair of the first two ATVA symposia, for providing valuable suggestions.

For the administrative support, we thank the Laboratory of Computer Science at the Institute of Software of the Chinese Academy of Sciences. We also thank Martin Karusseit from Metaframe for his help with the online conference server.

October 2006

Susanne Graf
Wenhui Zhang

Organization

Steering Committee

E. Allen Emerson	University of Texas at Austin
Oscar H. Ibarra	University of California at Santa Barbara
Insup Lee	University of Pennsylvania
Doron A. Peled	University of Warwick
Farn Wang	National Taiwan University
Hsu-Chun Yen	National Taiwan University

General Chair

Huimin Lin	Chinese Academy of Sciences

Sponsoring Organizations

National Natural Science Foundation of China
Institute of Software of the Chinese Academy of Sciences

Program Committee

Rajeev Alur	University of Pennsylvania
Christel Baier	University of Bonn
Jonathan Billington	University of South Australia
Sung-Deok Cha	Korea Advanced Inst. of Sci. and Techn.
Shing-Chi Cheung	Hong Kong Univ. of Sci. and Techn.
Ching-Tsun Chou	Intel
Jin Song Dong	National University of Singapore
E. Allen Emerson	University of Texas at Austin
Masahiro Fujita	University of Tokyo
Susanne Graf	VERIMAG
Wolfgang Grieskamp	Microsoft research
Teruo Higashino	Osaka University
Pei-Hsin Ho	Synopsys
Oscar H. Ibarra	University of California at Santa Barbara
Orna Kupferman	Hebrew University
Robert P. Kurshan	Cadence
Insup Lee	University of Pennsylvania
Xuandong Li	Nanjing University

Shaoying Liu	Hosei University
Zhiming Liu	IIST/United Nations University
Mila E. Majster-Cederbaum	University of Mannheim
Olaf Owe	University of Oslo
Doron A. Peled	University of Warwick
Zhong Shao	Yale University
Xiaoyu Song	Portland State University
Yih-Kuen Tsay	National Taiwan University
Irek Ulidowski	Leicester University
Bow-Yaw Wang	Academia Sinica
Farn Wang	National Taiwan University
Ji Wang	National U. of Techn. of China
Yi Wang	Uppsala University
Baowen Xu	Southeast University of China
Hsu-Chun Yen	National Taiwan University
Tomohiro Yoneda	Tokyo Institute of Technology
Wenhui Zhang	Chinese Academy of Sciences
Lenore Zuck	University of Illinois at Chicago

Local Organization Chair

Naijun Zhan Chinese Academy of Sciences

Reviewers

Hasan Amjad
Madhukar Anand
Dave Arney
Louise Avila
Ittai Balaban
Frederic Beal
Ritwik Bhattacharya
Howard Bowman
Marius Bozga
Victor Braberman
Thomas Brihaye
Lin-Zan Cai
Meeyoung Cha
Wen-Chin Chan
Chien-Liang Chen
Chunqing Chen
Liqian Chen
Xiaofang Chen
Yu-Fang Chen
Zhenbang Chen
Zhenyu Chen
Chih-Hong Cheng
Rance Cleaveland
Gavin Cox
Zhe Dang
Stephane Demri
Yuxin Deng
Jyotirmoy Deshmukh
Johan Dovland
Claude Dutheillet
Karsten Ehrig
Edith Elkind
Colin Fidge
Sebastian Fischmeister
Joern Freiheit
Felix Freiling
Xiang Fu
Guy Gallasch
Vijay Gehlot
Stephen Gorton
Zonghua Gu
Arie Gurfinkel
Ping Hao
Chris Hawblitzel
Holger Hermanns
Geng-Dian Huang
Samuel Hym
John Håkansson
Mengluo Ji
Li Jiao
Einar Broch Johnsen
Ferhat Khendek
Taeho Kim
Piotr Kosiuczenko
Maciej Kounty
Lars Kristensen
Sava Krstic

Georgios Lajios
Charles Lakos
François Laroussinie
Heungkyu Lee
Wenjun Lee
Tim Leonard
Guangyuan Li
Wenjun Li
Nimrod Lilith
Yih-Kai Lin
Zhi-Wei Lin
Lin Liu
Wanwei Liu
Yang Liu
Alessio Lomuscio
Bozena Wozna
Jih-Shien Lu
Yi Lu
Michael Luttenberger
Chammika Mannakkara
Moritz Martens
Michael May
Christoph Minnameier
Anders Moen
Armaghan Naik
Akio Nakata
Dinesh Nikhil
Carl I. Colombo Nilsen
Kozo Okano
Peter Ølveczky
Rotem Oshman
Joel Ouaknine
Chun Ouyang
Robert Palmer
Jun Pang
Bo-Yuan Peng
Paul Petterson
Nir Piterman
Amir Pnueli
Zdenek Sawa
Sven Schewe
Tzay-Farn Shih
Jeremy Sproston
Volker Stolz
Jun Sun
Jinsong Tan
Arild Torjusen
Gerardo Schneider
Ralf Treinen
Ming-Hsien Tsai
Emilio Tuosto
Somsak Vanit-Anunchai
Thomas Wahl
Jun Wei
Verena Wolf
Bozena Wozna
Baohua Wu
Kang-Nien Wu
Ke-Ren Wu
Gaoyan Xie
Chang Xu
Jin Yang
Tuba Yavuz-Khaveci
Chunyang Ye
Xiaodong Yi
Hong Qing Yu
Ingrid Chieh Yu
Lien-Po Yu
Naijun Zhan
Tian Zhang
Jianhua Zhao
Liang Zhao
Conghua Zhou
Xiaocong Zhou

Table of Contents

Keynote Speeches

Regular Papers

Analysis of Recursive Probabilistic Models

Mihalis Yannakakis

Department of Computer Science, Columbia University
mihalis@cs.columbia.edu

In this talk we will discuss recent work on the modeling and analysis of systems that involve recursion and probability. Both, recursion and probability, are fundamental constructs that arise in a wide variety of settings in computer science and other disciplines.

There has been extensive work over the years in the verification community on the algorithmic analysis of finite state probabilistic models and their properties (eg. [10,11,13,30,33,36,43]). *Markov chains* serve as the standard basic model for systems that evolve probabilistically in a wide variety of domains, including in particular, as a model for (finite-state abstractions of) probabilistic programs. The probabilities of the transitions may either reflect randomizing steps of the program or the system under study; or they may reflect statistical assumptions on the branching of the program or the evolution of the system. *Markov Decision Processes* (MDP) and *Stochastic Games* (SG) model systems that contain both probabilistic and nonprobabilistic actions that are controlled by one agent (entity) or by two (or more) agents respectively; these models serve in particular to capture open systems that interact with their environment. In the case of games (among two or more agents), a distinction is usually made between *turn-based* (or *simple*) games where the agents take turns, i.e. only one agent acts at a time, and the more general case of *concurrent* games where several agents may act at the same time.

Another line of verification research has extended finite-state model checking methods to models that correspond to (abstractions of) recursive programs with procedures ([2,3,14]. *Recursive State Machines* (RSM) and *Pushdown Systems* (PDS) are two equivalent models for this purpose. Informally, a RSM is a finite collection of finite-state machines that can call each other in a potentially recursive manner (similar to a recursive program); a PDS is a machine with a finite control equipped with a pushdown store (a stack). The two models are expressively and computationally equivalent, but they represent somewhat different views as modeling formalisms. Their relation is analogous to the relation between a program that is written as a set of procedures that call each other, and a nonrecursive (single-procedure) program that uses a stack to perform an equivalent computation. *Hierarchical State Machines* (HSM) form a subclass of Recursive State Machines, in which the calling relation between the component machines is acyclic (hierarchical); they are useful in modularizing and representing succinctly larger finite state systems.

In the last few years there has been a lot of activity in the study of systems that involve both recursion and probability [4,5,6,15,16,17,18,19,20,21,22].

S. Graf and W. Zhang (Eds.): ATVA 2006, LNCS 4218, pp. 1–5, 2006.

The primary motivation comes from the analysis of probabilistic programs with procedures, but such systems have arisen also in various other domains. In the presence of recursive procedures, a natural model for (purely) probabilistic programs is *Recursive Markov Chains* (RMCs): Informally, a RMC consists of a collection of finite state component Markov chains that can call each other in a potentially recursive manner [17]. An equivalent model is *Probabilistic Pushdown Automata* (pPDA) [15]. These models are essentially a succinct, finite representation of an infinite state Markov chain, which captures the global evolution of the system.

More generally, if some steps of the program/system are probabilistic while other steps are not, but rather are controllable by the system or the environment, then such a system can be naturally modeled by a *Recursive Markov Decision Process* (RMDP) or a *Recursive Stochastic Game* (RSG)[19,22]. In a RMDP all the nonprobabilistic actions are controlled by the same agent (the controller, or the environment), while in a RSG (simple or concurrent), different nonprobabilistic actions are controlled by two opposing agents (eg. some by the designer and some by the environment).

Recursive Markov chains encompass as special cases several other basic stochastic models that have been studied in various other domains. *Branching processes* are an important class of stochastic processes [29], introduced first by Galton and Watson in the 19th century to study population dynamics, and generalized later on in the mid 20th century to the multitype case by Kolmogorov and Sevastyanov [32,40]. A branching process specifies the probability distributions of the set of offsprings of each species (type) from one generation to the next. They have been applied in a wide variety of contexts such as population genetics [28], biology[31], and nuclear chain reactions [23]. Another related model is that of *stochastic context-free grammars* which have been studied extensively since the 1970's especially in the Natural Language Processing community (see eg. [34]), and in other contexts (for example, RNA modeling [39]). In a certain formal sense, (multitype) branching processes and stochastic context-free grammars correspond to a subclass of recursive Markov chains, namely the class of "1-exit RMCs", where each component Markov chain has a single exit state where it can terminate and return control to the component that called it. Another example that is also included in the subclass of 1-exit RMCS is a model of web-surfing, called "Markov chain with back-button", that was introduced and analyzed thoroughly by [24].

Recursive Markov chains, and their extension to Recursive Markov Decision Processes and Stochastic Games, have a rich theory and pose a lot of challenging problems. Even in the 1-exit case, recursive Markov chains introduce several difficulties not encountered in the case of standard finite Markov chains. For example, in the case of standard Markov chains, *qualitative questions* concerning events holding with probability 1 or 0, such as, "starting at state s will we reach state t almost surely?', or "does a given temporal logic property hold a.s. in an execution?" do not depend on the actual values of the probabilities on the edges, but only on which transitions are present (have nonzero probability). This is not true anymore in the case of recursive Markov chains: the actual values of the probabilities matter. Furthermore, in a finite Markov chain with rational transition probabilities, the probabilities of the events that we are interested in (for example, the probability that a trajectory satisfies a given LTL property) are also rational, and moreover have polynomially bounded complexity in the size of the Markov chain and can be computed efficiently. In recursive Markov chains this is not true any more: the probability of simple events (eg. termination, reachability) can be irrational and thus cannot be computed exactly.

The analysis of recursive probabilistic models involves combinatorial, algebraic, and numerical aspects. There are connections to various areas, such as the existential theory of the reals [8,38,7], multidimensional Newton's method, matrix theory, and many others. There are connections also with several well-known open problems, such as the square root sum problem [27,42] (a 30-year old intriguing, simple problem that arises often in the numerical complexity of geometric computations, and which is known to be in PSPACE, but it is not known even whether it is in NP), and the value of simple stochastic games [9] and related games (parity game etc.), which are in NP∩coNP, but it is not known whether they are in P.

In this talk we will present some of this theory, and the related algorithmic results and methods.

Acknowledgement. Work partially supported by NSF Grant CCF-04-30946.

References

1. R. Alur, M. Yannakakis. Model checking of hierarchical state machines. *ACM Trans. Prog. Lang. Sys.*, 23(3), pp. 273-303, 2001.
2. R. Alur, M. Benedikt, K. Etessami, P. Godefroid, T. W. Reps, and M. Yannakakis. Analysis of recursive state machines. In *ACM Trans. Progr. Lang. Sys.*, 27, pp. 786-818, 2005.
3. A. Bouajjani, J. Esparza, and O. Maler. Reachability analysis of pushdown automata: Applications to model checking. In *Proc. CONCUR'97*, pages 135–150, 1997.
4. T. Brázdil, V. Brozek, V. Forejt, A. Kučera. Reachability in recursive Markov decision processes. *Proc. CONCUR*, 2006.
5. T. Brázdil, A. Kučera, and J. Esparza. Analysis and prediction of the long-run behavior of probabilistic sequential programs with recursion. In *Proc. of FOCS'05*, pp. 521-530, 2005.
6. T. Brázdil, A. Kučera, and O. Stražovský. Decidability of temporal properties of probabilistic pushdown automata. In *Proc. of STACS'05*, 2005.
7. S. Basu, R. Pollack, and M. F. Roy. On the combinatorial and algebraic complexity of quantifier elimination. *J. ACM*, 43(6):1002–1045, 1996.
8. J. Canny. Some algebraic and geometric computations in PSPACE. In *Prof. of 20th ACM STOC*, pages 460–467, 1988.
9. A. Condon. The complexity of stochastic games. *Inf. & Comp.*, 96(2):203–224, 1992.
10. C. Courcoubetis and M. Yannakakis. The complexity of probabilistic verification. *Journal of the ACM*, 42(4):857–907, 1995.

11. C. Courcoubetis and M. Yannakakis. Markov decision processes and regular events. *IEEE Trans. on Automatic Control*, 43(10):1399–1418, 1998.
12. L. de Alfaro, M. Kwiatkowska, G. Norman, D. Parker, and R. Segala. Symbolic model checking of probabilistic processes using MTBDDs and the kronecker representation. In *Proc. of 6th TACAS*, pages 395–410, 2000.
13. L. de Alfaro, R. Majumdar. Quantitative solution of omega-regular games. *J. Comp. Sys. Sc.*, 68(2), pp. 374-397, 2004.
14. J. Esparza, D. Hansel, P. Rossmanith, and S. Schwoon. Efficient algorithms for model checking pushdown systems. In *Proc. 12th CAV*, volume 1855, pp. 232–247. Springer, 2000.
15. J. Esparza, A. Kučera, and R. Mayr. Model checking probabilistic pushdown automata. In *Proc. of 19th IEEE LICS'04*, 2004. Full version in *Logical Methods in Computer Science* 2(1), 2006.
16. J. Esparza, A. Kučera, and R. Mayr. Quantitative analysis of probabilistic pushdown automata: expectations and variances. *Proc. of 20th IEEE LICS*, 2005.
17. K. Etessami and M. Yannakakis. Recursive Markov chains, stochastic grammars, and monotone systems of non-linear equations. *Proc. of 22nd STACS'05*. Springer, 2005. Full, expanded version available from http://homepages.inf.ed.ac.uk/kousha/bib_index.html.
18. K. Etessami and M. Yannakakis. Algorithmic verification of recursive probabilistic state machines. In *Proc. 11th TACAS*, vol. 3440 of LNCS, 2005.
19. K. Etessami and M. Yannakakis. Recursive Markov Decision Processes and Recursive Stochastic Games. In *Proc. 32nd ICALP*, pp. 891-903, Springer, 2005.
20. K. Etessami and M. Yannakakis. Checking LTL Properties of Recursive Markov Chains. In *Proc. 2nd Intl. Conf. on Quantitative Evaluation of Systems*, IEEE, 2005.
21. K. Etessami and M. Yannakakis. Efficient Analysis of Classes of Recursive Markov Decision Processes and Stochastic Games. *Proc. 23rd STACS*, pp. 634-645, 2006.
22. K. Etessami and M. Yannakakis. Recursive concurrent stochastic games. *Proc. 33rd ICALP*, vol. 2, pp. 324-335, 2006.
23. C. J. Everett and S. Ulam. Multiplicative systems, part i., ii, and iii. Technical Report 683,690,707, Los Alamos Scientific Laboratory, 1948.
24. R. Fagin, A. Karlin, J. Kleinberg, P. Raghavan, S. Rajagopalan, R. Rubinfeld, M. Sudan, and A. Tomkins. Random walks with "back buttons" (extended abstract). In *ACM Symp. on Theory of Computing*, pages 484–493, 2000.
25. E. Feinberg and A. Shwartz, editors. *Handbook of Markov Decision Processes.* Kluwer, 2002.
26. J. Filar and K. Vrieze. *Competitive Markov Decision Processes.* Springer, 1997.
27. M. R. Garey, R. L. Graham, and D. S. Johnson. Some NP-complete geometric problems. In *8th ACM Symp. on Theory of Computing*, pages 10–22, 1976.
28. P. Haccou, P. Jagers, and V. A. Vatutin. *Branching Processes: Variation, Growth, and Extinction of Populations.* Cambridge U. Press, 2005.
29. T. E. Harris. *The Theory of Branching Processes.* Springer-Verlag, 1963.
30. A. Hinton, M. Z. Kwiatkowska, G. Norman, D. Parker. PRISM: A tool for automatic verification of probabilistic systems. *Proc. TACAS*, pp. 441-444, 2006.
31. P. Jagers. *Branching Processes with Biological Applications.* Wiley, 1975.
32. A. N. Kolmogorov and B. A. Sevastyanov. The calculation of final probabilities for branching random processes. *Dokl. Akad. Nauk SSSR*, 56:783–786, 1947. (Russian).
33. M. Kwiatkowska. Model checking for probability and time: from theory to practice. In *18th IEEE LICS*, pages 351–360, 2003.

34. C. Manning and H. Schütze. *Foundations of Statistical Natural Language Processing.* MIT Press, 1999.
35. A. Paz. *Introduction to Probabilistic Automata.* Academic Press, 1971.
36. A. Pnueli and L. D. Zuck. Probabilistic verification. *Inf. and Comp.*, 103(1):1–29, 1993.
37. M. L. Puterman. *Markov Decision Processes.* Wiley, 1994.
38. J. Renegar. On the computational complexity and geometry of the first-order theory of the reals, parts I-III. *J. Symb. Comp.*, 13(3):255–352, 1992.
39. Y. Sakakibara, M. Brown, R Hughey, I.S. Mian, K. Sjolander, R. Underwood, and D. Haussler. Stochastic context-free grammars for tRNA modeling. *Nucleic Acids Research*, 22(23):5112–5120, 1994.
40. B. A. Sevastyanov. The theory of branching processes. *Uspehi Mathemat. Nauk*, 6:47–99, 1951. (Russian).
41. L.S. Shapley. Stochastic games. *Proc. Nat. Acad. Sci.*, 39:1095–1100, 1953.
42. P. Tiwari. A problem that is easier to solve on the unit-cost algebraic ram. *Journal of Complexity*, pages 393–397, 1992.
43. M. Vardi. Automatic verification of probabilistic concurrent finite-state programs. In *Proc. of 26th IEEE FOCS*, pages 327–338, 1985.

Verification Challenges and Opportunities in the New Era of Microprocessor Design

Jin Yang, Ph.D.,
Principal Research Scientist

Validation Research Lab., Intel Corporation
jin.yang@intel.com

Microprocessor design continues to be driven by the economics of Moore's Law. Each new process generation doubles the number of transistors available to microprocessor architects and designers. Design complexity continues to increase, and so does verification complexity, in order to keep microprocessor performance scaling up with Moore's Law. Moving forward, we are facing even tougher challenges associated with the power scaling and reliability issues of future transistor devices. To build high performance, power efficient, reliable microprocessors using unreliable devices, we have to take a holistic approach, and deliver innovative technology solutions across the entire stack: circuit, micro-architecture, architecture, platform, and embedded software. Here we examine several future design trends and their implications on verification.

Multi-Core System-On-Chip Design. It is no longer possible to sorely rely on exploring micro-architectural level parallelism to maintain performance scaling without breaking the power wall. We need to explore architectural level parallelism by introducing multi-cores and advanced cache/memory hierarchy, and at the same time balance architectural and micro-architectural level parallelisms on a single chip. We need to have sophisticated embedded software to manage hardware resources to enable system and application softwares to keep Moore's Law alive for performance. We need to have a vertically integrated power management scheme to maintain power and energy efficiency. Because of this paradigm shift, there will be a much stronger emphasis on system-level verification such as software and hardware co-verification, protocol verification, embedded software verification, and feature integration verification.

High Level Design. Today, hardware design is done at the RTL level. RTL model complexity also scales roughly according to Moore's Law. Study shows that the number of bugs in a RTL model is proportional to the size of the model. This cannot be good news. Another closely related problem is that today we do not have a rigorous approach to capture architectural and micro-architectural designs and ensure their correctness. This creates a verification gap that is very hard to bridge with existing formal technologies. Architectural bugs are much more difficult and costly to detect and fix late in the design cycle. In order to turn the trend around, we need to raise the level of design abstraction. We need to strive hard to formally specify and verify architectural design, and tightly

S. Graf and W. Zhang (Eds.): ATVA 2006, LNCS 4218, pp. 6–7, 2006.

integrate verification into the design flow to enable correct-by-construction and a bug-free implementation. Last but not least, we need to make design cleaner and simpler.

IP Reuse. Another promising approach to combat design complexity is through IP reuse. This not only requires formally specifying the interface behavior of an IP component and verifying that it is implemented correctly, but also requires formally specifying the usage model of the component and verifying that other components in the system interact with this component in a compliant way. System level verification also needs to comprehend IP components. Furthermore, a true IP reuse in microprocessor design often requires the treatment of an IP component as a gray box rather than a black box, as the introduction of a new technology feature may cut across a large portion of the design hierarchy, including the IP component. Therefore, the reusable IP component needs to be made customizable and extensible without compromising its correctness promise.

DFx, Reliability and Fault Tolerance. Due to the underlying device physics, a functionally correct design is far from ensuring a correctly-functioning chip. The reliability of transistor devices will get worse in the future due to the continuous scaling of device size into the deep sub-micron world. There will be more manufacturing defects due to process variation, and more circuit marginality problems and soft errors due to their increasing sensitivity to the changes in operation conditions. At the same time, the human resource and equipment cost for post-silicon validation, debug and bug fix and debug is skyrocketing. Even more, the increasingly worse device aging problem will make a chip more likely to fail on the field during its lifetime, even though the chip has been fully verified in the factory. These challenges call for DFx features (design for test, design for verification, and design for debug, etc.) and unconventional post-silicon verification technologies to keep the cost down. They also call for technology innovations to build a reliable, fault tolerant system using unreliable components, i.e., to build sophisticated runtime verification and recovery mechanism across the entire system to ensure that a chip will function correctly on the field even if some devices fail. These DFx and reliability features must be verified against their specifications to make sure they work correctly as promised.

In summary, to keep Moore's Law alive in the new era of microprocessor design requires disruptive thinkings, and innovations in design and verification technologies and methodologies. We are entering an exciting period full of challenges and opportunities.

Automated Abstraction of Software

Thomas Ball

Software Reliability Research, Microsoft Research
tball@microsoft.com

Automatically proving that a program has some property requires the discovery of appropriate abstractions. Such abstractions simplify the proof task and make it tractable. One approach is for a human to identify an appropriate abstraction. Another approach is to use the computer to search for an appropriate abstraction, based on the program and property under consideration. I will explain how the techniques of predicate abstraction and analysis of spurious error paths can guide the search for appropriate abstractions. These techniques are embedded in the SLAM analysis engine, which forms the core of a recently released Microsoft tool for checking Windows device drivers, called Static Driver Verifier.

S. Graf and W. Zhang (Eds.): ATVA 2006, LNCS 4218, p. 8, 2006.

Symmetry Reduction for Probabilistic Model Checking Using Generic Representatives

Alastair F. Donaldson* and Alice Miller

Department of Computing Science
University of Glasgow
Glasgow, Scotland
{ally,alice}@dcs.gla.ac.uk

Abstract. Generic representatives have been proposed for the effective combination of symmetry reduction and symbolic representation with BDDs in non-probabilistic model checking. This approach involves the translation of a symmetric source program into a *reduced* program, in which counters are used to *generically* represent states of the original model. Symmetric properties of the original program can also be translated, and checked directly over the reduced program. We extend this approach to apply to probabilistic systems with Markov decision process or discrete time Markov chain semantics, represented as MTBDDs. We have implemented a prototype tool, GRIP, which converts a symmetric PRISM program and $PCTL$ property into reduced form. Model checking results for the original program can then be inferred by applying PRISM, unchanged, to the smaller model underlying the reduced program. We present encouraging experimental results for two case studies.

1 Introduction

Symmetry reduction techniques can be effective at combatting the state space explosion problem for model checking [4,5,9,12,13,22]. Replication in the structure of a distributed system can give rise to symmetries, or *automorphisms*, of a Kripke structure modelling the system: bijections of the states of the structure which preserve its transition relation. The most common type of Kripke structure automorphisms are *component symmetries* – permutations of the set of component identifiers which preserve the transition relation when applied to all states. A group of automorphisms gives rise to a partition of the states of a structure into equivalence classes, or *orbits*, and a *quotient* Kripke structure can be constructed by choosing a single representative from each orbit. If the group is non-trivial this structure is smaller than the original, and they are bisimilar. Thus temporal logic properties which are symmetrically invariant can be checked over the smaller quotient structure.

The obvious approach to combining symmetry reduction techniques with symbolic representation is to represent the quotient Kripke structure using a binary

* Supported by the Carnegie Trust for the Universities of Scotland.

S. Graf and W. Zhang (Eds.): ATVA 2006, LNCS 4218, pp. 9–23, 2006.

decision diagram (BDD). However, this approach requires a BDD to be constructed for the *orbit relation* — for a symmetry group G this is the set of pairs of symmetrically equivalent states under G. It has been shown that for a large class of commonly occurring symmetry groups construction of such a BDD representation is intractable [6]. A promising approach which avoids computing the orbit relation for the case of full component symmetry uses *generic representatives* [12]. Here an equivalence class of states is represented by a state which *counts* the number of components in each local state, ignoring the specific component identities. This state is a *generic* representative. Using mutual exclusion as a canonical example, if the local state of a component belongs to $\{N, T, C\}$ (Non-critical, Trying and Critical), the global states for a 4-component model include (N, T, N, C), (C, T, N, N) and (N, C, N, T), which are symmetrically equivalent and are all represented generically by $(2N, 1T, 1C)$. The attraction of this approach is that symmetry can be exploited at the source code level: a fully symmetric source program and fully symmetric property can be translated into a *reduced* program and property. The Kripke structure for the reduced program is isomorphic to the quotient structure of the original under full symmetry, and the generic property is equivalent to the original. Thus the benefits of symmetry reduction can be obtained by applying standard symbolic model checking algorithms to the reduced program.

Recently there has been much interest in probabilistic model checking [1,18,25], and some work on extending symmetry reduction techniques to a probabilistic setting [8,20]. In this paper we extend the generic representatives approach to apply to symbolic model checking of probabilistic systems. We define a symmetric subset of the PRISM modelling language, SP, and show how SP programs with Markov decision process (MDP) or discrete time Markov chain (DTMC) semantics, together with symmetric PCTL properties, can be translated into a reduced form. As in the non-probabilistic case, the time complexity of this translation is polynomial in the size of the input program. We describe a software tool, GRIP, which automates the translation of an SP program to generic form, and illustrate our approach using two case studies.

2 Background

2.1 Symmetry Reduction for Non-probabilistic Model Checking

We use a simple model to represent the computation of a system comprised of n communicating components, interleaving concurrently [11]. Let $I = \{1, 2, \ldots, n\}$ be the set of component identifiers, and for some $k \geq 0$, let $L = \{0, 1, 2, \ldots, k\}$ denote the possible local states of the components. A Kripke structure is a pair $\mathcal{K} = (S, R)$, where $S \subseteq L^n$, is a non-empty set of states, and $R \subseteq S \times S$ is a total transition relation. The usual lexicographical ordering of vectors provides a total ordering on S. If $s = (l_1, l_2, \ldots, l_n) \in S$ then we use $s(i)$ to denote l_i, the local state of component i. Communication between components is via inspection of local states.

The set of all permutations of I forms a group under composition of mappings, denoted S_n (the symmetric group on n points). Let $\mathcal{K} = (S, R)$ be a Kripke structure, and let $\alpha \in S_n$. Then α acts on a state $s = (l_1, l_2, \ldots, l_n) \in S$ in the following way: $\alpha(s) = (l_{\alpha^{-1}(1)}, l_{\alpha^{-1}(2)}, \ldots, l_{\alpha^{-1}(n)})$. If $(\alpha(s), \alpha(t)) \in R \; \forall \; (s,t) \in R$, α is an *automorphism* of $\mathcal{K}$. The set of all automorphisms of $\mathcal{K}$ forms a group $Aut(\mathcal{K}) \leq S_n$ under composition of mappings.

A subgroup G of $Aut(\mathcal{K})$ induces an equivalence relation $\theta = \{(s, \alpha(s)) : s \in S, \alpha \in G\}$ on the states of $\mathcal{K}$. The equivalence class under θ of a state $s \in S$, denoted $[s]$, is called the *orbit* of s under the action of G, and θ is the *orbit relation*. The *smallest* element of $[s]$ under the total ordering described above is denoted $min[s]$. The quotient Kripke structure for $\mathcal{K}$ with respect to G is a pair $\overline{\mathcal{K}} = (\overline{S}, \overline{R})$ where $\overline{S} = \{min[s] : s \in S\}$, and $\overline{R} = \{(min[s], min[t]) : (s,t) \in R\}$. If G is non-trivial $\overline{\mathcal{K}}$ is a smaller structure than $\mathcal{K}$, but $\overline{\mathcal{K}}$ and $\mathcal{K}$ are equivalent in the sense that they satisfy the same set of temporal logic properties which are *invariant* under the group G. Thus by choosing a suitable symmetry group G, model checking can be performed over $\overline{\mathcal{K}}$ instead of $\mathcal{K}$, potentially resulting in considerable savings in memory and verification time.

2.2 Symmetry Reduction and Symbolic Representation

Our definition of a quotient structure in the previous section involves the selection of the *smallest* state of an equivalence class as a representative. However, any representative function which maps all elements of a class on to the same unique representative could be used. Symmetry reduction techniques can in principle be combined with symbolic representation by constructing a BDD for such a representative function, and applying the function during fixpoint iterations. This is described in detail in [6], and summarised in [12]. Unfortunately, constructing the representative function requires a BDD for the orbit relation which, for many commonly occurring symmetry groups, has size exponential in $min(k+1, n)$ [6].

Several alternative approaches to combining symmetry reduction and symbolic model checking have been proposed, including the use of multiple representatives [5]; under-approximation [3]; dynamic symmetry reduction [13]; and generic representatives [11,12,14]. Summaries of these approaches can be found in [20,22]. In this paper, we restrict our attention to the generic representatives approach, which we now describe.

In order to avoid constructing a BDD for the orbit relation when exploiting full component symmetry, a fully symmetric source program can be translated into a reduced program, which can be checked using standard symbolic model checking algorithms and has a state space isomorphic to the symmetric quotient structure of the model underlying the original program. A program with n components and $k+1$ local states per component is translated into a program with $k+1$ *counter* variables, each with domain $I \cup \{0\}$ [11]. A state of this program indicates *how many* processes are in each local state of the original program, but does not refer to individual processes (see the mutual exclusion example in Section 1). This approach is extended [12] to include systems with global shared variables. The translation of a program into reduced form is polynomial in the length of the program and the approach compares well to those using unique or multiple representatives.

Details of the translation of a fully symmetric program into reduced form can be found in [12], and the approach is similar to the one we present for fully symmetric PRISM programs with MDP semantics in Section 5. The approach is limited as it only applies to fully symmetric systems and requires a somewhat restrictive input language. However, full component symmetry is the most common kind of symmetry in model checking problems, and promises the best state space reduction of any kind of symmetry.

3 Symmetry Reduction for Probabilistic Models

We now consider systems comprised of n *stochastic* components which interleave concurrently. Once again, communication between components is achieved by inspection of local states. Let I and L be as before. A Markov decision process (MDP) is a pair $\mathcal{M} = (S, \mathit{Steps})$, where $S \subseteq L^n$, and $\mathit{Steps} : S \rightarrow 2^{\mathit{Dist}(S)}$ maps each state s to a finite, non-empty set of probability distributions over S. A discrete time Markov chain (DTMC) is a pair $\mathcal{D} = (S, P)$ where S is as for an MDP, and $P : S \times S \rightarrow [0, 1]$ is a *transition probability matrix*. An MDP can model systems which exhibit both nondeterminism and probabilistic behaviour (e.g. nondeterministic scheduling of processes in a randomised distributed algorithm), whereas DTMCs can be used to model purely probabilistic systems.

For either type of model, a total ordering on states is provided as before by the usual lexicographic ordering on vectors, and the action of a permutation $\alpha \in S_n$ on states is the same as that described in Section 2.1. Recall that Kripke structure automorphisms preserve the transition relation of the structure. Automorphisms of probabilistic structures preserve the *probabilistic* transition relation. The following definitions are adapted from [20].

Definition 1. *Let $\mathcal{M} = (S, \mathit{Steps})$ and $\mathcal{M}' = (S', \mathit{Steps}')$ be MDPs, and let $\alpha : S \rightarrow S'$ be a bijection. Suppose that for all $s \in S$ and for all $\mu \in \mathit{Steps}(s)$, there exists $\mu' \in \mathit{Steps}(\alpha(s))$ such that, for all $t \in S$, $\mu(t) = \mu'(\alpha(t))$. Then α is an isomorphism from $\mathcal{M}$ to $\mathcal{M}'$, and $\mathcal{M}$ and $\mathcal{M}'$ are said to be isomorphic. If $\mathcal{M} = \mathcal{M}'$, α is an automorphism of $\mathcal{M}$.*

Definition 2. *Let $\mathcal{D} = (S, P)$ and $\mathcal{D}' = (S', P')$ be DTMCs, and let $\alpha : S \rightarrow S'$ be a bijection. Suppose that for all $s, t \in S$, $P(s, t) = P'(\alpha(s), \alpha(t))$. Then α is an isomorphism from $\mathcal{D}$ to $\mathcal{D}'$, and $\mathcal{D}$ and $\mathcal{D}'$ are said to be isomorphic. If $\mathcal{D} = \mathcal{D}'$, α is an automorphism of $\mathcal{D}$.*

In both cases, the set of all automorphisms forms a group under composition, denoted $\mathit{Aut}(\mathcal{D})$ or $\mathit{Aut}(\mathcal{M})$, and a subgroup of this group induces orbits on the state space as before. Taking the minimum element of each orbit as a representative, a quotient DTMC/MDP can be defined analogously to the non-probabilistic case [20].

The quotient DTMC $\overline{\mathcal{D}} = (\overline{S}, \overline{P})$ is defined by $\overline{S} = \{\underline{min[s]} : s \in S\}$, and $\overline{P}(min[s], min[t]) = \sum_{x \in [t]} P(min[s], x)$. For a quotient MDP $\overline{\mathcal{M}} = (\overline{S}, \overline{\mathit{Steps}})$,

$\overline{S}$ is defined similarly and, if $min[s] \in \overline{S}$ then $\overline{\mu} \in \overline{Steps}(min[s])$ iff there is some $\mu \in Steps(min[s])$ such that, for all $min[t] \in \overline{S}$, $\overline{\mu}(min[t]) = \sum_{x \in [t]} \mu(x)$. It is easy to show using results on probabilistic bisimulation [21,26] that, as in the non-probabilistic case, the quotient models preserve the truth of temporal properties which are *invariant* under symmetry. This means that for each maximal propositional subformula f of a property ϕ, and for all $\alpha \in G$, $s \models f \Leftrightarrow \alpha(s) \models f$. To express properties of MDPs or DTMCs we use $PCTL$ (Probabilistic Computation Tree Logic) [17].

Theorem 1. *Let ϕ be a $PCTL$ property which is invariant under G. Then, for all $s \in S$,*

$$\mathcal{M}, s \models \phi \Leftrightarrow \overline{\mathcal{M}}, min[s] \models \phi.$$

Formulas in the sub-logic $SPCTL$, described in Section 4.1, are invariant under full symmetry.

The following theorem establishes a correspondence between properties of isomorphic MDPs under an appropriate transformation of atomic propositions. We omit the proof, which is straightforward using induction on the structure of $PCTL$ formulas.

Theorem 2. *Let $\mathcal{M} = (S, Steps)$ and $\mathcal{M}' = (S', Steps')$ be MDPs, F and F' sets of propositions over the local states of components of $\mathcal{M}$ and $\mathcal{M}'$ respectively, and $\gamma : F \to F'$ a bijection. For a $PCTL$ formula ϕ with maximal propositional subformulas taken from F, $\gamma(\phi)$ is the $PCTL$ formula with maximal propositional subformulas taken from F', obtained from ϕ by replacing every subformula f with $\gamma(f)$. Let δ be an isomorphism from $\mathcal{M}$ to $\mathcal{M}'$ such that, for all $s \in S$ and $f \in F$, $s \models f \Leftrightarrow \delta(s) \models \gamma(f)$. Then for any $PCTL$ formula ϕ over F and $s \in S$,*

$$\mathcal{M}, s \models \phi \Leftrightarrow \mathcal{M}', \delta(s) \models \gamma(\phi).$$

Analogous versions of Theorems 1 and 2 hold for DTMCs.

As with non-probabilistic symbolic model checking, construction of a quotient model as a multi-terminal BDD (MTBDD) is intractable for commonly occurring symmetry groups. We now define a subset of the PRISM modelling language for specification of fully symmetric MDP or DTMC models. In Section 5 we show how the generic representatives approach of [11,12] can be extended to exploit the symmetry inherent in these models.

4 Symmetric PRISM

We now define an input language for specifying fully symmetric programs. The language defined is a subset of the PRISM modelling language, which we call *Symmetric PRISM* (SP). An SP program consists of a module `process1`, and $n-1$ renamed copies of this module, denoted `process2`,..., `process`n. Each module has a single variable, `s`i, which has domain L and is initialised to 0. For ease of presentation, we sometimes refer to $\mathtt{s}_i$ rather than `s`i. Every statement of a module consists of a compound guard, followed by a probabilistic choice of

```
spec              ::= nondeterministic main_module other_modules |
                      probabilistic main_module other_modules
main_module       ::= module process1
                      s1 : [0..k] init l; statements
                      endmodule   (l ∈ L)
statements        ::= statement | statement statements
statement         ::= [] local_guard & guard -> stochastic_update;
local_guard       ::= s1=j   (j ∈ L)
stochastic_update ::= λ1:(s1'=j1) + λ2:(s1'=j2) + ... + λv:(s1'=jv)
                      (v > 0, λi ∈ [0,1], ji ∈ L)
other_modules     ::= module process2 = process1 [s1=s2, s2=s1] endmodule
                        ⋮
                      module processn = process1 [s1=sn, sn=s1] endmodule
```

Fig. 1. Syntax of Symmetric PRISM

updates to $\mathtt{s}_i$ (a *stochastic* update). The compound guard is a conjunction of a *local guard*, which has the form $\mathtt{s}_i\mathtt{=}j$, for some $j \in L$, and an optional guard over the variables $\mathtt{s}_1,\mathtt{s}_2,\ldots,\mathtt{s}_n$.

The core grammar of SP is given in Figure 1, while the form of optional guards is presented in Table 1. The *generic form* column of Table 1 will be explained in Section 5. For conciseness, the quantifiers $\forall$ and $\exists$ are used to denote conjunctions and disjunctions over all (or all but one) components. For example, the guard ($\mathtt{s1=}j\,\&\,\mathtt{s2=}j\,\&\ldots\&\,\mathtt{s}n\mathtt{=}j$) is denoted by $\forall_i\ \mathtt{s}_i\mathtt{=}j$ in the table. The last four forms of guard in Table 1, together with module renaming, allow conditions on just the state of *other* modules than that in which the guard appears. This extends the form of guards allowed in [11,12], and requires more complex rules for translation into generic form (see Section 5). In Figure 1, the keywords `nondeterministic` and `probabilistic` indicate that the underlying model is an MDP or DTMC respectively, and we say that $\mathcal{P}$ is a *nondeterministic* or *probabilistic* program, using $\mathcal{M}(\mathcal{P})/\mathcal{D}(\mathcal{P})$ to denote the model. Each statement in an SP program consists of a guard followed by a *stochastic update*. The stochastic update is a probabilistic choice over local updates of the form $\lambda_i\mathtt{:(s1'=}j_i\mathtt{)}$, where $\lambda_i \in [0,1]$ is the probability of this local update being chosen, and $\sum_{i=1}^{v} \lambda_i = 1$. Note that SP programs cannot include multiple local variables in modules, multiple module types, or communication by synchronisation.

We illustrate the syntax of SP by modelling a minimum space shared memory leader election protocol [7]. The protocol is carried out by a set of n processors, each with a single-writer multi-reader binary register (the *leader* register). Eventually, all of these registers apart from one will be set to zero (the *election condition* will be satisfied). The process for whom the associated register is non zero is chosen as the leader. At each stage of the protocol, if the election condition is not satisfied then for each processor P_i such that P_i has associated register value 1, or P_i has register value 0 and *every* other processor also has register value 0, P_i updates its register to 0 or 1 with equal probability.

Table 1. Forms of guard, with their generic versions, where the associated SP statement has local guard s1=i (for some $i \in L$)

guard ::=	generic form $\widehat{guard}$	
(*guard*)	$(\widehat{guard})$	
!*guard*	$!\widehat{guard}$	
$guard_1$ & $guard_2$	$\widehat{guard_1}$ & $\widehat{guard_2}$	
$guard_1$ | $guard_2$	$\widehat{guard_1}$ | $\widehat{guard_2}$	
$\forall_i$ s_i=j	no_j=n	
$\forall_i$ s_i!=j	no_j=0	
$\exists_i$ s_i=j	no_j > 0	
$\exists_i$ s_i!=j	no_j < n	
$\exists_i$ (s_i=j & ($\forall_{k \neq i}$ s_k!=j))	no_j=1	
	$j = i$	$j \neq i$
$\forall_{i>1}$ s_i=j	no_j=n	no_j = $n - 1$
$\forall_{i>1}$ s_i!=j	no_j=1	no_j=0
$\exists_{i>1}$ s_i=j	no_j >1	no_j >0
$\exists_{i>1}$ s_i!=j	no_j < n	no_j < $n - 1$

To model all possible initial configurations, in our specification processors start in default state 2, from which they move to state 0 or 1 nondeterministically. The protocol begins once all processors have state 0 or 1. Below we give the SP specification for a system of 3 processors.

```
nondeterministic
module process1
  s1 : [0..2] init 2;
  [] s1=2 -> 1:(s1'=0);
  [] s1=2 -> 1:(s1'=1);
  [] s1=0 & (s1!=2 & s2!=2 & s3!=2) & (s1=0 & s2=0 & s3=0) ->
                                     0.5:(s1'=0) + 0.5:(s1'=1);
  [] s1=0 & (s1!=2 & s2!=2 & s3!=2) & (s2=1 | s3=1) -> 1:(s1'=0);
  [] s1=1 & (s1!=2 & s2!=2 & s3!=2) & (s2=1 | s3=1) ->
                                     0.5:(s1'=0) + 0.5:(s1'=1);
  [] s1=1 & (s1!=2 & s2!=2 & s3!=2) & (s2=0 & s3=0) -> 1:(s1'=1);
endmodule

module process2 = process1 [ s1 = s2, s2 = s1 ] endmodule
module process3 = process1 [ s1 = s3, s3 = s1 ] endmodule
```

We now show that if $\mathcal{M}(\mathcal{P})$ is the MDP associated with a nondeterministic SP program $\mathcal{P}$ then any permutation of components is an automorphism of $\mathcal{M}(\mathcal{P})$ when lifted to states. Note that if $t \in S$ then $t(i)$ is the value of variable s_i. The proof of the following lemma (which applies to both MDPs and DTMCs) is straightforward, using structural induction on the form of guards given in Table 1.

Lemma 1. *Let σ be a statement in module* processi *of an SP program $\mathcal{P}$ ($1 \leq i \leq n$), let t be a state in the associated MDP or DTMC and let $\alpha \in S_n$. If σ' is the corresponding statement in module* process$\alpha(i)$ *then σ is executable in $t \Leftrightarrow \sigma'$ is executable in $\alpha(t)$.*

Theorem 3. *Let $\mathcal{P}$ be a nondeterministic SP program. Then $Aut(\mathcal{M}(\mathcal{P})) = S_n$.*

Proof. By definition, $Aut(\mathcal{M}(\mathcal{P})) \subseteq S_n$. Let $\alpha \in S_n$ and $\mu \in Steps(t)$ for some $t \in S$. By the definition of an MDP automorphism (Definition 1), we must show that $\alpha(t) \in S$, and there exists $\mu' \in Steps(\alpha(t))$ such that $\mu(u) = \mu'(\alpha(u))$ for all $u \in S$. Suppose first that $t = t_0$, the initial state of $\mathcal{M}(\mathcal{P})$. Since each variable $\mathtt{s}_i$ is initialised to l for some $0 \leq l \leq k$, $t_0 = (l, l, \ldots, l)$, so clearly $\alpha(t_0) = t_0$.

Now let t be arbitrary in S, and suppose that $\alpha(t) \in S$. The distribution μ arises from the stochastic update of a statement, σ say, in module processi, for some $i \in I$, in which the value of $\mathtt{s}_i$ is updated. Module process$\alpha(i)$ is a renaming of processi where $\mathtt{s}_i$ and $\mathtt{s}_{\alpha(i)}$ are interchanged, so process$\alpha(i)$ has a corresponding statement σ' in which $\mathtt{s}_{\alpha(i)}$ is updated. By Lemma 1, σ' is executable in $\alpha(t)$.

Let $\mu' \in Steps(\alpha(t))$ be the probability distribution associated with σ'. Since σ only updates $\mathtt{s}_i$, for any $u \in S$, if $t(j) \neq u(j)$ for some $i \neq j$ then $\mu(u) = 0$. As $\alpha(t)(j) \neq \alpha(u)(j)$, by a similar argument $\mu'(\alpha(u)) = 0$. Now suppose that $t(j) = u(j)$ for all $j \neq i$. Suppose $u(i) = k \in L$. Then $\mu(u)$ is the probability of updating $\mathtt{s}_i$ to k in σ, and $\mu'(u)$ is the probability of updating $\mathtt{s}_{\alpha(i)}$ to k in σ'. Thus $\mu(u) = \mu'(\alpha(u))$.

Finally, for any $t \in S$, we *must* have $\alpha(t) \in S$, since if $t_0, t_1, \ldots, t$ is a path from the initial state to t, by the above argument there is a corresponding path $t_0 = \alpha(t_0), \alpha(t_1), \ldots, \alpha(t)$ from the initial state to $\alpha(t)$.

The proof of the analogous result for probabilistic SP programs is similar.

Theorem 4. *Let $\mathcal{P}$ be a probabilistic SP program. Then $Aut(\mathcal{D}(\mathcal{P})) = S_n$.*

4.1 Symmetric PCTL

The temporal logic *PCTL* (probabilistic computation tree logic), presented in detail in [25], can be used to specify properties of MDP and DTMC models which can be verified using the PRISM model checker.

We define *SPCTL*, a subset of *PCTL* for reasoning about SP programs. A *symmetric guard* is a guard of the form described in Table 1 which *does not* include sub-expressions of the last four forms in the table. A symmetric guard g has the property that, if $\alpha \in S_n$, the guard $\alpha(g)$ obtained by replacing $\mathtt{s}_i$ with $\mathtt{s}_\alpha(i)$ is identical to g (modulo order of operands to commutative operators). A *PCTL* property ϕ is in *SPCTL* iff every maximal propositional subformula of ϕ is a symmetric guard. Formulas of *SPCTL* are, by construction, invariant under full symmetry.

For the leader election example, the property

$$P_{\geq 1}\left[\, true\, U\,\texttt{(((s1=1 \& s2!=1 \& s3!=1) | (s2=1 \& s1!=1 \& s3!=1) |} \right. \quad (1)$$
$$\left. \texttt{(s3=1 \& s1!=1 \& s2!=1)) \& (s1!=2 \& s2!=2 \& s3!=2))}\,\right]$$

is in $SPCTL$, and asserts that with probability 1 a leader will eventually be elected.

5 Symmetry Reduction by Counter Abstraction

We now show how a nondeterministic SP program $\mathcal{P}$ can be translated into a reduced program $\widehat{\mathcal{P}}$ and an $SPCTL$ formula ϕ into a reduced formula $\widehat{\phi}$. The translation process is polynomial in the size of $\mathcal{P}$. We then show that $\overline{\mathcal{M}(\mathcal{P})}$ and $\mathcal{M}(\widehat{\mathcal{P}})$ are isomorphic, and apply Theorem 2 to show that $SPCTL$ properties of $\overline{\mathcal{M}(\mathcal{P})}$ can be inferred by checking reduced properties of $\mathcal{M}(\widehat{\mathcal{P}})$. As $\mathcal{M}(\mathcal{P})$ and $\overline{\mathcal{M}(\mathcal{P})}$ are bisimilar (Theorem 1), $PCTL$ properties of the *original* model can be inferred in this way. As $\overline{\mathcal{M}(\mathcal{P})}$ and $\mathcal{M}(\widehat{\mathcal{P}})$ are isomorphic, the state space reduction associated with model checking over $\mathcal{M}(\widehat{\mathcal{P}})$ is the same as that gained by building a quotient structure.

5.1 Translating SP into Generic Form

Let $\mathcal{P}$ be an SP program. The corresponding reduced program $\widehat{\mathcal{P}}$ consists of a single module, `generic_process`. Recall that each module `process`i of $\mathcal{P}$ has a local variable $\mathtt{s}_i$ with domain $L = \{0, 1, \ldots, k\}$, for some $k \geq 0$. The module `generic_process` has $k+1$ local variables, `no_0`, `no_1`,...,`no_`k, each with domain $I \cup \{0\}$, where `no_`j indicates the number of components of the original system which are in local state $j \in L$. For any $j \in L$, `no_`j is initialised to n if j is the initial value of the variable `s1` in the original program, and to 0 otherwise.

For nondeterministic programs, the `generic_process` module has one statement corresponding to each statement of `process1` in $\mathcal{P}$. Suppose a statement of $\mathcal{P}$ has the following form:

$$\texttt{[] s\_1=}j\texttt{ \& }guard\texttt{ -> }\lambda_1\texttt{:(s1'=}j_1\texttt{) + }\lambda_2\texttt{:(s1'=}j_2\texttt{) + ... + }\lambda_v\texttt{:(s1'=}j_v\texttt{);} \quad (2)$$

where *guard* is a guard of the form specified in Table 1. Then the corresponding statement of `generic_process` is as follows:

$$\begin{aligned}\texttt{[] no\_}j\texttt{>0 \& }\widehat{guard}\texttt{ -> } & \lambda_1\texttt{:(no\_}j\texttt{'=no\_}j\texttt{-1)\&(no\_}j_1\texttt{'=no\_}j_1\texttt{+1)} \\ & \texttt{+ }\lambda_2\texttt{:(no\_}j\texttt{'=no\_}j\texttt{-1)\&(no\_}j_2\texttt{'=no\_}j_2\texttt{+1)} \\ & \vdots \\ & \texttt{+ }\lambda_v\texttt{:(no\_}j\texttt{'=no\_}j\texttt{-1)\&(no\_}j_v\texttt{'=no\_}j_v\texttt{+1);}\end{aligned} \quad (3)$$

with the exception that if one of the j_i in the original stochastic update equals j, the corresponding component of the generic update is (`no_`j_i`'=no_`j_i) (otherwise the update would be (`no_`j_i`'=no_`j_i`-1)&(no_`j_i`'=no_`j_i`+1)`, which intuitively should have the same effect, but is not legal in PRISM). The guard $\widehat{guard}$ in $\widehat{\mathcal{P}}$ is the *generic form* of *guard*. Details of the translation of guards are given in the *generic form* column of Table 1. Note that, for the last four forms of guard in the table, the translation to generic form depends on the local guard associated with the statement.

Translation of statements is less straightforward for probabilistic programs, due to the absence of nondeterminism. Let *update* denote the right hand side of -> in (3). The probability of some module executing their copy of statement (2) in a given state is proportional to the number of modules for which this statement is executable. Thus, in the reduced program, statement (2) is translated to n statements as follows:

$$\texttt{[] no\_}j\texttt{>0 \& } \widehat{guard} \texttt{ -> } update$$

$$\texttt{[] no\_}j\texttt{>1 \& } \widehat{guard} \texttt{ -> } update$$

$$\vdots$$

$$\texttt{[] no\_}j\texttt{>} n-1 \texttt{ \& } \widehat{guard} \texttt{ -> } update$$

Thus if d modules can execute a statement equivalent to (2) in a given state of the *original* model ($0 \leq d \leq n$), exactly d of the statements above will be executable in the corresponding state of the *reduced* model.

Recall that the states of $\mathcal{M}(\mathcal{P})/\mathcal{D}(\mathcal{P})$ are a subset of L^n. Clearly for the MDP/DTMC $\mathcal{M}(\widehat{\mathcal{P}}) = (\widehat{S}, \widehat{Steps})/\mathcal{D}(\widehat{\mathcal{P}}) = (\widehat{S}, \widehat{P})$, we have $\widehat{S} \subseteq I^{k+1}$.

Below we give the generic form of the leader election example introduced in Section 4.

```
nondeterministic module generic_process
  no_0 : [0..3] init 0;
  no_1 : [0..3] init 0;
  no_2 : [0..3] init 3;
  [] no_2>0 -> 1:(no_2'=no_2-1)&(no_0'=no_0+1);
  [] no_2>0 -> 1:(no_2'=no_2-1)&(no_1'=no_1+1);
  [] no_0>0 & no_2=0 & no_0=3 -> 0.5:(no_0'=no_0) +
                                   0.5:(no_0'=no_0-1)&(no_1'=no_1+1);
  [] no_0>0 & no_2=0 & no_1>0 -> 1:(no_0'=no_0);
  [] no_1>0 & no_2=0 & no_1>1 -> 0.5:(no_1'=no_1-1)&(no_0'=no_0+1)
                                  + 0.5:(no_1'=no_1);
  [] no_1>0 & no_2=0 & no_0=2 -> 1:(no_1'=no_1);
endmodule
```

5.2 Translation of *SPCTL* Properties

Since the states of $\mathcal{M}(\mathcal{P})/\mathcal{D}(\mathcal{P})$ relate to the local states of components, whereas those of $\mathcal{M}(\widehat{\mathcal{P}})/\mathcal{D}(\widehat{\mathcal{P}})$ relate to *how many* components are in each local state, it is necessary to convert an $SPCTL$ formula ϕ into a *reduced form*.

Let ϕ be an $SPCTL$ formula. Recall from Section 4.1 that the maximal propositional subformulas of ϕ are symmetric guards. The reduced form of ϕ, denoted

$\widehat{\phi}$, is identical to ϕ except that every maximal propositional formula g occurring in ϕ is replaced with $\widehat{g}$, using the translation rules of Table 1.

The generic form of the *election* property (property (1) in Section 4.1) is

$$P_{\geq 1}\,[\,\mathit{true}\; U\, \texttt{(no\_1=1 \& no\_2=0)}\,].$$

Note that this concise property is independent of the number of processors participating in the protocol, whereas in the unreduced program, a variant of (1) is required for every protocol configuration.

5.3 Relationship Between $\overline{\mathcal{M}(\mathcal{P})}$ and $\mathcal{M}(\widehat{\mathcal{P}})$

Recall that $\overline{S} = \{min[s] : s \in S\}$. Since components of $\mathcal{P}$ are fully interchangeable, $\overline{S} = \{s \in S : i < j \Rightarrow s(i) \leq s(j)\}$. Then a state $s \in \overline{S}$ has the form

$$s = (\underbrace{0,0,\ldots,0}_{m_0},\underbrace{1,1,\ldots,1}_{m_1},\ldots,\underbrace{k,k,\ldots,k}_{m_k}),$$

where m_i denotes the number of entries equal to i, and $\sum_{i=0}^{k} m_i = n$. With $s \in \overline{S}$ as above, define a mapping $\delta : \overline{S} \to \widehat{S}$ by $\delta(s) = (m_0, m_1, \ldots, m_k)$.

Lemma 2. *The mapping δ is an isomorphism from $\overline{\mathcal{M}(\mathcal{P})}$ to $\mathcal{M}(\widehat{\mathcal{P}})$.*

Let SG be the set of all symmetric guards. The translation rules of Table 1 define a bijection $\widehat{\ } : SG \to SG'$, where SG' is the set of reduced forms of symmetric guards.

Lemma 3. *Let $g \in SG$ be a symmetric guard. Then, for all $s \in \overline{S}$, $s \models g \Leftrightarrow \delta(s) \models \widehat{g}$.*

Proof. Suppose $g =$ `(s1=`d `& s2=`d `& ... & sn=`d`)` for some $d \in L$. Then $\widehat{g} =$ `no_`d`=`n. Clearly g only holds at the state $t = (d, d, \ldots, d)$, and $\widehat{g}$ only holds at the state

$$\delta(t) = (\underbrace{0,0,\ldots,0}_{d}, n, \underbrace{0,\ldots,0}_{k-(d+1)}).$$

The other base cases are similar, and the result follows by structural induction on the form of symmetric guards.

We can now apply Theorem 2 to deduce:

Theorem 5. *For any SPCTL property ϕ and $s \in \overline{s}$,*

$$\overline{\mathcal{M}}, s \models \phi \Leftrightarrow \mathcal{M}(\widehat{\mathcal{P}}), \delta(s) \models \widehat{\phi}.$$

Further, combining Theorem 1 and Theorem 5 we get

Corollary 1. *For any SPCTL property ϕ and $s \in \overline{S}$,*

$$\mathcal{M}, s \models \phi \Leftrightarrow \overline{\mathcal{M}}, min[s] \models \phi \Leftrightarrow \mathcal{M}(\widehat{\mathcal{P}}), \delta(min[s]) \models \widehat{\phi}.$$

It is thus possible to infer *SPCTL* properties of $\mathcal{M}(\mathcal{P})$ by checking corresponding reduced properties of $\mathcal{M}(\widehat{\mathcal{P}})$. Analogous results to those in this section hold for probabilistic programs.

6 Experimental Results for Case Studies

We have implemented GRIP (Generic Representatives In PRISM), a Java tool which takes an SP program as input, and outputs the corresponding reduced version. A parser for SP was generated using SableCC [15]. In this section we present experimental results for two case studies – the leader election protocol from [7] which we have used as a running example within this paper, and a probabilistic mutual exclusion protocol adapted from a case study supplied with the PRISM distribution [23], and analysed in [24].

Proving property (1) of Section 4.1 for the leader election example requires the imposition of fairness constraints. It is well known for non-probabilistic model checking that fairness and symmetry reductions cannot be directly combined since the path of an individual process cannot be traced in the quotient structure [10]. Thus for this example we use PRISM to prove that the *maximum* probability of a leader being elected is 1, using the original specification and its generic form. Expressing the mutual exclusion protocol in SP required some straightforward syntactic modifications to the original PRISM code. The property here is that the maximum probability of the critical section becoming clear once occupied approaches 1.

Table 2. Experimental results for various configurations of the leader election (leader) and mutual exclusion (mutex) protocols

	original				reduced			
system	**states**	**nodes**	**build**	**check**	**states**	**nodes**	**build**	**check**
leader 20	3.5×10^{9}	5300	0.4	1	231	1144	0.1	0.04
leader 40	1.2×10^{19}	20240	2	26	861	2563	0.2	0.2
leader 60	4.2×10^{28}	44780	4	109	1891	3735	0.4	0.2
leader 80	1.5×10^{38}	78920	10	669	3321	5706	0.7	0.5
leader 100	5.2×10^{47}	122660	19	2754	5151	7054	1	0.7
leader 120	1.8×10^{57}	176888	30	o/m	7381	8378	1	1
leader 140	6.3×10^{66}	238940	53	o/m	10011	11133	2	2
mutex 4	26600	3591	0.7	0.2	1691	4069	1	0.2
mutex 12	4.9×10^{12}	40687	22	14	892542	25670	5	2
mutex 20	7.1×10^{20}	114647	137	86	3.3×10^{7}	59202	18	7
mutex 28	9.4×10^{28}	225471	552	499	4.2×10^{8}	90381	64	20
mutex 36	1.2×10^{37}	373159	14,003	3262	3.1×10^{9}	138006	322	44
mutex 44	-	-	o/t	-	1.6×10^{10}	175990	604	112
mutex 52	-	-	o/t	-	6.3×10^{10}	214045	1805	162

Table 2 shows, for various configurations of each case study, the number of states (**states**) and MTBDD nodes (**nodes**) for each model. Time taken (in seconds) for model building (**build**) and checking the associated SPCTL property (**check**) are given for each case. Cases where PRISM did not complete model building within 24 hours, and where our memory limit (500 Mb) was exceeded, are denoted by o/t and o/m respectively. All experiments were performed using a PC with a 2.4 GHz Intel Pentium 4 processor, running PRISM version 3.0.beta1 under Red Hat Linux.

Symmetry reduction with generic representatives works particularly well for the leader election example, with significant reductions in both state space and MTBDD sizes, and much shorter times for model building and checking. This is expected, as the approach has been shown to work well in the non-probabilistic case when there are a small number of local states. Here there are 3 local states, and the number of reachable states is reduced from 3^n to $\frac{1}{2}(n+1)(n+2)$ – the theoretical maximum factor of reduction.

Results for the mutual exclusion case study show a saving in MTBDD nodes for larger configurations, but the original model for 4 processes actually requires *fewer* nodes than the generic version (there are 16 process local states so the generic program always uses 16 variables, whereas a configuration with 4 processes only uses 4 variables). It is unsurprising that the benefit of symmetry reduction is not as striking here as there are more local states. Nevertheless, larger configurations exhibit an encouraging reduction in time for both model building and checking, and GRIP enabled us to verify configurations which were previously intractable.

GRIP, together with PERL scripts to generate SP programs and SPCTL properties for both case studies, can be downloaded from our website [16].

7 Related Work

Generic representatives and fully symmetric program transformations were first proposed in [11]. This approach is extended to programs which include global variables [12] and optimised using techniques from compiler optimisation (static reachability analysis and dead variable elimination) in [14], where a prototype generic model checker, *UTOOL* is described. Preliminary results on extending these ideas to probabilistic model checking were presented in [8].

Another approach to combining symmetry reduction with symbolic representation is proposed in [13], where representative states are determined dynamically during fixpoint iterations. This approach has some advantages over using generic representatives (including fewer restrictions on the form of of input programs), but requires significant modifications to a symbolic model checking algorithm. A related approach has been used for symmetry reduction in the PRISM model checker [20]. Here the state space explosion problem is partially avoided: construction of an MTBDD for the full model is still required, but probabilistic temporal properties can be checked over a quotient structure. This approach is useful as, in many cases, it is possible to represent a very large model as an MTBDD, but not to check properties of this model. The problem of combining symmetry reduction with fairness assumptions is discussed in [10], where an automata theoretic approach applicable to explicit state model checking is presented. To our knowledge, the problem of combining symmetry, fairness and symbolic representation has not been investigated.

Other methods for combining symmetry reduction with non-probabilistic symbolic model checking are given in [3,6]. Numerous approaches for exploiting symmetry in non-probabilistic explicit state model checking have been proposed (see [22] for a recent survey), but the application of these techniques to probabilistic explicit state model checking [1] has not been investigated.

8 Conclusions and Future Work

We have shown that an approach to symmetry reduction for non-probabilistic symbolic model checking, based on generic representatives, can be applied in the probabilistic setting. Our techniques are applicable to symmetric PRISM programs with MDP or DTMC semantics, and the translation of an SP program to its reduced form is implemented by the GRIP tool. Experimental results for two protocol case studies – minimum space leader election and mutual exclusion – show that the technique can be effective.

Future work includes extending the approach to allow model checking of CSL properties over continuous time Markov chain models, and using techniques proposed in [14] to allow a less restrictive input language for symmetric programs. It will also be useful to carry out an experimental comparison with alternative symmetry reduction techniques for PRISM [20] based on dynamic symmetry reduction [13].

Acknowledgements. The authors would like to thank Douglas Graham for many useful discussions relating to this work, and Dave Parker for providing an advance copy of [20].

References

1. C. Baier, F. Ciesinski and M. Größer. ProbMela and verification of Markov decision processes. *SIGMETRICS Performance Evaluation Review*, 32(4): 22-27, 2005.
2. C. Baier, M. Kwiatkowska. Model checking for a probabilistic branching time logic with fairness. *Distributed Computing*, 11:125–155, 1998.
3. S. Barner and O. Grumberg. Combining symmetry reduction and under-approximation for symbolic model checking. *Formal Methods in System Design*, 27(1–2):29–66, 2005.
4. D. Bosnacki, D. Dams, and L. Holenderski. Symmetric spin. *International Journal on Software Tools for Technology Transfer*, 4(1):65–80, 2002.
5. E.M. Clarke, E.A. Emerson, S. Jha, and A.P. Sistla. Symmetry reductions in model checking. In *CAV'98*, LNCS 1427, pages 147–158. Springer, 1998.
6. E.M. Clarke, R. Enders, T. Filkhorn, and S. Jha. Exploiting symmetry in temporal logic model checking. *Formal Methods in System Design*, 9(1–2):77–104, 1996.
7. S. Dolev, A. Israeli and S. Moran. Analysing expected time by scheduler-luck games. *IEEE Transactions on Software Engineering*, 21(5):429–439, 1995.
8. A.F. Donaldson and A. Miller Symmetry reduction for probabilistic systems. In *Proc. 12th Workshop on Automated Reasoning*, pages 17–18, 2005.

9. A.F. Donaldson and A. Miller Exact and approximate strategies for symmetry reduction in model checking. In *FM'06*, LNCS 4085, pages 541–556. Springer, 2006.
10. E.A. Emerson and A.P. Sistla. Utilizing symmetry when model-checking under fairness assumptions: an automata-theoretic approach. *ACM Transactions on Programming Languages and Systems*, 19(4):617–638, 1997.
11. E.A. Emerson and R.J. Trefler. From asymmetry to full symmetry: new techniques for symmetry reduction in model checking. In *CHARME'99*, LNCS 1703, pages 142–156. Springer, 1999.
12. E.A. Emerson and T. Wahl. On combining symmetry reduction and symbolic representation for efficient model checking. In *CHARME'03*, LNCS 2860, pages 216–230. Springer, 2003.
13. E.A. Emerson and T. Wahl. Dynamic symmetry reduction. In *TACAS'05*, LNCS 3440, pages 382–396. Springer, 2005.
14. E.A. Emerson and T. Wahl. Efficient reduction techniques for systems with many components. *Electronic Notes in Theoretical Computer Science*, 130:379–399, 2005.
15. E. Gagnon and L. J. Hendren. SableCC, an object-oriented compiler framework. In *TOOLS'98*, pages 140–154. IEEE Computer Society Press, 1998.
16. GRIP website. http://www.dcs.gla.ac.uk/people/personal/ally/grip/.
17. H. Hansson and B. Jonsson. A logic for reasoning about time and reliability. *Formal Aspects of Computing*, 6(4):512–535, 1994.
18. A. Hinton, M. Kwiatkowska, G. Norman and D. Parker. PRISM: a tool for automatic verification of probabilistic systems. In *TACAS'06*, LNCS 3920, pages 441–444. Springer, 2006.
19. C.N. Ip and D.L. Dill. Better verification through symmetry. *Formal Methods in System Design*, 9(1/2): 41–75, 1996.
20. M. Kwiatkowska, G. Norman and D. Parker. Symmetry reduction for probabilistic model checking. To appear in *CAV'06*, LNCS. Springer, 2006.
21. K. Larsen and A. Skou. Bisimulation through probabilistic testing. *Information and Computation*, 94: 1–28, 1991.
22. A. Miller, A. Donaldson and M. Calder. Symmetry in temporal logic model checking. To appear in *Computing Surveys*, 2006.
23. PRISM website. http://www.cs.bham.ac.uk/~dxp/prism/.
24. A. Pnueli and L. Zuck. Verification of multiprocess probabilistic protocols. *Distributed Computing*, 1(1):53–72, 1986.
25. J.J.M.M. Rutten, M. Kwiatkowska, G. Norman and D. Parker. Mathematical Techniques for Analyzing Concurrent and Probabilistic Systems. *CRM Monograph Series* 23. American Mathematical Society 2004.
26. R. Segala and N. Lynch. Probabilistic simulations for probabilistic processes. *Nordic Journal of Computing*, 2(2):250–273, 1995.

Eager Markov Chains

Parosh Aziz Abdulla[1], Noomene Ben Henda[1], Richard Mayr[2], and Sven Sandberg[1]

[1] Uppsala University, Sweden
parosh@it.uu.se, Noomene.BenHenda@it.uu.se, svens@it.uu.se
[2] NC State University, USA
mayr@csc.ncsu.edu

Abstract. We consider infinite-state discrete Markov chains which are *eager*: the probability of avoiding a defined set of final states for more than n steps is bounded by some exponentially decreasing function $f(n)$. We prove that eager Markov chains include those induced by Probabilistic Lossy Channel Systems, Probabilistic Vector Addition Systems with States, and Noisy Turing Machines, and that the bounding function $f(n)$ can be effectively constructed for them. Furthermore, we study the problem of computing the expected reward (or cost) of runs until reaching the final states, where rewards are assigned to individual runs by computable reward functions. For eager Markov chains, an effective path exploration scheme, based on forward reachability analysis, can be used to approximate the expected reward up-to an arbitrarily small error.

1 Introduction

A lot of research effort has been devoted to developing methods for specification and analysis of stochastic programs [28,25,16,31]. The motivation is to capture the behaviors of systems with uncertainty, such as programs with unreliable channels, randomized algorithms, and fault-tolerant systems; and to analyze quantitative aspects such as performance and dependability. The underlying semantics of such a program is usually defined as a *finite-state* Markov chain. Then, techniques based on extensions of finite-state model checking can be used to carry out verification [17,8,12,27].

One limitation of such methods is the fact that many systems that arise in computer applications can only be faithfully modeled as Markov chains which have *infinite* state spaces. A number of recent works have therefore considered the challenge of extending model checking to systems which induce infinite-state Markov chains. Examples include *probabilistic pushdown automata* (recursive state machines) which are natural models for probabilistic sequential programs with recursive procedures [19,20,22,21,18,23]; and *probabilistic lossy channel systems* which consist of finite-state processes communicating through unreliable and unbounded channels in which messages are lost with a certain probability [1,6,9,10,13,26,29].

In a recent paper [3], we considered a class of infinite-state Markov chains with the property that any computation from which the set F of *final* states is always reachable, will almost certainly reach F. We presented generic algorithms for analyzing both qualitative properties (checking whether F is reached with probability one), and quantitative properties (approximating the probability by which F is reached from a given state).

S. Graf and W. Zhang (Eds.): ATVA 2006, LNCS 4218, pp. 24–38, 2006.

A central problem in quantitative analysis is to compute the *expectations*, *variances* and higher moments of random variables, e.g., the reward (or cost) for runs until they reach F. We address this problem for the subclass of *eager Markov chains*, where the probability of avoiding F for n or more steps is bounded by some exponentially decreasing function $f(n)$. In other words, computations that reach F are likely to do so in "few" steps. Thus, eagerness is a strengthening of the properties of the Markov chains considered in [3].

Eagerness trivially holds for all finite state Markov chains, but also for several classes of infinite-state ones. Our main result (see Section 4 and 5) is that the following classes of infinite-state systems induce eager Markov chains and that the bounding function $f(n)$ can be effectively constructed.

- Markov chains which contain a finite *eager attractor*. An *attractor* is a set of states which is reached with probability one from each state in the Markov chain. An attractor is *eager*, if the probability of returning to it in more than n steps decreases exponentially with n. Examples of such Markov chains are those induced by *probabilistic lossy channel systems (PLCS)*. This is shown in two steps. First, we consider systems that contain *GR-attractors*, defined as generalizations of the classical *gambler's ruin* problem, and show that each GR-attractor is eager. Then, we show that each PLCS induces a Markov chain which contains a GR-attractor.
- Markov chains which are *boundedly coarse*: there is a K such that if F is reachable then F will be reached within K steps with a probability which is bounded from below. We give two examples of boundedly coarse Markov chains, namely those induced by *Probabilistic Vector Addition Systems with States (PVASS)* and *Noisy Turing Machines (NTM)*.

Decidability of the eagerness property is not a meaningful question: for finite MC the answer is always yes, and for infinite MC the instance is not finitely given, unless one restricts to a special subclass like PLCS, PVASS or NTM.

For any eager Markov chain, and any computable reward function, one can effectively approximate the expectation of the reward gained before a state in F is reached. In Section 3 we present an exploration scheme, based on forward reachability analysis, to approximate the expected reward up-to an arbitrarily small error $\epsilon > 0$. We show that the scheme is guaranteed to terminate in the case of eager Markov chains.

Related Work. There has been an extensive work on model checking of finite-state Markov chains [17,11,8,12,27].

Recently, several works have considered probabilistic pushdown automata and probabilistic recursive state machines [19,20,22,21,18,23]. However, all the decidability results in these papers are based on translating the relevant properties into formulas in the first-order theory of reals. Using results from [3], it is straightforward to show that such a translation is impossible to achieve for the classes of Markov chains we consider.

The works in [1,6,10,13,29,9] consider model checking of PLCS. In particular, [3] gives a generic theory for verification of infinite-state Markov chains including PLCS and PVASS. However, all these works concentrate on computing probabilities, and do not give algorithms for analysis of expectation properties.

The work closest to ours is a recent paper by Brázdil and Kučera [14] which considers the problem of computing approximations of the accumulated reward (and gain) for some classes of infinite-state Markov chains which satisfy certain preconditions (e.g., PLCS). However, their technique is quite different from ours and their preconditions are incomparable to our eagerness condition. The main idea in [14] is to approximate an infinite-state Markov chain by a sequence of effectively constructible finite-state Markov chains such that the obtained solutions for the finite-state Markov chains converge toward the solution for the original infinite-state Markov chain. Their preconditions [14] include one that ensures that this type of approximation converges, which is not satisfied by, e.g., PVASS. Furthermore, they require decidability of model checking for certain path formulas in the underlying transition system.

In contrast, our method is a converging path exploration scheme for infinite-state Markov chains, which only requires the eagerness condition. It is applicable not only to PLCS but also to other classes like PVASS and noisy Turing machines. We also do not assume that reachability is decidable in the underlying transition system. Finally, we solve a somewhat more general problem. We compute approximations for the *conditional* expected reward, consider possibly infinite sets of final states (rather than just a single final state) and our reward functions can be arbitrary (exponentially bounded) functions on runs (instead of cumulative state-based linear-bounded functions in [14]).

In a recent paper [5], we extend the theory of Markov chains with eager attractors and show that the steady state distribution and limiting average expected reward can be approximated for them. This provides additional motivation for studying Markov chains with eager attractors.

Proofs omitted due to space limitations can be found in [4].

2 Preliminaries

Transition Systems. A *transition system* is a triple $\mathcal{T} = (S, \longrightarrow, F)$ where S is a countable set of *states*, $\longrightarrow \subseteq S \times S$ is the *transition relation*, and $F \subseteq S$ is the set of *final states*. We write $s \longrightarrow s'$ to denote that $(s, s') \in \longrightarrow$. We assume that transition systems are deadlock-free, i.e., each state has at least one successor. If this condition is not satisfied, we add a self-loop to states without successors – this does not affect the properties of transition systems considered in this paper.

A *run* ρ is an infinite sequence $s_0 s_1 \ldots$ of states satisfying $s_i \longrightarrow s_{i+1}$ for all $i \geq 0$. We use $\rho(i)$ to denote s_i and say that ρ is an s-run if $\rho(0) = s$. We assume familiarity with the syntax and semantics of the temporal logic CTL^* [15]. We use $(s \models \phi)$ to denote the set of s-runs that satisfy the CTL^* path-formula ϕ. For instance, $(s \models \bigcirc F)$ and $(s \models \Diamond F)$ are the sets of s-runs that visit F in the next state resp. eventually reach F. For a natural number n, $\bigcirc^{=n} F$ denotes a formula which is satisfied by a run ρ iff $\rho(n) \in F$. We use $\Diamond^{=n} F$ to denote a formula which is satisfied by ρ iff ρ reaches F first in its nth step, i.e., $\rho(n) \in F$ and $\rho(i) \notin F$ when $0 \leq i < n$. Similarly, for $\sim \in \{<, \leq, \geq, >\}$, $\Diamond^{\sim n} F$ holds for a run ρ if there is an $m \in \mathbb{N}$ with $m \sim n$ such that $\Diamond^{=m} F$ holds.

A *path* π is a finite sequence $s_0, \ldots, s_n$ of states such that $s_i \longrightarrow s_{i+1}$ for all $i : 0 \leq i < n$. We let $|\pi| := n$ denote the number of transitions in a path. Note that a path is a prefix of a run. We use ρ^n for the path $\rho(0)\rho(1) \cdots \rho(n)$ and $Path_F^{=n}(s)$ for the set $\{\rho^n | \rho \in (s \models \Diamond^{=n} F)\}$. In other words, $Path_F^{=n}(s)$ is the set of paths of length n starting from s and reaching F first in the last state.

A transition system $\mathcal{T} = (S, \longrightarrow, F)$ is said to be *effective* if it is finitely branching and for each $s \in S$, we can explicitly compute all successors, and check if $s \in F$.

Reward Functions. A *reward function* (with respect to a state s) is a mapping $f : (s \models \Diamond F) \to \mathbb{R}$ which assigns a *reward* $f(\rho)$ to any s-run that visits F. A reward function is *tail-independent* if its value only depends on the prefix of the run up-to the first state in F, i.e., if $\rho_1, \rho_2 \in (s \models \Diamond^{=n} F)$ and $\rho_1^n = \rho_2^n$ then $f(\rho_1) = f(\rho_2)$. In such a case (abusing notation), we write $f(\pi)$ to denote $f(\rho)$ where $\pi = \rho^n$. We say that f is *computable* if we can compute $f(\pi)$.

We will place an exponential limit on the growth of reward functions: A reward function is said to be *exponentially bounded* if there are $\alpha, k \in \mathbb{R}_{>0}$ s.t. $|f(\rho)| \leq k\alpha^n$ for all $n \in \mathbb{N}$ and $\rho \in (s \models \Diamond^{=n} F)$. We call (α, k) the *parameter* of f.

Markov Chains. A *Markov chain* is a triple $\mathcal{M} = (S, P, F)$ where S is a countable set of *states*, $P : S \times S \to [0, 1]$ is the *probability distribution*, satisfying $\forall s \in S. \sum_{s' \in S} P(s, s') = 1$, and $F \subseteq S$ is the set of *final states*.

A Markov chain induces a transition system, where the transition relation consists of pairs of states related by a positive probability. Formally, the *underlying transition system* of $\mathcal{M}$ is $(S, \longrightarrow, F)$ where $s_1 \longrightarrow s_2$ iff $P(s_1, s_2) > 0$. In this manner, concepts defined for transition systems can be lifted to Markov chains. For instance, a run or a reward function in a Markov chain $\mathcal{M}$ is a run or reward function in the underlying transition system, and $\mathcal{M}$ is effective, etc, if the underlying transition system is so.

A Markov chain $\mathcal{M} = (S, P, F)$ and a state s induce a probability space on the set of runs that start at s. The probability space $(\Omega, \Delta, \mathcal{P}_{\mathcal{M}})$ is defined as follows: $\Omega = sS^\omega$ is the set of all infinite sequences of states starting from s and Δ is the σ-algebra generated by the basic cylindric sets $\{D_u = uS^\omega : u \in sS^*\}$. The probability measure $\mathcal{P}_{\mathcal{M}}$ is first defined on finite sequences of states $u = s_0 \ldots s_n \in sS^*$ by $\mathcal{P}_{\mathcal{M}}(u) = \prod_{i=0}^{n-1} P(s_i, s_{i+1})$ and then extended to cylindric sets by $\mathcal{P}_{\mathcal{M}}(D_u) = \mathcal{P}_{\mathcal{M}}(u)$; it is well-known that this measure is extended in a unique way to the entire σ-algebra. Let $\mathcal{P}_{\mathcal{M}}(s \models \phi)$ denote the measure of the set $(s \models \phi)$ (which is measurable by [31]).

Given a Markov chain $\mathcal{M} = (S, P, F)$, a state $s \in S$, and a reward function f on the underlying transition system, define the random variable $X_f : \Omega \to \mathbb{R}$ as follows: $X_f(\rho) = 0$ if $\rho \notin (s \models \Diamond F)$, and $X_f(\rho) = f(\rho)$ if $\rho \in (s \models \Diamond F)$. Then $E(X_f | s \models \Diamond F)$ is the conditional expectation of the reward from s to F, under the condition that F is reached.

A Markov chain $\mathcal{M}$ is said to be *eager with respect to* $s \in S$ if there are $\alpha < 1$ and $k \in \mathbb{R}_{>0}$ s.t. $\forall n \in \mathbb{N}. \mathcal{P}_{\mathcal{M}}(s \models \Diamond^{\geq n} F) \leq k\alpha^n$. Intuitively, $\mathcal{M}$ is eager with respect to s if the probability of avoiding F in n or more steps (starting from the initial state s) decreases exponentially with n. We call (α, k) the *parameter* of $(\mathcal{M}, s)$.

3 Approximating the Conditional Expectation

In this Section, we consider the *approximate conditional expectation problem* defined as follows:

APPROX_EXPECT

Instance

- An effective Markov chain $\mathcal{M} = (S, P, F)$, a state $s \in S$ such that $s \models \exists\Diamond F$, $\mathcal{M}$ is eager w.r.t. s, and $(\mathcal{M}, s)$ has parameter (α_1, k_1).
- An exponentially bounded and computable tail-independent reward function f with parameter (α_2, k_2) such that $\alpha_1 \cdot \alpha_2 < 1$.
- An error tolerance $\epsilon \in \mathbb{R}_{>0}$

Task Compute a number $r \in \mathbb{R}$ such that $r \leq E(X_f | s \models \Diamond F) \leq r + \epsilon$.

Note that the instance of the problem assumes that F is reachable from s. This is because the expected value is undefined otherwise. We observe that the condition $\alpha_1 \cdot \alpha_2 < 1$ can always be fulfilled if the reward function f is bounded by a polynomial, since $\alpha_2 > 1$ can then be chosen arbitrarily close to 1. Many natural reward functions are in fact polynomial. For instance, it is common to assign a reward $g(s)$ to each state and consider the reward of a run to be the sum of state rewards up to F: if $\rho \models \Diamond^{=n} F$ then $f(\rho) = \sum_{i=0}^{n} g(\rho(i))$. If there is a bound on the state reward, i.e., $\exists M \in \mathbb{R}. \forall \rho. \forall i. |g(\rho(i))| < M$, then such a reward function is linearly bounded in the length of the run. Another important case is state rewards that depend on the "size" of the state which can grow at most by a constant in every step, e.g., values of counters in a Petri net (or VASS) or the number of messages in an unbounded communication channel. In this case, the reward function is at most quadratic in the length of the run.

Remark. If $\alpha_1 \cdot \alpha_2^k < 1$, the kth moment X_f^k can also be approximated as it satisfies the conditions above. In particular, all moments can be approximated for polynomially bounded reward functions. Using the formula $V(X_f) = E(X_f^2) - E(X_f)^2$, we can also approximate the variance. □

Algorithm. We present a path enumeration algorithm (Algorithm 1) for solving APPROX_EXPECT (defined in the previous section), and then show that it terminates and computes a correct value of r.

In Algorithm 1, since $s \models \exists\Diamond F$ by assumption, we know that $\mathcal{P}_\mathcal{M}(s \models \Diamond F) > 0$, and therefore:

$$E(X_f | s \models \Diamond F) = \frac{E(X_f)}{\mathcal{P}_\mathcal{M}(s \models \Diamond F)} = \frac{E(X_f)}{E(X_R)},$$

where $R(\rho) = 1$ if $\rho \in (s \models \Diamond F)$, and $R(\rho) = 0$ otherwise. The algorithm tries to approximate the values of $E(X_f)$ and $E(X_R)$ based on the observation that $E(X_f) = \sum_{i=0}^{\infty} \sum_{\pi \in Path_F^{=i}(s)} \mathcal{P}_\mathcal{M}(\pi) \cdot f(\pi)$ and $E(X_R) = \sum_{i=0}^{\infty} \sum_{\pi \in Path_F^{=i}(s)} \mathcal{P}_\mathcal{M}(\pi)$.

The algorithm maintains four variables: E_f and E_R which contain approximations of the values of $E(X_f)$ and $E(X_R)$; and ε_f and ε_R which are bounds on the errors in the current approximations. During the nth iteration, the values of E_f and E_R are modified by $\sum_{\pi \in Path_F^{=n}(s)} \mathcal{P}_\mathcal{M}(\pi) \cdot f(\pi)$ and $\sum_{\pi \in Path_F^{=n}(s)} \mathcal{P}_\mathcal{M}(\pi)$. This maintains the invariant that each time we arrive at line 7, we have

$$E_f = \sum_{i=0}^{n} \sum_{\pi \in Path_F^{=i}(s)} \mathcal{P}_\mathcal{M}(\pi) \cdot f(\pi), \qquad E_R = \sum_{i=0}^{n} \sum_{\pi \in Path_F^{=i}(s)} \mathcal{P}_\mathcal{M}(\pi). \tag{1}$$

The algorithm terminates in case two conditions are satisfied:

- F is reached, i.e., $E_R > 0$.
- The difference between the upper and lower bounds $\frac{E_f+\varepsilon_f}{E_R}$ and $\frac{E_f-\varepsilon_f}{E_R+\varepsilon_R}$ on the conditional expectation (derived in the proof of Theorem 1), is below the error tolerance ϵ.

Algorithm 1 – APPROX_EXPECT
Input: An instance of the problem as described in Section 3.
Variables: $E_f, E_R, \varepsilon_f, \varepsilon_R$: $\mathbb{R}$
1. $n \leftarrow 0, \quad E_f \leftarrow 0, \quad E_R \leftarrow 0$
2. **repeat**
3. $\quad E_f \leftarrow E_f + \sum_{\pi \in Path_{\overline{F}}^{=n}(s)} \mathcal{P}_{\mathcal{M}}(\pi) \cdot f(\pi)$
4. $\quad E_R \leftarrow E_R + \sum_{\pi \in Path_{\overline{F}}^{=n}(s)} \mathcal{P}_{\mathcal{M}}(\pi)$
5. $\quad \varepsilon_f \leftarrow k_1 \cdot k_2 \cdot (\alpha_1 \cdot \alpha_2)^{n+1}/(1-\alpha_1 \cdot \alpha_2)$
6. $\quad \varepsilon_R \leftarrow k_1 \cdot \alpha_1^{n+1}/(1-\alpha_1)$
7. $\quad n \leftarrow n+1$
8. **until** $(E_R > 0) \wedge \left(\frac{E_f+\varepsilon_f}{E_R} - \frac{E_f-\varepsilon_f}{E_R+\varepsilon_R} < \epsilon\right)$
9. **return** $\left(\frac{E_f-\varepsilon_f}{E_R+\varepsilon_R}\right)$

Observe that the parameters (α_1, k_1) and (α_2, k_2) are required by Algorithm 1, and hence they should be computable for the Markov chains to be analyzed by the algorithm. This is possible for the classes of Markov chains we consider in this paper.

Theorem 1. *Algorithm 1 terminates and returns a correct value of* r.

Proof. Clearly, each time the algorithm is about to execute line 7, the values of E_f and E_R are described by (1). The error in E_f as an approximation to $E(X_f)$ is thus

$$|E(X_f) - E_f| = \left| \sum_{i=n+1}^{\infty} \sum_{\pi \in Path_{\overline{F}}^{=i}(s)} \mathcal{P}_{\mathcal{M}}(\pi) \cdot f(\pi) \right| \leq \left| \sum_{i=n+1}^{\infty} k_2 \cdot \alpha_2^i \sum_{\pi \in Path_{\overline{F}}^{=i}(s)} \mathcal{P}_{\mathcal{M}}(\pi) \right|$$

$$\leq \left| \sum_{i=n+1}^{\infty} k_1 \cdot k_2 \cdot \alpha_1^i \cdot \alpha_2^i \right| = k_1 \cdot k_2 \cdot (\alpha_1 \cdot \alpha_2)^{n+1}/(1-\alpha_1 \cdot \alpha_2) = \varepsilon_f.$$

Here, the first equality follows by definition, and the inequalities follow from the fact that f is exponentially bounded and $\mathcal{M}$ is eager.

The inequality $|E(X_R) - E_R| \leq \varepsilon_R$ is obtained similarly. By assumption, $\alpha_1 \cdot \alpha_2 < 1$ and $\alpha_2 < 1$, so $\lim_{n\to\infty} \varepsilon_f = \lim_{n\to\infty} \varepsilon_R = 0$. This implies that the algorithm terminates.

Now, we show correctness of the algorithm. It is clear that $0 \leq E_R \leq E(X_R)$ since E_R increases each iteration. Hence, we have the two inequalities $E_f - \varepsilon_f \leq E(X_f) \leq E_f + \varepsilon_f$ and $E_R \leq E(X_R) \leq E_R + \varepsilon_R$. If $E_R > 0$, we can invert the second inequality and multiply it with the first to obtain

$$\frac{E_f - \varepsilon_f}{E_R + \varepsilon_R} \leq \frac{E(X_f)}{E(X_R)} \leq \frac{E_f + \varepsilon_f}{E_R}.$$

Hence, when the algorithm terminates, $\frac{E_f-\varepsilon_f}{E_R+\varepsilon_R}$ is a correct value of r.

Remark 1. If reachability is decidable in the underlying transition system (as for the classes of Markov chains we consider in this paper), we can explicitly check whether the condition $s \models \exists\Diamond F$ is satisfied before running the algorithm. □

Remark 2. When computing the sums over $Path_{\overline{F}}^{=n}(s)$ on lines 3 and 4, the algorithm can use either breadth-first search or depth-first search to find the paths in the transition system. Breadth-first search has the advantage that it computes $Path_{\overline{F}}^{=n}(s)$ explicitly, which can be reused in the next iteration to compute $Path_{\overline{F}}^{=n+1}(s)$. With depth-first search, on the other hand, the search has to be restarted from s in each iteration, but it only requires memory linear in n. □

4 Eager Attractors

We consider Markov chains that contain a *finite attractor*, and prove that certain weak conditions on the attractor imply eagerness of the Markov chain. Consider a Markov chain $\mathcal{M} = (S, P, F)$. A set $A \subseteq S$ is said to be an *attractor* if $\mathcal{P}_{\mathcal{M}}(s \models \Diamond A) = 1$ for each $s \in S$. In other words, a run from any state will almost certainly return back to A. We will only work with attractors that are *finite*; therefore we assume finiteness (even when not explicitly mentioned) for all the attractors in the sequel.

Eager Attractors. We say that an attractor $A \subseteq S$ is *eager* if there is a $\beta < 1$ and a $b \geq 1$ s.t. for each $s \in A$ and $n \geq 0$ it is the case that $\mathcal{P}_{\mathcal{M}}\left(s \models ((\Diamond^{\geq n} A)\right) \leq b\beta^n$. In other words, for every state $s \in A$, the probability of first returning to A in $n + 1$ (or more) steps is exponentially bounded in n. We call (β, b) the *parameters* of A. Notice that it is not a restriction to have β, b independent of s, since A is finite.

Theorem 2. *Let $\mathcal{M} = (S, P, F)$ be a Markov chain that contains an eager attractor $A \subseteq S$ with parameters (β, b). Then $\mathcal{M}$ is eager with respect to any $s \in A$ and the parameters (α, k) of $\mathcal{M}$ can be computed.*

We devote the rest of this section to the proof of Theorem 2. Fix a state $s \in A$, let $n \geq 1$, and define

$$U_s(n) := \mathcal{P}_{\mathcal{M}}\left(s \models \Diamond^{=n} F\right).$$

We will compute an upper bound on $U_s(n)$, where the upper bound decreases exponentially with n. To do that, we partition the set of runs in $(s \models \Diamond^{=n} F)$ into two subsets R_1 and R_2, and show that both have "low" probability measures:

- R_1: the set of runs that visit A "seldom" in the first n steps. Such runs are not probable since A is eager. In our proof, we use the eagerness of A to compute an upper bound $U_s^1(n)$ on the measure of R_1, where $U_s^1(n)$ decreases exponentially with n.
- R_2: the set of runs that visit A "often" in the first n steps. Each time a run enters a state in A, it will visit F with a probability, which is bounded from below, before it returns back to A. The runs of R_2 are not probable, since the probability of avoiding F between the "many" re-visits of A is low. We use this observation to compute an upper bound $U_s^2(n)$ on the measure of R_2, that also decreases exponentially with n.

A crucial aspect here is to define the border between R_1 and R_2. We consider a run to re-visit A often (i.e., belong to the set R_2) if the number of re-visits is at least n/c, where c is a constant, defined later, that only depends on (β, b).

To formalize the above reasoning, we need the following definition. For natural numbers $n, t : 1 \leq t \leq n$, we define the formula $A^{\#}_{n,t}$, which is satisfied by an s-run ρ iff ρ^n contains exactly t occurrences of elements in A before the last state in ρ^n, i.e., the very last state $\rho(n)$ does not count toward t even if it is in A. Then:

$$U_s(n) = \mathcal{P}_{\mathcal{M}}\left(s \models \Diamond^{=n} F\right) = \sum_{t=1}^{n} \mathcal{P}_{\mathcal{M}}\left(s \models \Diamond^{=n} F \wedge A^{\#}_{n,t}\right) = U^1_s(n) + U^2_s(n),$$

where

$$U^1_s(n) := \sum_{t=1}^{\lfloor \frac{n}{c} \rfloor} \mathcal{P}_{\mathcal{M}}\left(s \models \Diamond^{=n} F \wedge A^{\#}_{n,t}\right), \quad U^2_s(n) := \sum_{t=\lfloor \frac{n}{c} \rfloor + 1}^{n} \mathcal{P}_{\mathcal{M}}\left(s \models \Diamond^{=n} F \wedge A^{\#}_{n,t}\right).$$

Below, we derive our bounds on $U^1_s(n)$ and $U^2_s(n)$.

Bound on $U^1_s(n)$. The proof is based on the following idea. Each run $\rho \in R_1$ makes a number of visits (say t visits) to A before reaching F. We can thus partition ρ into t segments, each representing a part of ρ between two re-visits of A. To reason about the segments of ρ, we need a number of definitions.

For natural numbers $1 \leq t \leq n$, let $n \oplus t$ be the set of vectors of positive natural numbers of the form $(x_1, \ldots, x_t)$ such that $x_1 + \cdots + x_t = n$. Intuitively, the number x_i represents the length of the ith segment of ρ. Observe that the set $n \oplus t$ contains $\binom{n-1}{t-1}$ elements.

For paths $\pi = s_0 s_1 \cdots s_m$ and $\pi' = s'_0 s'_1 \cdots s'_n$ with $s_m = s'_0$, let $\pi \bullet \pi'$ denote the path $\pi = s_0 s_1 \cdots s_m s'_1 \cdots s'_n$. For a set $A \subseteq S$ and $v = (x_1, \ldots, x_t) \in (n \oplus t)$, a run ρ satisfies $A^{\#}_{n,v}$ if $\rho^n = \pi_1 \bullet \pi_2 \bullet \cdots \bullet \pi_t$ and for each $i : 1 \leq i \leq t$: (i) $|\pi_i| = x_i$, (ii) $\pi_i(0) \in A$, and (iii) $\pi_i(j) \notin A$, for each $j : 0 < j < |\pi_i|$. Eagerness of $\mathcal{M}$ gives the following bound on the measure of runs satisfying $A^{\#}_{n,v}$.

Lemma 1. *For each $n, t : 1 \leq t \leq n$, $v \in (n \oplus t)$, and $s \in A$, it is the case that $\mathcal{P}_{\mathcal{M}}\left(s \models A^{\#}_{n,v}\right) \leq b^t \beta^{n-t}$.*

Recalling the definition of $U^1_s(n)$ and using Lemma 1: $U^1_s(n) \leq$

$$\sum_{t=1}^{\lfloor \frac{n}{c} \rfloor} \mathcal{P}_{\mathcal{M}}\left(s \models A^{\#}_{n,t}\right) = \sum_{t=1}^{\lfloor \frac{n}{c} \rfloor} \sum_{v \in (n \oplus t)} \mathcal{P}_{\mathcal{M}}\left(s \models A^{\#}_{n,v}\right) \leq \sum_{t=1}^{\lfloor \frac{n}{c} \rfloor} \sum_{v \in (n \oplus t)} b^t \beta^{n-t} = \sum_{t=1}^{\lfloor \frac{n}{c} \rfloor} \binom{n-1}{t-1} b^t \beta^{n-t}$$

To bound the last sum, we use the following lemma.

Lemma 2. *For all $n \geq 2c$, $c \geq 2$ and $b \geq 1$*

$$\sum_{t=1}^{\lfloor n/c \rfloor} \binom{n-1}{t-1} b^t \beta^{n-t} \leq \left(\left(\frac{c}{c-1} \right) (2c)^{1/c} \left(\frac{1}{c} + \frac{b}{\beta} \right)^{1/c} \cdot \beta \right)^n.$$

Choose $c > \max\left(1 + \frac{1}{\beta^{-1/3}-1}, 7, \frac{9}{\log^2 \beta}, \frac{-3\log(\frac{1}{7}+b/\beta)}{\log \beta}\right)$. Define $\alpha_1 := \left(\frac{c}{c-1}\right) \cdot (2c)^{1/c} \cdot \left(\frac{1}{c} + \frac{b}{\beta}\right)^{1/c} \cdot \beta$. It is not difficult to prove that we have $\beta < \alpha_1 < 1$. For $n \geq 2c$, Lemma 2 yields $U_s^1(n) \leq \alpha_1^n$. For $n < 2c$ we have $U_s^1(n) \leq b\beta^{n-1} \leq (b/\beta)\beta^n \leq (b/\beta)\alpha_1^n$. Let $k_1 := (b/\beta) > 1$. We obtain, $\forall n \in \mathbb{N}. U_s^1(n) \leq k_1 \alpha_1^n$.

Bound on $U_s^2(n)$. Let B be the subset of A from which F is reachable, i.e., $B := \{s \in A | \; s \models \exists \Diamond F\}$. If $s \in A - B$ then trivially $U_s^2(n) = 0$. In the following we consider the case when $s \in B$. Let $w := |B|$.

The bound on $U_s^2(n)$ is computed based on the observation that runs in R_2 visit A many times before reaching F. To formalize this, we need a definition. For a natural number k and sets of states S_1, S_2, we define $\left(s \models S_1^k \; \underline{Before} \; S_2\right)$ to be the set of s-runs ρ that make at least k visits to S_1 before visiting S_2 for the first time. Formally, an s-run satisfies the formula if there are $0 \leq i_1 < i_2 < \cdots < i_k \leq n$ such that $\rho(i_j) \in S_1$ for each $j : 1 \leq j \leq k$, and $\rho(i) \notin S_2$ for each $i : 0 \leq i \leq n$. We write $S_1 \; \underline{Before} \; S_2$ instead of $S_1^1 \; \underline{Before} \; S_2$, $S_1^k \; \underline{Before} \; s_2$ instead of $S_1^k \; \underline{Before} \; \{s_2\}$, and $s_1^k \; \underline{Before} \; S_2$ instead of $\{s_1\}^k \; \underline{Before} \; S_2$.

Notice that $(s \models \Diamond^{=n} F \wedge A_{n,t}^{\#}) = (s \models \Diamond^{=n} F \wedge B_{n,t}^{\#}) \subseteq (s \models B^t \; \underline{Before} \; F)$. It follows that $U_s^2(n) \leq \sum_{t=\lfloor \frac{n}{c} \rfloor + 1}^{n} \mathcal{P}_{\mathcal{M}} \left(s \models B^t \; \underline{Before} \; F\right)$.

Any run from s that makes t visits to B before visiting F must have the following property. By the Pigeonhole principle there exists at least one state $s_B \in B$ that is visited at least $\lceil t/w \rceil$ times before visiting F. This means that

$$\left(s \models B^t \; \underline{Before} \; F\right) \subseteq \bigcup_{s_B \in B} \left(s \models s_B^{\lceil t/w \rceil} \; \underline{Before} \; F\right),$$

and hence

$$U_s^2(n) \leq \sum_{t=\lfloor \frac{n}{c} \rfloor + 1}^{n} \sum_{s_B \in B} \mathcal{P}_{\mathcal{M}} \left(s \models s_B^{\lceil t/w \rceil} \; \underline{Before} \; F\right).$$

By cutting runs at the first occurrence of s_B, we see that $\mathcal{P}_{\mathcal{M}}(s \models s_B^{\lceil t/w \rceil} \; \underline{Before} \; F) = \mathcal{P}_{\mathcal{M}}(s \models s_B \; \underline{Before} \; F) \cdot \mathcal{P}_{\mathcal{M}}(s_B \models s_B^{\lceil t/w \rceil} \; \underline{Before} \; F)$ and in particular $\mathcal{P}_{\mathcal{M}}(s \models s_B^{\lceil t/w \rceil} \; \underline{Before} \; F) \leq \mathcal{P}_{\mathcal{M}}(s_B \models s_B^{\lceil t/w \rceil} \; \underline{Before} \; F)$. Consider the runs in the set $(s_B \models s_B^{\lceil t/w \rceil} \; \underline{Before} \; F)$. In such a run, there are $\lceil t/w \rceil$ parts that go from s_B to s_B and avoid F. The following lemma gives an upper bound on such runs. To capture this upper bound, we introduce the parameter μ which is defined to be positive and smaller than the minimal probability, when starting from some $s \in B$, of visiting F before returning to s. In other words, $0 < \mu \leq \min_{s \in B} \mathcal{P}_{\mathcal{M}} \left(s \models ((F \; \underline{Before} \; s)\right)$. Note that μ is well-defined since F is reachable from all $s \in B$ and $\mu > 0$ since B is finite.

Lemma 3. $\mathcal{P}_{\mathcal{M}} \left(s_B \models s_B^x \; \underline{Before} \; F\right) \leq (1-\mu)^{x-1}$, *for each* $s_B \in B$.

Since μ only needs to be a lower bound, we can assume $\mu < 1$. From Lemma 3 it follows that

$$U_s^2(n) \leq \sum_{t=\lfloor \frac{n}{c} \rfloor+1}^{n} \sum_{s_B \in B} (1-\mu)^{\lceil t/w \rceil - 1} \leq \frac{w}{1-\mu} \cdot \sum_{t=\lfloor \frac{n}{c} \rfloor+1}^{n} (1-\mu)^{t/w}$$

$$= \frac{w}{1-\mu} \cdot \frac{(1-\mu)^{(\lfloor \frac{n}{c} \rfloor+1)/w} - (1-\mu)^{(n+1)/w}}{1-(1-\mu)^{1/w}} < \frac{w}{(1-\mu)(1-(1-\mu)^{1/w})} \cdot \left((1-\mu)^{\frac{1}{cw}}\right)^n.$$

Let $\alpha_2 := (1-\mu)^{\frac{1}{cw}} < 1$ and $k_2 := \frac{w}{(1-\mu)(1-(1-\mu)^{1/w})}$. Thus $\forall n \in \mathbb{N}.\, U_s^2(n) \leq k_2 \alpha_2^n$.

Remark 3. The reason why we do not use *equality* in the definition of μ, i.e., define $\mu = \min_{s \in B} \mathcal{P}_{\mathcal{M}}\left(s \models ((F \ \underline{Before} \ s)\right)$, is that (as it will later be explained for PLCS) it is in general hard to compute $\min_{s \in B} \mathcal{P}_{\mathcal{M}}\left(s \models ((F \ \underline{Before} \ s)\right)$ exactly. However, we can compute a non-zero lower bound, which is sufficient for the applicability of our algorithm. □

Eagerness of $\mathcal{M}$ with respect to $s \in A$. From the bounds on $U_s^1(n)$ and $U_s^2(n)$, we derive the parameters (α, k) of $(\mathcal{M}, s)$ as follows. Let $\alpha_3 := \max(\alpha_1, \alpha_2) < 1$ and $k_3 := k_1 + k_2$. Then $U_s(n) \leq U_s^1(n) + U_s^2(n) \leq k_1\alpha_1^n + k_2\alpha_2^n \leq (k_1+k_2)\alpha_3^n = k_3\alpha_3^n$. Finally,

$$\mathcal{P}_{\mathcal{M}}\left(s \models \diamond^{\geq n} F\right) = \sum_{i=n}^{\infty} U_s(i) \leq k_3 \frac{\alpha_3^n}{1-\alpha_3}$$

Choose $\alpha := \alpha_3$ and $k := k_3/(1-\alpha_3)$. It follows that $\forall n \in \mathbb{N}.\, \mathcal{P}_{\mathcal{M}}\left(s \models \diamond^{\geq n} F\right) \leq k\alpha^n$. This concludes the proof of Theorem 2. □

4.1 GR-Attractors

We define the class of *gambler's ruin-like attractors* or *GR-attractors* for short, show that any GR-attractor is also eager (Lemma 4), and that any PLCS contains a GR-attractor (Lemma 7).

Let $\mathcal{M} = (S, P, F)$ be a Markov chain that contains a finite attractor $A \subseteq S$. Then A is called a *GR-attractor*, if there exists a "distance" function $h : S \to \mathbb{N}$ and a constant $q > 1/2$ such that for any state $s \in S$ the following conditions hold.

1. $h(s) = 0 \iff s \in A$.
2. $\sum_{\{s' \mid h(s') < h(s)\}} P(s, s') \geq q$, for all s with $h(s) \geq 1$.
3. $P(s, s') = 0$, if $h(s') > h(s) + 1$.

Let $p := 1 - q$. We call (p, q) the parameter of A. Intuitively, h describes the distance from A. This condition means that, in every step, the distance to A does not increase by more than 1, and it decreases with probability uniformly $> 1/2$. In particular, this implies that A is an attractor, i.e., $\forall s \in S.\, \mathcal{P}_{\mathcal{M}}(s \models \diamond A) = 1$, but not every attractor has the distance function. As we will see below, a Markov chain with a GR-attractor generalizes the classical "gambler's ruin" problem [24], but converges at least as quickly. We devote the rest of Section 4.1 to show the following Lemma.

Lemma 4. *Let $\mathcal{M}$ be a Markov chain. Every finite GR-attractor with parameter (p, q) is an eager attractor with parameters $\beta = \sqrt{4pq}$ and $b = 1$.*

To prove this, we need several auxiliary constructions.

For a state $s \in S$ with $h(s) = k$, we want to derive an upper bound for the probability of reaching A in n or more steps. Formally, $f(k,n) := \sup_{h(s)=k} \mathcal{P}_{\mathcal{M}}\left(s \models \Diamond^{\geq n} A\right)$.

To obtain an upper bound on $f(k,n)$, we relate our Markov chain $\mathcal{M}$ to the Markov chain $\mathcal{M}^G$ from the gambler's ruin problem [24], defined as $\mathcal{M}^G = (\mathbb{N}, P_G, \{0\})$ with $P_G(x, x-1) = q$, $P_G(x, x+1) = p := 1 - q$ for $x \geq 1$ and $P_G(0,0) = 1$. Let $g(k,n) := \mathcal{P}_{\mathcal{M}^G}\left(k \models \Diamond^{\geq n}\, 0\right)$.

The following Lemma shows that f is bounded by g, so that any upper bound for the gambler's ruin problem also applies to a GR-attractor.

Lemma 5. *If* $0 \leq k \leq n$ *then* $f(k,n) \leq g(k,n)$.

Next, we give an upper bound for the gambler's ruin problem.

Lemma 6. *For all* $n \geq 2$, $g(1,n) \leq \frac{3q}{\sqrt{\pi}}(4pq)^{\lfloor \frac{n}{2} \rfloor}$.

Proof. **(of Lemma 4)** Let $\beta := \sqrt{4pq}$. For $n = 0$, we have $\mathcal{P}_{\mathcal{M}}\left(s \models ((\Diamond^{\geq n} A)\right) \leq 1 = \beta^0$. For $n = 1$, we have $\mathcal{P}_{\mathcal{M}}\left(s \models ((\Diamond^{\geq n} A)\right) \leq p \leq \beta^1$. For $n \geq 2$, Lemma 5 gives $\mathcal{P}_{\mathcal{M}}\left(s \models ((\Diamond^{\geq n} A)\right) \leq p \cdot g(1,n)$, so by Lemma 6, $\mathcal{P}_{\mathcal{M}}\left(s \models ((\Diamond^{\geq n} A)\right) \leq \frac{3pq}{\sqrt{\pi}}\,(4pq)^{\lfloor \frac{n}{2} \rfloor} = \frac{3}{4\sqrt{\pi}}\,(4pq)^{\lfloor \frac{n}{2} \rfloor + 1} \leq \frac{3}{4\sqrt{\pi}}(4pq)^{\frac{n}{2}} \leq \left(\sqrt{4pq}\right)^n = \beta^n$.

4.2 Probabilistic Lossy Channel Systems

As an example of systems with finite GR-attractors, we consider *Probabilistic lossy channel systems (PLCS)*. These are probabilistic processes with a finite control unit and a finite set of channels, each of which behaves as a FIFO buffer which is unbounded and unreliable in the sense that it can spontaneously lose messages. There exist several variants of PLCS which differ in how many messages can be lost, with which probabilities, and in which situations. We consider the relatively realistic PLCS model from [6,13,29] where each message in transit independently has the probability $\lambda > 0$ of being lost in every step, and the transitions themselves are subject to probabilistic choice.

Remark 4. The definition of PLCS in [6,13,29] assumes that messages can be lost only after discrete steps, but not before them. Thus, since no messages can be lost before the first discrete step, the set $\{s \in S : s \models \exists\Diamond F\}$ of predecessors of a given set F of target states is generally not upward closed. It is more realistic to assume that messages can be lost before and after discrete steps, in which case $\{s \in S : s \models \exists\Diamond F\}$ is upward closed. However, for both versions of the definition, it follows easily from the results in [2] that for any effectively representable set F, the set $\{s \in S : s \models \exists\Diamond F\}$ is decidable. □

In [6,13,9], it was shown that each Markov chain induced by a PLCS contains a finite attractor. Here we show a stronger result.

Lemma 7. *Each Markov chain induced by a PLCS contains a GR-attractor.*

Proof. For any configuration c, let $\#c$ be the number of messages in transit in c. We define the attractor A as the set of all configurations that contain at most m messages in transit, for a sufficiently high number m (to be determined). $A := \{c \mid \#c \leq m\}$. Since there are only finitely many different messages and a finite number of control-states, A is finite for every fixed m. The distance function h is defined by $h(c) := \max\{0, \#c - m\}$. Now we show that h satisfies the requirements for a GR-attractor. The first condition, $h(c) = 0 \iff c \in A$, holds by definition of h and A. The third condition holds, because, by definition of PLCS, at most one new message can be added in every single step. Consider now a configuration c with at least m messages. For the second condition it suffices to show that, for sufficiently large m, the probability of losing at least two messages in transit is at least $q > 1/2$ (and thus the new configuration contains at least one message less than the previous one, since at most one new message is added). The probability q of losing at least 2 messages (of at least $m+1$) satisfies $q \geq 1 - ((1-\lambda)^{m+1} + (m+1)\lambda(1-\lambda)^m) = 1 - (1-\lambda)^m(1+\lambda m))$. Since $\lambda > 0$, we can choose m s.t. $q > 1/2$. It suffices to take $m \geq \frac{2}{\lambda}$.

Theorem 3. *The problem* APPROX_EXPECT *is computable for PLCS.*

Proof. By Lemma 7 the Markov chain induced by a PLCS contains a GR-attractor, which is an eager attractor by Lemma 4. Then, by Theorem 2 the Markov chain is eager and Algorithm 1 can in principle solve the problem APPROX_EXPECT. However, to apply the algorithm, we first need to know (i.e., compute) the parameters (α, k), or at least sufficient upper bounds on them.

Given the parameter λ for message loss in the PLCS, we choose the parameter m and the GR-attractor A such that $q > 1/2$, as in the proof of Lemma 7. This attractor is eager with parameters $\beta = \sqrt{4(1-q)q} < 1$ and $b = 1$ by Lemma 4. For any effectively representable set of target states F of a PLCS, the set $\{s \in S : s \models \exists \Diamond F\}$ is decidable by Remark 4. Thus we can compute $B = A \cap \{s \in S : s \models \exists \Diamond F\}$ and obtain the parameter $w = |B|$. Since B is known and finite, we can compute an appropriate μ, i.e., a μ such that $0 < \mu \leq \min_{s \in B} \mathcal{P}_{\mathcal{M}}\left(s \models .(F\ \underline{\mathit{Before}}\ s)\right)$, by path exploration. When A, w, μ, β and b are known, we can compute, in turn, c, α_1, k_1, α_2, k_2, and finally α and k, according to Section 4.

Remark 5. Choosing a larger m (and thus larger attractor A) has advantages and disadvantages. The advantage is that a larger m yields a larger q and thus a smaller parameter $\beta = \sqrt{4pq}$ and thus possibly faster convergence. The disadvantage is that a larger attractor A possibly yields a smaller parameter μ and a larger parameter w (see Section 4) and both these effects cause slower convergence. □

5 Bounded Coarseness

In this section, we consider the class of Markov chains that are *boundedly coarse*. We first give definitions and a proof that boundedly coarse Markov chains are eager with respect to any state, and then examples of models that are boundedly coarse.

A Markov chain $\mathcal{M} = (S, P, F)$ is *boundedly coarse* with *parameter* (β, K) if, for every state s, either $s \not\models \exists \Diamond F$, or $\mathcal{P}_{\mathcal{M}}(s \models \Diamond^{\leq K} F) \geq \beta$.

Lemma 8. *If a Markov Chain $\mathcal{M}$ is boundedly coarse with parameter (β, K) then it is eager with respect to all states in $\mathcal{M}$ and the eagerness parameter (α, k) can be computed.*

Sufficient Condition. We give a sufficient condition for bounded coarseness. A state s is said to be of *coarseness* β if, for each $s' \in S$, $P(s, s') > 0$ implies $P(s, s') \geq \beta$. We say that $\mathcal{M}$ is of *coarseness* β if each state is of coarseness β, and $\mathcal{M}$ is *coarse* if it is of coarseness β, for some $\beta > 0$. Notice that if $\mathcal{M}$ is coarse then the underlying transition system is finitely branching; however, the converse is not necessarily true.

A transition system is *of span* K if for each $s \in S$, either $s \not\models \exists\Diamond F$ or $s \models \exists\Diamond^{\leq K} F$, i.e., either F is unreachable or it is reachable in at most K steps. A transition system is finitely spanning if it is of span K for some K and a Markov chain is finitely spanning (of span K) if its underlying transition system is so. The following result is immediate.

Lemma 9. *If a Markov chain is coarse (of coarseness β), and finitely spanning (of span K), then it is boundedly coarse with parameter (β^K, K).*

Probabilistic VASS. A *Probabilistic Vector Addition System with States (PVASS)* (see [3] for details) is an extended finite-state automaton which operates on a finite set of variables ranging over the natural numbers. The variables behave as weak counters (weak in the sense that they are not compared for equality with 0). Furthermore, each transition has a *weight* defined by a natural number. A PVASS $\mathcal{V}$ induces an (infinite-state) Markov chain $\mathcal{M}$ in a natural way where the states of $\mathcal{M}$ are configurations of $\mathcal{V}$ (the local state of the automaton together with the counter values), and the probability of performing a transition from a given configuration is defined by the weight of the transition relative to the weights of other transitions enabled in the same configuration.

It was shown in [3] that each Markov chain induced by a PVASS where the set F is *upward closed* (with respect to the standard ordering on configurations) is effective, coarse, and finitely spanning (with the span being computable). This, together with Lemmas 9 and 8, yields the following theorem.

Theorem 4. APPROX_EXPECT *is solvable for* PVASS *with an upward closed set of final configurations.*

Noisy Turing Machines. Noisy Turing Machines (NTMs) were recently introduced by Asarin and Collins [7]. They study NTMs from a theoretical point of view, considering the computational power as the noise level tends to zero, but motivate them by practical applications such as computers operating in a hostile environment where arbitrary memory bits can change with some small probability. We show that NTMs with a fixed noise level are boundedly coarse, so by Lemma 8, they induce eager Markov chains.

An NTM is like an M-tape Turing Machine (with a finite control part and a given final control state), except that prior to a transition, for each cell on each tape, with probability λ it is *subjected to noise*. In this case, it changes to one of the symbols in the alphabet (possibly the same as before) uniformly at random.

An NTM induces a Markov chain $\mathcal{M} = (S, P, F)$ as follows. A state in S is a triple: the current time, the current control state, and an M-tuple of *tape configurations*. A tape configuration is represented as a triple: the head position; a finite word w over the alphabet representing the contents of all cells visited by the head so far; and a $|w|$-tuple of natural numbers, each representing the last point in time when the head visited the corresponding cell.

These last-visit times allow us to add noise "lazily": cells not under the head are not modified. Since it is known when the head last visited each cell, we compensate for the missing noise by a higher noise probability for the cell under the head. If the cell was last visited k time units ago, we increase the probability of noise to $1 - (1 - \lambda)^k$, which is the probability that the cell is subject to noise in any of k steps. Then the last-visit time for the cell under the head is updated to contain the current time, and the next configuration is selected according to the behavior of the control part. The final states F are those where the control state is final.

Lemma 10. *The Markov chain induced by a Noisy Turing Machine is coarse and finitely spanning.*

By Lemmas 8, 9, and 10, NTMs are eager, and we have:

Theorem 5. APPROX_EXPECT *is solvable for NTMs.*

Remark 6. A somewhat simpler way to generate a Markov chain from an NTM avoids the need for a counter per tape cell. Instead, all cells ever visited by a head are subject to noise in each step. When a cell is visited for the first time, say after k steps, the probability of noise is increased to $1 - (1 - \lambda)^k$. This is an example of a Markov chain that is boundedly coarse but not coarse (the probability of a successor obtained by changing n tape cells is λ^n). □

6 Conclusion, Discussion, and Future Work

We have described a class of discrete Markov chains, called *eager Markov chains*, for which the probability of avoiding a defined set of final states F for more than n steps is bounded by some exponentially decreasing function $f(n)$. Finite-state Markov chains are trivially eager for any set of final states F.

Our main result is that several well-studied classes of *infinite-state* Markov chains are also eager, including PLCS, PVASS, and NTM. Furthermore, the bounding function $f(n)$ is effectively constructible for Markov chains in these classes.

We have presented a path exploration algorithm for approximating the conditional expected reward (defined via computable reward functions) up-to an arbitrarily small error. This algorithm is guaranteed to terminate for any eager Markov chain.

Directions for future work include extending our results to Markov decision processes and stochastic games.

References

1. P. A. Abdulla, C. Baier, P. Iyer, and B. Jonsson. Reasoning about probabilistic lossy channel systems. In *Proc. CONCUR 2000*, 2000.
2. P. A. Abdulla, K. Čerāns, B. Jonsson, and T. Yih-Kuen. Algorithmic analysis of programs with well quasi-ordered domains. *Information and Computation*, 160:109–127, 2000.
3. P. A. Abdulla, N. B. Henda, and R. Mayr. Verifying infinite Markov chains with a finite attractor or the global coarseness property. In *Proc. LICS '05*, pp. 127–136, 2005.
4. P. A. Abdulla, N. B. Henda, R. Mayr, and S. Sandberg. Eager Markov chains. Technical Report 2006-009, Department of Information Technology, Uppsala University, 2006.
5. P. A. Abdulla, N. B. Henda, R. Mayr, and S. Sandberg. Limiting behavior of Markov chains with eager attractors. In *Proc. QEST '06*. IEEE Computer Society Press, 2006. To appear.
6. P. A. Abdulla and A. Rabinovich. Verification of probabilistic systems with faulty communication. In *Proc. FOSSACS '03*, vol. 2620 of *LNCS*, pp. 39–53, 2003.
7. E. Asarin and P. Collins. Noisy Turing machines. In *Proc. ICALP '05*, pp. 1031–1042, 2005.

8. A. Aziz, K. Sanwal, V. Singhal, and R. Brayton. Model-checking continuous-time Markov chains. *ACM Trans. on Computational Logic*, 1(1):162–170, 2000.
9. C. Baier, N. Bertrand, and P. Schnoebelen. A note on the attractor-property of infinite-state Markov chains. *Information Processing Letters*, 97(2):58–63, 2006.
10. C. Baier and B. Engelen. Establishing qualitative properties for probabilistic lossy channel systems. In Katoen, editor, *ARTS '99, Formal Methods for Real-Time and Probabilistic Systems, 5th Int. AMAST Workshop*, vol. 1601 of *LNCS*, pp. 34–52. Springer Verlag, 1999.
11. C. Baier, B. Haverkort, H. Hermanns, and J.-P. Katoen. Model checking meets performance evaluation. *ACM Performance Evaluation Review*, 32(2):10–15, 2005.
12. C. Baier, B. R. Haverkort, H. Hermanns, and J.-P. Katoen. Automated performance and dependability evaluation using model checking. In *Proc. Performance 2002*, pp. 261–289, 2002.
13. N. Bertrand and P. Schnoebelen. Model checking lossy channels systems is probably decidable. In *Proc. FOSSACS03*, vol. 2620 of *LNCS*, pp. 120–135, 2003.
14. T. Brázdil and A. Kučera. Computing the expected accumulated reward and gain for a subclass of infinite Markov chains. In *Proc. FSTTCS '05*, vol. 3821 of *LNCS*, pp. 372–383, 2005.
15. E. Clarke, O. Grumberg, and D. Peled. *Model Checking*. MIT Press, Dec. 1999.
16. C. Courcoubetis and M. Yannakakis. The complexity of probabilistic verification. *Journal of the ACM*, 42(4):857–907, 1995.
17. L. de Alfaro, M. Z. Kwiatkowska, G. Norman, D. Parker, and R. Segala. Symbolic model checking of probabilistic processes using mtbdds and the Kronecker representation. In *Proc. TACAS '00*, vol. 1785 of *LNCS*, pp. 123–137, 2000.
18. J. Esparza and K. Etessami. Verifying probabilistic procedural programs. In *Proc. FSTTCS '04*, pp. 16–31, 2004.
19. J. Esparza, A. Kučera, and R. Mayr. Model checking probabilistic pushdown automata. In *Proc. LICS '04*, pp. 12–21, 2004.
20. J. Esparza, A. Kučera, and R. Mayr. Quantitative analysis of probabilistic pushdown automata: Expectations and variances. In *Proc. LICS '05*, pp. 117–126, 2005.
21. K. Etessami and M. Yannakakis. Algorithmic verification of recursive probabilistic state machines. In *Proc. TACAS '05*, vol. 3440 of *LNCS*, pp. 253–270, 2005.
22. K. Etessami and M. Yannakakis. Recursive Markov chains, stochastic grammars, and monotone systems of non-linear equations. In *Proc. STACS '05*, vol. 2996 of *LNCS*, pp. 340–352, 2005.
23. K. Etessami and M. Yannakakis. Recursive Markov decision processes and recursive stochastic games. In *Proc. ICALP '05*, vol. 3580 of *LNCS*, pp. 891–903, 2005.
24. W. Feller. *An Introduction to Probability Theory and Its Applications*, vol. 1. Wiley & Sons, second edition, 1966.
25. S. Hart and M. Sharir. Probabilistic temporal logics for finite and bounded models. In *Proc. STOC '84*, pp. 1–13, 1984.
26. P. Iyer and M. Narasimha. Probabilistic lossy channel systems. In *TAPSOFT '97: Theory and Practice of Software Development*, vol. 1214 of *LNCS*, pp. 667–681, 1997.
27. M. Kwiatkowska, G. Norman, and D. Parker. Probabilistic model checking in practice: Case studies with PRISM. *ACM Performance Evaluation Review*, 32(2):16–21, 2005.
28. D. Lehmann and S. Shelah. Reasoning with time and chance. *Information and Control*, 53:165–198, 1982.
29. A. Rabinovich. Quantitative analysis of probabilistic lossy channel systems. In *Proc. ICALP '03*, vol. 2719 of *LNCS*, pp. 1008–1021, 2003.
30. P. Stănică. Good lower and upper bounds on binomial coefficients. *Journal of Inequalities in Pure and Applied Mathematics*, 2(3), 2001.
31. M. Vardi. Automatic verification of probabilistic concurrent finite-state programs. In *Proc. FOCS '85*, pp. 327–338, 1985.

A Probabilistic Learning Approach for Counterexample Guided Abstraction Refinement*

Fei He[1,2], Xiaoyu Song[3], Ming Gu[2], and Jiaguang Sun[2]

[1] Dept. Computer Science & Technology, Tsinghua University, Beijing, China
hef02@mails.tsinghua.edu.cn
[2] School of Software, Tsinghua University, Beijing, China
[3] Dept. ECE, Portland State University, Oregon, USA

Abstract. The paper presents a novel probabilistic learning approach to state separation problem which occurs in the counterexample guided abstraction refinement. The method is based on the sample learning technique, evolutionary algorithm and effective probabilistic heuristics. Compared with the previous work by the sampling decision tree learning solver, the proposed method outperforms 2 to 4 orders of magnitude faster and the size of the separation set is 76% smaller on average.

1 Introduction

Abstraction is one of the most important techniques when applying model checking to large scale systems. The hypostasis of abstraction is to eliminate the irrelevant information to reduce the system model. The counterexample-guided abstraction refinement (CEGAR) [1] is an effective strategy in application of abstraction. In CEGAR, the verification is performed in an abstract-check-refine fashion, and the refinement is guided by counterexamples. The counterexample contains the critical clues about the cause of the violation. If there exists a real path in the concrete model that simulates the counterexample, one can find a real bug, otherwise the counterexample is spurious and one has to refine the abstract model to eliminate such a spurious path.

Many counterexample-guided abstraction refinement strategies have been proposed [2, 3, 4, 5, 6, 7]. Some recent methods on automatic abstraction [8, 6, 9, 10] employ the unsatisfiable core saved in the SAT solver, and the abstraction is based on the proofs provided by the SAT solver, but not on refuting the counterexamples. In [3], the abstraction is performed by making a set of state variables invisible. If the counterexample is spurious, we need to refine the abstract model. State separation problem poses the main hurdle during the refinement.

* This work was supported in part by the Chinese National 973 Plan under grant No. 2004CB719406 and NSF of China under grant No. 60553002.

S. Graf and W. Zhang (Eds.): ATVA 2006, LNCS 4218, pp. 39–50, 2006.

In this paper, we propose a novel probabilistic learning approach to state separation problem (SSP) which occurs in the abstraction refinement. Our approach incorporates sample learning technique, evolutionary algorithm and effective heuristics in a synergistic way. Experimental results demonstrate the promising performance of our approach. In comparison with the previous work by the sampling decision tree learning solver [3], the proposed method outperforms 2 to 4 orders of magnitude faster and the size of the separation set is 76% smaller on average.

The remainder of the paper is organized as follows. In Section 2, we introduce some preliminaries. In Section 3, we formally define the problem. In Section 4, we present our probabilistic learning approach. The experimental results are reported in Section 5. Finally, Section 6 concludes the paper.

2 Preliminaries

We use state transition systems to model systems. Given a non-empty set of atomic propositions AP, let $M = \langle S, S_0, R, L\rangle$ be a transition system where

- S is the set of states.
- $S_0 \subseteq S$ is the set of initial states.
- $R \subseteq S \times S$ is the transition relation.
- $L : S \rightarrow 2^{AP}$ is the labeling function.

Let $V = \{v_1, v_2, \ldots v_{|V|}\}$ be the universal domain of system variables. We assume that the variables in V range over a finite set D. A valuation for V corresponds to a state in S.

As in [3], we think of V as two parts: the set of *visible* variables (denoted as V_S) and the set of *invisible* variables (denoted as V_N). Invisible variables are those that we will ignore when build the model. For example, consider a digital system with latches. The subset of the latches in which we are interested is considered as visible variables, while the remaining latches are regarded as invisible.

In the original (non-abstracted) model, all system variables are visible. The abstraction process is essentially equivalent to selecting and setting some of the visible variables as invisible. Oppositely, the refinement process is to make some of the invisible variables as visible.

Let M be the original model. We use $\tilde{M} = \langle \tilde{S}, \tilde{S_0}, \tilde{R}, \tilde{L}\rangle$ to denote the abstract model, where the definitions of $\tilde{S}$, $\tilde{S_0}$ $\tilde{R}$ and $\tilde{L}$ follow those in M.

Notice that we require our abstraction to be conservative, that is: $\tilde{R}(\tilde{s_1}, \tilde{s_2})$ holds if and only if there exist s_1 in $h^{-1}(\tilde{s_1})$ and s_2 in $h^{-1}(\tilde{s_2})$, such that $R(s_1, s_2)$ holds, where h is the abstract function from S to $\tilde{S}$. Such a conservative translation may introduce additional behaviors into the abstract model. Consider the example shown in Fig. 1, after mapping the concrete states 7, 8, 9 to III, and 10 to IV, respectively, the additional transitions $7 \rightarrow 10$, $8 \rightarrow 10$ are added implicitly to the abstract model.

Given an abstract path $\tilde{P} = \langle \tilde{s_1}, \tilde{s_2}, \ldots \tilde{s_m}\rangle$ in $\tilde{M}$ and a concrete path $P = \langle s_1, s_2, \ldots s_m\rangle$ in M, we define the simulation relation $\sim$ as follows:

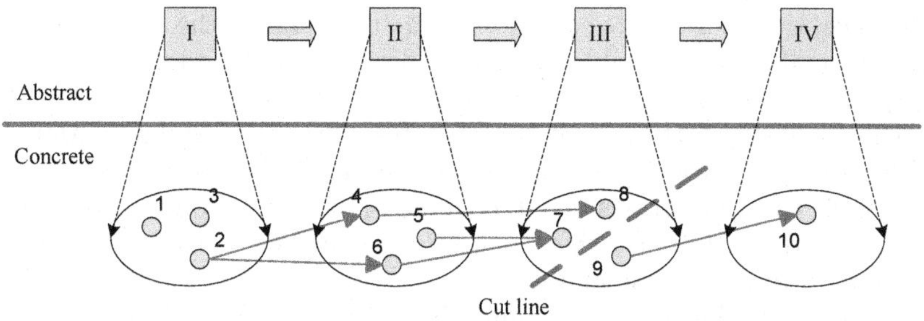

Fig. 1. A spurious counterexample

$$P \sim \tilde{P} \iff s_1 \in S_0 \text{ and } s_1 \in h^{-1}(\tilde{s_1}), s_2 \in h^{-1}(\tilde{s_2}), \ldots s_m \in h^{-1}(\tilde{s_m}). \quad (1)$$

In the counterexample-guided approach, if we find a counterexample $\tilde{P}$ in the abstract model, we check if there is a concrete path P in M such that $P \sim \tilde{P}$. If it is true, we find a real bug. Otherwise, the counterexample is spurious. In the case of the spurious counterexample, we need to compute the *failure index* i_F, i.e. the maximal index i_F, $i_F < m$, such that there exists a concrete path in M which simulates the i_F prefix of $\tilde{P}$. With the failure index, we define the *failure states* to be the group of concrete states $F = \{s | s \in h^{-1}(\tilde{s_{i_F}})\}$ in M. Consider the example in Fig. 1, the failure index is III, and the failure states are 7, 8 and 9.

The failure states can be partitioned into three sets.

1. the set of deadend states F_d: $s \in F_d$ if and only if
   - $s \in F$;
   - there exists a concrete path to s which simulates the i_F prefix of $\tilde{P}$.
2. the set of bad states F_b: $s \in F_b$ if and only if
   - $s \in F$;
   - there exists no concrete path to s which simulates the i_F prefix of $\tilde{P}$;
   - there exists a transition from s to some states in $h^{-1}(s_{i_F+1})$.
3. $F - F_d - F_b$.

3 State Separation Problem

The State Separation Problem (SSP) [3] is to find a subset Λ of the invisible variables in V_N such that

$$\forall s_i \in F_d, \forall t_j \in F_b, \exists v_r \in \Lambda, s_i(v_r) \neq t_j(v_r). \quad (2)$$

The set Λ is named as *separation set.* We usually want the separation set to be as minimal as possible so that the corresponding refined model is minimal. This problem is known as the *minimal state separation problem* (MSSP).

Consider the abstract counterexample $\hat{P} = \langle \text{I, II, III, IV} \rangle$ shown in Fig. 1. It is spurious since there is no corresponding path in the concrete model. For this instance, the failure states are 7, 8 and 9. To eliminate the counterexample, we need to make some variables visible to distinguish the sets of states $\{7, 8\}$ and $\{9\}$.

In realistic systems, the size of failure states is usually very large. Moreover, since the state separation problem is embedded in the abstract-check-refine iteration, each time a spurious counterexample is found, a solution to the SSP needs to be provided. Thus, there is a strong demand for the effectiveness of SSP solvers in terms of time and memory.

In [3], an integer linear programming (ILP) model for the minimal state separation problem (MSSP) has been presented, and both an ILP solver and a decision tree learning (DTL) solver are employed for solving this problem. The general ILP solver attempts to enumerate the solution space to find the optimal solution for the state separation problem. However, since the minimal state separation problem is NP-hard, it is infeasible for the ILP solver to find the solution when the problem size is large. Note that we do not necessarily need the solution to be minimal. An approximate optimum may still good enough for the refinement process, nevertheless, the resulting refined model may be slightly bigger. In [3], an improved solver was proposed, which is based on the decision tree learning. The DTL algorithm trains the decision tree based on the input examples. It utilizes the well-trained decision tree to classify data. With some adjustments on the parameters, the DTL algorithm is used to solve the state separation problem, and the structure of its decision tree just gives a possible solution. Obviously, the DTL approach is an approximate method. Its solution precision relies on the number of input examples. If there are a sufficient number of examples, the solution could be guaranteed. However, if the input examples are too many, the time cost is extremely high. Thus, there is a trade-off between the solution precision and the solving cost. Furthermore, in coping with the large problem size, an efficient sampling technique has been applied to the DTL solver. Experimental results show that DTL solver with efficient sampling technique (for short, SDTL) outperforms the ordinary DTL solver [2].

3.1 Problem Formulation

In this section, we first prove the NP-hardness of MSSP by reducing it to the set covering problem. Then we present a new mathematical model for MSSP.

Definition 1. *Given a pair of states* $\langle s, t\rangle$, $s \in F_d$, $t \in F_b$, *if there exists a variable* v, *such that* $s(v) \neq t(v)$, *we say that the state pair* $\langle s, t\rangle$ *is* covered *by the variable* v.

Proposition 1. *The MSSP is reducible to the set covering problem.*

Proof. Consider $F_d \times F_b$ as the universal set. Obviously, each variable in V_N covers a subset of elements in $F_d \times F_b$, i.e. each variable corresponds to a subset of $F_d \times F_b$. Then according to the definition, the MSSP is essentially to find a minimal collection of subsets of $F_d \times F_b$ such to cover all the elements in $F_d \times F_b$. Obviously, it is a set covering problem. □

Given a MSSP instance, assume there are n invisible variables and m state pairs. For simplicity, we use $p_j, 1 \leq j \leq m$, to denote a state pair in $F_d \times F_b$, i.e. $F_d \times F_b = \{p_1, p_2, \dots, p_m\}$. We define the decision variables as follows:

$$x_i = \begin{cases} 1, \text{ if } v_i \in \Lambda, \\ 0, \text{ else.} \end{cases}$$

Assume $p_j = \langle s^{p_j}, t^{p_j} \rangle$, where

$$s^{p_j} = \langle s_1^{p_j}, s_2^{p_j}, \dots, s_n^{p_j} \rangle$$

and

$$t^{p_j} = \langle t_1^{p_j}, t_2^{p_j}, \dots, t_n^{p_j} \rangle.$$

According to (2), p_j must be covered by certain variable in the separation set, i.e.

$$\exists i \in \Lambda, s_i^{p_j} \neq t_i^{p_j}.$$

It is equivalent to:

$$\sum_{i=1 \text{ to } n} (s_i^{p_j} \oplus t_i^{p_j}) \cdot x_i \geq 1, \tag{3}$$

where $\oplus$ is the *exclusive or* operator, and x_i the decision variable of v_i.

Let $A = \{a_{ij}\}_{m \times n}$ be a coefficient matrix where

$$a_{ij} = s_i^{p_j} \oplus t_i^{p_j}, \text{ for } 1 \leq i \leq n, 1 \leq j \leq m.$$

Obviously, a_{ij} equals 1 if and only if the state pair p_j is covered by the variable v_i. Then the MSSP can be formulated as:

$$\min \sum_{i=1}^{n} x_i, \text{ where}$$

$$\sum_{i=1}^{n} a_{ij} x_i \geq 1, \qquad j = 1, \dots, m \tag{4}$$

$$x_i = \{0, 1\}, \qquad i = 1, \dots, n \tag{5}$$

where equations (4) and (5) characterize the feasible solutions.

4 Our Approach

In the verification process, note that we do not necessarily need the solutions of SSP to be minimal. Thus, it is possible for us to use some approximate method to solve this problem. In [3], a decision tree learning solver is proposed. In this paper, we present a novel learning approach based on the sample learning technique, evolutionary algorithm and efficient heuristics. Experimental results show the better performance of our solver.

4.1 Sample Learning Technique

In practice, the number of failure states of SSP is very large. It is not easy to determine the separation set for large scale systems. In [3], an idea of inferring the separation set by learning from some selected samples, instead of the entire sets, was introduced.

The main procedure of our Sample Learning Approach (SLA) is shown in Alg. 1.. The method avoids the complexity of SSP by considering only samples of the set of state pairs. This algorithm is iterative. By adjusting the parameters *MAX_ITER* and *MAX_SAM*, we set the maximal number of iterations and the maximal number of samples picked in every iteration. A sample here is a pair of states $\langle s, t\rangle \in F_d \times F_b$. The algorithm randomly picks *MAX_SAM* samples in every iteration, among which only those that are not covered by the present separation set (we call them efficient samples) can be added into the set *SAMPLE*. The *REQ_SIZE* is a preassigned parameter. When there are enough efficient samples generated, the set of samples will be renewed, and then the separation set is computed.

Note that we use the covering concept to judge the validity of the given samples. The samples that are already covered by the present separation set will be directly discarded. Given an appropriate value to the *REQ_SIZE*, many samples will be discarded directly according to their coverage to the present separation set, and thus the number of invoking EA solver will be greatly reduced.

Let $A_j = \langle a_{0j}, a_{1j}, \ldots, a_{nj}\rangle$ be the coefficient vector corresponding to p_j. According to (3), it is not difficult to determine the coverage of p_j to the present separation set Λ. It is equivalent to testing true value of the following formula:

$$\sum_{i=1 \text{ to } n} a_{ij} \cdot x_i \geq 1.$$

4.2 Probabilistic Evolutionary Algorithm

Evolutionary algorithm (EA) [11] is a powerful search and optimization paradigm. It utilizes the principles of natural evolution and "survival of the fittest". The EA elaborates on many solutions at the same time. The main characteristic of an evolutionary algorithm is population-based. Starting with a set of initial solutions, evolutionary algorithms explore the solution space through the simulated evolution. Solutions are evaluated by their fitness. The more suitable they are, the more chances they have to survive and be reproduced.

There are many studies on applying evolutionary algorithms to the set covering problem [12,13,14,15]. The experimental results listed in the above literatures show the good performance of applying EA to the set covering problem. However, we cannot apply EA directly to the SSP, since the huge number of failure states. Essentially, SSP is a special case of set covering problem, where the number of constraints is much more than the number of variables. By applying the sample learning technique, we avoid the complexity of such huge number of constraints.

Algorithm 1. Outline of the sample learning algorithm

```
Λ := φ
SAMPLE := φ
NEWSAMPLE := φ
for i := 1 to MAX_ITER do
  for i := 1 to MAX_SAM do
    randomly pick ⟨s,t⟩ from F_d × F_b
    if ⟨s,t⟩ cannot be covered by Λ then
      NEWSAMPLE := NEWSAMPLE ∪⟨s,t⟩
    end if
  end for
  if sizeof(NEWSAMPLE) ≥ REQ_SIZE then
    SAMPLE := SAMPLE ∪ NEWSAMPLE
    call solver to compute Λ based on SAMPLE
    NEWSAMPLE := φ
  end if
end for
```

Algorithm 2. Evolutionary algorithm

```
1: Generate a initial population
2: while not (terminal condition) do
3:   Update the chromosomes by crossover and mutation operations
4:   Evaluate the fitness of each chromosome
5:   Select chromosomes to form a new population
6: end while
```

We use EA as the central solver embedded in the learning structure and used for computing the separation set. The EA procedure is shown in Alg. 2..

We reinforce the basic EA in a way such that problem-specific knowledge is incorporated. We observe following properties in SSP, which derive the effective heuristics:

1. For a state pair, there may be multiple variables that can cover it.
2. If the variables in a separation set cover all state pairs in $F_d \times F_b$, then the corresponding solution is already a feasible solution.

In order to get a feasible solution more quickly, an effective strategy is to assign larger probabilities to the variables which cover more state pairs. Denote $EV(v)$ as the number of state pairs covered by variable v. Based on the statistic analysis on the sets of states F_d and F_b, the $EV(v)$ values for all variables can be evaluated easily in advance of the execution of our algorithm.

Probabilistic Initialization. We use a n-bit binary string as the chromosome structure where n is the number of invisible variables. A value of 1 for the i-th bit implies that the variable v_i is selected into the separation set.

We generate *pop_size* chromosomes to initialize the population. To obtain a random chromosome, the involved method acts as follows:

1. randomly generate an integer e $(0 \leq e \leq n)$, and use it as the size of the separation set.
2. randomly select e variables into the separation set.
3. the probability of each variable to be selected is proportional to the number of state pairs it covers.

Probabilistic Mutation. Let P_m be the probability of mutation. We adopt the two-point mutation. For a traditional two-point mutation, it randomly selects two points r_1 and r_2 in the chromosome, and then replaces the value of every character between sites r_1 and r_2 with a random value (0 or 1).

In our probabilistic two-point mutation, the mutation sites r_1 and r_2 are selected similarly, however, the value of each character between site r_1 and r_2 are replaced in a heuristic way as follows:

1. randomly generate a integer e $(0 \leq e < r_2 - r_1)$.
2. randomly select e genes between sites r_1 and r_2 into the separation set.
3. the probability of each gene between sites r_1 and r_2 to be chosen is proportional to the number of state pairs it covers.

Probabilistic Crossover. We let P_c be the probability of crossover. We adopt the uniform crossover operator. It is claimed that the uniform crossover has a better recombination potential to combine smaller building blocks into larger ones [16,17]. The uniform crossover works with a crossover mask which is created at random. The mask has the same length as the chromosome structure, and the parity of the bits indicates the corresponding parent.

We follow the probabilistic crossover operator defined in [12]. Empirical studies show that this crossover operator is suitable for the set covering problem. Probabilistic crossover is derived from the standard uniform crossover. For the probabilistic crossover operator, the probability of a parent to be chosen for contributing its variable to the offspring is proportional to its fitness value. Formally, given parents $P = \langle P_1 P_2 \ldots P_n \rangle$ and $Q = \langle Q_1 Q_2 \ldots Q_n \rangle$, the crossover mask $M = \langle M_1 M_2 \ldots M_n \rangle$ is generated as follows:

$$M_i = 0 \text{ with the probability } p = \frac{fitness(Q)}{fitness(P) + fitness(Q)}$$

$$M_i = 1 \text{ with the probability } 1 - p$$

Solution Improvement. When applying evolutionary operators to the chromosomes, the resulting solutions are no longer guaranteed to be feasible. We implemented two strategies to deal with infeasible solutions.

The first strategy is to apply penalty function to deteriorate the optimality of an infeasible solution by adding a penalty cost to its objective function. In our approach, after the penalty function applied, the optimization model becomes:

$$\text{Minimize} \sum_{i=1}^{n} x_i + \sum_{j=1}^{m} f(\sum_{i=1}^{n} a_{ij} x_j \geq 1),$$

where $f(\cdot)$ is the penalty function for unsatisfying the constraints (4). The penalty function has a strong influence on the performance of the whole algorithm. In our approach, we implement a simple and efficient penalty function as follows:

$$f(x) = \begin{cases} 0, & \text{if } x \text{ is true}, \\ \text{BIGVALUE}, & \text{otherwise}. \end{cases}$$

The second strategy way is to apply a heuristic operator to transform the infeasible solution into feasible solution. We implemented the heuristic feasibility operator proposed in [12] with minor modifications. By applying this heuristic operator, not only can the infeasible solutions be transformed into feasible solutions, but also the feasible solutions can be improved by eliminating the redundant variables. Algorithm 3. gives the framework of the operator.

Algorithm 3. Heuristic feasibility operator

1: for each A_j, compute the number of variables that are in the separation set and can cover this row, i.e.

$$n_j = \sum_{i=1}^{n} a_{ij} x_i, \text{ for } 1 \le j \le m.$$

2: **while** $(\exists j \in [1, m], n_j = 0)$ **do**

3: find the best variable v^* which is not in the separation set and can cover maximal number of uncovered rows, i.e.

$$\max_{i=1}^{n} \left\{ \sum_{j=1}^{m} (n_i = 0) \wedge (x_j = 0) \wedge (a_{ij} = 1) \right\}.$$

4: add v^* into the solution and renew n_j for each A_j.

5: eliminate the redundant variables, i.e. the variables satisfying:

$$\forall j \in [1, m], (a_{ij} = 1) \wedge (x_i = 1) \rightarrow n_j \ge 2.$$

6: **end while**

5 Experimental Results

To validate our approach, we implemented our probabilistic learning approach using C++ language and ran on a PC with Intel® Celeron® 2.4GHz CPU and 512M RAM. All benchmarks are created using a random generator. The parameters are set as: *pop_size* = 40, *MaxIter* = 1000, $P_m = 0.25$, $P_c = 0.5$, where *pop_size* is the size of the population, *MaxIter* is the maximal number of generations, P_m and P_c are the probabilities of mutation and crossover, respectively.

The experiment compares the performance of our solver to the latest published sampling decision tree learning (SDTL) solver [2,3]. The results are listed

Table 1. Our solver vs. SDTL

Benchmark	Our solver		SDTL	
	time	|SepSet|	time	|SepSet|
ran_k10_m150_n120	0.141	7	15.954	10
ran_k20_m150_n120	0.422	7	30.594	20
ran_k30_m150_n120	0.594	6	35.891	28
ran_k40_m150_n120	0.656	7	51.813	31
ran_k50_m150_n120	2.953	6	53.312	38
ran_k20_m500_n300	0.515	7	1197.562	20
ran_k30_m500_n300	1.281	7	1836.203	30
ran_k40_m500_n300	1.454	7	2664.453	40
ran_k50_m500_n300	3.907	7	3476.797	46
ran_k60_m500_n300	2.89	7	4360.484	55
ran_k30_m150_n200	0.719	6	78.485	29
ran_k30_m500_n1000	1.985	8	4028.937	30
ran_k30_m3000_n4000	3.813	8	timeout	
ran_k30_m5000_n4000	3.922	8	timeout	
ran_k40_m200_n250	1.735	7	470.078	36
ran_k40_m1000_n2000	4.703	8	timeout	
ran_k40_m2000_n5000	5.734	8	timeout	
ran_k40_m8000_n7000	8.859	8	timeout	
ran_k50_m200_n300	1.891	7	1026.672	43
ran_k50_m1000_n2000	8.672	7	timeout	
ran_k50_m2000_n5000	12.687	8	timeout	
ran_k50_m8000_n7000	23.515	9	timeout	
ran_k60_m200_n300	1.125	6	1595.594	47
ran_k60_m1000_n2000	7.578	8	timeout	
ran_k60_m2000_n5000	11.625	8	timeout	

in Table 1. *Benchmark* is the name of the tested benchmark. The benchmark's name implies the parameters. For example, the name "$ran\_k30\_m500\_n300$" indicates that the number of invisible variables is 30, the number of deadend states is 500, and the number of bad states is 300, respectively. The *time* column lists the runtime in seconds, and the |SepSet| column gives the size of the resulting separation set. We evaluate the efficiency of the solver by its runtime, and the solution quality by the size of the separation set. In order to force termination, we impose a limit of two hours on the running time. We denote by 'timeout' in the *time* column the examples that could not be solved in this time limit.

The results in Table 1 are arranged into six groups. In the former two groups, we let the numbers of deadend states and bad states be fixed, and let the number of invisible variables increase, we observed that all the solvers' run times increase in most of cases. In the latter four groups, we fixed the number of invisible variables, and let the number of deadend states and bad states increase, we observed that the SDTL solver quickly blows up, whereas our solver still works well. Even for the benchmarks that are solvable by both the solvers, the runtime of our solver are 2 to 4 orders of magnitude smaller than that of the SDTL solver. Regarding the separation set size, the separation set found by our solver is smaller 76% than that by the SDTL solver on average.

6 Conclusion

We investigated the state separation problem in this paper. A novel probabilistic learning approach was presented for solving this problem. Experimental results showed the efficiency and power of our approach. Compared with the latest work using the sampling decision tree learning (SDTL) solver, the proposed approach outperforms 2 to 4 orders of magnitude faster and the size of the separation set is 76% smaller on average.

References

1. Clarke, E.M., Grumberg, O., Jha, S., Lu, Y., Veith, H.: Counterexample-guided abstraction refinement. In: Computer Aided Verification. (2000) 154–169
2. Clarke, E.M., Gupta, A., Kukula, J.H., Strichman, O.: SAT based abstraction-refinement using ILP and machine learning techniques. In: CAV. (2002) 265–279
3. Clarke, E., Gupta, A., Strichman, O.: SAT based counterexample-guided abstraction-refinement. IEEE Transactions on Computer Aided Design **23**(7) (2004) 1113–1123
4. Henzinger, T.A., Jhala, R., Majumdar, R., Sutre, G.: Lazy abstraction. In: Symposium on Principles of Programming Languages. (2002) 58–70
5. Glusman, M., Kamhi, G., Mador-Haim, S., Fraer, R., Vardi, M.Y.: Multiple-counterexample guided iterative abstraction refinement: an industrial evaluation. In: TACAS. (2003) 176–191
6. Gupta, A., Strichman, O.: Abstraction refinement for bounded model checking. In: Computer Aided Verification. (2005) 112–124
7. Govindaraju, S.G., Dill, D.L.: Counterexample-guided choice of projections in approximate symbolic model checking. In: ICCAD. (2000) 115–119
8. McMillan, K.L., Amla, N.: Automatic abstraction without counterexamples. In: TACAS. (2003) 2–17
9. Gupta, A., Ganai, M.K., Yang, Z., Ashar, P.: Iterative abstraction using SAT-based BMC with proof analysis. In: ICCAD. (2003) 416–423
10. Wang, C., Jin, H., Hachtel, G.D., Somenzi, F.: Refining the SAT decision ordering for bounded model checking. In: DAC. (2004) 535–538
11. Dumitrescu, D., Lazzerini, B., Jain, L., Dumitrescu, A.: Evolutionary Computation. CRC Press (2000)
12. Beasley, J., Chu, P.: A genetic algorithm for the set covering problem. European Journal of Operational Research **94** (1996) 392–404
13. Sen, S.: Minimal cost set covering using probabilistic methods. In: Proceedings of the 1993 ACM/SIGAPP symposium on Applied computing, Indianapolis, Indiana, United States, ACM Press (1993) 157–164
14. Aickelin, U.: An indirect genetic algorithm for set covering problems. Journal of the Operational Research Society **53**(10) (2002) 1118–1126
15. Marchiori, E., Steenbeek, A.: An evolutionary algorithm for large scale set covering problems with application to airline crew scheduling. In: EvoWorkshops. Volume 1803 of Lecture Notes in Computer Science., Springer (2000) 367–381

16. Syswerda, G.: Uniform crossover in genetic algorithms. In: Proceedings of the 3rd International Conference on Genetic Algorithms, San Mateo, California, USA, Morgan Kaufmann Publishers Inc. (1989) 2–9
17. Spears, W.M., De Jong, K.A.: On the virtues of parameterized uniform crossover. In Belew, R., Booker, L., eds.: Proceedings of the Fourth International Conference on Genetic Algorithms, San Mateo, CA, Morgan Kaufman (1991) 230–236

A Fine-Grained Fullness-Guided Chaining Heuristic for Symbolic Reachability Analysis*

Ming-Ying Chung, Gianfranco Ciardo, and Andy Jinqing Yu

Department of Computer Science and Engineering
University of California, Riverside
{chung, ciardo, jqyu}@cs.ucr.edu

Abstract. Chaining can reduce the number of iterations required for symbolic state-space generation and model-checking, especially in Petri nets and similar asynchronous systems, but requires considerable insight and is limited to a static ordering of the events in the high-level model. We introduce a two-step approach that is instead fine-grained and dynamically applied to the decision diagrams nodes. The first step, based on a precedence relation, is guaranteed to improve convergence, while the second one, based on a notion of node fullness, is heuristic. We apply our approach to traditional breadth-first and saturation state-space generation, and show that it is effective in both cases.

1 Introduction

BDD-based symbolic model checking [17] is one of the most successful techniques to verify industrial hardware and embedded software systems, and symbolic reachability analysis is a fundamental step in symbolic model checking. It is well-known that the peak number of BDD nodes is often much larger than the final number of BDD nodes for symbolic reachability analysis. In this paper, we propose a new *chaining* technique to reduce this peak number.

For asynchronous concurrent systems, such as distributed software, network protocols, and various classes of Petri nets, *chaining* [22] can reduce the peak memory usage and speed-up symbolic state-space generation by exploring events in a particularly favorable order. Chaining is normally applied as a modification of a strict breadth-first search (BFS), but it is also one of the factors behind the efficiency of the *saturation* algorithm [6]. As introduced, however, chaining is limited to finding a good order in which to apply the high-level model events during the symbolic iterations.

In this paper, we propose a general and effective heuristic that uses a partial-order relation and the concept of decision diagram node *fullness* to guide the chaining order, independent of the high-level formalism used to model the system. Our definition of node fullness is related to, but different from, the BDD node *density* defined in [20]. A detailed comparison can be found in Sect. 6.

* Work supported in part by the National Science Foundation under grants CNS-0501747 and CNS-0501748.

S. Graf and W. Zhang (Eds.): ATVA 2006, LNCS 4218, pp. 51–66, 2006.

Sect. 2 gives background on structured models, decision diagrams, BFS-based and saturation-based symbolic state-space generation, and chaining. Sect. 3 details our main contribution, where a fine-grained chaining is applied dynamically using the current structure of the decision diagram, rather than the model events. Sect. 4 describes the modified symbolic state-space generation algorithms incorporating our heuristic and gives implementation details. Sect. 5 provides numerical results on a suite of models showing that our heuristic reduces the runtime and memory requirements of both BFS-based and saturation-based algorithms. Sect. 6 compares the newly proposed chaining heuristics with some related work. Finally, Sect. 7 concludes with directions for future research.

2 Preliminaries

We consider a discrete-state model $(\widehat{\mathcal{S}}, \mathcal{S}^{init}, \mathcal{R})$, where $\widehat{\mathcal{S}}$ is a finite set of states, $\mathcal{S}^{init} \subseteq \widehat{\mathcal{S}}$ are the initial states, and $\mathcal{R} \subseteq \widehat{\mathcal{S}} \times \widehat{\mathcal{S}}$ is a transition relation. We assume the (*global*) model state to be a tuple of K *local state* variables, $(x_K, ..., x_1)$, where, for $K \geq l \geq 1$, $x_l \in \mathcal{S}_l = \{0, 1, ..., n_l - 1\}$, with $n_l > 0$, is the the lth *local* state variable. Thus, $\widehat{\mathcal{S}} = \mathcal{S}_K \times \cdots \times \mathcal{S}_1$ and we write $\mathcal{R}(\mathbf{i}[K], ..., \mathbf{i}[1], \mathbf{j}[K], ..., \mathbf{j}[1])$, or $\mathcal{R}(\mathbf{i}, \mathbf{j})$, if the model can move from *current state* $\mathbf{i}$ to *next state* $\mathbf{j}$ in one step.

2.1 Symbolic Encoding of State Space and Transition Relation

State-space generation consists of building the smallest set of states $\mathcal{S} \subseteq \widehat{\mathcal{S}}$ satisfying $\mathcal{S} \supseteq \mathcal{S}^{init}$ and $\mathcal{S} \supseteq Img(\mathcal{S}, \mathcal{R})$, where the *image computation* function gives the set of successor states: $Img(\mathcal{S}, \mathcal{R}) = \{\mathbf{j} : \exists \mathbf{i} \in \mathcal{S}, \mathcal{R}(\mathbf{i}, \mathbf{j})\}$. Most symbolic approaches to store the state space encode x_l using $\lceil \log n_l \rceil$ boolean variables and a set of states $\mathcal{Z}$ using a BDD with $\sum_{K \geq l \geq 1} \lceil \log n_l \rceil$ levels.

We prefer to discuss our approach in terms of *ordered multi-way decision diagrams* (MDDs) [14], where each variable x_l is directly encoded in a single level, using a node with n_l outgoing edges. MDDs can be implemented directly, the approach taken in our tool SMART [3], or as an interface to BDDs [25].

Definition 1. An MDD over $\widehat{\mathcal{S}}$ is an acyclic edge-labeled multi-graph where:
- Each node p belongs to a *level* in $\{K, ..., 1, 0\}$, denoted $p.lvl$.
- There is a single *root* node $r^\star$.
- Level 0 can contain only the *terminal* nodes, **0** and **1**.
- A node p at level $l > 0$ has n_l outgoing edges, labeled from 0 to $n_l - 1$. The edge labeled by $i \in \mathcal{S}_l$ points to node q, with $p.lvl > q.lvl$; we write $p[i] = q$.

Then, to ensure canonicity, *duplicate* nodes are forbidden:
- Given nodes p and q at level l, if $p[i] = q[i]$ for all $i \in \mathcal{S}_l$, then $p = q$,

and we must use either the *fully-reduced* rule [1] that forbids *redundant* nodes:
- No node p at level l can exist such that, $p[i] = q$ for all $i \in \mathcal{S}_l$,

or the *quasi-reduced* rule [15] that restricts arcs spanning multiple levels:
- The root is at level K.
- Given a node p at level l, $p[i].lvl$ is either $l - 1$ or 0, for all $i \in \mathcal{S}_l$. □

Definition 2. The set encoded by MDD node p at level k w.r.t. level $l \geq k$ is $\mathcal{B}(l,p) = \mathcal{S}_l \times \cdots \times \mathcal{S}_{k+1} \times \left(\bigcup_{i \in \mathcal{S}_k} \{i\} \times \mathcal{B}(k-1, p[i])\right)$, where $\forall \mathcal{X} \subseteq \mathcal{S}_l \times \cdots \times \mathcal{S}_1$, $\mathcal{X} \times \mathcal{B}(0, \mathbf{0}) = \emptyset$ and $\mathcal{X} \times \mathcal{B}(0, \mathbf{1}) = \mathcal{X}$. If $l = k$, we write $\mathcal{B}(p)$ instead of $\mathcal{B}(k,p)$. □

MDDs vs. BDDs. We use MDDs to implicitly encode the state space $\mathcal{S}$ and transition relation $\mathcal{R}$, instead of using $\lceil \log_2 \mathcal{S}_l \rceil$ bits for the local state variable x_l, and encoding $\mathcal{S}$ and $\mathcal{R}$ with BDDs. Compared with BDDs, MDDs have the disadvantage of resulting in larger and less shareable nodes when the variable domains $\mathcal{S}_l$ are very large (which is however not the case in our applications). On the other hand, MDDs have also advantages. First, many real-world models (e.g., non-safe Petri nets and software protocols) have variable domains with a priori unknown or very large upper bounds. These bounds must then be discovered "on the fly" during the symbolic iterations [10], and MDDs are preferable to BDDs when using this approach, due to the ease with which MDD nodes and variable domains can be extended. A second advantage, related to the present paper, is that our chaining heuristics applied to the MDD state variables more closely reflect structural information of the model behavior, which is instead spread on multiple levels in a BDD.

Most symbolic model checkers, e.g., NuSMV [11], generate the state space with BFS iterations, each consisting of an image computation. Set $\mathcal{X}^{[0]}$ is initialized to $\mathcal{S}^{init}$ and, after the dth iteration, set $\mathcal{X}^{[d]}$ contains all the states at distance up to d from $\mathcal{S}^{init}$. When using MDDs, $\mathcal{X}^{[d]}$ is encoded as a K-level MDD and $\mathcal{R}$ as a $2K$-level MDD whose current and next state variables are normally interleaved for efficiency. We use this order too. Also, the transition relation is often conjunctively partitioned into a set of *conjuncts* or disjunctively partitioned into a set of *disjuncts* [2], stored as a set of MDDs that can share nodes instead of a single monolithic MDD. Heuristically, these partitionings have been shown to be effective for both synchronous and asynchronous systems.

In the following, we use the data-types mdd and mdd2 to indicate quasi-reduced MDDs encodings sets and relations, respectively, and, for readability, we let $\mathcal{X}$ indicate both a set and the root of the MDD encoding that set.

2.2 Disjunctive Partition of $\mathcal{R}$ and Chaining

Both asynchronous and synchronous behaviors may be present in many systems. We focus on *globally-asynchronous locally-synchronous* behaviors. Thus, we assume the high-level model specifies a set of asynchronous events $\mathcal{E}$, where each event $\alpha \in \mathcal{E}$ can be further specified as a set of small synchronous components.

For example, a guarded command language model specifies a set of commands of the form "$guard \rightarrow assignment_1 \parallel assignment_2 \parallel \cdots \parallel assignment_m$", where, whenever the boolean predicate *guard* evaluates to *true*, the m parallel atomic assignments can be executed concurrently (synchronously). Each command is an asynchronous events in the system and for each command, each assignment of the parallel assignments is a synchronous component of the event. Similarly, for Petri net models, the set of transitions in the net are the asynchronous events in the system and the firing of a transition synchronously updates all the places connected to it. We use extended Petri nets as the input formalism in SMART [3].

We encode the transition relation as $\mathcal{R} \equiv \bigvee_{\alpha\in\mathcal{E}} \mathcal{D}_\alpha$, where each disjunct $\mathcal{D}_\alpha$ corresponds to an asynchronous event α. Each $\mathcal{D}_\alpha$ is further conjunctively partitioned, where each conjunct $\mathcal{C}_{\alpha,l}$ represents a synchronous component of α, thus we can write $\mathcal{R} \equiv \bigvee_{\alpha\in\mathcal{E}} \mathcal{D}_\alpha \equiv \bigvee_{\alpha\in\mathcal{E}}(\bigwedge_l \mathcal{C}_{\alpha,l})$.

Chaining [22] was introduced to speed up symbolic BFS-based state-space generation and similar symbolic fixed-point computations for asynchronous systems. The idea of chaining is based on the observation that the number of symbolic iterations might be reduced if the effect of exploring various events on a given set of states is compounded sequentially. More precisely, in a strict BFS symbolic iteration, the set $\mathcal{X}^{[d]}$ of states at distance up to d from $\mathcal{S}^{init}$ is built in exactly d iterations starting from $\mathcal{X}^{[0]} = \mathcal{S}^{init}$. The dth iteration applies the monolithic $\mathcal{R}$, or each disjunct $\mathcal{D}_\alpha$ corresponding to a distinct event α, to the set of states $\mathcal{X}^{[d-1]}$ reachable in up to $d-1$ steps. However, when we have the individual disjuncts $\mathcal{D}_\alpha$ at our disposal, we can instead apply them in an incremental fashion. If the event set is $\mathcal{E} = \{\alpha_1, \alpha_2, ..., \alpha_m\}$ and $\mathcal{Y}^{[d-1]}$ is the set of states found at the end of iteration d–1 with chaining, this approach computes

- $\mathcal{Y}^{[d;1]} \leftarrow \mathcal{Y}^{[d-1]} \cup Img(\mathcal{Y}^{[d-1]}, \mathcal{D}_{\alpha_1})$,
- $\mathcal{Y}^{[d;2]} \leftarrow \mathcal{Y}^{[d;1]} \cup Img(\mathcal{Y}^{[d;1]}, \mathcal{D}_{\alpha_2})$, and so on, until
- $\mathcal{Y}^{[d;m]} \leftarrow \mathcal{Y}^{[d;m-1]} \cup Img(\mathcal{Y}^{[d;m-1]}, \mathcal{D}_{\alpha_m})$, which becomes our next $\mathcal{Y}^{[d]}$.

Clearly, this will not discover states in strict BFS order, but it guarantees that the set of states discovered with chaining at the dth (outer) iteration is at least as large as those discovered in strict BFS order: $\mathcal{Y}^{[d]} \supseteq \mathcal{X}^{[d]}$. Thus, chaining may reach the fixed point, i.e., compute $\mathcal{S}$, in fewer iterations. Of course, the efficiency of state-space generation is determined not just by the *number* of symbolic iterations, but also by their *cost*, which is strictly related to the number of nodes in the decision diagrams being manipulated. While chaining could in principle result in larger intermediate decision diagrams and even slow down the computation, in practice. the opposite is often true: chaining has been shown to be quite effective in many asynchronous models.

To maximize the effectiveness of chaining, however, we must employ some heuristic to decide the order in which events should be explored. For example, [22] uses a topological sort on the gates of a circuit modeled as a Petri net. The intuition is that, if firing Petri net transition α adds tokens to a place that is input to another Petri net transition β, then the corresponding disjunct $\mathcal{D}_\alpha$ should be applied before $\mathcal{D}_\beta$ within each iteration, as this increases the chances that β will be enabled, thus discover more states, in the larger set of states obtained by considering also the effect of α. If the Petri net has cycles, they need to be "opened" by arbitrarily picking one transition in the cycle to fire first, and then firing the remaining transitions in order.

A different, not model-based, chaining order heuristic can also be employed. Given an event α, define $\mathcal{V}_M(\alpha) = \{x_l : \exists \mathbf{i}, \mathbf{j} \in \widehat{\mathcal{S}}, \mathcal{D}_\alpha(\mathbf{i}, \mathbf{j}) \wedge \mathbf{i}[l] \neq \mathbf{j}[l]\}$, and

mdd *BfsChaining*( )
1 $\mathcal{S} \leftarrow \mathcal{S}^{init}$;
2 **repeat**
3   **for** $l = 1$ **to** K **do**
4   **foreach** $\alpha \in \mathcal{E}_l$ **do**
5          $\mathcal{S} \leftarrow Union(\mathcal{S}, Image(\mathcal{S}, \mathcal{D}_\alpha))$
6 **until** $\mathcal{S}$ does not change;
7 **return** $\mathcal{S}$;

Fig. 1. Symbolic BFS-based state-space generation with chaining

$\mathcal{V}_D(\alpha) = \{x_l : \exists \mathbf{i}, \mathbf{i}' \in \widehat{\mathcal{S}}, \forall k \neq l, \mathbf{i}[k] = \mathbf{i}'[k] \wedge \exists \mathbf{j} \in \widehat{\mathcal{S}}, \mathcal{D}_\alpha(\mathbf{i}, \mathbf{j}) \wedge \nexists \mathbf{j}' \in \widehat{\mathcal{S}}, \mathcal{D}_\alpha(\mathbf{i}', \mathbf{j}')\}$, the variables that can be modified by α, or can disable, α, respectively. Letting

$$Top(\alpha) = \max\{l : x_l \in \mathcal{V}_M(\alpha) \cup \mathcal{V}_D(\alpha)\}, Bot(\alpha) = \min\{l : x_l \in \mathcal{V}_M(\alpha) \cup \mathcal{V}_D(\alpha)\},$$

we can then partition the events according to the value of *Top*, by defining the subsets of events $\mathcal{E}_l = \{\alpha : Top(\alpha) = l\}$, for $K \geq l \geq 1$ (some of these sets can be empty, of course). In [7] we observed that a chaining order that applies these subsets to the MDD in bottom-up fashion, as shown in Fig. 1, results in good speedups with respect to a strict BFS symbolic state-space generation.

Recognizing this *event locality* also lets us store $\mathcal{D}_\alpha$ with an MDD over just the current and next state variables having index k, for $Top(\alpha) \geq k \geq Bot(\alpha)$. Then, when computing the image of event α with $Top(\alpha) = l$, statement 5 in *BfsChaining* requires to access only MDD nodes at level l or below and to modify *in-place* [5] only MDD nodes at level l, without having to traverse the MDD from the root. Exploiting identity transformations in $\mathcal{D}_\alpha$ for variables strictly between $Top(\alpha)$ and $Bot(\alpha)$ is not as critical for the efficiency of the saturation approach, and therefore we do not discuss it in the rest of the paper, for simplicity's sake. However, it does contribute to the experimental results in Sect. 5.

2.3 Saturation Algorithm

An MDD node p at level l is said to be *saturated* [6] if it encodes a fixed point:

$$\forall \alpha \in \mathcal{E}, Top(\alpha) \leq l, \; \mathcal{B}(K, p) \supseteq Img(\mathcal{B}(K, p), \mathcal{D}_\alpha).$$

To saturate node p once its descendants are saturated, we compute the effect of firing α on p for each α such that $Top(\alpha) = l$, recursively saturating any nodes at lower levels that might be created in the process, and add the result to $\mathcal{B}(p)$ using in-place updates. One advantage of this approach is that it stores only saturated nodes in the cache and unique table; these are the only "potentially useful" nodes, since nodes in the MDD encoding $\mathcal{S}$ are saturated by definition.

Fig. 2 shows the saturation algorithm in its most general form, as presented in [10]. Its fixed-point iterations constitute an extreme form of chaining. Saturation has been shown to reduce memory and runtime requirements by several orders of magnitude with respect to BFS-based algorithms when applied to asynchronous systems, for both state-space generation and CTL model-checking [8].

---

void *Saturation*( )

  1 **for** $l = 1$ **to** K **do**
  2   **foreach** node p at level l in the MDD $\mathcal{S}^{init}$ **do**
  3   *Saturate*(p);   ●*Bottom-up sub-fixpoint computation by DD node*

---

void *Saturate*(mdd p)

  1 $l \leftarrow p.lvl$;
  2 **repeat**
  3   choose $\alpha \in \mathcal{E}_l, i \in \mathcal{S}_l, j \in \mathcal{S}_l$ s.t. $p[i] \neq \mathbf{0}$ and $\mathcal{D}_\alpha[i][j] \neq \mathbf{0}$;
  4      $p[j] \leftarrow Union(p[j], ImageSat(p[i], \mathcal{D}_\alpha[i][j]))$;
  5 **until** p does not change;

---

mdd *ImageSat*(mdd q, mdd2 f)

  1 **if** $q = \mathbf{0}$ or $f = \mathbf{0}$ **then return** $\mathbf{0}$;
  2 $k \leftarrow q.lvl$;   ●*given our quasi-reduced form, $f.lvl = k$ as well*
  3 $s \leftarrow$ a new MDD node at level k with all edges set to $\mathbf{0}$;
  4 **foreach** $i \in \mathcal{S}_k, j \in \mathcal{S}_k$ s.t. $q[i] \neq \mathbf{0}$ and $f[i][j] \neq \mathbf{0}$ **do**
  5      $s[j] \leftarrow Union(s[j], ImageSat(q[i], f[i][j]))$;
  6 *Saturate*(s);
  7 **return** s.

Fig. 2. Saturation-based state-space generation

As an example, Fig. 3 shows a Petri net, and its equivalent guarded command language expression, modeling a gated-service queue with a limited pool of customers. New arrivals wait at the gate until it is opened, then all the waiting customers enter the service queue. Customers return to the pool after service. A state of the model can be represented as an evaluation of the integer variable vector (p, w, i), where p stands for *pool*, w for *wait* and i for *in-service*. Assuming a pool of two customers, the model has an initial state $(2, 0, 0)$ and six reachable states: $\mathcal{S} = \{(2, 0, 0), (1, 1, 0), (0, 2, 0), (1, 0, 1), (0, 0, 2), (0, 1, 1)\}$. Fig. 4 shows the execution of the saturation algorithm on this example. We use a for *arrive*, g for *gate*, and s for *service* to denote the transitions.

In Fig. 4, snapshot (a) shows the $2K$-level MDDs encoding the disjunctively partitioned transition relation. Snapshots from (b) to (k) show the evolution of the encoding of the state space, from the initial state to the final state space, where the key procedure calls are shown. For readability, node edges leading to terminal $\mathbf{0}$ are omitted. We denote each MDD node encoding the state space with a capital letter (A to I in the example), and color a node black after it becomes saturated. Not all procedure calls are shown, e.g., *ImageSat*$(C[1], \mathcal{D}_s[1][2])$ is called in snapshot (k) before node C becomes saturated, but it is not shown since no new nodes (states) are generated from the call.

3   Node-Wise Fine-Grained Chaining

Previously introduced chaining heuristics are *event-based*, thus *coarse-grained* (they define an order in which to explore the model-level events) and *static* (the order is derived from the high-level model prior to state-space generation). Our

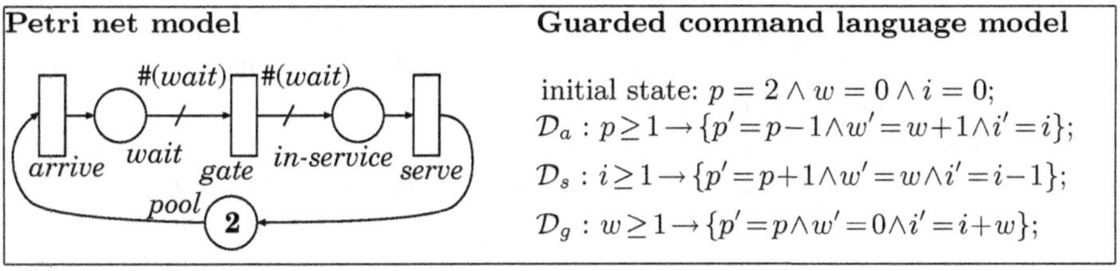

Fig. 3. A limited-arrival gated-service model with marking-dependent arc cardinalities

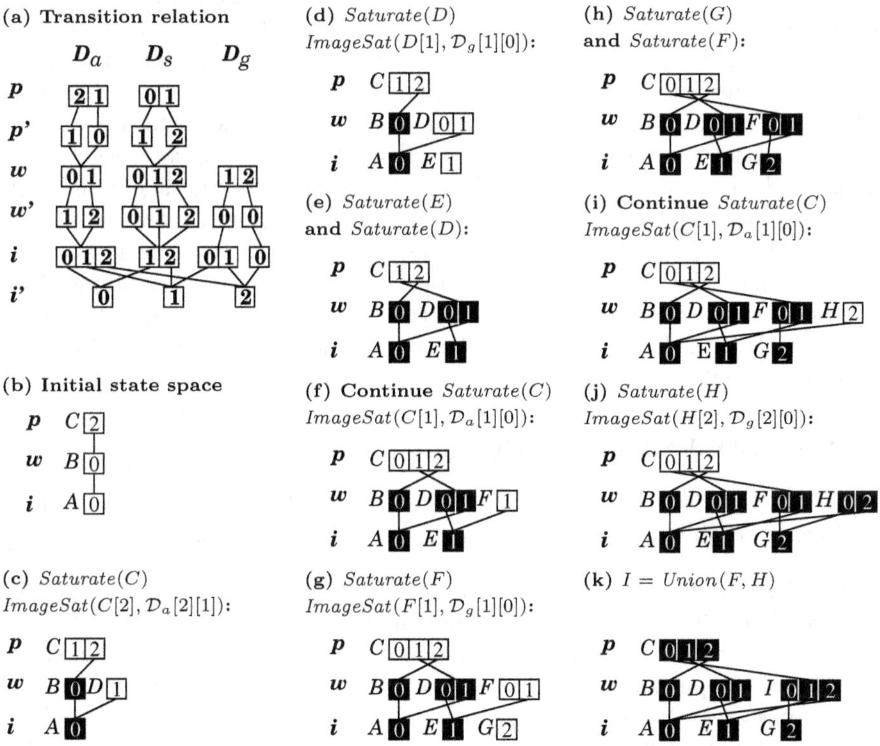

Fig. 4. Saturation applied to the limited-arrival gate-service model

heuristic is instead *decision-diagram-node-based*, thus *fine-grained* (it defines the order of descent for the decision diagram nodes during image computation) and *dynamic* (the order is decided on a per-node basis during state-space generation). Such a dynamic policy has the potential to be more flexible and efficient than a static policy, but also the risk of higher runtime costs. In fact, Sect. 5 shows that our heuristic can achieve substantial improvements and has small overhead.

Before presenting our heuristic, we rewrite the transition relation by grouping the disjuncts according to the value of $Top(\alpha)$, i.e., $\mathcal{R} \equiv \bigvee_{K \geq l \geq 1} \mathcal{R}_l$, where

$\mathcal{R}_l \equiv \bigvee_{\alpha \in \mathcal{E}_l} \mathcal{D}_\alpha \equiv \bigvee_{\alpha \in \mathcal{E}_l} (\bigwedge_j \mathcal{C}_{\alpha,j})$. Thus, $\mathcal{R}$ is described by a set of K MDDs where, for $K \geq l \geq 1$, the root $r_l^\star$ of the MDD encoding $\mathcal{R}_l$ is at level l (some of these MDDs can be empty).

We then seek good chaining by determining an order for the exploration of the children of a node p at level l and of $r_l^\star$, when computing $Image(p, r_l^\star)$ and using in-place updates. More precisely, we repeatedly choose a pair of local states $(i, j) \in \mathcal{S}_l \times \mathcal{S}_l$, compute $Image(p[i], r_l^\star[i][j])$, and use the result to update $p[j]$. Intuitively, pair (i', j') is preferred over (i'', j'') if there is a chance that updating j' can eventually "benefit" i'', i.e., increase $\mathcal{B}(p[i''])$, but no chance that updating j'' can benefit i'. Sect. 3.1 formalizes this concept by defining an equivalence relation on $\mathcal{S}_l$ that implies a partial order on the equivalence classes. This is the same rationale as for the original chaining heuristic, but at a much finer level. To further refine the order within each equivalence class, we use the "fullness" of the MDD nodes. Intuitively, if $p[i]$ encodes more substates than $p[j]$, we want to compute $Image(p[i], r_l^\star[i][j])$ and use it to update $p[j]$ before computing $Image(p[j], r_l^\star[j][i])$ to update $p[i]$. The same is true if $p[i]$ and $p[j]$ encode the same number of substates, but $r_l^\star[i][j]$ encodes more transitions than $r_l^\star[j][i]$. Sect. 3.2 formalizes this idea by assigning a *score* to each pair (i, j). We stress that, while the first observation is based on logical conditions that are *guaranteed* to improve chaining, i.e., the best (total) chaining order must be compatible with the partial order, the second one is just a heuristic *likely* to improve chaining.

3.1 Partial-Order-Based Chaining

Definition 3. Given node p at level l, $K \geq l \geq 1$, its *dynamic transition graph* is a directed graph $G_p = (\mathcal{S}_l, \mathcal{T}_p)$, where $\mathcal{T}_p = \{(i, j) : r_l^\star[i][j] \neq \mathbf{0} \wedge p[j] \neq \mathbf{1}\}$. □

An edge $(i, j) \in \mathcal{T}_p$, if $p[i] \neq \mathbf{0}$, corresponds to an $Image(p[i], r_l^\star[i][j])$ that must eventually be computed when applying $r_l^\star$ to p. Obviously, if $p[i] = \mathbf{0}$ or $r_l^\star[i][j] = \mathbf{0}$, the image is $\mathbf{0}$, thus no computation is needed. Less obviously, we can avoid computation also when $p[j] = \mathbf{1}$, i.e., when $p[j]$ already encodes all possible substates; this new optimization could have been used in our original saturation algorithm [6], but was not (in other words, condition "$p[j] \neq \mathbf{1}$" should be added to the test in statement 3 of *Saturate* in Fig. 2).

Our heuristic chooses the pairs (i, j) respecting the partial order implied by graph: (i', j') is chosen before (i'', j'') if there is a path from j' to i'' but not from j'' to i', and $p[i'] \neq \mathbf{0}$. Note that computing $Image(p[i], r_l^\star[i][j])$ and using it to update $p[j]$ might change $p[j]$ from $\mathbf{0}$ to some other node, or it may make $p[j]$ become $\mathbf{1}$ (in which case we remove any of its incoming edges).

This first part of our heuristic considers the strongly connected components (SCCs) of the dynamic transition graph, and explores the edges according to their position in the resulting quotient graph. However, to discriminate between edges within the same SCCs, we need to refine our heuristic, which we do next.

3.2 Heuristic Node-Fullness-Guided Chaining

We define the *fullness* of a node as the ratio of the number of substates it encodes over the maximum number of substates it could encode, $n_{l:1} =_{\mathrm{df}} \prod_{l \geq k \geq 1} n_k$.

Definition 4. The fullness of the terminal nodes is $\phi(\mathbf{0})=0$ and $\phi(\mathbf{1})=1$. The fullness of an MDD node p at level $l > 0$ is $\phi(p) = |\mathcal{B}(p)|/n_{l:1}$. □

For models with boolean variables, the node fullness is the number of on-set minterms of the boolean function encoded by the BDD node over all the possible minterms. Our definition of node fullness is related to, but different from, the concept of node *density* proposed in [20]. We compare the two in Sect. 6.

Given p at level $l > 0$, we have $1/n_{l:1} \leq \phi(p) \leq 1$. If we store the value of ϕ with each node, or in a separate cache, we can compute it recursively bottom-up as $\phi(p) = \sum_{i \in \mathcal{S}_l} \phi(p[i])/n_l$. This definition can be applied also to the MDD encoding the transition relation $\mathcal{R}$ or of the disjuncts $\mathcal{D}_\alpha$. In practice, $\phi(p)$ is extremely small, and Sect. 4.1 addresses how to avoid floating point underflows.

To choose the next pair (i, j) to be explored when computing $Image(p, r_l^\star)$ if the partial order of Sect. 3.1 does not suffice, i.e., if there are edges (i', j') and (i'', j'') in the dynamic transition graph, with $p[i'] \neq \mathbf{0}$, $p[i''] \neq \mathbf{0}$, and paths from j' to i'' and from j'' to i', for each MDD node, we assign a *score* corresponding to each pair (i, j) and explore the pair with the highest score.

3.3 Scoring Function Based on Probability

In this section, we restrict ourselves to a particular SCC of the dynamic transition graph. Using probabilistic arguments, we define the "score" of the pair (i, j) in node p at level l as $\sigma(p, i, j) = \phi(p[i]) \cdot \phi(r_l^\star[i][j]) \cdot (1 - \phi(p[j]))$. Then, in the image computation, we choose to explore next the pair with the highest score.

Assume that, for any i and j, the sets $\mathcal{B}(p[i])$, $\mathcal{B}(r_l^\star[i][j])$, and $\mathcal{B}(p[j])$ are independent and uniformly distributed random variables, i.e., that any of the $C_{n_{l-1:1}}^{|\mathcal{B}(p[i])|}$, $C_{n_{l-1:1}^2}^{|\mathcal{B}(r_l^\star[i][j])|}$, and $C_{n_{l-1:1}}^{|\mathcal{B}(p[j])|}$ possible choices for them are equally likely. The score of (i, j) could then be set to the expected fraction of new states found (ignoring the effect of saturating newly created nodes at lower levels): $\phi_{new} = E\left[|\mathcal{B}(Image(p[i], r_l^\star[i][j])) \setminus \mathcal{B}(p[j])|\right]/n_{l-1:1}$.

Consider the problem: given $A \in \mathbb{B}^n$, $R \in \mathbb{B}^{n \times m}$, and $B \in \mathbb{B}^m$, respectively with a, r, and b ones, compute $E[|\{j | B[j]=0 \wedge \exists i, A[i]=1 \wedge R[i,j]=1\}|]/m$. Thanks to linearity, we can write this as $\rho(m-b)/m$, where ρ is the probability that, for a given j s.t. $B[j] = 0$, there is an i s.t. $A[i] = 1$ and $R[i, j] = 1$. We can compute the complementary probability $1 - \rho$ by observing that, if $A[i] = 0$, $R[i, j]$ can be either 0 or 1 but, if $A[i] = 1$, $R[i, j]$ must be 0. Thus, $1 - \rho$ is the probability that none of the ones in matrix R is in one of the "taboo" positions of column j corresponding to $A[i] = 1$, i.e., $1 - \rho = C_{nm-a}^r / C_{nm}^r$.

In our case, $n = m = n_{l-1:1}$, $a = |\mathcal{B}(p[i])| = n\phi(p[i])$, $r = |\mathcal{B}(r_l^\star[i][j])| = n^2\phi(r_l^\star[i][j])$, $b = |\mathcal{B}(p[j])| = n\phi(p[j])$, and ϕ_{new} is given by

$$\left[1 - \frac{C_{nm-a}^r}{C_{nm}^r}\right]\frac{m-b}{m} = \left[1 - \frac{(n^2 - n\phi(p[i]))!(n^2 - n^2\phi(r_l^\star[i][j]))!}{(n^2)!(n^2 - n^2\phi(r_l^\star[i][j]) - n\phi(p[i]))!}\right][1 - \phi(p[j])].$$

Let $G = \phi(p[i])$, and $H = \phi(r_l^\star[i][j])$, then ϕ_{new} can be written as:

$$\begin{aligned}
\phi_{new} &= \left[1 - \frac{(n^2 - nG)!(n^2 - n^2H)!}{(n^2)!(n^2 - n^2H - nG)!}\right][1 - \phi(p[j])] \\
&= \left[1 - \frac{(n^2 - n^2H)! \;/\; (n^2 - n^2H - nG)!}{(n^2)! \;/\; (n^2 - nG)!}\right][1 - \phi(p[j])] \\
&= \left[1 - \frac{n^2 - n^2H}{n^2} \cdot \frac{n^2 - n^2H - 1}{n^2 - 1} \cdots \frac{n^2 - n^2H - (nG-1)}{n^2 - (nG-1)}\right][1 - \phi(p[j])] \\
&= \left[1 - \left(1 - \frac{n^2H}{n^2}\right) \cdot \left(1 - \frac{n^2H}{n^2 - 1}\right) \cdots \left(1 - \frac{n^2H}{n^2 - (nG-1)}\right)\right][1 - \phi(p[j])] \\
&\approx \left[1 - (1 - H)^{nG}\right][1 - \phi(p[j])] && \text{(since } nG - 1 \ll n^2\text{)} \\
&\approx \left[1 - (1 - nGH + o(nGH))\right][1 - \phi(p[j])] && \text{(assuming } nGH \ll 1\text{)} \\
&\approx [nGH][1 - \phi(p[j])] && \text{(ignoring the higher order terms).}
\end{aligned}$$

We then use ϕ_{new}/n, i.e., $\phi(p[i]) \cdot \phi(r_l^\star[i][j]) \cdot (1 - \phi(p[j]))$, as the value of the scoring function $\sigma(p, i, j)$, since n is the same for all the nodes at level l. Observe that, just as ϕ_{new}, $\sigma(p, i, j)$ lies between 0 and 1, increases with $\phi(p[i])$ and $\phi(r_l^\star[i][j])$, decreases with $\phi(p[j])$, and evaluates to 0 when $p[i] = \mathbf{0}$, $r_l^\star[i][j] = \mathbf{0}$, or $p[j] = \mathbf{1}$, as it should be expected.

4 Fine-Grained Chaining Symbolic State-Space Generation

Fig. 5 and 6 show the modified BFS-based and saturation-based symbolic state-space generation algorithms with our fullness-guided chaining. Unlike the algorithm of Fig. 1 that applies each event α with $Top(\alpha) = l$, for $l = 1, ..., K$, once, the one in Fig. 5 leaves level l only when further applications of $\mathcal{R}_l$ do not add states. To distinguish between the different aggressiveness in chaining, we indicate them as Top and Top*. The modified saturation-based algorithm is as in Fig. 2, except that *SaturateFineGrainedChaining* replaces *Saturate*.

Both chaining algorithms use a dynamic transition graph $(\mathcal{S}_l, \mathcal{T}_p)$ to repeatedly explore transitions, corresponding to edges (i, j), until no new substates can be added. The edges of the graph are marked if they need to be explored. Function *InitTransGraph*$(p, r_l^\star)$ initializes this graph according to Def. 3 and marks any edge leaving a node i, if $p[i]$ encodes some substates. Function *UpdateTransGraph*$(p, j, \mathcal{T}_p)$ updates the set of edges according to Def. 3 after $p[j]$ has been modified, i.e., it removes any edge directed to node j, if $p[j] = 1$, and marks the edges leaving node j, since they need to be explored.

The algorithms call a function *ChooseEdge* which, given an mdd p, an mdd2 $r_l^\star$, and a set of edges $\mathcal{T}_p$, returns the (marked) edge (i, j) to explore next, based on the partial order and scoring function heuristics. The marking of edges is essential since, once (i, j) has been explored, there is no need to explore it again unless $p[i]$ changes.

set of (int,int) *InitTransGraph*(mdd p, mdd2 $r_l^\star$)
  $\mathcal{T}_p \leftarrow \{(i,j) \in \mathcal{S}_l \times \mathcal{S}_l : r_l^\star[i][j] \neq \mathbf{0} \wedge p[j] \neq \mathbf{1}\}$; *•Definition 3*
  mark edges $\{(i,j) \in \mathcal{T}_p : p[i] \neq \mathbf{0}\}$; *•transitions to be explored*
  return $\mathcal{T}_p$;

set of (int,int) *UpdateTransGraph*(mdd p, int j, set of (int,int) $\mathcal{T}_p$)
  mark edges $\{(j,h) \in \mathcal{T}_p : p[h] \neq \mathbf{1}\}$; *•edges leaving j must be (re-)explored*
  if $p[j] = \mathbf{1}$ **then** *•no new substates can be added to $\mathcal{B}(p[j])$*
    $\mathcal{T}_p \leftarrow \mathcal{T}_p \setminus \mathcal{S}_l \times \{j\}$; *•remove all edges directed toward node j*
  return $\mathcal{T}_p$;

mdd *BfsFineGrainedChaining*( )
  $\mathcal{S} \leftarrow \mathcal{S}^{init}$;
  repeat
    for $l = 1$ **to** K **do**
      foreach node p at level l in the MDD of $\mathcal{S}$ **do**
        $\mathcal{T}_p \leftarrow InitTransGraph(p, r_l^\star)$; *•build graph $(\mathcal{S}_l, \mathcal{T}_p)$ and mark its edges*
        while there is a marked edge in $\mathcal{T}_p$ **do**
          $(i,j) \leftarrow ChooseEdge(p, r_l^\star, \mathcal{T}_p)$;
          unmark edge (i,j);
          $u \leftarrow Union(p[j], Image(p[i], r_l^\star[i][j]))$; *•image computation*
          if $u \neq p[j]$ **then** *•new substates found*
            $p[j] \leftarrow u$; *•in-place update p to add the new substates*
            $\mathcal{T}_p \leftarrow UpdateTransGraph(p, j, \mathcal{T}_p)$;
  until no node in the MDD encoding $\mathcal{S}$ has changed; *•fixed-point computation*
  return $\mathcal{S}$; *•the reachable state space*

Fig. 5. Fine-grained chaining variant of *BfsChaining*

void *SaturateFineGrainedChaining*(mdd p)
  $l \leftarrow p.lvl$;
  $\mathcal{T}_p \leftarrow InitTransGraph(p, r_l^\star)$; *•build graph $(\mathcal{S}_l, \mathcal{T}_p)$ and mark its edges*
  while there is a marked edge in $\mathcal{T}_p$ **do**
    $(i,j) \leftarrow ChooseEdge(p, r_l^\star, \mathcal{T}_p)$;
    unmark edge (i,j);
    $u \leftarrow Union(p[j], ImageSat(p[i], r_l^\star[i][j]))$; *•image computation*
    if $u \neq p[j]$ **then** *•new substates found*
      $p[j] \leftarrow u$; *•in-place update p to add the new substates*
      $\mathcal{T}_p \leftarrow UpdateTransGraph(p, j, \mathcal{T}_p)$;

Fig. 6. Fine-grained chaining variant of *Saturate* for the algorithm in Fig. 2

The quotient graph and score computations for our heuristic can be implemented efficiently. Using the execution profiler `gprof` on the benchmarks described in the next section, we can experimentally conclude that the total runtime overhead incurred by calling *ChooseEdge* is less than 1%. To achieve this low overhead, we initially build a static transition graph $(\mathcal{S}_l, \mathcal{T}_l)$ for each level l, based on the information in $r_l^\star$ alone, and compute its quotient graph. Then, when applying $r_l^\star$ to a node p during state-space generation, we build the dynamic graph transition as a subgraph of the static one (removing edges to any node j such that $p[j] = \mathbf{1}$) and its quotient graph as a refinement of the static one. We store the "marked" flag and the score in an adjacency matrix, restricted to the current SCC for efficiency. After a call *UpdateTransGraph*$(p, j, \mathcal{T}_p)$, the score of all edges incident to j is recomputed. The element with maximum score in each row of the adjacency matrix is recorded, so that *ChooseEdge* can efficiently find the maximum without searching the entire matrix.

4.1 Implementation Details

One interesting issue is how to recognize the condition $\phi(p[j]) = 1$ appearing in our heuristic. As presented so far, we simply need to test whether $p[j] = \mathbf{1}$ but, in the past, we have proposed symbolic state-space generation algorithms where the actual ranges of the state variables are initially unknown, so that the sets $\mathcal{S}_l$, for $K \geq l \geq 1$, are built "on the fly" during the symbolic iterations [10]. In this case, only non-terminal nodes at level 1 can point to node $\mathbf{1}$, since the meaning of $\mathcal{B}(l, \mathbf{1})$, and the value of $\phi(p)$, change every time one of the sets $\mathcal{S}_k$, for $l \geq k \geq 1$, changes. In this setting, it is best to store the absolute substate count $|\mathcal{B}(p)|$ instead of $\phi(p)$. Our tool SMART [3] provides an arbitrary precision integer state counting capability, but this is relatively expensive in terms of memory and time for large MDDs, so we store $|\mathcal{B}(p)|$ using a floating-point value, appropriately scaled. Then, however, recognizing that $p[j]$ encodes all (so far) possible substates, i.e., that $\phi(p[j]) = 1$, is feasible only if the value of $|\mathcal{B}(p[j])|$ is stored with enough precision that the comparison $|\mathcal{B}(p[j])| = n_{l-1:1}$ is reliable. Testing whether $\phi(p[i]) = 0$ or $\phi(r_l^\star[i][j]) = 0$, instead, is always possible, since it is equivalent to testing whether $p[i] = \mathbf{0}$ or $r_l^\star[i][j] = \mathbf{0}$, respectively, and edges to $\mathbf{0}$ from non-terminal nodes at any level can be present even if the variable ranges are not known a priori.

5 Experimental Results

We now report results on a suite of asynchronous benchmarks parametrized by an integer N. We compare three different fine-grained chaining orders applied to the Top* and saturation algorithms: (1) a random order, (2) the order used in [7], where set of edges to explore is initialized using the order in which local states are discovered during symbolic state-space generation, then managed as a FIFO queue, and (3) the proposed fullness-guided order, respectively denoted $\mathsf{Top}^\star_r$, $\mathsf{Top}^\star_d$, $\mathsf{Top}^\star_g$, Sat_r, Sat_d, Sat_g, and compare them with (4) pure BFS without chaining and (5) Top, the coarse-grained chaining of Fig. 1. All algorithms are implemented in our tool SMART [3], run on a 3 Ghz Pentium IV workstation with 1GB memory. In all our experimental benchmarks, we use the best MDD variable order known to us, which is either obtained from the variable ordering heuristic described in [23] or derived manually in the high-level model.

The columns of Table 1 report the value of the parameter N, the size $|\mathcal{S}|$ of the state space, the runtime and peak number of MDD nodes for each approach, and the final number of MDD nodes. For each benchmark, we provide the number

N	$\|\mathcal{S}\|$	Runtime (sec)								Peak Nodes (in thousands)								Final
		BFS	Top	Top^*_r	Top^*_d	Top^*_g	Sat_r	Sat_d	Sat_g	BFS	Top	Top^*_r	Top^*_d	Top^*_g	Sat_r	Sat_d	Sat_g	Nodes
Bounded open queuing network (BQ) [12]										N is the number of customers and $K = 8$								
20	$2.3{\cdot}10^7$	1,865	1,739	72	124	23	0.22	0.24	0.09	46	16	10	12	7	6	7	2	88
30	$2.4{\cdot}10^7$	-	-	996	1,667	217	0.7	0.73	0.28	-	-	24	30	18	13	15	5	128
200	$1.7{\cdot}10^{13}$	-	-	-	-	-	257	220	65	-	-	-	-	-	537	646	168	808
Aloha network protocol (Aloha) [4]										N is the number of nodes in the network and $K = N + 3$								
18	$2.6{\cdot}10^6$	21	20	10	20	9	0.07	0.09	0.05	6	6	5	6	5	5	6	5	551
24	$2.1{\cdot}10^8$	1,669	1,670	875	1,666	735	0.16	0.22	0.12	13	13	12	13	10	12	12	10	950
180	$1.4{\cdot}10^{56}$	-	-	-	-	-	76	103	53	-	-	-	-	-	4,410	4,925	3,954	49,232
Kanban manufacturing system (Kanban) [24]										N is the number of each type of parts and $K = 16$								
7	$4.1{\cdot}10^7$	2,016	899	3	4	3	0.04	0.03	0.03	38	6	2	3	2	0.94	1	0.92	107
15	$4.7{\cdot}10^{13}$	-	-	836	1,020	535	0.28	0.16	0.15	-	-	9	9	8	4	4	4	211
150	$1.4{\cdot}10^{21}$	-	-	-	-	-	396	121	90	-	-	-	-	-	338	364	309	1,966
Leader election protocol (Leader) [13]										N is the number of processors in the ring and $K = 11N$								
5	$5.9{\cdot}10^5$	218	139	48	46	45	3	3	2	1,495	977	376	373	372	121	123	108	18,401
6	$9.8{\cdot}10^6$	-	-	1,083	1,067	1,020	16	16	14	-	-	2,390	2,368	2,352	631	661	557	66,967
7	$1.3{\cdot}10^8$	-	-	-	-	-	53	50	45	-	-	-	-	-	1,895	1,872	1,594	142,412
Slotted ring network protocol (Slot) [19]										N is the number of nodes in the network and $K = N$								
7	$6.2{\cdot}10^6$	367	132	34	30	30	0.01	0.01	0.01	19	4	0.38	0.37	0.37	0.11	0.1	0.08	31
8	$6.8{\cdot}10^7$	-	1,622	378	347	347	0.01	0.01	0.01	-	7	0.95	0.89	0.89	0.18	0.2	0.16	40
200	$8.4{\cdot}10^{211}$	-	-	-	-	-	207	149	86	-	-	-	-	-	1,692	1,408	732	20,200
Distributed mutual exclusion circuit (DME) [16]										N is the number of cells in the protocol and $K = 18N$								
4	$7.5{\cdot}10^4$	309	113	3	3	3	0.01	0.01	0.01	751	228	18	18	18	3	3	3	1,422
5	$8.0{\cdot}10^5$	-	-	34	36	34	0.14	0.14	0.16	-	-	29	29	29	4	4	4	1,955
350	$8.8{\cdot}10^{324}$	-	-	-	-	-	15	15	16	-	-	-	-	-	391	391	391	185,840

Table 1. Experimental results ("-" indicates that the runtime is over 3600 seconds)

of state variables K as a function of the model parameter N, and give a reference where a detailed description of the model can be found. These benchmarks include network protocols (Aloha, Leader, Slot), generalized queueing/Petri net models (BQ, Kanban), and a speed-independent asynchronous circuit model (DME) from the NuSMV [11] distribution.

From this table, we see a separation by several orders of magnitude in terms of efficiency, with BFS at the lowest end, followed by Top, then Top*, and finally Sat. Comparing different fine-grained chaining heuristics in the Top* and saturation algorithms, the chaining heuristic has significant impact on five out of the six benchmarks. In the DME benchmark, the "r", "d", and "g" orders result in exactly the same peak MDD nodes; as the runtimes are similar, this confirms that our fullness-guided heuristic has a small overhead.

Compared with random-order chaining, discovery-order chaining has worse performance for Top* in three cases and similar performance in the remaining four cases, while, for Sat, it has better performance in three cases, worse performance in one case, and similar performance in four cases. Compared with random-order or discovery-order chaining, the newly proposed fullness-guided chaining heuristic achieves better (by a factor of up to four) or similar runtime and memory consumption for both Top* and Sat in all benchmarks.

We conclude from our experiments that the newly proposed fullness-guided chaining heuristic is more efficient and stable than both discovery chaining order and random chaining order. In particular, the Sat_g algorithm is by far the most efficient among the eight algorithms we considered.

6 Related Work

Ravi and Somenzi [20] defined the *density* of a BDD node p as the ratio of the number of substates encoded by p over the number of BDD nodes reachable from p, and used it to make decisions about which nodes to explore during state-space generation, with the goal of reducing memory consumption. In particular, their algorithm could ignore low-density nodes and explore just high-density ones, at the price of computing a (hopefully good) under-approximation of the exact state space. In contrast, our definition of node fullness does not take into account the number of decision diagram nodes needed to encode the node's function. Most importantly, we use it for a fundamentally different purpose. Instead of exploring only dense nodes and computing an under-approximation of the state space, we look for asynchronous transition from high-fullness nodes to low-fullness nodes with the goal of reducing the number of symbolic iterations required to reach the exact fixed-point via chaining.

In another related work, *hints* [21] were proposed with the same intent to guide the symbolic traversal of the state space and avoid intermediate BDD blow-ups in symbolic invariance checking and model checking. Hints are constraints which are added to the transition relation before the start of symbolic state-space exploration, and later removed from the transition relation to compute the exact solution, with the hope to avoid the peak memory consumption. However, this is orthogonal to our approach, since hints were designed to be dependent on the high-level model (as well as on the properties being verified), and either provided by model checker users [21] or automatically generated from the input model [26], while our approach lies in the symbolic back-end solver and is completely independent of the high-level model.

7 Conclusion and Future Work

We introduced a new approach to exploit *chaining* during symbolic state-space generation. Unlike previous heuristics that operate on a high-level model and decide in which order to explore events, ours considers low-level information extracted from the decision diagrams encoding the current state space and the transition relation, thus it is applicable to any globally-asynchronous locally-synchronous system, regardless of the formalism used to model it. We implemented our heuristic in both BFS-based and saturation-based algorithms, and experimentally demonstrated that runtimes and memory requirements can improve by a factor up to four. Having established the soundness of the approach, we plan in the future to investigate further refinements of the proposed heuristic.

References

1. R. E. Bryant. Graph-based algorithms for boolean function manipulation. *IEEE Trans. Comp.*, 35(8):677–691, Aug. 1986.
2. J. R. Burch, E. M. Clarke, and D. E. Long. Symbolic model checking with partitioned transition relations. *Proc. Int. Conference on Very Large Scale Integration*, pages 49–58, Aug. 1991. IFIP Transactions, North-Holland.
3. G. Ciardo, R. L. Jones, A. S. Miner, and R. Siminiceanu. Logical and stochastic modeling with SMART. *Perf. Eval.*, 63:578-608, 2006.
4. G. Ciardo and Y. Lan. Faster discrete-event simulation through structural caching. *Proc. PMCCS*, pages 11–14, Sept. 2003.
5. G. Ciardo, Lüttgen, Gerald and G. Ciardo, G. Lüttgen, and R. Siminiceanu. Efficient symbolic state-space construction for asynchronous systems. *Proc. ICATPN*, LNCS 1825, pages 103-122, Jun. 2000. springer.
6. G. Ciardo, G. Lüttgen, and R. Siminiceanu. Saturation: An efficient iteration strategy for symbolic state space generation. *Proc. TACAS*, LNCS 2031, pages 328–342, Apr. 2001. Springer.
7. G. Ciardo, R. Marmorstein, and R. Siminiceanu. The saturation algorithm for symbolic state space exploration. *STTT*, 8(1):4-25, Feb. 2006.
8. G. Ciardo and R. Siminiceanu. Structural symbolic CTL model checking of asynchronous systems. *Proc. CAV*, LNCS 2725, pages 40–53, July 2003. Springer.
9. G. Ciardo and K. S. Trivedi. A decomposition approach for stochastic reward net models. *Perf. Eval.*, 18(1):37–59, 1993.
10. G. Ciardo and A. J. Yu. Saturation-based symbolic reachability analysis using conjunctive and disjunctive partitioning. *Proc. CHARME*, LNCS 3725, pages 146–161, Oct. 2005. Springer.
11. A. Cimatti, E. Clarke, F. Giunchiglia, and M. Roveri. NuSMV: A new symbolic model verifier. *Proc. CAV*, LNCS 1633, pages 495–499, 1999. Springer.

12. P. Fernandes, B. Plateau, and W. J. Stewart. Efficient descriptor-vector multiplication in stochastic automata networks. *J. ACM*, 45(3):381–414, 1998.
13. A. Itai and M. Rodeh. Symmetry breaking in distributed networks. *Proc. FOCS*, pages 150–158. IEEE Comp. Soc. Press, Oct. 1981.
14. T. Kam, T. Villa, R. Brayton, and A. Sangiovanni-Vincentelli. Multi-valued decision diagrams: theory and applications. *Multiple-Valued Logic*, 4(1–2):9–62, 1998.
15. S. Kimura and E. M. Clarke. A parallel algorithm for constructing binary decision diagrams. *Proc. ICCD*, pages 220–223, Sept. 1990. IEEE Comp. Soc. Press.
16. A. J. Martin. The design of a self-timed circuit for distributed mutual exclusion. *Proc. Chapel Hill Conference on VLSI*, pages 245–260, 1985.
17. K. L. McMillan. *Symbolic Model Checking*. Kluwer, 1993.
18. A. S. Miner and G. Ciardo. Efficient reachability set generation and storage using decision diagrams. *Proc. ICATPN*, LNCS 1639, pages 6–25, June 1999. Springer.
19. E. Pastor, O. Roig, J. Cortadella, and R. Badia. Petri net analysis using boolean manipulation. *Proc. ICATPN*, LNCS 815, pages 416–435, June 1994. Springer.
20. K. Ravi and F. Somenzi. High-density reachability analysis. *Proc. ICCAD*, pages 154–158. IEEE Comp. Soc. Press, 1995.
21. K. Ravi and F. Somenzi. Hints to accelerate Symbolic Traversal. *Proc. CHARME*, pages 250–264 , 1999.
22. O. Roig, J. Cortadella, and E. Pastor. Verification of asynchronous circuits by BDD-based model checking of Petri nets. *Proc. ICATPN*, LNCS 935, pages 374–391. Springer, June 1995.
23. R. Siminiceanu and G. Ciardo. New metrics for static variable ordering in decision diagrams. *Proc. TACAS*, LNCS 2031, pages 328–342. Springer, March 2006.
24. M. Tilgner, Y. Takahashi, and G. Ciardo. SNS 1.0: Synchronized Network Solver. *Proc. 1st Int. Workshop on Manuf. and Petri Nets*, pages 215–234, June 1996.
25. The VIS Group. VIS: A system for verification and synthesis. *Proc. CAV*, LNCS 1102, pages 428–432, Springer, July 1996.
26. D. Ward and F. Somenzi. Automatic Generation of Hints for Symbolic Traversal. *Proc. CHARME*, pages 207–221 , 2005.

Model Checking Timed Systems with Urgencies

Pao-Ann Hsiung, Shang-Wei Lin, Yean-Ru Chen, Chun-Hsian Huang, Jia-Jen Yeh, Hong-Yu Sun, Chao-Sheng Lin, and Hsiao-Win Liao

Department of Computer Science and Information Engineering,
National Chung Cheng University, Chiayi, Taiwan−621, ROC
hpa@computer.org

Abstract. Computation tree logic (CTL) model checkers either allow modeling of only *lazy* semantics in the timed system model or consider at most a simple *as soon as possible* semantics. However, the design of real-time systems requires different types of urgencies, which have been modeled by several urgency variants of the timed automata model. Except for the IF toolset that model checks timed automata with urgency against observers, the urgency variants of timed automata have not yet been used for verifying the satisfaction of CTL properties in real-time systems. This work is targeted at proposing a zone-based urgency semantics that is time-reactive and at model checking timed automata models that have been extended with such urgency semantics for *delayable* and *eager* transition types. Interactions among these different types of transition urgencies are also investigated. The proposed verification methods were implemented in the SGM CTL model checker and applied to real-time and embedded systems. Several experiments, comparing the state space sizes produced by SGM with that by the IF toolset, show that SGM produces much smaller state-spaces.

1 Introduction

A popular model for real-time systems is *Timed Automata* (TA) [2], for which several model checkers such as SGM [15], RED [14], UPPAAL [4], and Kronos [16] have been developed. However, timed automata models assume a *lazy* semantics, that is, an enabled state transition need not be taken as long as the invariant condition of the state is not violated. Lazy transition semantics are too general to model the urgent behavior found in many real-world systems such as medical devices, home appliances, robotics, and others. Thus, the TA model was extended with urgency semantics such as the *Timed Automata with Deadlines* (TAD) [5], *Timed Automata with Urgent Transitions* [3], *Timed I/O Automata with Stopping Condition* [11], and *Timed I/O Automata with Urgency* [10]. These extended variants incorporate different syntax for accurately modeling urgency. However, system verification using such extended variants have not received as much attention in the area of *Computation Tree Logic* (CTL) model checking [8] . This work focuses on proposing zone-based urgency semantics to a class of TA with urgencies and how they can be model checked and how different types of urgencies affect verification results.

Before urgency semantics were defined for timed automata, state invariants were used to model urgent behavior by forcing a TA to transit to successor states before

S. Graf and W. Zhang (Eds.): ATVA 2006, LNCS 4218, pp. 67–81, 2006.

the invariants are violated due to time elapse. However, the invariant-based method was only applicable to hard deadlines, where the stopping of time due to urgency and the non-existence of any transition to take when time is stopped resulted in a *timelock*. Stopping conditions associated with timed I/O automata also result in similar timelocks. Different methods were proposed to avoid timelocks such as associating a transition with a deadline predicate [5], with an urgency predicate [10], or with a positive rational parameter representing deadline [3]. However, there is very little research on how such models with urgent semantics are to be verified using CTL model checking [8]. There is also no CTL model checker that can directly model check these models. The IF toolset [7] can model check timed automata with urgency against properties written as *observers*, which are IF processes that monitor and guide simulation.

The expressivities of deadline predicates, urgency predicates, and deadline parameters are all same [10,3]. Further, it has also been shown that deadline predicates can be simplified into urgency types, namely *lazy*, *delayable*, and *eager*. We thus decided that we need only address the model checking of timed automata having transitions associated with urgency types. We call this model as *Urgent Timed Automata* (UTA). The major issue in this work is how do we restrict time progress so that the enabled urgent transitions are taken as required by their semantics and the models can be model checked.

Our major contribution in this work is the proposal of a method by which a conventional TA model checker can be used to model check a system modeled by a set of UTA. A novel *zone capping* operation is proposed for enforcing urgency. Other contributions include the investigation of the interactions amongst different urgencies in terms of model checking.

The remaining portion is organized as follows. Section 2 describes previous work related to urgency modeling and verification. Basic definitions used in our work are given in Section 3. Section 4 will formulate the solutions to solve the above described issues in model checking urgent timed automata. Section 5 describes the algorithm and implementation of the proposed method. The article is concluded and future research directions are given in Section 6.

2 Related Work

The majority of work that has extended the timed automata model with urgency semantics is focused on the modeling aspects [3,5,10] such as expressivity and compositionality. Except for the IF toolset, little attention has been paid to the verification of systems modeled by these urgency extended models.

Timed automata with deadlines (TAD) [5] proposed by Sifakis et al. were among the first models that extended TA with urgency. An urgent transition was associated with a *deadline predicate*, which represents the condition when time progress must stop to allow for the urgent transition to be taken. Once the urgent transition is taken, time progress can continue. TADs are *time-reactive* or *timelock-free*, that is, the system never comes to a complete halt due to the violation of a deadline and some enabled transition can always be taken when time progress is stopped. Semantically, a TAD state s is associated with a *time progress condition* (TPC) $c_s = \neg \bigvee_{i \in I} d_i$, where d_i

is the deadline predicate of transition $i \in I$ and I is the set of all outgoing transitions from state s [5]. However, TPC is not suitable for model checking because it results in non-convex clock zones which require further post-processing such as zone partitioning [12]. It was also shown that any TAD can be transformed into an equivalent TAD with only eager and lazy transitions [5].

A recent extension is called *Timed Automata with Urgent Transitions* (TAUT) [3], which associates a rational number *deadline parameter*, $l \in \mathcal{Q}^+$, with a TA such that urgent transitions must be taken within l time units after they are enabled. The expressiveness of TAUT is the same as that of TAD, but TAUT allows shorter deadline specifications. Another improvement is that TAUT allows right-closed TPC, which cannot be handled by TAD.

The deadline predicates have also been applied to *Timed I/O Automata* (TIOA) [11] which orginally had only a stopping condition for specifying deadlines. As noted earlier, similar to state invariants, stopping conditions may result in timelocks. This extension of TIOA associated urgent transitions with an *urgency predicate*, which made them time-reactive by construction and closed under composition. Invariant properties are proved by constructing time progress predicates for each urgent transition and then taking the conjunction of these time progress predicates as the condition for time progress. However, a time progress predicate is the negation of urgency predicate, which would result in non-convex clock zones and thus make model checking difficult. The authors of [10] remarked that by restricting the clock zones in urgency predicates one can avoid non-convex time progress predicates, however this is too strict a restriction.

From the above descriptions, we can observe that TAD and TIOA with urgency use time progress conditions (predicates) that can result in non-convex clock zones, while TAUT adopts a TA transformation approach. Our work is similar to the transformation approach of TAUT, however we do not need the deadline parameter l and our approach is much simpler in terms of conformance with the original TA model and region semantics. Similar to TAUT, we allow left-open transition enabling time intervals (zones), which are not allowed by TAD and TIOA with urgency. Further, unlike all the other models, TAD, TAUT, and TIOA with urgency, we separate prioritization from urgency, which constitutes a more general and useful semantics. Our previous work on prioritization of TA transitions [12] is applicable to the UTA model in this work, so we do not repeat them again here.

Support for modeling urgency in systems and verifying them has been incorporated in tools such as IF [7] and UPPAAL [4]. The IF toolset is an environment for modeling and validation of heterogeneous real-time systems using TAD. It consists of two parts: a syntactic transformer, which provides language level access to IF descriptions and has been used to implement static analysis and optimization techniques, and an open exploration platform, which gives access to the graph of possible executions. IF has been connected to some state-of-art model checkers and test-case generators. IF can also model check directly using observers. UPPAAL uses urgent channels that are taken as soon as they are enabled, however time constraints cannot be associated with urgent channels. We pose no such restriction on urgent transitions.

Fig. 1 shows how an eager transition is enforced using invariants, TPC, and the newly proposed zone capping. We find that only zone capping succeeds in associating the

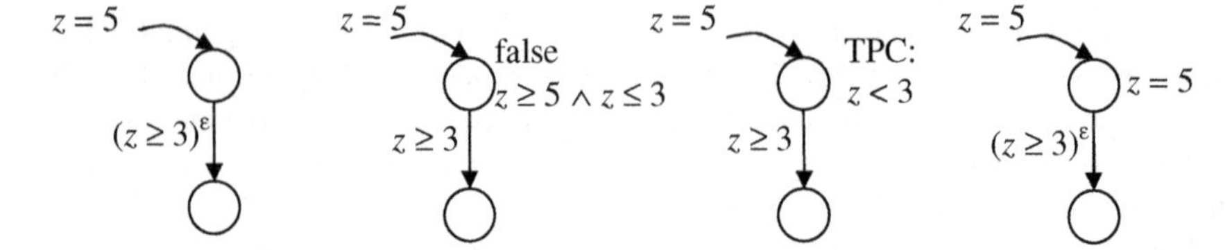

Fig. 1. Enforcing Urgency using Different Methods

model with a correct and intuitive semantics. If a user specified an invariant of $z \leq 3$ to enforce the eager transition with trigger $z \geq 3$ to be taken as soon as enabled, then we might end up with some runs being eliminated because if the mode clock zone is $z \geq 5$, then when conjuncted with the invariant $z \leq 3$, would be false. Thus, invariants fail to enforce correct urgency semantics. Since a TPC is constructed from the deadline predicates in transition triggers, in this example, the TPC would be $z < 3$. However, when time stops progressing at $z = 3$, the mode is not yet entered so there is a timelock. Originally, TPC guaranteed time-reactivity only under the condition that when time stops the transition is enabled. We have violated this assumption to produce a timelock. Zone capping takes the mode clock zone $z \geq 5$ also into consideration when stopping time progress (bounding or capping the zone), thus no such assumption is required. Zone capping thus provides a correct and intuitive urgency semantics.

3 Preliminaries

Given a set C of clock variables and a set D of discrete variables, the syntax of a *mode predicate* η over C and D is defined as: $\eta := \mathit{false} \mid x \sim c \mid x - y \sim c \mid d \sim c \mid \eta_1 \wedge \eta_2 \mid \neg\beta_3$, where $x, y \in C$, $\sim \in \{\leq, <, =, \geq, >\}$, $c \in \mathcal{N}$, the set of non-negative integers, $d \in D$, η_1, η_2 are mode predicates, and β_3 is a discrete variable constraint. A mode predicate η can be expressed as a conjunction of a clock constraint ζ and a Boolean condition β on the discrete variables, that is, $\eta = \zeta \wedge \beta$, where the clock constraint is also called a clock zone.

Definition 1. Urgent Timed Automaton
An *Urgent Timed Automaton* (UTA) is a tuple $\mathcal{A}_i = (M_i, m_i^0, C_i, D_i, L_i, \chi_i, T_i, \psi_i, \tau_i, \mu_i, \rho_i)$ such that: M_i is a finite set of modes. $m_i^0 \in M$ is the initial mode. C_i is a set of clock variables. D_i is a set of discrete variables. L_i is a set of synchronization labels, and $\alpha \in L_i$ is a special label that represents asynchronous behavior (i.e. no need of synchronization). $\chi_i : M_i \mapsto B(C_i, D_i)$ is an *invariance* function that labels each mode with a condition true in that mode. $T_i \subseteq M_i \times M_i$ is a set of transitions. $\psi_i : T_i \mapsto L_i$ associates a synchronization label with a transition. $\tau_i : T_i \mapsto B(C_i, D_i)$ defines the transition triggering conditions, where $\tau_i(t) = \zeta_{\tau_i(t)} \wedge \beta_{\tau_i(t)}$ gives the clock zone and the Boolean condition associated with the transition's trigger, respectively. $\mu_i : T_i \mapsto \{\lambda, \delta, \alpha\}$ associates an urgency type with a transition, including *lazy*, *delayable*, and *eager*, respectively, whose semantics are given in Section. 4.1. $\rho_i : T_i \mapsto 2^{C_i \cup (D_i \times \mathcal{N})}$

is an *assignment* function that maps each transition to a set of assignments such as resetting some clock variables and setting some discrete variables to integer values. □

The semantics of a UTA can be defined by its state and computation run as follows.

Definition 2. State and Run
A pair $s = (m, \nu)$ is called a *state* of a UTA $\mathcal{A}_i = (M_i, m_i^0, C_i, D_i, L_i, \chi_i, T_i, \psi_i, \tau_i, \mu_i, \rho_i)$ if $m \in M_i$ is a mode and ν maps each clock from C_i and each discrete variable from D_i to a real number in $\mathcal{R}$. A sequence of state-transition pairs $\langle s_0 \xrightarrow{t_0} s_1 \ldots s_n \rangle$ is called a *computation run* if s_{i+1} is reachable from s_i either through a mode transition $t_i \in T_i$ or a time transition. A time transition represents the elapse of time without changing mode. A state s is said to be *reachable* if there exists a computation run $\langle s_0 \xrightarrow{t_0} s_1 \ldots s \rangle$, where $s_0 = (m_i^0, \nu_0)$ is an initial state of $\mathcal{A}_i$. □

States can be grouped into zones and the infinite number of states can be classified into a finite number of regions as defined in the following.

Definition 3. Region
Let c_{max} be the largest constant integer that is compared with any clock. Two states $s = (m, \nu)$ and $s' = (m, \nu')$ are said to be in the same *region* if either $\nu(x) > c_{max}$ and $\nu'(x) > c_{max}$ for all $x \in C_i$ or $\lfloor \nu(x) \rfloor = \lfloor \nu'(x) \rfloor$ and $(\nu(x) - \lfloor \nu(x) \rfloor > \nu(y) - \lfloor \nu(y) \rfloor) \Longleftrightarrow (\nu'(x) - \lfloor \nu'(x) \rfloor > \nu'(y) - \lfloor \nu'(y) \rfloor), \forall x, y \in C_i$, and $\nu(d) = \nu'(d), \forall d \in D_i$. We use the notation $[s]$ to denote the region to which s belongs. □

Definition 4. Clock Zone and Zone
A convex union of regions is called a *clock zone*. Given a mode m, a clock zone ζ_m, and a Boolean constraint β_m, the tuple (m, ζ_m, β_m) is called a *zone*. A state $s = (m, \nu)$ is in a zone $z = (m, \zeta_m, \beta_m)$ if $\zeta_m \to \nu(C_i)$ and $\beta_m \to \nu(D_i)$. □

In most model checkers, the clock constraints are represented by *Difference Bound Matrices* (DBM) [9]. Since our solutions for modeling transition urgencies focus on the manipulation of clock zones, we give the definition of DBM as follows.

Definition 5. Difference Bound Matrix (DBM)
A clock zone ζ that represents a clock constraint on n clocks in $C_i = \{x_1, x_2, \ldots, x_n\}$ can be implemented as a $(n+1) \times (n+1)$ matrix Δ, where $\Delta(i,j) = (\sim, c), \sim \in \{<, \leq\}, c \in \mathcal{N} \cup \{\infty\}$, represents the constraint $x_i - x_j \sim c$, $0 \leq i, j \leq n$. $x_0 = 0$. □

Given a DBM Δ representing a clock zone ζ, $\Delta(0,i)$ and $\Delta(i,0)$ are respectively the lower and upper bounds for clock x_i. Given two DBM elements $\Delta(i,j) = (\sim, c)$ and $\Delta(i',j') = (\sim', c')$, we can compare them by saying $\Delta(i,j) < \Delta(i',j')$ if either (1) $c < c'$ or (2) $c = c'$ and $\sim$ is $<$ and $\sim'$ is $\leq$. The other relational comparisons between $\Delta(i,j)$ and $\Delta(i',j')$ can be similarly defined.

Given two lower bound DBM elements $\Delta(0,j) = (\sim, c)$ and $\Delta'(0,j') = (\sim', c')$, a difference operator between the two DBM elements can be defined as follows, where the exponents $+$ and $-$ are used to represent infinitesimally larger and smaller numbers than those in the brackets, respectively.

$$\text{diff}(\Delta(0,j),\Delta'(0,j')) = \begin{cases} c'-c & \text{if } \sim \text{ and } \sim' \text{ are the same} \\ (c'-c)^+ & \text{if } \sim \in \{<\}, \sim' \in \{\leq\} \\ (c'-c)^- & \text{if } \sim \in \{\leq\}, \sim' \in \{<\} \end{cases}$$

For an integer c, we have the following relation: $c^- < c < c^+$. Similarly, given two upper bound DBM elements $\Delta(i,0) = (\sim, c)$ and $\Delta'(i',0) = (\sim', c')$, a difference operator can be defined as follows.

$$\text{diff}(\Delta(i,0),\Delta'(i',0)) = \begin{cases} c-c' & \text{if } \sim \text{ and } \sim' \text{ are the same} \\ (c-c')^+ & \text{if } \sim \in \{\leq\}, \sim' \in \{<\} \\ (c-c')^- & \text{if } \sim \in \{<\}, \sim' \in \{\leq\} \end{cases}$$

Intuitively, the difference operator between two lower bound DBM elements represents the time lag between *entering* the two zones represented by the DBMs and that between two upper bound DBM elements represent the time lag between *leaving* the two zones. The difference considers only a single clock at a time, so for actually entering or leaving a zone, we need to define zone lag that considers all clocks. The difference operator will be used to define zone lag in Definition 6.

Definition 6. Zone Entry Lag and Zone Exit Lag
Given two clock zones ζ_1 and ζ_2 for clocks in C, represented by DBMs Δ_1 and Δ_2, respectively, the zone entry lag and zone exit lag between the two zones are denoted by $\text{enlag}(\Delta_1, \Delta_2)$ and $\text{exlag}(\Delta_1, \Delta_2)$ as defined in the following.

$$\begin{aligned} \text{enlag}(\Delta_1,\Delta_2) &= \max_{1\leq j\leq |C|}\{\text{diff}(\Delta_1(0,j),\Delta_2(0,j))\} \\ \text{exlag}(\Delta_1,\Delta_2) &= \min_{1\leq i\leq |C|}\{\text{diff}(\Delta_1(i,0),\Delta_2(i,0))\} \end{aligned}$$ □

When $\text{enlag}(\Delta_1, \Delta_2)$ is positive, it means Δ_1 is entered later than Δ_2; when zero, it means they are entered at the same time; and when negative, it means Δ_1 is entered earlier than Δ_2. When $\text{exlag}(\Delta_1, \Delta_2)$ is positive, it means Δ_1 is exited later than Δ_2; when zero, it means they are exited at the same time; and when negative, it means Δ_1 is exited earlier than Δ_2.

Given an urgent timed system $\mathcal{S}$ with n components modeled by UTA $\mathcal{A}_i = (M_i, m_i^0, C_i, D_i, L_i, \chi_i, T_i, \psi_i, \tau_i, \mu_i, \rho_i)$, $1 \leq i \leq n$, the system model is defined as a state graph represented by $\mathcal{A}_1 \times \ldots \times \mathcal{A}_n = \mathcal{A}_{\mathcal{S}} = (M, m^0, C, D, L, \chi, T, \psi, \tau, \mu, \rho)$, where $\times$ is the parallel composition operator, such as the merge manipulator in SGM, except for the urgency of synchronized transitions that is resolved as shown in Table 1.

Table 1. Urgency Resolution for Synchronized Transitions

$\mu_i(e_i)$	λ	λ	δ	λ	δ	ϵ
$\mu_j(e_j)$	λ	δ	δ	ϵ	ϵ	ϵ
$\mu(e)$	λ	δ	δ	ϵ	ϵ	ϵ

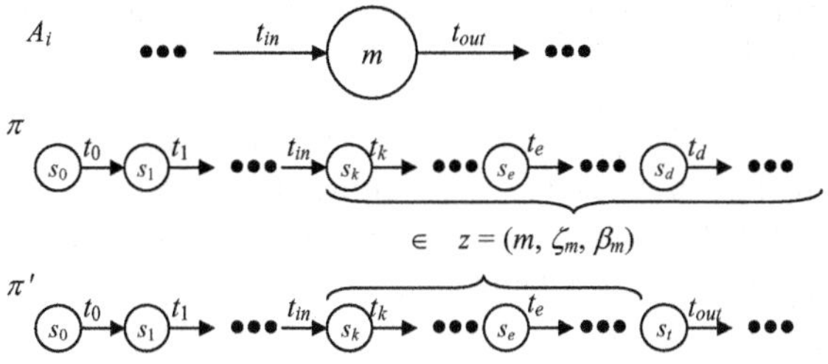

Fig. 2. Computation Runs

4 Model Checking Urgent Timed Systems

Our target problem is to model and verify urgent timed systems such as real-time embedded systems. A set of urgent timed automata is used to model such a system and model checking is used to verify if the urgent timed system state graph, obtained by merging the set of UTA, satisfies user-given CTL properties.

4.1 Semantics of Urgent Timed Automata

The syntax of urgencies was given as symbols $\{\lambda, \delta, \epsilon\}$ associated with transitions, as defined by $\mu_i(t)$ in Definition 1. As shown in Figure 2, consider a non-initial mode $m \in M_i$ of an urgent timed automaton $\mathcal{A}_i = (M_i, m_i^0, C_i, D_i, L_i, \chi_i, T_i, \psi_i, \tau_i, \mu_i, \rho_i)$, which has an incoming mode transition t_{in} and an outgoing mode transition t_{out}. For simplicity, we first assume that m has a single incoming and a single outgoing transition. From the two computation runs in Figure 2, we can make the following observations, where each state $s_j = (m_j, \nu_j)$.

State sequence $\langle s_0, \ldots, s_{k-1} \rangle$ leads to zone $z = (m, \zeta_m, \beta_m)$. s_k is the first reachable state in zone z, that is, $m_j \neq m, \forall j, 0 \leq j < k$ and $m_k = m$. s_e is the first reachable state in zone z in which transition t_{out} is enabled. Transition t_{out} may be taken anytime starting from state s_e before it is disabled, as in run π', and s_d is the first reachable state in zone z in which transition t_{out} is disabled before it is taken, as in π.

In Figure 2, there are two kinds of computation runs π and π' as follows. Transition t_{out} is enabled and then disabled, without being taken:
$\pi = \langle s_0 \xrightarrow{t_0} s_1 \ldots \xrightarrow{t_{in}} s_k \xrightarrow{t_k} s_{k+1} \xrightarrow{t_{k+1}} \ldots s_e \xrightarrow{t_e} s_{e+1} \xrightarrow{t_{e+1}} \ldots s_d \xrightarrow{t_d} s_{d+1} \xrightarrow{t_{d+1}} \ldots \rangle$, where starting from state s_k, all states are in the zone $z = (m, \zeta_m, \beta_m)$, that is, $\zeta_m \rightarrow \nu_j(C_i)$ and $\beta_m \rightarrow \nu_j(D_i)$ for all $j \geq k$. Let Π be set of all such computation runs π, where t_{out} is never taken. Transition t_{out} is enabled and is taken before being disabled: $\pi' = \langle s_0 \xrightarrow{t_0} s_1 \ldots \xrightarrow{t_{in}} s_k \xrightarrow{t_k} s_{k+1} \xrightarrow{t_{k+1}} \ldots s_e \xrightarrow{t_e} s_{e+1} \xrightarrow{t_{e+1}} \ldots s_t \xrightarrow{t_{out}} \ldots \rangle$, where the states $s_k, \ldots, s_{t-1}$ are in the zone $z = (m, \zeta_m, \beta_m)$. Let Π' be the set of all such computation runs, where t_{out} is enabled and taken before being disabled.

Since there are infinite number of states in which transition t_{out} may be enabled and taken, let us consider clock regions as defined in Definition 3. Given a region R, let $\Pi'_R \subseteq \Pi'$ be the subset of computation runs where t_{out} is taken in region R, that is, $s_t \in R$. The semantics of the transition behavior differ according to the urgency $\mu_i(t_{out})$ associated with the transition as follows.

- Lazy Transition (λ): If t_{out} is a lazy transition, that is, $\mu_i(t_{out}) = \lambda$, then the set of reachable computation runs that passes through mode m is $\Pi(m, t_{out}) = \Pi \cup \Pi'$, which means all runs where t_{out} after being enabled is either taken or not taken before being disabled are reachable.
- Delayable Transition (δ): If t_{out} is a delayable transition, that is, $\mu_i(t_{out}) = \delta$, then the set of runs through mode m is $\Pi(m, t_{out}) = \Pi'$, which means all runs where t_{out} after being enabled is taken latest before being disabled.
- Eager Transition (ϵ): If t_{out} is an eager transition, that is, $\mu_i(t_{out}) = \epsilon$, then the set of reachable computation runs that passes through mode m is $\Pi(m, t_{out}) = \bigcup_R \Pi'_R, R = [s_e]$, where $[s_e]$ is the region in which t_{out} is enabled.

4.2 Capping Zones

When a system is in a zone $z = (m, \zeta_m, \beta_m)$ such that the clock zone has no upper bound, that is, $\Delta_m(i, 0) = (<, \infty)$ for some clock $x_i \in C_i$, or the upper bound allows the system to stay in the mode m beyond that allowed by a delayable or an eager transition outgoing from the mode m, then we need to restrict the upper bound of the zone, which we term as *capping zones*. By capping a zone, a system is forced to exit the mode before the upper bound is violated due to time elapse, otherwise the behavior of the system will be undefined. Before defining zone capping, since the upper bounds for delayable and eager transitions are different, we need to first define the *subzones* that will be used as upper bounds for zone capping.

Definition 7. Earliest Subzone
Given a clock zone ζ, represented by a DBM Δ, the earliest subzone ESub(ζ) is a subspace of ζ such that the DBM Δ_e representing ESub(ζ) is defined as follows.

$$\Delta_e(i,0) = \begin{cases} (\leq, -c) & \text{if } \Delta(0,i) = (\leq, c) \\ (<, -c+1) & \text{if } \Delta(0,i) = (<, c) \end{cases}$$
$$\Delta_e(i,j) = \Delta(i,j), j \neq 0$$
□

Definition 8. Final Subzone
Given a clock zone ζ, represented by a DBM Δ, the final subzone FSub(ζ) is a subspace of ζ such that the DBM Δ_f representing FSub(ζ) is defined as follows.

$$\Delta_f(0,j) = \begin{cases} (\leq, -c) & \text{if } \Delta(j,0) = (\leq, c) \\ (<, -c+1) & \text{if } \Delta(j,0) = (<, c) \\ \Delta(0,j) & \text{if } \Delta(j,0) = (<, \infty) \end{cases}$$
$$\Delta_f(i,j) = \Delta(i,j), i \neq 0$$
□

A zone is called a *subzone* when it is the earliest subzone or the final subzone for some clock zone. Zone capping can be defined using a subzone as upper bound for a clock zone.

Definition 9. **Zone Capping**
Given a clock zone ζ for clocks in C and a subzone ζ_s, represented respectively by DBMs Δ and Δ_s, the zone ζ can be capped by ζ_s into a new zone denoted by ZCap(ζ, ζ_s) which is defined by its DBM $\Delta_{(\zeta,\zeta_s)}$ as follows.

$$\begin{aligned} \Delta_{(\zeta,\zeta_s)}(i,0) &= \min(\Delta(i,0), \Delta_s(i,0)) \\ \Delta_{(\zeta,\zeta_s)}(i,j) &= \Delta(i,j), j \neq 0 \end{aligned} \qquad (1)$$

□

It must be noted here that after zone capping, we need to canonicalize the DBM $\Delta_{(\zeta,\zeta_s)}$ before they can used for further processing in model checking.

4.3 Enforcing Urgencies

We now show how urgency is enforced in UTA by applying the zone capping operation using the earliest and final subzones. Given a mode m with zone (m, ζ_m, β_m), zero or more delayable transitions $\{t_d\}$, zero or more eager transitions $\{t_e\}$, and zero or more lazy transitions, urgency is enforced by modifying the clock zone ζ_m as shown in Table 2. If there is no urgent transition ($p = q = 0$), then the mode clock zone ζ_m is not modified.

Table 2. Zone Capping for Different Types of Urgencies

Urgency	Newly Capped Zone (ζ'_m)
$p=q=0$	ζ_m
$p>0, q=0$	ZCap$(\zeta_m, \text{FSub}(\zeta_m \cap \zeta_{\tau(t_d)}))$, for some $t_d \in \{t_d \mid \text{exlag}(\Delta_{t_d}, \Delta_m) = \min_{t_d}(\text{exlag}(\Delta_{t_d}, \Delta_m))\}$
$p=0, q>0$	ZCap$(\zeta_m, \text{ESub}(\zeta_m \cap \zeta_{\tau(t_e)}))$, for some $t_e \in \{t_e \mid \text{enlag}(\Delta_{t_e}, \Delta_m) = \min_{t_e}(\text{enlag}(\Delta_{t_e}, \Delta_m))\}$
$p>0, q>0$	ZCap$(\zeta_m, \text{ESub}(\zeta_m \cap \zeta_{\tau(t_e)}))$ if $\text{exlag}(\Delta_{t_d}, \Delta_m) \geq \text{enlag}(\Delta_{t_e}, \Delta_m)$ undefined, otherwise. $t_d \in \{t' \mid \text{exlag}(\Delta_{t'}, \Delta_m) = \min_t(\text{exlag}(\Delta_t, \Delta_m))\}$ $t_e \in \{t' \mid \text{enlag}(\Delta_{t'}, \Delta_m) = \min_t(\text{enlag}(\Delta_t, \Delta_m))\}$

$p = |\{t_d\}|, q = |\{t_e\}|$

The intuitions behind the modifications are as follows. When there are only delayable transitions, we need to force the system to leave mode m latest in the last subzone before t_d becomes disabled and this is the final subzone (FSub) of the intersection of ζ_m and $\zeta_{\tau(t_d)}$. However, for multiple delayable transitions, we need to select the one that becomes disabled the earliest, which is the one with the minimum zone exit lag, that is, the transition t_d with $\min_{t_d}(\text{exlag}(\Delta_{t_d}, \Delta_m))$.

When there are only eager transitions, we need to force the system to leave mode m latest in the first subzone when t_e becomes enabled and this is the earliest zubzone (ESub) of the intersection of ζ_m and $\zeta_{\tau(t_e)}$. However, for multiple eager transitions, we need to select the one that becomes enabled the earliest, which is the one with the minimum zone entry lag, that is, the transition t_e with $\min_{t_e}(\text{enlag}(\Delta_{t_e}, \Delta_m))$.

When there are delayable and eager transitions, in order to satisfy the semantics of both types of transitions, we need to ensure that the earliest disabled delayable transition becomes disabled in the same subzone or later than the earliest enabled eager transition. This also results in time-reactivity or the absence of timelocks as is desired of urgency extensions for timed automata. Hence, the condition $\text{exlag}(\Delta_{t_d}, \Delta_m) \geq \text{enlag}(\Delta_{t_e}, \Delta_m)$, where t_d and t_e are the earliest disabled delayable and earliest enabled eager transitions, respectively. When the condition is not satisfied, we have chosen to leave it as undefined because capping the zone either using the deadline of the earliest disabled delayable transition or the enabling time of the earliest enabled eager transition, would result in violating the semantics of the other urgent transition. This is a limitation of our proposed method, which we leave for investigation in the future.

5 Implementation and Application Examples

The proposed method for model checking urgent timed automata (UTA) is implemented in the *State-Graph Manipulators* (SGM) model checker [15], which is a high-level compositional model checker for real-time systems. For verifying an urgent timed system modeled by a set of UTA, the system properties are specified in the *Computation Tree Logic* (CTL) [1]. As described in Section 5.1, UTA can be input to SGM and they are model checked automatically against user-specified CTL properties. Theoretical results such as time reactivity and semantics equivalence are proved in Section 5.2. This is the first known implementation and handling of urgency for timed automata in a model checker itself. Other tools such as UPPAAL does not support the urgency semantics described in this work, while the IF toolset [7] supports modeling of urgency, exhaustive simulation, and model checking using observers. Labeled transition systems (LTS) generated by IF could blow up in size and even not terminate, as detailed in Section 5.3.

5.1 Urgency Processing Algorithm

The methods proposed in Section 4 were all implemented into SGM. The main algorithm for processing urgency assumes that we already have a system state graph which represents the concurrent behavior of a set of timed automata. This state graph can be obtained through the *merge* manipulator in SGM. The urgency processing algorithm is then applied to the merged state-graph.

Due to page limit, the algorithm is not shown here. However, it is described briefly as follows. For each mode, we count the number of delayable and eager outgoing transitions. Then, for each delayable transition, we calculate its zone exit lag with respect to the mode clock zone Z_m and for each eager transition, we calculate its zone entry lag with respect to the mode clock zone. During the zone lag calculations, we also record the delayable transition (t_{minx}) that has the minimum zone exit lag and the eager transition (t_{mine}) that has the minimum zone entry lag. Next, we check if the minimum zone exit lag is smaller than the minimum zone entry lag, which is the *undefined* case in Table 2 and we exit the algorithm if such a case is encountered. Finally, the zone operations `ZCap`, `ESub`, `FSub`, `Intersect` are used to modify the mode clock zone Z_m according to Table 2.

For an urgent system state graph $G = \mathcal{A}_{\mathcal{S}} = (M, m^0, C, D, L, \chi, T, \psi, \tau, \mu, \rho)$ for a system $\mathcal{S}$, the complexity of the algorithm is $\mathcal{O}(|M| \times |T| \times |C|)$. For each mode in M, we need to calculate the zone exit lag for each outgoing delayable transition and the zone entry lag for each outgoing eager transition. The zone lag computations have $\mathcal{O}(|C|)$ time complexity. Hence, the complexity of the algorithm is $\mathcal{O}(|M| \times |T| \times |C|)$. It is noted here that the zone capping, the subzone computation, and the intersect operations all require $|C|^2$ time complexity. However, we can assume that $|C| = \mathcal{O}(|T|)$ because the number of clocks is usually much smaller than the number of transitions in real-world system models.

5.2 Theoretical Results

We give some theoretical results pertaining to our proposed zone capping method for enforcing zone-based urgency semantics. We first state that zone-based urgency semantics is equivalent to absolute urgency semantics as advocated by the previous work on urgency modeling [10,3,5]. Next, we state that our method preserves time-reactivity for urgent timed automata.

Theorem 1. *Semantics Equivalence*
Zone-based urgency semantics and absolute urgency semantics give the same model checking results.

Proof: For left closed, right open, and right closed time intervals on urgent transitions, the two semantics are similar. However, for left open time intervals (c, ∞) on an eager transition, absolute urgency semantics require the transition to be taken at c^+, while zone-based urgency semantics require the transition to be taken in the clock zone $(c, c+1)$. Since $c^+ \in (c, c+1)$ and any two time points in $(c, c+1)$ are in the same region, the two semantics give the same model checking results. □

Theorem 2. *Time-Reactivity*
The proposed zone capping method for enforcing zone-based urgency semantics preserves time-reactivity for urgent timed automata.

Proof: The zone capping method stops time progress either in an earliest subzone $\text{ESub}(\zeta_m \cap \zeta_{\tau(t_e)})$ for an eager transition t_e or in a final subzone $\text{FSub}(\zeta_m \cap \zeta_{\tau(t_d)})$ for a delayable transition t_d. However, since we have taken the triggers of the urgent transitions into consideration, at least one transition is enabled when time is stopped. Hence, the zone capping method preserves time-reactivity for urgent timed automata. □

5.3 Application Examples

Besides SGM, there are no other known CTL model checkers that have implemented the proposed urgency semantics. The closest work that we have found is the IF toolset [7], which performs model checking using observers. The UPPAAL model checker has implemented urgent channels and committed locations, however these cannot be used to model the urgency semantics described in this work. We first show why urgent channels and state invariants cannot model the urgency semantics. Then, we compare SGM with

Table 3. Application Examples

No.	System	$n(\|M_i\|/\|T_i\|)$	Urgency	#Del	#Eager
1	Water Sprinkler	2 (2/2, 2/2)	Single Delayable	1	0
2	Heating Apparatus	2 (2/2, 2/2)	Concurrent Eager	0	4
3	Error Checker	2 (2/3, 2/2)	Branching Eager	0	4
4	Priority Arbiter	3 (3/4, 3/4, 3/4)	Branching Eager/Delayable	1	9
5	Periodic Processes	2 (3/3, 3/3)	Single Eager/Delayable	2	4
6	Lip Synchronization (VF)	4 (2/2, 1/1, 5/5, 4/5)	Complex Eager/Delayable	1	10
7	Lip Synchronization (SF)	3 (1/1, 2/2, 6/7)	Complex Eager/Delayable	2	7

n: # of UTA, VF: Video First, SF: Sound First
Models and input files: "http://embedded.cs.ccu.edu.tw/~esl_web/Project/Ch/SGM/"

IF using six examples from the embedded real-time systems domain, which show that our approach as implemented in SGM always terminates and is more efficient.

We found two problems while modeling urgency in UPPAAL, as follows: (1) an eager transition with time constraints could not be modeled by an urgent channel because an urgent channel cannot be associated with any time constraint, and (2) a delayable transition when forced out of a state using invariants in UPPAAL could result in timelocks. Out of the six examples we tried, as shown in Table 3, only one could be modeled in UPPAAL using state invariants, namely the periodic processes system, because there was no communication between the periodic processes.

We compared our urgency semantics implementation in SGM with that in IF using six typical examples as summarized in Table 3, which have various combinations of eager and delayable transitions. For each example, we also specified a few CTL properties to verify the urgency semantics, which could not have been possible if we used UPPAAL or any other model checker without urgency semantics. Due to page-limits, we describe the most complex example, namely Lip Synchronization, and use a toy example to illustrate the differences between SGM, UPPAAL, and IF.

The Lip Synchronization algorithm was first described in the synchronous language Esterel [13]. Then specifications in a number of different formalisms were presented. The lip synchronization algorithm tries to synchronize audio and video streams as long as their arrival times are within certain time intervals. It is a typical real-time protocol for distributed multimedia systems. Bowman et al. [6] verified the lip synchronization algorithm using the UPPAAL model checker. However, they also described the limitations in UPPAAL in detecting timelocks and in the "hand-wired" construction of timeout operators and watchdog timers, which could easily lead to timelocks. Since the lip synchronization algorithm distinguished between the initial arrival of video or sound, it was easy to partition the algorithm into two parts for verification. The models for initial arrival of video and sound are given in Fig. 3. The main job of lip synchronization is to compute $vmins$, the difference between the rate of the sound stream and the video stream. If $vmins$ is out of some predefined range, it means that the streams are out of synchronization. We verified the following property, where mode $v07$ represents out of synchronization: AG($!mode(VideoSync) = v07$).

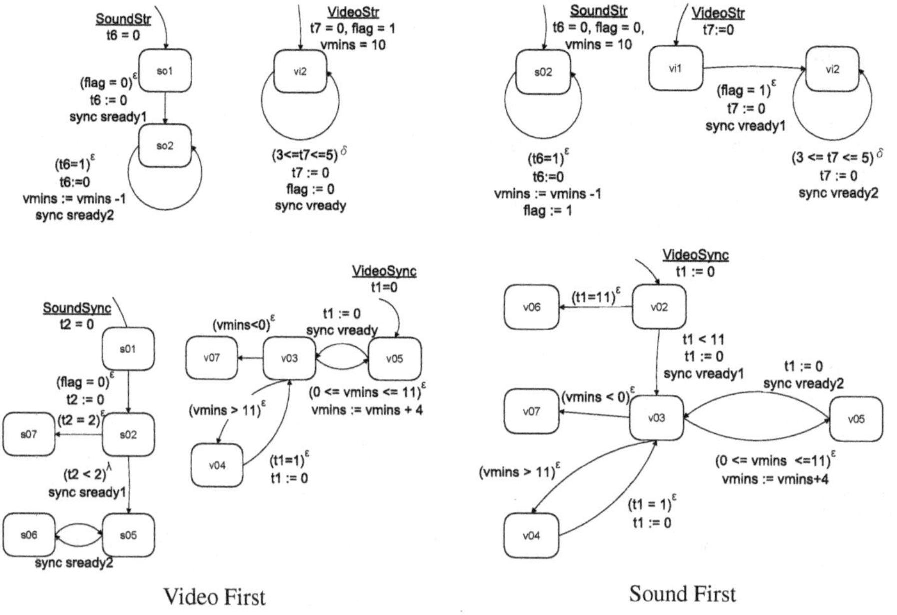

Fig. 3. Lip Synchronization Algorithm

In Fig. 3, we can see that it is much straightforward to model systems with urgency using UTA in SGM, compared to the construction of timeout operators and of watchdog timers, using UPPAAL committed locations and urgent channels as in [6]. As shown in Table 4, we experimented with different video input streams for the lip synchronization algorithm, by restricting the video input clock such as $t7 \in [3, 4]$, that is a video frame comes every 3 to 4 time units. The results of comparing SGM with IF for the six examples are given in Table 4. We can observe that the state-graphs with urgency handling as generated by SGM are all smaller in size than the labeled transition systems generated by IF. For the larger examples such as the priority arbiter and the lip synchronization algorithm, the exhaustive simulation in IF does not terminate, while SGM can generate manageable state graphs that can be model checked.

To show how the LTS generated by IF differs from our zone-based urgency handling in SGM, we use a small example, as illustrated in Fig. 4, where the delayable transition with time trigger $x \leq 20$ in the first UTA when simulated in IF, using `-tf -dfs -po` parameters, results in an LTS with 5 states and 8 transitions. In comparison, the zone-based urgency semantics in SGM produces a state-graph with only 2 states and 3 transitions. Moreover, using state invariants in UPPAAL results in only a single initial state due to timelock as shown in Fig. 4.

From the above experiments, we can observe that our zone-based urgency semantics as implemented in SGM has the following advantages. First, compared to the state-of-the-art CTL model checkers, modeling and verifying systems with urgency semantics has become feasible, straightforward, flexible, and consistent with model checking. Second, compared to the IF toolset, the urgency handling is more symbolic and the sizes of the state graphs are thus much reduced, which makes model checking more efficient.

Table 4. State Graph Sizes Produced by SGM and IF

Example ($t7$)	1		2		3		4		5		6 [3, 4]		6 [3, 5]		7 [3, 4]		7 [3, 5]	
Size	$\|M\|$	$\|T\|$	$\|M\|$	$\|T\|$	$\|M\|$	$\|T\|$	$\|M\|$	$\|T\|$	$\|M\|$	$\|T\|$	$\|M\|$	$\|T\|$	$\|M\|$	$\|T\|$	$\|M\|$	$\|T\|$	$\|M\|$	$\|T\|$
IF*	31	65	12	17	8	14	N/T		341	759	N/T		N/T		N/T		N/T	
IF**	17	28	10	13	7	11	N/T		339	673	N/T		N/T		N/T		N/T	
SGM†	9	11	8	9	4	5	200	327	116	194	178	184	700	892	155	165	506	594

$t7$: Video Clock, *Using DBM and DFS traversal with partial order reduction (`-dfs -po`), **Using DBM and `-tf -dfs -po` parameters, †No reduction, N/T: Non-Terminating

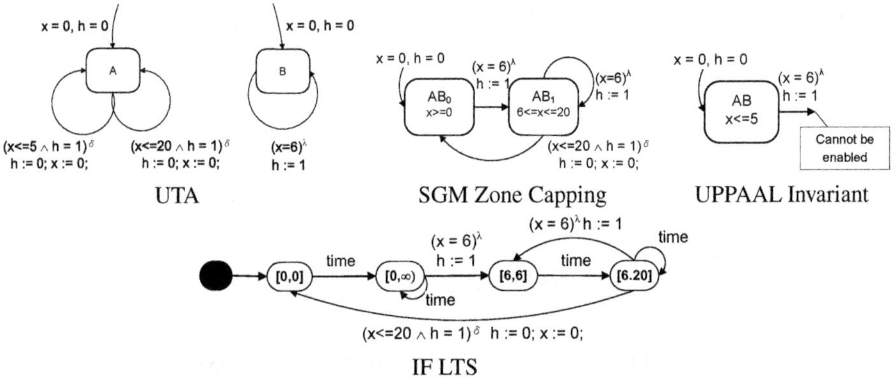

Fig. 4. Comparing Between Zone Capping, State Invariant, and IF LTS

Third, timelocks are naturally avoided due to the UTA semantics and urgency handling, thus we need not use invariants for enforcing urgency now. Nevertheless, a current limitation of the proposed zone-based urgency semantics in SGM, as described in Section 4.3, is an undefined composition of urgency transitions that have no time overlaps.

6 Conclusions

We have shown how a zone-based urgency semantics of the urgent timed automata model can be used for verifying real-time embedded systems based on the CTL model checking paradigm. We have proposed a novel zone capping operation, which enforces the semantics of urgency types in urgent timed automata. The proposed zone-based urgency semantics is equivalent to the absolute urgency semantics and advantageous for model checking. The method also preserves time-reactivity. Several application examples illustrate how our method for verifying real-time embedded systems with urgency is more symbolic and efficient compared to state-of-the-art model checkers. Future work will consist of making the approach more complete.

References

1. R. Alur, C. Courcoubetis, and D.L. Dill. Model-checking for real-time systems. In *Proceedings of the 5th Annual Symposium on Logic in Computer Science*, pages 414–425. IEEE Computer Society Press, 1990.
2. R. Alur and D.L. Dill. A theory of timed automata. *Theoretical Computer Science*, 126(2):183–235, 1994.
3. R. Barbuti and L. Tesei. Timed automata with urgent transitions. *Acta Informatica*, 40(5):317–347, 2004.
4. J. Bengtsson, K. Larsen, F. Larsson, P. Pettersson, and Y. Wang. UPPAAL: a tool suite for automatic verification of real-time systems. In *Proceedings of Workshop on Verification and Control of Hybrid Systems III, LNCS*, volume 1066, pages 232–243, October 1995.
5. S. Bornot, J. Sifakis, and S. Tripakis. Modeling urgency in timed systems. In *Compositionality, LNCS*, volume 1536. Springer Verlag, 1997.
6. H. Bowman, G. Faconti, J-P. Katoen, D. Latella, and M. Massink. Automatic verification of a lip synchronisation algorithm using UPPAAL -extended version-. *Third Internatinoal Workshop on Formal Methods for Industrial Critical Systems*, pages 97–124, May 1998.
7. M. Bozga, J. Cl. Fernandez, L. Ghirvu, S. Graf, J.P. Krimm, and L. Mounier. IF: An intermediate representation and validation environment for time asynchronous systems. In *Proceedings of the Formal Methods Conference (FM)*, 1999.
8. E.M. Clarke and E.A. Emerson. Design and sythesis of synchronization skeletons using branching time temporal logic. In *Proceedings of the Logics of Programs Workshop*, volume 131 of *LNCS*, pages 52–71. Springer Verlag, 1981.
9. David L. Dill. Timing assumptions and verification of finite-state concurrent systems. In *Proceedings of Workshop on Automatic Verification Methods for Finite State Systems*, volume 407 of *LNCS*, pages 197–212. Springer-Verlag, 1989.
10. B. Gebremichael and F. Vaandrager. Specifying urgency in timed I/O automata. In *Proceedings of the 3rd IEEE International Conference on Software Engineering and Formal Methods (SEFM)*, pages 5–9, September 2005.
11. D. K. Kaynar, N. Lynch, R. Segala, and F. Vaandrager. Timed I/O automata: A mathematical framework for modeling and analyzing real-time systems. In *Proceedings of the 24th IEEE International Real-Time Systems Symposium (RTSS)*, pages 166–177. IEEE CS Press, December 2003.
12. S.-W. Lin, P.-A. Hsiung, C.-H. Huang, and Y.-R. Chen. Model checking prioritized timed automata. In *Proceedings of the 3rd International Symposium on Automated Technology for Verification and Analysis (ATVA, Taipei, Taiwan), LNCS*, volume 3707. Springer Verlag, October 2005.
13. J-B Stefani, L. Hazard, and F.Horn. Computational model for distributed multimedia application based on a synchronous programming language. *Computer Communications (Special Issue on FDTs)*, 15(2), 1992.
14. F. Wang. RED: Model-checker for timed automata with clock-restriction diagram. In *Proceedings of the Workshop on Real-Time Tools*, August 2001. Technical Report 2001-014, ISSN 1404-3203, Department of Information Technology, Uppsala University.
15. F. Wang and P.-A. Hsiung. Efficient and user-friendly verification. *IEEE Transactions on Computers*, 51(1):61–83, January 2002.
16. S. Yovine. Kronos: A verification tool for real-time systems. *International Journal of Software Tools for Technology Transfer*, 1(1/2):123–133, October 1997.

Whodunit? Causal Analysis for Counterexamples*

Chao Wang[1], Zijiang Yang[2], Franjo Ivančić[1], and Aarti Gupta[1]

[1] NEC Laboratories America
4 Independence way, Princeton, NJ 08540, USA
{chaowang,ivancic,agupta}@nec-labs.com
[2] Department of Computer Science
Western Michigan University, Kalamazoo, MI 49008, USA
zijiang.yang@wmich.edu

Abstract. Although the counterexample returned by a model checker can help in reproducing the symptom related to a defect, a significant amount of effort is often required for the programmer to interpret it in order to locate the cause. In this paper, we provide an automated procedure to zoom in to potential software defects by analyzing a single concrete counterexample. Our analysis relies on extracting from the counterexample a syntactic-level proof of infeasibility, i.e., a minimal set of word-level predicates that contradict with each other. The procedure uses an efficient weakest pre-condition algorithm carried out on a single concrete execution path, which is significantly more scalable than other model checking based approaches. Unlike most of the existing methods, we do not need additional execution traces other than the buggy one. We use public-domain examples to demonstrate the effectiveness of our new algorithm.

1 Introduction

One of the major advantages of model checking [5, 22] is the production of a counterexample when verification fails. However, the counterexample only shows a symptom of the defect; users still need to spend a considerable amount of time scrutinizing the potentially lengthy trace in order to find the cause of the failure. In principle, an observable *failure* is caused by a *defect* in the code after the infection propagates through a sequence of relevant statements (also called the *infection chain* [26]). In this paper we present an efficient procedure for identifying this infection chain, i.e., the cause-effect segments from the given counterexample that eventually lead to a failure.

The problem of fault localization for software programs has been the attention of recent research. Testing based methods [16, 23] rely on availability of a good test suite; they compare a large set of failing executions with successful ones to find out points in the failing executions that may (statistically) be responsible for the failure. Usually, they assume that a large number of successful executions are available to be chosen as a comparison to failing executions.

* A *whodunit*, for "who done it?", is a plot-driven variety of detective story in which the reader is provided with clues from which the identity of the perpetrator of the crime may be deduced. Examples are the Sherlock Holmes stories by Conan Doyle.

S. Graf and W. Zhang (Eds.): ATVA 2006, LNCS 4218, pp. 82–95, 2006.

Model checking based methods [3, 11, 10] seek additional execution traces by deploying the same model checker again with additional constraints. A representative approach is the work by Groce *et al.* [10], which uses a SAT based bounded model checker to produce the counterexample, and then uses a pseudo-Boolean constraint solver (called PBS [2]) on a constrained version of the same bounded model checking instance to search for a "closest" successful execution trace. The difference between these two traces is considered as potential cause of failure. A drawback of model checking based method is their limited scalability in dealing with large systems or long counterexamples. Furthermore, the difference between a successful run and the counterexample does not always provide a good explanation of the failure.

Delta debugging as in [26, 6] uses automated testing to isolate relevant variables and values of the program by systematically narrowing the state difference between a passing run and a failing run. Note that this method also requires alternative runs in addition to the given counterexample. The method is based on *trial and error*, by assessing the outcome of altered executions to determine whether a change in the program state makes a difference in the test outcome. The alternative runs also determine the quality of results that Delta debugging can infer: a variable can be isolated as a failure cause only if its value differs in the two runs. This method is purely empirical, which is quite different from methods based on formal/static analysis. As is stated in [26], Delta debugging may require a large number of tests to find a difference that can no longer be narrowed.

A problem closely related to fault localization is program repair, which has been studied in [25, 15, 9]. They take the view that a system component may be responsible for a failure if replacing it by an alternative can make the system correct. The program repair problem is cast into a two-player reachability game on a finite-state machine extended from the system, by assuming any component can be replaced by an arbitrary function in terms of inputs and the system state. An algorithm that computes a winning strategy for the game effectively solves the program repair problem. However, program repair in general is significantly more costly than standard model checking.

In general, accurately locating the faulty code requires a complete specification of the system behavior (the same argument also holds for automated program repair). Unfortunately, such specifications are often missing in realistic software development settings. Without a complete specification, it is not possible to determine whether a particular line in the code is faulty or not. What can be done (a view shared by many previous works as well as this paper) is to locate portions of the program where a defect may reside, and to provide an explanation how a defect triggers the failure. In this paper, we try to identify the infection chain in the failed execution path, with the belief that the defect resides in one of the chain segments.

The new causal analysis algorithm presented in this paper differs from previous works in that: (1) it does not require additional successful or failing executions other than the given counterexample; (2) it does not use expensive model checking or constraint solving algorithms. Instead, we use a path-based syntactic-level weakest precondition computation algorithm to aid the analysis. It produces a concise proof of infeasibility for the given counterexample, which is a minimal set of word-level predicates extracted from the failed execution that explains why the execution fails. Since the pre-condition computations are cheap and are restricted to a single execution path (less chance to blow up), our method is significantly more scalable than other model checking based methods.

2 Motivating Examples

We provide two small examples to illustrate a shortcoming of some existing fault localization methods. The main assumption of the method in [10] is that, one can locate the defect by comparing a successful run with a buggy run. A similar assumption is also made in Delta debugging [26] although automatic testing is used to get alternative runs. The unique feature of [10] is defining a distance metric with respect to the given counterexample and then searching for a "closest" successful run with respect to that metric. Since a program is deterministic, the only change they make in searching for a successful run is the input values. By changing the input values and minimizing the difference caused by these changes, they try to find an execution trace that does not violate the property. In other words, they try to find ways to dodge the observable failure instead of fixing it.

```
   find_max (x1, x2, x3)
   {
1:   max = x1;
     ...
2:   if ( max <= x2 )
3:      max = x2 ;
     ...
4:   if ( max >= x3 )
5:      max = x3 ;
     ...
6:   assert ( max >= x1 ) ;
7:   assert ( max >= x2 ) ;
8:   assert ( max >= x3 ) ;
   }
```

(a) the maximum of three inputs;

```
   compute_diff (x1, x2)
   {
1:   if ( x1 != x2 ) {
2:      if ( x1 < x2 )
3:         diff = x1 - x2 ;
4:      else
5:         diff = x2 - x1 ;
     }
6:   else {
7:      diff = 0 ;
        ...
     }
8:   assert ( diff > 0 ) ;
   }
```

(b) the difference of two inputs;

Fig. 1. Two examples to illustrate fault localization algorithms

First, we note that it is not always possible to dodge the failure by merely changing input values. When a failure exists regardless of any particular input value, the algorithm in [10] fails since there is no valid solution for the constraint solver to optimize. Even if a successful run can be found, the difference between the two runs does not necessarily offer enough hints to locate the defect. This can be illustrated by the C program in Figure 1-(a), which is supposed to find the maximum of three inputs. The input `(0,1,0)` can trigger an execution that fails the assertion check at Line 7. The assertion failure is caused by Lines 4-5 where the conditional expression should have been different.

Table 1 lists the variable assignments at different execution steps for the original counterexample and a closest successful run. Each row in the table shows the names of variables or conditional expressions, their program locations (`max @3` corresponds to Line 3), their values, and the distance according to the metric in [10]. Since there are only two different assignments: `x2 @0` and `max @3`, it would classify Line 3 as cause of the failure. However, both Line 3 and Line 2 (the guard of Line 3) are correct, and the real error is in Lines 4-5.

Table 1. Counterexample and successful executions for `find_max`

variables/predicates	variable/predicate valuations in		distance
	counterexample	a successful run	
x1 @ 0	0	0	
x2 @ 0	1	0	1
x3 @ 0	0	0	
max @ 1	0	0	
(max<=x2) @ 2	true	true	
max @ 3	1	0	1
(max>=x3) @ 4	true	true	
max @ 5	0	0	
(max>=x1) @ 6	true	true	
(max>=x2) @ 7	false	true	

Our second example, Figure 1-(b), is a program to compute $|x1 - x2|$ when the two inputs have different values. There is a bug at Line 2 and the correct version should be `(x1 > x2)`. A counterexample can be produced with the input `(0,1)`, under which the program goes through Lines 1-3 and 8. Since there is no way to avoid the failure as long as `(x1 != x2)`, a closest successful run would be with the input `(0,0)`. The successful run goes through lines 6-8. As a result, all lines within the if-branch and else-branch are different between the two runs, and would be marked as potential causes of the failure.

In these two examples, the inaccuracy of the algorithm is due to its way of analyzing causality, which we believe is very different from the actual debugging practice by programmers. Given an execution trace exhibiting some erroneous behavior, a programmer will not keep changing the input values until the bug disappears. Instead, the programmer will keep the same input and try to find out *how this particular input value leads to the failure*. When there is an assertion check in the code, it often means that the program is expected to work at this location all the time, regardless of which path it has taken to reach here and regardless of the input values. Therefore, we choose to focus on the given counterexample and tackle the problem from a different angle; in particular, we want to explain why this particular run fails.

3 Preliminaries

We provide some needed notations before introducing the definition of transforming statement and the notion of minimal proof of infeasibility, which are the foundation of our counterexample causal analysis algorithm. We focus on the class of failures that can be captured using assertions. In a C program, for instance, `assert(!crash)` represents the property that `crash` should never be true at this program location. A counterexample is a particular execution path of the program that violates the assertion.

An *execution path* $\pi = s_1, s_2, \ldots$ is a sequence of simple program statements, each of which has one of the following types:

- assignment statement `s: v := e`, where v is a variable and e is an expression; we assume that the statement has no side-effects.
- branching statement `s: assume(c)`, where c is a predicate. It may come from statements like `if(c)...else` or successfully executing of `assert(c)`.

Given an execution path π, we use $\pi^i = s_i, \ldots$ to represent the suffix starting from $i \geq 1$; we also use $\pi^{i,j} = s_i, \ldots, s_j$ to represent the segment between i and j.

A *counterexample* is a tuple $\langle I, \pi^{1,n} \rangle$, where I is an input valuation and $\pi^{1,n}$ is the corresponding execution path leading to failure at s_n:`assert(c)`. A counterexample is a concrete execution of the program. Given a set I of initial values to input variables, the execution of a deterministic program is completely fixed. It is easy to map a counterexample back to an execution path π. Complex data structures and language constructs do not pose a problem, because everything is completely determined in a concrete trace. For pointers, the locations that they point to are fixed at every step; similarly for arrays, the indexes are also fully determined. Since a counterexample is of finite length, recursive functions and statements involving data in dynamically allocated memory can be rewritten into simple but equivalent statements.

The set of input variables of the program induces an *input space*, in which each particular input valuation corresponds to a point. In general, an execution path $\pi^{1,n}$ corresponds to more than one counterexamples, each of which maps to a distinct point in the input space. The input subspace related to $\pi^{1,n}$ can be represented by the *weakest pre-condition* of $\neg c$ with respect to $\pi^{1,n-1}$; that is, the weakest condition before $\pi^{1,n-1}$ that entails the failure at s_n. The definition of weakest pre-condition is given below, where we use $f(V/W)$ to denote the simultaneous substitution of W with V in function $f(W)$.

Definition 1 (cf.[8]). *Given $\pi^{i,j} = s_i, \ldots, s_j$ and a propositional formula ϕ, the weakest pre-condition of ϕ with respect to $\pi^{i,j}$, denoted by $WP(\pi^{i,j}, \phi)$, is defined as follows,*

- *For a statement* `s: v = e`, $WP(s, \phi) = \phi(e/v)$;
- *For a statement* `s: assume(c)`, $WP(s, \phi) = \phi \wedge c$;
- *For a sequence of statements* `s1; s2`, $WP(s1 : s2, \phi) = WP(s1, WP(s2, \phi))$.

Weakest pre-condition computation has been used in several recent predicate abstraction algorithms [20, 13, 14], where it is applied to an infeasible counterexample in the abstract model in order to find relevant predicates that can eliminate the trace in the refined model. However, in this paper the purpose of computing weakest pre-conditions is quite different, since the counterexample here is a feasible trace in the concrete program, as opposed to an infeasible trace in an abstract model.

We use this computation to find a minimal set of conditions for the program to stay on the same path without violating the assertion. The result is a set of predicates that should hold at each step of the path. By comparing how these predicates contradict with each other and with the given set of input values, we can locate part of the original code responsible for this particular assertion failure.

4 Analyzing the Infection Chain

Given a counterexample $\langle I, \pi^{1,n} \rangle$, we identify a set of statements in $\pi^{1,n}$ constituting the infection chain, i.e., cause-effect segments that lead eventually to a failure in s_n. We accomplish this by computing $WP(\pi^{1,n-1}, c)$. According to the definition, the weakest precondition over a path is a conjunction of predicates. That is,

$$WP(\pi^{i,j}, c) = c' \wedge (c'_1 \wedge c'_2 \ldots \wedge c'_k) \ ,$$

where c' is transformed from the given formula c through (possibly transitive) variable substitutions, and each c'_l is transformed from a condition in s_l: `assume(`c_l`)` such that $i \leq l \leq j$. More formally, given a formula ϕ, we use ϕ' to denote the formula in WP that is transformed from ϕ. The definition is transitive in that both $\phi' = \phi(e/v)$ and $\phi'(e_2/v_2)$ are *transformed formulae* from ϕ.

Definition 2. *A* transforming statement *of ϕ is an assignment statement* `s: v = e` *such that variable v appears in the transitive support of formula ϕ.*

For example, statement `s1:x = y+1` is a transforming statement of ϕ:`(x > 0)`, since $WP(s1, \phi)$ produces ϕ':`(y+1 > 0)`; statement `s2:y = z*10` is also a transforming statement of ϕ, since $WP(s2, \phi')$ produces `(z*10+1 > 0)`. During weakest precondition computations, only assignment statements can transform an existing conjunct c into a new conjunct c'. Branching statements can only add new conjuncts to the existing formulae, but cannot transform them. Given an execution path $\pi^{i,j} = s_i, \ldots, s_j$, we use the subset $TS(\pi^{i,j}, c) \subseteq \{s_i, \ldots, s_j\}$ to denote the transforming statements for the predicate c. Transforming statements are the foundation of our causal analysis algorithm.

For a failed execution path $\pi^{1,n}$ where the statement s_n is `assert(c)`, the three pre-conditions, $WP(\pi^{1,n-1}, true)$, $WP(\pi^{1,n-1}, c)$, and $WP(\pi^{1,n-1}, \neg c)$, have the following relationships:

1. $WP(\pi^{1,n-1}, true) = WP(\pi^{1,n-1}, c) \vee WP(\pi^{1,n-1}, \neg c)$;
2. $WP(\pi^{1,n-1}, c) \wedge WP(\pi^{1,n-1}, \neg c) = \emptyset$;

This is illustrated by Figure 2. Also note that the three pre-conditions share a common subformula $(c'_1 \wedge \cdots \wedge c'_k)$, which is the same as $WP(\pi^{1,n-1}, true)$. We now introduce the notion of proof of infeasibility.

Theorem 1. *Given a counterexample $\langle I, \pi^{1,n} \rangle$, we have $I \subseteq WP(\pi^{1,n-1}, \neg c)$, meaning that*

$$I \wedge WP(\pi^{1,n-1}, c) = \emptyset \ .$$

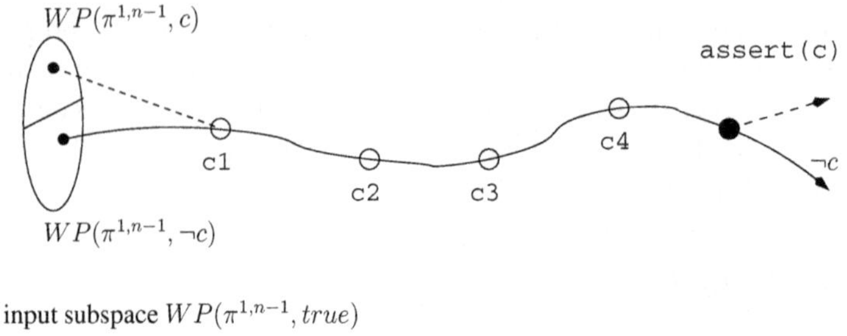

Fig. 2. Partitioning of the input subspace $WP(\pi^{1,n-1}, true)$

The input valuation I is a conjunction set of predicates $I = I_1 \wedge \ldots \wedge I_m$, where I_i, for instance, can be the valuation of an input variable `x = 10`. Given that

$$(I_1 \wedge \ldots \wedge I_m) \wedge c' \wedge (c'_1 \wedge \ldots \wedge c'_k) = \emptyset \ ,$$

there exist a minimal subset of conjuncts in I and a minimal subset of conjuncts in $WP(\pi^{1,n-1}, c)$, denoted by I_{sub} and WP_{sub}, respectively, such that $I_{sub} \wedge WP_{sub} = \emptyset$. The point here is that only some conjuncts are responsible for the empty intersection (which is the reason of the assertion failure). We call $I_{sub} \wedge WP_{sub}$ a minimal *proof of infeasibility*.

In general, one can find a minimal set of contradicting predicates as follows,

1. initialize $I_{sub} = I$ and $WP_{sub} = WP(\pi^{1,n-1}, c)$;
2. minimize WP_{sub} by dropping each conjunct c'_i in WP_{sub}, and then checking whether $I_{sub} \wedge WP_{sub} = \emptyset$: if the result remains empty, drop c'_i permanently; otherwise, add it back.
3. minimize I_{sub} by dropping each I_i in I_{sub}, and then checking whether $I_{sub} \wedge WP_{sub} = \emptyset$: if the result remains empty, drop I_i permanently; otherwise, add it back.

For this particular application, however, we note that WP_{sub} always contains c'. This is because other conjuncts c'_i come from `assume` statements and are all consistent with I, but c' comes from the failed assertion condition c. Therefore, we can skip the test for c' when minimizing WP_{sub}. It is often the case that c' contradicts to some other conjuncts in WP and I_{sub} is not needed in the proof of infeasibility. However, if WP does not have conflicting conjuncts by itself, then a minimal proof is of the form $I_{sub} \wedge c'$.

The intuition behind this definition is that: given a concrete counterexample, our proof of infeasibility provides a succinct explanation about the cause of the assertion failure at s_n. The choice of computing a syntactic-level proof of infeasibility, as opposed to other forms including interpolation [19], is due to the need of eventually mapping the proof back to the source code program. In our case, the explanation can be mapped back to the source code by finding the transforming statements with respect to predicates in WP_{sub}.

5 The Causal Analysis Procedure

In this section we present the entire causal analysis procedure and then explain how it can be applied to the two working examples.

5.1 The Algorithm

Given a counterexample $\langle I, \pi^{1,n} \rangle$, we compute the weakest precondition $WP(\pi^{1,n-1}, c)$ by starting backward from c. (Recall that c comes from the failed `assert(c)` at s_n.) During this process, we also record in $TS(c)$ all transforming statements of c. At each pre-condition computation step, we check whether the intermediate result $WP(\pi^{i,n-1}, c)$ is empty. There are two possibilities:

- there exists an index $1 \leq i < n$ such that $WP(\pi^{i,n-1}, c) = \emptyset$;
- no such index exists and the computation of $WP(\pi^{1,n-1}, c)$ completes.

We consider the first case as a special case, since it implies emptiness of $WP(\pi^{1,n-1}, c)$ and hence emptiness of its intersection with I.

1. In the first case, we take the set of conjuncts in $WP(\pi^{i,n-1}, c)$ right after it becomes empty and compute a minimal subset WP_{sub}. We consider all conjuncts in WP_{sub} as responsible for triggering the failure. In the source code, we mark only transforming statements in $\{s \mid s \in TS(\phi)$ such that $\phi' \in WP_{sub}\}$ as explanation of the failure.
2. In the second case, we take all conjuncts in I and $WP(\pi^{1,n-1}, c)$ and compute a minimal proof $I_{sub} \wedge WP_{sub}$. We consider I_{sub} and all conjuncts in WP_{sub} as responsible for triggering the failure. As is illustrated in Figure 3-(a), WP_{sub} has only one subformula in this case; that is, $WP_{sub} = c'$. In the source code, we mark only transforming statements in $TS(c)$ as explanation of the failure. The marked source code shows how I_{sub} leads to the failure at s_n:`assert(c)` through the execution of the transforming statements.

The result in the first case is a stronger condition for explaining the failure—an empty $WP(\pi^{i,n}, c)$ means that any execution path with the same suffix $(s_i, ..., s_{n-1})$ would fail at s_n. As is illustrated in Figure 3-(b), the relevant input subspace in this case becomes $WP(\pi^{i,n-1}, true)$, which is large than $WP(\pi^{1,n-1}, true)$ in general. (In the figure, with a little abuse of notation, we have used $WP_{sub} \setminus c'$ to represent the removal of c' from the set of conjuncts in WP_{sub}.) By focusing on WP_{sub} only, we can explain the cause of failure common to all these execution paths.

Our algorithm aims at explaining why the given execution path fails by focusing on the infection chain (i.e., set of transforming statements) leading to the failure. We do not attempt to answer the question *which segment in the infection chain contains the faulty code* or *how to fix the bug by changing a particular segment.* We believe that the latter two problems in general require a relatively complete specification of the intended program behavior in order for them to be solved effectively. Unfortunately, complete specifications are often missing in realistic software development settings.

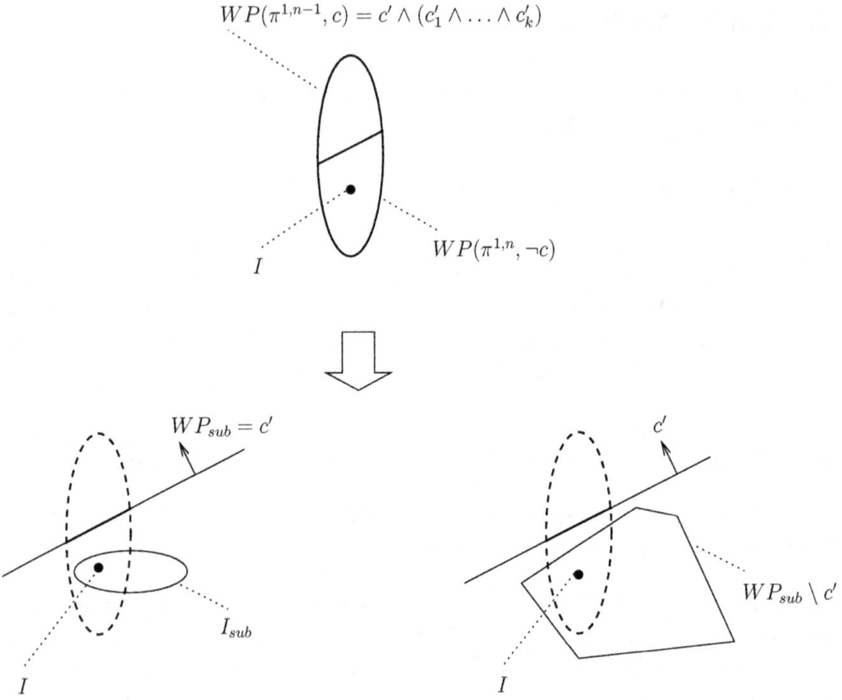

(a) When $I_{sub} \wedge WP_{sub} = \emptyset$ (b) $WP_{sub} = \emptyset$ before reaching s_1

Fig. 3. The minimal proof of infeasibility. WP_{sub} consists of a subset of conjuncts of $WP(\pi^{i,n-1}, c)$, and thus $WP(\pi^{i,n-1}, c) \subseteq WP_{sub}$. Similarly, $I \subseteq I_{sub}$.

5.2 The Working Examples

We now demonstrate that our new method can produce better results than existing algorithms. We first apply the new algorithm to `find_max` in Figure 1-(a). We start the weakest pre-condition computation with the failed assertion condition `(max >= x2)`. The sequence of intermediate results are listed in Table 2, where the first column gives the line numbers, the second column gives the subformulae whose conjunction is WP, the third column indicates whether the statement belongs to $TS(max \geq x2)$; for instance, a "yes" for Line 5 means that s_5 :`max = x3` is a transforming statement of the predicate $(max \geq x2)$. The last column shows whether the weakest pre-condition is an empty set.

Table 2 shows that the weakest pre-condition becomes empty only after the intersection with initial input values `x1=0, x2=1, x3=0`. The minimal subset is

$$(x2 = 1) \wedge (x3 = 0) \wedge (x3 \geq x2)$$

In the source code, we highlight all transforming statements of predicates in $TS(max \geq x2)$ as responsible for the failure. Thus, Line 5 is marked as explanation of the

Table 2. Analyzing the cause of failure in `find_max`

Line	Predicates in the WP	in $TS(max \geq x2)$	empty WP?
7	(max≥x2)		
6	max≥x1, (max≥x2)		
5	x3≥x1, (x3≥x2)	yes	
4	max≥x3, x3≥x1, (x3≥x2)		
3	x2≥x3, x3≥x1, (x3≥x2)		
2	max≤x2, x2≥x3, x3≥x1, (x3≥x2)		
1	x1≤x2, x2≥x3, x3≥x1, (x3≥x2)		
0	0≤1, 1≥0, 0≥0, (0≥1)		empty

Table 3. Analyzing the cause of failure in `compute_diff`

Line	Predicates in WP	in $TS(diff > 0)$	empty WP
8	(diff>0)		
3	(x1-x2>0)	yes	
2	x1<x2, (x1-x2>0)		empty
1	x1≠x2, x1<x2, (x1-x2>0)		empty
0	0≠1, 0<1, (0-1>0)		empty

failure cause; this is significantly more accurate than the algorithm of [10] (which instead would mark Line 3).

Next, we apply our algorithm to `compute_diff` in Figure 1-(b). We start weakest precondition computation with the failed assertion condition `(diff > 0)`. The sequence of intermediate results are given in Table 3. The statement in Line 3 transforms the initial predicate into `(x1-x2 > 0)`, which then contradicts to `(x1 < x2)`, the new predicate added at Line 2. Since $WP(\pi^{i,n-1}, (diff > 0)) = \emptyset$, we compute the minimal proof of infeasibility at this point. The result is as follows,

$$(x1 < x2) \wedge (x1 - x2 > 0) \ .$$

In the source code, we mark all transforming statements in $TS(diff > 0)$ and $TS(x1 < x2)$, as well as the source statement of c'_1, which is `assume(x1 < x2)`. Thus, our algorithm reports Lines 2-3 of Figure 1-(b) as the failure cause. The fact that weakest pre-condition becomes empty in the middle of a counterexample strongly indicates that the error may happen in the common suffix. In contrast, the algorithm in [10] is ineffective on this example since the first `else`-branch is the only possible successful run; as a result, it would mark the code in both branches.

6 Further Discussion

6.1 About Delta-Debugging

The notion of cause transition in [26, 6] is similar to transforming statements in our method. A cause transition points to the connecting points of execution path where a change of the previous state would lead the execution to a different branch. To find the defect, the method in [26, 6] traces forward in the program to identify the chain of cause transitions, by running an additional set of tests. Their idea of empirically comparing state difference between successful and failing runs is significantly different from ours; the notion of minimal proof of infeasibility is not used. In our method, the set of predicates produced by weakest pre-condition computations at each individual program location represents an *abstract* program state.

As is pointed out in [6], for each infection $\mathcal{F}'$, there is either an earlier infection $\mathcal{F}$ that causes $\mathcal{F}'$, or no earlier infection—in which case $\mathcal{F}'$ is the defect. Therefore, given the observable failure, tracing back the infection chain requires two proofs:

1. to prove that $\mathcal{F}$ and $\mathcal{F}'$ are "infected";
2. to prove that $\mathcal{F}$ causes $\mathcal{F}'$.

Without a complete specification, in general it is not possible to determine whether a program state is infected (and therefore not possible to determine where the very first infection is). However, we note that the actual defect ought to be in one of the chain segments. By our definition, each transforming statement of the failed assertion condition (i.e., the last infection) is a proof that a previous infection $\mathcal{F}$ causes $\mathcal{F}'$.

6.2 About Distance Metric in Explain [10]

Compared to the `explain` tool in [10], our method answers the question why a specific execution path fails, instead of *how the failure can be avoided.* In general, it is hard to answer the latter question in a useful way unless one has a complete specification. The reason is that there can be multiple ways of avoiding a particular failure, each of which corresponds to a different program intent. (Program intent in principle can only be provided by human.)

For example, the failed property in our first working example is, "all runs that go through Lines 1-8 should pass the assertion check at Line 9." This is only a partial specification of the program behavior. When being represented in linear temporal logic, this property is of the form $\mathbf{G}(P \rightarrow Q)$, where

- P: the execution actually goes through lines 1-8;
- Q: the execution fails assertion check at line 9.

A counterexample of this property is an execution on which $(P \wedge \neg Q)$ holds. One can avoid this particular failure by satisfying $\neg(P \wedge \neg Q)$ under the same input condition, which is the same as

$$(\neg c'_1 \vee \ldots \vee \neg c'_k) \vee c' \ .$$

Unfortunately, any one of the disjunctive subformulae entails the entire formula. Note that in our causal analysis, we focus only on c' (i.e., the assertion check at s_n should pass) by assuming that P holds.

More Related Work: The property $P \rightarrow Q$ has also been studied in the context of vacuity detection in [4, 18, 21], where $P \rightarrow Q$ is said to be vacuously satisfied whenever P is false. This is because Q is often the property that the user intends to check, while P is only a pre-condition. We believe that the same argument also applies to counterexample explanation or fault localization.

6.3 About Dynamic Slicing

Our method is also different from dynamic slicing [17, 1, 12], which is a variant of program slicing with the restriction to an execution path. Although dynamic slicing often gives more accurate data dependencies between variables than normal static analysis, it is inferior to our weakest pre-condition based causal analysis in explaining cause of failed assertions. Consider the following example,

```
1:    x1 = 10;
2:    x3 = 5;
3:    ...
4:    x2 = 0 ;
5:    if ( x1 == 10) {
6:      x2 = x2 * x3 ;
7:      ...
8:    }
9:    else {
10:     x2 = x2 * x4;
11:   }
12:   assert( x2 != 0 );
```

If only Lines 1-8 and 12 are executed, dynamic slicing with respect to line 12 can remove the irrelevant variable $x4$, which could not have been removed by static program slicing without knowing which path will be executed. However, it could not remove variable $x1$ since whether line 6 gets executed or not depends on the condition `(x1==10)`. In contrast, our analysis algorithm would remove `(x1==10)` because it is not in the minimal proof of infeasibility (lines 4, 6, and 12).

7 Experiments

In this section, we apply our procedure to public benchmark programs in the Siemens suite [24]. The Siemens suite provides a set of C programs, each of which has a number of test vectors as well as a correct version of the program. The examples we used in this study are from the TCAS (Traffic Collision Avoidance System) example, which is a model of the aircraft conflict detection system. The assertion checks (or properties) used in our experiment originated from a previous study using symbolic execution [7].

A faulty TCAS version differs from the correct one in Line 100, where the relational operator $>$ is used when it should be $\geq$.

```
  result = !( Own_Below_Thread()) || ((Own_Below_Threat())
           && (!(Down_Separation >= ALIM())))) ;    // correct
---
  result = !( Own_Below_Thread()) || ((Own_Below_Threat())
           && (!(Down_Separation >  ALIM())))) ;    // buggy
```

The counterexample used in our study has been generated from a software model checker, and it has a length of 90. (The counterexample may also come from other software testing tools—our causal analysis procedure would be equally applicable as long as the counterexample is a fully determined execution path.) When our causal analysis procedure is used, the weakest pre-condition becomes empty right after the computation passes Line 100. This gives a succinct explanation of the actual failure down the stretch.

We compare our results with the previous results in [10]. Given the same counterexample, the initial explanation by this previous algorithm was not particularly useful. In fact, their tool dodged the failure by making the antecedent of the implication false. As is stated in [10], to coerce it into reporting a more meaningful explanation, they had to manually add some additional constraints (e.g. the antecedent should not be true). After that, their tool reports a similar result as ours. We argue, however, that this kind of manual intervention requires the user to have a deep understanding of the counterexample as well as the software program. In contrast, our method does not need additional hints from the programmer, but still achieves the same accuracy as [10] combined with manually provided assumptions.

8 Conclusions

We have addressed the problem of locating the failure cause of a program given a concrete counterexample trace, and demonstrated the effectiveness of our approach using several examples. Our automated procedure relies on the minimal proof of infeasibility to generate succinct failure explanations. Since the computations are performed at the syntactic level and are restricted to a single concrete path, there is no foreseeable difficulty in applying it to long counterexamples in large production-quality software. As future work, we will pursue a more detailed experimental study of the proposed technique and comparison with existing tools.

References

[1] H. Agrawal, R. A. DeMillo, and E. H. Spafford. Debugging with dynamic slicing and backtracking. *Software - Practice and Experience*, 23(6):589–616, 1993.

[2] F. A. Aloul, B. D. Sierawski, and K. A. Sakallah. Satometer: How much have we searched? In *Proceedings of the Design Automation Conference*, pages 737–742, New Orleans, LA, June 2002.

[3] T. Ball, M. Naik, and S. K. Rajamani. From symptom to cause: Localizing errors in counterexample traces. In *Symposium on Principles of Programming Languages (POPL'03)*, pages 97–105, January 2003.

[4] I. Beer, S. Ben-David, C. Eisner, and Y. Rodeh. Efficient detection of vacuity in ACTL formulas. In *Computer Aided Verification (CAV'97)*, pages 279–290. Springer, 1997. LNCS 1254.

[5] E. M. Clarke and E. A. Emerson. Design and synthesis of synchronization skeletons using branching time temporal logic. In *Proceedings Workshop on Logics of Programs*, pages 52–71, Berlin, 1981. Springer-Verlag. LNCS 131.

[6] H. Cleve and A. Zeller. Locating causes of program failures. In *ACM/IEEE International Conference on Software Engineering*, 2005.

[7] A. Coen-Porisini, G. Denaro, C. Ghezzi, and M. Pezze. Using symbolic execution for verifying safety-critical systems. In *European Software Engineering Conference/Foundations of Software Engineering*, pages 142–151, 2001.

[8] E. Dijkstra. *A Discipline of Programming*. Pretice Hall, NJ, 1976.
[9] A. Griesmayer, R. Bloem, and B. Cook. Repair of boolean programs with an application to c. In *Computer Aided Verification (CAV'06)*. Springer, 2006. LNCS series.
[10] A. Groce, S. Chaki, D. Kroening, and O. Strichman. Error explanation with distance metrics. *International Journal on Software Tools for Technology Transfer*, 2005.
[11] A. Groce and W. Visser. What went wrong: Explaining counterexamples. In *Model Checking of Software: 10th International SPIN Workshop*, pages 121–135. Springer-Verlag, May 2003. LNCS 2648.
[12] T. Gyimóthy, Á. Beszédes, and I. Forgács. An efficient relevant slicing method for debugging. In *7th European Software Engineering Conference (ESEC/FSE'99)*, pages 303–321. Springer, 1999. LNCS 1687.
[13] H. Jain, F. Ivančić, A. Gupta, and M. Ganai. Localization and register sharing for predicate abstraction. In *Tools and Algorithms for the Construction and Abnalysis of Systems (TACAS'05)*, pages 394–409. Springer, 2005. LNCS 3440.
[14] H. Jain, F. Ivančić, A. Gupta, I. Shlyakhter, and C. Wang. Using statically computed invariants inside the predicate abstraction and refinement loop. In *Computer Aided Verification (CAV'06)*. Springer, 2006. LNCS series.
[15] B. Jobstmann, A. Griesmayer, and R. Bloem. Program repair as a game. In *Computer Aided Verification (CAV '05)*, pages 226–238. Springer, 2005. LNCS 3576.
[16] J. A. Jones, M. J. Harrold, and J. Stasko. Visualization of test information to assist fault localization. In *ACM/IEEE International Conference on Software Engineering*, 2002.
[17] B. Korel and J. W. Laski. Dynamic slicing of computer programs. *Journal of Systems and Software*, 13(3):187–195, 1990.
[18] O. Kupferman and M. Y. Vardi. Vacuity detection in temporal model checking. In *Correct Hardware Design and Verification Methods (CHARME'99)*, pages 82–96, Berlin, September 1999. Springer-Verlag. LNCS 1703.
[19] K. L. McMillan and N. Amla. Automatic abstraction without counterexamples. In *Tools and Algorithms for Construction and Analysis of Systems (TACAS'03)*, pages 2–17, April 2003. LNCS 2619.
[20] K. S. Namjoshi and R. P. Kurshan. Syntactic program transformations for automatic abstraction. In *Computer Aided Verification (CAV'00)*, pages 435–449. Springer, 2000. LNCS 1855.
[21] M. Purandare and F. Somenzi. Vacuum cleaning CTL formulae. In *Computer Aided Verification (CAV'02)*, pages 485–499. Springer-Verlag, July 2002. LNCS 2404.
[22] J. P. Quielle and J. Sifakis. Specification and verification of concurrent systems in CESAR. In *Proceedings of the Fifth Annual Symposium on Programming*, 1981.
[23] M. Renieris and S. P. Reiss. Fault localization with nearest neighbor queries. In *International Conference on Automated Software Engineering*, pages 30–39, Montreal, Canada, October 2003.
[24] G. Rothermel and M.J. Harrold. Empirical studies of a safe regression test selection technique. *Software Engineering*, 24:401–419, 1999.
[25] S. Staber, B. Jobstmann, and R. Bloem. Finding and fixing faults. In *Correct Hardware Design and Verification Methods (CHARME '05)*, pages 35–49. Springer, 2005. LNCS 3725.
[26] A. Zeller. Isolating cause-effect chains from computer programs. In *Symposium on the Foundations of Software Engineering (FSE'02)*, pages 1–10, November 2002.

On the Membership Problem for Visibly Pushdown Languages*

Salvatore La Torre, Margherita Napoli, and Mimmo Parente

Facoltà di Scienze Matematiche, Fisiche e Naturali
Università degli Studi di Salerno, Italy
{slatorre,napoli,parente}@unisa.it

Abstract. Visibly pushdown languages are a subclass of deterministic context-free languages that can model nonregular properties of interest in program analysis. This class properly contains typical classes of parenthesized languages like "balanced" and "input-driven" languages. Visibly pushdown languages are closed under boolean operations and some decision problems, such as inclusion and universality, are decidable. In this paper, we study the membership problem for this class of languages and show that it can be solved in time linear in the size of the input grammar and in the length of the input word. The algorithm consists of a reduction to the reachability problem on game graphs. The same approach can be efficiently applied when the input language is given as a visibly pushdown automaton, moreover we also show time complexities of the same problem using other approaches. We further motivate our result showing an application to XML schema.

1 Introduction

Context-free languages are a very interesting class of languages that have been intensively studied by many researchers from different areas. Via their recursive characterization (the context-free grammars) they have played a central role in the development of compiler technologies, and recently, they are also used to describe document formats over the Web (Document Type Definitions) [14]. The automaton-like characterization of this class of formal languages, the pushdown automata, is a natural model for the control flow of sequential programs of typical procedural programming languages. Thus, program analysis, compiler optimizations, and program verification can be rephrased as decision problems for pushdown automata. As sample references on these topics see [2,8,5,9,11,13,19].

The relevance of context-free languages often cannot be fully exploited due to the intractability of many fundamental problems. In a recent paper Alur and Madhusudan [4] have introduced the class of *visibly pushdown languages* (VPLs). Visibly pushdown languages are context-free languages accepted by pushdown automata in which the input symbols determine the stack operations. They have

* Work partially supported by funds for the research from MIUR 2006, grant "Metodi Formali per la verifica di sistemi chiusi ed aperti", Università di Salerno.

S. Graf and W. Zhang (Eds.): ATVA 2006, LNCS 4218, pp. 96–109, 2006.

been also characterized by the so-called *visibly pushdown grammars* (VPGs) [4]. This class of languages is rich enough to model nonregular properties and is also tractable and robust like the class of regular languages. In fact, VPLs are closed under all the boolean operations and decision problems, such as inclusion and universality, are EXPTIME-complete while they are in general undecidable for the context-free languages. In [3], syntactic congruences on words and the problem of finding a minimal canonical deterministic pushdown automaton for VPLs are studied.

In this paper, we focus on the *membership problem*: "given a word w and a VPL language L, is $w \in L$?" While w is represented explicitely, L can be represented by an automaton or a grammar and this leads to different approaches. When the VPL is represented by a VPA a simple algorithm for testing membership can be obtained by determinizing the visibly pushdown automaton by the construction given in [4] and then running the deterministic automaton on the input word. Clearly, it is not needed to compute the whole deterministic automaton (that would require exponential time) but the determinization can be carried out directly (on-the-fly) getting an $O(|w| \cdot |Q|^3)$ time upper bound, where Q is the state set of the pushdown automaton accepting the input language.

On the other hand, it is interesting to have an efficient algorithm also when the language is given by a VPG. It is known that for context-free languages, represented by grammars in Chomsky-Normal-Form, an efficient algorithm is the CYK algorithm. This algorithm runs in time cubic in the size of the word and linear in the size of the grammar. Time complexity improves on to quadratic if the grammar is not ambiguous [14]. More efficient algorithms have been given for particular subclasses of unambiguous grammars [1].

Here we give a solution to the membership problem for VPLs that takes time linear in both the size of the input word w and the size of the input visibly pushdown grammar G. Non-null productions of this kind of grammars are either of the form $X \to aY$ or of the form $X \to aYbZ$ where X, Y, Z are variables, a, b are terminal symbols, and in the second production a and b correspond respectively to a push and its matching pop of the stack. The main idea of our algorithm is to reduce this problem to a two-player game H where: a player (the existential player) claims that she can show a derivation for a word and gives the next step in her proof; the other player (the universal player) challenges her to proceed in her proof on a portion of the remaining part of the word. Note that when a production of the form $X \to aY$ is picked by the existential player as next step in the proof of av, then the only claim on which the universal player can challenge her is on generating v from Y. Instead, when a production of the form $X \to aYbZ$ is picked as next step in the proof of $avbz$, then the universal player can challenge the existential player both on generating v from Y and on generating z from Z. Clearly, the proof is completed when the existential player is asked to show that the empty word is generated from a variable X such that $X \to \varepsilon$ is a production of G. Therefore, if S is the start variable of G, we have that $w \in L(G)$ if and only if the existential player can prove the claim $S \Rightarrow^* w$ independently from the objections of the universal player.

The above game can be modeled as a reachability problem on a game graph of size linear in the size of w and G. Therefore, our result follows from the fact that the game-graph reachability problem can be solved in linear time (see [20]).

Classical applications of the membership problem for formal languages have concerned with the parsing of programs and thus is strictly related to the design of compilers. In such a context, a language generator/acceptor is constructed and then it is used to parse several programs. Therefore, the size of the grammar or the automaton can be considered constant and the efficiency of the algorithms is measured in terms of the length of the document (i.e., word) to parse. Also, the possibility of computing a deterministic model that captures the languages of interest guarantees efficient parsing independently of the complexity of the determinization procedure (determinization is done once for all). Clearly, such observations do not apply when the language acceptor/generator may vary and this is the case of the type conformity checking of XML documents [22,23]. In this paper, we show that the synctactic structure of a Document Type Definition (DTD) and of an XML schema can be efficiently captured by a visibly pushdown grammar, and thus our algorithm solving the membership problem for visibly pushdown languages can be used for efficiently checking the type of XML documents.

The rest of the paper is organized as follows. In the next section we give all the definitions and some known result on VPL languages. In Section 3, we give our solution to the membership problem for VPLs. In Section 4, we show that our result can be used in type-checking XML documents. In Section 5, we report a thorough discussion on the presented result and the related research. Finally, we conclude the paper with few remarks.

2 Preliminaries

In this section we give some definitions and some preliminary results, mostly following the notation of [4].

2.1 Visibly Pushdown Languages

A *pushdown alphabet* is a tuple $\tilde{\Sigma} = \langle \Sigma_c, \Sigma_r, \Sigma_\ell \rangle$ consisting of three disjoint alphabets: Σ_c is a finite set of *calls*, Σ_r is a finite set of *returns* and Σ_ℓ is a finite set of *local actions*.

Call, return and local symbols determine the stack operations of a Visibly Pushdown Automata over $\tilde{\Sigma}$, defined as follows.

Definition 1 (Visibly Pushdown Automata). *A (nondeterministic) Visibly Pushdown Automaton (*VPA*) on finite words over $\langle \Sigma_c, \Sigma_r, \Sigma_\ell \rangle$ is a tuple $M = (Q, Q_{in}, \Gamma, \delta, Q_F)$ where Q is a finite set of states, $Q_{in} \subseteq Q$ is a set of initial states, Γ is a finite stack alphabet that contains a special bottom-of-stack symbol $\perp$, $\delta \subseteq (Q \times \Sigma_c \times Q \times (\Gamma \setminus \{\perp\})) \cup (Q \times \Sigma_r \times \Gamma \times Q) \cup (Q \times \Sigma_\ell \times Q)$, and $Q_F \subseteq Q$ is a set of final states.*

Let us remark that the acceptance is only on final states (not by *empty-stack*) and ϵ-transitions are not allowed. The languages accepted by a VPA over $\tilde{\Sigma}$ is a context-free language over an alphabet $\Sigma = (\Sigma_c \cup \Sigma_r \cup \Sigma_\ell)$.

Definition 2. *A language of finite words $L \subseteq \Sigma^*$ is a visibly pushdown language (VPL) with respect to $\tilde{\Sigma}$ (a $\tilde{\Sigma}$-VPL) if there is a VPA M over $\tilde{\Sigma}$ such that $L(M) = L$.*

Visibly pushdown languages are characterized also by a context-free grammar.

Definition 3 (Visibly Pushdown Grammar). *A context-free grammar $G = (V, S, P)$, over an alphabet Σ, is a Visibly Pushdown Grammar (VPG) with respect to the partitioning $\tilde{\Sigma} = (\Sigma_c, \Sigma_r, \Sigma_\ell)$, if the set V of variables is partitioned into two disjoint sets V^0 and V^1, such that the production in P are of one the following forms*

- $X \to \epsilon$
- $X \to aY$ *such that if* $X \in V^0$ *then* $a \in \Sigma_\ell$ *and* $Y \in V^0$*;*
- $X \to aYbZ$ *such that* $a \in \Sigma_c$ *and* $b \in \Sigma_r$ *and* $Y \in V^0$ *and if* $X \in V^0$ *then* $Z \in V^0$.

A word w is *well-matched* if either $w \in \Sigma_\ell^*$ or $w = xaybz$ where x, y, z are well-matched, $a \in \Sigma_c$ and $b \in \Sigma_r$. In a word $w = uaxbv$, where $u, v, x \in \Sigma^*$ and x is well-matched, $a \in \Sigma_c$ and $b \in \Sigma_r$ are called *matching symbols*, thus in any word for each *call* symbol there is at most one matching *return* symbol and vice-versa.

Directly from the definition, we can prove that from variables in V^0 only well-matched words can be derived. While words that can be derived from variables in V^1 are not necessarily well-matched.

Example 1. Consider the grammar $G = (V, S, P)$ over $\tilde{\Sigma} = \langle\{a\}, \{b\}, \{d\}\rangle$ where $V^0 = \{X, Y\}$, $V^1 = \{S\}$ and P has the following rules:
$S \to \epsilon \mid aS \mid bS \mid aXbS$; $X \to \epsilon \mid aYbY$; $Y \to \epsilon \mid dY$.

It is easy to see that the word $w = a^3bdba \in L(G)$. Note that in w the first and the last occurrences of a are *unmatched*, while the others match with the b's. Note also that G is ambiguous (consider for example the word ab). □

Now we recall some known results about VPL languages which will be used in the rest of the paper.

Theorem 1. *[4] For a pushdown alphabet $\tilde{\Sigma}$, a language L is VPL if and only if it can be generated by a visibly pushdown grammar.*

Theorem 2. *[4] For any VPA M over $\tilde{\Sigma}$, there is a deterministic VPA M' over $\tilde{\Sigma}$ such that $L(M') = L(M)$. Moreover, if M has n states, we can construct M' with $O(2^{n^2})$ states and with stack alphabet of size $O(2^{n^2} \cdot |\Sigma_c|)$.*

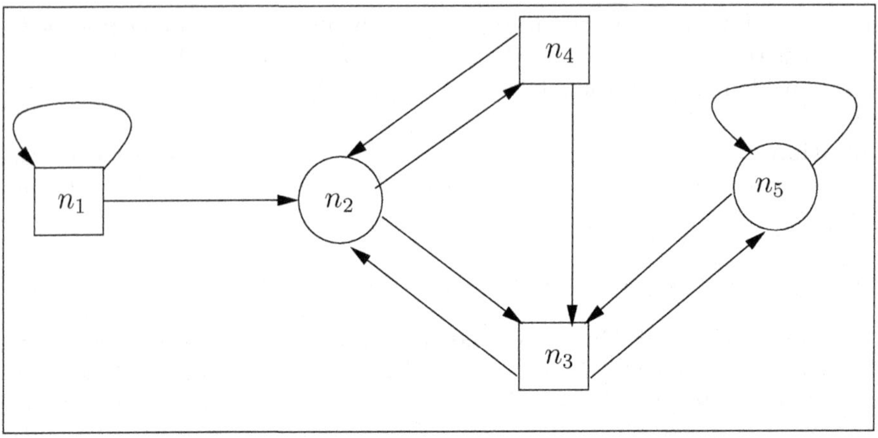

Fig. 1. An example of a game graph, where the ∃-nodes are circles and the ∀-nodes are boxes

2.2 Game Graphs

A *game graph* is a graph $H = (N, E)$ where N is a finite set of nodes partitioned into two sets $N_\exists$ and $N_\forall$, and $E \subseteq N \times N$ is the set of edges. A node of $N_\exists$ is called an ∃*-node* and a node of $N_\forall$ is called a ∀*-node.* A *strategy tree* from a node n_0 of H is a labeled tree obtained from H as follows. The root is labeled with n_0, and for each *internal* node u of the tree: if u is labeled with an ∃-node n_1 of H, then it has only a child which is labeled with a node n_2 such that $(n_1, n_2) \in E$; if u is labeled with a ∀-node n_1 of H, then for each n_2 such that $(n_1, n_2) \in E$ it has a child that is labeled with n_2. Note that nodes n_2 may be leaves of the strategy tree.

Given a game graph H, a starting node n_0 and a set T of nodes of H (called the *target set*), the reachability problem in H consists of determining if there exists a finite strategy tree from n_0 whose leaves are all labeled with nodes of T. We call such a strategy tree a *winning strategy.*

In Figure 1, a simple game graph is shown. We have used a circle to denote an ∃-node and a box to denote a ∀-node. If we consider as target set $T = \{n_5\}$ then there are no strategy trees from n_1 whose leaves are all in T, that is the reachability problem is not satisfied. If instead we set $T = \{n_1, n_4\}$, the reachability problem is satisfied.

Reachability in game graphs can be solved at a cost of a depth-first search of the graph. Therefore, we have the following theorem.

Theorem 3. *The reachability problem on a game graph H can be solved in $O(|H|)$ time.*

3 Membership Problem

Given a string w and a language L, the *membership problem* consists of establishing whether w is in L. While w is represented explicitely, L can be represented

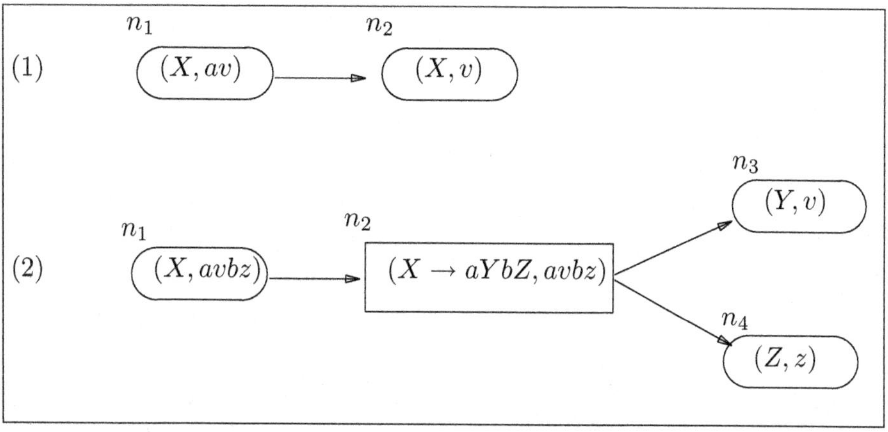

Fig. 2. Graphical representation of the construction rules of the game graph H_w^G

by an automaton, a grammar, or an expression. For each of these representations a different algorithm, hence different time and space complexities, corresponds.

In this section we present an algorithm to decide whether a word $w \in \Sigma^*$ belongs to a language generated by a given VPG $G = (V, S, P)$. The main idea of this algorithm is to reduce our membership problem to reachability in game graphs.

The construction of the game graph. Let G be a VPG (V, S, P) over $\tilde{\Sigma} = \langle \Sigma_c, \Sigma_r, \Sigma_\ell \rangle$ and $w \in \Sigma^*$. Define $H_w^G = (N, E)$ with $N = N_\forall \cup N_\exists$ and $N_\exists \subset (V \times \Sigma^*)$ and $N_\forall \subset (P \times \Sigma^*)$. The sets N and E are defined constructively as follows:

Let $(S, w) \in N_\exists$. Consider a node $n_1 = (X, u)$ in $N_\exists$, then

1. if $u = av$ and $(X \to aY) \in P$, then $n_2 = (Y, v) \in N_\exists$ and the edge $(n_1, n_2) \in E$ (see part (1) of Figure 2);
2. if $u = avbz$ such that $a \in \Sigma_c$ and $b \in \Sigma_r$ are matching symbols and $(X \to aYbZ) \in P$, then
   - $n_2 = (X \to aYbZ, u) \in N_\forall$ and $(n_1, n_2) \in E$,
   - $n_3 = (Y, v) \in N_\exists$ and $(n_2, n_3) \in E$,
   - $n_4 = (Z, z) \in N_\exists$ and $(n_2, n_4) \in E$.

   (See part (2) of Figure 2.)

The target set T consists of the nodes (X, ϵ), such that $X \to \epsilon$ is a rule in P. Note that the graph H_w^G is a directed acyclic graph, having just one node with no incoming edges and the nodes in T do not have outgoing edges. Moreover each $\forall$-node has only one incoming edge (stemming from an $\exists$-node) and at most two outgoing edges (going into $\exists$-nodes).

Example 2. Given G as in the Example 1 and $w = a^3bdba$ the corresponding graph H_w^G is given in Fig. 3. It is immediate to see that $w \in L(G)$ and there

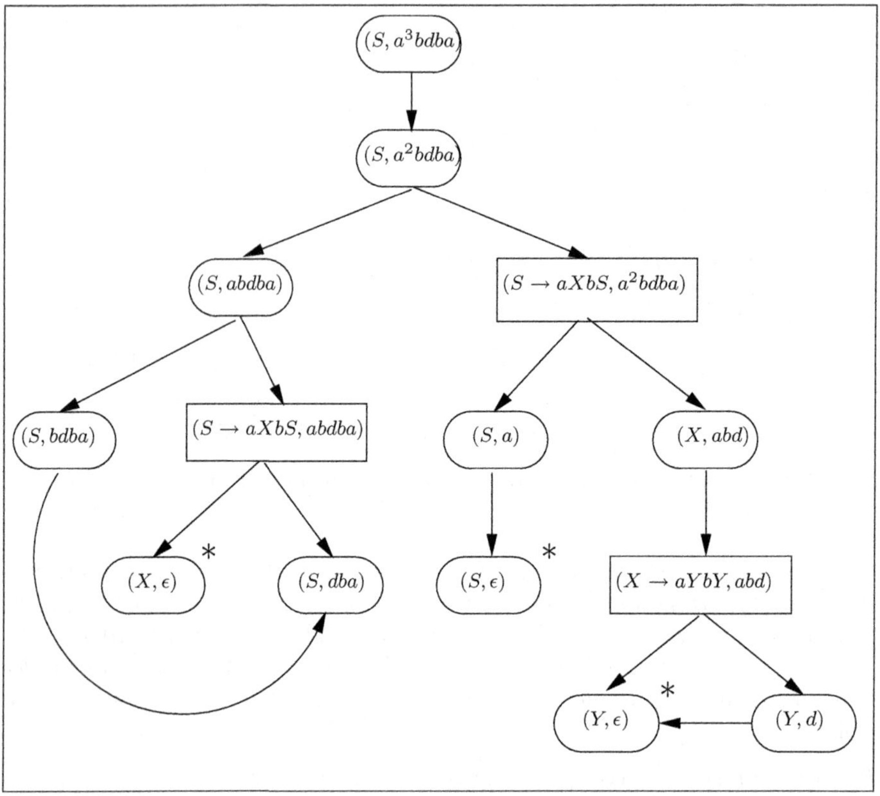

Fig. 3. The ∃-nodes are circles and the ∀-nodes are boxes. The nodes in the target-set are starred.

is a strategy tree, from (S, w), whose leaves are all in the target set (the two uppermost starred nodes). □

In the above construction, it is clear that the words denoting the second component of the ∃-nodes and ∀-nodes are all subwords of w. Since all these subwords are $O(|w|^2)$, we get an $O(|w|^2 \cdot |V|)$ upper bound on the number of ∃-nodes and $O(|w^2| \cdot |P|)$ for the ∀-nodes. We will show that indeed the number of the nodes in the graph is $O(|w| \cdot |P|)$. To this aim, in the next lemma we give a careful characterization of the forms of the subwords effectively used in the construction of H_w^G.

Lemma 1. *If* $(Y, v) \in N_\exists$ *then*

1. *either* v *is a suffix of* w
2. *or* $Y \in V^0$, v *is well-matched and there is a subword* w' *of* w *such that*
   2.1 *either* $w' = a_1 \alpha v b_1$, *where* a_1, b_1 *are matching symbols and* $\alpha \in \Sigma_\ell^*$
   2.2 *or* $w' = a_1 x_1 a_2 x_2 b_2 \alpha v b_1$, *where* a_1, b_1 *and* a_2, b_2 *are matching symbols,* $x_1, x_2 \in \Sigma^*$ *and* $\alpha \in \Sigma_\ell^*$.

Proof. The proof is by structural induction on the definition of $N_\exists$. If $(Y, v) = (S, w)$ then clearly v is a suffix of w. Suppose now that (Y, v) has an incoming edge then three cases can occur:

i) The incoming edge comes from the $\exists$-node (X, u), and this implies that $X \to aY \in P$ and $u = av$. If u is a suffix of w then v is a suffix as well. Otherwise, from the inductive hypothesis, u is well-matched and $X \in V^0$. Then, from the definition of G, $a \in \Sigma_\ell$. Moreover, there exists a subword w' of w such that either $w' = a_1\alpha u b_1 = a_1\alpha a v b_1$ or $w' = a_1 x_1 a_2 x_2 b_2 \alpha u b_1 = a_1 x_1 a_2 x_2 b_2 \alpha a v b_1$, where $\alpha a \in \Sigma_\ell^*$ and thus 2 holds.
ii) The incoming edge comes from a $\forall$-node $(X \to aYbZ, u)$ and in turn this has an incoming edge from the $\exists$-node (X, u) where $u = avbz$, for some $z \in \Sigma^*$. Since a, b are matching symbols, then $Y \in V^0$ and v is well-matched. From inductive hypothesis u is a subword of w and then $w' = avb$ is a subword of w as well (case 2.1 holds).
iii) The incoming edge comes from a $\forall$-node $(X \to aZbY, u)$ and this in turn has an incoming edge from the $\exists$-node (X, u) where $u = azbv$, for some $z \in \Sigma^*$. If u is a suffix of w then v is a suffix of w as well. Otherwise u is well-matched and there exists a subword w' of w such that either $w' = a_1\alpha u b_1 = a_1\alpha azbvb_1$ or $w' = a_1 x_1 a_2 x_2 b_2 \alpha u b_1$ which can be written as $a_1 x' azbvb_1$ where $x' = x_1 a_2 x_2 b_2 \alpha$. Moreover $X \in V^0$ implies that $Y \in V^0$ too and thus case 2 holds. □

Note that the second component of a $\forall$-node is identical to the second component of the $\exists$-nodes which precedes it. From the above lemma a simpler property of the subwords in the second component of the nodes can be obtained. A well-matched subword v of w is called *right maximal* if $w = uvx$, $u \neq \epsilon$, and, for each prefix $x' \neq \epsilon$ of x, the subword vx' is not well-matched. This implies that if $x \neq \epsilon$, then it begins with a return symbol whose matching call does not appear in v. The words v characterized in Lemma 1 are of this kind and thus the following corollary holds.

Corollary 1. *If $(\cdot, v) \in N$ then v either is a suffix of w or a right maximal well-matched subword of w.*

We can thus compute the size of H_w^G.

Lemma 2. *The graph H_w^G has $O(|w| \cdot |G|)$ nodes and edges.*

Proof. Consider first the $\exists$-nodes. Fix $w = w_1 \dots w_n$ and denote by $w(i, j)$ the subword of w from the i-th through the j-th position (i.e., $w(i, j) = w_i \dots w_j$). From Corollary 1, we have that if $(Y, v) \in N_\exists$ then v is either a suffix of w or a right maximal well-matched subword of w. Thus, for $i = 1, \dots, n$, if $v = w(i, h)$ for some $i \leq h \leq n$ and $(Y, v) \in N_\exists$ then one of the following cases holds:

– $i > 0$ and w_i is either a matched call or a local action: then v is either $w(i, n)$ or the right maximal well-matched subword starting at position i;
– else $i = 0$ or w_i is either an unmatched call or a return: then $v = w(i, n)$.

Therefore, the number of $\exists$-nodes is bounded by $|V| \cdot (2|w| - n_{uc} - n_r - 1)$, where n_{uc} is the number of unmatched calls in w and n_r is the number of returns. Similarly, from the definition of H_w^G and the above counting, the $\forall$-nodes and the edges are $O(|P| \cdot |w|)$ and thus the lemma follows. □

In the next Lemma we prove that a strategy tree from (S, w) to nodes of the target set exists if and only if $w \in L(G)$ (cf. Example 2).

Lemma 3. *For every $(X, u) \in N_\exists$ there is a strategy tree from (X, u) to the target set T if and only if there is a derivation from X to u in G.*

Proof. We prove the assert by induction on the definition of $N_\exists$, using the nodes with no outgoing edges as base case. Let (X, u) be one of these nodes. If $u = \epsilon$ then clearly a derivation from X to u exists if and only if $(X, u) \in T$. If $u \neq \epsilon$ then $(X, u) \notin T$. As (X, u) has no outgoing edges, there are no productions of G from X that can start a derivation to u. Thus, a derivation from X to u does not exist. For the induction step we prove first the *only-if* part and let e be the outgoing edge branching off the root (X, u) of the strategy tree. If e is added in the H_w^G construction for a production of the form $X \to aY$, then an $\exists$-node (Y, v) exists having e as an incoming edge and $u = av$. Then by induction hypothesis there is a derivation from Y to v, and thus a derivation from X to u. If, on the other hand, e is added for a production of the form $X \to aYbZ$, then a $\forall$-node having e as an incoming edge exists. In H_w^G, each $\forall$-node is followed by two $\exists$-nodes within a strategy tree, let (Y, v) and (Z, z), with $u = avbz$, be the labels of such nodes. By induction, $Y \Rightarrow^* v$ and $Z \Rightarrow^* z$ holds. Thus, the following derivation exists: $X \Rightarrow aYbZ \Rightarrow^* avbZ \Rightarrow^* avbz$.

The *if* part can be easily proved analogously, by constructing the strategy tree from the derivation of u from X. □

From Lemmas 2 and 3 our main result follows.

Theorem 4. *The membership problem for a* VPG *$G = (V, S, P)$ over Σ and a word $w \in \Sigma^*$ is decidable in $O(|w| \cdot |G|)$.*

4 XML Grammars and XML Document Processing

In this section, we describe an interesting application of the membership problem of VPLs for processing XML documents. We start recalling the definition of an XML grammar which captures the synctactic structure of a Document Type Definition (DTD) and of an XML schema [6].

Let Σ be a finite alphabet, we define by $\bar{\Sigma}$ the set of symbols $\bar{\sigma}$ such that $\sigma \in \Sigma$. A symbol $\sigma \in \Sigma$ denotes an "open tag" and $\bar{\sigma}$ its matching "close tag". Fix $\hat{\Sigma} = \Sigma \cup \bar{\Sigma}$. *XML grammars* are defined over symbols of $\hat{\Sigma}$.

Definition 4 (XML Grammar). *An XML grammar $G = (V, S, P, R)$, over an alphabet $\hat{\Sigma}$, is such that:*

- $V = \{X_\sigma \mid \sigma \in \Sigma\}$, *i.e., each non-terminal symbol is in a one-to-one correspondence to an open tag;*
- $S \in V$ *is the axiom;*
- $R = \{R_\sigma \mid \sigma \in \Sigma\}$, *where* R_σ *denotes a regular language over* V*;*
- *productions in* P *are of the form* $X_\sigma \to \sigma\alpha\bar{\sigma}$ *where* $\alpha \in R_\sigma$*. (Note that each pair of open and close tags is produced from just one grammar variable.)*

An *XML language* is the language generated by an XML grammar. In the following, we assume that each regular language is represented by a right-linear grammar that generates it. We will comment on the generality of such assumption in Section 5.

Any XML language can be seen as a visibly pushdown language where open tags correspond to call symbols and close tags to their matching return symbols. Thus, an XML language over $\hat{\Sigma}$ can be generated by a visibly pushdown grammar over the alphabet $\tilde{\Sigma} = (\Sigma, \bar{\Sigma}, \emptyset)$ as shown in the following lemma.

Lemma 4. *Given an XML grammar* G_{XML} *over an alphabet* $\hat{\Sigma}$*, there exists a visibly pushdown grammar* G *over* $\tilde{\Sigma} = (\Sigma, \bar{\Sigma}, \emptyset)$ *such that* $L(G) = L(G_{XML})$ *and* $|G| = O(|G_{XML}|)$*.*

Proof. Let G_{XML} be the XML grammar $(V_{XML}, S_{XML}, P_{XML}, R_{XML})$. For each set R_σ, let $G_\sigma = (V_\sigma, S_\sigma, P_\sigma)$ be a regular right-linear grammar over Σ such that $L(G_\sigma) = R_\sigma$. Assume that for each $\sigma \in \Sigma$ the sets V_σ are pairwise disjoint.

We construct a visibly pushdown grammar $G = (V, S, P)$ such that $L(G) = L(G_{XML})$ as follows. The set V is $\{S\} \cup \bigcup_{\sigma\in\Sigma}\{X' \mid X \in V_\sigma\}$ where S denotes a fresh symbol. The set of productions P is the smallest set containing:

- a production $S \to \theta S'_\theta\bar{\theta}$, if $S_{XML} \to \theta\alpha\bar{\theta}$ is a production in P_{XML} (i.e., S_{XML} is the non-terminal symbol corresponding to θ), and
- a production $X' \to \tau S'_\tau\bar{\tau}Y'$ for each open tag σ and production $X \to \tau Y$ of G_σ;
- a production $X' \to \epsilon$ for each open tag σ and production $X \to \epsilon$ of G_σ.

The cardinality of V is $1 + \sum_{\sigma\in\Sigma}|V_\sigma|$, and the number of productions in P is $1 + \sum_{\sigma\in\Sigma}|P_\sigma|$. Therefore, we obtain the claimed bound. □

Given an XML document D and a DTD (or an XML schema) S, the *XML type-checking problem* is the problem of checking if D syntactically conforms to S. This problem can be formalized as a membership problem for XML languages. From the above lemma and Theorem 4, we have the following corollary.

Corollary 2. *The type-checking problem for XML documents is decidable in time linear in the length of the document and in the size of the DTD (or XML schema).*

5 Discussion

A VPL can be represented either as a grammar or a (non)deterministic automaton. In this section, we briefly discuss on the computational complexity of other solutions to the membership problem for VPLs considering as a starting representation both VPGs and VPAs. We also comment on the complexity of the type-checking problem for XML languages and the assumption made in Section 4. Finally, we recall some related works.

In what follows, we fix a VPG $G = (V, S, P)$ over an alphabet Σ, a VPA $A = (Q, Q_{in}, \Gamma, \delta, Q_F)$ and a word $w = w_1 w_2 \ldots w_n$, where $w_i \in \Sigma$ for $i = 1, \ldots, n$ and $n \geq 0$.

When a VPL is given as a VPA A, since this class of automata is determinizable (see Theorem 2), we can use the determinization construction on-the-fly while checking for language membership. This approach leads to an algorithm that takes cubic time in the number of states of the nondeterministic automaton: $O(|Q|^2 \cdot |\Gamma| + |Q|^3)$, see [4].

Alternatively, we could transform the VPA A into an equivalent VPG G_A and this, again using the construction given in [4], amounts to a set of rules P of size $|Q|^4 \cdot |\Gamma|^2 \cdot |\Sigma_c| \cdot |\Sigma_r|$.

Consider now the case when a VPL is represented by a VPG. The membership problem can be solved using an algorithm which resembles the well known CYK algorithm [1]. Recall that in the original CYK algorithm the grammar is in Chomsky Normal Form. Since VPGs have productions with at most two variables (nonterminals) on the right hand side, we can develop a similar procedure: a bottom-up parsing to fill in a lookup table whose entry (i, j) represents the set of all the variables from which the subword $w_i, \cdots, w_{i+j-1}$ can be derived. The overall time complexity of this algorithm is $O(|P| \cdot n^2)$ (recall that the CYK algorithm for a generic context-free grammar runs in time $O(|P| \cdot n^3)$).

Alternatively, one can think of translating the VPG into an equivalent VPA, but this turns out to be quite expensive in general. In fact, by the construction given in [4], translating a VPG into a VPA costs $O(|P| + |P_\epsilon| \cdot |\Sigma_r| \cdot |V|)$ time, where $|P_\epsilon|$ is the subset of the *nullable* productions (productions of the form $X \to \epsilon$). The size of the set of states and the size of the stack alphabet of the VPA are respectively $|V|$ and $|V \cdot \Sigma_r|$.

Concerning to the type checking problem presented in Section 4, a comment on the linearity of the complexity of Corollary 2 is needed. In the Document Type Definitions (DTD) and XML schemas, the regular sets R_σ are given as regular expressions. Therefore, in the proof of Lemma 4 we have to take into account also a translation from regular expressions to right-linear grammars that might cause a quadratic blow-up in the size of the DTD, or equivalently of the XML schema. However, according to W3C recommendation [22], such regular languages are required to admit a deterministic regular expression (cf. also [6]). Therefore, it is reasonable to assume that the size of right-linear grammars G_σ generating languages R_σ have linear size in the size of the regular expression used in the DTD (or XML schema).

Related research

Several kinds of grammars generating subsets of Dyck languages have been studied in the past and they are strictly related to VPG grammars. The best known examples are the *parenthesis* grammars, defined by Mc Naughton in 1967 [18] and the *bracketed* grammars, introduced by Ginsburg and Harrison [12]. A parenthesis grammar is a context-free grammar with set of variables V and alphabet $\Sigma \cup \{(,)\}$, where each rule is of the form $X \to (\alpha)$, $\alpha \in (\Sigma \cup V)^*$.

One of the most relevant result for this class was obtained by Knuth [15] who showed the existence of an algorithm for determining whether a context-free language admits a parenthesis grammar (actually the class of languages considered by Knuth is slightly larger than that defined by Mc Naughton since a word in a language does not needed to be surrounded by parenthesis). In 1977, Lynch [17] studied the membership problem for parenthesis language and showed that it is in LOGSPACE in the size of the input word.

A bracketed grammar differs from a parenthesis grammar because of a set of indexed parentheses and a bijection between parentheses and production rules. In fact, any rule i of a bracketed grammar is of the form $X \to (_i\alpha)_i$, $\alpha \in (\Sigma \cup V)*$, and $(_i \neq (_j$ for $i \neq j$.

More recently, the class of so called *balanced* grammars has been introduced [6] which extends both parenthesis and bracketed grammars. In these grammars the set of productions for each variable is a regular set (as in the XML grammars, studied in [7] and considered in Section 4). Many interesting properties of this class have been studied such as inclusion, equivalence, intersection, canonical form and testing context-free languages for membership to the class of XML-languages.

The classes of languages defined by the above described grammars are strictly included in the class of VPLs. They all are deterministic context-free languages and the membership problem can thus be solved in time which is linear with respect to the length of the input word, but the complexity of the membership problem with respect to size of the language representation has not been addressed.

In [21,10], the class of *input-driven* languages has been introduced, which coincides with well matched VPLs. In these papers the space complexity of the membership problem is analysed when the languages are given as automata (instead of grammars).

The use of visibly push-down automata for solving problems for XML that involve processing of documents from left to right (such as the type-checking problem we have considered in this paper) has been recently proposed in [16]. There, the authors give an automaton counterpart to XML-grammars that they call XVPA (a variant of visibly push-down automata) and rephrase some typing and streaming problems for XML (including the type-checking problem) as automata decision problems.

6 Conclusions

The membership problem is a central decision problem in the formal languages theory. The time complexity of the membership problem for subclasses of context-free languages has been largely studied, mainly because of its importance in parsing (see also [1]).

In this paper, we have addressed the membership problem for visibly pushdown languages, a sub-class of deterministic context-free languages. Using the visibly pushdown grammars from [4], we have given an algorithm to solve this problem in time linear in both the length of the input word and the size of the grammar. Thus, checking for membership in visibly pushdown grammars can be done faster than for general context-free grammars (even in the case of unambiguous grammars [14]). (Recall that the membership problem in regular languages is linear both in the size of the automaton/grammar and the length of the input word.) As for the other decision problems, the complexity of the membership one confirms that visibly pushdown languages have nice features in terms of tractability and robustness, and thus from this point of view are more alike to the class of regular languages than to the class of context-free languages. As shown in Section 4, our result on the membership problem for VPLs has a natural application in the processing of XML documents.

Acknowledgments. We would like to thank Rajeev Alur and Parthasarathy Madhusudan for fruitful discussions.

References

1. A. Aho and J. Ullman. "The theory of Parsing, Traslation and Compiling, vol. I, Prentice-Hall, Englewood Cliffs, NJ, 1973
2. R. Alur, M. Benedikt, K. Etessami, P. Godefroid, T. W. Reps, and M. Yannakakis. "Analysis of recursive state machines", in *ACM Trans. Program. Lang. Syst.*, 27(4):786–818, 2005.
3. R. Alur, V. Kumkar, P. Madhusudan and M. Viswanathan. "Congruences for visibly pushdown languages" in *Proc. of the 32nd Intl. Coll. of Automata and Languages (ICALP'05)*, LNCS 3580:1102–1114, 2005.
4. R. Alur and P. Madhusudan. "Visibly Pushdown Languages", *www.cis.upenn.edu/˜alur/*. A preliminary version appears in *Proc. of the 36th ACM Symp. on Theory of Computing (STOC'04)*, 201–211, 2004.
5. T. Ball and S. Rajamani. "Bebop: A Symbolic Model Checker for Boolean Programs", in *Proc. of the 7th Intern. Workshop on Model Checking of Software (SPIN 2000)*, LNCS 1885: 113–130, 2000.
6. J. Berstel and L. Boasson. "Balanced Grammars and Their Languages", in *Formal & Natural Computing: Essay dedicated to Grzegorz Rozenberg* , LNCS 2300:3–25,2002.
7. J. Berstel and L. Boasson. "Formal Properties of XML Grammars and Languages", in *Acta Informatica*, 38 :649–671,2002.
8. A. Bouajjani, J. Esparza, and O. Maler. "Reachability analysis of pushdown automata: Application to model-checking", in *Proc. of the 8th Inter. Conf. on Concurrency Theory (CONCUR'97)*, LNCS 1243: 135–150, 1997.
9. O. Burkart and B. Steffen. "Model Checking for Context-Free Processes", in *Proc. of the 3rd Inter. Conf. on Concurrency Theory (CONCUR'92)*, LNCS 620:123–137, 1992.

10. P. W. Dymond. "Input-driven languages are Recognized in Log n Space", in *IPL* , 26:247250, 1988.
11. J. Esparza, A. Kucera, and S. Schwoon. "Model checking LTL with regular valuations for pushdown systems", *Information and Computation,* 186(2): 355–376 2003.
12. S. Ginsburg and M. A. Harrison. "Bracketed Context-free languages", *J. Computer and System Sci.*, 1:1-23, 1967.
13. T. A. Henzinger, R. Jhala, R. Majumdar, G. C. Necula, G. Sutre, and W. Weimer. "Temporal-Safety Proofs for Systems Code", in *Proc. of the 14th Inter. Conf. on Comp.-Aided Verif. (CAV 2002)*, LNCS 2404: 526–538, 2002.
14. J.E. Hopcroft, R. Motwani and J.D. Ullman "Introduction to Automata Theory, Languages, and Computation" Addison Wesley, 2001.
15. D.E. Knuth. "A characterization of parenthesis languages", *Information and Control,* 11(3):269–289,1967.
16. V. Kumkar, P. Madhusudan and M. Viswanathan. "Visibly Pushdown Languages for XML". Technical Report UIUCDCS-R-2006-2704, UIUC, 2006.
17. N. Lynch. "Log Space Recognition and Traslation of Parenthesis Languages", *J. ACM,* 24(4):583–590,1977.
18. R. McNaughton. "Parenthesis grammars", *J. ACM,* 14(3):490–500,1967.
19. T. W. Reps, S. Horwitz, and S. Sagiv. "Precise Interprocedural Dataflow Analysis via Graph Reachability", in *Proc. of the 22nd Symposium on Principles of Programming Languages (POPL'95)*, 49–61, 1995.
20. W. Thomas, "On the synthesis of strategies in infinite games", in *12th Annual Symposium on Theoretical Aspects of Computer Science, STACS'95*, LNCS 900: 1–13, 1995.
21. B. von Braunmhl and R. Verbeek. "Input-driven languages are Recognized in Log n Space", in *Proc. of FCT* , LNCS 158:4051, 1983.
22. W3C Recommendation. Extensible Markup Language (XML) 1.0 (Second Edition), 6 October 2000. http://www.w3.org/TR/REC-xml
23. W3C Recommendation. XML Schema Part 0,1 and 2, 2 May 2001. http://www.w3.org/TR/xmlschema-0,1,2

On the Construction of Fine Automata for Safety Properties

Orna Kupferman and Robby Lampert

Hebrew University, School of Engineering and Computer Science, Jerusalem 91904, Israel
{orna,robil}@cs.huji.ac.il

Abstract. Of special interest in formal verification are *safety* properties, which assert that the system always stays within some allowed region. Each safety property ψ can be associated with a set of *bad prefixes*: a set of finite computations such that an infinite computation violates ψ iff it has a prefix in the set. By translating a safety property to an automaton for its set of bad prefixes, verification can be reduced to reasoning about finite words: a system is correct if none of its computations has a bad prefix. Checking the latter circumvents the need to reason about cycles and simplifies significantly methods like symbolic fixed-point based verification, bounded model checking, and more.

A drawback of the translation lies in the size of the automata: while the translation of a safety LTL formula ψ to a nondeterministic Büchi automaton is exponential, its translation to a tight bad-prefix automaton — one that accepts all the bad prefixes of ψ, is doubly exponential. Kupferman and Vardi showed that for the purpose of verification, one can replace the tight automaton by a fine automaton — one that accepts at least one bad prefix of each infinite computation that violates ψ. They also showed that for many safety LTL formulas, a fine automaton has the same structure as the Büchi automaton for the formula. The problem of constructing fine automata for general safety LTL formulas was left open. In this paper we solve this problem and show that while a fine automaton cannot, in general, have the same structure as the Büchi automaton for the formula, the size of a fine automaton is still only exponential in the length of the formula.

1 Introduction

Today's rapid development of complex and safety-critical systems requires reliable verification methods. In formal verification, we verify that a system meets a desired property by checking that a mathematical model of the system meets a formal specification that describes the property. Of special interest are properties asserting that observed behavior of the system always stays within some allowed region, in which nothing "bad" happens. For example, we may want to assert that every message received was previously sent. Such properties of systems are called *safety properties*. Intuitively, a property ψ is a safety property if every violation of ψ occurs after a finite execution of the system. In our example, if in a computation of the system a message is received without previously being sent, this occurs after some finite execution of the system.

In order to formally define what safety properties are, we refer to computations of a nonterminating system as infinite words over an alphabet Σ. Typically, $\Sigma = 2^{AP}$,

S. Graf and W. Zhang (Eds.): ATVA 2006, LNCS 4218, pp. 110–124, 2006.

where AP is the set of the system's atomic propositions. Consider a language L of infinite words over Σ. A finite word x over Σ is a *bad prefix* for L iff for all infinite words y over Σ, the concatenation $x \cdot y$ of x and y is not in L. Thus, a bad prefix for L is a finite word that cannot be extended to an infinite word in L. A language L is a *safety language* if every word not in L has a finite bad prefix. Linear properties of nonterminating systems are often specified using nondeterministic Büchi automata on infinite words (NBW) or linear temporal logic (LTL) formulas. We say that an NBW is a safety NBW if it recognizes a safety language. Similarly, an LTL formula is a safety formula if the set of computations that satisfy it form a safety language.

In addition to proof-based methods for the verification of safety properties [MP92, MP95], there is extensive work on model checking of safety properties. General methods for model checking of linear properties are based on a construction of an NBW $\mathcal{A}_{\neg\psi}$ that accepts exactly all the infinite computations that violate the property ψ [VW94]. Verification of a system M with respect to ψ is reduced to checking the emptiness of the product of M and $\mathcal{A}_{\neg\psi}$ [VW86]. This check can be performed on-the-fly and symbolically [BCM+92, CVWY92]. When ψ is an LTL formula, the size of $\mathcal{A}_\psi$ is exponential in the length of ψ, and the complexity of verification that follows is PSPACE, with a matching lower bound [SC85].

When ψ is a safety property, the NBW $\mathcal{A}_{\neg\psi}$ can be replaced by *bad-pref*$(\mathcal{A}_\psi)$ – an automaton on finite words (NFW) that accepts exactly all the bad prefixes of ψ [KV01a]. This has several advantages, as reasoning about finite words is simpler than reasoning about infinite words: symbolic reasoning (in particular, bounded model checking procedures) need not look for loops (cf. [HKSV97]) and can, instead, apply backward or forward reachability analysis [BCM+92, IN97, CBRZ01, Hol04]. In fact, the construction of *bad-pref*$(\mathcal{A}_\psi)$ reduces the model-checking problem to the problem of invariance checking [MP92], which is amenable to both model-checking techniques [BCM+92, IN97] and deductive verification techniques [BM83, OSR95, MAB+94]. In addition, using *bad-pref*$(\mathcal{A}_\psi)$, we can return to the user a finite error trace, which is a bad prefix, and which is often more helpful than an infinite error trace.

The construction of *bad-pref*$(\mathcal{A}_\psi)$ is studied in [KV01a]. As shown there, while the translation of ψ to the NBW $\mathcal{A}_{\neg\psi}$ involves an exponential blow-up, the NFW *bad-pref*$(\mathcal{A}_\psi)$ may be doubly-exponential in the length of ψ. This discouraging blow-up is reflected in the fact that practitioners have restricted attention to invariance checking [GW91, McM92, Val93, MR97], have assumed that a general safety property is given by the set of its bad prefixes [GW91], or have worked with variants of $\mathcal{A}_{\neg\psi}$ that approximate the set of bad prefixes [GH01].

Such an approximation is also studied in [KV01a], which relaxes the requirement on *bad-pref*$(\mathcal{A}_\psi)$ and seek, instead, an NFW that need not accept all the bad prefixes, yet must accept at least one bad prefix of every infinite computation that does not satisfy ψ. Such an NFW is said to be *fine* for ψ. For example, an NFW that accepts all the finite words in $0^* \cdot 1 \cdot (0+1)$ does not accept all the bad prefixes of the safety language $\{0^\omega\}$; in particular, it does not accept the minimal bad prefixes in $0^* \cdot 1$. Yet, such an NFW is fine for $\{0^\omega\}$. Indeed, every infinite word that is different from 0^ω has a prefix in $0^* \cdot 1 \cdot (0+1)$. In practice, almost all the benefit that one obtains from *bad-pref*$(\mathcal{A}_\psi)$

can also be obtained from a fine automaton. It is shown in [KV01a] that for many safety formulas ψ, a fine automaton has the same structure as the NBW $\mathcal{A}_{\neg\psi}$, and can be constructed by redefining its set of accepting states.

The construction in [KV01a] has been optimized and implemented in [Lat03], which also describes an implementation of the algorithm for checking whether an LTL formula ψ is such that a fine automaton for it can be easily constructed from $\mathcal{A}_{\neg\psi}$. The problem of constructing fine automata for general safety LTL formulas was left open in both papers. We note that the problem was left open not due to a lack of interest; to the contrary – in practice we do come across formulas for which the constructions in [KV01a, Lat03, GH01] do not work, and a fine automaton is desirable. In this paper we solve this problem and show how to construct, for every LTL formula, a fine automaton of size only exponential in the length of the formula. We also show that while a fine automaton for ψ cannot, in general, have the same structure as the NBW $\mathcal{A}_{\neg\psi}$, its construction is similar to that of $\mathcal{A}_{\neg\psi}$. The key idea behind our construction is that even though it is impossible to bound the length of a good prefix, it is possible to bound the number of visits that a good prefix has to the set of accepting states. In addition to the above positive result, we give negative results about fine automata constructed from $\mathcal{A}_{\psi}$ (rather than $\mathcal{A}_{\neg\psi}$), and about the possibility of using properties of the NBWs obtained from LTL formulas (c.f., reverse determinism, single accepting run, obtained by alternation removal of a very weak alternating automaton) in order to define a fine automaton with the same structure as $\mathcal{A}_{\psi}$.

From a theoretical point of view, we find our result very interesting: the "fine-automaton" problem belongs to a class of long-standing open problems that refer to the power of nondeterminism, and this work is the first to solve a problem from this class. To get the flavor of this class, consider an NBW $\mathcal{A}$, and assume we want to translate it to an equivalent nondeterministic co-Büchi automaton[1] (NCW). The best known procedure for doing it is to determinize $\mathcal{A}$ to a Streett automaton and then define the co-Büchi condition on top of the deterministic automaton. This involves an exponential blow-up, with no matching lower bound, and the question about the existence of an efficient NBW-to-NCW translation that avoids determinization and goes directly to an NCW is open. More problems in this class include a translation of an NBW to an automaton on finite words (accepting a language whose limit is the language of the original automaton, see [Lan69]), a translation of nondeterministic tree automata for a derivable language to a word automaton for the language that derives it (see [KSV96]), and more. The "fine-automaton" problem is the first problem in this class to which we are able to avoid determinization. Indeed, the existing solution, from [KV01a], applies the subset construction. We hope the solution would shed light on the other problems in this class. In particular, we believe that the idea used here, of using the complementary nondeterministic automaton instead of a deterministic automaton would be useful for the other problems: both determinization and complementation involves an exponential blow-up. Nevertheless, when the language is given in terms of an LTL formula, complementation

[1] Such a translation is not always possible, and attention is restricted to languages for which it is possible. The need for such a translation arises from the fact that the transition from NCW to the alternation-free μ-calculus is linear, whereas the transition from NBW to the alternation-free μ-calculus is exponential. For details, see [KV05a].

is for free. Thus, as is the case with fine-automata, a construction that uses the complementing automaton rather than the deterministic one is exponentially better.

From a practical point of view, our solution shows that reasoning about all safety formulas can be done symbolically with a single exponential blow-up and a single nested fixed-point. In Section 5, we discuss the application of our result in run-time verification and bounded model checking.

2 Preliminaries

Safety and Co-safety Languages. Consider a language $L \subseteq \Sigma^\omega$ of infinite words over the alphabet Σ. A finite word $x \in \Sigma^*$ is a *bad prefix* for L iff for all $y \in \Sigma^\omega$, we have $x \cdot y \notin L$. Thus, a bad prefix is a finite word that cannot be extended to an infinite word in L. Note that if x is a bad prefix, then all the finite extensions of x are also bad prefixes. A language L is a *safety* language iff every infinite word $w \notin L$ has a finite bad prefix. For a safety language L, we denote by *bad-pref*(L) the set of all bad prefixes for L.

For a language $L \subseteq \Sigma^\omega$ (Σ^*), we use *comp*(L) to denote the complement of L; i.e., *comp*$(L) = \Sigma^\omega \setminus L$ ($\Sigma^* \setminus L$, respectively). We say that a language $L \subseteq \Sigma^\omega$ is a *co-safety* language iff *comp*(L) is a safety language. (The term used in [MP92] is *guarantee* language.) Equivalently, L is co-safety iff every infinite word $w \in L$ has a *good prefix* $x \in \Sigma^*$: for all $y \in \Sigma^\omega$, we have $x \cdot y \in L$. For a co-safety language L, we denote by *good-pref*(L) the set of good prefixes for L. Note that for a safety language L, we have that *good-pref*$($*comp*$(L)) =$ *bad-pref*(L). Thus, in order to construct the set of bad prefixes for a safety property, one can construct the set of good prefixes for its complementary language.

Word Automata. Given an alphabet Σ, an *infinite word over* Σ is an infinite sequence $w = \sigma_1 \cdot \sigma_2 \cdots$ of letters in Σ. We denote by w^l the suffix $\sigma_l \cdot \sigma_{l+1} \cdot \sigma_{l+2} \cdots$ of w. A *nondeterministic Büchi word automaton* (NBW, for short) is $\mathcal{A} = \langle \Sigma, Q, \delta, Q_0, F \rangle$, where Σ is the input alphabet, Q is a finite set of states, $\delta : Q \times \Sigma \to 2^Q$ is a transition function, $Q_0 \subseteq Q$ is a set of initial states, and $F \subseteq Q$ is a set of accepting states. If $|Q_0| = 1$ and δ is such that for every $q \in Q$ and $\sigma \in \Sigma$, we have that $|\delta(q, \sigma)| = 1$, then $\mathcal{A}$ is a *deterministic* Büchi word automaton (DBW, for short).

Given an input word $w = \sigma_0 \cdot \sigma_1 \cdots$ in Σ^ω, a *run* of $\mathcal{A}$ on w is a sequence $r_0, r_1, \ldots$ of states in Q, such that $r_0 \in Q_0$ and for every $i \geq 0$, we have $r_{i+1} \in \delta(r_i, \sigma_i)$; i.e., the run starts in one of the initial states and obeys the transition function. Note that a nondeterministic automaton can have many runs on w. In contrast, a deterministic automaton has a single run on w.

For a run r, let $inf(r)$ denote the set of states that r visits infinitely often. That is, $inf(r) = \{q \in Q : r_i = q \text{ for infinitely many } i \geq 0\}$. As Q is finite, it is guaranteed that $inf(r) \neq \emptyset$. The run r is *accepting* iff $inf(r) \cap F \neq \emptyset$. That is, iff there exists a state in F that r visits infinitely often. A run that is not accepting is *rejecting*. An NBW $\mathcal{A}$ accepts an input word w iff there exists an accepting run of $\mathcal{A}$ on w. The *language* of an NBW $\mathcal{A}$, denoted $\mathcal{L}(\mathcal{A})$, is the set of words that $\mathcal{A}$ accepts. We assume that a given NBW $\mathcal{A}$ has no empty states (that is, at least one word is accepted from each state – otherwise we can remove the state).

We say that the automaton $\mathcal{A}$ over infinite words is a safety (co-safety) automaton iff $\mathcal{L}(\mathcal{A})$ is a safety (co-safety) language. We use *bad-pref*$(\mathcal{A})$, *good-pref*$(\mathcal{A})$, and *comp*$(\mathcal{A})$ to abbreviate *bad-pref*$(\mathcal{L}(\mathcal{A}))$, *good-pref*$(\mathcal{L}(\mathcal{A}))$, and *comp*$(\mathcal{L}(\mathcal{A}))$.

Linear Temporal Logic. The logic *LTL* is a linear temporal logic. Formulas of LTL are constructed from a set AP of atomic propositions using the usual Boolean operators and the temporal operators G ("always"), F ("eventually"), X ("next time"), and U ("until"). Formulas of LTL describe computations of systems over AP. For example, the LTL formula $G(req \rightarrow Fack)$ describes computations in which every position in which req holds is eventually followed by a position in which ack holds. For the detailed syntax and semantics of LTL, see [Pnu81]. The *model-checking problem* for LTL is to determine, given an LTL formula ψ and a system M, whether all the computations of M satisfy ψ.

General methods for LTL model checking are based on translation of LTL formulas to nondeterministic Büchi word automata:

Theorem 1. [VW94] *Given an LTL formula ψ, one can construct an NBW $\mathcal{A}_\psi$ that accepts exactly all the computations that satisfy ψ. The size of $\mathcal{A}_\psi$ is, in the worst case, exponential in the length of ψ.*

Given a system M and a property ψ, model checking of M with respect to ψ is reduced to checking the emptiness of the product of M and $\mathcal{A}_{\neg\psi}$ [VW94]. This check can be performed on-the-fly and symbolically [BCM$^+$92, CVWY92], and the complexity of model checking that follows is PSPACE, with a matching lower bound [SC85].

3 Detecting Bad and Good Prefixes

Recall that the model-checking problem for an LTL formula ψ involves the construction of an NBW that accepts infinite computations that violate ψ. As discussed in Section 1, when ψ is a safety property, it is desirable to construct, instead, a *nondeterministic automaton on finite words* (NFW, for short) for the bad prefixes of ψ. In this section we recall the relevant results from [KV01a], and the problem that has been left open there.

Consider a safety NBW $\mathcal{A}$. If $\mathcal{A}$ is deterministic, we can construct a *deterministic automaton on finite words* (DFW, for short) for *bad-pref*$(\mathcal{A})$ by defining the set of accepting states to be the set of states s for which $\mathcal{A}$ with initial state s is empty. Likewise, if $\mathcal{A}$ is a co-safety automaton, we can construct a DFW for *good-pref*$(\mathcal{A})$ by defining the set of accepting states to be the set of states s for which $\mathcal{A}$ with initial state s is universal.

When $\mathcal{A}$ is nondeterministic, the story is more complicated. Even if we are after a nondeterministic, rather than a deterministic, automaton for the bad or good prefixes, the transition from infinite words to finite words involves an exponential blow-up. Formally, we have the following.

Theorem 2. [KV01a] *Consider an NBW $\mathcal{A}$ of size n.*

1. *If $\mathcal{A}$ is a safety automaton, the size of an NFW for bad-pref$(\mathcal{A})$ is $2^{\Theta(n)}$.*
2. *If $\mathcal{A}$ is a co-safety automaton, the size of an NFW for good-pref$(\mathcal{A})$ is $2^{\Theta(n)}$.*

The lower bound in Theorem 2 for the case $\mathcal{A}$ is a safety automaton is not surprising. Essentially, it follows from the fact that *bad-pref*$(\mathcal{A})$ refers to words that are not accepted by $\mathcal{A}$. Hence, it has the flavor of complementation, and complementation of nondeterministic automata involves an exponential blow-up [MF71]. The second blow-up, however, in going from a co-safety automaton to a nondeterministic automaton for its good prefixes is surprising. Since its proof in [KV01a] highlights our contribution here, we describe it below.

For $n \geq 1$, let $\Sigma_n = \{1, \ldots, n, \&\}$. We define L_n as the language of all words $w \in \Sigma_n^\omega$ such that w contains at least one & and the letter after the first & is either & or it has already appeared somewhere before the first &. The language L_n is a co-safety language. Indeed, each word in L_n has a good prefix (e.g., the one that contains the first & and its successor). We can recognize L_n with an NBW with $O(n)$ states (the NBW guesses the letter that appears after the first &). Obvious good prefixes for L_n are 12&&, 123&2, etc. That is, prefixes that end one letter after the first &, and their last letter is either & or has already appeared somewhere before the &. We can recognize these prefixes with an NFW with $O(n)$ states. But L_n also has some less obvious good prefixes, like $1234 \cdots n\&$ (a permutation of $1 \ldots n$ followed by &). These prefixes are indeed good, as every suffix we concatenate to them would start in either & or a letter in $\{1, \ldots, n\}$, which has appeared before the &. To recognize these prefixes, an NFW needs to keep track of subsets of $\{1, \ldots, n\}$, for which it needs 2^n states. Consequently, an NFW for *good-pref*(L_n) must have at least 2^n states.

As described in the proof, some good prefixes for L_n (the "obvious prefixes") can be recognized by a small NFW. What if we give up the non-obvious prefixes and construct an NFW $\mathcal{A}'$ that accepts only the "obvious subset" of L_n? It is not hard to see that each word in L_n has an obvious prefix. Thus, while $\mathcal{A}'$ does not accept all the good prefixes, it accepts at least one prefix of every word in L. This useful property of $\mathcal{A}'$ is formalized below.

Consider a safety language L. We say that a set $X \subseteq$ *bad-pref*(L) is a *trap* for L iff every word $w \notin L$ has at least one bad prefix in X. Thus, while X need not contain all the bad prefixes for L, it must contain sufficiently many prefixes to "trap" all the words not in L. Dually, a trap for a co-safety language L is a set $X \subseteq$ *good-pref*(L) such that every word $w \in L$ has at least one good prefix in X. We denote the set of all the traps, for an either safety or co-safety language L, by *trap*(L).

An NFW $\mathcal{A}$ is *fine* for a safety or a co-safety language L iff $\mathcal{A}$ accepts a trap for L. For example, an NFW that accepts $0^* \cdot 1 \cdot (0+1)$ does not accept all the bad prefixes of the safety language $\{0^\omega\}$; in particular, it does not accept the minimal bad prefixes in $0^* \cdot 1$. Yet, such an NFW is fine for $\{0^\omega\}$. Indeed, every infinite word that is different from 0^ω has a prefix in $0^* \cdot 1 \cdot (0+1)$. Likewise, the NFW is fine for the co-safety language $0^* \cdot 1 \cdot (0+1)^\omega$. In practice, almost all the benefit that one obtains from an NFW that accepts all the bad/good prefixes can also be obtained from a fine automaton. It is shown in [KV01a] that for natural safety formulas ψ, the construction of an NFW fine for ψ is as easy as the construction of $\mathcal{A}_{\neg\psi}$. In more details, if we regard $\mathcal{A}_{\neg\psi}$ as an NFW, with an appropriate definition of the set of accepting states, we get an automaton fine for ψ. For general safety formulas, the problem of constructing small fine automata was left open:

Open question [KV01a]: *Are there feasible constructions of fine automata for general safety and co-safety formulas?*

In the rest of the paper, we solve the question and discuss our solution.

4 Fine Automata for Safety and Co-safety Properties

In this section we study the size of fine automata for safety and co-safety properties. We start with the case the property is given by means of an NBW and show that then, the size of a fine automaton is polynomial in the sizes of the NBWs for the property and its negation. Since for LTL, the sizes of the NBWs for a formula and its negation are both exponential in the length of the formula, we conclude that LTL formulas have exponential fine automata.

4.1 Fine Automata for Safety NBW

We start with fine automata for safety NBWs. It is shown in [KV01a] that the transition from an NBW to a tight NFW for its bad prefixes is exponential, and that the exponential blow-up follows from the fact that a complementing NBW can be constructed from a tight NFW. When we consider fine automata, things are more complicated, as the fine NFW need not accept all bad prefixes. As we show below, however, a construction of fine automata still has the flavor of complementation, and must involve an exponential blow-up.

Theorem 3. *Given a safety NBW $\mathcal{A}$ of size n, the size of an NFW fine for $\mathcal{A}$ is exponential in n.*

Proof: Since every tight NFW is fine, the upper bound follows from Theorem 2.

The lower bound follows from the exponential lower bound for NFW complementation [SS78]. As detailed below, given an NFW $\mathcal{U}$, one can construct an NBW $\mathcal{U}'$ of size linear in the size of $\mathcal{U}$, such that $\mathcal{L}(\mathcal{U}')$ is safety and an NFW fine for $\mathcal{U}'$ can be turned into an NFW for *comp*$(\mathcal{L}(\mathcal{U}))$ of the same size. It follows that a sub-exponential construction of fine automata would lead to a sub-exponential complementation construction, which is known to be impossible.

For an alphabet Σ with $\# \notin \Sigma$ and an NFW $\mathcal{U}$ for a language $L \subseteq \Sigma^*$, we define the language $L' = \{u\#^\omega : u \in L\} \cup \Sigma^\omega$ over the alphabet $\Sigma' = \Sigma \cup \{\#\}$. Note that every word $y \in (\Sigma')^\omega$ that is not in L' must contain at least one $\#$. Indeed, otherwise $y \in \Sigma^\omega$, which is contained in L'. Nevertheless, L' is a safety language, as every word $y \notin L'$ is of the form ht, where t is some string in $(\Sigma')^\omega$ and h is either $v\#$ for $v \in \Sigma^* \setminus L$, or $v\#^+a$ for $v \in (\Sigma')^\omega$ and $a \neq \#$. In both cases, h is a bad prefix.

Given $\mathcal{U}$, we construct the NBW $\mathcal{U}'$ for L' by adding to $\mathcal{U}$ two new states, which are going to be the only accepting states of $\mathcal{U}'$. The first state (which accepts Σ^ω) has a σ transition from the initial state and from itself, for every $\sigma \in \Sigma$. The second state (which accepts $\#^\omega$ and is reachable by traversing $v\#$ for $v \in L$) has a $\#$ transition from every accepting state of $\mathcal{U}$ and from itself. It is not hard to see that $\mathcal{L}(\mathcal{U}') = L'$.

Let $\mathcal{A}$ be an NFW fine for $\mathcal{U}'$. We now show how an NFW $\overline{\mathcal{U}}$ for *comp*(L) can be obtained from $\mathcal{A}$. Given $\mathcal{A}$, we make the following two changes. First, we define the set of accepting states to be the set of states of $\mathcal{A}$ from which we can reach an accepting state by reading a string $t \in \#^+$. Then, we delete from $\mathcal{A}$ all $\#$ transitions.

We prove that $\overline{\mathcal{U}}$ indeed accepts $comp(L)$. Consider a word $w \in \Sigma^*$. Assume first that $w \in comp(L)$. Then, $w \notin L$ and $w\#^\omega \notin L'$. Therefore, as $\mathcal{A}$ is fine, a prefix of $w\#^\omega$ is accepted by $\mathcal{A}$. Let h be the minimal prefix of $w\#^\omega$ accepted by $\mathcal{A}$, and let $|h| = l$. Since $\Sigma^\omega \subseteq L'$, the prefix h must contain at least one $\#$. Thus, $h = w\#^k$ for some $k \geq 1$. Let $r_0 r_1 \ldots r_l$ be an accepting run of $\mathcal{A}$ on h. Since we can reach the accepting state r_l from r_{l-k} by reading $\#^k$, then, by the definition of $\overline{\mathcal{U}}$, the state r_{l-k} is accepting in $\overline{\mathcal{U}}$, thus $r_0 r_1 \ldots r_{l-k}$ is an accepting run of $\overline{\mathcal{U}}$ on w, and $w \in \mathcal{L}(\overline{\mathcal{U}})$. Assume now that $w \in \mathcal{L}(\overline{\mathcal{U}})$. Let $|w| = m$ and let $r_0 r_1 \ldots r_m$ be an accepting run of $\overline{\mathcal{U}}$ on w. Then, by the definition of $\overline{\mathcal{U}}$, there is an accepting run $r_0 r_1 \ldots r_m r_{m+1} \ldots r_{m+k}$ of $\mathcal{A}$ on $h = w\#^k$ for some $k \geq 1$, which means that $h \in$ *bad-pref*(L'). As stated above, $h \in$ *bad-pref*(L') if either $h = v\#t$ for $v \in \Sigma^* \setminus L$, or $h = v\#^+ at$ for $v \in (\Sigma')^\omega$ and $a \neq \#$ (Note that since h need not be a minimal bad prefix, t may be a finite string over Σ'). Since h consists of w, which contains only letters from Σ, followed by $\#^k$, no letter $a \neq \#$ appears after the first $\#$ in h. Thus, h must have the form $v\#t$ for $v \notin L$. As the part of h preceding the first $\#$ is w, we have that $w \notin L$, and we are done. □

The proof of Theorem 3 shows that constructing a fine NFW for a safety NBW has the flavor of complementation. In Theorem 5, we show that the size of the complementary automaton is indeed the bottleneck in the construction of fine NFW for safety NBW, and that a fine automaton can be constructed with a blow-up that depends on the size of the complementary automaton.

4.2 Fine Automata for Co-safety NBW

We now move on to consider co-safety NBWs. We start with bad news and show that a fine NFW for a co-safety NBW cannot, in general, have the same structure as the co-safety NBW. We then present our main result and show that a fine NFW for a co-safety property can be constructed from the NBWs for the property and its negation. Note that by dualizing this result, we get a similar bound also for safety NBWs.

NBWs Are Not Fine-Type. The notion of *typeness* arises in the context of translations between different types of automata on infinite words [KPB94, KMM04]. For an acceptance condition γ (say, Büchi), an automaton $\mathcal{A}$ is said to be γ-type if whenever there is a γ-automaton equivalent to $\mathcal{A}$, there is also a γ-automaton $\mathcal{A}'$ equivalent to $\mathcal{A}$ with the same structure as $\mathcal{A}$. Thus, $\mathcal{A}'$ is obtained from $\mathcal{A}$ by redefining its acceptance condition. It is shown, for example, in [KPB94] that deterministic Rabin automata are Büchi type: if a deterministic Rabin automaton $\mathcal{A}$ recognizes a language that can be recognized by a deterministic Büchi automaton, then $\mathcal{A}$ has an equivalent deterministic Büchi automaton on the same structure. On the other hand, Streett automata are not Büchi type: there is a deterministic Streett automaton $\mathcal{A}$ that recognizes a language that can be recognized by a deterministic Büchi automaton, but all the possibilities of defining a Büchi acceptance condition on the structure of $\mathcal{A}$ result in an automaton recognizing a different language.

For a co-safety NBW $\mathcal{A}$, we say that $\mathcal{A}$ is *fine-type* if a fine automaton for $\mathcal{A}$ can be defined on the structure of $\mathcal{A}$. It is shown in [KV01a] that the NBWs for many co-safety LTL formulas are fine-type: by taking the NBW $\mathcal{A}_\psi$ for ψ and defining only accepting sinks to be accepting[2], one gets an NFW fine for ψ. Intuitively, each state of $\mathcal{A}_\psi$ is associated with a set S of subformulas of ψ. A word w is accepted by $\mathcal{A}_\psi$ from state S iff w satisfies all the formulas in S. For natural LTL formulas and for constructions of $\mathcal{A}_\psi$ (c.f., [GPVW95]) that keep in S only formulas that are essential for the satisfaction, the set S would become empty after reading some prefix of a word that satisfies ψ. Unfortunately, this is not true for all formulas. The reason for this is the fact that known constructions for LTL proceed according to the syntax of the formulas, and the co-safetyness of a formula may hide. We demonstrate this in the examples below, which also show that NBWs are not fine type.

The NBW $\mathcal{A}_\varphi$ in Figure 1 is the union of two NBWs. The NBW on the left accepts all words over the alphabet $\{a, b\}$ that satisfy $Fa \wedge GFb$ ("eventually a and infinitely many b's"). The NBW on the right accepts all words satisfying $Fb \wedge GFa$. While each of these languages is neither safe nor co-safe, their union is the co-safety language of all words satisfying $Fa \wedge Fb$ ("eventually a and eventually b"). The formula $\varphi = (Fa \wedge GFb) \vee (Fb \wedge GFa)$ is *pathologically* co-safe [KV01a], which means intuitively that it is hard to tell that it is co-safe just from its syntax: a computation that satisfies φ has no *informative prefix* [KV01a] — a prefix in which all the syntactic eventualities in the formulas are satisfied. Indeed, only the combination of the two NBWs in the union reveals the co-safetyness of φ.

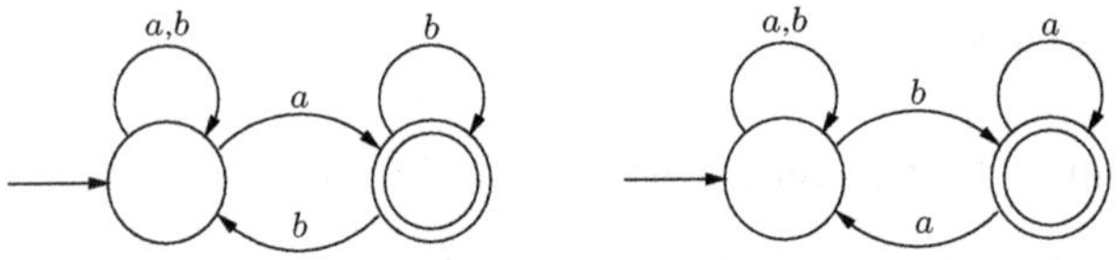

Fig. 1. An NBW for $\varphi = (Fa \wedge GFb) \vee (Fb \wedge GFa)$

The above analysis is reflected in the fact that the NBW $\mathcal{A}_\varphi$ is not fine type; i.e., there is no way to define a fine NFW on its structure, by just redefining the accepting states. To see this, observe that every state in $\mathcal{A}_\varphi$ can be reached after reading a prefix of length at most 1. Since every such prefix can be extended to one of the infinite words a^ω or b^ω, which do not satisfy $Fa \wedge Fb$, an NFW with the structure of $\mathcal{A}_\varphi$ is either empty or accepts words that are not good prefixes for φ.

The above example refers to general co-safety NBWs. In Appendix A, we describe two stronger examples, in the sense that they show the non-fine-typeness of restricted classes of NBWs — classes that correspond to the NBWs obtained by translating LTL formulas to NBWs. The first class of NBWs we consider is *single run* NBWs; i.e., every word that is accepted by the NBW has a single accepting run. The NBWs whose construction is described in [VW94] are single run. The second class we consider is

[2] The details in [KV01a] are for alternating automata, and the argument refers to the NBW obtained by translating these automata to nondeterministic ones via the construction of [MH84].

of NBWs obtained by applying the Miyano-Hayashi procedure for alternation removal [MH84] on top of the alternating Büchi automaton obtained from the LTL formula.

A Construction of Fine NFWs. While general co-safety NBWs are not fine-type, we can still construct an NFW fine for a co-safety NBW $\mathcal{A}$ and whose size depends on the sizes of $\mathcal{A}$ and *comp*($\mathcal{A}$). The idea is that it is possible to bound the number of times that a run of $\mathcal{A}$ visits the set of accepting states, when it runs on a word not in $\mathcal{L}(\mathcal{A})$. Formally, we have the following:

Lemma 1. *Consider a co-safety NBW $\mathcal{A}$. Let F be the set of accepting states of $\mathcal{A}$ and let $\overline{\mathcal{A}}$ be an NBW with $\overline{n}$ states such that $\mathcal{L}(\overline{\mathcal{A}}) = comp(\mathcal{L}(\mathcal{A}))$. If a run of $\mathcal{A}$ on a finite word $h \in \Sigma^*$ visits F more than $|F| \cdot \overline{n}$ times, then h is a good prefix for $\mathcal{L}(\mathcal{A})$.*

Proof: Since $\mathcal{A}$ is a co-safety NBW, $\overline{\mathcal{A}}$ is a safety NBW. Recall that no state of $\overline{\mathcal{A}}$ is empty. Therefore, by [Sis94], every infinite run of $\overline{\mathcal{A}}$ is accepting[3]. Let $r = r_0 r_1 \ldots r_l$ be a run of $\mathcal{A}$ on h that visits F more than $|F| \cdot \overline{n}$ times. Assume, by way of contradiction, that h is not a good prefix. Then, h can be extended to a word accepted by $\overline{\mathcal{A}}$, and thus, there is a (finite) run $r' = r'_0 r'_1 \ldots r'_l$ of $\overline{\mathcal{A}}$ on h. Since r visits F more than $|F| \cdot \overline{n}$ times, there exist $0 \leq i < j \leq l$ such that $r_j = r_i \in F$ and $r'_j = r'_i$. Let $w = h_1 \ldots h_i (h_{i+1} \ldots h_j)^\omega$. Since $r_j = r_i \in F$, the run $r_0 r_1 \ldots r_i (r_{i+1} \ldots r_j)^\omega$ is an accepting run of $\mathcal{A}$ on w. On the other hand, $r'_0 r'_1 \ldots r'_i (r'_{i+1} \ldots r'_j)^\omega$ is an accepting run of $\overline{\mathcal{A}}$ on w. Hence, w is accepted by both $\mathcal{A}$ and $\overline{\mathcal{A}}$, and we have reached a contradiction. □

Theorem 4. *Consider a co-safety NBW $\mathcal{A}$ with n states, m of them accepting. Let $\overline{\mathcal{A}}$ be an NBW with $\overline{n}$ states such that $\mathcal{L}(\overline{\mathcal{A}}) = comp(\mathcal{L}(\mathcal{A}))$. There exists an NFW $\mathcal{A}'$ with $n \cdot (m \cdot \overline{n} + 1)$ states such that $\mathcal{A}'$ is fine for $\mathcal{L}(\mathcal{A})$.*

Proof: Let $t = m \cdot \overline{n}$. The NFW $\mathcal{A}'$ consists of $t + 1$ copies of $\mathcal{A}$. The transition function is such that when a run of $\mathcal{A}'$ visits F in the j-th copy of $\mathcal{A}$, it moves to the $(j + 1)$-th copy. The accepting states of $\mathcal{A}'$ are the states of F in the $(t + 1)$-th copy. Thus, there is a run of $\mathcal{A}$ on an infinite word $w \in \Sigma^\omega$ that has $t + 1$ visits in F iff there is a run of $\mathcal{A}'$ on w that reaches an accepting state in the $t + 1$-th copy of $\mathcal{A}$. Formally, given $\mathcal{A} = \langle \Sigma, Q, \delta, Q_0, F \rangle$, we define $\mathcal{A}' = \langle \Sigma, Q', \delta', Q'_0, F' \rangle$ as follows.

- $Q' = Q \times \{0, 1, \ldots, t\}$.
- For every $q \in Q$, $a \in \Sigma$, and $0 \leq i \leq t$ the transition function δ' is defined as follows.
$$\delta'(\langle q, i \rangle, a) = \begin{cases} \delta(q, a) \times \{i + 1\} & \text{if } q \in F \text{ and } i < t, \\ \delta(q, a) \times \{i\} & \text{if } q \notin F. \end{cases}$$
- $Q'_0 = Q_0 \times \{0\}$.
- $F' = F \times \{t\}$. Note that there are no transitions from states in F'.

Clearly, the number of states in $\mathcal{A}'$ is $n \cdot (t + 1)$.

[3] Note that $\overline{\mathcal{A}}$ is equivalent to the nondeterministic word automaton obtained by making all its states accepting. Such automata are termed *looping*.

For every run $r = r_0 r_1 \ldots$ of $\mathcal{A}$ on an infinite word $w \in \Sigma^\omega$ we define a single (possibly finite) corresponding run $s = s_0 s_1 \ldots$ of $\mathcal{A}'$ on w such that for all $i \geq 0$, we have that $s_i = \langle r_i, j_i \rangle$ for some $0 \leq j_i \leq t$, and in addition, the following hold.

1. $j_0 = 0$.
2. If $r_i \in F$, then $j_{i+1} = j_i + 1$; otherwise, $j_{i+1} = j_i$.
3. If $s_i = \langle r_i, t \rangle$ and $r_i \in F$, then the run s ends at s_i.

In order to prove that $\mathcal{A}'$ is fine for $\mathcal{L}(\mathcal{A})$, we first prove the following proposition, relating the runs r and s.

Proposition 1. *For every $i \geq 0$ and state $s_i = \langle r_i, j_i \rangle$ in s, the prefix $r_0 \ldots r_{i-1}$ of r has j_i visits in F.*

Proof: The proof proceeds by an induction on i. For $i = 0$, the prefix $r_0 \ldots r_{0-1}$ is empty, so it does not visit F at all, and indeed, by Condition 1 in the definition of s, we have that $j_0 = 0$. For $i > 0$, the induction hypothesis for $i - 1$ implies that $r_0 \ldots r_{i-2}$ has j_{i-1} visits in F. If $r_{i-1} \in F$, then, by Condition 2 of the definition of s, we have that $j_i = j_{i-1} + 1$, and indeed $r_0 \ldots r_{i-1}$ has $j_{i-1} + 1$ visits in F. Otherwise, $r_{i-1} \notin F$, and, by Condition 2 of the definition of s, we have that $j_i = j_{i-1}$, and indeed $r_0 \ldots r_{i-1}$ has j_{i-1} visits in F. □

We can now prove that $\mathcal{A}'$ is fine for $\mathcal{L}(\mathcal{A})$. That is, we prove that for every $w \in \Sigma^\omega$, it holds that $w \in \mathcal{L}(\mathcal{A})$ if and only if $\mathcal{A}'$ accepts some prefix of w.

Assume first that $w \in \mathcal{L}(\mathcal{A})$. Then, there exists a run r of $\mathcal{A}$ on w that visits F infinitely many times. By Proposition 1, when r makes its $(t + 1)$-th visit to F, the corresponding run of $\mathcal{A}'$ on w visits a state in F'. Thus, $\mathcal{A}'$ accepts a prefix of w, and we are done.

For the other direction, assume that there is an accepting run $s = s_0 s_1 \ldots s_k$ of $\mathcal{A}'$ on a prefix of w. The run s ends in some state in F'. Therefore, by Proposition 1, since $s_k \in F \times \{t\}$, the run s corresponds to a prefix $r_0 \ldots r_k$ of a run r of $\mathcal{A}$ on w such that $r_0 \ldots r_{k-1}$ has t visits in F. In addition, since $r_k \in F$, we have that $r_0 \ldots r_k$ has $t + 1$ visits in F. Thus, by Lemma 1, $w \in \mathcal{L}(\mathcal{A})$, and we are done. □

Given a safety NBW, its complement NBW is co-safety. Thus, dualizing Theorem 4, we get the following.

Theorem 5. *Consider a safety NBW $\mathcal{A}$ with n states. Let $\overline{\mathcal{A}}$ be an NBW with $\overline{n}$ states, $\overline{m}$ of them accepting, such that $\mathcal{L}(\overline{\mathcal{A}}) = comp(\mathcal{L}(\mathcal{A}))$. There exists an NFW $\mathcal{A}'$ with $\overline{n} \cdot (\overline{m} \cdot n + 1)$ states such that $\mathcal{A}'$ is fine for $\mathcal{L}(\mathcal{A})$.*

4.3 Fine Automata for Safety and Co-safety LTL Formulas

By Theorem 1, given an LTL formula ψ, we can construct NBWs $\mathcal{A}_\psi$ and $\mathcal{A}_{\neg\psi}$ for ψ and $\neg\psi$, respectively. The number of states in each of the NBWs is at most $2^{O(|\psi|)}$. Hence, by Theorem 4, we can conclude:

Theorem 6. *Consider a safety LTL formula φ of length n. There exists an NFW fine for φ with at most $2^{O(n)}$ states.*

5 Discussion

We have answered to the positive the question about the existence of exponential fine automata for general safety LTL formulas. This improves the doubly-exponential construction in [KV01a]. Essentially, our construction adds a counter on top of the NBW for the formula. The counter is increased whenever the NBW visits an accepting state, and a computation is accepted after the counter reaches a bound that depends on the size of the formula. While we have focused on LTL, it is possible to extend our results to all specification formalisms that can be translated to NBWs and for which negation involves no blow-up. Thus, small fine automata can be defined also for specifications described in recent industrial property-specification languages like PSL and SVA.

Our results give a better understanding of the relationship between safety and *bounded* properties. A property ψ is bounded if there is a bound $k \geq 0$ such that every word of length k is either a good or a bad prefix for ψ. Thus, satisfaction of ψ can be determined after reading a prefix of length k of the computation. It is known that a property ψ is bounded iff ψ is both safety and co-safety [KV01b]. For a bounded property with bound k, we know that if a word of length k is not a bad prefix, then it must be a good prefix. Accordingly, if the NBW $\mathcal{A}_\psi$ does not get stuck during its run on a prefix of a computation of length k, the computation satisfies ψ. Moreover, k depends on the size of the NBW for ψ [KV01b]. This enables simple application of bounded model-checking procedures [CBRZ01] for the verification of bounded properties. For a co-safety property, there is no such bound k: while we know that a computation that satisfies ψ has a good prefix, we cannot point to a k such that if the NBW $\mathcal{A}_\psi$ does not get stuck during its run on the prefix of a computation of length k, then the computation satisfies ψ. Our results here show that co-safety properties (and hence, also reasoning about safety properties) do have a bounded nature, only that the bound depends not only on the length of the prefix, but also on the number of visits to the set of accepting states that the NBW $\mathcal{A}_\psi$ makes on its run on the prefix. Indeed, there is a bound k such that if the NBW $\mathcal{A}_\psi$ has a run on a computation and the run visits the set of accepting states k times, then the computation satisfies ψ. Interestingly, the bound on k is similar to the one known for bounded properties [KV01b].

This result is helpful in the context of run-time verification and bounded model checking. Run-time verification does not store the entire state space of the system. Instead, it observes finite executions. In [GH01], the authors describe a semantics for LTL formula with respect to finite words. In this semantics, eventualities have to be satisfied within the finite prefix. Thus, as with the "informative prefixes" of [KV01a], a prefix never satisfies a pathologically safe formula ψ, even if it is a good prefix. By counting visits to the set F of accepting state of the NBW for $\neg\psi$, the semantics can be made tighter, and a prefix accepted by the fine automaton can be declared as violating ψ. The same technique, applied to richer specification formalisms, enables the run-time verification algorithm in [AKT$^+$06], which also follows finite prefixes, to return a definite answer for more properties. Counting visits to F can help also in SAT-based bounded model checking. Recall that SAT-based model checking of a safety property ψ tries to find a path that satisfies $\neg\psi$ and uses a bounded semantics for LTL: the formula $\neg\psi$ is checked with respect to prefixes of some bounded length k, possibly with a loop back. The method is complete in the sense that if some computation satisfies $\neg\psi$, then there is some prefix as above, where k depends on both the size of the checked system and ψ [CBRZ01]. The need to specify the fact that the prefix may have a loop back makes the formula whose satisfaction we check much more complex, and complicates the verification procedure. Our results imply an alternative approach, which prevents the need to consider loops and suggests, instead, to count sufficiently many visits to the set F of accepting state of the NBW for $\neg\psi$. We note that for many co-safety formulas, the states in F are accepting sinks, thus while k is a bound for the number of transitions needed to reach F for the first time, we can expect successive visits to be made within a single transition.

Finally, while we solved the problem of constructing exponential fine automata for LTL formulas, the problem of constructing polynomial fine automata for co-safety NBW is still open. The challenge here is similar to other challenges in automata-theoretic constructions in which one needs both the NBW and its complementing NBW — something that is easy to have in the context of LTL, but difficult in the context of NBW. For a discussion of more problems in this status, see [KV05b]. From a practical point of view, however, the problem of going from a co-safety automaton to a fine NFW is of less interest, as users that use automata as their specification formalism are likely to start with an automaton for the bad or the good prefixes anyway. Thus, the problem about the size of fine automata is interesting mainly for the specification formalism of LTL, which we did solve.

Acknowledgment. We thank Moshe Vardi for helpful discussions.

References

[AKT+06] R. Armoni, D. Korchemny, A. Tiemeyer, M.Y. Vardi, and Y. Zbar Deterministic dynamic monitors for linear-Time assertions. In *Proc FATES/RV*, LNCS, 2006.

[BCM+92] J.R. Burch, E.M. Clarke, K.L. McMillan, D.L. Dill, and L.J. Hwang. Symbolic model checking: 10^{20} states and beyond. *I& C*, 98(2):142–170, June 1992.

[BM83] R.S. Boyer and J.S. Moore. Proof-checking, theorem-proving and program verification. Technical Report 35, Institute for Computing Science and Computer Applications, University of Texas at Austin, January 1983.

[CBRZ01] E. M. Clarke, A. Bierea, R. Raimi, and Y. Zhu. Bounded model checking using satisfiability solving. *Formal Methods in System Design*, 19(1):7–34, 2001.

[CVWY92] C. Courcoubetis, M.Y. Vardi, P. Wolper, and M. Yannakakis. Memory efficient algorithms for the verification of temporal properties. *Formal Methods in System Design*, 1:275–288, 1992.

[GH01] D. Giannakopoulou and K. Havelund. Automata-based verification of temporal properties on running programs. In *Proc. 16th International Conference on Automated Software Engineering*, pages 412–416. IEEE Computer Society, 2001.

[GPVW95] R. Gerth, D. Peled, M.Y. Vardi, and P. Wolper. Simple on-the-fly automatic verification of linear temporal logic. In P. Dembiski and M. Sredniawa, editors, *Protocol Specification, Testing, and Verification*, pages 3–18. Chapman & Hall, August 1995.

[GW91] P. Godefroid and P. Wolper. Using partial orders for the efficient verification of deadlock freedom and safety properties. In *Proc. 3rd CAV*, LNCS 575, pages 332–342, 1991.

[Hol04] G.J. Holzmann. The Spin Model Checker: primer and reference manual. Addison-Wesley, 2004.

[HKSV97] R.H. Hardin, R.P. Kurshan, S.K. Shukla, and M.Y. Vardi. A new heuristic for bad cycle detection using BDDs. In *Proc. 9th CAV*, LNCS 1254, pages 268–278, 1997.

[IN97] H. Iwashita and T. Nakata. Forward model checking techniques oriented to buggy designs. In *Proc. ICCAD*, pages 400–404, 1997.

[KMM04] O. Kupferman, G. Morgenstern, and A. Murano. Typeness for ω-regular automata. In *Proc. 2nd ATVA*, LNCS 3299, pages 324–338. Springer-Verlag, 2004.

[KPB94] S.C. Krishnan, A. Puri, and R.K. Brayton. Deterministic ω-automata vis-a-vis deterministic Büchi automata. In *Algorithms and Computations*, LNCS 834, pages 378–386. Springer-Verlag, 1994.

[KSV96] O. Kupferman, S. Safra, and M.Y. Vardi. Relating word and tree automata. In *Proc. 11th LICS*, pages 322–333, DIMACS, June 1996.

[KV01a] O. Kupferman and M.Y. Vardi. Model checking of safety properties. *Formal methods in System Design*, 19(3):291–314, November 2001.

[KV01b] O. Kupferman and M.Y. Vardi. On bounded specifications. In *Proc. 8th LPAR*, LNCS 2250, pages 24–38. Springer-Verlag, 2001.

[KV05a] O. Kupferman and M.Y. Vardi. From linear time to branching time. *ACM Trans. on Computational Logic*, 6(2):273–294, April 2005.

[KV05b] O. Kupferman and M.Y. Vardi. Safraless decision procedures. In *Proc. 46th FOCS*, pages 531–540, Pittsburgh, October 2005.

[Lan69] L.H. Landweber. Decision problems for ω–automata. *Mathematical Systems Theory*, 3:376–384, 1969.

[Lat03] T. Latvala. Efficient model checking of safety properties. In *Proc. 10th SPIN Workshop on Model Checking of Software*, LNCS 2648, pages 74–88, 2003.

[MAB$^+$94] Z. Manna, A. Anuchitanukul, N. Bjorner, A. Browne, E. Chang, M. Colon, L. De Alfaro, H. Devarajan, H. Sipma, and T. Uribe. STeP: The Stanford Temporal Prover. TR STAN-CS-TR-94-1518, Dept. of Computer Science, Stanford University, 1994.

[McM92] K.L. McMillan. Using unfolding to avoid the state explosion problem in the verification of asynchronous circuits. In *Proc. 4th CAV*, LNCS 663, pages 164–174, Montreal, June 1992. Springer-Verlag.

[MF71] A.R. Meyer and M.J. Fischer. Economy of description by automata, grammars, and formal systems. In *Proc. 12th IEEE Symp. on Switching and Automata Theory*, pages 188–191, 1971.

[MH84] S. Miyano and T. Hayashi. Alternating finite automata on ω-words. *Theoretical Computer Science*, 32:321–330, 1984.

[MP92] Z. Manna and A. Pnueli. *The Temporal Logic of Reactive and Concurrent Systems: Specification.* Springer-Verlag, Berlin, January 1992.

[MP95] Z. Manna and A. Pnueli. *The Temporal Logic of Reactive and Concurrent Systems: Safety.* Springer-Verlag, New York, 1995.

[MR97] S. Melzer and S. Roemer. Deadlock checking using net unfoldings. In *Proc. 9th CAV*, LNCS 1254, pages 364–375. Springer-Verlag, 1997.

[OSR95] S. Owre, R.E. Shankar, and J.M. Rushby. *User guide for the PVS specification and verification system.* CSL, 1995.

[Pnu81] A. Pnueli. The temporal semantics of concurrent programs. *Theoretical Computer Science*, 13:45–60, 1981.

[SC85] A.P. Sistla and E.M. Clarke. The complexity of propositional linear temporal logic. *Journal ACM*, 32:733–749, 1985.

[Sis94] A.P. Sistla. Safety, liveness and fairness in temporal logic. *Formal Aspects of Computing*, 6:495–511, 1994.

[SS78] W. Sakoda and M. Sipser. Non-determinism and the size of two-way automata. In *Proc. 10th STOC*, pages 275–286, 1978.

[Val93] A. Valmari. On-the-fly verification with stubborn sets. In *Proc. 5th CAV*, LNCS 697. Springer-Verlag, 1993.

[VW86] M.Y. Vardi and P. Wolper. An automata-theoretic approach to automatic program verification. In *Proc. 1st LICS*, pages 332–344, Cambridge, June 1986.

[VW94] M.Y. Vardi and P. Wolper. Reasoning about infinite computations. *Information and Computation*, 115(1):1–37, November 1994.

A NBWs for LTL Formulas Are Not Fine-Type

The NBW $\mathcal{A}_\theta$ in Figure 2 consists of two NBWs too. The left one accepts all words satisfying $Fa \wedge FGb$ and the right one accepts words satisfying $Fb \wedge GFa$. Thus, $\mathcal{A}_\theta$, their union, accepts all words satisfying $\theta = (Fa \wedge FGb) \vee (Fb \wedge GFa)$. It is not hard to see that $\mathcal{A}_\theta$ is a single-run automaton (in particular, it is the union of two disjoint languages) that accepts exactly the words satisfying the formula $Fa \wedge Fb$. Also, by the same considerations we had in Section 4.2 for $\mathcal{A}_\varphi$, for $\varphi = (Fa \wedge GFb) \vee (Fb \wedge GFa)$, it is not fine-type.

We note that the single-run NBW obtained for φ by following the translation procedure in [VW94] is not fine-type either.

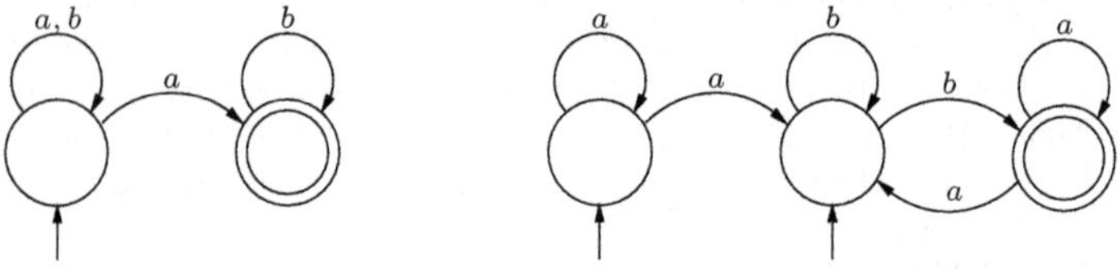

Fig. 2. A single run NBW for $\theta = (Fa \wedge FGb) \vee (Fb \wedge GFa)$

In the full version, we describe an NBW $\mathcal{A}_\xi$ for the formula $\xi = (GFa \wedge F(b \wedge XFb)) \vee (GFb \wedge F(a \wedge XFa))$. The formula ξ is equivalent to the formula $F(b \wedge XFb) \wedge F(a \wedge XFa)$. Thus, the language of $\mathcal{A}_\xi$ is the co-safety language of all infinite words that contain at least two a's and at least two b's. The NBW $\mathcal{A}_\xi$ is obtained from ξ by translating ξ to an alternating Büchi word automaton (ABW) and translating this automaton to a nondeterministic one [MH84]. Thus, $\mathcal{A}_\xi$ is obtained by a translation that is more optimized than the one in [VW94]. Still, $\mathcal{A}_\xi$ is not fine type. To see this, note that each of $\mathcal{A}_\xi$'s states can be reached after reading a prefix of length at most 3. Since every such prefix can be extended to an infinite word in which a or b appear at most once, and thus does not satisfy ξ, an NFW with the structure of $\mathcal{A}_\xi$ is either empty or accepts words that are not good prefixes for ξ.

On the Succinctness of Nondeterminism

Benjamin Aminof and Orna Kupferman

Hebrew University, School of Engineering and Computer Science, Jerusalem 91904, Israel
{benj,orna}@cs.huji.ac.il

Abstract. Much is known about the differences in expressiveness and succinctness between nondeterministic and deterministic automata on infinite words. Much less is known about the relative succinctness of the different classes of nondeterministic automata. For example, while the best translation from a nondeterministic Büchi automaton to a nondeterministic co-Büchi automaton is exponential, and involves determinization, no super-linear lower bound is known. This annoying situation, of not being able to use the power of nondeterminism, nor to show that it is powerless, is shared by more problems, with direct applications in formal verification.

In this paper we study a family of problems of this class. The problems originate from the study of the expressive power of deterministic Büchi automata: Landweber characterizes languages $L \subseteq \Sigma^\omega$ that are recognizable by deterministic Büchi automata as those for which there is a regular language $R \subseteq \Sigma^*$ such that L is the *limit* of R; that is, $w \in L$ iff w has infinitely many prefixes in R. Two other operators that induce a language of infinite words from a language of finite words are *co-limit*, where $w \in L$ iff w has only finitely many prefixes in R, and *persistent-limit*, where $w \in L$ iff almost all the prefixes of w are in R. Both co-limit and persistent-limit define languages that are recognizable by deterministic co-Büchi automata. They define them, however, by means of nondeterministic automata. While co-limit is associated with complementation, persistent-limit is associated with universality. For the three limit operators, the deterministic automata for R and L share the same structure. It is not clear, however, whether and how it is possible to relate nondeterministic automata for R and L, or to relate nondeterministic automata to which different limit operators are applied. In the paper, we show that the situation is involved: in some cases we are able to describe a polynomial translation, whereas in some we present an exponential lower bound. For example, going from a nondeterministic automaton for R to a nondeterministic automaton for its limit is polynomial, whereas going to a nondeterministic automaton for its persistent limit is exponential. Our results show that the contribution of nondeterminism to the succinctness of an automaton does depend upon its semantics.

1 Introduction

Finite *automata on infinite objects* were first introduced in the 60's, and were the key to the solution of several fundamental decision problems in mathematics and logic [5,17,21]. Today, automata on infinite objects are used for *specification* and *verification* of nonterminating systems. The automata-theoretic approach to verification reduces questions about systems and their specifications to questions about automata [13,26].

S. Graf and W. Zhang (Eds.): ATVA 2006, LNCS 4218, pp. 125–140, 2006.

Recent industrial-strength property-specification languages such as Sugar [3], ForSpec [2], and PSL 1.01 [7] include regular expressions and/or automata, making specification and verification tools that are based on automata even more essential and popular.

There are many ways to classify an automaton on infinite words. One is the class of its acceptance condition. For example, in *Büchi* automata, some of the states are designated as accepting states, and a run is accepting iff it visits states from the accepting set infinitely often [5]. Dually, in *co-Büchi* automata, a run is accepting iff it visits states from the accepting set only finitely often. Another way to classify an automaton is by the type of its branching mode. In a *deterministic* automaton, the transition function maps the current state and input letter to a single successor state. When the branching mode is *nondeterministic*, the transition function maps the current state and letter to a set of possible successor states. Thus, while a deterministic automaton has a single run on an input word, a nondeterministic automaton may have several runs on an input word, and the word is accepted by the automaton if at least one of the runs is accepting.

The different classes of automata have different *expressive power*. For example, unlike automata on finite words, where deterministic and nondeterministic automata have the same expressive power, deterministic Büchi automata (DBW) are strictly less expressive than nondeterministic Büchi automata (NBW). That is, there exists a language L over infinite words such that L can be recognized by a nondeterministic Büchi automaton but cannot be recognized by a deterministic Büchi automaton. It also turns out that some classes of automata may be more *succinct* than other classes. For example, translating a nondeterministic co-Büchi automaton (NCW) into a deterministic co-Büchi automaton (DCW) is possible [20], but involves an exponential blow up.

There has been extensive research on the expressiveness and succinctness of automata on infinite words [25]. In particular, since reasoning about deterministic automata is simpler than reasoning about nondeterministic ones, questions like deciding whether a nondeterministic automaton has an equivalent deterministic one, and the blow up involved in determinization, are of particular interest [8,16,12]. These questions get further motivation with the discovery that many natural specifications correspond to the deterministic fragments. In particular, it is shown in [12] that given a linear temporal logic (LTL) formula ψ, there is an alternation-free μ-calculus (AFMC) formula equivalent to $\forall\psi$ iff ψ can be recognized by a DBW. Evaluating specifications in the alternation-free fragment of μ-calculus can be done with linearly many symbolic steps, so coming up with an optimal translation of LTL to AFMC is a problem of great practical importance.

Let us elaborate on the LTL to AFMC example, as it highlights the open problems that have led to our research. Current translations translate the LTL formula ψ to a DBW, which can be linearly translated to an AFMC formula for $\forall\psi$. The translation of LTL to DBW, however, is doubly exponential, thus the overall translation is doubly-exponential, with only an exponential matching lower bound. A promising direction for tightening the upper bound was suggested in [12]: instead of translating an LTL formula ψ to a DBW, one can translate $\neg\psi$ to an NCW. Then, the NCW can be linearly translated to an AFMC formula for $\exists\neg\psi$, whose negation is equivalent to $\forall\psi$. The fact that the translation can go through a nondeterministic rather than a deterministic automaton is very promising, as nondeterministic automata are typically exponentially more succinct than deterministic ones. Nevertheless, the problem of translating LTL formulas to NCWs of exponential size[1] is still open. The best translation that is known today involves a doubly-exponential blow up, and it actually results in a DCW, giving up the idea that the translation of LTL to AFMC can be exponentially more efficient by using intermediate nondeterministic automata.

This unfortunate situation of not being able to use the power of nondeterminism is shared by more problems. One that is strongly related to the LTL to AFMC problem described above is the open problem of translating NBWs to NCWs (when possible). Despite continuous efforts, the best translation that is known first determinizes the NBW. Accordingly, starting with an NBW with n states, we end up with an NCW with $2^{O(n \log n)}$ states [22]. This is particularly annoying as even no super-linear lower bound is known, and in fact, only recently were we able to come up with an example that an NCW cannot be defined on top of the state space and transitions of the NBW [9]. The class of open problems of this nature expands also to the branching setting. For a language L of infinite words, let $der(L)$ be the language of infinite trees that contain exactly all trees all of whose paths are in L. It is known that $der(L)$ can be recognized by a nondeterministic Büchi tree automaton (NBT) iff L can be recognized by a DBW [10]. Given an NBT for $der(L)$, the most efficient construction that is known for generating from it an NBW for L is exponential, and it actually constructs a DBW for L. Also here, no super-linear lower bound is known, and yet it is not clear how nondeterminism, and its succinctness with respect to the deterministic model, can be used.

In this paper we study a family of problems in this class. Recall that DBWs are less expressive than NBWs. Landweber characterizes languages $L \subseteq \Sigma^\omega$ that can be recognized by a DBW as those for which there is a regular language $R \subseteq \Sigma^*$ such that L is the *limit* of R. Formally, w is in the limit of R iff w has infinitely many prefixes in R [14]. It is not hard to see that a DBW for L, when viewed as a deterministic finite automaton (DFW), recognizes a language whose limit is L, and vice versa – a DFW for R, when viewed as a DBW, recognizes the language that is the limit of R. What about the case in which R and L are given by nondeterministic automata? It is not hard to see that the simple transformation between the two formalisms no longer holds. For example, the NBW $\mathcal{A}$ in Figure 1 recognizes the language L of all words with infinitely many 1s, yet when viewed as a nondeteministic finite automaton (NFW), it recognizes $(0+1)^+$, whose limit is $(0+1)^\omega$. As another example, the language of the NBW $\mathcal{A}'$ is empty, yet when viewed as an NFW, it recognizes the language $(0+1)^* \cdot 1$, whose limit is L. As demonstrated by the examples, the difficulty of the nondeterministic case originates from the fact that different prefixes of the infinite word may follow different accepting runs of the NFW, and there is no guarantee that these runs can be merged into a single run of the NBW. Accordingly, the best translation that is known for going from an NFW to an NBW accepting its limit, or from an NBW to a limit NFW, is to first determinize the given automaton. This involves a $2^{O(n \log n)}$ blow up and gives up the potential succinctness of the nondeterministic model. On the other hand, no lower bound above $\Omega(n \log n)$ is known.

[1] As mentioned above, not all LTL formulas can be translated to NCWs. When we talk about the blow up in a translation, we refer to formulas for which a translation exists.

Fig. 1. Relating NBWs and limit NFWs

In addition to the limit operator introduced by Landweber, we introduce and study two more ways to induce a language of infinite words from a language of finite words: the *co-limit* of R is the set of all infinite words that have only finitely many prefixes in R. Thus, co-limit is dual to Landweber's limit. Also, the *persistent limit* of R is the set of all infinite words that have only finitely many prefixes not in R. Thus, eventually all the prefixes are in R.

We study the succinctness of NFWs for R with respect to DBWs, DCWs, NBWs, and NCWs recognizing languages induced by each of the three limit operators, and the succinctness of the Büchi and co-Büchi automata with respect to the NFWs. In particular, we prove that while the translation from an NFW to an NBW for its limit is cubic (thus, nondeterminism is helpful, and the traditional "determinize first" approach is beaten!), the translations from an NFW to an NCW for its co-limit or its persistent limit are exponential, thus determinization is legitimate. We also study succinctness among NFWs to which different limit operators are applied. For example, we prove that going from a persistent limit NFW to a limit NFW involves an exponential blow up. In other words, given an NFW $\mathcal{A}$ whose persistent limit is L, translating $\mathcal{A}$ to an NFW whose limit is L may involve an exponential blow up. Note that persistent limit and limit are very similar – both require the infinite word to have infinitely many prefixes in $L(\mathcal{A})$, only that the persistent limit requires, in addition, that only finitely many prefixes are not in $L(\mathcal{A})$. This difference, which is similar to the difference between NBW and NCW, makes persistent limit exponentially more succinct. Technically, it follows from the fact that persistent limit NFWs inherit the power of alternating automata. In a similar, though less surprising way, co-limit NFWs inherit the power of complementation, and are also exponentially more succinct. In cases where we are not able to describe a lower bound, we prove that the translations are not *type* [8,9], namely that an equivalent NFW cannot be defined on top of the same transition structure.

The study of the limit operators checks behaviors in the limit. We examine how our results are affected by limiting attention to *safety*, *co-safety*, and *bounded* languages [1,24,11]. In these languages, the behavior in the limit is not restricted. In particular, in bounded languages, membership in the language depends on a bounded prefix of the word. We show that most of our lower bounds apply even in the restricted setting of the limited fragments, yet for some cases we are able to describe upper bounds that do not hold in the general case. Finally, recall that the difficulty of the nondeterministic case originates from the fact that the accepting runs on different prefixes of the infinite word may not be merged into one infinite accepting run of the NBW. We describe a sufficient structural condition on NFWs that guarantees that accepting runs can be merged. We call NFWs that satisfy this condition *continuous NFWs*. We show that while the limit of a continuous NFW $\mathcal{A}$ is the language of $\mathcal{A}$ when viewed as an NBW, continuous NFWs are exponentially more succinct than DBWs.

2 Preliminaries

2.1 Automata on Finite and Infinite Words

Given an alphabet Σ, a *word* over Σ is a sequence $w = \sigma_1 \cdot \sigma_2 \cdot \sigma_3 \cdots$ of letters in Σ. A word may be either finite or infinite. An *automaton* is a tuple $\mathcal{A} = \langle \Sigma, Q, \delta, Q_0, \alpha \rangle$, where Σ is the input alphabet, Q is a finite set of states, $\delta : Q \times \Sigma \to 2^Q$ is a transition function, $Q_0 \subseteq Q$ is a set of initial states, and $\alpha \subseteq Q$ is an acceptance condition. We define several acceptance conditions below. The automaton $\mathcal{A}$ may have several initial states and the transition function may specify many possible transitions for each state and letter, and hence we say that $\mathcal{A}$ is *nondeterministic*. In the case where $|Q_0| = 1$ and for every $q \in Q$ and $\sigma \in \Sigma$, we have that $|\delta(q, \sigma)| = 1$, we say that $\mathcal{A}$ is *deterministic*.

The automaton may run on finite or infinite words. A *run* of $\mathcal{A}$ on a finite word $w = \sigma_1 \cdot \sigma_2 \cdots \sigma_k \in \Sigma^*$ is a function $r : \{0, \ldots, k\} \to Q$ where $r(0) \in Q_0$, and for every $0 \leq i < k$, we have that $r(i+1) \in \delta(r(i), \sigma_{i+1})$. The run is *accepting* iff $r(k) \in \alpha$. Otherwise, it is rejecting. When the input word is infinite, and thus $w = \sigma_0 \cdot \sigma_1 \cdots \in \Sigma^\omega$, a run of $\mathcal{A}$ on w is a function $r : \mathbb{N} \to Q$ with $r(0) \in Q_0$, and for every $i \geq 0$, we have that $r(i+1) \in \delta(r(i), \sigma_{i+1})$. Acceptance is defined with respect to the set of states $inf(r)$ that the run r visits infinitely often. Formally, $inf(r) = \{q \in Q : \text{ for infinitely many } i \in \mathbb{N}, \text{ we have } r(i) = q\}$. As Q is finite, it is guaranteed that $inf(r) \neq \emptyset$. The run r is *accepting* iff the set $inf(r)$ satisfies the acceptance condition α. We consider here the *Büchi* and the *co-büchi* acceptance conditions. A set S satisfies a Büchi acceptance condition $\alpha \subseteq Q$ if and only if $S \cap \alpha \neq \emptyset$. Dually, S satisfies a *co-Büchi* acceptance condition $\alpha \subseteq Q$ if and only if $S \cap \alpha = \emptyset$.

We sometimes view a run r as a (finite or infinite) word over the alphabet Q. For example, $r = q_0, q_5, q_5$ indicates that $r(0) = q_0$ whereas $r(1) = r(2) = q_5$. Note that while a deterministic automaton has a single run on an input word, a nondeterministic automaton may have several runs on w or none at all. An automaton accepts a word iff it has an accepting run on it. The language of an automaton $\mathcal{A}$, denoted $L(\mathcal{A})$, is the set of words that $\mathcal{A}$ accepts. For a language L, the complement of L, denoted $comp(L)$, is the set of words not in L. Thus, for $L \subseteq \Sigma^*$ we have $comp(L) = \Sigma^* \setminus L$, and for $L \subseteq \Sigma^\omega$ we have $comp(L) = \Sigma^\omega \setminus L$.

We denote the different classes of automata by three letter acronyms in $\{\text{D}, \text{N}\} \times \{\text{F}, \text{B}, \text{C}\} \times \{\text{W}\}$. The first letter stands for the branching mode of the automaton (deterministic or nondeterministic); the second letter stands for the acceptance-condition type (finite, Büchi, or co-Büchi). The third letter indicates that the automaton runs on words.

For two automata $\mathcal{A}$ and $\mathcal{A}'$, we say that $\mathcal{A}$ and $\mathcal{A}'$ are *equivalent* if $L(\mathcal{A}) = L(\mathcal{A}')$. For a class γ of automata, we say that an automaton $\mathcal{A}$ is γ *realizable* iff $\mathcal{A}$ has an equivalent automaton in the class γ. Similarly, a language L is γ *realizable* iff there is an automaton $\mathcal{A}$ in the class γ whose language is L. In the case of finite words, NFWs can be determinized, thus all NFWs are DFW realizable. In the case of infinite words, different classes of automata have different expressive power. In particular, while NBWs recognize all ω-regular language [17], DBWs are strictly less expressive than NBW, and so are DCW [14]. In fact, a language L is DBW-realizable iff $comp(L)$ is DCW-realizable. Indeed, by viewing a DBW as a DCW, we get an automaton for the complementing language, and vice versa. The expressiveness superiority of the nondeterministic model with respect to the deterministic one does not apply to the co-Büchi acceptance condition. There, NCWs can be determinized[2], thus all NCWs are DCW realizable.

2.2 Limits of Languages of Finite Words

Studying the expressive power of DBWs, Landweber characterizes languages $L \subseteq \Sigma^\omega$ that are DBW-realizable as those for which there is a regular language $R \subseteq \Sigma^*$ such that $w \in L$ iff w has infinitely many prefixes in R. Thus, each language of finite words induces a language of infinite words. In Definition 1 below, we introduce two additional ways to induce a language of infinite words from a language on finite words. Given a word $w = \sigma_1, \sigma_2, \cdots \in \Sigma^\omega$, we denote the i-th letter of w by $w[i]$, the sub-word $\sigma_i, \cdots, \sigma_j$ by $w[i,j]$ and the sub-word $\sigma_i, \cdots, \sigma_{j-1}$ by $w[i,j)$.

Definition 1. *Consider a language $R \subseteq \Sigma^*$. We define three languages of infinite words induced by R.*

1. **[limit]** *$lim(R) \subseteq \Sigma^\omega$ is the set of all words that have infinitely many prefixes in R. I.e., $lim(R) = \{w \mid w[1,i] \in R$ for infinitely many i's$\}$* [14].
2. **[co-limit]** *$co\text{-}lim(R) \subseteq \Sigma^\omega$ is the set of all words that have only finitely many prefixes in R. I.e., $co\text{-}lim(R) = \{w \mid w[1,i] \in R$ for finitely many i's$\}$.*
3. **[persistent limit]** *$plim(R) \subseteq \Sigma^\omega$ is the set of all words that have only finitely many prefixes not in R. I.e., $plim(R) = \{w \mid w[1,i] \in R$ for almost all i's$\}$.*

For example, for $R = (a + b)^*b$, the language $lim(R)$ consists of all words that have infinitely many b's, $co\text{-}lim(R)$ is the language of words that have finitely many b's, and $plim(R)$ is the language of words that have finitely many a's. For an NFW $\mathcal{A}$, we use $lim(\mathcal{A})$, $co\text{-}lim(\mathcal{A})$, and $plim(\mathcal{A})$, to denote $lim(L(\mathcal{A}))$, $co\text{-}lim(L(\mathcal{A}))$, and $plim(L(\mathcal{A}))$, respectively.

The three limit operators are dual in the following sense:

Lemma 1. *For every $R \subseteq \Sigma^*$, we have $comp(lim(R)) = co\text{-}lim(R) = plim(comp(R))$.*

Recall that a language $L \subseteq \Sigma^\omega$ is DBW realizable iff $L = lim(R)$ for some regular $R \subseteq \Sigma^*$ [14]. By Lemma 1 and the duality between DBW and DCW, it follows that L is DCW realizable iff $L = co\text{-}lim(R)$ for some regular $R \subseteq \Sigma^*$, or, equivalently, $L = plim(R)$ for some regular $R \subseteq \Sigma^*$. A direct way to prove the above expressiveness results is to consider the deterministic Büchi or co-Büchi automaton $\mathcal{A}$ for L. Let $\mathcal{A}_{fin}$ be $\mathcal{A}$ when viewed as a DFW, and let $\tilde{\mathcal{A}}_{fin}$ be $\mathcal{A}_{fin}$ with a dualized accepting set. In case $\mathcal{A}$ is a DBW, then $L(\mathcal{A}) = lim(\mathcal{A}_{fin})$. Similarly, if $\mathcal{A}$ is a DCW, then $L(\mathcal{A}) = co\text{-}lim(\mathcal{A}_{fin}) = plim(\tilde{\mathcal{A}}_{fin})$. Thus, in the deterministic setting, the transitions among

[2] When applied to universal Büchi automata, the translation in [20], of alternating Büchi automata into NBW, results in DBW. By dualizing it, one gets a translation of NCW to DCW.

the automata for L and R involve no blow up, and are even done on top of the same structure. Our goal in this paper is to study the blow up between the automata in the nondeterministic setting. In order to avoid lower bounds that are inherited directly from the exponential blow up of complementation, we study both co-limit and persistent-limit. Note that only the former has the flavor of complementation.

Finally, note that for all of the three limit operators, different regular languages may induce the same limit language. For example, if L is the language of all finite words of length at least 7, L' the language of all finite words of length at least 20, and L'' the language of all finite words of even length, then $L \neq L'$ and yet $lim(L) = lim(L') = plim(L) = plim(L') = \Sigma^\omega$, and $co\text{-}lim(L) = co\text{-}lim(L') = \emptyset$. Also, even though $L'' \neq comp(L)$, we still have that $co\text{-}lim(L) = plim(L'')$.

3 Succinctness of NFW with Respect to Büchi and Co-Büchi Automata

In this section we study the succinctness of the NFW for R with respect to the Büchi and co-Büchi automata that recognize the ω-regular languages induced by applying each of the three limit operators to R. We start with the case the Büchi and co-Büchi automata are deterministic, and show that then, the succinctness of the nondeterministic model in the case of finite words carries over to the limit setting. We then proceed to the case the Büchi and co-Büchi automata are nondeterministic and show that there, the situation is more involved. First, the exponential blow up in NFW complementation is carried over to an exponential blow up in a translation of co-limit NFW to an NCW. More surprising are the results for limit and persistent limit NFW: by analyzing the structure of an NFW, we are able to translate an NFW to an NBW for its limit with only a cubic blow up. On the other hand, while persistent limit involves no complementation, it enables a universal reference to the prefixes of the input word. Consequently, we are able to prove that the exponential succinctness of *alternating* automata on finite words with respect to NFW carries over to an exponential lower bound on the translation of an NFW to a NCW for its persistent limit.

We start with DBW and DCW. Recall that limit is associated with DBW whereas co-limit and persistent limit are associated with DCW. We are still able to describe a bound for the translation to both DBW and DCW.

Theorem 1. [lim NFW $\rightarrow$ DBW, plim NFW $\rightarrow$ DCW, clim NFW $\rightarrow$ DCW]

- *For every $n \geq 1$, there is $L_n \subseteq \Sigma^\omega$ such that there is an NFW $\mathcal{A}$ with $O(n)$ states such that $lim(\mathcal{A}) = plim(\mathcal{A}) = L_n$, but L_n cannot be recognized by a DBW or a DCW with less than 2^n states.*
- *For every $n \geq 1$, there is $L_n \subseteq \Sigma^\omega$ such that there is an NFW $\mathcal{A}$ with $O(n)$ states such that $co\text{-}lim(\mathcal{A}) = L_n$, but L_n cannot be recognized by a DBW or a DCW with less than 2^n states.*

Proof: We start with limit and persistent limit. For $n \geq 1$, let $R_n \subseteq \Sigma^*$ be such that an NFW for R_n has $O(n)$ states, whereas a DFW for it must have at least 2^n states. By [18], such R_n exist. Let # be a letter not in Σ, and let $L_n = R_n \cdot \#^\omega$. In the full version, we show that there is an NFW $\mathcal{A}$ with $O(n)$ states such that $lim(\mathcal{A}) = plim(\mathcal{A}) = L_n$, but a DBW or a DCW for L_n must have at least 2^n states.

We now turn to co-limit. For $n \geq 1$, let $R_n \subseteq \Sigma^*$ be such that an NFW for R_n has $O(n)$ states whereas a DFW for $comp(R_n)$ must have at least 2^n states. By [18], such R_n exist. In the full version, we show that there is an NFW $\mathcal{A}$ with $O(n)$ states such that $co\text{-}lim(\mathcal{A}) = L_n$, but there is no DBW or DCW for L_n with less than 2^n states. □

The results proved in Theorem 1 are not surprising, as they meet our expectation from the finite-word case. We now turn to study the succinctness of NFWs with respect to NBWs and NCWs. Here, we can no longer apply the known succinctness of NFWs.

We first show that in the case of the limit operator, it is possible to translate an NFW $\mathcal{A}$ to an NBW $\mathcal{A}'$ of cubic size such that $lim(\mathcal{A}) = L(\mathcal{A}')$. Thus, while the limit operator enables each prefix of the run to be accepted by following different nondeterministic choices, this flexibility does not lead to an exponential succinctness.

We first need some notations. Given an NFW $\mathcal{A} = \langle \Sigma, Q, \delta, Q_0, \alpha \rangle$ and two sets of states $P, S \subseteq Q$, we denote by $L_{P,S}$ the language of $\mathcal{A}$ with initial set P and accepting set S. Formally, $L_{P,S}$ is the language accepted by the NFW $\langle \Sigma, Q, \delta, P, S \rangle$. If S or P are singletons we omit the curly braces; so instead of $L_{\{p\},S}$ we simply write $L_{p,S}$, etc.

Theorem 2. *For every NFW* $\mathcal{A} = \langle \Sigma, Q, \delta, Q_0, \alpha \rangle$,

$$lim(\mathcal{A}) = \bigcup_{p \in Q} L_{Q_0,p} \cdot (L_{p,p} \cap L_{p,\alpha})^\omega.$$

Proof: Assume first that w can be partitioned into sub-words $w = u_0 \cdot u_1 \cdot u_2 \cdots$ such that for some $p \in Q$, we have $u_0 \in L_{Q_0,p}$, and for every $i \geq 1$, the word u_i is in $L_{p,p} \cap L_{p,\alpha}$. It follows that there is a run r_0 of $\mathcal{A}$ on u_0 that starts in Q_0 and ends in p, and that for every $i \geq 1$ there are runs r_i and r'_i of $\mathcal{A}$ on u_i such that r_i starts in p and ends in p while r'_i starts in p and ends in some state in α. Then, for every $i \geq 1$ the run $r_0 \cdot r_1 \cdots r_{i-1} \cdot r'_i$ is an accepting run of $\mathcal{A}$ on the prefix $u_0 \cdot u_1 \cdots u_i$ of w, thus $w \in lim(\mathcal{A})$.

For the other direction, assume that $w \in lim(\mathcal{A})$. For technical simplicity assume first that $\mathcal{A}$ has a single initial state q_0. We construct a tree T in which each node is labeled by a state in Q. For a node x of T, let $|x|$ denote the level of x in the tree, and let $state(x)$ be the state with which x is labeled. The tree T embodies all the possible accepting runs of $\mathcal{A}$ on prefixes of w. The root of T is labeled by q_0. Consider a node x in the tree. All the successors of x have different labels, and y is a successor of x iff $|y| = |x| + 1$, and there is an accepting run r of $\mathcal{A}$ on a prefix of w of length at least $|y|$ such that $r(|x|) = state(x)$ and $r(|y|) = state(y)$. Observe that every node in the tree has at most $|Q|$ successors and that the tree is infinite since $\mathcal{A}$ accepts infinitely many prefixes of w. Also note that every node in the tree is part of at least one accepting run of $\mathcal{A}$ on some prefix of w.

By König's Lemma the tree has an infinite path π. We associate with every node π_i on this path two nodes y_i and z_i such that y_i is some node labeled by an accepting state that is reachable in zero or more steps from π_i, and z_i is the node on π that is at the same level as y_i. Since Q is finite, there are two states $p \in Q, q \in \alpha$ such that $state(y_j) = q$ and $state(z_j) = p$ for infinitely many indices j. By taking a sub-sequence of these indices we can get an infinite set of indices $0 < j_0 < j_1 < \ldots$ such that for every $k \geq 0$ not only $state(y_{j_k}) = q$ and $state(z_{j_k}) = p$, but also $|z_{j_k}| < |\pi_{j_{k+1}}|$. It follows that $w[0, |z_{j_0}|)$ is a word in $L_{q_0,p}$. Also, for every $k \geq 0$ the tree has a path from z_{j_k} to $\pi_{j_{k+1}}$ and from there to $y_{j_{k+1}}$ implying that $w[|z_{j_k}|, |y_{j_{k+1}}|)$ is in $L_{p,\alpha}$. Similarly, the tree has a path from z_{j_k} to $z_{j_{k+1}}$ implying that $w[|z_{j_k}|, |z_{j_{k+1}}|)$ is in $L_{p,p}$. Recalling that $|y_{j_{k+1}}| = |z_{j_{k+1}}|$ we obtain that $w \in L_{q_0,p} \cdot (L_{p,p} \cap L_{p,\alpha})^\omega$.

When Q_0 is not a singleton, we may have instead of a single tree T, a forest of trees, with one tree for each state in Q_0. Since Q_0 is finite, one of the trees in the forest is infinite, and the proof proceeds with that tree. □

Given $\mathcal{A} = \langle \Sigma, Q, \delta, Q_0, \alpha \rangle$ with n states, constructing an NBW accepting $\bigcup_{p \in Q} L_{Q_0,p} \cdot (L_{p,p} \cap L_{p,\alpha})^\omega$, involves n intersections of NFWs, n applications of the ω operation to an NFW, n concatenations of an NFW to an NBW, and finally, obtaining the union of the resulting n NBWs. Accordingly, the characterization in Theorem 2 implies the following upper bound.

Corollary 1. [lim NFW → NBW] *Given an NFW $\mathcal{A}$ with n states, there is an NBW $\mathcal{A}'$ with $O(n^3)$ states such that $L(\mathcal{A}') = lim(\mathcal{A})$.*

We now turn to study co-limit and persistent limit. In the first case, the exponential blow up in NFW complementation and the complementing nature of the co-limit operator hint that an exponential lower bound is likely to exist also for the translation of NFW to an NCW or an NBW for its co-limit. In the case of persistent limit, however, we expect the translation to be similar to the one for limit: the NFW enables the prefixes to be accepted each by following a different nondeterministic choice, and, as with the limit operator, an NCW that is polynomially larger should be able to merge these choices into a single nondeterministic choice. This expectation is refuted: the persistence of the plim operator adds to the NFW the power of universal branching, which makes it exponentially more succinct.

Theorem 3. [co-lim NFW → NCW / NBW, plim NFW → NCW/ NBW] *For every $n \geq 1$, there is a language $L_n \in \Sigma^\omega$ such that there are NFW $\mathcal{A}$ and $\mathcal{A}'$, both with $O(n)$ states, such that $plim(\mathcal{A}) = co\text{-}lim(\mathcal{A}') = L_n$, but L_n cannot be accepted by an NCW or an NBW with less than 2^n states.*

Proof: Let $\Sigma = \{0, 1\}$. Every word w over Σ can be viewed as a word in $(\Sigma^n)^\omega$, that is, as an infinite sequence of n-bit vectors. The language L_n is the language of sequences that are almost everywhere identical. Formally, $L_n = \{w \mid$ there is $u \in (\Sigma^n)^*$ and $v \in \Sigma^n$ such that $w = uv^\omega\}$.

In the full version, we describe an NFW $\mathcal{A}$ with $O(n)$ states such that $plim(\mathcal{A}) = L_n$. On the other hand, by [23], the language L_n cannot be accepted by a nondeterministic Streett automaton with less than 2^n states. Since NBWs and NCWs are a special case of nondeterministic Streett automata, we are done. □

4 Succinctness Among the Different Limit Operators

In the previous section, we related NFWs with Büchi and co-Büchi automata. In this section we study the blow ups involved in translating an NFW that induces a language of infinite words by a limit operator (*lim*, *co-lim*, or *plim*) to an NFW that induces the same language by a different limit operator.

We first show that the exponential blow up in NFW complementation can be lifted to an exponential blow up in the translation of a *lim* or a *plim* NFW to a *co-lim* NFW.

Theorem 4. [lim NFW $\to$ co-lim NFW, plim NFW $\to$ co-lim NFW] *For every $n \geq 1$, there is $L_n \subseteq \Sigma^\omega$ such that there is an NFW $\mathcal{A}$ with $O(n)$ states such that lim$(\mathcal{A})$ = plim$(\mathcal{A}) = L_n$, but an NFW $\mathcal{A}'$ such that co-lim$(\mathcal{A}') = L_n$, must have at least 2^n states.*

Proof: For $n \geq 1$, let $R_n \subseteq \Sigma^*$ be such that an NFW for R_n has $O(n)$ states, whereas an NFW for *comp*(R_n) must have at least 2^n states. By [18], such R_n exist. We can construct from an NFW $\mathcal{A}$ for R_n, an NFW $\mathcal{A}'$ with one extra state for $R_n \cdot \#^+$. Then, *lim*$(\mathcal{A}')$ = *plim*$(\mathcal{A}') = R_n \cdot \#^\omega$. In the full version, we prove that there is no NFW $\mathcal{A}$ with less than 2^n states, such that *co-lim*$(\mathcal{A}) = R_n \cdot \#^\omega$. □

We note that similar arguments can be used to show that NCWs (and thus also NBWs, as NCWs are linearly translatable to NBWs) are exponentially more succinct than *co-lim* NFWs. To see this, note that the NCW obtained from the NFW $\mathcal{A}'$ for $R_n \cdot \#^+$ by letting all states but the $\#$-sink to be in α, accepts $R_n \cdot \#^\omega$.

Theorem 5. [co-lim NFW $\to$ lim NFW, plim NFW $\to$ lim NFW] *For every $n \geq 1$, there is a language $L_n \subseteq \Sigma^\omega$ such that there are NFWs $\mathcal{A}$ with $O(n)$ states, and $\mathcal{A}'$ with $O(n^2)$ states, such that co-lim$(\mathcal{A})$ = plim$(\mathcal{A}') = L_n$ but an NFW $\mathcal{A}''$ such that lim$(\mathcal{A}'') = L_n$ must have at least 2^n states.*

Proof: Consider the language $L_n \subseteq \{0,1\}^\omega$ of all words w such that $w = uuz$, with $|u| = n$. In the full version, we prove that an NFW $\mathcal{A}''$ such that *lim*$(\mathcal{A}'') = L_n$ must remember subsets of size n, and thus must have at least 2^n states.

In order to construct small NFW for the co-limit and persistent limit operators, we observe that a word w is in L_n iff $\bigwedge_{i=1}^{n}(w[i] = w[n+i])$. In the case of co-limit, we can check that only finitely many (in fact, 0) prefixes h of an input word are such that $h[i] \neq h[i+n]$ for some $1 \leq i \leq n$. This is done by letting $\mathcal{A}$ guess a position $1 \leq i \leq n$, remember $h[i]$, and accept a word iff the letter that comes n positions after it (that is, in $h[i+n]$) is different. It is easy to see that $\mathcal{A}$ requires only $O(n)$ states. A word w has finitely many prefixes in $L(\mathcal{A})$ iff $w \in L_n$. Hence, *co-lim*$(\mathcal{A}') = L_n$.

The case of persistent limit is much harder, as we cannot use the implicit complementation used in the co-limit case. Instead, we use the universal nature of persistence. We define the NFW $\mathcal{A}'$ as a union of n gadgets $\mathcal{A}'_1, \ldots, \mathcal{A}'_n$. The gadget $\mathcal{A}'_i$ is responsible for checking that $w[i] = w[n+i]$. In order to make sure that the conjunction on all $1 \leq i \leq n$ is satisfied, we further limit $\mathcal{A}'_i$ to accept only words of length i mod n. Hence, $\mathcal{A}'_i$ accepts a word $u \in \Sigma^*$ iff $u[i] = u[n+i] \wedge |u| = i \bmod n$. Consequently, if $w[i] \neq w[n+i]$, then all the prefixes of w of length i mod n are rejected by $\mathcal{A}'$. On the other hand, if only a finite number of prefixes of an infinite word are not accepted by $\mathcal{A}'$, then for all $1 \leq i \leq n$, only a finite number of prefixes of length i mod n are not accepted by $\mathcal{A}'_i$. Thus, a word w is in *plim*$(\mathcal{A}')$ iff for every $1 \leq i \leq n$, almost all the prefixes of w of length i mod n are accepted by $\mathcal{A}'_i$. Hence, $w \in plim(\mathcal{A}')$ iff for all $1 \leq i \leq n$ we have that $w[i] = w[n+i]$, and we are done. Since each of the gadgets has $O(n)$ states, and $\mathcal{A}'$ needs n gadgets, it has $O(n^2)$ states. □

The notion of *typeness* for automata was introduced in [8] in the context of DBW. It is shown there that if a deterministic Rabin automaton $\mathcal{A}$ recognizes a language that is DBW realizable, then $\mathcal{A}$ has an equivalent DBW on the same structure. Typeness in general was studied in [9]. For example, it is shown in [9] that an NBW that is NCW realizable need not have an NCW on the same structure. Here, we study typeness for NFWs to which the limit operators are applied. For two limit operators β and γ (*lim*, *co-lim*, or *plim*) we say that an NFW $\mathcal{A} = \langle \Sigma, Q, \delta, Q_0, \alpha \rangle$ is (β, γ)*-type* if there is $\alpha' \subseteq Q$ such that the NFW $\mathcal{A}' = \langle \Sigma, Q, \delta, Q_0, \alpha' \rangle$ satisfies $\gamma(\mathcal{A}') = \beta(\mathcal{A})$. Thus, we can apply the limit operator γ to an NFW obtained by only modifying the set of accepting states of $\mathcal{A}$, and get the same language obtained by applying to $\mathcal{A}$ the limit operator β. Finally, we say that β is γ-type if all NFWs $\mathcal{A}$ are (β, γ)-type.

The exponential lower bounds in Theorems 4 and 5 imply that *lim* and *plim* are not *co-lim*-type, and that *co-lim* and *plim* are not *lim*-type. Two lower bounds that we miss are from *co-lim* and *lim* to *plim*. Below we show that polynomial translations to a *plim* NFW, even if exist, cannot be done in general on the same structure.

Theorem 6. *lim and co-lim are not plim-type.*

Proof: We start with limit. Consider the NFW $\mathcal{A}$ in Figure 2. Note that $lim(A) = a^+b^\omega$. As such, $ab^\omega \in lim(\mathcal{A})$. It is not hard to see that if we change the set of accepting states in such a way that only a finite number of prefixes of ab^ω are rejected, then all prefixes of the word a^ω are accepted. Hence, no NFW $\mathcal{A}'$ with $plim(\mathcal{A}') = a^+b^\omega$ can be defined on the same structure as $\mathcal{A}$.

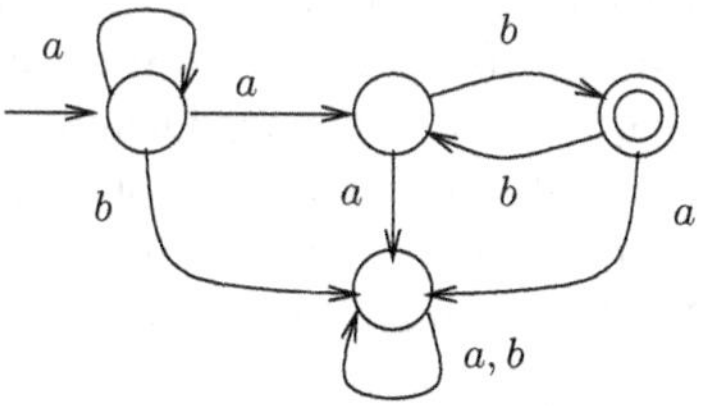

Fig. 2. An NFW $\mathcal{A}$ with $lim(\mathcal{A}) = a^+b^\omega$ and $co\text{-}lim(\mathcal{A}) = \Sigma^\omega \setminus a^+b^\omega$

We now turn to co-limit. Consider again the NFW $\mathcal{A}$. Note that $co\text{-}lim(\mathcal{A}) = \Sigma^\omega \setminus a^+b^\omega$. As such, $b^\omega \in co\text{-}lim(\mathcal{A})$. Thus, an NFW $\mathcal{A}'$ with $plim(\mathcal{A}') = co\text{-}lim(\mathcal{A})$ should reject only finitely many prefixes of b^ω. The only way for $\mathcal{A}'$ with the same structure as $\mathcal{A}$ to do so, is to let the sink be accepting. Then, however, all but two prefixes of the word aab^ω are also accepted, contradicting the fact that $aab^\omega \notin co\text{-}lim(A)$. □

5 Succinctness in Safety, Co-safety, and Bounded Properties

The study of limit operators checks behaviors in the limit. In this section we restrict attention to properties that refer to a bounded prefix of the computation. We show that even though such properties can be recognized by automata of very restricted type, almost all the lower bounds that hold in the general case, hold also in this restricted case. We consider *safety*, *co-safety*, and *bounded* properties. We start with some definitions. Let L be a language of infinite words over Σ. A finite word $x \in \Sigma^*$ is a *bad prefix* for L if for all infinite words $y \in \Sigma^\omega$, the concatenation $x \cdot y$ of x and y is not in L. Thus, a bad prefix for L is a finite word that cannot be extended into an infinite word in L. In a similar fashion, a finite word $x \in \Sigma^*$ is a *good prefix* for L, if for all infinite words $y \in \Sigma^\omega$, the concatenation $x \cdot y$ of x and y is in L.

Definition 2. *A language L is*

- *a* safety language *if every word not in L has a bad prefix,*
- *a* co-safety language *if every word in L has a good prefix,*
- *a* bounded *language if it is both safety and co-safety.*

Note that a language L is bounded iff every word $w \in \Sigma^\omega$ has either a good or a bad prefix [11]. Accordingly, evaluation of bounded properties can be done by traversing a bounded prefix of the computation, making bounded properties suitable for bounded model checking [6].

From an automata-theoretic point of view [24,11], safety properties correspond to looping automata (Büchi automata where all states are accepting), co-safety properties to co-looping automata (Büchi automata with a single accepting state that is a loop), and bounded properties to cycle-free automata (automata whose transition function contains no cycle, except possibly a self loop in an accepting sink). Accordingly, we expect the differences between the limit operators to vanish.

Examining the results in the previous sections, however, we see that most of the succinctness results established for the general case were actually proven with a bounded language, making them valid also for the bounded fragment. An exception is Theorem 3, which makes a heavy use of the unbounded nature of the language L_n. Nevertheless, the language we have used in Theorem 5 is bounded and cannot be recognized by a sub-exponential NCW or NBW. Hence, we also have exponential lower bounds for the co-lim NFW $\rightarrow$ NCW/NBW and plim NFW $\rightarrow$ NCW/NBW transformations in the bounded case.

In some cases, however, safetyness (and hence also boundedness) makes things simpler. We start with the *plim*-typeness of *lim* NFWs:

Lemma 2. *When restricted to safety properties, lim is plim-type.*

Proof: Consider an NFW $\mathcal{A} = \langle \Sigma, Q, \delta, Q_0, \alpha \rangle$ such that *lim*$(\mathcal{A})$ is a safety language. We prove that there is $\mathcal{A}' = \langle \Sigma, Q, \delta, Q_0, \alpha' \rangle$ such that *plim*$(\mathcal{A}')$ = *lim*$(\mathcal{A})$.

By Theorem 2, we have that *lim*$(\mathcal{A}) = \bigcup_{p \in Q} L_{Q_0,p} \cdot (L_{p,p} \cap L_{p,\alpha})^\omega$. Let $S \subseteq Q$ be the set of states in $\mathcal{A}$ that are not reachable from Q_0 or from which no state p such that $L_{p,p} \cap L_{p,\alpha} \neq \emptyset$ is reachable. The NFW $\mathcal{A}'$ is obtained from $\mathcal{A}$ by defining the accepting set to be $\alpha' = Q \setminus S$. In the full version, we prove that *lim*$(\mathcal{A})$ = *lim*$(\mathcal{A}')$ = *plim*$(\mathcal{A}')$.
□

Note that, in the construction above, removing all the states in S from $\mathcal{A}'$ does not change the language *lim*$(\mathcal{A}')$, and results in an NFW in which all the states are accepting. It is not hard to prove that if $\mathcal{A}$ is an NFW in which all states are accepting, then it is always the case that *lim*$(\mathcal{A}) = L(\mathcal{A}_{inf})$, where $\mathcal{A}_{inf}$ is $\mathcal{A}$ when viewed as a Büchi automaton. Thus, in the case of safety properties, the above simple linear construction gives a transformation from *lim* NFWs to NBWs, and the cubic construction in Section 3 can be circumvented. In addition, if $\mathcal{A}$ is a looping NBW, then it is always the case that $L(\mathcal{A}) =$ *lim*$(\mathcal{A}_{fin})$, where $\mathcal{A}_{fin}$ is $\mathcal{A}$ when viewed as an NFW. Hence, we have the following.

Theorem 7. *When restricted to safety properties, the transformations from an NBW to a limit NFW and from a limit NFW to an NBW are linear.*

It is not hard to see that *co-lim* is not *plim* type also in the context of bounded properties. Indeed, the non-typeness there has to do with the non-typeness of NFW complementation (that is, the fact that NFW complementation cannot always be done on top of the same structure). More difficult is to show that *lim* is not *plim* type for co-safety properties:

Lemma 3. *lim is not plim-type, even for co-safety properties.*

Proof: Consider the NFW $\mathcal{A}$ in Figure 3. Note that *lim*$(\mathcal{A}) = \Sigma^\omega \setminus \{a^\omega, b^\omega\}$. Observe that there is no way to define the accepting states in such a way that only a finite number of prefixes of ab^ω are rejected, while maintaining the requirement that infinitely many prefixes of a^ω and b^ω are rejected. □

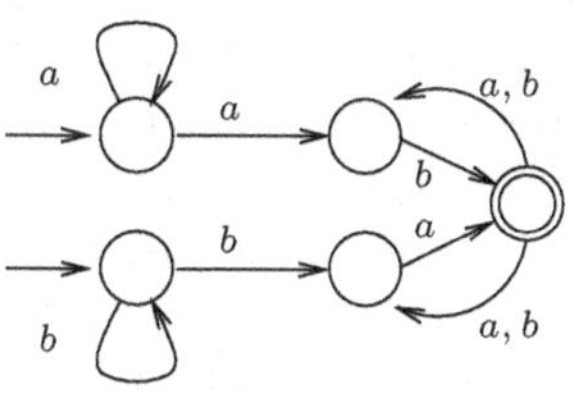

Fig. 3. An NFW $\mathcal{A}$ with *lim*$(\mathcal{A}) = \Sigma^\omega \setminus \{a^\omega, b^\omega\}$

6 Discussion

In Figure 4, we summarize most of our results. All the lower bounds in the table, with the exception of *plim* NFW $\rightarrow$ *co-lim* NFW, are tight.

Below we discuss the cases that were left open and our efforts to solve them. In addition to the results described in Figure 4, Theorem 4 describes an exponential lower bound for the translation of NBW and NCW to *co-lim* NFW. A translation of an NBW to a *lim* NFW was left open (the considerations for the NCW to *plim* NFW case are similar). Recall that an NBW $\mathcal{A}$ can be transformed to an NFW $\mathcal{A}'$ with $L(\mathcal{A}) =$ *lim*$(\mathcal{A}')$ iff $L(\mathcal{A})$ can be accepted by a DBW. As demonstrated in Section 1, even in cases where the transformation is possible, the NFW $\mathcal{A}'$ may not be defined on the same structure

	lim NFW	*co-lim* NFW	*plim* NFW
DBW	$2^{\Omega(n)}$ [Theorem 1]		
DCW	$2^{\Omega(n)}$ [Theorem 1]		
NBW	$O(n^3)$ [Corollary 1]	$2^{\Omega(n)}$ [Theorem 3]	
NCW	?	$2^{\Omega(n)}$ [Theorem 3]	
lim NFW	-	$2^{\Omega(n)}$ [Theorem 5]	$2^{\Omega(\sqrt{n})}$ [Theorem 5]
co-lim NFW	$2^{\Omega(n)}$ Theorem 4	-	$2^{\Omega(n)}$ [Theorem 4]
plim	? (not type [Theorem 6], type for safety [Lemma 2])	? (not type [Theorem 6])	-

Fig. 4. Main Results Summary

as $\mathcal{A}$. This follows from the fact that different prefixes of an infinite word may follow different accepting runs, and there is no guarantee that these runs can be merged into a single infinite accepting run. Since a deterministic automaton has a single run on every input, it does not suffer from this problem, and indeed the transformation from a DBW to a *lim* DFW can be done on the same structure. This suggests an exponential upper bound for the NBW to *lim* NFW transformation, and also hints that an exponential lower bound may follow from the exponential lower bound on determinization. On the other hand, similar considerations apply to the reverse transformation — of a *lim* NFW to an NBW, and there, as we have seen in Section 3, we are able to avoid determinization and have a polynomial transformation. Another related observation is that an exponential lower bound, if exists, cannot follow easily from the exponential lower bound on NFW determinization. Indeed, as we have noted in Section 5, the transformation from an NBW to a *lim* NFW is linear for safety languages (and hence also for ω-regular languages that are based on regular languages).

It follows that the most promising direction for obtaining an exponential lower bound in the NBW to *lim* NFW case is one that makes use of the combinatorial properties of the Büchi condition and relies on the $2^{O(n \log n)}$ lower bound for NBW determinization. A natural candidate for a family of languages with which a lower bound can be proved is therefore the family L_n defined by Michel in the context of NBW complementation and later used by Löding in the context of NBW determinization [19,15]. As we show, however, in the full version, even though there is no DFW $\mathcal{A}$ with less than $2^{\Omega(n \log n)}$ states such that $lim(\mathcal{A}) = L_n$, there is an NFW $\mathcal{A}$ with only $O(n^2)$ states, such that $lim(\mathcal{A}) = L_n$. The NFW $\mathcal{A}$ belongs to a special class of NFWs we call *continuous* NFWs. The main property of continuous NFW is that the language they accept as NBWs coincides with their limit. I.e., for a continuous NFW, the different accepting runs over prefixes of an infinite word do merge into an accepting run on the infinite word. Formally, we have the following. Consider an NFW $\mathcal{A} = \langle \Sigma, Q, \delta, Q_0, \alpha \rangle$. For sets $P, S \subseteq Q$, we use $L^{\neg\alpha}_{P,S}$ to denotes the language of all words that $\mathcal{A}$ can read along a run disjoint from α that start in P and ends in S (the runs may start and/or end in a state in α, but states of α are not allowed in the middle of the run).

Definition 3. *An NFW $\mathcal{A} = \langle \Sigma, Q, \delta, Q_0, \alpha \rangle$ is* continuous *if the languages $lim(L^{\neg\alpha}_{Q_0,\alpha})$ and $lim(L^{\neg\alpha}_{\alpha,\alpha})$ are both empty.*

In the full version, we show that all DFWs are continuous and that if $\mathcal{A}$ is a continuous NFW, then $L(\mathcal{A}) = lim(\mathcal{A}_{inf})$, when $\mathcal{A}_{inf}$ is $\mathcal{A}$ viewed as an NBW. As detailed in the full version, the proof makes use of the characterization described for limit languages in Theorem 2 — the characterization that was the key to the polynomial *lim* NFW to NBW transformation. Our conjecture is that a polynomial translation from NBW to lim NFW is possible also in the general case.

We now discuss another problem that was left open: the transformation from a *lim* NFW to a *plim* NFW. Note that a "*lim* to *plim*" transformation is possible only for languages that are recognizable by both DBW and DCW, and hence are also recognizable by a deterministic *weak* automaton [4] (a similar challenge is the "*lim* to NCW" transformation, which was also left open). Our initial conjecture was that *lim* is *plim* type. The examples in Theorem 6 and Lemma 3 have made us realize that the fact a *lim* NFW does not have to eventually accept all prefixes enables it to classify states that are the only destination of some prefixes as rejecting ones. As demonstrated in the examples, this enables the NFW to use these states in cycles that are traversed along runs of words that are not in the limit. On the one hand, this points to an advantage of *lim* NFWs over *plim* NFWs. Note that a dual advantage enabled us to prove an exponential lower bound in the reverse "*plim* to *lim*" transformation. On the other hand, this advantage of *lim* seems to help it only with a bounded number of prefixes. Technically, it may be (and this is the case in both examples), that by unwinding the graph of the NFW some fixed number of times, we get a new NFW that is *plim* type. Thus, here too, our conjecture is that a polynomial transformation exists.

Acknowledgment. We thank Annielo Murano for many helpful discussions.

References

1. B. Alpern and F.B. Schneider. Defining liveness. *IPL*, 21:181–185, 1985.
2. R. Armoni, L. Fix, A. Flaisher, R. Gerth, B. Ginsburg, T. Kanza, A. Landver, S. Mador-Haim, E. Singerman, A. Tiemeyer, M.Y. Vardi, and Y. Zbar. The ForSpec temporal logic: A new temporal property-specification logic. In *8th TACAS*, LNCS 2280, pages 296–211, 2002.
3. I. Beer, S. Ben-David, C. Eisner, D. Fisman, A. Gringauze, and Y. Rodeh. The temporal logic Sugar. In *Proc. 13th CAV*, LNCS 2102, pages 363–367, 2001.
4. B. Boigelot, S. Jodogne, and P. Wolper. On the use of weak automata for deciding linear arithmetic with integer and real variables. In *IJCAR*, LNCS 2083, pages 611–625, 2001.
5. J.R. Büchi. On a decision method in restricted second order arithmetic. In *Proc. International Congress on Logic, Method, and Philosophy of Science. 1960*, pages 1–12, Stanford, 1962.
6. E. M. Clarke, A. Bierea, R. Raimi, and Y. Zhu. Bounded model checking using satisfiability solving. *Formal Methods in System Design*, 19(1):7–34, 2001.
7. Accellera Organization Inc. http://www.accellera.org.
8. S.C. Krishnan, A. Puri, and R.K. Brayton. Deterministic ω-automata vis-a-vis deterministic Büchi automata. In *Algorithms and Computations*, LNCS 834, pages 378–386, 1994.
9. O. Kupferman, G. Morgenstern, and A. Murano. Typeness for ω-regular automata. In *Proc. 2nd ATVA*, LNCS 3299, pages 324–338, 2004.
10. O. Kupferman, S. Safra, and M.Y. Vardi. Relating word and tree automata. In *Proc. 11th LICS*, pages 322–333, DIMACS, June 1996.
11. O. Kupferman and M.Y. Vardi. On bounded specifications. In *Proc. 8th LPAR*, LNCS 2250, pages 24–38, 2001.

12. O. Kupferman and M.Y. Vardi. From linear time to branching time. *ACM TOCL*, 6(2):273–294, April 2005.
13. R.P. Kurshan. *Computer Aided Verification of Coordinating Processes*. Princeton Univ. Press, 1994.
14. L.H. Landweber. Decision problems for ω–automata. *Mathematical Systems Theory*, 3:376–384, 1969.
15. C. Löding. Optimal bounds for the transformation of omega-automata. In *Proc. 19th FSTTCS*, LNCS 1738, pages 97–109, 1999.
16. C. Löding. Efficient minimization of deterministic weak omega-automata. *IPL*, 79(3):105–109, 2001.
17. R. McNaughton. Testing and generating infinite sequences by a finite automaton. *I& C*, 9:521–530, 1966.
18. A.R. Meyer and M.J. Fischer. Economy of description by automata, grammars, and formal systems. In *Proc. 12th SSAT*, pages 188–191, 1971.
19. M. Michel. Complementation is more difficult with automata on infinite words. CNET, Paris, 1988.
20. S. Miyano and T. Hayashi. Alternating finite automata on ω-words. *TCS*, 32:321–330, 1984.
21. M.O. Rabin. Decidability of second order theories and automata on infinite trees. *Transaction of the AMS*, 141:1–35, 1969.
22. S. Safra. On the complexity of ω-automata. In *Proc. 29th FOCS*, pages 319–327, 1988.
23. S. Safra and M.Y. Vardi. On ω-automata and temporal logic. In *Proc. 21st ACM STOC*, pages 127–137, 1989.
24. A.P. Sistla. Safety, liveness and fairness in temporal logic. *Formal Aspects of Computing*, 6:495–511, 1994.
25. W. Thomas. Automata on infinite objects. *Handbook of Theoretical Computer Science*, pages 133–191, 1990.
26. M.Y. Vardi and P. Wolper. Reasoning about infinite computations. *I& C*, 115(1):1–37, 1994.

Efficient Algorithms for Alternating Pushdown Systems with an Application to the Computation of Certificate Chains*

Dejvuth Suwimonteerabuth, Stefan Schwoon, and Javier Esparza

Institut für Formale Methoden der Informatik, Universität Stuttgart,
Universitätsstr. 38, 70569 Stuttgart, Germany
{suwimodh,schwoosn,esparza}@informatik.uni-stuttgart.de

Abstract. Motivated by recent applications of pushdown systems to computer security problems, we present an efficient algorithm for the reachability problem of alternating pushdown systems. Although the algorithm is exponential, a careful analysis reveals that the exponent is usually small in typical applications. We show that the algorithm can be used to compute winning regions in pushdown games. In a second contribution, we observe that the algorithm runs in polynomial time for a certain subproblem, and show that the computation of certificate chains with threshold certificates in the SPKI/SDSI authorization framework can be reduced to this subproblem. We present a detailed complexity analysis of the algorithm and its application, and report on experimental results obtained with a prototype implementation.

1 Introduction

Pushdown systems are a concept from formal-language theory that has turned out to be useful in computer-aided verification. They naturally model the behaviour of programs with possibly recursive procedures, and therefore model-checking for pushdown systems has been the subject of recent research. Burkhard and Steffen [1] and Walukiewicz [2] have studied the problem for the modal μ-calculus. Other papers [3,4,5] have investigated specialised algorithms for LTL model checking and both forward and backward reachability on pushdown systems. Concrete algorithms for these tasks with a precise complexity analysis were proposed in [5] and subsequently implemented in the Moped tool. Moreover, [3] has shown that a similar approach can be used to solve the *backward* reachability problem in alternating pushdown systems. This can be used to solve the model-checking problem for the alternation-free μ-calculus on (non-alternating) pushdown systems.

More recently, pushdown systems have also been applied in the field of computer security. In the authorization framework SPKI/SDSI [6], certificates are used to assign permissions to groups of principals, which are defined using local,

* This work was partially supported by the DFG project *Algorithms for Software Model Checking* and SFB 627 Nexus, Project A6.

S. Graf and W. Zhang (Eds.): ATVA 2006, LNCS 4218, pp. 141–153, 2006.

hierarchical namespaces. In order to prove that a principal may access a certain resource, he/she needs to produce a chain of certificates that, taken together, provide a proof of authorisation. Jha and Reps [7] showed that a set of certificates can be seen as a pushdown system, and that certificate-chain discovery reduces to pushdown reachability. The SPKI/SDSI specification also provides for so-called *threshold certificates*, allowing specifications whereby a principal can be granted access to a resource if he/she can produce authorisations from multiple sources. We observe that this extension reduces to reachability on *alternating* pushdown systems.

Motivated by the applications in verification and authorisation, we study reachability algorithms for alternating pushdown systems (APDS) in more detail. The algorithm proposed in [3] is abstract (i.e. only the saturation rule is given), and its complexity is given as "exponential", without further details. Here, we provide a concrete algorithm for solving the problem together with a precise complexity analysis. Moreover, inspired by the work of [7], we show that the algorithm is very efficient for a special class of instances. Then, we consider two applications. The first one is straightforward: We show that the algorithm immediately leads to a procedure for computing winning regions in pushdown reachability games, and derive a complexity bound improving a previous analysis by [8]. The second application is perhaps more interesting. In [7], Jha and Reps observed that, for a restricted form of threshold certificates, the certificate-chain-discovery problem can be solved in polynomial, rather than exponential time. We prove this result again by showing that the existence of certificate chains can be reduced to the special class of instances of the reachability problem that we have identified. We perform a detailed complexity analysis, and report on a prototype implementation on top of the Nexus platform for context-aware systems [9].

We proceed as follows: Section 2 introduces alternating pushdown systems and other concepts used in the paper. Section 3 presents an algorithm for solving the reachability problem on APDS and analyzes its complexity. Section 4 studies the special class of instances mentioned above. Section 5 presents new upper bounds for computing winning regions in reachability pushdown games. Section 6 presents our application to certificate-chain discovery, and Section 7 reports experimental results.

Due to lack of space, all proofs have been omitted from this paper. A complete version that contains all the proofs has been published as a technical report [10].

2 Preliminaries

An *alternating pushdown system* (APDS) is a triplet $\mathcal{P} = (P, \Gamma, \Delta)$, where P is a finite set of *control locations*, Γ is a finite *stack alphabet*, and $\Delta \subseteq (P \times \Gamma) \times 2^{(P \times \Gamma^*)}$ is a set of *transition rules*. A *configuration* of $\mathcal{P}$ is a pair $\langle p, w \rangle$, where $p \in P$ is a control location and $w \in \Gamma^*$ is a *stack content*. If $((p, \gamma), \{(p_1, w_1), \ldots, (p_n, w_n)\}) \in \Delta$, we write $\langle p, \gamma \rangle \hookrightarrow \{\langle p_1, w_1 \rangle, \ldots, \langle p_n, w_n \rangle\}$ instead. We call a rule *alternating* if $n > 1$, or *non-alternating* otherwise. We also write $\langle p, \gamma \rangle \hookrightarrow \langle p_1, w_1 \rangle$ (braces omitted) for a non-alternating rule. Moreover, for every $w \in \Gamma^*$, the configuration $\langle p, \gamma w \rangle$ is an *immediate predecessor* of the set $\{\langle p_1, w_1 w \rangle, \ldots, \langle p_n, w_n w \rangle\}$.

A *computation tree* of $\mathcal{P}$ is a directed tree whose nodes are labelled by configurations and where every node n is either a leaf or an internal node labelled with c such that n has one outgoing hyperedge whose set of target nodes is labelled with configurations $C = \{c_1, \ldots, c_n\}$, where c is an immediate predecessor of C. We define the *reachability relation* $\Rightarrow$ as $c \Rightarrow C$ if there exists a computation tree such that c labels the root and C is the set of labels of the leaves. If $c \Rightarrow C$, then C is *reachable* from c. Given a set of configurations C, we define the set of *predecessors*, $pre^*(C) = \{c \mid \exists C' \subseteq C \colon c \Rightarrow C'\}$, as the set of configurations that are reachable backwards from subsets of C via the reachability relation.

Let us fix an APDS $\mathcal{P} = (P, \Gamma, \Delta)$. An alternating $\mathcal{P}$-automaton is a quintuple $\mathcal{A} = (Q, \Gamma, \delta, P, F)$, where $Q \supseteq P$ is a finite set of *states*, $F \subseteq Q$ is the set of *final states*, and $\delta \subseteq Q \times \Gamma \times 2^Q$ is a set of *transitions*. The *initial states* of $\mathcal{A}$ are the control locations of $\mathcal{P}$. We define the *transition relation* $\rightarrow \subseteq Q \times \Gamma^* \times 2^Q$ as the smallest relation satisfying:

- $q \xrightarrow{\varepsilon} \{q\}$ for every $q \in Q$,
- if $(q, \gamma, Q') \in \delta$ then $q \xrightarrow{\gamma} Q'$, and
- if $q \xrightarrow{w} \{q_1, \ldots, q_m\}$ and $q_i \xrightarrow{\gamma} Q_i$ for each $1 \leq i \leq m$, then $q \xrightarrow{w\gamma} (Q_1 \cup \ldots \cup Q_m)$.

$\mathcal{A}$ *accepts* or *recognizes* a configuration $\langle p, w \rangle$ if $p \xrightarrow{w} Q'$ for some $Q' \subseteq F$. The set of configurations recognized by $\mathcal{A}$ is denoted by $L(\mathcal{A})$.

In [3], it has been shown that given a set of configurations C of $\mathcal{P}$, recognized by an alternating automaton $\mathcal{A}$, we can construct another automaton $\mathcal{A}_{pre^*}$ such that $L(\mathcal{A}_{pre^*}) = pre^*(C)$.

The procedure of [3] assumes w.l.o.g. that $\mathcal{A}$ has no transition leading to an initial state. $\mathcal{A}_{pre^*}$ is computed by means of a saturation procedure, which adds new transitions to $\mathcal{A}$, according to the following rule:

> If $\langle p, \gamma \rangle \hookrightarrow \{\langle p_1, w_1 \rangle, \ldots, \langle p_m, w_m \rangle\} \in \Delta$ and $p_1 \xrightarrow{w_1} P_1, \ldots, p_m \xrightarrow{w_m} P_m$ holds, then add $p \xrightarrow{\gamma} (P_1 \cup \ldots \cup P_m)$.

3 An Implementation for *pre**

In this section we present an implementation, as shown in Fig. 1, of the abstract algorithm from Sect. 2. Without loss of generality, the algorithm imposes two restrictions on every rule $\langle p, \gamma \rangle \hookrightarrow R$ in Δ:

> (R1) if $R = \{\langle p', w' \rangle\}$, then $|w'| \leq 2$, and
> (R2) if $|R| > 1$, then $|R| = 2$ and $\forall \langle p', w' \rangle \in R \colon |w'| = 1$.

Note that any APDS can be converted into an equivalent one that satisfies (R1) and (R2) with only a linear increase in size (i.e. the converted automaton executes the same sequences of actions, modulo the fact that one step may be refined into a sequence of steps).

In the rest of the paper we conduct a careful analysis in terms of certain parameters of the input, which are listed below:

- $\Delta_a, \Delta_0, \Delta_1, \Delta_2$ denote the sets of alternating rules and non-alternating rules with $0, 1, 2$ stack symbols in their right-hand side, respectively.
- The set of *pop control locations*, denoted by P_ε, is the set of control locations $p_1 \in P$ such that Δ_0 contains some rule $\langle p, \gamma \rangle \hookrightarrow \langle p_1, \varepsilon \rangle$.
- Given an alternating automaton, we define Q_{ni} as the set of its non-initial states, i.e., $Q_{ni} = Q \setminus P$.

Algorithm 1 computes $\mathcal{A}_{pre^*}$ by implementing the saturation rule. The sets *rel* and *trans* contain the transitions that are known to belong to $\mathcal{A}_{pre^*}$; *rel* contains those that have already been examined. Lines 1–4 initialize the algorithm. The rules $\langle p, \gamma \rangle \hookrightarrow \langle p_1, \epsilon \rangle$ are dealt with first, as in the *pre** algorithm of the non-alternating case [5]. All rules are copied to Δ' (line 3), and the auxiliary function $\mathcal{F}(r)$ is assigned to set of empty set for each rule r (line 4). The algorithm then proceeds by iteratively removing transitions from *trans* (line 6), adding them to *rel* if necessary (lines 7–8), and examining whether they generate other transitions via the saturation rule (lines 9–22). The idea of the algorithm is to avoid unnecessary operations. Imagine that the saturation rule allows to add transition t if transitions t_1 and t_2 are already present. Now, if t_1 is taken from *trans* but t_2 has not been added to $\mathcal{A}_{pre^*}$, we do not put t_1 back to *trans* but store the following information instead: if t_2 is added, then we can also add t. It turns out that these implications can be stored in the form of "fake pushdown rules" (like those added in line 18 or 21) and in the form of the auxiliary sets $\mathcal{F}(r)$.

Let us now look at the lines 9–22 in more detail. Lines 9–10 are as in [5]. Push rules (lines 11–19) and alternating rules (lines 20–22), however, require a more delicate treatment. At line 11 we know that $q \xrightarrow{\gamma} Q'$ is a transition of $\mathcal{A}_{pre^*}$ (because it has been popped from *trans*) and that $\langle p_1, \gamma_1 \rangle \hookrightarrow \langle q, \gamma\gamma_2 \rangle$ is a rule of the APDS. So we divide the states $q' \in Q'$ into those for which there is some rule $q' \xrightarrow{\gamma_2} Q''$ in *rel* and the rest. If there is no rest then we can add new rules to *trans* (lines 14–15). Otherwise we add the "fake rule" of line 18. At line 20 we know that $q \xrightarrow{\gamma} Q'$ is a transition of $\mathcal{A}_{pre^*}$ and $\langle p_1, \gamma_1 \rangle \hookrightarrow \{\langle q, \gamma \rangle\} \cup R$ is an alternating rule. So we add the "fake rule" $\langle p_1, \gamma_1 \rangle \hookrightarrow R$.

Note that the algorithm obviously runs with exponential time, since the number of transitions of A_{pre^*} can be exponential in the number of states. However, a closer look at the complexity reveals that the algorithm is exponential only in a proper subset of states, which can be small depending on the instance.

Lemma 1. *Algorithm 1 takes* $O(|\delta_0| + |\Delta_0| + |\Delta_1| 2^n + (|\Delta_2| n + |\Delta_a|) 4^n)$ *time, where* $n = |P_\varepsilon| + |Q_{ni}|$.

In typical applications, we start with a small automaton, i.e. δ_0 and Q_{ni} will be small. In that case, n will be dominated by $|P_\varepsilon|$, therefore the complexity can be simplified to $O(|\Delta_0| + |\Delta_1| 2^{|P_\varepsilon|} + (|\Delta_2||P_\varepsilon| + |\Delta_a|) 4^{|P_\varepsilon|})$

Theorem 1. *Let* $\mathcal{P} = (P, \Gamma, \Delta)$ *be an alternating pushdown system and* $\mathcal{A} = (Q, \Gamma, \delta_0, P, F)$ *be an alternating automaton. There exist an alternating automaton* $\mathcal{A}_{pre^*}$ *that recognizes* $pre^*(L(\mathcal{A}))$*. Moreover, if the restrictions R1 and R2 are met,* $\mathcal{A}_{pre^*}$ *can be constructed in* $O(|\delta_0| + |\Delta_0| + |\Delta_1| 2^n + (|\Delta_2| n + |\Delta_a|) 4^n)$ *time, where* $n = |P_\varepsilon| + |Q_{ni}|$.

Algorithm 1
Input: an APDS $\mathcal{P} = (P, \Gamma, \Delta)$;
an alternating $\mathcal{P}$-automaton $\mathcal{A} = (Q, \Gamma, \delta_0, P, F)$ without transitions into P
Output: the set of transitions of $\mathcal{A}_{pre^*}$

$rel := \emptyset$;
$trans := \delta_0 \cup \{ (p, \gamma, p') \mid \langle p, \gamma \rangle \hookrightarrow \langle p', \varepsilon \rangle \in \Delta \} \cup \{ (p, \gamma, \emptyset) \mid \langle p, \gamma \rangle \hookrightarrow \emptyset \in \Delta \}$;
$\Delta' := \Delta$;
$\mathcal{F} := \lambda x.\{\emptyset\}$;
while $trans \neq \emptyset$ **do**
  pop $t := (q, \gamma, Q')$ from $trans$;
  if $t \notin rel$ **then**
    add t to rel;
    for all $r := \langle p_1, \gamma_1 \rangle \hookrightarrow \langle q, \gamma \rangle \in \Delta'$ **and** $Q'' \in \mathcal{F}(r)$ **do**
      add $(p_1, \gamma_1, Q' \cup Q'')$ to $trans$;
    for all $\langle p_1, \gamma_1 \rangle \hookrightarrow \langle q, \gamma\gamma_2 \rangle \in \Delta'$ **do**
      $S := \{ q' \in Q' \mid \exists Q'' : (q', \gamma_2, Q'') \in rel \}$;
      $\mathcal{Q}_1 := \{ \bigcup_{q' \in S} Q_{q'} \mid \forall q' \in S \colon (q', \gamma_2, Q_{q'}) \in rel \}$;
      if $S = Q'$ **then**
        add $\{(p_1, \gamma_1, Q_1) \mid Q_1 \in \mathcal{Q}_1\}$ to $trans$;
      else
        $r := \langle p_1, \gamma_1 \rangle \hookrightarrow \{\langle q', \gamma_2 \rangle \mid q' \in Q' \setminus S\}$;
        add r to Δ';
        add $\mathcal{Q}_1$ to $\mathcal{F}(r)$;
    for all $r := \langle p_1, \gamma_1 \rangle \hookrightarrow \{\langle q, \gamma \rangle\} \cup R \in \Delta'$ s.t. $R \neq \emptyset$ **do**
      add $\langle p_1, \gamma_1 \rangle \hookrightarrow R$ to Δ';
      add $\{Q'' \cup Q' \mid Q'' \in \mathcal{F}(r)\}$ to $\mathcal{F}(\langle p_1, \gamma_1 \rangle \hookrightarrow R)$;
return rel;

Fig. 1. An algorithm for computing pre^*

Given an APDS $\mathcal{P}$, a configuration c of $\mathcal{P}$, and a set of configurations C, the *backward reachability* problem for $\mathcal{P}$, c, and C is to check whether $c \in pre^*_{\mathcal{P}}(C)$. By Theorem 1, the problem is in EXPTIME. The following theorem shows a corresponding lower bound. It is a rather straightforward modification of a theorem of [11].

Theorem 2. *The backward reachability problem for alternating pushdown systems is* ***EXPTIME****-complete, even if C is a singleton.*

4 A Special Case

Recall the saturation rule of the abstract algorithm for the computation of pre^*: for every transition rule $\langle p, \gamma \rangle \hookrightarrow \{\langle p_1, w_1 \rangle, \ldots, \langle p_m, w_m \rangle\}$ and every set $p_1 \xrightarrow{w_1} P_1, \ldots, p_m \xrightarrow{w_m} P_m$, add a new transition $p \xrightarrow{\gamma} (P_1 \cup \ldots \cup P_m)$. The exponential complexity of the algorithm is due to the fact that the target of the new transition can be an arbitrary set of states, and so we may have to add an exponential number of new rules in the worst case. We now consider a special class of instances in which a new transition $p \xrightarrow{\gamma} Q$ need only be added if Q is a singleton, and show that a suitable modification of Algorithm 1 has polynomial running time.

Definition 1. *Let $\mathcal{P} = (P, \Gamma, \Delta)$ be an APDS, and let $R \subseteq P\Gamma^*$ be a set of configurations. We say that $(\mathcal{P}, R)$ is a* good *instance for the computation of pre* if for every $\langle p, d\rangle \hookrightarrow \{\langle p_1, w_1\rangle, \ldots, \langle p_n, w_n\rangle\} \in \Delta$ with $n \geq 2$ and for every $i \in \{1, \ldots, n\}$: $p_i w_i w \in pre^*(R)$ implies $w = \varepsilon$.*

I.e., if the set R can be reached from $p_i w_i$, then it cannot be reached from any $p_i w_i w$, where w is a nonempty word. As mentioned above, we introduce the following modification to the saturation rule: a new transition $p \xrightarrow{\gamma} Q$ is added only if Q is a singleton.

Theorem 3. *Let $\mathcal{P} = (P, \Gamma, \Delta)$ and R be a good instance, and let $\mathcal{A}$ be a nondeterministic automaton recognizing R. Assume w.l.o.g. that $\mathcal{A}$ has one single final state. Then, the modified saturation procedure produces a nondeterministic automaton recognizing the same language as $\mathcal{A}_{pre^*}$.*

Algorithm 1 implements the modified procedure after the following change to line 9: **for all** $r := \langle p_1, \gamma_1\rangle \hookrightarrow \langle q, \gamma\rangle \in \Delta'$ **and** $Q'' \in \mathcal{F}(r) \cap \{\emptyset, Q'\}$ **do.**

Lemma 2. *The modified Algorithm 1 takes $O(|\delta_0| + |\Delta_0| + (|\Delta_1| + |\Delta_a|)n + |\Delta_2|n^2)$ time, where $n = |P_\varepsilon| + |Q_{ni}|$, when applied to a good instance.*

Note that Algorithm 1, when applied to a *non-alternating* PDS (i.e. one with $\Delta_a = \emptyset$), has the same complexity as the algorithm from [5] that was specially designed for non-alternating PDS.

5 Computing Attractors in Pushdown Games

In [8] Cachat provided an algorithm for computing the winning positions of a player in a pushdown reachability game. It is straightforward to reformulate the algorithm in terms of *pre** computations for alternating pushdown automata. We do this, and apply the results of Sect. 3 to provide very precise upper bounds for the complexity of these problems.

A *pushdown game system* (PGS) is a tuple $\mathcal{G} = (P, \Gamma, \Delta_\mathcal{G}, P_0, P_1)$, where $(P, \Gamma, \Delta_\mathcal{G})$ is a PDS and P_0, P_1 is a partition of P. A PGS defines a pushdown game graph $G_\mathcal{G} = (V, \rightarrow)$ where $V = P\Gamma^*$ is the set of all configurations, and $p\gamma v \rightarrow qwv$ for every $v \in \Gamma^*$ iff $(p, \gamma, q, w) \in \Delta_\mathcal{G}$. P_0 and P_1 induce a partition $V_0 = P_0\Gamma^*$ and $V_1 = P_1\Gamma^*$ on V. Intuititively, V_0 and V_1 are the nodes at which players 0 and 1 choose a move, repectively. Given a start configuration $\pi_0 \in V$, a play is a maximal (possibly infinite) path $\pi_0\pi_1\pi_2\ldots$ of $G_\mathcal{G}$; the transitions of the path are called *moves*; a move $\pi_i \rightarrow \pi_{i+1}$ is made by player 0 if $\pi_i \in V_0$; otherwise it is made by player 1.

The winning condition of a reachability game is a regular *goal set* of configurations $R \subseteq P\Gamma^*$. Player 0 wins those plays that visit some configuration of the goal set and also those that reach a deadlock for player 1. Player 1 wins the rest. We wish to compute the winning region for player 0, denoted by $Attr_0(R)$, i.e. the set of nodes from which player 0 can always force a visit to R or a deadlock for player 1. Formally [8]:

$$\begin{aligned} Attr_0^0(R) &= R \ , \\ Attr_0^{i+1}(R) &= Attr_0^i(R) \cup \{u \in V_0 \mid \exists v : u \to v, v \in Attr_0^i(R)\} \\ &\cup \{u \in V_1 \mid \forall v : u \to v \Rightarrow v \in Attr_0^i(R)\} \ , \\ Attr_0(R) &= \bigcup_{i \in \mathbb{N}} Attr_0^i(R) \ . \end{aligned}$$

Given a PGS $\mathcal{G} = (P, \Gamma, \Delta_{\mathcal{G}}, P_0, P_1)$, we define an APDS $\mathcal{P} = (P, \Gamma, \Delta)$ as follows. For every $p \in P$ and $\gamma \in \Gamma$: if $p \in P_0$, then for every rule $\langle p, \gamma \rangle \hookrightarrow \langle q, w \rangle$ of $\Delta_{\mathcal{G}}$ add the rule $\langle p, \gamma \rangle \hookrightarrow \{\langle q, w \rangle\}$ to Δ; if $p \in P_1$ and S is the set of right-hand-side configurations of rules with $\langle p, \gamma \rangle$ as left-hand-side, then add $\langle p, \gamma \rangle \hookrightarrow S$ to Δ. It follows immediately from the definitions that $Attr_0(R) = pre^*_{\mathcal{P}}(R)$ (intuitively, if $c \in pre^*_{\mathcal{P}}(R)$ then $c \Rightarrow C$ for some $C \subseteq R$, and so player 0 can force the play into the set C). So we can use Algorithm 1 to compute $Attr_0(R)$. To derive the complexity bound, we apply Lemma 1:

Theorem 4. *Let $\mathcal{G} = (P, \Gamma, \Delta_{\mathcal{G}}, P_0, P_1)$ be a PGS and a goal set R recognized by an alternating automaton $\mathcal{A}_R = (Q, \Gamma, \delta_0, P, F)$. An alternating automaton accepting the winning region can be computed in $O(|\delta_0| + |\Delta_0| + |\Delta_1| 2^n + (|\Delta_2| n + |\Delta_a|) 4^n)$ time, where $n = |P_\varepsilon| + |Q_{ni}|$.*

In [8] an upper bound of $O(|\Delta| \cdot 2^{c \cdot |Q|^2})$ is given. Our algorithm runs in $O(|\Delta| \cdot 2^{c \cdot |Q|})$ time, and in fact Theorem 4 further reduces the exponent $c \cdot |Q|$ to $|P_\varepsilon| + |Q_{ni}|$. Typically, $|P_\varepsilon| + |Q_{ni}|$ is much smaller than $|Q|$. First, recall that, because of the definition of $\mathcal{P}$-automaton, we have $P \subseteq Q$. Moreover, goal sets often take the form $p_1 \Gamma^* \cup \ldots \cup p_n \Gamma^*$, i.e., player 0 wins if the play hits one of the control states $p_1, \ldots, p_n$. In this case we can construct $\mathcal{A}_R$ with $|Q_{ni}| = 1$. Since $|P_\varepsilon|$ is typically much smaller than $|P|$, the parameter n is much smaller than $|Q|$.

6 Computing Certificate Trees in SPKI/SDSI

In access control of shared resources, authorization systems allow to specify a security policy that assigns permissions to principals in the system. The *authorization problem* is, given a security policy, should a principal be allowed access to a specific resource? In frameworks such as SPKI/SDSI [6] and RT_0 [12], the security policy is expressed as a set of certificates, and the authorization problem reduces to discovering a subset of certificates proving that a given principal is allowed to access a given resource.

The SPKI/SDSI standard provides for so-called *threshold certificates*. Jha and Reps already observed in [7] that the authorization problem in the presence of such certificates can be reduced to the APDS reachability problem, and that a special case had polynomial complexity. In this paper, we observe that the special case corresponds to *good instances* of APDS reachability, as defined in Sect. 4, and provide a detailed complexity analysis. Moreover, we report on experimental results for a prototype implementation of the algorithm as an extension of the Nexus platform [9] with distributed access control.

The expressiveness of RT_0 is very similar to that of SPKI/SDSI and also allows for role intersection. We note, therefore, that the authorization problem for RT_0 also reduces to APDS reachability. In [12], a specialised certificate-chain-discovery algorithm for RT_0 was proposed to which our solution provides an alternative. A comparison between the two algorithms is a little involved, however, and can be found in [10].

We proceed in two steps. First, we consider "simple" SPKI/SDSI, a subset of SPKI/SDSI that has been considered in most of the work on this topic. Simple SPKI/SDSI does not handle threshold certificates, which we present in the second part.

6.1 Simple SPKI/SDSI

In this paper, we introduce only the basic notations that are required to understand SPKI/SDSI and its connections with alternating PDS. A more thorough explanation can be found in [7].

In SPKI/SDSI, the principals (individuals, resources, or any other entities) are represented by their public keys. We denote by $\mathcal{K}$ the set of public keys (or principals), specific keys are denoted by K, K_A, K', etc. An *identifier* is a word over some alphabet Σ (usually denoted by typewriter font such as `A`, `B`, ...). The set of identifiers is denoted by $\mathcal{A}$. A *local name* is of the form K `A`, where $K \in \mathcal{K}$ and $\mathtt{A} \in \mathcal{A}$. For example, K_X `Customer` is a local name. A *term* is a key followed by zero or more identifiers. For example, K `Area Customer` is a term. SPKI/SDSI has two types of certificates, or "certs":

Name Certificates. A name cert provides a definition of a local name in the issuer's local name space. Simply speaking, it can be understood as a rewrite rule of the form $K\ \mathtt{A} \to S$, where $K\ \mathtt{A}$ is a local name and and S is a term. Intuitively, this defines a meaning for `A` in the local name space of principal K, and only K may issue and sign such a cert.

Imagine, for instance, that X is a telecommunication company with multiple divisions, including the mobile phone division Xm. Alice is a customer with the mobile phone division. Consider the following certificates:

$$K_{Xm}\ \mathtt{customer} \to K_{Alice} \tag{1}$$

$$K_X\ \mathtt{customer} \to K_{Xm}\ \mathtt{customer} \tag{2}$$

Here, (1) intuitively declares Alice to be a customer of Xm, while (2) says that customers of Xm are also customers of the company X as a whole.

Authorization Certificates. An auth cert grants or delegates a specific authorization from an issuer to a subject. It can be understood as a rewrite rule of the form

$K_R \, \Box \rightarrow S \, b$, where $b \in \{\Box, \blacksquare\}$. If K_R is the owner of some resource R, then this certificate grants access to R to all principals described by term S. Only K_R may issue such a certificate. If $b = \Box$, then authorized principals may delegate this authorization to other principals, otherwise delegation is not permitted. The following certificate grants access to resource R to all of X's customers, without delegation:

$$K_R \, \Box \rightarrow K_X \, \texttt{customers} \, \blacksquare \tag{3}$$

Certificate Chains. In order for Alice to prove that she has access to some resource, she needs to provide a list of certificates that lead from the public key to herself by applying left-prefix rewriting. Such a list of certificates is called a *certificate chain*. In the example, Alice is granted authorisation to access R if she can produce the certificate chain (3),(2),(1), because applying them (in this order) shows that:

$$K_R \, \Box \overset{(3)}{\rightarrow} K_X \, \texttt{customers} \, \blacksquare \overset{(2)}{\rightarrow} K_{Xm} \, \texttt{customers} \, \blacksquare \overset{(1)}{\rightarrow} K_{Alice} \, \blacksquare$$

Since this chain leads from $K_R \, \Box$ to $K_{Alice} \, \blacksquare$, Alice is authorised to access R, the "$\blacksquare$" indicating that she is unable to delegate that access further.

It was observed in [7] that a set of name and auth certs can be interpreted as a pushdown system; therefore, the authorization problem reduces to the problem of pushdown reachability and can be solved using the algorithms from [3,5].

6.2 SPKI/SDSI with Threshold Certificates

The SPKI/SDSI standard [6] provides for so-called *threshold subjects*. A threshold subject is a pair $(\mathcal{S}, k)$ where $\mathcal{S}$ is a set of terms and $k \leq |\mathcal{S}|$. A threshold certificate is a name or auth cert where the right-hand side is a threshold subject. If threshold certificates are involved, proofs of authorisation can no longer be done purely by certificate chains. Instead, a proof of authorisation for Alice to access resource R becomes a *certificate tree*, where the nodes are labelled with terms and the edges are labelled with rewrite rules that can be applied to the term labelling their source nodes. The root is $K_R \, \Box$, and if $K \; \texttt{A} \rightarrow (\mathcal{S}, k)$ is used to rewrite a node n, then the children of n are the elements of $\mathcal{S}$. The tree is considered a valid proof of authorisation for Alice if at least k of the children can be rewritten to $K_{Alice} \, b$, where $b \in \{\Box, \blacksquare\}$.

We observe that it is sufficient to consider threshold certificates with subject $(\mathcal{S}, k)$ such that $k = |\mathcal{S}|$. (Any certificate where $k < |\mathcal{S}|$ can be simulated by $\binom{|\mathcal{S}|}{k}$ threshold certificates for each subset of $\mathcal{S}$ with exactly k elements.) Therefore, we will omit the number k from now on, silently assuming that it is equal to the cardinality of $\mathcal{S}$.

It can now easily be seen that in the presence of threshold certificates, the certificate set can be interpreted as an *alternating* pushdown system, and that the authorisation problem reduces to APDS reachability. In other words, Alice is granted access to resource R if she can prove that $K_R \, \Box \Rightarrow \{K_{Alice} \, \Box, K_{Alice} \, \blacksquare\}$.

In [13,7] the use of threshold subjects is restricted to just authorization certificates, claiming that the use of threshold subjects in name certificates would make the semantics "almost surely too convoluted". Moreover, [7] observes that under this restriction the authorisation problem can be solved without incurring (asymptotic) run-time penalties for threshold subjects and gives an informal algorithm. Within our framework, we note that the restriction of threshold subjects to auth certs allows one to obtain a good instance and to apply the algorithm from Sect. 4 to solve the authorisation problem.

Theorem 5. *Let C_t, C_0, C_1, and C_2 be sets of certificates, where C_t contains the auth certs with threshold subjects, C_0 contains the name certs in which terms have zero identifiers, C_1 contains the name and auth certs in which terms have one and zero identifiers, respectively, and C_2 consists of the rest. Let n be the number of different terms in C_0. The authorization problem can be solved in $O(|C_0| + (|C_1| + |C_t|)n + |C_2|n^2)$ time.*

7 Implementation and Experiments

We have implemented a prototype of the *pre** algorithm for APDS (in fact, a dedicated version for good instances) inside the Nexus platform [9]. An application can use Nexus "middleware" in order to obtain context data about mobile objects registered at the platform, like the position of an object or whether it enjoys a given relation to another object.

Nexus is based on an *Augmented World Model* (AWM). AWM can contain both real world objects (e.g. rooms or streets) and virtual objects (e.g. websites). Furthermore, Nexus defines a language called *Augmented World Modeling Language* (AWML). This XML-based language is used for exchanging Nexus objects between the platform and data repositories.

Our prototype extends the AWM and AWML with name and authorization relations, which can be viewed as name and authorization certificates in the case of SPKI/SDSI, respectively. In other words, we model relations as virtual objects in the Nexus context. Moreover, we extend the platform so that it can serve applications querying relations between entities. Note that, normally, the base information about objects is contained in a Nexus database (the so-called context server) and returned in the form of AWML documents. Our prototype is not yet connected to such a database; instead, all data is kept directly in AWML.

7.1 A Scenario

Consider a scenario where company X takes part in a trade fair. The exhibition center consists of 2 exhibitions. An exhibition's area is a hierarchical structure with 3 exhibition halls, divided into 4 floors with 5 booths each. The structure can be written by pushdown rules as follows, given that $1 \leq i \leq 2, 1 \leq j \leq 3, 1 \leq k \leq 4, 1 \leq l \leq 5$:

$$E_i \; \texttt{Area} \rightarrow E_i \; \texttt{Hall Floor Booth} \tag{4}$$

$$E_i \; \texttt{Hall} \rightarrow H_{[i,j]} \tag{5}$$

$$H_{[i,j]} \; \texttt{Floor} \rightarrow F_{[i,j,k]} \tag{6}$$

$$F_{[i,j,k]} \; \texttt{Booth} \rightarrow B_{[i,j,k,l]} \tag{7}$$

Now, company X launches a promotion for visitors of the exhibition center to freely download ringtones for their mobile phones. The following visitors are allowed to download: (1) customers of X who are currently in the area of exhibition 1; (2) non-customers to whom the right has been delegated by one of X's customers; (3) customers who are currently not in the area of exhibition 1, but have received delegation from another visitor of exhibition 1. This is expressed by the following rule:

$$K_X \; \square \rightarrow \{E_1 \; \texttt{Area Visitor} \; \square, K_X \; \texttt{Customer} \; \square\} \tag{8}$$

The facts that Alice is visiting a booth in exhibition 1, and that she delegates her right to Bob, who is a customer of X, can be written as:

$$B_{[1,j,k,l]} \; \texttt{Visitor} \rightarrow K_{Alice}, \qquad \text{for some } j, k, l \tag{9}$$

$$K_{Alice} \; \square \rightarrow K_{Bob} \; \blacksquare \tag{10}$$

$$K_X \; \texttt{customer} \rightarrow K_{Bob} \tag{11}$$

When Bob wants to download a ringtone, we can efficiently compute the set $pre^*(\{\langle K_{Bob}, \square\rangle, \langle K_{Bob}, \blacksquare\rangle\})$ by noting the fact that the rules (4)–(11) and $\{\langle K_{Bob}, \square\rangle, \langle K_{Bob}, \blacksquare\rangle\}$ form a good instance. Bob's request is granted in this case because $\langle X, \square\rangle \in pre^*(\{\langle K_{Bob}, \square\rangle, \langle K_{Bob}, \blacksquare\rangle\})$. Note that Bob can only download as long as Alice stays in booths in the exhibition 1. As soon as she moves away (i.e. the rule (9) is removed), a request from Bob can no longer be granted even though he is a customer of X.

7.2 Experiments

The scenario explained above is implemented as an application of the Nexus platform. We report on the running time for some experiments. The experiments should give a rough idea of the size of problems that can be handled in reasonable time.

We randomly add visitors to the exhibition center, and let them randomly issue certificates. We consider a base case with 1000 visitors in the exhibition center, 100 of them are customers of the company X, and the visitors issue 1000 authorization certificates. The issuer of a certificate decides randomly whether the right can be further delegated or not. The series were conducted on a 2 GHz PC with 256 MB RAM.

7.3 Experiment 1

In the base case, 10 % of visitors are customers of X, and a visitor issues one certificate on average. In our first experiment we keep these two ratios constant, and increase the number of visitors (for example, if there are 2000 visitors, there will be 200 customers that authorize 2000 times). We ran the experiment five times for each set of parameters. In each run 1000 random download requests are made. Table 1 displays the average results for 1000, 2000, 5000, and 10000 visitors (V). The table shows how often the request was granted (G) and rejected (R), the average time of a certificate search (T), and average time for granted (T(G)) and rejected (T(R)) searches. All measurements are in milliseconds.

In a realistic scenario, solving the authorisation problem requires to query databases (e.g. databases containing the positions of objects) and transmit data over a network, which are comparatively expensive operations. We kept relations of various types in different AWML files and whenever a piece of data was needed, we retrieved it from there. Since opening and reading files is also a comparatively expensive operation, this gives some insight as to the overhead such operations would incur in practice. The table shows the number of times AWML files (F) needed to be opened in average. For comparison, the numbers for granted (F(G)) and rejected (F(R)) requests are also displayed.

Table 1. Results of Experiment 1

V	G	R	T	T(G)	T(R)	F	F(G)	F(R)
1000	229.8	770.2	18.71	29.09	15.49	13.84	22.54	11.19
2000	195.6	804.4	19.23	28.76	16.92	13.14	21.25	11.16
5000	202.2	797.8	18.62	29.33	15.90	12.99	21.10	10.93
10000	199.4	800.6	24.90	38.25	21.60	13.00	22.00	10.77

This experiment allows to draw a first conclusion: The average time of a search does not depend on the number of visitors per se. When a visitor requests a download, the algorithm has to search for the issuers of its certificates. Since the number of certificates is equal to the number of visitors, each visitor has one certificate in average.

7.4 Experiment 2

In this experiment, we kept the number of visitors constant, and increased the number of certificates they issue, shown in column C in Table 2. The other columns are as in Experiment 1. Again, we ran the experiment five times for each value of C. Each run consisted of 100 random requests.

Table 2. Results of Experiment 2

C	G	R	T	T(G)	T(R)	F	F(G)	F(R)
1000	23.0	77.0	18.71	29.09	15.49	13.84	22.54	11.19
2000	56.2	43.8	120.72	193.93	21.96	74.68	118.50	15.83
3000	86.4	13.6	1477.35	1704.21	33.66	625.41	721.69	12.91
4000	95.2	4.8	2279.13	2393.81	13.40	898.01	942.94	9.64

We see that the running time grows rapidly with the number of certificates issued. The explanation is the larger number of certificates received by each visitor, which leads to many more certificate chains. Observe also that the number of granted requests increases.

The overall conclusion of the two experiments is that the algorithm scales well to realistic numbers of visitors and certificates. Notice that in the intended application a user will be willing to wait for a few seconds.

8 Conclusions

We have provided an efficient implementation of the saturation algorithm of [3] for the computation of pre^* in alternating pushdown systems. Following [8], we have applied the algorithm to the problem of determining the winning region in reachability pushdown games, improving the complexity bound of [8]. We have shown that the algorithm has very low complexity for certain good instances, and provided an application: The computation of certificate chains with threshold subjects in the SPKI/SDSI authorization framework can be reduced to these instances. We have implemented the algorithm within the Nexus platform [9], and shown that it scales up to realistic scenarios.

References

1. Burkart, O., Steffen, B.: Model checking the full modal mu-calculus for infinite sequential processes. In: Proc. ICALP. LNCS 1256, Springer (1997) 419–429
2. Walukiewicz, I.: Pushdown processes: Games and model checking. In: Proc. CAV. LNCS 1102 (1996) 62–74
3. Bouajjani, A., Esparza, J., Maler, O.: Reachability analysis of pushdown automata: Application to model-checking. In: Proc. CONCUR. LNCS 1243 (1997) 135–150
4. Finkel, A., Willems, B., Wolper, P.: A direct symbolic approach to model checking pushdown systems. ENTCS **9** (1997)
5. Esparza, J., Hansel, D., Rossmanith, P., Schwoon, S.: Efficient algorithms for model checking pushdown systems. In: Proc. CAV. LNCS 1855 (2000) 232–247
6. Ellison, C., Frantz, B., Lampson, B., Rivest, R., Thomas, B., Ylönen, T.: RFC 2693: SPKI Certificate Theory. The Internet Society. (1999)
7. Jha, S., Reps, T.: Model checking SPKI/SDSI. JCS **12**(3–4) (2004) 317–353
8. Cachat, T.: Symbolic strategy synthesis for games on pushdown graphs. In: Proc. ICALP. LNCS 2380 (2002) 704–715
9. Hohl, F., Kubach, U., Leonhardi, A., Rothermel, K., Schwehm, M.: Nexus - an open global infrastructure for spatial-aware applications. Technical Report 1999/02, Universität Stuttgart: SFB 627 (1999)
10. Suwimonteerabuth, D., Schwoon, S., Esparza, J.: Efficient algorithms for alternating pushdown systems: Application to certificate chain discovery with threshold subjects. Technical report, Universität Stuttgart (2006)
11. Chandra, A., Kozen, D., Stockmeyer, L.: Alternation. JACM **28**(1) (1981) 114–133
12. Li, N., Winsborough, W., Mitchell, J.: Distributed credential chain discovery in trust management. In: Proc. CCS, ACM Press (2001) 156–165
13. Clarke, D., Elien, J., Ellison, C., Fredette, M., Morcos, A., Rivest, R.: Certificate chain discovery in SPKI/SDSI. At `http://theory.lcs.mit.edu/~rivest/` (1999)

Compositional Reasoning for Hardware/Software Co-verification*

Fei Xie[1], Guowu Yang[1], and Xiaoyu Song[2]

[1] Dept. of Computer Science, Portland State Univ., Portland, OR 97207
{xie, guowu}@cs.pdx.edu
[2] Dept. of Electrical & Computer Engineering, Portland State Univ., Portland, OR 97207
song@ece.pdx.edu

Abstract. In this paper, we present and illustrate an approach to compositional reasoning for hardware/software co-verification of embedded systems. The major challenges in compositional reasoning for co-verification include: (1) the hardware/software semantic gaps, (2) lack of common property specification languages for hardware and software, and (3) lack of compositional reasoning rules that are applicable across the hardware/software boundaries. Our approach addresses these challenges by (1) filling the hardware/software semantic gaps via translation of hardware and software into a common formal language, (2) defining a unified property specification language for hardware, software, and entire systems, and (3) enabling application of existing compositional reasoning rules across the hardware/software boundaries based on translation, developing a new rule for compositional reasoning with components that share sub-components, and extending the applicability of these rules via dependency refinement. Our approach has been applied to co-verification of networked sensors. The case studies have shown that our approach is very effective in enabling application of compositional reasoning to co-verification of non-trivial embedded systems.

1 Introduction

Embedded systems are pervasive in the infrastructure of our society. They are often mission-critical, therefore, must be highly trustworthy. Embedded systems often support concurrency intensive operations such as simultaneous monitoring, computation, and communication. Thus, to build trustworthy embedded systems, they must be extensively verified. Due to strict design constraints of embedded systems, to achieve better performance, hardware and software components must closely interact and the trade-off between hardware and software must be exploited. This demands hardware/software co-design and, therefore, hardware/software co-verification of embedded systems.

Model checking [1,2] is a powerful formal verification method which has great potential in hardware/software co-verification of embedded systems. It provides exhaustive state space coverages for the systems being verified. However, a stumbling block to scalable application of model checking to co-verification is the intrinsic complexity of model checking. The number of possible states and execution paths in a real-world

* This research was supported by Semiconductor Research Corporation, Contract 1356.001.

S. Graf and W. Zhang (Eds.): ATVA 2006, LNCS 4218, pp. 154–169, 2006.

system can be extremely large, which makes naive application of model checking intractable and requires state space reduction. Compositional reasoning [3,4,5,6,7,8,9], as applied in model checking, is a powerful state space reduction algorithm. Using compositional reasoning, model checking of a property on a system is accomplished by decomposing the system into components, model checking the component properties locally on the components, and deriving the system property from the component properties.

Co-verification of an embedded system involves both its hardware and software components, which leads to the following major challenges to compositional reasoning:

1. *Hardware/software semantic gaps.* Hardware usually follows synchronous clock-driven semantics while software semantics are more diversified, e.g., asynchronous interleaving message-passing semantics and event-driven call-return semantics.
2. *Lack of unified property specification languages.* Effective compositional reasoning can benefit greatly from uniform specification of properties of both hardware and software components and, furthermore, properties of entire embedded systems.
3. *Lack of appropriate rules for co-verification.* Existing compositional reasoning rules do not readily address the special needs of co-verification: compositional reasoning involving components of different semantics and components that share sub-components, e.g., an execution scheduler shared by software components.

In this paper, we present and illustrate an approach to compositional reasoning for hardware/software co-verification of embedded systems. This approach addresses the above challenges as follows:

1. The hardware/software semantic gaps are filled via translation of both hardware and software components into a formal language whose semantics serves as the common semantic basis for co-verification and compositional reasoning.
2. A unified property specification language is defined, which supports property specification for hardware components, software components, and furthermore entire embedded systems. This unification of property specification facilitates compositional reasoning across the hardware/software semantic boundaries.
3. A new compositional reasoning rule supports compositional reasoning for components that share sub-components. The new rule and the existing rules are applied across the hardware/software boundaries based on translation. The applicability of these rules is further extended through dependency refinement.

Our approach has been applied to co-verification of networked sensors, an emerging type of embedded systems. Hardware components of sensors are specified in Verilog while software components are specified in C following an asynchronous event-driven call-run semantics of TinyOS [10] or in xUML [11], an executable dialect of UML, following the asynchronous interleaving message-passing semantics. The case studies have shown that our approach enables compositional reasoning of non-trivial embedded systems and achieves order-of-magnitude reduction on verification complexities.

Related Work. There has been much research on compositional reasoning [9]. Particularly relevant is assume-guarantee compositional reasoning, which was introduced by

Chandy and Misra [3] and Jones [4] for analyzing safety properties. Abadi and Lamport [5], Alur and Henzinger [6], and McMillan [7] extended assume-guarantee compositional reasoning to liveness properties. However, these extensions are incomplete, i.e., there exist properties of systems which are true but not provable under these extensions [12]. Amla, Emerson, Namjoshi, and Trefler [8] proposed a sound and complete compositional reasoning rule for both safety and liveness properties. Our approach builds on the previous work on compositional reasoning and enables application of compositional reasoning across the hardware/software boundaries. This is based on translating hardware and software into the same formal model-checkable language.

The rest of this paper is organized as follows. In Section 2, we provide the background of this work. We discuss how translation fills the hardware/software semantic gaps in Section 3. In Section 4, we define a unified property specification language. We present compositional reasoning for co-verification in Section 5. In Section 6, we illustrate our approach with case studies on networked sensors. We conclude in Section 7.

2 Background

2.1 A Formal Semantics: ω-Automaton Semantics

We adopt the L-process model of ω-automaton semantics. Details of this model can be found in [13]. Only the concepts essential for understanding this paper are given below.

Definition 1. *For an L-process, ω, its language, $\mathcal{L}(\omega)$, is the set of all infinite sequences accepted by ω.*

Definition 2. *For an L-process, ω, $\mathcal{L}_*(\omega)$ denotes the set of all finite prefixes of $\mathcal{L}(\omega)$.*

Definition 3. *For L-processes, $\omega_1, \ldots, \omega_n$, their synchronous parallel composition, $\omega = \omega_1 \otimes \ldots \otimes \omega_n$, is also an L-process and $\mathcal{L}(\omega) = \cap \mathcal{L}(\omega_i)$.*

Definition 4. *For L-processes, $\omega_1, \ldots, \omega_n$, their Cartesian sum, $\omega = \omega_1 \oplus \ldots \oplus \omega_n$, is also an L-process and $\mathcal{L}(\omega) = \cup \mathcal{L}(\omega_i)$.*

For a language $\mathcal{L}$ of infinite sequences over a set of variables, V, the safety closure [14] of $\mathcal{L}$, denoted by $cl(\mathcal{L})$, is defined as the set of infinite sequences over V where $x \in cl(\mathcal{L})$ iff for each finite prefix y of x, there exists an infinite sequence z, $y : z \in \mathcal{L}$. ($y : z$ denotes the concatenation of y and z where y and z are sequences over V.) In [13], $cl(\mathcal{L})$ is termed as the smallest limit prefix-closed language containing $\mathcal{L}$.

Definition 5. *The safety closure $CL(\omega)$ of an L-process ω is an L-process whose language is the safety closure of the language of ω, $\mathcal{L}(CL(\omega)) = cl(\mathcal{L}(\omega))$.*

$CL(\omega)$ can be derived from ω by changing the fairness condition of ω to true.

Definition 6. *For a set S of finite sequences over a set of variables V, the limit of S, denoted by $lim(S)$, is the set of infinite sequences whose finite prefixes are all in S.*

Notations. Given two languages $\mathcal{L}_1$ and $\mathcal{L}_2$, $\mathcal{L}_1 \Rightarrow \mathcal{L}_2$ denotes $\mathcal{L}_1 \subseteq \mathcal{L}_2$, and $\mathcal{L}_1 \equiv \mathcal{L}_2$ denotes $\mathcal{L}_1 \subseteq \mathcal{L}_2$ and $\mathcal{L}_2 \subseteq \mathcal{L}_1$.

Lemma 1. $cl(\mathcal{L}(\omega)) \equiv lim\, \mathcal{L}_*(\omega)$

Proof of Lemma 1: Follows from the definitions of cl and lim. □

Under the ω-automaton semantics model checking is reduced to checking L-process language containment. Suppose a system is modeled by the composition $\omega_1 \otimes \ldots \otimes \omega_n$ of L-processes, $\omega_1, \ldots, \omega_n$, and a property to be checked on the system is modeled by an L-processes, ω. The property holds on the system if and only if the language of $\omega_1 \otimes \ldots \otimes \omega_n$ is contained by the language of ω, $\mathcal{L}(\omega_1 \otimes \ldots \otimes \omega_n) \subseteq \mathcal{L}(\omega)$.

Definition 7. *Given two L-processes ω_1 and ω_2, ω_1 implements ω_2 (denoted by $\omega_1 \models \omega_2$) if $\mathcal{L}(\omega_1) \subseteq \mathcal{L}(\omega_2)$.*

2.2 S/R Language: A Realization of ω-Automaton Semantics

The S/R language is the input formal language of the COSPAN model checker [15]. In S/R, a system P is composed of synchronously interacting processes, conceptually ω-automata. A process consists of state variables, selection variables, inputs, state transition rules, and selection rules. Selection variables define the outputs of the process. Each process inputs a subset of all the selection variables of other processes. State transition rules update state variables as functions of the current state, selection variables, and inputs. Selection rules assign values to selection variables as functions of state variables. Such a function is non-deterministic if several values are possible for a selection variable in a state. The "selection/resolution" execution model of S/R is synchronous clock-driven, under which a system of processes behaves in a 2-phase procedure every logical clock cycle: *[1: Selection Phase]* Every process "selects" a value possible in its current state for each of its selection variables. The values of the selection variables of all the processes form the global selection of the system. *[2: Resolution Phase]* Every process "resolves" the current global selection simultaneously by updating its state variables according to its state transition rules. In S/R, a property to be checked is also modeled by an ω-automaton T. COSPAN performs the verification by checking the language containment, $\mathcal{L}(P) \subseteq \mathcal{L}(T)$, using either an explicit state space enumeration algorithm or a symbolic (BDD-based or SAT-based) search algorithm.

2.3 A Hardware Semantics: Synchronous Clock-Driven Semantics of Verilog

In the IEEE standard, the semantics of the Verilog hardware description language is defined informally by means of a discrete event simulator. We adopt the semantics of a Verilog subset that can be formalized via translation to the S/R language. The translation has been implemented in FormalCheck [16]. Abstractly, a Verilog model consists of a number of modules. The sequential portion of a module consists of flip-flops that keep the states of the module. The outputs of a flip-flop can be updated based on its inputs at the positive edge or the negative edge of the system clock. The outputs of combinational circuits are updated based on their inputs instantly if zero delay is assumed.

2.4 Two Software Semantics

Asynchronous Event-Driven Call-Return Semantics of TinyOS. TinyOS [10] is an operating system for networked sensors. It is component-based and is readily extensible and configurable via developing new components and including only the necessary components in the system configuration for a given mission. A complete TinyOS system configuration consists of a scheduler and a graph of components. A component has four interrelated parts: a set of command handlers, a set of event handlers, a fixed-size data frame, and a bundle of tasks. Command handlers, event handlers, and tasks execute in the context of the frame and operate on its state and are implemented as functions which are invoked following the call-return semantics. Higher level components issue commands to lower level components and lower level components signal events to the higher level components. The lowest level of components abstracts physical hardware.

Event handlers are invoked to deal with hardware events, either directly or indirectly. The lowest level components have handlers connected directly to hardware interrupts. An event handler can deposit information into its frame, post tasks, signal higher level events or call lower level commands. A hardware event triggers a fountain of processing that goes upward through events and can bend downward through commands. In order to avoid cycles in the command/event chain, commands cannot signal events. Commands and events are intended to perform a small, fixed amount of work.

Tasks perform the primary work. They are atomic with respect to other tasks, though they can be preempted by events. Tasks can call lower level commands, signal higher level events, and post other tasks within a component. The semantics of tasks make it possible to allocate a single stack that is assigned to the currently executing task. Tasks allow concurrency since they execute asynchronously with respect to events. However, tasks must never block or spin wait or they will prevent progress in other components. While events and commands approximate light-weight instantaneous computations, task bundles provide a way to incorporate arbitrary computations into the event-driven model. The task scheduler is FIFO, utilizing a bounded size scheduling queue.

Asynchronous Interleaving Message-Passing (AIM) Semantics of Executable UML. Executable UML (xUML) [11] is an executable dialect of UML supporting model-driven development of embedded software. System models in xUML can be simulated with execution simulators and can also be automatically compiled into C/C++. xUML features an asynchronous interleaving message-passing semantics. Under this semantics, a system consists of a set of interacting object instances. The behavior of each object instance is specified by an extended Moore state model in which each state may be associated with a state action. A state action is a program segment that executes upon entry to the state. Object instances communicate with each other through asynchronous message-passing. In a system execution, at any given moment only one object instance can progress by executing a state transition or a state action in its extended Moore state model. The execution of a state transition or a state action is run-to-completion.

3 Translations of Hardware and Software

For practical reasons, hardware and software components of an embedded system are often specified in various languages with different semantics, for instance, the ones given in Section 2. However, to formally verify correctness properties of the entire system, a common formal semantic basis is needed, upon which events in hardware and software components can be precisely defined and, furthermore, related to one another. This enables meaningful specification and reasoning of system-level properties which often span across the hardware and software boundaries.

Leveraging the formal semantic basis to fill the hardware/software semantic gaps requires translations of the hardware and software languages to the formal language. The translations formalize the hardware and software semantics by simulating them with the formal semantics. (Restrictions are applied to the software semantics to ensure software components be finite-state.) The translations enable reuse of model checkers and compositional reasoning rules that have been developed for the formal semantics.

The translation from Verilog to S/R has been implemented in FormalCheck [16], which simulates the synchronous clock-driven semantics of Verilog with the selection/resolution semantics of S/R. The xUML-to-S/R translation has been implemented in ObjectCheck [17], which simulates the AIM semantics with the selection/resolution semantics of S/R. In this section, we briefly discuss the translation from TinyOS to S/R.

3.1 Translation from TinyOS to S/R

The TinyOS-to-S/R translation simulates the asynchronous event-driven call-return semantics of TinyOS with the selection/resolution semantics of S/R and is currently being implemented. Each component in a TinyOS system is mapped to multiple automata in the resulting S/R system: the fixed-size data frame is modeled by an automaton which keeps the state of the data frame and each event handler, command handler, or task is also modeled as an automaton which updates the data frame by interacting with the data frame automaton. An additional automaton, *scheduler*, is introduced in the S/R system and it determines which event handler, command handler, or task should be executed. The *scheduler* exports a selection variable, *choice*, imported by the automata corresponding to event handlers, command handlers, and tasks. At any given moment, the *scheduler* selects an automaton corresponding to an event handler, command handler, or task by setting *choice* to a particular value. Only the chosen automaton executes a state transition corresponding to the execution of a C language statement in the event handler, command handler, or task. Other automata follow a self-loop transition back to their current states.

Event handlers, command handlers, and tasks are implemented as C functions in TinyOS. The call-return semantics is simulated with the semantics of S/R as follows. The caller exports a Boolean selection variable which is set to true when the call is made. The callee imports this variable and responds to the call if the variable is set to true. Parameters of the call are passed via additional selection variables. The callee exports a selection variable which indicates the call return and is imported by the caller. The return value of the call is passed via additional selection variables of the callee.

In TinyOS, tasks are atomic with respect to other tasks, but can be preempted by events. We assume that a task can be preempted in between the execution of two consecutive C language statements. The preemption is implemented through the *scheduler* adjusting the value of the *choice* variable. In between the execution of two consecutive C language statements in a task, the *scheduler* checks for hardware interrupts. If there exists an interrupt, the *choice* is set to the automaton simulating the event handler of the interrupt. The *choice* is set back to the task when the interrupt handling is done.

4 Unified Property Specification Language

Co-verification examines both hardware and software components, and entire embedded systems. It is highly desirable to have a unified property specification language for both hardware and software components, and entire systems. We have developed such a language based on ω-automata, which extends the hardware property specification language of FormalCheck [16]. This unified language is presented in terms of a set of property templates shown in Figure 1, which have intuitive meanings and also rigorous

Always/Never (f) After (e) Always/Never (f) [Unless[After] (d)] After (e) Always/Never (f) [Until[After] (d)] Always/Never (f) Unless[After] (d) Always/Never (f) Until[After] (d)
After (e) Eventually (f) [Unless (d)] Eventually (f) [Unless (d)] IfRepeatedly (e) Repeatedly/Eventually (f) IfRepeatedly (e) EventuallyAlways (f) After (e) EventuallyAlways (f) [Unless (d)] EventuallyAlways (f) EventuallyAlways (f) Unless (d) After (e) Repeatedly (f) [Unless (d)] Repeatedly (f) [Unless (d)] IfEventuallyAlways (e) Repeatedly/Eventually (f) IfEventuallyAlways (e) EventuallyAlways (f)

Fig. 1. A list of available property templates

mappings to property templates written in S/R. (Note that in S/R, both systems and properties are formulated as ω-automata.) An example of such templates is

$$\texttt{After}(e)\ \texttt{Eventually}(d)$$

where the *enabling* condition e and the *discharging* condition d are Boolean propositions declared over semantic entities of hardware or software. The semantic meaning is that after each occurrence of e there eventually follows an occurrence of d. Although similar to the LTL formula $G(e \rightarrow XF(d))$, our property does not require a second d in case the discharge condition d is accompanied by a second e, whereas an initial e is not discharged by an accompanying d. This asymmetry meets many requirements of software specification. (On account of this asymmetry, our property cannot be expressed in LTL.) The formal semantics of a property instantiating this template can be precisely defined based on the mappings from the hardware and software semantics to the semantics of S/R and the mapping of this template to a template written in S/R. The property can be automatically translated into S/R based on these mappings.

Our property specification language is linear-time, with the expressiveness of ω-automata [13]. The templates define parameterized automata. The language is readily extensible: new templates can be formulated as needed. A property in this language consists of (1) declarations of Boolean propositions over software or hardware semantic entities, and (2) declarations of temporal assertions. A temporal assertion is declared through instantiating a property template: each argument of the template is realized by a Boolean expression composed from the declared Boolean propositions.

5 Compositional Reasoning for Co-verification

5.1 Previous Work: Translation-Based Compositional Reasoning for Software

In [18], we developed translation-based compositional reasoning (TBCR), an approach to application of compositional reasoning in model checking software systems based on translation. If a translation can be shown to preserve the validity of properties (e.g., for the xUML-to-S/R translation, we established that the translation is linear-monotonic with respect to language containment), then given a software system and a property to be checked, compositional reasoning in the software semantics is conducted as follows. (1) The system is decomposed into components on the software semantics level. (2) The component properties are formulated. The components and their properties are translated into the formal semantics. A compositional reasoning rule in the formal semantics is reused. The conditions of the rule are checked. (3) If the conditions hold, then it can be concluded on the software semantics level that the system property holds.

TBCR has been realized for software specified in xUML. The xUML-to-S/R translation implements the semantic mapping from the AIM semantics to the ω-automaton semantics. Based on this translation, we have reused, for verification of xUML models, a rule [8] that has been established in the ω-automaton semantics, Rule 1.

Rule 1. *For ω-automata P_1 and P_2 modeling two components of a system, and Q modeling a property of the system, to show that $P_1 \otimes P_2 \models Q$, find ω-automata Q_1 and Q_2 modeling the component properties such that the following conditions are satisfied.*[1]

C1: $P_1 \otimes Q_2 \models Q_1$ *and* $P_2 \otimes Q_1 \models Q_2$
C2: $Q_1 \otimes Q_2 \models Q$
C3: *Either* $P_1 \otimes CL(Q) \models (Q \oplus Q_1 \oplus Q_2)$ *or* $P_2 \otimes CL(Q) \models (Q \oplus Q_1 \oplus Q_2)$

5.2 Translation-Based Compositional Reasoning for Co-verification

The translation-based nature of TBCR enables its natural extension to support compositional reasoning for co-verification. Given an embedded system and a system property in the unified property specification language, compositional reasoning for co-verification can be conducted as follows: (1) The system is partitioned into its hardware and software components. (2) The properties of the hardware and software components

[1] An additional condition of Rule 2 is that Q_1 (or Q_2) does not block P_2 (or P_1). A process Q does not block process P iff (i) any initial state of P can be extended to an initial state of $P \otimes Q$, and (ii) for any reachable state of $P \otimes Q$, any transition of P from that state can be extended to a transition of $P \otimes Q$. The condition holds trivially in the ω-automaton semantics.

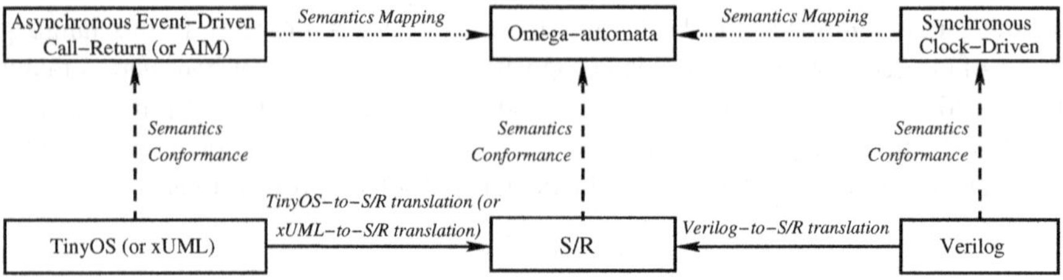

Fig. 2. Model translations realize semantic mappings for co-verification

are formulated. The hardware and software components and their properties are translated into a formal language with their corresponding translators. The conditions of a compositional reasoning rule in the formal semantics are checked. (3) If the conditions hold, it can be concluded that the system property holds. As shown in Figure 2, the Verilog-to-S/R translation and the TinyOS-to-S/R (or xUML-to-S/R, respectively) translation realize the semantic mappings from the synchronous clock-driven semantics and the asynchronous event-driven call-return semantics (or the AIM semantics) to the ω-automaton semantics, therefore, enables compositional reasoning for systems with hardware in Verilog and with software in the C subset for TinyOS (or in xUML).

This extension of TBCR requires that the hardware and software translations preserve the validity of the hardware and software properties, e.g., TinyOS-to-S/R and Verilog-to-S/R translations are linear-monotonic with respect to language containment.

5.3 Compositional Reasoning with Components That Share Sub-components

Compositional reasoning for co-verification requires new rules that support reasoning about components that share sub-components. Simulating a software semantics with the common formal semantics often requires modeling of a scheduler in the formal semantics. The translation of a TinyOS system into S/R inserts in the resulting S/R system a scheduler that interacts with the automata simulating each software component. The translation of an xUML system into S/R inserts a scheduler that interacts with each automaton simulating an object instance. (A component in xUML may contain multiple object instances.) These schedulers make scheduling decisions based on interactions with hardware. When each software component is verified, it is often the case that the scheduler must be included in the verification since using assumptions to abstract the scheduler is often difficult. Therefore, the scheduler becomes a shared sub-component. Rule 1 does not apply here since it does not allow components to share sub-components.

We propose a new compositional reasoning rule, Rule 2, addressing this problem:

Rule 2. *For ω-automata P_1 and P_2 modeling two components of a system, S modeling a common component, and Q modeling the system property, to show that $S \otimes P_1 \otimes P_2 \models Q$, find ω-automata Q_1 and Q_2 modeling the component properties such that the following conditions are satisfied.*

C1': $S \otimes P_1 \otimes Q_2 \models Q_1$ *and* $S \otimes P_2 \otimes Q_1 \models Q_2$
C2': $S \otimes Q_1 \otimes Q_2 \models Q$
C3': *Either* $S \otimes P_1 \otimes CL(Q) \models (Q \oplus Q_1 \oplus Q_2)$ *or* $S \otimes P_2 \otimes CL(Q) \models (Q \oplus Q_1 \oplus Q_2)$

Lemma 2. $\mathcal{L}_*(S \otimes P_1 \otimes P_2) \Rightarrow \mathcal{L}_*(S \otimes Q_1 \otimes Q_2)$

Proof of Lemma 2: Follows from C1' by induction on length of finite prefixes. □

Theorem 1. *(Soundness) For ω-automata S, P_1, P_2, Q_1, Q_2, and Q satisfying the conditions of Rule 2, $S \otimes P_1 \otimes P_2 \models Q$.*

We decompose the proof of Theorem 1 into a safety proof and a liveness proof according to the decomposition of $\mathcal{L}(Q)$ into its safety part and liveness part, $\mathcal{L}(Q) \equiv cl(\mathcal{L}(Q)) \wedge (\neg cl(\mathcal{L}(Q)) \vee \mathcal{L}(Q))$. The safety proof shows that $\mathcal{L}(S \otimes P_1 \otimes P_2) \Rightarrow cl(\mathcal{L}(Q))$ while the liveness proof shows that $\mathcal{L}(S \otimes P_1 \otimes P_2) \wedge cl(\mathcal{L}(Q)) \Rightarrow \mathcal{L}(Q)$.

Proof of Safety Part of Theorem 1:

$$
\begin{aligned}
&\mathcal{L}(S \otimes P_1 \otimes P_2) \\
\Rightarrow\ & cl(\mathcal{L}(S \otimes P_1 \otimes P_2)) \quad \{\text{Closure is weakening}\} \\
\equiv\ & lim\ \mathcal{L}_*(S \otimes P_1 \otimes P_2) \quad \{\text{Lemma 1}\} \\
\Rightarrow\ & lim\ \mathcal{L}_*(S \otimes Q_1 \otimes Q_2) \quad \{lim \text{ is monotonic; Lemma 2}\} \\
\equiv\ & cl(\mathcal{L}(S \otimes Q_1 \otimes Q_2)) \quad \{\text{Lemma 1}\} \\
\Rightarrow\ & cl(\mathcal{L}(Q)) \quad \{\text{Closure is monotonic; Condition C2'}\}
\end{aligned}
$$

□

Proof of Liveness Part of Theorem 1:

$$
\begin{aligned}
&\mathcal{L}(S \otimes P_1 \otimes P_2) \wedge cl(\mathcal{L}(Q)) \\
\equiv\ & \mathcal{L}(S \otimes P_1 \otimes P_2) \wedge \mathcal{L}(CL(Q)) \quad \{\text{Closure represents language closure}\} \\
\equiv\ & \mathcal{L}(S) \wedge \mathcal{L}(P_1) \wedge \mathcal{L}(P_2) \wedge \mathcal{L}(CL(Q)) \\
& \{\text{Composition is conjunction of languages}\} \\
\Rightarrow\ & \mathcal{L}(S) \wedge \mathcal{L}(P_1) \wedge \mathcal{L}(P_2) \wedge \mathcal{L}(Q \oplus Q_1 \oplus Q_2) \quad \{\text{Condition C3'}\} \\
\equiv\ & \mathcal{L}(S) \wedge \mathcal{L}(P_1) \wedge \mathcal{L}(P_2) \wedge (\mathcal{L}(Q) \vee \mathcal{L}(Q_1) \vee \mathcal{L}(Q_2)) \\
& \{\text{Cartesian sum is disjunction of languages}\} \\
\Rightarrow\ & \mathcal{L}(Q) \vee (\mathcal{L}(S) \wedge \mathcal{L}(P_1) \wedge (\mathcal{L}(Q_2)) \vee (\mathcal{L}(S) \wedge \mathcal{L}(P_2) \wedge \mathcal{L}(Q_1)) \\
& \{\text{Distribution of } \wedge \text{ over } \vee\text{; dropping conjuncts}\} \\
\Rightarrow\ & \mathcal{L}(Q) \vee (\mathcal{L}(S) \wedge \mathcal{L}(Q_1) \wedge \mathcal{L}(Q_2)) \quad \{\text{Condition C1'}\} \\
\Rightarrow\ & \mathcal{L}(Q) \quad \{\text{Condition C2'}\}
\end{aligned}
$$

□

Theorem 2. *(Completeness) For ω-automata S, P_1, P_2, and Q, if $S \otimes P_1 \otimes P_2 \models Q$, there exist Q_1 and Q_2 that satisfy the conditions of Rule 2.*

Proof of Theorem 2: By choosing P_1 and P_2 as Q_1 and Q_2, the proof is trivial. □

5.4 Dependency Refinement

Both Rule 1 and Rule 2 share the same intuition: using Conditions C3 and C3' to prevent circular reasoning by showing that at least one component will take the first step voluntarily. However, naive application of these rules will fail to establish system properties in many cases where the interaction between the two components of a system has more than two steps which form a dependency cycle. Suppose that a system has two components, M_1 and M_2, as shown in Figure 3(a). The property of M_1 (or M_2, respectively), Q_1 (or Q_2), is actually the conjunction of a set of sub-properties, Q_{11}, Q_{12}, and Q_{13} (or Q_{21}, Q_{22}, and Q_{23}), each of which asserts on a step of the interaction. The circular dependency among Q_1 and Q_2, in fact, consists of more complicated dependencies among Q_{11}, Q_{12}, Q_{13}, Q_{21}, Q_{22}, and Q_{23} as shown in Figure 3(b). If Q_1 and Q_2 are used straightforwardly in Rule 1 (or Rule 2, respectively), C3 (or C3') does not hold since the left-hand side of C3 (or C3') implies the sub-properties of Q_1 or Q_2 asserted on the first step of the interaction, but not those asserted on the other steps.

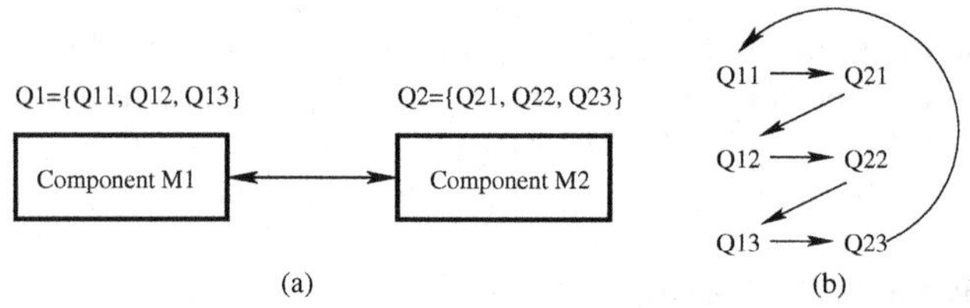

Fig. 3. A motivating example for dependency refinement

Our solution to the above problem is dependency refinement: (1) decompose the component properties into their sub-properties, derive the refined dependency graph of the sub-properties, and identify the cycles in the refined graph; (2) apply C3 or C3' to break each of the identified cycles; (3) if all cycles in the refined dependency graph can be broken, the compositional reasoning is sound and the component properties can be established. For the example in Figure 3, suppose that we can establish C3 for Q_{11}, i.e., M_1 takes the first step. We can then conclude that the component properties Q_1 and Q_2 hold since there is a single cycle. Currently, manual efforts are required to decompose the component properties into their sub-properties, refine the dependency graph, and identify the first sub-property in a dependency cycle for which the conditions C3 or C3' should be checked first. We are exploring heuristics that can automate these steps.

6 Case Studies

Our approach to compositional reasoning for co-verification has been applied to networked sensors with hardware specified in Verilog and software specified in xUML following the asynchronous interleaving message-passing semantics or in C following the asynchronous event-driven call-return semantics. In this section, we illustrate our

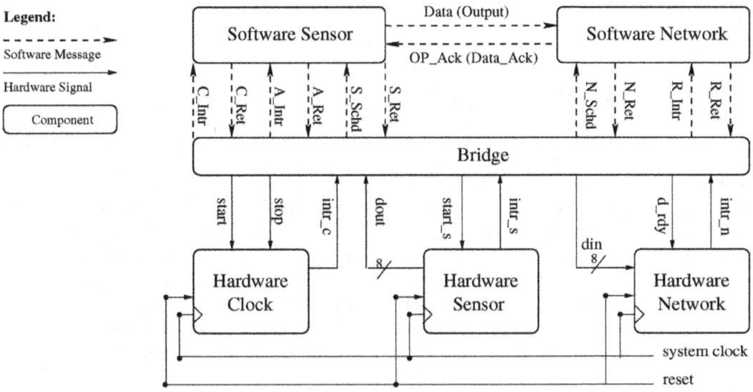

Fig. 4. Architecture of a sensor instance with software in xUML and hardware in Verilog

approach with its application to a sensor instance with software in xUML. The approach is applied to sensor instances with software in C the same way. (Translation of sensor software in C to S/R currently requires manual efforts due to the unfinished translator.)

The architecture of the sensor instance with software in xUML is shown in Figure 4. Its software is partitioned into two components: software sensor (*S-SEN*) and software network (*S-NET*) and its hardware is partition into three components: hardware clock (*H-CLK*), hardware sensor (*H-SEN*), and hardware network (*H-NET*). The software components execute on a generic processor while the hardware components are implemented as application specific integrated circuits (ASICs). The software and hardware components are connected through a bridge component (*BRDG*) which interacts with the software components following the software semantics and with the hardware components following the hardware semantics and propagates events such as software messages and hardware interrupts across the hardware/software boundary.

The property shown in Figure 5 is to be verified on the entire system. This property

Repeated (H-NET.flag = true); **Repeated** (H-NET.flag = false);

Fig. 5. Repeated transmission property

asserts that the sensor system transmits on the network repeatedly. Repeated setting and clearing of a flag in *H_NET* indicates repeated transmission. The system property is manually decomposed into the properties of its components as shown in Figure 6. Note that as *S-SEN* and *S-NET* are composed, the *Output* (or *Output_Ack*, respectively) message type of *S-SEN* is mapped to the *Data* (or *Data_Ack*) message type of *S-NET*. The *ADC.Pending* variable in *S-SEN* and the *RFM.Pending* variable in *S-NET* are mapped to the *start_s* signal in *H-SEN* and the *d_rdy* signal in *H-NET* via BRDG, respectively. *STQ.Empty* (or *NTQ.Empty*, respectively) is a variable in *S-SEN* (or *S-NET*).

We verify the system property with compositional reasoning in two steps. In Step 1, we establish the property of the composite component *S&B* that is composed of *S-SEN*,

Property of S-SEN, P_{SS}*:*
$P_{SS}(1)$:
IfRepeatedly (C_Intr) **Repeatedly** (Output);
$P_{SS}(2)$:
After (C_Intr) **Eventually** (C_Ret); **After** (A_Intr) **Eventually** (A_Ret); **After** (S_Schd) **Eventually** (S_Ret);
$P_{SS}(3)$:
After (Output) **Never** (Output) **UnlessAfter** (OP_Ack);
Never (Output) **UnlessAfter** (S_Schd); **After** (Output) **Never** (Output) **UnlessAfter**(S_Schd);
Never (S_Ret) **UnlessAfter** (OP_Ack); **After** (S_Ret) **Never** (S_Ret) **UnlessAfter**(OP_Ack);
Never (C_Ret) **UnlessAfter** (C_Intr); **After** (C_Ret) **Never** (C_Ret) **UnlessAfter** (C_Intr);
Never (A_Ret) **UnlessAfter** (A_Intr); **After** (A_Ret) **Never** (A_Ret) **UnlessAfter** (A_Intr);
After (ADC.Pending) **Never** (ADC.Pending) **UnlessAfter** (A_Ret);
Never (S_Ret) **UnlessAfter** (S_Schd); **After** (S_Ret) **Never** (S_Ret) **UnlessAfter** (S_Schd);
After (STQ.Empty=False) **Never** (STQ.Empty=False) **UnlessAfter**(S_Ret);

Property of S-NET, P_{SN}*:*
$P_{SN}(1)$:
IfRepeatedly (Data) **Repeatedly** (RFM.Pending); **IfRepeatedly** (Data) **Repeatedly** (RFM.Pending=False);
$P_{SN}(2)$:
After (Data) **Eventually**(Data_Ack); **After** (N_Schd) **Eventually** (N_Ret); **After** (R_Intr) **Eventually** (R_Ret);
$P_{SN}(3)$:
Never (Data_Ack) **UnlessAfter** (Data); **After** (Data_Ack) **Never** (Data_Ack) **UnlessAfter** (Data);
Never (N_Ret) **UnlessAfter** (N_Schd); **After** (N_Ret) **Never** (N_Ret) **UnlessAfter** (N_Schd);
After (NTQ.Empty=False) **Never**(NTQ.Empty=False) **UnlessAfter**(N_Ret);
Never (R_Ret) **UnlessAfter** (R_Intr); **After** (R_Ret) **Never** (R_Ret) **UnlessAfter** (R_Intr);
After (RFM.Pending) **Never** (RFM.Pending) **UnlessAfter** (R_Ret);

Property of BRDG, P_B*:*
$P_B(1)$:
IfRepeatedly (intr_c) **Repeatedly** (C_Intr);
IfRepeatedly (RFM.Pending) **Repeatedly** (d_rdy);
IfRepeatedly (RFM.Pending=False) **Repeatedly** (d_rdy=False);
$P_B(2)$:
After (ADC.Pending) **Eventually** (A_Intr); **After** (STQ.Empty=False) **Eventually** (S_Schd);
After (NTQ.Empty=False) **Eventually** (N_Schd); **After** (RFM.Pending) **Eventually** (R_Intr);
$P_B(3)$:
After (C_Intr) **Never** (C_Intr + A_Intr + S_Schd + N_Schd + R_Intr) **UnlessAfter** (C_Ret);
Never (A_Intr) **UnlessAfter** (ADC.Pending);
After (A_Ret) **Never** (A_Intr) **UnlessAfter** (ADC.Pending);
After (A_Intr) **Never** (C_Intr + A_Intr + S_Schd + N_Schd + R_Intr) **UnlessAfter** (A_Ret);
Never (S_Schd) **UnlessAfter** (STQ.Empty=False);
After (S_Ret) **Never** (S_Schd) **UnlessAfter** (STQ.Empty=False);
After (S_Schd) **Never** (C_Intr + A_Intr + S_Schd + N_Schd + R_Intr) **UnlessAfter** (S_Ret);
Never (N_Schd) **UnlessAfter** (NTQ.Empty=False);
After (N_Ret) **Never** (N_Schd) **UnlessAfter** (NTQ.Empty=False);
After (N_Schd) **Never** (C_Intr + A_Intr + S_Schd + N_Schd + R_Intr) **UnlessAfter** (N_Ret);
Never (R_Intr) **UnlessAfter** (RFM.Pending);
After (R_Ret) **Never** (R_Intr) **UnlessAfter** (RFM.Pending);
After (R_Intr) **Never** (C_Intr + A_Intr + S_Schd + N_Schd + R_Intr) **UnlessAfter** (R_Ret);

Property of H-CLK, P_{HC}*:*
$P_{HC}(1)$: **Repeatedly** (intr_c);

Property of H-SEN, P_{HS}*:*
$P_{HS}(1)$:
After (start_s) **Eventually** (intr_s);
Never (intr_s) **UnlessAfter** (start_s); **After** (intr_s) **Never** (intr_s) **UnlessAfter** (start_s);

Property of H-NET, P_{HN}*:*
$P_{HN}(1)$:
IfRepeatedly (d_rdy) **Repeatedly** (flag); **IfRepeatedly** (d_rdy=False) **Repeatedly** (flag=False);
$P_{HN}(2)$:
After (d_rdy) **Eventually** (intr_n);
Never (intr_n) **UnlessAfter** (d_rdy); **After** (intr_n) **Never** (intr_n) **UnlessAfter** (d_rdy);

Fig. 6. Component properties and their sub-properties

S-NET, and *BRDG*. In this step, we apply Rule 2 since although not shown in Figure 4, *S-SEN*, *S-NET*, and *BRDG* share a scheduler that schedules the execution of the xUML object instances in each component. The scheduler is inserted when the xUML model is translated into S/R. The properties of *S-SEN*, *S-NET*, and *BRDG* can be directly verified by assuming the properties of the others hold. (*BRDG* also has assumptions on the hardware components.) Therefore, Condition C1' holds. Since we define the property of *S&B* as the conjunction of the properties of its sub-components, Condition C2' holds trivially. The dependencies among the sub-properties of the component properties are shown in Figure 7. It can be observed that on the component property level, there is

$$
\begin{aligned}
&P_{SS}(1) \rightarrow \{P_{SN}(2), P_{SN}(3), P_B(2), P_B(3)\}\\
&P_{SS}(2) \rightarrow \{P_{SN}(2), P_{SN}(3), P_B(3)\}\\
&P_{SS}(3) \rightarrow \{P_{SN}(3), P_B(3)\}\\
\\
&P_{SN}(1) \rightarrow \{P_{SS}(3), P_B(2), P_B(3)\}\\
&P_{SN}(2) \rightarrow \{P_{SS}(3), P_B(3)\}\\
&P_{SN}(3) \rightarrow \{P_{SS}(3), P_B(3)\}\\
\\
&P_B(1) \rightarrow \{P_{SS}(2), P_{SS}(3), P_{HS}(1), P_{HN}(2)\}\\
&P_B(2) \rightarrow \{P_{SS}(2), P_{SS}(3), P_{SN}(2), P_{SN}(3), P_{HS}(1), P_{HN}(2)\}\\
&P_B(3) \rightarrow \{P_{SS}(3), P_{SN}(3), P_{HS}(1), P_{HN}(2)\}
\end{aligned}
$$

Fig. 7. Dependencies among component sub-properties

a dependency cycle among the property P_{SS} of *S-SEN*, the property P_{SN} of *S-NET*, and the property P_B of *BRDG*. If P_{SS}, P_{SN}, and P_B are used straightforwardly in Rule 2, Condition C3' does not hold. However, if we conduct dependency refinement and examine the dependencies among the component sub-properties, we can successfully establish the property of *S&B* using Rule 2. $P_{SS}(3)$, $P_{SN}(3)$, and $P_B(3)$ forms a dependency cycle on which C3' holds since $P_{SS}(3)$, $P_{SN}(3)$, and $P_B(3)$ are safety properties. Thus, $P_{SS}(3)$, $P_{SN}(3)$, and $P_B(3)$ holds. Following the dependencies backward, we can show all other sub-properties hold. Therefore, the property of *S&B* holds.

In Step 2, we derive the system property by applying Rule 1 to *S&B*, *H-CLK*, *H-SEN*, and *H-NET* since these components do not share any sub-component. The properties of *H-CLK*, *H-SEN*, and *H-NET* are verified directly, thus C1 holds. Since the system property is implied by $P_{HC}(1)$, $P_B(1)$, $P_{SS}(1)$, $P_{SN}(1)$, and $P_{HN}(1)$, C2 holds. There is no need to check C3 since there are no circular dependencies among the properties of *S&B*, *H-CLK*, *H-SEN*, and *H-NET*. Therefore, the system property holds.

If the system property is verified using the straightforward translation-based co-verification approach in [19]: translating the entire system into S/R and verify it using COSPAN, 50800 seconds and 730.54 megabytes are needed. The time and memory usages for establishing C1' in Step 1 and C1 in Step 2: model checking the component properties, are shown in Table 1. In Step 1, C2' holds trivially and since the sub-properties for which C3' must be checked are safety properties, C3' also holds trivially. In step 2, C2 can be established by checking the system property on the component

Table 1. Time and memory usages for model checking the component properties

Components	Time (Seconds)	Memory (MBytes)
S-SEN	18.66	8.49
S-NET	18.06	9.11
BRDG	86.05	15.83
H-CLK	0.21	3.38
H-SEN	0.22	3.38
H-NET	0.22	3.38

properties using 0.1 seconds and 3.4 megabytes. It can be observed that our component-based approach to co-verification achieved order-of-magnitude reduction on verification complexities over the translation-based approach in verifying this sensor instance.

7 Conclusions and Future Work

In this paper, we have presented a novel approach to compositional reasoning for co-verification. Its key contributions include integration of compositional reasoning for hardware and software based on translation, development of a new compositional reasoning rule allowing components to share sub-components, and extending applicability of compositional reasoning rules via dependency refinement. Case studies on networked sensors have shown that our approach is very effective. Future work will be focused on automation of compositional reasoning with heuristics that explore architectural patterns of embedded systems to formulate system and component properties, decompose system properties into component properties, and facilitate dependency refinement.

References

1. Clarke, E.M., Emerson, E.A.: Design and synthesis of synchronization skeletons using branching time temporal logic. In: Proc. of Logic of Programs Workshop. (1981)
2. Quielle, J.P., Sifakis, J.: Specification and verification of concurrent systems in CESAR. In: Proc. of Symposium on Programming. (1982)
3. Chandy, K.M., Misra, J.: Proofs of networks of processes. IEEE Transaction on Software Engineering **7**(4) (1981)
4. Jones, C.B.: Development methods for computer programs including a notion of interference. PhD thesis, Oxford University (1981)
5. Abadi, M., Lamport, L.: Conjoining specifications. TOPLAS **17**(3) (1995)
6. Alur, R., Henzinger, T.: Reactive modules. FMSD **15**(1) (1999)
7. McMillan, K.L.: A methodology for hardware verification using compositional model checking. Cadence Design Systems Technical Reports (1999)
8. Amla, N., Emerson, E.A., Namjoshi, K.S., Trefler, R.: Assume-guarantee based compositional reasoning for synchronous timing diagrams. In: Proc. of TACAS. (2001)
9. de Roever, W.P., de Boer, F., Hanneman, U., Hooman, J., Lakhnech, Y., Poel, M., Zwiers, J.: Concurrency Verification: Introduction to Compositional and Non-compositional Proof Methods. Cambridge University Press (2001)
10. Hill, J., Szewczyk, R., Woo, A., Hollar, S., Culler, D.E., Pister, K.S.J.: System architecture directions for networked sensors. In: Proc. of ASPLOS. (2000)

11. Mellor, S.J., Balcer, M.J.: Executable UML: A Foundation for Model Driven Architecture. Addison Wesley (2002)
12. Namjoshi, K.S., Trefler, R.J.: On the completeness of compositional reasoning. In: Proc. of CAV. (2000)
13. Kurshan, R.P.: Computer-Aided Verification of Coordinating Processes: The Automata-Theoretic Approach. Princeton University Press (1994)
14. Alpern, B., Schneider, F.: Defining liveness. Information Processing Letters **21**(4) (1985)
15. Hardin, R.H., Har'El, Z., Kurshan., R.P.: COSPAN. In: Proc. of CAV. (1996)
16. Kurshan, R.P.: FormalCheck User Manual. Cadence (1998)
17. Xie, F., Levin, V., Browne, J.C.: Objectcheck: A model checking tool for executable object-oriented software system designs. In: Proc. of FASE. (2002)
18. Xie, F., Browne, J.C., Kurshan, R.P.: Translation-based compositional reasoning for software systems. In: Proc. of FME. (2003)
19. Xie, F., Song, X., Chung, H., Nandi, R.: Translation-based co-verification. In: Proc. of MEMOCODE. (2005)

Learning-Based Symbolic Assume-Guarantee Reasoning with Automatic Decomposition*

Wonhong Nam and Rajeev Alur

Dept. of Computer and Information Science
University of Pennsylvania
{wnam, alur}@cis.upenn.edu

Abstract. Compositional reasoning aims to improve scalability of verification tools by reducing the original verification task into subproblems. The simplification is typically based on the assume-guarantee reasoning principles, and requires decomposing the system into components as well as identifying adequate environment assumptions for components. One recent approach to automatic derivation of adequate assumptions is based on the L^* algorithm for active learning of regular languages. In this paper, we present a fully automatic approach to compositional reasoning by automating the decomposition step using an algorithm for hypergraph partitioning for balanced clustering of variables. We also propose heuristic improvements to the assumption identification phase. We report on an implementation based on NuSMV, and experiments that study the effectiveness of automatic decomposition and the overall savings in the computational requirements of symbolic model checking.

1 Introduction

To enhance the scalability of analysis tools, compositional verification suggests a "divide and conquer" strategy to reduce the verification task into simpler subtasks. The assume-guarantee based compositional reasoning to verify that a system S satisfies a requirement φ typically consists of the following three steps: (1) *System Decomposition*: decompose the system S into components $M_1, \cdots, M_n$, (2) *Assumption Discovery*: find an environment assumption A_i for each component M_i, and (3) *Assumption Checking*: verify that the assumptions A_i are adequate for proving or disproving the satisfaction of φ by S. The last step involves a number of verification subtasks, and while the exact nature of these subtasks depends on the specific compositional rule used, each subtask involves only one of the components M_i, and can be implemented using model checkers as it can be computationally less demanding than the original verification task.

The success of compositional reasoning depends on discovering appropriate assumptions for all the components so that the assumption checking phase will succeed, and one promising approach for automating this step is based on learning [9,5,3,11]. If a component M_i communicates with its environment via a set X_i

* This research was partially supported by ARO grant DAAD19-01-1-0473, and NSF grants ITR/SY 0121431 and CCR0306382.

S. Graf and W. Zhang (Eds.): ATVA 2006, LNCS 4218, pp. 170–185, 2006.

of boolean variables, then the assumption A_i can be viewed as a language over the alphabet 2^{X_i}, and the assumption checking constraints impose a lower and an upper bound on this language. The assumptions are constructed by adopting the L^* algorithm for learning a regular language using membership and equivalence queries [4,17]. The membership query (whether a trace belongs to the desired assumption), and the equivalence query (whether the current assumption is adequate for the assumption checking phase) are implemented by invoking a model checker.

In this paper, we develop a fully automated framework for assume-guarantee based compositional reasoning by automating the decomposition phase also. While a modular description of a system can suggest a natural decomposition, an automated approach may be necessary for a variety of reasons: the description of a system, particularly when compiled from a high-level language to the input language of a model checker, is often monolithic; the decomposition suggested by the syntactic description need not be the one suitable for compositional reasoning, either in terms of the number of components or the partitioning of functionality among components. Our solution is based on an algorithm for partitioning of hypergraphs [14,13]. Given a system S consisting of a set X of variables, and a desired number n of components, we partition the set X into n disjoint subsets $X_1, \cdots, X_n$ so that each set X_i contains approximately the same number of variables while keeping the number of communication variables (i.e. variables whose update depends on or affects a variable in another cluster) small. Each such variable partition X_i corresponds to a component M_i that controls these variables.

We describe an implementation of the automated compositional reasoning using parts of the state-of-the-art symbolic model checker NuSMV [7]. In our application, the alphabet size of the language being learnt itself grows exponentially with the number of communication variables. Consequently, in [3] we have developed a symbolic implementation of the L^* algorithm where the data structures for recording the membership information, and the assumption automaton, are maintained compactly using binary decision diagrams (BDDs) [6]. As described in Section 5, we have enhanced our implementation with several additional heuristics, in particular, one aimed at early falsification, and one aimed at deleting edges from the conjecture machine to force rapid convergence without violating the correctness of the learning algorithm.

In Section 6, we report on some examples where the original model contains around 100 variables, and the computational requirements of NuSMV are significant. The experiments are aimed at understanding the following tradeoffs: (1) how does our strategy for automatic decomposition compare with respect to the experiments we had performed earlier with manually chosen decomposition? (2) what is the impact of the number of components on the overall computational requirements? (3) how do the revised and more general assume-guarantee rule, and the new heuristics impact the performance? and (4) how does the integrated tool, *automatic symbolic compositional verifier* (ASCV), compare with NuSMV? It turns out the automatic decomposition strategy works pretty well, and manual (or structure-directed) decomposition seems unnecessary. No conclusions can be drawn regarding whether small or large number of components should be preferred in this approach. In terms of comparisons of the integrated tool with NuSMV, excellent gains are observed in some cases either reducing the required time or memory by two or three orders of magnitude, or converting infeasible problems into feasible ones. However, in some cases the number of states of the assumption is too large, and our learning-based strategy performs poorly.

Related Work. While program slicing [20] is a technique to extract, from an original program, program statements relevant to a particular computation, compositional verification is to reduce a large verification problem into smaller subproblems. Compositional reasoning using assume-guarantee rules has a long history in formal verification literature (c.f. [19,12,1,2,16]). The use of learning algorithms for automatic discovery of assumptions was first reported in [9,5], and has been further developed by many researchers: [18] considers the problem of substituting one component with another and how to reuse the conjecture machines computed in the original version while checking properties of the revised version; [8] reports several experiments to test whether assumptions with small DFA (deterministic finite automaton) representations exist. Our work is based on the symbolic implementation of learning-based compositional reasoning in [3]. The contributions of this paper include an automatic decomposition strategy, use of a more general assume-guarantee rule that is applicable to multiple components, heuristic improvements in computing the conjecture assumptions, and experiments to study several tradeoffs.

2 Preliminaries

We formalize the notions of a symbolic transition system and decomposition into its modules, and explain the assume-guarantee rule we use in this paper.

2.1 Symbolic Transition Systems

In the following, for any set of boolean variables X, we will denote the set of primed variables of X as $X' = \{x' \mid x \in X\}$. For a valuation q for X, q' denotes the valuation for X' such that $q'(x') = q(x)$ for every $x' \in X'$. A predicate $\varphi(X)$ is a boolean formula over X, and for a valuation q of variables in X, we write $\varphi(q)$ to mean that q satisfies the formula φ. We denote, given a predicate φ, a set of unprimed variables appearing in φ as $Var(\varphi)$.

A *symbolic transition system*, shortly a transition system, is a tuple $S(X, Init, T)$ with the following components:

- X is a finite set of boolean *variables*,
- $Init(X) = \bigwedge_{x \in X} Init_x(X)$ is an *initial predicate* over X, where $Init_x(X)$ is an initial predicate for the variable x,
- $T(X, X') = \bigwedge_{x \in X} T_x(X, X')$ is a *transition predicate* over $X \cup X'$ (X' represents a set of variables encoding the successor states), where $T_x(X, X')$ is a transition predicate for the variable x.

A *state* q of S is a valuation of the variables in X; i.e. $q : X \to \{true, false\}$. Let Q denote the set of all states q of S. For a state q over a set X of variables, let $q[Y]$, where $Y \subseteq X$ denote the valuation over Y obtained by restricting q to Y. The semantics of a transition system is defined in terms of the set of runs it exhibits. A *run* of $S(X, Init, T)$ is a sequence $q_0 q_1 \cdots$ where every $q_i \in Q$, such that $Init(q_0)$ holds, and for every $i \geq 0$, $T(q_i, q'_{i+1})$ holds. A *safety property* for a transition system $S(X, Init, T)$ is a predicate over X. For a transition system $S(X, Init, T)$ and a safety property $\varphi(X)$, we define $S \models \varphi$ if, for each run $q_0 q_1 \cdots$ of S, $\varphi(q_i)$ holds for each $i \geq 0$. Finally, given a transition system $S(X, Init, T)$ and a safety property $\varphi(X)$, an *invariant checking problem* is to check $S \models \varphi$.

2.2 Decomposition into Modules

A *module* is a tuple $M(X_M, I_M, O_M, Init_M, T_M)$ with the following components:

- X_M is a finite set of boolean variables controlled by the module M,
- I_M is a finite set of boolean *input variables* that the module reads from its environment; I_M is disjoint from X_M,
- $O_M \subseteq X_M$ is a finite set of boolean *output variables* that are observable to the environment of M; let IO_M denote $I_M \cup O_M$,
- $Init_M(X_M, I_M)$ is an initial predicate over $X_M \cup I_M$,
- $T_M(X_M, I_M, X'_M)$ is a transition predicate over $X_M \cup I_M \cup X'_M$.

Given modules $M_1, \cdots, M_n$, where each $M_i = (X_{M_i}, I_{M_i}, O_{M_i}, Init_{M_i}, T_{M_i})$, we can compose them if for every i, X_{M_i} is disjoint from $X_{M_j} (j \neq i)$. We denote this composition as $M_1 \| \cdots \| M_n$, and a set of all input variables and output variables as IO (i.e. $IO = \bigcup_i IO_{M_i}$). As a symbolic transition system, the semantics for $M_1 \| \cdots \| M_n$ is defined in terms of the set of runs it exhibits. A *run* of $M_1 \| \cdots \| M_n$ is a sequence $q_0 q_1 \cdots$, where each q_i is a state over $X_{M_1} \cup \cdots \cup X_{M_n}$, such that for every $1 \leq j \leq n$, $Init_{M_j}(q_0[X_{M_j}], q_0[I_{M_j}])$ holds and for every $i \geq 0$ and $1 \leq j \leq n$, $T_{M_j}(q_i[X_{M_j}], q_i[I_{M_j}], q'_{i+1}[X'_{M_j}])$ holds. Again, given a composition of modules $M_1 \| \cdots \| M_n$ and a safety property φ over $X_{M_1} \cup \cdots \cup X_{M_n}$, we define $M_1 \| \cdots \| M_n \models \varphi$ if for every run $q_0 q_1 \cdots$ of $M_1 \| \cdots \| M_n$, $\varphi(q_i)$ holds for every $i \geq 0$.

Given a symbolic transition system $S(X, Init, T)$ and a set $Y \subseteq X$ of variables, we define a module $M[S, Y]$, shortly $M[Y]$, as a tuple $(X_{M[Y]}, I_{M[Y]}, O_{M[Y]}, Init_{M[Y]}, T_{M[Y]})$ as follows:

- $X_{M[Y]} = Y$,
- $Init_{M[Y]} = \bigwedge_{x \in Y} Init_x(X)$ where each $Init_x(X)$ is acquired from S,
- $T_{M[Y]} = \bigwedge_{x \in Y} T_x(X, X')$ where each $T_x(X, X')$ is also obtained from S,
- $I_{M[Y]} = \{x \in X \setminus Y \mid x \in Var(Init_{M[Y]}) \cup Var(T_{M[Y]})\}$,
- $O_{M[Y]} = \{x \in Y \mid \exists y \in X \setminus Y.\ x \in Var(Init_y) \cup Var(T_y)\}$.

Now, we can decompose a transition system $S(X, Init, T)$ into modules $M[X_1]$, $\cdots, M[X_n]$ by partitioning X into $X_1, \cdots, X_n$ where $X = \bigcup_i X_i$ and every X_i is disjoint from each other. In addition, we can denote this decomposition as

$S \stackrel{dec}{=} M[X_1]\|\cdots\|M[X_n]$ using the composition operator $\|$, since every X_i is disjoint from each other. For the sake of simplicity, we will use $=$ instead of $\stackrel{dec}{=}$.

For a transition system $S(X, \mathit{Init}, T)$ decomposed into $M[X_1], \cdots, M[X_n]$ where each $M[X_i] = (X_{M[X_i]}, I_{M[X_i]}, O_{M[X_i]}, \mathit{Init}_{M[X_i]}, T_{M[X_i]})$, each run of S is obviously a run of $M[X_1]\|\cdots\|M[X_n]$ and each run of $M[X_1]\|\cdots\|M[X_n]$ is also a run of S, since $X = \bigcup_i X_i$, and *Init* and T of S are equivalent to the conjunction of every $\mathit{Init}_{M[X_i]}$ and $T_{M[X_i]}$, respectively. Finally, given $S(X, \mathit{Init}, T)$ and a partition of X into disjoint subsets $X_1, \cdots, X_n$, $M[X_1]\|\cdots\|M[X_n] \models \varphi$ iff $S \models \varphi$.

2.3 Assume-Guarantee Rule

Given a module $M(X_M, I_M, O_M, \mathit{Init}_M, T_M)$, a *run* of M is, similarly with a run of a transition system, a sequence $q_0 q_1 \cdots$ where every q_i is a state over $X_M \cup I_M$ such that $\mathit{Init}(q_0[X_M], q_0[I_M])$ holds and for every $i \geq 0$, $T(q_i[X_M], q_i[I_M], q'_{i+1}[X'_M])$ holds. For a run $q_0 q_1 \cdots$ of M, the *trace* is a sequence $q_0[IO_M] q_1[IO_M] \cdots$. Let us denote the set of all the traces of M as $L(M)$, and the complement of the set as $L^C(M)$ (formally, $L^C(M) = Q_M^{IO*} \setminus L(M)$ where Q_M^{IO} is a set of all the states over IO_M). For a trace set L over a variable set IO_M and a safety property φ over IO_M, we can extend the notion of $\models$ to trace sets as following: $L \models \varphi$ if, for every trace $q_0 q_1 \cdots \in L$, $\varphi(q_i)$ holds for every $i \geq 0$. In addition, the composition operator $\|$ can be extend to trace sets which have the same alphabet (i.e. the same set of input/output variables) as following: for L_1 and L_2 with the same I/O variable set, $L_1 \| L_2 = L_1 \cap L_2$.

Now, we use the following assume-guarantee rule to prove that a composition of modules, $M_1\|\cdots\|M_n$ satisfies a safety property φ over IO where for every module A_i, IO_{A_i} equals to IO of $M_1\|\cdots\|M_n$ ($IO = \bigcup_i IO_{M_i}$).

$$\frac{\begin{array}{lr} M_1\|A_1 \models \varphi, \cdots, M_n\|A_n \models \varphi & (\mathbf{Pr1}) \\ L^C(A_1)\|\cdots\|L^C(A_n) \models \varphi & (\mathbf{Pr2}) \end{array}}{M_1\|\cdots\|M_n \models \varphi}$$

The rule above says that if there exist assumption modules $A_1, \cdots, A_n$ such that for each i, the composition of M_i and A_i is safe (i.e. satisfies the property φ) and the composition of the complements of every A_i satisfies φ, then $M_1\|\cdots\|M_n$ satisfies φ. Intuitively, the first premise **Pr1** makes every assumption strong enough to keep each M_i safe, and the second premise **Pr2** makes the assumptions weak enough to cover all the traces which can violate φ (i.e., for every trace violating φ, **Pr2** requires at least one assumption to contain it). This rule is sound and complete [5]. Our aim is to construct such assumptions $A_1, \cdots, A_n$ to show that $M_1\|\cdots\|M_n$ satisfies φ, and the smaller assumptions can save the more in terms of searching state space.

Given a symbolic transition system $S(X, \mathit{Init}, T)$, an integer $n \geq 2$ and a safety property φ, the *model-checking problem* we consider in this paper is, instead of checking $S \models \varphi$, to partition X into disjoint subsets $X_1, \cdots, X_n$, and to check $M[X_1]\|\cdots\|M[X_n] \models \varphi$ using the above assume-guarantee rule. Note that we are assuming that the safety property φ is a predicate over IO, but this is not a restriction: to check a property that refers to private variables of a module, we can simply declare them as output variables. Finally, the challenges of this paper are (1) how to find a variable partition and (2) how to find assumptions satisfying both of the above premises.

3 Automatic Partitioning

Automatic partitioning is, given a transition system $S(X, \mathit{Init}, T)$ and an integer $n \geq 2$, to decompose X into disjoint subsets $X_1, \cdots, X_n$, and there exist about $n^{|X|}$ possible partitions. Among them, we want a partition to minimize memory usage for assumption construction and commitment in our assume-guarantee reasoning. The memory usage, however, cannot be formulated. Therefore, we roughly fix our goal to find a partition that has small number of variables required in each step of the assume-guarantee reasoning because a state space for each step is exponential in the number of variables. More precisely, the alternative goal is to find a partition that minimizes $max_i(|X_i \cup IO_{M_i}|)$ where IO_{M_i} is the set of I/O variables of module $M[X_i]$. This partitioning problem is NP-complete.

We reduce our problem into a well-known partitioning problem called the *hypergraph partitioning problem* which can be used for directed-graph partitioning. For the reduction, we relax our goal as following; given a transition system $S(X, \mathit{Init}, T)$, and an integer $n \geq 2$, our automatic partitioning is to find a partition decomposing X into n disjoint subsets such that (1) the number of variables in each module is in some bound (near even distribution) and (2) modules corresponding to each variable subset have as few input/output variables as possible.

A *hypergraph* $G(V, E)$ is defined as a set of vertices V and a set of *hyperedges* E where each hyperedge is a set of arbitrary number of vertices in V. Thus, an ordinary graph is a special case of hypergraphs such that every edge is a pair of two vertices. Given a hypergraph $G(V, E)$ and an overall load imbalance tolerance $c \geq 1.0$, the *k-way hypergraph partitioning problem* is to partition the set V into k disjoint subsets, $V_1, \cdots, V_k$ such that the number of vertices in each set V_i is bounded by $|V|/(c \cdot k) \leq |V_i| \leq |V|(c/k)$, and the size of *hyperedge-cut* of the partition is minimized where the hyperedge-cut is a set of hyperedges e such that there exist v_1 and v_2 in e which belong to different partitions.

Now, our partitioning problem can be reduced to the k-way hypergraph partitioning problem. Given a transition system $S(X, \mathit{Init}, T)$, we construct a hypergraph $G(V, E)$ as follows. $V = \{v_x \mid x \in X\}$. For each $x \in X$, we have a hyperedge e_x that immediately contains the corresponding vertex v_x and also vertices v_y such that $x \in \mathit{Var}(\mathit{Init}_y) \cup \mathit{Var}(T_y)$. Intuitively, e_x represents the corresponding variable x and all the variables to read x. Finally, E is the set of all e_x. Then, after hypergraph partitioning, $V_1, \cdots, V_k$ correspond with $X_1, \cdots, X_n$ in our problem. If we have a hyperedge e_x in the hyperedge-cut (let us assume that the corresponding vertex v_x belongs to V_i), then there exist some vertex $v_y \in e_x$ which belongs to $V_j (i \neq j)$. Since y is dependent on x but they are in different partitions, x should be an input variable of $M[X_j]$ and also an output variable of $M[X_i]$. For the overall load imbalance tolerance c, a large value for c can reduce the number of I/O variables but it causes larger imbalance among each module. On the other hand, a small value for c increases I/O variables. Therefore, we perform partitioning with six different values (i.e. 1.0, 1.2, $\cdots$, 2.0) and pick the partition that has the minimum value as $max_i(|X_i \cup IO_{M_i}|)$.

Many researchers have studied this problem and developed tools, and among them we use hMETIS [14]. hMETIS is one of the state-of-the-art hypergraph partitioning tools which uses a multilevel k-way partitioning algorithm. The multilevel partitioning algorithm has three phases; (1) it first reduces the size of a given hypergraph by collapsing vertices and edges until the hypergraph is small enough (*coarsening phase*), (2) the algorithm partitions it into k sub-hypergraphs (*initial partitioning phase*), and (3) the algorithm uncoarsens them to construct a partition for the original hypergraph (*uncoarsening and refinement phase*). Experiments on a large number of hypergraphs arising in various domains including VLSI, databases and data mining show that hMETIS produces partitions that are consistently better than those produced by other widely used algorithms, such as KL [15] and FM [10]. In addition, it is so fast as to produce high quality bisections of hypergraphs with 100,000 vertices in 3 minutes [13].

4 Learning Assumptions

In this section, we define the *weakest safe assumption tuple* which is a witness for the truth of a given invariant, and briefly explain an algorithm for learning regular languages, called *L^* algorithm*. We then establish that our verification algorithm based on the L^* algorithm converges to the weakest safe assumption tuple or, before that, concludes with a witness for the invariant.

4.1 Weakest Safe Assumptions

After partitioning, our aim is, given a set of modules $M[X_1], \cdots, M[X_n]$ (obtained from automatic partitioning) and a safety property $\varphi(IO)$, to verify that $M[X_1] \| \cdots \| M[X_n] \models \varphi$ by finding assumption modules $A_1, \cdots, A_n$ that satisfy both premises of our assume-guarantee rule. A tuple $(A_1, \cdots, A_n)$ of assumptions is called a *safe assumption tuple* (ST) if the assumptions $A_1, \cdots, A_n$ satisfy **Pr1**, and a tuple $(A_1, \cdots, A_n)$ of assumptions is called an *appropriate assumption tuple* (AT) if the assumptions $A_1, \cdots, A_n$ satisfy both of **Pr1** and **Pr2**. For every $M[X_i]$, the *weakest safe assumption* W_i is a module such that $M[X_i] \| W_i \models \varphi$ and $L(W_i) \supseteq L(A_i)$ for every A_i such that $M[X_i] \| A_i \models \varphi$. We denote such a tuple $(W_1, \cdots, W_n)$ as the *weakest safe assumption tuple* (WT). Now, we show that the WT is a witness for the truth of $M[X_1] \| \cdots \| M[X_n] \models \varphi$.

Lemma 1. *If $M[X_1] \| \cdots \| M[X_n] \models \varphi$, the WT $(W_1, \cdots, W_n)$ is a witness of $M[X_1] \| \cdots \| M[X_n] \models \varphi$.*

Proof. If $M[X_1] \| \cdots \| M[X_n]$ does indeed satisfy φ, then there exists an AT $(A_1, \cdots, A_n)$ since the composition rule is complete. By definition, $(W_1, \cdots, W_n)$

satisfies **Pr1**. For the above AT $(A_1, \cdots, A_n)$, since for every i, $L^C(W_i) \subseteq L^C(A_i)$ and $L^C(A_1)\|\cdots\|L^C(A_n) \models \varphi$, $L^C(W_1)\|\cdots\|L^C(W_n) \models \varphi$ (**Pr2**). Finally, the WT $(W_1, \cdots, W_n)$ is one of ATs and a witness of $M[X_1]\|\cdots\|M[X_n] \models \varphi$.

Lemma 2. *If $M[X_1]\|\cdots\|M[X_n] \not\models \varphi$, the WT $(W_1, \cdots, W_n)$ is a witness of $M[X_1]\|\cdots\|M[X_n] \not\models \varphi$.*

Proof. If $M[X_1]\|\cdots\|M[X_n]$ does not satisfy φ, then there is no AT; i.e., if an assumption tuple $(A_1, \cdots, A_n)$ satisfies **Pr1**, there exists a trace $\tau \in L^C(A_1)\|\cdots\| L^C(A_n)$ violating φ. Again, since $(W_1, \cdots, W_n)$ satisfies **Pr1** by definition, there exists $\tau \in L^C(W_1)\|\cdots\|L^C(W_n)$ violating φ. For every $(A_1, \cdots, A_n)$ that satisfies **Pr1**, since for every i, $L^C(W_i) \subseteq L^C(A_i)$ and $L^C(W_1)\|\cdots\|L^C(W_n) \subseteq L^C(A_1)\|\cdots\|L^C(A_n)$, the above trace τ violating φ also belongs to $L^C(A_1)\|\cdots\| L^C(A_n)$. Thus, the WT $(W_1, \cdots, W_n)$ is a witness of $M[X_1]\|\cdots\|M[X_n] \not\models \varphi$.

The WT $(W_1, \cdots, W_n)$ can be represented by a tuple of DFAs with the alphabet Q^{IO} (where Q^{IO} is a set of all states over IO) as each $M[X_i]$ is finite. Therefore, we can learn the WT which a witness for truth of $M[X_1]\|\cdots\|M[X_n] \models \varphi$, using the L^* algorithm for learning regular languages.

4.2 L^* Algorithm

The L^* *algorithm* learns an unknown regular language U (let Σ be its alphabet) and generates a minimal DFA that accepts the regular language. This algorithm was introduced by Angluin [4], but we use an improved version by Rivest and Schapire [17]. The algorithm infers the structure of the DFA by asking a teacher, who knows the unknown language, membership and equivalence queries. Membership queries ask whether a given string $\sigma \in \Sigma^*$ is in the language U, and the answer for the queries is yes or no. Equivalence queries ask whether a given conjecture DFA C represents the language U, and the answer is yes or no with a counter-example that is a symmetric difference between $L(C)$ and U.

At any given time, the L^* algorithm has, in order to construct a conjecture machine, information about a finite collection of strings over Σ, classified either as members or non-members of U based on membership queries. This information is maintained in an *observation table* (Rs, Es, Mp) which represents the conjecture DFA; Rs is a set of representative strings for states in the DFA such that each representative string $r_q \in Rs$ for a state q leads from the initial state (uniquely) to the state q, and Es is a set of experiment suffix strings that are used to distinguish states. Mp maps strings σ in $(Rs \cup Rs{\cdot}\Sigma) \cdot Es$ to 1 if σ is in U, and to 0 otherwise. Once a conjecture machine C is built, the algorithm asks an equivalence query. Finally, if the answer is 'yes', it returns the current conjecture DFA C; otherwise, a counter-example $cex \in ((L(C) \setminus U) \cup (U \setminus L(C))$ is provided by the teacher. In the latter case, the algorithm updates the current conjecture using the counter-example cex.

If a teacher for two kinds of queries is provided, the L^* algorithm is guaranteed to construct a minimal DFA for the unknown regular language using only $O(|\Sigma|n^2 + n\log m)$ membership queries and at most $n-1$ equivalence queries, where n is the number of states in the final DFA and m is the length of the longest counter-example provided by the teacher for equivalence queries.

4.3 Automatic Symbolic Compositional Verification

Now, we present our verification algorithm. Given a transition system $S(X, Init, T)$, an invariant property φ, and an integer $n \geq 2$, our *automatic symbolic compositional verification* (ASCV) algorithm decomposes X into n disjoint subsets $X_1, \cdots, X_n$ and then checks $M[X_1] \| \cdots \| M[X_n] \models \varphi$ by learning the WT (weakest safe assumption tuple), which is a witness for the truth of the invariant. For learning the WT, the ASCV algorithm provides teachers who answer membership and equivalence queries, which correspond with the WT $(W_1, \cdots, W_n)$.

Given a string $\tau \in Q^{IO^*}$ and a module $M[X_i]$, a teacher for membership queries answers whether there is an execution of $M[X_i]$ consistent with τ, which violates φ; that is, whether $\tau \in L(W_i)$. The ASCV algorithm constructs a conjecture assumption A_i for each module $M[X_i]$, based on the results of membership queries, and after this phase, it asks an equivalence query. The equivalence query consists of two sub-queries: checking **Pr1** and **Pr2** of the assume-guarantee rule. If a given assumption tuple satisfies both premises, we conclude $S = M[X_1] \| \cdots \| M[X_n] \models \varphi$; otherwise, the teacher produces a counter-example. More precisely, the teacher checking **Pr1** answers, given an assumption A_i for a module $M[X_i]$, whether $M[X_i] \| A_i \models \varphi$; if not, it returns $\tau \in L(A_i)$ violating φ (i.e. $\tau \in L(A_i) \setminus L(W_i)$). The teacher for **Pr2** checks, given $A_1, \cdots, A_n$, whether $L^C(A_1) \| \cdots \| L^C(A_n) \models \varphi$; if not, it returns $\tau \in L^C(A_i)$ for every i which violates φ. For **Pr1** queries, τ is immediately used to update A_i, but for **Pr2** queries, we need an additional analysis. That is, when we execute every $M[X_i]$ corresponding to τ, if every $M[X_i]$ reaches a state violating φ, then τ is a counter-example of the original problem, $S = M[X_1] \| \cdots \| M[X_n] \models \varphi$; otherwise, τ is used to update A_i such that $M[X_i]$ correspondent with A_i does not violate the invariant φ (i.e. $\tau \in L(W_i) \setminus L(A_i)$).

In the ASCV algorithm, since all answers from teachers are always consistent with the WT (for equivalence queries, counter-examples are checked with each W_i), our ASCV algorithm will converge to the WT which a witness for the truth of $S \models \varphi$, in the polynomial number of queries by the property of the L^* algorithm. However, there can be early termination with a counter-example or an AT satisfying both premises. In addition, the algorithm will not generate any assumption A_i with more states than W_i.

Figure 1 illustrates our ASCV algorithm. Given a transition system S, a safety property φ, and an integer n, the ASCV algorithm first decomposes S into n modules and assigns them to an array $M[\,]$ (line 1), and it constructs the initial conjecture machines according to the rule of the L^* algorithm (line 2). Then, we repeat asking two sub-queries for equivalence and updating the current conjecture machines; if either of them returns a counter-example *cex*, the algorithm updates the conjecture machines using *cex* (lines 4–18). In more detail, we check that for every i, the current $A[i]$ is a safe assumption such that $M[i] \| A[i] \models \varphi$ by a function `SafeAssumption()`. If so, we have $A[1], \cdots, A[n]$

```
    Boolean ASCV(S, φ, n)
1:  M[ ] := AutomaticPartitioning(S, φ, n);
2:  A[ ] := InitializeAssumptions(M[1], ···, M[n], φ);
3:  repeat:
4:      foreach(1 ≤ i ≤ n){
5:          while((cex := SafeAssumption(M[i], A[i], φ)) ≠ null){
6:              UpdateAssumption(M[i], A[i], cex);
7:      } }
8:      if((cex := DischargeAssumptions(A[1], ···, A[n], φ)) = null){
9:          return true;
10:     } else {
11:         IsRealCex := true;
12:         foreach(1 ≤ i ≤ n) {
13:             if(SafeTrace(M[i], cex)) {
14:                 UpdateAssumption(M[i], A[i], cex);
15:                 IsRealCex := false;
16:         } }
17:         if(IsRealCex) return false;
18:     }
```

Fig. 1. Automatic symbolic compositional verification algorithm

satisfying **Pr1**; otherwise (i.e., for some i, we have a counter-example *cex*), we update $A[i]$ with respect to *cex* (line 6). Once we have $A[1], \cdots, A[n]$ satisfying **Pr1**, the algorithm checks **Pr2** by a function `DischargeAssumptions()`. If the function returns *null*, then we conclude $S \models \varphi$ since $A[1], \cdots, A[n]$ satisfy both premises; otherwise, we are provided a counter-example *cex*. Lines 11–17 analyze whether *cex* is a real counter-example for the invariant; if *cex* indeed violates φ for every $M[i]$, then we conclude $S \not\models \varphi$. Otherwise, it is a spurious counter-example and we update $A[i]$ that is the conjecture for $M[i]$ not violating φ.

5 Symbolic Implementation

The ASCV algorithm can be implemented explicitly as well as implicitly. However, as input/output variables increase, the number of the alphabet symbols of the languages we want to learn also increases exponentially. In explicit implementations [9,11], the large alphabet size poses crucial problems: (1) the constructed assumption DFAs have too many edges when represented explicitly, (2) the size of the observation tables for each assumption gets very large, and (3) the number of membership queries needed to fill each entry in the observation tables also increases. In [3] we introduced a symbolic implementation for learning-based compositional verification and we, in this paper, extend the technique.

5.1 Data Structures and Functions

For symbolic implementation, we already defined a symbolic transition system and decomposition to modules implicitly in Section 2. Here, we present the rest of important symbolic data structures used in the ASCV algorithm.

- Each conjecture assumption A_i is also a module $A_i(X_{A_i}, I_{A_i}, O_{A_i}, Init_{A_i}, T_{A_i})$ that can be constructed using BDDs. Each A_i represents a conjecture DFA in the L^* algorithm: X_{A_i} encodes a set of states, IO_{A_i} represents its alphabet, and $Init_{A_i}$ and T_{A_i} encode an initial state and a transition function, respectively.
- Observation table (Rs, Es, Mp) for each conjecture assumption A_i is maintained using BDDs. Each representative string $r \in Rs$ is encoded by a BDD representing a set of states of $M[X_i]$ reachable by r (i.e. $PostImage(Init_{M[X_i]}, r)$). Every experiment string $e \in Es$ is also represented by a BDD encoding a set of states of $M[X_i]$ from which some state violating φ is reachable by e (i.e. $PreImage(\neg\varphi, e)$). Mp is maintained by a set of boolean arrays.
- A counter-example *cex* is a finite sequence of states over IO, and it is represented by a list of BDDs.

All functions in the ASCV algorithm are implemented using symbolic computation as following (where all the parameters are already represented by BDDs).

- `SafeAssumption`$(M[X_i], A_i, \varphi)$ checks $M[X_i] \| A_i \models \varphi$. It can be achieved by an ordinary symbolic reachability test.
- `DischargeAssumptions`$(A_1, \cdots, A_n, \varphi)$ checks $L^C(A_1) \| \cdots \| L^C(A_n) \models \varphi$. For every A_i, we first construct a module encoding a complement DFA of A_i. This complementing can be easily performed even in our symbolic implementation. We then check that the composition of the complement DFAs satisfies φ, which is also handled by the symbolic reachability test.
- `UpdateAssumption`$(M[X_i], A_i, cex)$ reconstructs the conjecture assumption A_i for the module $M[X_i]$ to be used in the next iteration. It first finds a new experiment string that is the longest suffix of *cex* which can demonstrate the difference between the current conjecture and the goal language. We then update the observation table for A_i by adding the new experiment string. This addition introduces new states and edges. We identify a set of edges between states by BDD computation.
- `SafeTrace`$(M[X_i], cex)$ checks, by the reachability test, that there exists any trace of $M[X_i]$ corresponding with *cex*, which violates φ.

5.2 Early Falsification

In the previous implementations of learning-based compositional verification [9,11] including ours [3], we have found a possible optimization that allows us to conclude earlier $S \not\models \varphi$ with a counter-example. In Figure 1, if *cex* acquired from `DischargeAssumptions()` reaches some state violating φ for every $M[X_i]$, then we conclude that the invariant is false (line 17). That is, in the case that the invariant is indeed false, the algorithm cannot terminate until encountering safe assumptions for each module and checking `DischargeAssumptions()`. On the other hand, *cex* provided from `SafeAssumption()` is immediately used for updating the current conjecture (line 6) even though it is a candidate of evidence for $S \not\models \varphi$. In our new implementation, if *cex* obtained from `SafeAssumption()` is a feasible trace for every other module $M[X_j] (j \neq i)$, then we declare *cex* as a counter-example for $S \models \varphi$. Otherwise (*cex* violates φ in $M[X_i]$, but it is infeasible for some other module), we update the current assumption for $M[X_i]$ to rule out *cex* as the original algorithm. We believe that the additional feasibility checking adds a little effort in terms of time and memory, but sometimes this function can falsify the invariant earlier. We will present examples where we can conclude much earlier than experiments without *early falsification* in Section 6. The function `EarlyFalsify()` is implemented as below:

```
EarlyFalsify(Trace τ, int MNum){
    foreach (j ≠ MNum)
        if (¬ FeasibleTrace(M[j], τ)) return false;
    return true;
}
```

Finally, we add the function `EarlyFalsify()` between line 5 and 6 in the ASCV algorithm (see Figure 1).

```
5:    while((cex := SafeAssumption(M[i], A[i], φ)) ≠ null){
5′:       if(EarlyFalsify(cex, i)) return false;
6:        UpdateAssumption(M[i], A[i], cex);
```

5.3 Edge Deletion for Safe Assumptions

The ultimate goal of our model-checking problem is to quickly discover a small AT (appropriate assumption tuple) or a counter-example for $S \models \varphi$. The ASCV algorithm, however, only guarantees that we can eventually learn the WT (weakest safe assumption tuple) whose size is, in theory, exponential in the size of each module in the worst case. That is, the ASCV algorithm based on the L^* algorithm may keep introducing new states for conjecture machines until converging on a very large WT, even though there may exist smaller ATs than the WT. We have experienced many cases where our algorithm needs many iterations to converge on the WT (lines 5–6). The optimal solution for this problem is to learn the smallest AT in terms of the number of states rather than the WT, but this is a computationally hard problem.

Instead, we propose a simple heuristic called *edge deletion* for this problem where we retry, without introducing new states, to check **Pr1** and **Pr2** after eliminating some edges from the current assumption. More precisely, when we are given a counter-example *cex* from `SafeAssumption`$(M[X_i], A_i, \varphi)$, *cex* is a list of BDDs encoding a set of counter-examples to reach some state violating φ. Each counter-example is a sequence of states of $M[X_i] \| A_i$, and we can extract the edge of A_i from the last transition of the sequence which immediately leads to the state violating φ. By disallowing the edges from A_i, we can rule out *cex* from the current conjecture machine A_i. Then, we check `SafeAssumption()` again; if we get a safe assumption by the retrial, we proceed to the next step. If we cannot conclude using this stronger assumption, then we replace it with the original assumption and update the original one for the next iteration. This replacement ensures the convergence to the WT. Intuitively, our heuristic *edge deletion* searches, with the same number of states, more broadly in solution candidate space, while the original L^* algorithm keeps searching deeply by introducing new states. We believe that sometimes this heuristic also can encounter a smaller AT than the original algorithm. Section 6 shows evidence of this benefit.

6 Experiments

We have implemented our automatic symbolic compositional verification algorithm with the BDD package in a symbolic model checker NuSMV. For experiment, we have six sets of examples where five sets are collected from the NuSMV package and one is artificial. For the artificial examples, we know that small assumptions exist, and for examples from NuSMV package, we added some variables or scaled them up as tools finished fast with the original models. All experiments have been performed on a Sun-Blade-1000 workstation using a 750MHz UltraSPARC III processor, 1GB memory and SunOS 5.10. First, we compare our *automatic symbolic compositional verifier* (ASCV) with our previous implementation in [3]. We then present effects of the number of partitions and new features (early falsification and edge deletion in Section 5). Finally, we compare our ASCV with the invariant checking (with early termination) of NuSMV 2.3.0. Each result table has the number of variables in total (tv), I/O variables, $max_i(|X_i \cup IO_{M_i}|)$ (mx), execution time in seconds, the peak BDD size and the number of states in the assumptions we learn (asm). The running time includes time to perform partitioning as well. Entries denoted by '–' mean that a tool did not finish within 2 hours. In addition, columns denoted by 'F/D' mean that early falsification or edge deletion contributes to concluding earlier, and 'np' means the number of partitions.

ASCV vs. SCV. Compared with the previous implementation SCV in [3], ASCV has the following new features: automatic partitioning, a symmetric compositional rule, early falsification and edge deletion. Table 1 presents that ASCV shows better performance in 10 over 14 examples. However, since the examples in Table 1 were selected in [3] so as to explain that SCV worked well, they may be favorable to SCV. Also, in all the examples, automatic partitioning is as good as manual partitioning in terms of $max_i(|X_i \cup IO_{M_i}|)$, and in 5 cases it reduces the numbers by 20–40%.

The Number of Partitions. Table 2 shows how the number of partitions affects the performance. In two cases, increasing the number of partitions saves significantly in terms of time and BDD usage by keeping generating small assumptions. However, other two cases need more time and BDDs due to large assumptions. Therefore, one has to experiment with the different number of partitions for better results.

Early Falsification and Edge Deletion. In Table 3, we present how our new features help to conclude earlier. In case of that given invariants are true, our edge deletion heuristic saves the number of states of assumptions in many examples.

Table 1. Comparison between SCV and ASCV

example name	spec	tot var	SCV mx	SCV IO	SCV time	SCV peak BDD	ASCV np	ASCV mx	ASCV IO	ASCV time	ASCV peak BDD	F/D
simple1		69	37	4	19.2	607,068	2	36	4	4.9	605,024	D
simple2	true	78	42	5	106	828,842	2	41	5	31.3	620,354	D
simple3		86	46	5	754	3,668,980	2	46	5	223	2,218,762	D
simple4		94	50	5	4601	12,450,004	2	50	5	1527	9,747,836	D
guidance1	false	135	118	23	124	686,784	2	89	18	–	–	–
guidance2	true	122	105	22	196	1,052,660	4	59	18	6.6	359,744	D
guidance3	true	122	93	46	357	619,332	2	76	15	–	–	–
barrel1	false	60	35	10	20.3	345,436	2	35	10	–	–	–
barrel2	true	60	35	10	23.4	472,164	2	35	10	–	–	–
msi1		45	37	25	2.1	289,226	2	37	19	0.3	50,078	D
msi2	true	57	49	25	37.0	619,332	2	49	22	1.8	524,286	D
msi3		70	62	26	1183	6,991,502	2	60	25	31.9	2,179,926	D
robot1	false	92	89	12	1271	4,169,760	2	52	5	283	1,905,008	F
robot2	true	92	75	12	1604	2,804,368	2	50	7	9.5	427,196	D

Table 2. Effect of the number of partitions

np	simple4 spec	tv	mx	IO	time	peak BDD	asm	guidance2 spec	tv	mx	IO	time	peak BDD	asm
2			49	5	1526	9,747,836	2,2			82	18	1680	612,178	2,2
3	true	94	61	37	1.8	497,714	2,2,2	true	122	61	23	34	614,222	2,2,2
4			53	37	0.7	217,686	2,2,2,2			59	33	6.6	359,744	2,2,2,2

np	robot1 spec	tv	mx	IO	time	peak BDD	asm	syncarb4 spec	tv	mx	IO	time	peak BDD	asm
2			52	5	283	1,905,008	3,2			21	21	332	7,700,770	131,131
3	false	92	62	30	–	–	too many	true	21	21	21	643	14,870,100	35,19,35
4			64	46	–	–	too many			21	21	4520	31,234,364	11,11,19,19

Table 3. With/without Early falsification and edge deletion

example name	spec	tot var	np	mx	IO var	Without F/D time	Without F/D peak BDD	Without F/D asm	With F/D time	With F/D peak BDD	With F/D asm	F/D
simple1		69	2	36	4	10.3	605,024	2,3	4.9	605,024	2,2	D
simple2	true	78	2	41	5	58.3	624,442	2,3	31.3	620,354	2,2	D
simple3		86	2	45	5	441	2,997,526	3,2	223	1,849,462	2,2	D
simple4		94	2	49	5	3044	9,747,836	2,3	1526	9,747,836	2,2	D
guidance2	true	122	2	105	18	1634	1,066,968	2,37	1603	612,178	2,2	D
msi1		45	2	37	19	–	–	too many	0.3	49,056	2,2	D
msi2	true	57	2	49	22	–	–	too many	1.8	524,286	2,2	D
msi3		70	2	60	25	–	–	too many	31.9	2,179,926	2,2	D
robot1	false	92	2	52	5	529	2,275,994	3,58	283	1,905,008	3,2	F
robot2	true	92	2	50	7	10.4	529,396	2,3	9.5	427,196	2,2	D
syncarb1	false	18	2	18	18	28.2	1,384,810	67,67	125	1,536,066	67,67	–
syncarb2	true	18	2	18	18	30.4	1,274,434	67,67	86.6	1,280,566	67,67	–

In case of false, early falsification helps to save. In two examples (`syncarb1` and `syncarb2`), however, these features affect performance adversarially.

ASCV vs. NuSMV. Finally, Table 4 presents the comparison between ASCV (with the heuristics) and NuSMV. In 10 examples, ASCV is significantly better than NuSMV where we have found small assumptions. In `syncarb3` and `syncarb4`, however, the assumptions we have learnt are relatively large (with more than 100 states for each) and we believe that the large size of assumptions

Table 4. Comparison between ASCV and NuSMV

example name	spec	tot var	ASCV					NuSMV	
			np	mx	IO	time	peak BDD	time	peak BDD
simple1	true	69	2	36	4	4.9	605,024	269	3,993,976
simple2		78	2	41	5	31.3	620,354	4032	32,934,972
simple3		86	4	50	37	1.0	330,106	–	–
simple4		94	4	53	37	0.7	217,686	–	–
guidance2	true	122	4	59	18	6.6	359,744	–	–
msi1	true	45	2	37	19	0.3	50,078	157	1,554,462
msi2		57	2	49	22	1.8	524,286	3324	16,183,370
msi3		70	2	60	25	31.9	2,179,926	–	–
robot1	false	92	2	52	5	283	1,905,008	654	2,729,762
robot2	true	92	2	50	7	9.5	427,196	1039	1,117,046
syncarb3	false	21	2	21	21	351	9,948,148	0.1	5,110
syncarb4	true	21	2	21	21	332	7,700,770	0.1	3,066
barrel1	false	60	–	–	–	–	–	1201	28,118,286
barrel2	true	60	–	–	–	–	–	4886	36,521,170

is a main reason of negative results in these examples. Also, it can explain why ASCV cannot complete in the timeout in `barrel1` and `barrel2`. More details about the examples are available at `http://www.cis.upenn.edu/~wnam/ASCV/`.

References

1. M. Abadi and L. Lamport. Conjoining specifications. *ACM TOPLAS*, 17:507–534, 1995.
2. R. Alur and T.A. Henzinger. Reactive modules. *Formal Methods in System Design*, 15(1):7–48, 1999. A preliminary version appears in *Proc. 11th LICS, 1996.*
3. R. Alur, P. Madhusudan, and W. Nam. Symbolic compositional verification by learning assumptions. In *Proc. CAV 2005*, pages 548–562, 2005.
4. D. Angluin. Learning regular sets from queries and counterexamples. *Information and Computation*, 75:87–106, 1987.
5. H. Barringer, C.S. Pasareanu, and D. Giannakopolou. Proof rules for automated compositional verification through learning. In *Proc. 2nd SVCBS*, 2003.
6. R.E. Bryant. Graph-based algorithms for boolean-function manipulation. *IEEE Transactions on Computers*, C-35(8):677–691, 1986.
7. A. Cimatti, E. Clarke, E. Giunchiglia, F. Giunchiglia, M. Pistore, M. Roveri, R. Sebastiani, and A. Tacchella. NuSMV Version 2: An OpenSource Tool for Symbolic Model Checking. In *Proc. CAV 2002*, LNCS 2404, pages 359–364, 2002.
8. J.M. Cobleigh, G.S. Avrunin, and L.A. Clarke. Breaking up is hard to do: an investigation of decomposition for assume-guarantee reasoning. *Technical Report UM-CS-2004-023*, 2005.
9. J.M. Cobleigh, D. Giannakopoulou, and C.S. Pasareanu. Learning assumptions for compositional verification. In *Proc. 9th TACAS*, LNCS 2619, pages 331–346, 2003.
10. C.M. Fiduccia, R.M. Mattheyses. A linear time heuristic for improving network partitions. In *Proc. of 19th DAC*, pages 175–181, 1982.
11. D. Giannakopoulou, C.S. Pasareanu. Learning-based assume-guarantee verification. In *Proc. of SPIN 2005*, pages 282–287, 2005.
12. O. Grümberg and D.E. Long. Model checking and modular verification. *ACM Transactions on Programming Languages and Systems*, 16(3):843–871, 1994.

13. G. Karypis, R. Aggarwal, V. Kumar, and S. Shekhar. Multilevel hypergraph partitioning: applications in VLSI domain. *IEEE Trans. VLSI Systems*, 7(1):69–79, 1999.
14. G. Karypis and V. Kumar. Multilevel k-way hypergraph partitioning. *In Proc. of 36th Design Automation Conference*, pages 343–348, 1999.
15. B.W. Kernighan and S. Lin. An efficient heuristic procedure for partitioning graphs. *The Bell System Technical Journal*, 49(2):291–307, 1970.
16. K.L. McMillan. A compositional rule for hardware design refinement. In *CAV 97: Computer-Aided Verification*, LNCS 1254, pages 24–35, 1997.
17. R.L. Rivest and R.E. Schapire. Inference of finite automata using homing sequences. *Information and Computation*, 103(2):299–347, 1993.
18. N. Sharygina, S. Chaki, E.M. Clarke, and N. Sinha. Dynamic component substitutability analysis. In *Proc. of FM 2005*, LNCS 3582, pages 512–528, 2005.
19. E.W. Stark. A proof technique for rely-guarantee properties. In *FST & TCS 85*, LNCS 206, pages 369–391, 1985.
20. M. Weiser. Program slicing. IEEE Trans. on Software Engineering, 10:352–357, 1984.

On the Satisfiability of Modular Arithmetic Formulae

Bow-Yaw Wang*

Institute of Information Science
Academia Sinica
Taiwan

Abstract. Modular arithmetic is the underlying integral computation model in conventional programming languages. In this paper, we discuss the satisfiability problem of propositional formulae in modular arithmetic over the finite ring $\mathbf{Z}_{2^\omega}$. Although an upper bound of $2^{2^{O(n^4)}}$ can be obtained by solving alternation-free Presburger arithmetic, it is easy to see that the problem is in fact **NP**-complete. Further, we give an efficient reduction to integer programming with the number of constraints and variables linear in the length of the given linear modular arithmetic formula. For non-linear modular arithmetic formulae, an additional factor of ω is needed. With the advent of efficient integer programming packages, our algorithm could be useful to software verification in practice.

1 Introduction

Modular arithmetic is widely used in the design of cryptosystems and pseudo random number generators [22,12]. Since integers use a finite binary representation in conventional programming languages such as C, modular arithmetic is often required in software verification as well. Indeed, many algorithms are designed to avoid overflow in modular arithmetic explicitly. Verification tools therefore need to support modular arithmetic to check these algorithms.

In this paper, we discuss the satisfiability problem of propositional formulae in modular arithmetic. All arithmetic computation in the formulae is over the finite ring $\mathbf{Z}_{2^\omega}$ for some fixed ω. In addition to linear terms, non-linear terms such as multiplications and modulo operations of arbitrary terms are allowed. We show that the satisfiability problem is **NP**-complete for formulae of linear modular arithmetic. The problem is still in **NP** for full modular arithmetic.

We give an efficient reduction to integer programming to have a practical decision procedure for modular arithmetic. Several issues have to be addressed in our construction. Firstly, modular computation must be simulated by linear constraints, as well as all logical operations. Furthermore, non-linear multiplications and modulo operations need to be expressed in the form of linear constraints. Most importantly, we would not like our reduction to increase the size of the

* This work was partly supported by NSC under grants NSC 94-2213-E-001-003- and NSC 95-2221-E-001-024-MY3.

S. Graf and W. Zhang (Eds.): ATVA 2006, LNCS 4218, pp. 186–199, 2006.

problem significantly. Our construction should not use more than a linear number of constraints and variables in the length of the modular arithmetic formula.

It is well-known that the first-order non-linear arithmetic theory is undecidable [8]. Presburger arithmetic is a decidable first-order linear arithmetic theory [6,15,19]. In [15], Oppen shows an upper bound of $2^{2^{2^{O(n \lg n)}}}$ for determining the truth of Presburger arithmetic formula of length n. If the number of quantifier alternation is m, the problem can be solved in time $2^{2^{O(n^{m+4})}}$ and space $2^{O(n^{m+4})}$ [19]. Although Presburger arithmetic can express first-order linear arithmetic properties, it does not allow modular arithmetic nor non-linear operations.

Integer programming optimizes a given linear objective function subject to a set of linear constraints [16]. The problem is known to be **NP**-complete. Unlike Presburger arithmetic, it does not allow arbitrary logical combinations of constraints but their conjunction. It does not allow modular arithmetic either.

Other decision procedures for linear arithmetic are available. In [4], a survey of the automata-theoretic approach is given. For a special class of quantifier-free Presburger arithmetic, [21] gives an efficient reduction to Boolean satisfiability. The tool CVC Lite [2] contains a decision procedure to check validity of linear arithmetic formula. Similar to [6,15,19], none of them considers modular arithmetic nor non-linear operations. In [1], a decision procedure for systems of modular arithmetic inequalities is proposed. Although the authors use an algebraic approach to check the satisfiability of (in)equalities in a system. It is unclear whether the logical and modulo operations can be added within their framework.

We note that our reduction may serve as a reduction to Presburger arithmetic. Since Presburger arithmetic does not allow modular arithmetic, encoding it in linear constraints allows us to solve the problem by various decision procedures for Presburger arithmetic. However, solving the corresponding Presburger arithmetic formula requires $2^{2^{O(n^4)}}$ in the length of the modular arithmetic formula. Our reduction is more efficient asymptotically.

The remaining of paper is organized as follows. Section 2 contains the background. It is followed by the syntax and semantics of linear modular arithmetic in Section 3. The algorithm for the satisfiability of linear modular arithmetic is presented in Section 4. The syntax and semantics of modular arithmetic formulae are defined in Section 5. Section 6 discusses the satisfiability problem for non-linear modular arithmetic. Applications of our algorithm are discussed in Section 7. We report our preliminary experimental results in Section 8. Finally, Section 9 concludes the paper.

2 Preliminaries

Let $\mathbf{Z}$ be the set of integers, $\mathbf{Z}^+$ the set of positive integers, and $\mathbf{Z}^\times$ the set of non-zero integers. In the following exposition, we will fix the set X of integer variables and $m = 2^\omega$ where $\omega \in \mathbf{Z}^+$.

Definition 1. *([11], for example) For any $a \in \mathbf{Z}, b \in \mathbf{Z}^\times$, there are $q, r \in \mathbf{Z}$ such that $a = bq + r$ and $0 \leq r < |b|$.*

The numbers q and r are called *a quotient b* ($a \operatorname{quo} b$) and *a modulo b* ($a \bmod b$) respectively. We also define *signed quotient* and *signed modulo* as follows.

$$a \operatorname{smod} b \triangleq \begin{cases} a \bmod b & \text{if } 0 \leq a \bmod b < \lfloor \frac{|b|}{2} \rfloor \\ a \bmod b - |b| & \text{if } \lfloor \frac{|b|}{2} \rfloor \leq a \bmod b < |b| \end{cases}$$

$$a \operatorname{squo} b \triangleq \frac{a - (a \operatorname{smod} b)}{b}$$

For example, -7 quo $-3 = 3$ and -7 mod $-3 = 2$, but -7 squo $-3 = 2$ and -7 smod $-3 = -1$ for $-7 = -3 \times 3 + 2$. We say a is *congruent to b modulo m*, $a \equiv b \pmod{m}$, if $(a - b) \bmod m = 0$. For any $a \in \mathbf{Z}$, the *residue class of a modulo m* is the set $[a] \triangleq \{x | x \equiv a \pmod{m}\}$. It is easy to verify that the *residue class system* $\mathbf{Z}_m = (\{[0], [1], \ldots, [m-1]\}, +, [0], \cdot, [1])$ is a commutative ring with identity [11].

Since $\mathbf{Z}_m$ consists of residue classes of integers modulo m, several representations of the equivalence classes are possible. Particularly, we call $\{-\frac{m}{2}, \ldots, -1, 0, 1, \frac{m}{2} - 1\}$ the *signed representation* and $\{0, 1, \ldots, m-1\}$ the *unsigned representation*. To emulate integral computation in conventional languages, we use the signed representation if not mentioned otherwise. If $c \in \mathbf{Z}$, the notation $c \in \mathbf{Z}_m$ denotes that c is an element in the signed representation of $\mathbf{Z}_m$.

Let $c, a_{i,j} \in \mathbf{Z}$ and $x_j \in X$ for $0 \leq i < M$, $0 \leq j < N$. Given a set of M *linear constraints* $\sum_{j=0}^{N-1} a_{i,j} x_j \sim_i c_i$ where $\sim_i \in \{\leq, <, =, >, \geq\}$, and a linear objective function $\sum_{j=0}^{N-1} b_j x_j$, the *integer programming problem* is to find a *valuation* $\rho : X \to \mathbf{Z}$ such that ρ satisfies all linear constraints and attains the maximum value of the objective function. We denote an instance of integer programming problem as follows.

$$\begin{array}{ll} \text{maximize } \sum_{j=0}^{N-1} b_j x_j & \\ & \sum_{j=0}^{N-1} a_{0,j} x_j \sim_0 c_0 \\ \text{subject to} & \sum_{j=0}^{N-1} a_{1,j} x_j \sim_1 c_1 \\ & \vdots \\ & \sum_{j=0}^{N-1} a_{M-1,j} x_j \sim_{M-1} c_{M-1} \end{array}$$

It is known that the integer programming problem is **NP**-complete [16].

3 Linear Modular Arithmetic

For any $c \in \mathbf{Z}_m$ and $x \in X$, the syntax of the Linear Modular Arithmetic Formula over $\mathbf{Z}_m$ is defined in Figure 1. We use the symbols % and $\div$ for the modulo and quotient operators respectively in our object language to avoid confusion. Also, we do not use syntactic translation for equality nor any of the logical connectives. A more efficient reduction can be attained by treating each operator separately, although it does not improve the performance asymptotically.

$$\text{Term } t \triangleq c \mid c \cdot t \mid t \,\%\, c \mid t \div c \mid t + t'$$
$$\text{Atomic Proposition } l \triangleq \mathsf{ff} \mid t \leq t' \mid t = t'$$
$$\text{Formula } f \triangleq l \mid \neg f \mid f \wedge f' \mid f \vee f'$$

Fig. 1. Syntax of Linear Modular Arithmetic Formula over $\mathbf{Z}_m$

$$\begin{aligned} [\![c]\!]_\rho &\triangleq c \\ [\![c \cdot t]\!]_\rho &\triangleq c[\![t]\!]_\rho \,\mathrm{smod}\, m \\ [\![t + t']\!]_\rho &\triangleq [\![t]\!]_\rho + [\![t']\!]_\rho \,\mathrm{smod}\, m \end{aligned} \qquad \begin{aligned} [\![t \,\%\, c]\!]_\rho &\triangleq [\![t]\!]_\rho \bmod c \\ [\![t \div c]\!]_\rho &\triangleq [\![t]\!]_\rho \,\mathrm{quo}\, c \end{aligned}$$

$$\begin{aligned} [\![\mathsf{ff}]\!]_\rho &\triangleq \mathsf{false} \\ [\![t \leq t']\!]_\rho &\triangleq [\![t]\!]_\rho \leq [\![t']\!]_\rho \\ [\![t = t']\!]_\rho &\triangleq [\![t]\!]_\rho = [\![t']\!]_\rho \end{aligned} \qquad \begin{aligned} [\![\neg f]\!]_\rho &\triangleq \neg [\![f]\!]_\rho \\ [\![f \wedge f']\!]_\rho &\triangleq [\![f]\!]_\rho \wedge [\![f']\!]_\rho \\ [\![f \vee f']\!]_\rho &\triangleq [\![f]\!]_\rho \vee [\![f']\!]_\rho \end{aligned}$$

Fig. 2. Semantics of Linear Modular Arithmetic Formula over $\mathbf{Z}_m$

Finally, only constants in $\mathbf{Z}_m$ are allowed. Overflowed constants cause compilers to generate warnings; they can be identified rather easily.[1]

For any valuation ρ, the semantic function $[\![\bullet]\!]_\rho$ for linear modular arithmetic formulae over $\mathbf{Z}_m$ is defined in Figure 2. Since $c \in \mathbf{Z}_m$, it is unnecessary to compute the signed representations for constants, modulo and quotient operations. For the others, their semantic values are obtained by the signed modulo m.

Assume each integral and logical computation in conventional languages takes $O(1)$ time. We can now phrase the *satisfiability problem* as follows.

Problem 1. (Satisfiability) Given a linear modular arithmetic formula f over $\mathbf{Z}_m$ with variables $\bar{x}$, determine whether there is a valuation ρ such that $[\![f]\!]_\rho = \mathsf{true}$.

Since the evaluation of any linear modular arithmetic formula is in **P**, we immediately have the following upper bound for the satisfiability problem.

Proposition 1. *The satisfiability problem for any linear modular arithmetic formula f can be decided in **NP**.*[2]

The lower bound of the problem can be obtained by reduction from **3CNF**. Although Boolean variables are not allowed in linear modular arithmetic, they can be simulated by the parity of integer variables fairly easily.

Proposition 2. *The satisfiability problem for any linear modular arithmetic formula f is **NP**-hard.*

Corollary 1. *The satisfiability problem for linear modular arithmetic formula is **NP**-complete.*

[1] In gcc 4.0.2, the warning message "integer constant is too large for its type" is shown.
[2] Please refer to [23] for all proofs of the propositions and theorems in this paper.

4 Solving the Satisfiability Problem for Linear Modular Arithmetic

Since modular arithmetic is the default integral computation in conventional languages, deciding the satisfiability of linear modular arithmetic formula could be useful in software verification. One may, of course, use binary encoding and solve the problem in the Boolean domain. But it would disregard the nature of the problem. We are therefore looking for alternatives capable of exploiting the underlying mathematical structure of the problem.

Given an instance of any syntactic class (terms, atomic propositions, or formulae), we translate it to an integer variable and a set of constraints. Intuitively, the integer variable has the semantic value of the given instance for any valuation subject to the set of constraints. For terms, the integer variable has a value in $[-\frac{m}{2}, \frac{m}{2} - 1]$. For atomic propositions and formulae, it has values 0 or 1.

$$\sigma(c) \triangleq (p, p = c) \qquad \sigma(c \cdot t) \triangleq \begin{pmatrix} & \alpha \\ p, & -\frac{m}{2} \leq p < \frac{m}{2} \\ & cp' - mq = p \end{pmatrix} \text{ where } (p', \alpha) = \sigma(t)$$

$$\sigma(t_0 + t_1) \triangleq \begin{pmatrix} & \alpha_0 \\ & \alpha_1 \\ p, & -\frac{m}{2} \leq p < \frac{m}{2} \\ & p_0 + p_1 - mq = p \end{pmatrix} \text{ where } \begin{matrix} (p_0, \alpha_0) = \sigma(t_0) \\ (p_1, \alpha_1) = \sigma(t_1) \end{matrix} \qquad \sigma(t \,\%\, c) \triangleq \begin{pmatrix} & \alpha \\ p, & 0 \leq p < |c| \\ & p' - cq = p \end{pmatrix} \text{ where } (p', \alpha) = \sigma(t)$$

$$\sigma(t \div c) \triangleq \begin{pmatrix} & \alpha \\ p, & 0 \leq p' - cp < |c| \end{pmatrix} \text{ where } (p', \alpha) = \sigma(t)$$

Fig. 3. Linear Constraints for Terms

Consider, for example, the following translation of $t \,\%\, c$ (Figure 3).

$$\begin{pmatrix} & \alpha \\ p, & 0 \leq p < |c| \\ & p' - cq = p \end{pmatrix} \text{ where } (p', \alpha) = \sigma(t)$$

The semantic value p' and constraints α of t are obtained by $\sigma(t)$ recursively. Since the semantic value p of $t \,\%\, c$ is equal to $p' \,\%\, c$, we add the constraints $0 \leq p < |c|$ and $p' - cq = p$. The following proposition shows that the semantics of terms is still retained in spite of the constraints in Figure 3.

Proposition 3. *Let t be a term in linear modular arithmetic. Then, there is a valuation ρ such that $[\![t]\!]_\rho = d \Leftrightarrow$ there is a valuation η such that η satisfies α and $\eta(p) = d$ where $(p, \alpha) = \sigma(t)$.*

$$\lambda(\mathsf{ff}) \triangleq (p, p = 0) \qquad \lambda(t_0 \leq t_1) \triangleq \begin{pmatrix} & \alpha_0 \\ & \alpha_1 \\ p, & 0 \leq p \leq 1 \\ & p_0 - p_1 - (m-1)(1-p) \leq 0 \\ & p_0 - p_1 + mp > 0 \end{pmatrix} \text{ where } \begin{array}{l} (p_0, \alpha_0) = \sigma(t_0) \\ (p_1, \alpha_1) = \sigma(t_1) \end{array}$$

$$\lambda(t_0 = t_1) \triangleq \begin{pmatrix} & \alpha_0 \\ & \alpha_1 \\ & 0 \leq q_0 + q_1 \leq 1 \\ p, & p_0 - p_1 + m(1-q_0) - q_0 \geq 0 \\ & p_0 - p_1 - m(1-q_1) + q_1 \leq 0 \\ & p_0 - p_1 - m(q_0+q_1) \leq 0 \\ & p_0 - p_1 + m(q_0+q_1) \geq 0 \\ & 1 - q_0 - q_1 = p \end{pmatrix} \text{ where } \begin{array}{l} (p_0, \alpha_0) = \sigma(t_0) \\ (p_1, \alpha_1) = \sigma(t_1) \end{array}$$

Fig. 4. Linear Constraints for Atomic Propositions

For atomic propositions, observe

$$-m < -m+1 = -\frac{m}{2} - (\frac{m}{2} - 1) \leq [\![t_0]\!]_\rho - [\![t_1]\!]_\rho \leq (\frac{m}{2} - 1) - (-\frac{m}{2}) = m - 1 < m.$$

Consider the atomic proposition $t_0 \leq t_1$. From Figure 4, we have

$$\begin{pmatrix} & \alpha_0 \\ & \alpha_1 \\ p, & 0 \leq p \leq 1 \\ & p_0 - p_1 - (m-1)(1-p) \leq 0 \\ & p_0 - p_1 + mp > 0 \end{pmatrix} \text{ where } \begin{array}{l} (p_0, \alpha_0) = \sigma(t_0) \\ (p_1, \alpha_1) = \sigma(t_1) \end{array}.$$

Since the variables p_0 and p_1 have the semantic values of the terms t_0 and t_1 respectively, we have $-m < p_0 - p_1 \leq m - 1$. If $p_0 \leq p_1$, it is easy to verify that the constraints are satisfied if the semantic value p is 1. Conversely, if the variable p has the value 1, $p_0 - p_1 - (m-1)(1-p) = p_0 - p_1 \leq 0$ is enforced by the constraints. Thus $p_0 \leq p_1$.

For equality, one could use a less efficient construction by conjunction and comparison. But we have a slightly better translation in Figure 4. Intuitively, the variables q_0 and q_1 denote $p_0 > p_1$ and $p_0 < p_1$ respectively. Note that q_0 and q_1 must be 0 or 1 by the constraint $0 \leq q_0 + q_1 \leq 1$. If $q_0 = 1$, then $p_0 - p_1 - 1 \geq 0$ by the constraint $p_0 - p_1 + m(1 - q_0) - q_0 \geq 0$. Hence $p_0 > p_1$. Conversely, suppose $p_0 > p_1$ but $q_0 = 0$. There are two cases. If $q_1 = 0$, we have $p_0 - p_1 \leq 0$ by the constraint $p_0 - p_1 + m(q_0 + q_1) \leq 0$, a contradiction. If $q_1 = 1$, $p_0 - p_1 + 1 \leq 0$ by the constraint $p_0 - p_1 - m(1 - q_1) + q_1 \leq 0$, also a contradiction. Hence, $q_0 = 1$ if and only if $p_0 > p_1$ for any valuation satisfying the constraints. And the semantic value of $t_0 = t_1$ is 1 if and only if $q_0 = q_1 = 0$, namely, $1 - q_0 - q_1$.

The following proposition shows that we can replace the semantics values of atomic propositions by 0 or 1.

Proposition 4. *Let l be an atomic proposition in linear modular arithmetic. Then, (1) there is a valuation ρ such that $[\![l]\!]_\rho = \textsf{true} \Leftrightarrow$ there is a valuation η such that η satisfies α and $\eta(p) = 1$ where $(p, \alpha) = \lambda(l)$; (2) there is a valuation ρ such that $[\![l]\!]_\rho = \textsf{false} \Leftrightarrow$ there is a valuation η such that η satisfies α and $\eta(p) = 0$ where $(p, \alpha) = \lambda(l)$.*

Let p_0 and p_1 be the semantic values of the subformulae f_0 and f_1 respectively. Consider the constraints $p_0 + p_1 \geq p$ and $p_0 + p_1 \leq 2p$ in the translation of their disjunction (Figure 5). We would like the semantic value p of their disjunction to be 0 when both p_0 and p_1 are 0. It is achieved by the constraint $p_0 + p_1 \geq p$. On the other hand, the constraint $p_0 + p_1 \leq 2p$ is added to enforce $p = 1$ when any of the disjuncts is true.

$$\phi(l) \triangleq \lambda(l) \qquad \phi(\neg f) \triangleq \begin{pmatrix} p, & \begin{matrix} \alpha \\ 1 - p' = p \end{matrix} \end{pmatrix} \text{ where } (p', \alpha) = \phi(f)$$

$$\phi(f_0 \wedge f_1) \triangleq \begin{pmatrix} & \alpha_0 \\ & \alpha_1 \\ p, & 0 \leq p \leq 1 \\ & p_0 + p_1 \geq 2p \\ & p_0 + p_1 \leq 1 + p \end{pmatrix} \text{ where } \begin{matrix} (p_0, \alpha_0) = \phi(f_0) \\ (p_1, \alpha_1) = \phi(f_1) \end{matrix} \qquad \phi(f_0 \vee f_1) \triangleq \begin{pmatrix} & \alpha_0 \\ & \alpha_1 \\ p, & 0 \leq p \leq 1 \\ & p_0 + p_1 \geq p \\ & p_0 + p_1 \leq 2p \end{pmatrix} \text{ where } \begin{matrix} (p_0, \alpha_0) = \phi(f_0) \\ (p_1, \alpha_1) = \phi(f_1) \end{matrix}$$

Fig. 5. Linear Constraints for Formulae

Note that we do not rearrange the input formula to canonical forms. Since the rearrangement could increase the length of the formula significantly, it would not be efficient. In order to have linear number of constraints and variables, it is crucial not to transform the input formula to canonical forms.

Given a formula in linear modular arithmetic, there is a set of constraints such that the semantic value of the formula is denoted by the designated variable in our construction. Our progress is summarized in the following proposition.

Proposition 5. *Let f be a formula in linear modular arithmetic. Then, (1) there is a valuation ρ such that $[\![f]\!]_\rho = \textsf{true} \Leftrightarrow$ there is a valuation η such that η satisfies α and $\eta(p) = 1$ where $(p, \alpha) = \phi(f)$; and (2) there is a valuation ρ such that $[\![f]\!]_\rho = \textsf{false} \Leftrightarrow$ there is a valuation η such that η satisfies α and $\eta(p) = 0$ where $(p, \alpha) = \phi(f)$.*

To solve the satisfiability problem of a linear modular arithmetic formula f, we first obtain an integer variable p and a set of constraints α from the translation $\phi(f)$. It is not difficult to see that the satisfiability problem can be solved by optimizing the objective function p with respect to α.

Our translation is constructed recursively. A recursive call is invoked for each subformula in the input formula. Further, a constant number of constraints and variables are added in each recursion. Since the number of subformulae is linear in the length of the input formula, the corresponding integer programming problem has the number of variables and constraints linear in the length of the input formula. The following theorem summarizes our result on the satisfiability problem for linear modular arithmetic formulae.

Theorem 1. *Given a formula f in linear modular arithmetic, the satisfiability problem can be solved by an instance of the integer programming problem with the number of constraints and variables linear in $|f|$.*

5 Modular Arithmetic

The syntax and semantics of modular arithmetic extend those of linear modular arithmetic by multiplication, $t \cdot t'$, and modulo operation, $t \,\%\, t'$, of terms (Figure 6). Similar to linear terms, the semantic value of term multiplication uses the signed modulo to reflect the semantics of conventional programming languages. On the other hand, it is unnecessary to compute the signed representation for modulo operations of terms since overflow could not occur.

$$\text{Term } t \triangleq \ldots \mid t \cdot t' \mid t \,\%\, t'$$

$$[\![t \cdot t']\!]_\rho \triangleq [\![t]\!]_\rho [\![t']\!]_\rho \operatorname{smod} m$$
$$[\![t \,\%\, t']\!]_\rho \triangleq [\![t]\!]_\rho \bmod [\![t']\!]_\rho$$

Fig. 6. Syntax and Semantics of Modular Arithmetic over $\mathbf{Z}_m$

The lower bound of the satisfiability problem for modular arithmetic formula follows from Proposition 2. Additionally, the evaluation of any modular arithmetic formula can also be done in polynomial time, we immediately have the following theorem.

Theorem 2. *The satisfiability problem for modular arithmetic formula is* ***NP****-complete.*

6 Solving the Satisfiability Problem for Modular Arithmetic

Based on the translation of linear modular arithmetic formulae, multiplications and modulo operations of arbitrary terms can be emulated in integer programming. Of course, one could use the binary representation and encode a multiplier circuit in linear modular arithmetic. But it would introduce too many temporary variables. Besides, the mathematical nature of the problem would not be preserved by Boolean circuits. We hereby propose a more efficient translation.

In order to compute non-linear terms, we will use the binary representations of operands' semantic values. But it becomes complicated for negative numbers. However, it is safe to use the unsigned representation in this context. Observe

$$ab \equiv (a+m)b \equiv a(b+m) \equiv (a+m)(b+m) \pmod{m}.$$

We therefore assume the unsigned representation, compute the result, then convert it back to the signed representation for multiplications of terms. Thus, only the linear constraints of the unsigned multiplication is needed.

$$\chi(p_0, p_1) \triangleq \left(c, \begin{array}{r} p_1 < m \\ 0 \le b_i \le 1 \text{ for } 0 \le i < \omega \\ \sum_{i=0}^{\omega-1} 2^i b_i = p_0 \\ 0 \le c_i \le 2^i p_1 \text{ for } 0 \le i < \omega \\ 2^i p_1 - 2^i m(1-b_i) \le c_i \text{ for } 0 \le i < \omega \\ 2^i m b_i \ge c_i \text{ for } 0 \le i < \omega \\ \sum_{i=0}^{\omega-1} c_i = c \end{array} \right)$$

Fig. 7. Linear Constraints for Unsigned Multiplication

More concretely, suppose $0 \le p_0 < m$. The constraints $0 \le b_0, \ldots, b_{\omega-1} \le 1$ and $\sum_{i=0}^{\omega-1} 2^i b_i = p_0$ compute the unsigned representation of p_0 (Figure 7). Intuitively, the bit string $b_{\omega-1}b_{\omega-2}\cdots b_1 b_0$ is the binary representation for p_0.

To compute the partial result $c_i = 2^i b_i p_1$, we use the constraints $0 \le c_i \le 2^i p_1$, $2^i p_1 - 2^i m(1-b_i) \le c_i$, and $2^i m b_i \ge c_i$. If $b_i = 0$, we have $2^i m b_i = 0 \ge c_i \ge 0$. On the other hand, we have $2^i p_1 - 2^i m(1-b_i) = 2^i p_1 \le c_i \le 2^i p_1$ when $b_i = 1$. Thus, $c_i = 2^i b_i p_1$.

Proposition 6. *Let p_0, p_1 be variables. Then, there is a valuation ρ such that $0 \le \eta(p_0) = d_0, \rho(p_1) = d_1 < m$, and $\rho(p_0)\rho(p_1) = d \Leftrightarrow$ there is a valuation η such that η satisfies α, $\eta(p_0) = d_0$, $\eta(p_1) = d_1$, and $\eta(p) = d$ where $(p, \alpha) = \chi(p_0, p_1)$.*

$$\zeta(p') \triangleq \left(p, \begin{array}{c} 0 \le a \le 1 \\ \frac{m}{2}(a-1) \le p' \le \frac{m}{2}a - 1 \\ -ma \le p + p' \le ma \\ -m(1-a) \le p - p' \le m(1-a) \end{array} \right)$$

Fig. 8. Linear Constraints for Absolute Value

For modulo operations of terms, note

$$a \bmod b = a \bmod |b| = \begin{cases} |a| \bmod |b| & \text{if } a \ge 0 \\ (-|a|) \bmod |b| = |b| - (|a| \bmod |b|) & \text{if } a < 0. \end{cases}$$

We can therefore perform the modulo operations of terms by their absolute values. Consider the constraints $0 \le a \le 1$ and $\frac{m}{2}(a-1) \le p' \le \frac{m}{2}a - 1$ in Figure 8, where

p' has the semantic value of any term. Intuitively, p' is non-negative if and only if $a = 1$. Suppose $p' \geq 0$ and $a = 0$. We would have $-\frac{m}{2} \leq p' \leq -1$, a contradiction. Conversely, $a = 1$ implies $0 \leq p' \leq \frac{m}{2} - 1$. Hence $p' \geq 0$.

Proposition 7. *Let p' be a variable. Then, there is a valuation ρ such that $-m \leq \rho(p') = d' \leq m$ and $|\rho(p')| = d \Leftrightarrow$ there is a valuation η such that η satisfies α, $\eta(p') = d'$, and $\eta(p) = d$ where $(p, \alpha) = \zeta(p')$.*

We can now describe the linear constraints for non-linear terms. For multiplication $t_0 \cdot t_1$, we first get the unsigned representation p'_0 and p'_1 of the semantic values of t_0 and t_1 respectively. This is done by the constraints $p'_0 = p_0 + ma$, $0 \leq p'_0 < m$, $p'_1 = p_1 + mb$, and $0 \leq p'_1 < m$ where $(p_0, \alpha_0) = \sigma(t_0)$ and $(p_1, \alpha_1) = \sigma(t_1)$ respectively. Then we compute the unsigned result p' by $\chi(p'_0, p'_1)$. Finally, the result is converted to the signed representation p by $p' - md = p$ and $-\frac{m}{2} \leq p < \frac{m}{2}$ (Figure 9).

To compute the semantic value of $t_0 \% t_1$, we first get the absolute values p'_0 and p'_1 of the semantic values of t_0 and t_1 by $\zeta(p_0)$ and $\zeta(p_1)$ respectively. The constraints $p'_0 - r = p'$ and $0 \leq p' < p'_1$ give $p' = |p_0| \bmod |p_1|$ where r is a multiple of $|p_1|$. Suppose $p_0 \geq 0$. Then $a = 1$ by the constraint $\frac{m}{2}(a-1) \leq p_0 \leq \frac{m}{2}a - 1$. Hence $p = p' = |p_0| \bmod |p_1|$ by the constraint $-2m(1-a) \leq p - p' \leq m(1-a)$. On the other hand, $p_0 < 0$ implies $a = 0$. Hence $p = p'_1 - p' = |p_1| - (|p_0| \bmod |p_1|)$ by the constraint $-ma \leq p - p'_1 + p' \leq 2ma$ (Figure 9).

Proposition 8. *Let t be a non-linear term in modular arithmetic. Then, there is a valuation ρ such that $[\![t]\!]_\rho = d \Leftrightarrow$ there is a valuation η such that η satisfies α and $\eta(p) = d$ where $(p, \alpha) = \sigma(t)$.*

$$\sigma(t_0 \cdot t_1) \triangleq \left(p, \begin{array}{c} \alpha_0 \\ \alpha_1 \\ \alpha_2 \\ p'_0 = p_0 + ma \\ 0 \leq p'_0 < m \\ p'_1 = p_1 + mb \\ 0 \leq p'_1 < m \\ p' - md = p \\ -\frac{m}{2} \leq p < \frac{m}{2} \end{array} \right) \quad \text{where } \begin{array}{r} (p_0, \alpha_0) = \sigma(t_0) \\ (p_1, \alpha_1) = \sigma(t_1) \\ (p', \alpha_2) = \chi(p'_0, p'_1) \end{array}$$

$$\sigma(t_0 \% t_1) \triangleq \left(p, \begin{array}{c} \alpha_0 \\ \alpha_1 \\ \alpha_2 \\ \alpha_3 \\ \alpha_4 \\ p'_0 - r = p' \\ 0 \leq p' < p'_1 \\ 0 \leq a \leq 1 \\ \frac{m}{2}(a-1) \leq p_0 \leq \frac{m}{2}a - 1 \\ -2m(1-a) \leq p - p' \leq m(1-a) \\ -ma \leq p - p'_1 + p' \leq 2ma \end{array} \right) \quad \text{where } \begin{array}{r} (p_0, \alpha_0) = \sigma(t_0) \\ (p_1, \alpha_1) = \sigma(t_1) \\ (p'_0, \alpha_2) = \zeta(p_0) \\ (p'_1, \alpha_3) = \zeta(p_1) \\ (r, \alpha_4) = \chi(p'_1, p'') \end{array}$$

Fig. 9. Linear Constraints for Non-linear Terms

Since the number of constraints and variables in the unsigned multiplication is $O(\omega)$, our translation requires $O(\omega)$ constraints and variables for non-linear terms. In summary, the satisfiability problem for modular arithmetic formula can be reduced to an instance of integer programming with $O(\omega|f|)$ constraints and variables.

Theorem 3. *Given a formula f in modular arithmetic over $\mathbf{Z}_m$ where $m = 2^\omega$, the satisfiability problem can be solved by an instance of the integer programming problem with the number of constraints and variables linear in $\omega|f|$.*

7 Applications

Our decision procedure may be useful in software verification, especially for programs in conventional programming languages. For hardware verification, our reduction may work as a non-linear constraint solver which accepts control signals from other decision procedures. Particularly, we find that the following areas may benefit from our algorithm.

Modern proof assistants allow external decision procedures to discharge proof obligations [13,17,10]. Although modular arithmetic is essential to many number theoretic and cryptographic algorithms, there is no proof assistant which provides decision procedures for modular arithmetic to the best of our knowledge. Since it is rather tedious to deal with modular arithmetic in each integral computation, verifiers simply assume the infinite-precision integer model in software verification. Subsequently, algorithms certified by proof assistants are not exactly the same as their implementations. Our procedure may help verifiers work in a more realistic computational model.

If a proof assistant is used to determine the truth values of predicates, abstract models constructed in predicate abstraction [7,20] may be inadequate for the same reason. In the presence of non-linear modular arithmetic, our integer programming-based procedure may also be more efficient than, say, SAT-based technique used in predicate abstraction [5] (see Section 8). The new technique refines the abstraction and may perform better in such circumstances.

Another possible application of our algorithm is SAT-based model checking ([3], for instance). Our word-level decision procedure may be better for models with modular arithmetic, but it does not seem to fare well on Boolean satisfiability. However, modern integer programming packages support distributed computation [18]. Our approach gives a parallel SAT solver indirectly.

8 Experimental Results

We have implemented the algorithm to solve the satisfiability problem of modular arithmetic formulae. Our implementation generates instances of integer programming problems in the MPS format [14]. These files are then sent to the SYMPHONY package [18] as inputs. SYMPHONY is an open-sourced mixed integer programming solver. In addition to the conventional execution model,

Experiment	Uni-process solution	time	Multi-process solution	time
(i)	$x = 53, y = 51$	183.97	$x = 13, y = 11$	1.90
(ii)	-	> 600	$x = y = 0, z = 253$	0.39
(iii)	-	> 600	$x = y = 0, z = 3$	0.92
(iv)	$x = y = 0, z = 128$	0.84	$x = 42, y = 0, z = 6$	0.61
(v)	$x = y = 0, z = 128$	1.12	$x = y = 0, z = 128$	1.60

(a) with Integer Programming Package

Experiment	solution	time
(i)	x = 15, y = 129	0.19
(ii)	x = 64, y = 254, z = 255	2.08
(iii)	x = y = 0, z = 3	1.53
(iv)	x = y = 0, z = 128	1.52
(v)	x = y = 0, z = 128	1.52

(b) with SAT Solver

Fig. 10. Experimental Results

the SYMPHONY package also supports Parallel Virtual Machine [9]. We therefore conduct our experiments with both the uni- and multi-process versions. The uni-process version runs on an Intel Pentium 4 2.8GHz Linux 2.6.17 workstation with 2GB memory. The multi-process version runs on a PC cluster consisting of fifteen AMD Athlon MP 2000+ Linux 2.4.22 workstations with 1GB memory. For comparison, we repeat the experiments by the SAT solver zchaff on the workstation of the same configuration as the uni-process version.[3] We are interested in solving the following problems in $\mathbf{Z}_{256}$ (that is, $\omega = 8$).

i. $(x \cdot y = 143) \wedge (x \leq 143) \wedge (y \leq 143) \wedge ((x \neq 1 \wedge y \neq 1))$
ii. $x \cdot y \cdot z + y \cdot z + 2 \cdot x \cdot z + 2 \cdot z + 3 \cdot x \cdot y + 3 \cdot y + 6 \cdot x + 6 = 0$
iii. $x \cdot y \cdot z - y \cdot z - 2 \cdot x \cdot z + 2 \cdot z - 3 \cdot x \cdot y + 3 \cdot y + 6 \cdot x - 6 = 0$
iv. $((x \neq 0) \vee (y \neq 0) \vee (z \neq 0)) \wedge x \cdot y \cdot z + y \cdot z + 2 \cdot x \cdot z + 2 \cdot z + 3 \cdot x \cdot y + 3 \cdot y + 6 \cdot x = 0$
v. $((x \neq 0) \vee (y \neq 0) \vee (z \neq 0)) \wedge x \cdot y \cdot z - y \cdot z - 2 \cdot x \cdot z + 2 \cdot z - 3 \cdot x \cdot y + 3 \cdot y + 6 \cdot x = 0$

Our first experiment is to factorize 143. Although it is easy to see that $11 \times 14 = 143$ is a solution, other solutions may be possible in $\mathbf{Z}_{256}$. Other experiments find roots to three-variable polynomials of degree three. In Experiment (ii) and (iii), the polynomials have constant terms. Hence their roots are always non-trivial. For polynomials without constant terms, trivial solutions can easily be found. We therefore look for non-trivial solutions in Experiment (iv) and (v).

Figure 10 shows the solution and the user time (in seconds) for each experiment. The multi-process solver does improve the performance significantly. For

[3] Unfortunately, we have not conducted all the experiments in the same platform at the time of writing. Each workstation in our PC cluster is a bit outdated than the workstation used in the uni-version version.

example, the factorization is done in less than two seconds by the multi-process solver. But it takes more than three minutes with the uni-process solver. Another interesting observation is that the solutions are not necessarily obvious. The factorization found by the uni-process solver is somewhat unexpected. Instead of the unique factorization in $\mathbf{Z}$, we have $53 \times 51 \equiv 143$ in $\mathbf{Z}_{256}$. Similarly, the solution found by the multi-process solver in Experiment (iv) is correct only in $\mathbf{Z}_{256}$. These unexpected solutions are precisely the reasons why bugs may occur. On the other hand, the SAT solver performs rather stably. Although it may not always outperform the uni-process integer programming package, it does solve all problems in seconds. The multi-process integer programming package is able to finish and outperform the SAT solver in three of the five problems. More thorough experiments are still needed to compare both techniques.

9 Conclusion

Deciding the satisfiability of modular arithmetic formula is essential in software verification. We have characterized the complexity of its satisfiability problem and provided an efficient reduction to the integer programming problem. Our result shows that it is more efficient to develop specialized algorithms than apply more general algorithms for Presburger arithmetic. Additionally, the number of constraints and variables is linear in the length of the input formula in our reduction. With heuristics like relaxation and rounding, the satisfiability problem could be solved efficiently by modern integer programming packages in practice.

It would be interesting to compare our algorithm with other techniques [4,21,1], especially those with the binary encoding scheme. Since the satisfiability problem of modular arithmetic formula is **NP**-complete, one could also build a decision procedure based on SAT solvers. But the binary encoding would eliminate the mathematical nature of the problem. Although our preliminary experimental results suggest that our approach may be useful in finding solutions to multi-variant low-degree polynomials, it is unclear which approach will prevail in practice.

There are still a few missing pieces in our construction. Our translation of the unsigned multiplication is not satisfactory. It would be more useful if our construction used only $O(\lg \omega)$ variables and constraints. Additionally, the quotient and remainder operations of arbitrary terms are not allowed. Although it is possible to encode them in modular arithmetic formula, an efficient construction similar to non-linear terms is certainly welcome.

Acknowledgement. The author would like to thank anonymous referees for their constructive comments in improving the paper.

References

1. Babić, D., Musuvathi, M.: Modular arithmetic decision procedure. Technical Report MSR-TR-2005-114, Microsoft Research (2005)
2. Barrett, C., Berezin, S.: CVC Lite: A new implementation of the cooperating validity checker. In Alur, R., Peled, D.A., eds.: Computer Aided Verification. Volume 3114 of LNCS., Springer-Verlag (2004) 515–518

3. Biere, A., Cimatti, A., Clarke, E.M., Fujita, M., Zhu, Y.: Symbolic model checking using SAT procedures instead of BDDs. In: Design Automation Conference, ACM Press (1999) 317–320
4. Boigelot, B., Wolper, P.: Representing arithmetic constraints with finite automata: An overview. In Stuckey, P.J., ed.: International Conference on Logic Programming. Volume 2401 of LNCS., Springer-Verlag (2002) 1–19
5. Clarke, E., Kroening, D., Sharygina, N., Yorav, K.: Predicate abstraction of ANSI-C programs using SAT. Formal Methods in System Design **25**(2–3) (2004) 105–127
6. Cooper, D.C.: Theorem proving in arithmetic without multiplication. Machine Intelligence **7** (1972)
7. Cousot, P., Cousot, R.: Abstract interpretation: a unified lattice model for static analysis of programs by construction or approximation of fixpoints. In: ACM Symposium on Principles of Programming Languages. (1977) 238–252
8. Enderton, H.: A Mathematical Introduction to Logic. Academic Press (1972)
9. Geist, A., Beguelin, A., Dongarra, J., Jiang, W., Manchek, R., Sunderam, V.: PVM: Parallel Virtual Machine – A Users' Guide and Tutorial for Networked Parallel Computing. The MIT Press (1994)
10. Huet, G., Kahn, G., Paulin-Mohring: The Coq proof assistant: a tutorial: version 6.1. Technical Report 204, Institut National de Recherche en Informatique et en Automatique (1997)
11. Hungerford, T.W.: Algebra. Volume 73 of Graduate Texts in Mathematics. Springer-Verlag (1980)
12. Knuth, D.E.: The Art of Computer Programming. Volume II, Seminumerical Algorithms. Addison-Wesley (1997)
13. Melham, T.F.: Introduction to the HOL theorem prover. University of Cambridge, Computer Laboratory. (1990)
14. Murtagh, B.A.: Advanced Linear Programming: Computation and Practice. McGrawHill (1981)
15. Oppen, D.C.: Elementary bounds for presburger arithmetic. In: ACM Symposium on Theory of Computing, ACM (1973) 34–37
16. Papadimitriou, C.H.: Computational Complexity. Addison-Wesley (1994)
17. Paulson, L.C., Nipkow, T.: Isabelle tutorial and user's manual. Technical Report TR-189, Computer Laboratory, University of Cambridge (1990)
18. Ralphs, T.K., Guzelsoy, M.: The SYMPHONY callable library for mixed integer programming. In: INFORMS Computing Society. (2005)
19. Reddy, C.R., Loveland, D.W.: Presburger arithmetic with bounded quantifier alternation. In: ACM Symposium on Theory of Computing, ACM (1978) 320–325
20. Saídi, H., Graf, S.: Construction of abstract state graphs with PVS. In Grumberg, ed.: Computer Aided Verification. Volume 1254 of LNCS., Springer Verlag (1997) 72–83
21. Seshia, S.A., Bryant, R.E.: Deciding quantifier-free presburger formulas using parameterized solution bounds. In: Logic in Computer Science, IEEE Computer Society (2004) 100–109
22. Stinson, D.R.: Cryptography: Theory and Practice. CRC Press, Inc (1995)
23. Wang, B.Y.: On the satisfiability of modular arithmetic formula. Technical Report TR-IIS-06-001, Institute of Information Science, Academia Sinica (2006) http://www.iis.sinica.edu.tw/LIB/TechReport/tr2006/tr06.html.

Selective Approaches for Solving Weak Games

Malte Helmert[1], Robert Mattmüller[1], and Sven Schewe[2]

[1] Albert-Ludwigs-Universität Freiburg
79110 Freiburg, Germany
{helmert,mattmuel}@informatik.uni-freiburg.de
[2] Universität des Saarlandes
66123 Saarbrücken, Germany
schewe@cs.uni-sb.de

Abstract. Model-checking alternating-time properties has recently attracted much interest in the verification of distributed protocols. While checking the validity of a specification in alternating-time temporal logic (ATL) against an *explicit* model is cheap (linear in the size of the formula and the model), the problem becomes EXPTIME-hard when *symbolic* models are considered. Practical ATL model-checking therefore often consumes too much computation time to be tractable.

In this paper, we describe a novel approach for ATL model-checking, which constructs an explicit weak model-checking game on-the-fly. This game is then evaluated using heuristic techniques inspired by efficient evaluation algorithms for and/or-trees.

To show the feasibility of our approach, we compare its performance to the ATL model-checking system MOCHA on some practical examples. Using very limited heuristic guidance, we achieve a significant speedup on these benchmarks.

1 Introduction

Alternating-time temporal logics like ATL [2] have recently attracted much interest in the multi-agent community [15,16,14,17]. A typical application of alternating-time model-checking is the verification of distributed protocols. In the design of such protocols, we are often interested in the strategic abilities of certain agents (cf. [15,16,3]). For example, in a contract-signing protocol, it is important to ensure that while Alice and Bob can cooperate to sign a contract, Alice is never able to obtain Bob's signature unless Bob can also obtain Alice's signature, and vice versa. Such properties can be expressed in ATL, which extends the branching-time temporal logic CTL [7] with modalities that quantify over the strategic choices of groups of agents.

As in the case of CTL, the model-checking problem for ATL reduces to solving weak games [2]. Weak games are a particular simple version of parity games, where all vertices within a strongly connected component have the same color. ATL model-checking therefore seems to be simple: Given an alternating transition system $\mathcal{A}$ (i. e., an *explicit* model for ATL) and a specification φ, the size of the weak model-checking game is in $O(|\mathcal{A}| \cdot |\varphi|)$, where $|\mathcal{A}|$ denotes the size of $\mathcal{A}$ and $|\varphi|$ the

S. Graf and W. Zhang (Eds.): ATVA 2006, LNCS 4218, pp. 200–214, 2006.

number of subformulas of φ. The resulting weak game can be solved in time linear in its size. It thus seems, at first glance, that ATL inherits the model-checking complexity from CTL. Indeed, MOCHA [3], the only available tool for ATL model-checking, generalizes a symbolic backward approach for CTL model-checking [5].

In light of these similarities, it might appear somewhat surprising that the performance of ATL model checking does not seem to meet the high standards set by CTL model checking. Kremer and Raskin, for example, observed exceptionally large time consumption (and, partly, abortions) when model checking simple properties of small protocols [15]. One possible explanation for this discrepancy is that, despite the identical model-checking complexity of $O(|\mathcal{A}|\cdot|\varphi|)$ for explicit models, the model-checking complexities of CTL and ATL do *not* coincide for symbolic models: while symbolic model-checking is PSPACE-complete for CTL, it becomes EXPTIME-complete for ATL, as recently shown by van der Hoek et al. [18]. In practice, model-checkers use succinct symbolic representations for models, such as RML for MOCHA [3] or PROMELA for SPIN [12], so that the symbolic model checking complexity is of paramount importance.

In addition to the increased complexity of ATL model-checking, there is a significant structural difference between model-checking ATL and CTL formulas. When we model-check a CTL formula, it is not unusual that the *complete* (reachable) state space needs to be explored (consider, e.g., a proof that φ holds during all computations, $\mathsf{AG}\varphi$). For many ATL formulas, there is no such necessity of complete exploration: to prove that a group A of agents can enforce that φ globally holds ($\langle\!\langle A\rangle\!\rangle\mathsf{G}\varphi$), we only need to consider a fragment of the states, defined by the strategies followed by these agents.

We therefore propose an approach that constructs the explicit model-checking game from a symbolic representation of the model-checking problem on-the-fly. Different from a forward-backward approach, we do not start by constructing the *complete* set of forward reachable states. Instead, we adopt heuristic best-first search methods for solving reachability games in and/or-trees to weak games, and finish a model-checking run as soon as we can prove that the considered set of states is sufficiently large for one of the players to have a winning strategy. Our adoption takes into account that, unlike and/or-trees, weak games can not only be won by a player by reaching winning states, but also by forcing the game to stay in vertices with a winning color. It turns out that selectively exploring the space of game vertices is a powerful method for obtaining small proof graphs and fast evaluation results.

Organization of the Paper. The following section introduces weak games, followed by Section 3 describing our approach for their solution. We then discuss the application of these techniques to ATL model-checking in Section 4. We close with a presentation (Section 5) and discussion (Section 6) of our results.

2 Weak Games

A *weak game* is a tuple $\mathcal{G} = \langle V_{even}, V_{odd}, E, v_0, \alpha\rangle$, where

- $V = V_{even} \uplus V_{odd}$ is a finite set of vertices, partitioned into V_{even} and V_{odd}, with a designated initial vertex $v_0 \in V$.

- $E \subseteq V \times V$ is a set of edges.
- $\alpha : V \to \mathbb{N}$ is a coloring function, satisfying $(v, w) \in E \Rightarrow \alpha(v) \leq \alpha(w)$.

Each vertex $v \in V$ has outdegree at least 1 in the directed graph (V, E). For a vertex $v \in V_{even}$ we say that *even* is the owner of v ($owner(v) = even$) and for a vertex $v \in V_{odd}$ we say that *odd* is the owner of v ($owner(v) = odd$). We say that the level of v is *even* ($level(v) = even$) iff $\alpha(v)$ is even and that that the level of v is *odd* ($level(v) = odd$) iff $\alpha(v)$ is odd. For each natural number $n \in \alpha(V)$ in the mapping of α, the vertices $\alpha^{-1}(n)$ colored with n are called a *level.*

The winning condition for weak games is defined in terms of runs. A *run* of a game is an infinite sequence $v_0v_1v_2\ldots$ in V^ω such that $(v_i, v_{i+1}) \in E$ is an edge if v_{i+1} is a successor of v_i. A run is *winning* for player *even* (*odd*) iff the highest color of vertices occurring infinitely often in the run is even (odd). Due to the monotonicity condition for vertex colors, almost all vertices in a run have the same color, and every run is winning either for player *even* or *odd.*

Weak games are a special form of parity games, and consequently one player wins with a memoryless strategy [9]. A (memoryless) *strategy* for player $p \in \{odd, even\}$ is a mapping $s_p : V_p \to V$ such that $(v, v') \in E$ whenever $s_p(v) = v'$. A run $v_0v_1v_2\ldots$ is in accordance with a strategy s_p iff, for all $i \in \mathbb{N}$, $v_i \in V_p \Rightarrow v_{i+1} = s_p(v_i)$ holds. A strategy s_p is *winning* for player p, iff all runs in accordance with s_p are winning for player p.

A vertex v is winning for player p iff she has a winning strategy in the game $\langle V_{even}, V_{odd}, E, v, \alpha\rangle$, and a game is *won* by player p iff the initial vertex is winning for her. *Solving a game* means determining by which player it is won.

3 Solving Weak Games

Weak games with n vertices and e edges can be solved in time $O(n+e)$ following a simple backward approach. For player $p \in \{even, odd\}$ and a given (partial) labeling of the game vertices as winning for *even* or winning for *odd*, define the *p-attractor* to be the minimal set V_p such that:

- a vertex $v \in V$ with $owner(v) = p$ belongs to V_p if some successor $w \in succ(v)$ is labeled as winning for p or belongs to V_p (player p can choose to play into a vertex winning for p), and
- a vertex $v \in V$ with $owner(v) \neq p$ belongs to V_p if each successor $w \in succ(v)$ is labeled as winning for p or belongs to V_p (the opponent of p is forced to play into a vertex winning for p).

The backward algorithm proceeds in phases, iterating until the initial vertex is labeled as winning for either player. In every phase, it considers the set of unlabeled vertices V_{max} whose color is maximal among all unlabeled vertices and labels the vertices in V_{max} as winning for p, where p is *even* (*odd*) if the color of the vertices in V' is even (odd). It then computes the p-attractor V_p and labels the vertices in V_p as winning for p. The algorithm can easily be implemented in such a way that every vertex and edge is considered only once (cf. [8,4]), proving the $O(n + e)$ complexity bound.

A disadvantage of this approach is that usually almost all vertices of the game need to be considered. On the other hand, only a small fragment of the state space is forward reachable in most model-checking games. An obvious improvement in such situations is to construct all forward reachable states in a first phase, and then solve the smaller resulting game using a standard backward algorithm. The complexity of this approach is linear in the size of the forward reachable sub-game.

For larger examples, this is still unsatisfactory: knowing a winning strategy beforehand, it suffices to consider only the fragment of the forward reachable vertices defined by this strategy. For example, in games corresponding to and/or-trees of uniform outdegree $b \geq 2$ and depth d, exploiting the knowledge of a winning strategy reduces the number of vertices that need to be considered from $O(b^d)$ to $O(b^{d/2})$ [13]. In other words, the number of vertices to consider is reduced to its square root.

This raises the question whether we can identify winning states without the need of completely exploring the game graph. This is obviously the case for vertices which are won because they belong to the attractor of a previously labeled set of vertices: If all successors of a vertex are winning for p, or if the vertex is owned by p and has at least one winning successor, then it is winning. However, it is also possible to define a winning criterion for vertices which are winning for a player because they belong to a level of that player and the opponent cannot force a run to leave this level without playing into a losing vertex. For this purpose, we define a *force-set* of player $p \in \{even, odd\}$ to be a set F of vertices in the same level $level(F) = \{p\}$ with the following properties:

- each vertex $v \in F$ with $owner(v) = p$ has some successor $w \in succ(v)$ which belongs to F or is already labeled as winning for p, and
- each vertex $v \in F$ with $owner(v) \neq p$ only has successors $w \in succ(v)$ which belong to F or are already labeled as winning for p.

Vertices in a force-set F of player p are winning for player p, following a strategy which maps vertices in F to vertices in F or to vertices labeled as winning for p.

3.1 A Strategic Forward-Backward Approach

Our algorithm for solving weak games incrementally constructs the game graph. Different from a forward-backward approach, we do not start by constructing the *complete* set of forward reachable states, but rather aim at an early (partial) evaluation of the constructed fragment.

The central data structure of the algorithm is the *partial game graph*, which represents a subgraph of the game graph (V, E) of the weak game to be solved. At any time during the execution of the algorithm, vertices in the partial game graph are partitioned into three groups:

```
Procedure ExpandFringeVertex(v: Vertex):
    change the status of v from "fringe" to "pending"
    for all outgoing edges (v, v') ∈ E:
        add (v, v') to the partial game graph
        if v' is unconstructed:
            add v' to the fringe
    if v has an evaluated successor v' ∈ succ(v) with winner(v') = owner(v):
        EvaluatePendingVertex(v, owner(v))
    else if all successors v' ∈ succ(v) are evaluated:
        EvaluatePendingVertex(v, opponent(owner(v)))
```

Fig. 1. Expanding a vertex moves it from the fringe to the set of pending vertices and add its outgoing edges to the graph, creating new fringe vertices where necessary. The new vertex is immediately evaluated if possible.

- An *evaluated* vertex v has already been classified as winning for *even* or winning for *odd*, and all outgoing edges $(v, w) \in E$ are represented in the partial game graph.
- A *pending* vertex v has not yet been classified, but all outgoing edges $(v, w) \in E$ are represented in the partial game graph.
- A *fringe* vertex v has not yet been classified, and none of its outgoing edges are is represented in the partial game graph.

Evaluated, pending and fringe vertices are called *constructed*, while vertices not represented in the partial game graph at all are called *unconstructed*.

The central primitive operations of the algorithm are *expanding a fringe vertex*, which transforms a fringe vertex into a pending vertex and adds its unconstructed successors to the fringe, and *evaluating a pending vertex*, which transforms a pending vertex into an evaluated vertex. Both operations can lead to the evaluation of further vertices. The overall *solving procedure* repeatedly expands vertices and identifies force-sets, triggering the ensuing vertex evaluations until the initial vertex of the game is evaluated. At this point, the algorithm stops. We now explain these three parts of the algorithm in sequence.

Expanding a Fringe Vertex. When a fringe vertex is expanded, it is removed from the fringe and becomes a pending vertex. Pending vertices must have their outgoing edges represented in the partial game graph, so they are added at this step, which may lead to the creation of new fringe vertices.

It may be the case that the winner for the expanded vertex can be determined immediately: If the owner of the vertex can play into a winning vertex, she wins the expanded vertex. Conversely, if the owner of the vertex is forced to play into a losing vertex for lack of other possibilities, she loses the expanded vertex. In either situation, procedure EvaluatePendingVertex is called to mark the vertex as evaluated and propagate the evaluation result upwards in the partial game graph where possible. The pseudo-code for the expansion procedure is depicted in Figure 1.

```
Procedure EvaluatePendingVertex(v: Vertex, p: Player):
    change the status of v from "pending" to "evaluated"
    set winner(v) to p
    for all pending predecessors v' ∈ pred(v):
        if owner(v') = p:
            EvaluatePendingVertex(v', p)
        else if v' has no unevaluated successors:
            EvaluatePendingVertex(v', p)
```

Fig. 2. Whenever a vertex is evaluated as winning for either player, the evaluation result is propagated up the partial game graph until no further evaluations are possible

Evaluating a Pending Vertex. The evaluation procedure moves a vertex v from the set of pending vertices to the set of evaluated vertices and stores the winning player p in $winner(v)$.

Evaluating a vertex may lead to further winning vertices being found: If the partial game graph contains a pending predecessor v' of v which is owned by p, then p can choose to play into v from there and consequently also wins v'. A pending predecessor v' owned by the opponent of p is winning for p if all its successors are winning for p. In the evaluation procedure, it suffices to test that such a vertex v' has no pending or fringe successors; it cannot have evaluated successors won by the opponent of p, because in that case it would have been evaluated as winning for the opponent in an earlier call to the evaluation procedure.

In either case where a winning predecessor v' is found, the evaluation procedure is called recursively to mark v' as winning and propagate the evaluation result. The pseudo-code for the evaluation procedure is depicted in Figure 2.

Overall Solution Algorithm. To solve a weak game, the overall solution algorithm starts with an empty game graph, which only contains the initial vertex as a fringe vertex.

It then proceeds iteratively by locating force-sets of pending vertices and evaluating the contained vertices as won by their owner, or if no force-set can be found, expanding a fringe vertex which can be selected with an arbitrary selection strategy. This process is repeated until the initial vertex is evaluated (pseudo-code in Figure 3).

The algorithm is guaranteed to terminate: In each iteration, either a force-set can be identified or a fringe vertex can be expanded. In particular, if there are no fringe vertices left, the complete reachable part of the game graph has been constructed, in which case the set of all pending vertices of maximal color forms a force-set. (If no pending vertices remain, the initial vertex must already be evaluated.) It is thus not possible for the overall search procedure to arrive in a situation where it is impossible to proceed further. It is clear that the algorithm must terminate after at most $2|V|$ iterations of the main loop, because each iteration either moves a vertex from the fringe to the set of pending vertices or from there to the set of evaluated vertices.

```
Procedure SolveWeakGame():
    initialize the sets of evaluated and pending vertices with ∅
    initialize the set of fringe vertices with {v0}
    while v0 is not evaluated:
        if we can locate a force-set F among the set of pending vertices:
            for all v ∈ F:
                EvaluatePendingVertex(v,level(v))
        else:
            pick a fringe vertex v
            ExpandFringeVertex(v)
```

Fig. 3. Starting from a partial game graph containing only the initial vertex, expand vertices and evaluate force-sets until the initial vertex is evaluated

The remaining open question is how the algorithm locates force-sets. A complete – but expensive – method to identify force-sets is to continuously test if a force-set exists using a strategy similar to that used by the pure backward algorithm. However, the complexity of this approach is too high, scaling with the *product* of the size of the constructed sub-game and the maximal size of a single level.

Thus, the algorithm pursues the less ambitious approach of only searching for force-sets that consist of *all pending vertices within a given level*. Testing this property can be performed very efficiently, as we will now discuss. Although it cannot find all force-sets, it already provides good results (cf. Section 5).

Efficient Implementation. We assume that the basic set operations of adding an element, removing an element and testing membership can be performed in constant time. Hash tables with randomized hash functions can achieve this in the *expected* case. (If we do not want to resort to randomization, we can instead use AVL trees, in which case a logarithmic factor needs to be added to our complexity result.)

We also assume that it is possible to enumerate the set of successor vertices $succ(v)$ of a given vertex v in time linear in $|succ(v)|$.

Under these assumptions, procedure ExpandFringeVertex only requires time $O(|succ(v)|)$ for a given vertex v (excluding any time spent within EvaluatePendingVertex), and as it is called at most once for each vertex in the partial game graph, the total time spent in this procedure is $O(|E'|)$, where E' is the set of edges in the partial game graph upon termination.

To efficiently determine the pending predecessors of a vertex, we can maintain sets $pred(v)$ for all constructed vertices, adding each vertex v' to the predecessor set of all its successors as it is constructed. (We never need to refer to predecessors which are not part of the partial game graph.) To efficiently determine whether a vertex has unevaluated successors, we can keep track of the *number* of such successors for all vertices in the partial game graph. Maintaining the consistency of these numbers is easy to achieve without increasing the complexity of the search procedures. Excluding recursive invocations, procedure EvaluatePendingVertex thus runs in time linear in the number of constructed predecessors of a given vertex v, again leading to an overall bound of $O(|E'|)$ because each vertex in the partial game graph is evaluated at most once.

To efficiently track whether the pending vertices of a given level form a force set, we maintain a single counter for each level which tracks the number of *violating* vertices in this level, and a set of levels for which this counter is currently 0. A pending vertex v violates the force-set condition iff it is owned by the level owner and has no pending successors in the same level or is owned by the other player and has a fringe successor or a pending successor with a higher color. (Note that we can ignore evaluated successors for testing the force-set condition because the propagation of evaluation results is already adequately taken care of by procedure EvaluatePendingVertex.) We thus only need to keep track of one additional number for each constructed vertex, which either counts the number of pending successors in the same level (for vertices v with $owner(v) = level(v)$), or the combined number of fringe successors and pending successors with a higher color (for other vertices). Again, keeping track of these numbers does not increase the asymptotical run-time of the algorithm.

If, finally, we also maintain a hash table which maps each color in the partial game graph to the corresponding set of pending vertices, procedure SolveWeakGame can be implemented in such a way that the overhead for each call to EvaluatePendingVertex or ExpandFringeVertex is constant, leading to the following result.

Theorem 1. *Procedure SolveWeakGame is a sound and complete algorithm for the problem of solving weak games. Its runtime is bounded by $O(|E'|)$, where E' is the set of edges constructed.*

The theorem follows from the previous discussion. In particular, termination and the run-time bound have already been been established, and for soundness, observe that vertices are only evaluated if they belong to a force-set or if their evaluation immediately follows from that of already evaluated successors.

4 Games and ATL

4.1 ATL

Alternating-time temporal logic (ATL) extends the classical computation tree logic (CTL) with path quantifiers $\langle\langle A\rangle\rangle$ and $[\![A]\!]$, expressing that a group A of agents has a strategy to accomplish a goal (defined by the respective path formula). For a definition of ATL formulas, we first introduce the structures over which a formula is interpreted. An alternating transition system (ATS) is a tuple

$$\mathcal{A} = \langle \Pi, \Sigma, Q, q_0, \pi, \delta \rangle,$$

consisting of a finite set Π of atomic propositions, a finite set Σ of agents, a finite set Q of states with a designated initial state q_0, a labeling function $\pi : Q \rightarrow 2^{\Pi}$ that decorates each state with a subset of the atomic propositions, and a transition function $\delta : Q \times \Sigma \rightarrow 2^{2^Q}$. Intuitively, δ maps a state q and an agent a to the choices available to a at q. For any state $q \in Q$ and set of agents $A \subseteq \Sigma$, we define the set of *joint decisions* $\Delta(q, A)$ of A in state q as $\Delta(q, A) = \{\bigcap_{a \in A} Q_a \mid Q_a \in \delta(q, a) \text{ for all } a \in A\}$. Once all agents $a \in \Sigma$ have made their choice $Q_a \in \delta(q, a)$ in a state q, the successor state must be uniquely determined. We thus require δ to be defined such that, in any state q, all joint decisions in $\Delta(q, \Sigma)$ are singletons.

ATL formulas are interpreted over an alternating transition system $\mathcal{A} = \langle \Pi, \Sigma, Q, q_0, \pi, \delta \rangle$. An ATL formula can be formed using the following grammar:

$$\varphi ::= \mathit{true} \mid \mathit{false} \mid p \mid \neg p \mid \varphi \wedge \varphi \mid \varphi \vee \varphi \mid \langle\!\langle A \rangle\!\rangle \bigcirc \varphi \mid [\![A]\!] \bigcirc \varphi \mid \\ \langle\!\langle A \rangle\!\rangle \varphi \mathsf{U} \varphi \mid [\![A]\!] \varphi \mathsf{U} \varphi \mid \langle\!\langle A \rangle\!\rangle \varphi \mathsf{W} \varphi \mid [\![A]\!] \varphi \mathsf{W} \varphi,$$

where $p \in \Pi$ is an atomic proposition, and $A \subseteq \Sigma$ is a set of agents. (Note that this definition deviates slightly from the original definition of ATL. The variant we use is strictly more expressive; e. g., in the original definition of ATL $\langle\!\langle A \rangle\!\rangle \varphi \mathsf{W} \psi$ cannot be expressed.) Intuitively, a formula $\langle\!\langle A \rangle\!\rangle \tau$ expresses the capability of the agents in A to enforce the path formula τ if they always have to make their choices before the other agents, while $[\![A]\!]\tau$ is the weaker requirement expressing that the agents in A can enforce the path formula τ if they only need to fix their decisions after their opponents made their choices.

For an ATL formula φ with atomic propositions Π and an alternating transition system $\mathcal{A} = \langle \Pi, \Sigma, Q, q_0, \pi, \delta \rangle$, $\|\varphi\|_{\mathcal{A}} \subseteq Q$ denotes the set of states where φ holds. The set $\|\varphi\|_{\mathcal{A}}$ is defined inductively along the structure of φ:

- Atomic propositions are interpreted as follows: $\|\mathit{true}\|_{\mathcal{A}} = Q$, $\|\mathit{false}\|_{\mathcal{A}} = \emptyset$, $\|p\|_{\mathcal{A}} = \{q \in Q \mid p \in \pi(q)\}$ and $\|\neg p\|_{\mathcal{A}} = \{q \in Q \mid p \notin \pi(q)\}$.
- As usual, conjunction and disjunction are interpreted as intersection and union, respectively: $\|\varphi \wedge \psi\|_{\mathcal{A}} = \|\varphi\|_{\mathcal{A}} \cap \|\psi\|_{\mathcal{A}}$ and $\|\varphi \vee \psi\|_{\mathcal{A}} = \|\varphi\|_{\mathcal{A}} \cup \|\psi\|_{\mathcal{A}}$.
- A state $q \in Q$ is in $\|\langle\!\langle A \rangle\!\rangle \bigcirc \varphi\|_{\mathcal{A}}$ if the agents A can make a joint decision $Q_A \in \Delta(q, A)$ such that, for all joint decisions $Q_{\Sigma \smallsetminus A} \in \Delta(q, \Sigma \smallsetminus A)$ of the other agents, φ holds in the successor state ($Q_A \cap Q_{\Sigma \smallsetminus A} \subseteq \|\varphi\|_{\mathcal{A}}$).
- A state $q \in Q$ is in $\|[\![A]\!] \bigcirc \varphi\|_{\mathcal{A}}$ if for all joint decisions $Q_{\Sigma \smallsetminus A} \in \Delta(q, \Sigma \smallsetminus A)$ of the other agents, the agents A can make a joint decision $Q_A \in \Delta(q, A)$ such that φ holds in the successor state ($Q_A \cap Q_{\Sigma \smallsetminus A} \subseteq \|\varphi\|_{\mathcal{A}}$).
- The remaining temporal operators are defined as fixed points.
  - $\|\langle\!\langle A \rangle\!\rangle \varphi \mathsf{U} \psi\|_{\mathcal{A}}$ ($\|\langle\!\langle A \rangle\!\rangle \varphi \mathsf{W} \psi\|_{\mathcal{A}}$) is the smallest (greatest) set X satisfying $\|\psi\|_{\mathcal{A}} \subseteq X \subseteq \|\varphi \vee \psi\|_{\mathcal{A}}$ with the following property: For all $q \in X \smallsetminus \|\psi\|_{\mathcal{A}}$, the agents in A can make a joint decision $Q_A \in \Delta(q, A)$ such that, for all joint decisions $Q_{\Sigma \smallsetminus A} \in \Delta(q, \Sigma \smallsetminus A)$ of the other agents, the successor state is in X ($Q_A \cap Q_{\Sigma \smallsetminus A} \subseteq X$), and
  - $\|[\![A]\!] \varphi \mathsf{U} \psi\|_{\mathcal{A}}$ ($\|[\![A]\!] \varphi \mathsf{W} \psi\|_{\mathcal{A}}$) is the smallest (greatest) set X satisfying $\|\psi\|_{\mathcal{A}} \subseteq X \subseteq \|\varphi \vee \psi\|_{\mathcal{A}}$ with the following property: For all $q \in X \smallsetminus \|\psi\|_{\mathcal{A}}$ and all joint decisions $Q_{\Sigma \smallsetminus A} \in \Delta(q, \Sigma \smallsetminus A)$ of the other agents, the agents A can make a joint decision $Q_A \in \Delta(q, A)$ such that the successor state is in X ($Q_A \cap Q_{\Sigma \smallsetminus A} \subseteq X$).

$\mathcal{A}$ is a *model* of a specification φ iff φ holds in the initial state ($q_0 \in \|\varphi\|_{\mathcal{A}}$).

4.2 Weak Games for ATL Model-Checking

Given an ATS $\mathcal{A}$ and an ATL formula φ, model-checking $\mathcal{A}$ naturally reduces to solving a weak model-checking game $\mathcal{G}_{\mathcal{A}}^{\varphi}$. The vertices of this game essentially consist of pairs of states of $\mathcal{A}$ and subformulas of φ.

Constructing the Game Graph. Intuitively, an ATL model-checking game is concurrently played on the formula tree and on the alternating transition system. It is technically more convenient to identify an until or wait-for formula $\psi = ((A))\psi' \mathsf{V} \psi''$ ($((A)) \in \{\langle\langle A\rangle\rangle, [\![A]\!]\}, \mathsf{V} \in \{\mathsf{U}, \mathsf{W}\}$) with the equivalent formula $\psi'' \vee \psi' \wedge ((A)) \bigcirc ((A))\psi' \mathsf{V} \psi''$. The extended set Φ of subformulas of a formula φ thus consists of the following formulas:

- each subformula ψ of φ,
- for each subformula $\psi = \langle\langle A\rangle\rangle \psi' \mathsf{U} \psi''$ or $\psi = \langle\langle A\rangle\rangle \psi' \mathsf{W} \psi''$ of φ, the formulas $\overline{\psi} = \langle\langle A\rangle\rangle \bigcirc \psi$ and $\widehat{\psi} = \psi' \wedge \langle\langle A\rangle\rangle \bigcirc \psi$, and
- for each subformula $\psi = [\![A]\!] \psi' \mathsf{U} \psi''$ or $\psi = [\![A]\!] \psi' \mathsf{W} \psi''$ of φ, the formulas $\overline{\psi} = [\![A]\!] \bigcirc \psi$ and $\widehat{\psi} = \psi' \wedge [\![A]\!] \bigcirc \psi$.

The formulas ψ, $\overline{\psi}$ and $\widehat{\psi}$ are called *connected* (with the intuition that they form a strongly connected component in a subformula graph), and formulas of the form $\langle\langle A\rangle\rangle \bigcirc \psi$ and $[\![A]\!] \bigcirc \psi$ are called *temporal.*

The model checking game has two types of vertices:

- For each state $q \in Q$ of the model $\mathcal{A}$ and formula $\psi \in \Phi$ in the extended set of subformulas of φ, there is a *full-move* vertex (q, ψ), representing the situation where q is the current state in the model and formula ψ must be proved.
- For each *temporal* formula $\langle\langle A\rangle\rangle \bigcirc \psi \in \Phi$ or $[\![\Sigma \smallsetminus A]\!] \bigcirc \psi \in \Phi$ in the extended set of subformulas of φ, state $q \in Q$ and joint decision $Q' \in \Delta(q, A)$, there is a *half-move* vertex (q, ψ, A, Q'), representing the situation where q is the current state in the model, formula ψ must be proved, and the agents in A have already made their next joint decision Q'.

It is computationally more convenient to use a variant of weak games where some vertices, namely those which refer to literals, have no successors, but are evaluated immediately. Such vertices appear as sinks in the game graph.

The weak model-checking game has the following transitions:

- There is a transition from (q, ψ) to (q, ψ') if ψ' is a direct subformula of ψ, where until and wait-for formulas $((A))\psi \mathsf{V} \psi'$ are again interpreted as disjunctions $\psi' \vee \psi \wedge ((A)) \bigcirc ((A))\psi \mathsf{V} \psi'$.
- There is a transition from (q, ψ) to (q, ψ, A, Q') if ψ is a temporal formula.
- There is a transition from (q, ψ, A, Q') to (q', ψ') if $q' \in Q' \cap Q_{\Sigma \smallsetminus A}$ for some joint decision $Q_{\Sigma \smallsetminus A} \in \Delta(q, \Sigma \smallsetminus A)$ of the agents not in A, and $\psi = ((A)) \bigcirc \psi'$.

Game Construction. To construct a weak game $\mathcal{G}_{\mathcal{A}}^{\varphi} = \langle V_{even}, V_{odd}, E, v_0, \alpha \rangle$, we only need to partition the set V of vertices into two sets V_{even} and V_{odd} of vertices, owned by the two players *even* and *odd*, find a suitable coloring function, and define the initial vertex. We assume that the objective of *even* is to prove that the model satisfies the formula, while the objective of *odd* is to disprove this.

The initial vertex is given by the pair (q_0, φ) consisting of the initial state q_0 of the model and the formula φ to be checked. A proper partition of V follows from the ATL semantics: Vertices (q, ψ) of the model-checking game whose formula part ψ is a conjunction or a temporal formula of the form $[\![A]\!] \bigcirc \psi'$, and vertices (q, ψ, A, Q') whose formula part ψ is a temporal formula of the form $\langle\!\langle A \rangle\!\rangle \bigcirc \psi'$ are owned by player *odd*; the remaining vertices are owned by player *even*. A proper coloring function maps a state $(q, \langle\!\langle A \rangle\!\rangle \psi \mathsf{U} \psi')$ or $(q, [\![A]\!] \psi \mathsf{U} \psi')$ to an odd color, and a state $(q, \langle\!\langle A \rangle\!\rangle \psi \mathsf{W} \psi')$ or $(q, [\![A]\!] \psi \mathsf{W} \psi')$ to an even color.

While the algorithm is sound and complete for every proper coloring function, the chosen coloring function can have a significant impact on the performance of the algorithm introduced in Section 3. The “standard” coloring is designed to create a *small* number of colors, which depend only on the formula. While this is convenient in a pure backwards analysis, it makes finding force-sets more difficult. In an optimal setting each strongly connected component of the game graph has a color of its own. While partitioning the game graph into strongly connected components is not cheaper than a complete evaluation, significant information can often be drawn from the *symbolic* representation of an alternating transition system.

A simple analysis of an RML specification suffices to identify counters that are only counted up (or down) and flags that are only set (or reset). Such situations naturally arise, e. g., in the definition of protocols. This allows for a simple construction of a ranking function γ on the abstract states, which is preserved by the concretization. Using such a ranking function results in a significant reduction of the size of levels, and therefore accelerates model-checking (cf. Section 5).

To achieve small levels, we create a coloring function which assigns the same color to two states (q, ψ) and (q', ψ') if and only if q and q' have the same rank and ψ and ψ' are equivalent or connected. In the protocol benchmark discussed in Section 5, this increases the number of colors from 2 colors in the standard coloring to about $5.3 \cdot 10^{33}$ colors, leaving the single levels in an accessible size.

5 Benchmarks and Results

To evaluate our algorithm, we implemented it in Java and tested it on some ATL properties of the Garay and MacKenzie multi-party contract signing protocol [10], using the RML formalization by Chadha et al. [6].

In particular, we considered the case of five agents (four contract-signing parties $P_1, \ldots, P_4$ and a trusted third party T) and the property of *protocol fairness*: A protocol is fair for an agent P_i following the protocol iff, whenever some other agent P_j obtains the signature of P_i, then P_i can obtain the signatures of the other agents, even if they are all dishonest (i. e., do not follow the protocol) and do not cooperate. In ATL, we can express this property as

$$\mathsf{AG}\Big(\Big(\bigvee_{j\neq i} has\_sig(P_j, P_i)\Big) \rightarrow \langle\!\langle P_i \rangle\!\rangle \mathsf{F} \bigwedge_{j\neq i} has\_sig(P_i, P_j)\Big)$$

(The common G and F modalities can be expressed in ATL using W and U in the usual way [5]. The A path quantifier is synonymous with $\langle\!\langle \emptyset \rangle\!\rangle$.) Because the Garay and MacKenzie protocol is asymmetric, protocol fairness must be proved or disproved separately for each of the four contract-signing parties P_i.

As we observed in the introduction, selective explicit-state methods are only useful when checking properties which *can* be verified or refuted without considering the complete reachable state space. Given that the protocol fairness property is of the form $\mathsf{AG}\varphi$, *verifying* it requires constructing all reachable states. However, as originally shown by Chadha et al. [6], fairness is *violated* in the Garay and MacKenzie protocol for the case of $i \neq 4$, and thus in this case the property can serve as a useful benchmark for selective methods. The protocol is fair for agent P_4, so selective algorithms do not work well in this case.

We have model-checked the protocol fairness property for each agent using three different approaches:

- First, we used the MOCHA model checker, which solves the weak game corresponding to an ATL formula by a symbolic backward computation.
- Second, we implemented a standard explicit-state forward-searching evaluation strategy, exploring the game graph in depth-first order.
- Third, we considered our strategic forward-backward approach. As a selection strategy for choosing the next fringe vertex to expand, we employed a variant of the proof-number search algorithm used for evaluating and/or-trees [1].

A symbolic (non-strategic) forward-backward algorithm would have been a good fourth candidate approach, but it appears that no efficient implementation of such an algorithm is available. To at least compute a lower bound on the performance of such an algorithm, we performed a complete symbolic forward exploration – the first stage of a symbolic forward-backward algorithm – of the game graph using MOCHA's symbolic forward exploration capabilities (which are distinct from its ATL model-checking algorithm and can only be used to model-check invariants).

To initialize proof numbers for fringe vertices within our strategic forward-backward approach, we used the FF heuristic [11] with a *problem-dependent* goal formula, i. e., for each of the three properties we specified a collection of literals that we considered to be likely to be satisfied near "interesting" vertices in the game graph, which biases the exploration towards such vertices. Using such problem-dependent heuristics of course means that this is merely a *semi-automatic* approach: while the algorithm is sound and complete for all possible heuristics, a reasonable choice of heuristics is important for good performance. Using hand-tuned heuristic information is sufficient for the purposes of this investigation, in which our objective is to demonstrate the usefulness of selective game-solving approaches in general rather than the development of game-solving heuristics; however, the latter certainly remains as an important open problem.

	MOCHA	forward	SFB	strategic
fairness for P_1	21:15:07	failure	> 04:19:52	00:01:22
fairness for P_2	failure	failure	> 02:41:45	00:01:46
fairness for P_3	10:57:07	failure	> 06:25:33	00:01:26
fairness for P_4	00:39:14	failure	> 10:44:13	failure

Fig. 4. Run-time results for the protocol-fairness property. The four algorithms considered are MOCHA, explicit forward search, symbolic forward-backward search (SFB; only forward exploration counted), and strategic forward-backward search. Time is measured in hours, minutes and seconds (hh:mm:ss).

	evaluated	pending	fringe	reachable
fairness for P_1	130	934	37036	$2.4 \cdot 10^{14}$
fairness for P_2	298	2098	51814	$7.6 \cdot 10^{15}$
fairness for P_3	628	4765	31952	$7.4 \cdot 10^{17}$

Fig. 5. Numbers of evaluated, pending and fringe vertices generated by the strategic forward-backward algorithm. The total number of forward-reachable vertices is shown for comparison.

The results of our experiment are shown in Figure 4.[1] We clearly see that selectivity pays off on this suite of benchmarks. Simple-minded explicit search methods like standard forward search cannot cope with this state space at all, and exhaustive symbolic methods require many hours of solution time where the selective approach terminates within a few minutes. In particular, it dramatically improves on a symbolic forward-backward exploration, which would require several hours for computing the set of forward reachable states alone. All this only applies to agents P_1, P_2 and P_3, however. For agent P_4, the complete reachable state space must be considered to prove protocol fairness, and there is no hope of achieving this with an explicit-state method.

Compared to traditional approaches, one advantage of our algorithm is that proofs (or refutations) of the checked properties are generated as part of the search. In particular, the subgraph of the partial game graph induced by the set of evaluated vertices forms an explicit proof of the property. In comparison, MOCHA only reports whether a given ATL formula holds or does not hold in a model, without providing further information. Figure 5 offers some statistics on the size of the explored state spaces, showing that the generated proofs are indeed very selective.

6 Discussion

We have presented a new algorithm for solving weak games, such as those arising from ATL model-checking problems, which is based on the idea of selectively generating only those parts of the game graph which are relevant to proving

[1] Experiments were conducted on a standard Linux PC with a 3 GHz CPU and using a heap limit of 512 MB. All failures are due to running out of memory.

or disproving the hypothesized property. Using a combination of forward exploration to extend a partially constructed game graph and backward propagation of evaluation results, including the efficient detection of *force-sets* for situations where a player can force a run of the game to stay in a given level of the game graph indefinitely, the algorithm can solve a weak game in time which is linear in the *size of the subgame considered*, rather than linear in the size of the game. In the best case, this can lead to dramatic speedups compared to exhaustive approaches. In the worst case, the algorithm is still asymptotically optimal.

One significant advantage of the selective search method we present is that, unlike traditional methods for solving weak games symbolically, it generates a verifiable proof of the model-checking result. What is more, due to the selective nature of the search, we can expect such proofs to be comparatively small, because they are explicitly represented within the algorithm as subgraphs of the partial game graph that serves as a main data structure.

Of course, the flip side of this advantage is that selective search techniques only make sense for games where short proofs exist, i. e., where one player can force the game to remain in a comparatively small fragment of the overall game graph. If the complete game graph needs to be explored, there is little point in using a selective method, and one can expect better performance from a systematic symbolic algorithm.

Future Work. In the current form, the algorithm only finds force-sets that cover all pending vertices within a level. One might consider strengthening this approach by initiating an exhaustive evaluation after each expansion, but this is too expensive to be pursued. An interesting alternative is to use approximative methods based on the weak or strong connectivity structure of the pending vertices in a level. Both structures provide useful information since finding a force-set within a strongly or weakly connected component coincides with finding a force-set in a level.

Weak connectedness, in particular, can be efficiently tracked using classical union-find data structures. Thus, distinguishing weakly connected components within a level promises a good trade-off between (expensive) continuous re-evaluations and the coarse approximation of the basic method. Using this method, worst-case runtime is still quasi-linear in the number $|E'|$ of edges constructed by the algorithm, while the constructed subgraph is potentially smaller.

Another method to speed up the detection of force-sets is to use *thresholding forward-backward search*, where a *complete* backward evaluation is initiated after $c, c^2, c^3, \dots$ steps (for some constant $c > 1$). On a finer granularity, one could initiate the evaluation of a *level* after $c, c^2, c^3, \dots$ vertices of the level have been constructed. One strength of such a thresholding approach is that it retains the asymptotically optimal behavior of the basic algorithm.

Acknowledgement

This work was partly supported by the German Research Council (DFG) as part of the Transregional Collaborative Research Center "Automatic Verification and

Analysis of Complex Systems" (SFB/TR 14 AVACS). See www.avacs.org for more information.

References

1. L. V. Allis, M. van der Meulen, and H. J. van der Herik. Proof-number search. *Artificial Intelligence*, 66(1):91–124, 1994.
2. R. Alur, T. A. Henzinger, and O. Kupferman. Alternating-time temporal logic. *Journal of the ACM*, 49(5):672–713, 2002.
3. R. Alur, T. A. Henzinger, F. Y. C. Mang, S. Qadeer, S. K. Rajamani, and S. Tasiran. Mocha: Modularity in model checking. In *Proc. CAV*, pages 521–525, 1998.
4. H. R. Andersen. Model checking and boolean graphs. *Theor. Comput. Sci.*, 126(1):3–30, 1994.
5. J. R. Burch, E. M. Clarke, K. L. McMillan, D. L. Dill, and L. J. Hwang. Symbolic model checking: 10^{20} states and beyond. *Information and Computation*, 98(2):142–170, 1992.
6. R. Chadha, S. Kremer, and A. Scedrov. Analysis of multi-party contract signing. Technical Report 516, Université Libre de Bruxelles, 2004.
7. E. M. Clarke and E. A. Emerson. Design and synthesis of synchronization skeletons using branching time temporal logic. In *Proc. IBM Workshop on Logics of Programs*, pages 52–71, 1981.
8. R. Cleaveland and B. Steffen. A linear-time model-checking algorithm for the alternation-free modal μ-calculus. In *Proc. CAV '91*, pages 48–58, 1992.
9. E. A. Emerson and C. S. Jutla. Tree automata, μ-calculus and determinacy. In *Proc. FOCS*, pages 368–377, 1991.
10. J. A. Garay and P. D. MacKenzie. Abuse-free multi-party contract signing. In *International Symposium on Distributed Computing*, volume 1693 of *LNCS*, pages 151–165, 1999.
11. J. Hoffmann and B. Nebel. The FF planning system: Fast plan generation through heuristic search. *Journal of Artificial Intelligence Research*, 14:253–302, 2001.
12. G. J. Holzmann. The model checker SPIN. *Software Engineering*, 23(5):279–295, 1997.
13. D. E. Knuth and R. W. Moore. An analysis of alpha-beta pruning. *Artificial Intelligence*, 6(4):293–326, 1975.
14. S. Kremer. *Formal Analysis of Optimistic Fair Exchange Protocols*. PhD thesis, Université Libre de Bruxelles, Brussels, Belgium, Dec. 2003.
15. S. Kremer and J.-F. Raskin. A game-based verification of non-repudiation and fair exchange protocols. *Journal of Computer Security*, 11(3):399–430, 2003.
16. A. Mahimkar and V. Shmatikov. Game-based analysis of denial-of-service prevention protocols. In *IEEE Computer Security Foundations Workshop*, pages 287–301, 2005.
17. M. Ryan and P.-Y. Schobbens. Agents and roles: Refinement in alternating-time temporal logic. In *Proc. ATAL*, pages 100–114, 2001.
18. W. van der Hoek, A. Lomuscio, and M. Wooldridge. On the complexity of practical ATL model checking. In *Proc. AAMAS*, 2006.

Controller Synthesis and Ordinal Automata*

Thierry Cachat

LIAFA/CNRS UMR 7089 & Université Paris 7, France

Abstract. Ordinal automata are used to model physical systems with Zeno behavior. Using automata and games techniques we solve a control problem formulated and left open by Demri and Nowak in 2005. It involves partial observability and a new synchronization between the controller and the environment.

1 Introduction

Controller Synthesis. The synthesis of controller is today one of the most important challenges in computer science. Since [RW89] different formalisms have been considered to model (un)controllable and (un)observable actions. The problem is well understood for finite systems admitting infinite behavior (indexed by ω) [PR89]. Recent developments concern extensions to e.g. infinite state systems or timed systems [BDMP03].

Transforming control problems into two-player games have provided efficient solutions [Tho95]. In this setting the controller is modeled by a player and the environment by her opponent. Determining whether a controller exists falls down to determine the winner and computing a winning strategy is equivalent to synthesizing a controller.

Ordinal Automata. A Büchi or Muller automaton, after reading an ω-sequence, simply accepts or rejects, depending on the states visited infinitely often. In an ordinal automaton there is a limit transition to a new state, also depending on the states visited infinitely often and the run goes on from this state. This allows to model a system preforming ω actions in a finite time and reaching a limit state.

Systems with Zeno Behaviors. When modeling physical systems we face the problem that different components can have different time scales. For example the controller of an anti-lock braking system (ABS) is supposed to react much quicker than the physical environment. In the opposite one can consider physical systems admitting Zeno behavior —infinitely many actions in a finite amount of time— whereas the controller is a computer with constant clock frequency. A simple example is a bouncing ball. Another one is the physical description of an electronic circuit which evolves much quicker than its logical description in

* The author acknowledges partial support by the ACI "Sécurité et Informatique" CORTOS. `http://www.lsv.ens-cachan.fr/aci-cortos/`

S. Graf and W. Zhang (Eds.): ATVA 2006, LNCS 4218, pp. 215–228, 2006.

VHDL. The speeds are so different that one can consider that the former one evolves infinitely quicker than the latter one.

Following this idea Demri and Nowak [DN05] have proposed to model physical systems by ordinal automata, thus admitting ordinal sequences as behavior (typically of length ω^k). They define a logic LTL(ω^k) as an extension of LTL to express properties of such systems. The controller should be a usual automaton whose execution is an ω-sequence. The synchronization between controller and environment is the following: environment makes ω^{k-1} steps "alone", then controller and environment makes one step together, and so on.

Particularly in the context of timed systems, different techniques have been proposed to forbid or restrict Zeno behaviors, see introduction of [AFH$^+$03] for an overview. Our claim is that we want to allow Zeno behavior, to model them and express properties about them, and finally to control such systems.

Our Contribution. The main contribution of our article is a solution to the control problem stated and left open in [DN05]. Given a physical system modeled by an ordinal automaton and a formula ψ of LTL(ω^k) we want to determine whether a controller exists and synthesize one. The technique used is to transform the control problem into a game problem. Because of the unobservable actions and also because of the different time scales, the controller can not fully observe the current state of the system. For that reason we construct a game of imperfect information. Another difficulty is that the length of the interaction is greater than ω, but fortunately one can summarize ω^{k-1} steps done by the environment "alone". Several games and automata techniques are used.

Related Work. It is known that games of imperfect information have higher computational complexity [Rei84]. Zeno behavior have already been considered in the literature. In [BP00] languages of ordinal words accepted by timed automata are studied. In the framework of hybrid systems [AM98, Bou99] or cellular automata on continuous time and space [DL05] it is known that allowing Zeno behaviors gives rise to highly undecidable problems. In [DN05] Demri and Nowak solve the satisfiability and the model-checking problem for LTL(ω^k): given an ordinal automaton reading ω^k-sequences and a formula ψ, determine whether every run of the automaton satisfies ψ. For this they use a "succinct" form of ordinal automata to have better complexity bounds.

Plan of the Paper. In the next section we present the temporal logic LTL(ω^k), ordinal automata and the control problem. We show a translation to first order logic. In Section 3 we solve our main problem. We first explain how to translate it to a game and why the controller has imperfect information about the system. An example is provided in Section 4.

2 Reasoning About Transfinite Sequences

We assume basic knowledge about ordinals less than ω^ω, see e.g. [Ros82]. An *ordinal* is a well and totally ordered set. It is either 0 or a successor ordinal of the form $\beta+1$ or a limit ordinal. The first limit ordinal is denoted ω. For all ordinal α, $\beta < \alpha \Leftrightarrow \beta \in \alpha$ and $\alpha = \{\beta : \beta < a\}$. In this article we restrict ourselves to ordinals less or equal than ω^ω. By the Cantor Normal Form theorem, for all $\alpha < \omega^\omega$ there exists unique integers $p, n_1, \ldots, n_p$ and $k_1, \ldots, k_p$ such that $k_1 > k_2 > \cdots > k_p$ and $\alpha = \omega^{k_1} n_1 + \omega^{k_2} n_2 + \cdots + \omega^{k_p} n_p$. Recall e.g. that $2\omega = \omega$ and $\omega + \omega^2 = \omega^2$. An ordinal α is said to be closed under addition whenever $\beta, \beta' < \alpha$ implies $\beta + \beta' < \alpha$. In particular for every $\alpha \leq \omega^\omega$, α is closed under addition iff α is equal to ω^β for some $\beta \leq \omega$ or $\alpha = 0$. In the following we will consider a logic whose models are ω^k sequences for some $k < \omega$.

2.1 Temporal Logic

We recall the definition of the logic LTL(α) introduced in [DN05]. For every ordinal α closed under addition, the models of LTL(α) are precisely sequences of the form $\sigma : \alpha \to 2^{\mathrm{AP}}$ for some countably infinite set AP of atomic propositions. The formulas of LTL(α) are defined as follows: $\phi ::= p \mid \neg\phi \mid \phi_1 \wedge \phi_2 \mid \mathtt{X}^\beta \phi \mid \phi_1 \mathtt{U}^{\beta'} \phi_2$, where $p \in \mathrm{AP}$, $\beta < \alpha$ and $\beta' \leq \alpha$. The satisfaction relation is inductively defined below where σ is a model for LTL(α) and $\beta < \alpha$:

- $\sigma, \beta \models p$ iff $p \in \sigma(\beta)$,
- $\sigma, \beta \models \phi_1 \wedge \phi_2$ iff $\sigma, \beta \models \phi_1$ and $\sigma, \beta \models \phi_2$, $\sigma, \beta \models \neg\phi$ iff not $\sigma, \beta \models \phi$,
- $\sigma, \beta \models \mathtt{X}^{\beta'} \phi$ iff $\sigma, \beta + \beta' \models \phi$,
- $\sigma, \beta \models \phi_1 \mathtt{U}^{\beta'} \phi_2$ iff there is $\gamma < \beta'$ such that $\sigma, \beta + \gamma \models \phi_2$ and for every $\gamma' < \gamma$, $\sigma, \beta + \gamma' \models \phi_1$.

Closure under addition of α guarantees that $\beta + \beta'$ and $\beta + \gamma$ above are strictly smaller than α. Usual LTL is expressively equivalent to LTL(ω): $\mathtt{X}$ is equivalent to $\mathtt{X}^1$ and $\mathtt{U}$ is equivalent to $\mathtt{U}^\omega$, conversely $\mathtt{X}^n$ and $\mathtt{U}^n$ can be expressed in LTL. Standard abbreviations are also extended: $\mathtt{F}^\beta \phi \stackrel{\text{def}}{=} \top \mathtt{U}^\beta \phi$ and $\mathtt{G}^\beta \phi \stackrel{\text{def}}{=} \neg \mathtt{F}^\beta \neg \phi$. Using Cantor Normal Form it is easy to effectively encode an LTL(ω^k) formula for $k < \omega$. We provide below properties dealing with limit states that can be easily expressed in LTL(ω^k) ($k \geq 2$).
"p holds in the states indexed by limit ordinals strictly less than ω^k":

$$\mathtt{G}^{\omega^k}(\mathtt{X}^\omega p \wedge \cdots \wedge \mathtt{X}^{\omega^{k-1}} p).$$

For $1 \leq k' \leq k-2$, "if p holds infinitely often in states indexed by ordinals of the form $\omega^{k'} \times n$, $n \geq 1$, then q holds in the state indexed by $\omega^{k'+1}$":

$$(\mathtt{G}^{\omega^{k'+1}} \mathtt{F}^{\omega^{k'+1}} \mathtt{X}^{\omega^{k'}} p) \Rightarrow (\mathtt{X}^{\omega^{k'+1}} q).$$

2.2 Translation to First Order Logic

In [DN05] it is proved that LTL(ω^ω) (hence also LTL(ω^k)) can be translated to the monadic second order theory of $\langle \omega^\omega, < \rangle$, which gives a non-elementary decision procedure for satisfiability [BS73]. We improve this result by showing that LTL(ω^ω) can be translated even to the first order theory (FO) of $\langle \omega^\omega, < \rangle$.

Proposition 1. *For every* LTL(ω^ω) *formula there exists an equivalent first order formula over* $\langle \omega^\omega, < \rangle$.

It is open whether the converse also holds, extending Kamp's theorem [Kam68].

Proof (sketch). The main point is the definition of a formula $+_\beta(x,y)$ for some $\beta < \omega^\omega$ such that $\langle \omega^\omega, < \rangle \models_v +_\beta(x,y)$ with $v : \{x,y\} \to \omega^\omega$ iff $v(y) = v(x) + \beta$. The relation $\models_v$ is the standard satisfaction relation under the valuation v. The formulas of the form $+_\beta(x,y)$ with $\beta < \omega^\omega$ are inductively defined as:

1. $+_0(x,y) \stackrel{\text{def}}{=} (x = y)$,
2. $+_1(x,y) \stackrel{\text{def}}{=} (x < y) \wedge \forall\, z\ (z > x \Rightarrow y \leq z)$,
3. $+_{\omega^k n+\beta}(x,y) \stackrel{\text{def}}{=} \exists\, z\ +_{\omega^k}(x,z) \wedge +_{\omega^k(n-1)+\beta}(z,y)$ $(n \geq 1,\ k \geq 0)$,
4. $+_{\omega^k}(x,y) \stackrel{\text{def}}{=} (x < y) \wedge \forall z (x \leq z < y \Rightarrow \exists z' (+_{\omega^{k-1}}(z,z') \wedge z' < y)) \wedge$ $\forall y' [((x < y') \wedge \forall z (x \leq z < y' \Rightarrow \exists z' (+_{\omega^{k-1}}(z,z') \wedge z' < y'))) \Rightarrow y \leq y']$ $(k \geq 1)$.

For $k = 1$, the latter formula is written in the following way. The ordinal y such that $+_\omega(x,y)$ holds is greater than x, greater than every finite step successors of x, and y is the least ordinal satisfying this two conditions. By induction one can show that $y > x + n$ for every $n < \omega$. Analogously for $k > 1$, the formula implies that $y > x + \omega^{k-1} n$ for every $n < \omega$. □

The first order theory of $\langle \omega^\omega, + \rangle$ has a non-elementary decision procedure [Mau96]. We are not aware of the exact complexity of the more restricted first order theory of $\langle \omega^\omega, < \rangle$. We use ordinal automata, both to model physical systems and to represent specifications.

2.3 Ordinal Automata

Since Büchi in the 1960s and Choueka in the 1970s, different forms of ordinal automata have been proposed. A particular class of ordinal automata is well suited to solve our problem. See [Bed98] for the equivalence between different definitions. Ordinal automata has two kinds of transitions: usual one-step transition for successor ordinals and limit transitions for limit ordinals where the state reached is determined by the set of states visited again and again "before" that ordinal. An ordinal automaton is a tuple $(Q, \Sigma, \delta, E, I, F)$ where:

- Q is a finite set of states,
- Σ is a finite alphabet,
- $\delta \subseteq Q \times \Sigma \times Q$ is a one-step transition relation,
- $E \subseteq 2^Q \times Q$ is a limit transition relation,
- $I \subseteq Q$ is a finite set of initial states,
- $F \subseteq Q$ is a finite set of final states.

We write $q \xrightarrow{a} q'$ whenever $\langle q, a, q' \rangle \in \delta$ and $P \to q$ whenever $\langle P, q \rangle \in E$. A *path* of length $\alpha + 1$ is an $(\alpha + 1)$-sequence $r : \alpha + 1 \to Q$ labeled by an

α-sequence $\sigma : \alpha \to \Sigma$ such that for every $\beta \in \alpha$, $r(\beta) \xrightarrow{\sigma(\beta)} r(\beta+1)$ and for every limit ordinal $\beta \in \alpha + 1$, there is $P \to r(\beta) \in E$ s.t. $P = \mathit{cofinal}(\beta, r)$ with $\mathit{cofinal}(\beta, r) \stackrel{\text{def}}{=} \{q \in Q$: for every $\gamma \in \beta$, there is γ' such that $\gamma < \gamma' < \beta$ and $r(\gamma') = q\}$. The set $\mathit{cofinal}(\beta, r)$ is the set of states visited again and again arbitrary close to β (hence infinitely often).
If moreover $r(0) \in I$, it is a *run*. If moreover $r(\alpha) \in F$, it is accepting.

Example 1. We present here an example of ordinal automaton $\mathcal{A}$ with limit transitions $\{0\} \to 1$ and $\{0,1\} \to 2$. One can show that $\mathrm{L}(\mathcal{A})$ contains only ω^2-sequences and $\mathrm{L}(\mathcal{A}) = (a^\omega \cdot b)^\omega$.

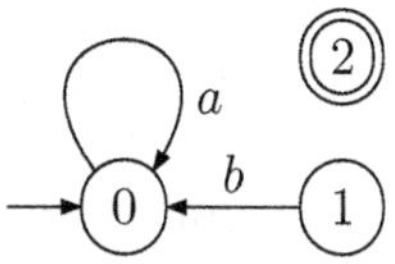

For all $k < \omega$ there exists an ordinal automaton accepting exactly the sequences of length ω^k, using $k+1$ states. But if an ordinal automaton accepts a sequence of length ω^ω, then it must also accept longer sequences. That is a second reason, beside closure under addition, why we restrict ourselves to ordinals less than ω^ω.

Level. An ordinal automaton $\mathcal{A} = \langle Q, \Sigma, \delta, E, I, F\rangle$ is of *level* $k \geq 1$ iff there is a map $l : Q \to \{0, \dots, k\}$ such that:

- for every $q \in F$, $l(q) = k$;
- $q \xrightarrow{a} q' \in \delta$ implies $l(q') = 0$ and $l(q) < k$;
- $P \to q \in E$ implies $l(q) \geq 1$, for every $q' \in P$, $l(q') < l(q)$, and there is $q' \in P$ such that $l(q') = l(q) - 1$.

The idea is that a state of level i is reached at positions $\beta + \omega^i.j$, $j < \omega$. Since [VW86], different techniques for translating logic formulas to automata are widely used.

Proposition 2 ([DN05]). *For all* $\mathrm{LTL}(\omega^k)$ *formula, there exists an equivalent ordinal automaton.*

This result can be obtain by translating an $\mathrm{LTL}(\omega^k)$ formula into an equivalent first order formula (or even monadic second order) and applying results from [BS73]. In [DN05] a succinct version of ordinal automata is defined to improve the complexity of the translation from non-elementary to polynomial (resp. exponential) space when integers in the formulas are encoded in unary (resp. binary).

2.4 Control Problem

Before we recall the control problem from [DN05] we need some preliminary definitions. In order for the physical system to evolve much faster than the controller we need a particular synchronization between them.

Synchronous Product. We define below the synchronous product of two ordinal automata having possibly different alphabets. They synchronize only on the common actions. This is used later to model unobservable actions. Let $\Sigma_i = 2^{Act_i}$

for $i = 1, 2$, a letter from Σ_i is a set of actions. Given two ordinal automata $\mathcal{A}_i = \langle Q_i, \Sigma_i, \delta_i, E_i, I_i, F_i \rangle$, for $i = 1, 2$, their synchronous product is defined as $\mathcal{A}_1 \times \mathcal{A}_2 = \langle Q, \Sigma, \delta, E, I, F \rangle$ where:

- $Q = Q_1 \times Q_2, \qquad \Sigma = 2^{Act_1 \cup Act_2}$.
- $\langle q_1, q_2 \rangle \xrightarrow{a} \langle q_1', q_2' \rangle \in \delta$ iff $q_1 \xrightarrow{a \cap Act_1} q_1'$ and $q_2 \xrightarrow{a \cap Act_2} q_2'$.
- $P \to \langle q_1, q_2 \rangle \in E$ iff there exists $P_1 \to q_1 \in E_1$ and $P_2 \to q_2 \in E_2$ such that $\{q : \langle q, q' \rangle \in P\} = P_1$ and $\{q' : \langle q, q' \rangle \in P\} = P_2$.
- $I = I_1 \times I_2, \qquad F = F_1 \times F_2$.

Lifting. In order to synchronize the system with a controller working on ω-sequences, we need to transform the controller so that its product with $\mathcal{S}$ only constraints states on positions $\omega^{k-1} \times n$, $n < \omega$. The other positions are not constrained.

Let $\mathcal{A} = \langle Q, \Sigma, \delta, E, I, F, l \rangle$ be an automaton of level 1. We define its lifting $\mathit{lift}_k(\mathcal{A})$ at level $k \geq 2$ to be the automaton $\langle Q', \Sigma, \delta', E', I', F', l' \rangle$ by:

- $Q' = \{0, \ldots, k\} \times Q, \qquad I' = \{k-1\} \times I, \qquad F' = \{k\} \times F$
- $l'(\langle i, q' \rangle) = i$,
- $\delta' = \{\langle k-1, q \rangle \xrightarrow{a} \langle 0, q' \rangle \ : \ q \xrightarrow{a} q' \in \delta\} \cup$
  $\{\langle i, q \rangle \xrightarrow{a} \langle 0, q \rangle \ : \ 0 \leq i \leq k-2,\ a \in \Sigma,\ q \notin F\}$,
- $E' = \{\{\langle 0, q \rangle, \ldots, \langle i-1, q \rangle\} \to \langle i, q \rangle \ : \ 1 \leq i < k,\ q \in Q\} \cup \{\{\langle 0, q_1 \rangle, \ldots, \langle k-1, q_1 \rangle, \ldots, \langle 0, q_n \rangle, \ldots, \langle k-1, q_n \rangle\} \to \langle k, q \rangle \ | \ \{q_1, \ldots q_n\} \to q \in E\}$.

Example 2. We present below an example of ordinal automaton $\mathcal{A}$ with limit transition $\{q_0, q_1\} \to q_2$ and the corresponding automaton $\mathit{lift}_2(\mathcal{A})$ with limit transitions $\{\langle 0, q_0 \rangle\} \to \langle 1, q_0 \rangle$, $\{\langle 0, q_1 \rangle\} \to \langle 1, q_1 \rangle$, and $\{\langle 0, q_0 \rangle, \langle 1, q_0 \rangle, \langle 0, q_1 \rangle, \langle 1, q_1 \rangle, \} \to \langle 2, q_2 \rangle$. We omit useless transitions.

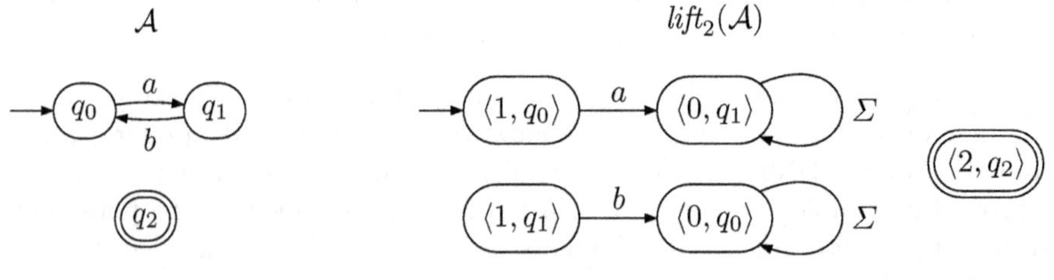

Proposition 3 ([DN05]). *For all $w \in \Sigma^{\omega^k}$, $w \in \mathrm{L}(\mathit{lift}_k(\mathcal{A}))$ iff the word $w' \in \Sigma^\omega$, defined by $w'(i) = w(\omega^{k-1} \times i)$, is in $\mathrm{L}(\mathcal{A})$.*

A physical system $\mathcal{S}$ is modeled as a structure

$$\langle \mathcal{A}_\mathcal{S}, Act_C, Act_O, Act \rangle$$

where $\mathcal{A}_\mathcal{S}$ is an ordinal automaton of level k with alphabet 2^{Act} where Act is a finite set of actions, $Act_O \subseteq Act$ is the set of observable actions, $Act_C \subseteq Act_O$ is the set of controllable actions. The set $Act \backslash Act_C$ of uncontrollable actions is denoted by $Act_{\mathcal{NC}}$. A specification of the system $\mathcal{S}$ is naturally an LTL(ω^k) formula ψ. A controller $\mathcal{C}$ for the pair $\langle \mathcal{S}, \psi \rangle$ is a system whose complete executions are ω-sequences (typically ordinal automata of level 1) verifying the properties below.

(obs) Only observable actions are present in the controller. Hence, thanks to the synchronization mode, in the product system between $\mathcal{S}$ and $\mathcal{C}$, unobservable actions do not change the $\mathcal{C}$-component of the current state. So the alphabet of $\mathcal{C}$ is $2^{Act_{\mathcal{O}}}$. Moreover for every state q of $\mathcal{C}$ there is a transition $q \xrightarrow{\emptyset} q$.

(unc) From any state of $\mathcal{C}$, uncontrollable actions can always be executed: $\forall q \cdot \forall a \subseteq Act_{\mathcal{O}} \setminus Act_{\mathcal{C}}$, there is a transition $q \xrightarrow{b} q'$ in $\mathcal{C}$ such that $b \cap Act_{\mathcal{NC}} = a$.

(prod) Finally, the system $\mathcal{S}$ controlled by $\mathcal{C}$ satisfies ψ. Because $\mathcal{S}$ and $\mathcal{C}$ work on sequences of different length, the controlled system is in fact equal to $lift_k(\mathcal{C}) \times \mathcal{S}$. So $lift_k(\mathcal{C}) \times \mathcal{S} \models \psi$ should hold. This is equivalent to the emptiness of the language of the product automaton $lift_k(\mathcal{C}) \times \mathcal{S} \times \mathcal{A}_{\neg\psi}$.

We say that $\mathcal{C}$ is a controller for $\mathcal{S}$ (without mentioning ψ) if $\mathcal{C}$ fulfills the first two conditions. The notion of final state is not relevant for the controller or the physical system. To conform with previous definitions we require that every $(\omega + 1)$-run of the controller and $(\omega^k + 1)$-run of $\mathcal{S}$ end in a final state.

The *control problem for* LTL(ω^k) is defined as follows:
input: a system $\mathcal{S} = \langle \mathcal{A}_{\mathcal{S}}, Act_{\mathcal{C}}, Act_{\mathcal{O}}, Act \rangle$ with ordinal automaton $\mathcal{A}_{\mathcal{S}}$ of level k and an LTL(ω^k) formula ψ over atomic formulas in Act.
output: an ordinal automaton $\mathcal{C}$ of level 1 satisfying the conditions (obs), (unc) and (prod) above if there exists one. Otherwise the answer "no controller exists".

3 Solving the Control Problem

Given a physical system $\mathcal{S}$ modeled by an ordinal automaton $\mathcal{A}_{\mathcal{S}}$ of level k and an LTL(ω^k)-formula ψ, we are looking for a controller $\mathcal{C}$ such that $lift_k(\mathcal{C}) \times \mathcal{A}_{\mathcal{S}} \models \psi$ and $\mathcal{C}$ has the expected properties about uncontrollable and unobservable actions.

From Control Problem to Game. Let $\mathcal{B} = lift_k(\mathcal{C}) \times \mathcal{A}_{\mathcal{S}} \times \mathcal{A}_{\neg\psi}$. At a given point in a run of $\mathcal{B}$ the controller is in a state q. From q and for all $o \subseteq Act_o \cap Act_{nc}$ it must have at least one transition labeled by $o \cup c$ for some $c \subseteq Act_{\mathcal{C}}$. The most general form of a controller (possibly with infinite memory) is a function $f : (2^{Act_o})^* \times (2^{Act_o \cap Act_{nc}}) \to 2^{Act_c}$, because the current state of the controller shall only depend on the past observable actions. This function is exactly a strategy in a game that we will define. A controller for $\langle \mathcal{S}, \psi \rangle$ is such that every run according to f is winning.

Let $\mathcal{A} = \mathcal{A}_{\mathcal{S}} \times \mathcal{A}_{\neg\psi}$. It is also an ordinal automaton of level k : $\mathcal{A} = \langle Q, \Sigma, \delta, E, I, F, l \rangle$. We are looking for a controller $\mathcal{C}$ such that the language of $lift_k(\mathcal{C}) \times \mathcal{A}$ is empty. We will consider a game where the environment tries to build an accepting run of $\mathcal{A}$, whereas the controller tries to avoid that, using the controlled actions. In fact the environment plays both for the system $\mathcal{S}$ and for the automaton of $\neg\psi$, as we will see later.

3.1 Some Definitions from Game Theory

We recall some definitions about games. See for example [Tho95, GTW02] for an introduction. An *arena*, or *game graph*, is a triple (V_0, V_1, G), where $V = V_0 \cup V_1$ is the set of vertices and $G \subseteq V \times V$ is the set of edges. The vertices of V_0 belongs to Player 0, those of V_1 to Player 1 ($V_0 \cap V_1 = \emptyset$). A *play* from $v_0 \in V$ proceeds as follows: if $v \in V_0$, Player 0 chooses a successor v_1 of v_0, else Player 1 does. Again from $v_1 \in V_i$, Player i chooses a successor v_2 of v_1, and so on.

A play $\pi = v_0, v_1, v_2, \ldots$ is a finite or infinite sequence of vertices such that $\forall i, (v_i, v_{i+1}) \in G$. If the play is finite, the convention is that the player who belongs the last vertex loses (he is stuck). If the play is infinite, the winner is determined by a *winning set*, $Win \subseteq V^\omega$: Player 0 wins an infinite play π if and only if $\pi \in Win$. Usually Win is an ω-regular set, defined by a Büchi, Rabin, parity or Muller automaton. One speaks also of *winning condition*. A *game* (V_0, V_1, G, Win) is an arena together with a winning condition and possibly an initial vertex $v_0 \in V$.

For a game or an automaton, a Büchi condition is given by a set $F \subseteq V$ of "final" vertices and $\pi \in Win$ if and only if $\forall i > 0, \exists j > i, \pi_i \in F$. A Muller condition is given by $\mathcal{F} \subseteq 2^V$, $\mathcal{F} = \{F_1, \cdots, F_n\}$, and $\pi \in Win$ if and only if the set of states visited infinitely often along π is equal to one of the F_i's.

A *strategy* for Player 0 is a (partial) function $f_0 : V^*V_0 \mapsto V$ such that for every prefix $v_0, v_1, v_2, \cdots v_i$ of a play, where $v_i \in V_0$, $f(v_0v_1v_2 \cdots v_i)$ is a vertex v_{i+1} such that $(v_i, v_{i+1}) \in G$. A play π is played according to a strategy f_0 if $\forall i, v_i \in V_0 \Rightarrow v_{i+1} = f(v_0v_1v_2 \cdots v_i)$. A strategy for Player 1 is defined analogously. A strategy of Player 0 is *winning* if every play according to it is winning for Player 0. An important case in practice is when the strategy is *positional*: it depends only on the current vertex, not on the past of the play, *i.e.*, for all $v_0, v_1, v_2, \cdots v_i$, $f(v_0v_1v_2 \cdots v_i) = f(v_i)$.

From [Mar75] we know that every zero-sum two-player turn based game of complete information with Borel winning condition (including ω-regular and many more) is determined: from a given initial configuration, one of the players has a winning strategy.

In the case of incomplete information, the players do not in general know exactly the current position of the game. They only know that the position belongs to a certain set of uncertainty. The move chosen by a player (by his strategy) shall depend on this set, but not on the precise position of the play. As we will see in some cases one can transform such a game into a game of complete information, where a vertex represents a set of positions of the original game.

3.2 A Solution with Incomplete Information

Summarizing ω^{k-1} Steps. From the definition of $lift_k$ we see that the controller can act only every ω^{k-1} steps of the environment. Our aim is to summarize ω^{k-1} steps of the environment in a single step. One can compute a relation $\mathcal{R} \subseteq Q \times 2^Q \times Q$ such that $(q, P, q') \in \mathcal{R}$ iff there exists in $\mathcal{A}$ a path from q to q' of length $\omega^{k-1} + 1$ where the set of states seen along this path is exactly P.

Note that to determine $\mathcal{R}$, one has to look for cycles in $\mathcal{A}$ and states that are seen infinitely often, but in $\mathcal{R}$ itself we only need to know states that are ever visited. The reason is that (considering $cofinal(\omega^k, r)$) it is not relevant to know that some state is visited infinitely often between e.g. $\omega^{k-1}3$ and $\omega^{k-1}4$ and no more visited after $\omega^{k-1}4$. Relation $\mathcal{R}$ can be computed in time $2^{\mathcal{O}(|Q|)}$ [Car02].

Game. We introduce a game ($\mathcal{G}$) modeling the interaction between the controller (Cont) and the environment (Env). It is not possible in general for Cont to know exactly the current state of the system for several reasons.

- Cont cannot know the ω^{k-1} steps done by the environment without control.
- As Env act, by choosing $v \subseteq Act_{nc}$, Cont can only observe the actions that are in Act_o.
- Moreover $\mathcal{A}$ is not necessarily deterministic. In particular it is possible that $\mathcal{A}_{\neg\psi}$ is not deterministic and Env has to "choose" which subformulas of $\neg\psi$ he wants to make true.
- Also Cont cannot know exactly the initial state chosen by Env.

In the game $\mathcal{G}$ Cont has partial information: a position of the game is a subset Q_i of Q, such that Cont knows that the current state of the system is in Q_i, but does not know which state exactly. The game is defined by the following steps:

1. $i = 0$ and the initial position is $Q_0 = I$, the set of initial states of $\mathcal{A}$
2. Env chooses $o_i \subseteq Act_o \cap Act_{nc}$,
3. Cont chooses $c_i \subseteq Act_c$,
4. there is a one step transition to

$$Q'_i = \{q' \in Q : \exists u \subseteq Act \backslash Act_o, \exists q \in Q_i, q \xrightarrow{c_i \cup o_i \cup u} q'\},$$

5. there is a jump to Q_{i+1}, summarizing ω^{k-1} steps

$$Q_{i+1} = \{q \in Q : \exists q' \in Q'_i, \exists (q', P, q) \in \mathcal{R}\},$$

6. $i = i + 1$, continue at point 2.

In this game the knowledge of Cont about the current state is exactly what a controller can compute in the original problem, based on the observable actions. A play is essentially a sequence $Q_0, Q'_0, Q_1, Q'_1, \dots$ (a more precise definition of the game graph is given below) and now it is more intricate to determine the winner. The sequence $Q_0, Q'_0, Q_1, Q'_1, \dots$ represents the point of view of the controller, and we call it an abstract play. After the game is played a *referee* has to choose inside this abstract play a concrete path (if it exists one) $q_0, q'_0, q_1, q'_1, \dots$ such that $q_i \in Q_i, q'_i \in Q'_i$ and compatible to the sequence of c_i's and o_i's. That is to say one has to choose $q_0 \in Q_0$, a sequence of elements $u_i \in Act \backslash Act_o$ such that $q_i \xrightarrow{c_i \cup o_i \cup u_i} q'_i$ and elements $(q'_i, P_i, q_i) \in \mathcal{R}$. The sequence $q_0, q'_0, P_0, q_1, q'_1, P_1, \dots$ summarizes a run in $\mathcal{A}$ and we can determine if it is accepting, in which case Env wins the play. Note that for the acceptance condition of $\mathcal{A}$ it is relevant to know whether some $q \in Q$ appears in infinitely many P_i's. Therefore the set of winning plays of Env can be defined by a *non deterministic* Muller automaton searching a concrete path, as we will see below, after we make some comments.

The advantage that Env plays "abstractly" the game, and one selects a concrete path only afterward is not unfair. Again we want a controller that is secure, and we worry if the environment *could have* won. And in the case that the controller does not have a winning strategy, it does not necessarily mean that the environment has one, but it means that there is a risk that the environment wins. This is related to the fact that games of incomplete information are not determined in general: it is possible that no player has a winning strategy.

We now describe the automaton defining the set of winning plays and then the arena in more details. Note that the sequence $Q_0, Q'_0, Q_1, Q'_1, \ldots$ above is uniquely determined by the sequence $o_0, c_0, o_1, c_1, \ldots$ of actions chosen by Cont and Env. The state space of the automaton $\mathcal{A}_{Win}$ recognizing the winning plays for Env is $Q \times 2^Q$. For all $P \neq \emptyset$ there is a transition $(q, P) \xrightarrow{c \cup o} (q', \emptyset)$ if and only if $\exists u \subseteq Act \backslash Act_o$, $\exists q \xrightarrow{c \cup o \cup u} q'$ in $\mathcal{A}$ and there is a transition $(q', \emptyset) \xrightarrow{\epsilon} (q, P)$ if and only if $\exists\, (q', P, q) \in \mathcal{R}$.

The automaton $\mathcal{A}_{Win}$ non-deterministically guesses a run in $\mathcal{A}$ conforming to the sequence $o_0, c_0, o_1, c_1, \ldots$ The acceptance condition of $\mathcal{A}_{Win}$ is the same as those of $\mathcal{A}$: it can be seen as a Muller condition depending on the states appearing infinitely often in a run. It is given by a set of sets $\mathcal{F} \subseteq 2^Q$. The usual way to handle such a non-deterministic Muller automaton is to transform it into a non-deterministic Büchi automaton [GTW02, Ch. 1]. The Büchi automaton $\mathcal{B}_{Win}$ simulates $\mathcal{A}_{Win}$ and guesses at some point which subset of states are going to be visited infinitely often and that other states are no longer visited. The state space of $\mathcal{B}_{Win}$ is $Q \cup Q \times \mathcal{F} \times (Q \cup \{q_f\})$. It checks in turn that each state of the chosen acceptance component $F \in \mathcal{F}$ is visited infinitely often and it is not necessary to remember the whole $(q, P) \in Q \times 2^Q$ of $\mathcal{A}_{Win}$. Using e.g. Safra's construction [GTW02, Ch. 3] one can transform the Büchi automaton $\mathcal{B}_{Win}$ into a *deterministic* Rabin automaton $\mathcal{C}_{Win}$. Then the Index Appearance Record allows to have a deterministic parity automaton $\mathcal{D}_{Win}$ [GTW02, p.86] [Löd98].

For defining the arena, we see that Cont and Env essentially choose the actions c_i and o_i:

$$V_{Env} = 2^{Act_c}, \quad V_{Cont} = 2^{Act_o \cap Act_{nc}}, \quad G = (V_{Env} \times V_{Cont}) \cup (V_{Cont} \times V_{Env})$$

Now the product of the arena (V_{Env}, V_{Cont}, G) by the parity automaton $\mathcal{D}_{Win}$ gives rise to a parity game on a finite graph. One can determine the winner and compute a positional winning strategy [GTW02, Ch.6,7] [JPZ06]. Due to the synchronization between the arena and $\mathcal{D}_{Win}$, the set V_{Env} can be merged to a single vertex: it is not needed to remember the move of Cont because its effect on $\mathcal{D}_{Win}$ is sufficient. In fact the successive sets $Q_0, Q'_0, Q_1, Q'_1, \ldots$ of the above description are computed by $\mathcal{D}_{Win}$ (thanks to Safra's construction already in $\mathcal{C}_{Win}$).

Theorem 1. *The control problem defined in Section 2.4 can be solved in* 2EXPTIME. *Moreover if a controller exists, then there is one with finite memory of double exponential size.*

The complexity is measured in the number $|Q|$ of states of $\mathcal{A} = \mathcal{A}_{\mathcal{S}} \times \mathcal{A}_{\neg\psi}$. Recall that the usual control problem is 2EXPTIME-complete [PR89] in the size of the system and the length of the formula.

See Appendix for the proof. The idea is to prove the following facts. If the game $\mathcal{G}$ is won by Cont then a controller for $\langle \mathcal{S}, \psi \rangle$ exists, and it can be constructed. Conversely if a controller for $\langle \mathcal{S}, \psi \rangle$ exists then $\mathcal{G}$ is won by Cont. By construction a strategy for Cont in $\mathcal{G}$ is a finite state automaton with expected properties about (un)observable and (un)controllable actions. Moreover if that strategy is winning, it defines a controller for $\langle \mathcal{S}, \psi \rangle$: every run of $\mathit{lift}_k(\mathcal{C}) \times \mathcal{S}$ fulfills ψ. Conversely, if a controller for $\langle \mathcal{S}, \psi \rangle$ exists, possibly with infinite memory, then this controller provides a winning strategy for Cont in $\mathcal{G}$. From the analysis above we know that if there is a controller for $\langle \mathcal{S}, \psi \rangle$, then there is one with finite memory, and one can compute it.

4 Example

We illustrate our construction by a (slightly modified) example from [DN05]. The system is a bouncing ball with three actions *lift-up*, *bounce* and *stop*, where only *lift-up* is controllable, and only *stop* and *lift-up* are observable. The law of the ball is described by the following LTL(ω^2) formula:

$$\phi = \mathtt{G}^{\omega^2}(\mathit{lift\text{-}up} \Rightarrow \mathtt{X}^1(\mathtt{G}^{\omega}\mathit{bounce} \wedge \mathtt{X}^{\omega}\mathit{stop})) .$$

Informally, ϕ states that when the ball is lifted-up, it bounces an infinite number of times in a finite time and then stops. Equivalently the behavior of the system is modeled by the following ordinal automaton of level 2.

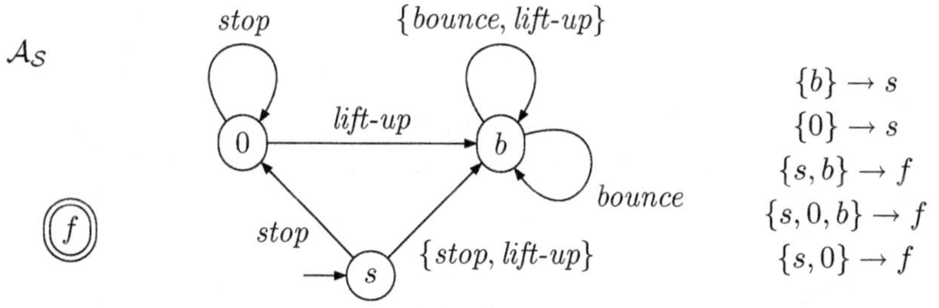

The specification is given by the LTL(ω^2) formula:

$$\psi = \mathtt{G}^{\omega^2}\mathtt{X}^1\mathit{bounce}$$

Informally, ψ states that the ball should almost always be bouncing. In the following picture of the automaton $\mathcal{A}_{\neg\psi}$, the star ($*$) stands for any subset of actions of *Act*.

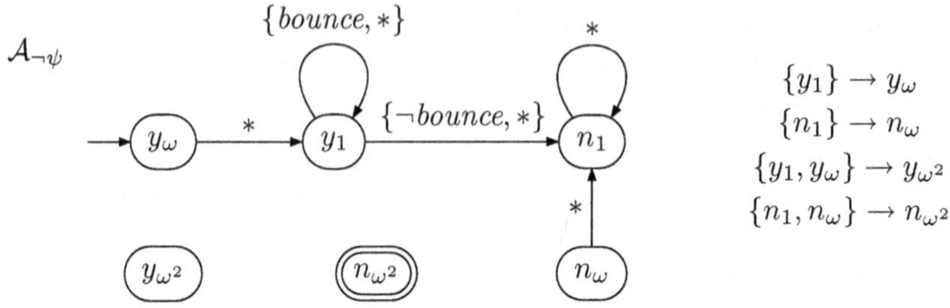

The automaton $\mathcal{A} = \mathcal{A}_\mathcal{S} \times \mathcal{A}_{\neg\psi}$ is then

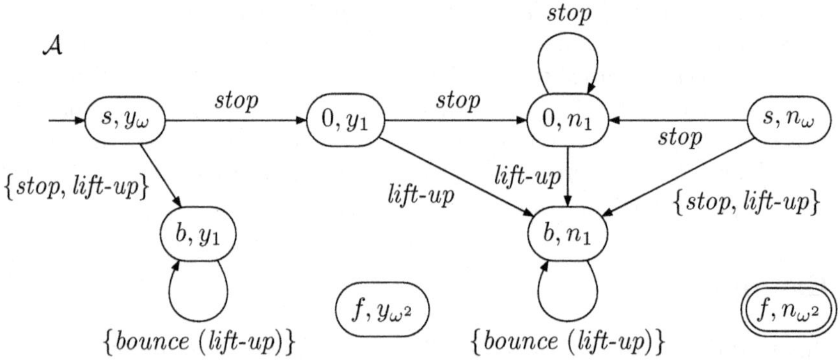

We omit here the limit transitions. In the relation $\mathcal{R} \subseteq Q \times 2^Q \times Q$ the relevant elements are

$$
\begin{array}{ll}
(\langle b, y_1\rangle, \{\langle b, y_1\rangle\}, \langle s, y_\omega\rangle) & (\langle 0, y_1\rangle, \{\langle 0, n_1\rangle\}, \langle s, n_\omega\rangle) \\
(\langle b, n_1\rangle, \{\langle b, n_1\rangle\}, \langle s, n_\omega\rangle) & (\langle 0, n_1\rangle, \{\langle 0, n_1\rangle\}, \langle s, n_\omega\rangle) \\
 & (\langle 0, n_1\rangle, \{\langle 0, n_1\rangle, \langle b, n_1\rangle\}, \langle s, n_\omega\rangle)
\end{array}
$$

If we construct the automaton $\mathcal{A}_{Win}$, we see that its (Muller) acceptance condition can be reduced to a Büchi condition. In the next figure the automaton $\mathcal{D}_{Win}$ is simplified, and some unnecessary transitions are omitted.

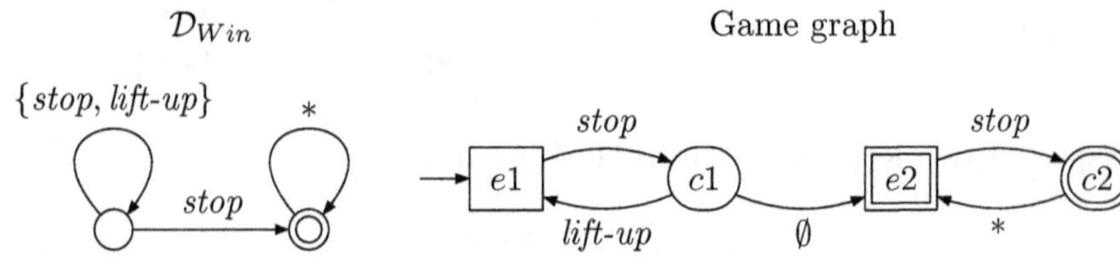

The winning strategy for Cont is: from $c1$ always go to $e1$. The corresponding controller for $\langle \mathcal{S}, \psi\rangle$ has essentially two loops on its initial state: one labeled $\{stop, lift\text{-}up\}$ and one labeled $\{lift\text{-}up\}$.

5 Perspectives

It is open whether the upper bounds of Theorem 1 are tight, and whether one can find LTL-fragments or restrictions on the physical system such that the complexity of the control problem is lower.

We would like to extend the previous results in two directions: to timed systems and to other linear orderings. Given a timed automaton, it is possible to determine whether it has Zeno behaviors. Our motivation is to extend the semantics such that after ω transitions there is a limit transition to a new control state and the new clock values are the limit of the former ones (see [BP00]).

A Zeno behavior is not necessarily an ordinal sequence, it can be a more general linear ordering (see [BC05]). One should extend the results to this more general class of automata.

Acknowledgments. Great thanks to Stéphane Demri and David Nowak for many interesting discussions, helpful comments on previous versions and for their help.

References

[AFH$^+$03] L. de Alfaro, M. Faëlla, T. A. Henzinger, R. Majumdar, and M. Stoelinga. The element of surprise in timed games. *CONCUR'03*, LNCS 2761, pp. 142–156. 2003.

[AM98] E. Asarin and O. Maler. Achilles and the tortoise climbing up the arithmetical hierarchy. *JCSS* 57(3), pp. 389–398. 1998.

[BC05] A. Bès and O. Carton. A Kleene theorem for languages of words indexed by linear orderings. *DLT'05*, LNCS 3572, pp. 158–167. 2005.

[BDMP03] P. Bouyer, D. D'Souza, P. Madhusudan, and A. Petit. Timed control with partial observability. *CAV'03*, LNCS 2725, pp. 180–192. 2003.

[Bed98] N. Bedon. *Langages reconnaissables de mots indexés par des ordinaux.* PhD thesis, Université de Marne-la-Vallée. 1998.

[Bou99] O. Bournez. Achilles and the tortoise climbing up the hyper-arithmetical hierarchy. *TCS*, 210(1):21–71. 1999.

[BP00] B. Bérard and C. Picaronny. Accepting Zeno words: A way toward timed refinements. *Acta Informatica*, 37(1):45–81. 2000.

[BS73] J. R. Buchi and D. Siefkes. *The monadic second order theory of all countable ordinals, Lect. Notes in Math.* 328 Springer. 1973.

[Car02] O. Carton. Accessibility in automata on scattered linear orderings. *MFCS'02*, LNCS 2420, pp. 155–164. 2002.

[DL05] J. Durand-Lose. Abstract geometrical computation for black hole computation (extended abstract). In *Machines, computations, and universality*, LNCS 3354, pp. 176–187. 2005.

[DN05] S. Demri and D. Nowak. Reasoning about transfinite sequences (extended abstract). *ATVA'05*, LNCS 3707, pp. 248–262. 2005.

[GTW02] E. Grädel, W. Thomas, and T. Wilke, editors. *Automata, Logics, and Infinite Games: A Guide to Current Research*, *LNCS* 2500. 2002.

[GW94] P. Godefroid and P. Wolper. A partial approach to model checking. *Inform. and Comput.*, 110(2):305–326. 1994.

[JPZ06] M. Jurdzinski, M. Paterson, and U. Zwick. A deterministic subexponential algorithm for solving parity games. *SODA*, pp. 117–123, 2006.

[Kam68] H. Kamp. *Tense Logic and the Theory of Linear Order.* PhD thesis, University of California at Los Angeles, 1968.

[Löd98] C. Löding. Methods for the transformation of omega-automata: Complexity and connection to second order logic. Master's thesis, Christian-Albrechts-University of Kiel, 1998.

[Mar75] D. A. Martin. Borel Determinacy. *Annals of Math.*, 102:363–371, 1975.

[Mau96] Françoise Maurin. Exact complexity bounds for ordinal addition. *Theor. Comput. Sci.*, 165(2):247–273, 1996.

[PR89] A. Pnueli and R. Rosner. On the synthesis of a reactive module. In *POPL'89*, pp. 179–190. ACM, 1989.

[Rei84] J. H. Reif. The complexity of two-player games of incomplete information. *J. Comput. System Sci.*, 29(2):274–301. 1984.

[Ros82] J. G. Rosenstein. *Linear orderings.* Academic Press Inc. 1982.

[RW89] P. J. Ramadge and W. M. Wonham. The control of discrete event systems. *Proceedings of IEEE 77(1)*, pp. 81–98. 1989.

[Tho95] W. Thomas. On the synthesis of strategies in infinite games. *STACS'95*, LNCS 900, pp. 1–13. 1995.

[VW86] M. Y. Vardi and P. Wolper. An automata-theoretic approach to automatic program verification. LICS'86, pp. 332–344. 1986.

Effective Contraction of Timed STGs for Decomposition Based Timed Circuit Synthesis

Tomohiro Yoneda[1] and Chris J. Myers[2]

[1] National Institute of Informatics
yoneda@nii.ac.jp
[2] University of Utah
myers@ece.utah.edu

Abstract. This paper presents a way to contract timed STGs effectively for a decomposition based logic synthesis of timed circuits. In the decomposition based synthesis method, a sufficient input signal set for each output is first obtained, and the timed STG is contracted to include only transitions on this input signal set and the output of interest, from which the circuit for the output is synthesized. Care is, however, needed for the contraction of timed STGs. A simple contraction algorithm used for the untimed version can result in the loss of important timing information, causing it to synthesize non-optimal circuits. On the other hand, exact contraction that preserves the timing information precisely is applied only to a small class of transitions, which degrades the performance of the decomposition based synthesis method. This paper proposes a way to contract timed STGs effectively without losing the optimality of the synthesized circuits, and shows some experimental results.

1 Introduction

Logic synthesis [1,2,3] from *signal transition graphs* (STGs) is one of the major approaches to the automated synthesis of asynchronous circuits. The cost required by this approach to enumerate the full state space of the given STG has, however, limited the size of STGs to which it can be successfully applied. The decomposition based synthesis method, which was originally suggested by Chu [4], has recently been used with sophisticated algorithms to determine *relevant input sets* (or *CSC supports*) based on the *complete state coding* (CSC) violation trace analysis [5] or the incidence matrix solver by the integer linear programming technique [6], and is reported to succeed in synthesizing large asynchronous circuits that the previous logic synthesis methods cannot handle. The idea is that for each output signal x, it first finds a set of input signals relevant to x, and then contracts (or projects) the STG to include only transitions on those signals as well as x, and finally synthesizes a sub-circuit for x from the reduced STG. Since the relevant input signal set is usually much smaller than the set of all signals in the given STG, the reduced STG is very small, and so, the cost for logic synthesis is reduced dramatically.

On the other hand, in order to satisfy the requirements of high performance, designers are interested in optimization based on timing information, and aggressively timed

S. Graf and W. Zhang (Eds.): ATVA 2006, LNCS 4218, pp. 229–244, 2006.

circuit design styles are sometimes used (e.g., RAPPID [7] and GasP [8]). It is, however, not easy to perform such optimization based on timing or to design aggressively timed circuits by hand. Thus, it is desirable to synthesize such optimized circuits automatically using timing information given. Fortunately, the above decomposition based synthesis by CSC violation trace analysis can be extended for handling timed circuits [9]. This is because its original untimed algorithm can be utilized almost as is, i.e., only the state space exploration and the STG contraction must be replaced with their timed versions. Care, however, should be taken for the timed extension of STG contraction. If one wants to contract as many transitions as in the untimed case, the contraction algorithm should be conservative in dealing with time bounds. It still synthesizes a correct circuit, but the circuit may be less optimal due to the conservative timing information. In order to avoid this problem, timed contraction should be performed so that timing information is preserved exactly. Exact contraction, however, results in inefficiency of the synthesis process because only a small class of transitions can be contracted.

This paper proposes a way to contract timed STGs effectively without a significant loss in circuit quality. It finds portions of timed STGs that should be exactly contracted from the structural information of the timed STG, and thus, the other portion can be contracted conservatively without affecting optimality. Our algorithm currently pursues the heuristics for deciding trigger and context signals precisely.

Untimed net contractions for Petri nets have had a long history [10,11,12]. More recently, Vogler and Wollowski formalized the contraction algorithm for untimed STGs using a bisimulation relation in [13]. Zheng et al. developed a timed contraction algorithm in [14] and applied it to perform modular synthesis in [15]. This method, however, requires user-specified hierarchy information to guide the decomposition of the synthesis algorithm. Therefore, it cannot be used on flat designs or large modules. This method also preserves timing in a conservative fashion which may sacrifice circuit optimality.

2 Definitions

This section reviews the definitions and theorems needed for the discussion in this paper, which are taken from [9].

A time Petri net is a Petri net, where each transition t is annotated with two firing times, denoted by $\mathsf{Eft}(t)$ and $\mathsf{Lft}(t)$. Intuitively, a transition t cannot fire before being enabled for $\mathsf{Eft}(t)$ and must fire before it has been enabled for longer than $\mathsf{Lft}(t)$. A timed STG is a time Petri net, where each transition t is further annotated with a labeling function l that maps a transition to either an input or output signal change, denoted by $w+$ or $w-$ for a signal w, or a symbol λ. In figures of this paper, a transition is shown either by its name (as shown in Figure 2) or by its signal change (e.g., transitions except for t_1 and t_2 in Figure 7 (a)). If a transition is related to an output signal change, it is called an *output transition*. An *input transition* is defined similarly. If a transition is related to the change of a signal w, the transition is sometimes called a w*-transition*. A transition that is related to λ is called a *dummy transition*. For a transition t, a set of places connected to t (i.e., *source places*) is denoted by $\bullet t$, and a set of places connected from t (i.e., *destination places*) is denoted by $t\bullet$. For a place p, $\bullet p$ and $p\bullet$ are defined similarly. Transitions t and t' such that $\bullet t \cap \bullet t' \neq \emptyset$ are said to be in *conflict*. Let *conflict*$(t) = \{t' \mid \bullet t \cap \bullet t' \neq \emptyset\} - \{t\}$.

A timed state of a timed STG is defined by a marking and a clock function, where the latter associates each transition with the time for which it has been enabled. Let $\sigma \xrightarrow{t_f} \sigma'$ denote that a timed state σ' is obtained from a timed state σ by first passing some time and then firing a transition t_f. For a sequence $v = t_1 t_2 \cdots$ of transitions, $\sigma \xrightarrow{v} \sigma'$ is defined similarly (σ is equal to σ' for an empty v). If in any reachable timed state, a token is never produced into a place that already has a token, then the timed STG is called *one-safe*. Furthermore, a timed STG is *consistent*, if in every transition sequence v, every signal alternates. (e.g., $\cdots w+ \cdots w- \cdots$).

A *timed state graph* of an STG G is a graph $\langle V, E\rangle$ with an initial timed state σ^0, denoted by $\mathcal{G}_G = (\langle V, E\rangle, \sigma^0)$, such that V is the set of all reachable timed states of G, and E is the timed state transition relation of G, that is, $\{(\sigma, t, \sigma') \mid \sigma \in V, \sigma \xrightarrow{t} \sigma'\}$. An output signal w is *excited* in a timed state σ, if there exists a (possibly empty) sequence $u_1 u_2 \cdots u_n$ of dummy transitions such that $(\sigma, u_1 u_2 \cdots u_n, \sigma_2) \in E^*$, and t with $l(t) = w+$ or $l(t) = w-$ is enabled (i.e., every place in $\bullet t$ is marked) in σ_2. Let $\mathsf{out\_excited}(\sigma)$ be a set of output signals that are excited in σ. A *dummy-free timed state graph* of $\mathcal{G}_G$ is a graph $\langle V', E'\rangle$ with an initial timed state σ^0, denoted by $\mathcal{G}_G^{df} = (\langle V', E'\rangle, \sigma^0)$, satisfying, $V' = \{\sigma \mid (\sigma', t, \sigma) \in E, l(t) \neq \lambda\} \cup \{\sigma^0\}$ and $E' = \{(\sigma, t, \sigma_3) \mid \sigma \in V', (\sigma, u_1 u_2 \cdots u_n, \sigma_2) \in E^*, n \geq 0, \forall i.l(u_i) = \lambda, (\sigma_2, t, \sigma_3) \in E, l(t) \neq \lambda\}$. This dummy-free timed state graph is constructed based on the fact that timed state transitions by a (possibly empty) sequence of dummy transitions followed by a nondummy transition can be replaced by the single nondummy transition.

A timed state in a dummy-free timed state graph is mapped to a *signal state*, which is a binary vector representing the values of signals. Different timed states may be mapped to the same signal state. For an output signal x, *ES*$(x+)$ denotes a set of signal states mapped from timed states where x is excited for rising, and *QS*$(x+)$ denotes a set of similar signal states except that x has the value 1 and is not excited. *ES*$(x-)$ and *QS*$(x-)$ are defined similarly. The other signal states are unreachable, and the set of unreachable signal states is denoted by *UR*.

There are two important properties for synthesizability. Suppose that two timed states have a common signal state, but the excitation of some output signals is different. This situation is called a *CSC violation*. If an STG has a CSC violation, we say that the STG does not have CSC. Otherwise, it has CSC. If an STG does not have CSC, a circuit cannot be synthesized from the STG without modifying the STG. The property called *output semi-modularity* is also necessary to synthesize a circuit from an STG. This paper uses the following simplified definition of output semi-modularity for timed STGs. A timed STG G is output semi-modular, if for any conflicting transitions that are enabled in the same timed state of $\mathcal{G}_G$, every (possibly empty) path of dummy transitions starting from each of them on the STG ends with an input transition. Intuitively, if an output transition conflicts with some other transition directly or indirectly (i.e., through dummy transitions), the excitation of the output signal can be lost without changing the output signal itself. This violates output semi-modularity.

Although one-safeness of STGs is not required for synthesis, our timed state space enumeration algorithm supports only one-safe STGs like other tools such as atacs [16].

Furthermore, the consistency requirement significantly simplifies the analysis and synthesis algorithms. Thus, we say that an STG G is *synthesizable*, if G is one-safe, consistent, output semi-modular, and has CSC.

There is another property needed especially for timed circuit synthesis. The timed circuit synthesis method assumes that a synthesized logic function for an output is implemented with a delay within the firing time bounds (i.e., $[\mathsf{Eft}(t), \mathsf{Lft}(t)]$) of the corresponding output transitions in the given timed STG. This assumption, however, may not make sense, if the output transitions related to the same output signal have different firing time bounds, or even a dummy transition that precedes those output transitions has a non-zero delay. In order to simplify the problem, this paper considers a class of timed STGs satisfying the following timed-implementability. A timed STG G is *timed implementable*, if for every output signal x of G, every x-transition has the same firing time bounds, and in any path of dummy transitions on G that ends with an output transition, all dummy transitions have [0,0] bounds. In this paper, it is assumed that a given timed STG is always both synthesizable and timed implementable.

From different STGs, circuits that behave similarly under the given environment can be synthesized. Thus, from this point of view, the correctness of an STG with respect to the original STG can be defined. A circuit is defined by a set of logic functions, and a logic function is specified by a *cover*, which is a set of signal states where the logic function is changed to or kept at the value 1. In the *atomic gate implementation*, for each output signal x, an STG G defines a cover, denoted by $C(x)$, satisfying $C(x) - \mathit{UR} = \mathit{ES}(x+) \cup \mathit{QS}(x+)$. An STG G_1 is *cover-correct* with respect to G, if for each output signal of G_1, the cover $C_1(x)$ for G_1 satisfies the above condition of the cover for G. That is, $C_1(x)$ satisfying $C_1(x) - \mathit{UR}_1 = \mathit{ES}_1(x+) \cup \mathit{QS}_1(x+)$ must satisfy $C_1(x) - \mathit{UR} = \mathit{ES}(x+) \cup \mathit{QS}(x+)$.

In order that a correct delay can be assigned to the synthesized circuit, another property is needed for the correctness of G_1. An STG G_1 is *delay-correct* with respect to G, if G_1 is timed implementable, and for every output signal x of G_1, every x-transition of G_1 has the same firing time bounds (i.e., $[\mathsf{Eft}(t), \mathsf{Lft}(t)]$) as x-transitions in G. If G_1 is both cover-correct and delay-correct with respect to G, G_1 is *correct* with respect to G.

In order to decide the cover-correctness more directly, the following notion is introduced. For STGs G_1 and G_2 with the same input and output signal sets, a *simulation* from G_1 to G_2 is a relation S between timed states of $\mathcal{G}^{df}_{G_1} = (\langle V'_1, E'_1\rangle, \sigma^0_1)$ and $\mathcal{G}^{df}_{G_2} = (\langle V'_2, E'_2\rangle, \sigma^0_2)$ satisfying

1. $(\sigma^0_1, \sigma^0_2) \in S$,
2. for any $(\sigma_1, \sigma_2) \in S$, $\mathsf{out\_excited}(\sigma_1) = \mathsf{out\_excited}(\sigma_2)$ holds, and
3. for any $(\sigma_1, \sigma_2) \in S$ and any $(\sigma_1, t_1, \sigma'_1) \in E'_1$, there exists some t_2 and σ'_2 such that $l(t_2) = l(t_1)$, $(\sigma_2, t_2, \sigma'_2) \in E'_2$, and $(\sigma'_1, \sigma'_2) \in S$ hold.

Let $G_1 \rightsquigarrow G_2$ denote that G_1 and G_2 have the same input and output signal sets, and that there exists a simulation from G_1 to G_2 (i.e., G_2 can simulate G_1).

For an STG G with a signal set W, an output signal x of G, and $V \subseteq W$ with $x \in V$, let $G\,|_{V,x}$ denote an STG, which has the input signal set $V - \{x\}$ and the output signal set $\{x\}$, and is obtained from G by replacing w-transitions by dummy transitions for signals w with $w \in W - V$. Let $\mathsf{abs}(G, V, x)$ be any STG such that

$G\,|_{V,x}\!\rightsquigarrow$ $\mathsf{abs}(G,V,x)$. Furthermore, $\mathsf{trigger}(x)$ denotes the set of all possible trigger signals for an output x, where a signal w is a *possible trigger signal* of x, if some of w-transitions can reach some x-transitions on G either directly or through only dummy transitions. The following theorem is proved in [9].

Theorem 1. *If* $\mathsf{abs}(G,V,x)$ *has CSC and* $\mathsf{trigger}(x) \subseteq V$ *holds, then* $\mathsf{abs}(G,V,x)$ *is cover-correct with respect to G.*

Transforming $G\,|_{V,x}$ to as small $\mathsf{abs}(G,V,x)$ as possible is one of the keys of the decomposition based synthesis method. This is done by the contraction described in the next section.

3 Contraction of Timed STGs

3.1 Basic Algorithm

The contraction of timed STGs consists of the transformation of the net structure and the modification of time bounds (the earliest and latest firing times). The former is the same as that for untimed nets (e.g., [13]). The algorithm for this transformation with respect to a transition t is **transform_net**(t) shown in Figure 1. In this algorithm, for each pair (p,p') such that $p \in \bullet t$ and $p' \in t\bullet$, a new place p_{new} is created, and the incoming arcs to p and p' are redirected to p_{new}, and the outgoing arcs from p and p' are originated from p_{new}. If p or p' initially has a token, so does p_{new}. Then, t, its preset and postset, and the arcs connected from/to them are removed. Finally, duplicated places that are introduced by this transformation are removed.

The modification of time bounds is performed by **modify_bounds**(t). It basically transfers the delay of the contracted transition to its successor transitions. That is, when t is contracted, $\mathsf{Eft}(t)$ is added to $\mathsf{Eft}(x)$ and $\mathsf{Lft}(t)$ is added to $\mathsf{Lft}(x)$ for $x \in t\bullet\bullet$. This modification of time bounds, however, does not work when x has a source place that has a source transition other than t, i.e., $\bullet\bullet(t\bullet\bullet)$ is not equal to $\{t\}$. For example, in Figure 2 (a), $\bullet\bullet(t\bullet\bullet)$ is $\{t,y\}$. In this case, when u fires much earlier than v, x can fire 3 time units after the firing of v in the original STG. If both $\mathsf{Eft}(t)$ and $\mathsf{Lft}(t)$ are added to x as shown in the STG labeled by [incorrect] in the figure, then it takes at least 13 time units for x to fire after the firing of v, which means that the contracted STG cannot simulate the original STG. A similar situation occurs when arcs merge at a place. Thus, in such cases, the time bounds of the successor transitions are enlarged conservatively as shown in the right-hand side of the figure. In this STG, the earliest firing time of x is kept at its original value 2. This preserves the behavior of the original STG that x fires 3 time units after the firing of v. When v fires early enough, x fires 2 time units after the firing of u, which is an extra behavior that is not included in the original STG. But, this is not a problem, because the contracted STG can now simulate the original STG.

This modification of timed bounds is not appropriate when t conflicts with some other transitions. For example, in Figure 2 (b), t and then x can fire in the original STG. In this case, $\bullet\bullet(t\bullet\bullet) = \{t\}$ holds. Thus, the above algorithm simply adds both the earliest and latest firing times to those of x, which results in the STG shown in the middle of Figure 2 (b). In this STG, however, x can no longer fire due to a too small

timed_contract(t) {
modify_bounds(t);
transform_net(t);
}

transform_net(t) {
forall $p \in \bullet t$ and $p' \in t\bullet$ {
add new place p_{new} to the net;
forall $u \in \bullet p \cup \bullet p' - \{t\}$
add u to $\bullet p_{new}$;
forall $v \in p \bullet \cup p' \bullet - \{t\}$
add v to $p_{new}\bullet$;
if (p or p' is marked) mark p_{new};
}
remove t and $\bullet t \cup t\bullet$ from the STG;
remove duplicate places from the STG;
}

modify_bounds(t) {
max_orig_Lft $= \max\{\mathsf{Lft}(x) \mid x \in t \bullet \bullet\}$;
forall $x \in t \bullet \bullet$
$\mathsf{Lft}(x) = \mathsf{Lft}(x) + \mathsf{Lft}(t)$;
if $(\bullet \bullet (t \bullet \bullet) == \{t\})$
forall $x \in t \bullet \bullet$
$\mathsf{Eft}(x) = \mathsf{Eft}(x) + \mathsf{Eft}(t)$;
forall $u \in$ *conflict*(t)
$\mathsf{Lft}(u) = \mathsf{Lft}(u) +$ *max_orig_Lft*;
}

Fig. 1. Contraction algorithm for a transition

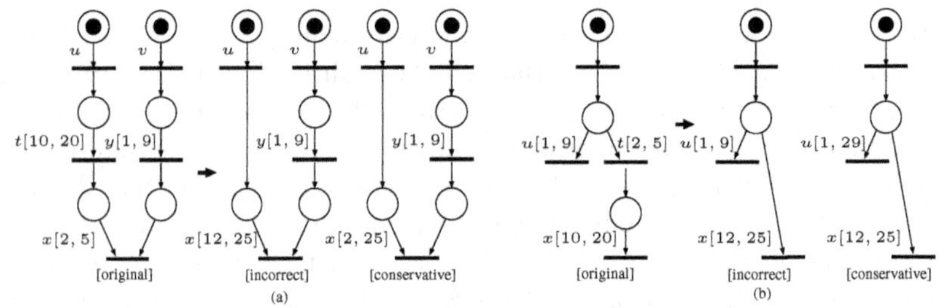

Fig. 2. Modification of time bounds

latest firing time 9 of u, which again means that the contracted STG cannot simulate the original STG. To avoid this situation, the latest firing time of u should be increased by the latest firing time of x in the original STG, because u is now conflicting with x, whose firing time can be larger, by at most the latest firing time of x, than the originally conflicting transition t. Thus, from the original STG in Figure 2 (b), the STG in the right-hand side is obtained. **modify_bounds**(t) shows this modification of time bounds.

There are still several issues to be discussed about the above contraction algorithm. First, a self-loop (i.e., the case that $\bullet t \cap t\bullet \neq \emptyset$ holds) cannot be handled correctly by the above contraction algorithm. Second, if both $(\bullet t)\bullet$ and $\bullet(t\bullet)$ includes transitions other than t, contracting t may add additional untimed behavior to the STG. For example, in an STG shown in the right-hand side of Figure 3 (a), which is obtained by contracting t using the above contraction algorithm, u can be enabled when v fires. It is, however, impossible in the original STG. Since our simulation relation requires the exact excitation ($\mathsf{out\_excited}(\sigma_1) = \mathsf{out\_excited}(\sigma_2)$), such a contraction should be avoided. Third, some conflicting transitions cannot be contracted appropriately. Consider an STG shown in the left-hand side of Figure 3 (b). In this STG, if $\mathsf{Eft}(t) \leq \mathsf{Lft}(u)$ holds, t can fire, and then x fires after v fires. On the other hand, if t is contracted, x never fires in the case that v fires too late. This problem cannot be solved by introducing conservativeness, because it is hard to estimate what value should be added to $\mathsf{Lft}(u)$ without checking the whole state

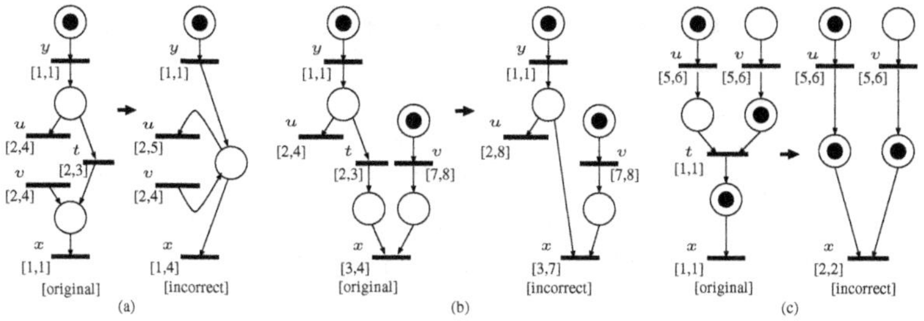

Fig. 3. Illegal contraction

space. Finally, if both source and destination places of t have tokens in the initial marking as shown in Figure 3 (c), then a correct contracted STG can be obtained by putting two tokens in the right source place of x, which, however, violates the one-safeness. Thus, our method prohibits the contraction in the above four cases[1].

Hence, in our method, the contraction is applied to a transition t only when t satisfies the following conditions.

(1) t is dummy, i.e., $l(t) = \lambda$.
(2) t has no self-loops.
(3) Either $(\bullet t)\bullet = \{t\}$ or $\bullet(t\bullet) = \{t\}$.
(4) Either *conflict*$(t) = \emptyset$ or $\forall x \in t \bullet \bullet . |\bullet x| = 1$.
(5) Either $\bullet t \cap \mu^0 = \emptyset$ or $t \bullet \cap \mu^0 = \emptyset$.

We say that a transition t is *contractable* if t satisfies the above (1), (2), (3), (4) and (5).

Suppose that G is a timed STG and t is one of its contractable transitions. Let G' denote a timed STG obtained by applying the above contraction algorithm to t. The following theorem holds.

Theorem 2. *If G' is one-safe, then $G \rightsquigarrow G'$ holds.*

From the transitivity of $\rightsquigarrow$, the contraction algorithm can be applied to contractable transitions repeatedly while preserving the relation $\rightsquigarrow$ as long as one-safeness is preserved. Thus, for $G|_{V,x}$ (defined in the last paragraph of Section 2), a STG G'' obtained by contracting contractable transitions in $G|_{V,x}$ one by one satisfies $G|_{V,x} \rightsquigarrow G''$, and thus G'' can be $\mathsf{abs}(G, V, x)$. Therefore, if $\mathsf{trigger}(x) \subseteq V$ holds and V is chosen such that G'' has CSC, Theorem 1 guarantees that G'' is cover-correct with respect to G. The outline of the algorithm to choose V such that G'' has CSC is shown in Section 4.1. Furthermore, from the output semi-modularity and the timed implementability of the original STG, the delay-correctness of G'' is easily achieved by disallowing the contraction of w-transitions with $w \in \mathsf{trigger}(x)$. This is because the time bound of a transition t is modified, only when t is in conflict with some other transition, or some other transition in $\bullet \bullet t$ with non-zero bound is contracted, but neither case can happen, because no output transition conflicts with other transitions (from output semi-modularity), any non-dummy transition reached through only dummy transitions from each output transition cannot be contracted (i.e., those non-dummy transitions are related to possibly

[1] This does not guarantee that the contracted STG is always one-safe. As mentioned in the end of this subsection, a recovery action is needed when one-safeness violation is detected during the state space exploration process.

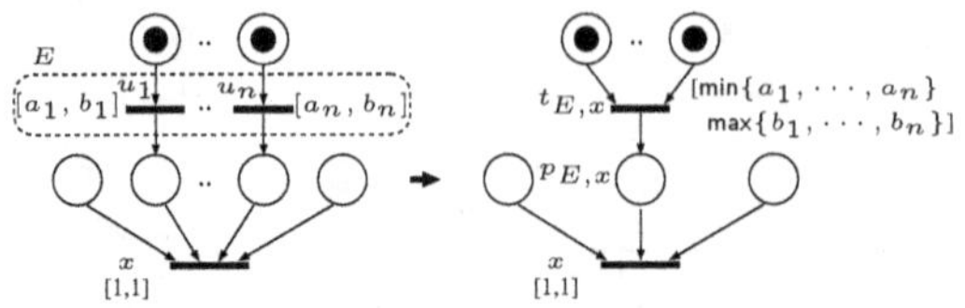

Fig. 4. Transformation $\mathcal{F}_{E,x}$

trigger signals), and all dummy transitions between them have zero bound (from timed implementability). In order not to contract w- transitions with $w \in \mathsf{trigger}(x)$, it is only needed to choose V with $\mathsf{trigger}(x) \subseteq V$, which coincides with the second condition of Theorem 1. Hence, it can be concluded that the above G'' is correct with respect to G. Note that this discussion for proving the delay-correctness implies that the time bounds of output transitions are never modified. This is one of the properties required by our correctness definition.

As for one-safeness, it is unavoidable that contracting some transition may cause a one-safeness violation when the one-safeness of the original STG is guaranteed by timing. It is, however, usually easy to detect such a problem during the state space exploration process needed in the synthesis algorithm. When a one-safeness violation is detected at the firing of transition u, it is mainly caused by contracting transitions t of the original STG satisfying $t \in u \bullet \bullet$. Thus, if such transitions exist, they are flagged to be non-contractable, and the contraction and the state space exploration process are repeated. Otherwise, reducing the contraction of other transitions is necessary.

3.2 Optimization

The contraction algorithm of Figure 1 sometimes widens time bounds of transitions unnecessarily. For example, if t and then y are contracted in the original net of Figure 2 (a), the time bounds [2,34] is finally obtained for x. However, for enabling x, both t and y must fire. Thus, at least one time unit needs to pass, and passing 20 time units is enough, even if either t or y fires later. Hence, the time bound [3,25] is sufficient for x.

To formalize this optimization, another transformation is considered. A transition t is a *simple trigger* of a transition x, if t is contractable, $t\bullet = \{p\}$ with $p\bullet = \{x\}$ and $\bullet p = \{t\}$ holds, and p is not marked initially. For example, in the original STG of Figure 2 (a), both t and y are simple triggers of x. For a set E of simple triggers of x, let $\mathcal{F}_{E,x}$ denote a transformation of an STG such that every $u \in E$ is removed with its postset, and a new transition $t_{E,x}$ and its single destination place $p_{E,x}$ are introduced connecting every source place of u to $t_{E,x}$ and $p_{E,x}$ to x, where $\mathsf{Eft}(t_{E,x}) = \mathsf{min}_{u \in E}\{\mathsf{Eft}(u)\}$ and $\mathsf{Lft}(t_{E,x}) = \mathsf{max}_{u \in E}\{\mathsf{Lft}(u)\}$ (See Figure 4). Similar optimizations for the cases that arcs merge at a place or even more complicated cases are possible but omitted here.

Let G' denote a timed STG obtained by applying $\mathcal{F}_{E,x}$ to G. The following holds.

Theorem 3. *If G' is one-safe, then $G \rightsquigarrow G'$ holds and $t_{E,x}$ is contractable in G'.*

Since $t_{E,x}$ is contractable in G', the contraction algorithm shown in Figure 1 can be applied to $t_{E,x}$. Let G'' be the resultant STG. Then, G'' also satisfies $G \rightsquigarrow G''$. This G''

conservative_STG_contract(C) {
1:   while (C has contractable transitions) {
2:       $t \leftarrow$ a contractable transition in C;
3:       if ($\bullet\bullet(t \bullet\bullet) == \{t\}$) {
4:           $C = C - \{t\}$;
5:           timed_contract(t);
6:       }
7:   }
8:   while (C has contractable transitions) {
9:       $t \leftarrow$ a contractable transition in C;
10:      $x \leftarrow$ a transition in $t \bullet\bullet$;
11:      if ($\forall t' \in \bullet\bullet x$. [$t'$ is a simple
                             trigger of x]) {
12:          $C = C - \bullet\bullet x$;
13:          perform $\mathcal{F}_{E,x}$ for $E = \bullet\bullet x$;
14:          timed_contract($t_{E,x}$);
15:      }
16: }

17: while (C has contractable transitions) {
18:      $t \leftarrow$ a contractable transition in C;
19:      $C = C - \{t\}$;
20:      timed_contract(t);
21: }
}

exact_STG_contract(C) {
1:   while (C has exactly-contractable
                   transitions) {
2:       $t \leftarrow$ an exactly-contractable transition
                   in C;
3:       $C = C - \{t\}$;
4:       timed_contract(t);
5:   }
}

Fig. 5. Conservative and exact contraction algorithms for timed STGs

has the same net structure as the timed STG G''' obtained by applying the contraction algorithm to each $u \in E$ one by one, but the time bounds of x in G'' are tighter than those in G'''.

One simple heuristic for obtaining a better (i.e., less conservative) STG is to apply the contraction algorithm to the transitions in the following order. (1) A contractable transition t satisfying $\bullet\bullet(t \bullet\bullet) = \{t\}$. (2) A transition $t_{E,x}$ obtained by $\mathcal{F}_{E,x}$, if for a transition x, every transition in $E = \bullet\bullet x$ is a simple trigger of x. If every transition in $\bullet\bullet x$ can be transformed by $\mathcal{F}_{E,x}$, introducing unnecessary conservativeness can be avoided. (3) Any remaining contractable transition.

Figure 5 shows an overall contraction algorithm for timed STGs based on this heuristic. C is initially given a set of all dummy transitions in a timed STG. Since this algorithm introduces conservativeness, it is called **conservative_STG_contract(C)**.

On the other hand, it is possible to consider a restricted version of the above contraction algorithm by which no conservativeness is introduced. It can be seen that the above STG contraction algorithm introduces conservative time bounds, only if a transition t satisfying one of the following conditions is contracted.

(a) $conflict(t) \neq \emptyset$.   (c) $|t \bullet| > 1$.
(b) $\bullet\bullet(t \bullet\bullet) \neq \{t\}$.

Some explanation may be necessary for the third condition. If transition t has two destination places, and two transitions x and y have each of them as their source place, x and y are enabled by t at the same time. If t is contracted, however, this information that both x and y are enabled at the same time is lost. This may introduce additional behavior. We say that a transition t is *exactly-contractable*, if it is contractable and satisfies none of the above (a) $\cdots$ (c). Our second STG contraction algorithm that never introduces conservativeness is **exact_STG_contract(C)**, and it is shown in Figure 5.

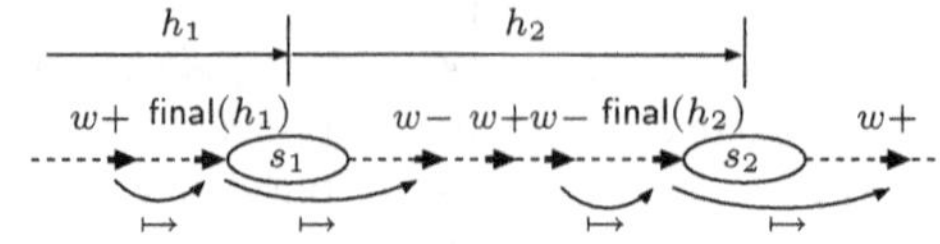

Fig. 6. Causality relation needed for w to solve the CSC violation

4 Effective Contraction

4.1 Overview of Decomposition Based Synthesis

For a given timed STG G, our timed circuit synthesis method is performed in the following 5 steps for each output x [9].

Step 1. The initial input set for x is defined by trigger(x), the set of the possible trigger signals of x.

Step 2. The transitions that are not related to either x or the signals in the input signal set for x are contracted from G if possible, and a reduced STG G' is obtained.

Step 3. The timed state space of G' is explored. The partial order reduction [17] and the POSET method [18] are used in this step in order to avoid interleaving non-signal (i.e., dummy) transitions in G'. If this state graph has CSC, then a correct circuit for x is synthesized from this state graph from Theorems 1, 2, and 3.

Step 4. Otherwise, the state graph is examined, and traces that cause the CSC violations are extracted. Note that these traces are on G', but the corresponding traces on G are necessary for our purpose. Thus, G is simulated guided by the traces on G', and real traces on G are obtained. Then, they are analyzed to find signals that should be added to the input set for x. The idea is that for each CSC violation trace, a signal in G but not in G' that occurs in odd times between the CSC violation state pair in the trace is found. The occurrence order in the trace, however, does not guarantee a (timed) causality relation. Thus, the four pairs of transitions shown in Figure 6 are further checked if one actually causes the other, where w is the candidate signal, s_1 and s_2 are the CSC violation pair, final(h) denotes the last transition of the subtrace h, and $\mapsto$ denotes the causality relation.

Step 5. The input set for x is updated by adding the signals found in the above step, and the steps from Step 2 are performed again.

The key issue addressed in this section is how to perform Step 2. If **conservative_STG_contract**(C) is used for this step, the synthesized circuits may lose the additional performance that is supposed to be obtained from the timed circuit synthesis, due to the conservative timing information. On the other hand, if the contraction is done only by **exact_STG_contract**(C), only a restricted class of transitions can be contracted. As a result, the advantage of the above approach to reduce the synthesis cost is lost. Hence, the contraction of timed STGs should be performed very carefully in order to avoid degrading the performance of the synthesized circuits while keeping the efficiency of the approach.

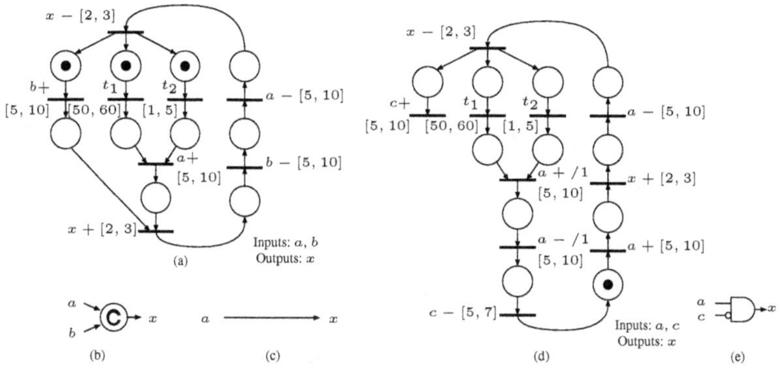

Fig. 7. Influence on synthesis

Contracting inappropriate transitions conservatively affects the synthesis process in the following aspects.

(1) Circuit performance: In timed circuit synthesis, if some trigger signals of an output x always occur too early, then they are automatically excluded from the circuit for x, which makes the circuit simple and fast. If the time bounds of trigger transitions (or some of their near ancestors) are enlarged by inappropriate conservative contraction, this advantage of timed circuit synthesis may be lost. Hence, the relative firing times between trigger transitions for each output transition should be preserved after contraction. For example, in the timed STG shown in Figure 7 (a), if the transitions t_1 and t_2 are contracted by **conservative_STG_contract**(C), the time bounds for $a+$ is modified to [6,70]. From the contracted STG, the circuit shown in Figure 7 (b) is synthesized. This is because in the contracted STG, $a+$ can fire earlier than $b+$. It is, however, impossible in the original STG, because $a+$ actually fires much later than $b+$ due to the earliest firing time 50 of t_1. Using this timing information, the circuit (just a wire) shown in Figure 7 (c) is actually synthesized from the original STG. Hence, to avoid synthesizing such redundant circuits, the relative firing times between trigger transitions for each output transition should be preserved by restricting the application of contraction to them and some of their ancestors.

(2) CSC: Besides the trigger signals, the circuit input contains the context signals to satisfy the CSC property. Such context transitions must satisfy the causality relation between some other transitions. In timed circuit synthesis, such a causality relation may be established by timing, not by the net structure. In the timed STG shown in Figure 7 (d), c is a context signal, which distinguishes the state where $a+$ (or $a-$) triggers $x+$ (or $x-$) and the state where $a+$ or $a-$ triggers nothing. The circuit synthesized from this STG is shown in Figure 7 (e). For c to be a context signal, $c+$ must fire before $a+/1$, but the causality between $c+$ and $a+/1$ is guaranteed by the delay of t_1. In such cases, the inappropriate conservative contraction may destroy the causality relation. This makes it impossible to synthesize a circuit from the contracted STG, or causes the circuit to use more context signals, which again degrades the advantage of the timed circuit synthesis. In this example, if t_1 and t_2 are contracted conservatively, the synthesis becomes impossible. Hence, when a context signal is chosen in Step 4 of

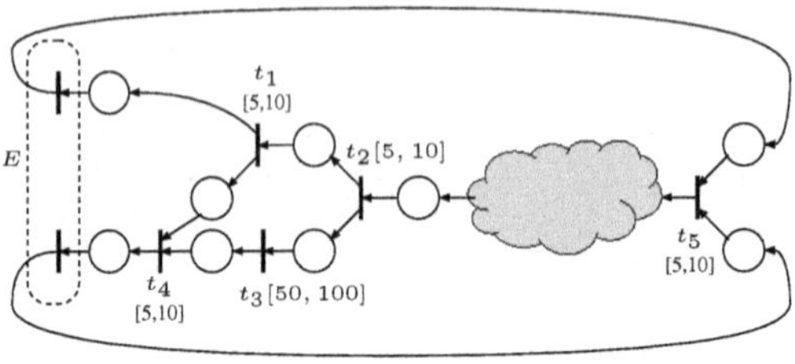

Fig. 8. A timed STG with a cone $\langle t_2, \{t_1, t_2, t_3, t_4\} \cup E \rangle$

the previous subsection, the transitions such that the causality relation is required between them should be identified, and the relative firing times between them should be preserved after the contraction (by restricting contraction).

4.2 Selecting Contraction Methods

Let a *target transition set* denote a set of transitions such that the relative firing times should be preserved after the contraction. For each target transition set, our algorithm computes a set of transitions that should not be contracted conservatively, and marks them. Then, the marked transitions are contracted by **exact_STG_contract**(C), while the others are contracted by **conservative_STG_contract**(C).

For this purpose, we define the following notion. For a transition a and b of a timed STG, let $a \overset{P}{\rightsquigarrow} b$ denote that the transition b is reached from a on the STG via a sequence P of transitions. It is assumed that $a \notin P$ and $b \notin P$. Note that $a \overset{P}{\rightsquigarrow} a$ holds with $P = \emptyset$. A *cone* for a set E of transitions is a pair $\langle cone\_top, B \rangle$, where

- $E \subseteq B$, and $cone\_top \in B$,
- for any $a \in B$, there exists some P such that $cone\_top \notin P$ and $a \overset{P}{\rightsquigarrow} x$ with some $x \in E$,
- for any $a \in \overline{B}$, every P such that $a \overset{P}{\rightsquigarrow} x$ with $x \in E$ satisfies $cone\_top \in P \cup \{x\}$.

Intuitively, every path to the transitions in E from the outside of the cone certainly passes through *cone_top* as shown in Figure 8. Thus, the firing times of the transition outside of B do not affect the relative firing times of the transitions in E. Hence, for each target transition set, if its cone is computed, and the transitions in B are marked such that they should be exactly contracted, appropriate conservative contraction can be performed. For example, in the timed STG shown in Figure 8, $\langle t_1, \{t_1, t_4\} \cup E \rangle$ cannot be a cone for E, because t_3, which is outside of $\{t_1, t_4\} \cup E$, can reach an element of E without passing through t_1. Actually, if t_3 is contracted conservatively, the information that t_1 always fires earlier than t_4 is lost. In this example, $\langle t_2, \{t_1, t_2, t_3, t_4\} \cup E \rangle$ is a cone for E. Note that for a cone $\langle cone\_top, B \rangle$ for E, a different pair $\langle t, B' \rangle$ satisfying $t \in \overline{B}$ and $B \subseteq B'$ may also be a cone for E. Thus, it is desirable to find a cone with the smallest B. A cone may seem to be a notion similar to a dominator (e.g, [19]). However, a dominator is usually considered in directed graphs where start nodes or terminal nodes are defined. On the other hand, STGs have no such nodes in general. This makes it more difficult to compute cones.

```
compute_cone(E) {
1:  i = 0;
2:  forall t ∈ E {
3:      E_i = T_i = {t};
4:      i = i + 1;
5:  }
6:  while(true) {
7:      forall 0 ≤ i ≤ |E| {
8:          E_i = •• E_i − T_i;
9:          T_i = T_i ∪ E_i;
10:     }
11::    C = ∩_{0≤i≤|E|} T_i;
12:     forall can ∈ C {
13:         B = construct_cone_body(can, E, ∅);
14:         if (|B| ≤ threshold) return ⟨can, B⟩;
15:         else keep ⟨can, B⟩;
16:     }
17:     if (every E_i is empty)
18:         return ⟨can, B⟩ with smallest B;
19: }
}
```

```
construct_cone_body(can, F, B) {
    F = F − B;
    if (F = ∅) return B;
    B = B ∪ F;
    F = •• (F − {can});
    construct_cone_body(can, F, B);
}
```

```
top_level_contract(x, in_signals, ℰ) {
    change transitions not related to
        x or in_signals to dummies;
    Let C be the set of dummy transitions;
    exact_STG_contract(C);
    Let C be the set of dummy transitions
        of the resulting STG;
    forall E ∈ ℰ {
        ⟨c, B⟩ = compute_cone(E);
        C = C − B;
    }
    conservative_STG_contract(C);
}
```

Fig. 9. Algorithms to compute a cone

This paper proposes the following heuristics to compute relatively good cones. Our algorithm is based on a backward breadth-first-search from each element of E in parallel. The algorithm **compute_cone**(E) shown in Figure 9 uses two sets E_i and T_i for each element of E, where E_i keeps frontiers and T_i stores reached transitions during the backward breadth-first-search. In the second `forall` block (lines 7–10), these sets are updated. In each backward step, the conjunction C of all T_i is obtained. The elements in this conjunction C are the candidates of *cone_top*, because they are reached backwardly from every element of E. Some of them, however, may not be a good cone. To check it, **construct_cone_body**() constructs B with respect to a candidate can by the simple backward breadth-first-search from E except that the backward search cannot go beyond can. If the constructed set B is small enough, it is decided that the candidate is a *cone_top* for a good cone. This decision is based on $threshold$, which is set to, for example, one tenth of the number of transitions of the given STG. If it is not a good cone, the parallel backward breadth-first-search is continued in **compute_cone**(E). In the case that no good cone can be found, a cone with smallest B is returned.

The remaining task of our algorithm is to obtain the target transition sets properly for each of the above cases (1) and (2). This is done as follows.

(1) For each output transition x, its possible trigger transitions form a target transition set. For example, for the timed STG shown in Figure 7 (a), transitions $a+$ and $b+$ are the possible trigger transitions for x, and so, $\{a+, b+\}$ is a target transition set. From it, a cone $\langle x-, B\rangle$ is obtained, where $B = \{x-, a+, b+, t_1, t_2\}$. Hence, neither t_1 nor t_2 is contracted.

(2) When a signal a is chosen as a candidate of newly added input signals, its corresponding transitions are supposed to satisfy the causality relation shown in Figure 6. If some of them are satisfied by timing, not by the net structure, then the pair of transitions concerned is recorded with respect to a. When every CSC violation trace is analyzed, and signals added to the input are decided, each pair of transitions recorded with respect to the signals that are actually added to the input set form a target transition set. For example, in the timed STG shown in Figure 7 (d), the initial input set is $\{a\}$ because the possible trigger signal for x is a, and a CSC violation trace

$$a+,\ x+,\ a-,\ x-,\ t_2,\ c+,\ t_1,\ a+/1$$

is obtained by the guided simulation, where the state after firing $a+$ and the final state cause the CSC violation (i.e. both signal states are $(ax) = (10)$). Since the transition for signal c fires in odd times between the CSC violation pair, c is chosen as an additional input signal. In this case, the causality between $c+$ and $a+/1$ holds by timing. Thus, $\{c+, a+/1\}$ is obtained as a target transition set. From it, $x-$ is chosen as a *cone_top* and $B = \{x-, c+, t_1, t_2, a+/1\}$ is obtained. Hence, neither t_1 nor t_2 is contracted.

When a timed STG is contracted for the first time, only the target transition sets for the first category (i.e., for the possible trigger transitions) are used. After the CSC violation trace analysis, if the target transition sets for the second category are obtained, they are used for the next contraction. Let $\mathcal{E}$ denote the set of the target transition sets obtained as above. For an output x, the input signal set $in\_signals$, and this $\mathcal{E}$, the top level algorithm for contraction is shown in Figure 9.

5 Experimental Results

The proposed method has been implemented, and experiments are performed on a 3.0 GHz Pentium 4 workstation with 4 gigabytes of memory. Table 1 shows the synthesis results for the examples that are taken from [20]. They are specifications for an IIR filter, an FIR filter, and a portion of the Discrete Cosine Transform (DCT) circuit obtained from SpecC/Balsa high-level specifications. All of these timed STGs satisfy CSC. "#T" and "#W" show the number of transitions and the number of input and output signals in each STG. The columns "Exact" show the values when only the exact contraction is used. The numbers in parentheses in "CPU" columns show the CPU times for the contraction and the state space exploration of the reduced STGs (Step 2 and Step 3 in Subsection 4.1), which the proposed method mainly improves. "sp. up" shows their speed-up ratios. "#Lit" shows the total number of literals of the synthesized circuits. "Red" columns show how the STG sizes are reduced from the original ones by the decomposition based synthesis method, that is

$$\text{Red} = \left(1 - \frac{\sum_{x \in \mathit{Out}} (\text{size of reduced STG for } x)}{(\text{size of original STG}) \times |\mathit{Out}|}\right) \times 100,$$

where *Out* is the set of output signals of the original STG. The sizes are evaluated by the average number of transitions in the reduced STG used for each output. Note that these "Red" values are used to compare the effectiveness of the proposed method over

Table 1. Experimental results

STG	#T	#W	CPU (s)					#Lit		Red (%)	
			Exact		Proposed		sp. up	Exact	Proposed	Exact	Proposed
IIR_a	370	126	9.56	(5.28)	5.45	(1.22)	4.1	391	391	26.9	84.7
IIR_b	362	128	54.69	(49.76)	37.54	(32.45)	1.5	462	462	27.7	84.8
FIR_a	872	293	142.75	(67.12)	87.34	(12.47)	5.4	923	923	28.7	90.0
FIR_b	848	291	820.41	(749.67)	545.35	(468.18)	1.6	1116	1116	30.6	91.2
DCT_a	1763	533	2396.03	(628.28)	1497.79	(46.15)	13.6	1872	1871	33.4	94.3
DCT_b	1774	507	2612.57	(1107.54)	1486.19	(147.76)	7.5	1902	1902	38.1	94.3

the exact contraction method. These results show that the proposed method succeeds in effectively reducing the sizes of STGs (about 90% of transitions are projected out) and accordingly improving the CPU times while keeping the quality of the synthesized circuits.

6 Conclusion

This paper presents a method to contract timed STGs effectively without losing optimality of the synthesized circuits. It first formalizes the contraction algorithm for timed STGs and justifies its correctness. Then, the algorithm to find portions of the given STGs that should be contracted exactly for deciding the trigger and context signals precisely is shown. The remaining part of the STGs can be contracted conservatively, which makes the decomposition based timed synthesis approach more applicable to larger classes of designs. The experimental results show that significant reduction in the size of STGs is obtained by the proposed method. Our tool `nutas` implemented based on the proposed ideas is available at `http://research.nii.ac.jp/~yoneda`.

References

1. J. Cortadella, M. Kishinevsky, A. Kondratyev, L. Lavagno, and A. Yakovlev. Petrify: a tool for manipulating concurrent specifications and synthesis of asynchronous controllers. *IEICE Trans. on Information and Systems*, E80-D(3):315–325, 1997.
2. P. A. Beerel, C. J. Myers, and T. H.-Y. Meng. Covering conditions and algorithms for the synthesis of speed-independent circuits. *IEEE Trans. on Computer-Aided Design*, 1998.
3. R. M. Fuhrer, S. M. Nowick, M. Theobald, N. K. Jha, B. Lin, and L. Plana. Minimalist: An environment for the synthesis, verification and testability of burst-mode asynchronous machines. Technical Report TR CUCS-020-99, Columbia University, NY, 1999.
4. Tam-Anh Chu. *Synthesis of Self-Timed VLSI Circuits from Graph-Theoretic Specifications.* PhD thesis, MIT Laboratory for Computer Science, 1987.
5. T. Yoneda, H. Onda, and C. Myers. Synthesis of speed independent circuits based on decomposition. In *Proc. International Symposium on Advanced Research in Asynchronous Circuits and Systems*, pages 135–145. IEEE Computer Society Press, 2004.
6. J. Carmona and J. Cortadella. ILP models for the synthesis of asynchronous control circuits. *Proc. of the IEEE/ACM International Conference on Computer Aided Design*, pages 818–825, 2003.

7. K. Stevens, S. Rotem, R. Ginosar, P. Beerel, C. Myers, K. Yun, R. Kol, C. Dike, and M. Roncken. An asynchronous instruction length decoder. *IEEE Journal of Solid-State Circuits*, 35(2):217–228, February 2001.
8. Ivan Sutherland and Scott Fairbanks. GasP: A minimal FIFO control. In *Proc. International Symposium on Advanced Research in Asynchronous Circuits and Systems*, pages 46–53. IEEE Computer Society Press, 2001.
9. Tomohiro Yoneda and Chris Myers. Synthesis of timed circuits based on decomposition. *NII Technical Report*, NII-2006-001E, 2006.
10. I. Suzuki and T. Murata. *Stepwise refinements for transitions and places.* New York: Springer-Verlag, 1982.
11. G. Berthelot. Checking properties of nets using transformations. In *Lecture Notes in Computer Science, 222*, pages 19–40, 1986.
12. T. Murata. Petri nets: Properties, analysis, and applications. In *Proceedings of the IEEE 77(4)*, pages 541–580, 1989.
13. Walter Vogler and Ralf Wollowski. Decomposition in asynchronous circuit design. In J. Cortadella, A. Yakovlev, and G. Rozenberg, editors, *Concurrency and Hardware Design*, volume 2549 of *Lecture Notes in Computer Science*, pages 152–190. Springer-Verlag, 2002.
14. H. Zheng, E. Mercer, and C. J. Myers. Modular verification of timed circuits using automatic abstraction. *IEEE Trans. on Computer-Aided Design*, 22(9), 2003.
15. H. Zheng. *Modular Synthesis and Verification of Timed Circuits Using Automatic Abstraction.* PhD thesis, University of Utah, 2001.
16. Chris J. Myers. *Computer-Aided Synthesis and Verification of Gate-Level Timed Circuits.* PhD thesis, Dept. of Elec. Eng., Stanford University, 1995.
17. T. Yoneda, E. G. Mercer, and C. J. Myers. Modular synthesis of timed circuits using partial order reduction. *Proc. of The 10th Workshop on Synthesis And System Integration of Mixed Technologies*, pages 127–134, 2001.
18. E. G. Mercer, C. J. Myers, and T. Yoneda. Improved POSET timing analysis in timed Petri nets. *Proc. of The 10th Workshop on Synthesis And System Integration of Mixed Technologies*, pages 151–158, 2001.
19. L. Georgiadis, R. E. Tarjan, S. Triantafyllis, and D. August. Finding dominators in practice. *In Proceedings of the 12th Annual European Symposium on Algorithms*, LNCS 3221:677–688, 2004.
20. T. Yoneda, A. Matsumoto, M. Kato, and C. Myers. High level synthesis of timed asynchronous circuits. In *Proc. International Symposium on Advanced Research in Asynchronous Circuits and Systems*, pages 178–189. IEEE Computer Society Press, 2005.

Synthesis for Probabilistic Environments*

Sven Schewe

Universität des Saarlandes, 66123 Saarbrücken, Germany
schewe@cs.uni-sb.de

Abstract. In synthesis we construct finite state systems from temporal specifications. While this problem is well understood in the classical setting of non-probabilistic synthesis, this paper suggests the novel approach of open synthesis under the assumptions of an environment that chooses its actions randomized rather than nondeterministically. Assuming a randomized environment inspires alternative semantics both for linear-time and branching-time logics. For linear-time, natural acceptance criteria are *almost-sure* and *observable* acceptance, where it suffices if the probability measure of accepting paths is 1 and greater than 0, respectively.

We distinguish 0-environments, which can freely assign probabilities to each environment action, from ε-environments, where the probabilities assigned by the environment are bound from below by some $\varepsilon > 0$. While the results in case of 0-environments are essentially the same as for nondeterministic environments, the languages occurring in case of ε-environments are topologically different from the results for nondeterministic and 0-environments (in case of LTL, recognizable by weak alternating automata vs. recognizable by deterministic automata). The complexity of open synthesis is, in both cases, EXPTIME and 2EXPTIME-complete for CTL and LTL specifications, respectively.

1 Introduction

Among the most important developments in verification is the development of model-checking algorithms, which test whether or not a finite-state program satisfies a temporal specification. However, this method suffers from two significant drawbacks: First, it can only be applied *after* much effort has been invested to the (manual) construction of the system. And second, model-checking cannot distinguish unrealizable specifications from erroneous implementations. The natural approach to circumvent these drawbacks is to construct finite-state systems directly from the specification. Such an approach is called synthesis.

Early works consider *closed systems* that do not interact with an environment [3,18]. Closed synthesis is in this sense a constructive extension of satisfiability checking. This approach is not suitable for *open systems*, which interact with a predefined environment, since the synthesized system cannot restrict the

* This work was partly supported by the German Research Foundation (DFG) as part of the Transregional Collaborative Research Center "Automatic Verification and Analysis of Complex Systems" (SFB/TR 14 AVACS).

S. Graf and W. Zhang (Eds.): ATVA 2006, LNCS 4218, pp. 245–259, 2006.

behavior of its environment. Later works therefore concentrate on the synthesis of open systems from linear-time specifications [15,16,1]. These fundamental works on open synthesis required that the system satisfies its specification for *all* possible behaviors of the environment, i.e., an LTL formula φ is interpreted as the CTL* formula $A\varphi$. Pnueli and Rosner [15] demonstrated that the LTL synthesis problem is 2EXPTIME-complete in this setting. Kupferman and Vardi [10] extended open synthesis to branching-time specifications and incomplete information, and established EXPTIME and 2EXPTIME-completeness results for the CTL and CTL* synthesis problem, respectively.

In the view of the attractiveness of synthesis, it is alluring to extend its applicability as far as possible. A particular interesting extension is the treatment of probabilistic systems. Probabilistic randomization has, e.g., successfully been introduced into protocols (cf. [13]). In synthesis, we want to construct systems which, under reasonable assumptions about the probabilistic behavior of the environment, satisfy a linear-time specification with probability 1 (*almost-surely*) or with probability greater than 0 (*observably*).

System synthesis is more complex than model-checking probabilistic systems (Markov decision processes). There, a probabilistic measure is defined a priori on the set of computations, usually by assigning fixed probabilities to the single transitions. In synthesis, on the other hand, we do not have a transition-system to start with (this situation is comparable with the problem occurring in the treatment of transition fairness in system synthesis, cf. [2]).

When restricting the scope to almost-sure and observable satisfaction of linear-time properties, the concrete probabilities of single transitions play a minor role; in finite systems it is only of interest whether or not a probability is 0 or 1. It turns out that these properties are preserved when the probabilities of the single transitions are uncertain, as long as an (arbitrary) lower bound $\varepsilon > 0$ on their probability is guaranteed. This allows for considering synthesis for environments, which only guarantee the *existence* of some lower bound on the probability of each single action. We call such environments *ε-environments.* They are closely related to probabilistic fair systems [5] (with the distinction that systems discussed in this paper necessarily have a predefined *constant* set of environment actions) and inherit their semantical benefits: they provide a simple way of representing probabilistic choices while abstracting from the numerical value of probability. The LTL synthesis problem remains 2EXPTIME complete in almost-sure and observable semantics for ε-environments.

The decidability of almost-sure and observable acceptance gives rise to a redefinition of the semantics for the branching-time logic CTL*. CTL* allows for universal ($A\pi$) and existential ($E\pi$) path quantification. A natural analogy is to interpret universal path quantification as the property that the probability measure of the paths satisfying π is 1 (i.e., that a path almost-surely satisfies π), and existential path quantification as the property that the probability measure of the paths satisfying π is greater than 0 [8]. This paper provides a constructive method to solve the synthesis problem for CTL* in 3EXPTIME in the length of the specification, whereas a 2EXPTIME lower bound is inherited from the

LTL synthesis problem. While the exact complexity remains open for CTL*, the synthesis problem is EXPTIME-complete for CTL.

Under the assumption of stronger environments, which can reduce the probability of each single event arbitrarily, synthesis for almost-sure/observable semantics is essentially equivalent to synthesis for classical semantics.

2 Preliminaries

Synthesis algorithms automatically construct, for a given class of environments, systems that are correct by construction from a given specification. The environment is an external part of the system, which is not under the control of the synthesis algorithm. Intuitively, the environment provides the system with inputs from a finite input-alphabet Υ. The system reacts on each input by emitting an output symbol from a finite output-alphabet Σ. When the specifications are provided as temporal logics, the input- and output alphabet consist of the possible valuations of boolean input- and output-variables, respectively [15,10,11], which also serve as atomic propositions in the specification. A system is modeled as a finite transition-system, which defines a mapping $m : \Upsilon^* \to \Sigma$ from histories of input-signals to output-signals. This paper addresses synthesis for linear- and branching-time specifications for environments with an uncertain probabilistic behavior.

Environments. In general, the concrete behavior of the environment is unknown or too complex to represent. The uncertainty with respect to the concrete behavior of the environment is expressed by the power of the environment to choose, in every step, a probability distribution of its single input letters.

An environment is called an *ε-environment* if, in each step, the probability $p(\upsilon) \in [\varepsilon, 1]$ that the environment chooses a particular input letter $\upsilon \in \Upsilon$ is bound from below by some $\varepsilon > 0$. It is called a *0-environment*, if the probability that the environment chooses a particular input letter $\upsilon \in \Upsilon$ is not bound from below ($p(\upsilon) \in]0, 1]$ or $p(\upsilon) \in [0, 1]$).

Transition Systems. A system is implemented as a finite *Σ-labeled Υ-transition-system* $\mathcal{T} = (S, s_0, \tau, l)$, where S is a set of states with initial state $s_0 \in S$, $\tau : S \times \Upsilon \to S$ is a transition function and $l : S \to \Sigma$ is a labeling function. A Σ-labeled Υ-transition-system is called *input-preserving*, if $\Sigma = \Upsilon \times \Sigma'$ for some Σ' and the Υ-projection of $l(\tau(s, \upsilon))$ is υ for all $s \in S$ (i.e., the Υ-part of the label reflects the previous input from the environment).

Parity Automata. An *alternating automaton* is a tuple $\mathcal{A} = (\Sigma, Q, q_0, \delta, \alpha)$, where Σ denotes a finite set of labels, Q denotes a finite set of states, $q_0 \in Q$ denotes a designated initial state, δ denotes a transition function, and $\alpha : Q \to C \subset \mathbb{N}$ is a coloring function. The transition function $\delta : Q \times \Sigma \to \mathbb{B}^+(Q \times \Upsilon)$ maps a state and an input letter to a positive boolean combination of states and directions. In our context, an alternating automaton runs on Σ-labeled

Υ-transition-systems. The acceptance mechanism of alternating automata is defined in terms of run trees.

As usual, a Ξ-tree is a prefixed closed subset $Y \subseteq \Xi^*$ of the finite words over a predefined set Ξ of directions. For given sets Σ and Ξ, a *Σ-labeled Ξ-tree* is a pair $\langle Y, l \rangle$, consisting of a tree $Y \subseteq \Xi^*$ and a labeling function $l : Y \to \Sigma$ that maps every node of Y to a letter of Σ. If Υ and Σ are not important or clear from the context, $\langle Y, l \rangle$ is called a tree.

A *run tree* $\langle R, r \rangle$ on a given transition-system $\mathcal{T} = (S, s_0, \tau, l)$ is a $Q \times S$-labeled tree where the root is labeled with (q_0, s_0) and where, for each node n with label (q, s), there is a set $\mathfrak{A}_n \subseteq Q \times \Upsilon$ which satisfies $\delta(q, l(s))$ such that $(q', \upsilon) \in \mathfrak{A}_n$ iff a child of n is labeled with $(q', \tau(s, \upsilon))$.

An infinite path fulfills the *parity condition*, if the highest color of the states appearing infinitely often on the path is even. A run tree is *accepting* if all infinite paths fulfill the parity condition. A transition-system is accepted if it has an accepting run tree.

The set of transition-systems accepted by an alternating automaton $\mathcal{A}$ is called its *language* $\mathcal{L}(\mathcal{A})$. An automaton is empty, if its language is empty.

The acceptance of a transition-system can also be viewed as the outcome of a game, where player *accept* chooses, for a pair $(q, \sigma) \in Q \times \Sigma$, a set of atoms of $\delta(q, \sigma)$, satisfying $\delta(q, \sigma)$, and player *reject* chooses one of these atoms, which is executed. The input tree is accepted iff player *accept* has a strategy enforcing a path that fulfills the parity condition. One of the players has a memoryless winning strategy, i.e., a strategy where the moves only depend on the state of the automaton and the state of the transition-system, and, for player *reject*, on the choice of player *accept* in the same move.

A *nondeterministic* automaton is a special alternating automaton, where the image of δ consists only of such formulas that, when rewritten in disjunctive normal form, contain exactly one element of $Q \times \{\upsilon\}$ for all $\upsilon \in \Upsilon$ in every disjunct. For nondeterministic automata, every node of a run tree corresponds to a node in the input tree (the unrolling of the transition-system). Emptiness can therefore be checked with an *emptiness game*, where player *accept* also chooses the letter of the input alphabet. A nondeterministic automaton is empty iff the emptiness game is won by *reject*.

A nondeterministic automaton is called *deterministic* if the image of δ consists only of such formulas that, when rewritten in disjunctive normal form, contain exactly one disjunct. An automaton is called a *word* automaton if Υ is singleton; in this case, Υ is omitted in the notation. An automaton is called *weak* if, for every path on every run tree for every transition-system, the color increases monotonously, i.e, if δ maps each pair (q, σ) of states and input letters to positive boolean combination over pairs of states and directions, where the color of the respective state is not smaller than the color of q. An automaton is called a *Büchi* automaton iff the image of α is contained in $\{1, 2\}$.

The Synthesis Problem. For trace languages, we distinguish *almost-sure* and *observable* acceptance of transition-systems. A transition-system $\mathcal{T}$ satisfies a specification

- *almost-surely* iff the probability measure of the set of infinite paths defined by $\mathcal{T}$ that satisfy the specification is 1, and
- *observably* iff the probability measure of the set of infinite paths defined by $\mathcal{T}$ that satisfy the specification is greater than 0.

In case of temporal logics, the input-alphabet 2^I and output-alphabet 2^O represent the possible assignments to boolean input and output variables, which also serve as atomic propositions in the specification.

For CTL* specifications, all subformulas of the form $A\pi$ and $E\pi$ are interpreted as state formulas with the semantics that the path formula π is satisfied almost-surely and observably, respectively. The *synthesis problem* is to either construct, for a given input-alphabet Υ, a given output-alphabet Σ and a specification φ, an input-preserving $\Upsilon \times \Sigma$-labeled Υ-transition-system which satisfies the specification, or to prove that no such transition-system exists.

3 Synthesis for Trace Languages

Following an automata-theoretic approach to open synthesis, the synthesis problem is decomposed into two parts: finding an automaton, which accepts a transition-system iff it is input-preserving and satisfies the specification, and constructing a transition-system accepted by this automaton (or demonstrating its emptiness). In this section, we consider synthesis for specifications provided as deterministic word automata under the assumption of ε-environments.

Structural Acceptance Criteria. Testing whether a transition-system $\mathcal{T}$ almost-surely (observably) satisfies a deterministic word automaton $\mathcal{D}$ can be reduced to a simple structural argument over the composition of $\mathcal{T}$ and $\mathcal{D}$. The result of their composition is a colored graph, and it suffices to check if the highest color in all (some) reachable strongly connected components of $\mathcal{G}_{\mathcal{D}}^{\mathcal{T}}$ that are leaves in the SCC-graph of $\mathcal{G}_{\mathcal{D}}^{\mathcal{T}}$ is even.

The composition $\mathcal{G}_{\mathcal{D}}^{\mathcal{T}} = \mathcal{T} \| \mathcal{D}$ of a transition-system $\mathcal{T} = (S, s_0, \tau, l)$ and a deterministic word automaton $\mathcal{D} = (\Sigma, Q, q_0, \delta, \alpha)$ is a colored graph $\mathcal{G}_{\mathcal{D}}^{\mathcal{T}} = (S \times Q, (s_0, q_0), \tau', \alpha')$ with transition function $\tau' : ((s,q), \upsilon) \mapsto (\tau(s,\upsilon), \delta(q, l(s)))$ and coloring function $\alpha' : (s,q) \mapsto \alpha(q)$.

Lemma 1. *An Υ-transition-system $\mathcal{T}$ almost-surely (observably) satisfies a specification provided as a deterministic word automaton $\mathcal{D}$ iff the highest color in all (some) reachable leaf-SCCs of $\mathcal{G}_{\mathcal{D}}^{\mathcal{T}} = \mathcal{T} \| \mathcal{D}$ is even.*

Proof. For all ε-environments, the probability of every single transition is bound from below by some $\varepsilon \in]0,1]$. This implies the following attributes of the computations:

- Almost-surely almost all states of a computation are in a single leaf of the SCC-tree of $\mathcal{G}_{\mathcal{D}}^{\mathcal{T}}$, which is reachable from the initial state of $\mathcal{G}_{\mathcal{D}}^{\mathcal{T}}$:
  If $\mathcal{G}_{\mathcal{D}}^{\mathcal{T}}$ has n states, then, from every state of $\mathcal{G}_{\mathcal{D}}^{\mathcal{T}}$, the probability *not* to reach some leaf-SCC within the next n steps is bound from above by $\varepsilon' = 1 - \varepsilon^n < 1$, which implies a probability of 0 to stay forever out of reachable leaf-SCCs.

- Every reachable leaf-SCC of $\mathcal{G}_{\mathcal{D}}^{\mathcal{T}}$ is reached with some positive probability (which is bound from below by ε^n).
- For traces that eventually reach a leaf-SCC L, the highest color occurring infinitely often is almost-surely the highest color of the states of L:
  The probability *not* to reach some state s in L within the next n steps is again bound from above $\varepsilon' = 1 - \varepsilon^n < 1$. This implies, for every position in the trace, a probability of 0 that s occurs never again; this holds in particular for a state s whose color is maximal in L.

The first (second) and third attribute imply the claim for almost-sure (observable) satisfaction. □

Game Construction. These structural criteria can be transformed into (weak) *acceptance games* deciding almost-sure and observable acceptance, respectively. These games are played on $\mathcal{G}_{\mathcal{D}}^{\mathcal{T}}$, starting in (s_0, q_0), and consist of three phases. For almost-sure (observable) acceptance the game is played according to the following rules:

- In the first phase, player *reject* (*accept*) either chooses to proceed to the second phase or picks a transition in $\mathcal{G}_{\mathcal{D}}^{\mathcal{T}}$. Picking a transition means that, in a state (s, q), she chooses a direction υ and the game proceeds in $\tau'((s, q), \upsilon)$. Intuitively, she can use this phase to move to a leaf-SCC of her choice.
- In the second phase, player *accept* (*reject*) either picks a transition in $\mathcal{G}_{\mathcal{D}}^{\mathcal{T}}$ or chooses to proceed to the third phase, but with the restriction that he can only move to the third phase if the color of the current node is even (odd). In case he moves to the third phase, the color c of the current node is stored. This phase is to prevent player *reject* (*accept*) from "cheating" by terminating the first phase in a state of $\mathcal{G}_{\mathcal{D}}^{\mathcal{T}}$, which is no element of any leaf-SCC. Player *accept* could, in such a case, move on to a vertex with highest color in a leaf-SCC of his choice (reachable from υ), or even pick any arbitrary state reachable from υ.
- In the last phase, player *reject* (*accept*) again chooses the transitions. She wins immediately upon reaching a state with an odd (even) color greater than c.

Infinite plays of the game are won by player *accept* (*reject*) if the game always stays in the first phase and if the game eventually stays forever in the third phase, while player *reject* (*accept*) wins otherwise.

Lemma 2. *The acceptance game on $\mathcal{G}_{\mathcal{D}}^{\mathcal{T}}$ is won by player* accept *if, and only if, $\mathcal{T}$ satisfies $\mathcal{D}$ almost-surely (observably).*

Proof. To prove the claim for almost-sure acceptance, first assume that $\mathcal{T}$ does not satisfies $\mathcal{D}$ almost-surely. In this case, the highest color in some reachable leaf-SCC L of $\mathcal{G}_{\mathcal{D}}^{\mathcal{T}}$ is odd by Lemma 1. Player *reject* can direct the game towards such a leaf-SCC L and then let the game proceed to the second phase.

If player *accept* ever moves on to the third phase, he must do so from a state in L. Since L is cyclic, player *reject* can then move to a state with maximal (odd) color and wins directly. If, on the other hand, player *accept* never moves to the third phase, player reject wins since the third phase is never reached.

To prove the "if" direction, recall that almost-sure satisfaction of $\mathcal{D}$ by $\mathcal{T}$ entails that the highest color in all reachable leaf-SCCs of $\mathcal{G}_{\mathcal{D}}^{\mathcal{T}}$ is even. If player *reject* never leaves the first phase, player *accept* wins due to the winning condition for infinite plays. If player *reject* eventually changes in some state v to the second phase, then player *accept* can move to *some* leaf-SCC L. Since L is cyclic by definition, he can reach a state v' in L, whose (even) color is maximal in L. After having moved on to v', player *accept* changes to the third phase (storing the color of v'). Since the color of v' is maximal in L, player *reject* cannot win directly in the third phase, and consequently loses by the winning condition for infinite plays.

The proof for observable acceptance runs accordingly. □

From Acceptance Games to Automata. It is only a small step from the acceptance games of the previous paragraph to weak alternating automata over transition-systems. A given deterministic word automaton $\mathcal{D}$ can be turned into weak alternating automata, which accept a transition-system iff it satisfies $\mathcal{D}$ almost-surely or observably, respectively. The states of these automata are constructed from the states and colors of $\mathcal{D}$, and the transition function reflects the transitions of the game introduced in the previous paragraph.

Theorem 1. *Given a deterministic word automaton $\mathcal{D} = (\Sigma, Q, q_0, \delta, \alpha)$ we can construct weak alterating tree automata $\mathcal{A}_{\mathcal{D}}$ and $\mathcal{O}_{\mathcal{D}}$ which accept a Σ-labeled Υ-transition-system if it almost-surely and observably satisfies $\mathcal{D}$, respectively. If $\mathcal{D}$ has n states and c colors, $\mathcal{A}_{\mathcal{D}}$ and $\mathcal{O}_{\mathcal{D}}$ have at most $n \cdot \lceil 2 + \frac{c}{2} \rceil$ states.*

Proof. $\mathcal{A}_{\mathcal{D}} = (\Sigma, Q', q_0', \delta', \alpha')$ is defined as follows:

- The set of states is set to $Q' = Q \times (\{f, s\} \cup C_e)$ and initial state $q_0' = (q_0, f)$, where C_e denotes the set of even colors of $\mathcal{D}$.
- The transition function is defined by:
  - $\delta' : ((q, f), \sigma) \mapsto \delta'((q, s), \sigma) \wedge \bigwedge_{\upsilon \in \Upsilon}((\delta(q, \sigma), f), \upsilon)$,
  - $\delta' : ((q, s), \sigma) \mapsto \delta'((q, \alpha(q)), \sigma) \vee \bigvee_{\upsilon \in \Upsilon}((\delta(q, \sigma), s), \upsilon)$ if $\alpha(q)$ is even and
  - $\delta' : ((q, s), \sigma) \mapsto \bigvee_{\upsilon \in \Upsilon}((\delta(q, \sigma), s), \upsilon)$ if $\alpha(q)$ is odd,
  - $\delta' : ((q, c), \sigma) \mapsto$ *false* if $\alpha(q)$ is an odd number greater then c, and
  - $\delta' : ((q, c), \sigma) \mapsto \bigwedge_{\upsilon \in \Upsilon}((\delta(q, \sigma), c), \upsilon)$ otherwise.
- The coloring function α' maps $Q \times \{f\}$ to 0, $Q \times \{s\}$ to 1, and $Q \times C_e$ to 2.

Likewise, $\mathcal{O}_{\mathcal{D}} = (\Sigma, Q'', q_0'', \delta'', \alpha'')$ is defined as follows:

- The set of states is set to $Q'' = Q \times (\{f, s\} \cup C_o)$ and initial state $q_0'' = (q_0, f)$, where C_o denotes the set of odd colors of $\mathcal{D}$.
- The transition function is defined by:
  - $\delta'' : ((q, f), \sigma) \mapsto \delta''((q, s), \sigma) \vee \bigvee_{\upsilon \in \Upsilon}((\delta(q, \sigma), f), \upsilon)$,
  - $\delta'' : ((q, s), \sigma) \mapsto \delta''((q, \alpha(q)), \sigma) \wedge \bigwedge_{\upsilon \in \Upsilon}((\delta(q, \sigma), s), \upsilon)$ if $\alpha(q)$ is odd and
  - $\delta'' : ((q, s), \sigma) \mapsto \bigwedge_{\upsilon \in \Upsilon}((\delta(q, \sigma), s), \upsilon)$ if $\alpha(q)$ is even,

  - $\delta'' : ((q, c), \sigma) \mapsto \mathit{true}$ if $\alpha(q)$ is an even number greater then c, and
  - $\delta'' : ((q, c), \sigma) \mapsto \bigwedge_{\upsilon \in \Upsilon}((\delta(q, \sigma), c), \upsilon)$ otherwise.
- The coloring function α'' maps $Q \times \{f\}$ to 1, $Q \times \{s\}$ to 2, and $Q \times C_o$ to 3.

The states $Q \times \{f\}$ refer to the first phase of the acceptance game, the states $Q \times \{s\}$ to the second and the remaining states $Q \times C_e$ and $Q \times C_o$, respectively, refer to the third phase of the acceptance game. A winning strategy for either player in the acceptance game on $\mathcal{G}_{\mathcal{D}}^{\mathcal{T}}$ can easily be transformed into a winning strategy in the acceptance game of the respective alternating automaton. □

Efficient Nondeterminization. Weak alternating automata are well suited for model-checking, but synthesis (or its non-constructive equivalent, checking non-emptiness) usually contains an exponential blow-up due to a nondeterminization step. A closer look on the special weak alternating automata of Theorem 1 reveals that this is not the case here: Most decisions can easily be guessed by a nondeterministic automaton. The crucial point in the nondeterminization is the single decision of player *reject* when to proceed from the first to the second phase (in case of almost-sure acceptance) and from the second to the third phase (in case of observable acceptance), respectively. It turns out that this single decision can be left uncertain in the construction of a nondeterministic automaton, avoiding the blow-up.

Theorem 2. *Given deterministic word automaton $\mathcal{D} = (\Sigma, Q, q_0, \delta, \alpha)$ we can construct nondeterministic Büchi tree automata $\mathcal{A}_{\mathcal{D}}'$ and $\mathcal{O}_{\mathcal{D}}'$ which accept a Σ-labeled Υ-transition-system if it almost-surely and observably satisfies $\mathcal{D}$, respectively. If $\mathcal{D}$ has n states and c colors, $\mathcal{A}_{\mathcal{D}}'$ and $\mathcal{O}_{\mathcal{D}}'$ have at most $2n \cdot \lfloor 1 + \frac{c}{2} \rfloor + 1$ and $n \cdot \lfloor 2 + \frac{c}{2} \rfloor$ states, respectively.*

Proof. The nondeterministic Büchi tree automaton $\mathcal{O}_{\mathcal{D}}' = (\Sigma, Q'', q_0'', \delta'', \alpha'')$ for testing observable acceptance is defined as follows:

- The set of states is set to $Q'' = Q \cup Q \times C_o^-$ and the initial state $q_0'' = q_0$ is the initial state from $\mathcal{D}$. C_o^- denotes the set of odd colors of $\mathcal{D}$, plus an additional color $e_{min} = o_{min} - 1$, where o_{min} denotes the smallest odd color of $\mathcal{D}$.
- The transition function is defined by:
  - $\delta'' : (q, \sigma) \mapsto \bigvee_{\upsilon \in \Upsilon}(\delta(q, \sigma), \upsilon) \vee \delta''(q, e_{min}), \sigma)$,
  - $\delta'' : ((q, c), \sigma) \mapsto \bigvee_{\upsilon \in \Upsilon}\Big(((\delta(q, \sigma), \max\{c, \alpha(q)\}), \upsilon)$
    $\wedge \bigwedge_{\upsilon \neq \upsilon' \in \Upsilon}((\delta(q, \sigma), e_{min}), \upsilon)\Big)$ if $\alpha(q)$ is odd,
  - $\delta'' : ((q, c), \sigma) \mapsto \bigwedge_{\upsilon \in \Upsilon}((\delta(q, \sigma), e_{min}), \upsilon)$
    if $\alpha(q) > c$ is even and greater than c, and
  - $\delta'' : ((q, c), \sigma) \mapsto \bigvee_{\upsilon \in \Upsilon}\Big(((\delta(q, \sigma), c), \upsilon) \wedge \bigwedge_{\upsilon \neq \upsilon' \in \Upsilon}((\delta(q, \sigma), e_{min}), \upsilon)\Big)$
    if $\alpha(q) < c$ is even and smaller than c.
- The coloring function α'' maps the states $Q \times \{e_{min}\}$ to 2 and the remaining states to 1.

The states in Q reflect the first phase of the acceptance game on $\mathcal{G}_{\mathcal{D}}^{\mathcal{T}}$: player accept moves to a position of her choice ($\bigvee_{\upsilon \in \Upsilon}(\delta(q,\sigma),\upsilon)$) and eventually moves on to the second phase ($(\delta''(q,e_{min}),\sigma)$). The color 1 for these states reflect the winning condition on infinite plays (player *accept* looses if she stays for ever in the first phase).

In the second phase, the situation is more involved, since rather than guessing the action of player *accept*, the automaton needs to cover all possible actions of player *reject*. Intuitively, the option of player *reject* to stay in the second phase is covered by sending, from a state (q,c), a copy (q',e_{min}) (with $q' = \delta(q,\sigma)$) to each direction. Since player *reject* looses when staying in the second phase indefinitely, the color of these states is 2. Additionally, if $\alpha(q)$ is odd, player *reject* could move to the third phase, which could be reflected by sending a copy $(q,\alpha(q))$ to some direction ($\alpha(q)$ denotes the color to be stored). Concurrently, we must consider the possibility that the game is in the third phase. If $\alpha(q)$ is even and greater than c, then player *accept* wins immediately (no successor send), otherwise (q',c) is sent to some successor. Since player *accept* loses by staying in the third phase indefinitely, the color of a state (q,c) with $c \neq e_{min}$ is 1. Since the situation of player *reject* becomes strictly better when the stored color c increases, we can, instead of sending (q',c) *and* (q',c') into the same direction, send only $(q',\max\{c,c'\})$. This results in the *nondeterministic* automaton $\mathcal{O}_{\mathcal{D}}{}'$.

The nondeterministic Büchi tree automaton $\mathcal{A}_{\mathcal{D}}{}' = (\Sigma, Q', q_0', \delta', \alpha')$ for testing almost-sure acceptance is defined as follows:

- The set of states is set to $Q' = Q \times \mathbb{B} \times C_e^+ \cup \{\bot\}$ with initial state $q_0' = (q_0, \mathit{true}, e_{max})$, where C_e^+ denotes the set of even colors of $\mathcal{D}$, plus, if the highest color of $\mathcal{D}$ is an odd number o_{max}, $o_{max}+1$. e_{max} denotes the highest number in C_e^+.
- The transition function is defined by:
  - $\delta' : ((q,*,c),\sigma) \mapsto \bigvee_{\upsilon \in \Upsilon}\Big(((\delta(q,\sigma),\mathit{true},c),\upsilon)$
    $\wedge \bigwedge_{\upsilon \neq \upsilon' \in \Upsilon}((\delta(q,\sigma),\mathit{false},c),\upsilon)\Big)$
    $\vee \bigwedge_{\upsilon \in \Upsilon}(\delta(q,\sigma),\mathit{false},\min\{c,\alpha(q)\}),\upsilon)$ if $\alpha(q)$ is even,
  - $\delta' : ((q,*,c),\sigma) \mapsto \bigwedge_{\upsilon \in \Upsilon}(\bot,\upsilon)$ if $\alpha(q) > c$ is odd and greater than c,
  - $\delta' : ((q,*,c),\sigma) \mapsto \bigvee_{\upsilon \in \Upsilon}\Big(((\delta(q,\sigma),\mathit{true},c),\upsilon)$
    $\wedge \bigwedge_{\upsilon \neq \upsilon' \in \Upsilon}((\delta(q,\sigma),\mathit{false},c),\upsilon)\Big)$ otherwise, and
  - $\delta' : (\bot,\sigma) \mapsto \bigwedge_{\upsilon \in \Upsilon}(\bot,\upsilon)$.
- The coloring function α' maps $Q \times \{\mathit{true}\} \times C_e^+$ and the error state $\bot$ to 1 and $Q \times \{\mathit{false}\} \times C_e^+$ to 2.

In almost-sure acceptance, the situation is slightly more involved. The states keep three pieces of information: the state of the deterministic word automaton, the information, if the game *could* be in the second phase, and a color, which reflects that the third phase could have been entered from a state in this color. The color is initialized to e_{max}, which is greater than all odd colors. From every point of the computation tree, one or no successor can refer to the second phase: No successor, if player *accept* would move to the third phase, and one successor otherwise. Player *accept* loses iff there is a trace where he eventually stays indefinitely in the second phase, or if there is a trace where he eventually moves to the third phase in a state $(q,*,*)$ and then reaches a state $(q',*,*)$ with odd color $\alpha(q') > \alpha(q)$. The latter is modelled by moving to the designated error state $\bot$. The remaining information can be handled by storing the (even) color $\alpha(q)$ every time player *accept* would move to the third phase $(\bigwedge_{\upsilon\in\Upsilon}((\delta(q,\sigma), \mathit{false}, \min\{c,\alpha(q)\}),\upsilon))$ *or* by marking the direction player accept would choose when staying in the second phase $(\bigvee_{\upsilon\in\Upsilon}((\delta(q,\sigma), \mathit{true}, c),\upsilon) \wedge \bigwedge_{\upsilon\neq\upsilon'\in\Upsilon}((\delta(q,\sigma), \mathit{false}, c),\upsilon))$.

Obviously, a transition-system is rejected by $\mathcal{A}_{\mathcal{G}}{}'$ iff the acceptance game on $\mathcal{G}_{\mathcal{D}}^{\mathcal{T}}$ is won by player *reject*. □

These automata additionally have the pleasant property that their transition tables are short (at most $|\Upsilon| + 1$ entries for each state/input-letter pair).

The step to input-preserving transition-systems is a small one. The respective automaton can be multiplied with a deterministic safety automaton that checks if the label always agrees with the direction. The small transition table property is preserved by this transformation.

Theorem 3. *[11] Given an alternating tree automaton $\mathcal{A}$ over $\Upsilon \times \Sigma$-labeled Υ-transition-systems, we can construct an alternating tree automaton $\mathcal{A}'$ over $\Upsilon \times \Sigma$-labeled Υ-transition-systems that accepts a transition-system $\mathcal{T}$ iff it is input-preserving and accepted by $\mathcal{A}$. If $\mathcal{A}$ has n states, $\mathcal{A}'$ has at most $n \cdot |\Upsilon| + 1$ states, and if $\mathcal{A}$ is a (non)deterministic, weak or Büchi automaton, so is $\mathcal{A}'$.* □

4 Temporal Logics

While Section 3 provided basic techniques for trace languages and ε-environments, these results are transferred to temporal logics in this section. For the linear-time temporal logic LTL the techniques from the previous section can easily be applied: It suffices to translate an LTL formula into an equivalent deterministic word automaton, and then use the results of Section 3.

For probabilistic systems, the almost-sure/observable semantics for LTL inspire a redefinition of CTL* semantics [8]: Universal path quantification $(A\pi)$ can be interpreted as the property that the probability measure of the paths satisfying π is 1, and existential path quantification can be interpreted as the property that the probability measure of the paths satisfying π is greater than 0.

Liner-Time Logic. Converting LTL formulas to deterministic word automata is well established.

Theorem 4. *[15,7] Given an LTL specification φ, we can construct a deterministic word automaton $\mathcal{D}_\varphi$ that accepts exactly the models of φ. The number of states of $\mathcal{D}_\varphi$ is doubly exponential in the length of φ.* □

Given an LTL specification φ, we can, by the Theorems 4, 2 and 3, construct a nondeterministic Büchi tree automaton $\mathcal{N}_\varphi$ that accepts an input-preserving

$2^I \times 2^O$-labeled 2^I-transition-system iff it almost-surely (observably) satisfies φ, such that the number of states of $\mathcal{N}_\varphi$ is doubly exponential in the length of φ. Checking $\mathcal{N}_\varphi$ for emptiness and, if $\mathcal{N}_\varphi$ is non-empty, constructing a transition-system accepted by $\mathcal{N}_\varphi$ reduces to solving a Büchi game, whose states intuitively consist of the states of $\mathcal{N}_\varphi$ and the entries in the transition-table of $\mathcal{N}_\varphi$.

Corollary 1. *Given an LTL specification φ we can, in time doubly-exponential in the length of φ, construct an input-preserving $2^I \times 2^O$-labeled 2^I-transition-system which almost-surely (observably) satisfies φ, or show that no such transition-system exists, in time doubly-exponential in the length of φ.* □

It turns out that this upper bound is sharp.

Theorem 5. *The LTL synthesis problem is 2EXPTIME complete.*

Proof. The upper bound is established by Corollary 1. To establish a matching lower bound, consider the ω-regular trace language

$$\mathcal{L}_n = \{\{0,1,2,3\}^* \cdot 3 \cdot \{0,1,2\}^* \cdot 2 \cdot v \cdot 2 \cdot \{0,1,2\}^* \cdot 3 \cdot v \cdot \{0,1,2\}^\omega \mid v \in \{0,1\}^n\}.$$

While $\mathcal{L}_n$ can be expressed by an LTL formula with size quadratic in n, any automaton accepting $\mathcal{L}_n$ necessarily has at least 2^n states [9] (since it must continously update the set of *subsets* of $\{0,1\}$ words of length n that have occurred between two 2 symbols since the last 3).

Consider a system with two boolean input variables i_1 and i_2, and a single output variable o. One can use i_1 and i_2 to encode the letters $0,\ldots,3$, and represent the language $\mathcal{L}_n$ by a formula φ_n (of length quadratic in n).

The specification $\psi_n = \varphi_n \leftrightarrow FGo$ can only be satisfied by a transition-system with at least $O(2^n)$ states, regardless if in classical, almost-sure or observable semantics, since the transition-system *always* needs to react on an additional 3 (e.g., by setting the value of the output variable to *true* or *false* n steps after a 3 was read and keeping it constant otherwise). □

Branching-Time. In the branching-time case, one can use the fact that $E\psi$ and $A\psi$ are state-formulas. We call the strict subformulas of a CTL* specification φ of this special form the *basic* subformulas of φ, denoted *basic*(φ). Testing if a transition-system $\mathcal{T}$ satisfies a CTL* formula φ can be reduced to testing if the labels of $\mathcal{T}$ can be extended with suitable truth values for the basic subformulas of φ. The correct labels can be guessed on the fly.

Theorem 6. *Given a CTL* specification φ we can construct a weak alternating tree automaton $\mathcal{A}$ which accepts an $2^I \times 2^O$-labeled 2^I-transition-system iff it satisfies φ. The number of states of $\mathcal{A}$ is doubly-exponential in the length of φ.*

Proof. In our construction, the values of the basic formulas are guessed. Let $\mathcal{A}_\psi = (\Sigma^\psi, Q^\psi, q_0^\psi, \delta^\psi, \alpha^\psi)$ denote the weak alternating tree automaton that accepts the models of a basic formula $\psi = E\psi'$ or $\psi = A\psi'$ of φ (or of φ itself), where the basic subformulas of ψ are provided as atomic proposions.

$\mathcal{A}_\psi$ can be constructed by the method introduced in Theorem 1. The number of states of $\mathcal{A}_\psi$ is doubly exponential in the number of states of ψ. Let $\mathcal{A}_{\overline{\psi}} = (\Sigma^\psi, Q^{\overline{\psi}}, q_0^{\overline{\psi}}, \delta^{\overline{\psi}}, \alpha^{\overline{\psi}})$ denote the weak alternating automaton dual to $\mathcal{A}_\psi$.

We assume w.l.o.g. that φ is basic (otherwise we can replace the state formula φ by $A\varphi$ or $E\varphi$ without changing the semantics) and define the weak alternating tree automaton $\mathcal{A} = (2^I \times 2^O, Q, q_0, \delta, \alpha)$ as follows: The states $Q = Q^\varphi \cup \bigcup_{\psi \in basic(\varphi)} (Q^\psi \cup Q^{\overline{\psi}})$ are formed by the states of the single weak alternating automata $\mathcal{A}_\psi$, and the initial state $q_0 = q_0^\varphi$ is the initial state of $\mathcal{A}_\varphi$. The transition function is defined such that

$$\delta(q^\psi, \sigma) = \bigvee_{\Psi \subseteq basic(\psi)} \Big(\delta^\psi(q^\psi, \sigma \cup \Psi) \wedge \bigwedge_{\psi' \in \Psi} \delta(q_0^{\psi'}, \sigma) \wedge \bigwedge_{\psi' \in basic(\psi) \smallsetminus \Psi} \delta(q_0^{\overline{\psi'}}, \sigma)\Big)$$

holds true. The coloring function maps a state q^ψ with even (odd) color $\alpha^\psi(q^\psi)$ in $\mathcal{A}_\psi$ to an even (odd) color, such that the weakness criterion is preserved.

Intuitively, the truth of the single basic subformulas is guessed on the fly. To demonstate that guessing these values is safe, we show that player *accept* has a winning strategy in the acceptance game if, and only if, he as a winning strategy where he always guesses the validity of all basic subformulas correctly. This can be demonstrated by induction along the structure of φ: Assume that player *accept* has a winning strategy where the truth value of some subformula is guessed incorrectly. Then there is a basic subformula ψ whose truth value is eventually guessed *incorrectly*, but the truth values of the basic subformulas of ψ are always guessed correctly. Then, for a state s in the transition-system $\mathcal{T}$ where the truth of ψ was eventually guessed incorrectly (w.l.o.g. to *true*), player accept has a winning strategy from (q_0^ψ, s) in the acceptance game, such that all values of basic subformulas of ψ are guessed correctly. Then player *accept* has a winning strategy in $\mathcal{A}_\psi$ when the labeling of $\mathcal{T}$ are enriched by the correct values for the basic subformulas of ψ (the winning strategy is the winning strategy from $\mathcal{A}$, with the simplification that the correct values need not be guessed). But in this case ψ *is* valid in s. □

The automaton $\mathcal{A}_\varphi$ constructed by Theorem 6 can be turned into an equivalent nondeterministic Büchi tree automaton $\mathcal{N}_\varphi$ [14] with exponentially more states than $\mathcal{A}_\varphi$. The language of $\mathcal{N}_\varphi$ can be restricted to input-preserving transition-systems (Theorem 3). A transition-system accepted by $\mathcal{A}_\varphi$ can be constructed via solving the emptiness game for the resulting automaton.

Corollary 2. *Given a CTL* specification φ we can construct an input-preserving $2^I \times 2^O$-labeled 2^I-transition-system, or proof that no such system exists, in time triply exponential in the length of φ.*

Theorem 5 provides a 2EXPTIME lower bound, which leaves the exact characterization of the complexity of the CTL* synthesis problem open. For its important sub-logic CTL, the complexity coincides with the synthesis complexity for classical semantics.

Theorem 7. *The CTL synthesis problem is EXPTIME complete.*

Proof. In CTL, each path quantifier refers to a path formula of the form $\psi_1 U \psi_2$, $G\psi_1$, or $X\psi_1$, where ψ_1 and ψ_2 are propositional (when basic formulas are viewed as propositions). For such path formulas (and their negations) acceptance of a path can be tested by a deterministic word automaton with three, two, or three states, respectively. The alternating automaton constructed by Theorem 6 is therefore only *linear* in the length of the specification, and emptiness can be checked (via nondeterminization [14] of this automaton) in time exponential in the length of the specification.

To demonstrate EXPTIME-hardness, we reduce solving the two player game PEEK-G_4 [17] to CTL synthesis. An instance of this game is a four-tuple $\langle X, Y, Z, \varphi\rangle$, where X and Y are disjoint sets of boolean variables with the intuition that X is under the control of the system and Y is under the control of the environment. $Z \subseteq X \cup Y$ denotes the variables which initially hold true and φ is a propositional formula over the variables $X \cup Y$. The game is played in rounds where first the system can change the value of at most one variable in X, followed by a decision of the environment to change the value of at most one variable in Y. The system wins the game iff φ is eventually satisfied (after the move of the system). To determine the winner of such games is EXPTIME-hard [17].

An instance of this game can be reduced to the synthesis problem for a system with one input-variable i, two output variables o_1 and o_2, and a CTL specification ψ quadratic in $|X|+|Y|$ and linear in φ. $\psi = \psi_0 \wedge \psi_1 \wedge \psi_2 \wedge \psi_3 \wedge \psi_\varphi$ is a conjunction of the following five CTL formulas:

- ψ_0 requires that the first $|X|$ values of o_1 reflect (on every path) the initial truth value of the variables in X (defined by $X \cap Z$) and the following $|Y|$ values of o_1 reflect the initial truth value of the variables in Y.
- ψ_1 requires that o_2 is *true* exactly every $|X| + |Y|$ steps (and initially) on every path.
- ψ_2 requires that at most one value of the variables o_1 within $|X| - 1$ steps after o_2 was last set to *true* (including the current step) differs from the value of o_1 $|X| + |Y|$ steps earlier.
- ψ_3 states that within $|X|$ to $|X| + |Y| - 1$ steps after o_2 was set true, the value of the variable o_1 is different from its value $|X| + |Y|$ steps earlier iff (1) the value of the input variable is *true* and (2) the values of the previous input variables since $|X|$ steps after o_2 was last set to *true* were all *false*.
- ψ_φ requires that, for all paths, there is eventually a position where o_2 is *true* and along the path where i is *false* for the following $|X| + |Y|$ steps, the following $|X| + |Y|$ values of o_1 (including the current value) satisfy φ.

ψ_2 and ψ_3 refer to the changing of at most one assignment for the variables of X and Y by the system and the environment, respectively, ψ_0 initializes the game and ψ_1 guarantees that o_2 can be used as a flag, indicating that a round starts. ψ_φ reflects the winning condition of the game. An input-preserving transition-system that satisfies ψ (in classical semantics as well as in almost-sure/observable semantics) defines a winning strategy for $\langle X, Y, Z, \varphi\rangle$ and vice versa. □

5 0-Environments

0-environments can "emphasize" each single path by assigning a probability measure of 1 (if the probability of each single action can be chosen from $[0, 1]$) or arbitrarily close to 1 (if the probability of each single action can be chosen from $]0, 1]$). For the latter consider an assignment of the probability $1 - 2^i \cdot \varepsilon$ for staying on the path desired by the environment in the i-th step for some $\varepsilon > 0$[1]. Consequently, the LTL synthesis problem coincides for almost-sure and observable semantics with the LTL synthesis problem for classical semantics, which is 2EXPTIME-complete [15].

For almost-sure/observable CTL* semantics this implies that existential and universal path quantifiers coincide. Consequently, a transition-system $\mathcal{T}$ is a model of a CTL* specification φ iff $\mathcal{T}$ is a model of a specification φ' in classical semantics, where φ' is obtained from φ by replacing all existential path quantifiers by universal path quantifiers. This implies EXPTIME and 2EXPTIME upper bounds for the CTL and CTL* synthesis problem [11], respectively.

On the other hand, in classical semantics each specification ψ can be translated to an equivalent specification ψ' by replacing each occurrence of an existential path quantifier E by the sequence $\neg A \neg$. Since the length of ψ' is linear in the length of ψ and the classical semantics for ψ' coincides with the almost-sure/observable semantics, the matching lower bounds for the CTL and CTL* synthesis problem [11] are preserved as well.

6 Conclusions

This paper suggests constructive decision procedures for the LTL, CTL and CTL* synthesis problems under the assumption of 0-environments and ε-environments. While the semantics for 0-environments essentially reflect the classical semantics and practically all established results trivially carry over, the results for ε-environments provide interesting new insights.

The results of this paper show that the complexity of synthesizing transition-systems satisfying an LTL or CTL specification φ in almost-sure/observable semantics is, under the assumption of ε-environments, equivalent to the complexity in classical semantics. While the complexity coincides, the language classes for LTL are at the same time simpler and more involved than for classical semantics: They are simpler in the sense that the languages are recognizable by *weak* alternating automata, and more involved since they cannot be recognized by deterministic automata.

Two interesting questions deserve further study: the exact complexity of CTL* synthesis in almost-sure/observable semantics, and the influence of incomplete information on the complexity of the LTL[2] synthesis problem. These problems

[1] The probability measure of the path is, in this case, greater than $1 - \varepsilon$, and can therefore be chosen arbitrarily close to 1 by the 0-environment.

[2] For CTL and CTL* synthesis, incomplete information can be handled using established automata-based techniques [10].

may be closely interrelated: In classical semantics, both problems can be solved through the existence of alternating automata that are only exponential in the length of a CTL* formula φ, which accept the models of φ. It does not seem unlikely that similar solutions exist for almost-sure/observable semantics, taking into account that model-checking remains PSPACE-complete (Yannakakis PSPACE result for LTL model-checking [4] trivially extends to CTL*).

An interesting side effect of using an automata-based synthesis algorithm is the possibility to extend the results for single-process synthesis directly to multi-process synthesis [12,6].

References

1. M. Abadi, L. Lamport, and P. Wolper. Realizable and unrealizable concurrent program specifications. In *Proc. ICALP*, pages 1–17. Springer-Verlag, July 1989.
2. A. Anuchitanukul and Z. Manna. Realizability and synthesis of reactive modules. In *Proc. CAV*, pages 156–168. Springer-Verlag, June 1994.
3. E. M. Clarke and E. A. Emerson. Design and synthesis of synchronization skeletons using branching time temporal logic. In *Proc. IBM Workshop on Logics of Programs*, pages 52–71. Springer-Verlag, 1981.
4. C. Courcoubetis and M. Yannakakis. The complexity of probabilistic verification. *J. ACM*, 42(4):857–907, 1995.
5. L. de Alfaro. From fairness to chance. In *Proc. PROBMIV'98*, 1999.
6. B. Finkbeiner and S. Schewe. Uniform distributed synthesis. In *Proc. LICS*, pages 321–330. IEEE Computer Society Press, June 2005.
7. Y. Gurevich and L. Harrington. Trees, automata and games. 14:60–65, 1982.
8. H. Hansson and B. Jonsson. A logic for reasoning about time and reliability. *Formal Aspects of Computing*, 6(5):512–535, 1994.
9. O. Kupferman and M. Vardi. Freedom, weakness, and determinism: From linear-time to branching-time. In *Proc. LICS*, June 1995.
10. O. Kupferman and M. Y. Vardi. Synthesis with incomplete informatio. In *Proc. ICTL*, pages 91–106, Manchester, July 1997.
11. O. Kupferman and M. Y. Vardi. Church's problem revisited. *The bulletin of Symbolic Logic*, 5(2):245–263, June 1999.
12. O. Kupferman and M. Y. Vardi. Synthesizing distributed systems. In *Proc. LICS'01*, pages 389–398. IEEE Computer Society Press, July 2001.
13. D. Lehmann and M. O. Rabin. On the advantages of free choice: a symmetric and fully distributed solution to the dining philosophers problem. In *Proc. POPL '81*, pages 133–138. ACM Press, 1981.
14. D. E. Muller and P. E. Schupp. Simulating alternating tree automata by nondeterministic automata: new results and new proofs of the theorems of Rabin, McNaughton and Safra. *Theor. Comput. Sci.*, 141(1-2):69–107, 1995.
15. A. Pnueli and R. Rosner. On the synthesis of a reactive module. In *Proc. POPL*, pages 179–190. ACM Press, 1989.
16. A. Pnueli and R. Rosner. On the synthesis of an asynchronous reactive module. In *Automata, Languages and Programming*, pages 652–671. Springer-Verlag, 1989.
17. L. J. Stockmeyer and A. K. Chandra. Provably difficult combinatorial games. *SIAM J. Comput.*, 8(2):151–174, 1979.
18. P. Wolper. *Synthesis of Communicating Processes from Temporal-Logic Specifications.* PhD thesis, Stanford University, 1982.

Branching-Time Property Preservation Between Real-Time Systems*

Jinfeng Huang[1], Marc Geilen[1], Jeroen Voeten[1,2], and Henk Corporaal[1]

[1] Eindhoven University of Technology, The Netherlands
[2] Embedded systems institute, The Netherlands
J.Huang@tue.nl

Abstract. In the past decades, many formal frameworks (e.g. timed automata and temporal logics) and techniques (e.g. model checking and theorem proving) have been proposed to model a real-time system and to analyze real-time properties of the model. However, due to the existence of ineliminable timing differences between the model and its realization, real-time properties verified in the model often cannot be preserved in its realization. In this paper, we propose a branching representation (timed state tree) to specify the timing behavior of a system, based on which we prove that real-time properties represented by Timed CTL^* ($TCTL^*$ in short) formulas can be preserved between two neighboring real-time systems. This paper extends the results in [1][2], such that a larger scope of real-time properties can be preserved between real-time systems.

1 Introduction

Real-time systems have been widely used in various control applications, such as robotic control and consumer electronics. The timing behaviors of these systems have to satisfy critical timing constraints (real-time properties) for correct functioning. To this end, a model of the system can be constructed and formal verification techniques (e.g. model-checking or theorem proving) can be used to check whether the desired real-time properties are satisfied by the model. However, in practice the timing behavior of a model is not always identical to that of its realization. It has been shown that a small timing perturbation in the timing behavior of the model can invalidate formal verification results. Therefore, real-time properties satisfied by the model may not hold in its realization.

To address this problem, the robustness of the model has been investigated in literature. In [3], a subclass of timed automata is examined, whose properties are robust w.r.t. infinitesimal timing errors. In [4], an algorithm is given to extend the behavior of a timed automaton to tolerate infinitesimal clock drifts. Consequently, properties of the extended behavior are robust w.r.t. the infinitesimal clock drifts. Based on a similar technique proposed in [4], [5] shows that for a given property, the upper bound of timing errors on guards of the timed

* This research is supported by PROGRESS project TES.7020, "Predictable co-design for distributed embedded mechatronic control systems".

S. Graf and W. Zhang (Eds.): ATVA 2006, LNCS 4218, pp. 260–275, 2006.

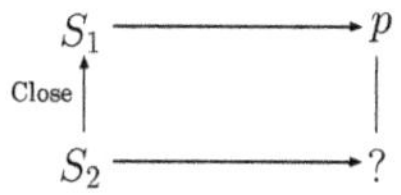

Fig. 1. The objective of property preservation

automaton can be calculated. Consequently, the timed automaton incorporating these timing errors is still robust w.r.t. the given property.

Different from the above mentioned work, the problem mentioned previously can also be addressed by investigating property relations between two timing behaviors (e.g. of a model and its realization). The core question of this work is illustrated in Figure 1. When real-time system S_1 is *close* to S_2, then the properties of S_2 can be predicted from those of S_1. For instance, in [1], we demonstrate that linear real-time properties (*MTL* formulas [6]) of two neighboring real-time systems can be predicted from one to the other based on their relative and absolute timing differences. In [7], authors showed that the same property relations also hold for *TCTL* formulas. Consequently, real-time properties of the realization can be predicted from those of the model. In this framework, a model and its realization with a small distance between them satisfy similar properties. Furthermore, the closer is the model and its realization, the more similar their properties are. This is different from [3],[4] and especially [5], which look into the conditions under which properties satisfied by the model hold in the realization.

In this paper, we extend previous work in [1] [7] to achieve more general property-preservation results. To this end, we first propose a branching representation (called timed state trees) to specify the timing behavior of a system (Section 2). Following that, we introduce *TCTL** as a generalisation of *TCTL* [8] to express real-time properties (Section 3). Subsequently, we prove that *TCTL** formulas can be preserved between these branching-timing behaviors (Section 4). Since *TCTL** is more expressive than *MTL*, a larger scope of real-time properties can be preserved between real-time systems.

2 Representation of System Behaviors

A commonly-used branching representation of a system is a computation tree $\langle s_0, S, \rightarrow \rangle$, where s_0 is the root of the tree, S is a countable set of states and $\rightarrow$ is a binary relation over states. Starting from state s_0, the computation tree is recursively formed by attaching each state s with a set of computation trees rooted by its successors. However, this discrete branching representation of the system is not always sufficient. For instance, in a continuous time domain, the state of the system *continuously* changes during the time progress. Furthermore, the system may have different choices for the evolution at each state of these continuous states. In [8], a *TCTL*-structure is proposed to specify the continuous behavior in a branching structure, in which each sequence (called a run) records the states at time instances in a continuous time domain along an execution, and the branching structure is defined by the fusion and suffix closure properties.

In our context, the same system behavior may have different timing observations. For example, suppose two persons measure the duration of the same traffic light using different clocks. If the clock of the first person is 1.2 faster than that of the second person, the time duration observed by the first person should be 1.2 longer than that observed by the second person. This simple example illustrates that the same untimed behavior observed in different time domains could result in different time behaviors. In this case, using the *TCTL*-structure to represent the branching behavior of a system in different time domains has two limitations. 1)We assume that the same untimed behavior can be observed in different time domains, which results in different timing behaviors. In the assumption, we consider that the untimed behavior specifies the *qualitative ordering relations* between system states, while the timing behavior defines the *quantitative ordering relations* between states. In the *TCTL*-structure, both qualitative and quantitative ordering relations between states are defined in the same formalism. Hence, the untimed behavior cannot be specified directly by the *TCTL*-structure.
2) According to the fusion closure property of the *TCTL*-structure, once a state s is observed during the system evolution, its possible succeeding timing sequences are always the same. The *TCTL*-structure is not sufficient for specifying a system observed in different time domains. For instance, suppose the behavior of system S is observed in two different time domains D_1 and D_2, where the time progress of D_2 is faster than that of D_1 by varying factors. If the timing behavior of S observed in D_1 is a *TCTL*-structure, then the timing behavior of S observed in D_2 may not be a *TCTL*-structure any more, because the succeeding possible timing behavior of a state can be varying according to the time progress of D_2.

In the following, we first propose a formalism (state trees) to express the untimed behavior of the system, which is independent from its time observations. Afterwards, the timing behavior of the system is specified by labelling times on the states of the state tree.

2.1 Untimed Behaviors

In many formal frameworks, an execution of the untimed behavior is represented by a sequence of *discrete* states. If continuous states can be observed along an execution of the system, the untimed behavior cannot be expressed by a finite or countable finite sequence of states. In the following, we introduce *state segment* to represent a sequence of continuous states. Correspondingly, an execution of the system can be represented by a finite or countable infinite sequence of state segments.

Proposition set. *Prop* is a set of atomic propositions. An observable state of a system can be associated with a subset of *Prop* which contains all propositions that hold in that state. Notice that two states with the same interpretation are not necessarily identical.

Index interval. I is a set of continuous positions defined over $\mathbb{R}^{\geq 0}$. I has the form $[0, t]$, where $t \in \mathbb{R}^{\geq 0}$. $|I|$ $(= t)$ represents the length of interval I.

State segment. Intuitively, state segment $\hat{s}$ is a sequence of continuous states. More formally, it can be viewed as a function mapping each position x in index interval I to a state. $|\hat{s}|$ represents the length of $\hat{s}$, which equals $|I|$. For any $0 \leq x \leq |\hat{s}|$, $\hat{s}(x)$ represents the state observed at position x of $\hat{s}$. Two state segments $\hat{s}$ and $\hat{s'}$ are equal iff $|\hat{s}| = |\hat{s'}|$ and for any $0 \leq x \leq |\hat{s}|$, $\hat{s}(x) = \hat{s'}(x)$. $\hat{s}$ is singular iff $|\hat{s}| = 0$.

Example 1 shows the application of state segments in a timed automaton.

Example 1. Consider a timed automaton [9] $A = \langle l_0, L, X, E \rangle$, where l_0 is the initial location, L is the set of locations, X is an ordered set of n *local clocks*[1] and E is a set of edges. The state of a timed automaton with clocks X is $(l, \mathbf{x})$ where l is a location and $\mathbf{x} \in \mathbb{R}^n$ is an assignment of clocks in X. $\mathbf{x} + t$ denotes that each clock assignment in $\mathbf{x}$ is increased by t. An edge e from location l to location l' is (l, g, r, l') where g is the guard and $r \subseteq \{1, ...n\}$ are clocks which are reset during the jump from l to l'. Guard $g \subseteq \mathbb{R}^n$ is defined inductively by $g := x \leq c \mid x \geq c \mid \neg g \mid g_1 \wedge g_2$, where $x \in X$ and c is a constant.

We consider that the semantics of a timed automaton A is given by a transition system $T = \langle s_0, Q_T, \rightarrow, \Sigma \rangle$ [4], where s_0 is the initial state $(l_0, \mathbf{0})$, Q_T is the state space of A, $\rightarrow \subseteq Q_T \times (\mathbb{R}^+ \cup \{d\}) \times Q_T$ is the set of discrete and continuous transitions. Continuous transition $((l, \mathbf{x}), t, (l, \mathbf{y})) \in \rightarrow$ represents that the timed automaton A resides in the same location and lets the time elapse, where $t > 0$ and $\mathbf{y} = \mathbf{x} + t$. Discrete transition $((l, \mathbf{x}), d, (l', \mathbf{y})) \in \rightarrow$ represents that A jumps from one location l to another l', when there exists an edge $(l, g, r, l') \in E$ such that $\mathbf{x} \in g$, $y_k = 0$ when $k \in r$ and $y_k = x_k$ for $k \notin r$.

Given a timed automaton A, each of its states $(l, \mathbf{x})$ can be denoted by a singular state segment $\hat{s} = \langle l, \mathbf{x}, 0 \rangle$, where 0 represents the length of $\hat{s}$. The continuous states observed during continuous transition $((l, \mathbf{x}), t, (l, \mathbf{y}))$ can be represented by a state segment $\hat{s} = \langle l, \mathbf{x}, t \rangle$, where t is the length of the state segment. For any position $0 \leq t' \leq t$, the mapping from t' to a state is given by $\hat{s}(t') = (l, \mathbf{x} + t')$.

We consider that the positions of a state segment $\hat{s}$ only specify qualitative ordering relations between continuous states of $\hat{s}$. Quantitative ordering relations between states derived from positions are not of our interest. In our context, the quantitative ordering relations between states are derived from the time tags of states, which are determined by the time progress of a time domain.

Two state segments $\hat{s}$ and $\hat{s'}$ are contiguous iff $\hat{s}(|\hat{s}|) = \hat{s'}(0)$. Two operations are defined over state segments.

(1) **Concatenation:** if two state segments $\hat{s}$ and $\hat{s'}$ are contiguous, the concatenation of state segments $\hat{s}$ and $\hat{s'}$ is a state segment $\hat{s} \cdot \hat{s'}$ given by:

$$\hat{s} \cdot \hat{s'}(x) = \begin{cases} \hat{s}(x); & \text{if } 0 \leq x \leq |\hat{s}|, \\ \hat{s'}(x - |\hat{s}|); & \text{if } |\hat{s}| < x \leq |\hat{s}| + |\hat{s'}|). \end{cases}$$

(2) **Extraction:** for state segment $\hat{s}$ and interval $[a, b] \subset [0, |\hat{s}|]$, an extraction $\hat{s}_{[a,b]}$ of state segment $\hat{s}$ is given by $\hat{s}_{[a,b]}(t) = \hat{s}(t + a)$, if $0 \leq t \leq b - a$.

[1] To distinguish from the clock concept used to measure the time progress of a time domain, we call clocks of a timed automaton as local clocks.

Given a set of state segments $\hat{S}$, we call $\hat{S}$ *closed under concatenation* iff for any two contiguous state segments $\hat{s_1}, \hat{s_2} \in \hat{S}$, $\hat{s_1} \cdot \hat{s_2} \in \hat{S}$. Similarly, we call $\hat{S}$ *closed under extraction* iff for any state segment $\hat{s} \in \hat{S}$ and $[a,b] \subseteq [0,|\hat{s}|]$, state segment $\hat{s}_{[a,b]} \in \hat{S}$. We can verify that the set of state segments of a timed automaton given in Example 1 is closed under both concatenation and extraction. In the sequel, we assume that state segment set $\hat{S}$ is closed under both concatenation and extraction, unless explicitly stated otherwise.

State path. $\overline{\rho}$ of state segment set $\hat{S}$ is a finite or countable infinite sequence of state segments in $\hat{S}$, $\hat{s_0}, \hat{s_1}, \hat{s_2}, ...$, which satisfies the stutter-free constraint: for any two adjacent state segments $\hat{s_i}$ and $\hat{s_{i+1}}$, $\hat{s_i}(|\hat{s_i}|) \neq \hat{s_{i+1}}(0)$. According to this, a continuous state segment should not be split into two or more segments in a state path. $N(\overline{\rho})$ represents the length (the number of the state segments) of $\overline{\rho}$. $\overline{\rho}(i)$ represents the i-th state segment of $\overline{\rho}$, and $\overline{\rho}(i,x)$ represents the state at position x of the i-th state segment of $\overline{\rho}(i)$. Given a state path $\overline{\rho}$, the set of its positions are defined by $\Phi^{\overline{\rho}} = \{(i,x) \mid i < N(\overline{\rho}) \wedge 0 \leq x \leq |\overline{\rho}(i)|\}$. $\overline{\rho}$, therefore, can be viewed as a function which maps each position (i,x) in $\Phi^{\overline{\rho}}$ to a state. A total order is defined over $\Phi^{\overline{\rho}}$. $(i,x) < (j,y)$ iff $i < j$ *or* $i = j$ and $x < y$.

Example 2. A state path $\overline{\rho}$ of a timed automaton T is a sequence of state segments $\hat{s}_0\hat{s}_1...$, which satisfies the stutter-free property. Namely, for any $i \leq |\overline{\rho}|$, there exists a discrete transition $(\hat{s}_i(|\hat{s}_i|), d, \hat{s}_{i+1}(0)) \in \rightarrow$. Furthermore, the state path $\overline{\rho}$ of T is diverging, i.e. for any $t > 0$, there exists $i \leq N(\overline{\rho})$ such that $\sum_{k=0}^{i} |\overline{\rho}(k)| > t$. Actually, the state path of a timed automaton is similar to the *s-path* concept defined in [8] by removing its time tags on states.

In the following, we define operations *suffix*, *prefix* and *concatenation* for state paths. For any $(i,x) \in \Phi^{\overline{\rho}}$, the (i,x)-*suffix* of $\overline{\rho}$ (denoted as $\overline{\rho}^{(i,x)}$) represents a path:

$$\overline{\rho}^{(i,x)}(j,y) = \begin{cases} \overline{\rho}(i, x+y), & \text{if } j = 0 \text{ and } (i, x+y) \in \Phi^{\overline{\rho}} \\ \overline{\rho}(i+j, y) & \text{if } j > 0 \text{ and } (i+j, y) \in \Phi^{\overline{\rho}}. \end{cases}$$

The (i,x)-*prefix* of $\overline{\rho}$ (denoted as $\overline{\rho}_{(i,x)}$) is defined by a function which maps position (j,y) in $\{(j,y) \mid (j,y) \leq (i,x), (j,y) \in \Phi^{\overline{\rho}}\}$ to state $\overline{\rho}(j,y)$.

Given a (i,x)-prefix of path $\overline{\rho}$ and a path $\overline{\rho}'$, the concatenation of $\overline{\rho}_{(i,x)}$ with $\overline{\rho}'$ (denoted as $\overline{\rho}_{(i,x)} \cdot \overline{\rho}'$) is a path $\overline{\rho}^*$. To ensure $\overline{\rho}^*$ to be stutter-free, $\overline{\rho}^*$ is defined differently according to the relation between $\overline{\rho}(i,x)$ and $\overline{\rho}'(0,0)$.

$$\overline{\rho}(i,x) \neq \overline{\rho}'(0,0) : \begin{cases} \overline{\rho}^*(j,y) = \overline{\rho}(j,y); & \text{if } (j,y) \leq (i,x) \text{ and } (j,y) \in \Phi^{\overline{\rho}} \\ \overline{\rho}^*(i+j+1,y) = \overline{\rho}'(j,y); & \text{if } (j,y) \in \Phi^{\overline{\rho}'}. \end{cases}$$

$$\overline{\rho}(i,x) = \overline{\rho}'(0,0) : \begin{cases} \overline{\rho}^*(j,y) = \overline{\rho}(j,y); & \text{if } (j,y) \leq (i,x) \text{ and } (j,y) \in \Phi^{\overline{\rho}} \\ \overline{\rho}^*(i,x+y) = \overline{\rho}'(0,y); & \text{if } (0,y) \in \Phi^{\overline{\rho}'} \\ \overline{\rho}^*(i+j,y) = \overline{\rho}'(j,y); & \text{if } j > 0 \text{ and } (j,y) \in \Phi^{\overline{\rho}'}. \end{cases}$$

If Θ is a set of paths, then $\overline{\rho}_{(t,m)} \cdot \Theta$ is the set of paths $\{\overline{\rho}_{(t,m)} \cdot \overline{\rho}' \mid \overline{\rho}' \in \Theta\}$.

It is easy to see that if $\overline{\rho}$ is a state path of $\hat{S}$, so is its suffix $\overline{\rho}^{(i,x)}$. Similarly, if $\overline{\rho}$ and $\overline{\rho}'$ are state paths of $\hat{S}$, so is $\overline{\rho}_{(i,x)} \cdot \overline{\rho}'$. In the following, we define the branching structure of the untimed behavior based on state paths.

Definition 1. ***state tree***
A state tree M is a tuple $\langle s_0, S, \hat{S}, \mu, f\rangle$ where $s_0 \in S$ is the initial state, S is a set of states, $\hat{S}$ is a set of state segments defined over S, μ maps each state $s \in S$ to a set of atomic propositions and f maps each state $s \in S$ to a set of state paths of $\hat{S}$ starting with s. $f(s)$ satisfies the following constraints.
1) Fusion closure: for all $\overline{\rho} \in f(s)$, $\overline{\rho}_{(i,x)} \cdot f(\overline{\rho}(i,x)) \subseteq f(s)$.
2) Suffix closure: for all $\overline{\rho} \in f(s)$, $\overline{\rho}^{(i,x)} \in f(\overline{\rho}(i,x))$.

As we have mentioned previously, the state path of a timed automaton is similar to the *s-path* concept of a *TCTL*-structure by removing its time tags. Correspondingly, a state tree can roughly be considered as a *TCTL*-structure by removing its time tags.

2.2 Timing Behaviors

In the previous section, we have introduced a branching representation to specify the untimed behavior for a real-time system, where only qualitative order relations between states are specified. When the untimed behavior is observed in a time domain, quantitative timing relations between states can be specified based on their observation times. In the following, we define a time observation of a state tree.

Definition 2. *Given a state tree $M = \langle s_0, S, \hat{S}, \mu, f\rangle$, a time observation D of M maps each path prefix $\overline{\rho}$ of $f(s_0)$ to a non-negative real and $D(\overline{\rho}_{(0,0)}) = 0$. Furthermore, D is weakly monotonically increasing such that if $(i,x) \leq (j,y)$, $D(\overline{\rho}_{(i,x)}) \leq D(\overline{\rho}_{(j,y)})$. The pair (D, M) is called a* timed state tree.

The following example shows a timed state tree of a timed automaton.

Example 3. Consider a timed automaton $T = \langle l_0, L, X, E\rangle$, whose untimed behavior is given by a state tree $M = \langle s_0, S, \hat{S}, \mu, f\rangle$. s_0 is the initial state of T. S is the state space of T. $\hat{S}$ is the set of state segments of T, which is defined as in Example 1. f maps each state $s \in S$ to the set of state paths of $\hat{S}$, which start from s. It can be verified that f satisfies fusion and suffix closure.

Assume that M is observed in the model time domain, where the domain clock is always consistent with the progress of local clocks in the timed automaton. For instance, an increase of the local clock value by 5 at a location indicates that the model time also progresses 5 time units. During the location jump, each local clock either remains unchanged or is reset, which implies that the model time does not progress. Therefore, the time observation of M in the model time domain is defined as below. For any state path $\overline{\rho} \in f(s_0)$ and $(i,x) \in \Phi^{\overline{\rho}}$,

- $D_m(\overline{\rho}_{(0,0)}) = 0$;
- if $i > 0$ and $x = 0$, then $D_m(\overline{\rho}_{(i,0)}) = D_m(\overline{\rho}_{(i-1,0)}) + |\overline{\rho}(i-1)| = \sum_{k=0}^{i-1} |\overline{\rho}(i)|$;
- if $i > 0$ and $0 < x \leq |\overline{\rho}(i)|$, then $D_m(\overline{\rho}_{(i,x)}) = D_m(\overline{\rho}_{(i,0)}) + x$.

It is easy to see that D_m is a time observation of M. Furthermore, if we consider $D_m(\overline{\rho}_{(i,x)})$ to be the time tag labelled on the state $\overline{\rho}(i,x)$, this timed state tree can be considered as a *TCTL*-structure.

A state tree with different time observations results in different timed state trees. For example, assume that the realization of a system have the same qualitative relations between states as the model, e.g. the untimed behaviors of both is specified by the same state tree. However, the timing behavior of the model is observed in a continuous model time domain, while that of the realization is observed in a digital hardware time domain. Consequently, the same path prefix of the state tree is labelled with different values in the two time domains. To capture the difference between timed state trees, in the following, we introduce two proximity measures: *absolute time deviation* and *relative time drift*. The absolute time deviation refers to the absolute differences between the times of corresponding path prefix in two timed state trees. The relative time drift refers to the ratio between the corresponding time differences of path prefixes in two timed state trees.

Definition 3. ***Absolute time deviation***
Let $M = \langle s_0, S, \hat{S}, \mu, f\rangle$ be a state tree and let D and D' be two of its time observations. Further let $\epsilon \in \mathbb{R}^{\geq 0}$. (D', M) is ***absolute*** ***ϵ-close*** *to (D, M), iff for any path $\overline{\rho} \in \overline{f}(s_0)$ and $(i, x) \in \Phi^{\overline{\rho}}$, $|D'(\overline{\rho}_{(i,x)}) - D(\overline{\rho}_{(i,x)})| \leq \epsilon$.*

Definition 4. ***Relative time drift***
Let $M = \langle s_0, S, \hat{S}, \mu, f\rangle$ be a state tree and let D and D' be two of its time observations. Further let $\epsilon \in \mathbb{R}^{\geq 1}$. (D', M) is ***relative*** ***ϵ-close*** *to (D, M), iff for any path $\overline{\rho} \in f(s_0)$, $(i, x), (j, y) \in \Phi^{\overline{\rho}}$ such that $(i, x) < (j, y)$*

$$\frac{D'(\overline{\rho}_{(j,y)}) - D'(\overline{\rho}_{(i,x)})}{D(\overline{\rho}_{(j,y)}) - D(\overline{\rho}_{(i,x)})} \in [\frac{1}{\epsilon}, \epsilon].$$

In the case that both $D'(\overline{\rho}_{(i,x)}) - D'(\overline{\rho}_{(j,y)})$ and $D(\overline{\rho}_{(i,x)}) - D(\overline{\rho}_{(j,y)})$ are zero, then $\frac{D'(\overline{\rho}_{(i,x)}) - D'(\overline{\rho}_{(j,y)})}{D(\overline{\rho}_{(i,x)}) - D(\overline{\rho}_{(j,y)})}$ is not defined.

In practice, the observation times of a state tree in a time domain is determined by the time progress measured by a domain clock. Correspondingly, we can also use the deviation/drift between domain clocks to estimate the deviation/drift between timed state trees. For instance, given two clocks C_1 and C_2, if clock C_1 is at most 2 and at least -2 seconds faster than C_2, then we can estimate that the timed state tree (D_1, M) observed in the time domain of C_1 is absolute 2-close to (D_2, M) observed in the time domain of C_2. Similarly, if the change rate of C_1 is at most twice faster and at least 0.5 faster than that of C_2 at any moment, then we can estimate that timed state tree (D_1, M) is relative 2-close to (D_2, M).

3 Representations of Real-Time Properties

Temporal logics have been widely applied to the formalization of real-time properties of a system. Typical examples include *LTL*, *CTL* and *CTL**. When timeliness becomes a major concern, it is necessary to incorporate quantitative timing constraints into temporal logics to express desired quantitative real-time properties. A common way to do so is to extend qualitative temporal logics by attaching time bounds to their temporal operators. Typical examples include metric temporal logic MTL (a time-bounded extension of LTL) [6] and branching time-bounded temporal logic RTCTL (real-time CTL) [10]. In this paper, due to the rich expressiveness of *CTL**, we use a time-bounded extension *TCTL** of *CTL** to express the quantitative timing constraints. In the following, we first introduce the syntax of *TCTL** and give its semantics w.r.t. timed state trees defined in the previous section. Then, we investigate the weakening relations between *TCTL** formulas, and define two specific weakening functions over *TCTL** formulas. These weakening functions are used to establish property relations between neighboring timed state trees in the next section.

3.1 Quantitative Temporal Logic *TCTL**

In this paper, a time-bounded extension of *CTL** is used to express the quantitative timing constraints. The extension of its syntax is similar to that from *CTL* to *TCTL*, which has been proposed in [8]. Hence, his extension is denoted as *TCTL**. A *TCTL** formula is defined by the following state formulas α and path formulas β.

$$\alpha := p \mid \neg p \mid \alpha_1 \wedge \alpha_2 \mid \alpha_1 \vee \alpha_2 \mid E\beta \mid A\beta;$$

$$\beta := \alpha \mid \beta_1 \wedge \beta_2 \mid \beta_1 \vee \beta_2 \mid \beta_1 \mathsf{U}_I \beta_2 \mid \beta_1 \mathsf{V}_I \beta_2,$$

where **time bound** I is an interval of non-negative reals. We use $l(I)$ and $r(I)$ to represent the left end and right end of I respectively.

We choose a set of dual operators: $\wedge$ ("and") and $\vee$ ("or"), A ("all paths") and E ("for some path"), U ("until") and V ("unless") to define a "negation-free" *TCTL** logic, where negation only appears in front of atomic propositions. However, it is also possible to choose another set of operators $\neg$ ("not") $\wedge$, A and U to define the *TCTL** logic. The two definitions are equivalent. The choice of negation-free *TCTL** can facilitate the establishment of the property-preservation relation between different timed state trees later. In the following, we define the semantics of *TCTL** w.r.t. a timed state tree.

Definition 5. ***Semantics of*** *TCTL**
For any state tree $M = \langle s_0, S, \hat{S}, \mu, f \rangle$, *time observation* D, *state* $s \in S$, *path* $\overline{\rho} \in f(s_0)$, *state formula* α *of TCTL* and path formula* β *of TCTL*, the satisfaction relations* $(M, s) \models_D \alpha$ *and* $(M, (\overline{\rho}, (i, x))) \models_D \beta$ *are inductively defined as follows (M is omitted, whenever it is implicitly understood.).*

- $s \models_D p$ *iff* $p \in \mu(s)$;
- $s \models_D \neg p$ *iff* $p \notin \mu(s)$;
- $s \models_D \alpha_1 \wedge \alpha_2$ *iff* $s \models_D \alpha_1$ *and* $s \models_D \alpha_2$;
- $s \models_D \alpha_1 \vee \alpha_2$ *iff* $s \models_D \alpha_1$ *or* $s \models_D \alpha_2$;
- $s \models_D E\beta$ *iff for any* $\overline{\rho} \in f(s_0)$ *and* $(i, x) \in \Phi^{\overline{\rho}}$ *such that* $\overline{\rho}(i, x) = s$, *there exists* $\overline{\rho}' \in f(s)$ *such that* $(\overline{\rho}_{(i,x)} \cdot \overline{\rho}', (i, x)) \models_D \beta$.

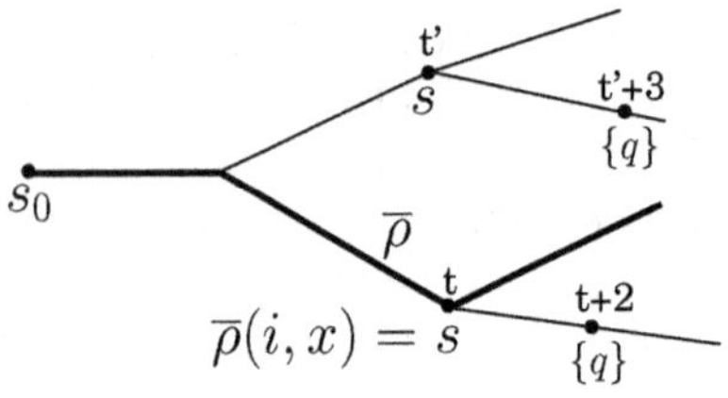

Fig. 2. A timed state tree

Table 1. Syntactic abbreviations

true	$T \equiv p \vee \neg p$
false	$F \equiv p \wedge \neg p$
eventually	$\Diamond_I \beta \equiv T \mathsf{U}_I \beta$
always	$\Box_I \beta \equiv F \mathsf{V}_I \beta$
weakly until	$\beta_1 \mathcal{U}_I \beta_2 \equiv (\beta_1 \mathsf{U}_I \beta_2) \vee \Box_I \beta_1$
implication	$\beta_1 \rightarrow \beta_2 \equiv \neg \beta_1 \vee \beta_2$

- $s \models_D A\beta$ *iff for any* $\overline{\rho} \in f(s_0)$ *and* $(i,x) \in \Phi^{\overline{\rho}}$ *such that* $\overline{\rho}(i,x) = s$ *and for any* $\overline{\rho}' \in f(s)$, $(\overline{\rho}_{(i,x)} \cdot \overline{\rho}', (i,x)) \models_D \beta$.
- $(\overline{\rho},(i,x)) \models_D \alpha$ *iff one of the following conditions is satisfied*
  - $(\alpha = p$ *or* $\alpha = \neg p)$ *and* $\overline{\rho}(i,x) \models_D \alpha$;
  - $\alpha = \alpha_1 \wedge \alpha_2$ *and* $((\overline{\rho},(i,x)) \models_D \alpha_1$ *and* $(\overline{\rho},(i,x)) \models_D \alpha_2)$;
  - $\alpha = \alpha_1 \vee \alpha_2$ *and* $((\overline{\rho},(i,x)) \models_D \alpha_1$ *or* $(\overline{\rho},(i,x)) \models_D \alpha_2)$;
  - $\alpha = E\beta$ *and there exists* $\overline{\rho}' \in f(\overline{\rho}(i,x))$ *such that* $(\overline{\rho}_{(i,x)} \cdot \overline{\rho}', (i,x)) \models_D \beta$;
  - $\alpha = A\beta$ *and for any* $\overline{\rho}' \in f(\overline{\rho}(i,x))$, $(\overline{\rho}_{(i,x)} \cdot \overline{\rho}', (i,x)) \models_D \beta$;
- $(\overline{\rho},(i,x)) \models_D \beta_1 \wedge \beta_2$ *iff* $(\overline{\rho},(i,x)) \models_D \beta_1$ *and* $(\overline{\rho},(i,x)) \models_D \beta_2$;
- $(\overline{\rho},(i,x)) \models_D \beta_1 \vee \beta_2$ *iff* $(\overline{\rho},(i,x)) \models_D \beta_1$ *or* $(\overline{\rho},(i,x)) \models_D \beta_2$;
- $(\overline{\rho},(i,x)) \models_D \beta_1 \mathsf{U}_I \beta_2$ *iff there exists* $(j,y) \geq (i,x)$ *such that* $D(\overline{\rho}_{(j,y)}) - D(\overline{\rho}_{(i,x)}) \in I$, $(\overline{\rho},(j,y)) \models_D \beta_2$ *and for any* $(i,x) \leq (k,z) < (j,y)$, $(\overline{\rho},(k,z)) \models_D \beta_1$;
- $(\overline{\rho},(i,x)) \models_D \beta_1 \mathsf{V}_I \beta_2$ *iff for any* $(j,y) \geq (i,x)$ *such that* $D(\overline{\rho}_{(j,y)}) - D(\overline{\rho}_{(i,x)}) \in I$, *either* $(\overline{\rho},(j,y)) \models_D \beta_2$ *or there exists* $(i,x) \leq (k,z) < (j,y)$ *such that* $(\overline{\rho},(k,z)) \models_D \beta_1$.

In the case that I is $[0,\infty)$, we omit the time bound I of temporal operators. Several other useful abbreviations are defined in Table 1.

Once a state s is observed during the system evolution, its possible succeeding state paths are always the same (the fusion closure of the state tree). However, the quantitative timing relations between states in the succeeding state paths can vary for different occurrences of s. Therefore, if a state formula α is satisfied by a state s, we require that α is satisfied by all possible occurrences of s in the timed state tree. On the other hand, if a state formula α is satisfied by a path $\overline{\rho}$ at its position (i,x) $(\overline{\rho}(i,x) = s)$, we only require that the particular occurrence of s in the particular $\overline{\rho}$ satisfies α. For instance, property $E\Diamond_{[0,3]}q$ is satisfied by state s in the timed state tree in Figure 2, but $E\Diamond_{[0,2]}q$ is not. However, $E\Diamond_{[0,2]}q$ is satisfied by path $\overline{\rho}$ at its position (i,x) where $\overline{\rho}(i,x) = s$.

3.2 Weakening Formulas

In this subsection, we first introduce the weakening relation between $TCTL^*$ formulas, based on which two specific functions, the absolute-weakening function and the relative-stretching function, are defined over *TCTL** formulas. These two functions are used to establish property relations between two neighboring real-time systems.

Weakening Relation. Formula φ is weaker than φ', if the satisfaction of φ' by a timed state tree always implies the satisfaction of φ. For example, formula $p \vee q$ is weaker than formula p. The weakening relation between negation-free *TCTL** formulas can be derived from the weakening relation between their sub-formulas and/or the inclusion relation between their time bounds. This is briefly summarised as the following lemmas, which proofs are straightforward.

Lemma 1. *For any TCTL* formula φ and sub-formula ϕ of φ, if ϕ' is a weaker formula than ϕ and φ' is the formula obtained by replacing one occurrence of ϕ with ϕ' in φ, then φ' is a weaker formula than φ.*

Lemma 2. *Let I and I' be two time bounds. Further let φ_1, φ_2 be two TCTL* formulas. If $I \subseteq I'$, then $\varphi_1 \mathsf{U}_{I'} \varphi_2$ ($\varphi_1 \mathsf{V}_I \varphi_2$) is a weaker formula than $\varphi_1 \mathsf{U}_I \varphi_2$ ($\varphi_1 \mathsf{V}_{I'} \varphi_2$).*

Weakening Functions. We have shown that the inclusion of time bounds implies the weakening of formulas. Now we define several operators for modifying the size of time bounds. More specifically, operators $\oplus$ and $\ominus$ change time bounds with absolute values, while operators $\otimes$ and $\oslash$ change time bounds with scale factors. Correspondingly, the absolute-weakening function and the relative-stretching function are defined by modifying the time bounds of *TCTL** formulas.

Operators $\oplus$ and $\ominus$. For any $\epsilon \in \mathbb{R}^{\geq 0}$ and time-bound I, $I \oplus \epsilon$ represents an interval, which has the same form as I and has left end-point $l(I) + \epsilon$ and right end-point $r(I) - \epsilon$. $I \ominus \epsilon$ is an interval, which has the same form as I and has left end-point $l(I)+\epsilon$ and right end-point $r(I)-\epsilon$. For instance, $[2, 4] \oplus 0.5 = [1.5, 4.5]$, $(3, 9) \oplus 1 = (2, 10)$ and $[1.5, 3) \ominus 1 = [2.5, 2] = \emptyset$.

Operators $\otimes$ and $\oslash$. For any $\epsilon \subseteq \mathbb{R}^{\geq 1}$ and time-bound I, $I \otimes \epsilon$ represents an interval, which has the same form as I and has left end-point $l(I) \cdot \frac{1}{\epsilon}$ and right end-point $r(I) \cdot \epsilon$. $I \oslash \epsilon$ represents an interval, which has the same form as I and has left end-point $l(I) \cdot \epsilon$ and right end-point $r(I) \cdot \frac{1}{\epsilon}$. For instance, $[2, 4] \otimes 2 = [1, 8]$, $(3, \infty) \otimes 1.5 = (2, \infty)$ and $[2, 3) \oslash 2 = [4, 1.5) = \emptyset$.

The following lemmas reveal the relations between I, $I \ominus \epsilon \oplus \epsilon$ and $I \oslash \epsilon \otimes \epsilon$, which are useful for the proofs of property preservation in the next section.

Lemma 3. *Let I be a non-empty time bound. For any $\epsilon \in \mathbb{R}^{\geq 0}$, if $I \ominus \epsilon \neq \emptyset$ then $I \ominus \epsilon \oplus \epsilon = I \oplus \epsilon \ominus \epsilon = I$.*

Lemma 4. *Let I be a non-empty time bound. For any $\epsilon \in \mathbb{R}^{\geq 1}$, if $I \oslash \epsilon \neq \emptyset$ then $I \oslash \epsilon \otimes \epsilon = I \otimes \epsilon \oslash \epsilon = I$.*

Absolute ϵ-weakening function. The absolute ϵ-weakening function over *TCTL** formulas is defined based on operators $\oplus$ and $\ominus$. In the next section, the absolute ϵ-weakening function is used to establish the property relations between two timed state trees, where their proximity is measured based on the absolute time deviation.

Definition 6. *Weakening function* $R^{\epsilon}_{\mathbf{a}} : TCTL^* \to TCTL^*$ *is inductively defined by:*

$$
\begin{array}{ll}
R^{\epsilon}_{\mathbf{a}}(p) = p; & R^{\epsilon}_{\mathbf{a}}(\neg p) = \neg p; \\
R^{\epsilon}_{\mathbf{a}}(\alpha_1 \vee \alpha_2) = R^{\epsilon}_{\mathbf{a}}(\alpha_1) \vee R^{\epsilon}_{\mathbf{a}}(\alpha_2); & R^{\epsilon}_{\mathbf{a}}(\alpha_1 \wedge \alpha_2) = R^{\epsilon}_{\mathbf{a}}(\alpha_1) \wedge R^{\epsilon}_{\mathbf{a}}(\alpha_2); \\
R^{\epsilon}_{\mathbf{a}}(A\alpha) = AR^{\epsilon}_{\mathbf{a}}(\alpha); & R^{\epsilon}_{\mathbf{a}}(E\alpha) = ER^{\epsilon}_{\mathbf{a}}(\alpha); \\
R^{\epsilon}_{\mathbf{a}}(\beta_1 \vee \beta_2) = R^{\epsilon}_{\mathbf{a}}(\beta_1) \vee R^{\epsilon}_{\mathbf{a}}(\beta_2); & R^{\epsilon}_{\mathbf{a}}(\beta_1 \wedge \beta_2) = R^{\epsilon}_{\mathbf{a}}(\beta_1) \wedge R^{\epsilon}_{\mathbf{a}}(\beta_2); \\
R^{\epsilon}_{\mathbf{a}}(\beta_1 \mathsf{U}_I \beta_2) = R^{\epsilon}_{\mathbf{a}}(\beta_1) \mathsf{U}_{I \oplus \epsilon \cap [0,\infty]} R^{\epsilon}_{\mathbf{a}}(\beta_2); & R^{\epsilon}_{\mathbf{a}}(\beta_1 \mathsf{V}_I \beta_2) = R^{\epsilon}_{\mathbf{a}}(\beta_1) \mathsf{V}_{I \ominus \epsilon} R^{\epsilon}_{\mathbf{a}}(\beta_2).
\end{array}
$$

In the absolute ϵ-weakening function $R^{\epsilon}_{\mathbf{a}}(\varphi)$, ϵ is a parameter giving the extent to which the time bounds of φ are elongated (or shrunk). Since $I \oplus \epsilon$ may elongate I to negative reals, we avoid this by using the intersection of $I \oplus \epsilon$ and $[0, \infty]$ in the definition of $R^{\epsilon}_{\mathbf{a}}$. $R^{\epsilon}_{\mathbf{a}}(\varphi)$ relaxes the quantitative timing constraints in formula φ and is called the *absolute ϵ-weakened* formula of φ. For instance, $R^{0.01}_{\mathbf{a}}(p \vee q) = p \vee q$, and $R^{0.5}_{\mathbf{a}}(p\mathsf{U}_{[1.2,5)}q) = p\mathsf{U}_{[1.2,5)\oplus 0.5}q = p\mathsf{U}_{[0.7,5.5)}q$. The following proposition shows that formula $R^{\epsilon}_{\mathbf{a}}(\varphi)$ is indeed weaker than formula φ. Since for any time bound I, it is easy to see that $I \subseteq (I \oplus \epsilon) \cap [0, \infty)$ and $I \ominus \epsilon \subseteq I$. Proposition 1 can be proved by induction on the structure of formula $R^{\epsilon}_{\mathbf{a}}(\varphi)$ and using Lemma 1 and 2.

Proposition 1. *For any* $\epsilon_1, \epsilon_2 \in \mathbb{R}^{\geq 0}$ *such that* $\epsilon_1 \leq \epsilon_2$ *and* $\varphi \in TCTL^*$, $R^{\epsilon_2}_{\mathbf{a}}(\varphi)$ *is weaker than* $R^{\epsilon_1}_{\mathbf{a}}(\varphi)$.

It is easy to see from Proposition 1 that for any $\epsilon \geq 0$, $R^{\epsilon}_{\mathbf{a}}(\varphi)$ is always weaker than φ.

Relative ϵ-stretching function. For the relative timing difference case, we use the relative ϵ-stretching function $R^{\epsilon}_{\mathbf{r}}$ which is defined over $TCTL^*$ formulas based on operators $\otimes$ and $\oslash$. Function $R^{\epsilon}_{\mathbf{r}}$ is defined similar to function $R^{\epsilon}_{\mathbf{a}}$. The only differences between the definitions are *unless* and *until* formulas.

$$R^{\epsilon}_{\mathbf{r}}(\beta_1 \mathsf{U}_I \beta_2) = R^{\epsilon}_{\mathbf{r}}(\beta_1) \mathsf{U}_{I \otimes \epsilon} R^{\epsilon}_{\mathbf{r}}(\beta_2);\ R^{\epsilon}_{\mathbf{r}}(\beta_1 \mathsf{V}_I \beta_2) = R^{\epsilon}_{\mathbf{r}}(\beta_1) \mathsf{V}_{I \oslash \epsilon} R^{\epsilon}_{\mathbf{r}}(\beta_2).$$

Similar to the absolute case, we also have the weakening relation for relative ϵ-stretching functions.

Proposition 2. *For any* $\epsilon_1, \epsilon_2 \in \mathbb{R}^{\geq 1}$ *such that* $\epsilon_1 \leq \epsilon_2$ *and* $\varphi \in TCTL^*$, $R^{\epsilon_2}_{\mathbf{r}}(\varphi)$ *is weaker than* $R^{\epsilon_1}_{\mathbf{r}}(\varphi)$.

4 Property Preservation Between Timed State Trees

In this section, we complete the diagram illustrated in Figure 1. Intuitively speaking, when a timed tree (D_2, M) is close to (D_1, M), we expect that properties of (D_2, M) are close to those of (D_1, M) as well. This intuition can be conformed in two ways as shown in Figure 3. First we consider the case when two timed state trees are absolute close.

(a) Absolute case (b) Relative case

Fig. 3. Property-preservation results

Lemma 5. *Let $M = \langle s_0, S, \hat{S}, \mu, f\rangle$ be a state tree, and let D_1 and D_2 be two of its time observations such that (D_2, M) is absolute ϵ-close to (D_1, M). For any path $\overline{\rho} \in f(s_0)$, $(i, x), (j, y) \in \Phi^{\overline{\rho}}$ such that $(i, x) < (j, y)$, and interval $I \subseteq \mathbb{R}^{\geq 0}$, if $D_1(\overline{\rho}_{(j,y)}) - D_1(\overline{\rho}_{(i,x)}) \in I$ then $D_2(\overline{\rho}_{(j,y)}) - D_2(\overline{\rho}_{(i,x)}) \in I \oplus 2\epsilon \cap [0, \infty]$.*

Proof. Note that $D_2(\overline{\rho}_{(j,y)}) - D_2(\overline{\rho}_{(i,x)}) = (D_2(\overline{\rho}_{(j,y)}) - D_1(\overline{\rho}_{(j,y)})) - (D_2(\overline{\rho}_{(i,x)}) - D_1(\overline{\rho}_{(i,x)})) + (D_1(\overline{\rho}_{(j,y)}) - D_1(\overline{\rho}_{(i,x)}))$, where $-\epsilon \leq D_2(\overline{\rho}_{(j,y)}) - D_1(\overline{\rho}_{(j,y)}) \leq \epsilon$, $-\epsilon \leq D_2(\overline{\rho}_{(i,x)}) - D_1(\overline{\rho}_{(i,x)}) \leq \epsilon$, and $(D_1(\overline{\rho}_{(j,y)}) - D_1(\overline{\rho}_{(i,x)})) \in I$. The rest of the proof is straightforward by the definition of operator $\oplus$ and the monotonic property of D_2.

Theorem 1. *Let $M = \langle s_0, S, \hat{S}, \mu, f\rangle$ be a state tree, and let D_1 and D_2 be two of its time observations such that (D_2, M) is absolute ϵ-close to (D_1, M). For any state $s \in S$, path $\overline{\rho} \in f(s_0)$, state formula α and path formula β of TCTL*, if $s \models_{D_1} \alpha$ then $s \models_{D_2} R_{\mathbf{a}}^{2\epsilon}(\alpha)$ and if $(\overline{\rho}, (i, x)) \models_{D_1} \beta$ then $(\overline{\rho}, (i, x)) \models_{D_2} R_{\mathbf{a}}^{2\epsilon}(\beta)$.*

Proof. We show that $s \models_{D_2} R_{\mathbf{a}}^{2\epsilon}(\alpha)$ and $(\overline{\rho}, (i, x)) \models_{D_2} R_{\mathbf{a}}^{2\epsilon}(\beta)$ by induction on the structure of formulas α and β. In the following, we only give the proof for cases that $\alpha = E\beta$, $\beta = \beta_1 \mathsf{U}_I \beta_2$, and $\beta = \beta_1 \mathsf{V}_I \beta_2$. The other cases are straightforward or can be proven in a similar way.

- **Case** $\alpha = E\beta$. By the interpretation of *TCTL** logic, for any $\overline{\rho} \in f(s_0)$ and $(i, x) \in \Phi^{\overline{\rho}}$ such that $\overline{\rho}(i, x) = s$, there exists $\overline{\rho}' \in f(\overline{\rho}(i, x))$ such that $(\overline{\rho}_{(i,x)} \cdot \overline{\rho}', (i, x)) \models_{D_1} \beta$. By induction, we know that $(\overline{\rho}_{(i,x)} \cdot \overline{\rho}', (i, x)) \models_{D_2} R_{\mathbf{a}}^{2\epsilon}(\beta)$. Therefore, $s \models_{D_2} ER_{\mathbf{a}}^{2\epsilon}(\beta) = R_{\mathbf{a}}^{2\epsilon}(E\beta)$.
- **Case** $\beta = \beta_1 \mathsf{U}_I \beta_2$. There exists $(j, y) \geq (i, x)$ such that $D_1(\overline{\rho}_{(j,y)}) - D_1(\overline{\rho}_{(i,x)}) \in I$, $(\overline{\rho}, (j, y)) \models_{D_1} \beta_2$ and for any $(i, x) \leq (k, z) < (j, y)$, $(\overline{\rho}, (k, z)) \models_{D_1} \beta_1$. By Lemma 5, $D_2(\overline{\rho}_{(j,y)}) - D_2(\overline{\rho}_{(i,x)}) \in I \oplus 2\epsilon$. By induction, $(\overline{\rho}, (j, y)) \models_{D_2} R_{\mathbf{a}}^{2\epsilon}(\beta_2)$ and for any $(i, x) \leq (k, z) < (j, y)$, $(\overline{\rho}, (k, z)) \models_{D_2} R_{\mathbf{a}}^{2\epsilon}(\beta_1)$. Thus, $(\overline{\rho}, (i, x)) \models_{D_2} R_{\mathbf{a}}^{2\epsilon}(\beta_1 \mathsf{U}_I \beta_2)$.
- **Case** $\beta = \beta_1 \mathsf{V}_I \beta_2$. For any (j, y) such that $D_2(\overline{\rho}_{(j,y)}) - D_2(\overline{\rho}_{(i,x)}) \in I \ominus 2\epsilon$, by Lemma 3 and Lemma 5, $D_1(\overline{\rho}_{(j,y)}) - D_1(\overline{\rho}_{(i,x)}) \in I$. Then, either $(\overline{\rho}, (j, y)) \models_{D_1} \beta_2$ or there exists $(i, x) \leq (k, z) < (j, y)$ such that $(\overline{\rho}, (k, z)) \models_{D_1} \beta_1$. By induction, either $(\overline{\rho}, (j, y)) \models_{D_2} R_{\mathbf{a}}^{2\epsilon}(\beta_2)$ or there exists $(i, x) \leq (k, z) < (j, y)$ such that $(\overline{\rho}, (k, z)) \models_{D_2} R_{\mathbf{a}}^{2\epsilon}(\beta_1)$. Therefore, $(\overline{\rho}, (i, x)) \models_{D_2} R_{\mathbf{a}}^{2\epsilon}(\beta_1 \mathsf{V}_I \beta_2)$.

Similarly, we can prove the property relation between timed trees based on their relative time drift. This is given by the following lemma and theorem.

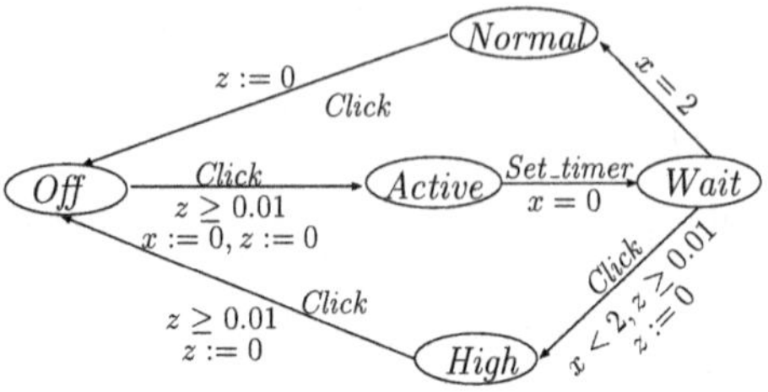

Fig. 4. The behavior of the intelligent light controller

Lemma 6. *Let* $M = \langle s_0, S, \hat{S}, \mu, f \rangle$ *be a state tree, and let* D_1 *and* D_2 *be two of its time observations such that* (D_2, M) *is relative* ϵ*-close to* (D_1, M)*. For any path* $\overline{\rho} \in f(s_0)$*,* $(i, x), (j, y) \in \Phi^{\overline{\rho}}$ *such that* $(i, x) < (j, y)$*, and non-negative interval* $I \subseteq \mathbb{R}^{\geq 0}$*, if* $D_1(\overline{\rho}_{(j,y)}) - D_1(\overline{\rho}_{(i,x)}) \in I$ *then* $D_2(\overline{\rho}_{(j,y)}) - D_2(\overline{\rho}_{(i,x)}) \in I \otimes \epsilon$*.*

Theorem 2. *Let* $M = \langle s_0, S, \hat{S}, \mu, f \rangle$ *be a state tree, and let* D_1 *and* D_2 *be two of its time observations such that* (D_2, M) *is relative* ϵ*-close to* (D_1, M)*. For any state* $s \in S$*, path* $\overline{\rho} \in f(s_0)$*, state formula* α *and path formula* β *of TCTL*, if* $s \models_{D_1} \alpha$ *then* $s \models_{D_2} R^{\epsilon}_{\mathbf{r}}(\alpha)$ *and if* $(\overline{\rho}, (i, x)) \models_{D_1} \beta$ *then* $(\overline{\rho}, (i, x)) \models_{D_2} R^{\epsilon}_{\mathbf{r}}(\beta)$*.*

5 An Example

In this section, we apply the property-preservation results proven in the previous sections to the design of a real-time system. We consider the design process starting from the model of a real-time system, proceeding with the transformation of the model into a realization on a digital target platform and ending with a realization observed in a continuous environment time domain.

Example 4. Consider an intelligent light controller, which can adjust light intensity according to different input action sequences. The timing behavior of the system is modeled by a timed automaton T_c visualised in Figure 4. We assume that there is at least 0.01 seconds delay between two consecutive clicks. If a click action occurs at the initial location (*Off*), the controller goes into location (*Active*) where a timer with duration 2 seconds is activated. Then the controller switches immediately to another location (*Wait*) to wait for the time-out or another click action. If a second click occurs within 2 seconds, the light intensity is set to high. If the timer expires, the light intensity is set to normal. When the light is on (with either normal or high intensity), another click turns the light off.

5.1 The Model in the Continuous Model Time Domain

Here we define an atomic proposition set AP with four atomic propositions.
1) *Active*: The controller detects the first click when the light is off.
2) *Wait*: The controller is waiting for the next action.

3) *Normal*: The light intensity is normal.
4) *High*: The light intensity is high.

The location set L of T_c is defined by $\{Off, Active, Wait, Normal, High\}$. Each location is associated with a set of atomic propositions. *Off* is associated with $\emptyset$ and the other locations are associated with the corresponding atomic propositions e.g. *Active* with $\{Active\}$. In this example, we use two clocks x and z to specify timing constraints of the controller, where x is used to specify the constraint of the timer and z specifies the timing constraint between two consecutive clicks. The initial location of the system is *Off* and the initial state of the system is $(Off, (0,0))$, where clocks x and z are initialised to 0. The edge set E is illustrated in Figure 4. For instance, the edge from location *Off* to *Active* is $(Off, z \geq 0.01, \{1,2\}, Active)$.

The state segments of T_c are defined in the same way as in Example 1. Several state segments of timed automaton T_c are $\langle Wait, (0,0), 1.5\rangle$, $\langle High, (1.2, 1.2), 3\rangle$ and $\langle Active, (0,0), 0\rangle$. A state path of the intelligent light controller can be

$$\overline{\rho} = \langle Off, (0,0), 1\rangle, \langle Active, (0,0), 0\rangle, \langle Wait, (0,0), 1\rangle, \langle High, (1,0), 2\rangle....$$

The state tree M_c of T_c can be defined as in Example 3. Furthermore, the time observation D_m of M_c in the model time domain is also the same as that in Example 3. For instance, we have that $D_m(\overline{\rho}_{(0,0.5)}) = 0.5$ and $D_m(\overline{\rho}_{(3,1.5)}) = 1 + 0 + 1 + 1.5 = 3.5$.

A real-time property of the model

Consider a real-time property of the controller stating that *it is always possible to switch the light to the high intensity within 0.1 seconds.* This property can be expressed by *TCTL** formula $P = A\Box(E\Diamond_{[0,0.1]}High)$. In the model of the intelligent light controller, we can see a stronger property $P_m = A\Box(E\Diamond_{[0,0.02]}High)$ is satisfied.

5.2 The Realization in the Digital Hardware Time Domain

Typically, a real-time system is deployed on a certain platform, where the time is measured by a digital hardware clock. We cannot ensure that the timing relations specified in the model completely hold in the realization. For instance, two simultaneous actions in the model are observed with a small delay between them in the digital hardware time domain. Furthermore, since digital hardware clocks measure time progress in a discrete way, it is obvious that the time labelling of each state path in a continuous time domain (the model time domain) is not always consistent with that in the digital hardware time domain. Consequently, the real-time properties verified in the model may not hold in the realization.

However, if the timing behavior of the controller in the digital hardware time domain is absolute-close to that in the model time domain, the real-time properties of the realization can still be predicted. In the example of intelligent light controller, we introduce an additional clock y to timed automaton T_c. The value of clock y is initialised to 0 and keeps on increasing during the execution of T_c. It is easy to see that for any state path prefix of T_c, the value of clock y in the last state of the prefix equals the observation time of the prefix in the model time domain. During the execution of timed automaton T_c in the digital hardware time domain, T_c evolves based on the same execution semantics as in the model. The only difference is that the values of clock y are synchronised with/mapped to the values of the digital clock such that their deviations are always less than 0.01 seconds. In this way, the observation time of each state path prefix in the state tree in the digital time domain deviates no more than 0.01 seconds from that in the model time domain. That is, the timed state tree (D_d, M) in the digital hardware time domain is absolute 0.01-close to (D_m, M). Therefore, we can predict the controller satisfies an absolute 0.02-weakened property of P_m: $P_d = A\Box(E\Diamond_{[0,0.04]} High)$[2].

5.3 The Realization in the Continuous Time Domain

The realization on the hardware platform has to react to the stimuli (clicks) from the environment. In general the behavior of the realization has to be reasoned about in the time domain of the environment instead of the digital hardware clock. Assume that the environment time is measured by a continuous clock. This clock may have infinitely large absolute deviation from the digital hardware clock in a long term. However, if we assume that the average relative change rate between two clocks within any 0.01 second interval is less than 1%, then we can construct an auxiliary continuous time domain, whose time absolute time deviation from the digital hardware time domain is always within 0.001 seconds. The relative time drift from environment time domain to the auxiliary time domain is within $[\frac{1}{1.01}, 1.01]$. In this case, we can predict that the controller satisfies property $P_a = R_{\mathbf{a}}^{0.01}(P_d) = A\Box(E\Diamond_{[0,0.05]} High)$ in the auxiliary time domain, and it satisfies property $P_e = R_{\mathbf{r}}^{1.01}(P_a) = A\Box(E\Diamond_{[0,0.0505]} High)$ in the environment time domain. It is easy to see that P_e is stronger than the required property P.

6 Conclusion

During real-time system design, the timing behavior of the model is not identical to that of its realization. Consequently, properties of the model cannot be always satisfied by its realization. To address this problem, in this paper, we have first proposed a formalism (timed state trees) to specify the timing behavior of real-time systems in a branching structure. On one hand, the proposed formalism is "compatible" to the existing formal frameworks such as timed automata and timed transition systems. On the other hand, it is more flexible to capture

[2] The 0.02-weakened property of P_m should be $A\Box_{[0.02,\infty]}(E\Diamond_{[0,0.04]} High)$. However, when the time interval of operator U (or $\Box$) starts from 0, the left end of the time interval is unchanged in the preserved properties. Lemma 7.9 and Theorem 7.11 in [2] state a similar result for the preservation of *MTL* formulas between real-time systems.

the timing behaviors observed in different time domains. Based on the timed state trees, we have proven the theoretical results to build up property relations between two neighboring real-time systems. Together with existing formal verification techniques, these property-preservation results can be applied to real-time system design. By estimating the absolute and relative differences between the model and its realization, we can predict the properties of the realization from those of the model. A design example has been given to illustrate our method.

For brevity, we use one parameter ϵ to capture the proximity between real-time systems in this paper. However, we can also use two parameters to capture the upper and lower bounds of absolute time deviation (or relative time drift) respectively, which results in tighter property-preservation results. Interested readers are referred to [2], where we proved property-preservation for MTL logics using two parameters to capture proximities between real-time systems.

References

1. Huang, J., Voeten, J., Geilen, M.: Real-time property preservation in approximations of timed systems. In: Proceedings of 1st ACM & IEEE International Conference on Formal Methods and Models for Codesign, IEEE Computer Society Press (2003) 163–171
2. Huang, J.: Predictability in Real-time System Design. PhD thesis, Eindhoven University of Technology, The Netherlands (Aug. 2005)
3. Gupta, V., Henzinger, T., Jagadeesan, R.: Robust timed automata. In Maler, O., ed.: Hybrid and Real-Time Systems, Proceedings of International Workshop HART'97, Grenoble, France, Springer Verlag, LNCS 1201 (1997) 331–345
4. Puri, A.: Dynamical properties of timed automata. Discrete Event Dynamic Systems **10**(1-2) (2000) 87–113
5. Wulf, M.D., Doyen, L., Raskin, J.F.: Almost asap semantics: From timed models to timed implementations. Formal Aspects of Computing **17**(3) (2005) 319–341
6. Koymans, R.: Specifying real-time properties with metric temporal logic. Real-Time Systems **2**(4) (1990)
7. Henzinger, T.A., Majumdar, R., Prabhu, V.: Quantifying similarities between timed systems. In: Proceedings of the Third International Conference on Formal Modeling and Analysis of Timed Systems (FORMATS), Lecture Notes in Computer Science 3829, Springer, 2005. (2005) 226–241
8. Alur, R., Courcoubetis, C., Dill, D.: Model-checking in dense real-time. Information and Computation **104**(1) (1993) 2–34
9. Alur, R., Dill, D.L.: A theory of timed automata. Theoretical Computer Science **126**(2) (1994) 183–235
10. Emerson, E., Mok, A., Sistla, A., Srinivasan, J.: Quantitative temporal reasoning. In: Proceedings of the 2nd International Workshop on Computer Aided Verification, Springer-Verlag (1991) 136–145

Automatic Verification of Hybrid Systems with Large Discrete State Space*

Werner Damm[1,2], Stefan Disch[3], Hardi Hungar[2], Jun Pang[1], Florian Pigorsch[3], Christoph Scholl[3], Uwe Waldmann[4], and Boris Wirtz[1]

[1] Carl von Ossietzky Universität Oldenburg
Ammerländer Heerstraße 114-118, 26111 Oldenburg, Germany
[2] OFFIS e.V., Escherweg 2, 26121 Oldenburg, Germany
[3] Albert-Ludwigs-Universität Freiburg
Georges-Köhler-Allee 51, 79110 Freiburg, Germany
[4] Max-Planck-Institut für Informatik
Stuhlsatzenhausweg 85, 66123 Saarbrücken, Germany

Abstract. We address the problem of model checking hybrid systems which exhibit nontrivial discrete behavior and thus cannot be treated by considering the discrete states one by one, as most currently available verification tools do. Our procedure relies on a deep integration of several techniques and tools. An extension of AND-Inverter-Graphs (AIGs) with first-order constraints serves as a compact representation format for sets of configurations which are composed of continuous regions and discrete states. Boolean reasoning on the AIGs is complemented by first-order reasoning in various forms and on various levels. These include implication checks for simple constraints, test vector generation for fast inequality checks of boolean combinations of constraints, and an exact subsumption check for representations of two configurations.

These techniques are integrated within a model checker for universal CTL. Technically, it deals with discrete-time hybrid systems with linear differentials. The paper presents the approach, its prototype implementation, and first experimental data.

1 Introduction

The analysis of hybrid systems faces the difficulty of having to address not only the continuous dynamics of mechanical, electrical and other physical phenomena, but also the intricacies of discrete switching. Both of these two constituents of hybrid systems alone often pose a major challenge for verification approaches, and their combination is of course by no means simpler. For instance, the behavior of a car or airplane is usually beyond the scope of mathematically precise assessment, even if attention is restricted to only one particular aspect like the functioning of a braking assistant. Even though the continuous behavior might

* This work was partly supported by the German Research Council (DFG) as part of the Transregional Collaborative Research Center "Automatic Verification and Analysis of Complex Systems" (SFB/TR 14 AVACS, `http://www.avacs.org/`).

S. Graf and W. Zhang (Eds.): ATVA 2006, LNCS 4218, pp. 276–291, 2006.

in such a case be rather simple – at least after it has been simplified by introducing worst-case assumptions to focus on the safety-critical aspects –, through the interaction with discrete-state control the result is in most cases unmanageable by present-day techniques.

In this work, we address the analysis of hybrid systems with a focus on the discrete part. Systems with non-trivial discrete state spaces arise naturally in application classes where the overall control of system dynamics rests with a finite-state supervisory control, and states represent knowledge about the global system status. Examples of such global information encoded in states are phases of a cooperation protocol in inter-vehicle communication (such as in platooning maneuvers or in collision-avoidance protocols), knowledge about global system states (e. g., on-ground, initial ascent, ascent, cruising, ... for an aircraft), and/or information about the degree of system degradation (e. g., due to occurrence of failures). States of the control determine the selection of appropriate continuous maneuvers, and conditions on the continuous state (reached thresholds, for instance) trigger changes in the control. But while there might be tens or hundreds of boolean state variables, often there are only very few different maneuvers and continuous trigger conditions, so that much of the discrete switching happens independently of the continuous evolution.

In our approach, we intend to profit from the independence of the supervisory control and the continuous sections, using adequate techniques for each of the two constituents in a hybrid procedure. We do so by representing discrete states *symbolically*, as in symbolic model checking [5], and combine this with a first-order logic representation of the continuous part. In that way, unnecessary distinctions between discrete states can be avoided and efficiency gained.

This idea, which has already been pursued in a different setting in [14,3], can be seen as combining symbolic model checking with Hoare's program logic [13]. The discrete part of the state is encoded in bit vectors of fixed length. Sets of discrete states are represented in an efficient format for boolean functions, in our case functionally reduced AND-Inverter graphs (FRAIGs) [15]. The state vectors are extended by additional components referring to linear (first-order) constraints. Model checking works essentially as in [5,17] on the discrete part, while in parallel for the continuous part a Hoare-like calculus is applied. An important detail is that the set of constraints is dynamic: computing the effect of a system step usually entails the creation of new constraints. So it is not just model checking a finite-state encoding of the hybrid verification problem.

To make an automatic proof procedure out of this, we add diverse reasoning procedures for the first-order constraints. Of central importance is the ability to perform a subsumption check on our hybrid state-set representation in order to detect whether a fixpoint has been reached during model checking. HySAT [9] is one of the tools we use for that purpose. However, a key point of our approach is the idea to avoid expensive applications of decision procedures as much as possible. Test vector generation for fast inequality checks of boolean combinations of constraints, implication checks for linear constraints, and advanced boolean reasoning are examples for methods which provide some lightweight and inexpensive reasoning and are used both in the context of subsumption checks and for keeping state set representations as compact as possible.

In its current form, our approach is applicable to checking universal temporal logic in discrete-time hybrid systems, where conditions and transitions contain linear terms over the continuous variables. These correspond to a time discretization of systems whose evolution is governed by linear differential equations, of which the linear hybrid automata from [11] form a subset.

We present our class of models formally in Section 2. Section 3 explains our procedure on a semantical and logical level. The implementation is described in Section 4, followed by a report on first experiments with our current prototype in Section 5. Sections 6 and 7 discuss related work and possible future extensions.

2 System Model

2.1 Time Discretization

As mathematical model we use discrete-time hybrid automata, which in each time step of fixed duration update a set of real-valued variables as determined by assignments occurring as transition labels. Since assignments and transition guards may use linear arithmetical expressions, this subsumes the capability to describe the evolvement of plant variables by difference equations. Steps of the automata are assumed to take a fixed time period (also called cycle-time), intuitively corresponding to the sampling period of the control unit, and determine the new mode and new outputs (corresponding to actuators) based on the sampled inputs (from sensors).

The decision to base our analysis on discrete-time models of hybrid systems is motivated from an application perspective. Industrial design flows for embedded control software typically entail a transition from continuous time models in early analysis addressing control-law design, to discrete-time models in modeling tools such as Scade^{TM}, ASCET^{TM}, or MATLAB/Simulink-StateFlow^{TM}, as a basis for subsequent autocode generation. We address the latter class of models, from which the production code can be generated. Note that the discrete complexity of our systems results mainly from the control logic, discretization of time only adds one more dimension to the complexity.

In this paper, we analyze closed-loop systems with only discrete inputs, e. g., corresponding to discrete set points.

2.2 Formal Model

Our analysis is based on discrete-time models of hybrid systems. Time is modeled implicitly, in that each step corresponds to a fixed unit delay δ, as motivated in the previous section.

We assume that a hybrid system operates over two disjoint finite sets of variables D and C. The elements of $D = \{d_1, \dots, d_n, d_{n+1}, \dots, d_p\}$ $(n \leq p)$ are discrete variables, which are interpreted over finite domains; $D_{in} = \{d_{n+1}, \dots, d_p\}$ $\subseteq D$ is a finite set of discrete inputs. The elements of $C = \{c_1, \dots, c_m\}$ are continuous variables, which are interpreted over the reals $\mathbb{R}$. Let $\mathbf{D}$ denote the set of all valuations of D over the respective domains, $\mathbf{C} = \mathbb{R}^m$ the set of all valuations of C. The state space of a hybrid system is presented by the set $\mathbf{D} \times \mathbf{C}$; a valuation $(\mathbf{d}, \mathbf{c}) \in \mathbf{D} \times \mathbf{C}$ is a state of the hybrid system.

A set of states of a hybrid system can be represented symbolically using a suitable (quantifier-free) first-order logic formula over D and C. We assume that the data structure for the discrete variables D is given by a signature $\mathcal{S}_D$ which introduces typed symbols for constants and functions, and by $\mathcal{I}_D$ which assigns a meaning to symbols. We denote by $\mathcal{T}_D(D)$ the set of terms over D, and by $\mathcal{B}(D)$ the set of boolean expressions over D. The first-order part on continuous variables is restricted to linear arithmetic of $\mathbb{R}$, which has the signature $\{\mathbb{Q}, +, -, \times, =, <, \leq\}$, where $\mathbb{Q}$ is the set of rational numbers appearing as constants, $\{+, -, \times\}$ is the set of function symbols, and $\{=, <, \leq\}$ is the set of predicate symbols. The interpretation $\mathcal{I}_C$ assigns meanings to these symbols as usual. We define

- $\mathcal{T}_C(C)$ as the set of linear terms over C,
- $\mathcal{L}(C)$ as the set of linear constraints, with the syntax $t \sim 0$, where $\sim \in \{=, <, \leq\}$ and $t \in \mathcal{T}_C(C)$, and
- $\mathcal{P}(D, C)$, the set of first-order predicates, as boolean combinations of expressions in $\mathcal{B}(D)$ and linear constraints.

We use $\phi(D, C)$, $g(D)$, $t(C)$, and $\ell(C)$, possibly with subscripts, to denote first-order predicates in $\mathcal{P}(D, C)$, terms in $\mathcal{T}_D(D)$, terms in $\mathcal{T}_C(C)$, and linear constraints in $\mathcal{L}(C)$, respectively; D and C may be omitted, if they are clear from the context. We use $\mathcal{I}_{D,C} \models \phi(\mathbf{d}, \mathbf{c})$ to denote that ϕ is true under the valuations $\mathbf{d}$ and $\mathbf{c}$. Thus ϕ represents the sets of states of a hybrid system such that $\{ (\mathbf{d}, \mathbf{c}) \mid \mathcal{I}_{D,C} \models \phi(\mathbf{d}, \mathbf{c}) \}$. Assignments to the variables D and C are given in the form of $(d_1, \ldots, d_n) := (g_1, \ldots, g_n)$ and $(c_1, \ldots, c_m) := (t_1, \ldots, t_m)$; they may leave some variables unchanged.

Definition 1. A discrete-time hybrid system *DTHS contains four components:*

- $D = \{d_1, \ldots, d_n, d_{n+1}, \ldots, d_p\}$ *($n \leq p$) is a finite set of discrete variables,* $D_{in} = \{d_{n+1}, \ldots, d_p\} \subseteq D$ *is a finite set of discrete inputs;*
- $C = \{c_1, \ldots, c_m\}$ *is a finite set of continuous variables;*
- *Init is a set of initial states, given in the form of* $\phi_0(D - D_{in}, C)$*;*
- *Trans is a union of a finite number of guarded assignments, each guarded assignment* ga_i *($i = 1, \ldots, k$ and $k \geq 1$) is in the form of*

$$\phi_i(D, C) \to (d_1, \ldots, d_n) := (g_{i,1}, \ldots, g_{i,n}); (c_1, \ldots, c_m) := (t_{i,1}, \ldots, t_{i,m}).$$

The assignment of ga_i *transforms a state* $(\mathbf{d}, \mathbf{c})$ *to* $(\mathbf{d}', \mathbf{c}')$*. Moreover, such* $(\mathbf{d}', \mathbf{c}')$ *exists if and only if* $\mathcal{I}_{D,C} \models \phi_i(\mathbf{d}, \mathbf{c})$.

We assume that the guards of the assignments defining the transition relation are exclusive and exhaustive. This is no restriction of the set of systems we consider, as nondetermism can be eliminated from the transition relation by introducing *resolution* variables $R \subseteq D$. These are discrete inputs which are used like r in the following illustration of the case of two overlapping guards:

$$\left.\begin{array}{l}\phi_1 \rightarrow \mathit{assignment}_1\\ \phi_2 \rightarrow \mathit{assignment}_2\end{array}\right\} \rightsquigarrow \left\{\begin{array}{l}\phi_1 \wedge (\neg\phi_2 \vee r = 1) \rightarrow \mathit{assignment}_1\\ \phi_2 \wedge (\neg\phi_1 \vee r = 2) \rightarrow \mathit{assignment}_2\end{array}\right.$$

A trajectory of a DTHS is a discrete-time sequence $(\mathbf{d}_i, \mathbf{c}_i)$ satisfying the conditions (i) $(\mathbf{d}_0, \mathbf{c}_0) \in \mathit{Init}$ and (ii) $((\mathbf{d}_i, \mathbf{c}_i), (\mathbf{d}_{i+1}, \mathbf{c}_{i+1})) \in \mathit{Trans}$ for all $i \in \{0, 1, \ldots\}$. Given a DTHS, we define the reachable set of states to be the set of all states that are reachable by a trajectory of the DTHS. The purpose of verification is to determine whether all possible behaviors of a system satisfy some property, which is specified as formula in a temporal logic.

3 Approach

3.1 Specification Logic

We sketch a model checker for a temporal logic over discrete and quantifier-free first-order atoms. Though we could build, from our basic ingredients, a procedure handling full CTL (or a linear-time logic), we restrict ourselves to its universal fragment ACTL with the temporal operators $\mathbf{AX}\cdot$ (next), $\mathbf{A}[\cdot\,\mathbf{U}\,\cdot]$ (until) and $\mathbf{A}[\cdot\,\mathbf{W}\,\cdot]$ (unless), with $\mathbf{AG}\cdot$ (globally) and $\mathbf{AF}\cdot$ (finally) as derived operators.

In practice, we expect the valuations of continuous variables to come from bounded subsets of $\mathbb{R}$. In other words, for each $c \in C$ we assume a lower and an upper bound l_c and u_c. Such restrictions can be captured in *global constraints* GC. With global constraints present, the formula operators are interpreted as follows:

$$\begin{aligned}\mathbf{A}_{GC}\mathbf{X}\phi &= \neg GC \vee \mathbf{AX}(\phi \vee \neg GC)\\ \mathbf{A}_{GC}[\phi\,\mathbf{W}\,\psi] &= \mathbf{A}[\phi\,\mathbf{W}\,(\psi \vee \neg GC)]\\ \mathbf{A}_{GC}[\phi\,\mathbf{U}\,\psi] &= \mathbf{A}[\phi\,\mathbf{U}\,(\psi \vee \neg GC)]\end{aligned}$$

3.2 Logical Representation of State Sets

Our model-checking procedure operates on logical representations of state sets. For ease of exposition we assume that discrete variables are encoded by sets of boolean variables, i. e., we consider D as a set of boolean variables. Then, a state-set representation is a boolean formula over D and $\mathcal{L}(C)$, the set of linear constraints. To be able to use advanced data structures for boolean formulas, we introduce a set of new (boolean) *constraint variables* Q as encodings for linear constraints, where each occurring $\ell \in \mathcal{L}(C)$ is represented by some $q_\ell \in Q$. Thus we arrive at boolean formulas over $D \cup Q$, together with a mapping of Q into $\mathcal{L}(C)$.

3.3 Step Computation

Our procedure works backwards, which means that it has to compute pre-images of state sets. Since we are going to check ACTL, we compute

$$pre(S) =_{\text{df}} \{ s \mid \forall s'. s \rightarrow s' \Rightarrow s' \in S \} ,$$

which corresponds to the temporal operator **AX** ($\Rightarrow$ stands for logical implication, $\rightarrow$ for the transition relation). On the logical level, for the transitions of our DTHSs consisting of conditions, assignments and input, this can be expressed by substitution for assignments and universal quantification for input, see [3]. Since we have restricted ourselves to closed-loop systems, there are no continuous inputs. Therefore, there is no need for first-order quantification, only boolean quantification has to be performed. In the following, we describe in detail how to compute *pre* for our state-set representations, given a DTHS. The variables in D and Q are treated rather differently.

A discrete variable $d_j \in D - D_{in}$ is updated according to the transitions in the following set.

$$\{ \phi_i(D, C) \;\rightarrow\; d_j := g_{i,j}(D) \mid i = 1, \ldots k \}$$

This translates to the (logical) update function:

$$pre(d_j) \;=\; \bigwedge_{i=1}^{k} (\phi_i(D, C) \;\Rightarrow\; g_{i,j}(D))$$

For the continuous part, we have to update the variables Q. The transitions

$$\{ \phi_i(D, C) \;\rightarrow\; (c_1, \ldots, c_m) := (t_{i,1}(C), \ldots, t_{i,m}(C)) \mid i = 1, \ldots k \}$$

induce

$$pre(q_\ell) \;=\; \bigwedge_{i=1}^{k} (\phi_i(D, C) \;\Rightarrow\; q_{\ell[c_1, \ldots, c_m / t_{i,1}(C), \ldots t_{i,m}(C)]})$$

as an update for a constraint variable q_ℓ occurring in the state-set description. That is, each q_ℓ gets replaced by a boolean combinations of constraint variables. In this formula, $q_{\ell[c_1, \ldots, c_m / t_{i,1}(C), \ldots, t_{i,m}(C)]}$ is a (possibly new) constraint variable which represents the linear constraint resulting from ℓ by replacing the variables c_j by the terms $t_{i,j}(C)$.

Finally, the pre-image of a set of states S is computed by substituting in parallel the pre-images for the respective variables, and afterwards universally quantifying over the discrete inputs.

$$\begin{aligned} &pre(S) = \\ &\quad \forall D_{in}.\, S[d_1, \ldots, d_n, q_{\ell_1}, \ldots, q_{\ell_v} \,/\, pre(d_1), \ldots, pre(d_n), pre(q_{\ell_1}), \ldots, pre(q_{\ell_v})] \end{aligned}$$

Note that the pre-image of a boolean variable is described by a quantifier-free formula which does not change during model checking – it can be computed once and for all. The same holds for each single constraint variable: The right-hand side remains constant. But the RHS may contain a constraint not already present in the formula. This necessitates to add constraint variables to the state representations during model checking, and also to add corresponding components to the step function. This corresponds to the semantical view of model-checker steps: Semantically, an occurring constraint is a hyperplane serving as a bound to define a polyhedron in the continuous state space. The pre-image of the polyhedron then is bounded by other hyperplanes, whose descriptions are derived via substitution from the existing bounding conditions.

3.4 Model Checking

The computation of the effect of a step is one main ingredient of CTL model checking. Besides that, one needs the ability to check whether two sets of states are equal, to detect that a fixpoint has been reached. In explicit or symbolic model checking, the criterion is simple: Two successive approximations must be the same. Here, where constraints enter the state-set descriptions, one has to check for *semantical* equality. Since our constraints are linear, this problem is decidable. This check for implication between two state-set representation completes the model-checking procedure.

In the following section we will present how we realized the conceptual procedure of this section, explaining the concrete representation format, how we perform logical operations and test for semantical implication.

Remark 2. Note the procedure described above can be applied to a broad class of systems. The logical treatment of the step function permits arbitrary *linear* terms on the right-hand sides of assignments, like $c_1 := \alpha_1 c_1 + \alpha_2 c_2 + \alpha_0$. Discretization of the linear hybrid automata from [11] yields the more restricted format $c := c + \alpha$.

4 Realization

In order to implement the approach described in the previous section, we use a new data structure for representing sets of states, the so-called First-Order AND-Inverter-Graphs (FO-AIGs) (see Fig. 1 for an illustration).

Using efficient methods for keeping this representation as compact as possible is a key point for our approach. This goal is achieved by a rather complex interaction of various methods. In the following we give some more details on these concepts. The methods are divided into three classes:

- methods dealing with the boolean part,
- methods dealing with the first-order part, and
- methods dealing with the interaction of the boolean and the first-order part.

Note that to implement the model-checking algorithm we need only boolean operations, substitution and first-order implication. Our description focuses on the the first-order part and on how to keep our data structures small.

4.1 Methods Dealing with the Boolean Part

In FO-AIGs boolean formulas are represented by Functionally Reduced AND-Inverter Graphs (FRAIGs) [15,17]. FRAIGs are basically boolean circuits consisting only of AND gates and inverters. In contrast to BDDs as used in [3], they are not a canonical representation for boolean functions, but they are "semi-canonical" in the sense that every node in the FRAIG represents a unique boolean function. To achieve this goal several techniques like structural hashing, simulation and SAT solving are used:

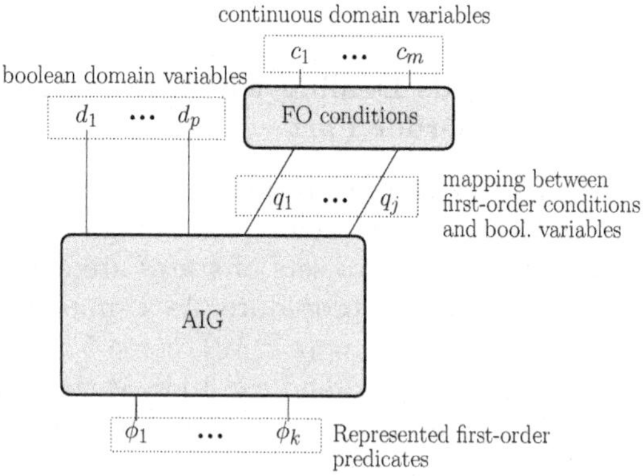

Fig. 1. The FO-AIG structure

First, simple local transformation rules are used for node minimization. For instance, we apply structural hashing for identifying isomorphic AND nodes which have the same pairs of inputs.

Moreover, we maintain the so-called "functional reduction property": Each node in the FRAIG represents a unique boolean function (up to complementation). We use a SAT solver to check for equivalent nodes while constructing a FRAIG and to merge equivalent nodes immediately.

Of course, checking each possible pair of nodes would be quite inefficient. However, *simulation* using test vectors of boolean values restricts the number of candidates for SAT check to a great extent: If for a given pair of nodes simulation is already able to prove non-equivalence (i. e., the simulated values are different for at least one test vector), the more time consuming SAT checks are not needed. The simulation vectors are initially random, but they are updated using feedback from satisfied SAT instances (i. e., from proofs of non-equivalence).

For the pure boolean case, enhanced with other techniques such as quantifier scheduling, node selection heuristics and BDD sweeping, FRAIGs proved to be a promising alternative to BDDs in the context of CTL model checking, avoiding in many cases the well-known memory explosion problem which may occur during BDD-based symbolic model checking [17].

4.2 Methods Dealing with the First-Order Part

The second component of FO-AIGs is a representation of linear constraints ℓ connected to the boolean part by constraint variables q_ℓ. These constraints are of the form $\sum_{i=1}^{n} \alpha_i c_i + \alpha_0 \sim 0$ with rational constants α_j, real variables c_i, and $\sim \in \{=, <, \leq\}$. When new linear constraints are computed by substitution during the step computation (see Sect. 3), we avoid introducing linear constraints which are equivalent to existing constraints. The restriction to *linear* constraints makes this task simple, since it reduces to the application of (straightforward) normalization rules.

4.3 Methods Dealing with the Interaction of the Boolean and the First-Order Part

Of course, a strict separation between the boolean part and the first-order part of FO-AIGs gives us usually not enough information, for instance when we have to check whether two sets of states are equivalent during the fixpoint check of the model checking procedure. As a simple example consider the two predicates $\phi_1 = (c < 5)$ and $\phi_2 = (c < 10) \wedge (c < 5)$. If $c < 5$ is represented by the boolean constraint variable q_1 and $c < 10$ by variable q_2, then the corresponding boolean formulas q_1 and $q_1 \wedge q_2$ are not equivalent, whereas ϕ_1 and ϕ_2 are certainly equivalent. Both as a means for further compaction of our representations and as a means for detecting fixpoints we need methods for transferring knowledge from the first-order part to the boolean part. (In the example above this may be the information that $q_1 = 1$ and $q_2 = 0$ can not be true at the same time or that ϕ_1 and ϕ_2 are equivalent when replacing boolean variables by their first-order interpretations.)

Computing Implications Between Linear Constraints. In our first method we consider dependencies between linear constraints that are easy to detect a priori and transfer them to the boolean part. It is not known initially, which dependencies are actually needed in the rest of the computation; for this reason we restrict to two simple cases: First, we compute unconditional implications between linear constraints $\alpha_1 c_1 + \ldots + \alpha_n c_n + \alpha_0 \leq 0$ and $\alpha_1 c_1 + \ldots + \alpha_n c_n + \alpha_0' \leq 0$, where $\alpha_0 > \alpha_0'$ (and analogously implications involving negations of linear constraints). Second, we use a sound but incomplete method to detect implications modulo global constraints, where a linear constraint $\alpha_1' c_1 + \ldots + \alpha_n' c_n + \alpha_0' \leq 0$ follows from $\alpha_1 c_1 + \ldots + \alpha_n c_n + \alpha_0 \leq 0$ and the global lower and upper bounds $l_i \leq c_i \leq u_i$ for the first-order variables.

Using Implications Between Linear Constraints. Suppose we have found a pair of linear constraints ℓ_1 and ℓ_2 with $\ell_1 \Rightarrow \ell_2$, and in the boolean part ℓ_1 is represented by the constraint variable q_1, ℓ_2 by variable q_2. Then we know that the combination of values $q_1 = 1$ and $q_2 = 0$ is inconsistent w. r. t. the first-order part, i. e., it will never be applied to inputs q_1 and q_2 of the boolean part. We transfer this knowledge to the boolean part by a modified behavior of the FRAIG package: First we adjust our test vectors, such that they become consistent with the found implications (potentially leading to the fact that proofs of non-equivalence by simulation will not hold any longer for certain pairs of nodes) and second we introduce the implication $q_1 \Rightarrow q_2$ as an additional clause in every SAT problem checking equivalence of two nodes depending on q_1 and q_2. In that way non-equivalences of AIG nodes which are only caused by differences w. r. t. inconsistent input value combinations with $q_1 = 1$ and $q_2 = 0$ will be turned into equivalences, removing redundant nodes in the AIG.

Using a Decision Procedure for Deciding Equivalence. In addition to the eager dependency check for linear constraints above, we use HySAT [9] as a decision procedure for the equivalence of nodes in FO-AIGs (representing boolean combinations of linear constraints). If two nodes are proven to be equivalent (taking the linear constraints into account), then these nodes can be merged, leading to a compaction of the representation or leading to the detection of a fixpoint in the model checking computation.

In principle, we could use HySAT in an eager manner every time when a new node is inserted into the FO-AIG representation, just like SAT (together with simulation) is used in the FRAIG representation of the boolean part. This would lead to a FO-AIG representation where different nodes in the FRAIG part always represent different first-order predicates. However, we decided to use HySAT only in a lazy manner in order to avoid too many potentially expensive applications of HySAT (taking the linear constraints into account): In our first implementation HySAT is only invoked by explicit equivalence checks and fixpoint checks of the model checking procedure.

Using Test Vectors to Increase Efficiency. As in the boolean case (see Sect. 4.1), we use simulation with test vectors as an incomplete but cheap method to show the non-equivalence of FO-AIG nodes, thus reducing the number of expensive calls to HySAT. However, note that the boolean simulation vectors which we apply to the boolean variables corresponding to linear constraints must now be *consistent with respect to the linear constraints*, since otherwise our proof of non-equivalence could be incorrect. For this reason we use an appropriate set of test vectors in terms of real variables such that we can compute consistent boolean valuations of linear constraints based on the real valued test vectors.

Trying to find an optimal set of test vectors that allows us to distinguish between any two boolean combination of linear constraints is at least as hard as solving our main problem, the implication check between such boolean combinations, and therefore unpractical. On the other hand, if test vectors are picked randomly with a uniform distribution over the polyhedron of permitted values, a large number of them fall into "uninteresting regions" of this polyhedron.

Our solution is to choose test vectors randomly *in the proximity of relevant hyperplanes:* Assume that every variable c_i has a global lower and upper bound $l_i \leq c_i \leq u_i$, so that the polyhedron of permitted values is $P = \{\vec{c} \mid \vec{c} = (c_1, \ldots, c_n), l_i \leq c_i \leq u_i\}$. For each linear constraint $f(\vec{c}) \leq 0$ with $f(\vec{c}) = \alpha_1 c_1 + \ldots + \alpha_n c_n + \alpha_0$, we determine first the vertices $\vec{r}$ and $\vec{s}$ of P for which f is maximal or minimal, respectively (without loss of generality, $f(\vec{r}) > 0 > f(\vec{s})$). Second, we compute random points $\vec{t} \in P$, and finally, for each of these random points, we use linear interpolation between $\vec{t}$ and $\vec{r}$ (if $f(\vec{t}) < 0$) or $\vec{t}$ and $\vec{s}$ (otherwise) to obtain a point on the straight line between $\vec{t}$ and $\vec{r}$ (or $\vec{t}$ and $\vec{s}$) that is close to the hyperplane defined by $f(\vec{c}) = 0$.

Satisfied HySAT instances (i. e., proofs of non-equivalence for boolean combinations of linear constraints) are another source of boolean simulation vectors which are consistent w. r. t. linear constraints. The satisfying assignments computed by HySAT are guaranteed to be consistent w. r. t. linear constraints and they are able to separate at least the pair of nodes which are currently proven to be non-equivalent. (Learning from HySAT corresponds to learning from SAT in the pure Boolean case.)

5 Application

We implemented a prototype model checker based on the concepts mentioned above and applied it both to several small examples and to a model derived from an industrial case study. In this section we report on results for the case study.

5.1 The Case Study

General Description. Our sample application is derived from a case study for Airbus, a controller for the flaps of an aircraft [4]. The flaps are extended during take-off and landing to generate more lift at low velocity. They are not robust enough for high velocity, so they must be retracted for cruising period. It is the controller's task to correct the pilot's commands if he endangers the flaps. However, the flap controller is not supposed to guarantee safety under all circumstances, but only if the pilot acts "reasonably". To enable manoeuvres risking aircraft integrity in critical situations, the controller is limited to only modify the pilot's command by one notch.

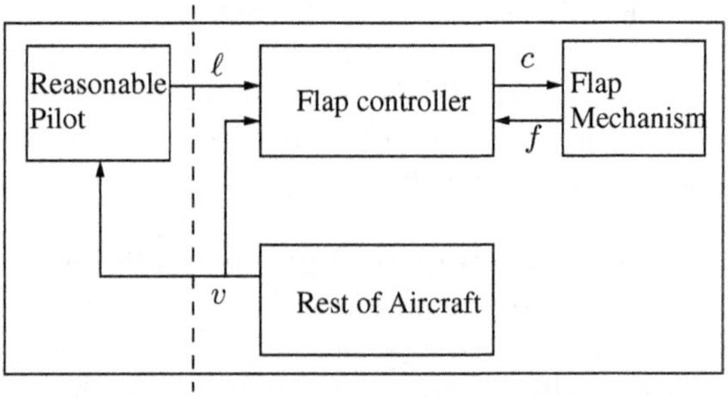

Fig. 2. Components in the flap controller example

Model Structure. Our simplified system consists of four components to model, i. e., the pilot behavior, the controller, the flap mechanism, and the rest of the aircraft. It contains two continuous variables v (velocity) and f (flap angle), and two discrete variables ℓ (lever position set by the pilot) and c (corrected position, set by the controller). For each lever position, there is a pre-defined flap position and a pre-defined nominal velocity $nominal(f)$.

Property. The property "safe" to establish for our model is the following: "For the current flap setting f, the aircraft's velocity v shall not exceed the nominal velocity $nominal(f)$ plus 7 knots". Whether this requirement holds for our model depends on a "race" between flap retraction and speed increase. The controller is correct, if it initiates flap retraction (by correcting the pilot) early enough.

Model Details. The pilot component in our model ensures reasonable lever positions, by guaranteeing that the lever is at most one notch too high. The behavior of the controller depends on both ℓ and v: When the velocity is greater than the nominal max value ($nominal(f) + 2.5$ knots), the modification of the pilot behavior is activated ($c = \ell - 1$); when the velocity has changed to less than the nominal min value ($nominal(f) - 2.5$ knots), the modification is turned off ($c = \ell$). The flap mechanism controls the continuous variable f, and depends on the discrete variable c. It models the mechatronic which adapts the physical flap angle f to the position commanded by c. This is a process which takes time. f has a range from 0 to 55.0. At each discrete time step (the sampling rate is $\delta = 100$ ms in this example), the flap angle may change by $\Delta_f = 0.15625$. At the same time, the rest of the aircraft might increase the velocity by 0.5 knots within a range from 150.0 to 340.0 knots. This defines the "races" mentioned above. Our specification of the model is simply **AG** *safe*.

5.2 Experimental Results

Our prototype successfully model checked the flap controller with 3 lever positions, $220.0 \le v \le 340.0$, and $0.0 \le f \le 20.0$, showing that the system remains in the safe region. Using all the concepts presented in Section 4 our model checking run was completed after 46 steps within 4.7 minutes of CPU time.[5]

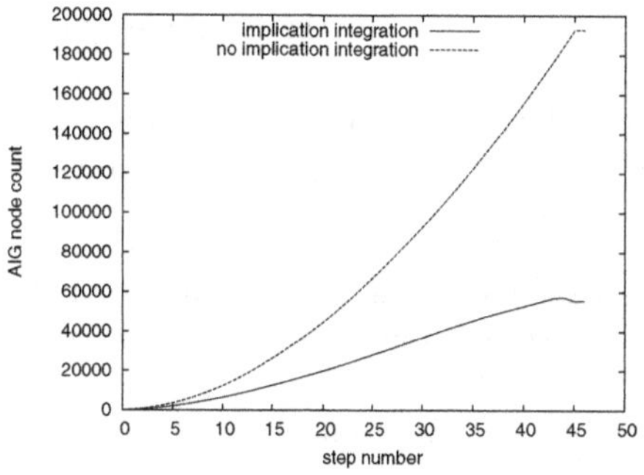

Fig. 3. Number of AIG nodes

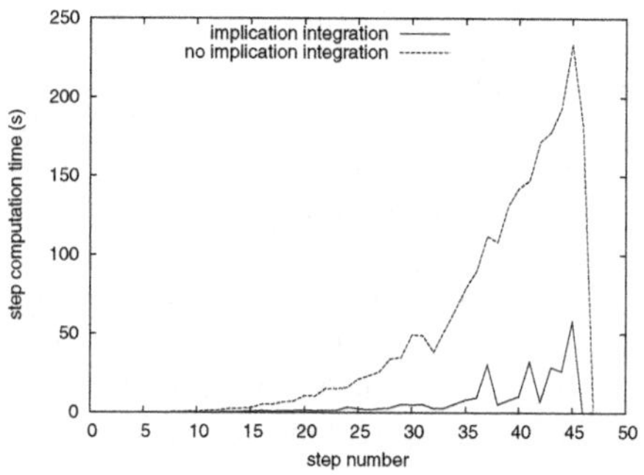

Fig. 4. CPU times for different steps

In a first experiment we evaluated the effect of integrating knowledge of implications between linear constraints into the FO-AIG representation. We compared two cases: Case *no_impl* when no implications were computed and integrated and case *impl* when implications were computed and integrated as described in Section 4.3. Figure 3 depicts the number of AIG nodes used during the different steps of the model checking procedure both for case *no_impl* (dashed line) and case *impl* (solid line). For case *no_impl* the maximal number of active AIG nodes was 192, 630 whereas for case *impl* the maximal number was only 59, 372. This clearly shows that integrating knowledge of linear constraints pays off in terms of node counts: By using implications it was possible to simplify the representation to a great extent, since AIG nodes were identified which were equivalent taking the

[5] All experiments were performed on a dual Opteron 250, 2.4 GHz with 4 GB memory.

linear constraints into account. Figure 4 shows that making use of implications not only improves node counts, but run times as well: It presents the run times needed for the different steps in both cases. The total run time for case *no_impl* was 37.9 CPU minutes whereas the total run time for case *impl* was 4.7 CPU minutes. (The total number of implications between linear constraints computed by our tool was 622 (implications due to transitivity not taken into account).)

In the following we will confine ourselves to case *impl* and we will perform a more detailed analysis of the behavior of our representation of states containing discrete and continuous variables. The efficiency of our FO-AIGs relies both on efficient methods for boolean manipulations and on efficient methods for integrating knowledge of linear constraints avoiding the application of more expensive calls to a linear constraint solver as much as possible.

We could observe that the number of SAT checks divided by the total number of attempts to insert a node into the FRAIG was only 0.24 % in our experiment. The fraction of SAT checks which led to the result that the compared nodes were functionally equivalent was 59 %. This means that – although we are always maintaining the functional reduction property of FRAIGs – the assistance of SAT by simulation and structural hashing as described in Sect. 4.1 assures that SAT is applied only for a small fraction of all node insertions. Moreover, the high percentage of SAT checks proving functional equivalence of two nodes shows the effectiveness of simulation in avoiding unnecessary SAT checks for nodes which are not equivalent.

In a last experiment we analyzed how often the application of calls to the linear constraint solver HySAT was saved by incomplete (but inexpensive) methods. In our method HySAT calls can be saved for two reasons:

1. The equivalence of two boolean combinations of linear constraints can be proven just by considering the boolean part (without interpreting the variables representing linear constraints).
2. The non-equivalence of two boolean combinations of linear constraints can be proven by simulation with test vectors as described in Section 4.3.

Our model checking run involved 5374 equivalence checks for boolean combinations of linear constraints. However, for only 22 out of these 5374 checks it turned out to be necessary to call the linear constraint solver in HySAT (i. e., in 0.41 % of all cases). In 42.91 % of all cases the call to HySAT could be avoided due to reason (1) and in 56.68 % of all cases due to reason (2).

Although we believe that the complex interaction of different methods in our approach to first-order model checking still leaves room for improvement, our first experiments provide promising results confirming our idea of increasing efficiency by incomplete but inexpensive methods.

6 Related Work

We address hybrid systems consisting not only of a continuous part, but also of a potentially complex discrete part. Tools like HyTech [12], `d/dt` [1], PHAver [10] based on the notion of hybrid automaton [11] fail when dealing with complex hybrid controllers, since only the continuous part of the system is represented symbolically, while the discrete states are represented explicitly. Thus, these tools cannot take advantage of the breakthrough achieved for symbolic model checkers [5]. In this section, we discuss those verification tools which can (potentially) deal with hybrid systems with large discrete parts, and compare them with our work in the end of this section.

CheckMate [19] is a MATLAB-based tool for simulation and verification of *threshold-event driven hybrid systems* (TEDHSs). A TEDHS has a clear separation between purely continuous blocks representing the dynamics in a given mode and discrete controllers. The changes in the discrete state can occur only when continuous state variables encounter specified thresholds. CheckMate converts the TEDHS model into a *polyhedral-invariant hybrid automaton* [6], computes the sets of reachable states for the continuous dynamics using *flowpipe* approximations [7], and performs search in a completely constructed *approximate quotient transition system.* This approach was adapted for discrete-time controllers with fixed sampling rate [18], where the sampled behavior only applies to conditions for discrete-state transitions.

Separation of continuous dynamics and control by observing threshold predicates as guards of transitions was also taken in [3,2], which extended symbolic model checking with dynamically generated first-order predicates. Those predicates express sets of valuations over large data domains like reals. BDDs are used to encode discrete states, and specific variables within the BDDs are used to represent those first-order formulas, which are maintained separately.

The SAL verification tool [16] for hybrid systems builds on a symbolic representation of polynomial hybrid systems in PVS, the guards on discrete transitions and the continuous flows in all modes can be specified using arbitrary polynomial expressions over the continuous variables. SAL applies *hybrid abstraction* [20] to construct a sound discrete approximation using a set of polynomial expressions to partition the continuous state space into *sign-invariant zones.* This abstract discrete system is passed to a symbolic model checker. SAL also uses other techniques like quantifier elimination and invariant generation.

HySAT [9] is a bounded model checker for linear hybrid systems. It combines Davis-Putnam style SAT solving techniques with linear programming, and implements state of the art optimizations such at nonchronological backjumping, conflict driven learning and lazy clause evaluation.

HYSDEL [21] is a model language for describing discrete-time hybrid systems by interconnections of linear dynamic systems, finite-state automata, if-then-else and propositional logic rules. The description can be transformed into a Mixed Logical Dynamical (MLD) system. HYSDEL uses mathematical programming to perform reachability analysis for MLD systems. The algorithms determines the reachable set by solving a mixed-integer optimization problem.

Both CheckMate and SAL construct a discrete approximation in order to perform model checking. Our approach checks properties directly on a computed reachable state space, which includes both discrete and continuous parts, without using any approximation. Moreover, instead of using BDDs as in [3,2], we use FO-AIGs as symbolic representation of hybrid state spaces. Various techniques like implication test and test vector generation are tightly integrated to identify equivalent and non-equivalent linear constraints efficiently. This approach allows us to deal with large discrete state spaces, while smoothly incorporating reasoning about continuous variables (linear constraints). From this perspective, our approach is different with all the aforementioned works. Unlike bounded model checking in HySAT, we perform verification on a completely constructed state space. Tools like CheckMate and SAL deal with continuous-time hybrid systems. Our approach focuses on discrete-time hybrid systems as HYSDEL, but the analysis procedure in HYSDEL is different from ours.

7 Conclusions and Future Work

In this paper, we have proposed an approach for model checking safety propreties of discrete-time hybrid systems. It uses a first-order extension of AIGs as a compact representation for sets of configurations, which are composed of both continuous regions and discrete states. Several efficient methods for keeping this representation as compact as possible have been tightly integrated. For instance, we have implemented techniques to keep the discrete part functionally reduced, to detect implications between linear constraints, to use a decision procedure to perform equivalence checks on our hybrid state-set representation, to generate test vectors to distinguish between any two boolean combination of linear constraints. The typical application domain of our approach is hybrid systems with non-trivial discrete state spaces.

So far, the preliminary implementation of our approach has been used to check an industrial case study with limited size and several small examples. In the future we will apply our approach to more sophisticated examples for further evaluation and for comparisons with other tools (see Sect. 6). Moreover, it seems that an integration of predicate abstraction to derive a finite-state abstraction of the hybrid system either on-the-fly or at a separate initial abstraction step (as in [3,2]) can be achieved without much difficulties. We expect that for larger examples the exectution time of our approach will heavily rely on time discretization. For this reason, currently techniques like *acceleration* to speed up step computation are under our investigation. We also plan to use counter-example guided abstraction refinement, as it has been added to CheckMate [8] recently.

References

1. E. Asarin, T. Dang, and O. Maler. The d/dt tool for verification of the hybrid systems. In *Proc. CAV 2002, LNCS 2404*, pp. 365–370. Springer.
2. T. Bienmüller, J. Bohn, H. Brinkmann, U. Brockmeyer, W. Damm, H. Hungar, and P. Jansen. Verification of the automotive control units. In *Correct System Design – Recent Insights and Advances*, 1999, *LNCS 1710*, pp. 319–341. Springer.
3. J. Bohn, W. Damm, O. Grumberg, H. Hungar, and K. Laster. First-order-CTL model checking. In *Proc. FST&TCS 1998, LNCS 1530*, pp. 283–294. Springer.

4. M. Bretschneider, H.-J. Holberg, E. Böde, I. Brückner, T. Peikenkamp, and H. Spenke. Model-based safety analysis of a flap control system. In *Proc. 14th Annual INCOSE Symposium*, 2004.
5. J. R. Burch, E. M. Clarke, K. L. McMillan, D. L. Dill, and J. Hwang. Symbolic model checking: 10^{20} states and beyond. In *Proc. LICS 1990*, pp. 428–439.
6. A. Chutinan and B. H. Krogh. Computing polyhedral approximations to flow pipes for dynamic systems. In *Proc. IEEE CDC 1998.*
7. A. Chutinan and B. H. Krogh. Verification of the polyhedral-invariant hybrid automata using polygonal flowpipe approximations. In *Proc. HSCC 1999, LNCS 1569*, pp. 76–90. Springer.
8. E. M. Clarke, A. Fehnker, Z. Han, B. H. Krogh, J. Ouaknine, O. Stursberg, and M. Theobald. Abstraction and counterexample-guided refinement in model checking of hybrid systems. *Foundations of Computer Science*, 14(4):583–604, 2003.
9. M. Fränzle and C. Herde. Efficient proof engines for bounded model checking of hybrid systems. *ENTCS*, 133:119–137, 2005.
10. G. Frehse. PHAVer: Algorithmic verification of hybrid systems past HyTech. In *Proc. HSCC 2005, LNCS 3414*, pp. 258–273. Springer.
11. T. A. Henzinger. The theory of hybrid automata. In *Proc. LICS 1996*, pp. 278–292.
12. T. A. Henzinger, P.-H. Ho, and H. Wong-Toi. HyTech: A model checker for hybrid systems. *Software Tools for Technology Transfer*, 1(1-2):110–122, 1997.
13. C. A. R. Hoare. An axiomatic basis for computer programming. *Communication of the ACM*, 12:576–583, 1969.
14. H. Hungar, O. Grumberg, and W. Damm. What if model checking must be truly symbolic. In *Proc. CHARME 1995, LNCS 987*, pp. 1–20. Springer.
15. A. Mishchenko, S. Chatterjee, R. Jiang, and R. K. Brayton. FRAIGs: A unifying representation for logic synthesis and verification. Technical report, EECS Dept., UC Berkeley, 2005.
16. L. de Moura, S. Owre, H. Rueß, J. Rushby, N. Shankar, M. Sorea, and A. Tiwari. SAL 2. In *Proc. CAV 2004, LNCS 3114*, pp. 496–500. Springer.
17. F. Pigorsch, C. Scholl, and S. Disch. Advanced unbounded model checking by using AIGs, BDD sweeping and quantifier scheduling. In *Proc. FMCAD 2006.*
18. B. I. Silva and B. H. Krogh. Modeling and verification of hybrid system with clocked and unclocked events. In *Proc. IEEE CDC 2001.*
19. B. I. Silva, K. Richeson, B. H. Krogh, and A. Chutinan. Modeling and verification of hybrid dynamical system using CheckMate. In *Proc. 4th Conference on Automation of Mixed Processes*, 2000.
20. A. Tiwari and G. Khanna. Series of the abstractions for hybrid automata. In *Proc. HSCC 2002, LNCS 2289*, pp. 465–478. Springer.
21. F. D. Torrisi and A. Bemporad. HYSDEL - A tool for generating computational hybrid models. *IEEE Transactions on Control Systems Technology*, 12(2):235–249, 2004.

Timed Unfoldings for Networks of Timed Automata

Patricia Bouyer[1], Serge Haddad[2], and Pierre-Alain Reynier[1]

[1] LSV, CNRS & ENS Cachan, France
[2] LAMSADE, CNRS & Université Paris-Dauphine, France
{bouyer,reynier}@lsv.ens-cachan.fr, haddad@lamsade.dauphine.fr

Abstract. Whereas partial order methods have proved their efficiency for the analysis of discrete-event systems, their application to timed systems remains a challenging research topic. Here, we design a verification algorithm for networks of timed automata with invariants. Based on the unfolding technique, our method produces a branching process as an acyclic Petri net extended with *read arcs*. These arcs verify conditions on tokens without consuming them, thus expressing concurrency between conditions checks. They are useful for avoiding the explosion of the size of the unfolding due to clocks which are compared with constants but not reset. Furthermore, we attach *zones* to events, in addition to markings. We then compute a complete finite prefix of the unfolding. The presence of invariants goes against the concurrency since it entails a global synchronization on time. The use of read arcs and the analysis of the clock constraints appearing in invariants helps increasing the concurrency relation between events. Finally, the finite prefix can be used to decide reachability properties, and transition enabling.

1 Introduction

Partial-order methods for discrete-event systems. In the last decades, major advances in the analysis of distributed systems were based on two paradigms: the *independence* and the *locality* of actions. Whereas *partial-order* methods mainly take advantage of the independence (see e.g. [20]), the *unfolding* methods rely on both concepts [13,17]. Furthermore from a semantical point of view, system unfoldings are a theoretical well-defined alternative to the usual interleaving semantics. It must be emphasized that this semantics is more discriminant than the classical one and may be applied for other purposes than verification like observation and diagnosis (see e.g. [9]).

Timed systems. Several timed models have been proposed for representing real-time systems, e.g. various extensions of Petri nets, but the most studied and well-established model is the one of timed automata (TA for short). It has been defined in [1] and since then much investigated, with the development of several tools based on this model.

Partial-order methods for timed systems. If this approach led to efficient tools and algorithms in the untimed case, no counterpart has so far been achieved for *timed systems*. The main reason is that time synchronization of actions in the standard timed models is essentially *global* and thus yields numerous conceptual and technical difficulties for adapting or extending the previous methods. We discuss in Section 5 existing works.

Our contribution. In this paper, we design an efficient verification algorithm for *networks of timed automata with invariants* (NTA). Our algorithm is based on the unfolding technique, and produces an acyclic Petri net with *read arcs*. Conditions (*i.e.* places

S. Graf and W. Zhang (Eds.): ATVA 2006, LNCS 4218, pp. 292–306, 2006.

of the net) are labeled either by locations or by clocks, and events (*i.e.* transitions of the net) represent the transitions of the NTA. Read arcs are convenient for modeling clock testing with no clock reset (see for instance [7]), and, though they add some complexity to the building of the unfoldings [21,22], they increase the independence relation between events.

More precisely, we define a timed unfolding of an NTA close to the untimed case, by attaching *zones* (a classical symbolic representation in the framework of timed systems) to events, in addition to markings. Roughly the zone attached to an event t will capture all relevant timing informations of possible configurations reached after having fired all events belonging to the minimal causal past of t. It must be emphasized that the dimension of the zones that we attach to events is small (and constant while the NTA is unfolded): it is equal to three times the number of clocks plus twice the number of TA.

The main problem encountered by previous works is that urgency requirements (for instance due to invariants) entail global synchronization between *a priori* independent transitions. When a clock appears in an invariant, we use read arcs to express dependencies of the transitions w.r.t. this invariant. This increases the concurrency relation between events, even in the presence of invariants and enables a local decision of the firability of an event (*i.e.* only by looking at its cut).

Finally, we prove that we can build a complete finite prefix which can be used, as in the untimed case, for deciding in linear time (w.r.t. the size of the finite prefix) reachability (as well as transition firing) properties in NTA.

Due to lack of space, proofs are omitted, but can be found in [8]

2 Networks of Timed Automata

Let X be a finite set of variables, called *clocks*. We write $\mathcal{C}(X)$ for the set of *constraints* over X, which consist of conjunctions of atomic formulae of the form $x \bowtie c$ and $x - y \bowtie c$ for $x, y \in X$, $c \in \mathbb{Z}$ and $\bowtie \in \{<, \leq, =, \geq, >\}$. We write *Clocks*$(\gamma)$ for the set of clocks involved in γ. We define the proper subset $\mathcal{C}_{df}(X)$ of *diagonal-free* constraints over X where constraints $x - y \bowtie h$ (called *diagonal constraints*) are not allowed. Similarly, we define the proper subset $\mathcal{C}_{ub}(X)$ of *upper-bounded* constraints over X where only constraints $x \prec h$ with $\prec \in \{<, \leq\}$ are allowed.

Let s be a mapping from X to elementary expressions over some set X' (*i.e.* x, $x - y$ or $x - c$). Then the substitution of s in a diagonal-free constraint γ, denoted $\gamma[\{x \leftarrow s(x)\}_{x \in X}]$ is defined as the expression obtained by replacing in γ every occurrence of x by the term $s(x)$, for any clock x. Note that the resulting expression belongs to $\mathcal{C}(X')$.

We will use as timed domain the set $\mathbb{R}_{\geq 0}$ of nonnegative real numbers. A *valuation* over the set X of clocks is an element of $\mathbb{R}_{\geq 0}^X$. For $R \subseteq X$, the valuation $v[R \leftarrow 0]$ is the valuation v' such that $v'(x) = 0$ when $x \in R$ and $v'(x) = v(x)$ otherwise. For $d \in \mathbb{R}_{\geq 0}$, the valuation $v + d$ is defined by $(v + d)(x) = v(x) + d$ for every $x \in X$. Constraints of $\mathcal{C}(X)$ are interpreted in a natural way over valuations: we write $v \models \gamma$ when the constraint γ is satisfied by v.

We use the classical notion of zones to represent symbolically infinite sets of valuations [12]. A *zone* over a set of variables Y is defined as a constraint of $\mathcal{C}(Y)$. We assume the reader to be familiar with the following operations on zones (see [6]):

conjunction, extension of the set of variables, elimination of a set of variables (we write $\exists V.Z$), and emptiness checking. The *extrapolation* of zone Z w.r.t. constant M is the smallest zone containing Z defined with constants in $\{-M, \ldots, 0, \ldots, M\}$.

Definition 1 (Timed Automaton (TA) [1]). *A* timed automaton $\mathcal{A}$ *over* Σ *is a tuple* $(L, \ell_0, X, \Sigma, E, Inv)$ *where* L *is a finite set of* locations, $\ell_0 \in L$ *is the* initial location, X *is a finite set of* clocks, Σ *is a finite alphabet of actions,* $E \subseteq L \times \mathcal{C}_{df}(X) \times \Sigma \times 2^X \times L$ *is a finite set of* edges *and* $Inv \subseteq \mathcal{C}_{ub}(X)^L$ *associates to each location an* invariant *given as an upper bound constraint. An edge* $(\ell, g, a, R, \ell') \in E$ *(or* $\ell \xrightarrow{g,a,R} \ell'$*) represents a transition from location* ℓ *to location* ℓ' *labeled by* a*, with the guard* g *defined by a constraint and reset* $R \in 2^X$.

Definition 2 (Network of TA (NTA)). *A partial function* $f : (\Sigma \cup \{\bot\})^n \to \Sigma$ *is called an* n*-ary* synchronization function. *A* network of timed automata *is a finite family* $(\mathcal{A}_i)_{1 \leq i \leq n}$ *of* n *TA, whose sets of locations are pairwise disjoint, together with an* n*-ary synchronization function* f.

Note that we do not assume that clocks are local to each TA of an NTA. Before giving the semantics of an NTA, we first give some notation and definitions which will be useful in the rest of the paper. We fix an NTA $\mathcal{A}$, and we assume that $\mathcal{A}$ is given by $(\mathcal{A}_i)_{1 \leq i \leq n}$, and f a synchronization function. We write $\mathcal{A}_i = (L_i, \ell_{i,0}, X_i, \Sigma, E_i, Inv_i)$ for every $1 \leq i \leq n$. We then denote by X (resp. L) the set $\bigcup_{1 \leq i \leq n} X_i$ (resp. $\bigcup_{1 \leq i \leq n} L_i$). We extend naturally the function *Inv* over the set L.

Finally, we consider a synchronization function $f : (\Sigma \cup \{\bot\})^n \to \Sigma$. In the sequel, we denote $\overline{\Sigma_\bot}$ (resp. $\overline{E}$) the set $(\Sigma \cup \{\bot\})^n$ (resp. the set $\prod_i (E_i \cup \{\bot\})$). We use a similar notation for their elements: we denote $\overline{a}$ (resp. $\overline{e}$) an n-uple $(a_1, \ldots, a_n) \in \overline{\Sigma_\bot}$ (resp. $(e_1, \ldots, e_n) \in \overline{E}$). We define the function *Lab* from $\overline{E}$ to $\overline{\Sigma_\bot}$ which maps an element $\overline{e}$ to the element $\overline{a}$ defined for every $1 \leq i \leq n$ by $a_i = b$ if $e_i = \ell_i \xrightarrow{g,b,R} \ell'_i$, and by $a_i = \bot$ otherwise. We define the subset $Sync = Lab^{-1}(f^{-1}(\Sigma))$ of $\overline{E}$, which is the set of possible synchronizations of edges, *i.e.* the set of transitions of the NTA. Given $\overline{e} \in Sync$, assuming $e_i = \ell_i \xrightarrow{g_i, a_i, R_i} \ell'_i$, for all i such that $e_i \neq \bot$, we define $I(\overline{e})$ the set $\{1 \leq i \leq n \mid e_i \neq \bot\}$, $g(\overline{e})$ the constraint $\bigwedge_{i \in I(\overline{e})} g_i$ and $R(\overline{e})$ the set $\bigcup_{i \in I(\overline{e})} R_i$. Finally, given an n-tuple $\overline{\ell}$, we note $Inv(\overline{\ell}) = \bigwedge_{1 \leq i \leq n} Inv(\ell_i)$.

Definition 3 (Semantics of an NTA). *Let* $\mathcal{A} = ((\mathcal{A}_i)_{1 \leq i \leq n}, f)$ *be an NTA. The semantics of* $\mathcal{A}$ *is the transition system* $\mathcal{S}_\mathcal{A} = (Q, q_0, \to)$ *where* $Q = (\Pi_{1 \leq i \leq n} L_i) \times (\mathbb{R}_{\geq 0})^X$,[1] $q_0 = (\overline{\ell}_0, \mathbf{0})$ *and* $\to$ *is defined by:*

$$\begin{cases} (\overline{\ell}, v) \xrightarrow{d} (\overline{\ell}, v + d) \text{ if } d \in \mathbb{R}_{\geq 0} \text{ and } v + d \models Inv(\overline{\ell}) \text{ (delay moves);} \\ (\overline{\ell}, v) \xrightarrow{a} (\overline{\ell}', v') \quad \text{if } \exists \overline{e} \in Lab^{-1}(f^{-1}(\{a\})) \text{ s.t. } v \models g(\overline{e}), v' = v[R(\overline{e}) \leftarrow 0] \text{ and} \\ \qquad \ell'_i \text{ is given by } e_i \text{ if } i \in I(\overline{e}) \text{ and by } \ell_i \text{ otherwise (discrete moves).} \end{cases}$$

Finally, an element $\sigma = (\bar{e}_i, d_i)_{i \geq 0} \in (Sync \times \mathbb{R}_{\geq 0})^*$ *is a* timed sequence *of* $\mathcal{A}$ *if the sequence of moves* $q_0 \xrightarrow{d_0} \ldots \xrightarrow{d_i - d_{i-1}} \xrightarrow{f(Lab(\bar{e}_i))} \ldots \xrightarrow{f(Lab(\bar{e}_n))}$ *is in* $\mathcal{S}_\mathcal{A}$.

[1] We denote $\overline{\ell}$ an n-tuple of $\Pi_{1 \leq i \leq n} L_i$, and $\overline{\ell}_0 = (\ell_{i,0})_{1 \leq i \leq n}$.

W.l.o.g. we assume that the constraints and resets associated with edges syntactically ensure that the invariants associated with the output locations of every edge are satisfied when a discrete move following that edge is performed.

Important and unusual definitions. We define several other notions, which will be fundamental for defining our unfolding. Let $\mathcal{A}$ be an NTA. Let X be its set of clocks, then X_{inv} is the subset of clocks occurring in the invariant of some location of L. Given an edge $\bar{e} = \bar{\ell} \xrightarrow{g,\bar{a},R} \bar{\ell}'$, and a clock $x \in X$, we say that x is *redefined* by $\bar{e}$ if x is not reset by $\bar{e}$, and if the constraints $Inv(\overline{\ell})$ and $Inv(\overline{\ell'})$ are not equivalent w.r.t. x. We denote by *Redefined*$(\bar{e})$ the set of clocks redefined by $\bar{e}$. Given a clock $x \in X$, we say that x is *modified* by $\bar{e}$ if $x \in R(\bar{e}) \cup \mathit{Redefined}(\bar{e})$. This means that x has either been reset by one of the edges, or an invariant constraint over x has been redefined. Moreover, we say that x is *tested* by $\bar{e}$ if $x \in \mathit{Clocks}(g(\bar{e})) \cup X_{inv}$. This means that the clock x is either tested in one of the constraints, or used in some invariant of the NTA. It is worth noticing that we include here the whole set X_{inv}. This latter point will be discussed later. Finally, we note:

$$\begin{cases} \mathsf{Pre}(\overline{e}) = \{\ell_i \mid i \in I(\overline{e})\} \cup \{x \in X \mid x \text{ is modified by } \overline{e}\} \\ \mathsf{Read}(\overline{e}) = \{x \in X \mid x \text{ is tested but not modified by } \overline{e}\} \\ \mathsf{Post}(\overline{e}) = \{\ell_i' \mid i \in I(\overline{e})\} \cup \{x \in X \mid x \text{ is modified by } \overline{e}\} \end{cases}$$

3 Unfoldings of NTA

3.1 Untimed Nets

We first define the untimed structures we use. These are classical structures defined e.g. in [17,13], extended with read arcs [21,22]. Even if read arcs do not add expressiveness to (untimed) Petri nets (w.r.t. reachability), they improve quite a lot unfolding techniques, since they increase the concurrency relation between events. However, their unfolding is more involved.

Definition 4 (Read Arc Petri Net). *A* read arc Petri net *is a tuple* $\mathcal{N} = (P, T, \mathit{Pre}, \mathit{Post}, \mathit{Read}, M_0)$ *where P is a (finite) set of* places, *T is a (finite) set of* transitions *with $P \cap T = \emptyset$, Pre, Post and Read are three mappings from T to 2^P called resp.* backward, forward *and* read *incidence mapping. Finally, $M_0 \in 2^P$ is the* initial *marking.*

The untimed structure associated with the unfolding of a NTA is a particular kind of read arc Petri net. Before giving the structure, we first define precedence, strong precedence and conflict relations between nodes of a net. We first give some notation. Let t be a transition and p be a place of a net $\mathcal{N} = (P, T, \mathsf{Pre}, \mathsf{Post}, \mathsf{Read}, M_0)$:

- ${}^\bullet t$ denotes the set $\mathsf{Pre}(t)$, $t^\bullet$ denotes the set $\mathsf{Post}(t)$, ${}^\circ t$ denotes the set $\mathsf{Read}(t)$,
- ${}^\bullet p$ denotes the set $\{t' \in T \mid p \in t'^\bullet\}$, $p^\bullet$ denotes the set $\{t' \in T \mid p \in {}^\bullet t'\}$.

We extend the notation to set of nodes as usual. We now define relations between nodes:

- Let $<$ (the *precedence relation*) be the minimal transitive relation over $P \cup T$ satisfying for every $t, t' \in T$, for every $p \in P$,
  if $p \in {}^\bullet t$ then $p < t$, if $t \in {}^\bullet p$ then $t < p$, if $p \in {}^\circ t$ and $p \in t'^\bullet$ then $t' < t$.
  We denote $\leq$ the reflexive closure of $<$.

- Let $\prec$ (the *stong precedence relation*) be the minimal transitive relation over $P \cup T$ satisfying for every $t, t' \in T$, for every $p \in P$, and for every nodes x and y, if $x < y$ then $x \prec y$, if $p \in {}^\circ t$ and $p \in {}^\bullet t'$ then $t \prec t'$.
  We denote $\preceq$ the reflexive closure of $\prec$.
- Let $\#$ (the *conflict relation*) be defined by $x \# y$ iff $\exists p \in P,\ \exists t, t' \in p^\bullet$ s.t. $t \neq t' \wedge t \leq x \wedge t' \leq y$.

These definitions are those given in [22] which are a slight variant of those in [21].

Definition 5 (Occurrence Net). *An* occurrence net *is a net* $\mathcal{N} = (P, T, \mathsf{Pre}, \mathsf{Post}, \mathsf{Read}, M_0)$ *fulfilling the following conditions.* $|{}^\bullet p| \leq 1$ *for every* $p \in P$. *The precedence relation* $<$ *of* $\mathcal{N}$ *is a finitary partial order (*i.e. *every item of* $P \cup T$ *has a finite number of predecessors). For every item* $x \in P \cup T$, *the strong precedence relation restricted to the set of predecessors of* x *w.r.t.* $<$ *is a partial order. No element is in conflict with itself.* $M_0 = \mathit{Min}(P)$, *where* $\mathit{Min}(P)$ *denotes the set* $\{p \mid {}^\bullet p = \emptyset\}$.

In an occurrence net, elements of P are called *conditions* and elements of T *events*. We define the branching process associated with an NTA as a labeled occurrence net:

Definition 6 (Branching Process of an NTA). *Let* $\mathcal{A}$ *be the* NTA *given as a family* $(\mathcal{A}_i)_{1\leq i\leq n}$ *of* n TA *and an* n*-ary function* f. *A* branching process *of* $\mathcal{A}$ *is defined as a pair of an occurrence net* $\mathcal{N} = (P, T, \mathsf{Pre}, \mathsf{Post}, \mathsf{Read}, M_0)$ *and a labeling function* λ *ranging over* $P \cup T$ *such that:*

- $\lambda(P) \subseteq \bigcup_{1\leq i\leq n}(L_i \cup X_i)$ *(conditions correspond to locations or clocks of* $\mathcal{A}$*),*
- $\lambda(T) \subseteq \mathit{Sync}$ *(events correspond to possible transitions of* $\mathcal{A}$*),*
- λ *is a one-to-one mapping from* M_0 *to* $\bigcup_{1\leq i\leq n} \ell_{i,0} \cup X$ *(initially, the marking consists in initial locations plus the clocks),*
- *for every element* $t \in T$ *with* $\lambda(t) = \bar{e} \in \mathit{Sync}$, λ *is a one-to-one mapping from* ${}^\bullet t$ *(resp.* ${}^\circ t$, $t^\bullet$*) to* $\mathsf{Pre}(\bar{e})$ *(resp. to* $\mathsf{Read}(\bar{e})$, $\mathsf{Post}(\bar{e})$*).*
- $\forall t, t' \in T,\ \lambda(t) = \lambda(t') \wedge {}^\bullet t = {}^\bullet t' \wedge {}^\circ t = {}^\circ t' \Rightarrow t = t'$ *(no redundancy)*

We use read-arcs in our unfoldings for increasing the concurrency relation between events: indeed, when firing a transition, there is no need to create a new place for a clock which is not modified, that's thus relevant to test its value using a read-arc, and not a pre-arc.

In [21,22], a prefix relation is defined between branching processes of an NTA and it is shown that these processes form a complete lattice w.r.t. this relation which implies that there is a maximal branching process. The branching processes differ on "how much they unfold". The *untimed unfolding of an* NTA is defined as its maximal branching process.

Example 1. An example of branching process is depicted on Figure 1. Conditions are represented by circles, and events by boxes, as usual for Petri nets. Labels are written close to the nodes. A read arc is represented by an arc with no arrow (for instance there is a read arc from the top-most condition labeled x to the top-most event labeled a_1: for being fired, event a_1 will check that there is a token in condition x, since x is involved in an invariant). The dashed part of the branching process represents an event that will be considered by our algorithm but whose timing constraints are unconsistent, and thus which will not be built (see Subsection 3.2).

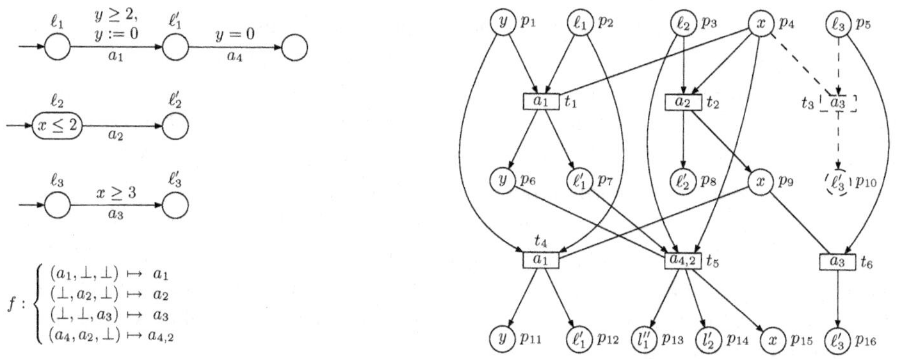

(a) A NTA $\mathcal{A}$ (b) A branching process of $\mathcal{A}$

Fig. 1. An example of branching process of an NTA

We introduce more or less classical notions concerning branching processes. Note that these definitions take into account read arcs.

Definition 7 (Non-branching Process, Configuration, Cut, Causal Past). *Let $\beta = (\mathcal{N}, \lambda)$ be a branching process of an NTA $\mathcal{A}$. We write T (resp. P) for the set of events (resp. of conditions) of $\mathcal{N}$. We consider the occurrence net $(P', T') \subseteq (P, T)$ obtained as a restriction $\mathcal{N}'$ of $\mathcal{N}$, and the labeling function λ' defined as the restriction of λ to $\mathcal{N}'$. Then $\beta' = (\mathcal{N}', \lambda')$ is called a* non-branching process *of β if it satisfies the five following conditions:*

- $\forall t \in T, \forall p \in {}^\bullet t \cup {}^\circ t \cup t^\bullet, t \in T' \Rightarrow p \in P'$ *(events are consistent with β),*
- $\forall p \in P, \forall t \in {}^\bullet p, p \in P' \Rightarrow t \in T'$ *(conditions are consistent with β),*
- *Relation $\prec$ restricted to $P' \cup T'$ is a partial order,*
- $\forall x, y \in P' \cup T', \neg(x \# y)$ *($\mathcal{N}'$ is conflict-free),*
- $Min(P') = Min(P)$.

We fix a non-branching process β'. The configuration *C of β' is the set of events of β'. A set of conditions is a* co-set *if it is an antichain w.r.t. $\prec$ in β'* (i.e. *where items are pairwise incomparable). A* cut *is a maximal co-set. If C is the configuration of β', we associate with C the cut $Cut(C)$ defined by $Cut(C) = (Min(P) \cup C^\bullet) \setminus {}^\bullet C$. We also define the cut of a non-branching process as the cut of its configuration.*

Given a non-branching process β' of β, and an event t belonging to β', we denote $[t]_{\beta'}$ the causal past *of t relative to β' defined as the set of events $\{t' \in T' \mid t' \preceq t\}$. The minimal causal past* [2] *of t, denoted $[t]$, is $\bigcap_{\beta'} [t]_{\beta'}$ where β' ranges over the set of non-branching processes of β containing t. $[t]$ is a configuration and we denote by β_t its associated non branching process.*

Finally, we say that a non-branching process β^+ extends a non-branching process β, denoted by $\beta \sqsubseteq \beta^+$ if the events of β are events of β^+ and if given any event t of β and any event t^+ of $\beta^+ \setminus \beta$, we do not have $t^+ \prec t$ in β^+.

[2] Note that $[t]$ may be inductively defined by $[t] = \{t\} \cup \bigcup_{t' \in {}^\bullet({}^\bullet t \cup {}^\circ t)} [t']$. Due to the lattice structure of branching processes of a read arc Petri net, $[t]$ does not depend on β.

Example 1 continued. Let β be the branching process of Figure 1. Then the subgraph underlied by nodes $\{p_i\}_{i=1..9} \cup \{t_1, t_2\}$ is a non branching process (say β'); its associated configuration is $\{t_1, t_2\} = [t_2]_{\beta'} \neq [t_2] = \{t_2\}$. Let β_1 (resp. β_2) be the non branching process corresponding to $\{t_1, t_2, t_3\}$ (resp. $\{t_1, t_2, t_6\}$). Then $\beta' \subseteq \beta_i$ for $i = 1, 2$ and $\beta' \sqsubseteq \beta_2$ but $\beta' \not\sqsubseteq \beta_1$ due to the arc between p_4 and t_3 (implying $t_3 \prec t_2$).

Important remark. It is worth noticing that if C is a configuration of an NTA, the set $Cut(C) \cap \lambda^{-1}(X)$ is in bijection (by λ) with the set X of clocks of the NTA and that λ maps the set $Cut(C) \cap \lambda^{-1}(L)$ to a set consisting of one location per TA of the NTA. Indeed, each time a clock place is consumed, it is produced back and each time a place whose label is a location of a TA is consumed another place whose label is a location of the same TA is produced.

We use the notation of [21] to present the (semi-)algorithm (Algorithm 1.) for the construction of the untimed unfolding of an NTA. In the algorithm, a condition of the unfolding is encoded as a pair (p, t) where p is the label of this condition, and t is the unique input event of this condition (t equals to $\emptyset$ if the condition has an empty preset). An event is represented with three fields $(\bar{e}, Y_{in}, Y_r)$ where $\bar{e}$ is the label of this event (a synchronized edge), Y_{in} and Y_r are two lists of pointers to conditions (respectively the input and read conditions).

Definition 8 (Possible Extensions (PE)). *Let $\beta = (\mathcal{N}, \lambda)$ be a branching process of an NTA $\mathcal{A}$. The* possible extensions *of β are the triples $t = (\bar{e}, Y_{in}, Y_r)$ where $\bar{e}$ is an element of Sync such that there exists a non branching process β' with $Y_{in} \cup Y_r$ being a co-set of β', such that λ is a one-to-one mapping from Y_{in} (resp. Y_r) to Pre$(\bar{e})$ (resp. Read$(\bar{e})$), and such that $(\bar{e}, Y_{in}, Y_r)$ does not already belong to β.*

In this case, we define the extension of β by t, obtained by the operation Extend(β, t) as the branching process β' obtained from β by adding an event labeled by $\bar{e}$, connected to conditions in Y_{in} with pre-arcs and to conditions in Y_r with read arcs, and with new conditions, according to Post$(\bar{e})$.

Algorithm 1. Building the (eventually infinite) untimed unfolding (semi-algorithm)

Require: An NTA $\mathcal{A}$.
Ensure: The unfolding *Unf* of $\mathcal{A}$.

```
Unf := {(ℓ_{1,0}, ∅), ..., (ℓ_{n,0}, ∅)} ∪ {(x, ∅) | x ∈ X};      (Initialization)
pe := PE(Unf);                                                     (Possible Extensions)
while pe ≠ ∅ do
    Choose an event t = (ē, Y_in, Y_r) in pe.                      (ē is the label of t)
    Extend(Unf, t);
    pe := PE(Unf);
end while
```

3.2 Adding Timing Constraints to the Untimed Unfolding

Our objective is to add timing information in the untimed structure described before for getting a new symbolic representation of the set of timed sequences of an NTA.

This will also reduce the size of the untimed structure, by removing extensions with unfeasible timed part (see the dashed part of Example 1).

Timed executions. In order to define and compute the timed unfolding of an NTA, we first add time to a non-branching process. We associate an absolute date, written $\mathbf{d}$, with every event corresponding to its occurrence and two or three dates with every condition. The first one corresponds to its production (or birth), written $\mathbf{d_b}$. The second date corresponds to the consumption (or end) of the condition (it may be $+\infty$), written $\mathbf{d_e}$. A third date is associated with a condition corresponding to a clock, and represents the date at which the clock has been reset the last time (written $\mathbf{d_r}$).

Definition 9 (Timed Valuation of a Non-branching Process). *Let β be a branching process, and β' a non-branching process of β. A* timed valuation *of β' is a mapping $\mathbf{d}$ from T' to $\mathbb{R}_{\geq 0}$, a mapping $\mathbf{d_b}$ from P' to $\mathbb{R}_{\geq 0}$, a mapping $\mathbf{d_e}$ from P' to $\mathbb{R}_{\geq 0} \cup \{+\infty\}$ and a mapping $\mathbf{d_r}$ from $P' \cap \lambda^{-1}(X)$ to $\mathbb{R}_{\geq 0}$.*

We want to characterize the timed valuations of a non-branching process corresponding to a real timed execution of the NTA. In order to obtain such a characterization, we introduce some additional notation. Let t be an event, $\mathcal{C}^+(t)$ (resp. $\mathcal{C}^-(t)$) is the cut corresponding to configuration $[t]$ (resp. $[t]\setminus\{t\}$). We denote by $L(t) = \mathcal{C}^-(t) \cap \lambda^{-1}(L)$. Given a clock x, there is a unique place p_x^+ (resp. p_x^-) in cut $\mathcal{C}^+(t)$ (resp. $\mathcal{C}^-(t)$) whose label is x. Given a timed valuation of a non-branching process including t, we note $v(t)_x = \mathbf{d}(t) - \mathbf{d_r}(p_x^-)$ and $v'(t)_x = \mathbf{d}(t) - \mathbf{d_r}(p_x^+)$.

Definition 10 (Feasibility of a Timed Valuation). *Let β be a branching process of an NTA, and β' a non-branching process of β. A* timed valuation $(\mathbf{d}, \mathbf{d_b}, \mathbf{d_e}, \mathbf{d_r})$ *of β' is* feasible *iff it satisfies the following (in)equations: for every $t \in T'$,*

Causal (in)equations:	*Timed (in)equations:*
- $\forall p \in t^\bullet$, $\mathbf{d_b}(p) = \mathbf{d}(t)$	- $g(\lambda(t))[\{x \leftarrow v(t)_x\}_{x\in X}]$
- $\forall p \in {}^\bullet t$, $\mathbf{d_e}(p) = \mathbf{d}(t)$	- $\bigwedge_{\ell \in L(t)} \mathit{Inv}(\ell)[\{x \leftarrow v(t)_x\}_{x\in X}]$
- $\forall p \in {}^\circ t$, $\mathbf{d_b}(p) \leq \mathbf{d}(t) \leq \mathbf{d_e}(p)$	- $\bigwedge_{x\in R(\lambda(t))} v'(t)_x = 0$
- $\forall p \in P'$, $\mathbf{d_b}(p) \leq \mathbf{d_e}(p)$	- $\bigwedge_{x \in \mathit{Redefined}(\lambda(t))} v'(t)_x = v(t)_x$
- $\forall p \in \mathit{Min}(P')$, $\mathbf{d_b}(p) = \mathbf{d_r}(p) = 0$	

Definition 11. *Let $\mathcal{A}$ be an NTA and σ a timed sequence of $\mathcal{A}$. Its* timed non-branching process *$(\beta, \mathbf{d}, \mathbf{d_b}, \mathbf{d_e}, \mathbf{d_r})$ is inductively defined as follows:*

- *If σ is the empty sequence then β is $\mathit{Min}(P)$, $\forall p \in \mathit{Min}(P)$, $\mathbf{d_b}(p) = 0$, $\mathbf{d_e}(p) = \infty$, and for every $p \in \mathit{Min}(P) \cap \lambda^{-1}(X)$, $\mathbf{d_r}(p) = 0$.*
- *If $\sigma = \sigma'(\bar{e}, d)$ (d represents the date of the occurrence of $\bar{e}$) and $(\beta', \mathbf{d}', \mathbf{d_b}', \mathbf{d_e}', \mathbf{d_r}')$ is the timed non-branching process of σ' then, denoting $\mathcal{C}$ the cut associated with β', there is a unique possible extension of β' from $\mathcal{C}$ by an event t labeled by $\bar{e}$. β is this extension.*
  - *The timed valuation on places and transitions of β' is preserved except for the places $p \in {}^\bullet t$, for which we set $\mathbf{d_e}(p) = d$.*
  - *We set $\mathbf{d}(t) = d$, and for every place $p \in t^\bullet$, we set $\mathbf{d_b}(p) = d$ and $\mathbf{d_e}(p) = \infty$.*
  - *If $p \in t^\bullet$ is s.t. $\lambda(p) = x \in X$, if x is reset by e, we set $\mathbf{d_r}(p) = d$; otherwise let p' be the unique place of $\mathcal{C}$ whose label is x, then $\mathbf{d_r}(p) = \mathbf{d_r}(p')$.*

The next proposition shows the close relation between timed sequences and feasible timed non-branching processes, *i.e.* admitting a feasible timed valuation.

Proposition 1 (Feasibility is Equivalent to Execution). *Let $\mathcal{A}$ be an NTA. Then:*

1. *If σ is a timed sequence of $\mathcal{A}$ then its timed non-branching process is feasible.*
2. *If β is a non-branching process of $\mathcal{A}$ and $(\mathbf{d}, \mathbf{d_b}, \mathbf{d_e}, \mathbf{d_r})$ a feasible time valuation of β, then there is a timed sequence σ of $\mathcal{A}$ whose timed non-branching process is $(\beta, \mathbf{d}, \mathbf{d_b}, \mathbf{d_e}, \mathbf{d_r})$.*

We obtain as a corollary that the set of configurations obtained after firing a shuffle of concurrent transitions is a zone, a result also proved in [3] by other means.

The proof of this proposition (see [8]) heavily relies on the way invariants are handled: since transitions are connected by read arcs or pre arcs to a single condition per clock involved in some invariant, two concurrent transitions *must share these conditions and be connected to them by a read arc*. Thus, given an event t of the non-branching process β of σ, the satisfaction of the invariant constraint by t in σ is equivalent to the satisfaction of the invariant equation in $\lceil t \rceil$. If an event t is not firable in $\lceil t \rceil$ (its non-branching process β is not feasible) then it is firable in no extension of β. We illustrate this point in Example 1. Every event is connected to one place labeled by x by a read arc. Since the firing of a_2 redefines the invariant on clock x, there are two places labeled by x. This leads to two different occurrences of a_1 and a_3, depending on their ordering with a_2, which are necessary since they yield different behaviors. Firing a_3 before a_2 is unfeasible (see the dashed event), whereas a_3 is firable after a_2 with the constraint $x = y \wedge x \geq 3$. For a_1, we get similarly different timing constraints over clocks x and y.

Remark. It is worth noticing that we could increase slightly the locality of events by restricting connections to invariants clocks. Indeed, given a global edge $\bar{e}$, we could perform an offline untimed analysis of the system to restrict the possible set of undetermined locations, thus restricting the set of invariants to consider. That way to proceed would be similar to the method of *active* clocks [11].

Symbolic representation of timed executions. If we interpret the dates of a non-branching process β as variables and the (in)equations of Definition 10 as a system of linear inequations, we obtain a zone, denoted $Eq(\beta)$. As stated by Proposition 1, this zone characterizes the set of timed sequences of β and β admits a timed sequence iff $Eq(\beta)$ is satisfiable. The set of variables of $Eq(\beta)$ is $\{\mathbf{d}(t) \mid t \in T\} \cup \{\mathbf{d_b}(p), \mathbf{d_e}(p) \mid p \in P\} \cup \{\mathbf{d_r}(p) \mid p \in P \cap \lambda^{-1}(X)\}$, whose size is larger than that of β. Since the complexity of operations on zones heavily depends on the number of variables, we will reduce the number of variables as much as possible. We thus keep only variables which are necessary to decide whether one can extend the non-branching process. To this aim, we state the following proposition, which is a key ingredient to compute incrementally timed feasibility of non-branching processes, and whose proof follows by examining the inequations of Definition 10.

Proposition 2. *Let β, β^+ be non-branching processes of some NTA such that $\beta \sqsubseteq \beta^+$, let C be the cut associated with β. We partition the variables of $Eq(\beta^+)$ into three sets: V_C the variables associated with places of C, V^- the variables of $Eq(\beta)$ different* *from* $V_{\mathcal{C}}$ *and* V^+ *the remaining variables. Then* $Eq(\beta^+)$ *can be decomposed as the conjunction* $Eq(\beta) \wedge Eq'(\beta^+ \setminus \beta)$*, where the set of variables of* $Eq(\beta^+)$ *(resp.* $Eq(\beta)$ *and* $Eq'(\beta^+ \setminus \beta)$*) is the disjoint union* $V^- \cup V_{\mathcal{C}} \cup V^+$ *(resp.* $V^- \cup V_{\mathcal{C}}$ *and* $V_{\mathcal{C}} \cup V^+$*).*

Given a non-branching process β, we now define the zone Z_β as the zone $\exists V^-.Eq(\beta)$, with the notation of Proposition 2. If t is an event, Z_t denotes Z_{β_t}. By previous proposition, the set of variables of Z_t is equal to $V_{\mathcal{C}}$. We have $V_{\mathcal{C}} = \{\mathbf{d_b}(p), \mathbf{d_e}(p) \mid p \in \mathcal{C}\} \cup \{\mathbf{d_r}(p) \mid p \in \mathcal{C} \cap \lambda^{-1}(X)\}$, where $\mathcal{C}$ denotes the cut *Cut*$([t])$ (note that variable $\mathbf{d}(t)$ has been eliminated). It is worth noticing that the size[3] of $V_{\mathcal{C}}$ is equal to $2n + 3|X|$.

Timed unfolding. We can now propose a (semi-)algorithm, namely Algorithm 2., which builds the (possibly infinite) timed unfolding of an NTA such that an event occurs in the unfolding iff there is at least one timed sequence whose branching process includes this event. This algorithm is an extension of Algorithm 1., in which we associate with each event t of the unfolding the zone Z_t defined above. By previous study, we thus add the event t if and only if Z_t admits a solution (line 6). If Z is a zone, we write $\langle Z \rangle$ for the set of valuations satisfying Z. We also need to record the possible extensions already considered but leading to empty zones (line 7). The remaining point is the computation of the zone Z_t (line 5).

Algorithm 2. Building the (eventually infinite) timed unfolding (semi-algorithm)

Require: An NTA $\mathcal{A}$.
Ensure: The timed unfolding *T-Unf*$(\mathcal{A})$ of $\mathcal{A}$.

1: *T-Unf* $:= \{(\ell_{1,0}, \emptyset), \ldots, (\ell_{n,0}, \emptyset)\} \cup \{(x, \emptyset) \mid x \in X\}$;
2: *pe* $:= PE($*T-Unf*$)$;
3: **while** *pe* $\neq \emptyset$ **do**
4:     Choose an event $t = (\bar{e}, X, Y)$ in *pe*.
5:     Compute the zone Z_t associated with the firing of t
6:     **if** $\langle Z_t \rangle \neq \emptyset$ **then** $Extend($*T-Unf*$, t)$; *pe* $:= PE($*T-Unf*$)$;
7:         **else** Mark t as useless event. **end if**   (In order to not consider t again)
8: **end while**

Since we do not keep the entire equation system of the non-branching process yielding an event t but only a projection of it, the computation of a new zone Z_t is a difficult task. To solve this problem, we compute additional zones associated with intermediate non branching processes. A first remark is that given the zone Z_β corresponding to some non-branching process β, and an extension β^+ of β consisting of a set of concurrent events, it is easy to compute the zone $Z_{\beta+}$, simply by applying Definition 10 (see [8]).

Let T be the set of maximal events of configuration $C = [t] \setminus \{t\}$ and β_T be the non branching process associated with C. Using previous remark, it is easy, given the zone Z_T corresponding to β_T, to compute the zone Z_t. Our goal is thus to compute Z_T. Let $t_0 \in C$. A topological sort of $C \setminus [t_0]$ w.r.t. $\prec$ gives sets of concurrent events, which we call “slices”. If we can apply the previous remark from β_{t_0} to these successive

[3] We obtain the bound claimed in the introduction.

slices, then we can compute iteratively, for each of these slices, the zone resulting from the firing of a slice, and thus get the desired zone. To apply the remark, the different intermediate non-branching processes have to extend each other. Because of read arcs, given a non-branching process β and an event $t' \in \beta$, this may be the case that β does not extend $\beta_{t'}$. This happens exactly when $[t']_\beta \setminus [t'] \neq \emptyset$. In this case, a transition t'' of this difference set reads a place belonging to $\beta' \setminus Cut(\beta')$. Using this characterization, we can compute correctly the initial event t_0. The previous discussion is formalized in [8], providing an algorithm for the computation of the zone Z_t.

As a direct consequence of the previous developments, we obtain the following theorem, which states properties of our (infinite) timed unfolding.

Theorem 1. *Algorithm 2. is correct: if $\mathcal{A}$ is an* NTA*, an event t occurs in the timed unfolding T-Unf($\mathcal{A}$) iff there is at least one timed sequence whose non-branching process is β_t, and Z_t is the set of possible values for the variables associated with $Cut([t])$ obtained by timed sequences whose non-branching process is β_t.*

4 Algorithm for the Construction of a Finite Prefix

The construction of a complete finite prefix for read arcs Petri nets is much more involved that in classical Petri nets. It has been first studied in [21] where the problem is solved for a subclass of read arcs Petri nets, and a solution for the general class has then been proposed in [22]. All the algorithms rely on the detection of *cut-off events*: the cut obtained from every non-branching process including a cut-off event can be obtained by a non-branching process built from another already computed event.

In the timed framework, we must take into account the zones associated with the cut-off event and the previously computed event for checking whether the current cut-off event is redundant also w.r.t. timing constraints. In the context of TA, it is well-known that there are infinitely many incomparable zones. Thus, an *extrapolation* operator has been designed, which bounds the number of zones which can be computed. This extrapolation is an over-approximation, but is correct for checking reachability properties [6].

However, to compare the configurations reached by two non-branching processes $[t]$ and $[t']$, we cannot use directly the zones Z_t and $Z_{t'}$ computed in the previous section: indeed, the (unbounded) dates of occurrence of t and t' are irrelevant w.r.t. to the corresponding configurations reached in the NTA. Thus, we compute from zone Z_t a new zone corresponding to the possible valuations of the clocks reached in the NTA after firing all possible timed sequences corresponding to the non-branching process of $[t]$. To enforce termination, we then apply the classical extrapolation operator on this last zone and get the so-called *clock zone* $Test_t$. Unfortunately, two events whose clock zones and cuts are identical can lead to different processes: indeed, it must be noticed that a configuration $[t]$ may be extended by an event t' whose timed occurrence precedes the one of t! This may occur if the new event added t' is concurrent with t. Then, the date of t' may be smaller than that of t, which implies that classical extrapolation may induce mistakes, and thus that we can no more "forget the past" by comparing only clock zones and cuts. We will thus use a subclass of *synchronized events*, which have the desired property of "forgettable past". Indeed, when an event t synchronizes all the TA of an NTA $\mathcal{A}$, the timing occurrences of all events extending configuration $[t]$ will follow the one of t. This is the key ingredient which enables us to obtain a finite prefix, see Lemma 2. Note that this observation is quite similar to the one of [16] (operator \$). Note also that our algorithm avoids using the sophisticated algorithm of [22]. We now define an *unavoidable* subset of edges of an NTA.

Definition 12. *Let $\mathcal{A} = ((\mathcal{A}_i)_{1 \leq i \leq n}, f)$ be an NTA and E' be a subset of global edges of $\mathcal{A}$ (i.e. a subset of Sync), then E' is* unavoidable *iff for every i, every circuit of the underlying graph of $\mathcal{A}_i$ intersects E': there is some e_i belonging to the circuit such that if e_i occurs in $\bar{e} \in Sync$ then $\bar{e} \in E'$.*

Obviously, any NTA has at least one *unavoidable* subset of edges. However the efficiency of the method will depend on two characteristics of the selected subset: its size and the *synchronization factor* of its edges (*i.e.* $|I(\bar{e})|$). Now we transform the NTA in such a way that when one fires an edge of E', one synchronizes the whole NTA.

Definition 13. *Let $\mathcal{A} = ((\mathcal{A}_i)_{1 \leq i \leq n}, f)$ and E' be an unavoidable set of edges, then*

- *if $\bar{e} \in E'$, its synchronized version is $Sync(\bar{e}) = \{\bar{e'} \mid \forall i \in I(\bar{e}),\ e'_i = e_i \text{ and } \forall i \notin I(\bar{e}),\ \exists \ell_i \in L_i \text{ s.t. } e'_i = idle(\ell_i)\}$ with $idle(\ell_i) = \ell_i \xrightarrow{true,\varepsilon,\emptyset} \ell_i$.*
- *$\mathcal{A}(E')$ is the NTA where E' has been replaced by $\bigcup_{\bar{e} \in E'} Sync(\bar{e})$.*

Note that $\mathcal{A}(E')$ is not defined *via* a synchronization function but directly with its set of edges. However all previous results equally apply on such NTA. Note also that $\mathcal{A}$ and $\mathcal{A}(E')$ have the same set of (finite or infinite) timed sequences with the same intermediate configurations and so any property expressible in terms of these extended timed sequences is equivalent for $\mathcal{A}$ and $\mathcal{A}(E')$. This is in particular the case for reachability, and event occurrence which are the usual properties checked by the unfolding method. Note that if for all $\bar{e} \in E'$, $I(\bar{e}) = \{1, \ldots, n\}$ then $\mathcal{A}(E') = \mathcal{A}$.

Let us now explain how we build the finite prefix of the timed unfolding of $\mathcal{A}(E')$ (Algorithm 3., page 304). When we fire a synchronized event t, we build the clock zone $Test_t$ as follows. We project the last zone (corresponding to Z_t of the previous section before elimination of variable $\mathbf{d}(t)$) over the variables $\mathbf{d}(t)$ and $\{\mathbf{d_r}(p) \mid p \in Cut([t]) \cap \lambda^{-1}(X)\}$. Then we relativise the result w.r.t. variable $\mathbf{d}(t)$, *i.e.* we replace variables $\mathbf{d_r}(p)$ by $\mathbf{d}(t) - \mathbf{d_r}(p)$, and we eliminate variable $\mathbf{d}(t)$. We note W_t this new zone.

Lemma 1. *The zone W_t corresponds to the set of valuations v such that there exists a timed sequence whose non-branching process β_t, and such that in $\mathcal{A}(E')$, the clock valuation after having fired the above timed sequence is v.*

We close zone W_t by time elapsing and intersect it with the invariant specified by $Cut([t])$, *i.e.* the conjunction of invariants of locations appearing in $Cut([t])$. At last we extrapolate the result, yielding the zone $Test_t$. We then check whether there exists a synchronized event $t' \lhd t$ [4] with $\lambda(Cut([t'])) = \lambda(Cut([t]))$ and $\langle Test_t \rangle \subseteq \langle Test_{t'} \rangle$. If this is the case, we mark t as useless and we do not produce its output places.

---

[4] $\lhd$ denotes an *adequate order*, as required by [13,17] for proving completeness of the finite prefix construction. A possible such order is $Card([t']) < Card([t])$.

It is worth noticing that diagonal constraints appearing in zones Z_t do not induce wrong extrapolation results as in timed automata using diagonal constraints [6]. Indeed, the zones $Test_t$ are related to the NTA $\mathcal{A}(E')$, which does not have diagonal constraints, the extrapolation operator can thus safely be used.

Algorithm 3. Building a finite and complete prefix of the timed unfolding

Require: An NTA $\mathcal{A}$.
Ensure: A finite and complete prefix *Fin* of *T-Unf*($\mathcal{A}$).

$Fin := \{(\ell_{1,0}, \emptyset), \ldots, (\ell_{n,0}, \emptyset)\} \cup \{(x, \emptyset) \mid x \in X\}$; $pe := PE(Fin)$;
while $pe \neq \emptyset$ **do**
  Choose an event $t = (\bar{e}, Y_{in}, Y_r)$ in pe.
  if t is not a synchronized event **then**
    Compute the zone Z_t associated with the firing of t
    if $\langle Z_t \rangle \neq \emptyset$ **then** $Extend(Fin, t)$; $pe := PE(Fin)$;
      else Mark t as useless event; **end if** (In order to not consider t again)
  else (t is a synchronized event)
    Compute the extrapolated zone $Test_t$ of clock values.
    if $\exists$ a synchronized event $t' \lhd t \mid \lambda(Cut([t'])) = \lambda(Cut([t])) \wedge \langle Test_t \rangle \subseteq \langle Test_{t'} \rangle$ **then**
      Mark t as useless event. (In order to not consider t again)
    else if $\langle Z_t \rangle \neq \emptyset$ **then** $Extend(Fin, t)$; $pe := PE(Fin)$;
      else Mark t as useless event; **end if** (In order to not consider t again)
  end if
end while

Synchronized events enjoy the following nice property, proved in [8].

Lemma 2 (Forgettable Past of Synchronized Events). *Let t be a synchronized event of a branching process of an NTA. It is equivalent to extend β_t and to build a non-branching process from Cut([t]) with constraints on variables $\{\mathbf{d_r}(p) \mid p \in Cut([t]) \cap \lambda^{-1}(X)\}$ given by $Test_t$.*

Finally the following theorem states the termination and soundness of Algorithm 3..

Theorem 2. *Algorithm 3. terminates and the computed finite prefix Fin is such that: (1) a transition t can become firable in $\mathcal{A}(E')$ iff an event labeled by t occurs in Fin; (2) a configuration is reachable in $\mathcal{A}(E')$ iff an equivalent configuration (w.r.t. strong time bisimulation) is reachable by a timed sequence whose non-branching process is included in Fin.*

We have thus constructed for any NTA $\mathcal{A}$ a finite prefix which is complete for checking reachability properties, and transition enabling.

5 Related Work

Partial order method for TA with ample sets. During the state exploration, partial-order methods select a subset of transitions rather than developping all the state successors. This subset, called an *ample* set, fulfills some properties relying on an independence relation between transitions (see [19] for more details). Thus the efficiency of these methods is closely related to the size of the independence relation. So introducing time (and its implicit synchronizations) will necessarily restrict the corresponding relation for the associated untimed model. In [4,18], the authors define an alternative semantics for NTA based on local time elapsing. Despite the fact that this semantics allows more behaviours than the standard semantics, the reachability relation associated with the usual semantics can be checked on the system corresponding to the new one. Moreover, the independence relation is enlarged when considering local time elapsing. Clearly, the efficiency of this method depends on two opposite factors: local time semantics generate more states but the independence relation restricts the exploration.

Partial order method for TA with Mazurkiewicz trace. In [16], the independence between transitions of a TA are exploited in a different way: the occurrences of two independent transitions do no need to be ordered (and consequently nor the occurrences of the clock resets). Thus a symbolic state in this framework is defined by a location and constraints between variables related to both the clock resets and the transition occurrences. When two sequences ab and ba are developped from a state with a and b independent, they will lead to the same symbolic state whereas with the ordinary construction they would generally yield two different states. However this method does not exploit the independence relation for limiting the exploration.

Partial order method for time Petri nets with ample (or stubborn) sets. In Petri nets, ample sets are denoted as stubborn sets [20]. Stubborn sets are similar to ample sets but their definition takes advantage of the "locality" of the firing rule. In [23], the authors generalise this concept to time Petri nets (TPN) calling it *a ready set* and applying it to the class graph construction of [5] where a class is similar to a symbolic state of a TA. Given a symbolic state, a ready set is a stubborn set with an additional constraint relative to the timing occurrences of enabled transitions. Thus the efficiency of the method depends on the weakness of the timing coupling between transitions.

Partial order method for TPNs with unfoldings. Depending on the Petri net to be analysed, the unfolding and stubborn set methods behave very differently. For instance, the former one outperforms the latter one when the net presents "confusion", (*i.e.* when the firing of a transition may influence the conflict set of another unrelated transition of the net). The generalisation of the unfoldings for TPNs has been developed by different searchers. First, in [2] the authors have studied the realisability of a non-branching process in a TPN showing that the temporal mechanism of these nets requires a global analysis of the process in order to check the firing of a transition in such a process. Starting from this analysis, [10] has recently designed a finite complete prefix for TPNs. In another direction, [15] proposes a method controlling the class graph construction with an unfolding of the untimed net. However this unfolding may be infinite whereas the TPN is bounded. In [14] the authors propose a discrete-time semantics for TPNs equivalent to the dense-time one w.r.t. reachability. The net include a special transition of the net modelling time elapsing but the occurrence of this transition in the unfolding requires a complete cut drastically decreasing the locality of the unfolding. Furthermore, this method suffers the combinatorial explosion related to the discrete time approach.

References

1. R. Alur and D. Dill. A theory of timed automata. *Theor. Comp. Sci.*, 126(2):183–235, 1994.
2. T. Aura and J. Lilius. A causal semantics for time Petri nets. *Theor. Comp. Sci.*, 243(1–2):409–447, 2000.
3. R. Ben Salah, M. Bozga, and O. Maler. On interleaving in timed automata. In *17th Int. Conf. Concur. Theory (CONCUR'06)*, LNCS 4137. Springer, 2006. To appear.
4. J. Bengtsson, B. Jonsson, J. Lilius, and W. Yi. Partial order reductions for timed systems. In *9th Int. Conf. Concur. Theory (CONCUR'98)*, LNCS 1466, 485–500. Springer, 1998.
5. B. Berthomieu and M. Diaz. Modeling and verification of time dependent systems using time Petri nets. *IEEE Trans. Softw. Engineering*, 17(3):259–273, 1991.
6. P. Bouyer. Forward analysis of updatable timed automata. *Formal Methods in Syst. Design*, 24(3):281–320, 2004.
7. P. Bouyer, S. Haddad, and P.-A. Reynier. Timed Petri nets and timed automata: On the discriminating power of Zeno sequences. In *33rd Int. Coll. Automata, Languages and Programming (ICALP'06)*, LNCS 4052, 420–431. Springer, 2006.
8. P. Bouyer, S. Haddad, and P.-A. Reynier. Timed unfoldings for networks of timed automata. Research Rep. LSV-06-09, Lab. Spécification et Vérification, ENS de Cachan, France, 2006.
9. Th. Chatain and C. Jard. Time supervision of concurrent systems using symbolic unfoldings of time Petri nets. In *3rd Int. Conf. Formal Modeling and Analysis of Timed Syst. (FORMATS'05)*, LNCS 3829, 196–210. Springer, 2005.
10. Th. Chatain and C. Jard. Complete finite prefixes of symbolic unfoldings of time Petri nets. In *27th Int. Conf. Appl. and Theory of Petri Nets (ICATPN'06)*, LNCS 4024, 125–145. Springer, 2006.
11. C. Daws and S. Tripakis. Model-checking of real-time reachability properties using abstractions. In *4th Int. Conf. Tools and Algo. for the Construction and Analysis of Syst. (TACAS'98)*, LNCS 1384, 313–329. Springer, 1998.
12. D. Dill. Timing assumptions and verification of finite-state concurrent systems. In *of the Work. Automatic Verification Methods for Finite State Systems (1989)*, LNCS 407, 197–212. Springer, 1990.
13. J. Esparza, S. Römer, and W. Vogler. An improvement of McMillan's unfolding algorithm. *Formal Methods in Syst. Design*, 20(3):285–310, 2002.
14. H. Fleischhack and C. Stehno. Computing a finite prefix of a time Petri net. In *23rd Int. Conf. Appl. and Theory of Petri Nets (ICATPN'02)*, LNCS 2369, 163–181. Springer, 2002.
15. J. Lilius. Efficient state space search for time Petri nets. ENTCS 18, 1998.
16. D. Lugiez, P. Niebert, and S. Zennou. A partial order semantics approach to the clock explosion problem of timed automata. In *10th Int. Conf. Tools and Algo. for the Construction and Analysis of Syst. (TACAS'04)*, LNCS 2988, 296–311. Springer, 2004.
17. K. McMillan. A technique of state space search based on unfolding. *Formal Methods in Syst. Design*, 6(1):45–65, 1995.
18. M. Minea. Partial order reduction for model checking of timed automata. In *10th Int. Conf. Concur. Theory (CONCUR'99)*, LNCS 1664, 431–446. Springer, 1999.
19. D. Peled. All from one, one for all: on model checking using representatives. In *5th Int. Conf. Computer Aided Verif. (CAV'93)*, LNCS 697, 409–423. Springer, 1993.
20. A. Valmari. Stubborn sets for reduced state space generation. In *10th Int. Conf. Appl. and Theory of Petri Nets (ICATPN'89)*, LNCS 483, 491–515. Springer, 1989.
21. W. Vogler, A. L. Semenov, and A. Yakovlev. Unfolding and finite prefix for nets with read arcs. In *9th Int. Conf. Concur. Theory (CONCUR'98)*, LNCS 1466, 501–516. Springer, 1998.
22. J. Winkowski. Reachability in contextual nets. *Fundam. Inform.*, 51(1-2):235–250, 2002.
23. T. Yoneda and B.-H. Schlingloff. Efficient verification of parallel real-time systems. *Formal Methods in Syst. Design*, 11(2):187–215, 1997.

Symbolic Unfoldings for Networks of Timed Automata

Franck Cassez[1,*], Thomas Chatain[2], and Claude Jard[3]

[1] CNRS/IRCCyN, Nantes, France
franck.cassez@cnrs.irccyn.fr
[2] IRISA/INRIA, Campus de Beaulieu, Rennes, France
Thomas.Chatain@irisa.fr
[3] IRISA/ENS Cachan, Campus de Kerlann, Bruz, France
Claude.Jard@irisa.fr

Abstract. In this paper we give a symbolic concurrent semantics for network of timed automata (NTA) in terms of *extended symbolic nets*. Extended symbolic nets are standard occurrence nets extended with *read arcs* and *symbolic constraints* on places and transitions. We prove that there is a *complete finite prefix* for any NTA that contains at least the information of the simulation graph of the NTA but keep explicit the notions of concurrency and causality of the network.

1 Introduction

Concurrent Semantics for Finite State Systems. The analysis of *distributed* or *concurrent* finite state systems has been dramatically improved thanks to *partial-order* methods (see e.g. [21]) that take advantage of the *independence* between actions, and to the *unfolding* based methods [11,16] that improve the partial order methods by taking advantage of the *locality* of actions.

Timed Systems. The main models that include timing information and are used to specify distributed timed systems are networks of timed automata (NTA) [1], and time Petri nets (TPN) [17]. There are a number of theoretical results about NTA and TPN and efficient tools to analyze them have been developed. Nevertheless the analysis of these models is always based on the exploration of a graph which is a single large automaton that produces the same behaviours as the NTA or the TPN; this induces an exponential blow up in the size of the system to be analysed.

Related Work. In [13,18], the authors define an alternative semantics for NTA based on local time elapsing. The efficiency of this method depends on two opposite factors: local time semantics generate more states but the independence relation restricts the exploration. In [15] (a generalization of [22]), the independence between transitions in a TA is exploited in a different way: the key observation is that the occurrences of two independent transitions do no need to be ordered and consequently nor do the occurrences of the clock resets. The relative drawback of the method is that, before their exploration, the symbolic states include more variables than the clock variables. Partial order methods for TPNs are studied in [20], where the authors generalize the concept

* Work supported by the project CORTOS, a program of the French government.

S. Graf and W. Zhang (Eds.): ATVA 2006, LNCS 4218, pp. 307–321, 2006.

of *stubborn set* to time Petri nets, calling it a *ready set*. They apply it to the *state class graph* construction of [5]. The efficiency of the method depends on whether the (dynamical) timing coupling between transitions is weak or not. Unfortunately the urgent semantics of this model entails a strong timing coupling. The previous *partial order* methods only take advantage of the independence of actions and not of any locality property. We are interested in a true concurrent semantics for NTA and this has not been developed in the aforementioned work.

Process semantics for time Petri nets which is a generalization of the unfolding semantics for time Petri nets has been developed by different researchers. From a semantical point of view, Aura and Lilius have studied in [19] the *realizability problem* of a non branching process in a TPN. They build an unfolding of the untimed Petri net underlying a safe TPN, and add constraints on the dates of occurrence of the events. It is then possible to check that a timed configuration is valid or not. In [12] the authors consider bounded TPN and a discrete time domain: the elapsing of one time unit is a special transition of the net. Thus the global synchronization related to this transition heavily decreases the locality property of the unfolding. Furthermore, when the intervals associated with the transitions involve large integers, this method suffers the usual combinatorial explosion related to the discrete time approach.

Section 3 of this paper can be viewed as the counterpart of the work of Aura and Lilius [19] in the framework of NTA: we define similar notions for NTA and build a *symbolic unfolding* which is a *symbolic net*. We have to extend the results of Aura and Lilius because there is no urgency for firing a transition[1] in a NTA. As stated in [19] those unfoldings are satisfactory for *free choice nets* which are a strict subclass of TPN. Our NTA are not free choice nets and in section 4 we refine our symbolic unfolding to obtain an *extended symbolic unfolding* which is a symbolic net with *read arcs*.

Following our recent approach [9] using the notion of symbolic unfolding to capture the partial order behaviors of TPN, we propose in this paper a similar notion for NTA, but we cannot directly apply the framework of [9]. Indeed TA and TPN have different expressive powers [4,8] and as stated earlier NTA do not have the nice *urgency* features that TPN have.

Up to our knowledge, this is the first attempt to equip NTA with a concurrent semantics, which can be finitely represented by a prefix of an unfolding. In this paper we answer the following questions:

1. What can be a good model for a *concurrent semantics* of NTA? The result is an extension of the model of symbolic nets we have proposed in [9];
2. How to define a *concurrent semantics* for NTA, *i.e.* how to define a *symbolic unfolding* that captures the essential properties of a NTA while preserving concurrency information? This is achieved in two steps: first build a *symbolic unfolding* and use this object to build a proper *extended symbolic unfolding* of the NTA. By *proper* unfolding, we mean a symbolic Petri net on which we can check that a *local configuration* is valid using only the *extended causal* past of an event.
3. Is there a *complete finite prefix* for NTA? This result is rather easy to obtain on the symbolic unfolding object and carries over to the extended symbolic unfolding.

[1] *invariants* and *guards* can be independent and a transition is not bound to fire before its deadline given by the *guard*.

About point 3 above, we are not addressing the problem of building such a prefix efficiently but our work is concerned with identifying the key issues in the construction of a prefix for NTA. The solution proposed in [9] builds a complete finite prefix for safe TPNs, but with no guarantee that this prefix is one of the smallest, which is a very difficult problem to solve. Based on this work, we address more basic questions about NTA, which are in a sense easier to study than safe TPNs because the concurrent structure is explicit.

Key Issues. In this section we present informally the problem and the key issues raised by the three previous questions. In the case of networks of finite automata, *finite complete prefixes* exist. For example, for the network[2] of Fig. 1(a), a finite complete prefix is given on Fig. 1(b). Finite complete prefixes contain full information about the reachable states of the network and about the set of events that are *feasible* in the network. A set of events (labels) is feasible iff it is a word that can be generated by the network. For example, $\{t_1\}$ is not a feasible set of events in the network $\mathcal{N}_1$, because t_1 must be

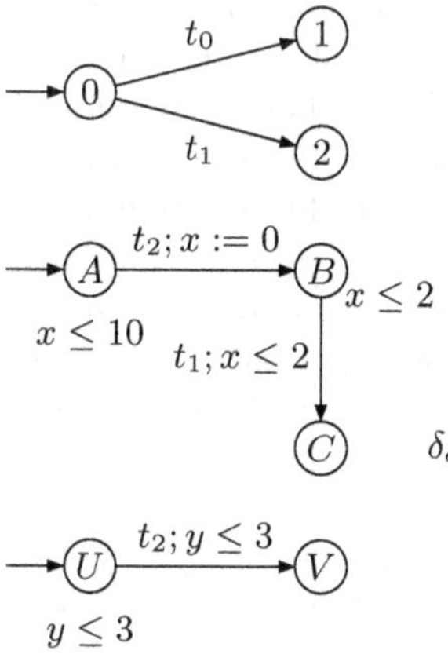

(a) The NTA $\mathcal{N}_1$

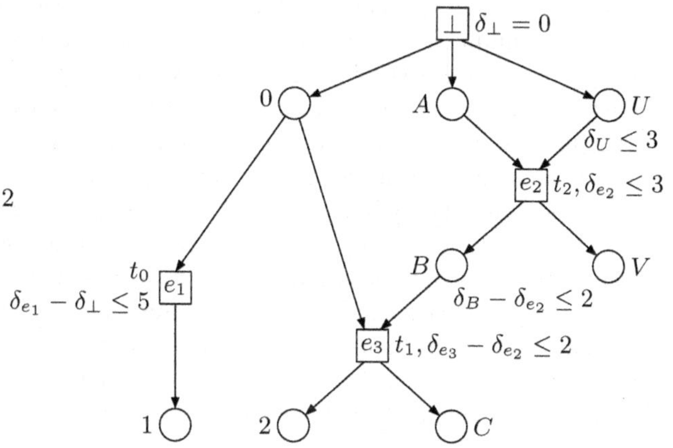

(b) Symbolic unfolding for the network $\mathcal{N}_1$

Fig. 1. A NTA and its Symbolic Unfolding

preceded by t_2. And this appears in the unfolding as event e_3 (labelled by t_1) must be preceded by e_2 (labelled by t_2). In an unfolding, a set of events K is a *configuration* if there is a reachable marking obtained by firing each event in K. For example $\{\perp, e_1\}$ is a configuration, $\{\perp, e_1, e_2\}$ as well, but $\{\perp, e_3\}$ is not as e_3 must be preceded by e_2 before it occurs. The minimal set of events necessary for an event e to occur is called the *causal past* (or *local configuration*) of e. Note that by definition a configuration contains the causal past of each of its event. A *complete* prefix is an unfolding that satisfies property (P): a set of events is feasible in the NTA iff it is a configuration of the

[2] The automata synchronize on common labels. Labels of the events and places represent the corresponding location and transition in the network of automata. The constraints appearing near each node are explained later and can be ignored at this stage.

unfolding[3]. This property of unfoldings is the key point in the untimed case and allows one to do model-checking on the complete finite prefix. This unfolding can also be used for *fault diagnosis* purposes which is a very important application area.

In the case of networks of timed automata, we deal with *timed events* which are pairs (e, δ) where $\delta \in \mathbb{R}_{\geq 0}$. A set of timed events E is feasible iff there is a run in the NTA that generates a timed word that contains all the timed events in E. To decide whether a set of timed events is feasible in a network of timed automata, we can build a *symbolic unfolding*. For this, we add a symbolic timing constraint $g(e)$ to each event of the previous unfolding. For example, with e_1 we can associate the constraint $g(e_1) \stackrel{def}{=} \delta_{e_1} - \delta_\perp \leq 5$, where δ_e is the variable that represents the date of occurrence of e. A set of timed events $\{(e_1, d_1), \cdots, (e_k, d_k)\}$ is a *timed configuration* if $\{e_1, e_2, \cdots, e_k\}$ is a configuration and the constraint $g(e_1) \wedge \cdots \wedge g(e_k)$ is satisfied when replacing each δ_{e_i} by d_i. For example $\{(\perp, 0), (e_1, 4)\}$ is a timed configuration with $g(\perp) \stackrel{def}{=} \delta_\perp = 0$. Thus the property we would like to have for symbolic unfoldings is (P'): $\{(e_1, d_1), \cdots, (e_k, d_k)\}$ is a timed configuration iff there is a run $(e_{f(1)}, d_{f(1)}), \cdots, (e_{f(k)}, d_{f(k)})$ in the NTA with f a one-to-one mapping from $1..k$ to $1..k$. In the untimed case, one can check that an event is fireable in the unfolding using only the causal past of the event. We want this property to hold for the timed unfoldings as well and then a formula associated with an event e should only involve variables that are associated with events in the causal past of e (the local configuration of e). Now assume we want to decide whether $\{(\perp, 0), (e_1, d_1), (e_2, d_2)\}$ is a timed configuration. It is actually if $d_1 - d_2 \leq 2$. But this cannot be captured by any conjunction $g(\perp) \wedge g(e_1) \wedge g(e_2)$ because e_1 is not in the causal past of e_2 and e_2 not in the causal past of e_1. A symbolic unfolding built by associating constraints with each event e, with the property that each constraint $g(e)$ uses only variables in the causal past of e, does not always contain enough information for property (P') to hold. In this paper we show 1) how to build an unfolding that contains enough information so that (P') holds; 2) how to build a finite and complete prefix of the unfolding satisfying (P').

Organization of the Paper. The paper is organized as follows. Section 2 presents the model of NTA and its usual sequential semantics. Section 3 gives a concurrent semantics for NTA in terms of *symbolic branching processes* (SBP) and proves the existence of complete finite prefixes. The SBP is a first step towards a complete finite prefix having property (P'). In section 4, we show how to build an *extended* SBP, using *read-arcs*, which is a complete finite prefix satisfying property (P'). Section 5 gives a summary of the paper and directions for future work. The proofs of the theorems are omitted and can be found in the extended version of the paper [7].

2 Networks of Timed Automata

Notations . Given a set B we use B^ε for the set $B \cup \{\varepsilon\}$ (assuming $\varepsilon \notin B$). Let $X = \{x_1, \cdots, x_n\}$ be a finite set of *clock* variables. A *valuation* ν is a mapping from X to $\mathbb{R}_{\geq 0}$. Let $X' \subseteq X$. The valuation $\nu[X']$ is defined by: $\nu[X'](x) = 0$ if $x \in X'$

[3] Actually we should write "it is a labeling" of a configuration of the unfolding.

and $\nu[X'](x) = \nu(x)$ otherwise. $\nu_{|X'}$ is the restriction (projection) of ν to X' and is defined by $\nu_{|X'}(x) = \nu(x)$ for $x \in X'$. We denote $\mathbf{0}$ the valuation defined by $\mathbf{0}(x) = 0$ for each $x \in X$. For $\delta \in \mathbb{R}$, $\nu + \delta$ is the valuation defined by $(\nu + \delta)(x) = \nu(x) + \delta$. $\mathcal{C}(X)$ is defined to be the set of conjunctions of terms of the form $x - x' \bowtie c$ or $x \bowtie c$ for $x, x' \in X$ and $c \in \mathbb{N}$ and $\bowtie \in \{<, \leq, =, \geq, >\}$. $\mathcal{C}(X)$ is called the set of *diagonal constraints* over X. The set of *rectangular* constraints, $\mathcal{C}_r(X)$ is the subset of $\mathcal{C}(X)$ where only constraints of the form $x \bowtie c$ appear. Given a formula $\varphi \in \mathcal{C}(X)$ and a valuation $\nu \in \mathbb{R}^X_{\geq 0}$, we use $\varphi[x/\nu(x)]$ for φ where x is replaced by $\nu(x)$. we denote $\varphi(\nu) \in \{\mathsf{tt}, \mathsf{ff}\}$ the truth value of $\varphi[x/\nu(x)]$. We let $[\![\varphi]\!] = \{\nu \in \mathbb{R}_{\geq 0} \mid \varphi(\nu) = \mathsf{tt}\}$. A subset Z of $\mathbb{R}^X_{\geq 0}$ is a zone if $Z = [\![\varphi_Z]\!]$ for some $\varphi_Z \in \mathcal{C}(X)$. Note that the intersection of two zones is a zone. Two operators are defined on zones: the *time successor* operator, $Z^{\nearrow} = \{v + \delta \mid v \in Z, \delta \in \mathbb{R}_{\geq 0}\}$ and the *R-reset* operator, $Z[R] = \{v \mid \exists v' \in Z \text{ s.t. } v = v'[R]\}$. Both $Z^{\nearrow}$ and $Z[R]$ are zones if Z is a zone.

Timed Automata. *Timed automata* were introduced in [1] to model systems which combine *discrete* and *continuous* evolutions.

Definition 1. *A* timed automaton *$\mathcal{A}$ is a tuple $(L, \ell_0, \Sigma, X, T, \mathrm{Inv})$ where: L is a finite set of* locations*; ℓ_0 is the* initial *location; Σ is a finite set of* discrete *actions; $X = \{x_1, \cdots, x_n\}$ is a finite set of (positive real-valued)* clocks*; $T \subseteq L \times \mathcal{C}_r(X) \times \Sigma \times 2^X \times L$ is a finite set of* transitions*: $(\ell, g, a, R, \ell') \in T$ represents a transition from the location ℓ to ℓ', labeled by a, with the guard g and the reset set $R \subseteq X$; we write $\mathrm{SRC}(t) = \ell$, $\mathrm{TGT}(t) = \ell'$, $\mathrm{G}(t) = g$, $\lambda(t) = a$ and $\mathrm{R}(t) = R$. $\mathrm{Inv} \in \mathcal{C}_r(X)^L$ assigns an* invariant *to any location. We require that* Inv *be a conjunction of terms of the form $x \bowtie c$ with $\bowtie \in \{<, \leq\}$ and $c \in \mathbb{N}$.*

A *state* of a timed automaton is a pair $(\ell, v) \in L \times \mathbb{R}^X_{\geq 0}$. A timed automaton is *bounded* if there exists a constant $k \in \mathbb{N}$ s.t. for each $\ell \in L$, $\mathrm{Inv}(\ell) \subseteq [\![0 \leq x_1 \leq k \wedge \cdots \wedge 0 \leq x_n \leq k]\!]$. Examples of timed automata are given in Fig. 1(a). In the sequel we require that for any valuation v and any transition $t = (\ell, g, a, R, \ell')$, $g(v) \implies \mathrm{Inv}(\ell')(v[R])$.

Definition 2. *The semantics of a timed automaton $\mathcal{A} = (L, \ell_0, \Sigma, X, T, Inv)$ is a labeled timed transition system (TTS) $S_{\mathcal{A}} = (Q, q_0, T \cup \mathbb{R}_{\geq 0}, \to)$ with $Q = L \times (\mathbb{R}_{\leq 0})^X$, $q_0 = (\ell_0, \mathbf{0})$ is the initial state and $\to$ consists of the discrete and continuous transition relations: i) the discrete transition relation is defined for all $t \in T$ by: $(\ell, v) \xrightarrow{t} (\ell', v') \iff \exists t = (\ell, g, a, R, \ell') \in T$ s.t. $g(v) = \mathsf{tt}$, $v' = v[R \mapsto 0]$; ii) the continuous transition relation is defined for all $\delta \in \mathbb{R}_{\geq 0}$ by: $(\ell, v) \xrightarrow{\delta} (\ell', v')$ iff $\ell = \ell'$, $v' = v + \delta$ and $\forall 0 \leq \delta' \leq \delta$, $Inv(\ell)(v + \delta') = \mathsf{tt}$. A* run *of a timed automaton $\mathcal{A}$ is a path in $S_{\mathcal{A}}$ starting in q_0 where continuous and discrete transitions alternate*[4]*. The set of runs of $\mathcal{A}$ is denoted by $[\![\mathcal{A}]\!]$. A state q is* reachable *in $\mathcal{A}$ if there is a run from q_0 to q. $\mathrm{REACH}(\mathcal{A})$ is the set of reachable states of $\mathcal{A}$. A timed word $w \in (T \times \mathbb{R}_{\geq 0})^*$ is* accepted *by $\mathcal{A}$ if there is a run $\rho \in [\![\mathcal{A}]\!]$ s.t. the trace of ρ is w.*

The analysis of timed automata is based on the exploration of a (finite) graph, the *simulation graph*, where the nodes are *symbolic states*. A symbolic state is a pair (ℓ, Z) where ℓ is a location and Z a *zone* over the set $\mathbb{R}^X_{\geq 0}$.

[4] In our definition runs are labeled by transitions.

Definition 3. *The* simulation graph $SG(\mathcal{A})$ *of a timed automaton* $\mathcal{A}$ *is given by: i) the set of states is the set of symbolic states of the form* (ℓ, Z) *where* Z *is a zone; ii) the initial state is* (ℓ_0, Z_0) *with* $Z_0 = \mathbf{0}^{\nearrow} \cap [\![\text{Inv}(\ell_0)]\!]$*; iii)* $(\ell, Z) \xrightarrow{a} (\ell', Z')$ *if there is a transition* (ℓ, g, a, R, ℓ') *in* $\mathcal{A}$ *s.t.* $Z \cap [\![g]\!] \neq \emptyset$ *(this ensures* Z' *is not empty) and* $Z' = ((Z \cap [\![g]\!])[R])^{\nearrow} \cap [\![\text{Inv}(\ell')]\!]$.

We assume that the timed automata are bounded *i.e.* in each location ℓ, $\text{Inv}(\ell)$ is bounded[5]. In this case the number of zones of the simulation graph is finite [14,6].

Network of Timed Automata. We use the classical composition notion based on a *synchronization function*. Let $\mathcal{A}_1, \ldots, \mathcal{A}_n$ be n timed automata with $\mathcal{A}_i = (L_i, l_{i,0}, \Sigma_i, X_i, T_i, Inv_i)$. We assume that for each $i \neq j$, $L_i \cap L_j = \emptyset$ and $X_i \cap X_j = \emptyset$ (clocks are not shared). A *synchronization constraint* I is a subset of $\Sigma_1^\varepsilon \times \Sigma_2^\varepsilon \cdots \times \Sigma_n^\varepsilon \backslash (\varepsilon, \cdots, \varepsilon)$. The (synchronization) vectors of a synchronization constraint I indicate which actions synchronize. For $(t_1, \cdots, t_n) \in T_1^\varepsilon \times \cdots T_n^\varepsilon$ we write $\lambda(t_1, \cdots, t_n) = (\lambda_1(t_1), \cdots, \lambda_n(t_n))$ with $\lambda_i(\varepsilon) = \varepsilon$. $\lambda^{-1}(I) \subseteq T_1^\varepsilon \times \cdots T_n^\varepsilon$ indicates how the transitions synchronize. For $t \in \lambda^{-1}(I)$, we let: $\text{SRC}^*(t) = \{l \in \text{SRC}(t[i]) \,|\, t[i] \neq \varepsilon\}$, $\text{TGT}^*(t) = \{l \in \text{TGT}(t[i]) \,|\, t[i] \neq \varepsilon\}$, $\text{R}(t) = \{x \,|\, x \in \text{R}(t[i]) \text{ and } t[i] \neq \varepsilon\}$, $\text{G}(t) = \wedge_{t[i] \neq \varepsilon} \text{G}(t[i])$.

Definition 4. *The network of timed automata (NTA)* $(\mathcal{A}_1 | \ldots | \mathcal{A}_n)_I$ *is the timed automaton* $\mathcal{B} = (L, \mathbf{l}_0, \Sigma, X, T, \text{Inv})$ *defined by:* $L = L_1 \times \cdots \times L_n$, $\mathbf{l}_0 = (\ell_{1,0}, \cdots, \ell_{n,0})$, $\Sigma = \Sigma_1 \times \cdots \times \Sigma_n$, $X = \cup_{i=1}^n X_i$*;* $(\mathbf{l}, g, a, R, \mathbf{l}') \in T$ *iff* $\exists t \in \lambda^{-1}(I)$ *s.t.: (1) if* $t[i] \neq \varepsilon$ *then* $\mathbf{l}_i = \text{SRC}(t[i])$ *and otherwise* $\mathbf{l}'_i = \text{TGT}(t[i])$*, (2)* $a = \lambda(t)$*,* $g = \text{G}(t)$ *and* $R = \text{R}(t)$ *and* $\text{Inv}(\mathbf{l}) = \wedge_{i=1}^n \text{Inv}_i(\ell_i)$ *if* $\mathbf{l} = (\ell_1, \cdots, \ell_n)$.

This definition implies that if each $\mathcal{A}_i$ is bounded (resp. simple) then the NTA is bounded (resp. simple).

3 Symbolic Unfolding for Network of Timed Automata

In this section we define the symbolic semantics of a NTA in terms of *symbolic branching processes*. Those processes contain timing constraints both on places and events. We do not recall the definitions of *occurrence nets*, *branching processes (BP)* for untimed network of automata. The reader is referred to [10] for a detailed presentation of these notions.

Let $(\mathcal{A}_1 | \ldots | \mathcal{A}_n)_I$ be a synchronous product of TA. In a first step, we build the *untimed branching processes* (UBPs) of $(\mathcal{A}_1 | \ldots | \mathcal{A}_n)_I$. For each timed automaton $\mathcal{A}_i$ we let $\text{UNTIME}(\mathcal{A}_i)$ be the automaton obtained by removing all the timing constraints and clocks in $\mathcal{A}_i$. An UBP of a NTA is a BP of the network of untimed automata $(\text{UNTIME}(\mathcal{A}_1) | \ldots | \text{UNTIME}(\mathcal{A}_n))_I$ in the sense of [10]. The set of UBPs is defined inductively over two sets $\mathcal{E}$ and $\mathcal{P}$ by: i) $\bot \in \mathcal{E}$, ii) if $e \in \mathcal{E}$ and $s \in L$ then $(e, s) \in \mathcal{P}$, iii) if $S \subseteq \mathcal{P}$ and $t \in \lambda^{-1}(I)$ then $(S, t) \in \mathcal{E}$. On those two sets we define the mappings ${}^\bullet(), ()^\bullet$:

[5] Any timed automaton can be transformed into an equivalent (behaviours) bounded automaton [2].

- for $\mathcal{E}$, ${}^\bullet\bot = \emptyset$, and if $e = (S, t)$, ${}^\bullet e = S$; and $e^\bullet = \{s \,|\, (e, s) \in \mathcal{P}\}$;
- for $\mathcal{P}$: ${}^\bullet(e, s) = e$ and $(e, s)^\bullet = \{e \,|\, {}^\bullet e \cap s \neq \emptyset\}$.

By definition of E and P a SBP is completely determined by E ans P as ${}^\bullet()$ and $()^\bullet$ are implicitly defined. Let x, y be two nodes (place or transitions). If $x \in {}^\bullet y$ or $y \in x^\bullet$ there is an *arc from* x to y and we write $x \longrightarrow y$. This enables us to refer to the *directed graph of a net* which is simply the graph $(E \cup P, \longrightarrow)$. The reflexive and transitive closure of $\longrightarrow$ is denoted $\preceq$. x, y are *causally related* if either $x \preceq y$ or $y \preceq x$. x is in the (strict) *causal past* of y if $x \preceq y$ and $x \neq y$, *i.e.* $x \prec y$. x, y are in *conflict*, noted $x\#y$, if there is a place $p \in P$ such that $p \longrightarrow w \preceq x$ and $p \longrightarrow u \preceq y$ with $u \neq w$. x and y are *concurrent* if x and y are neither causally related nor in conflict. If J is a set of events then $\uparrow J = \big(\cup_{e \in J} e^\bullet\big) \backslash \big(\cup_{e \in J} {}^\bullet e\big)$. For a set $J \subseteq E \cup P$ $\lceil J \rceil = \{e' \in E \cup P \,|\, e' \preceq e \text{ for some } e \in J\}$. A set of events J is *causally closed* if $\lceil J \rceil = J$. A *configuration* of a BP is a set of events $K \subseteq E$ which is causally closed and conflict-free. A set A is a *co-set* iff $A \subseteq \uparrow K$ where K is a configuration. A *cut* $S \subseteq P$ is a set of places which is a maximal co-set. To each configuration K, we can associate a unique cut $\uparrow K$ which is denoted $\text{CUT}(K)$. A place $p = (e, s) \in \mathcal{P}$ is a i-place if $s \in L_i$. We can define the union of two branching processes (E_1, P_1) and (E_2, P_2) component-wise on events and places. BPs are closed under countable union and the *unfolding* of $(\text{UNTIME}(\mathcal{A}_1)| \ldots |\text{UNTIME}(\mathcal{A}_n))_I$ is be the maximal branching process. The next two properties are taken from [10]:

Proposition 1. *Two i-places of a UBP are either causally related or in conflict.*

Proposition 2. *Let C be a cut of a UBP. C contains one i-place for each $1 \leq i \leq n$.*

Thus given a configuration K, $\text{CUT}(K)$ corresponds to a unique state of the product of untimed automata.

The *symbolic* branching processes of a NTA are built from the UBP. The intuition is that we associate with places and events a time variable. For an event e, the variable δ_e stands for the (global) time at which event e fired. For a place p, δ_p stands for the most recent (global) time for which a token was in p. We define $\delta(E \cup P)$ to be the set of variables $\{\delta_x \,|\, x \in E \cup P\}$. A *symbolic branching process (SBP)* (E, P, γ) of $(\mathcal{A}_1| \ldots |\mathcal{A}_n)_I$ is a UBP (E, P) of $(\text{UNTIME}(\mathcal{A}_1)| \ldots |\text{UNTIME}(\mathcal{A}_n))_I$ with $\gamma : E \cup P \longrightarrow \mathcal{C}(\delta(E \cup P))$ a mapping that associates to each node a timing constraint. The constraint on a node x should only refer to variables in $\lceil x \rceil$.

The constraint $\gamma(x)$ is computed by rewriting the timing constraints of the NTA in terms of the variables δ_y for $y \in \lceil x \rceil$. For the event $\bot$ we just set $\delta_\bot = 0$ stating that the system started at time 0. On the example of Fig. 1(b), to compute the timing constraint $\gamma(U)$ we just rewrite the invariant $y \leq 3$ in terms of the firing times of the events in the past of place U: if the current (global) time at which a token is in U is δ_U we must have $x = \delta_U - \delta_\bot \leq 3$ *i.e.* $\delta_U \leq 3$. For event e_3, we must have $x \leq 2$ and the value of x is given by $\delta_{e_3} - \delta_{e_2}$ which yields $\delta_{e_3} - \delta_{e_2} \leq 2$. The result for the NTA of Fig. 1(a) is depicted on Fig. 1(b). The important point is that each constraint $\gamma(x)$ is entirely determined by x. Hence to each UBP (E, P) we can associate a unique SBP (E, P, γ). We can thus define the *symbolic unfolding* $\text{TBP}(\mathcal{A}_1| \ldots |\mathcal{A}_n)_I$ of $(\mathcal{A}_1| \ldots |\mathcal{A}_n)_I$ to be the symbolic branching process associated with the unfolding of $(\text{UNTIME}(\mathcal{A}_1)| \ldots |\text{UNTIME}(\mathcal{A}_n))_I$.

To define cuts for SBP we need to take into account the timing constraints: for instance in Fig. 1(b), $(0, A, U)$ is a cut iff $\delta_0 = \delta_A = \delta_U \leq 3$ meaning that the global time in each place is the same and the constraints on the places are satisfied. For an event the same strategy applies. We can define a formula that characterizes all the timed cuts of a SBP:

Definition 5. *(M, Φ) is a* symbolic co-set *of (E, P, γ) if: 1) M is a co-set of (E, P), 2) $\Phi = \Phi_1(M) \wedge \Phi_2(M) \wedge \Phi_3(M) \wedge \Phi_4(M)$ with:*

$$\Phi_1(M) = \bigwedge_{x \in \lceil M \rceil} \gamma(x) \quad (1) \qquad \Phi_3(M) = \bigwedge_{p \in M} (\delta_{\bullet p} \leq \delta_p) \quad (3)$$

$$\Phi_2(M) = \bigwedge_{e \in \lceil M \rceil \cap E} (\wedge_{p \in {}^\bullet e} \delta_p = \delta_e) \quad (2) \qquad \Phi_4(M) = (\bigwedge_{p, p' \in M} \delta_p = \delta_{p'}) \quad (4)$$

If M is a cut of (E, P), (M, Φ) is a symbolic cut. The meaning of formula (2) is that the last date δ_p at which a token was in p is the time at which an event removed a token in p. (3) imposes that if a token is in p and p is in a co-set, the current time in p which is δ_p is larger than the date of occurrence of the event that put a token in p. Finally (4) requires that all the places in the co-set have reached the same global time. The reason why we need to use variables associated with places is because there is no urgency in NTA. Notice that the formula Φ of a symbolic co-set is entirely determined by the co-set M and unique; we denote it by Φ_M. Moreover the form of the constraints on $\delta(E \cup P)$ in the SBP is such that Φ_M is a zone for each symbolic cut M:

Theorem 1. *For each symbolic cut (M, Φ_M) Φ_M is a zone.*

Given a SBP (E, P, γ), a set $M \subseteq P$, and a mapping $\Theta : \delta(\lceil M \rceil) \rightarrow \mathbb{R}_{\geq 0}$ that associates with each node a date, (M, Θ) is a *timed cut* iff (M, Φ_M) is a symbolic cut and $\Theta \in [\![\Phi_M]\!]$. Given a timed cut (M, Θ) we can associate a unique state of the NTA $\text{GS}(M, \Theta)$: it suffices to compute the values of each clock variables in X from the values of the nodes variables in the SBP. Conversely, given a state $(\mathbf{l}, v)$ of the product, we can associate a timed cut to $(\mathbf{l}, v)$ as stated by Theorem 3 below.

Theorem 2. *If K is a configuration of $\text{TBP}(\mathcal{A}_1 | \ldots | \mathcal{A}_n)_I$ and $\Theta \in [\![\Phi_{\text{CUT}(K)}]\!]$ then a) $\text{GS}(\text{CUT}(K), \Theta) = (\mathbf{l}, v)$ for some $(\mathbf{l}, v)$ reachable in $(\mathcal{A}_1 | \ldots | \mathcal{A}_n)_I$, and b) if $K \cup \{e\}$ is a configuration and $\Theta \in [\![\Phi_{\text{CUT}(K)} \wedge \gamma(e) \bigwedge (\wedge_{p \in {}^\bullet e} \delta_p = \delta_e)]\!]$ then $(\mathbf{l}, v) \xrightarrow{\lambda(e)} (\mathbf{l}', v')$ with $\text{GS}(K \cup \{e\}, \Theta') = (\mathbf{l}', v')$ and $\Theta'_{|\text{CUT}(K)} = \Theta$ and $\Theta'(x) = \Theta(p)$ for some $p \in \text{CUT}(K)$ otherwise.*

The formula $\Phi_{\text{CUT}(K)} \wedge \gamma(e) \bigwedge (\wedge_{p \in {}^\bullet e} \delta_p = \delta_e)$ asserts that the global time is the same in every automata which is also equal to the firing time of e and that the guard of the transition t holds.

Theorem 3. *Let $(\mathbf{l}, v)$ be a reachable state in $(\mathcal{A}_1 | \ldots | \mathcal{A}_n)_I$. There is a configuration K of $\text{TBP}(\mathcal{A}_1 | \ldots | \mathcal{A}_n)_I$ and $\Theta \in [\![\Phi_{\text{CUT}(K)}]\!]$ s.t.: a) $\text{GS}(\text{CUT}(K), \Theta) = (\mathbf{l}, v)$, and b) if $(\mathbf{l}, v) \xrightarrow{t} (\mathbf{l}', v')$ there is a configuration $K \cup \{e\}$ s.t. $\lambda(e) = t$ and a valuation $\Theta' \in [\![\Phi_{\text{CUT}(K \cup \{e\})}]\!]$ s.t. $\text{GS}(K \cup \{e\}, \theta') = (\mathbf{l}', v')$.*

If a TBP $\mathcal{T}$ satisfies the conditions of Theorem 3, we say that $\mathcal{T}$ is *complete*. Theorem 2, corresponds to a *correctness* property. For network of finite untimed automata, complete and correct finite branching processes exist, and are called *complete finite prefixes* [16,10]. In the case of network of timed automata we can construct a finite complete prefix that preserves the reachability information of the simulation graph.

Theorems 3 and 2 have two consequences. They follow from the fact that each $\Phi_{\mathrm{CUT}(K)}$ is a zone for a configuration K. This means that the set of valuations reachable by all the linearizations of the events in K defines a zone as well. In the symbolic unfolding we construct, we obtain one zone for all the linearizations of the events in K whereas in $SG((\mathcal{A}_1|\dots|\mathcal{A}_n)_I)$ they could be two distinct states for two different linearizations. The first consequence is that the union of the zones reachable by all the linearization in $SG((\mathcal{A}_1|\dots|\mathcal{A}_n)_I)$ is a zone. Indeed computing global states preserves zones. This result was obtained recently by Ramzi Ben Salah, Marius Bozga and Oded Maler in [3] and has useful consequences. Our framework gives an alternative proof of this result and accounts for it in terms of partial order. The second consequence is that finite complete prefixes exist for NTA.

Assume the two configurations K_1 and K_2 lead to the same symbolic state $\mathrm{GS}(\mathrm{CUT}(K_1), \Phi_{\mathrm{CUT}(K_1)}) = \mathrm{GS}(\mathrm{CUT}(K_2), \Phi_{\mathrm{CUT}(K_2)})$, then they have the same future. Thus we can discard the events that extend one of them, for instance the smallest w.r.t. the order $\ll$ defined as: $K_1 \ll K_2$ iff $\mathrm{GS}(\mathrm{CUT}(K_1), \Phi_{\mathrm{CUT}(K_1)}) = \mathrm{GS}(\mathrm{CUT}(K_2), \Phi_{\mathrm{CUT}(K_2)}) \wedge |K_1| < |K_2|$. As the simulation graph contains a finite number of (union of) zones and because each $\Phi_{\mathrm{CUT}(K)}$ is a union of zones, we can not have an infinite number of different symbolic states. This allows us to construct a complete finite prefix by keeping only the events e such that there exists a configuration K that enables e and is minimal w.r.t. $\ll$. We let $\mathrm{PREF}((\mathcal{A}_1|\dots|\mathcal{A}_n)_I)$ be the complete symbolic finite prefix obtained from $(\mathcal{A}_1|\dots|\mathcal{A}_n)_I$. So far we are able to answer the question whether a set of timed events is a timed configuration: given the set of events K and the valuation Θ we can check whether $\Theta \in [\![\Phi_{\mathrm{CUT}(K)}]\!]$. What we would like to do is to check whether a set of events K can be extended to a configuration *i.e.* if $\uparrow(K)$ is a co-set. We cannot do this directly with the SBP we have constructed so far. In the next section we refine our unfolding so that we do not need to look at the global state of the system to decide whether a set of events can be extended to a timed configuration.

4 Extended Finite Complete Prefixes

In the case of finite automata, any cut containing a co-set that enables an event, still enables the same event. This is not the case for network of timed automata as can be seen on the example of Fig. 1(b). If e_2 has not fired, e_1 can fire because nothing can prevent it from doing so (e_3 is not enabled). The fact that e_2 has not fired can be inferred from the fact that either place A or U contains a token. But this implies that the date δ_{e_1} at which e_1 fires satisfies $\delta_{e_1} \leq 3$. If e_2 has fired at δ_{e_2}, e_3 and e_1 are in conflict. Thus e_1 can only occur at a date when a token can be in B, *i.e.* to fire we must have $\delta_B = \delta_{e_1}$ and the constraint on the date at which a token can be in B which is $\delta_B - \delta_{e_2} \leq 2$. This implies $\delta_{e_1} - \delta_{e_2} \leq 2$. Thus the timing constraints associated with e_1 are not the same in the cuts $(0, A, U)$ and $(0, B, V)$ although they are both cuts that contain ${}^\bullet e_1$.

To encode this timing dependency structurally we can use symbolic occurrence nets with *read arcs*. For instance the symbolic net of Fig. 1(b) can be "transformed" into the symbolic extended net of Fig. 2 (a read arc is a dash line). Read arcs enable us to point to the missing timing information in the net that is needed to ensure an event can fire. This also means that we duplicate the event e_1 into e_1 and e_1' because the constraints are different depending on whether e_2 has occurred or not. Read arcs enlarge the *causal past* of the events. In the extended occurrence net, the constraint between the dates of occurrence of e_1 and e_2 can be inferred from the past of e_1: indeed, to fire, we must have $\delta_{e_1} = \delta_B$ and thus $\delta_{e_1} - \delta_{e_2} \leq 2$. Read arcs enable us to differentiate the two cuts $(0, A, U)$ and $(0, B, V)$ that generate different timing constraints on e_1 and e_2.

Extended Branching Processes. An *extended net* $\mathcal{N}$ is a tuple $(E, P, {}^\bullet(), ()^\bullet, {}^\circ())$ where $(E, P, {}^\bullet(), ()^\bullet)$ is a net, and ${}^\circ() : E \rightarrow 2^P$. If ${}^\circ e = \emptyset$ for each $e \in E$ then $\mathcal{N}$ is a net. The set ${}^\circ e$ represents the input places of an event that are to be read without removing a token. The *Extended* symbolic branching processes (ESBP) of a network are defined as in section 3: the only change we need to do is to define the set of events so that it includes the *read-only* places of an event denoted ${}^\circ e$. To this end, if $S, S' \subseteq \mathcal{P}$ and $t \in T$, (S, S', t) is in $\mathcal{E}$ and if $e = (S, S', t)$, ${}^\circ e = S'$.

The causality relation is now defined by: $x \rightarrow y$ if $x \in {}^\bullet y \cup {}^\circ y$ or $y \in x^\bullet$. $\preceq$ is the reflexive and transitive closure of $\rightarrow$. The *weak* causality relation $\dashrightarrow$ is given by: $x \dashrightarrow y$ if either $x \rightarrow y$ or ${}^\circ x \cap {}^\bullet y \neq \emptyset$ (if x needs a token in one of the input place of y this implies a causality relation, even if x is not in the past of y in the sense of $\rightarrow$.). We let $\trianglelefteq$ the reflexive and transitive closure of $\dashrightarrow$. Two nodes x and y are *weakly causally related* if either $x \trianglelefteq y$ or $y \trianglelefteq x$. x and y are in conflict, $x \# y$, if there is a place p s.t. there exist w and u, $w \neq u$, $p \in {}^\bullet u \cap {}^\bullet w$ and $w \trianglelefteq x$ and $u \trianglelefteq y$. x and y are concurrent if they are not weakly causally related nor in conflict. For $J \subseteq E \cup P$, the definitions of $\uparrow J$ and $\lceil J \rceil$ are unchanged (we use the new $\preceq$). A set of events is now causally closed if $\lceil J \rceil = J$. Co-sets, configurations and cuts are defined as before.

Safe Co-sets. Let $\text{ENABLE}(e)$ denote the *enabling cuts* of $e \neq \bot$ in a finite symbolic branching process $\mathcal{N}$: $\text{ENABLE}(e) = \{C \mid {}^\bullet e \subseteq C \textit{ and } C \textit{ is a cut of } \mathcal{N}\}$. As a running example we take the prefix $\mathcal{N}_1$ built in Fig. 1(b) and $\delta_\bot$ is always replaced by 0 (zero). For this example the enabling cuts are: $\text{ENABLE}(e_1) = \{(0, A, U), (0, B, V)\}$, $\text{ENABLE}(e_2) = \{(0, A, U), (1, A, U)\}$, $\text{ENABLE}(e_3) = \{(0, B, V)\}$.

Now assume an event e is in conflict with another event e' in the symbolic unfolding. As we pointed out at the end of section 3, the timing constraints given by $\lceil {}^\bullet e \rceil$ on the firing time of e do not always contain enough information to ensure event e can fire: event e_1 in $\mathcal{N}_1$ can fire if a) e_2 has not fired (this must be at time $\delta \leq 3$), or b) e_2 has fired, and the time elapsed since it has occurred is less than 2 time units (*i.e.* at time δ with $\delta - \delta_{e_2} \leq 2$), or c) e_2 has been disabled by another event in conflict with it and cannot occur in the future. To ensure e can fire, we should add to the conditions in ${}^\bullet e$ some information about the events in conflict with e. This is the purpose of *safe co-sets*. They extend the co-sets of the symbolic unfolding with some information about the conflicting events. In terms of occurrence nets, a safe co-set for an event e will be the set of places ${}^\bullet e$, extended with a set a *read only* places, ${}^\circ e$. The information contained in a safe co-set should be such that, if the timing constraints obtained by $\Phi_{{}^\bullet e \cup {}^\circ e}$ are satisfied, then there is a cut $C \supseteq {}^\bullet e \cup {}^\circ e$ s.t. Φ_C is satisfied.

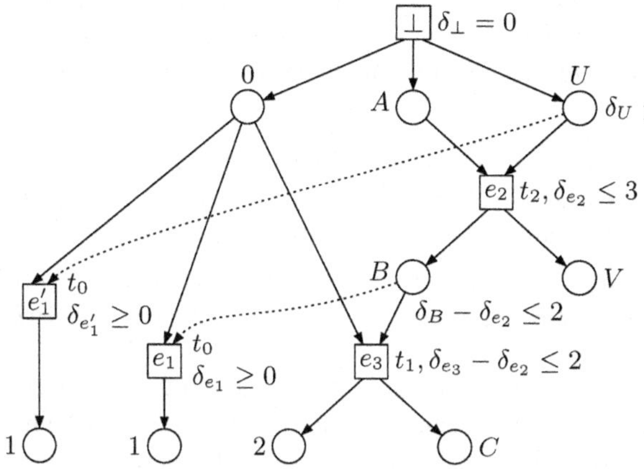

Fig. 2. Extended symbolic unfolding for the example of Fig. 1(a)

For any cut C, the formula Φ_C (Def. 5, equations (1)–(4)) is a formula over $\delta(C \cup (\lceil C \rceil \cap E))$. Indeed all the intermediate places p, not in the cut, are constrained by a formula of the form $\delta_e = \delta_p$ because of equation 2 of Def. 5. For instance $\Phi_{(0,B,V)} = \delta_B - \delta_{e_2} \leq 2 \wedge 0 \leq \delta_{e_2} \leq 3 \wedge \delta_B \geq \delta_{e_2} \wedge \delta_0 = \delta_B = \delta_V$.

Because of the term Φ_4, if we use an extra variable δ and the formula $(\delta = \delta_p) \wedge \Phi_C$ for any[6] $p \in C$, we obtain a formula over $\delta(\lceil C \rceil \cap E) \cup \{\delta\}$: δ stands for the current global time (since the system started) and the constraint on δ in Φ_C defines the set of instants for which the cut C is *reachable i.e.* there are tokens in each place $p \in C$. We write Φ^δ_C for the projection on $(\lceil C \rceil \cap E) \cup \{\delta\}$ of the formula $\Phi_C \wedge (\delta = \delta_p)$. In our example, $\Phi^\delta_{(0,A,U)} = \delta \leq 3$, $\Phi^\delta_{(1,A,U)} = \delta_{e_1} \leq 3 \wedge \delta_{e_1} \leq \delta \leq 3$ and $\Phi^\delta_{(0,B,V)} = \delta - \delta_{e_2} \leq 2 \wedge 0 \leq \delta_{e_2} \leq 3 \wedge \delta \geq \delta_{e_2}$. This last example is interesting because it shows that the set of dates s.t. a token is in $(0, B, V)$ depends on the time at which e_2 occurred. Finally we let $\Theta(e) = \{\Phi^\delta_C \mid C \in \text{ENABLE}(e)\}$ and in the previous example, we obtain: $\Theta(e_1) = \{\Phi^\delta_{(0,A,U)}, \Phi^\delta_{(0,B,V)}\}$, $\Theta(e_2) = \{\Phi^\delta_{(0,A,U)}, \Phi^\delta_{(1,A,U)}\}$, $\Theta(e_3) = \{\Phi^\delta_{(0,B,V)}\}$ $\Theta(e)$ represents the set of different constraints that can be generated by all the enabling cuts of event e.

Definition 6. *A set of places S is a* safe representative *of a pair (e, C) where $e \in E$ and $C \in$ ENABLE(e) if 1) $^\bullet e \subseteq S \subseteq C$ and 2) for all $\nu : \delta(\lceil C \rceil \cap E) \cup \{\delta\} \to \mathbb{R}_{\geq 0}$ if $\nu_{|\delta(\lceil S \rceil \cap E) \cup \{\delta\}} \in [\![\Phi^\delta_S]\!]$ and $\nu_{|\delta(\lceil C \setminus S \rceil \cap E) \cup \{\delta\}} \in [\![\Phi^\delta_{C \setminus S}]\!]$ then $\nu \in [\![\Phi^\delta_C]\!]$. S is a safe representative of e if S is a safe representative of each pair (e, C) with $C \in$ ENABLE(e).*

If S is a safe representative of (e, C), then if $\gamma(e)$ holds together with Φ_S, e can be added to the unfolding. For example, $(0, A)$ is not a safe representative of $(0, A, U)$ because $\Phi^\delta_{(0,A)} = \delta \geq 0$ and $\Phi^\delta_{(0,A,U)} = \delta \leq 3$. $(0, U)$ is a safe representative of $(0, A, U)$ as well as $(0, A, U)$ itself. $(0, B)$ is a safe representative of $(0, B, V)$. As

[6] As equation (4) already imposes $\delta_{p'} = \delta_p$ for $p, p' \in C$ we can add $\delta = \delta_p$ for any p in C.

each cut $C \in \textsc{Enable}(e)$ is a safe representative of itself, there is always one safe representatives for any C which is $\textsc{Enable}(e)$. We can state a theorem which is a variant of Theorem 2 using only safe representatives of an event (item *b)* of the theorem is altered):

Theorem 4. *If K is a configuration of* $\text{TBP}(\mathcal{A}_1|\dots|\mathcal{A}_n)_I$ *and* $\Theta \in [\![\Phi_{\textsc{Cut}(K)}]\!]$ *then a)* $\text{GS}(\textsc{Cut}(K),\Theta) = (\mathrm{l},v)$ *for some* (l,v) *reachable in* $(\mathcal{A}_1|\dots|\mathcal{A}_n)_I$*, and b) if* $K \cup \{e\}$ *is a configuration and S is a safe representative of* $\textsc{Cut}(K)$ *and* $\Theta \in [\![\Phi_S \wedge \gamma(e) \bigwedge(\wedge_{p\in {}^\bullet e}\delta_p = \delta_e)]\!]$ *then* $(\mathrm{l},v) \xrightarrow{\lambda(e)} (\mathrm{l}',v')$ *with* $\text{GS}(K\cup\{e\},\Theta') = (\mathrm{l}',v')$ *and* $\Theta'_{|\textsc{Cut}(K)} = \Theta$ *and* $\Theta'(x) = \Theta(p)$ *for some* $p \in \textsc{Cut}(K)$ *otherwise.*

This theorem is a direct consequence of Theorem 2 and Def. 6. It states that a safe representative for e contains enough information to decide whether event e can be fired or not. As a consequence, if whenever we add a new event e to a (finite) extended symbolic branching process of a NTA $(\mathcal{A}_1|\dots|\mathcal{A}_n)_I$, we use a safe representative $S = {}^\bullet e \cup {}^\circ e$ and add *read-arcs* to the places of ${}^\circ e$, then $\lceil e \rceil$ (including $\lceil S \rceil$) gives the accurate constraints on the date δ_e at which e can fire.

To build an extended complete finite prefix for a NTA we can proceed as follows: 1) build the symbolic net defined in section 3; this enables us to obtain the safe co-sets for each event; 2) build an extended net by adding an event to the unfolding using safe co-sets instead of simple co-sets. On the example of Fig. 1 this gives the unfolding of Fig. 2:

1. start with places $0, A, U$ and event $\perp$;
2. to add an event labelled t_0 use a safe co-set: we choose $(0,U)$ and add event e_1' with a read arc to U;
3. add e_2 and e_3;
4. now a new safe co-set has appeared: $(0,B)$; we can add an event e_1 labelled by t_0 with a read arc from place B.

This construction can be formally defined (see [7]). The result is a finite extended symbolic complete prefix $\textsc{EPref}((\mathcal{A}_1|\dots|\mathcal{A}_n)_I)$ that satisfies property (P'). Formally, we define *symbolic configurations*. Assume $\textsc{EPref}((\mathcal{A}_1|\dots|\mathcal{A}_n)_I) = (E,P,\gamma)$.

Definition 7. *(K,Ψ) is a* symbolic configuration *of (E,P,γ) if: 1) K is a configuration of (E,P), and 2) $\Psi = \Psi_1(K) \wedge \Psi_2(K)$ where $\Phi_i(M), 1 \le i \le 2$ are defined by:*

$$\Psi_1(K) = \bigwedge_{e\in\lceil K\rceil} \gamma(e) \quad (5) \quad \textit{and} \quad \Psi_2(K) = \bigwedge_{e\in K} \left(\wedge_{p\in {}^\bullet e \cup {}^\circ e}\delta_p = \delta_e\right) \quad (6)$$

Notice that Ψ uses only information in the past of K and is uniquely determined thus we can write it Ψ_K. Let $\nu : K \to \mathbb{R}_{\ge 0}$. (K,ν) is a *timed configuration* if $\nu \in [\![\Psi_K]\!]$.

Theorem 5. *If (K',Ψ') is a symbolic configuration of* $\textsc{EPref}((\mathcal{A}_1|\dots|\mathcal{A}_n)_I)$ *and* $\Theta' \in [\![\Psi']\!]$ *then: there exists a symbolic configuration (K,Ψ) with $K \supseteq K'$ and $\Theta \in [\![\Psi]\!]$ s.t. 1)* $\text{GS}(\textsc{Cut}(K),\Theta) = (\mathrm{l},v)$ *for some* (l,v) *reachable in* $(\mathcal{A}_1|\dots|\mathcal{A}_n)_I$*, and 2) if $(K'\cup\{e\},\Psi'')$ is a symbolic configuration and $[\![\Psi'']\!] \neq \emptyset$ then* $(\mathrm{l},v) \xrightarrow{\lambda(e)} (\mathrm{l}',v')$ *and* $\text{GS}(\textsc{Cut}(K'\cup\{e\}),\Theta') = (\mathrm{l}',v')$ *for some* $\Theta' \in [\![\Psi'']\!]$.

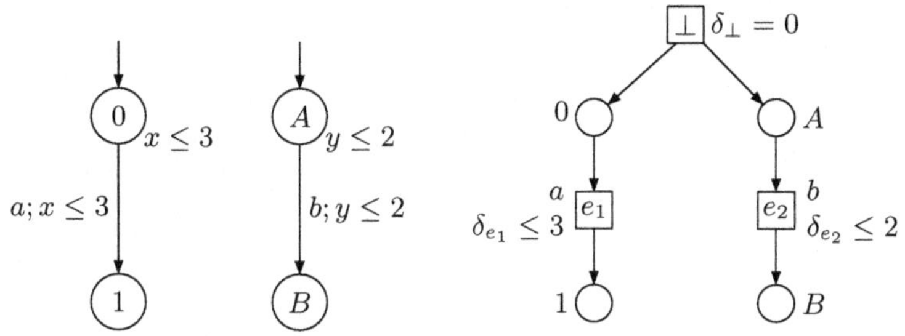

(a) Two Independent Automata (b) The Unfolding

Fig. 3. A Network of two Independent Timed Automata

On the example of Fig. 1(a), $\{(\bot, 0), (e_1, \delta_{e_1}), (e_2, \delta_{e_2})\}$ is a timed configuration iff $\delta_{e_1} - \delta_{e_2} \le 2$ and $\delta_{e_2} \le 3$.

Minimality for Safe Co-sets. The purpose of unfoldings is to keep explicit the concurrency of events. In the case of untimed network of automata, $^\bullet e$ is sufficient to ensure e can fire. For NTA, we have to use read arcs, but we should be concerned about the number of the new dependencies: for instance, if we use $\text{ENABLE}(e)$ as the set of safe representatives for each e, we require that the global state of the network is known each time we want to fire e. This means we do not keep explicit any concurrency in the unfolding. It is thus important to try and reduce the number of read arcs from each event. To this extent we define a notion of *minimality* for safe representatives.

We can define a partial order $\sqsubseteq$ on co-sets *i.e.* sets of places using the cardinality of the sets: $C_1 \sqsubseteq C_2$ iff $|C_1| \le |C_2|$. For each $C \in \text{ENABLE}(e)$ we can take one minimal element in the set of safe representatives of C. Given $e \in E$, $\text{SAFE}(e)$ denotes a set of minimal safe representatives, one for each $C \in \text{ENABLE}(e)$. In the example for $\mathcal{N}_1$ we can take the sets: $\text{SAFE}(e_1) = \{(0, U), (0, B)\}$, $\text{SAFE}(e_2) = \{(A, U)\}$, $\text{SAFE}(e_3) = \{(0, B)\}$. For the independent automata of Fig. 3(a), we obtain that 0 is a safe representative of e_1 (in Fig. 3(b)): indeed 0 is a safe representative of $(0, A)$ and a safe representative of $(0, B)$ which belongs to $\text{ENABLE}(e_1)$. For the NTA given by Fig. 3(a) we obtain the unfolding of Fig. 3(b).

The minimality criterion we have defined does not give a unique set of safe representatives. A consequence is that there is no smallest complete finite prefix for a NTA but rather a set of set of minimal complete finite prefixes. Moreover as we take at least one safe representative for each pair (e, C) the branching process we build is still complete.

Checking Validity of Timed Configuration. To complete the construction and provide a solution to the problem of checking whether a timed configuration is valid, we can define the constraint $\Gamma(e)$ associated with an event e by: $\Gamma(e) = \Psi(\lceil e \rceil)_{|\lceil e \rceil \cap E}$. This constraint gathers the constraints of all the past events. The branching process obtained this way is a *reduced* branching process with only constraints on events. For the network of timed automata of Fig. 1(a), the reduced branching process is given on Fig. 4. It

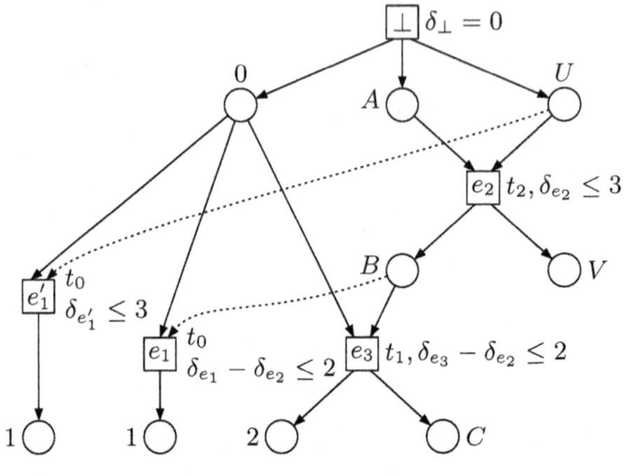

Fig. 4. Reduced Extended symbolic unfolding for the example of Fig. 1(a)

enables us to decide whether a closed set of events K is a prefix of an extended symbolic branching process.

5 Conclusion

In this paper we have defined a model, *extended symbolic branching process*, to define the concurrent semantics of timed systems. We have also proved that each NTA admits a *finite complete prefix* which is a symbolic extended branching process, and we have given an algorithm to compute such a prefix. Other interesting results are: 1) there is no unique complete finite prefix for a NTA but rather a set of complete finite prefixes; 2) building a *small* (optimal) complete finite prefix is very expensive as it requires the computation of information spread across the network; and 3) we have pointed out the difficulties arising in the construction of such a prefix, namely the need for *safe co-sets*. Our future work will consist in: a) define heuristics to determine when an event can be added to a prefix of an unfolding; this means having an efficient way of computing safe representatives, which are no more guaranteed to be minimal; b) when step 1 is developed, we can define algorithms to check properties of the NTA using the unfolding and assess the efficiency of these algorithms.

References

1. Rajeev Alur and David Dill. A theory of timed automata. *Theoretical Computer Science (TCS)*, 126(2):183–235, 1994.
2. Gerd Behrmann, Ansgar Fehnker, Thomas Hune, Kim G. Larsen, Paul Pettersson, Judi Romijn, and Frits Vaandrager. Minimum-cost reachability for priced timed automata. In *Proc. 4th International Workshop on Hybrid Systems: Computation and Control (HSCC'01)*, volume 2034 of *Lecture Notes in Computer Science*, pages 147–161. Springer, 2001.
3. Ramzi Ben Salah, Marius Bozga, and Oded Maler. On interleaving in timed automata. In *Proceedings of the* 17th *International Conference on Concurrency Theory (CONCUR'06)*, LNCS, aug 2006. To appear.

4. Béatrice Bérard, Franck Cassez, Serge Haddad, Olivier H. Roux, and Didier Lime. Comparison of the Expressiveness of Timed Automata and Time Petri Nets. In Paul Pettersson and Wang Yi, editors, *Proceedings of the third International Conference on Formal Modeling and Analysis of Timed Systems (FORMATS'05)*, volume 3829 of *Lecture Notes in Computer Science*, pages 211–225, Uppsala, Sweden, September 2005. Springer.
5. Bernard Berthomieu and Michel Diaz. Modeling and verification of time dependent systems using time Petri nets. *IEEE Trans. Software Eng.*, 17(3):259–273, 1991.
6. Patricia Bouyer. Forward analysis of updatable timed automata. *Formal Methods in System Design*, 24(3):281–320, 2004.
7. Franck Cassez, Thomas Chatain, and Claude Jard. Symbolic Unfoldings for Networks of Timed Automata. Technical Report RI-2006-4, IRCCyN/CNRS, Nantes, May 2006.
8. Franck Cassez and Olivier H. Roux. Structural translation from time petri nets to timed automata. *Journal of Systems and Software*, 2006. forthcoming.
9. Thomas Chatain and Claude Jard. Complete finite prefixes of symbolic unfoldings of safe time Petri nets. In *ICATPN*, volume 4024 of *LNCS*, pages 125–145, june 2006.
10. Javier Esparza and Stefan Römer. An unfolding algorithm for synchronous products of transition systems. In *CONCUR*, volume 1664 of *LNCS*, pages 2–20. Springer, 1999.
11. Javier Esparza, Stefan Römer, and Walter Vogler. An improvement of McMillan's unfolding algorithm. *Formal Methods in System Design*, 20(3):285–310, 2002.
12. Hans Fleischhack and Christian Stehno. Computing a finite prefix of a time Petri net. In *ICATPN*, pages 163–181, 2002.
13. J. Bengtsson, B. Jonsson, J. Lilius, W. Yi. Partial order reductions for timed systems. In *CONCUR 99*, volume 1466 of *LNCS*, pages 485–500, 1999.
14. Kim G. Larsen, Fredrik Larsson, Paul Pettersson, and Wang Yi. Efficient verification of real-time systems: Compact data structure and state-space reduction. In *Proc. 18th IEEE Real-Time Systems Symposium (RTSS'97)*, pages 14–24. IEEE Computer Society Press, 1997.
15. Denis Lugiez, Peter Niebert, and Sarah Zennou. A partial order semantics approach to the clock explosion problem of timed automata. In *Proc. 10th International Conference on Tools and Algorithms for the Construction and Analysis of Systems (TACAS'2004)*, volume 2988 of *Lecture Notes in Computer Science*, pages 296–311. Springer, 2004.
16. Kenneth L. McMillan. A technique of state space search based on unfolding. *Formal Methods in System Design*, 6(1):45–65, 1995.
17. P.M. Merlin and D.J. Farber. Recoverability of communication protocols – implications of a theorical study. *IEEE Transactions on Communications*, 24, 1976.
18. M. Minea. Partial order reduction for model checking of timed automata. In *CONCUR 99*, volume 1664 of *LNCS*, pages 431–446, 1999.
19. T. Aura and J. Lilius. A causal semantics for time petri nets. *Theoretical Computer Science*, 1–2(243):409–447, 2000.
20. T. Yoneda, B-H. Schlingloff. Efficient verification of parallel real-time systems. *Formal Methods in System Design*, 2(11):187–215, 1997.
21. A. Valmari. Stubborn sets for reduced state space generation. In *Applications and Theory of Petri Nets*, volume 483 of *LNCS*, pages 491–515, 1989.
22. W. Belluomini, C. J. Myers. Verification of timed systems using posets. In *CAV 98*, volume 1427 of *LNCS*, pages 403–415, 1998.

Ranked Predicate Abstraction for Branching Time: Complete, Incremental, and Precise*

Harald Fecher[1] and Michael Huth[2]

[1] Institut für Informatik, Christian-Albrechts-Universität zu Kiel, Germany
hf@informatik.uni-kiel.de
[2] Department of Computing, Imperial College London, United Kingdom
M.Huth@doc.imperial.ac.uk

Abstract. Predicate abstraction frameworks are a powerful means of combating the state explosion problem in model checking as they automatically synthesize abstract models that either verify compliance with a property, give rise to a genuine counter-example or produce a spurious counter-example that drives refinement of the abstract model. Prominent tools for safety (e.g. Blast) and termination (e.g. Terminator) checking rely on this approach. This paper presents such an abstraction framework for all properties of the modal μ-calculus based on ranked predicate abstraction. We show that our framework is incremental and confluent and should therefore allow good refinement heuristics. Moreover, ranked predicate abstractions are proved to be precise (i.e. optimal as abstractions) and also complete in that all properties true in a model are also true in a finite-state, ranked predicate abstraction of that model. This completeness relates to known characterizations of relative completeness for predicate abstraction with branching time.

1 Introduction

Model checking, invented 25 years ago [4,24], provides a framework for verifying properties of systems: a system is represented by a mathematical model M, a property of interest is coded within a formal language as some ϕ, and the satisfaction relationship is captured by a formal predicate $\models$ relating formal models and properties. Its instances $M \models \phi$ are then decided fully automatic (e.g. if M is finite-state) or semi-automatic (e.g. if M is abstracted first). Models often have infinite state space and this infinity can have a variety of sources: unbounded data-types, recursive process specifications, quantitative and continuous parameter values etc. Even if models are finite, their size is typically exponential in the number of system variables or communicating sub-models. This *state explosion problem* is a severe impediment to the scalability of this approach and its technology transfer into industrial research & development units even if the complexity of computing $M \models \phi$ is linear in the sizes of M and ϕ.

Abstraction of models, e.g. [20,5,7,8,3,16], is seen as a key aid in realizing scalable model checks: instead of checking $M \models \phi$ for a large model M, construct an abstract model A from a compact specification of M such that $A \models \phi$ always implies $M \models \phi$ for certain kinds of properties ϕ. Predicate abstraction [15] partitions the state space

* This work is in part financially supported by the DFG project *Refism* (FE 942/1-1).

S. Graf and W. Zhang (Eds.): ATVA 2006, LNCS 4218, pp. 322–336, 2006.

of a model M based on finitely many predicates of a suitable logic and then abstractly interprets [6] its transitions and labelings over that partition to render an abstract model A. If decidability of that logic is computable or can be approximated, this abstract model structure (if expressible in the logic) can be synthesized automatically with calls to a theorem prover. Predicate abstraction is highly successful as it allows the automatic computation of abstractions and an incremental refinement of the abstraction with new predicates in case that the current abstraction contains spurious information, i.e. that $A \not\models \phi$ erroneously suggests $M \not\models \phi$. Finding good heuristics for the choice of initial and refining predicates and proving relative completeness (i.e. possible termination) of this refinement process are two principal concerns in this line of research.

To enable finite-state model checking via abstractions in principle, we require that $M \models \phi$ implies $A \models \phi$ for some finite-state abstraction A of M; as is customary, we call such A *feasible* abstractions. The existence of such a reduction for *all* properties of a given formal language is termed "completeness" in [10], a terminology we will adopt in this paper. Given completeness one could somehow find a magic abstraction even though the original problem $M \models \phi$ may be undecidable. For Kripke structures and formulas of linear-time temporal logic completeness has been shown by Kesten & Pnueli in [17], where models where augmented with progress monitors to allow abstractions to preserve liveness properties.

Branching-time temporal logics are needed in important application settings. We mention multiple system observers that prevent a "linearization of time," and invariants of dynamical systems that mix different path quantifiers (e.g. whether all reachable states in a model of a biological system can reach a state from which a cyclic behavior is possible). Branching time may also aid in expressing process/environment interaction as seen in alternating-time temporal logic [1]. For branching time, Dams & Namjoshi have shown in [10] that Kripke structures are incomplete for Existential Computation Tree Logic (ECTL) but that completeness can be secured for the entire modal μ-calculus (including CTL and CTL*) if models are augmented to render tree-automata-like structures: focussed transition systems in [10], μ-automata in [11], etc. Completeness proofs share that they, in essence, construct a finite-state abstraction A of M with $A \models \phi$ from a proof that $M \models \phi$ holds. This completeness is an expressibility result and says nothing about how a feasible finite-state abstraction may be found.

Namjoshi [22] shows completeness for the modal μ-calculus through the abstraction of an alternating transition system $M \times \phi$, a product between a labeled transition system M and an alternating tree automata ϕ that represents the property to be checked. These abstractions use choice predicates at OR-states, and rank functions for monitoring progress. For this abstraction framework, and a set of predicates that contains the initially chosen ones and is closed under weakest preconditions, he shows that the abstraction is relatively complete iff (choices at OR-states are uniform and progress ranks are bounded). In [22] we therefore find a precise characterization of the kind of branching-time properties for which predicate abstraction can find a feasible abstraction within the abstraction framework of loc. cit.

Dams [7] considers a quality measure of an abstraction, precision, an optimality principle that is concerned with maximizing the number of properties being preserved by the abstraction, given that its state space and model signature are fixed. In [22] precision is not covered.

In this paper we draw from the ideas in [7,17,22,10] discussed above to develop an abstraction framework for Kripke structures and the modal μ-calculus (given here in the equivalent form of alternating tree automata) that meets the following objectives:

1. our framework is complete for the modal μ-calculus in the sense of [10]
2. our framework allows the construction of precise abstractions in the sense of [7]
3. our framework supports a notion of *ranked predicate abstraction*, a predicate abstraction that can deal with liveness properties as well
4. all abstractions, including those that prove completeness, are specified through ranked predicate abstractions that partition the state space they abstract
5. ranked predicate abstractions are incremental and thus open up the possibility of counter-example-guided abstraction refinement as familiar for linear time, and
6. ranked predicate abstractions are *confluent*: feasible abstractions, if they exist, can always be found in principle, regardless of the particular history of incremental refinements of an initially chosen abstraction

Although our models and methods are somewhat related to the work in [22], we highlight important differences. Abstractions in [22] are computed from a product of the model with the property to be checked. In contrast, our ranked predicate abstraction extends the state space partitions familiar from predicate abstraction with finitely many ranking functions and a set of slice predicates (Section 4). In [22] they find sufficient and necessary conditions for a feasible abstraction to be computed through predicate abstraction. In our framework we show that ranked predicate abstraction can indeed always express feasible abstractions (Section 6). We also show that our canonical ranked predicate abstraction is precise (Section 4) and that ranked predicate abstraction is incremental and confluent (Section 5).

The use of ranking functions, and their heuristics [9], for encoding fairness conditions is certainly not knew. This use is seen in the aforementioned [17], in the compositional verification of liveness properties [12], and in the context of efficient complementation of automata [19]. We merely combine ranking functions with existing abstraction formalisms to prove desirable results for branching-time model checking.

2 Hypermixed Kripke Structures

We define the models of interest, extensions of disjunctive modal transition systems [21]. Models with similar transition structure as those presented here, but with a different kind of acceptance condition, had already been proposed, and shown to be complete, in the technical report [13]. Without loss of generality, we won't consider action labels on models in this paper. Throughout, $|S|$ denotes the cardinality of a set S and $\mathbb{P}(S)$ denotes its power set.

Definition 1 (Models). *For a set of atomic propositions* AP, *a* hypermixed Kripke structure M *is a tuple* $(S, R^-, R^+, L^-, L^+, (E_\ell, F_\ell)_{\ell\in\mathcal{L}})$ *with finite* $\mathcal{L}$ *such that*

- $(s \in)S$ *is a set of states,*
- $R^-, R^+ \subseteq S \times \mathbb{P}(S)$ *the set of* must- *and* may-*transitions (respectively),*
- $L^-, L^+ \colon S \to \mathbb{P}(\mathrm{AP})$ *the* must- *and* may-*labelings (respectively) of states, and*
- $(E_\ell, F_\ell)_{\ell \in \mathcal{L}}$ *is a Streett acceptance condition with each* (E_ℓ, F_ℓ) *in* $\mathbb{P}(S) \times \mathbb{P}(S)$.

We often refer to hypermixed Kripke structures as 'models'. Furthermore, such a model is finite *if* $|S| + |\bigcup_{s \in S} L^-(s)| + |\mathrm{AP} \setminus (\bigcup_{s \in S} L^+(s))|$ *is finite.*

Kripke structures have straightforward representations as hypermixed Kripke structures: let $R^- = R^+$, $L^- = L^+$, $\mathcal{L} = \{\}$, and ensure that $(s, D) \in R^-$ implies that D is a singleton. A hypermixed Kripke structure is depicted in Figure 1 and a Kripke structure is presented in Figure 2. The interpretation of the labelings L^- and L^+ is standard [7,8]: $L^-(s)$ lists those atomic propositions that must hold in any refining states of s whereas $L^+(s)$ lists those propositions that may hold in some refinement of s. A *must*-transition $(s, D) \in R^-$ specifies that all refining states $\ddot{s}$ of s in a Kripke structure $\ddot{M}$ must have a transition $(\ddot{s}, \{\ddot{s}'\})$ in $\ddot{M}$ such that $\ddot{s}'$ refines *some* state in D [21]. Dually, a *may*-transition $(s, C) \in R^+$ specifies that all refining states $\ddot{s}$ of s in a Kripke structure $\ddot{M}$ may (but must not) have transitions in $\ddot{M}$ of form $(\ddot{s}, \{\ddot{s}'\})$ such that $\ddot{s}'$ refines *all* states in C. We formalize these intuitions in refinement games below.

The Streett acceptance condition for model M is a predicate $\mathcal{A}_M$ that characterizes the *allowed* infinite sequences of states, those $(s_n)_{n \in \mathbb{N}}$ satisfying "*for all* $\ell \in \mathcal{L}$, set $\{n \in \mathbb{N} \mid s_n \in E_\ell\}$ is infinite or set $\{n \in \mathbb{N} \mid s_n \in F_\ell\}$ is finite". For example in the model from Figure 1, the infinitely repeating sequence of states $(s^1_{00}\, s^2_{10})^\omega$ is accepted whereas $(s^0_{10}\, s^1_{11})^\omega$ is not, where the superscript 2 (resp., 1) denotes membership in E_ℓ (resp., F_ℓ). We chose a Streett condition over, say, a Rabin condition since its conjunctivity allows us to enforce *all* constraints of a ranking function; and since it guarantees that checking guarded formulas of the modal μ-calculus for such models is in NP as Player I will have a memoryless winning strategy.

We turn to defining abstraction between models through a refinement notion, using various acceptance conditions of regular games. Below we write π_i for the projection into the i-th component of an ordered tuple. Given a relation $\rho \subseteq B \times C$ with subsets $X \subseteq B$ and $Y \subseteq C$ we write $X.\rho$ for $\{c \in C \mid \exists b \in X \colon (b, c) \in \rho\}$ and $\rho.Y$ for $\{b \in B \mid \exists c \in Y \colon (b, c) \in \rho\}$ and abuse this notation whenever ρ is a function (viewed as a graph). For a sequence of tuples Φ we write $\Phi[i]$ for the sequence obtained from Φ through projection into the i-th coordinate. Let $\mathrm{map}(f, \Phi)$ be the sequence obtained from Φ by applying function f to all elements of Φ in situ.

Definition 2 (Refinement)

1. *Finite refinement plays for models M_1 and M_2 have the rules and winning conditions as stated in Table 1. An infinite play Φ is a* win *for Player I (the verifier) iff* $[\mathcal{A}_{M_1}(\Phi[1]) \Rightarrow \mathcal{A}_{M_2}(\Phi[2])]$ *holds; otherwise it is won by Player II (the refuter).*
2. *State* $s_1 \in S_1$ refines $s_2 \in S_2$ *(and then* s_2 abstracts s_1*) iff Player I has a winning strategy for all refinement plays started at* (s_1, s_2).
3. *Model* M_1 refines (is abstracted by) M_2 *iff Player I has a strategy for the corresponding refinement game between M_1 and M_2 such that any state in S_1 is abstracted by some state in S_2, and any state in S_2 is refined by some state in S_1.*

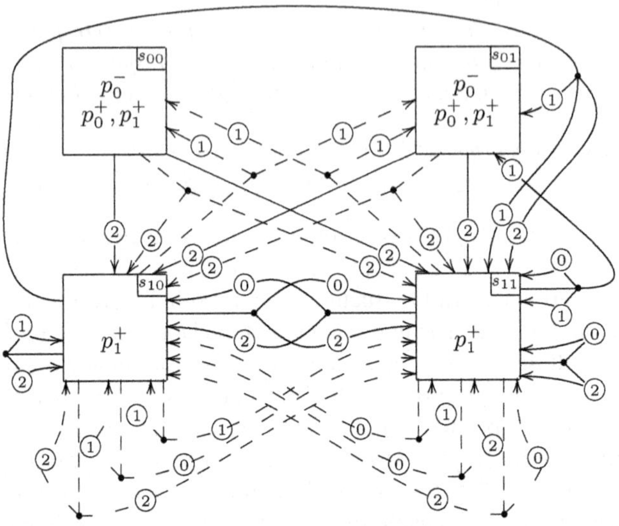

Fig. 1. A hypermixed Kripke structure. At state s, label p^- (resp., p^+) denotes $s \in L^-(p)$ (resp., $s \in L^+(p)$). Branching solid (resp., dashed) arrows model must-transitions (s, D) (resp., may-transitions (s, C)). Depicted states come in three versions — labeled with 0, 1, or 2 superscripts — that share outgoing transitions. Labels on transitions indicate the version of their source state. For example, the upper most depicted solid transition indicates $\{(s^i_{10}, \{s^1_{01}, s^1_{11}, s^2_{11}\}) \mid i \in \{0,1,2\}\} \subseteq R^-$. The state set of all versions labeled with 2, paired with the state set of all versions labeled with 1, yields the sole Streett acceptance condition of this model, here, $E = \{s^2_{00}, s^2_{01}, s^2_{10}, s^2_{11}\}$ and $F = \{s^1_{00}, s^1_{01}, s^1_{10}, s^1_{11}\}$.

Our ranked predicate abstraction defined below will ensure item 3. above by definition. Since this paper presents techniques that render abstractions by construction, we are not concerned with the complexity of checking refinement per se. We note that our refinement between two Kripke structures coincides with bisimulation [23].

Example 1 (Abstraction). The model in Figure 1 is an abstraction of the model from Figure 2 where all three versions of s_{00} and s_{01} abstract $\hat{s}$, and all three versions of s_{10} and s_{11} abstract all states of the Kripke structure other than $\hat{s}$.

3 Sound Satisfaction Relation

We will present the modal μ-calculus in its equivalent form of alternating tree automata [25]. All results in this section have standard proofs.

Definition 3 (Tree automata). *An* alternating tree automaton $A = (Q_A, \delta_A, \Theta_A)$ *has*

- *a finite, nonempty set of states* $(q \in)Q_A$
- *a transition relation* δ_A *mapping automaton states to one of the following forms, where* q, q_1, q_2 *are automaton states and* $p \in \mathrm{AP}$*:* $p \mid \neg p \mid q \mid q_1 \tilde{\wedge} q_2 \mid q_1 \tilde{\vee} q_2 \mid \mathbf{EX}\, q \mid \mathbf{AX}\, q$ *and*

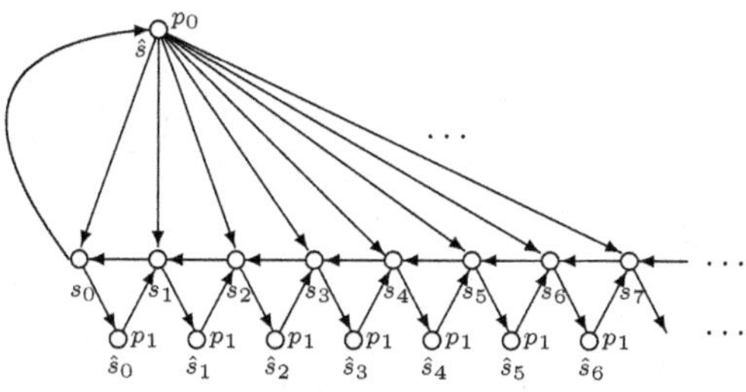

Fig. 2. A Kripke structure with $L^-(\hat{s}) = \{p_0\}$, $L^-(s_i) = \{\}$, and $L^-(\hat{s}_i) = \{p_1\}$ for all $i \geq 0$. Arrows $s \to s'$ denote $(s, \{s'\}) \in R^-$.

Table 1. Moves of refinement game at configuration (s_1, s_2). Refinement plays are sequences of configurations generated thus.

L^- labeling: Player II chooses p from $L^-(s_2)$; Player I wins iff p is in $L^-(s_1)$
L^+ labeling: Player II chooses p from AP $\setminus L^+(s_2)$; Player I wins iff p is not in $L^+(s_1)$
R^- transition: Player II chooses a set of states $D'_2 \in \{s_2\}.R_2^-$; Player I responds with $D'_1 \in \{s_1\}.R_1^-$; Player II chooses $s'_1 \in D'_1$; Player I responds with $s'_2 \in D'_2$; the next configuration is (s'_1, s'_2)
R^+ transition: Player II chooses a set of states $C'_1 \in \{s_1\}.R_1^+$; Player I responds with $C'_2 \in \{s_2\}.R_2^+$; Player II chooses $s'_2 \in C'_2$; Player I responds with $s'_1 \in C'_1$; the next configuration is (s'_1, s'_2)

- *an acceptance condition $\Theta_A \colon Q_A \to \mathbb{N}$ with finite image, where an infinite sequence of automata states is accepted iff the maximal acceptance number occurring infinitely often is even.*

An alternating tree automaton is depicted in Figure 3. Throughout this paper, we assume without loss of generality [18] that all automata correspond to guarded formulas of the modal μ-calculus, i.e. that every cycle in the underlying graph of automaton A has to contain an element that is labeled with **EX** or **AX**. Also, for any bounded sequence $\boldsymbol{n}$ of elements in $\mathbb{N}$ we write $\sup(\boldsymbol{n})$ for the largest m that occurs in $\boldsymbol{n}$ infinitely often.

Definition 4 (Satisfaction)

- *Finite satisfaction plays for model M and alternating tree automaton A have the rules and winning conditions as stated in Table 2. An infinite play Φ is a* win *for Player I iff $[\mathcal{A}_M(\Phi[1]) \Rightarrow \sup(\mathrm{map}(\Theta, \Phi[2]))$ is even$]$; otherwise it is won by Player II.*
- *Model M* satisfies *automaton A in configuration $(s, q) \in S \times Q$, written $(M, s) \models (A, q)$, iff Player I has a strategy for the corresponding satisfaction game between M and A such that Player I wins all satisfaction plays started at (s, q) with her strategy.*

The acceptance condition for satisfaction plays between a model M and an automata A is a variant of those familiar from the literature: An infinite play Φ is a win for Player I

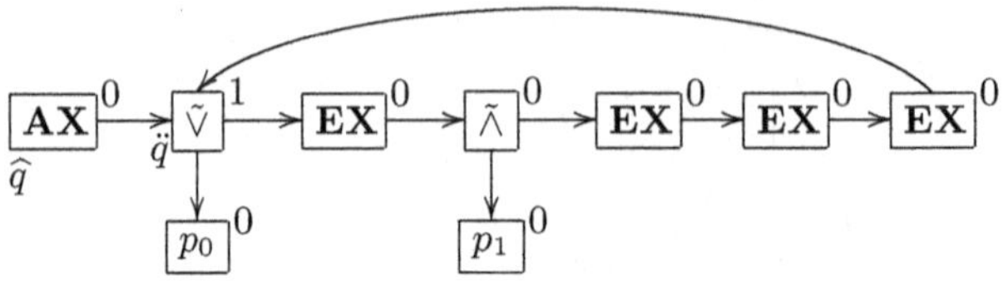

Fig. 3. An alternating tree automata. Accepting values are depicted next to states. At state $\ddot{q}$ it expresses that there is a run that reaches a p_0-state after $4n$ moves for some $n \geq 0$ (since the cycle has to be left to obtain an accepting sequence) such that p_1 always holds after $4m+1$ moves for every $m < n$ with $m \geq 0$. At $\widehat{q}$, it expresses that after any transition the property expressed at $\ddot{q}$ holds.

Table 2. Moves of satisfaction game at configuration (s, q), specified through a case analysis on the value of $\delta(q)$. Satisfaction plays are sequences of configurations generated thus.

p: Player I wins iff $p \in L^-(s)$
$\neg p$: Player I wins iff $p \notin L^+(s)$
q': the next configuration is (s, q')
$q_1 \tilde{\wedge} q_2$: Player II picks a q' from $\{q_1, q_2\}$; the next configuration is (s, q')
$q_1 \tilde{\vee} q_2$: Player I picks a q' from $\{q_1, q_2\}$; the next configuration is (s, q')
$\mathbf{EX}\, q'$: Player I picks $D' \in \{s\}.R^-$; Player II picks $s' \in D'$; the next configuration is (s', q')
$\mathbf{AX}\, q'$: Player II picks $C' \in \{s\}.R^+$; Player I picks $s' \in C'$; the next configuration is (s', q')

iff either the projection of Φ into the automata A is accepting in A ($\sup(\mathrm{map}(\Theta, \Phi[2]))$ is even) or the projection of Φ into M is non-accepting in M ($\neg \mathcal{A}_M(\Phi[1])$). We write $s \models q$ and Q, etc, whenever M and A are clear from the context. Note that $\models$ applied to Kripke structures corresponds to the usual satisfaction relation.

Example 2 (Satisfaction game). For the model of Figure 4 and the automaton from Figure 3 we have $s^0_{00} \models \widehat{q}$: at the $\widehat{q}$-state Player I chooses s^2_{10} or s^2_{20} in the $\mathbf{AX}$-move, depending on which may-transition from s^0_{00} is picked by Player II. In order to show $\ddot{q}$ at s^2_{10} or s^2_{20}, Player I chooses the $\mathbf{EX}$-automaton state in the $\tilde{\vee}$-move, then she chooses the must-transition pointing to $\{s^0_{31}\}$, (if Player II picks the $\mathbf{EX}$-state) Player I chooses the must-transition pointing to $\{s^0_{21}\}$, at the next $\mathbf{EX}$-move she chooses the one pointing to $\{s^1_{10}, s^0_{20}\}$, at the next $\mathbf{EX}$-move she chooses the one pointing to s^1_{01}, respectively the one pointing to $\{s^1_{10}, s^1_{20}\}$. Then in the latter case, a cycle has been reached and the game continues as described before. So either p_0 is reached or a sequence that contains no state labeled with 2 but infinitely many states labeled with 1 is generated, which contradicts the Streett acceptance condition.

The winning conditions for the satisfaction game are Rabin conditions as they have form [Streett $\Rightarrow$ RabinChain] which reduces to Rabin; so deciding $(M, s) \models (A, q)$ is in NP for finite-state models. We prove soundness of $(M, s) \models (A, q)$ as an approximation of the EXPTIME-hard relation which asks whether all pointed Kripke structures $(\ddot{M}, \ddot{s})$ that refine (M, s) satisfy A in $(\ddot{s}, q)$, the proof is completely standard. As usual,

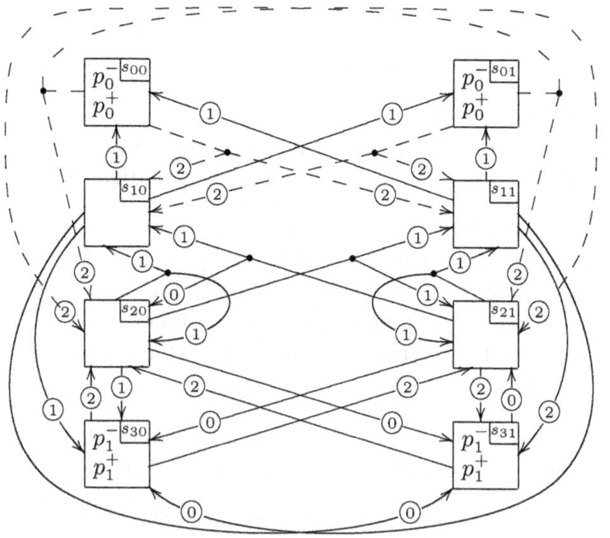

Fig. 4. Another hypermixed Kripke structure. For notational conventions we refer to Figure 1.

$(M, s) \not\models (A, q)$ does not imply $(M, s) \models (\neg A, q)$ where $\neg A$ recognizes the complement of A.

Theorem 1 (Soundness). *Suppose s_1 refines s_2. Then for any "guarded" automaton A and $q \in Q$, we have that $s_2 \models (A, q)$ implies $s_1 \models (A, q)$.*

4 Ranked Predicate Abstraction

Predicate abstraction computes a partition of a concrete state space by identifying states that have the same truth values for finitely many given formulas of some logic [15]. If that logic is decidable or if its decidability can be over-approximated, then model structure (e.g. a state transition relation) over this partition can be synthesized by means of such decision procedures without explicitly constructing the concrete model [15] — provided that model structure is expressible in the given logic.

We now adapt predicate abstraction to hypermixed Kripke structures and branching time and argue the suitability of that adaption. In doing so, we work with a function h that maps concrete states S to abstract states I. This function is derived from finitely many predicates $\phi_1, \phi_2, \ldots, \phi_n$ by the equivalence relation $\equiv \subseteq S \times S$, given by $s \equiv s'$ iff (for all $1 \leq i \leq n$, $s \models \phi_i \Leftrightarrow s' \models \phi_i$). Then I is the set of equivalence classes of $\equiv$ and $h(s)$ is defined to be the equivalence class of s.

Definition 5 (Ranked predicate abstraction). *A* ranked predicate abstraction $\aleph$ *of a state space S is a tuple $(I, h, J, (\leq^k)_{k \in K}, \wp)$ where*

- *$h: S \to I$ is a surjective function mapping concrete (S) to abstract (I) states*
- *J is a non-empty set of rank locations;*

- *for all* $k \in K$*, with* K *a (possible empty) index set,* $\leq^k \subseteq (S \times J) \times (S \times J)$ *is a pre-order with well-founded irreflexive version* $<^k$*; and*
- $\wp \subseteq \mathrm{AP}$ *is the set of* slice *predicates such that*
- $|I| + |J| + |K| + |\wp|$ *is finite.*

Ranked predicate abstraction $\aleph$ generalizes the familiar predicate abstraction [15] to the entire modal μ-calculus, and so to liveness properties in particular. In our approach

- precision and completeness require an acceptance condition: abstract runs that are infinitely descending and related (not necessarily state-wise) to concrete runs are rejected; "descending" is defined in terms of given pre-orders
- set J is used to allow more complex ranking pre-orders $\leq^k$
- set $\wp$ is used to restrict the predicates of the model to those which occur in properties one wishes to check.

Example 3 (Ranked predicate abstraction). Two ranked predicate abstractions for state space S of the Kripke structure in Figure 2 are $\widehat{\aleph} = (\{i_0, i_1\}, \widehat{h}, \{\ddot{\jmath}, \hat{\jmath}\}, (\leq^k)_{k \in \{0\}}, \{p_0\})$ and $\ddot{\aleph} = (\{i_0, i_1, i_2, i_3\}, \ddot{h}, \{\ddot{\jmath}, \hat{\jmath}\}, (\leq^k)_{k \in \{0\}}, \{p_0, p_1\})$ such that $\widehat{h}(\hat{s}) = \ddot{h}(\hat{s}) = i_0$, $\widehat{h}(s_0) = \ddot{h}(s_0) = i_1$, and for $n \in \mathbb{N}$, $\widehat{h}(s_{n+1}) = \widehat{h}(\hat{s}_n) = i_1$, $\ddot{h}(s_{n+1}) = i_2$, $\ddot{h}(\hat{s}_n) = i_3$, and $(s', j') \leq^0 (s, j) \Leftrightarrow \omega(s', j') \leq \omega(s, j)$ for $s, s' \in S, j, j' \in \{\ddot{\jmath}, \hat{\jmath}\}$ where $\omega(\hat{s}, \ddot{\jmath}) = \omega(\hat{s}, \hat{\jmath}) = 0$, $\omega(s_n, \hat{\jmath}) = \omega(\hat{s}_n, \ddot{\jmath}) = n + 1$, and $\omega(s_n, \ddot{\jmath}) = \omega(\hat{s}_n, \hat{\jmath}) = n + 2$.

We point out that a nontrivial J is required to obtain completeness of the abstraction framework, see Proposition 1 in Section 6 below. The $\aleph$-abstraction game involves two hypermixed Kripke structures M_1 and M_2 where $\aleph$ is a ranked predicate abstraction for the state space of M_1. The objective of Player I is to show that M_1 is abstracted by M_2 up to $\aleph$, meaning that Player II can switch between states of M_1 that map to the same elements via h as long as no contradiction to the acceptance condition of M_1 or to the ranking functions of $\aleph$ is produced. Therefore, the states of M_1 are represented in configurations via elements of $I \times J \times ((\mathcal{L} \cup K) \to \{0, 1, 2\})$, where J is under control of Player I such that soundness of the game is ensured, and $((\mathcal{L} \cup K) \to \{0, 1, 2\})$ is used to encode fairness constraints as follows: A Streett condition pair (E, F), represented by an element $k \in K$, is encoded via a function into $\{0, 1, 2\}$ where value 2 indicates that a state of E, respectively, a move not preserving $\leq^k$ happens; 1 indicates that a state of $F \setminus E$, respectively, a move that preserves $<^k$ happens; and 0 indicates that a state outside F or E, respectively, a move that preserves $\leq^k$ (but not strictly so) happens. Formally $\Omega^{M,\aleph} : (S \times J)^2 \to ((\mathcal{L} \cup K) \to \{0, 1, 2\})$ is given by

$$\Omega^{M,\aleph}_{(s',j',s,j)}(x) = \begin{cases} 2 & \text{if } (x \in \mathcal{L} \,\&\, s' \in E_x) \text{ or } (x \in K \,\&\, (s', j') \not\leq^x (s, j)) \\ 1 & \text{if } (x \in \mathcal{L} \,\&\, s' \in F_x \setminus E_x) \text{ or } (x \in K \,\&\, (s', j') <^x (s, j)) \\ 0 & \text{otherwise} \end{cases}$$

where we assume throughout that K and $\mathcal{L}$ are disjoint. For the completeness proof for $(M, s) \models (A, q)$ it is instructive to think of J as the set of automaton states Q_A. We write $\Phi(n)$ for the n-th configuration of play Φ.

Definition 6 (Ranked predicate abstraction game). *Let* $\aleph$ *be a ranked predicate abstraction for the state space of* M_1*.*

Table 3. Moves of $\aleph$-abstraction game at configuration $(i, j, g, s_2) \in I \times J \times ((\mathcal{L} \cup K) \to \{0,1,2\}) \times S_2$ where $\aleph$-abstraction plays are sequences of configurations generated thus.

L^- labeling: Player II chooses p from $L^-(s_2)$ and $s_1 \in h.\{i\}$; Player I wins iff $p \in L^-(s_1) \cap \wp$

L^+ labeling: Player II chooses p from $\mathrm{AP} \setminus L^+(s_2)$ and $s_1 \in h.\{i\}$; Player I wins iff $p \in \wp \setminus L^+(s_1)$

R^- transition: Player II chooses a set of states $D'_2 \in \{s_2\}.R_2^-$; Player I responds with $j' \in J$; Player II chooses $s_1 \in h.\{i\}$; Player I responds with $D'_1 \in \{s_1\}.R_1^-$; Player II chooses $s'_1 \in D'_1$; Player I responds with $s'_2 \in D'_2$; the next configuration is $(h(s'_1), j', \Omega^{M,\aleph}_{(s'_1,j',s_1,j)}, s'_2)$

R^+ transition: Player II chooses $s_1 \in h.\{i\}$ and $C'_1 \in \{s_1\}.R_1^+$; Player I responds with $C'_2 \in \{s_2\}.R_2^+$; Player II chooses $s'_2 \in C'_2$; Player I responds with $s'_1 \in C'_1$ and $j' \in J$; the next configuration is $(h(s'_1), j', \Omega^{M,\aleph}_{(s'_1,j',s_1,j)}, s'_2)$

- *Finite $\aleph$-abstraction plays for models M_1 and M_2 have the rules and winning conditions as stated in Table 3. An infinite play Φ is a* win *for Player I iff [(for all $x \in \mathcal{L} \cup K$, $\sup((\pi_3(\Phi(n))(x))_{n \in \mathbb{N}})$ is even) $\Rightarrow \mathcal{A}_{M_2}(\Phi[4])$] holds; otherwise it is won by Player II.*
- *The model M_1* is $\aleph$-abstracted by *M_2 iff Player I has a strategy for the corresponding $\aleph$-abstraction game between M_1 and M_2 such that for any $(i, j, g) \in I \times J \times ((\mathcal{L} \cup K) \to \{0,1,2\})$ there is $s_2 \in S_2$ (and, conversely, for all $s_2 \in S_2$ there is $(i, j, g) \in I \times J \times ((\mathcal{L} \cup K) \to \{0,1,2\})$) such that Player I wins with her strategy in all $\aleph$-abstraction plays started at (i, j, g, s_2).*

We show that $\aleph$-abstractions are indeed abstractions.

Theorem 2 (Consistency of ranked predicate abstractions). *Let $\aleph$ be a ranked predicate abstraction of the state space of M_1. If M_1 is $\aleph$-abstracted by M_2, then M_1 is abstracted by M_2.*

We now define an abstraction that is precise with respect to the $\aleph$-abstraction game.

Definition 7 (Precise ranked predicate abstraction). *Let $\aleph$ be a ranked predicate abstraction of the state space of M. The* precise $\aleph$-abstraction $M_\aleph$ of M *is defined to be the model $(S_\aleph, R_\aleph^-, R_\aleph^+, L_\aleph^-, L_\aleph^+, (E_x^\aleph, F_x^\aleph)_{x \in \mathcal{L} \cup K})$ where*

$$S_\aleph = \{(i', j', \Omega^{M,\aleph}_{(s',j',s,j)}) \in I \times J \times ((\mathcal{L} \cup K) \to \{0,1,2\}) \mid i' = h(s')\}$$

$$R_\aleph^- = \{((i,j,g), \widetilde{D}) \mid \exists j' \in J, f \colon S \to \mathbb{P}(S) : (\forall s \in h.\{i\} : f(s) \in \{s\}.R^-)\ \&$$
$$\widetilde{D} = \{(i', j', \Omega^{M,\aleph}_{(s',j',s,j)}) \mid s \in h.\{i\}\ \&\ s' \in h.\{i'\} \cap f(s)\}\}$$

$$R_\aleph^+ = \{((i,j,g), \widetilde{C}) \mid \exists s \in h.\{i\}, C \in \{s\}.R^+ :$$
$$\widetilde{C} = \{(i', j', \Omega^{M,\aleph}_{(s',j',s,j)}) \mid j' \in J\ \&\ s' \in C \cap h.\{i'\}\}\}$$

$$L_\aleph^-(i,j,g) = \wp \cap \bigcap_{s \in h.\{i\}} L^-(s) \qquad L_\aleph^+(i,j,g) = (\mathrm{AP} \setminus \wp) \cup \bigcup_{s \in h.\{i\}} L^+(s)$$

$$E_x^\aleph = \{(i,j,g) \mid g(x) = 2\} \qquad F_x^\aleph = \{(i,j,g) \mid g(x) = 1\}$$

In the $\aleph$-abstraction of M, the set of must-labelings (resp., may-labelings) is standard, except that it (resp., its complement) is restricted to predicates from $\wp$. The Streett conditions specify that value 1 must not occur infinitely often if value 2 occurs only finitely often. The state space is the reachable one occurring in the $\aleph$-abstraction game. The first component $h(s')$ corresponds to the abstract state, the second component j' corresponds to the rank location (the current automaton state if J is taken to be Q), and the third component corresponds to the acceptance encoded in the ranked predicate abstraction game.

A must-transition $((i, j, g), \widetilde{D}) \in R^-_\aleph$ is determined by choosing must-transitions $(s, f(s)) \in R^-$ for every related concrete state $s \in h.\{i\}$ and taking a ranked predicate location $j' \in J$. Note that Player I has control of the ranked predicate location in the satisfaction game, so she can always respond with the reached automaton state if J is taken to be Q. Set $\widetilde{D}$ is the union of the abstract states in $f(s)$ for $s \in h.\{i\}$ combined with j'. Furthermore, the g-component of a target in $\widetilde{D}$ may vary depending on the considered witnesses s and s' in M. A may-transition $((i, j, g), \widetilde{C}) \in R^+_\aleph$ is determined by taking a may-transition $(s, C) \in R^+$ for some s that is related to the abstract state i. The target set consists of all abstract states related to a state in C combined with any value from J. The g-component of a target in $\widetilde{C}$ may similarly vary depending on the witnesses for the abstract state in C.

Example 4. For $\widehat{\aleph}$ and $\ddot{\aleph}$ of Example 3, the $\widehat{\aleph}$-abstraction of the model in Figure 2 is shown in Figure 1 and the $\ddot{\aleph}$-abstraction of that same model is depicted in Figure 4. There the index of s_{ij} corresponds to the I-component (respectively J-component) and the g-component is encoded by the transition labels. These figures omit must-transitions that have matching must-transitions with a superset as target (these omission leads to refinement equivalent models). To enhance readability the must-transitions outgoing from states s_{00} and s_{01} as well as the outgoing may-transitions from other states are omitted in Figure 4.

We justify the adjective "precise" of Definition 7.

Theorem 3 (Precision). *The finite-state model $M_\aleph$ of Definition 7 is a precise $\aleph$-abstraction of M, i.e.,*

- *$M_\aleph$ is a $\aleph$-abstraction of M and*
- *if M_2 is a $\aleph$-abstraction of M, then M_2 abstracts $M_\aleph$.*

5 Incremental Analysis

In the case that an abstraction obtained by ranked predicate abstraction does not satisfy a property of interest, techniques for abstraction-refinement that reuse already verified sub-properties are called for. Such a technique, a generalization of adding predicates in the predicate or Cartesian abstraction approach [2,14], is introduced now:

Definition 8 (Extensions of ranked predicate abstractions). *Let $\aleph_1$ and $\aleph_2$ be ranked predicate abstractions of S. Then $\aleph_1$ is an* extension *of $\aleph_2$ if $h_2 = h_1 \circ h$ for some surjective function h, $J_2 \subseteq J_1$, $\wp_2 \subseteq \wp_1$, $K_2 \subseteq K_1$, and $\forall k \in K_2\colon \leq^k_1 = \leq^k_2$.*

For example, the ranked predicate abstraction $\ddot{\aleph}$ is an extension of $\widehat{\aleph}$, where $\ddot{\aleph}$ and $\widehat{\aleph}$ are given in Example 3. Extensions always enable incremental analysis.

Theorem 4 (Incremental analysis). *Let the ranked predicate abstraction $\aleph_1$ be an extension of the ranked predicate abstraction $\aleph_2$. Then $M_{\aleph_1}$ is abstracted by $M_{\aleph_2}$.*

Extensions should be confluent in the following sense: if a ranked predicate abstraction $\aleph_1$ for the state space of some model M yields an abstraction $M_{\aleph_1}$ satisfying the automaton (A, q), then any ranked predicate abstraction $\aleph_2$ for the state space of M should be extendable to a ranked predicate abstraction $\aleph$ such that $M_\aleph$ also satisfies (A, q). We define common extensions and show this desired confluence.

Definition 9 (Common extension). *Let $\aleph_1$ and $\aleph_2$ be ranked predicate abstractions for state space S, where we assume without loss of generality that K_1 and K_2 are disjoint. The ranked predicate abstraction $\aleph_1 \sqcap \aleph_2$ for S is $(S.h, h, J_1 \cup J_2, (\leq^k)_{k \in K_1 \cup K_2}, \wp_1 \cup \wp_2)$ where $h = \{(s, (i_1, i_2)) \in S \times (I_1 \times I_2) \mid s \in h_1.\{i_1\} \cap h_2.\{i_2\}\}$, and $\leq^k$ is $\leq^k_1$ if $k \in K_1$, but equals $\leq^k_2$ if $k \in K_2$.*

Theorem 5 (Confluence of extensions). *Let $\aleph_1$ and $\aleph_2$ be ranked predicate abstractions for state space S. Then $\aleph_1 \sqcap \aleph_2$ is an extension of $\aleph_1$ and of $\aleph_2$.*

6 Completeness

First we point out an issue of expressiveness: more than one rank location is needed in order to get a complete predicate abstraction.

Proposition 1 (Limited expressiveness). *There is no ranked predicate abstraction $\aleph$ of the Kripke structure from Figure 2 such that its J is a singleton and $(M_\aleph, h(\hat{s})) \models (A, \widehat{q})$ holds, where A is the automaton from Figure 3.*

We now construct ranked predicate abstractions that prove the desired completeness. Let $(M, s) \models (A, q)$ hold. The set of OR-states O_A and the set T_A of states that are targets of **EX** - or **AX** -states are defined:

$$O_A = \{q \in Q \mid \exists q_1, q_2 \in S \colon \delta(q) = q_1 \tilde{\vee} q_2\}$$
$$T_A = \{q' \in Q \mid \exists q \in Q \colon \delta(q) \in \{\mathbf{EX}\, q', \mathbf{AX}\, q'\}\}\,.$$

Without loss of generality, the automaton state q that describes the property we are interested in is in T_A (otherwise add a fresh automaton state q' with $\delta(q') = \mathbf{EX}\, q$; thus q' is unreachable and won't interfere with satisfaction games at other automaton states).

A *choice function* for A is a function $c_A \colon O_A \to \{1, 2\}$. Let $\mathtt{Ch}_A$ be the set of all choice functions for A. Let θ be a memoryless strategy for Player I for the satisfaction game between M and A. Then $c_A^{\theta,s}$ is the choice function whose choices on any $q \in O_A$ agree with those of θ on (s, q).

The ranked predicate abstraction that proves completeness with respect to a memoryless strategy θ is constructed as follows: States of M are equivalent iff

- they satisfy the same automaton states with respect to θ and
- θ behaves the same on every OR-state.

Relevant predicates are those that occur in the automaton. The set J is taken to be the set of automaton states T_A. The pre-orders $\leq^k$ are derived from ranking functions corresponding to odd automaton acceptance numbers: roughly speaking, the ranking function $\omega^{\theta,k}$ is determined (if possible, otherwise a default value κ is chosen) by the least number of unfoldings necessary to guarantee that no further $2k+1$ value can be reached by remaining below $2k+2$. This is formalized by counting the unfoldings of function $\mho_{\theta,k}$ applied to the empty set until the state of the model combined with the corresponding automaton state is obtained in the generated set (note that κ will be chosen such that it is always greater than any possible counting). Formally, $\mho_{\theta,k} \colon (S \times Q) \to (S \times Q)$ is given by

$$\mho_{\theta,k}(W) = W \cup \{(s,q) \mid \forall (s_n,q_n)_{n\in\mathbb{N}} \in \xi^{\theta}_{(s,q)}, r \in \mathbb{N}\colon \\ \Theta(q_{r+1}) = 1+2k \Rightarrow ((s_{r+1},q_{r+1}) \in W \text{ or } \exists r' \leq r\colon \Theta(q_{r'}) > 1+2k)\}$$

with $\xi^{\theta}_{(s,q)}$ as set of all plays started in configuration (s,q) and played via strategy θ.

Definition 10 (Complete ranked predicate abstraction). *Let θ be a memoryless strategy for Player I for the satisfaction game between M and automaton A. Then the θ-*ranked predicate abstraction *is $\aleph_\theta = (S.h_\theta, h_\theta, T_A, (\leq^k_\theta)_{k\in K_\theta}, \wp_\theta)$, where*

$$\begin{aligned}
&K_\theta = \{0,1,\ldots,\lfloor (max\{\Theta(q) \mid q \in Q\} - 1)/2 \rfloor\} \quad and \quad \kappa = |\mathbb{P}(\mathbb{P}(S \times Q))| \\
&h_\theta : S \to \mathbb{P}(T_A) \times \mathtt{Ch}_A \text{ with } h_\theta(s) = (\{q \in T_A \mid \theta \text{ wins in } (s,q)\}, c^{\theta,s}_A) \\
&\omega^{\theta,k}_{(s,q)} = min(\{\alpha \mid (s,q) \in \mho^{\alpha}_{\theta,k}(\{\})\} \cup \{\kappa\}) \\
&(s',q') \leq^k_\theta (s,q) \Leftrightarrow \omega^{\theta,k}_{(s',q')} \leq \omega^{\theta,k}_{(s,q)} \\
&\wp_\theta = \{p \mid \exists q \in Q\colon \delta(q) \in \{p, \neg p\}\}
\end{aligned}$$

Theorem 6 (Completeness). *Let M be a Kripke structure and θ be a memoryless strategy for Player I for $(M,s) \models (A,q)$ and $\aleph_\theta$ the θ-ranked predicate abstraction of M. Then $(M_{\aleph_\theta}, (h_\theta(s), q, g)) \models (A,q)$ holds whenever θ is winning for the satisfaction game at configuration (s,q).*

7 Discussion

Fairness constraints in models, the Streett acceptance conditions in our paper, are required for securing completeness as the property language is powerful enough to express such constraints. Such completeness can already be proved if R^+ has type $S \times S$ instead of our $S \times \mathbb{P}(S)$. But then abstractions for a given $\aleph$ may be less precise, and the completeness proof is likely to be harder; in fact, we don't know whether completeness for feasible abstractions restricted to state space partitions is then always realizable.

Our abstract models are closely related to the modal automata in [11], except that in our model

- only must-transitions point to OR-states, e.g., our must-transition (s, D) is graphically represented through an OR-state o that has exactly the outgoing transitions to all elements of D and s points to o; and
- may-transitions point to AND-states via a similar graphical representation.

Note that AND-states do not exist in modal automata; in our approach AND-states allow more compact abstractions and simplify our completeness proof. We did consider using modal automata but found that a definition and proof of precision would be more complex than for our choice of model, as indicated in the previous paragraph.

We also considered using the focussed transition systems in [10] as an alternative complete abstraction framework. We decided against its use as one of our key objectives was to maximize the reuse of tried and tested methods in predicate abstraction, notably the partition of a concrete state space through predicates and the computation of abstract transitions based on the existence of transitions between states of such partitions. The focus and defocus operations in focussed transition systems seem to make it difficult to reason about the existence of transitions in this manner. This is related to the fact that the model checking game $F \models \phi$ for property ϕ and focussed transition systems F in [10] does not satisfy conjunction elimination and disjunction introduction; e.g. there are F, ϕ_1, and ϕ_2 with $F \models \phi_1 \wedge \phi_2$ but $F \not\models \phi_1$. This also suggests that "most precise" abstractions may not exist or may be difficult to define for focussed transition systems.

Our completeness result, as all others, does not shed light on how to find feasible abstractions but it secures the existence of ranked predicate abstractions that are feasible, confluent, and incremental. So the design of an abstraction-refinement loop for predicate abstraction of branching time may be attainable in future work.

8 Conclusion

In this paper we developed an abstraction framework for Kripke structures that extends predicate abstraction to ranked predicate abstraction so that one can deal with all liveness properties as well. Specifically, whenever a Kripke structure M satisfies a property ϕ of the modal μ-calculus, there is a finite-state model computed through a ranked predicate abstraction that witnesses this truth, and so our framework is complete in the sense of Dams & Namjoshi [10]. We also proved that the abstractions synthesized in this way are precise in the sense of Dams [7]. Our ranked predicate abstractions correspond to state space partitions of the concrete model by definition. We demonstrated that these abstractions are incremental and confluent: new predicates may be added for abstraction-refinement, and feasible abstractions can be found no matter how, and how often, initial abstractions have been refined so far. In summary our results form a good foundation for the automated synthesis of abstractions and counter-example-guided abstraction-refinement for branching time, both subjects for future work.

References

1. R. Alur, Th. A. Henzinger, and O. Kupferman. Alternating-time temporal logic. *Journal of the ACM* 49(5):672–713, 2002.
2. Th. Ball, A. Podelski, and S. K. Rajamani. Boolean and Cartesian Abstraction for Model Checking C Programs. In *Proc. of TACAS'01*, LNCS 2031, pp. 268–283, Springer-Verlag, 2001.
3. G. Bruns and P. Godefroid. Model Checking Partial State Spaces with 3-Valued Temporal Logics. In *Proc. of CAV'99*, LNCS 1633, pp. 274–287, Springer-Verlag, 1999.

4. E. M. Clarke and E. A. Emerson. Synthesis of synchronization skeletons for branching time temporal logic. In *Logic of Programs Workshop*, LNCS 131, pp. 244–263. Springer-Verlag, 1981.
5. E. M. Clarke, O. Grumberg, and D. E. Long. Model checking and abstraction. *ACM TOPLAS* 16(5):1512–1542, 1994.
6. P. Cousot and R. Cousot. Abstract interpretation: a unified lattice model for static analysis of programs. In *Proc. of POPL'77*, pp. 238–252, ACM Press, 1977.
7. D. Dams. *Abstract interpretation and partition refinement for model checking*. PhD thesis, Technische Universiteit Eindhoven, The Netherlands, 1996.
8. D. Dams, R. Gerth, and O. Grumberg. Abstract interpretation of reactive systems. *ACM TOPLAS*, 19(2):253–291, 1997.
9. D. Dams, R. Gerth, and O. Grumberg. A Heuristic for the Automatic Generation of Ranking Functions. In *Proc. of the Workshop on Advances in Verification*, Chicago, July 2000.
10. D. Dams and K. Namjoshi. The Existence of Finite Abstractions for Branching Time Model Checking. In *Proc. of LICS'04*, pp. 335–344, IEEE Computer Society Press, 2004.
11. D. Dams and K. S. Namjoshi. Automata as Abstractions. In *Proc. of VMCAI'05*, LNCS 3385, pp. 216–232, Springer-Verlag, 2005.
12. Y. Fang, N. Piterman, A. Pnueli, and L. D. Zuck. Liveness with Incomprehensible Ranking. In *Proc. of TACAS'04*, LNCS 2988, pp. 482-496, Springer-Verlag, 2004.
13. H. Fecher and M. Huth. Complete abstractions through extensions of disjunctive modal transition systems. *Technical Report No. 0604, Institut für Informatik und Praktische Mathematik der Christian-Albrechts-Universität zu Kiel*, 31 pages, March 2006.
14. P. Godefroid, M. Huth, and R. Jagadeesan. Abstraction-based Model Checking using Modal Transition Systems. In *Proc. of CONCUR'01*, LNCS 2154, pp. 426–440, Springer-Verlag, 2001.
15. S. Graf and H. Saidi. Construction of abstract state graphs with PVS. In *Proc. of CAV'97*, LNCS 1254, pp. 72–83, Springer-Verlag, 1997.
16. M. Huth, R. Jagadeesan, and D. A. Schmidt. Modal transition systems: a foundation for three-valued program analysis. In *Proc. of ESOP'01*, LNCS 2028, pp. 155–169. Springer-Verlag, 2001.
17. Y. Kesten and A. Pnueli. Verification by Augmented Finitary Abstraction. *Inf. Comput.* 163(1):203-243, 2000.
18. D. Kozen. Results on the propositional μ-calculus. *Theoretical Computer Science* 27:333–354, 1983.
19. O. Kupferman and M. Y. Vardi. Complementation Constructions for Nondeterministic Automata on Infinite Words. In *Proc. of TACAS'05*, LNCS 3440, pp. 206–221, Springer-Verlag, 2005.
20. K. G. Larsen and B. Thomsen. A Modal Process Logic. In *Proc. of LICS'88*, pp. 203–210, IEEE Computer Society Press, 1988
21. K. G. Larsen and L. Xinxin. Equation Solving Using Modal Transition Systems. In *Proc. of LICS'90*, pp. 108–117, IEEE Computer Society Press, 1990.
22. K. Namjoshi. Abstraction for Branching Time Properties. In *Proc. of CAV'03*, LNCS 2725, pp. 288–300, Springer-Verlag, 2003.
23. D. M. R. Park. Concurrency and automata on infinite sequences. In *Proc. of the 5th GI Conference*, LNCS 104, pp. 167–183, Springer-Verlag, 1989.
24. J. P. Quielle and J. Sifakis. Specification and verification of concurrent systems in CESAR. In *Proc. of the 5th International Symposium on Programming*, 1981.
25. Th. Wilke. Alternating tree automata, parity games, and modal μ-calculus. *Bull. Soc. Math. Belg.*, 8(2):359–391, May 2001.

Timed Temporal Logics for Abstracting Transient States

Houda Bel Mokadem[1], Béatrice Bérard[2], Patricia Bouyer[1], and François Laroussinie[1]

[1] LSV, CNRS & ENS de Cachan, France
{mokadem,bouyer,fl}@lsv.ens-cachan.fr
[2] LAMSADE, CNRS & Université Paris-Dauphine, France
berard@lamsade.dauphine.fr

Abstract. In previous work, the timed logic TCTL was extended with an "almost everywhere" Until modality which abstracts *negligible* sets of positions (*i.e.* with a null duration) along a run of a timed automaton. We propose here an extension of this logic with more powerful modalities, in order to specify properties abstracting *transient* states, which are events that last for less than k time units. Our main result is that model-checking is still decidable and PSPACE-complete for this extension. On the other hand, a second semantics is defined, in which we consider the *total* duration where the property does not hold along a run. In this case, we prove that model-checking is undecidable.

1 Introduction

Timed Verification. Temporal logic is a convenient formalism for specifying systems and reasoning about them. Furthermore, model-cheking techniques lead to the automatic verification that a model of a system satisfies some temporal logic specification. These methods have been extended to real-time verification: systems are modeled with timed automata [4] and timed logics like TCTL [1] are used to express timed specification like "any problem is followed by an alarm within 3 seconds". Analysis tools have been developped [22,15,20] and successfully applied to numerous case studies.

Timed Temporal Logics and Duration Properties. Along with the study of timed automata, various timed logics have been defined to extend the classical temporal logics with quantitative modalities. For example, this was done with MTL [19,5,21], an extension of LTL, and TCTL [6,1,17], where CTL modalities are augmented with time comparisons of the form $\sim c$, where $\sim$ is a comparison operator. Another related logic is the Parametrized TCTL [13] where TCTL and the timed model are in turn extended with parameters.

In another direction, since the introduction of the *duration calculus* [14] in order to express duration properties, numerous works have been devoted to the algorithmic computation of such properties for timed systems. Since *clocks*, which evolve at the rate of time (as in timed automata), are sometimes not expressive enough, hybrid variables (with multiple slopes) have been considered. The

S. Graf and W. Zhang (Eds.): ATVA 2006, LNCS 4218, pp. 337–351, 2006.

resulting model of hybrid automata has been largely studied in the subsequent years [16]. However, while some decidability results could be obtained [3,18], using stopwatches (*i.e.* variables with slopes 0 and 1) already leads to undecidability for the reachability problem [2].

Further research has thus been devoted to weaker models where hybrid variables are only used as *observers*, *i.e.* are not tested in the automaton and thus play no role during a computation. These variables, sometimes called costs or prices in this context can be used in an optimization criterium [3,7,8,11] or as constraints in temporal logic formulas. For instance, the logic WCTL [12,10], interpreted over timed automata extended with costs, adds cost contraints on modalities: it is possible to express that a given state is reachable within a fixed cost bound.

Abstracting transient states. When practical examples are considered, the need for abstracting transient states often happens. For example, modeling the instantaneous changes of a variable may introduce artificial (and thus non pertinent) transient states in the model. This motivated the work in [9], where configurations with zero duration could be abstracted by introducing into TCTL the *almost everywhere* U^{a} modality. However, this is not sufficient in some cases.

Contribution. In this paper, we propose an extension of TCTL called TCTL^{Δ}, which brings out a powerful generalization of the results in [9]. We introduce a new modality U^k, where $k \in \mathbb{N}$ is a parameter, in order to abstract events that do not last continuously for at least k time units (t.u). For example, $\mathsf{AF}^2_{\leq 100}\, alarm$ expresses that for any execution, the atomic proposition *alarm* becomes true before 100 t.u and will hold for at least 2 time units. One also could express the fact that an event a precedes an event b along any run, an event being actually considered iff it lasts for at least k time units: the formula $\mathsf{A}\, request \mathsf{P}^3\, grant$ states that along any run where *grant* has occurred for a duration greater than 3, a *request* has been emitted continusously for a duration greater than 3. We prove that model-checking for TCTL^{Δ} is still PSPACE-complete. While the analogous result for TCTL or the extended version of [9] relies on the standard notion of equivalent runs, we have to define a stronger form for this equivalence, in order to obtain the consistency of TCTL^{Δ}-formulae on the regions of the timed automaton.

Finally, we also consider a *global* semantics, called $\mathsf{TCTL}^{\Delta}_{\Sigma}$, for which the global duration during which a property does not hold, is bounded by a fixed constant k. Although this semantics is more natural and uses only observer hybrid variables in the model, we prove that model-checking $\mathsf{TCTL}^{\Delta}_{\Sigma}$ is undecidable.

Outline. Section 2 recalls the main features of timed automata model and gives definitions for the syntax and semantics of our extended logics. Sections 3 and 4 are devoted to the model-checking of TCTL^{Δ} and, in the last section, we show that model-checking the extended logic $\mathsf{TCTL}^{\Delta}_{\Sigma}$ is undecidable.

2 Logic TCTL^{Δ}

Let $\mathbb{N}$ and $\mathbb{R}$ denote the sets of natural and non-negative real numbers, respectively. Let X be a set of real valued clocks. We write $\mathcal{C}(X)$ for the set of boolean expressions over atomic formulae of the form $x \sim k$ with $x \in X$, $k \in \mathbb{N}$, and $\sim \in \{<, \leq, =, \geq, >\}$. Constraints of $\mathcal{C}(X)$ are interpreted over *valuations* for clocks, i.e. mappings from X to $\mathbb{R}$. The set of valuations is denoted by $\mathbb{R}^X$. For every $v \in \mathbb{R}^X$ and $d \in \mathbb{R}$, we use $v+d$ to denote the time assignment which maps each clock $x \in X$ to the value $v(x) + d$. For every $r \subseteq X$, we write $v[r \leftarrow 0]$ for the valuation which maps each clock in r to the value 0 and agrees with v over $X \setminus r$. Let AP be a set of atomic propositions.

2.1 Timed Automata

Definition 1. *A* timed automaton *(TA) is a tuple $A = \langle X, Q_A, q_{init}, \rightarrow_A, \mathsf{Inv}_A, l_A\rangle$ where X is a finite set of clocks, Q_A is a finite set of* locations or control states *and $q_{init} \in Q_A$ is the* initial location. *The set $\rightarrow_A \subseteq Q_A \times \mathcal{C}(X) \times 2^X \times Q_A$ is a finite set of* action transitions*: for $(q, g, r, q') \in \rightarrow_A$, g is the enabling condition and r is a set of clocks to be reset with the transition (we write $q \xrightarrow{g,r}_A q'$). $\mathsf{Inv}_A \colon Q_A \rightarrow \mathcal{C}(X)$ assigns an* invariant *to each control state. Finally $l_A \colon Q_A \rightarrow 2^{\mathsf{AP}}$ labels every location with a subset of* AP.

A *state* (or *configuration*) of a TA A is a pair (q, v), where $q \in Q_A$ is the current location and $v \in \mathbb{R}^X$ is the current clock valuation. The initial state of A is (q_{init}, v_0) with $v_0(x) = 0$ for any x in X. There are two kinds of transition. From (q, v), it is possible to perform the *action transition* $q \xrightarrow{g,r}_A q'$ if $v \models g$ and $v[r \leftarrow 0] \models \mathsf{Inv}_A(q')$ and then the new configuration is $(q', v[r \leftarrow 0])$. It is also possible to let time elapse, and reach $(q, v + d)$ for some $d \in \mathbb{R}$ whenever the invariant is satisfied along the delay. Formally the semantics of a TA A is given by a Timed Transition System (TTS) $\mathcal{T}_A = (S, s_{\text{init}}, \rightarrow_{\mathcal{T}_A}, l)$ where:

- $S = \{(q, v) \mid q \in Q_A \text{ and } v \in \mathbb{R}^X \text{ s.t. } v \models \mathsf{Inv}_A(q)\}$ and $s_{\text{init}} = (q_{\text{init}}, v_0)$.
- $\rightarrow_{\mathcal{T}_A} \subseteq S \times S$ and we have $(q, v) \rightarrow_{\mathcal{T}_A} (q', v')$ iff
  - either $q' = q$, $v' = v + d$ and $v + d' \models \mathsf{Inv}_A(q)$ for any $d' \leq d$. This is a delay transition — we write $(q, v) \xrightarrow{d} (q, v + d)$ —,
  - or there exists $q \xrightarrow{g,r}_A q'$ s.t $v \models g$, $v' = v[r \leftarrow 0]$ and $v' \models \mathsf{Inv}_A(q')$. This is an action transition — we write $(q, v) \rightarrow_a (q', v')$.
- $l \colon S \rightarrow 2^{\mathsf{AP}}$ labels every state (q, v) with the subset $l_A(q)$ of AP .

An execution (or run) of A is an infinite path $s_0 \rightarrow_{\mathcal{T}_A} s_1 \rightarrow_{\mathcal{T}_A} s_2 \ldots$ in $\mathcal{T}_A$ such that (1) time diverges and (2) there are infinitely many action transitions. Note that an execution can be described as an alternating infinite sequence $s_0 \xrightarrow{d_1}\rightarrow_a s_1 \xrightarrow{d_2}\rightarrow_a \cdots$ for some $d_i \in \mathbb{R}$. Such an execution ρ goes through any configuration s' reachable from some s_i by a delay transition of duration $d \in [0, d_i]$. Let $\text{Exec}(s)$ be the set of all executions from s. With a run ρ : $(q_0, v_0) \xrightarrow{d_1}\rightarrow_a (q_1, v_1) \xrightarrow{d_2}\rightarrow_a \ldots$ of A, we associate the sequence of absolute dates defined by $t_0 = 0$ and $t_i = \sum_{j \leq i} d_j$ for $i \geq 1$, and in the sequel, we often write ρ as the sequence $((q_i, v_i, t_i))_{i \geq 0}$.

A state (q, v) can occur several times along a run ρ, the notion of *position* [1] allows us to distinguish them: every occurrence of a state is associated with a unique position. Given a position p, the corresponding state is denoted by s_p.

The standard notions of prefix, suffix and subrun apply to paths in TTS: given a position $p \in \rho$, $\rho^{\leq p}$ is the prefix leading to p, $\rho^{\geq p}$ is the suffix issued from p. Finally a subrun σ from p to p' is denoted by $p \overset{\sigma}{\mapsto} p'$.

Note that the set of positions along ρ is totally ordered by $<_\rho$. Given two positions p and p', we say that p *precedes strictly* p' along ρ (written $p <_\rho p'$) iff there exists a finite subrun σ of ρ s.t. $p \overset{\sigma}{\mapsto} p'$ and σ contains at least one non null delay transition or one action transition (*i.e.* σ is not reduced to $\xrightarrow{0}$). We write $\sigma <_\rho p$ when for any position p' in the subrun σ, we have $p' <_\rho p$.

Given a position $p \in \rho$, the prefix $\rho^{\leq p}$ has a *duration*, $\mathsf{Time}(\rho^{\leq p})$, defined as the sum of all delays along $\rho^{\leq p}$. Since time diverges along an execution, we have: for any $t \in \mathbb{R}$, there exists $p \in \rho$ such that $\mathsf{Time}(\rho^{\leq p}) > t$.

For a subset $P \subseteq \rho$ of positions in ρ, we define a natural measure $\hat{\mu}(P) = \mu\{\mathsf{Time}(\rho^{\leq p}) \mid p \in P\}$, where μ is Lebesgue measure on the set of real numbers. In the sequel, we only use this measure when P is a subrun of ρ: in this case, for a subrun σ such that $p \overset{\sigma}{\mapsto} p'$, we simply have $\hat{\mu}(\sigma) = \mathsf{Time}(\rho^{\leq p'}) - \mathsf{Time}(\rho^{\leq p})$.

2.2 Definition of TCTL^Δ

TCTL^Δ is obtained by adding to TCTL the modalities $\mathsf{E\_U}^k_{\sim c}\text{\_}$ and $\mathsf{A\_U}^k_{\sim c}\text{\_}$ with $k \in \mathbb{N}$:

Definition 2 (Syntax of TCTL^Δ). *TCTL^Δ formulae are given by the following grammar:*

$$\varphi, \psi ::= P_1 \mid P_2 \mid \ldots \mid \neg\varphi \mid \varphi \wedge \psi \mid \mathsf{E}\varphi\mathsf{U}_{\sim c}\psi \mid \mathsf{A}\varphi\mathsf{U}_{\sim c}\psi \mid \mathsf{E}\varphi\mathsf{U}^k_{\sim c}\psi \mid \mathsf{A}\varphi\mathsf{U}^k_{\sim c}\psi$$

where $P_i \in \mathsf{AP}$, $\sim$ belongs to the set $\{<, >, \leq, \geq, =\}$ and $c, k \in \mathbb{N}$.

Standard abbreviations include $\top, \bot, \varphi \vee \psi, \varphi \Rightarrow \psi, \ldots$ as well as:

$$\mathsf{EF}^k_{\sim c}\,\varphi \overset{def}{=} \mathsf{E}(\top\,\mathsf{U}^k_{\sim c}\,\varphi) \qquad \mathsf{AF}^k_{\sim c}\,\varphi \overset{def}{=} \mathsf{A}(\top\,\mathsf{U}^k_{\sim c}\,\varphi)$$
$$\mathsf{EG}^k_{\sim c}\,\varphi \overset{def}{=} \neg\mathsf{AF}^k_{\sim c}\neg\varphi \qquad \mathsf{AG}^k_{\sim c}\,\varphi \overset{def}{=} \neg\mathsf{EF}^k_{\sim c}\neg\varphi$$

Moreover U^k stands for $\mathsf{U}^k_{\geq 0}$.

Definition 3 (Semantics of TCTL^Δ). *The following clauses define when a state s of some TTS $\mathcal{T} = \langle S, s_{init}, \rightarrow, l\rangle$ satisfies a TCTL^Δ formula φ, written $s \models \varphi$, by induction over the structure of φ (the semantics of boolean operators is omitted).*

---

[1] Note that as it is possible to perform a sequence of action transitions in 0 t.u., we cannot replace the notion of positions by a function from f_ρ from $\mathbb{R}$ to S.

$s \models \mathsf{E}\varphi\mathsf{U}_{\sim c}\psi$ *iff* $\exists\, \rho \in Exec(s)$ *s.t.* $\rho \models \varphi\mathsf{U}_{\sim c}\psi$
$s \models \mathsf{A}\varphi\mathsf{U}_{\sim c}\psi$ *iff* $\forall\, \rho \in Exec(s)$ *we have* $\rho \models \varphi\mathsf{U}_{\sim c}\psi$
$s \models \mathsf{E}\varphi\mathsf{U}^k_{\sim c}\psi$ *iff* $\exists\, \rho \in Exec(s)$ *s.t.* $\rho \models \varphi\mathsf{U}^k_{\sim c}\psi$
$s \models \mathsf{A}\varphi\mathsf{U}^k_{\sim c}\psi$ *iff* $\forall\, \rho \in Exec(s)$ *we have* $\rho \models \varphi\mathsf{U}^k_{\sim c}\psi$

$\rho \models \varphi\mathsf{U}_{\sim c}\psi$ *iff* $\exists p \in \rho$ *s.t.* $\mathsf{Time}(\rho^{\leq p}) \sim c \;\wedge\; s_p \models \psi \;\wedge\; \forall p' <_\rho p,\ s_{p'} \models \varphi$
$\rho \models \varphi\mathsf{U}^k_{\sim c}\psi$ *iff there exists a subrun* σ *along* ρ, *a position* $p \in \sigma$ *s.t.*
$\mathsf{Time}(\rho^{\leq p}) \sim c \;\wedge\; \hat{\mu}(\sigma) > k \;\wedge\; \forall p' \in \sigma,\ s_{p'} \models \psi$
and for all subrun σ' *s.t.* $\sigma' <_\rho p \;\wedge\; \forall p' \in \sigma',\ s_{p'} \models \neg\varphi$
we have $\hat{\mu}(\sigma') \leq k$

The modality U^k allows us to abstract intervals with duration less than k t.u. where φ does not hold. Thus $\mathsf{AF}^2_{\leq 100}\, alarm$ states that along every run, there is an event *alarm* of duration greater than 2 t.u. that occurs before 100 t.u.

The precedence operator [2] P can be written as follows: $\mathsf{A}\varphi\mathsf{P}^k\psi \overset{\text{def}}{=} \neg\mathsf{E}(\neg\varphi)\mathsf{U}^k\psi$. For example, $\mathsf{A}\; request\; \mathsf{P}^3 grant$ states that a *request* of duration greater than 3 has to occur before an event *grant* (which must also last more than 3 t.u.).

Note that the semantics has to be handled carefully: $\Phi = \mathsf{AG}^k\varphi$ expresses that no event $\neg\varphi$ occurs, *i.e.* it is not possible to have $\neg\varphi$ continuously for more than k t.u. An execution where $\neg\varphi$ holds for everywhere except every k t.u. would satisfy Φ. This choice of semantics is also motivated by negation closure of the Until modality.

Note that the logic $\mathsf{TCTL}^{\mathsf{ext}}$ defined in [9] is the restriction of TCTL^{Δ} where the parameter k is always 0. As the modality $\mathsf{E\_U}^0\_$ cannot be expressed in TCTL[9], TCTL^{Δ} is clearly more expressive then TCTL.

The size of a timed automaton and the size of a TCTL^{Δ} formula are defined in the standard way with constants written in binary notation.

3 Equivalence of Runs

In this section, we show that the classical notion of region proposed by Alur, Courcoubetis and Dill [1] for TCTL is also correct for TCTL^{Δ}. Nevertheless we need a stronger notion of equivalence for the runs in order to preserve the truth value of TCTL^{Δ} formulae.

First let us recall the standard equivalence over valuations:

Definition 4 (Equivalence on valuations [1]). *Given a set X of clocks and $M \in \mathbb{N}$, two valuations $v, v' \in \mathbb{R}^X$ are* M-equivalent *(written $v \cong_M v'$) if:*

1. *for any $x \in X$ $\lfloor v(x) \rfloor = \lfloor v'(x) \rfloor$ or $(v(x) > M \wedge v'(x) > M)$,*
2. *for any $x, y \in X$ s.t. $v(x) \leq M$ and $v(y) \leq M$, we have:*
   $\mathsf{frac}(v(x)) \leq \mathsf{frac}(v(y)) \Leftrightarrow \mathsf{frac}(v'(x)) \leq \mathsf{frac}(v'(y))$ *and*
   $\mathsf{frac}(v(x)) = 0 \Leftrightarrow \mathsf{frac}(v'(x)) = 0$.

[2] This is a kind of release operator.

An equivalence class of $\cong$ is called a *region*; and a region is called a *boundary region* if it contains valuations v s.t. the fractional part of $v(x)$ is 0, for some clock x. Given a TA A, we use M_A to denote the maximal constant occurring in A (in its guards or invariants). We write simply $\cong$ instead of $\cong_M$ when M is clear from the context. The equivalence $\cong_{M_A}$ is consistent w.r.t. TCTL^Δ formulae:

Theorem 1 (Consistency of $\cong$). *Given a TA A, $\Phi \in \mathsf{TCTL}^\Delta$ and $v, v' \in \mathbb{R}^X$ s.t. $v \cong_{M_A} v'$, we have: $(q, v) \models \Phi \;\Leftrightarrow\; (q, v') \models \Phi$.*

Consider the formula $\Phi = \mathsf{E}\varphi\mathsf{U}^k_{\sim c}\psi$ and assume $(q, v) \models \Phi$, *i.e.* there exists a run $\rho = ((q_i, v_i, t_i))_{i\geq 0}$ from (q, v) satisfying $\varphi\mathsf{U}^k_{\sim c}\psi$. In order to prove the theorem, we need to show that there exists an *equivalent* run ρ' from (q, v') which also satisfies $\varphi\mathsf{U}^k_{\sim c}\psi$.

For this, we first extend $\cong$ to pairs (v_i, t_i) as follows: $(v_i, t_i) \cong (v'_i, t'_i)$ iff (1) $v_i \cong v'_i$, (2) $\lfloor t_i \rfloor = \lfloor t'_i \rfloor$ and $\mathsf{frac}(t_i) = 0$ iff $\mathsf{frac}(t'_i) = 0$ and (3) for each clock $x \in X$, (i) $\mathsf{frac}(v_i(x)) < \mathsf{frac}(t_i)$ iff $\mathsf{frac}(v'_i(x)) < \mathsf{frac}(t'_i)$ and (ii) $\mathsf{frac}(v_i(x)) = \mathsf{frac}(t_i)$ iff $\mathsf{frac}(v'_i(x)) = \mathsf{frac}(t'_i)$.

Now we define the equivalence over runs as follows:

Definition 5 (Equivalence on runs). *Given a TA A, two runs $\rho = ((q_i, v_i, t_i))_{i\geq 0}$ and $\rho' = ((q'_i, v'_i, t'_i))_{i\geq 0}$ are equivalent (written $\rho \cong^* \rho'$) if*

(ER a.) for all $i \geq 0$, $q_i = q'_i$,
(ER b.) for all $i \geq 0$, $(v_i, t_i) \cong_{M_A} (v'_i, t'_i)$,
(ER c.) for all $0 \leq j < i$, (i) $\mathsf{frac}(t_j) < \mathsf{frac}(t_i)$ iff $\mathsf{frac}(t'_j) < \mathsf{frac}(t'_i)$ and (ii) $\mathsf{frac}(t_j) = \mathsf{frac}(t_i)$ iff $\mathsf{frac}(t'_j) = \mathsf{frac}(t'_i)$.

The equivalence on runs used in [1] to prove that regions are compatible with TCTL formulae only requires conditions *(ER a)* and *(ER b)*. This is however not sufficient for proving Theorem 1. Indeed, let A be the automaton depicted below, with atomic proposition P and two clocks x and y, and consider the two following runs, which are equivalent in [1]:

$$\rho : (q_0, (0,0)) \xrightarrow{0.1}\!\!\rightarrow_a (q_1, (0.1, 0)) \xrightarrow{0.8}\!\!\rightarrow_a (q_2, (0.9, 0.8)) \xrightarrow{0.3}\!\!\rightarrow_a (q_3, (1.2, 0)) \ldots$$
$$\rho' : (q_0, (0,0)) \xrightarrow{0.8}\!\!\rightarrow_a (q_1, (0.8, 0)) \xrightarrow{0.1}\!\!\rightarrow_a (q_2, (0.9, 0.1)) \xrightarrow{1.05}\!\!\rightarrow_a (q_3, (1.95, 0)) \ldots$$

A :

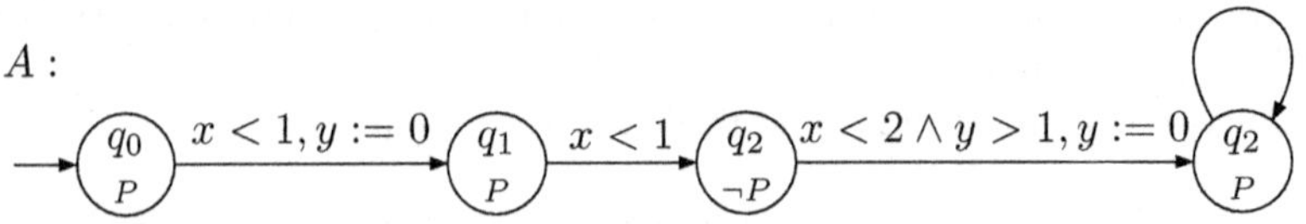

The runs ρ and ρ' satisfy conditions *(ER a)* and *(ER b)* but the delays spent in state q_2 where P does not hold are respectively 0.3 and 1.05, so that $\rho \models G^1 P$ whereas $\rho' \not\models G^1 P$.

This is why we need the stronger equivalence above which also requires condition *(ER c)*. Note that this condition *(ER c)* does not correspond to a splitting of the regions. Moreover, we will not prove that all equivalent paths satisfy the same until-formulae but rather that given a path ρ leaving from a configuration (q, v), we can build a path ρ', equivalent to ρ and which satisfies the formula we consider. The following proposition [3] then ensures the existence of equivalent runs:

Proposition 1. *Given a TA A, $q \in Q_A$, and $v, v' \in \mathbb{R}^X$ s.t. $v \cong_{M_A} v'$, then $\forall \rho \in Exec((q, v))$, there exists a run $\rho' \in Exec((q, v'))$ s.t. $\rho \cong^* \rho'$.*

We can now prove Theorem 1.

Proof (Theorem 1 – sketch). The proof is done by structural induction on Φ. We omit the basic cases and the TCTL operators (similar to [1]). Assume $(q, v) \models \mathsf{E}\varphi\mathsf{U}^k_{\sim c}\psi$. Let $\rho = ((q_i, v_i, t_i))_{i \geq 0}$ be a run from (q, v) s.t. $\rho \models \varphi\mathsf{U}^k_{\sim c}\psi$. Consider a run ρ' from (q, v') equivalent to ρ (its existence is ensured by Proposition 1).

Along ρ the truth value of φ and ψ depends on the current *region*. We know that ρ' goes through the same sequence of regions (as for TCTL) but we have also to show that the amounts of time spent in every sequence of consecutive regions in ρ and ρ' have the same integral part (less than or equal to k for $\neg\varphi$ and greater than k for ψ). Let σ be a subrun of ρ corresponding to an arrival in some region at time δ_1 until a departure from another region at time δ_2. Let δ'_1 and δ'_2 be the corresponding dates in ρ'. We want to prove that $\lfloor \delta_2 - \delta_1 \rfloor = \lfloor \delta'_2 - \delta'_1 \rfloor$.

A sufficient condition for this would be (1) $\lfloor \delta_i \rfloor = \lfloor \delta'_i \rfloor$ for $i = 1, 2$, (2) $\mathsf{frac}(\delta_1) < \mathsf{frac}(\delta_2)$ iff $\mathsf{frac}(\delta'_1) < \mathsf{frac}(\delta'_2)$ and (3) $\mathsf{frac}(\delta_1) = \mathsf{frac}(\delta_2)$ iff $\mathsf{frac}(\delta'_1) = \mathsf{frac}(\delta'_2)$.

Such a property would be ensured if the dates δ_i (and δ'_i) occurred as some t_j in ρ (and ρ'). But the t_js are the dates of *action* transitions. Consider the new TA $\bar{A}$ that extends A with loops on every control states, with no guard and no reset. In $\bar{A}$, there are additional runs (compared to A) but they induce no problem for checking $\mathsf{E\_U}^k_{\sim c}\text{\_}$ formulae.

Consider the run $\bar{\rho}$ in $\bar{A}$ that mimics ρ except that it performs a loop before entering/exiting a region [4]. Clearly $\bar{\rho}$ satisfies also $\varphi\mathsf{U}^k_{\sim c}\psi$. Now we consider a run $\bar{\rho}'$ from (q, v') equivalent to $\bar{\rho}$; then the property above over the δ_i is ensured by the definition of $\cong^*$. Clearly $\bar{\rho}' \models \varphi\mathsf{U}^k_{\sim c}\psi$. We can consider in A the run ρ' similar to $\bar{\rho}'$ without using the loops: ρ' satisfies $\varphi\mathsf{U}^k_{\sim c}\psi$. Then $(q, v') \models \mathsf{E}\varphi\mathsf{U}^k_{\sim c}\psi$.

Now consider the case of $\Phi = \mathsf{A}\varphi\mathsf{U}^k_{\sim c}\psi$. Assume $(q, v) \not\models \Phi$ and let ρ be a run from (q, v) s.t. $\rho \models \neg(\varphi\mathsf{U}^k_{\sim c}\psi)$. Thus we have either (1) there is no subrun σ of duration greater than k satisfying ψ and containing a position p located at duration $\sim c$, or (2) for any such σ and p, there exists a subrun $\sigma' <_\rho p$ s.t. σ' satisfies $\neg\varphi$ and $\hat{\mu}(\sigma') > k$. In both case, we can build a corresponding run from (q, v') witnessing $\neg(\varphi\mathsf{U}^k_{\sim c}\psi)$. □

4 Model-Checking Algorithm

In this section we show how to reduce the model-checking problem $A \models \Phi$ with a TA $A = \langle X, Q_A, q_{\text{init}}, \rightarrow_A, \mathsf{Inv}_A, l_A \rangle$ and $\Phi \in \mathsf{TCTL}^\Delta$, to a model-checking

[3] The omitted proofs are given in the long version of the paper.

[4] NB: when going into/out a non-boundary region, we consider the date corresponding to the previous/next boundary region.

problem $A' \models \Phi'$ where A' is a *region graph* (*i.e.* a finite Kripke structure) and Φ' is a CTL-like formula.

Let X^* be the set of clocks $X \cup \{z, z_r, z_{\bar{l}}\}$. The three extra clocks are used to verify timing constraints in the formula: z is used to handle subscripts $\sim c$ in U modalities (as in TCTL model checking) and the clock $z_{\bar{l}}$ (resp z_r) is used to measure time elapsing when the left (resp. right) part in U^k modalities is false (resp true). Thus these new clocks are used as observers and do not modify the behavior of A.

Let M_Φ be the maximal constant occurring in the timing constraints in Φ and k_m be the maximal k occurring in a modality U^k in Φ. Let M be $\max(M_A, M_\Phi + k_m)$.

The region graph $\mathcal{R}_{A,\Phi} = (V, \rightarrow, l, F)$ for A and Φ is defined as usual over X^* and M [1]: its set of states V is $\{(q,\gamma) \mid q \in Q_A \text{ and } \gamma \in \mathbb{R}^{X^*}/{\cong_M}\}$, the transitions correspond to action transitions ($\rightarrow_a$) in A or delay transitions ($\rightarrow_t$, leading to the *successor region* denoted by $succ(\gamma)$). The states are labeled with atomic propositions AP and we also use additional propositions for the extra clocks: a state (q,γ) is labeled with the proposition $(\!| y \sim a |\!)$ with $y \in \{z, z_{\bar{l}}, z_r\}$ and $0 \le a \le M$, when $\gamma \models y \sim a$. Moreover we use the proposition P_b to mark boundary regions. And F is a fairness constraint to enforce time divergence (see [1,9] for the detailed construction of $\mathcal{R}_{A,\Phi}$).

Labeling algorithm. We label the vertices of $\mathcal{R}_{A,\Phi}$ with the subformulae of Φ they satisfy, starting from the subformulae of length 1 and length 2 and so on. Here we only consider the U^k modalities.

Consider a formula Ψ of the form $\mathsf{E}\varphi_l \mathsf{U}^k_{\sim c} \varphi_r$ or $\mathsf{A}\varphi_l \mathsf{U}^k_{\sim c} \varphi_r$. At this step we know for every state (q,γ) of $\mathcal{R}_{A,\Phi}$ whether it satisfies (or not) φ_l and φ_r (*i.e.* whether any (q,v) with $v \in \gamma$ satisfies φ_l or/and φ_r). First we define a variant of $\mathcal{R}_{A,\Phi}$, called $\mathcal{R}^{\varphi_l,\varphi_r}_{A,\Phi}$, where some transitions are modified according to the truth value of φ_l and φ_r:

1. we replace the transitions $(q,\gamma) \rightarrow_t (q, succ(\gamma))$ by $(q,\gamma) \rightarrow_a (q, \gamma[z_{\bar{l}} \leftarrow 0])$ when $(q,\gamma) \models \varphi_l$, $(q, succ(\gamma)) \models \neg\varphi_l$ and $\gamma \not\models z_{\bar{l}} = 0$.
2. we replace the transitions $(q,\gamma) \rightarrow_a (q',\gamma')$ by $(q,\gamma) \rightarrow_a (q', \gamma'[z_{\bar{l}} \leftarrow 0])$ when $(q,\gamma) \models \varphi_l$, $(q',\gamma') \models \neg\varphi_l$.
3. we replace the transitions $(q,\gamma) \rightarrow_t (q, succ(\gamma))$ by $(q,\gamma) \rightarrow_a (q, \gamma[z_r \leftarrow 0])$ when $(q,\gamma) \models \neg\varphi_r$, $(q, succ(\gamma)) \models \varphi_r$ and $\gamma \not\models z_r = 0$.
4. we replace the transitions $(q,\gamma) \rightarrow_a (q',\gamma')$ by $(q,\gamma) \rightarrow_a (q', \gamma'[z_r \leftarrow 0])$ when $(q,\gamma) \models \neg\varphi_r$, $(q,\gamma') \models \varphi_r$.

Due to these changes, in $\mathcal{R}^{\varphi_l,\varphi_r}_{A,\Phi}$, the clock $z_{\bar{l}}$ (resp. z_r) measures the time elapsed since $\neg\varphi_l$ (resp. φ_r) is true : they are reset when the truth value of the corresponding formula changes. Thus given a path ρ in $\mathcal{R}^{\varphi_l,\varphi_r}_{A,\Phi}$ and a state (q,γ) along ρ, we have $(q,\gamma) \models \neg\varphi_l \wedge (\!| z_{\bar{l}} \le k |\!)$ iff there was (along ρ) a region satisfying φ_l "just before" (q,γ) where "just before" means "in less than k time units".

In the following we will use two abbreviations:

$$\overset{\leftarrow\cdots\dashv}{\varphi_l} \overset{\text{def}}{=} \varphi_l \vee (\!| z_{\bar{l}} \le k |\!) \qquad\qquad \overset{\longleftarrow\!\dashv}{\varphi_r} \overset{\text{def}}{=} \varphi_r \wedge (\!| z_r > k |\!)$$

The first one states that φ_l holds or did hold less than k t.u. ago. And the second one states that φ_r lasts for more than k t.u. We will also use the abbreviation to $\overleftarrow{\neg\varphi_l}$ to denote $\neg\varphi_l \wedge (\!|z_{\bar{l}} > k|\!)$: the formula $\neg\varphi_l$ has held for more than k t.u. And we use $\overset{\leftarrow\cdots}{\neg\varphi_r}$ for $\neg\varphi_r \vee (\!|z_r \leq k|\!)$. In this context, we have: $\overset{\leftarrow\cdots}{\varphi} \equiv \neg\overleftarrow{(\neg\varphi)}$. Thus the region graph $\mathcal{R}^{\varphi_l,\varphi_r}_{A,\Phi}$ allows us to decide $\overset{\leftarrow\cdots}{\varphi_l}$, $\overleftarrow{(\neg\varphi_l)}$, $\overleftarrow{\varphi_r}$ and $\overset{\leftarrow\cdots}{(\neg\varphi_r)}$.

Now we distinguish different cases depending on the modality rooted in Ψ:

- $\Psi \overset{\text{def}}{=} \mathsf{E}\varphi_l\mathsf{U}^k_{\sim c}\varphi_r$. We label a state (q,γ) of $\mathcal{R}_{A,\Phi}$ by Ψ iff $(q,\gamma[z,z_{\bar{l}},z_r \leftarrow 0])$ satisfies in $\mathcal{R}^{\varphi_l,\varphi_r}_{A,\Phi}$ the following CTL-formula:

$$\Psi_1 \overset{\text{def}}{=} \mathsf{E}\,\overset{\leftarrow\cdots}{\varphi_l}\,\mathsf{U}\Big((\!|z\sim c|\!) \wedge (\mathsf{after\text{-}a} \vee P_b \vee \overset{\leftarrow\cdots}{\varphi_l}) \wedge \mathsf{E}\,\varphi_r\,\mathsf{U}\overleftarrow{\varphi_r}\Big)$$

  where after-a holds for a state s along a path when the last transition performed (before reaching s) is an action transition. This is not, properly speaking, an atomic proposition since it depends on the way used to reach the state but it can easily be obtained either by using an EX modality or by changing $\mathcal{R}_{A,\Phi}$ in order to use an atomic proposition.
  Note that for labeling the TCTL formula $\mathsf{E}\varphi_l\mathsf{U}_{\sim c}\varphi_r$, one use the following formula: $\mathsf{E}\,\varphi_l\,\mathsf{U}\Big((\!|z\sim c|\!) \wedge \varphi_r \wedge (\mathsf{after\text{-}a} \vee P_b \vee \varphi_l)\Big)$. This formula states that there exists a path leading to a state s satisfying $(\!|z\sim c|\!)$ (*i.e.* the amount of elapsed time since $(q,\gamma[z,z_{\bar{l}},z_r \leftarrow 0])$ satisfies $\sim c$), φ_r and either after-a, P_b or φ_l: this last requirement is necessary because when s is not a boundary region and it has been reached via a delay transition, the formula φ_l has to hold also for this state [1].
  The formula Ψ_1 used for $\mathsf{E}\varphi_l\mathsf{U}^k_{\sim c}\varphi_r$ is based on the same structure, except that φ_l is replaced by $\varphi_l \vee (\!|z_{\bar{l}} \leq k|\!)$ (we allow short periods –of duration less than k – where $\neg\varphi_l$ holds) and we also specify that φ_r has to hold during more than k time units (*i.e.* $\varphi_r \wedge (\!|z_r > k|\!)$ has to hold).
  The notion of fair runs (used to ensure time divergence) is handled in the same manner as for TCTL.
- $\Psi \overset{\text{def}}{=} \mathsf{A}\varphi_l\mathsf{U}^k\varphi_r$. We label a state (q,γ) by Ψ iff $(q,\gamma[z,z_{\bar{l}},z_r \leftarrow 0])$ satisfies in $\mathcal{R}^{\varphi_l,\varphi_r}_{A,\Phi}$ the CTL-formula $\Psi_2 \overset{\text{def}}{=} \Psi_2' \wedge \Psi_2'' \wedge \Psi_3'''$ with:

$$\begin{aligned}
\Psi_2' &\overset{\text{def}}{=} \mathsf{AF}(\overleftarrow{\varphi_r})\\
\Psi_2'' &\overset{\text{def}}{=} \neg\mathsf{E}(\neg\,\overleftarrow{\varphi_r})\mathsf{U}\Big(\overleftarrow{(\neg\varphi_l)} \wedge \neg\mathsf{A}(\varphi_r\mathsf{U}\overleftarrow{\varphi_r})\Big)\\
\Psi_2''' &\overset{\text{def}}{=} \neg\mathsf{E}(\neg\,\overleftarrow{\varphi_r})\mathsf{U}\Big(P_b \wedge \neg\varphi_r \wedge \mathsf{EX}(\neg P_b \wedge \neg\overset{\leftarrow\cdots}{(\varphi_l)})\Big)
\end{aligned}$$

  Ψ_2' states that along any path, eventually φ_r holds for at least k t.u. Ψ_2'' expresses that it is not possible to have $\neg\varphi_l$ for more than k t.u. unless either φ_r has already been verified for k t.u. before, or the current state belongs to the interval σ witnessing $\overleftarrow{\varphi_r}$. Finally Ψ_2''' is used to specify that, in the last case, if the first region of σ is a not a boundary region and if it has been reached via a delay transition, then it also has to satisfy $\overset{\leftarrow\cdots}{\varphi_l}$ (for the same reason as for the E_U_ modality).

– $\Psi \stackrel{\text{def}}{=} \mathsf{A}\varphi_l \mathsf{U}^k_{<c} \varphi_r$. For dealing with this case, we first consider the formula $\mathsf{AF}^k_{<c}\varphi_r$ and more precisely we consider the dual modality $\mathsf{EG}^k_{<c}$.
The formula $\mathsf{EG}^k_{<c}\psi$ expresses that there exists an execution (from the current state s) where any subrun σ s.t. (1) $\hat{\mu}(\sigma) > k$ and (2) σ contains states located before c t.u. from s, contains a state satisfying ψ. Thus states satisfying ψ have to occur "often" (at least every k t.u.) during $c + k$ t.u. Therefore we label states (q, γ) by $\mathsf{EG}^k_{<c}\psi$ iff $(q, \gamma[z, z_{\bar{l}}, z_r \leftarrow 0])$ satisfies the CTL-formula $\mathsf{E}(\overset{\leftarrow\cdot\cdot|}{\psi})\mathsf{U}(\!|z = c + k|\!)$.
For labeling $\mathsf{AF}^k_{<c}\varphi_r$, we can then use: $\Psi_3 \stackrel{\text{def}}{=} \neg\mathsf{E}(\overset{\leftarrow\cdots\cdots|}{\neg\varphi_r})\ \mathsf{U}\ (\!|z = c+k|\!)$ for $(q, \gamma[z, z_{\bar{l}}, z_r \leftarrow 0])$ in $\mathcal{R}^{\varphi_l,\varphi_r}_{A,\Phi}$.
Therefore we label states (q, γ) by Ψ iff $(q, \gamma[z, z_{\bar{l}}, z_r \leftarrow 0])$ satisfies the CTL-formula $\Psi_3 \wedge \Psi_2'' \wedge \Psi_2'''$: compared with Ψ_2, we just have to require that φ_r holds before c t.u. (for more than k t.u.).

– $\Psi \stackrel{\text{def}}{=} \mathsf{A}\varphi_l \mathsf{U}^k_{\leq c} \varphi_r$. One just has to consider the following formula: $\Psi_4 \stackrel{\text{def}}{=} \neg\mathsf{E}(\overset{\leftarrow\cdots\cdots|}{\neg\varphi_r})\ \mathsf{U}\ (\!|z > c+k|\!)$. And we label states (q, γ) by Ψ iff $(q, \gamma[z, z_{\bar{l}}, z_r \leftarrow 0])$ satisfies the CTL-formula $\Psi_4 \wedge \Psi_2'' \wedge \Psi_2'''$ in $\mathcal{R}^{\varphi_l,\varphi_r}_{A,\Phi}$.

– $\Psi \stackrel{\text{def}}{=} \mathsf{A}\varphi_l \mathsf{U}^k_{\geq c} \varphi_r$. We label a state (q, γ) by Ψ iff $(q, \gamma[z, z_{\bar{l}}, z_r \leftarrow 0])$ satisfies in $\mathcal{R}^{\varphi_l,\varphi_r}_{A,\Phi}$ the formula: $\Psi_5 \stackrel{\text{def}}{=} \mathsf{A}\overset{\leftarrow\cdot\cdot|}{\varphi_l}\mathsf{U}\big((\!|z = c|\!) \wedge \mathsf{AF}(\overset{\leftarrow|}{\varphi_r}) \wedge \Psi_2'' \wedge \Psi_2'''\big)$. Ψ_5 states that along any run, φ_r will hold for more than k t.u. beyond a position where $z = c$, and that $\neg\varphi_l$ does not hold for more than k t.u. except after or in the interval witnessing $\overset{\leftarrow|}{\varphi_r}$ *etc.*

– $\Psi \stackrel{\text{def}}{=} \mathsf{A}\varphi_l \mathsf{U}^k_{>c} \varphi_r$. We label a state (q, γ) by Ψ iff $(q, \gamma[z, z_{\bar{l}}, z_r \leftarrow 0])$ satisfies the formula: $\Psi_6 \stackrel{\text{def}}{=} \mathsf{A}\big((\!|z \leq c|\!) \wedge \overset{\leftarrow\cdot\cdot|}{\varphi_l}\big)\mathsf{U}\big((\!|z > c|\!) \wedge \mathsf{AF}(\overset{\leftarrow|}{\varphi_r}) \wedge \Psi_2'' \wedge \Psi_2'''\big)$

– $\Psi \stackrel{\text{def}}{=} \mathsf{A}\varphi_l \mathsf{U}^k_{=c} \varphi_r$. If $c \geq k$, we label a state (q, γ) by Ψ iff $(q, \gamma[z, z_{\bar{l}}, z_r \leftarrow 0])$ satisfies in $\mathcal{R}^{\varphi_l,\varphi_r}_{A,\Phi}$ the following CTL-formula:

$$\Psi_7 \stackrel{\text{def}}{=} \mathsf{A}\overset{\leftarrow\cdot\cdot|}{\varphi_l}\mathsf{U}(\!|z = c|\!) \ \wedge\ \underbrace{\neg\mathsf{E}\ (\!|z < c|\!)\ \mathsf{U}\ \Big((\!|z = c|\!) \wedge \mathsf{E}\ \neg\overset{\leftarrow|}{\varphi_r}\ \mathsf{U}\ (\!|z > c+k|\!)\Big)}_{\Psi_8}$$

The first term ensures that $\neg\varphi_l$ does not hold for a duration greater than k before the position $z = c$. And the formula Ψ_8 states that it is not possible to avoid $\overset{\leftarrow|}{\varphi_r}$ between the position $z = c$ and the position $z > c + k$: thus any run has some interval (of duration greater than k) satisfying φ_r and containing a position located at duration c from the initial state.
If $c < k$, then we label (q, γ) by Ψ iff $(q, \gamma[z, z_{\bar{l}}, z_r \leftarrow 0])$ satisfies Ψ_8.

This algorithm is correct:

Lemma 1 (Correctness of the labeling algorithm). *Given a TA A, a* TCTL^{Δ} *formula Φ and Ψ a subformula of Φ, the labeling algorithm labels (q, γ) with Ψ in $\mathcal{R}_{A,\Phi}$ iff $(q, v) \models \Psi$ for any $v \in \gamma$.*

Proof (sketch). The proof is done by induction over the formulae. We only deal with the modalities $\mathsf{E\_U}^k_{\sim c}\mathsf{\_}$ and $\mathsf{A\_U}^k\mathsf{\_}$.

First consider $\Psi = \mathsf{E}\varphi_l \mathsf{U}^k_{\sim c}\varphi_r$.

$\Rightarrow$ Assume that the procedure labels (q, γ) with Ψ. Then in $\mathcal{R}^{\varphi_l,\varphi_r}_{A,\Phi}$, $(q, \gamma[z, z_l, z_r \leftarrow 0])$ satisfies $\Psi_1 \stackrel{\text{def}}{=} \mathsf{E}\, \overset{\leftarrow\cdot\cdot\mid}{\varphi_l}\, \mathsf{U}\Big((\!|z \sim c|\!) \wedge (\textsf{after-a} \vee P_b \vee \overset{\leftarrow\cdot\cdot\mid}{\varphi_l}) \wedge \mathsf{E}\,\varphi_r\, \mathsf{U}\overleftarrow{\varphi_r}\Big)$ Thus there exists a path $\bar{\rho}$ in $\mathcal{R}^{\varphi_l,\varphi_r}_{A,\Phi}$ leading to some (q', γ') satisfying the right-hand side of Ψ_1. From $\bar{\rho}$ one can build a run ρ in A from any (q, v) with $v \in \gamma$ (as it is done in the TCTL case). Before (q', γ'), the states along $\bar{\rho}$ verify $\overset{\leftarrow\cdot\cdot\mid}{\varphi_l}$, that is $\varphi_l \vee (\!|z_{\bar{l}} \leq k|\!)$: given the definition of $\mathcal{R}^{\varphi_l,\varphi_r}_{A,\Phi}$ this means that the durations of the corresponding $(\neg\varphi_l)$-subruns in ρ are less than k. Finally the state (q', γ') is located at duration $\sim c$ from the initial state ($\bar{\rho}$ starts from a region where z is equal to 0) and from this point, it is possible to verify φ_r for some time ensuring that (q', γ') belongs to an φ_r-subrun of duration greater than k. This ensures that the corresponding run in A satisfies $\varphi_l \mathsf{U}^k_{\sim c}\varphi_r$.

$\Leftarrow$ Assume $(q, v) \models \Psi$. From the run ρ witnessing $\varphi_l \mathsf{U}^k_{\sim c}\varphi_r$, on can build in $\mathcal{R}^{\varphi_l,\varphi_r}_{A,\Phi}$ a path $\bar{\rho}$ from $(q, \gamma[z, z^l, z^r \leftarrow 0])$ leading to a position located at duration $\sim c$ (then $(\!|z \sim c|\!)$ holds) and belonging to a φ_r-subrun of duration greater than k: then $\mathsf{E}\varphi_r \mathsf{U}(\varphi_r \wedge (\!|z_r > k|\!))$ holds. Moreover since the run ρ contains no $(\neg\varphi_l)$-subrun of duration greater than k, the path $\bar{\rho}$ never goes through a region where $\neg\varphi_l \wedge (\!|z_{\bar{l}} > c|\!)$ is true. This gives the result.

Now consider the case $\Psi = \mathsf{A}\varphi_l \mathsf{U}^k\varphi_r$.

$\Rightarrow$ Assume (q, γ) is labeled by Ψ. Thus $(q, \gamma[z, z_l, z_r \leftarrow 0])$ satisfies $\Psi_2' \wedge \Psi_2'' \wedge \Psi_2'''$. Let v be a valuation in γ. Any run ρ from (q, v) has a corresponding run $\bar{\rho}$ in $\mathcal{R}^{\varphi_l,\varphi_r}_{A,\Phi}$. From Ψ_2', we know that ρ has to contain an interval σ of duration greater than k satisfying φ_r.

Now Ψ_2'' states that before reaching σ, it is not possible to verify $\neg\varphi_l$ for a duration greater than k except if we have entered the interval σ witnessing $\overleftarrow{\varphi_r}$. In this last case, we also have to ensure that if the first region of σ is not a boundary region and if it has been reached via a delay transition, then it also has to satisfy $\overset{\leftarrow\cdot\cdot\mid}{\varphi_l}$: this is done by the formula Ψ_2'''.

$\Leftarrow$ Assume $(q, v) \models \mathsf{A}\varphi_l \mathsf{U}^k\varphi_r$. We clearly have $(q, \gamma[z, z_l, z_r \leftarrow 0]) \models \mathsf{AF}\overleftarrow{\varphi_r}$. Now assume $\neg\Psi_2''$ holds for $(q, \gamma[z, z_l, z_r \leftarrow 0])$. Then there exists a path $\bar{\rho}$ in $\mathcal{R}^{\varphi_l,\varphi_r}_{A,\Phi}$ satisfying $(\neg\overleftarrow{\varphi_r})\mathsf{U}(\overleftarrow{(\neg\varphi_l)} \wedge \neg\mathsf{A}\varphi_r\mathsf{U}\overleftarrow{\varphi_r})$. Thus the corresponding path ρ from (q, v) contains an interval σ' of duration greater than k where $\neg\varphi_l$ holds, and from σ' there is a run ρ' leading to some state satisfying $\neg\varphi_r$ before reaching the interval σ witnessing φ_r: the run $\rho \cdot \rho'$ does not satisfy $\varphi_l \mathsf{U}^k\varphi_r$ (σ' precedes strictly σ).

If $\neg\Psi_2'''$ holds for $(q, \gamma[z, z_l, z_r \leftarrow 0])$. Let (q', γ') be the region satisfying the right-hand side of the U, and let (q'', γ'') be its successor satisfying $\neg P_b \wedge \neg\overset{\leftarrow\cdots\mid}{(\varphi_l)}$ along a path $\bar{\rho}$. The transition from (q', γ') to (q'', γ'') is a delay transition (the truth value of P_b goes from $\top$ to $\bot$). Moreover the corresponding run ρ from (q, v) has to contain an interval σ witnessing $\overleftarrow{\varphi_r}$; in $\bar{\rho}$ this interval cannot be before (q', γ'), it is either after (q'', γ'') or it starts from (q'', γ''). Thus for any position p in σ along ρ, there will be states preceding p in the non-boundary region (q'', γ'') and since $\neg\varphi_l'$ holds for this region, the formula $\varphi_l \mathsf{U}^k \varphi_r$ cannot hold for ρ. □

Finally we have:

Theorem 2 (Complexity of model checking). *Given a TA A and a* TCTL^Δ *formula Φ, deciding whether Φ holds for A is a PSPACE-complete problem.*

PSPACE-hardness comes from TCTL, and the PSPACE-membership can be obtained by using an on-the-fly algorithm over the region graph.

5 Undecidability Result for the Global Semantics

In this section we propose an alternative semantics for the logic, denoted by $\mathsf{TCTL}^\Delta_\Sigma$, which can also be viewed as an extension of $\mathsf{TCTL}^{\mathsf{ext}}$ [9]. Now we require that the sum of all delays during which the property does not hold is bounded by some constant. The syntax of $\mathsf{TCTL}^\Delta_\Sigma$ is the same as for TCTL^Δ but $\varphi \mathsf{U}^k_{\sim c} \psi$ is now interpreted as follows:

$$\begin{aligned}\rho \models \varphi \mathsf{U}^k_{\sim c} \psi \text{ iff } & \text{there exists a subrun } \sigma \text{, a position p} \in \sigma \text{ s.t} \\ & \mathsf{Time}(\rho^{\leq p}) \sim c \wedge \hat{\mu}(\sigma) > k \wedge \forall p' \in \sigma\ s_{p'} \models \psi \\ & \text{and } \hat{\mu}(\{p' \mid p' <_\rho p \wedge s_{p'} \not\models \varphi\}) \leq k\end{aligned}$$

Consider the "leaking gas burner" example, often used for verification with hybrid automata. As depicted by the TA below, the system can be in one of two modes, either leaking or not leaking, and it is initially leaking. Leakages are detected and stopped within 1 second and, once a leakage has been stopped, the burner is guaranteed not to leak again until at least 30 seconds later. The usual requirement for the gas burner states that, if at least 60 seconds have passed, then the gas burner has been leaking for less than one fifth of the total elapsed time. Using the atomic proposition L for the leaking mode, we can express this property in $\mathsf{TCTL}^\Delta_\Sigma$ by the formula: $\mathsf{AG}(\mathsf{A}(\neg L)\mathsf{U}^{12}_{\geq 60} \top)$: any period of duration greater than 60s has to include less than 12s of leaking.

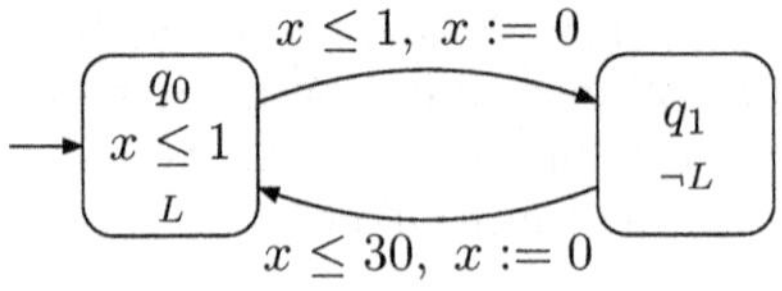

This problem is usually modeled with a stopwatch with respective slopes 1 in state q_0 and 0 in state q_1, in order to compute the leaking duration. But recall that model-checking is undecidable for hybrid automata. Moreover considering costs also makes verification undecidable (see for example the case of WCTL [10]). However, we need to be careful because of some positive results: for instance in [3,18,7,8,11], some duration-bounded reachability problems are proved to be decidable. Indeed, this kind of results can be obtained when the cost variables are only used as observers. Our case is even simpler because there is only one slope which is equal to the rate of time and $\mathsf{TCTL}^{\Delta}_{\Sigma}$ is clearly less expressive than a logic like WCTL. For example, deciding the formula $\mathsf{E}P_1\mathsf{U}^k P_2$ – with $P_1, P_2 \in \mathsf{AP}$ – interpreted with the global semantics can easily be done by using the procedure to check the *duration bounded reachability* proposed in [3]; the technique can also be adapted to handle formulas like $\mathsf{E}P_1\mathsf{U}^k_{\leq c}P_2$. Unfortunately, we still have the following result:

Theorem 3. *Model-checking* $\mathsf{TCTL}^{\Delta}_{\Sigma}$ *over timed automata is undecidable.*

The proof of this theorem consists in a reduction from the halting problem of a two-counter machine. The construction we present here is adapted from [10].

Let $\mathcal{M}$ be a two-counter machine. We build a timed automaton $\mathcal{A}_{\mathcal{M}}$ with initial location q_{init} and a $\mathsf{TCTL}^{\Delta}_{\Sigma}$ formula φ such that $\mathcal{M}$ halts iff $(q_{\text{init}}, v_{\text{init}}) \models \varphi$. The two counters c_1 and c_2 will be alternatively encoded by three clocks x, y and z. The value of c_1 and c_2 are encoded respectively by $h_1 = 1/2^{c_1}$ and $h_2 = 1/2^{c_2}$ with $h_1, h_2 \in \{x, y, z\}$. We use an extra clock t as a "tick".

We first explain how to encode the incrementation of counter c_1 with the module on the next figure (it corresponds to instruction i, going to instruction j after the counter operation). We assume that $x = 1/2^{c_1}$ and $y = 1/2^{c_2}$ when this module is entered (which means that counter c_1 is encoded by x and counter c_2 by y).

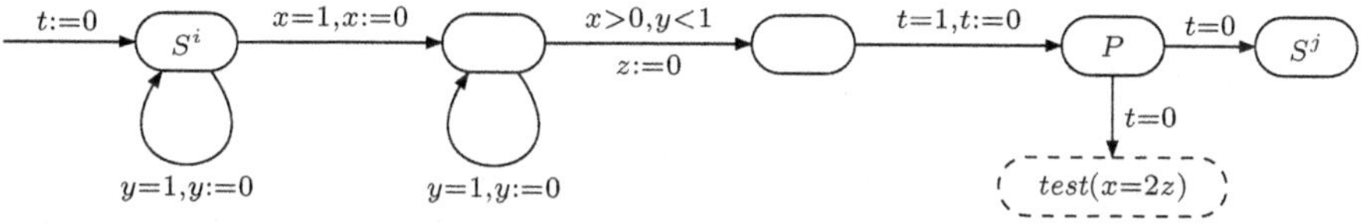

In this module, because of the constraints, it is easy to check that the values of the clocks when arriving in state labeled by P (or similarly S^j) are $x = 1/2^{c_1}$, $y = 1/2^{c_2}$, and $z = \gamma$ where $\gamma \in [0, 1)$ depends on the time at which the transition labeled by "$x > 0, y < 1, z := 0$" is taken. The test module "*test*($x = 2z$)" (described later) checks that γ is half the value of x, i.e. $\gamma = 1/2^{c_1+1}$ which will ensure that z correctly encodes the value of the first counter at the end of the incrementation instruction (whereas counter c_2 is correctly encoded by clock y).

Before describing the test module *test*($x = 2z$), we present the timed automaton *add*(x, z, p) below:

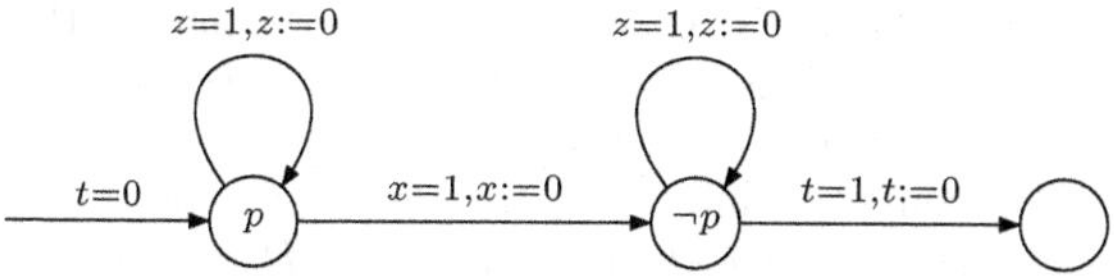

In this automaton, if $\alpha \in [0, 1]$ is the initial value of x when entering the module, then we stay $(1-\alpha)$ time units in the location labeled by atomic proposition p and α time units in the location labeled by $\neg p$.

Finally the test module "*test*($x = 2z$)" is depicted below:

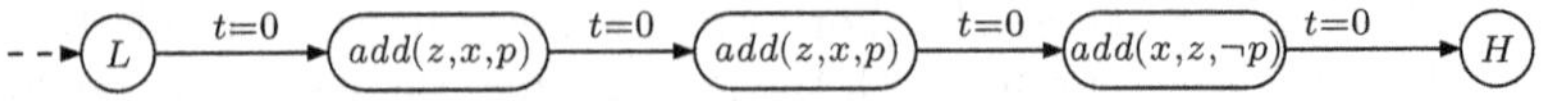

This test module has only one path which reaches the location labeled by H. If α and γ are the respective values of x and z on entering the module, this path will stay $2\cdot(1-\gamma)+\alpha$ time units in locations labeled by p and $2\cdot\gamma+(1-\alpha)$ time units in locations labeled by $\neg p$. Moreover the global time elapsed between L and H is exactly 3 time units. Thus, if formula $L \wedge \mathsf{E}(p\mathsf{U}^1 H) \wedge \mathsf{E}(\neg p \mathsf{U}^2 H)$ holds in state L, this will ensure that $2\cdot(1-\gamma)+\alpha \leq 2$ and $2\cdot\gamma+(1-\alpha) \leq 1$, which implies $2\cdot(1-\gamma)+\alpha = 2$ and $2\cdot\gamma+(1-\alpha) = 1$, thus $\gamma = \alpha/2$.

The simulation of a decrementation for a counter is very similar to the simulation of the incrementation, and we assume that we have constructed a module for every instruction (with the correct test module attached to state P, depending on what constraint we want to check) and that we have correctly glued the modules together. Then the formula that we want to check on the global automaton is $\mathsf{E}(\psi \mathsf{U} S^{\mathsf{Halt}})$ where ψ is equal to $P \Rightarrow \mathsf{E}\Big[(P \vee L)\mathsf{U}(L \wedge \mathsf{E}(p\mathsf{U}^1 H) \wedge \mathsf{E}(\neg p \mathsf{U}^2 H))\Big]$, which ensures that for each instruction we correctly store the value of the counter in the clocks. The correctness of the global reduction is a consequence of the previous discussion.

6 Conclusion

We have proposed an extension of TCTL in order to abstract transient events, where the notion of transient properties is parameterized by an integer k. We proved that model-checking for the new logic TCTL^{Δ} is still PSPACE-complete. We also proposed to interpret k-modalities with a global semantics but then we showed that model checking becomes undecidable. As future work, we plan to look for decidable fragments of $\mathsf{TCTL}^{\Delta}_{\Sigma}$, beyond the simple $\mathsf{E}P_1\mathsf{U}^k_{\leq c}P_2$.

References

1. R. Alur, C. Courcoubetis, and D. Dill. Model-checking in dense real-time. *Information and Computation*, 104(1):2–34, 1993.
2. R. Alur, C. Courcoubetis, N. Halbwachs, T. A. Henzinger, P.-H. Ho, X. Nicollin, A. Olivero, J. Sifakis, and S. Yovine. The algorithmic analysis of hybrid systems. *Theoretical Computer Science*, 138(1):3–34, 1995.
3. R. Alur, C. Courcoubetis, and T. A. Henzinger. Computing accumulated delays in real-time systems. *Formal Methods in System Design*, 11(2):137–156, 1997.
4. R. Alur and D. Dill. A theory of timed automata. *Theoretical Computer Science*, 126(2):183–235, 1994.
5. R. Alur, T. Feder, and Th. A. Henzinger. The benefits of relaxing punctuality. *J. ACM*, 43(1):116–146, 1996.

6. R. Alur and Th. A. Henzinger. Logics and models of real-time: a survey. In *Real-Time: Theory in Practice, Proc. REX Workshop, Mook, NL, June 1991*, vol. 600 of *LNCS*, p. 74–106. Springer, 1992.
7. R. Alur, S. La Torre, and G. J. Pappas. Optimal paths in weighted timed automata. In *Proc. 4th Int. Workshop Hybrid Systems: Computation and Control (HSCC 2001), Roma, Italy, Mar. 2001*, vol. 2034 of *LNCS*, p. 49–62. Springer, 2001.
8. G. Behrmann, A. Fehnker, Th. Hune, K. G. Larsen, P. Pettersson, J. Romijn, and F. Vaandrager. Minimum-cost reachability for priced timed automata. In *Proc. 4th Int. Workshop Hybrid Systems: Computation and Control (HSCC 2001), Roma, Italy, Mar. 2001*, vol. 2034 of *LNCS*, p. 147–161. Springer, 2001.
9. H. Belmokadem, B. Bérard, P. Bouyer, and F. Laroussinie. A new modality for almost everywhere propeties in timed automata. In *Proc. 16th International Conference on Concurrency Theory (CONCUR05)*, vol. 3653 of *LNCS*, p. 110–124. Springer, 2005.
10. P. Bouyer, T. Brihaye, and N. Markey. Improved Undecidability Results on Priced Timed Automata. *Information Processing Letters*, 98(5):188–194, 2006.
11. P. Bouyer, E. Brinksma, and K. G. Larsen. Staying alive as cheaply as possible. In *Proc. 7th Int. Workshop on Hybrid Systems: Computation and Control (HSCC 2004), Philadelphia, PA, USA, Mar. 2004*, vol. 2993 of *LNCS*, p. 203–218. Springer, 2004.
12. Th. Brihaye, V. Bruyère, and J.-F. Raskin. Model-checking for weighted timed automata. In *Proc. Joint Conf. Formal Modelling and Analysis of Timed Systems (FORMATS 2004) and Formal Techniques in Real-Time and Fault-Tolerant Systems (FTRTFT 2004), Grenoble, France, Sep. 2004*, vol. 3253 of *LNCS*, p. 277–292. Springer, 2004.
13. V. Bruyère, E. Dall'Olio, and J.-F. Raskin. Durations, parametric model-checking in timed automata with presburger arithmetic. In *Proc. 20th Ann. Symp. Theoretical Aspects of Computer Science (STACS 2003), Berlin, Germany, Feb. 2003*, vol. 2607 of *LNCS*, p. 687–698. Springer, 2003.
14. Z. Chaochen, C. Hoare, and A. Ravn. A calculus of duration. *Information Processing Letters*, 40(5):269–276, 1991.
15. T. A. Henzinger, P.-H. Ho, and H. Wong-Toi. HyTech: A model-checker for hybrid systems. *Journal of Software Tools for Technology Transfer*, 1(1–2):110–122, 1997.
16. Th. A. Henzinger. The theory of hybrid automata. In *Proc. 11th IEEE Symp. Logic in Computer Science (LICS '96), New Brunswick, NJ, USA, July 1996*, p. 278–292. IEEE Comp. Soc. Press, 1996.
17. Th. A. Henzinger, X. Nicollin, J. Sifakis, and S. Yovine. Symbolic model-checking for real-time systems. *Information and Computation*, 111(2):193–244, 1994.
18. Y. Kesten, A. Pnueli, J. Sifakis, and S. Yovine. Decidable integration graphs. *Information and Computation*, 150(2):209–243, 1999.
19. R. Koymans. Specifying real-time properties with metric temporal logic. *Real-Time Systems*, 2(4):255–299, 1990.
20. K. G. Larsen, P. Pettersson, and W. Yi. UPPAAL in a nutshell. *Journal of Software Tools for Technology Transfer*, 1(1–2):134–152, 1997.
21. J. Ouaknine and J. Worrell. On the decidability of Metric Temporal Logic. In *Proc. 20th IEEE Symp. Logic in Computer Science (LICS 2005), Chicago, IL, USA, June 2005*, p. 188–197. IEEE Comp. Soc. Press, 2005.
22. S. Yovine. Kronos: A verification tool for real-time systems. *Journal of Software Tools for Technology Transfer*, 1(1–2):123–133, 1997.

Predicate Abstraction of Programs with Non-linear Computation

Songtao Xia[1], Ben Di Vito[2], and Cesar Munoz[3]

[1] NASA Postdoc at NASA Langley Research Center, Hampton, VA
[2] NASA Langley Research Center, Hampton, VA
[3] National Institute of Aerospace, Hampton, VA

Abstract. Verification of programs relies on reasoning about the computations they perform. In engineering programs, many of these computations are non-linear. Although predicate abstraction enables model checking of programs with large state spaces, the decision procedures that currently support predicate abstraction are not able to handle such non-linear computations. In this paper, we propose an approach to model checking a class of data-flow properties for engineering programs that contain non-linear products and transcendental functions. The novelty of our approach is the integration of interval constraint solving techniques into the automated predicate discovery/predicate abstraction process, which extends the expressive power of predicate abstraction-based model checking. Using this approach, we construct a prototype model checker for C programs called VISA (Verification of Industrial-Strength Applications). VISA is built on top of Berkeley's BLAST and University of Nantes' Realpaver. We successfully apply VISA to scientific computation libraries and avionics applications to verify the absence of certain runtime arithmetic errors.

1 Introduction

Software systems are notoriously bug-ridden. Formal techniques have become increasingly popular in verification, bug-hunting, and automatic test case generation. In this paper, we are interested in safety properties of a particular set of engineering programs from the avionics industry. These programs have two distinct features. First, their state space consists of hundreds, or thousands of, inputs to the system. Second, these programs may perform non-linear computations. More specifically, in avionics systems, input variables participate in the computation of control signals to be sent to actuators. The laws of electronics, dynamics, and geometry on which these computations are based constantly involve mathematical expressions that include non-linear products and transcendental functions.

An example of the domain of interest is given in Figure 1, taken from KB3D, an aircraft conflict detection and resolution program [18]. We are interested in the ability to prove that the variable `a` is non-zero at Line 5 (We ignore the issues caused by floating point arithmetic for now.). A brief argument for the property

S. Graf and W. Zhang (Eds.): ATVA 2006, LNCS 4218, pp. 352–368, 2006.

is as follows: If a is zero, then both vx and vy have to be zero. Therefore, the first two terms in the assignment to d are zeros. The right hand side of the assignment is a subtraction from zero the sum of products of square numbers, which means d must be less than or equal to zero, which contradicts with the test in Line 4.

```
1: d = 2*sx*vx*sy*vy + sq(D)*(sq(vx)+sq(vy))
2:       - (sq(sx)*sq(vy) + sq(sy)*sq(vx));
3: a = sq(vx) + sq(vy);
4: if (d>0) {
5:       theta1 = 1/a;
6: }
```

Fig. 1. Code snippet from a conflict detection program

The challenge is to verify the kinds of properties automatically (with little or no human interaction) and accurately (with few or no false alarms). Among available techniques, some of which will be discussed in the related Section 7, we will focus on software model checking because it offers a high degree of automation. A major obstacle to software model checking is the large (infinite in most cases) state spaces. Predicate abstraction [21,10,19,7,15,40,36] has been successful in reducing the state explosion problem in model checking. This technique is particularly appealing when combined with counter-example driven predicate discovery techniques [6, 12, 16, 4, 25], because together they provide a (nearly) push-button process that, given a program and a property, will either verify the property or report a counter-example. The method is incomplete, but in practice, it has a high rate of success, especially when the cause of the bug (or the absence thereof) puts a virtual limit on the state space to be searched. Unfortunately, the decision procedures [9,17,20] used by predicate abstraction tools are not able to decide the satisfiability of formulas that contain non-linear computations.

This paper proposes a solution to predicate abstraction of programs with non-linear computations: instead of using a traditional cooperative decision procedure to answer the queries that occur during predicate abstraction and predicate discovery, we use constraint solvers based on interval analysis. Modern constraint solvers [28, 24, 34, 42] adopt a branch and prune strategy to search the solution space and apply interval computations [31,2,1] to reveal possible inconsistencies. Although incompleteness and slow convergence are intrinsic to these solvers, they are accurate, making them good candidates to be used in predicate abstraction.

Based on this approach, we extend Berkeley's BLAST [26] to construct a model checker for C programs with non-linear products and transcendental functions. Among possible applications, we present a prototype tool called VISA (Verification of Industrial-Strength Applications) that detects potential run-time violations such as division by zero and verifies the absence of these violations under certain conditions. Another application of this approach is in automated test case generation [43]. We have applied VISA to software (often of tens of thousands of lines of code) taken from the scientific computing community and from the avionics industry, including legacy code from a Boeing 737 autopilot simulator and KB3D. Our model checker is able to verify (or find a counter-example of) properties that involves non-linear computation fully automatically. This automation is not accomplished by any other tool to the best of our knowledge.

The rest of the paper is organized as follows. Technical background is introduced in Section 2, where we focus on software model checking based on predicate abstraction and predicate discovery based on counter-example analysis. The challenge posed by programs with non-linear computation and our resorting to numerical approaches are discussed in Section 3. The overview of our solution is presented in Section 4. This section also discusses the soundness and incompleteness issues relevant to different types and configurations of the numerical constraint solvers. The implementation of VISA is described in Section 5. Section 6 reports experimental results. We discuss related work in Section 7.

2 Background

We present predicate abstraction and counter-example based predicate discovery in a general framework that is not tied to a particular programming language. Most of the material presented in this section is a review of well-known concepts.

2.1 Definitions

A (concrete) *state* of a program is a type preserving value assignment to program variables, which includes artificial ones such as *pc*. We denote by $E[s]$ the value of expression E evaluated at state s. We also write $s \models P$ if the predicate P holds at state s.

A (concrete and later, abstract) program can be organized as a control flow graph (CFG) (N, E, M, A), where N is a set of nodes that correspond to program locations, E is a set of edges $N \times N$, M is a set of *moves*, and A is a mapping of edges to moves. A move, concrete or abstract, is an abstraction of one semantic step in the program that changes (a model checker's) knowledge of the current (abstract) state. For a program without function calls, there are two kinds of moves: *assignments* and *assumptions*. An assignment move represents one or more assignment statements in a program. Assumptions model branch conditions of an if statement. One assumption is represented by a predicate showing the result of testing the if- condition; it labels the edge from the testing to the corresponding branch in the CFG. Given a state and a move, executing the move will result in the next state. We write $\hookrightarrow(m, s)$ for the state after the move m is executed in state s.

The CFG for the code above is illustrated in Figure 2 with edges labeled with moves. Concrete (directly corresponding to C statements) and corresponding abstract moves (explained in the next section) are listed alongside.

To reason about moves, weakest preconditions are used. We write $\mathcal{WP}(m, P)$ for the weakest precondition of P with respect to move m. We write $\mathcal{WP}(\bar{m}, P)$ as the weakest precondition with respect to the sequence of moves $\bar{m}$. A *counter-example* $\bar{m}$ is a sequence of moves. A counter-example $\bar{m}$ is feasible if $\mathcal{WP}(\bar{m}, P)$

Move	Concrete	Abstract
E1:	d= 2*sx*vx*sy*vy +sq(D)*(sq(vx)+sq(vy)) -(sq(sx)*sq(vy)+ sq(sy)*sq(vx))	b1= 1
E2:	a = sq(vx) + sq(vy)	b2 = 1
E3:	d<=0	not b3
E4:	d>0	(b1 ∧ b2)? b3 ∧ ¬ b4 : b3
E5:	theta = 1/a	nop
E6, E7	nop	nop

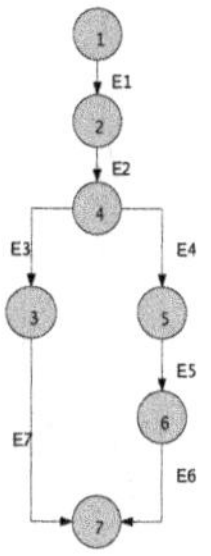

Fig. 2.

is *satisfiable.* A formula is satisfiable if there is a value assignment to the variables so that the formula is true under a certain interpretation.

2.2 Predicate Abstraction

We give an operational definition of predicate abstraction partially following that of Ball's [4]. Predicate abstraction accepts as input a move m and a set Φ of predicates, and outputs a function (called *abstraction transition*) that maps one abstract state to another. An abstract state is represented as a bit vector. Every bit[1] in the vector represents the truth value (plus another value $*$ representing a non-deterministic choice) of a predicate in Φ. We denote by s_Φ the abstract state of s with respect to the set of predicates Φ. We overload the operator $\hookrightarrow (m, s_\Phi)$ to denote the next abstract state of s_Φ after move m is followed (by a model checker). We extend this operator to sets of states (concrete and abstract) in the natural way.

The computation of the abstraction transition relation is performed for each move. Informally, the effect of a move m over a predicate $P_i \in \Phi$ can be written as an assignment [2] :

$$b_i = \mathcal{WP}'(m, P_i)$$

where we use b_i for the bit corresponding to P_i, $\mathcal{WP}'(m,P) = \mathcal{WP}(m,P)$ if m is an assignment, or $Q \Rightarrow P$ if m is assume(Q). Standard computation of predicate abstraction computes an approximation of $\mathcal{WP}(m,P)$ as $\mathcal{WP}_\Phi(m,P)$, which is implemented by calling a theorem prover to check the unsatisfiability of $Q \wedge \neg\mathcal{WP}(m,P)$.

The abstraction of our example with respect to four predicates (listed below) is shown on the right hand side of Figure 2.

[1] Strictly speaking not a bit, but a variable ranging over values from a free lattice over {true, false}.

[2] Conventionally, an assumption is represented by a predicate. But as far as model checking is concerned, it is equivalent to this assignment form.

$$b_1 : d = 2 * \texttt{sx} * \texttt{vx} * \texttt{sy} * \texttt{vy} + \texttt{sq(D)} * (\texttt{sq(vx)} + \texttt{sq(vy)}) - (\texttt{sq(sx} * \texttt{sq(vy)} + \texttt{sq(sy)} * \texttt{sq(vx))}$$
$$b_2 : a = \texttt{sq(vx)} + \texttt{sq(vy)}$$
$$b_3 : d > 0$$
$$b_4 : a = 0$$

Note that the branch of $d > 0$ is computed this way: $\mathcal{WP}'(d > 0, d > 0)$ is $d > 0 \Rightarrow d > 0$, so b_3 will always be true. $\mathcal{WP}(d > 0, \neg a = 0)$ is $d > 0 \Rightarrow \neg a = 0$, which is implied by:

$$a = \texttt{sq(vx)} + \texttt{sq(vy)} \wedge$$
$$d = 2 * \texttt{sx} * \texttt{vx} * \texttt{sy} * \texttt{vy} + \texttt{sq(D)} * (\texttt{sq(vx)} + \texttt{sq(vy)}) - (\texttt{sq(sx} * \texttt{sq(vy)} + \texttt{sq(sy)} * \texttt{sq(vx))}$$

Note that, because non-linear computation is involved, the implication above cannot be proven by the cooperative decision procedures used in previous predicate abstraction methods. We will return to this issue in Section 3.

2.3 Predicate Discovery

Based on counter-example feasibility testing, counter-example driven predicate discovery allows the model checker to incrementally discover a suitable set of predicates, starting with an initial value of Φ. This procedure is known as *predicate refinement* and is in general incomplete (c.f., [4]). Let $\bar{m} = m_1, \ldots, m_n$ be a counter-example. Iteratively, we compute the weakest preconditions $P_1, \ldots, P_n$:

$$P_1 = \mathcal{WP}(m_n, \phi)$$
$$P_{i+1} = \mathcal{WP}(m_{n-i+1}, P_i)$$

We check whether P_i is satisfiable. If, for some j, P_j is not satisfiable, we attempt to find new predicates from the path from m_j to m_n. One way to find new predicates is to collect all the predicates involved or use certain heuristics to select the new predicates. A better approach is to use Craig interpolation [29,25].

Again, in our example, we will need to check the satisfiability of non-linear formulas. The challenge and possible solutions are discussed in the next section.

3 Reasoning About Non-linear Computation

As revealed by the example in Section 2, reasoning about non-linear computation is an integral part of the abstraction and model checking mechanism. Unfortunately, the decision procedures used in counter-example driven predicate abstraction have trouble deciding the satisfiability of such formulas. They tend to work in a weaker theory of arithmetic. For example, in bug-hunting applications such as SLAM [7] and BLAST [26], the forms of the constraints are limited to propositional logic and quantifier free predicate logic with uninterpreted functions. When verifying hybrid systems, stronger decision procedures that accept linear equations and inequalities are used. For example, d/dt [3] uses the Lp_solve software package. Verification of non-linear programs in general is hard because non-linear arithmetic is not decidable over mixed (integer and real) variables and the satisfiability problem for formulas involving transcendental functions is not decidable even for reals.

3.1 Existing Tools

Existing decision procedures, such as ICS and CVC-lite [20, 9], also attempt to decide the satisfiability of non-linear products. Due to the nature of these cooperative decision procedures, such an attempt is made only during an early phase of an arithmetic sub-theory to rule out simple unsatisfiable cases. From our experience, the current versions of these tools cannot solve constraints that appear in our predicate abstraction.

Based on a variation of the simplex method [35] and computation of Gröbner basis [41], Tiwari's non-linear decision package [39] can solve many non-linear constraints very efficiently. Still the current version cannot handle unsatisfiable constraints that involve perfect squares.

None of these procedures mentioned above solves constraints that involve transcendental functions; in the best case, they can solve such constraints without interpreting these transcendental functions (for example, they can decide that formula $sin(x) = sin(x) + 1$ is not satisfiable).

3.2 Numeric Decision Procedures

Modern constraint solvers, pioneered by Numerica [24], adopt a branch-and-prune technique to either find a set of intervals that contain a solution or report that no solution is possible. In constraint solvers, the set of ranges where a variable is defined is called a *box*. The band-and-prune algorithm takes as arguments a set of constraints, an initial set of boxes for each variable appearing in the constraints, and a precision. If during the search, all the boxes contain intervals that are smaller than the precision, then the search stops. The internal loop of the algorithm consists of two stages: prune and branch. Prune removes boxes that are not in the solution space and branch splits one box into two or more boxes. The prune stage enforces local consistency conditions by reducing intervals associated with the variables. Typically, the constraints are evaluated using interval arithmetic [31].

A group of local constraint satisfaction techniques with polynomial time worst case complexity are also used. They can be applied to non-linear, non-square, and heterogeneous systems. Furthermore, numerical methods are adopted to process either a sub-problem or a sub-class of problems. For example, a Newton method can be used for an equation of the form $f(x) = 0$, where function f is square and differentiable [1]. Moreover, systems of inequalities can be handled by a version of the Simplex method [27].

4 Approach

The goal of VISA is to detect potential runtime safety bugs for C programs. Like BLAST, it allows a user to specify the property that she wants to check. The property specification is instrumented with the source code (at the CFG level) to form a new CFG where a violation will be reported when a special error node is reached during model checking.

The model checker will take this instrumented CFG as input. The model checking is based on the procedures described in Section 2. First, predicate abstraction is performed using an enhanced theorem prover, which will behave just like a traditional theorem prover if the candidate theorem (constraints) does not contain non-linear computation, and will behave like a wrapper of a constraint solver when attempting to prove a non-linear candidate theorem. Then, model checking is performed over the abstract model. When the model checker concludes the (artificial) error label is not reachable, VISA will report that the code is safe. Otherwise, if a counter example is discovered by the model checker, the same enhanced theorem prover will be used to determine its feasibility. If the error path is feasible, VISA will report an error. Otherwise, VISA attempts to refine the error trace to find a new predicate to repeat the abstraction/model checking process. Figure 3 illustrates the architecture of VISA.

4.1 Instrumentation

In VISA, a source program is first instrumented with respect to a property specification. In the instrumented program, an error node (in the CFG) is reachable if and only if the specified error condition is true in the source program.

We have designed a specification language that is similar to that of BLAST's [11]. A *cut-point* is a program location (strictly speaking, not a program location, but a node in CFG, see Section 5) where we may want to insert a check for a certain operation where we may insert a check; all cut-points that are pertaining to the operation are called (a not-entirely-misuse of term) *aspect.* A *pattern* is associated with a cut-point, which will match the actual expressions that participate in the operation of concern.

In VISA, the checking of division by zero is instrumented by first querying the patterns associated with division operations that we want to check. Such a pattern includes a divident and a divisor. We assert that this divisor must not be zero before division takes place. There is practically no restriction on the form of the formula being asserted. For example, a user may also choose to check whether the divisor's abstract value is less than a small positive constant.

Next, an instrumentor of VISA will scan the internal representation of the syntax tree (the CFG in BLAST), add an artificial test at an appropriate place per the specification, for example, before the division of interest. The assertion that specified by the user will be tested; if it is not true, an artificial error node is reached.

Once the code is instrumented, the model checker will check to see if the error node is reachable. The impact of using constraint solvers in such a model checker is discussed in the next subsection.

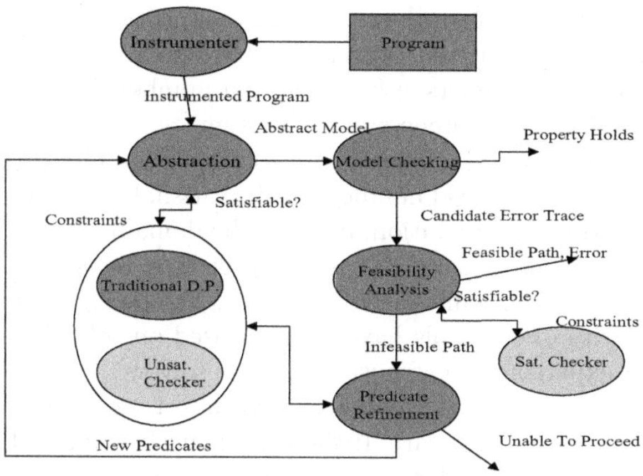

Fig. 3. Architecture of VISA

4.2 Using Constraint Solvers in Model Checking

In the approaches described above, the model checker uses the constraint solvers to process non-linear constraints at two different places (computing the abstract transition relation and testing/refining a candidate error trace). There are various configurations/types of numerical constraint solvers. Each solver behaves differently with regard to soundness, completeness or performance and is suitable only for certain applications.

Satisfiability vs. Unsatisfiability. Ideally, a constraint solver may return three possible answers: Satisfiable, Unsatisfiable, and Don't Know. In practice, a tool may return two answers (Satisfiable/Don't Know, or Unsatisfiable/Don't Know). For example, Realpaver, which is used in our prototype implementation, will either declare that a set of constraints is not satisfiable or give a set of boxes that might contain a solution. The latter should be considered as Don't Know. We will call a constraint solver that returns Satisfiable/Don't Know as a *satisfiability checker* while one that returns Unsatisfiable/Don't Know as an *unsatisfiability checker.*

- When testing whether an error path is feasible, an unsatisfiability checker may return a Don't know. Then we cannot detect an unfeasible path and can only raise a false alarm. Conversely, a satisfiability checker may return Don't know on a feasible path, which further contributes to the incompleteness of the system.
- When computing predicate abstraction, we should always use an unsatisfiability checker. As long as the Unsatisfiable answer is trusted, the soundness of predicate abstraction is preserved. Of course, Don't know answers further contributes to the imprecision that already exists in predicate abstraction.

It is also worth mentioning that the precision of a tool is adjustable. The more precise the tool is, the slower it is.

Floating Point vs. Real Numbers. It is also important to know exactly what satisfiability problem a particular solver aims to solve. In particular, whether the problem domain is real numbers or floating point numbers has a profound impact on the soundness and completeness of the system.

In theory, interval-based techniques can solve satisfiability problems for both floating point numbers and real numbers. If the satisfiability is interpreted as the existence of a floating point solution, because the domain is finite, the procedure always terminates; if the satisfiability is interpreted on reals, then the procedure may not terminate. But the unsatisfiability check can be highly accurate [22,34]. So far, the majority of the tools have been focused on solving real constraints. As a result, our experience has focused on these solvers.

When using a solver for real numbers, the result of both verification and bug-hunting must be treated with care. If the model checker signals that there is no error, then if we do not consider rounding errors, this answer is sound provided that the over-approximation condition is (as expected) satisfied. On the other hand, if the model checker finds a violation based on the fact that there is a real solution to a constraint, then this real solution may not correspond to a floating point number solution, in which case we have a false alarm.

It is hard for constraint solvers to maintain a semantics that exactly matches that of the floating point arithmetics of the machine; in reality, they rarely do. When an unsatisfiability checker decides that a particular set of boxes does not contain a solution, due to rounding error, there could still be a solution that causes the constraints to be satisfied. Here we must not confuse the interval arithmetic used in determining the unsatisfiability with the interval arithmetic used in controlling rounding error. In practice, a constraint solver extensively uses the former but seldom uses the latter.

The implication of this problem with rounding error is that we cannot claim full verification without the assumption of absence of rounding errors.

4.3 Example of VISA Approach

In Figure 2, suppose we are interested in Line 5, where a division takes place. To decide whether a could be zero, a counter-example driven approach will start the initial value of Φ to be $\{a = 0.0\}$. Line 1 does not affect this predicate. Line 3 assigns the sum of two square numbers to a. The precondition of $a = 0.0$, for example, will be:

$$0 = \mathtt{sq(vx)} + \mathtt{sq(vy)}$$

The predicate abstractor will attempt to decide whether combinations of predicates imply this precondition. This decision is made by calling an unsatisfiability checker. If the combination is $a = 0.0$, then we decide whether constraint:

$$\begin{aligned}&(a = 0.0)\ \wedge\\ &\neg(0 = \mathtt{sq(vx)} + \mathtt{sq(vy)})\end{aligned}$$

is satisfiable to see if $a = 0.0$ should be included in the approximation. The constraint is acquired as a conjunction of $a = 0.0$ and the negation of the precondition (the conclusion of the implication). This constraint is satisfiable, which means the implication does not hold. Repeating this for $\neg(a = 0.0)$, Line 3 will be translated into $b = *$, where b is the Boolean variable corresponding to $a = 0.0$.

Suppose that we have a test that checks whether a is 0 between Line 4 and Line 5. Because a is $*$, there will be a path in which $a = 0.0$ could be true. This way we have a counter-example. By analyzing this trace, we will find out that the following constraint, which is computed using weakest preconditions, is not satisfiable (note that the counter-example contains a test of a at the end, which is not reflected in the figure):

$$\begin{aligned}
\mathtt{a} &= 0.0 \wedge \\
0.0 &= \mathtt{sq(vx)} + \mathtt{sq(vy)} \wedge \\
0.0 &< \mathtt{d} \wedge \\
0.0 &< 2 * \mathtt{sx} * \mathtt{vx} * \mathtt{sy} * \mathtt{vy} + \mathtt{sq(D)} * (\mathtt{sq(vx)} + \mathtt{sq(vy)}) - \\
&\quad (\mathtt{sq}(\mathtt{sx} * \mathtt{sq(vy)} + \mathtt{sq(sy)} * \mathtt{sq}(Idvx))
\end{aligned}$$

A satisfiability constraint solver will decide that the constraint is not satisfiable. Thus the error trace is not feasible. Then related predicates (the four predicates described earlier) are added into Φ. This time, when the model checker reaches Line 4, in addition to $d > 0$, the predicate abstraction will also notice that $\neg(0.0 = a)$ must be true because the constraint below is not satisfiable. This constraint is the conjunction of the negation of formula above, that is, $a = 0.0$, the combination of predicates being tested and $d > 0$, which is introduced by computation of the precondition (details on how the constraints is computed are described earlier in Section 2.2).

$$\begin{aligned}
d = 2 * \mathtt{sx} * \mathtt{vx} * \mathtt{sy} * \mathtt{vy} + \mathtt{sq(D)} * (\mathtt{sq(vx)} + \mathtt{sq(vy)}) &- \\
(\mathtt{sq}(\mathtt{sx} * \mathtt{sq(vy)} + \mathtt{sq(sy)} * \mathtt{sq}(Idvx)) &\wedge \\
a = \mathtt{sq(vx)} + \mathtt{sq(vy)} \wedge d > 0 \wedge a &= 0.0
\end{aligned}$$

Then, between Line 4 and Line 5 the predicate abstractor will recognize that $a = 0.0$ must be false. Therefore the program will not cause division by zero.

5 Implementation of VISA

We implement our model checker based on two existing systems, BLAST from Berkeley [26] and Realpaver from University of Nantes [28]. BLAST provides a reachability test framework for a C program; Realpaver can be used to determine the unsatisfiability of a set of non-linear constraints. We extend Realpaver to a decision procedure of the Nelson and Oppen flavor. We then plug the new decision procedure into BLAST, replacing the decision procedures used there.

5.1 Extending BLAST

With C programs, many problems must be addressed before or during model checking. Function calls, pointers, various data types and a programmer's tendency to explore their flexibility are just some of them. Using CIL (C Intermediate Language) [30], BLAST handles full C syntax and represents different C syntax structure in a uniform and less ambiguous way. BLAST also provides context free analysis and alias analysis in a best-effort manner. Therefore, we do not focus on the issues mentioned above and rely on BLAST to cope with these for us, albeit pointers remain a major source of problems.

One extension (besides the interface to theorem provers, which will be covered in the next subsection) to BLAST is an instrumentation API that allows a user to specify the properties that they want to check. The specification language of VISA can be viewed as a front end using this API. A user can query about a cut-point and use the matching pattern to define a check using both the specfication language (as we have shown earlier) or equivalently, the API. Besides division, VISA supports the following aspects: addition, function call/return, array access, and assignment.

A cut-point in VISA is a finer-grained event that is of interest to a property comparing that in BLAST. For example, in BLAST, all function calls, are possible cut-points to verify the correct use of APIs. But this specification language cannot be used in VISA because the cut-points do not include arithmetic (and other) operations.

Other parts of BLAST that are particularly useful (some of which require re-programming) in VISA include:

- Lazy abstraction. The cost of predicate abstraction is exponential in the number of predicates. One of the important features of BLAST is lazy abstraction, where a predicate is included in the computation only in a part of the model checking tree where it is necessary. This is especially useful when clusters of predicates are locally relevant to the property only in certain parts of the search path. Such a pattern is found frequently in the programs of interest.
- Soundness issue. BLAST provides several options to compute the predicate abstraction. For speed considerations, the most commonly used ones are not conservative with respecct to aliases because alias-safe predicate abstraction is too expensive to be practical and alias analysis in general is not precise enough. Although the abstraction may be unsound and not suitable for strict verification, it is still good for bug-hunting.
- Trace Slicing. This is arguably one of the most useful features of BLAST. The idea is to slice the candidate error path to a portion of it that maintains same feasibility characteristics. Because the constraints generated in this stage are normal large and become a bottleneck for the constraint solver. Slicing the path will often generate a surprisingly small constraint. When combined with Craig interpolation, this feature is useful for dealing with counter-based loops (such as a for loop), which are sometimes used in initialization parts of the code and a major cause of unfeasible error trace.

5.2 Realpaver

We use Realpaver [28] as the numerical constraint solver. Based on interval computations, Realpaver solves non-linear formulas over the real numbers. The inputs to Realpaver are

- a finite list of real variables $\mathcal{V} = \{x_1, \ldots, x_n\}$,
- a list of constraints (that can contain nonlinear products and transcendental functions), and
- an initial set of of interval domains $\mathbf{x}_1, \ldots \mathbf{x}_n$ (called a *box*) for the variables in $\mathcal{V}$.

Under the assumption $x_i \in \mathbf{x}_i$, for $1 \leq i \leq m$, Realpaver returns either a *no solution in the initial box* message or a list of boxes, included in the initial box, that contain solutions to the conjunction of the constraints. Realpaver also returns a flag that indicates whether the resolution process was reliable or not. A non-reliable output means that some solutions may be lost during the process.

Realpaver is claimed to satisfy the following property [28].

Proposition 1 (Reliability). *Realpaver computes a union of boxes that contains all the solutions of the original constraint satisfaction problem. Therefore, if no box is computed by Realpaver, the constraint satisfaction problem has no solutions.*

This property means that Realpaver can be used as the basis for an unsatisfiability decision procedure.

We use an ad hoc method to integrate Realpaver into a cooperative decision procedure (cvc-lite [9]). Specifically, the core engine of a cooperative decision procedure uses variable abstraction to divide input formulas (of multiple theories) into formulas of different sub-theories. That is, these formulas do not contain sub-formulas that involve functions or predicates of a different theory. For each sub-theory, a combination of so-called solver and canonizer will find equalities and dis-equalities; this information is propagated to the core engine to find either a solution or inconsistency. Realpaver cannot be a solver as needed by such cooperative decision procedures because it cannot discover equality or dis-equality in an easy way. However, because it can discover inconsistencies, it is possible to put Realpaver into an arithmetic sub-theory before the solvers of this sub-theory is called and signal the core engine only when inconsistency is found. Modern cooperative decision procedures already use different heuristics to find simple inconsistency early at that stage (for speed considerations) [8]. In this sense, Realpaver can be considered as another heuristic.

6 Experience

In a preliminary case study, we apply VISA to a set of public domain scientific computation libraries. We choose these programs because 1) as scientific computation applications, they resemble the engineering programs in aviation industry, the domain of our interest; 2) these programs are actively maintained public domain program and are considered programs with reasonable quality; 3) they might not be as good in quality as the programs in the aviation industry, which makes them a good target to improve. We primarily look for division by zero violations. Table 4 below lists a few representative programs, their sizes, the number of divisions, model checking time, and the number of runs when the model checker fail to terminate (failure runs column in the table). The size of the program is measured by the numbers of lines of syntactically reachable functions with comments removed. The model checking time is the mean time in seconds for all terminating runs (we configure VISA to run once per division). The data reported here is on executing VISA on a commodity laptop (Pentium M 1.73GHz, 512Mb).

Program	Size	No. of Div.	MC Time	Failure Runs
anneal.c	12602	27	210	3
conjdir.c	24134	20	288	1
cube.c	1834	10	65	0
spmat.c	18517	11	60	0

Fig. 4. Representative Runs of VISA

We found division-by-zero traces for three of these programs (anneal.c, conjdir.c and cube.c). Human inspection of the error trace proves that these are all not false alarms. When there are no alarms, through reasoning about the source code (and the model checking trace produced by VISA) manually, we are able to double-justify the absence of division-by-zero.

Also, we apply VISA to KB3D. The correctness of this program, including the safety with regard to division-by-zero, has been previously verified using the theorem prover PVS [32]; thus the program is considered of high quality. KB3D is a small program of a few thousand lines and contains predominantly geometric computations. KB3D contains a number of good examples that demonstrate the capability of VISA. We are able to verify that this program is free of division-by-zero. The computation time is usually within a minute. We conjecture that other tools either are not be able to handle KB3D due to large number of non-linear computations or report false alarms.

VISA and its test suites are available on line at
http://www.nianet.org/m̃unoz/VISA.

7 Related Work and Conclusion

7.1 Program Analysis

In computer science folklore, data flow analysis has been treated as model checking over abstract domains [37]. Yet predicate abstraction can be viewed as a systematic way of designing abstract interpretation, and the counter-example driven approach is strongly connected with the widening operator. Abstraction based on interval analysis has been studied by Cousot's group to reduce runtime errors in C programs. Their tool, ASTREE [14], is based on such abstraction domains as octagon, ellipsoid and decision trees. ASTREE has been successfully applied to large embedded, command and control, safety critical real-time software. Differences between VISA and ASTREE are: First, VISA essentially provides an abstraction mechnism for a non-linear domain, which is a substantial (and practically useful) gain of expressive power; second, VISA does not handle the rounding errors, while ASTREE does; third, VISA is fully automatic (for all programs) while ASTREE needs to be trained to work on a family of programs; and fourth, VISA inherits unsound factors (such as pointers) and incompleteness from BLAST, which is not an issue with ASTREE because of its selected application domain.

Combining different aspects from VISA and ASTREE is a promising research direction. ASTREE researchers have pointed out that certain abstractions cannot be achieved using a counter-example based approaches; the problem that we had with counters is another example where other forms of abstract interpretation (different from predicate abstraction) are more efficient.

7.2 Decision Procedures

The decidability issue of real arithmetic dates back to the 1930's. Tarski [38] shows the first order theory of real numbers with addition and multiplication is decidable through quantifier elimination. Collins shows that quantifier elimination can be done through Cylindrical Algebraic Decomposition [13]. Adding different functions to the theory is different case by case. For example, adding periodic functions such as *sin* will cause the theory to be undecidable, while adding *exp* is decidable conditionally (if Schanuel's conjecture holds). Numerical decision procedures (for so-called stable formulas) are studied by Ratschan [33].

Cooperative decision procedures are mostly based on proposals by Shostak and by Nelson and Oppen. Various systems are used in practice, such as ICS [20], CVC-Lite [9], Simplify [17], Euclid, etc. Microsoft's Zapato [5] is designed specifically to solve formulas for predicate abstraction and is used in Microsoft's SLAM. Zapato uses Nelson and Oppen's method to combine a theory of uninterpreted functions with a solver for conjoined (linear) integer constraints based on Harvey and Stuckey's method [23], which is complete and linear in time. Zapato also takes advantage of fast propositional SAT solvers to first try an abstracted version of the original constraints.

8 Conclusion

This paper extends the current practice of automated software model checking to checking data-flow properties for real, engineering programs that contain non-linear products and transcendental functions. We propose the adoption of interval constraint solvers as the (un)satisfiability checkers used in predicate abstraction and predicate discovery. The soundness and completeness issues are discussed under both theoretical and practical settings. Factors that affect these issues are identified. Based on our proposed approach, a practical system is built for bug-hunting/verification. This prototype shows the potential applications of our model checking framework. The effectiveness of the prototype system is demonstrated on real programs from the avionics industry.

We feel that the framework of our method and the initial success of our prototypes constitute a reasonable contribution to state-of-the art in predicate abstraction research. Our preliminary case studies demonstrated the expressive power of this approach in verifying arithmetic safety. The prototypes that we implemented are valuable complements to the existing tools in the respective communities. We expect the approach to be integrated with other approaches as part of a collective method to prove or disprove run-time errors in an accurate and static way.

References

1. A. Neumaier. *Interval Methods for System of Equations.* Cambridge University Press, 1990.
2. G. Alefeld and J. Herzberger. *Introduction to Interval Computations.* Academic Press, 1983.
3. E. Asarin, T. Dang, and O. Maler. The d/dt tool for verification of hybrid systems. In *CAV*, pages 365–370, 2002.
4. T. Ball. Formalizing counter-example driven predicate refinement with weakest preconditions. Technical Report MSR-TR-2004-134, Microsoft Research, 2004.
5. T. Ball, B. Cook, S. K. Lahiri, and L. Zhang. Zapato: Automatic theorem proving for predicate abstraction refinement. In *CAV*, pages 457–461, 2004.
6. T. Ball, R. Majumdar, T. Millstein, and S. Rajamani. Automatic Predicate Abstraction of C Programs. In *Proceedings of Programming Languages Design and Implementation (PLDI) 2001*, pages 268–283. ACM, 2001.
7. T. Ball and S. Rajamani. Automatically Validating Temporal Safety Properties of Interfaces. In *SPIN2001, Lecture Notes in Computer Science 2057*, pages 103–122. Springer-Verlag, May 2001.
8. C. Barret and C. Tinelli. Theory and practice of decision procedures for combinations of theories. Slides of Talk Given at CAV 2005.
9. C. Barrett and S. Berezin. CVC Lite: A new implementation of the cooperating validity checker. In R. Alur and D. A. Peled, editors, *CAV*, Lecture Notes in Computer Science. Springer, 2004.
10. S. Bensalem, Y. Lakhnech, and S. Owre. Computing Abstractions of Infinite State Systems Compositionally and Automatically. In *Proceedings of Conference on Computer Aided Verification (CAV) 98, Lecture Notes in Computer Science 1427*, pages 319–331, June 1998.
11. D. Beyer, A. J. Chlipala, T. A. Henzinger, R. Jhala, and R. Majumdar. The BLAST query language for software verification. In *Proceedings of the 11th International Static Analysis Symposium (SAS 2004), LNCS 3148*, pages 2–18. Springer-Verlag, 2004.
12. E. Clarke, O. Grumberg, S. Jha, Y. Lu, and H. Veith. Counterexample-guided abstraction refinement. In *Proceedings of Conference on Computer Aided Verification (CAV) 00.* Springer-Verlag, 2000.
13. G. Collins. Quantifier elimination for real closed fields by cylindrical algebraic decomposition. In *Proceedings of the Second GI Conference on Automata Theory and Formal Languages*, volume 33 of *Lecture Notes in Computer Science*, pages 134–183. Springer-Verlag, 1975.

14. P. Cousot, R. Cousot, J. Feret, L. Mauborgne, A. Miné, D. Monniaux, and X. Rival. The ASTREE analyser. In *Proceedings of The European Symposium on Programming*, pages 21–30, 2005.
15. S. Das, D. Dill, and S. J. Park. Experience with Predicate Abstraction. In *Proceedings of Conference on Computer Aided Verification(CAV) 99, Lecture Notes in Computer Science 1633*, pages 160–171, Trento, Italy, July 1999.
16. S. Das and D. L. Dill. Counter-example based predicate discovery in predicate abstraction. In *Proceedings of Conference on Formal Methods in Computer-Aided Design*, Portland, Oregon, November 2002.
17. D. Detlefs, G. Nelson, and J. Saxe. Simplify: A theorem prover for program checking, 2003.
18. G. Dowek, A. Geser, and C. Muñoz. Tactical conflict detection and resolution in a 3-D airspace. In *Proceedings of the 4th USA/Europe Air Traffic Management R&DSeminar, ATM 2001*, Santa Fe, New Mexico, 2001. A long version appears as report NASA/CR-2001-210853 ICASE Report No. 2001-7.
19. M. Dwyer, J. Hatcliff, R. Joehanes, S. Laubach, C. Pasareanu, R. Visser, and H. Zheng. Tool-supported Program Abstraction for Finite-state Verification.
20. J.-C. Filliâtre, S. Owre, H. Rueß, and N. Shankar. ICS: Integrated Canonizer and Solver. In G. Berry, H. Comon, and A. Finkel, editors, *Proceedings of the 13th International Conference on Computer Aided Verification (Paris, France)*, volume 2102 of *Lecture Notes in Computer Science*, pages 246–249. Springer-Verlag, July 2001.
21. S. Graf and H. Saidi. Construction of Abstract State Graphs with PVS. In *Proceedings of Conference on Computer Aided Verification (CAV) 97, Lecture Notes in Computer Science 1254*, pages 72–83, Haifa, Israel, June 1997. Springer-Verlag.
22. L. Granvilliers. On the combination of interval constraint solvers. *Reliable Computing*, 7(6):467–483, 2001.
23. W. Harvey and P. J. Stuckey. Constraint representation for propagation. *Lecture Notes in Computer Science*, 1520:235–245, 1998.
24. P. V. Hentenryck, L. Michel, and Y. Deville. *Numerica, A Modeling Language for Global Optimization.* The MIT Press, 1997.
25. T. Henzinger, R. Jhala, R. Majumdar, and K. McMillan. Abstraction from Proofs. In *Proceedings of ACM SIGPLAN-SIGACT Conference on Principles of Programming Languages (POPL)*, pages 232–244, 2004.
26. T. Henzinger, R. Jhala, R. Majumdar, G. Necula, G. Sutre, and W. Weimer. Temporal-Safety Proofs for Systems Code. In *Proceedings of Conference on Computer-Aided Verification (CAV)*, pages 526–538, 2002.
27. K. Yamamura, H. Kawata and A. Tokue. Interval analysis using linear programming. *Proceedings of BIT 38*, pages 188–201, 1998.
28. L. Granvilliers and F. Benhamou. Realpaver: An interval solver using constraint satisfaction techniques. *ACM Transactions on Mathematical Software.* Accepted for publication.
29. K. L. McMillan. Craig interpolation and reachability analysis. In *SAS*, page 336, 2003.
30. S. McPeak, G. C. Necula, S. P. Rahul, and W. Weimer. CIL: Intermediate Languages and Tools for C Program Analysis and Transformation. In *Proceedings of Conference on Compiler Construction (CC'02)*, March 2002.
31. R. Moore. *Interval Analysis.* Prentice-Hall, 1966.
32. S. Owre, J. Rushby, and N. Shankar. Pvs: A prototype verification system, 1992.
33. S. Ratschan. Slides, available at `http://www.mpi-sb.mpg.de/řatschan/decproc1.pdf`.

34. S. Ratschan. Continuous first-order constraint satisfaction. In *Proceedings of Artificial Intelligence and Symbolic Computation*, LNCS. Springer, 2002.
35. W. Rudin. *Principles of Mathematical Analysis (Third Edition).* McGraw-Hill, 1976. Chapter 10.
36. H. Saidi and N. Shankar. Abstract and Model-check While You Prove. In *Proceedings of Conference on Computer Aided Verification (CAV) 99, Lecture Notes in Computer Science 1633*, pages 443–454. Springer-Verlag, July 1999.
37. D. Schmidt. Data Flow Analysis is Model Checking of Abstract Interpretation. In *Proceedings of SIGPLAN Symposium on Principles of Programming Languages (POPL) 98*, 1998.
38. A. Tarski. *Logic, Semantics, Metamathematics, papers from 1923 to 1938.* Hackett Publishing Company, 1983. English Version, original in Polish.
39. A. Tiwari. An algebraic approach for the unsatisfiability of nonlinear constraints. In L. Ong, editor, *Computer Science Logic, 14th Annual Conf., CSL 2005*, volume 3634 of *LNCS*, pages 248–262. Springer, Aug. 2005.
40. W. Visser, S. Park, and J. Penix. Applying Predicate Abstraction to Model Check Object-oriented Programs. In *Proceedings of the 33rd ACM SIGSOFT Workshop on Formal Methods in Software Practice.*
41. W. Adams and P. Loustaunau. *An Introduction to Gröbner Bases.* American Mathematical Society, 1994.
42. M. Wallace, S. Novello, and J. Schimpf. ECLiPSe: A platform for constraint logic programming, 1997.
43. S. Xia, B. D. Vito, and C. Muñoz. Automated test case generations for non-linear engineering programs. In *Proceedings of the Nineenth International Conference on Automated Software Engineering*, 2005.

A Fresh Look at Testing for Asynchronous Communication*

Puneet Bhateja[1], Paul Gastin[2], and Madhavan Mukund[1]

[1] Chennai Mathematical Institute, Chennai, India
{puneet,madhavan}@cmi.ac.in
[2] LSV, ENS de Cachan & CNRS, France
Paul.Gastin@lsv.ens-cachan.fr

Abstract. Testing is one of the fundamental techniques for verifying if a computing system conforms to its specification. We take a fresh look at the theory of testing for message-passing systems based on a natural notion of observability in terms of input-output relations. We propose two notions of test equivalence: one which corresponds to presenting all test inputs up front and the other which corresponds to interactively feeding inputs to the system under test. We compare our notions with those studied earlier, notably the equivalence proposed by Tretmans. In Tretmans' framework, asynchrony is modelled using synchronous communication by augmenting the state space of the system with queues. We show that the first equivalence we consider is strictly weaker than Tretmans' equivalence and undecidable, whereas the second notion is incomparable. We also establish (un)decidability results for these equivalences.

1 Introduction

Testing is a fundamental activity in verifying the correctness of systems. In this paper, we focus on testing in the restricted context of reactive systems. A theoretical foundation for testing labelled transition systems was laid in the framework of process algebra, where an operational notion of testing was defined and shown to have an extensional semantic characterization in terms of failures [7,8]. These ideas were expanded and elaborated in the work of Tretmans [16,17], in the form of an extensive theory of *conformance testing*—testing when an implementation conforms to its specification. This theory has been used to develop automated tools for testing, such as the TGV system [13].

The initial focus on formalizing testing for labelled transition systems was on synchronous communication, where the send and receive actions for each communication occur simultaneously. However, most communication protocols are based on asynchronous communication, or message-passing via buffers that can be modelled as queues. Many questions remain unanswered about the testing process for such systems. In addition to the usual problem of optimizing the size

* Partially supported by *Timed-DISCOVERI*, a project under the Indo-French Networking Programme.

S. Graf and W. Zhang (Eds.): ATVA 2006, LNCS 4218, pp. 369–383, 2006.

of test suites without sacrificing coverage, there are also additional issues to be considered, such as the possibility of distributing tests [12].

The first major effort to develop an effective theory of testing for asynchronous communication originated in the thesis of Tretmans [16], in which asynchronous communication is reduced to synchronous communication in a model augmented with infinite queues. A refined version of this theory is presented in [17], in terms of input-output transition systems that interact synchronously.

In parallel, asynchronous communication has also been an active area of study in the field of process algebra. A process algebra with asynchronous communication, whose semantics is given in terms of auxiliary data structures such as queues to store the channel state, has been formulated in [5,6]. The focus of this work is to identify semantic equivalences that are congruences with respect to process algebraic operators, rather than to formalize testing equivalence per se. Later papers have considered testing equivalence for process algebras with asynchronous communication [4,2]. In these approaches, there are no explicit channels between processes. Instead, all messages are emitted into a shared pool and can be consumed in any order by receiving processes. This approach towards modelling asynchronous communications is more suitable for name-passing calculi such as the π-calculus, but it is difficult to import any intuition or results to our setting in which processes with a fixed network topology exchange messages through point-to-point queues.

Our approach to testing is to consider a natural notion of observability for systems based on input-output pairs. Using this notion, we propose two notions of test equivalence. The first corresponds to presenting all test inputs up front while the other corresponds to interactively feeding inputs to the system under test. We show that the first equivalence is strictly weaker than Tretmans' equivalence, whereas the second notion is incomparable. Our work is closely related to the queued quiescent trace approach of [14], as explained in Section 4.

We also establish decidability results for these equivalences. We show that the weaker equivalence that we define is undecidable for finite-state systems, as is the equivalence proposed by Tretmans. However, the stronger equivalence is decidable for *well-structured* transition systems. We also show that our weaker notion of equivalence is decidable if we record the input-output behaviour of a system as an unlabelled message sequence chart [11].

The paper is organized as follows. In the next section, we introduce our formal model of asynchronously communicating systems. Three notions of asynchronous testing are introduced in Section 3. We describe the interrelationships between these notions in Section 4 and prove decidability and undecidability results in Section 5. We conclude with a brief discussion on directions for future work.

2 The Model

We work in the setting of labelled transition systems. A *labelled transition system* is a structure $TS = (S, I, \Sigma, \rightarrow)$ where S is a set of states with a subset I of initial states, Σ is an alphabet of actions and $\rightarrow \subseteq S \times \Sigma \times S$ is a labelled transition relation. We will write $s \xrightarrow{a} s'$ to denote that $(s, a, s') \in \rightarrow$.

We are interested in asynchronous systems that interact with their environment by sending and receiving messages. We represent this interaction abstractly by partitioning Σ into two sets: Σ_i, the set of input actions, and Σ_o, the set of output actions. We normally use a, b, c to denote input actions, x, y, z to denote output actions and Greek letters α, β to denote generic actions from Σ.

An action α is said to be *enabled* at a state $s \in S$ if there is some transition $s \xrightarrow{\alpha} s'$. We write $s \xrightarrow{\alpha}$ to denote that α is enabled at s and $s \not\xrightarrow{\alpha}$ to denote that α is not enabled at s. We can extend this to sets of actions: for $X \subseteq \Sigma$, $s \xrightarrow{X}$ if $s \xrightarrow{\alpha}$ for *some* $\alpha \in X$ and $s \not\xrightarrow{X}$ if $s \not\xrightarrow{\alpha}$ for *every* $\alpha \in X$. A state s is said to *refuse* a set $X \subseteq \Sigma$ of actions if $s \not\xrightarrow{X}$. A state s is *quiescent* if it refuses Σ_o.

A run of the transition system TS is a sequence of transitions of the form $s_0 \xrightarrow{\alpha_1} s_1 \xrightarrow{\alpha_2} \cdots \xrightarrow{\alpha_m} s_m$ where $s_0 \in I$. We call this a run of TS over the word $\alpha_1\alpha_2 \ldots \alpha_m$. Let $L(TS) = \{w \in \Sigma^* \mid TS \text{ admits a run over } w\}$. It is easy to see that $L(TS)$ is a prefix-closed language.

Without loss of generality, we assume that in the transition systems we consider, there is no loop $s_0 \xrightarrow{x_1} s_1 \xrightarrow{x_2} \cdots \xrightarrow{x_m} s_m = s_0$ labelled by a sequence of output labels $x_1 x_2 \ldots x_m \in \Sigma_o^*$. Such a loop would generate an unbounded behaviour of the system that does not require any input from the environment. This kind of spontaneous infinite behaviour is not normally expected from the class of systems we are interested in. In particular, this restriction implies that every transition system we consider has at least one quiescent state.

Asynchronous systems are normally assumed to be *receptive*—at each state s, every input action a should be possible. In practice, a system description will limit itself to providing moves for "useful" input actions at each state. One way to deal with missing inputs is to assume a dead state s_d that refuses Σ_o and has a self loop $s_d \xrightarrow{a} s_d$ for every input a. Whenever a state s refuses an input a, we add a move $s \xrightarrow{a} s_d$. In this interpretation of receptiveness, unexpected inputs cause the system to hang. Our semantics will implicitly capture this version of receptiveness, without requiring the explicit addition of such a dead state. An alternative approach, which we do not consider, is to allow the system to swallow unexpected inputs and continue with normal execution. This can be modelled by adding a self-loop labelled a at any quiescent state that refuses an input a.

In [3], Bourdonov et al study test equivalence for asynchronous systems with forbidden or refused inputs (for instance, an interactive form in which some buttons are disabled). They focus on adapting the testing formalism of [17] to such systems, with specific emphasis on compositionality. Here, on the other hand, we concentrate on expressiveness and decidability, rather than compositionality.

Queue semantics. In [16], a *queue semantics* is defined for transition systems with asynchronous communication which is used to transfer notions from the theory of testing for synchronous systems to the asynchronous framework.

Let $TS = (S, I, \Sigma, \rightarrow)$ be a transition system, where $\Sigma = \Sigma_i \uplus \Sigma_o$. A *configuration* of TS is a triple (s, σ_i, σ_o) where s is a state in S and $\sigma_i \in \Sigma_i^*$ and $\sigma_o \in \Sigma_o^*$ are the input and output queues associated with the system.

Initially, the system is in a configuration $(i, \varepsilon, \varepsilon)$, where i is an initial state and both queues are empty. Each input/output move of the original system breaks up into a visible move that alters the input/output queue without changing the internal state and an invisible move in which the input/output action updates the internal state as per the transition relation of the original system.

First, we have two rules describing how the queue based system reads inputs.

Input $(s, \sigma_i, \sigma_o) \xrightarrow{a} (s, \sigma_i a, \sigma_o)$ $\qquad \dfrac{s \xrightarrow{a} s'}{(s, a\sigma_i, \sigma_o) \xrightarrow{\tau} (s', \sigma_i, \sigma_o)}$

External inputs are appended to the input queue, leaving the internal state unchanged. The system can then silently consume the action at the head of the input queue and update its state using a transition of the original system.

Similarly, we have two rules for output actions.

Output $\dfrac{s \xrightarrow{x} s'}{(s, \sigma_i, \sigma_o) \xrightarrow{\tau} (s', \sigma_i, \sigma_o x)}$ $\qquad (s, \sigma_i, x\sigma_o) \xrightarrow{x} (s, \sigma_i, \sigma_o)$

Any output action of the original system results in a silent internal move that changes the state of the system and appends the action to the output queue. The system can then spontaneously emit the action at the head of output queue.

This semantics implies that, at the visible level, output actions can always be postponed. A path of the form $s \xrightarrow{a} s_1 \xrightarrow{x} s_2 \xrightarrow{b} s'$ in the original system may be observed asynchronously as a sequence abx by delaying the output x.

We denote by $Q(TS)$ the transition system whose states are the configurations of TS and whose transitions are governed by the queue semantics.

3 Asynchronous Testing Equivalence

Our main aim is to formalize what we can observe about the behaviour of an asynchronous system through testing. We define two natural notions of testing for asynchronous systems based on input-output pairs.

3.1 IO Behaviours

If $w \in \Sigma^*$ and $X \subseteq \Sigma$, we denote by $w{\downarrow_X}$ the subword obtained by erasing all letters not in X. We also write $\preceq$ for the prefix relation on words.

As usual, let $TS = (S, I, \Sigma, \rightarrow)$ be a transition system, where $\Sigma = \Sigma_i \uplus \Sigma_o$. A *maximal run* of TS is an execution sequence $i \xrightarrow{\alpha_1} s_1 \xrightarrow{\alpha_2} \cdots \xrightarrow{\alpha_n} s_n$ such that $i \in I$ and s_n is quiescent. If TS has a maximal run over a word w, we call w a δ-trace (sometimes referred to in the literature as a *quiescent trace*) of TS, written $\delta_{TS}(w)$. Let $\delta_{\text{traces}}(TS)$ denote the δ-traces of TS.

The IO-behaviour of TS corresponds to an operational model of testing where, for each test case, the tester generates a sequence of inputs, supplies them up front, and observes the effect. This corresponds, roughly, to static test generation. Formally, *IOBeh*(TS) is the set of pairs $(u, v) \in \Sigma_i^* \times \Sigma_o^*$ such that, in TS, there is a maximal run $i \xrightarrow{w} s$ labelled w with $w{\downarrow_{\Sigma_o}} = v$, and either $w{\downarrow_{\Sigma_i}} = u$ or $w{\downarrow_{\Sigma_i}} a \preceq u$ and s refuses a for some $a \in \Sigma_i$.

The condition that s refuses a for the case $w{\downarrow_{\Sigma_i}} a \preceq u$ implicitly captures the first notion of receptiveness, where unexpected inputs lead the system to hang. Formally, this means that if we add a dead state s_d to TS as described earlier, the resulting system will have the same IO-behaviours as the original system.

We can provide additional discriminating power to the tester by assuming that inputs are supplied incrementally, instead of being provided up front, analogous to on-the-fly test case generation.

A *block observation* of TS is a sequence $(u_1, v_1) \cdots (u_n, v_n) \in (\Sigma_i^* \times \Sigma_o^*)(\Sigma_i^+ \times \Sigma_o^*)^*$ such that there is a run $s_0 \xrightarrow{w_1} s_1 \cdots \xrightarrow{w_k} s_k$ with $1 \leq k \leq n$ starting from an initial state $s_0 \in I$ and going through quiescent states $s_1, \ldots, s_k$ with:

- $v_j = w_j{\downarrow_{\Sigma_o}}$ for all $1 \leq j \leq n$, and $v_j = \varepsilon$ for all $k < j \leq n$, and
- $u_j = w_j{\downarrow_{\Sigma_i}}$ for all $1 \leq j < k$, and either ($k = n$ and $u_n = w_n{\downarrow_{\Sigma_i}}$) or ($w_k{\downarrow_{\Sigma_i}} a \preceq u_k$ for some $a \in \Sigma_i$ such that s_k refuses a).

A block observation consists of supplying inputs in blocks $u_0 u_1 \ldots u_n$ and observing the incremental output associated with each block. The first input block is permitted to be empty, to account for a spontaneous initial output v_0. Let *IOBlocks*(TS) denote the set of block observations of TS.

Definition 1. *We define two testing equivalences on asynchronous systems, corresponding to IO-behaviours and block observations.*

$$TS \sim_{io} TS' \stackrel{def}{=} IOBeh(TS) = IOBeh(TS')$$
$$TS \sim_{ioblock} TS' \stackrel{def}{=} IOBlocks(TS) = IOBlocks(TS')$$

3.2 Synchronous Testing on Queues

In contrast to our direct definition of testing based on the observed input-output behaviour of asynchronous systems, the approach taken in [16] is to reduce asynchronous testing to synchronous testing via the queue semantics. Two systems are said to be testing equivalent in an asynchronous sense if the corresponding interpretations with queues are testing equivalent in a synchronous sense.

Let $\sim_Q$ denote asynchronous testing equivalence under the queue semantics and $\sim_{syn}$ denote the normal synchronous testing equivalence, which coincides with failures semantics [7,8]. Then,

$$TS \sim_Q TS' \stackrel{\text{def}}{=} Q(TS) \sim_{syn} Q(TS').$$

We do not recall the formal definition of synchronous testing equivalence, because we do not require this branching-time formulation of $\sim_Q$. Instead, it turns out that $\sim_Q$ admits a linear-time characterization (Corollary 5.15 in [16]).

Theorem 2. *$TS \sim_Q TS'$ iff $L(Q(TS)) = L(Q(TS'))$ and $\delta_{traces}(Q(TS)) = \delta_{traces}(Q(TS'))$.*

In the rest of this section, we define some notions related to $L(Q(TS))$ and $\delta_{\text{traces}}(Q(TS))$ that will prove useful in later analysis.

Tracks. We begin by defining an ordering @ on words. Intuitively, w @ w' (read as "w is *aped* by w'") if w can be observed as w' by postponing some outputs. In the process, w' could accept additional inputs. Formally, w @ w' if:

- $w{\downarrow}_{\Sigma_i} \preceq w'{\downarrow}_{\Sigma_i}$.
- $w{\downarrow}_{\Sigma_o} = w'{\downarrow}_{\Sigma_o}$.
- For every pair of prefixes w_j, w'_j of w, w' of length j, $w'_j{\downarrow}_{\Sigma_o} \preceq w_j{\downarrow}_{\Sigma_o}$.

The relation @ is a partial order on Σ^*. It is easy to see that $L(Q(TS))$, the prefix closed language of TS under the queue semantics, is upward-closed with respect to @: if $w \in L(Q(TS))$ and w @ w' then $w' \in L(Q(TS))$.

A *track* is an @-minimal word in $L(Q(TS))$. It is shown in [16] that every track is actually a word in $L(TS)$, the original transition system interpreted without the queue semantics. Moreover, since $L(Q(TS))$ is upward-closed with respect to @, the set of tracks completely determines the set of traces. Note that not every word in $L(TS)$ is a track: for instance, TS could explicitly have execution sequences $axby$ and $abxy$. Since $axby$ @ $abxy$, $abxy$ is not a track. Let Tracks(TS) denote the set of tracks of TS.

Empty and blocked deadlocks. We can classify quiescent traces into two groups. Recall that we have assumed a receptive model of asynchronous communication in which input actions are always enabled but unexpected inputs cause the system to hang. This gives rise to two possible scenarios when a system deadlocks. In the first scenario, the system is waiting for input with an empty input queue and can potentially make progress if a suitable input arrives. In the second scenario, the system has received an unexpected input and can never recover. We refer to these as empty and blocked deadlocks, respectively.

To define empty and blocked deadlocks formally, we need a new relation. We say that $w \in \Sigma^*$ is strictly aped by $w' \in \Sigma^*$, denoted w |@| w', if w @ w' and $|w| = |w'|$. We can then define the empty and blocked deadlocks of $Q(TS)$.

$$\delta_{\text{empty}}(Q(TS)) = \{w \in \Sigma^* \mid \exists\, i \xrightarrow{w'} s \text{ in } TS \text{ with } i \in I,\ s \text{ quiescent and } w' \mid@\mid w\}.$$

$$\delta_{\text{block}}(Q(TS)) = \{w \in \Sigma^* \mid \exists\, i \xrightarrow{w'} s \text{ in } TS \text{ with } i \in I, \exists\, a \in \Sigma_i \text{ such that } s \text{ refuses } \Sigma_o \cup \{a\} \text{ and } w'a \mathrel{@} w\}.$$

Observe that $\delta_{\text{empty}}(Q(TS))$ is |@|-upward closed and consists of traces w such that $(i, \varepsilon, \varepsilon) \xrightarrow{w} (s, \varepsilon, \varepsilon)$ in $Q(TS)$ with s quiescent. Similarly, $\delta_{\text{block}}(Q(TS))$ is @-upward closed and consists of traces w such that $(i, \varepsilon, \varepsilon) \xrightarrow{w} (s, a\sigma_i, \varepsilon)$ in $Q(TS)$ where s refuses $\Sigma_o \cup \{a\}$. It is not difficult to see that

$$\delta_{\text{traces}}(Q(TS)) = \delta_{\text{empty}}(Q(TS)) \cup \delta_{\text{block}}(Q(TS)).$$

However, note that the sets $\delta_{\text{empty}}(Q(TS))$ and $\delta_{\text{block}}(Q(TS))$ may overlap. In fact, it is even possible $TS_1 \sim_Q TS_2$ but $\delta_{\text{empty}}(Q(TS_1)) \neq \delta_{\text{empty}}(Q(TS_2))$ or $\delta_{\text{block}}(Q(TS_1)) \neq \delta_{\text{block}}(Q(TS_2))$ [16]. Despite these shortcomings, we will find these notions very useful.

4 Comparing the Three Equivalences

Our first set of results compare the three testing equivalences we have introduced earlier. We show that $\sim_{io}$ is strictly weaker than $\sim_Q$ and $\sim_{ioblock}$, but $\sim_Q$ and $\sim_{ioblock}$ are incomparable.

Proposition 3. *If $TS_1 \sim_{ioblock} TS_2$, then $TS_1 \sim_{io} TS_2$.*

Proof. This follows from the fact that $IOBeh(TS) = IOBlocks(TS) \cap (\Sigma_i^* \times \Sigma_o^*)$ for any transition system TS. □

Proposition 4. *If $TS_1 \sim_Q TS_2$, then $TS_1 \sim_{io} TS_2$.*

Proof. Let TS_1 and TS_2 be two transition systems such that $TS_1 \sim_Q TS_2$. We show that $TS_1 \sim_{io} TS_2$. Let $(u,v) \in IOBeh(TS_1)$ and let $i \xrightarrow{w} s$ be a maximal run in TS_1 labelled w, with $w{\downarrow_{\Sigma_o}} = v$, and either $w{\downarrow_{\Sigma_i}} = u$ or $w{\downarrow_{\Sigma_i}}a \preceq u$ and s refuses a for some $a \in \Sigma_i$.

Case 1: Suppose $w{\downarrow_{\Sigma_i}} = u$. By definition of the empty deadlocks, we obtain $w \in \delta_{\text{empty}}(Q(TS_1))$. Since $TS_1 \sim_Q TS_2$, we have $w \in \delta_{\text{traces}}(Q(TS_2))$.

If $w \in \delta_{\text{empty}}(Q(TS_2))$ then, in TS_2, there is a maximal run $i' \xrightarrow{w'} s'$ with $w' \;|@|\; w$. Since $w'{\downarrow_{\Sigma_i}} = w{\downarrow_{\Sigma_i}} = u$ and $w'{\downarrow_{\Sigma_o}} = w{\downarrow_{\Sigma_o}} = v$, we have $(u,v) \in IOBeh(TS_2)$.

If $w \in \delta_{\text{block}}(Q(TS_2))$ then, in TS_2, there is a maximal run $i' \xrightarrow{w'} s'$ where s' refuses $\Sigma_o \cup \{b\}$ and $w'b \;@\; w$ for some $b \in \Sigma_i$. Since $(w'b){\downarrow_{\Sigma_i}} \preceq w{\downarrow_{\Sigma_i}} = u$ and $w'{\downarrow_{\Sigma_o}} = w{\downarrow_{\Sigma_o}} = v$, we have $(u,v) \in IOBeh(TS_2)$.

Case 2: Suppose $w{\downarrow_{\Sigma_i}}a \preceq u$ and s refuses $a \in \Sigma_i$. As above, by definition of the blocked deadlocks we get $wa \in \delta_{\text{block}}(Q(TS_1))$. Let u' be such that $u = w{\downarrow_{\Sigma_i}}au'$. We have $wa \;@\; wau'$ and we obtain $wau' \in \delta_{\text{block}}(Q(TS_1))$ since this set is @-upward closed. Since $TS_1 \sim_Q TS_2$ we deduce $wau' \in \delta_{\text{traces}}(Q(TS_2))$.

If $wau' \in \delta_{\text{empty}}(Q(TS_2))$ then, in TS_2, there is a maximal run $i' \xrightarrow{w'} s'$ with $w' \;|@|\; wau'$. Since $w'{\downarrow_{\Sigma_i}} = w{\downarrow_{\Sigma_i}}au' = u$ and $w'{\downarrow_{\Sigma_o}} = w{\downarrow_{\Sigma_o}} = v$, we have $(u,v) \in IOBeh(TS_2)$.

If $wau' \in \delta_{\text{block}}(Q(TS_2))$ then, in TS_2, there is a maximal run $i' \xrightarrow{w'} s'$ where s' refuses $\Sigma_o \cup \{b\}$ and $w'b \;@\; wau'$ for some $b \in \Sigma_i$. Since $w'{\downarrow_{\Sigma_i}}b \preceq w{\downarrow_{\Sigma_i}}au' = u$ and $w'{\downarrow_{\Sigma_o}} = w{\downarrow_{\Sigma_o}} = v$, we have $(u,v) \in IOBeh(TS_2)$. □

The implications we have proved are strict. Below, we show two systems that are related by $\sim_{io}$ but not by $\sim_Q$. Here $\Sigma_i = \{a\}$ and $\Sigma_o = \{x\}$. For both systems, the IO-behaviours are given by $\{(\varepsilon,\varepsilon),(a,x),(a,xx)\} \cup \{(a^n,x),(a^n,x^2),(a^n,x^3) \mid n > 1\}$, so $TS_1 \sim_{io} TS_2$. However, notice that $axaxx \in \text{Tracks}(TS_1) \setminus \text{Tracks}(TS_2)$ because $axxax \in L(TS_2)$ and $axxax \;@\; axaxx$. Hence, $TS_1 \not\sim_Q TS_2$. This example also establishes that $\sim_{io}$ is strictly weaker than $\sim_{ioblock}$ since $(a,x)(a,xx) \in IOBlocks(TS_1) \setminus IOBlocks(TS_2)$.

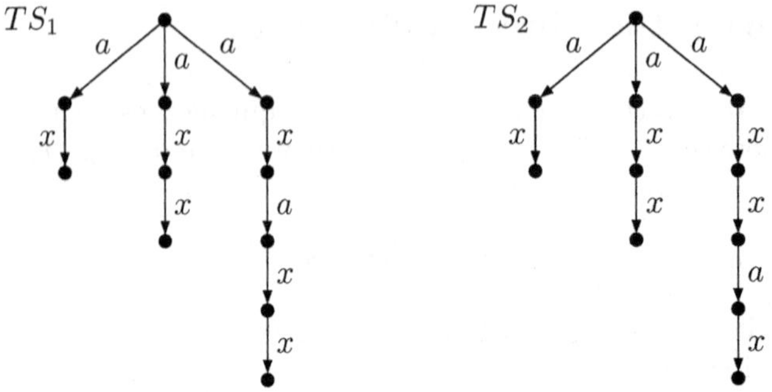

The equivalences $\sim_Q$ and $\sim_{ioblock}$ are incomparable. Below, we show two systems that are related by $\sim_Q$ but not by $\sim_{ioblock}$. Here, $\Sigma_i = \{a\}$ and $\Sigma_o = \{w, x, y, z\}$. We have $\text{Tracks}(TS_1) = \text{Tracks}(TS_2) = \{\varepsilon, ax, axy, axyaz, axaw\}$. Also, the set of empty deadlocks for both systems is the $|@|$-upper closure of $\{\varepsilon, ax, axy, axyaz, axaw\}$. Finally, the set of blocked deadlocks for both systems is the @-upper closure of $\{axyaza, axawa\}$. Hence $TS_1 \sim_Q TS_2$. However, $(a, x)(a, yz)$ is in $\mathit{IOBlocks}(TS_1) \setminus \mathit{IOBlocks}(TS_2)$, so $TS_1 \not\sim_{ioblock} TS_2$.

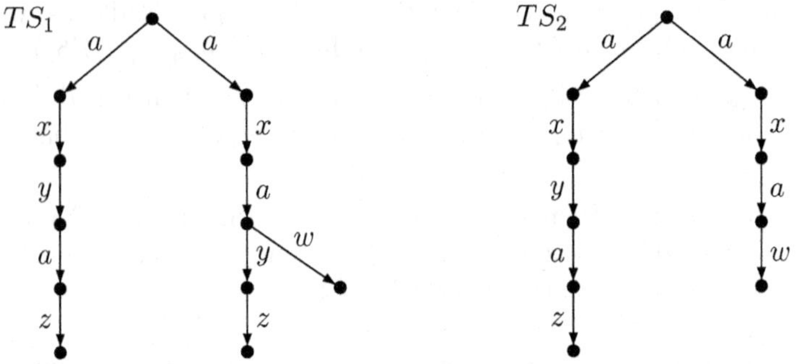

Similarly, we give below two systems that are related by $\sim_{ioblock}$ but not by $\sim_Q$. We have $axax \in \delta_{\text{traces}}(Q(TS_1)) \setminus \delta_{\text{traces}}(Q(TS_2))$, so $TS_1 \not\sim_Q TS_2$. On the other hand, $TS_1 \sim_{ioblock} TS_2$ since the block observations of TS_1 and TS_2 are

$$\begin{aligned}\{(\varepsilon,\varepsilon)\} &\cup \{(a^n, x), (a^n, xy), (aa^n, x^2) \mid n \geq 1\} \cdot (a^+ \times \{\varepsilon\}) \\ &\cup \{(\varepsilon,\varepsilon)\} \cdot \{(a^n, x), (a^n, xy), (aa^n, x^2) \mid n \geq 1\} \cdot (a^+ \times \{\varepsilon\})\end{aligned}$$

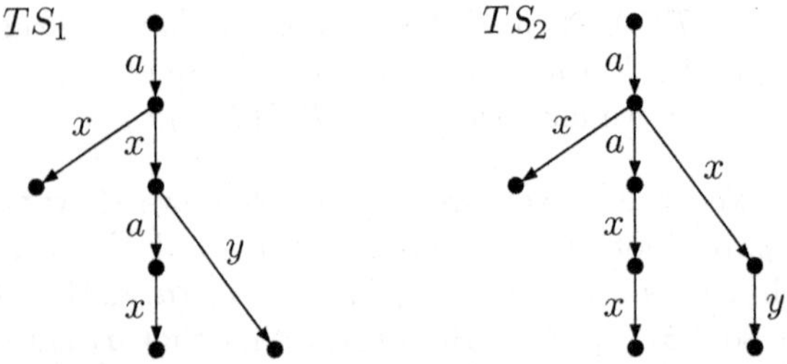

Queued Quiescent Traces. Our equivalences $\sim_{io}$ and $\sim_{ioblock}$ correspond to the notions queued quiescent trace equivalence and queued suspension trace equivalence, respectively, defined in [14]. While we directly provide extensional characterizations of these equivalences, the corresponding notions are developed in [14] via an intensional definition of testing that uses a variant of IO-automata with queues, from which an extensional definition is derived.

In [14], queued quiescent trace equivalence is compared with an equivalence called ioco, defined by Tretmans in [17], which differs slightly from the queue equivalence $\sim_Q$ that we consider here. It is shown, by examples, that some systems distinguished by ioco are equated by queued quiescent trace equivalence and that some systems equated by queued quiescent trace equivalence are distinguished by queued suspension trace equivalence. However, there is no formal characterization of the relative expressive powers of these three equivalences.

5 Decidability of Asynchronous Test Equivalence

We now examine the decidability of test equivalence for finite-state systems.

5.1 Undecidability of $\sim_{io}$

We prove this result using a reduction from the equivalence problem for rational relations [1,15]. We start by recalling some definitions. Let A, B be two finite alphabets. With componentwise concatenation, the set $A^* \times B^*$ is a monoid. A rational relation over A and B is a rational subset R of $A^* \times B^*$. Equivalently, R is a mapping from A^* to $\mathcal{P}(B^*)$ where $u \in A^* \mapsto R(u) = \{v \in B^* \mid (u,v) \in R\}$.

Le $(K, +, \times, 0, 1)$ be a semiring. A K-automaton over A is a tuple $\mathcal{A} = (S, \lambda, \mu, \gamma)$ with S a finite set of states, $\lambda, \gamma \in K^S$ and $\mu(a) \in K^{S\times S}$ for each $a \in A$. Intuitively, the automaton outputs λ_i when it is entered in state i, then it outputs $\mu(a)_{i,j}$ whenever a transition labelled a from i to j is taken and finally, it outputs γ_j when the input word has been completely read and we exit the automaton in state j. The value $(\mathcal{A}, u)$ computed by $\mathcal{A}$ on the input word $u = a_1 \cdots a_k \in A^*$ is the sum over all paths $i_0, \ldots, i_k \in S$ of the products $\lambda_{i_0}\mu(a_1)_{i_0,i_1} \cdots \mu(a_k)_{i_{k-1},i_k}\gamma_{i_k}$. Since K is a semiring, the set of matrices $K^{S\times S}$ equipped with matrix multiplication is a monoid and we can extend μ to a monoid morphism $\mu : A^* \to K^{S\times S}$. Viewing λ as a row vector and γ as a column vector, we have $(\mathcal{A}, u) = \lambda\mu(u)\gamma$ for each $u \in A^*$. Without loss of generality, we may assume that $\lambda_i \neq 0$ implies $\lambda_i = 1$ for each state $i \in S$.

The set $K = \mathrm{Rat}(B^*)$ equipped with union as addition and concatenation as multiplication is a semiring with $\emptyset$ as zero element and $\{\varepsilon\}$ as unit. A relation $R \subseteq A^* \times B^*$ is rational if and only if it can be realized by some $\mathrm{Rat}(B^*)$-automaton. We denote by $\mathcal{R}(\mathcal{A})$ the rational relation realized by $\mathcal{A}$ and for $u = a_1 \cdots a_k \in A^*$ we have $(u, v) \in \mathcal{R}(\mathcal{A})$ iff $v \in \lambda_{i_0}\mu(a_1)_{i_0,i_1} \cdots \mu(a_k)_{i_{k-1},i_k}\gamma_{i_k}$ for some $i_0, \ldots, i_k \in S$. The equivalence problem for rational relations given by $\mathrm{Rat}(B^*)$-automata is undecidable [1,15]. This undecidability holds even for rational relation for which $|B| = 1$ and given by a K-automaton where K is the semiring $\mathcal{P}_{\text{fin}}(B^*)$ of *finite* subsets of B^*. So in the following we assume that $B = \{b\}$ is a singleton and that $K = \mathcal{P}_{\text{fin}}(B^*)$.

We prefer to avoid ε-transitions. We call a K-automaton $\mathcal{A} = (S, \lambda, \mu, \gamma)$ *strict* if none of the sets $\mu(a)_{p,q}$ and γ_q contain the empty word ε. We show that the undecidability still holds for rational relations given by strict K-automata. Let $\mathcal{A} = (S, \lambda, \mu, \gamma)$ be a K-automaton. Define $\mathcal{A}^s = (S, \lambda, \mu^s, \gamma^s)$ by $\mu^s(a)_{p,q} = b\mu(a)_{p,q}$ and $\gamma^s_q = b\gamma_q$. Then, $\mathcal{A}^s$ is strict and for each $u \in A^*$ we have $\lambda\mu^s(u)\gamma^s = b^{|u|+1}\lambda\mu(u)\gamma$ (recall that $B = \{b\}$ so the semiring K is commutative). Then, $\mathcal{R}(\mathcal{A}) = \mathcal{R}(\mathcal{B})$ if and only if $\mathcal{R}(\mathcal{A}^s) = \mathcal{R}(\mathcal{B}^s)$. Therefore, equivalence is undecidable for rational relations given by strict K-automata.

We now associate to a strict K-automaton $\mathcal{A} = (S, \lambda, \mu, \gamma)$ a transition system $\mathcal{A}'$ over Σ with $\Sigma_i = A$ and $\Sigma_o = B \uplus \{\#\}$ where $\#$ is a new output letter. For each $(p, a, q) \in S \times A \times S$ we consider an automaton $\mathcal{A}_{p,a,q}$ recognizing $\mu(a)_{p,q}$ and such that $\mathcal{A}_{p,a,q}$ has a unique initial state $i_{p,a,q}$ with no ingoing transition, a unique final state $f_{p,a,q}$ with no outgoing transition and all other states have outgoing transitions. To construct $\mathcal{A}'$, we first take the disjoint union of the automata $\mathcal{A}_{p,a,q}$ for $(p, a, q) \in S \times A \times S$. Then, for each $q \in S$, we merge all states $f_{p,a,q}$ with $(p, a) \in S \times A$ into a single state denoted simply by q. Finally, for each $(p, a, q) \in S \times A \times S$, we add the transition $p \xrightarrow{a} i_{p,a,q}$. Thus we obtain the transition system $\mathcal{A}' = (S', I, \Sigma, \rightarrow)$ with $I = \{i \in S \mid \lambda_i \neq \emptyset\}$. Note that in $\mathcal{A}'$, all transitions leaving the states in S are labelled with input letters and all transitions leaving states in $S' \setminus S$ are labelled with output letters. Hence, the deadlocked states in $\mathcal{A}'$ are exactly those in S.

For each pair of states $p, q \in S$ we consider the relation

$$T_{p,q} = \{(w{\downarrow_A}, w{\downarrow_B}) \in A^* \times B^* \mid p \xrightarrow{w} q \text{ in } \mathcal{A}'\}.$$

The following lemma is a standard result from the theory of rational relations and K-automata.

Lemma 5. *For each $p, q \in S$, we have*

$$T_{p,q} = \{(u, v) \in A^* \times B^* \mid v \in \mu(u)_{p,q}\}.$$

For each $q \in S$ we consider an automaton $\mathcal{A}_q$ recognizing $\gamma_q\#$ and such that $\mathcal{A}_q$ has a unique initial state i_q with no ingoing transition, a unique final state f_q with no outgoing transition and all other states have outgoing transitions. We let $\mathcal{A}_q^+$ be $\mathcal{A}_q$ with the additional transitions $f_q \xrightarrow{a} f'_q$ for $a \in A$ and $f'_q \xrightarrow{\#} f_q$ so that f_q does not refuse any input letter. Finally, we let $\mathcal{A}''$ be the disjoint union of $\mathcal{A}'$ together with the automata $\mathcal{A}_q^+$ for $q \in S$ and the additional transitions $x \xrightarrow{b} i_q$ for each transition $x \xrightarrow{b} q$ of $\mathcal{A}'$. Note that the deadlocked states of $\mathcal{A}''$ are $S \cup \{f_q \mid q \in S\}$.

Lemma 6. $\mathit{IOBeh}(\mathcal{A}'') = \mathit{IOBeh}(\mathcal{A}') \cup \mathcal{R}(\mathcal{A}) \cdot \{(x, \#^{1+|x|}) \mid x \in A^*\}$.

Proof. First, maximal paths in $\mathcal{A}'$ are of the form $p \xrightarrow{w} q$ for $p \in I$ and $q \in S$. These are also maximal paths in $\mathcal{A}''$. Moreover, a state $q \in S$ refuses exactly the same input letters in $\mathcal{A}'$ and in $\mathcal{A}''$. Hence, $\mathit{IOBeh}(\mathcal{A}') \subseteq \mathit{IOBeh}(\mathcal{A}'')$. Conversely, the maximal paths in $\mathcal{A}''$ which do not use the letter $\#$ cannot enter one of the automata $\mathcal{A}_q$. Hence, they are also maximal paths in $\mathcal{A}'$ and we deduce that $IOBeh(\mathcal{A}'') \cap A^* \times B^* = IOBeh(\mathcal{A}')$.

Second, let $(u,v) \in \mathcal{R}(\mathcal{A})$. We have $v \in \lambda\mu(u)\gamma$ hence we find $p,q \in S$ with $v \in \lambda_p\mu(u)_{p,q}\gamma_q$. It follows that $\lambda_p \neq \emptyset$ (i.e., $p \in I$), which implies $\lambda_p = \{\varepsilon\}$ by our assumption on K-automata. Hence we can write $v = v'v''$ with $v' \in \mu(u)_{p,q}$ and $v'' \in \gamma_q$. By Lemma 5 we find a path $p \xrightarrow{w} q$ in $\mathcal{A}'$ with $u = w{\downarrow_A}$ and $v' = w{\downarrow_B}$. Replacing the last transition $x \xrightarrow{b} q$ of this path by $x \xrightarrow{b} i_q$ we find a path $p \xrightarrow{wv''\#} f_q$ in $\mathcal{A}''$. For $x = a_1 \cdots a_k$, this path can be extended with $f_q \xrightarrow{w'} f_q$ where $w' = a_1\# \cdots a_k\#$. We have $ux = (wv''\#w'){\downarrow_{\Sigma_i}}$ and $v\#^{1+|x|} = (wv''\#w'){\downarrow_{\Sigma_o}}$. Since f_q is a deadlocked state we deduce that $(ux, v\#^{1+|x|}) \in IOBeh(\mathcal{A}'')$.

Conversely, let $(u',v') \in IOBeh(\mathcal{A}'') \setminus A^* \times B^*$. Let $p \xrightarrow{w'} s$ be a run in $\mathcal{A}''$ with $p \in I$, s deadlocked, $w'{\downarrow_{\Sigma_o}} = v'$ and either $w'{\downarrow_{\Sigma_i}} = u'$ or $w'{\downarrow_{\Sigma_i}}a \preceq u'$ and s refuses $a \in \Sigma_i$. Since $v' \notin B^*$, we must have $s = f_q$ for some $q \in S$ and $w' = w\#a_1\# \cdots a_k\#$ with $w \in (A \cup B)^*$ and $x = a_1 \cdots a_k \in A^*$. Since $s = f_q$ does not refuse any input letter, we get $w'{\downarrow_{\Sigma_i}} = u'$. With $u = w{\downarrow_{\Sigma_i}}$ and $v = w{\downarrow_{\Sigma_o}}$ we have $v' = v\#^{1+k}$ and $u' = ux$. The path $p \xrightarrow{w'} f_q$ can be split in $p \xrightarrow{w_1} i_q \xrightarrow{w_2\#} f_q \xrightarrow{a_1\#\cdots a_k\#} f_q$ so that $p \xrightarrow{w_1} q$ is a path in $\mathcal{A}'$ and $i_q \xrightarrow{w_2\#} f_q$ is a path in $\mathcal{A}_q$ and $w = w_1w_2$. We deduce that $w_2 \in \gamma_q$, $u = w_1{\downarrow_A}$ and $v = (w_1{\downarrow_B})w_2$. By Lemma 5 we have $w_1{\downarrow_B} \in \mu(u)_{p,q}$. Therefore, $v \in \mu(u)_{p,q}\gamma_q$. Since $p \in I$ we have $\lambda_p = \{\varepsilon\}$ and we obtain $v \in \lambda\mu(u)\gamma = \mathcal{R}(\mathcal{A})(u)$. □

If we have another rational relation defined by a strict K-automaton $\mathcal{B}$ then we define similarly $\mathcal{B}'$ and $\mathcal{B}''$.

Theorem 7. *$\mathcal{A}' \uplus \mathcal{B}'' \sim_{io} \mathcal{A}'' \uplus \mathcal{B}'$ if and only if $\mathcal{R}(\mathcal{A}) = \mathcal{R}(\mathcal{B})$. Therefore, the $\sim_{io}$ equivalence is undecidable.*

Proof. The result follows from the following equations obtained from Lemma 6.

$$IOBeh(\mathcal{A}' \uplus \mathcal{B}'') = IOBeh(\mathcal{A}') \cup IOBeh(\mathcal{B}') \cup \mathcal{R}(\mathcal{B})\{(x, \#^{1+|x|}) \mid x \in A^*\}$$
$$IOBeh(\mathcal{A}'' \uplus \mathcal{B}') = IOBeh(\mathcal{A}') \cup IOBeh(\mathcal{B}') \cup \mathcal{R}(\mathcal{A})\{(x, \#^{1+|x|}) \mid x \in A^*\}$$

□

5.2 Undecidability of $\sim_Q$

Let A and B be two finite alphabets and let $f, g : A^+ \to B^+$ be two morphisms corresponding to an instance of Post's Correspondence Problem (PCP). The PCP instance has a solution if and only if we have $f(u) = g(u)$ for some $u \in A^+$.

We consider a new symbol $\$$ and define the input and output alphabets as $\Sigma_i = A \cup \{\$\}$ and $\Sigma_o = B$. We then construct two transition systems from the ingredients shown in the figure on the next page.

The transition system S_f corresponds to the morphism f and has one loop $ab_1b_2 \ldots b_k$ for each $a \in A$ such that $f(a) = b_1b_2 \ldots b_k$. Formally the set of states

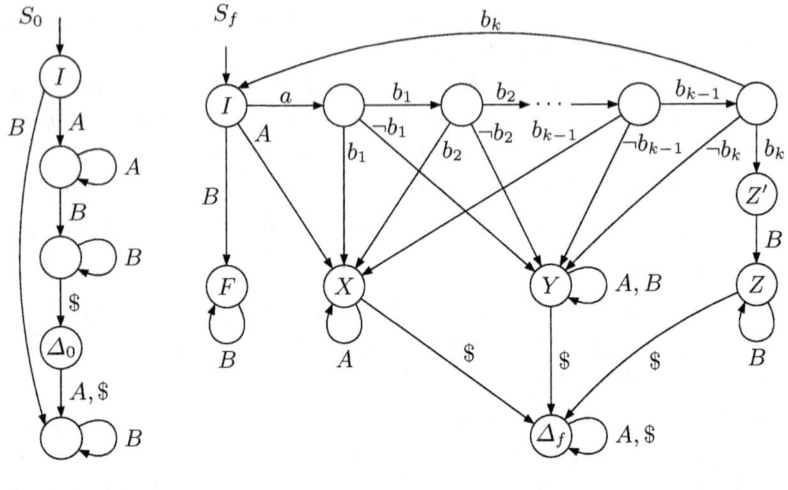

of S_f is $Q_f = \{I, F, X, Y, Z, Z', \Delta_f\} \cup \{(a, i) \mid a \in A, 0 < i \leq |f(a)|\}$ and its initial state is I. The transitions between states in $\{I, F, X, Y, Z, Z', \Delta_f\}$ are precisely given in the picture above, which also contains the intuition for the other transitions defined, for each $a \in A$ with $f(a) = b_1 b_2 \cdots b_k$, by:

- $I \xrightarrow{a} (a, 1) \xrightarrow{b_1} (a, 2) \xrightarrow{b_2} (a, 3) \quad \cdots \quad (a, k-1) \xrightarrow{b_{k-1}} (a, k) \xrightarrow{b_k} I$,
- $(a, i) \xrightarrow{b} Y$ if $1 \leq i \leq k$ and $b \in B \setminus \{b_i\}$,
- $(a, i) \xrightarrow{b_i} X$ if $1 \leq i < k$, and $(a, k) \xrightarrow{b_k} Z'$.

For the morphism g, we construct an analogous system S_g. We want to compare the following two systems, where $S_i + S_j$ denotes the disjoint union of the two systems with multiple initial states.

- $M_1 = S_0 + S_f + S_g$
- $M_2 = S_f + S_g$

The only deadlocked state in S_0 is Δ_0. Since this state does not refuse any input letter, $\delta_{\text{block}}(S_0) = \emptyset$. Similarly, the only deadlocked states in S_f are X and Δ_f and neither refuses any input letter, so $\delta_{\text{block}}(S_f) = \emptyset$. Therefore, $\delta_{\text{traces}}(M_1) = \delta_{\text{empty}}(S_0) \cup \delta_{\text{empty}}(M_2)$ and $\delta_{\text{traces}}(M_2) = \delta_{\text{empty}}(M_2)$ and $M_1 \sim_Q M_2$ if and only if $\text{Tracks}(M_1) = \text{Tracks}(M_2)$ and $\delta_{\text{empty}}(S_0) \subseteq \delta_{\text{empty}}(M_2)$.

Lemma 8. $\text{Tracks}(M_1) = \text{Tracks}(M_2) = \text{Tracks}(S_f) = B^*$.

Proof. First, let $v \in B^+$. Then v is @-minimal and $I \xrightarrow{v} F$ in S_f. Therefore, $B^* \subseteq \text{Tracks}(S_f)$. Since any word $w \in \Sigma^*$ apes its projection on the output alphabet B, we deduce that $\text{Tracks}(S_f) = B^*$. □

Lemma 9. *$\delta_{empty}(S_0)$ is the $|@|$-upper closure of $A^+B^+\$$.*

Proof. Follows from the definition of δ_{empty} and the fact that the set of words $w' \in \Sigma^*$ having a run $I \xrightarrow{w'} \Delta_0$ in S_0 is $A^+B^+\$$. □

Lemma 10. *Let $u \in A^+$ and $v \in B^+$. Then, $uv\$ \in \delta_{empty}(S_f)$ iff $v \neq f(u)$.*

Proof. If $v \neq f(u)$, the construction of S_f guarantees that there is some witnessing interleaving w of u and v that leads to one of the states X, Y or Z. Formally, assuming that $v \neq f(u)$ with $u = a_1 \cdots a_p$, we distinguish three cases:

1. If $v \prec f(u)$, let j be such that $f(a_1 \cdots a_{j-1}) \preceq v \prec f(a_1 \cdots a_j)$. Consider $w = a_1 f(a_1) \cdots a_{j-1} f(a_{j-1}) a_j (f(a_1 \cdots a_{j-1})^{-1} v) a_{j+1} \cdots a_p$. Then $w \;|@|\; uv$ and $I \xrightarrow{w} X$ in S_f.
2. If $v = f(a_1 \cdots a_{j-1}) v' b v''$ with $v' \prec f(a_j)$, $b \in B$ and $v'b \not\preceq f(a_j)$. Consider $w = a_1 f(a_1) \cdots a_{j-1} f(a_{j-1}) a_j v' b v'' a_{j+1} \cdots a_p$. Then $w \;|@|\; uv$ and $I \xrightarrow{w} Y$ in S_f.
3. If $f(u) \prec v$. Consider $w = a_1 f(a_1) \cdots a_p f(a_p)(f(u)^{-1} v)$. Then $w \;|@|\; uv$ and $I \xrightarrow{w} Z$ in S_f.

Hence, there is a run $I \xrightarrow{w\$} \Delta_f$ in S_f. Since $w\$ \;|@|\; uv\$$, $uv\$ \in \delta_{\text{empty}}(S_f)$.

Conversely, let $I \xrightarrow{w'} s$ be a run in S_f with s deadlocked and $w' \;|@|\; uv\$$. Since $\$$ must occur in w' we deduce that $s = \Delta_f$ and $w' = w\$$ with $w \;|@|\; uv$. Moreover, there is a run in S_f labelled w going from I to one of the states X, Y or Z. Let $u = a_1 \cdots a_p$.

1. If $I \xrightarrow{w} X$ then we have $w = a_1 f(a_1) \cdots a_{j-1} f(a_{j-1}) a_j (f(a_1 \cdots a_{j-1})^{-1} v) a_{j+1} \cdots a_p$ for some j such that $f(a_1 \cdots a_{j-1}) \preceq v \prec f(a_1 \cdots a_j)$ and we deduce that $v \neq f(u)$.
2. If $I \xrightarrow{w} Y$ then we have $w = a_1 f(a_1) \cdots a_{j-1} f(a_{j-1}) a_j v' b w''$ for some j such that $v' \prec f(a_j)$, $b \in B$ and $v'b \not\preceq f(a_j)$. We deduce that $v \neq f(u)$.
3. If $I \xrightarrow{w} Z$ then we have $w = a_1 f(a_1) \cdots a_p f(a_p) v'$ with $v' \in B^+$ and we deduce that $v \neq f(u)$. □

Theorem 11. *$M_1 \sim_Q M_2$ iff the PCP instance (f, g) has no solution.*

Proof. First, assume that the PCP instance (f, g) has a solution and let $u \in A^+$ be such that $v = f(u) = g(u)$. Then, $uv\$ \in \delta_{\text{empty}}(S_0) \setminus \delta_{\text{empty}}(M_2)$ by Lemmas 9 and 10. Therefore, $M_1 \not\sim_Q M_2$.

Conversely, if the PCP instance (f, g) has no solution, then for every $u \in A^+$ and $v \in B^+$ we have either $v \neq f(u)$ or $v \neq g(u)$. Hence, $uv\$ \in \delta_{\text{empty}}(M_2)$ by Lemma 10. Using Lemma 9 we deduce that $\delta_{\text{empty}}(S_0) \subseteq \delta_{\text{empty}}(M_2)$ since these sets are $|@|$-upward closed. Therefore, $M_1 \sim_Q M_2$. □

5.3 Decidability of $\sim_{ioblock}$ for Well Structured Systems

Let α and β be block-observations. We say that α is *finer than* β, denoted $\alpha \preceq \beta$, if β can be obtained from α by merging consecutive blocks. More precisely, if $\alpha = (u_1, v_1) \cdots (u_n, v_n)$ and $0 < j_1 < \cdots < j_p = n$ $(p \geq 1)$ then α is finer than $\beta = (u_1 \cdots u_{j_1}, v_1 \cdots v_{j_1}) \cdots (u_{1+j_{p-1}} \cdots u_{j_p}, v_{1+j_{p-1}} \cdots v_{j_p})$. Clearly, if $\alpha \in IOBlocks(TS)$ and $\alpha \preceq \beta$ then $\beta \in IOBlocks(TS)$.

We say that a block observation $\alpha = (u_1, v_1) \cdots (u_n, v_n)$ is *reduced* if $u_1 = \varepsilon$ and $u_j \in \Sigma_i$ for $1 < j \leq n$. A transition system is *well structured* (WS) if each state either refuses Σ_i or refuses Σ_o. A transition system is *receptive* if no quiescent state s refuses an input: $s \xrightarrow{a}$ for all $a \in \Sigma_i$.

Lemma 12. *Assume that TS is WS. If $\beta \in IOBlocks(TS)$ then there exists $\alpha \in IOBlocks(TS)$* reduced *with $\alpha \preceq \beta$. Therefore, $IOBlocks(TS)$ is characterized by its* reduced *block-observations.*

Let $L_\delta(TS)$ be the language accepted by TS with quiescent states as final.

Lemma 13.

1. *Assume that TS is WS. If $w = v_1 a_2 v_2 \cdots a_n v_n \in L_\delta(TS)$ with $v_j \in \Sigma_o^*$ and $a_j \in \Sigma_i$ then $(\varepsilon, v_1)(a_2, v_2) \cdots (a_n, v_n) \in IOBlocks(TS)$.*
2. *Let TS be WS and receptive. If $(\varepsilon, v_1)(a_2, v_2) \cdots (a_n, v_n) \in IOBlocks(TS)$ with $v_j \in \Sigma_o^*$ and $a_j \in \Sigma_i$ then $w = v_1 a_2 v_2 \cdots a_n v_n \in L_\delta(TS)$.*

We deduce from the lemmata above that $\sim_{ioblock}$ is decidable for WS and receptive transition systems since for these systems $\sim_{ioblock}$ amounts to language equivalence: $TS_1 \sim_{ioblock} TS_2$ iff $L_\delta(TS_1) = L_\delta(TS_2)$.

For $a \in \Sigma_i$, we define $L_{\delta,a}(TS)$ as the language accepted by TS when the final states are all the quiescent states that refuse a.

Lemma 14. *Assume that TS is WS. If $w = v_1 a_2 v_2 \cdots a_k v_k \in L_{\delta, a_{k+1}}(TS)$ with $v_j \in \Sigma_o^*$ for $1 \leq j \leq k$ and $a_j \in \Sigma_i$ for $2 \leq j \leq n$ $(k < n)$ then $(\varepsilon, v_1)(a_2, v_2) \cdots (a_n, v_n) \in IOBlocks(TS)$.*

From this we derive a sufficient condition for $\sim_{ioblock}$.

Lemma 15. *Assume that TS_1 and TS_2 are well-structured and that $L_\delta(TS_1) = L_\delta(TS_2)$ and $L_{\delta,a}(TS_1) = L_{\delta,a}(TS_2)$ for all $a \in \Sigma_i$. Then, $TS_1 \sim_{ioblock} TS_2$.*

5.4 Decidability of $\sim_{io}$ for Unlabelled MSC Tests

A message sequence chart, or MSC, visually represents a sequence of communications between a set of agents [11]. In an MSC, processes are represented by vertical lines, with time flowing downward, and messages are drawn as arrows connecting the vertical lines. One way of characterizing patterns of communications is in terms of the MSCs they generate. For these characterizations, message labels are often omitted, as in the treatment of regular MSC languages in [10]. When restricted to the communications between the tester and the system under test, this corresponds to a setting in which the input and output alphabets are both singletons, since all messages to and from the system under test are unlabelled. The reduction used to prove Theorem 7 allows us to model $\sim_{io}$ using rational relations. It is known that equality is decidable for rational relations over a pair of unary alphabets. Hence, we have the following.

Theorem 16. *For tests described using unlabelled MSCs, $\sim_{io}$ is decidable.*

6 Future Work

We have presented two intuitive notions of asynchronous testing and compared their expressive power with the definition due to Tretmans. Much work remains to be done to apply these new notions to make testing more effective. As mentioned in the introduction, the key problem remains that of identifying efficient yet exhaustive test sets for a given system. There is also the question of how to efficiently represent a family of such tests—see for instance [9]. Another interesting issue is to see how testing can be done in a distributed manner, extending the work reported in [12].

References

1. J. Berstel: *Transductions and Context-Free Languages*, Teubner Studienbücher, Informatik (1979).
2. M. Boreale, R. de Nicola and R. Pugliese: Trace and Testing Equivalence in Asynchronous Processes, *Inf. and Comput.*, **172** (2002), 139–164.
3. I.B. Bourdonov, A.S. Kossatchev and V.V. Kuliamin, : Formal Conformance Testing of Systems with Refused Inputs and Forbidden Actions, *MBT 2006*, Vienna, Austria, *ENTCS*, Elsevier (2006).
4. I. Castellani and M Hennessy: Testing Theories for Asynchronous Languages, *Proc. FSTTCS '98*, Springer LNCS **1530** (1998) 90–101.
5. F.S. de Boer, J.W. Klop and C. Palamidessi: Asynchronous communication in process algebra, *Proc. 7th IEEE Logics in Computer Science (LICS)*, IEEE Computer Society Press (1992) 137–147.
6. F.S. de Boer, J.N. Kok, C. Palamidessi and J.J.M.M. Rutten: The failure of failures: Towards a paradigm for asynchronous communication, *Proc. CONCUR 91*, Springer LNCS **527** (1991) 111–126.
7. R. de Nicola and M. Hennessy: Testing equivalences for processes, *Theor. Comput. Sci.*, **34** (1984) 83–133.
8. R.J. van Glabbeek: The linear time-branching time spectrum I: The semantics of concrete, sequential processes, in *Handbook of Process Algebra*, J.A. Bergstra, A. Ponse and S.A. Smolka, eds., Elsevier (2001) 3–99.
9. O. Henniger: On test case generation from asynchronously communicating state machines, *Proc. IWTCS'97* Cheju Island, South Korea, (1997).
10. J.G. Henriksen, M. Mukund, K. Narayan Kumar, M. Sohoni and P.S. Thiagarajan: A Theory of Regular MSC Languages, *Inf. and Comput.*, **202**(1) (2005) 1–38.
11. ITU-TS Recommendation Z.120: *Message Sequence Chart (MSC)*. ITU-TS, Geneva (1997).
12. C. Jard: Synthesis of distributed testers from true-concurrency models of reactive systems, *Information & Software Technology*, **45**(12) (2003) 805–814.
13. C. Jard and T. Jéron: TGV: theory, principles and algorithms, *Software Tools for Technology Transfer*, **7**(4)(2005) 297–315.
14. A. Petrenko, N. Yevtushenko and J.L. Huo: Testing Transition Systems with Input and Output Testers, *Proc TestCom 2003*, Sophia Antipolis, France, (2003) 129–145.
15. J. Sakarovitch: *Eléments de théorie des automates*, Vuibert (2003).
16. J. Tretmans: *A formal approach to conformance testing*, PhD Thesis, University of Twente, The Netherlands (1992).
17. J. Tretmans: Test Generation with Inputs, Outputs and Repetitive Quiescence, *Software—Concepts and Tools*, **17**(3) (1996) 103–120.

Proactive Leader Election in Asynchronous Shared Memory Systems

M.C. Dharmadeep and K. Gopinath

Computer Science and Automation,
Indian Institute of Science,
Bangalore 500012, India
dharma@csa.iisc.ernet.in, gopi@csa.iisc.ernet.in

Abstract. In this paper, we give an algorithm for fault-tolerant proactive leader election in asynchronous shared memory systems, and later its formal verification. Roughly speaking, a leader election algorithm is proactive if it can tolerate failure of nodes even after a leader is elected, and (stable) leader election happens periodically. This is needed in systems where a leader is required after every failure to ensure the availability of the system and there might be no explicit events such as messages in the (shared memory) system. Previous algorithms like DiskPaxos[1] are not proactive.

In our model, individual nodes can fail and reincarnate at any point in time. Each node has a counter which is incremented every period, which is same across all the nodes (modulo a maximum drift). Different nodes can be in different epochs at the same time. Our algorithm ensures that per epoch there can be at most one leader. So if the counter values of some set of nodes match, then there can be at most one leader among them. If the nodes satisfy certain timeliness constraints, then the leader for the epoch with highest counter also becomes the leader for the next epoch(stable property). Our algorithm uses shared memory proportional to the number of processes, the best possible. We also show how our protocol can be used in clustered shared disk systems to select a primary network partition. We have used the state machine approach to represent our protocol in Isabelle HOL[3] logic system and have proved the safety property of the protocol.

1 Introduction and Motivation

In certain systems, a leader is required after every failure to ensure progress of the system. This can be solved in shared memory systems by electing a leader every period. This problem admits a trivial solution: let $T \bmod n$ be the leader for T^{th} epoch, where n is the number of nodes. There are problems with this solution.

- Electing a different leader for each epoch is costly. For example, in clustered shared disk systems, recovery has to be done every time primary network partition changes. We need a "stable" leader election[7]: failures of nodes other than the leader should not change the leader.
- Failed nodes are also elected as leaders in some epochs.

S. Graf and W. Zhang (Eds.): ATVA 2006, LNCS 4218, pp. 384–398, 2006.

In this paper, we use the concept of a proactive leader election in the context of asynchronous shared memory systems. In such an election, a leader renews a lease every so often. The stable leader election[7], appropriate in asynchronous network systems, differs from proactive leader election, as in the latter no failures are needed to trigger leader election; leaders are "elected" on a regular beat. This is needed in the systems we are interested in such as clustered shared disk systems where there are no interrrupts to notify events that happen through the shared medium; all the communication is through shared disks.

Network partition is a possibility in a clustered shared disk system. A primary network partition is selected to ensure consistency of data on the shared disk. This is ensured by using a rule such as: the number of nodes in the primary network partition is atleast $\lfloor \frac{n}{2} \rfloor + 1$, where n is the total number of nodes in the cluster.

Another way of selecting a primary network partition is by the use of fence devices. Fencing is used in clustered shared disk systems to prevent nodes in the non-primary network partitions from accessing disks (to ensure mutual exclusion for shared resources such as disks). Examples of fencing methods are: reboot nodes not in primary partition, disable ports corresponding to nodes not in the primary partition in the network, etc. However, even in this case, there is still a chance that all nodes get fenced. Moreover, once a primary partition is selected, if the nodes in primary network partition fail, then the system comes to halt even if there are nodes that are alive in a different partition.

Consider a simple case of a network containing two nodes.

- Suppose we assign unequal weights to the nodes and require the total weight of nodes in the primary partition to be strictly greater than that of the smaller one. If the node with higher weight dies, the system comes to halt in spite of the node with lower weight being alive.
- Suppose fencing is used. Let us suppose fencing succeeds after a network partition and a primary partition is selected. Now if the only node in primary network partition dies, then the system comes to halt.

Networks with higher number of nodes can also run into similar situations.

In this paper, we give an algorithm for fault-tolerant proactive leader election in asynchronous shared memory systems, and later its formal verification. For example, in the second case, because of leases used in our algorithm, even if the node in the primary partition dies and the other node has already been fenced, in the subsequent epochs, the previously fenced node will get elected as the leader and the system becomes available again. Our work has been inspired by Paxos[2] and DiskPaxos[1] protocols; however, these protocols do not have the lease framework[1] incorporated into them.

We assume a model in which individual nodes can fail and reincarnate (this happens if the fencing method is reboot in clustered shared disk systems) at any point in time. Nodes have access to reliable shared memory[2]. There is no

[1] The Paxos paper mentions the use of leases but no details are given.

[2] We believe this not to be a serious constraint. There are methods for implementing fault tolerant wait free objects from atomic read/write registers[5]; they can be used

global clock accessible to all the nodes, but each node has access to a local counter which is incremented every T secs (whose accuracy has to be within the limits of a drift parameter) and restarts the protocol; for the current leader, this is extending the lease. The set of nodes which have the same counter value are said to be in the same epoch. It is quite possible that at a given instant, different nodes are in different epochs. In this paper, we propose a protocol that elects a leader for each epoch. We guarantee that there is at most one leader per epoch. Moreover, if the nodes in the system satisfy certain timeliness conditions, then the leader for the epoch with highest counter value also becomes the leader for the next epoch.

The rest of the paper is organized as follows. In section 2, we describe the related work. In section 3, we describe the model and algorithm informally. In section 4, we give details of the algorithm. In section 5, we discuss the encoding in Isabelle and the main invariant used in proving the safety property. In section 6, we discuss implementation issues. And we conclude with section 7.

2 Related Work

It is is well-known that there is no algorithm to solve consensus in asynchronous systems [13,14,15]. Failure detectors have been proposed to solve the problem in weaker models. The failure detector Ω for asynchronous network systems can be used to implement a leader oracle. Roughly speaking, the leader oracle running at each node outputs a node which it thinks is operational at that point in time. Moreover, if the network stabilizes after a point, then there is a time after which all operational nodes output the same value. Implementations of the the leader oracle and failure detectors in asynchronous network systems augmented with different kinds of assumptions are described in several works including [2,9,10,11].

The leader oracle (Ω) augmented with view numbers introduced in [7] is similar to the problem considered here. Here, in addition, a view changes if either the current leader, or the network links or both do not satisfy certain timeliness conditions. But we are interested in asynchronous shared memory systems that are more suited for clustered shared disk systems. Consensus in asynchronous shared memory systems with various failure detectors is studied in [12]. DiskPaxos[1], which has inspired this work, is similar to our protocol except that it does not have the lease framework.

Light weight leases for storage centric coordination is introduced in [6] that requires $O(1)$ shared memory (independent of the number of nodes). Their paper assumes a model similar to the timed asynchronous model [18] with the safety property involving certain timeliness conditions. We prove the safety property of our protocol assuming asynchronous shared memory model but it requires n units of shared memory. This matches the lower bound in Chockler and Malkhi[16], where they introduce a new abstract object called *ranked register*

for constructing reliable shared memory. Also, in clustered shared disk systems, shared "memory" can be realized with some extra effort by using hot swappable mirrored disk (RAID) devices with hot spares.

to implement the Paxos algorithm and show that it cannot be realized using less than n read/write atomic registers.

3 An Informal Description of the Model and Algorithm

We consider a distributed system with $n > 1$ processes. Each node has a area allocated in the shared memory (actually, a shared disk) to which only it can write and other nodes can read. Processes can fail and reincarnate at any point in time. We call a system stable[3] in $[s, t]$ if at all times between s and t the following hold:

- The drift rate between any two nodes or drift rate of any node from real time is bounded by δ.
- The amount of time it takes for a single node to read a block from the shared memory and process it or write a block to the shared memory is less than r secs.
- The time it takes to change the state after a read or write is negligible compared to r.

We require the second assumption, because in our case shared disk serves as the shared memory. We assume that the system is stable infinitely often and for a sufficient duration so that leader election is possible. We assume that each of the nodes know the value of δ and r. Each node has access to a local timer which times out every T secs. We assume $T >> 3nr(1 + \delta)$; this will be motivated later.

The counter value of each node is stored in local memory as well in the shared memory; it is first written to the shared memory area and then written to the local memory. The counter values of all nodes are initialized to 0. When a process reincarnates, it reads the counter value from its shared memory area and then starts the timer. When the timer at a node expires, it increments its counter value and restarts the timer.

Each node is associated with a node id which is drawn from the natural number set. We assume that each node knows the mapping *nodeid* between the shared memory addresses and the node ids. We assume that the shared memory is reliable[1].

3.1 Safety Property

The safety property of the protocol requires that if a node with counter value v becomes leader, the no other node with counter value v ever becomes leader.

3.2 Informal Description of Algorithm

Each block in shared memory allocated to a node consists of a counter value, a ballot number and proposed leader node id. When the counter of a node is

[3] Please note that this is different from the meaning of stable in "stable leader election". Context should make clear what is being meant.

incremented, it starts the protocol for the new epoch. During each of the phases, if a node finds a block with higher counter value, it sleeps for that epoch.

- In Phase 0, each node reads the disk blocks of all other nodes and moves to phase 1.
- In Phase 1, a node writes a ballot number to the disk. It chooses this ballot number that is greater than any ballot number read in the previous phase. If none of the blocks read after writing to the disk have a higher ballot number, the node moves to phase 2. If the node finds a block with higher ballot number, it restarts Phase1. This phase can viewed as selecting a node which proposes the leader node id.
- In Phase 2, a node proposes the node id of the leader and writes it to disk. This value is chosen so that all nodes that have finished the protocol for the current epoch agree on the same value. If none of the blocks read after writing the proposed value to the disk have a higher ballot number, the node completes the protocol for this epoch. If there is a block with a higher ballot number, it goes back to Phase1. If the proposed value is same as that of this node id, this node is the leader. Otherwise, it sleeps for this epoch.

4 The Algorithm

Each node's status (*nodestatus*) can be in one of the five states: *Suspended, Dead, Leader, PreviousLeader, Participant.*

- A node is in *Suspended* state, if it withdrew from the protocol for the current epoch.
- A node is in *Dead* state, if it has crashed.
- A node is in *Leader* state, if it is the leader for the current epoch.
- A node is in *PreviousLeader* state, if it was the leader for the previous epoch and is participating in the protocol for the current epoch.
- A node is in *Participant* state, if it is participating in the protocol for the current epoch and is not the leader for the previous epoch.

A block in the shared memory location allocated to a node is of form *(ctrv_d, pbal, bal, val)*, where *ctrv_d* is the counter value of the node (in the shared memory (actually, *disk*)) which has write permission to it, *pbal* is the proposed ballot number of that node, and *bal* is equal to the proposed ballot number *pbal* for which *val* was recently set. After each read or write to the shared memory, depending of whether some condition holds or not, the system moves from one phase to another. In each of the phases, *phase0*, *phase1* and *phase2*, before reading the blocks from the shared memory, each node clears its existing blocks read in the previous phase. To make our algorithm concise, we have used the phrase *"Node n rereads disk blocks of all nodes"* in each of the phases; this operation need not be atomic in our model.

We use *disk s n* to represent the block of node n in the shared memory in state s. Also, let *blocksRead s n* represent the blocks of nodes present at node n in state s. The state of the system is made up of: *state* of each of the nodes, *blocks* of each of the nodes in shared memory, *phase* of each of the nodes, the counter value of each of the nodes and *blocksRead* of each of the nodes.

Let $A(disk\ s\ n)$ denote the projection of component A of block *disk s n*. For example, $pbal(disk\ s\ n)$ denotes the *pbal* component of block *disk s n*. Similarly, $A(B :: set)$ denotes the set composed of projection of component A of all blocks in set B. We use *ctrv s n*, *nodestatus s n* and *phase s n* to denote the counter value, state and phase of node n in state s respectively. Note that *ctrv* is the value at the node whereas *ctrv_d* is the value at the disk.

There is an implicit extra action in each phase (omitted in the given specification for brevity): $Phase\{i\}Read\ s\ s'\ n\ m$, which says that node n in $phase\{i\}$ reads the block of node m and the system moves from state s to state s'. State variables not mentioned in a state transition below remain unchanged across the state transition.

For facilitating the proof, we use a history variable *LeaderChosenAtT*, but actually not needed in the algorithm: $LeaderChosenAtT\ s\ t = k$ if k is the leader for epoch t in state s. Also, $LeaderChosenAtT\ s'\ t = LeaderChosenAtT\ s\ t$ unless the value for t is changed explicitly.

Phase0

Action: Node n (re)reads disk blocks of all nodes including itself. Changes the state to *Suspended* if there exists a node with higher counter value. Otherwise, moves to phase 1. Formally,

Case: $\exists\ br \in blocksRead\ s\ n.\ ctrv\_d(br) > ctrv\ s\ n$
Outcome: $nodestatus\ s'\ n = Suspended.$

Case: $\neg\exists\ br \in blocksRead\ s\ n.\ ctrv\_d(br) > ctrv\ s\ n.$
Outcome: $phase\ s'\ n = 1$

Phase1

Action: Write a value greater than *pbal*s of all blocks read in previous phase to the disk. Formally,
$disk\ s'\ n = (ctrv\ s\ n,\ pbal',\ bal(disk\ s\ n),\ val(disk\ s\ n))$
where $pbal' = \text{Max}(pbal(blocksRead\ s\ n)) + 1.$
Node n rereads disk blocks of all the nodes.
If there exists a block with higher counter value, move to *Suspended* state. If there exists a block with higher *pbal*, restart phase 1. Otherwise, move to phase 2. Formally,

Case: $\exists\ br \in blocksRead\ s\ n.\ ctrv\_d(br) > ctrv\ s\ n.$
Outcome: $nodestatus\ s'\ n = Suspended.$

Case: $\exists\, br \in blocksRead\ s\ n.\ ctrv\_d(br) = ctrv\ s\ n$
$\quad \&\ ((pbal(br) > pbal(disk\ s\ n))$
$\quad\ \mid (pbal(br) = pbal(disk\ s\ n)$
$\quad\ \ \&\ nodeid(br) > n))$

Outcome: Node n restarts *Phase1*.

Case: $\neg\exists\, br \in blocksRead\ s\ n.\ ctrv\_d(br) > ctrv\ s\ n$
$\quad \mid ((ctrv\_d(br) = ctrv\ s\ n)$
$\quad\ \&\ (pbal(br) > pbal(disk\ s\ n)))$
$\quad \mid ((ctrv\_d(br) = ctrv\ s\ n)$
$\quad\ \&\ (pbal(br) = pbal(disk\ s\ n))$
$\quad\ \&\ (nodeid(br) > n))$

Outcome: $phase\ s'\ n = 2$.

Phase2

Action: Write the proposed leader node id to the disk, where the node id is chosen as follows: if no other node with same counter value has proposed a value, set it to this node id; otherwise, set it to the value of the block with highest *bal* whose proposed value is non-zero. Formally,

$disk\ s'\ n = (ctrv\ s\ n,\ pbal(disk\ s\ n),\ pbal(disk\ s\ n),\ proposedv)$

where $proposedv =$

n if $(\forall\, br \in blocksRead\ s\ n.\ ctrv\_d(br) = ctrv\ s\ n$
$\quad \longrightarrow val(br) = 0)$

else

m where $(m = val(br)$
$\quad \&\ bal(br) = \mathrm{Max}(bal(\{br \mid br \in blocksRead\ s\ n$
$\quad\quad \&\ ctrv\_d(br) = ctrv\ s\ n$
$\quad\quad \&\ val(br) \neq 0\})))$

Node n rereads the blocks of all the nodes. If there exists a node with higher counter value, move to *Suspended* state. If there exists a node with higher *pbal* restart from phase 1. Otherwise, if the proposed node id is same as the id of this node, this node is the leader. If the proposed node id is not same as the id of this node, move to *Suspended* state. Formally,

Case: $\exists\, br \in blocksRead\ s\ n.\ ctrv\_d(br) > ctrv\ s\ n.$
Outcome: $nodestatus\ s'\ n = Suspended.$

Case: $\exists\, br \in blocksRead\ s\ n.\ ctrv\_d(br) = ctrv\ s\ n$
$\quad \&\ ((pbal(br) > pbal(disk\ s\ n)$
$\quad\ \mid (pbal(br) = pbal(disk\ s\ n)$
$\quad\ \ \&\ nodeid(br) > n))$

Outcome: Node n restarts *Phase1*.

<u>Case:</u> $\neg\exists\ br \in blocksRead\ s\ n.\ ctrv\_d(br) > ctrv\ s\ n$
$\quad | \ ((ctrv\_d(br) = ctrv\ s\ n)$
$\quad\quad \& \ (pbal(br) > pbal(disk\ s\ n))$
$\quad | \ ((ctrv\_d(br) = ctrv\ s\ n)$
$\quad\quad \& \ (pbal(br) = pbal(disk\ s\ n))$
$\quad\quad \& \ (nodeid(br) > n))$

<u>Outcome:</u> if $val(disk\ s\ n) = n$
then $nodestatus\ s'\ n = Leader$
$\quad \& \ LeaderChosenAtT\ s'\ (ctrv\ s\ n) = n$
else $nodestatus\ s'\ n = Suspended$).

Fail

<u>Outcome:</u> $nodestatus\ s'\ n = Dead$

ReIncarnate

<u>Outcome:</u> $nodestatus\ s'\ n = Suspended$

IncrementTimer

<u>Case:</u>Node n timer expires.
If this node is the leader in previous epoch, update the counter value on disk and move to phase 2. Otherwise, update the counter value on disk, reset *bal* and *val* on disk and move to phase 0.Formally,

<u>Outcome:</u> if $nodestatus\ s\ n = Leader$
then $nodestatus\ s'\ n = PreviousLeader$
$\quad disk\ s'\ n =$
$\quad (ctrv\ s\ n + 1,\ pbal(disk\ s\ n),\ bal(disk\ s\ n),$
$\quad val(disk\ s\ n))$
$\quad \& \ ctrv\ s'\ n = ctrv\ s\ n + 1$
$\quad \& \ phase\ s'\ n = 2$
else $nodestatus\ s'\ n = Participant$
$\quad \& \ disk\ s'\ n = (ctrv\ s\ n + 1,\ pbal(disk\ s\ n),\ 0,\ 0)$
$\quad \& \ ctrv\ s'\ n = ctrv\ s\ n + 1$
$\quad \& \ phase\ s'\ n = 0$

Note that with our protocol, it is quite possible that a particular block on disk and the block corresponding to it in *blocksRead* of some node do not match. But this doesn't compromise the safety property mentioned below. However, for any node n, if the block corresponding to $disk\ s\ n$ is in its *blocksRead*, it will be same as that of $disk\ s\ n$.

safety property: $LeaderChosenAtT\ s\ t \neq 0 \longrightarrow$
$\quad \forall\ s',\ m.\ ((\ m \neq LeaderChosenAtT\ s\ t$
$\quad\quad \& \ ctrv\ s'\ m = t)$
$\quad\quad \longrightarrow nodestatus\ s'\ m \neq Leader)$

The safety property of the protocol says that if a node with counter value T becomes leader then no other node with counter value T ever becomes leader.

To ensure liveness of the protocol in Timed Asynchronous Model, one can use leader election oracle mentioned in [6] with Δ equal to T, and δ equal to r, to choose a node in *IncrementTimer*. If a node is not elected by the leader oracle, it sleeps for approximately $3nr(1+\delta)$ secs and then starts the protocol. If the leader oracle succeeds in electing a single leader, that particular node has to write to its block and read all other blocks, at most thrice, so the execution would take at most $3nr(1+\delta)$ in a stable period. Actually, this number can be reduced to $(n+1)r(1+\delta)$, if the output of the leader oracle in previous epoch is same as that of leader's id for current epoch. This is because the previous epoch leader directly moves to *phase2* after it increments its timer. So, if no other node is in *Participant* state when the previous epoch leader is participating in the protocol, it at most has to write to its block twice and read blocks of all other nodes once. This would take at most $(n+1)r(1+\delta)$ secs in a stable period. While proving the safety property of the protocol in asynchronous model, the timing constraints are not required. Hence, in the actual specification of the algorithm in Isabelle, we have not encoded the timing constraints.

5 Encoding in Isabelle and Its Proof

We have used the state machine approach to specify the protocol in Isabelle[3]. The encoding of the state machine in Isabelle is similar to the one given in [4]. Note that in *phase1* and *phase2*, we first write to the disk and then read the blocks of all nodes. Furthermore, in the specification of the algorithm above, we have used the phrase *"Node n restarts from phase1"*. We have realized this by associating a boolean variable $diskWritten$ with each node. We require it to be $true$, as a precondition for any of the cases to hold. When a node writes to the disk in *phase1* or *phase2*, it sets $diskWritten\ s'\ n$ to $true$ and sets $blocksReads'\ n$ to empty set. In addition, we require all blocks to be read as a precondition for any of the cases to hold. And by a node n restarting from phase 1, we mean that $diskWritten\ s'\ n$ is set to $false$ and $phase\ s'\ n$ is set to 1.

In the specification of the protocol in Isabelle, we have three phases while we had only two phases in the informal description. This is not essential, but we have done it for better readability of the specification. In the 3rd phase, a node does nothing except changing its state to *Leader* or *Suspended*. Furthermore, in the specification for *phase0*, we deliberately split the case 2 of *phase0* into two cases anticipating optimizations later.

The proof is by method of invariants and bottom-up. However unlike [1], the only history variable we have used is *LeaderChosenAtT*, where *LeaderChosenAtT(t)* is the unique leader, if any exists, for the epoch t, otherwise it is zero. The specification of the protocol, the invariants used and the lemmas can be found in [17]. The proof of the lemmas is quite straightforward, but lengthy because of the size of the protocol.

The main invariant used in the proof is the $AFTLE\_INV4$ & $AFTLE\_INV4k$. $AFTLE\_INV4$ requires that, if a node is in phase greater than 1 and has written its proposed value to the disk, then either $MaxBalInp$

is true or there exists a block br, either in $blocksRead$, or on disk which it is about to read, which will make this node to restart from $phase1$. Formally,

$$
\begin{aligned}
AFTLE\_INV4\ s \equiv\ & \\
& \forall\ p.\ ((phase\ s\ p\ >=\ 2) \\
& \quad \&\ (diskWritten\ s\ p\ =\ True)) \longrightarrow \\
& ((MaxBalInp\ s\ (bal(disk\ s\ p))\ p\ val(disk\ s\ p)) \\
& \mid (\exists\ br.\ ((br\ \in\ blocksRead\ s\ p) \\
& \qquad \&\ Greaterthan\ br\ (disk\ s\ p))) \\
& \mid (\exists\ n.\ ((\neg hasRead\ s\ p\ n) \\
& \qquad \&\ Greaterthan\ (disk\ s\ n)\ (disk\ s\ p)))
\end{aligned}
$$

where

- $Greaterthan\ br\ br' \equiv$
$$
\begin{aligned}
& ((ctrv\_d(br) > ctrv\_d(br')) \\
& \mid ((ctrv\_d(br) = ctrv\_d(br')) \\
& \quad \&\ (pbal(br) > pbal(br'))) \\
& \mid ((ctrv\_d(br) = ctrv\_d(br')) \\
& \quad \&\ (pbal(br) = pbal(br')) \\
& \quad \&\ (id(br) > id(br'))))
\end{aligned}
$$
- $MaxBalInp$ requires that, if the proposed value of node n is val, then any other node with same counter value as that of n and $(bal, nodeid)$ greater than that of node n, has val as its proposed value. Formally,

$$
\begin{aligned}
MaxBalInp\ s\ b\ m\ val \equiv\ & \\
& (\forall\ n.\ ((val > 0) \\
& \qquad \&\ (ctrv\ s\ n = ctrv\ s\ m) \\
& \qquad \&\ ((bal(disk\ s\ n) > b) \\
& \qquad\quad \mid ((bal(disk\ s\ n) = b) \\
& \qquad\qquad \&\ (n > m)))) \longrightarrow \\
& \qquad val(disk\ s\ n) = val) \\
& \&\ (\forall\ n.\ (\forall\ br.\ ((val > 0) \\
& \qquad\qquad \&\ (br\ \in\ blocksRead\ s\ n) \\
& \qquad\qquad \&\ (ctrv\ s\ m = ctrv\ s\ n) \\
& \qquad\qquad \&\ (ctrv\_d(br) = ctrv\ s\ n) \\
& \qquad\qquad \&\ ((bal(br) > b) \\
& \qquad\qquad\quad \mid ((bal(br) = b) \\
& \qquad\qquad\qquad \&\ (nodeid(br) > m))) \longrightarrow \\
& \qquad\qquad val(br) = val)))
\end{aligned}
$$

- $hasRead\ s\ p\ q \equiv$
$$(\exists\ br\ \in\ (blocksRead\ s\ p).\ nodeid(br)\ =\ q)$$

$AFTLE\_INV4k$ requires that, if a node n is not the leader in previous epoch, then for any node distinct from n which is in phase greater than 1 and whose counter value is less than that of n, one of the following hold: its *pbal* is less than *pbal* of n, it moves to $Suspendedor\ Dead$ state, moves to phase 1. Formally,

$$
\begin{aligned}
&AFTLE\_INV4k\ s\ \equiv \\
&\quad \forall\, p.\ (\forall\, n.\ ((n \neq p) \\
&\qquad\qquad \&\ (ctrv\ s\ n > ctrv\ s\ p) \\
&\qquad\qquad \&\ (phase\ s\ p >= 2) \\
&\qquad\qquad \&\ (diskWritten\ s\ p) \\
&\qquad\qquad \&\ (val(disk\ s\ p) = p) \\
&\qquad\qquad \&\ ((phase\ s\ n > 1) \\
&\qquad\qquad\quad \mid ((phase\ s\ n = 1) \\
&\qquad\qquad\qquad \&\ (diskWritten\ s\ n)))) \longrightarrow \\
&\qquad ((pbal(disk\ s\ n) > pbal(disk\ s\ p)) \\
&\qquad \mid (pbal(disk\ s\ n) = pbal(disk\ s\ p) \\
&\qquad\ \&\ (n > p)) \\
&\qquad \mid (\exists\ br\ \in\ blocksRead\ s\ p.\ Greaterthan\ br\ (disk\ s\ p)) \\
&\qquad \mid (\neg hasRead\ s\ p\ n)))
\end{aligned}
$$

First we proved that the invariant holds for the initial state and then we proved that if the invariant holds before a state transition, then it also holds after a state transition.

The first part of the invariant $AFTLE\_INV4$ is similar to the main invariant in [1]. The second part $AFTLE\_INV4k$ is new. We could not prove $AFTLE\_INV4$ by itself; we had to strengthen it by adding $AFTLE\_INV4k$ to be able to be prove it. The place where this invariant is needed is in *Increment-Timer*. The need for strengthening arises due to the one round optimization in the protocol. If a node A is the leader for epoch T, another node B is the leader for epoch $T+1$ with *pbal* smaller than that of A's and A increments its counter value and moves to *Phase2*, then this invariant could be violated. This is what is ruled out by $AFTLE\_INV4k$. $ATFLE\_INV4k$ says that if node A is the leader for a particular epoch, then any node other than A, which has a counter value greater than that of A and which had written to the disk in *Phase1*, has *pbal* greater than that of A. We could not prove $AFTLE\_INV4k$ alone either. When *incrementTimer* event occurs, if two nodes with same *ctrv_d* are leaders in s, then this invariant could be violated. This is exactly what is ruled out by $AFTLE\_INV4$.

The following are the only assumptions we used in the proof, apart from the axioms that each of the possible values of *nodestatus* are distinct from one another. Let us denote the set of all *nodeids* by S.

$$\boxed{S \neq \{\}, \quad finite\ S, \quad s \in S \longrightarrow s \neq 0}$$

Note that as a consequence, our protocol holds even if the number of nodes participating in the protocol is 1. But, in this case, leader election is trivial. We need the second assumption because we are often required to use the following rule which had that assumption as one of the premises.

$$finite\ A;\ A \neq \{\};\ x \in A \Longrightarrow x <= Max\ A$$

We have used HOL-Complex logic instead of just HOL logic of Isabelle anticipating use of *real set* later.

In the protocol specification, we chose *nodeids* from the natural number set. In spite of that, we had to state that none of the nodeid's is equal to 0 as a axiom. Futhermore, for each state transition, we had to mention the state variables that do not change along with those that change. There are some results which we could not prove using Isabelle, like

$$nodestatus\ s \neq (nodestatus\ s)(n := Leader) \Rightarrow nodestatus\ s\ n \neq Leader$$

which was created during the proof of a lemma by a method named *auto*. In such cases, we had to backtrack to find a alternate path which avoids such a situation. Futhermore, we had to explicitly prove and pass certain results to the theorem prover because it could not recognize these patterns. (The method *auto* could prove these results.)

One such example is the following.

$$(\forall\, x \in P.\ Q(x)) \Longrightarrow (\forall\, x.\ (x \in P) \longrightarrow Q(x))$$

More such examples can be found in the proof given in [17].

6 Selecting a Primary Network Partition in Clustered Shared Disk Systems

One can use the above protocol to select the primary network partition in clustered shared disk systems. In the following discussion, we assume that the nodes in the same network partition are loosely time synchronized, i.e., modulo the drift parameter. Once consensus is reached on node id of the leader, each node can check if the node id is present in its membership set. If it is present, it knows that it is part of the primary partition.

Note that in the asynchronous shared memory model, it is quite possible in our protocol that two different nodes in two different network partitions become leaders for different epochs at the same time instant (due to drift), although likely to happen only infrequently in practice. But, in clustered shared disk systems, once a primary partition is selected, nodes in network partitions other than the primary partition are fenced before the recovery is done. So even if two nodes from two different network partitions become leaders at the same time, at most one network partition would access the disk.

With existing methods, fencing does not work always correctly. In the process of implementing the protocol on Redhat Cluster GFS, we realized that there is a way in which fencing can always be made to work with Brocade fibre channel switches[4] that allow only one admin telnet login at a time. So each node can login into every switch first in a predefined order (for example in the order in which they appear in the configuration file), then check if it has been fenced in any switch, if so logout from all switches and return a error; otherwise fence all the nodes which are not in its partition, unfence ones in its partition, and once finished then logout of all the switches. Although this method works with Brocade switches, it need not work in general. Note that even this method can fail if the only node in the current primary partition fails in a two node cluster.

Our protocol requires some set of disks to be outside the fencing domain which it can use as the shared memory. We think such a scenario is not rare because when different nodes are accessing different disks, no fencing is required between them. If fencing uses the Brocade switch property, when a leader gets elected for a new epoch, it can use the fencing method mentioned above with the modification that before returning an error it unfences itself. Example two node network and the fencing method is illustrated in Figure 1.

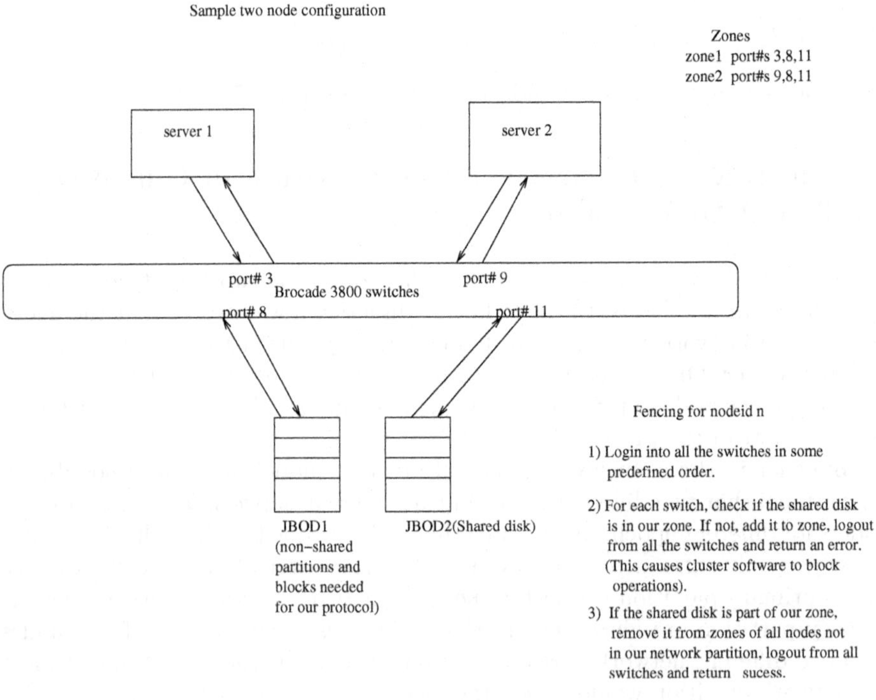

Fig. 1. Example two node cluster configuration

[4] Fibre Channel (FC) is a specialized data link layer for storage devices. FC switches are similar in function to gigabit ethernet switches.

Note as a consequence of the safety property, if the highest *ctrv_d* in the system is T, then recovery/fencing would have been done at most T times. Futhermore, once a primary partition is selected and the leader in the primary partition is in the epoch with highest counter value and no more partitions/failures occur in the primary partition, then the *leader* for this epoch will be elected as the leader for the next epoch if the system is in stable period. In this case, fencing and recovery need not be done again. Furthermore, one more optimization that could be done in *Phase0*: when a node finds that there exists a block with higher *pbal* or same *pbal* from a higher node id, it changes its state to *Suspended.* We believe similar optimizations can be done in *Phase1* and *Phase2* too. But this would require that once a node is selected as a leader, it inform the nodes in its partition through the network which otherwise can be avoided assuming nodes in same network partition are (loosely) time synchronized.

7 Conclusion

In this paper, we have given a protocol for proactive leader election in asynchronous shared memory systems. We have specified the protocol and proved the safety property of the protocol using Isabelle [3] theorem prover. We have also shown how one can use the protocol to choose a primary network partition in clustered shared disk systems. As a part of future work, we intend to specify the leader oracle protocol mentioned in [6] using Isabelle and also use it to prove the liveness property of our protocol with the the leader oracle in timed asynchronous model. We also intend to incorporate the fencing part in the protocol and prove its correctness. A prototype implementation is currently in progress and we intend to experimentally understand the relationship between δ, r and the number of nodes n. The complete theory files along with the technical report are accessible at *http://agni.csa.iisc.ernet.in/~dharma/ATVA06/*.

Acknowledgements

We thank V.H.Gupta for reviewing the earlier draft. We thank anonymous reviewers for their comments.

References

1. E. Gafni and L. Lamport. "Disk Paxos," In Proceedings of the International Symposium on Distributed Computing, pages 330-344,2000.
2. L. Lamport. "The part-time parliament," ACM Transactions on Computer systems *16* (1998) 133-169.
3. Tobias Nipkow, Lawrence C. Paulson, and Markus Wenzel. "Isabelle/HOL – A Proof Assistant for Higher-Order Logic," volume 2283 of LNCS. Springer, 2002.
4. "http://afp.sourceforge.net/browser_info/current/HOL/DiskPaxos/"
5. Prasad Jayanti, Tushar Deepak Chandra, and Sam Toueg. " Fault-tolerant wait-free shared objects," In Proceedings of the 33rd Annual Symposium on Foundations of Computer Science, 1992.

6. Chockler, Gregory and Dahlia Malkhi. "Light-Weight Leases for Storage-Centric Coordination," MIT-LCS-TR-934 Publication Date: 4-22-2004.
7. Marcos K. Aquilera, Carole Delporte-Gallet, Huques Fauconnier and Sam Toueg. "Stable Leader Election," In Proceedings of the 15th International Conference on Distributed Computing, 2001. Pages: 108-122.
8. Lampson, B. "How to build a highly available system using consensus," In *Distributed Algorithms*, ed. Babaoglu and Marzullo, LNCS 1151, Springer , 1996, 1-17.
9. R. De Prisco, B. Lampson, and N. Lynch. "Revisiting the Paxos algorithm," In Proceedings of the 11th Workshop on Distributed Algorithms (WDAG), pages 11-125,Saarbrücken, September 1997.
10. M. Larrea, A. Fernández, and S. Arévalo. "Optimal implementation of the weakest failure detector for solving consensus," In Proceedings of the 19th IEEE Symposium on Reliable Distributed Systems, SRDS 2000, pages 52-59, Nurenberg, Germany, October 2000.
11. F. Chu. "Reducing Ω to $\diamond W$," Information Processing Letters, 67(6):293-298, September 1998.
12. Wai-Kau Lo and Vassos Hadzilacos. "Using Failure Detectors to Solve Consensus in Asynchronous Shared-Memory Systems," In Proceedings of the 8th International Workshop in Distributed Algorithms, 1994. Pages: 280-295.
13. Michael J. Fischer, Nancy A. Lynch and Michael S. Paterson. "Impossibility of distributed consensus with one faulty process," Journal of the Association for Computing Machinery, 32(2): 374-382, April 1985.
14. Danny Dolev, Cynthia Dwork and Larry Stockmeyer. "On the minimal synchronism needed for distributed consensus," Journal of the ACM, 34(1):77-97 , January 1987.
15. Michael C. Loui and Hosame H. Abu-Amara. "Memory requirements for agreement among unreliable asynchronous processes," In advances in Computer Research, volume 4, pages 163-183. JAI Press Inc., 1987.
16. G. Chockler and D. Malkhi. "Active Disk Paxos with Infinitely Many Processes," Proceedings of the 21st ACM Symposium on Principles of Distributed Computing. (PODC), August 2002.
17. "http://agni.csa.iisc.ernet.in/~dharma/ATVA06/document.pdf"
18. F. Cristian and C. Fetzer. "The timed asynchronous system model," iin Proceedings of the 28th Annual International Symposium on Fault-Tolerant Computing, Munich, Germany, June 1998, pp. 140-149.

A Semantic Framework for Test Coverage

Laura Brandán Briones[1], Ed Brinksma[1,2], and Mariëlle Stoelinga[1]

[1] Faculty of Computer Science, University of Twente, The Netherlands
[2] Embedded Systems Institute, The Netherlands
{marielle,brandanl}@cs.utwente.nl, Ed.Brinksma@esi.nl

Abstract. Since testing is inherently incomplete, test selection has vital importance. Coverage measures evaluate the quality of a test suite and help the tester select test cases with maximal impact at minimum cost. Existing coverage criteria for test suites are usually defined in terms of syntactic characteristics of the implementation under test or its specification. Typical black-box coverage metrics are state and transition coverage of the specification. White-box testing often considers statement, condition and path coverage. A disadvantage of this syntactic approach is that different coverage figures are assigned to systems that are behaviorally equivalent, but syntactically different. Moreover, those coverage metrics do not take into account that certain failures are more severe than others, and that more testing effort should be devoted to uncover the most important bugs, while less critical system parts can be tested less thoroughly.

This paper introduces a semantic approach to black box test coverage. Our starting point is a weighted fault model (or WFM), which augments a specification by assigning a weight to each error that may occur in an implementation. We define a framework to express coverage measures that express how well a test suite covers such a specification, taking into account the error weight. Since our notions are semantic, they are insensitive to replacing a specification by one with equivalent behaviour. We present several algorithms that, given a certain minimality criterion, compute a minimal test suite with maximal coverage. These algorithms work on a syntactic representation of WFMs as fault automata. They are based on existing and novel optimization problems. Finally, we illustrate our approach by analyzing and comparing a number of test suites for a chat protocol.

1 Introduction

After years of limited attention, the theory of testing has now become a widely studied, academically respectable subject of research. In particular, the application of formal methods in the area of model-driven testing has led to a better understanding of the notion of conformance between an implementation and a specification. Automated generation methods for test suites from specifications [15,16,4,13] have been developed, which have lead to a new generation of powerful test generation and execution tools such as SpecExplorer[6], TorX[3] and TGV[8].

S. Graf and W. Zhang (Eds.): ATVA 2006, LNCS 4218, pp. 399–414, 2006.

A clear advantage of a formal approach to testing is the provable soundness of the generated test suites, i.e. the property that each generated test suite will only reject implementations that do not conform to the given specification. In many cases also a completeness or exhaustiveness result is obtained, i.e. the property that for each non-conforming implementation a test case can be generated that will expose its errors by rejecting it (cf. [15]).

In practice, the above notion of exhaustiveness is usually problematic, since exhaustive test suites will contain infinitely many tests. This raises the question of test selection, i.e. the selection of well-chosen, finite test suites that can be generated (and executed) within the available resources. Test case selection is naturally related to a measure of coverage, indicating how much of the required conformance is tested for by a given test selection. In this way, coverage measures can assist the tester in choosing test cases with maximal impact against some optimization criterion (i.e. number of tests, execution time, cost).

Typical coverage measures used in black-box testing are the number of states and/or transitions of the specification that would be visited by executing a test suite against it [17,9,12]; white-box testing often considers the number of statements, conditional branches, and paths through the implementation code that are touched by the test suite execution [10,11,1]. Although these measures do indeed help with the selection of tests and the exposure of faults, they share two shortcomings:

1. The approaches are based on syntactic model features, i.e. coverage figures are based on constructs of the specific model or program used as a reference. Therefore, we may get different coverage results when we replace the model in question with a behaviorally equivalent, but syntactically different one.
2. The approaches fail to account for the non-uniform gravity of failures, whereas it would be natural to select test cases in such a way that the most critical system parts are tested most thoroughly.

It is important to realize that the weight of a failure cannot be extracted from a purely behavioral model, as it may depend in an essential way on the particular application of the implementation under test (IUT). The importance of the same bug may vary considerably between, say, its occurrence as part of an electronic game, and that as part of the control of a nuclear power plant.

Overview. This paper introduces a semantic approach for test coverage that aims to overcome the two points mentioned above. Our point of departure is a WFM that assigns a weight to each potential error in an implementation. We define our coverage measures relative to these WFMs. Since WFMs are augmented specifications, our coverage framework qualifies as black box.

Since WFMs are infinite semantic objects, we need to represent them finitely if we want to model them or use them in algorithms. We provide such representations by fault automata (Section 4). Fault automata are rooted in ioco test theory [15] (recapitulated in Section 3), but their principles apply to a much wider setting.

We provide two ways of deriving WFMs from fault automata, namely the finite depth WFMs (Section 4.1) and the discounted WFMs (Section 4.2). The coverage measures obtained for these fault automata are invariant under behavioral equivalence. For both fault models, we provide algorithms that calculate and optimize test coverage (Section 5). These can all be studied as optimization problems in a linear algebraic setting. In particular, we compute the (total, absolute and relative) coverage of a test suite w.r.t. a weighted fault model (WFM).

We apply our theory to a small chat protocol (Section 6) and end by providing conclusions and suggestions for further research (Section 7). Due to space restrictions, we refer the reader to [5] for the full version of this paper.

2 Coverage Measures in Weighted Fault Models

Preliminaries. Let L be any set. Then L^* denotes the set of all finite sequences over L, which we also call *traces* over L. The empty sequence is denoted by ε and $|\sigma|$ denotes the length of a trace $\sigma \in L^*$. We use $L^+ = L^* \setminus \{\varepsilon\}$. For σ, $\rho \in L^*$, we say that σ is a *prefix* of ρ and write $\sigma \sqsubseteq \rho$, if $\rho = \sigma\sigma'$ for some $\sigma' \in L^*$. If σ is a prefix of ρ, then ρ is a *suffix* of σ. We call σ a *proper prefix* of ρ and ρ a *proper suffix* of σ if $\sigma \sqsubseteq \rho$, but $\sigma \neq \rho$.

We denote by $\mathcal{P}(L)$ the power set of L and for any function $f : L \to \mathbb{R}$, we use the convention that $\sum_{x\in\emptyset} f(x) = 0$ and $\prod_{x\in\emptyset} f(x) = 1$.

2.1 Weighted Fault Models

A weighted fault model specifies the desired behavior of a system by not only providing the correct system traces, but by also giving the severity of the erroneous traces. In this section, we work with a fixed action alphabet L.

Definition 1. *A* weighted fault model (WFM) *over L is a function $f : L^* \to \mathbb{R}^{\geq 0}$ such that* $0 < \sum_{\sigma\in L^*} f(\sigma) < \infty$.

Thus, a WFM f assigns a non-negative error weight to each trace $\sigma \in L^*$. If $f(\sigma) = 0$, then σ represents correct system behavior; if $f(\sigma) > 0$, then σ represents incorrect behavior and $f(\sigma)$ denotes the severity of the error. So, the higher $f(\sigma)$, the worse the error. We sometimes refer to traces $\sigma \in L^*$ with $f(\sigma) > 0$ as *error traces* and traces with $f(\sigma) = 0$ as *correct traces* in f.

We require the total error weight $\sum_{\sigma\in L^*} f(\sigma)$ to be finite and non-zero, in order to define coverage measures relative to the total error weight.

2.2 Coverage Measures

This section abstracts from the exact shape of test cases and test suites. Given a WFM f over action alphabet L, we only use that a test is a trace set, $t \subseteq L^*$; and a test suite is a collection of trace sets, $T \subseteq \mathcal{P}(L^*)$. In this way we define the absolute and relative coverage w.r.t. f of a test and for a test suite. Moreover, our coverage measures apply in all settings where test cases can be characterized as trace sets (in which case test suites can be characterized as collections of trace sets). This is a.o. true for tests in TTCN [7], ioco test theory [15] and FSM testing [17,9].

Definition 2. *Let $f : L^* \to \mathbb{R}^{\geq 0}$ be a WFM over L, let $t \subseteq L^*$ be a trace set and let $T \subseteq \mathcal{P}(L^*)$ be a collection of trace sets. We define*

- $abscov(t, f) = \sum_{\sigma \in t} f(\sigma)$ *and* $abscov(T, f) = abscov(\cup_{t \in T} t, f)$
- $totcov(f) = abscov(L^*, f)$
- $relcov(t, f) = \frac{abscov(t,f)}{totcov(f)}$ *and* $relcov(T, f) = \frac{abscov(T,f)}{totcov(f)}$

The coverage of a test suite T w.r.t. f measures the total weight of the errors that can be detected by tests in T. The absolute coverage $abscov(T, f)$ simply accumulates the weights of all error traces in T. Note that the weight of each trace is counted only once, since one test case is enough to detect the presence of an error trace in an IUT. The relative coverage $relcov(T, f)$ yields the error weight in T as a fraction of the weight of all traces in L^*. Since absolute (coverage) numbers have meaning only if they are put in perspective of a maximum or average; we advocate that the relative coverage yields a good indication for the quality of a test suite.

Completeness of a test suite can easily be expressed in terms of coverage.

Definition 3. *A test suite $T \subseteq \mathcal{P}(L^*)$ is* complete *w.r.t. a WFM $f : L^* \to \mathbb{R}^{\geq 0}$ if $relcov(T, f) = 1$.*

3 Test Cases in Labeled Input-Output Transition Systems

This section recalls some basic theory about test derivation from labeled input-output transition systems, following ioco testing theory [15]. It prepares for the next section that treats an automaton-based formalism for specifying WFMs.

3.1 Labeled Input-Output Transition Systems

Definition 4. *A* labeled input-output transition system (LTS) *$\mathcal{A}$ is a tuple $\langle S, s^0, L, \Delta \rangle$, where*

- *S is a finite set of states*
- *$s^0 \in S$ is the initial state*
- *L is a finite action alphabet. We assume that $L = L^I \cup L^O$ is partitioned (i.e. $L^I \cap L^O = \emptyset$) into a set L^I of* input labels *(also called input actions or inputs) and a set L^O of* output labels *L^O (also called output actions or outputs). We denote elements of L^I by $a?$ and elements of L^O by $a!$*
- *$\Delta \subseteq S \times L \times S$ is the transition relation. We require Δ to be deterministic, i.e. if $(s, a, s'), (s, a, s'') \in \Delta$, then $s' = s''$. The input transition relation Δ^I is the restriction of Δ to $S \times L^I \times S$ and the output transition relation Δ^O is the restriction of Δ to $S \times L^O \times S$. We write $\Delta(s) = \{(a, s') \mid (s, a, s') \in \Delta\}$ and similarly for $\Delta^I(s)$ and $\Delta^O(s)$. We denote by $outdeg(s) = |\Delta(s)|$ the outdegree of state s, i.e. the number of transitions leaving s*

We denote the components of $\mathcal{A}$ *by* $S_{\mathcal{A}}$, $s^0_{\mathcal{A}}$, $L_{\mathcal{A}}$, *and* $\Delta_{\mathcal{A}}$. *We omit the subscript* $\mathcal{A}$ *if it is clear from the context.*

We have required $\mathcal{A}$ to be deterministic only for technical simplicity. This is not a real restriction, since we can always determinize $\mathcal{A}$. We can also incorporate quiescence (i.e. the absence of outputs), by adding a self loop $s \xrightarrow{\delta} s$ labeled with a special label δ to each quiescent state s, i.e. each s with $\Delta^O(s) = \emptyset$ and considering δ as an output action. But, since quiescence is not preserved under determinization, we must first determinize and then add quiescence.

Example 1. Figure 1 a) presents a LTS of a MP3 player: if the user pushes the play-button, a song should be played. In b), we see the extension with quiescence. Since δ is not enabled in state q_1, we explicitly forbid the absence of outputs in q_1, i.e. a song must be played. The double circles represent the initial state.

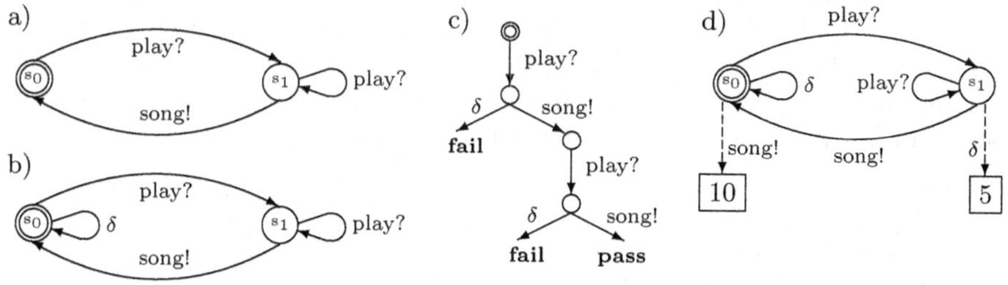

Fig. 1. A MP3 player: 1) its specification as a LTS; b) its extension with quiescence; c) a possible tests case t_1; and d) its fault automaton

We introduce the usual language theoretic concepts for LTSs.

Definition 5. *Let* $\mathcal{A}$ *be a LTS, then*

- *A* path *in* $\mathcal{A}$ *is a finite sequence* $\pi = s_0 a_1 s_1 \ldots s_n$ *such that* $s_0 = s^0$ *and, for all* $1 \leq i \leq n$, *we have* $(s_{i-1}, a_i, s_i) \in \Delta$. *We denote by* $paths_{\mathcal{A}}$ *the set of all paths in* $\mathcal{A}$ *and by* $last(\pi) = s_n$ *the last state of* π.
- *The* trace *of a path* π, $trace(\pi)$, *is the sequence* $a_1 a_2 \ldots a_n$ *of actions occurring in* π. *We write* $traces_{\mathcal{A}} = \{trace(\pi) | \pi \in paths_{\mathcal{A}}\}$ *for the set of all traces in* $\mathcal{A}$.
- *Let* $\sigma \in L^*$ *be any trace, not necessarily one from* $\mathcal{A}$. *We write* $reach^k_{\mathcal{A}}(\sigma)$ *for the set of states that can be reached in* $\mathcal{A}$ *in exactly* k *steps by following* σ, *i.e.* $s' \in reach^k_{\mathcal{A}}(s)$ *if* $|\sigma| = k$ *and there is a path* $\pi \in paths_{\mathcal{A}}$ *such that* $trace(\pi) = \sigma$ *and* $last(\pi) = s'$. *We write* $reach_{\mathcal{A}}(\sigma)$ *for the set of states that can be reached via trace* σ *in any number of steps, i.e.* $reach_{\mathcal{A}}(\sigma) = \bigcup_{k \in \mathbb{N}} reach^k_{\mathcal{A}}(\sigma)$; *we write* $reach^k_{\mathcal{A}}$ *for the set of states that can be reached in* k *number of steps, by following any trace, i.e.* $reach^k_{\mathcal{A}} = \bigcup_{\sigma \in L^*} reach^k_{\mathcal{A}}(\sigma)$; *and* $reach_{\mathcal{A}} = \bigcup_{\sigma \in L^*} reach_{\mathcal{A}}(\sigma)$ *for the set of all reachable states in* $\mathcal{A}$.

As before, we leave out the subscript $\mathcal{A}$ *if it is clear from the context.*

Definition 6. *Let $\mathcal{A}$ be a LTS and $s \in S$ be a state in $\mathcal{A}$, then $\mathcal{A}[s]$ denotes the LTS $\langle S, s, L, \Delta \rangle$.*

Thus, $\mathcal{A}[s]$ is the same as $\mathcal{A}$, but with s as initial state. This notation allows us to speak of paths, traces, etc, in $\mathcal{A}$ starting from a state that is not the initial state. For instance, $paths_{\mathcal{A}[s]}$ denotes the set of paths starting from state s.

3.2 Test Cases

Test cases for LTSs are based on ioco test theory [15]. As in TTCN, ioco test cases are adaptive. That is, the next action to be performed (observe the IUT, stimulate the IUT or stop the test) may depend on the test history, that is, the trace observed so far. If, after a trace σ, the tester decides to stimulate the IUT with an input $a?$, then the new test history becomes $\sigma a?$; in case of an observation, the test accounts for all possible continuations $\sigma b!$ with $b! \in L^O$ an output action. Ioco theory requires that tests are "fail fast", i.e. stop after the discovery of the first failure, and never fail immediately after an input. If $\sigma \in traces_{\mathcal{A}}$, but $\sigma a? \notin trace_{\mathcal{A}}$, then the behavior after $\sigma a?$ is not specified in s, leaving room for implementation freedom. Formally, a test case consists of the set of all possible test histories obtained in this way.

Definition 7.
- *A* test case *(or test) t for a LTS $\mathcal{A}$ is a finite, prefix-closed subset of $L^*_{\mathcal{A}}$ such that*
  - *if $\sigma a? \in t$, then $\sigma b \notin t$ for any $b \in L$ with $a? \neq b$*
  - *if $\sigma a! \in t$, then $\sigma b! \in t$ for all $b! \in L^O$*
  - *if $\sigma \notin traces_{\mathcal{A}}$, then no proper suffix of σ is contained in t*

  We denote the set of all tests for $\mathcal{A}$ by $\mathcal{T}(\mathcal{A})$.
- *The* length *$|t|$ of test t is the length of the longest trace in t, i.e. $|t| = \max_{\sigma \in t} |\sigma|$. We denote by $\mathcal{T}^k(\mathcal{A})$ the set of all tests for $\mathcal{A}$ with length k.*

Example 2. Figure 1 c) shows a test case for the MP3 player from Figure 1, represented as a tree and augmented with verdicts pass and fail. The prefix closed trace set is obtained by taking all traces in the tree.

Since each test of $\mathcal{A}$ is a set of traces, we can apply Definition 2 and speak of (absolute, total and relative) coverage of a test case (or a test suite) of $\mathcal{A}$, w.r.t to a WFM f. However, not all WFMs are consistent with the interpretation that traces of $\mathcal{A}$ represent correct system behavior, and that tests are "fail fast" and do not fail after an input.

Definition 8. *Let $\mathcal{A}$ be a LTS and let $f : L^* \to \mathbb{R}^{\geq 0}$ be a WFM. Then f is* consistent with $\mathcal{A}$ *if $L = L_{\mathcal{A}}$ and for all $\sigma \in L^*_{\mathcal{A}}$ we have*

- *If $\sigma \in traces_{\mathcal{A}}$, then $f(\sigma) = 0$ (correct traces have weight 0).*
- *$f(\sigma a?) = 0$ (no failure occurs after an input).*
- *If $f(\sigma) > 0$ then $f(\sigma\rho) = 0$ for all $\rho \in L^+_{\mathcal{A}}$ (at most one failure per trace).*

The following result states that the set containing all possible test cases has complete coverage.

Theorem 1. *Let $\mathcal{A}$ be a LTS and f be a WFM consistent with $\mathcal{A}$. Then, the set $\mathcal{T}(\mathcal{A})$ of all test cases for $\mathcal{A}$ is complete w.r.t. f.*

4 Fault Automata

Weighted fault models are infinite, semantic objects. This section introduces *fault automata*, which provide a syntactic format for specifying WFMs. A fault automaton is a LTS $\mathcal{A}$ augmented with a state weight function r. The LTS $\mathcal{A}$ is the behavioral specification of the system, i.e. its traces represent the correct system behaviors. Hence, these traces will be assigned error weight 0; traces not in $\mathcal{A}$ are erroneous and get an error weight through r, as explained below.

Definition 9. *A* fault automaton (FA) $\mathcal{F}$ *is a pair* $\langle \mathcal{A}, r \rangle$, *where* $\mathcal{A}$ *is a LTS and* $r : S \times L^O \to \mathbb{R}^{\geq 0}$. *We require that, if* $r(s, a!) > 0$, *then there is no* $a!$*-successor of* s *in* $\mathcal{F}$, *i.e. there is no* $s' \in S$ *such that* $(s, a!, s') \in \Delta$. *We define* $\overline{r} : S \to \mathbb{R}^{\geq 0}$ *as* $\overline{r}(s) = \sum_{a \in L^O(s)} r(s, a)$. *Thus,* $\bar{r}$ *accumulates the weight of all the erroneous outputs in a state. We denote the components of* $\mathcal{F}$ *by* $\mathcal{A}_{\mathcal{F}}$ *and* $r_{\mathcal{F}}$ *and leave out the subscripts* $\mathcal{F}$ *if it is clear from the context. We lift all concepts and notations (e.g. traces, paths, etcetera) that have been defined for LTSs to FAs.*

Example 3. Figure 1 d) presents a FA for our MP3 example. We give error weight 5 if in state q_0 a song is played; and weight 10 if in state q_1 no song occurs.

We wish to construct a WFM f from the FA $\mathcal{F}$, using r to assign weights to traces not in $\mathcal{A}$. If there is no outgoing $a!$-transition in s, then the idea is that, for a trace σ ending in s, the (incorrect) trace $\sigma a!$ gets weight $r(s, a!)$. Doing so, however, could cause the total error weight $totcov(f)$ to be infinite.

We consider two solutions to this problem. First, *finite depth WFMs* (Section 4.1) consider, for a given $k \in \mathbb{N}$, only faults in traces of length k or smaller. Second, *discounted WFMs* (Section 4.2) obtain finite total coverage through discounting, while considering error weight in all traces. The solution presented here are only two potential solutions, there are many other ways to derive a WFM from a fault automaton.

4.1 Finite Depth Weighted Fault Models

As said before, the finite depth model derives a WFM from a FA $\mathcal{F}$, for a given $k \in \mathbb{N}$, by ignoring all traces of length longer than k, i.e. by putting their error weight to 0. For all other traces, the weight is obtained via the function r. If σ is a trace of $\mathcal{F}$ ending in s, but $\sigma a!$ is not a trace in $\mathcal{F}$, then $\sigma a!$ gets weight $r(s, a!)$.

Definition 10. *Given a FA* $\mathcal{F}$, *and a number* $k \in \mathbb{N}$, *we define the function* $f^k_{\mathcal{F}} : L^* \to \mathbb{R}^{\geq 0}$ *by*

$$f^k_{\mathcal{F}}(\varepsilon) = 0 \qquad f^k_{\mathcal{F}}(\sigma a) = \begin{cases} r(s, a) & \text{if } s \in reach^k_{\mathcal{F}}(\sigma) \wedge a \in L^O \\ 0 & \text{otherwise} \end{cases}$$

Note that this function is uniquely defined because $\mathcal{F}$ is deterministic, so that there is at most one s with $s \in reach^k_{\mathcal{F}}(\sigma)$. Also, if $f^k_{\mathcal{F}}(\sigma a) = r(s, a) > 0$, then $\sigma \in traces_{\mathcal{F}}$, but $\sigma a \notin traces_{\mathcal{F}}$.

The following proposition states that $f^k_{\mathcal{F}}$ is a WFM consistent with $\mathcal{F}$, provided that $\mathcal{F}$ contains as most one state with a positive accumulated weight and that is reachable within k steps.

Proposition 1. *Let $\mathcal{F}$ be a FA, and $k \in \mathbb{N}$. If there is an $i \leq k$ and a state $s \in reach^i_{\mathcal{F}}$ with $\overline{r}(s) > 0$, then $f^k_{\mathcal{F}}$ is a WFM consistent with $\mathcal{F}$.*

Example 4. Given the FA $\mathcal{F}$ from Figure 1 d), Figure 2 shows the function $f^k_{\mathcal{F}}$ for $k = 3$. Using t the test presented in Figure 1 c), we can obtain $abscov(t, f^k_{\mathcal{F}}) = 5$.

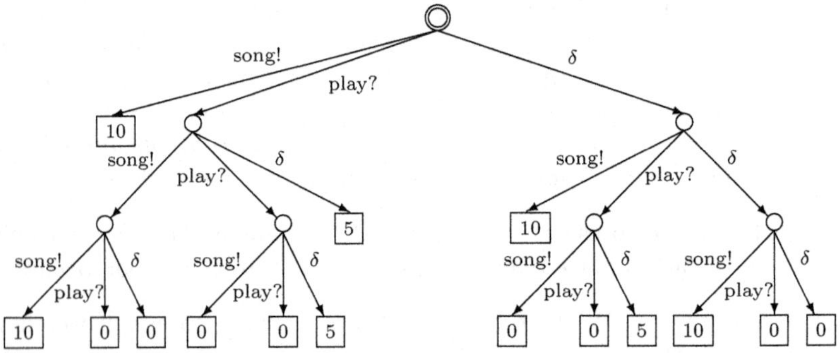

Fig. 2. Function $f^k_{\mathcal{F}}$, for $k = 3$ and $\mathcal{F}$ from Figure 1 b)

4.2 Discounted Weighted Fault Models

While finite depth WFMs achieve finite total coverage by considering finitely many traces, discounted WFMs take into account the error weights of all traces. To do so, only finitely many traces may have weight greater than ϵ, for any $\epsilon > 0$. One way to do this is by discounting: lowering the weight of a trace proportional to its length. The rationale behind this is that errors in the near future are worse than errors in the far future, and hence, the latter should have higher weights.

In its basic form, a discounted WFM f for an FA $\mathcal{F}$ sets the weight of a trace $\sigma a!$ to $\alpha^{|\sigma|} r(s, a!)$, for some discount factor $\alpha \in (0, 1)$. If we take α small enough, then one can easily show that $\sum_{\sigma \in L^*} f(\sigma) < \infty$. To be precise, we take $\alpha < \frac{1}{d}$, where d is the branching degree of $\mathcal{F}$ (i.e. $d = \max_{s \in S} outdeg(s)$). Indeed, let $\alpha d < 1$ and $M = \max_s r(s, a)/\alpha$. Then $f(\sigma) \leq \alpha^{|\sigma|} M$. Since there are at most d^k traces of length k in $\mathcal{F}$, it follows that

$$\sum_{\sigma \in L^*} f(\sigma) = \sum_{k \in \mathbb{N}} \sum_{\sigma \in L^k} \alpha^k M \leq \sum_{k \in \mathbb{N}} d^k \alpha^k M = \frac{M}{1 - d\alpha} < \infty$$

To obtain more flexibility, we allow the discount to vary per transition. That is, we work with a discount function $\alpha : S \times L \times S \to \mathbb{R}^{\geq 0}$ that assigns a positive weight to each transition of $\mathcal{F}$. Then we discount the trace $a_1 \dots a_k$ obtained from the path $s_0 a_1 s_1 \dots s_k$ by $\alpha(s_0, a_1, s_1)\alpha(s_1, a_2, s_2) \cdots \alpha(s_{k-1}, a_k, s_k)$. The requirement that α is small enough now becomes: $\sum_{a \in L, s' \in S} \alpha(s, a, s') < 1$, We can even be more flexible and, in the sum above, do not range over states in which all paths are finite, as in these states we have finite total coverage anyway. Thus, if $Inf_{\mathcal{F}}$ is the set of all states in $\mathcal{F}$ with at least one outgoing infinite path, we require for all states s: $\sum_{a \in L, s' \in Inf_{\mathcal{F}}} \alpha(s, a, s') < 1$.

Definition 11. *Let $\mathcal{F}$ be a FA. The set $Inf_{\mathcal{F}} \subseteq S_{\mathcal{F}}$ of states with at least one infinite path is defined as $Inf_{\mathcal{F}} = \{s \in S \mid \exists \pi \in paths_{\mathcal{F}[s]} \cdot |\pi| > |S|\}$.*

Definition 12. *Let $\mathcal{F}$ be a FA. Then a* discount function *for $\mathcal{F}$ is a function $\alpha : S_{\mathcal{F}} \times L_{\mathcal{F}} \times S_{\mathcal{F}} \to \mathbb{R}^{\geq 0}$ such that*

- *For all $s, s' \in S_{\mathcal{F}}$, and $a \in L_{\mathcal{F}}$ we have $\alpha(s, a, s') = 0$ iff $(s, a, s') \notin \Delta_{\mathcal{F}}$.*
- *For all $s \in S_{\mathcal{F}}$, we have: $\sum_{a \in L_{\mathcal{F}}, s' \in Inf_{\mathcal{F}}} \alpha(s, a, s') < 1$.*

Definition 13. *Let α be a discount function for the FA $\mathcal{F}$. Given a path $\pi = s_0 a_1 \ldots s_n$ in $\mathcal{F}$, we define $\alpha(\pi)$ as $\prod_{i=1}^{n} \alpha(s_{i-1}, a_i, s_i)$.*

Definition 14. *Let $\mathcal{F}$ be a FA, $s \in S$, and α a discount function for $\mathcal{F}$. We define the function $f_{\mathcal{F}}^{\alpha} : L^* \to \mathbb{R}^{\geq 0}$ by*

$$f_{\mathcal{F}}^{\alpha}(\varepsilon) = 0$$

$$f_{\mathcal{F}}^{\alpha}(\sigma a) = \begin{cases} \alpha(\pi) \cdot r(s, a) & \text{if } s \in reach_{\mathcal{F}}(\sigma) \wedge a \in L^O \wedge trace(\pi) = \sigma \\ 0 & \text{otherwise} \end{cases}$$

Since $\mathcal{F}$ is deterministic, there is at most one π with $trace(\pi) = \sigma$ and at most one $s \in reach(\sigma)$. Hence, the function above is uniquely defined.

The following proposition states that $f_{\mathcal{F}}^{\alpha}$ is a WFM consistent with $\mathcal{F}$, if $\mathcal{F}$ contains as most one reachable state with a positive accumulated weight.

Proposition 2. *Let $\mathcal{F}$ be a FA and α a discount function for $\mathcal{F}$. If there is a state $s \in reach_{\mathcal{F}}$ with $\overline{r}(s) > 0$, then $f_{\mathcal{F}}^{\alpha}$ is a WFM consistent with $\mathcal{F}$.*

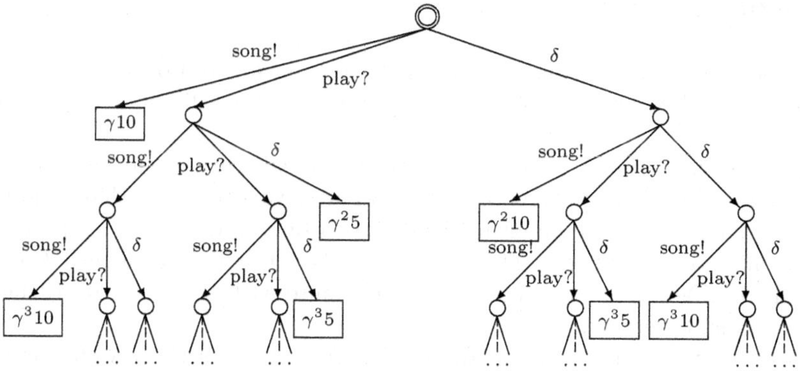

Fig. 3. Function $f_{\mathcal{F}}^{\alpha}$ for $\mathcal{F}$ from Figure 1 b) and $\alpha(s, a, s') = \gamma$

Example 5. Figure 3 presents function $f^{\alpha}_{\mathcal{F}}$ for $\mathcal{F}$ from Figure 1 b) and $\alpha(s,a,s') = \gamma$ for every transition $(s,a,s') \in \Delta$. Using t the test presented in Figure 1 c), we can obtain $abscov(t, f^{\alpha}_{\mathcal{F}}) = \gamma^2 5$.

It is not difficult to see that our coverage notions are truly semantic in that they are invariant under $\overline{r}$-preserving bisimilarity. More precisely, suppose states s, s' in $\mathcal{F}$ are bisimilar, and that bisimilar states are required to have the same $\overline{r}$-value (i.e. $\overline{r}(s) = \overline{r}(s')$). Then $f^{k}_{\mathcal{F}[s]} = f^{k}_{\mathcal{F}[s']}$ and $f^{\alpha}_{\mathcal{F}[s]} = f^{\alpha}_{\mathcal{F}[s']}$ for all α and k. We refer the reader to [5] for more details.

4.3 Calibration

Discounting weighs errors in short traces more than in long traces. Thus, if we discount too much, we may obtain very high test coverage just with a few short test cases. The calibration result (Theorem 2) presented in this section shows that, for any FA $\mathcal{F}$ and any $u > 0$, we can choose the discounting function in such a way that test cases of a given length k or longer are needed to achieve test coverage higher than a coverage bound $1 - u$. That is, we show that for any given k and u, there exists a discount function α such that the relative coverage of all test cases of length k or shorter is less than u. This means that, to get coverage higher than $1 - u$, one needs test cases longer than k.

For technical reasons, the weight assignment function of a FA have to be fair, i.e. all states in *Inf* must be able to reach some state with a positive weight.

Definition 15. *A FA $\mathcal{F}$ has* fair weight assignment *if for all $s \in Inf_{\mathcal{F}}$, there exists state $s' \in reach_{\mathcal{F}[s]}$ with $\overline{r}(s') > 0$.*

Theorem 2. *Let $\mathcal{F}$ be a FA with fair weight assignment. Then there exists a family of discount functions $\{\alpha_u\}_{u \in (0,1)}$ for $\mathcal{F}$ such that for all $k \in \mathbb{N}$ we have $\lim_{u \downarrow 0} relcov(\mathcal{T}^k(f^{\alpha_u}_{\mathcal{F}}), f^{\alpha_u}_{\mathcal{F}}) = 0$.*

5 Algorithms

This section represents various algorithms for computing and optimizing coverage for a given FA, interpreted under the finite depth or discounted weighted fault model.

In particular, Section 5.1 presents algorithms to calculate the absolute coverage in a test suite of a given FA. In Section 5.2 we give algorithms that yield the total coverage in a weighted fault model derived from a FA. Section 5.3 provides two optimization algorithms. The first one finds a test case of length k with maximal coverage; the second one finds a test suite with n test cases of length k and maximal coverage.

We use the following notation. Recall that $\mathcal{F}[s]$ denotes the FA that is the same as $\mathcal{F}$, but with s as initial state. When $\mathcal{F}$ is clear from the context, we write respectively f_s^k and f_s^α for the weighted fault models $f_{\mathcal{F}[s]}^k$ and $f_{\mathcal{F}[s]}^\alpha$ derived from $\mathcal{F}$. Moreover, given a FA $\mathcal{F} = \langle \mathcal{A}, r \rangle$, we write $A_\mathcal{F}$ for the multi-adjacency matrix of $\mathcal{A}$, containing at position (s, s') the number of edges between s and s', i.e. $(A_\mathcal{F})_{ss'} = \sum_{a:(s,a,s') \in \Delta} 1$. If α is a discount function for $\mathcal{F}$, then $A_\mathcal{F}^\alpha$ is a weighted version of $A_\mathcal{F}$, i.e. $(A_\mathcal{F}^\alpha)_{ss'} = \sum_{a \in L} \alpha(s, a, s')$. We omit the subscript $\mathcal{F}$ if it is clear from the context.

5.1 Absolute Coverage in a Test Suite

Given test suite T, a FA $\mathcal{F}$, and either a discounting function α for $\mathcal{F}$ or a number k, we desire to compute $abscov(T, f) = abscov(\cup_{t \in T} t, f)$, where $f = f_\mathcal{F}^k$ or $f_\mathcal{F}^\alpha$. Given two tests t and t' and an action a, we write at for $\{a\sigma \mid \sigma \in t\}$ and $t + t'$ for the union $t \cup t'$. We call a supertest (Stest) the union of any number of tests.

Now, we can write each test as $t = \varepsilon$; or $t = at_1$ in case a is an input; or $t = b_1t_1 + \cdots + b_nt_n$ when $b_1, \cdots, b_n$ are all output actions of $\mathcal{F}$. Each supertest can be written as $a_1t_1' + \cdots + a_kt_k' + b_1t_1'' + \cdots + b_nt_n''$ where a_i are inputs and b_i are all outputs and t_i', t_j'' are supertests.

To compute the union $\cup_{t \in T} t$, we recursively merge all tests in T into a supertest using the infix operator $\uplus : Stest \times$ test $\rightarrow Stest$. Then we add the error weights of all traces in $\cup_{t \in T} t$ via the function ac.

Merging of Tests. Let t' be a Stest, $t' = a_1t_1' + \cdots + a_kt_k' + b_1t_1'' + \cdots + b_nt_n''$ and t be a test, then $t = \varepsilon$ or $t = at_1$ or $t = b_1t_1' + \cdots + b_nt_n'$

$$t' \uplus t =$$

$$\begin{cases} a_1t_1' + \cdots + a_j(t_j' \uplus t_1) + \cdots + a_kt_k' + b_1t_1'' + \cdots + b_nt_n'' & \text{if } t = at_1 \wedge a = a_j \\ a_1t_1' + \cdots + a_kt_k' + b_1(t_1'' \uplus t_1) + \cdots + b_n(t_n'' \uplus t_n) & \text{if } t = b_1t_1' + \cdots + b_nt_n' \\ t' + t & \text{otherwise} \end{cases}$$

We write $\uplus\{t_1, t_2, \ldots t_n\}$ for $t_1 \uplus t_2 \uplus \ldots t_n$.

Absolute Coverage in a Stest. Given a Stest t of $\mathcal{F}$ and a state s on $\mathcal{F}$, then

$$ac(\varepsilon, s) = 0 \qquad ac(t, s) = \sum_{i=1}^n aux(a_it_i, s)$$

$$\text{where } aux(a_it_i, s) = \begin{cases} \alpha(s, a_i, \delta(s, a_i)) \cdot ac(t_i, \delta(s, a_i)) & \text{if } a_i \in \delta(s) \\ r(a_i, s) & \text{otherwise} \end{cases}$$

The correctness of this algorithm is stated in the following theorem.

Theorem 3. *Given a FA $\mathcal{F}$, a state $s \in V$, a number $k \in \mathbb{N}$, a function $\alpha : S \times L \times S \rightarrow [0, 1]$ and T a test suite, then*

- *If α is a discount function for $\mathcal{F}$, then $abscov(T, f_s^\alpha) = ac(\uplus T, s)$*
- *If $k \geq \max_{t \in T} |t|$ and $\alpha(s, a, s') = 1$ for all transitions (s, a, s') in $\mathcal{F}$, then $abscov(T, f_s^k) = ac(\uplus T, s)$.*

5.2 Total Coverage

Total Coverage in Discounted FA. Given a FA $\mathcal{F}$, a state $s \in S$ and a discounting function α for $\mathcal{F}$, we desire to calculate $totcov(f_s^\alpha) = \sum_{\sigma \in L^*} f_s^\alpha(\sigma)$. We assume that from each state in $\mathcal{F}$ we can reach at least one error state (i.e. $\forall s \in S : \exists s' \in reach_{\mathcal{F}[s]} : \overline{r}(s) > 0$). In this way, f_s^α is a WFM for every s.

The basic idea behind the computation method is that the function $tc : S \to [0,1]$ ("total coverage") given by $s \mapsto totcov(f_s^\alpha)$ satisfies the following set of equations.

$$tc(s) = \overline{r}(s) + \sum_{a \in L, s' \in S} \alpha(s,a,s') \cdot tc(s') = \overline{r}(s) + \sum_{s' \in S} A_s^\alpha s' \cdot tc(s') \qquad (*)$$

These equations express that the total coverage in state s equals the weight $\overline{r}(s)$ of all immediate errors in s, plus the weights in all successors s' in s, discounted by $\sum_{a \in L} \alpha(s,a,s')$. Using matrix-vector notation, we obtain $tc = \overline{r} + A^\alpha \cdot tc$. In [5] it is shown that the matrix $I - A^\alpha$ is invertible. Thus, we obtain the following result; in particular, tc is the unique solution of the equations (*) above.

Theorem 4. *Let $\mathcal{F}$ be a FA such that for all $s \in S$ there exists a state $s' \in reach_{\mathcal{F}[s]}$ with $\overline{r}(s') > 0$, and let α be a discount function for $\mathcal{F}$. Then $tc = (I - A^\alpha)^{-1} \cdot \overline{r}$.*

Complexity. The complexity of the method above is dominated by matrix inversion, which can be computed in $O(|S|^3)$ with Gaussian elimination, $O(|S|^{log_2 7})$ with Strassen's method or even faster with more sophisticated techniques.

Total Coverage in Finite Depth FA. Given a FA $\mathcal{F}$, a state $s \in S$ and a depth $k \in \mathbb{N}$, we desire to compute $totcov(f_s^k) = \sum_{\sigma \in L^*} f_s^k(\sigma)$. We assume that from each state, there is at least one error reachable in k steps (i.e. $\forall s \in S : \exists s' \in reach^k_{\mathcal{F}[s]} : \overline{r}(s') > 0$). This makes that f_s^k is a weighted fault model for any s.

The basic idea behind the computation method is that the function $tc_k : S \to [0,1]$ given by $s \mapsto totcov(f_s^k)$ satisfies the following recursive equations.

$$tc_0(s) = 0$$

$$tc_{k+1}(s) = \overline{r}(s) + \sum_{(a,s') \in \Delta(s)} tc_k(s') = \overline{r}(s) + \sum_{a \in L, s' \in S} A_{s,s'} \cdot tc_k(s')$$

Or, in matrix-vector notation, we have $tc_0 = 0$ and $tc_{k+1} = \overline{r} + A \cdot tc_k$.

Theorem 5. *Let $\mathcal{F}$ be a FA, a state $s \in S$ and $k \in \mathbb{N}$. If $\forall s \in S : \exists s' \in reach^k_{\mathcal{F}[s]} : \overline{r}(s') > 0$, then $tc_k = \sum_{i=0}^{k-1} A^i \cdot \overline{r}$.*

Complexity. Using Theorem 5 with sparse matrix multiplication, or iterating the equations just above it, tc_k can be computed in time $O(k \cdot |\Delta| + |S|)$.

Remark 1. A similar method to the one above can be used to compute the weight of all tests of length k in the discounted weighted fault model, i.e. $abscov(T^k, f_s^\alpha)$, for T^k (i.e. the set of all tests of length k in $\mathcal{F}$).

The recursive equations for computing $abscov(T^k, f_s^\alpha)$ are obtained by replacing A in Equation (*) by A_α. Since $I - A^\alpha$ is (unlike $I - A$) invertible, the analogon of Theorem 5 becomes $abscov(T^k, f_s^\alpha) = \sum_{i=0}^{k-1}(A_\alpha)^i \overline{r} = (I - A^\alpha)^{-1} \cdot (I - (A^\alpha)^k) \cdot \overline{r}$.

Relative Coverage. Combining the algorithms for computing total and absolute coverage from the previous sections, one easily computes $relcov(T, f) = \frac{abscov(T,f)}{totcov(f)}$ for a testsuite T and $f = f_s^k$ or $f = f_s^\alpha$.

5.3 Optimization

Optimal Coverage in a Test Case. Given a FA $\mathcal{F}$ and a length k, we compute the best test case with length k (i.e. the one with highest coverage). We treat the finite depth and discounted model at once by fixing, in the finite depth model $\alpha(s, a, s') = 1$ if (s, a, s') is a transition in Δ and $\alpha(s, a, s') = 0$ otherwise. A function *alpha* is call *extended discount function* if it is a discount function or it is obtained from a finite depth model in the presented previous way.

The optimization method is again based on recursive equations. We write $acopt_k(s) = \max_{t \in T^k}\{abscov(t, s)\}$ ("optimal absolute coverage"). Consider a test case of length $k+1$ that in state s applies an input $a?$ and in the successor state s' applies the optimal test of length k. The (absolute) coverage of this test case is $\alpha(s, a?, s') \cdot acopt_k(s')$. The best coverage that we can obtain by stimulating the IUT is given by $\max_{(a?,s') \in \Delta^I(s)} \alpha(s, a?, s') \cdot acopt_k(s')$.

Now, consider the test case of length $k+1$ that in state s observes the IUT and in each successor state s' applies the optimal test of length k. The coverage of this test case is $\overline{r}(s) + \sum_{(b!,s') \in \Delta^O(s)} \alpha(s, b!, s') \cdot acopt_k(s')$. The optimal test $acopt(s)$ of length $k+1$ is obtained from $acopt_k$ by selecting from these options (i.e. inputing an action $a?$ or observing) the one with the highest coverage.

Theorem 6. *Let $\mathcal{F}$ be a FA, α be an extended discount function, and $k \in \mathbb{N}$ test length. Then $acopt_k$ satisfies the following recursive equations. $acopt_0(s) = 0$ and $acopt_{k+1}(s) = \max\{\overline{r}(s) + \sum_{(b!,s') \in \Delta^O(s)} \alpha(s, b!, s') \cdot acopt_k(s'), \max_{(a?,s') \in \Delta^I(s)} \alpha(s, a?, s') \cdot acopt_k(s')\}$.*

Complexity. Based on Theorem 6, we can compute $acopt_k$ in time $O(k(|S|+|\Delta|))$.

Shortest Test Case with High Coverage. We can use the above method not only to compute the test case of a fixed length k with optimal coverage, but also to derive the shortest test case with coverage higher than a given bound c. We iterate the equations in Theorem 6 and stop as soon as we achieve coverage higher than c, i.e. at the first n with $acopt_k(s) > c$.

We have to take care that the bound c is not too high, i.e. higher than what is achievable with a single test case. In the finite depth model, this is easy: if the test length is the same as c then we can stop, since this is the longest test we can have. In the discounted model, however, we have to ensure that c is strictly smaller than the supremum of the coverage of all tests in single test case.

Let $mw(s) = supp_{t \in \mathcal{T}} abscov(t, s)$, i.e. the maximal absolute weight of a single test case. Then mw is again characterized by a set of equations.

Theorem 7. *Let $\mathcal{F}$ be a FA, and α be a discount function for $\mathcal{F}$. Then mw is the unique solution of the following set of equations:* $mw(s) = \max\{\max_{(a?,s') \in \Delta^I(s)} \alpha(s, a?, s') \cdot mw(s'), \overline{r}(s) + \sum_{(b!,s') \in \Delta^O(s)} \alpha(s, b!, s') \cdot mw(s')\}$.

The solution of these equations can be found by linear programming (LP).

Theorem 8. *Let $\mathcal{F}$ be a FA, and α be a discount function. Then mw is the optimal solution of the following LP problem: minimize $\sum_{s \in S} mw(s)$ subject to*

$$mw(s) \geq \alpha(s, a?, s') \cdot mw(s') \qquad (a?, s') \in \Delta^I(s)$$

$$mw(s) \geq r(s) + \sum_{(b!,s') \in \Delta^O(s)} \alpha(s, b!, s') \cdot mw(s') \qquad s \in S$$

Complexity. The above LP problem contains $|S|$ variables and $|S|+|\Delta^I|$ inequalities. Thus, solving this problem is polynomial in $|S|$, $|S| + |\Delta^I|$ and the length of the binary encoding of the coefficients [14]. In practice, the exponential time simplex method outperforms existing polynomial time algorithms.

Optimal Coverage in n Cases. The first algorithm in this section for computing the best test case of length k can be extended to a method for computing the best n test cases with optimal coverage: the previous algorithm picks the best test case with length k. To pick the second best test case, we apply the same procedure, except that we exclude the first choice from all possible options, for the third best choice, we exclude the previous two, etc. See [5] for more details.

6 Application: A Chat Protocol

This section applies our theory to a practical example, namely a chat protocol, also used as a conference protocol [2]. This protocol provides a multi-cast service to users engaged in a chat session. Each user can send messages to and receive messages from all other partners participating in the same chat session. The chat participants are dynamic, as the chat service allows them to join and leave the chat at any moment in time. Different chats can exist at the same time, but each user can only participate in at most one chat at a time.

Based on the LTS model in [2], we have created an FA $\mathcal{F}$ for this protocol. Our model considers two chat sessions and three users and has 39 states and 95 transitions. The complete model and the transition weight function can be found in [5]. We interpret $\mathcal{F}$ as a discounted WSM under different discount functions, α_1, α_2 and α_3. If $\theta = (s, a, s')$ is a transition in $\mathcal{F}$ leaving from state s with outdegree d, we use $\alpha_1(\theta) = \frac{1}{8}$; $\alpha_2(\theta) = \frac{1}{d} - \frac{1}{100}$; and $\alpha_3(\theta) = \frac{1}{d} - \frac{1}{10000}$.

	tc	tck, $k=2$	rck, $k=2$	tck, $k=4$	rck, $k=4$	tck, $k=50$	rck, $k=50$
α_1	99.134	89.750	91%	97.171	98%	99.134	100%
α_2	511.369	130.607	25%	239.025	47%	510.768	100%
α_3	743.432	132.652	18%	249.320	34%	733.540	99%

Fig. 4. Total coverage (tc); absolute (tck) and relative coverage (rck) of the test suite containing all tests of length k

	test t_1^k	test t_2^k	test t_3^k	test t_4^k	test t_5^k	test t_6^k	test t_7^k	test t_8^k	test t_9^k	test t_{10}^k	suite T^k
$k=30$	15.3%	4.6%	14.0%	5.3%	15.3%	4.6%	14.2%	8.5%	15.3%	4.9%	63.1%
$k=35$	14.1%	15.3%	15.3%	8.5%	8.6%	5.3%	15.3%	8.5%	8.5%	4.9%	69.1%
$k=40$	5.3%	14.0%	14.2%	15.3%	5.3%	14.1%	15.3%	5.3%	14.0%	15.3%	72.8%
$k=45$	5.0%	8.5%	14.0%	5.0%	8.5%	15.3%	4.9%	15.3%	4.5%	14.2%	47.2%
$k=50$	5.3%	14.2%	5.3%	4.9%	14.0%	5.3%	14.2%	5.3%	14.0%	15.3%	54.2%

Fig. 5. Relative coverage, as a percentage, of tests generated by TorX, using α_2

Figure 4 gives the total coverage in $\mathcal{F}$ (column 1) and the absolute (columns 2, 4, 6) and relative (columns 3, 5, 7) coverage of the test suites containing all tests of length k, for $k = 2, 4, 50$ and $\alpha_1, \alpha_2, \alpha_3$. These results were obtained by applying the first (total coverage in discounted FA) and third algorithm (Remark 1) from Section 5.2. We used Maple 9.5 to resolve the matrix equations in these algorithms.

Figure 5 displays the relative coverage for test suites that have been generated automatically with TorX, using discount function α_2. For test lengths $k = 30, 35, 40, 45, 50$, TorX has generated a test suite T^k, consisting of 10 tests $t_1^k, \ldots t_{10}^k$ of length k. We used Algorithm 5.1 to calculate the relative coverage of T^k. Figure 5 lists the coverage of each individual test t_i^k as well as for the test suites T^k.

The running times of all computations were very small, in the order of a few seconds. Note how the figures show the influence of the discount factor and the test length on the coverage numbers.

7 Conclusions and Future Research

Semantic notions of test coverage have long been overdue, while they are much needed in the selection, generation and optimization of test suites. In this paper, we presented semantic coverage notions based on WFMs. We introduced fault automata, FA, to syntactically represent (a subset of) WFMs and provided algorithms to compute and optimize test coverage. This approach is purely semantic since replacing a FA with a semantically equivalent one (i.e. $\overline{r}$-preserving bisimilar) leaves the coverage unchanged. Our experiments with the chat protocol indicate that our approach is feasible for small protocols. Larger case studies should evaluate the applicability of this framework for more complex systems.

Our weighted fault models are based on (adaptive) ioco test theory. We expect to be easy to adapt our approach to different settings, such as FSM testing or on-the-fly testing. Furthermore, our optimization techniques use test length as an optimality criterion. To accommodate more complex resource constraints (e.g time, costs, risks/probability) occurring in practice, it is relevant to extend our techniques with these attributes. Since these fit naturally within our model and optimization problems subject to costs, time and probability are well-studied, we expect that such extensions are both feasible and useful.

References

1. Ball, T. A theory of predicate-complete test coverage and generation. In *Proceedings of FMCO'04* (2004), pp. 1–22.
2. Belinfante, A., Feenstra, J., Vries, R., Tretmans, J., Goga, N., Feijs, L., Mauw, S., and Heerink, L. Formal test automation: A simple experiment. In *Int. Workshop on Testing of Communicating Systems 12* (1999), pp. 179–196.
3. Belinfante, A., Frantzen, L., and Schallhart, C. Tools for test case generation. In *Model-Based Testing of Reactive Systems* (2004), pp. 391–438.
4. Brandán Briones, L., and Brinksma, E. A test generation framework for *quiescent* real-time systems. In *FATES'04* (2004), pp. 64–78.
5. Brandán Briones, L., Brinksma, E., and Stoelinga, M. A semantic framework for test coverage (extended version). Tech. Rep. TR-CTIT-06-24, Centre for Telematics and Information Technology, University of Twente, 2006.
6. Campbell, C., Grieskamp, W., Nachmanson, L., Schulte, W., Tillmann, N., and Veanes, M. Model-based testing of object-oriented reactive systems. Tech. Rep. MSR-TR-2005-59, 2005.
7. ETSI. Es 201 873-6 v1.1.1 (2003-02). Methods for testing and specification (mts). In *The Testing and Test Control Notation version 3: TTCN-3 Control Interface (TCI). ETSI Standard* (2003).
8. Jard, C., and Jéron, T. TGV: theory, principles and algorithms. *STTT 7*, 4 (2005), 297–315.
9. Lee, D., and Yannakakis, M. Principles and methods of testing finite state machines - A survey. In *Proceedings of the IEEE* (1996), vol. 84, pp. 1090–1126.
10. Myers, G. *The Art of Software Testing.* Wiley & Sons, 1979.
11. Myers, G., Sandler, C., Badgett, T., and Thomas, T. *The Art of Software Testing.* Wiley & Sons, 2004.
12. Nachmanson, L., Veanes, M., Schulte, W., Tillmann, N., and Grieskamp, W. Optimal strategies for testing nondeterministic systems. In *International Symposium on Software Testing and Analysis* (2004), ACM Press, pp. 55–64.
13. Nicola, R., and Hennessy, M. Testing equivalences for processes. In *Proceedings ICALP* (1983), vol. 154.
14. Tardos, E. A strongly polynomial minimum cost circulation algorithm. *Combinatorica 5*, 3 (1985), 247–255.
15. Tretmans, J. Test generation with inputs, outputs and repetitive quiescence. *Software-Concepts and Tools 17*, 3 (1996), 103–120.
16. Tretmans, J., and Brinksma, E. TorX: Automated model-based testing. In *First European Conference on Model-Driven Software Engineering* (2003).
17. Ural, H. Formal methods for test sequence generation. *Computer Communications Journal 15*, 5 (1992), 311–325.

Monotonic Set-Extended Prefix Rewriting and Verification of Recursive Ping-Pong Protocols

Giorgio Delzanno[1], Javier Esparza[2,⋆], and Jiří Srba[3,⋆⋆]

[1] Dipartimento di Informatica e Scienze dell'Informazione
Università di Genova, Italy
[2] Institut für Formale Methoden der Informatik
Universität Stuttgart, Germany
[3] **BRICS**[⋆⋆⋆], Department of Computer Science
Aalborg University, Denmark

Abstract. Ping-pong protocols with recursive definitions of agents, but without any active intruder, are a Turing powerful model. We show that under the environment sensitive semantics (i.e. by adding an active intruder capable of storing all exchanged messages including full analysis and synthesis of messages) some verification problems become decidable. In particular we give an algorithm to decide control state reachability, a problem related to security properties like secrecy and authenticity. The proof is via a reduction to a new prefix rewriting model called Monotonic Set-extended Prefix rewriting (MSP). We demonstrate further applicability of the introduced model by encoding a fragment of the ccp (concurrent constraint programming) language into MSP.

1 Introduction

Motivation and Related Work. In recent years there has been an increasing interest in formal analysis of cryptographic protocols. Even under the *perfect encryption hypothesis* (an intruder cannot exploit weaknesses of the encryption algorithm itself) a number of protocols presented in the literature were flawed, which escalated the need for automatic verification of protocol properties like secrecy and authenticity. Unfortunately, the general problem for fully featured languages like the spi-calculus [1] is undecidable and hence finding a decidable yet reasonably expressive subset of such Turing-powerful formalisms is desirable. We contribute to this area by investigating the decidability borderline for protocols with a restricted set of cryptographic primitives while still preserving complex control-flow structures and with no restriction on the length of messages.

Recently, in [4,12,13] this kind of study has been carried out for models of cryptographic protocols with the basic *ping-pong behaviour* as introduced by Dolev

⋆ Partially supported by the DFG project "Algorithms for Software Model Checking".

⋆⋆ Partially supported by the research center ITI, project No. 1M0021620808, and by the grant MSM 0021622419 of Ministry of Education, Czech Republic.

⋆⋆⋆ **B**asic **R**esearch **I**n **C**omputer **S**cience, Danish National Research Foundation.

S. Graf and W. Zhang (Eds.): ATVA 2006, LNCS 4218, pp. 415–429, 2006.

and Yao [10]. In a ping-pong protocol a message is a single piece of data (plain text) possibly encrypted with a finite sequence of keys. Agents are memory-less. The ping-pong communication mechanism can be naturally modelled using prefix rewriting over finite words. The connection is based on the idea of representing a piece of data d encrypted, e.g., with k_1, k_2 and then k_3, as the word $k_3k_2k_1d$. On reception of a message, an agent can only apply a finite sequence of keys to decrypt the message, and then use another sequence of keys applied to the decrypted message to forge the reply. For example the prefix rewrite rule $k_3k_2 \to k_4$ transforms $k_3k_2k_1d$ into k_4k_1d (the suffix k_1d of the first word is copied into the reply).

In [9] Dolev, Even and Karp showed that secrecy properties are decidable in polynomial time for finite ping-pong protocols under an environment sensitive semantics (active attacker) used to model possibly malicious agents. (Where finite means that the length of all computations is syntactically bounded.) In the context of cryptographic protocols, the aim of the attacker is to augment his/her initial knowledge by listening on the communication channels, e.g., to learn some of the secrets exchanged by the honest agents. A general way of defining active attackers was introduced by Dolev and Yao in [10], now commonly known as the Dolev-Yao intruder model. In this model, the communication among the agents is asynchronous. The attacker can store and analyze all messages exchanged among the agents using the current set of *compromised keys*. The attacker can also synthesize new messages starting from the stored messages and compromised keys. In [4] Amadio, Lugiez and Vanackère extended the result of [9] by showing that secrecy is decidable in polynomial time for ping-pong protocols with replication. The replication operator $!P$ is peculiar of process algebraic languages. The agent $!P$ can generate an arbitrary number of identical copies of P operating in parallel. This work was later extended to protocols with a limited use of pairing [3,8].

A more powerful way of extending the class of finite ping-pong protocols is to allow for recursive process definitions, as in CCS. Loosely speaking, recursion allows to define processes with arbitrary flow-graphs; the finite case [10,9] corresponds to acyclic graphs. Recursive definitions are more powerful than replicative ones, in particular recursive protocols are not memory-less any more as every agent can be seen as an automaton with finite memory. This enables to verify not only secrecy but also authenticity. The combination of ping-pong behaviour with recursive definitions and finite memory enables us to encode several protocols studied in the literature, including features like a limited notion of pairing, public key encryption and others.

A process algebra for recursive ping-pong protocols was introduced in [12,13] where it was proved that the resulting model (without any notion of an attacker) is Turing powerful.

Novel Contribution. The results from [12,13] were obtained for protocols *in the absence of an attacker*. In this paper, we show that, maybe surprisingly, the control state reachability problem for recursive ping-pong protocols in the presence of a Dolev-Yao intruder is decidable (in particular, this new model is no longer Turing powerful). Since secrecy/authenticity properties can be reduced to the control state reachability problem by adding new control points that can be reached if and only if secrecy/authenticity is violated, this also implies the decidability of these properties.

Our main decidability result is consistent with the results on tail-recursive cryptographic protocols from [3]. Indeed the necessary (but not sufficient) conditions defined in [3] (locality, linearity and independency) for decidability of control state reachability are all satisfied by recursive ping-pong protocols.

Methodology: Reduction to a New Computational Model. In order to achieve this result, we first introduce a new model called *Monotonic Set-extended Prefix rewriting system (MSP)*. Configurations in MSPs have the form (p, T) where p is a control state and T is a *set* of words (the current store or pool). MSP rules enrich prefix rewrite rules with the update of the control state. Control states are partially ordered, and a state update can only lead to states that are greater or equal than the current one, like for instance in weak Büchi automata [17,14], or weak Process Rewrite Systems (wPRSs) [16]. Furthermore, when a rule is applied to a word w in the current store T with the result w', both w and w' are included in the new store. Thus, the store can only grow monotonically. In our application to ping-pong protocols, T represents the current knowledge of the attacker (modulo analysis and synthesis). More generally, it can be viewed as a monotonic store used for agent communication in languages like ccp [19].

Technical Contribution. As a main technical contribution, we will show that known results on prefix rewrite systems, namely the efficient representation of predecessor sets of words in prefix rewriting by nondeterministic finite automata [5], can be used to decide the control state reachability problem for MSPs. Furthermore, we will demonstrate how to reduce the control state reachability problem for recursive ping-pong protocols with Dolev-Yao attacker model to the control state reachability problem for MSPs. This reduction gives us an EXPTIME algorithm to decide the control state reachability problem for recursive ping-pong protocols. We also show that the problem is NP-hard. Closing the gap between both results is left for future research. Finally, we also demonstrate that an (infinite) fragment of the concurrent constraint programming language [19] can be naturally encoded into our MSP formalism.

Note. A full version of the paper, including complete proofs and examples of the modelling power of ping-pong protocols, is available as a BRICS technical report at `http://www.brics.dk/publications/`.

2 Facts About Prefix Rewriting on Words

Let us first state some standard facts about prefix rewriting.

Let Γ be a finite alphabet. A *prefix rewriting system* is a finite set R of *rules* such that $R \subseteq \Gamma^* \times \Gamma^*$. For an element $(v, w) \in R$ we usually write $v \longrightarrow w$. The system R generates a transition system via the standard prefix rewriting.

$$\frac{(v \longrightarrow w) \in R, \quad t \in \Gamma^*}{vt \longrightarrow_R wt}$$

Proposition 1 (see, e.g., [6,11]). *Let $T \subseteq \Gamma^*$ be a regular set of words. Then the sets $pre_R(T) \stackrel{\text{def}}{=} \{u' \in \Gamma^* \mid \exists u \in T.\ u' \longrightarrow_R u\}$ and $pre^*_R(T) \stackrel{\text{def}}{=} \{u' \in \Gamma^* \mid \exists u \in T.\ u' \longrightarrow^*_R u\}$ are also regular sets. Moreover, if T is given by a nondeterministic finite automaton A then we can in polynomial time construct the automata for $pre_R(T)$ and $pre^*_R(T)$ of polynomial size w.r.t. to A.*

3 Monotonic Set-Extended Prefix Rewriting

In this section we shall introduce a new computational model called *Monotonic Set-extended Prefix rewriting* (MSP). First, we provide its definition and then we argue for the decidability of control state reachability in MSP.

Let Γ be a finite alphabet and let Q be a finite set of control states together with a partial ordering relation $\leq \subseteq Q \times Q$. By $p < q$ we denote that $p \leq q$ and $p \neq q$. A *monotonic set-extended prefix rewriting system* (MSP) is a finite set R of rules of the form $pv \longrightarrow qw$ where $p, q \in Q$ such that $p \leq q$ and $v, w \in \Gamma^*$.

Assume a fixed MSP R. A *configuration* of R is a pair (p, T) where $p \in Q$ and $T \subseteq \Gamma^*$. The semantics is given by the following rule.

$$\frac{(pv \longrightarrow qw) \in R, \quad vt \in T}{(p, T) \longrightarrow_R (q, T \cup \{wt\})}$$

Let (p_0, T_0) be an *initial configuration* of MSP R such that $T_0 \neq \emptyset$ is a regular set and let $p_G \in Q$. The *control state reachability problem* is to decide whether $(p_0, T_0) \longrightarrow^*_R (p_G, T)$ for some T.

We will demonstrate the decidability of control state reachability for MSPs. From now on assume a fixed MSP R with an initial configuration (p_0, T_0) and a goal control state p_G. We proceed in three steps. First, we give some preliminaries on the relationship between MSPs and prefix rewriting systems. Then we introduce several notions: control path, π-scheme, and feasibility of a π-scheme. We show that the control state reachability problem reduces to the feasibility problem of π-schemes. Finally, we give an algorithm for feasibility of π-schemes, and give an upper bound on the complexity of the control state reachability problem.

Preliminaries. Given a rule $r = pv \rightarrow qw$ of R, we denote by $u_1 \longrightarrow_r u_2$ the fact that qu_2 can be obtained from pu_1 by applying r, i.e., that there is $t \in \Gamma^*$ such that $u_1 = vt$ and $u_2 = wt$. Furthermore, for every state $p \in Q$ we define the set R_p of rules from R that start from p and do not change the control state, i.e., $R_p \stackrel{\text{def}}{=} \{pv \longrightarrow pw \mid (pv \longrightarrow pw) \in R\}$, and write $v \longrightarrow^*_{R_p} w$ to denote that there is a sequence $v \longrightarrow_{r_1} v_1 \longrightarrow_{r_2} \cdots \longrightarrow_{r_n} w$ such that $r_i \in R_p$ for every $i \in \{1, \ldots, n\}$. We have the following obvious connection between $(p, T) \longrightarrow^*_{R_p} (p, T')$ and $v \longrightarrow^*_{R_p} w$.

Lemma 1. *If* $(p,T) \longrightarrow^*_{R_p} (p,T')$ *then for every* $w \in T'$ *there is* $v \in T$ *such that* $v \longrightarrow^*_{R_p} w$.

Control Paths and π*-Schemes.* Assume a given MSP R. A *control path* is a sequence $\pi = p_0 r_1 p_1 r_2 p_2 \dots p_{n-1} r_n p_n$, where $n \geq 0$, satisfying the following properties:

- $p_i \in Q$ for $i \in \{0,\dots,n\}$ and $r_j \in R$ for every $j \in \{1,\dots n\}$,
- $p_0 < p_1 < p_2 < \dots < p_n$, and
- for every $j \in \{1,\dots n\}$, r_j is a rule of the form $p_{j-1}v \longrightarrow p_j w$ for some v and w.

Note that the length of π is bounded by the length of the longest chain in $(Q,\leq)$. An execution of R starting at (p_0,T_0) *conforms to* π if the sequence of rules used in it belongs to the regular expression $\mathcal{E}(\pi) = R^*_{p_0} r_1 R^*_{p_1} \dots R^*_{p_{n-1}} r_n$ (for $n = 0$, to the regular expression ϵ). Obviously, p_G is reachable from (p_0,T_0) if and only if there is a control path $\pi = p_0 r_1 \dots r_{n-1} p_n$ such that $p_n = p_G$ and some execution of R ending in p_G conforms to π.

In the next lines, we will need to distinguish more precisely to which words the rules from a control path are applied in a particular computation of R. For this we introduce the notions of a π-scheme and feasibility of π-schemes.

A π*-scheme* is a labelled directed acyclic graph $S = (N,E,\lambda)$ where N is a finite set of nodes, $E \subseteq N \times N$ is a set of edges, and $\lambda \colon E \to X$ is a function that assigns to each edge e an element $\lambda(e)$ from the set $X = \{R^*_{p_0}, r_1, R^*_{p_1},\dots,R^*_{p_{n-1}}, r_n\}$. Moreover, S satisfies the following properties (where $\mathbf{n} \xrightarrow{l} \mathbf{n}'$ denotes that S has an edge from $\mathbf{n}$ to $\mathbf{n}'$ labelled by l):

(a) every node has at most one predecessor (i.e., S is a forest) and there are no isolated nodes,
(b) for every $i \in \{1,\dots,n\}$, there is exactly one edge labelled by r_i, and
(c) for every path $\mathbf{n}_0 \xrightarrow{l_1} \mathbf{n}_1 \dots \mathbf{n}_{k-1} \xrightarrow{l_k} \mathbf{n}_k$ leading from a root to a leaf, the sequence $l_1 \dots l_k$ can be obtained from $\mathcal{E}(\pi)$ by deleting 0 or more, but not all, of $r_1, r_2, \dots, r_n$, and there are no two different paths with the same sequence of labels.

Figure 1 shows a π-scheme for the control path $\pi = p_0 r_1 \dots p_3 r_4 p_4$. Intuitively, a π-scheme describes what type of words were necessary to perform the changes of control states described by a given control path. In our example, the first upper chain means that in order to employ the rule r_4 which changes a control state p_3 into p_4, we need to take some word from the initial pool T_0, modify it possibly by the rules from $R^*_{p_0}$, …, $R^*_{p_3}$ (in this order) and finally use the resulting word to enable the application of the rule r_4. In general, the situation can be more complicated as demonstrated in the lower part of Figure 1 for the remaining rules r_1, r_2 and r_3. A word resulting from an initial word taken from the set T_0 and possibly modified by $R^*_{p_0}$ is used to enable the application of the rule r_1. The resulting word is later on necessary for both the application of the rule r_2 and r_3.

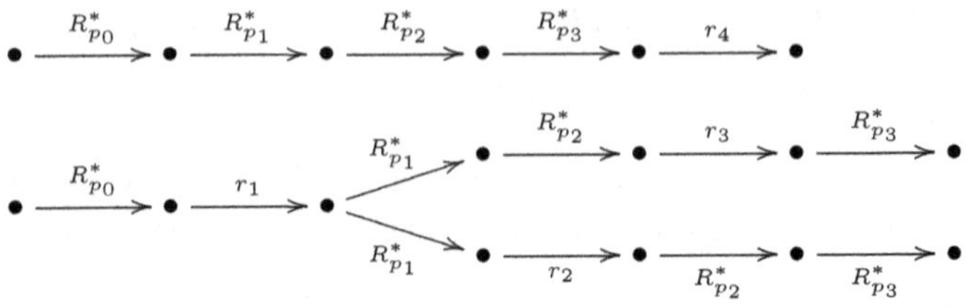

Fig. 1. A π-scheme for $\pi = p_0 r_1 \dots r_4 p_4$

Two π-schemes are *isomorphic* if they are equal up to renaming of the nodes. Note that every π-scheme is finite and there are only finitely many non-isomorphic π-schemes. We obtain a very rough upper bound on the number of π-schemes for a given control path π.

Lemma 2. *Let $\pi = p_0 r_1 p_1 r_2 p_2 \dots r_n p_n$ be a control path. There are at most $n^{O(n)}$ π-schemes up to isomorphism.*

We shall now formally define feasibility of π-schemes. A π-scheme is *feasible from* $T \subseteq \Gamma^*$ if there is a function $f \colon N \to \Gamma^*$ such that

(d) if $\mathbf{n}$ is a root, then $f(\mathbf{n}) \in T$, and

(e) if $\mathbf{n} \xrightarrow{R^*_{p_i}} \mathbf{n}'$, then $f(\mathbf{n}) \longrightarrow^*_{R_{p_i}} f(\mathbf{n}')$, and if $\mathbf{n} \xrightarrow{r_i} \mathbf{n}'$, then $f(\mathbf{n}) \longrightarrow_{r_i} f(\mathbf{n}')$.

Intuitively, the function f determines which particular words are used in order to realize a given π-scheme by some concrete execution in R.

Proposition 2. *Let π be a control path. There is an execution of R starting from (p_0, T_0) and conforming to π iff some π-scheme is feasible from T_0.*

Proposition 2 and Lemma 2 lead to the following algorithmic idea for deciding if there is a set T such that $(p_0, T_0) \longrightarrow^*_R (p_G, T)$:

- enumerate all control paths $\pi = p_0 r_1 \dots r_n p_n$ such that $p_n = p_G$ (their number is finite, because the length of a control path is bounded by the length of the longest $\leq$-chain in Q),
- for each control path π, enumerate all π-schemes (their number is finite by Lemma 2), and
- for each π-scheme S, decide if S is feasible.

Checking Feasibility of π-Schemes. To check feasibility of a π-scheme S, we first need to define the feasibility of a node $\mathbf{n}$ for a word $v \in \Gamma^*$. Let $\mathbf{n}$ be a node of S, and let $N_\mathbf{n}$ denote the set of all descendants of $\mathbf{n}$. We say that $\mathbf{n}$ is *feasible* for $v \in \Gamma^*$ if there is a function $f_n \colon N_\mathbf{n} \to \Gamma^*$ satisfying condition (e) of the definition of feasibility of a π-scheme, and such that $f_n(\mathbf{n}) = v$. Now, let $W(\mathbf{n})$ denote the set of all words v such that $\mathbf{n}$ is feasible for v. By Proposition 2, S is feasible from a set $T \subseteq \Gamma^*$ iff $T \cap W(\mathbf{n}) \neq \emptyset$ for every root $\mathbf{n}$ of S.

An apparent complication to compute the set $W(\mathbf{n})$ is the fact that it may be infinite, which prevents us from enumerating its elements in finite time. We solve this problem by showing that $W(\mathbf{n})$ is always a regular language, and that it is possible to effectively construct a nondeterministic automaton recognizing it. The key is the following characterization of W.

Proposition 3. *Let* $\mathbf{n}$ *be a node of a* π*-scheme* S*, then*

$$W(\mathbf{n}) = \Gamma^* \cap \bigcap_{\mathbf{n} \xrightarrow{R_p{}^*} \mathbf{n}'} pre^*_{R_p}(W(\mathbf{n}')) \cap \bigcap_{\mathbf{n} \xrightarrow{r} \mathbf{n}'} pre_r(W(\mathbf{n}'))$$

where $pre_r(T) \stackrel{\text{def}}{=} pre_{\{v \longrightarrow w\}}(T)$ *such that* r *is of the form* $pv \longrightarrow qw$.

Notice that if $\mathbf{n}$ is a leaf then $W(\mathbf{n}) = \Gamma^*$. Let $\mathbf{n}_0$ and $\mathbf{n}_1$ be the upper and lower root in the π-scheme of Figure 1. If we abbreviate the expression $pre^*_{R_{p_i}}(pre^*_{R_{p_{i+1}}}(\dots(pre^*_{R_{p_j}}(T))\dots)$ to $pre^*_{i\dots j}(T)$ for $i \leq j$, we get

$$\begin{aligned} W(\mathbf{n}_0) &= pre^*_{0123}(pre_{r_4}(\Gamma^*)) \\ W(\mathbf{n}_1) &= pre^*_0(pre_{r_1}(\ pre^*_{12}(pre_{r_3}(pre^*_3(\Gamma^*))) \cap pre^*_1(pre_{r_2}(pre^*_{23}(\Gamma^*)))\ )) \quad . \end{aligned}$$

Proposition 3 allows us to compute $W(\mathbf{n})$ bottom-up, starting at the leaves of S, and computing $W(\mathbf{n})$ after having computed $W(\mathbf{n}')$ for every immediate successor of $\mathbf{n}$. By Proposition 1, the pre^* and pre operations preserve regularity, and are effectively computable. Since regular languages are closed under intersection, $W(\mathbf{n})$ is effectively computable.

Hence control state reachability of monotonic set-extended prefix rewriting systems is decidable.

Theorem 1. *Control state reachability of monotonic set-extended prefix rewriting systems is decidable.*

Finally, we also establish a singly exponential upper bound of the running time of the algorithm.

Proposition 4. *Let* R *be an MSP over a finite alphabet* Γ *and a set of control states* $(Q, \leq)$ *and let* c *be the length of the longest* $\leq$*-chain. Let* m *be the maximum over all* $p, q \in Q$, $p \neq q$, *of the number of rules of the form* $pv \longrightarrow qw$ *in* R. *Let* $T_0 \subseteq \Gamma^*$ *be a regular set of words represented by a nondeterministic automaton of size* a. *We can decide if there is a set* T *such that* $(p_0, T_0) \longrightarrow^*_R (p_G, T)$ *for a given control state* p_G *in deterministic time* $(|Q| + m + |\Gamma|)^{O(c)} \cdot a$.

4 Recursive Ping-Pong Protocols

In this section we define the class of recursive ping-pong protocols.

Let $\mathcal{K}$ be a set of *symmetric encryption keys*. A word $w \in \mathcal{K}^*$ naturally represents an encrypted message with the outer-most encryption on the left hand-side.

For example k_1k_2k represents the plain text message (key) k encrypted first by the key k_2, followed by the key k_1. In the usual notation k_1k_2k hence stands for $\{\{k\}_{k_2}\}_{k_1}$. The *analysis* of a set of messages $T \subseteq \mathcal{K}^*$ is the least set $\mathcal{A}(T)$ satisfying

$$\mathcal{A}(T) = T \cup \{w \mid kw \in \mathcal{A}(T),\ k \in \mathcal{K} \cap \mathcal{A}(T)\}. \tag{1}$$

The *synthesis* of a set of messages $T \subseteq \mathcal{K}^*$ is the least set $\mathcal{S}(T)$ satisfying

$$\mathcal{S}(T) = T \cup \{kw \mid w \in \mathcal{S}(T),\ k \in \mathcal{K} \cap \mathcal{S}(T)\}. \tag{2}$$

Lemma 3. *Let n be a natural number, $T \subseteq \mathcal{K}^*$ and let $Q_i \in \{\mathcal{A}, \mathcal{S}\}$ for all i, $1 \leq i \leq n$. It holds that $Q_1(Q_2(\dots(Q_n(T))\dots)) \subseteq \mathcal{S}(\mathcal{A}(T))$.*

Proof. This standard fact (see also [4, Prop. 2.1]) follows directly from the following straightforward laws: $\mathcal{S}(\mathcal{S}(T)) = \mathcal{S}(T)$; $\mathcal{A}(\mathcal{A}(T)) = \mathcal{A}(T)$; $\mathcal{A}(\mathcal{S}(T)) \subseteq \mathcal{S}(\mathcal{A}(T))$; and $T_1 \subseteq T_2$ implies $\mathcal{S}(T_1) \subseteq \mathcal{S}(T_2)$. □

The set of *compromised keys* $C(T) \subseteq \mathcal{K}$ for a given set $T \subseteq \mathcal{K}^*$ of messages is defined by $C(T) \stackrel{\text{def}}{=} \mathcal{K} \cap \mathcal{A}(T)$. A *recursive ping-pong protocol* is a finite set Δ of *process definitions* over a finite set *Const* of *process constants* such that for every $P \in \mathit{Const}$ the set Δ contains exactly one process definition of the form

$$P \stackrel{\text{def}}{=} \sum_{i \in I} [?v_i \rhd .!w_i \rhd].P_i$$

where I is a finite index set such that $P_i \in \mathit{Const}$ and $v_i, w_i \in \mathcal{K}^*$ for all $i \in I$. We shall denote the empty sum as *Nil*. The intuition is that for any $i \in I$ the process P can input a message of the form $v_i t \in \mathcal{K}^*$, output $w_i t$, and behave as P_i. The symbol '?' represents the input prefix, '!' the output prefix, and '$\rhd$' the rest (suffix) of the communicated message.

A *configuration* of a ping-pong protocol Δ is a pair (P, T) where $P \in \mathit{Const}$ and $T \subseteq \mathcal{K}^*$. The set T is also called a *pool*. The reduction semantics is defined by the following rule.

$$\frac{P \stackrel{\text{def}}{=} \sum_{i \in I} [?v_i \rhd .!w_i \rhd].P_i, \quad i \in I, \quad v_i t \in \mathcal{S}(\mathcal{A}(T))}{(P, T) \longrightarrow_\Delta (P_i, T \cup \{w_i t\})}$$

Definition 1. *Let (P_0, T_0) be a given* initial configuration *such that $T_0 \neq \emptyset$ is a regular set and let $P_G \in \mathit{Const}$. The* control state reachability problem *is to decide whether $(P_0, T_0) \longrightarrow^*_\Delta (P_G, T)$ for some T.*

Example 1. Let Δ be a protocol consisting of $P_0 \stackrel{\text{def}}{=} [?k_1k_2 \rhd .!k_2k_1 \rhd].P_1$, $P_1 \stackrel{\text{def}}{=} [?k_2k_1 \rhd .!k_*k_2 \rhd].P_2$, and $P_2 \stackrel{\text{def}}{=} \mathit{Nil}$. Let $T_0 = \{k_*, k_1k_2\}$ be the initial pool in which k_* is the only compromised key. Then, $(P_0, T_0) \longrightarrow_\Delta (P_1, T_1) \longrightarrow_\Delta (P_2, T_2)$ where $T_1 = T_0 \cup \{k_2k_1\}$, and $T_2 = T_1 \cup \{k_*k_2\}$. At control point P_2 (but not before) the attacker can learn the keys k_1 and k_2. Indeed, he can use the compromised key k_* to extract k_2 from the last message k_*k_2 exchanged in the protocol, and k_2 to extract k_1 from the message k_2k_1. Thus, we have that $C(T_2) = \{k_*, k_1, k_2\}$. Suppose that messages are always terminated by the symbol $\perp$. In order to test if the attacker has uncovered, e.g., the key k_1, we can add (using $+$) to each process definition the observer process defined as $[?k_1\perp\rhd.!k_1\perp\rhd].Error$. Reachability of the control state *Error* denotes a violation of secrecy for our protocol.

Remark 1. Since we allow nondeterminism in the definitions of process constants, the control state reachability problem for a parallel composition of recursive ping-pong processes can be reduced (using a standard product construction) to control state reachability for a single recursive process. For example assume that $Const = \{P_1, P_2, P_2'\}$ such that $P_1 \stackrel{\text{def}}{=} [?k_1 \rhd .!k_2\rhd].P_1$, $P_2 \stackrel{\text{def}}{=} [?k_1\rhd .!\rhd].P_2' + [?k_2\rhd .!\rhd].P_2$, and $P_2' \stackrel{\text{def}}{=} [?k_1k_2\rhd .!k_2k_1\rhd].P_2$.

The parallel composition $P_1 \parallel P_2$ as defined e.g. in [3] can be modelled by the following protocol with $Const = \{(P_1, P_2), (P_1, P_2')\}$, where

$$(P_1, P_2) \stackrel{\text{def}}{=} [?k_1\rhd .!k_2\rhd].(P_1, P_2) + [?k_1\rhd .!\rhd].(P_1, P_2') + [?k_2\rhd .!\rhd].(P_1, P_2)$$

$$(P_1, P_2') \stackrel{\text{def}}{=} [?k_1\rhd .!k_2\rhd].(P_1, P_2') + [?k_1k_2\rhd .!k_2k_1\rhd].(P_1, P_2) \quad .$$

Note that by applying the reduction above, there is a possible exponential state-space explosion (however, it is exponential only in the number of parallel agents; in many protocols this number is fixed and small). In what follows we measure our complexity results in terms of the flat (single process) system.

5 Translating Recursive Ping-Pong Protocols to MSP

In this section we provide a reduction from control state reachability for recursive ping-pong protocols to control state reachability for MSP.

There are two main problems: (i) How can the analysis and synthesis be captured by prefix rewriting rules? and (ii) How to ensure that the control state unit is monotonic even for arbitrary recursive ping-pong protocols?

We shall now provide answers to these problems. Intuitively, problem (i) can be solved by keeping track of the set of compromised keys. The set of compromised keys grows monotonically and can be stored as a part of the control state. The rules for analysis and synthesis can then use the knowledge of the currently compromised keys and once a new compromised key is discovered, the control state unit is updated accordingly. Problem (ii) is more challenging. We cannot simply store the current process constant in the control state as this would destroy monotonicity (we allow arbitrary recursive behaviour in the protocol). Instead, we observe that a recursive ping-pong protocol is essentially a directed graph where nodes are process constants and edges are labelled by actions of the form $\alpha = [?v \rhd .!w\rhd]$. Once a certain action was taken due to some message present in the pool then it is permanently enabled also any time in the future (messages added to the pool T are persistent). Assume that there is a cycle of length ℓ (counting the number of edges) in the graph such that all the actions $\alpha_1, \ldots, \alpha_\ell$ on this cycle were already taken in the past. Then it is irrelevant in exactly which process constant on the cycle we are as we can freely move along the cycle as many times as needed. This essentially means that we can replace such a cycle with $!(\alpha_1) \parallel \cdots \parallel !(\alpha_\ell)$ where ! is the operator of replication. This observation can be further generalized to strongly connected components in the graph.

Let Δ be a recursive ping-pong protocol with a set of process constants *Const* and encryption keys $\mathcal{K}$. We shall formally demonstrate the reduction mentioned above. First, we introduce some notation. Let $\mathcal{T} \stackrel{\text{def}}{=} \{(P, \alpha_i, P_i) \mid P \in Const,\ P \stackrel{\text{def}}{=} \sum_{i \in I} \alpha_i.P_i,\ i \in I\}$ be a set of directed edges between process constants labelled by the corresponding actions. Let $E \subseteq \mathcal{T}$. We write $P \Longrightarrow_E P'$ whenever there is some α such that $(P, \alpha, P') \in E$. Assume that $P \in Const$ and $E \subseteq \mathcal{T}$. We define a strongly connected component in E represented by a process constant P as $\mathcal{S}cc(P, E) \stackrel{\text{def}}{=} \{P' \in Const \mid P \Longrightarrow_E^* P' \ \wedge\ P' \Longrightarrow_E^* P\}$.

Let us now define an MSP R. The alphabet is $\Gamma \stackrel{\text{def}}{=} \mathcal{K} \cup \{\bot\}$ where $\bot$ is a fresh symbol representing the end of messages. The control states of R are of the form $\langle S, E, C\rangle$ where

- $S \subseteq Const$ is the current strongly connected component,
- $E \subseteq \mathcal{T}$ is the set of already executed edges, and
- $C \subseteq \mathcal{K}$ is the set of compromised keys.

There are four types of rules in R called (analz), (synth), (learn) and (comm). The first three rules represent intruder's capabilities and the fourth rule models the communication with the environment.

(analz)	$\langle S, E, C\rangle k \longrightarrow \langle S, E, C\rangle \epsilon$	for all $k \in C$
(synth)	$\langle S, E, C\rangle \epsilon \longrightarrow \langle S, E, C\rangle k$	for all $k \in C$
(learn)	$\langle S, E, C\rangle k\bot \longrightarrow \langle S, E, C \cup \{k\}\rangle k\bot$	for all $k \in \mathcal{K}$
(comm)	$\langle S, E, C\rangle v \longrightarrow \langle \mathcal{S}cc(P', E'), E', C\rangle w$	where $E' = E \cup \{(P, \alpha, P')\}$ whenever there exists $P \in S$ and $(P, \alpha, P') \in \mathcal{T}$ such that $\alpha = [?v\rhd\ .!w\rhd]$

It is easy to define an ordering on states such that R is monotonic. The second and third component in the control states are non-decreasing w.r.t. $\subseteq$ and $\mathcal{T}$ and $\mathcal{K}$ are finite sets. For a fixed second coordinate E the strongly connected components (i.e. the values that the first coordinate S in the control state can take) form a directed acyclic graph. Let $T \subseteq \mathcal{K}^*$. By $T^\bot$ we denote the set $\{w\bot \mid w \in T\}$, i.e., the end symbol $\bot$ is appended to every message from T.

Lemma 4. *Let $P_0, P \in Const$ and $T_0 \subseteq \mathcal{K}^*$. If $(P_0, T_0) \longrightarrow_\Delta^* (P, T)$ for some T then $(\langle \{P_0\}, \emptyset, \emptyset\rangle, T_0^\bot) \longrightarrow_R^* (\langle S, E, C\rangle, T'^\bot)$ for some S, E, C and T' such that $P \in S$ and $T^\bot \subseteq T'^\bot$.*

We will now proceed to prove the other implication. In order to do that we will need the following straightforward proposition which essentially says that

(i) messages are persistent and once a certain step from a process constant P in the protocol was possible in the past then it is permanently enabled also in any future configuration in the control location P, and (ii) that the set C in the control state is always a subset of the compromised keys.

Proposition 5. *If* $(\langle\{P_0\},\emptyset,\emptyset\rangle, T_0^\perp) \longrightarrow_R^* (\langle S, E, C\rangle, T^\perp)$ *for some* S, E, C *and* T *then (i) for any* $(P,\alpha,P') \in E$ *there is some* T' *such that* $(P,T) \longrightarrow_\Delta (P',T')$ *by using the transition* (P,α,P')*, and (ii)* $C \subseteq C(T)$.

Lemma 5. *Let* $P_0 \in \mathit{Const}$ *and* $T_0 \subseteq \mathcal{K}^*$. *If we have* $(\langle\{P_0\},\emptyset,\emptyset\rangle, T_0^\perp) \longrightarrow_R^* (\langle S, E, C\rangle, T^\perp)$ *for some* S, E, C *and* T *then for all* $P \in S$ *also* $(P_0, T_0) \longrightarrow_\Delta^* (P, T')$ *such that* $T \subseteq \mathcal{S}(\mathcal{A}(T'))$.

The next theorem states the correctness of our reduction and follows directly from Lemma 4 and Lemma 5.

Theorem 2. *Let* $P_0, P \in \mathit{Const}$ *and* $T_0 \subseteq \mathcal{K}^*$. *It holds that* $(P_0, T_0) \longrightarrow_\Delta^* (P, T)$ *for some* T *if and only if* $(\langle\{P_0\},\emptyset,\emptyset\rangle, T_0^\perp) \longrightarrow_R^* (\langle S, E, C\rangle, T'^\perp)$ *for some* S, E, C *and* T' *such that* $P \in S$.

Hence control state reachability for recursive ping-pong protocols is reducible to control state reachability for monotonic set-extended prefix rewriting systems, which is decidable by Theorem 1. We also obtain the following complexity upper bound.

Corollary 1. *Control state reachability for recursive ping-pong protocols is decidable in deterministic time* $2^{O(n^4)} \cdot a$ *where* n *is the size of the protocol written as a string and* a *is the size of a nondeterministic automaton representing the pool* T_0.

Finally, we show that control state reachability for recursive ping-pong protocols is at least NP-hard.

Theorem 3. *Control state reachability of recursive ping-pong protocols is NP-hard.*

Proof. By reduction from the satisfiability problem of boolean formulae in CNF. Let $C = C_1 \wedge C_2 \wedge \ldots \wedge C_k$ be a formula over boolean variables $x_1, \ldots, x_n$ such that for all i, $1 \leq i \leq k$, C_i is a disjunction of literals. We shall construct a ping-pong protocol Δ where $\mathit{Const} \stackrel{\text{def}}{=} \{X_1, \ldots, X_{n+1}, Y_1, \ldots, Y_{k+1}\}$ and $\mathcal{K} = \{C_1, \ldots, C_k, \perp\}$. Let for all i, $1 \leq i \leq n$, t_i be the sequence of keys $C_{i_1} C_{i_2} \cdots C_{i_\ell}$ such that $1 \leq i_1 < i_2 < \cdots < i_\ell \leq k$ and $C_{i_1}, C_{i_2}, \ldots, C_{i_\ell}$ are all the clauses where x_i occurs positively, and let f_i be the sequence of keys $C_{i_1} C_{i_2} \cdots C_{i_\ell}$ such that $1 \leq i_1 < i_2 < \cdots < i_\ell \leq k$ and $C_{i_1}, C_{i_2}, \ldots, C_{i_\ell}$ are all the clauses where x_i occurs negatively. The set Δ of process definitions is given as follows.

$$X_i \stackrel{\text{def}}{=} [?\perp\rhd .!t_i\perp\rhd].X_{i+1} + [?\perp\rhd .!f_i\perp\rhd].X_{i+1} \qquad \text{for all } i,\ 1 \leq i \leq n$$
$$X_{n+1} \stackrel{\text{def}}{=} [?\perp\rhd .!\perp\rhd].Y_1$$
$$Y_i \stackrel{\text{def}}{=} [?C_i\rhd .!\rhd].Y_{i+1} + \sum_{1\leq j<i} [?C_j\rhd .!\rhd].Y_i \qquad \text{for all } i,\ 1 \leq i \leq k$$

It is now easy to observe that the given formula C is satisfiable if and only if $(X_1, \{\bot\}) \longrightarrow^* (Y_{k+1}, T)$ for some T. The computation from $(X_1, \{\bot\})$ starts by going through the sequence of control constants $X_1, \ldots, X_{n+1}$ where for every i, $1 \le i \le n$, there is a choice, whether $t_i\bot$ or $f_i\bot$ (but not both) is added to the pool of messages. This corresponds to selecting a truth assignment. Then the control constant is changed from X_{n+1} to Y_1 without modifying the pool and the second (verification) phase starts. The move from Y_i to Y_{i+1} is possible only if the key C_i is present somewhere in the pool (which means that the corresponding clause is satisfied). The second summand in the definition of Y_i enables to remove duplicate clauses from the messages in order to access C_i. The control constant is not changed if the second summand of Y_i is used. Observe that the operations of analysis and synthesis cannot add any of the keys $C_1, \ldots, C_k$ to the pool, unless the protocol does it itself. Hence we can reach the control constant Y_{k+1} if and only if it was possible to satisfy all the clauses by the given truth assignment generated during the first phase. □

6 MSP and Concurrent Constraint Programming

We shall now outline some further applicability of our model of monotonic set-extended prefix rewriting. The MSP model shares some similarities with the ccp (concurrent constraint programming) language [19]. The ccp language is based on the notion of a monotonic store which is used by a collection of agents as a common blackboard to communicate by means of two primitives: *ask* to query the store without removing information, and *tell* to add information to the store.

This feature of the ccp semantics is similar in spirit to the way we defined the semantics of MSP. In an MSP configuration (p, T) the component T can be viewed as the current store. Since prefix rules never remove information from T, we can view them as a special case of the *ask* and *tell* operations. To make the connection between ccp and MSP more informal, we define next a fragment of ccp whose semantics can be directly encoded in MSP.

For this purpose, given a finite alphabet A, we will consider an instance of the ccp framework in which the constraint store is a set of strings $T \subseteq A^*$. Furthermore, we consider only one type of constraint formula of the form $v \cdot x$ where v is a string and x is a variable. If T is a set of strings (the current store), then $T \models v \cdot x$ via the binding $x \rightsquigarrow w$ if $vw \in T$.

Concerning the syntax of our ccp instance, we will restrict ourselves to processes defined as follows. A process declaration is defined as $p \leftarrow A$ where p is a process constant taken from a finite set P, and A is an agent. Agents (and actions) are defined by the following grammar.

$$\begin{array}{ll} A & ::= \mathit{stop} \;\mid\; \Sigma_{i=1}^{k}\, \mathit{Act}_i \\ \mathit{Act} & ::= \mathit{ask}(v \cdot x) \rightarrow p \;\mid\; \mathit{ask}(v \cdot x) \rightarrow \mathit{tell}(w \cdot x) \rightarrow p \end{array}$$

Given a finite set of declarations $\mathcal{D} = \{D_1, \ldots, D_n\}$, a process P is defined as the (bounded) parallel compositions of ℓ agents, i.e., $P = A_1 \mid\mid \ldots \mid\mid A_\ell$. We assume that $\mid\mid$ is associative and commutative. The operational semantics of a process P is defined in accordance with the semantics of ccp. Configurations are pairs $\langle P, T\rangle$ where P is a process and T is a store. The transition relation is defined as follows.

1. $\langle P_1 || P_2, T\rangle \rightarrow \langle P_1' || P_2, T'\rangle$ *if* $\langle P_1, T\rangle \rightarrow \langle P_1', T'\rangle$
2. $\langle p, T\rangle \rightarrow \langle A, T\rangle$ *if* $p \leftarrow A \in \mathcal{D}$
3. $\langle \Sigma_{i=1}^{k} Act_i, T\rangle \rightarrow \langle p, T\rangle$ *if* $Act_i = ask(v \cdot x) \rightarrow p$ *and* $vz \in T$ *for* $1 \leq i \leq k$
4. $\langle \Sigma_{i=1}^{k} Act_i, T\rangle \rightarrow \langle p, T \cup \{wz\}\rangle$ *if* $Act_i = ask(v \cdot x) \rightarrow tell(w \cdot x) \rightarrow p$ *and* $vz \in T$ *for* $1 \leq i \leq k$

Remark 2. The seemingly nonstandard action $ask(v \cdot x) \rightarrow tell(w \cdot x) \rightarrow p$ can be in full ccp encoded as $ask(v \cdot x) \rightarrow \exists n.(tell(w \cdot x\ \&\ tok(n))\ ||\ ask(tok(n)) \rightarrow p)$ where $tok(x)$ is a new type of constraint with one argument x.

Following the reduction schemes of the recursive definition of ping-pong processes, we know that we can extract a set of partially ordered locations from the parallel control flow graph of n recursive processes (by using the idea of strongly connected components). Under this assumption, we can focus our attention on the way we can model ccp agents and actions. Actions can be naturally mapped into prefix rules:

- The definition $a \leftarrow ask(v \cdot x) \rightarrow b$ for the i-th thread is mapped to a rule like $pv \rightarrow qv$ in which p and q are related by the change of the local state of the i-th thread from a to b.
- The definition $a \leftarrow ask(v \cdot x) \rightarrow tell(w \cdot x) \rightarrow b$ for the i-th thread is mapped to a rule like $pv \rightarrow qw$ in which p and q are related by the change of the local state of the i-th thread from a to b.

Although quite limited with respect to the original ccp model (e.g. it is not possible to spawn new processes), this instance is still nontrivial since the constraint store can grow unboundedly during the execution of a process.

The decidability of the control reachability problem for this instance of the ccp framework follows then from our result for MSP. Further extensions of the restricted ccp formalism are left for future work.

7 Conclusion

We proved that the control state reachability problem for recursive ping-pong protocols with Dolev-Yao attacker is decidable in deterministic exponential time. This result may seem surprising when one observes that recursive ping-pong protocols without any attacker are Turing powerful [12,13]. However, a similar phenomenon occurs in FIFO-channel systems (automata whose transitions may add or retrieve items from channels, modelled as unbounded queues): if the channels are perfect, then the model is Turing powerful, but if one assumes that the channels are lossy, i.e., that the queues can spontaneously lose messages, then several important verification problems become decidable [7,2].

We have used our results to prove (in the full version of the paper, available as a BRICS technical report) the authenticity of Woo and Lam's protocol; to find a flaw in Otway and Rees' key distribution protocol and prove secrecy of a corrected version for arbitrarily many sessions; and to prove secrecy of Bull and Otway's recursive authentication protocol. To the best of our knowledge, no other method in the literature can deal simultaneously with these three problems in a fully automatic way. The approach of Rusinowitch and Turuani [18] can be used to prove authenticity of Woo and Lam's protocol, and Küsters has used regular transducers to automatically verify Bull and Otway's protocol [15]. However, these techniques can only deal with a bounded number of protocol sessions. In order to find the flaw in Otway and Rees' protocol they have to guess the right number of sessions, and they cannot directly prove secrecy of the corrected version. The replicative calculus of Amadio, Lugiez and Vanackère [4] can be used to model protocols with an unbounded number of sessions. However, the model over-approximates the semantics, i.e., there are executions of the model that do not correspond to executions of the protocol. Due to this over-approximation the secrecy or authenticity analysis can report false attacks.

Since our technique does not over-approximate the semantics, it is strictly more powerful than that of [4], at the price of a higher complexity (the algorithm of [4] runs in polynomial time), and it is incomparable with the techniques of [18,15]. On the one hand, it provides an exact analysis for an arbitrary number of sessions; on the other hand, it is restricted to prefix rewriting, which can only deal with very restricted forms of pairing. Our model also allows only a bounded number of nonces. The distinguishing feature of our technique seems to be the possibility to model open-ended protocols with messages of unbounded length, in combination with an unrestricted (cyclic) communication structure.

Our work also opens several venues for further research. MSPs are a rather natural computational model, which may have further applications, in particular in the area of coordination-based languages. To demonstrate this, we have presented an encoding of a fragment of the ccp language into MSP.

Acknowledgments. The second and the third author acknowledge a support from the Alexander von Humboldt Foundation.

References

1. M. Abadi and A.D. Gordon. A bisimulation method for cryptographic protocols. *Nordic Journal of Computing*, 5(4):267–303, 1998.
2. P.A. Abdulla and B. Jonsson. Verifying programs with unreliable channels. *Information and Computation*, 127(2):91–101, 1996.
3. R.M. Amadio and W. Charatonik. On name generation and set-based analysis in the Dolev-Yao model. In *Proceedings of the 13th International Conference on Concurrency Theory (CONCUR'02)*, volume 2421 of *LNCS*, pages 499–514. Springer-Verlag, 2002.
4. R.M. Amadio, D. Lugiez, and V. Vanackère. On the symbolic reduction of processes with cryptographic functions. *Theoretical Computer Science*, 290(1):695–740, October 2002.

5. A. Bouajjani, J. Esparza, and O. Maler. Reachability analysis of pushdown automata: Application to model-checking. In *Proceedings of the 8th International Conference on Concurrency Theory (CONCUR'97)*, volume 1243 of *LNCS*, pages 135–150. Springer-Verlag, 1997.
6. J.R. Büchi. Regular canonical systems. *Arch. Math. Logik u. Grundlagenforschung*, 6:91–111, 1964.
7. G. Cécé, A. Finkel, and S. Purushothaman Iyer. Unreliable channels are easier to verify than perfect channels. *Information and Computation*, 124(1):20–31, 1996.
8. H. Comon, V. Cortier, and J. Mitchell. Tree automata with one memory, set constraints, and ping-pong protocols. In *Proceedings of the 28th International Colloquium on Automata, Languages and Programming (ICALP'01)*, volume 2076 of *LNCS*, pages 682–693. Springer-Verlag, 2001.
9. D. Dolev, S. Even, and R.M. Karp. On the security of ping-pong protocols. *Information and Control*, 55(1–3):57–68, 1982.
10. D. Dolev and A.C. Yao. On the security of public key protocols. *Transactions on Information Theory*, IT-29(2):198–208, 1983.
11. J. Esparza, D. Hansel, P. Rossmanith, and S. Schwoon. Efficient algorithms for model checking pushdown systems. In *Proceedings of the 12th International Conference on Computer Aided Verification (CAV'00)*, volume 1855 of *LNCS*, pages 232–247. Springer-Verlag, 2000.
12. H. Hüttel and J. Srba. Recursive ping-pong protocols. In *Proceedings of the 4th International Workshop on Issues in the Theory of Security (WITS'04)*, pages 129–140, 2004.
13. H. Hüttel and J. Srba. Recursion vs. replication in simple cryptographic protocols. In *Proceedings of the 31st Annual Conference on Current Trends in Theory and Practice of Informatics (SOFSEM'05)*, volume 3381 of *LNCS*, pages 175–184. Springer-Verlag, 2005.
14. O. Kupferman and M. Vardi. Weak alternating automata are not that weak. *ACM Transactions on Computational Logic*, 2(3):408–429, 2001.
15. R. Küsters. On the decidability of cryptographic protocols with open-ended data structures. In *Proceedings of the 13th International Conference on Concurrency Theory (CONCUR'02)*, volume 2421 of *LNCS*, pages 515–530. Springer-Verlag, 2002.
16. M. Křetínský, V. Řehák, and J. Strejček. Extended process rewrite systems: Expressiveness and reachability. In *Proceedings of the 15th International Conference on Concurrency Theory (CONCUR'04)*, volume 3170 of *LNCS*, pages 355–370. Springer-Verlag, 2004.
17. D.E. Muller, A. Saoudi, and P.E. Schupp. Weak alternating automata give a simple explanation of why most temporal and dynamic logics are decidable in exponential time. In *Proceedings of the 3rd Annual IEEE Symposium on Logic in Computer Science (LICS'88)*, pages 422–427. IEEE Computer Society Press, 1988.
18. M. Rusinowitch and M. Turuani. Protocol insecurity with a finite number of sessions and composed keys is NP-complete. *TCS: Theoretical Computer Science*, 299, 2003.
19. V.A. Saraswat. *Concurrent Constraint Programming*. The MIT Press, Cambridge, Massachusetts, 1993.

Analyzing Security Protocols in Hierarchical Networks

Ye Zhang and Hanne Riis Nielson

Informatics and Mathematical Modelling, Technical University of Denmark
Richard Petersens Plads bldg 321, DK-2800 Kongens Lyngby, Denmark
{yez,riis}@imm.dtu.dk

Abstract. Validating security protocols is a well-known hard problem even in a simple setting of a single global network. But a real network often consists of, besides the public-accessed part, several sub-networks and thereby forms a hierarchical structure. In this paper we first present a process calculus capturing the characteristics of hierarchical networks and describe the behavior of protocols on such networks. We then develop a static analysis to automate the validation. Finally we demonstrate how the technique can benefit the protocol development and the design of network systems by presenting a series of experiments we have conducted.

1 Introduction

With the fast development of the communication technology, thousands of intranets of companies, colleges, etc. are connected via the Internet. The network structure may even change dynamically as exemplified when relocating a laptop from one place to another. Consider the example on the left of Figure 1 where gateways are inserted between local networks so that the locally exchanged messages are not available outside. A tree that represents the network structure is presented on the right of the figure; here the internal nodes denote the networks and the leaves represent the agents. The network hierarchy, therefore, requires that all messages sent between the server and the laptop must go through the office network.

The fact that the communication varies from place to place increases the complexity of protocol analysis. Also such networks present us with a new challenge of defining the attacker capabilities since the classical Dolev-Yao model [9] was originally proposed by assuming the existence of a single global network, the Internet. In this paper we shall present our approach to deal with these issues.

Overview of the Paper. In Section 2 we present a variant of the Ambient calculus [7,4,5] to model hierarchical networks as well as security protocols; in order to formalize authentication properties we syntactically add annotations for declaring authentication intentions of the protocol. In Section 3 we develop a control flow analysis [15,18] for tracking the interested property. Regarding the communication environment considered in this paper, we declare the attacker capability

S. Graf and W. Zhang (Eds.): ATVA 2006, LNCS 4218, pp. 430–445, 2006.

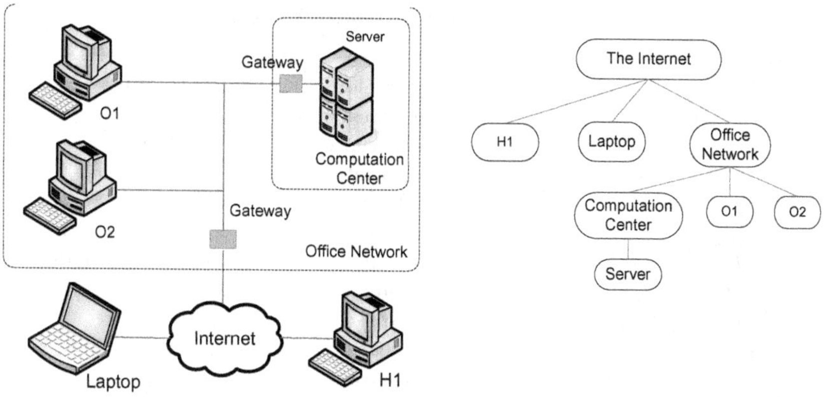

Fig. 1. Hierarchical network: an example

based on the Dolev-Yao conditions in Section 4. Our analysis is fully automatic and always terminating; in Section 5 we sketch the implementation and show its running-time is polynomial in the size of ambient processes. Section 6 reports our experimental results on a series of virtual networks and protocols. Finally we conclude with a brief assessment of our approach and a comparison with related work in Section 7.

2 ABoxed Ambients

We base ourselves on Boxed Ambients [4] and customize it in several ways. First we remove nil capability ϵ and concatenation $M_1.M_2$ from Boxed Ambients. Then we extend the calculus with annotations for specifying the authentication intentions of protocols explicitly. Finally our calculus deviates from all other ambient calculi, e.g. Mobile Ambients [7] and Discretionary Ambients [18], in having attacker processes that are used to declare the locations accessible to attackers.

The syntax of processes P, communication directions η, and capabilities M is given by Table 1. While most constructs are standard, the further explanation goes to the restriction and input primitives. The two restriction constructs have same effect on all processes except for attacker processes: suppose an attacker is inside P, restriction $(v\ n)P$ allows the value n to be part of initial knowledge of the attacker while secret restriction $(vk\ n)P$ keeps the value unknown to the attacker. For the simplicity of the presentation, we assume that a subset $\mathbf{C} \subseteq \mathbf{Name}$ of names is kept for constants and demand that the name introduced by two restriction constructs are constants. For input constructs we, inspired by Lysa [2], use a simple form of patterns, $(M'_1, \cdots, M'_j; x_{j+1}, \cdots, x_k)^\eta$, to be matched against a k-tuple of values $(M_1, \cdots, M_k)$. The idea is that the matching succeeds if the first $1 \le i \le j$ values M'_i pairwise correspond to the values M_i; if so, the remaining $k-j$ values are bound to the variables $x_{j+1}, \cdots, x_k$ respectively. For the sake of simplicity, we shall enforce that $x_i \in \mathbf{V}$ where $\mathbf{V} = \mathbf{Name} \setminus \mathbf{C}$.

Table 1. Syntax of ABoxed Ambients

$P ::= (v\ n)P$	restriction	$\eta ::= n$ child	
$\mid\ (vk\ n)P$	secretrestriction	$\mid\ \uparrow$ parent	
$\mid\ 0$	inactiveprocess	$\mid\ \circ$ local	
$\mid\ P_1 \mid P_2$	composition		
$\mid\ !P$	replication	$M ::=$ in n	enter n
$\mid\ n[P]$	ambient	$\mid$ out n	exit n
$\mid\ M.P$	movement	$\mid\ n$	name
$\mid\ \langle M_1, \cdots, M_k \rangle^\eta$	output		
$\mid\ (M_1, \cdots, M_j; x_{j+1}, \cdots, x_k)^\eta.P$	input		
$\mid\ \bullet$	attacker		

We assume perfect cryptography in this paper and make use of two processes, local-output and input-from-child, to model encryption and decryption respectively. The intuition is that in order to read the mailbox of a child a parent must have known his child's name (encryption key). To check protocol intentions, we syntactically annotate the pair by:

$$\langle M_1, \cdots, M_k \rangle^\circ_\ell [\text{dest } \mathcal{L}]$$
$$(M_1', \cdots, M_j'; x_{j+1}, \cdots, x_k)^n_\ell [\text{orig } \mathcal{L}]$$

where label ℓ (called crypt-point) is from some enumerable set $\mathcal{D}$ disjoint from **Name** and is added to program points where encryption and decryption happen. The assertion [dest $\mathcal{L}$] specifies a set of crypt-points $\mathcal{L} \subseteq \mathcal{D}$ where the message is intended to be decrypted. Similarly [orig $\mathcal{L}$] lists all desired crypt-points at which M is allowed to have been encrypted. A more detailed discussion on how to encode encryption and decryption with ambient calculus can be found in [19].

To simplify the analysis definition in Section 3, we shall suppose that each name has a *canonical name* $\lfloor n \rfloor \in$ **Name** and require the alpha-renaming preserves the canonical name; therefore only the canonical version of a name will be recorded in the analysis. Similarly we write $\lfloor M \rfloor$ for the *canonical capability* of M where the name or variable is replaced with its canonical version. To formulate protocols and networks more precisely and get better analysis results, we classify ambients into two classes: site ambients which formalize local networks and computers, and packet ambients which describe data objects moving between sites. The programs of interest are then ambients in the form of $n_\star[P_\star]$ where $n_\star \notin \text{fn}(P_\star)$ and the function $\text{fn}(P_\star)$ collects the free names of $P_\star$. Formally $P_\star$ satisfies the conjunction of the following conditions:

- any free name of $P_\star$ is from $\mathbf{C}$; formally $\lfloor \text{fn}(P_\star) \rfloor \subseteq \mathbf{C}$;
- $P_\star$ is well-formed with respect to $\mathbf{C}$; formally $\mathbf{C} \vdash wf_s(P_\star)$.

Here the canonicity operation $\lfloor \cdot \rfloor$ is extended in a pointwise manner; the well-formedness basically demands: (1) sites are not movable and thereby the network structure is static; (2) packets are simple data objects moving between sites, and

Table 2. Structural congruence: $P \equiv Q$ is the least congruence

Alpha – renaming :	Replication :
$P \equiv Q$ if P are disciplined α –equivalent to Q	$!P \equiv P\|!P$ $!0 \equiv 0$
Reordering of paralle processes :	Scope rules for name bindings :
$P\|Q \equiv Q\|P$ $(P\|Q)\|R \equiv P\|(Q\|R)$ $P\|0 \equiv P$	$(v\,n)0 \equiv 0$ $(v\,n)(v\,n')P \equiv (v\,n')(v\,n)P$ if $n \neq n'$ $(v\,n)(P\|Q) \equiv P\|(v\,n)Q$ if $n \notin \text{fn}(P)$ $(v\,n)(n[P]) \equiv n[(v\,n)P]$ if$n \notin \text{fn}(n)$ $(v\,n)P \equiv (v\,\text{m})(P\{n/m\})$ if $\text{m} \notin \text{fn}(P)$

(3) attacker processes are as expressive as sites. A formal definition of the well-formedness can be found in [19] for your reference.

Semantics. The semantics follows the approach of [7,4] and is specified by the structural congruence relation $P \equiv Q$ in Table 2 and the reduction relation $P \rightarrow_{\mathcal{R}} Q$ in Table 3; there are two variants of reduction semantics: (1) the standard semantics ($\rightarrow$) in which $\mathcal{R}$ is universally true and thus can be ignored; (2) the *reference monitor semantics* ($\rightarrow_{\mathsf{RM}}$) that deals with annotations by taking $\mathsf{RM}(\ell, \mathcal{L}', \ell', \mathcal{L}) = (\ell \in \mathcal{L}' \wedge \ell' \in \mathcal{L})$; thus decryptions may happen only at crypt-points designated when the corresponding encryptions were made, otherwise the execution is aborted. As stated in Table 2, the structural congruence relation allows rearranging the syntactic appearance of processes; especially we enforce that α – *renaming* preserves canonicity. The movement interactions give rise to re-structuring ambients while the communication interactions do not change their hierarchy but modify the process to reflect the new binding of names. Here we adopt the standard notion $P[M/x]$ for substitution. If reference monitor semantics is concerned, the condition $\mathsf{RM}(\ell, \mathcal{L}', \ell', \mathcal{L})$ is checked by some rules. While the syntax requires us to annotate every process of local-output and input-from-child, they may be used for non-cryptographic purposes. If that is the case, we reserve a special label ϵ for those processes and adopt the set $\mathcal{D}$ to ensure annotations are trivial ones, formally

$$\langle M_1, \cdots, M_k \rangle_{\epsilon}^{\circ}[\text{dest } \mathcal{D}]$$
$$(M_1', \cdots, M_j'; x_{j+1}, \cdots, x_k)_{\epsilon}^{n}[\text{orig } \mathcal{D}].P$$

Example 1. We consider the version of Wide Mouthed Frog (WMF) [6] below.

$$\begin{array}{lll} 1. & A \rightarrow S: & A,\ [B, K]_{K_A} \\ 2. & S \rightarrow B: & [A, K]_{K_B} \\ 3. & A \rightarrow B: & [M]_K \end{array}$$

It establishes a secret session key K between the initiator A and the responder B, who share master keys K_A and K_B with a trusted server S respectively. Its

Table 3. Transition relation: $P \rightarrow Q$

Movement of ambients

(In) $m\,[\text{in}\ n.\ P \mid Q] \mid n\,[R] \rightarrow_{\mathcal{R}} n\,[m\,[P \mid Q] \mid R]$

(Out) $n\,[m\,[\text{out}\ n.\ P \mid Q] \mid R] \rightarrow_{\mathcal{R}} m\,[P|Q] \mid n\,[R]$

Execution in context :

$$\frac{P \rightarrow_{\mathcal{R}} Q}{(\upsilon\ n)P \rightarrow_{\mathcal{R}} (\upsilon\ n)Q} \qquad \frac{P \rightarrow_{\mathcal{R}} Q}{(\upsilon k\ n)P \rightarrow_{\mathcal{R}} (\upsilon k\ n)Q} \qquad \frac{P \equiv P' \wedge P' \rightarrow_{\mathcal{R}} Q' \wedge Q' \equiv Q}{P \rightarrow_{\mathcal{R}} Q}$$

$$\frac{P \rightarrow_{\mathcal{R}} Q}{P \mid R \rightarrow_{\mathcal{R}} Q \mid R} \qquad \frac{P \rightarrow_{\mathcal{R}} Q}{n\,[P] \rightarrow_{\mathcal{R}} n\,[Q]}$$

Communication :

(Com 1) $$\frac{\wedge_{i=1}^{j} M_i = M_i' \ \wedge \mathcal{R}(\ell, \{\epsilon\}, \epsilon, \mathcal{L})}{\langle M_1, \cdots, M_k \rangle_{\ell}^{\circ}[\text{dest}\ \mathcal{L}] \mid (M_1', \cdots, M_j'; x_{j+1}, \cdots, x_k)^{\circ}.P \rightarrow_{\mathcal{R}} P\{M_{j+1}/x_{j+1}\} \cdots \{M_k/x_k\}}$$

(Com 2) $$\frac{\wedge_{i=1}^{j} M_i = M_i'}{\langle M_1, \cdots, M_k \rangle^{n} \mid n[(M_1', \cdots, M_j'; x_{j+1}, \cdots, x_k)^{\circ}.P|Q] \rightarrow_{\mathcal{R}} n[P\{M_{j+1}/x_{j+1}\} \cdots \{M_k/x_k\}|\ Q]}$$

(Com 3) $$\frac{\wedge_{i=1}^{j} M_i = M_i' \wedge \mathcal{R}(\ell, \{\epsilon\}, \epsilon, \mathcal{L})}{\langle M_1, \cdots, M_k \rangle_{\ell}^{\circ}[\text{dest}\ \mathcal{L}] \mid n[(M_1', \cdots, M_j'; x_{j+1}, \cdots, x_k)^{\uparrow}.P|Q] \rightarrow_{\mathcal{R}} n[P\{M_{j+1}/x_{j+1}\} \cdots \{M_k/x_k\}|\ Q]}$$

(Com 4) $$\frac{\wedge_{i=1}^{j} M_i = M_i'}{(M_1', \cdots, M_j'; x_{j+1}, \cdots, x_k)^{\circ}.P \mid n[\langle M_1, \cdots, M_k \rangle^{\uparrow}|R] \rightarrow_{\mathcal{R}} P\{M_{j+1}/x_{j+1}\} \cdots \{M_k/x_k\} \mid n[R]}$$

(Com 5) $$\frac{\wedge_{i=1}^{j} M_i = M_i' \wedge \mathcal{R}(\ell, \mathcal{L}', \ell', \mathcal{L})}{(M_1', \cdots, M_j'; x_{j+1}, \cdots, x_k)_{\ell'}^{n}[\text{orig}\ \mathcal{L}'].P \mid n[\langle M_1, \cdots, M_k \rangle_{\ell}^{\circ}[\text{dest}\ \mathcal{L}]|R] \rightarrow_{\mathcal{R}} P\{M_{j+1}/x_{j+1}\} \cdots \{M_k/x_k\} \mid n[R]}$$

ABoxed Ambients specification is then given by:

$$\begin{array}{l}
(\upsilon\ K_A)(\upsilon\ K_B) \\
(\ A[(\upsilon\ K)\ K_A[\text{out}\ A.\ \text{in}\ S.\ (\langle A \rangle^{\uparrow} | \langle B,\ K \rangle_{A_1}^{\circ}[\text{dest S}_1])] \mid \\
\qquad\qquad\qquad (\upsilon\ M)\ K[\text{out}\ A.\ \text{in} B.\ \langle M \rangle_{A_2}^{\circ}[\text{dest B}_2]] \\
\mid \\
\ S[(A;)^{\circ}.(B;\ y_K)_{S_1}^{K_A}[\text{orig A}_1]. \\
\qquad\qquad K_B[\text{out}\ S.\ \text{in}\ B.\langle A,\ y_K \rangle_{S_2}^{\circ}[\text{dest B}_1]] \\
\mid \\
\ B[(A;\ z_K)_{B_1}^{K_B}[\text{orig S}_2].(;z)_{B_2}^{z_K}[\text{orig A}_2]])
\end{array}$$

At first A generates a new session key K by the restriction $(v\ K)$ and then sends S a packet named by the key K_A. After the packet K_A moves into S, the plain message A is delivered to server's mailbox while the encrypted values (B, K) can be read only by the enclosing ambient knowing the master key K_A. On the other side, the server acquires and checks initiator's name A by local-input and then decrypts the encrypted part of the message with input-from-child where the reference monitor checks the authentication intentions. If the decryption succeeds, the server continues checking whether B is the responder's name; if that is the case, it stores the session key K in the placeholder y_K. The left part of the process is encoded in the similar way as illustrated above and the explanation, therefore, is straightforward. □

3 Control Flow Analysis

The aim of our analysis is to safely estimate when RM can cease the computation of a process. To achieve this goal, we shall develop an analysis for extracting the following information:

- γ: $\mathbf{C} \to \mathcal{P}(\mathbf{C} \cup \lfloor M \rfloor)$ that for every ambient name approximates which ambients and capabilities may be contained.
- κ: $\mathbf{C} \to \mathcal{P}((\mathbf{C} \cup \lfloor M \rfloor)^*)$ that for every ambient name records the tuples of messages that may show up in an ambient's mailbox.
- ρ: $\mathbf{V} \to \mathcal{P}(\mathbf{C} \cup \lfloor M \rfloor)$ that for every variable records the tuples of possible values including names and capabilities.
- φ: $\mathcal{P}(\mathcal{D} \times \mathcal{D})$ that describes the possible violation of authenticity.

The judgement of the analysis takes the form

$$(\gamma,\kappa,\rho) \models^{\mu} P : \varphi$$

and says that when the subprocess P (of $P_\star$) is enclosed within an ambient μ then as P evolves γ will reflect the contents of the ambients , κ will contain the messages of ambients' mail boxes, ρ will approximate all the bindings of names, and φ (of the form (ℓ, ℓ')) indicates something encrypted at ℓ was unexpectedly decrypted at ℓ'. The analysis is specified in Table 4 for all non-communication primitives and in Table 5 for communication related ones.

In Table 4 the rules for *restriction, replication* and *parallel composition* ensure the analysis is valid for the immediate subprocesses while the rule for the *inactive process* enforces no restriction on the analysis result.

For an ambient process the analysis first records that the ambient n is inside the ambient $*$ and then continues analyzing the process P within the updated environment. Here the auxiliary functions $\mathcal{M}_\rho : M \to \mathcal{P}(\lfloor M \rfloor)$ and $\mathcal{N}_\rho : \mathbf{Name} \to \mathcal{P}(\mathbf{C})$ map a variable to a set of canonical capabilities and values respectively

$\mathcal{N}_\rho(x) = \rho(\lfloor x \rfloor) \cap \mathbf{C}$	$\mathcal{N}_\rho(c) = \{\lfloor c \rfloor\}$
$\mathcal{M}_\rho(\text{in } n) = \{\text{in } \mu \mid \mu \in \mathcal{N}_\rho(n)\}$	$\mathcal{M}_\rho(x) = \rho(\lfloor x \rfloor)$
$\mathcal{M}_\rho(\text{out } n) = \{\text{in } \mu \mid \mu \in \mathcal{N}_\rho(n)\}$	$\mathcal{M}_\rho(c) = \{\lfloor c \rfloor\}$

Table 4. Analysis specification (1): $(\gamma, \kappa, \rho) \models^* P$

$(\gamma,\kappa,\rho) \models^* (\nu\ n)P : \varphi$	iff	$(\gamma,\kappa,\rho) \models^* P : \varphi$
$(\gamma,\kappa,\rho) \models^* (\nu k\ n)P : \varphi$	iff	$(\gamma,\kappa,\rho) \models^* P : \varphi$
$(\gamma,\kappa,\rho) \models^* 0 : \varphi$	iff	true
$(\gamma,\kappa,\rho) \models^* P_1 \mid P_2 : \varphi$	iff	$(\gamma,\kappa,\rho) \models^* P_1 : \varphi \wedge (\gamma,\kappa,\rho) \models^* P_2 : \varphi$
$(\gamma,\kappa,\rho) \models^* !P : \varphi$	iff	$(\gamma,\kappa,\rho) \models^* P : \varphi$
$(\gamma,\kappa,\rho) \models^* n[P] : \varphi$	iff	$\forall \mu \in \mathcal{N}_\rho(n) : \mu \in \gamma(*) \wedge (\gamma,\kappa,\rho) \models^\mu P : \varphi$
$(\gamma,\kappa,\rho) \models^* \text{in } n.P : \varphi$	iff	$\mathcal{M}_\rho(\text{in } n) \subseteq \gamma(*) \wedge (\gamma,\kappa,\rho) \models^* P : \varphi \wedge$ $\forall \text{in } \mu \in \mathcal{M}_\rho(\text{in } n) : \varphi_{\text{in}}(\mu)$
$(\gamma,\kappa,\rho) \models^* \text{out } n.P : \varphi$	iff	$\mathcal{M}_\rho(\text{out } n) \subseteq \gamma(*) \wedge (\gamma,\kappa,\rho) \models^* P : \varphi \wedge$ $\forall \text{out } \mu \in \mathcal{M}(\text{out } n) : \varphi_{\text{out}}(\mu)$
$(\gamma,\kappa,\rho) \models^* n.P : \varphi$	iff	$\mathcal{M}_\rho(n) \cap M \subseteq \gamma(*) \wedge (\gamma,\kappa,\rho) \models^* P : \varphi \wedge$ $\forall \text{in } \mu \in \mathcal{M}_\rho(n) : \varphi_{\text{in}}(\mu) \wedge$ $\forall \text{out } \mu \in \mathcal{M}_\rho(n) : \varphi_{\text{out}}(\mu)$

The last three clauses deal with prefixed processes. In each case all potential capabilities inside the current ambient are recorded by γ and then the continuation process is analyzed; the following closure conditions referred by the clauses serve the purpose of reflecting the semantics of in- and out- capabilities into the analysis.

$$\varphi_{\text{in}}(\mu) \quad \text{iff} \quad \forall \mu^a, \mu^p : \text{in } \mu \in \gamma(\mu^a) \wedge \mu^a \in \mathbf{C_p} \wedge \mu^a \in \gamma(\mu^p) \wedge \mu \in \gamma(\mu^p) \Rightarrow \mu^a \in \gamma(\mu)$$

$$\varphi_{\text{out}}(\mu) \quad \text{iff} \quad \forall \mu^a, \mu^p : \text{out } \mu \in \gamma(\mu^a) \wedge \mu^a \in \mathbf{C_p} \wedge \mu^a \in \gamma(\mu) \wedge \mu \in \gamma(\mu^g) \Rightarrow \mu^a \in \gamma(\mu^g)$$

Now turn to the clauses in Table 5. The clause for local-output first collects the potential values $\mathcal{M}(M_i)$ of every capability M_i in a message and records all k-tuples of such messages $\langle v_1, v_2, \cdots, v_k \rangle$ into the local mailbox. Compared to local-output, the clauses for output-to-parent and out-to-child do not update local mailbox but store messages into the mailboxes of possible parents and children of the current ambient respectively.

The clause for local-input $(M_1, \cdots, M_j; x_{j+1}, \cdots, x_k)^\circ.P$ retrieves the local mailbox to look for the k-tuple messages whose first j elements are pointwise inside $\mathcal{M}_\rho(M_i)$ for $1 \leq i \leq j$. Then the new bindings of names are recorded by the analysis component ρ for variables $x_{j+1}, \cdots, x_k$ respectively. Finally $\mathsf{RM}(\ell, \mathcal{D}, \epsilon, \mathcal{L})$ is checked for authentication; the special crypt-point ϵ and set $\mathcal{D}$ are inserted by the rule of local-input to check if any encrypted message may

Table 5. Analysis specification (2): $(\gamma,\ \kappa,\ \rho) \models^* P$

$$(\gamma,\kappa,\rho) \models^* \langle M_1,\cdots,M_k\rangle^{\circ}_{\ell}[\text{dest } \mathcal{L}] :\varphi \quad \text{iff} \quad \forall v_1,\cdots,v_k\colon \wedge_{i=1}^{k} v_i \in \mathcal{M}_\rho(M_i) \Rightarrow \langle v_1,\cdots,v_k\rangle_{\ell}[\text{dest } \mathcal{L}] \in \kappa(*)$$

$$(\gamma,\kappa,\rho) \models^* \langle M_1,\cdots,M_k\rangle^{N}:\varphi \quad \text{iff} \quad \forall \mu \in \mathcal{N}_\rho(N) : \mu \in \gamma(*) \wedge \forall v_1,\cdots,v_k\colon \wedge_{i=1}^{k} v_i \in \mathcal{M}_\rho(M_i) \Rightarrow \langle v_1,\cdots,v_k\rangle_{\epsilon}[\text{dest } \mathcal{D}] \subseteq \kappa(\mu)$$

$$(\gamma,\kappa,\rho) \models^* \langle M_1,\cdots,M_k\rangle^{\uparrow} : \varphi \quad \text{iff} \quad \forall \mu : * \in \gamma(\mu) \wedge \forall v_1,\cdots,v_k\colon \wedge_{i=1}^{k} v_i \in \mathcal{M}_\rho(M_i) \Rightarrow \langle v_1,\cdots,v_k\rangle_{\epsilon}[\text{dest } \mathcal{D}] \subseteq \kappa(\mu)$$

$$(\gamma,\kappa,\rho) \models^* (M_1,\cdots,M_j;x_{j+1},\cdots,x_k)^{\circ}.P:\varphi \quad \text{iff}$$
$$\langle v_1,\cdots,v_k\rangle_{\ell}[\text{dest } \mathcal{L}] \in \kappa(*)\colon \wedge_{i=1}^{j} v_i \in \mathcal{M}_\rho(M_i)$$
$$\Rightarrow \wedge_{i=j+1}^{k} v_i \in \rho(x_i) \wedge (\neg \mathsf{RM}(\ell,\mathcal{D},\epsilon,\mathcal{L}) \Rightarrow (\ell,\ \epsilon) \in \varphi) \wedge (\gamma,\kappa,\rho) \models^* P:\varphi$$

$$(\gamma,\kappa,\rho) \models^* (M_1,\cdots,M_j;x_{j+1},\cdots,x_k)^{N}_{\ell'}[\text{orig } \mathcal{L}'].P:\varphi \quad \text{iff}$$
$$\forall \mu \in \mathcal{N}_\rho(N) : \mu \in \gamma(*) \wedge \forall \langle v_1,\cdots,v_k\rangle_{\ell}[\text{dest } \mathcal{L}] \in \kappa(\mu) : \wedge_{i=1}^{j} v_i \in \mathcal{M}_\rho(M_i)$$
$$\Rightarrow \wedge_{i=j+1}^{k} v_i \in \rho(x_i) \wedge (\neg \mathsf{RM}(\ell,\mathcal{L}',\ell',\mathcal{L}) \Rightarrow (\ell,\ \ell') \in \varphi) \wedge (\gamma,\kappa,\rho) \models^* P:\varphi$$

$$(\gamma,\kappa,\rho) \models^* (M_1,\cdots,M_j;x_{j+1},\cdots,x_k)^{\uparrow}.P:\varphi \quad \text{iff}$$
$$\forall \mu : * \in \gamma(\mu) \wedge \forall \langle v_1,\cdots,v_k\rangle_{\ell}[\text{dest } \mathcal{L}] \in \kappa(\mu)) : \wedge_{i=1}^{j} v_i \in \mathcal{M}_\rho(M_i)$$
$$\Rightarrow v_{j+1} \in \rho(x_j) \wedge \cdots \wedge v_k \in \rho(x_k) \wedge (\neg \mathsf{RM}(\ell,\mathcal{D},\epsilon,\mathcal{L}) \Rightarrow (\ell,\epsilon) \in \varphi) \wedge (\gamma,\kappa,\rho) \models^* P:\varphi$$

be read unexpectedly. For the rule of input-from-parent and input-from-child we retrieve the mailboxes of possible parents and children of the current ambient respectively. The left part of the rule is quite similar to that of local-input except that no annotations are implicitly added in the rule of input-from-child as they have been declared explicitly. Especially we do not need a rule for the attacker process as it could be any processes (well-formed) whose analysis has been declared as above.

Semantic Properties. We prove the correctness of the analysis w.r.t. the operational semantics of ABoxed Ambients. It is convenient to prove the following lemmata. The first says that estimates keep valid for substitution of closed terms for variables. The second states that an estimate valid for a process P is also valid for every process congruent to P.

Lemma 1. *$(\gamma,\kappa,\rho) \models^{\mu} P : \varphi$ and $\lfloor M \rfloor \in \rho(\lfloor x \rfloor)$ imply $(\gamma,\kappa,\rho) \models^{\mu} P\{M/x\} : \varphi$.*

Lemma 2. *If $P \equiv Q$ then $(\gamma,\kappa,\rho) \models^{\mu} P : \varphi$ iff $(\gamma,\kappa,\rho) \models^{\mu} Q : \varphi$.*

We are now ready to state the subject reduction result, which says our analysis is semantically correct for both two variants of semantics:

Theorem 1. *If* $P \rightarrow_{\mathcal{R}} Q$ *and* $(\gamma,\kappa,\rho) \models^{\mu} P : \varphi$ *then* $(\gamma,\kappa,\rho) \models^{\mu} Q : \varphi$.

Finally we conclude that the analysis can correctly predict when we can safely remove the reference monitor:

Theorem 2. *If* $(\gamma,\kappa,\rho) \models^{\mu} P : \emptyset$ *then* RM *can not abort* P.

Example 2. For the ABoxed Ambients specification of WMF specified in Example 1, an estimate satisfying $(\gamma, \kappa, \rho) \models^{\star}$ WMF : φ is given by

$$
\begin{array}{llllll}
\gamma: & n_\star & \mapsto \{A, S, B, K_A, K_B, K\} & A & \mapsto & \{K_A, K\} \\
 & S & \mapsto \{K_A, K_B\} & B & \mapsto & \{K_B, K\} \\
 & K_A & \mapsto \{\text{out } A, \text{in } S\} & K & \mapsto & \{\text{out } A, \text{in } B\} \\
 & K_B & \mapsto \{\text{out } S, \text{in } B\} & & & \\
\kappa: & A & \mapsto \{\langle A\rangle_\epsilon[\text{dest } \mathcal{D}]\} & B & \mapsto & \emptyset \\
 & S & \mapsto \{\langle A\rangle_\epsilon[\text{dest } \mathcal{D}]\} & K_A & \mapsto & \{\langle B, K\rangle_{A_1}[\text{dest } S_1]\} \\
 & K & \mapsto \{\langle M\rangle_{A_2}[\text{dest } B_2]\} & K_B & \mapsto & \{\langle A, K\rangle_{S_2}[\text{dest } B_1]\} \\
\rho: & y_K & \mapsto \{K\} & z_K & \mapsto & \{K\} \\
 & z & \mapsto \{M\} & & &
\end{array}
$$

and $\varphi = \emptyset$ predicting that RM can not abort the process computation. □

4 Modelling Network Attacker

Protocols are executed in a multi-location environment where there may be malicious attackers in some of places. In a flat space of network, we usually take the form $n_\star[P \mid \bullet]$ in which P and $\bullet$ represent the implementation of a system and its working environment respectively. For the hierarchical network, however, there may be several local networks accessible to the attacker. Thus we must provide our assumption about which local networks the attacker may reside in. Suppose the attacker is on the network represented by the distinguished ambient $n_\star$ or a site ambient a, we declare attacker processes as one of top level processes of them, formally $n_\star[P \mid \bullet]$ or $a[Q \mid \bullet]$. Below we shall call a process without attackers inside *target process*. We can use $P_{sys}[0/\bullet]$ to get the target process from a system implementation P_{sys}.

To characterize all capabilities of network attackers, we aim at finding a parameterized formula $\mathcal{F}^{\text{A\_DY}}_{\text{RM}}(*)$; whenever an estimate $(\gamma, \kappa, \rho, \varphi)$ satisfies $\mathcal{F}^{\text{A\_DY}}_{\text{RM}}(*)$ then $(\gamma, \kappa, \rho) \models^{*} R : \varphi$ for all attackers R. Before we proceed to define such a formula, we must declare attackers' power on the network at first. The pioneering research in [9] describes the attacker capabilities as four conditions: (1) receiving messages by eavesdropping, (2) decrypting messages using the key they know, (3) constructing new messages (encrypted or plain), and (4) sending messages they have. Here the conditions (1) and (4) are not clear enough if the principal of local networks are concerned. For the first condition we need to provide assumption that which location(s) the attacker can overhear; for the fourth one we should clarify that which location(s) the attacker can send message to. We turn to the following adjusted Dolev-Yao condition; the design idea is that to guarantee any flaw of a protocol can be detected, the attacker should be able to control over any network resource he might gain in the real world.

a. Eavesdropping on any messages presenting in the attacker-nested location (declared by the attacker process);
b. Decrypting messages using the key the attacker knows;
c. Constructing both encrypted and plain messages;
d. Sending messages to any attacker-reachable sites;
e. Initially the attacker has some knowledge and a private channel is allocated for all attackers to share information with each other.

While the first three conditions are straightforward, we explain the last two in detail. The forth item declares that the attacker can deliver messages to any reachable site. We define the concept "reachable" based on the knowledge of the attacker: there is a route (consists of a series of sites) from attacker-nested place to a destination along which each name of the site is known by the attacker. For example, consider the network in Figure 1 again and suppose the attacker resides in the office. We then colored the tree in Figure 1 as below.

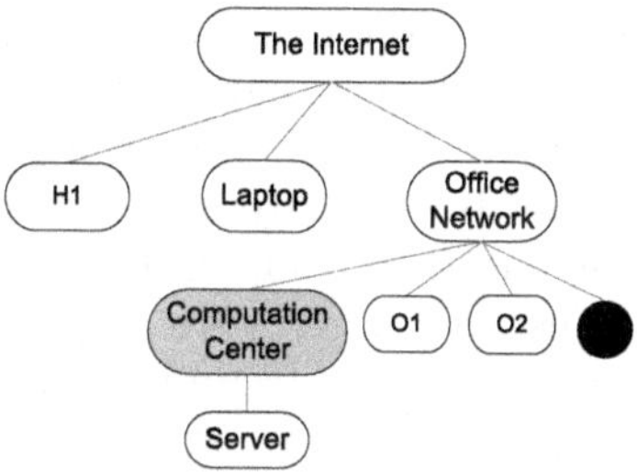

where grey nodes denotes attacker-invisible sites and white nodes represent the sites whose names are knowable to the attacker. As the figure shows, Computation Center is not reachable to the attacker-composed messages. Neither is Server although its name is known by the bad guy. Finally the fifth item allows attackers attack system by collusion. This is a strong assumption about attacker's capability: it always takes time to broadcast messages among attackers in reality; also we maximize attacker's power by assuming all malicious entities share information with each other. However, this only implies that we may get over-estimates but no flaw of a security protocol can be left over.

We follow the approach of [2] and state that a target process P is of type $(\mathcal{N}_{\mathsf{f}}, \mathcal{A}_{\mathcal{K}})$ whenever: (1) P is closed, (2) its free names are in $\mathcal{N}_{\mathsf{f}}$, and (3) all the arities used by input and output are in $\mathcal{A}_{\mathcal{K}}$. We can easily find minimal $\mathcal{N}_{\mathsf{f}}$ and $\mathcal{A}_{\mathcal{K}}$ so that P is of type $(\mathcal{N}_{\mathsf{f}}, \mathcal{A}_{\mathcal{K}})$. To charatacterise all attackers R, we have adopted a few assumptions and applied techniques to translate R into its semantically equivalent process $\overline{R}$ in order to have control over the infinite names and labels that attackers may have. Accordingly we have specified the formula $\mathcal{F}_{\mathsf{RM}}^{\mathsf{A\_DY}}(*)$; the idea is to add a series of constraints to an estimate so that the adjusted conditions can be implied from the estimate. For detailed description, please refer to [19].

We can establish the correctness of the adjusted Dolev-Yao condition for ABoxed Ambients in the following two theorems. The first state that estimates satisfying $\mathcal{F}_{\mathsf{RM}}^{\mathrm{A\_DY}}(*)$ are also valid for all attackers in site $*$.

Theorem 3. *If an estimate* $(\gamma,\kappa,\rho,\varphi)$ *satisfies* $\mathcal{F}_{\mathsf{RM}}^{\mathrm{A\_DY}}(*)$ *of type* $(\mathcal{N}_{\mathrm{f}},\mathcal{A}_{\mathcal{K}})$ *then* $(\gamma,\kappa,\rho) \models^{*} \overline{R}\colon \varphi$ *for all well-formed processes* R *of type* $(\mathcal{N}_{\mathrm{f}},\mathcal{A}_{\mathcal{K}})$.

Now assume $n_{\star}[P_{sys}]$ is the implementation of a system and a set of attacker-nesting places of P_{sys} is in the set I, we prove that estimates satisfying $\wedge_{*\in I}\mathcal{F}_{\mathsf{RM}}^{\mathrm{A\_DY}}(*)$ are valid for all attackers in the system:

Theorem 4. *If* $(\gamma,\kappa,\rho) \models^{\star} P_{sys}[0/\bullet] : \varphi$ *and* $(\gamma,\kappa,\rho,\varphi)$ *satisfies* $\wedge_{*\in I}\mathcal{F}_{\mathsf{RM}}^{\mathrm{A\_DY}}(*)$ *of type* $(\mathcal{N}_{\mathrm{f}},\mathcal{A}_{\mathcal{K}})$*, then* $(\gamma,\kappa,\rho) \models^{\star} P_{sys}[\overline{R}/\bullet] : \varphi$ *for all attackers* R.

5 ABox-Ambients Tool

We aim at developing an automatic tool to compute our control flow analysis correctly and efficiently. It can be shown that there always is a least estimate of γ, κ, ρ *and* φ for any process P such that $(\gamma,\kappa,\rho) \models^{\star} P : \varphi$. The aim of the tool is to compute such a least $(\gamma,\kappa,\rho,\varphi)$ for a given process. The generic strategy of implementing constraint-based analysis is to translate an analysis into a suitable constraint language and then compute the least estimate of these constraints with a standard constraint solver. We adopt Succinct Solver 2.0 [16], an expressive fragment of first-order predicate logic, as our constraint solver to obtain an efficient tool. The solver takes constraints encoded with Alternation-free Least Fixed Point logic (ALFP) as input and gives the least solution of a program analysis as output. The transforming of the analysis into ALFP proceeds in three steps. First we transform the analysis from succinct form into its verbose form [17] so that every analysis component has global scope. This is because the ALFP recognized by Succinct Solver can not provide scoping mechanisms for predicates. Second we translate the analysis and the attacker formulae into ALFP. This is conducted in a series of straightforward encodings, for instance, representing sets as predicates, and encoding annotations in communication primitives. Finally the analysis and the attacker formulae are turned into a generation function $\mathcal{G}$ that takes a process as argument and returns its analysis in the form of ALFP formulae.

As explained in [16], the time for solving a formula in Succinct Solver is polynomial in the size of a finite universe of atomic values, e.g. canonical names and capabilities, over which a formula is interpreted. Suppose the size of the universe is N, then a simple worst-case estimate of execution time is about $\mathcal{O}(N^{1+\tau})$ where τ is the maximal nesting depth of quantifiers in the clause. For our implementation, the depth of nesting is mainly given by the length of the sequences specified in communication.

6 Protocol Validation

Protocol validation is usually based on many assumptions. For instance, most formal techniques assume that cryptography is perfect, the master keys are always securely stored and retrieved. In this section we first discuss how to use our calculus to model key-store and key-retrieving and thereby protocols can be validated under fewer assumptions. By doing so, we expect that the approach can provide system designer more useful information. We then validate WMF and its two variants in a series of configurations, a set of assumptions about the network hierarchy, the locations of different roles and attackers. In all the experiments we have taken the number of each role (except server) to be 3 in order to ensure that the man-in-the-middle attack can be modeled.

Validating Protocol with Key-retrieving. Our first attempt is to model a data file storing master keys on the server in plain text. This can be formalised as:

$$\text{KeyTable} \;=\; \mathit{datafile}[!\langle n_1, K_1\rangle^{\circ}_{\epsilon}[\text{dest } \mathcal{D}]] | \cdots |!\langle n_m, K_{\text{m}}\rangle^{\circ}_{\epsilon}[\text{dest } \mathcal{D}]]$$

where n_i and K_i are the identity of a principle and its key respectively. Replication '!' is used to present the data of the table is persistent. Querying the table can be encoded as:

$$\text{Keytable}|(n_i; y_{\text{k}})^{\text{datafile}}_{\epsilon}[\text{dest}\mathcal{D}]. \cdots .y_{\text{k}} \cdots$$

where we take advantage of pattern match to check the name n_i in input and acquire its key by variable binding. Following this design idea, we can update the specification of Example 1 and validate WMF under the configuration whose ambient representation is visualized as:

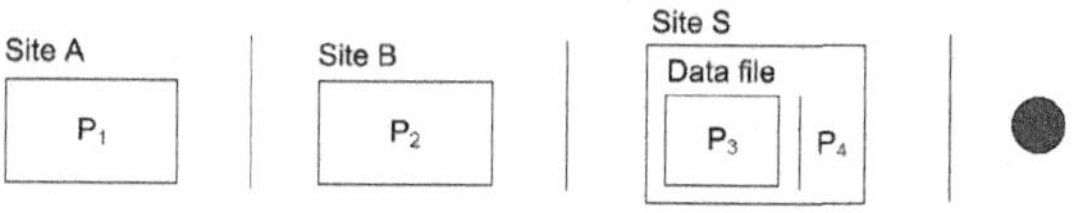

The experiment result shows no flaw is found in the system. Next suppose there are a large amount of secret keys to store and then a dedicated database server is assigned to support the service of an authentication server. In the real life the two servers are usually located in a secure area, e.g. a local network, to which no attackers can physically access. We then validate WMF on the network whose ambient structure is presented as below.

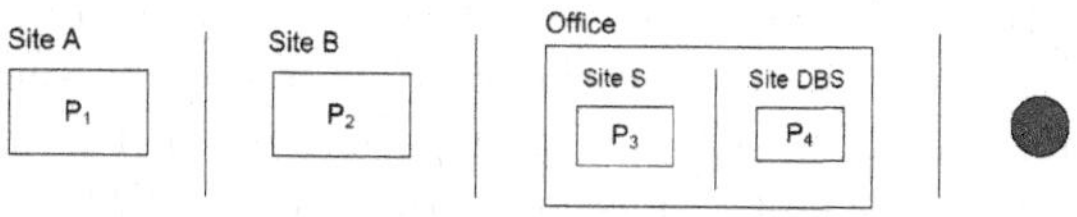

Here the database query is described by narration

$$\begin{array}{llll} 1. & S \;\rightarrow DBS: & & A \\ 2. & DBS \rightarrow S: & & A, K_A \end{array}$$

Our experiment result shows that the protocol may be flawed and φ is

$$\begin{array}{l}\{(A_{2i},\ell_\bullet)|1\le i\le n\}\cup\{(S_2,\ell_\bullet)\}\cup\{(\ell_\bullet,S_1)\}\\ \cup\{(\ell_\bullet,B_{1j})|1\le j\le n\}\cup\{(\ell_\bullet,B_{2j})|1\le j\le n\}\end{array}$$

Actually the protocol is flawed as illustrated by below two attacks.

$$\textbf{(i)}\ \begin{array}{lll} M_A & \to S: & A,[B,K_{M_1}]_{K_{M_2}}\\ M_{DB} & \to S: & A,K_{M_2}\\ S & \to B: & [A,K_{M_1}]_{K_B}\\ M_A & \to B: & [m]_{K_{M_1}}\end{array} \qquad \textbf{(ii)}\ \begin{array}{llll} A & \to S & : & A,[B,K]_{K_A}\\ M_{DB} & \to S & : & B,K_M\\ S & \to M_B & : & [A,K]_{K_M}\\ A & \to B & : & [m]_K\end{array}$$

For attack (i), B finally believes that he is getting message from A but he is actually reading messages composed by the attacker. For attack (ii) the attacker cheats the server S by sending it a fake master key K_M and finally the attacker can decrypt any message sent from A to B. The root cause of the flaw is that the authentication server can not distinguish the packets from the database server with those from attackers. We can fix the problem by either encrypting messages sent between the servers or simply modifying their communication as:

$$\begin{array}{llll} 1. & S & \to DBS: & A\\ 2. & DBS & \to S: & u,A,K_A\end{array}$$

where a new name u is introduced and initially known only by the two servers. Our experiment shows that the protocol is flawless for both the two solutions.

Optimizing Protocol in Hierarchical Networks. We now consider two variants of WMF: one where the first message ($A \to S$) is not encrypted and one where the second message ($S \to B$) is not encrypted; the protocol narration is as below.

$$\textbf{Variant 1}: \begin{array}{ll} A\to S: & u_1,A,B,K\\ S\to B: & [A,K]_{K_B}\\ A\to B: & [m]_K\end{array} \qquad \textbf{Variant 2}: \begin{array}{ll} A\to S: & A,[B,K]_{K_A}\\ S\to B: & u_2,A,K\\ A\to B: & [m]_K\end{array}$$

Here we assume u_1 is initially only known by A and S while u_2 is restricted over B and S. We validate the two protocols in a number of configurations; the experiment results are summarized in Table 6.

As shown in the first line of the table, the analysis reports that both the two variants are flawed since the session key K can be acquired by the attacker. For the second configuration, we assume the initiators and the server are located in the office that is not accessible to the attacker. Now the validation results show the first variant is still flawed but this time the second is secure. This is because the attacker can not overhear or intercept messages on the office network and that actually provides a private channel for the initiators and the server. Now we state Variant 2 has advantages over WMF in efficiency and space-consumption considering both of them are secure because (1) the variant saves time in encrypting and decrypting values that is usually the most time-consuming operations in security protocol, and (2) it sharply reduces the size of a data file or data base by storing much less master keys than before. Similarly we

Table 6. Experiments on validating protocols in hierarchical networks

Configuration	WMF-Variant 1	WMF-Variant 2
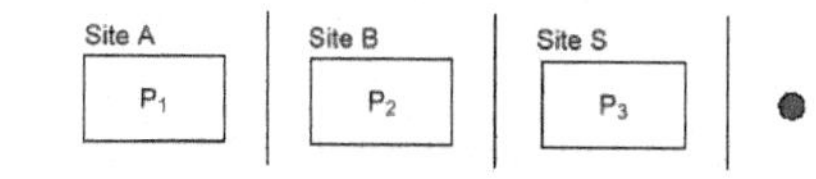	$\{(A_{1i},\ell_\bullet)\mid 1\le i\le n\}\cup\{(\ell_\bullet,B_{2j})\mid 1\le j\le n\}$	$\{(A_{2i},\ell_\bullet)\mid 1\le i\le n\}\cup\{(\ell_\bullet,B_{1j})\mid 1\le j\le n\}$
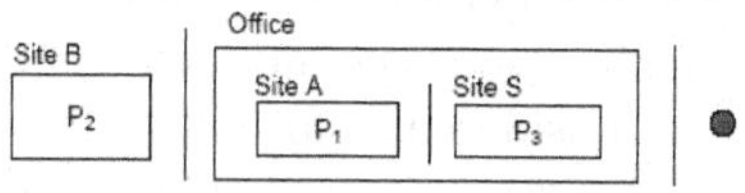	$\{(A_{1i},\ell_\bullet)\mid 1\le i\le n\}\cup\{(\ell_\bullet,B_{2j})\mid 1\le j\le n\}$	$\varnothing$
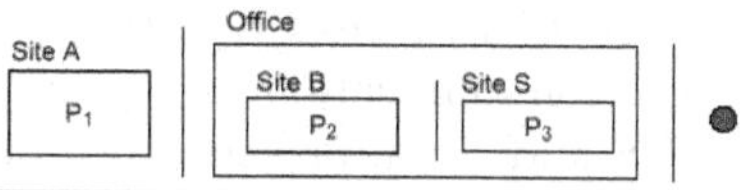	$\varnothing$	$\{(A_{2i},\ell_\bullet)\mid 1\le i\le n\}\cup\{(\ell_\bullet,B_{1j})\mid 1\le j\le n\}$
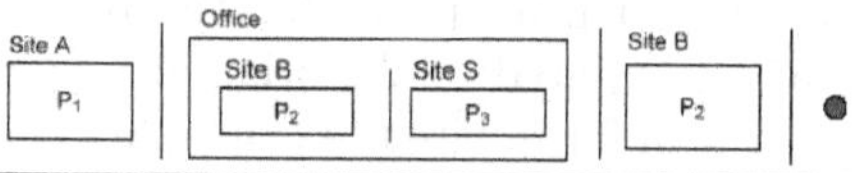	$\{(A_{2i},\ell_\bullet)\mid 1\le i\le n\}\cup\{(\ell_\bullet,B_{1j})\mid 1\le j\le n\}$	$\{(A_{2i},\ell_\bullet)\mid 1\le i\le n\}\cup\{(\ell_\bullet,B_{1j})\mid 1\le j\le n\}$
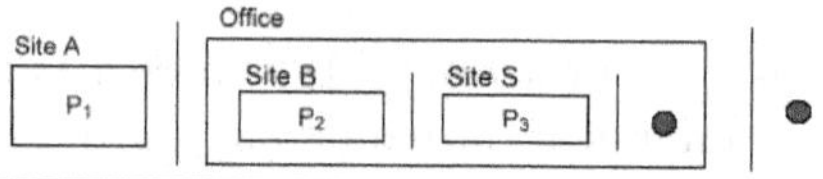	$\{(A_{2i},\ell_\bullet)\mid 1\le i\le n\}\cup\{(\ell_\bullet,B_{1j})\mid 1\le j\le n\}$	$\{(A_{2i},\ell_\bullet)\mid 1\le i\le n\}\cup\{(\ell_\bullet,B_{1j})\mid 1\le j\le n\}$

switch the position of the initiators for the responders in the third configuration; this time the first variant is secure as expected (see third row of Table 6).

The fourth configuration assumes the responders may appear on both the Internet and the office while the last one supposes a malicious guy gain access to the office. In both the two cases the variants are flawed as the attacker can acquire the session key K and thus the security of the protocols is compromised.

Summarizing the results of the experiment, we conclude that it is possible to optimize a protocol by considering network structures and principals' locations; in particular, the analysis can help system designers check whether the adapted protocol still guarantee authentication and provide information to track flaws if there are any.

7 Conclusion

We have shown that hierarchical networks and protocols applied on such networks may be formalized as ABoxed Ambients processes so that a static analysis can pinpoint a wide-variety of errors in security protocols. We have also presented a new attacker model based on the Dolev-Yao model in order to comply with the special network considered in this paper. We have argued that the model gives the attacker reasonable abilities to conduct passive and positive attack to protocols.

The analysis has been implemented using the Succinct Solver 2.0 and has then been applied to a number of examples. We would like to extend our calculus to deal with asymmetric cryptography. Also it would be interesting to see how the approach scales to a large protocol which is developed for the environment of hierarchial networks.

Comparison with related work. A number of formal methods have been developed in the field of protocol analysis. We shall compare them with our work in two aspects: the approaches of protocol formalism and the analysis techniques used to validate protocols. Many papers have considered to formulate protocols with process calculi such as CSP [12], CCS [10], Lysa [2,3] and ambient calculus [18]. We consider ambient calculi as a proper choice with regard to the network of interest; the scope of the message of local communication is clearly given by the boundary of ambients. With CSP, CCS and Lysa, one may use private channels to model local communication between principals. But the resulting specification would be harder to understand compared to the original topology of the modelled network. Ambients, however, can formulate the principle of local networks in a quite nature way.

Boxed Ambients is first used to model security protocol in [18] where a control flow analysis is also developed to track communication happening on different locations. But there is no attacker defined to model the realistic environment. We also have modified the calculus for the purpose of protocol validation specially, e.g. extending the input with a pattern match to model value-checking, adding annotations to declare protocol intentions explicitly.

Based on formal protocol specification, a lot of techniques have been developed to analyze protocols automatically. Two of main trends close to our approach are type systems and model checking. Type systems have been developed for security protocol analysis, e.g. by Abadi [1] and by Gordon and Jeffery [11]. The results show that type checking in these systems can be done in polynomial time while type inference takes exponential time. In comparison, the control flow analysis presented here retains polynomial time.

Model checking is a method that explores each state in a protocol; see e.g. FDR [13], Interrogator [14] and Brutus [8]. Since the state space for security protocol is usually infinite, the approach based on state space exploration can not guarantee termination while our approach adopts approximation to deal with arbitrarily long execution sequences. On the other hand, model checking techniques are often quite efficient in finding flaws if there is any in a protocol. Thus it can be seen as complementary to control flow analysis techniques.

The major advantages of static analysis approach taken here can be summarized as: first, the least solution always exists and can be computed in low polynomial time; second, the approach is operational oriented so that the correctness of the analysis can be established w.r.t. a formal operation semantics; last but not least, the approach can be fully automated.

References

1. M. Abadi. Secrecy by typing in security protocols. *Journal of the ACM*, 46(5):749–786, 1999.
2. C. Bodei, M. Buchholtz, P. Degano, F. Nielson, and H. R. Nielson. Static validation of security protocols. *Journal of Computer Security*, 13(3):347–390, 2005.
3. M. Buchholtz, H. R. Nielson, and F. Nielson. A calculus for control flow analysis of security protocols. *Int. J. Inf. Sec.*, 2(3-4):145–167, 2004.
4. M. Bugliesi, G. Castagna, and S. Crafa. Boxed Ambients. In *TACS*, pages 38–63, 2001.
5. M. Bugliesi, G. Castagna, and S. Crafa. Reasoning about security in mobile ambients. In *CONCUR*, pages 102–120, 2001.
6. M. Burrows, M. Abadi, and R. M. Needham. A logic of authentication. In *SOSP*, pages 1–13, 1989.
7. L. Cardelli and A. D. Gordon. Mobile ambients. *Theor. Comput. Sci.*, 240(1):177–213, 2000.
8. E. M. Clarke, S. Jha, and W. Marrero. Verifying security protocols with Brutus. *ACM Transactions on Software Engineering and Methodology*, 9(4):443–487, 2000.
9. D. Dolev and A. C. Yao. On the security of public key protocols. *IEEE Transactions on Information Theory*, 29(2):198–207, 1983.
10. R. Focardi and R. Gorrieri. A taxonomy of security properties for process algebras. *Journal of Computer Security*, 3(1):5–34, 1995.
11. A. D. Gordon and A. Jeffrey. Authenticity by typing for security protocols. *Journal of Computer Security*, 11(4):451–520, 2003.
12. G. Lowe. An attack on the Needham-Schroeder public-key authentication protocol. *Inf. Process. Lett.*, 56(3):131–133, 1995.
13. G. Lowe. Breaking and fixing the needham-schroeder public-key protocol using FDR. In *TACAS*, pages 147–166, 1996.
14. J. K. Millen. The interrogator: A tool for cryptographic protocol security. In *IEEE Symposium on Security and Privacy*, pages 134–141, 1984.
15. F. Nielson, H. R. Nielson, and R. R. Hansen. Validating firewalls using flow logics. *Theor. Comput. Sci.*, 283(2):381–418, 2002.
16. F. Nielson, H. Seidl, and H. R. Nielson. A succinct solver for ALFP. *Nord. J. Comput.*, 9(4):335–372, 2002.
17. H. R. Nielson and F. Nielson. Flow Logic: A multi-paradigmatic approach to static analysis. In *The Essence of Computation*, pages 223–244, 2002.
18. H. R. Nielson, F. Nielson, and M. Buchholtz. Security for Mobility. In *FOSAD*, pages 207–265, 2002.
19. Y. Zhang. Static analysis for protocol validation in hierarchical networks. Master's thesis, Technical University of Denmark, 2005.

Functional Analysis of a Real-Time Protocol for Networked Control Systems

Colin Fidge and Yu-Chu Tian

School of Software Engineering and Data Communications
Queensland University of Technology
Australia

Abstract. Traditional real-time control systems are tightly integrated into the industrial processes they govern. Now, however, there is increasing interest in networked control systems. These provide greater flexibility and cost savings by allowing real-time controllers to interact with industrial processes over existing communications networks. New data packet queuing protocols are currently being developed to enable precise real-time control over a network with variable propagation delays. We show how one such protocol was formally modelled using timed automata, and how model checking was used to reveal subtle aspects of the control system's dynamic behaviour.

1 Introduction

Process controllers for automated industrial plants must sample data from sensors, calculate appropriate responses, and send signals to actuators, all within strict timing bounds. The computations performed by such controllers implicitly rely on the assumptions that sensor data is received, and the controller software is invoked, periodically with very little 'jitter' (timing variability). Traditional control theory [4] assumes that the controller and the industrial process it governs are co-located, allowing communication between the sensors, controller and actuators to be treated as instantaneous.

Now, however, there is increasing interest in the greater flexibility and cost savings made possible by distributing the system's components, with the computer-based controller connected to the physical sensor and actuator devices via a standard communications network [12]. In practice, doing this introduces two significant problems. Firstly, transmission of data between the controller and the devices may suffer variable propagation delays. This can affect the accuracy of timing-dependent calculations in the control software. Secondly, communication over the network may be unreliable. Occasional data packet 'dropouts' can leave the controller with little or no information on which to base its control decisions. Both problems can significantly degrade the controller's performance [11].

As part of a project developing real-time protocols for networked control systems we needed to evaluate data packet queuing mechanisms intended to compensate for the effects of network-induced delays and data packet dropouts. In previous work we successfully analysed the timing characteristics of one such protocol using a network simulator [14,13], but these performance profiles did not tell us how the proposed protocol affects the functionality of the whole system.

S. Graf and W. Zhang (Eds.): ATVA 2006, LNCS 4218, pp. 446–460, 2006.

In this paper we explain how we used a real-time model checker to evaluate the behaviour of a proposed control algorithm for networked systems. To do this we constructed a simple finite-state model of the control system and a discrete approximation of its physical environment. The resulting model proved to be a highly effective and efficient way of discovering potential system behaviours. In particular, it quickly revealed situations in which the controller can become unstable.

2 Previous Work

Our goal in this research was to use model checking to analyse the functional behaviour of a networked control system. In this section we briefly review some relevant prior work on model checking and analysis of real-time control systems.

Model checking [6] involves constructing a model of a system from one or more finite state automata and then exploring the model's reachable states. Each automaton in the model consists of a number of locations and transitions between them. Transitions are guarded by predicates which determine when they may fire, and assignments to variables may be performed during the transition from one state to the next. Automata are nondeterministic when more than one transition is ready to fire at the same time.

Model checkers analyse such a model by exploring its state space, looking for particular states, or state sequences, of interest. The user usually describes states of interest using temporal logic formulæ. The model checker then performs proofs by refutation—it searches for a counterexample to a claimed property [9]. Since it is impractical to exhaustively explore models with large state spaces, much of the research in model checking has been on ways of optimising this process. Even so, users of model checkers are obliged to ensure that their model captures the essential properties of the system of interest, but without producing a state space that is too large to analyse.

Since we were concerned with real-time systems we decided to use the UPPAAL model checker [3], which is based on timed automata theory. It extends traditional state-machine notations with time-valued 'clock' variables. All clocks progress synchronously, which allows implicit synchronisation between automata. Explicit synchronisation is supported via shared 'channels'. UPPAAL has been optimised for analysis of time-dependent systems through the use of continuous intervals for modelling clocks, rather than discrete 'ticks' [2]. The UPPAAL toolkit has been used to analyse many real-time systems [10], including proposed real-time protocols for wireless networks [15], although not the kind of networked control system we consider here.

Analysis of real-time control systems is, of course, a well-explored topic. 'Hybrid' approaches are often used to account for the fact that a digital controller's behaviour is discrete, whereas its physical environment is continuous. Recently, for instance, Dubey *et al.* described a toolkit for analysis of real-time control systems [7]. They distinguish 'symbolic' analysis approaches, which construct executable models for directly simulating continuous behaviours, from 'reductionist' methods, which produce a discretized approximation to the continuous behaviour. Their ReachLab toolkit takes the former approach whereas, as explained below, we adopt the latter model. In their conclusion, Dubey *et al.* note that modelling 'networked hybrid automata' is an area for future work in their system [7]. Rather than attempting to devise an entirely new hybrid approach for networked control systems, we show below that a carefully constructed discrete model is sufficient to produce useful experimental results.

With respect to analysis of networked control systems, Martí *et al.* discuss the effects of network-induced timing delays on real-time controllers [11]. They stress the importance of integrating the controller model with that of the physical environment when analysing such systems. Their studies showed how network delays can create instability in the control system's responses. As shown in Section 4 below, our model confirms these findings.

Most recently, Andersson *et al.* used their TrueTime network simulator to analyse the behaviour of wireless networked control systems communicating with a continuous environment [1]. In our own work, we have similarly profiled the performance of a proposed networked control system protocol using the NS2 simulator [14,13]. However, our interest in this paper is in automatic exploration of all possible states through model checking, rather than examining individual traces using simulation.

In this paper we combine the lessons learned from all of this previous work. Mindful of the requirements of networked control system analysis [11], and informed by previous models of real-time systems [1,8,7], we develop a simple model that allows efficient and accurate exploration of possible networked control system behaviours using an off-the-shelf model checker.

3 Modelling a Networked Control System

In this section we explain how we modelled a proposed real-time queuing protocol for a networked control system as a set of timed automata. UPPAAL's timed-automata syntax is introduced as needed. Firstly, we briefly describe the proposed protocol (Section 3.1). The model then comprises three parts: a simple abstraction of the network's ability to deliver packets in time (Section 3.2); the components of the real-time controller itself (Section 3.3); and a discrete approximation of the physical environment (Section 3.4).

3.1 A Proposed Real-Time Queuing Protocol

In a previous paper [14] we outlined a simple queuing protocol for a 'smart' process controller which communicates with an industrial processing plant via an unreliable communications network with significant propagation delays. The controller receives sensor readings as data packets sent over the network and calculates responses to be sent to an actuator. As usual in such systems we assume that the controller's software is implemented as a simple computational 'task', or 'process', which is invoked at fixed intervals. The start of each such period is called the task invocation's 'arrival' time.

To allow for the possibility that a data packet arrives earlier than expected, the controller has a buffer, *sample*, which stores each data packet received until needed. (This could be implemented in latching hardware or using a software interrupt handler.) To allow for the possibility that a data packet arrives too late or not at all, the controller also has a queue, *previous*, which holds several previous data packets. These can be used to calculate responses when packets 'drop out'. Typically queue *previous* would hold at least three previous data values, to allow meaningful extrapolations to be calculated. The way in which this queue is updated and used depends on the particular control algorithm.

The controller performs various actions within fixed intervals relative to the arrival (starting) time of each period. These intervals are bounded by four constants.

1. *Earliest* is the earliest time at which a data packet sent from the sensor to the controller could possibly arrive.
2. *Latest* is the latest time at which a data packet is expected. Packets arriving after this time are ignored.
3. *Compute* is the time at which the controller will start using the received data packets to compute an output to send to the actuator.
4. *Deadline* is the time by which the controller must send its response to the actuator.

These constants are related as follows.

$$\mathit{Earliest} < \mathit{Latest} \leq \mathit{Compute} < \mathit{Deadline}$$

Our previous work on performance profiling of the protocol considered how to calibrate these constants [14,13], but did not analyse the system's overall functionality.

3.2 Finite State Model of the Communications Network

To formally analyse such a system our aim was to model its essential features without introducing irrelevant detail that would create a state-space 'explosion' during model checking. Although we could have modelled the passage of data packets from the sensor to the controller in detail, the only aspect of the network's behaviour that actually concerns us is whether or not packets arrive in time.

Therefore, our models of different network behaviours were simple state machines which indicate the status of each data packet. One such model is shown in Fig. 1. This particular model was one of several constructed to describe different network behaviours. Others included a relatively uncongested network in which each tardy packet is separated from the next by at least two punctual packets. The simplest model was of a totally reliable network which delivers all packets on time.

The particular automaton in Fig. 1 uses synchronisation channels **OnTime** and **TooLate** to say whether or not the packet for the current period arrived in time, respectively. The '!' decorations mean that these are 'output' synchronisations [3]. The corresponding inputs can be seen in Fig. 2. The finite state machine in Fig. 1 comprises three locations, denoted by circles, and several transitions, indicated by arrows [3]. Distinguished location **NetworkOK**, marked by a double circle, is the initial one in which the model begins. Transitions are annotated with the synchronisation events that allow them to fire. Since this (untimed) automaton is fully synchronised with the timed automaton in Fig. 2, there is no need for any explicit timing constraints in Fig. 1.

The particular network model in Fig. 1 represents a heavily congested network in which two consecutive data packets may arrive late. If the network is in location **NetworkOK**, a packet can be delivered late, leaving the network in location **Congested**. A second packet can then be delivered late, leaving the network in location **StillCongested**. After this, however, the next packet must arrive on time. The other network

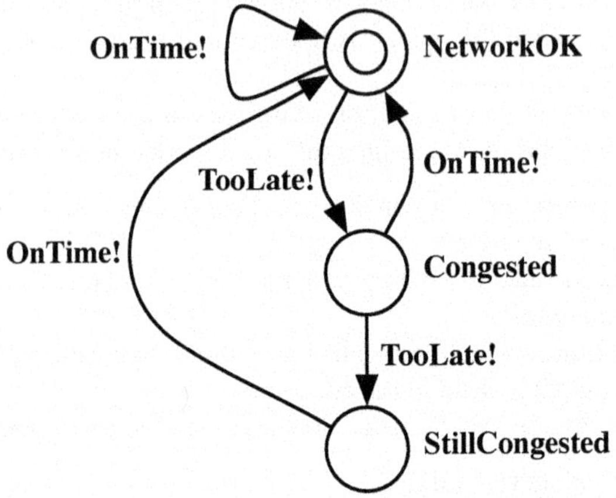

Fig. 1. Finite state machine model (one of several) of a heavily congested network

models used during the experiments made different assumptions about the separation between packet 'dropout' events and the number of consecutive dropouts allowed.

3.3 Timed Automata Model of the Real-Time Control System

As explained in Section 3.1, there are two consecutive phases of the controller's operation in each period: queuing received data packets and computing values to send to the actuator based on the available data. We chose to model these two phases as two distinct timed automata (Figs. 2 and 3), since this allowed us to experiment with different combinations of queuing protocols and response calculations.

Correct interleaving of the transitions performed by the two automata is guaranteed by the timing constraints on their transitions. Each automaton maintains its own clock variable, *time*, and uses this to determine when to perform transitions. Thanks to UPPAAL's synchronous time model there was no need to explicitly synchronise the two automata. However, the two automata share global state variables *sample* and *previous*.

Fig. 2 shows the automaton that models how the controller queues data packets. It has a single location **QueuesReady** and two transitions, both of which are synchronised with those of the network model in Fig. 1. The uppermost transition may occur when the network model says that a data packet arrives on time and the lower transition may occur when the packet arrives too late. Time-valued variable *arrival* is used to determine the time at which transitions may fire.

In UPPAAL's semantics time progresses while automata are in locations; transitions are instantaneous. Locations can be annotated with predicates which must be true for the automaton to remain in the location. Transitions may be guarded by predicates which must be true for the transition to fire, and may perform assignments to state and clock variables. Here we write guarded assignments as '*guard* → *assignments*' and individual assignments as '*variable* := *expression*'.

In Fig. 2 location **QueuesReady** is accompanied by an invariant which says that the automaton may stay in this location no later than the arrival time of the current period,

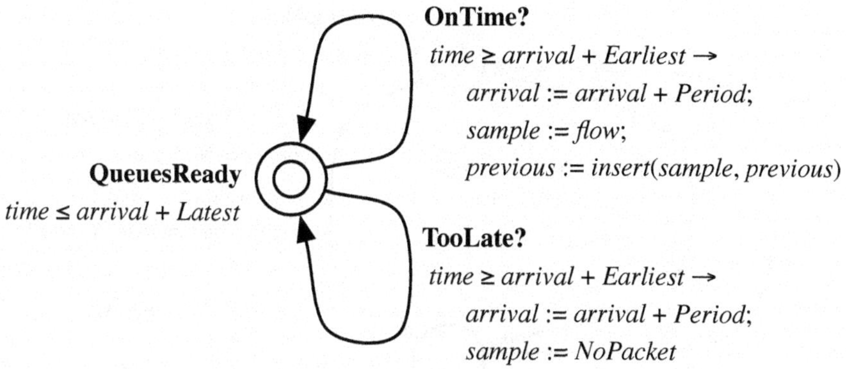

Fig. 2. Timed automaton model of the controller's data queues

represented by variable *arrival*, plus constant *Latest*. Both transitions are guarded by a predicate that says that they may fire no earlier than the arrival time of the period plus constant *Earliest*. In effect, the invariant combined with the guards ensures that the transitions fire between *Earliest* and *Latest* seconds from the arrival time of the period. When they fire, both transitions add constant *Period*, the separation between task invocations, to the arrival time in readiness for the next task invocation.

Importantly, the automaton in Fig. 2 models the way the data packet queues in the networked controller are updated [14]. If the data packet arrives on time the sampled sensor reading, *flow* (see Section 3.4), is both stored in buffer *sample* and inserted onto the front of queue *previous*. If the data packet arrives too late the only action is to store the special constant *NoPacket* in buffer *sample*.

The timed automaton which models the way the controller calculates responses for the actuator, shown in Fig. 3, uses its own local *time* and *arrival* variables to model its periodic invocation. In this case the invariants associated with the locations and the guards attached to transitions ensure that the automaton leaves location **AwaitingData** exactly *Compute* seconds after the arrival time of the period, and leaves location **PreparingOutput** at *Deadline* seconds after arrival.

When in location **AwaitingData** there are two transitions the controller can take, depending on whether or not a data packet was successfully received in this period, as indicated by the absence or presence of constant *NoPacket* in buffer *sample*. The specific assignments performed depend on which type of controller algorithm we are modelling, as discussed in Section 4. In general, though, if no packet has arrived (rightmost transition in Fig. 3), we need to update buffer *sample* and queue *previous* with some default or calculated value. If a data packet has arrived (middle transition in Fig. 3) no special action is required because we can use the value placed in variable *sample* by the queuing automaton in Fig. 2. In both transitions we may calculate an *error* value, for use when computing a response when packets are dropped, as discussed in Section 4.

When the automaton leaves location **PreparingOutput** it means that the calculation is complete and the value in buffer *sample* can be sent to the actuator (leftmost transition in Fig. 3). The arrival time is then set to the beginning of the next period.

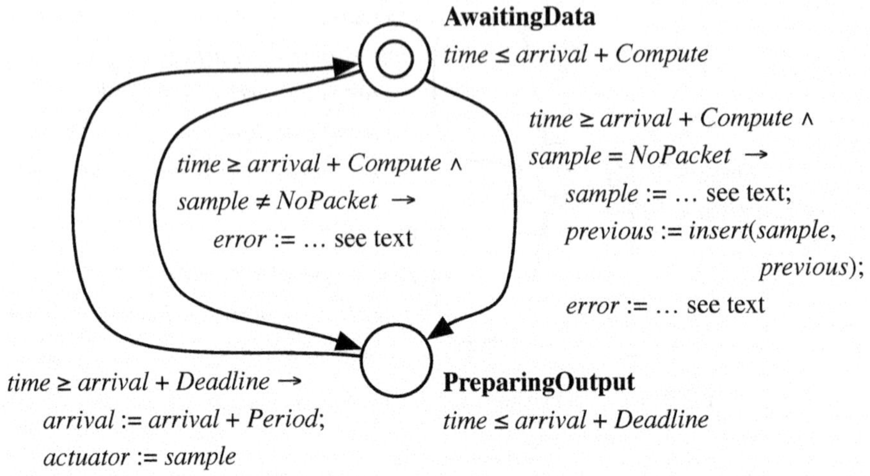

Fig. 3. Timed automaton model of the controller's main computation

3.4 Timed Automaton Model of the Physical Environment

To demonstrate the actual behaviour of a given controller algorithm we need to put it in the context of its anticipated physical environment. Consider a controller for a chemical processing plant which is required to monitor the flow of liquid through a pipe. A flow meter embedded within the pipe measures the (instantaneous) rate of flow of liquid through the pipe and this data is sent periodically to the controller, via a network. The controller uses the flow readings received to generate a suitable output to an actuator or display device.

When modelling such an environment we must devise a discrete approximation of its continuous dynamic properties. Brinksma and Mader, in their own work on model checking a chemical plant controller, noted the difficulty of devising a suitable discretization of the plant's continuous behaviour [5]. Based on our previous experience in modelling control systems and their environments [8], we resolved to develop a model which allowed us to precisely control the range, velocity and acceleration of the observed physical property.

As shown in Fig. 4, the model's main purpose is to update variable *flow*, which represents the rate at which liquid is currently flowing through the pipe, measured in litres per second. (Global variable *flow* is read by the controller model in Fig. 2.) Clock variable *delay* is used to determine when this variable is updated. Since the controller samples sensor readings periodically, it is sufficient to update *flow* at the same rate. Thus, each location in Fig. 4 has an invariant which says that the automaton may remain in the location for no longer than the period, and each transition is guarded by a condition that allows it to fire no later than the period's duration since the last transition. When each transition occurs, the *delay* variable is reset to zero. In effect, transitions in Fig. 4 fire exactly every *Period* seconds.

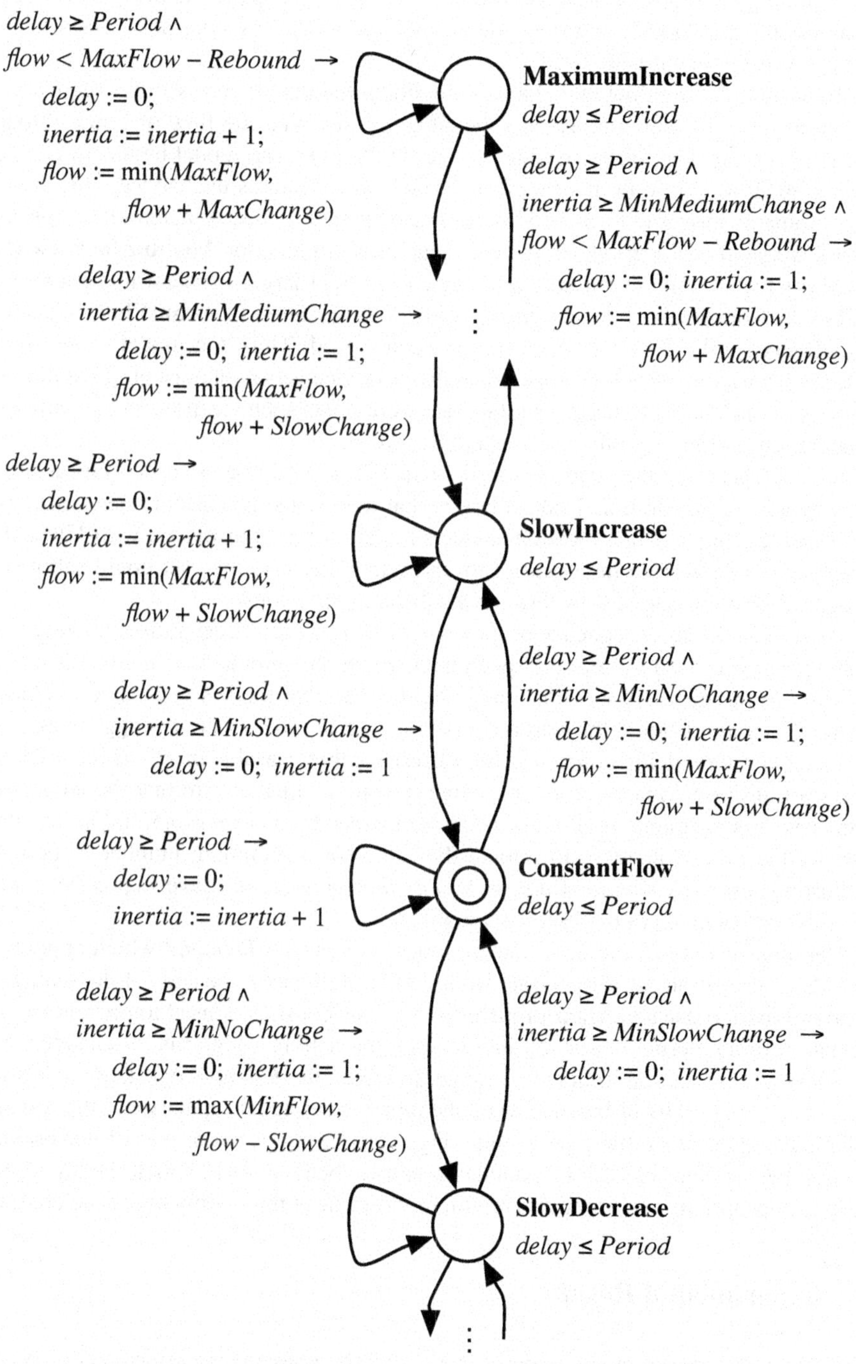

Fig. 4. Part of the timed automaton model of the physical environment

Bounding the range of the observed flow of liquid was achieved easily by ensuring that variable *flow* does not go outside an interval defined by constants *MinFlow* and *MaxFlow* each time it is updated.

To ensure that the flow rate changes smoothly, the model consists of a sequence of locations, each of which represents the situation in which the flow of liquid through the pipe is increasing or decreasing at a particular rate. The model begins in location **ConstantFlow**. While in this location, variable *flow* remains unchanged. However, if the automaton moves to location **SlowIncrease** the rate of flow is increased by constant *SlowChange* in each period. From here it can move to location **MediumIncrease** (not shown) which results in variable *flow* increasing by a larger constant in each period, and so on. Conversely, if the automaton moves from location **ConstantFlow** to location **SlowDecrease** the flow rate decreases in each period. Thus, the model cannot jump directly from a low rate of increase to a high one or vice versa—it must progress through a series of intermediate stages. In total there were seven such locations in the particular model used for the experiments shown in Section 4.

Strictly speaking, the separate locations in Fig. 4 could be collapsed into a single one, by adding an additional state variable that represents the current rate of increase. However, having separate locations made simulation traces displayed with UPPAAL's graphical user interface much easier to understand because the user could follow the progression of the rate of flow through the different locations.

As well as the strict sequence of locations which governs acceleration, counter variable *inertia* was used to limit the speed with which the automaton can move from one location to the next. As its name suggests, this variable models resistance to change in the flow rate of liquid through the pipe, i.e., the liquid's inherent sluggishness. For instance, if the model is in location **SlowIncrease** then variable *inertia* is incremented at each transition. Guards on the outgoing transitions then ensure that the automaton can leave this location only if *inertia* equals or exceeds constant *MinSlowChange*, thus forcing the rate of increase to remain the same for a minimum number of periods. Adjusting constants *MinSlowChange*, *MinMediumChange*, etc, gave us precise control over the rate of changes to observed variable *flow*.

The final feature of the environment model is constant *Rebound* which appears in guards on transitions leading to the two locations at the extreme ends of the sequence, **MaximumIncrease** and **MaximumDecrease**. This constant is used to prevent the automaton from entering or staying in a location modelling a high rate of change when the flow rate is near the limits of its range. In effect, the *Rebound* constant models the 'pushback' caused by turbulence when the pipe is nearing its capacity and the residual trickle of liquid when the pipe is emptying. This feature was not part of our original model, but we introduced it to exclude unrealistic behaviours in which the liquid was seen to approach its maximum and minimum flow rate at impossibly high accelerations.

4 Experimental Results

Our goal in this research was to develop a model for assessing the effectiveness of proposed controller algorithms (Figs. 2 and 3) given particular behaviours of the physical environment (Fig. 4) and of the network connecting the two (Fig. 1). In this section we

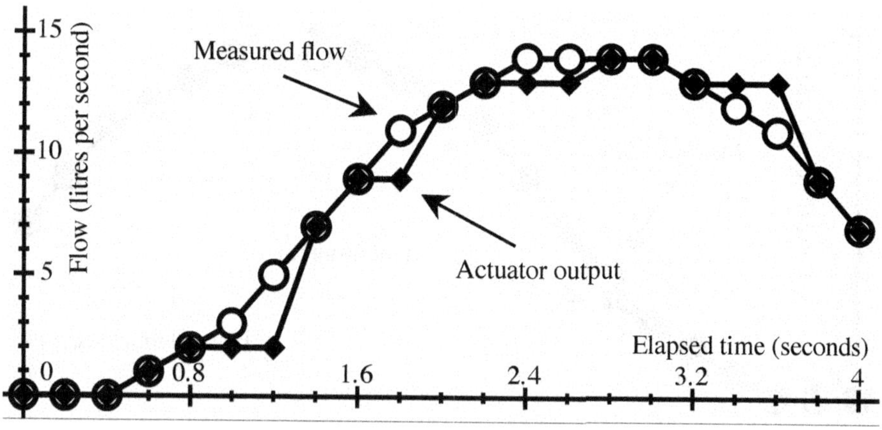

Fig. 5. Simulation showing poor behaviour of the simple controller due to packet dropouts

describe the results of a variety of experiments conducted with the model in Section 3.3 using UPPAAL's simulator and model checker. For ease of comparison between the controller's inputs and outputs, we assume here that our controller is merely required to forward sampled flow measurements to a display device. More generally, though, the controller's output would be some function of its inputs.

As a benchmark, we began with the simplest possible form of controller, one which merely reuses the last value seen when a sensor reading fails to arrive in time. In the rightmost transition in Fig. 3 this means that buffer *sample* is assigned the value at the head of queue *previous*, i.e.,

$$sample := previous[0]$$

where index zero accesses the first item the queue. (The *error* variable is not used yet.)

A typical simulation in this situation is shown in Fig 5, assuming a controller running at a frequency of 5 hertz, and a maximum rate of flow through the pipe of 15 litres per second. In the particular trace shown the measured flow of liquid begins at zero litres per second, quickly approaches the maximum capacity of the pipe, and then begins to decrease. The networked control system attempts to mirror this behaviour but cannot due to packet dropouts that occur in the periods beginning at times 1.0, 1.2, 1.8, 2.4, 2.6, 3.4 and 3.6 seconds after the start of the simulation. This causes the actuator's output to be lower than the actual flow when the rate is increasing and to exceed the true flow when the rate is decreasing, as we would expect.

To compensate for the effects of packet dropouts, we then developed a model of a controller which calculates a new value to replace a dropped one by extrapolating from the most recent values seen. In Fig. 3 the update to buffer *sample* in this case is

$$sample := previous[0] + (previous[0] - previous[1]) .$$

In other words, this 'extrapolating' controller adds the difference between the last two sensor readings displayed to the most recently displayed value when a sample is not received.

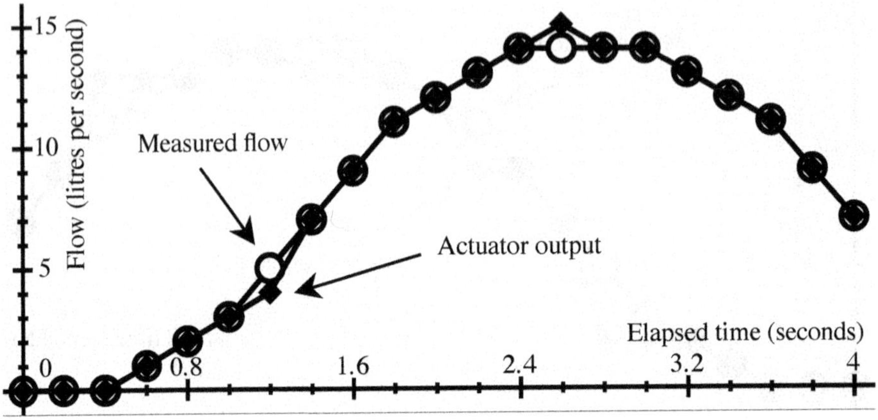

Fig. 6. Improved behaviour by the 'extrapolating' controller in the same circumstances as Fig. 5

To confirm the effectiveness of this control strategy we then simulated the revised system's behaviour as shown in Fig. 6. As hoped, the extrapolating controller's output is a much closer fit to the desired behaviour than that of the simple controller. It successfully compensates for dropped data packets except in situations where two successive packets are dropped while the rate of flow is changing.

Although this single simulation would seem to suggest that the extrapolating controller is adequate for our needs, the true advantage of using a model checking tool such as UPPAAL is that we can ask it to automatically explore a wide range of possible behaviours. Therefore, we asserted (using an appropriate temporal logic expression) that the controller's output will always stay within 4 litres per second of the actual flow of liquid and challenged the model checker to find a counterexample. Fig. 7 shows the result.

Here the model checker has found a particular network behaviour that causes the controller's output to become unstable. Even though there are no long sequences of consecutive packet dropouts, the counterexample reveals that a particular pattern of dropped packets can cause the extrapolating controller to successively overestimate and underestimate the flow values. Even worse, it can be made to do so with a cumulative error. Thus a dropped packet at time 1.2 caused the controller to underestimate the flow by one litre per second (extrapolating from the samples at times 0.8 and 1.0). The next packet dropout, at time 1.6, caused the controller to overestimate the value by 2 litres per second (extrapolating from the estimated value at time 1.2 and the sampled value at time 1.4), and so on.

With hindsight, it is apparent that the extraordinary controller behaviour in Fig. 7 is due to the presence of estimated values in queue *previous*. Each time a packet is dropped, an estimated replacement value is produced. This value is placed in queue *previous* in lieu of the missing packet (rightmost transition in Fig. 3), and can thus lead to a cumulative error in the next such calculation. Indeed, this kind of instability is well known in control theory, confirming the accuracy of our model.

Next we resolved to define a more sophisticated form of controller, to overcome the undesirable effects just seen. The new controller 'adapts' its behaviour by calculating

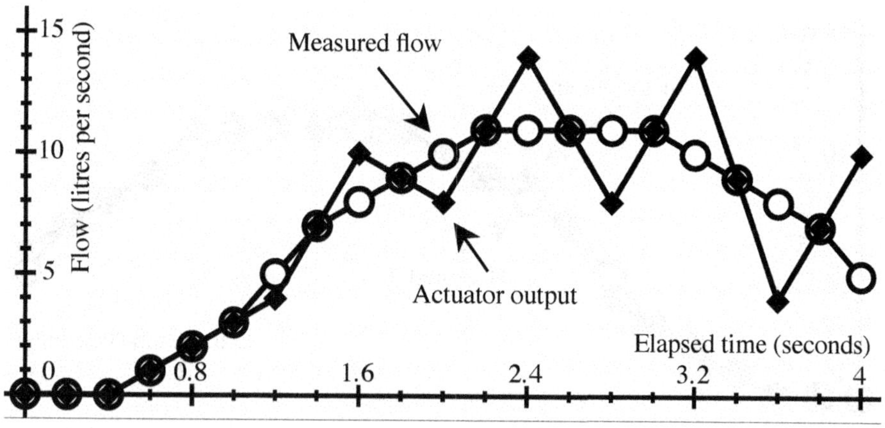

Fig. 7. Counterexample produced by the model checker showing instability in the 'extrapolating' controller caused by a repetitive pattern of dropped packets

the error between its own estimates and actual samples received. This error measurement is then used to adjust the extrapolated values when packets are dropped.

In the middle transition in Fig. 3, which models the controller's actions when a data packet has been successfully received, the error value is calculated as follows.

$$error := sample - (previous[1] + (previous[1] - previous[2]))$$

Here term '$previous[1] + (previous[1] - previous[2])$' is an extrapolation from previously-displayed values and '*sample*' is the actual value received. The error is thus the difference between the two.

For the rightmost transition in Fig. 3, which models the controller's actions when a data packet is dropped, the calculations of the replacement sample value and the error are as follows.

$$sample := \max((previous[0] + (previous[0] - previous[1]) - (error/2)), 0)$$
$$error := 0$$

The controller's output value is calculated by extrapolating from the previously-displayed values, as before, but corrected by a proportion of the error found in the preceding extrapolation. Through experimentation we found that using one half of the *error* value worked well. The *error* value for the next period is set to zero in this case since there is no actual sample to compare with the extrapolation.

To confirm that this control strategy has the desired effect we then simulated the 'adaptive' controller in the same situation that caused the unstable behaviour using a simple extrapolation. As shown in Fig. 8 the results were encouraging. The adaptive controller successfully avoided the cumulative oscillations that occurred previously.

As a final check, however, we once again challenged the model checker to find a counterexample to our assertion that the controller's output always stays close to the sampled input values. As shown in Fig. 9, the model checker responded with a remarkable counterexample where a particular pattern of dropped packets again causes the

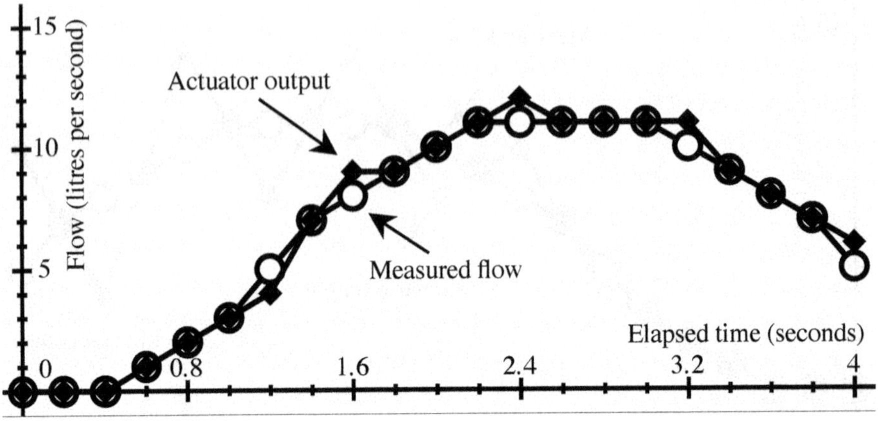

Fig. 8. Improved behaviour by the 'adaptive' controller in the same circumstances as Fig. 7

controller's output to oscillate with cumulative error around the desired values. Unlike Fig. 7, however, this behaviour could not be produced by isolated dropouts, but only by having sequences of two successive dropped packets, combined with a particular pattern of variations in the flow rate.

Once again the root cause of the problem is the presence of estimated, rather than actual, values in queue *previous*. To create instability in the adaptive controller, however, it proved necessary for the queue to contain at least two estimated values, in effect meaning that the majority of the values used to perform calculations were estimates. Thus, although the adaptive controller was shown to be more robust than the extrapolating one, it was still found to be vulnerable to certain extreme environmental behaviours.

Although obvious with hindsight, this result surprised us at first since it revealed that the relatively sophisticated 'adaptive' controller can have *worse* behaviour than the 'simple' one we began with. In Fig. 5 the simple controller performs comparatively well when the network drops sequences of packets, even when the rate of increase is steep, whereas Fig. 9 shows that the adaptive controller can become unstable even when the flow is increasing slowly overall.

Of course, a network that is dropping as many packets as shown in Fig. 9 would not be used in practice as a basis on which to make critical control calculations. Normally a separate fail-safe mechanism in the overall system design would shut the plant down or set it to some neutral state if the network was seen to be behaving like this.

5 Conclusion

Networked control systems are an emerging and increasingly important technology for governing industrial processes. Given that many such systems are safety-critical, it is important that their dynamic behaviours can be predicted before they are deployed. Model checking offers the ability to automatically explore a system's state space, potentially revealing extreme behaviours that could be overlooked during manually-guided simulations.

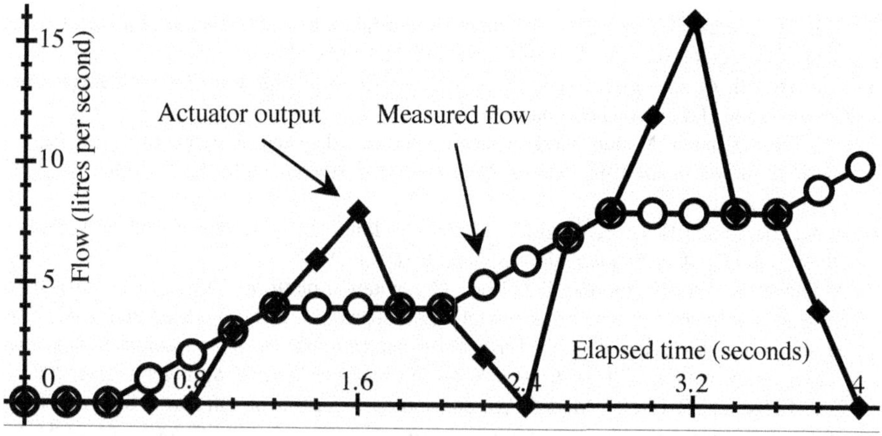

Fig. 9. Counterexample produced by the model checker showing instability in the 'adaptive' controller due to consecutive sequences of dropped packets

We have shown how we used model checking to explore the behaviour of a proposed 'smart' controller for networked control systems. This was done by modelling significant characteristics of the controller, network and physical environment. The network and controller models were fairly simple, although linked rather intricately by shared variables, channels and timing characteristics, while the environment model was comparatively large, due to the need to approximate a continuous behaviour, but had a simple regular structure. The UPPAAL model checker proved highly effective and efficient at finding undesirable system behaviours. All of the model checking results presented above were produced in a few minutes of processor time.

The approach can be adapted easily to analysis of other time-dependent systems. At the time of writing we are working on a model which will allow two different versions of a periodic software task to be directly compared by simulating both versions simultaneously within the same environment. This will be used to determine if a newly-developed controller is an adequate replacement for a legacy one.

Acknowledgements. We wish to thank the anonymous ATVA 2006 reviewers for their many helpful comments and corrections. This work was supported by Australian Research Council Discovery-Projects grants DP0449773, *Verified Emulation of Legacy Mission Computer Systems*, and DP0559111, *Wavelet-Based Modelling And Model Predictive Control Of Complex Multidimensional Crystallisation Processes*.

References

1. M. Andersson, D. Henriksson, A. Cervin, and K.-E. Årzén. Simulation of wireless networked control systems. In *Proceedings of the 44th IEEE Conference on Decision and Control and the European Control Conference (CDC-ECC 2005)*, pages 476–481. IEEE, 2005.
2. G. Behrmann, J. Bengtsson, A. David, K. G. Larsen, P. Petterson, and W. Yi. UPPAAL implementation secrets. In *Proceedings of the Seventh International Symposium on Formal Techniques in Real-Time and Fault Tolerant Systems (FTRTFT'02)*, 2002.

3. G. Behrmann, A. David, and K. G. Larsen. A tutorial on UPPAAL. Technical report, Department of Computer Science, Aalborg University, November 2004.
4. C. C. Bissell. *Control Engineering*, volume 15 of *Tutorial Guides in Electronic Enginering*. Chapman and Hall, second edition, 1994.
5. E. Brinksma and A. Mader. Model checking embedded system designs. In *Proceedings of the Sixth International Workshop on Discrete Event Systems (WODES'02)*, October 2002. Extended Abstract.
6. E. M. Clarke and B.-H. Schlingloff. Model checking. In A. Robinson and A. Voronkov, editors, *Handbook of Automated Reasoning*. Elsevier, 1999.
7. A. Dubey, X. Wu, H. Su, and T. J. Koo. Computation platform for automatic analysis of embedded software systems using model based approach. In D. A. Peled and Y.-K. Tsay, editors, *Automated Technology for Verification and Analysis: Third International Symposium (ATVA 2005)*, volume 3707 of *Lecture Notes in Computer Science*. Springer-Verlag, 2005.
8. C. J. Fidge and P. Cook. Model checking interrupt-dependent software. In *Proceedings of the Twelfth Asia-Pacific Software Engineering Conference (APSEC 2005)*, pages 51–58. IEEE Computer Society Press, 2005.
9. M. Huth and M. Ryan. *Logic in Computer Science: Modelling and Reasoning About Systems*. Cambridge University Press, second edition, 2004. ISBN 0-521-54310-X.
10. T. K. Iversen, K. J. Kristoffersen, K. G. Larsen, M. Laursen, R. G. Madsen, S. K. Mortensen, P. Pettersson, and C. B. Thomasen. Model-checking real-time control programs: Verifying LEGO MINDSTORMS systems using UPPAAL. In H. Toetenel, editor, *Twelfth EuroMicro Conference on Real-Time Systems (ECRTS'00)*, pages 147–156. IEEE Computer Society Press, 2000.
11. P. Martí, J. M. Fuertes, and G. Fohler. An integrated approach to real-time distributed control systems over fieldbuses. In *Eighth IEEE International Conference on Emerging Technologies and Factory Automation (ETFA 2001)*, pages 177–182, 2001.
12. P. Martí, R. Villá, J. M. Fuertes, and G. Fohler. Networked control systems overview. In R. Zurawski, editor, *The Industrial Information Technology Handbook*. CRC Press, 2005.
13. Y.-C. Tian, Q.-L. Han, C. J. Fidge, M. Tadé, and T. Gu. Communication architecture design for real-time networked control systems. In *Proceedings of the Fourth IEEE International Conference on Communications, Circuits and Systems (ICCCAS 2006)*, pages 1840–1845, 2006.
14. Y.-C. Tian, D. Levy, M. Tadé, T. Gu, and C. J. Fidge. Queuing packets in communication networks for networked control systems. In *Proceedings of the Sixth World Congress on Intelligent Control and Automation (WCICA 2006)*, pages 205–209. IEEE Computer Society Press, 2006.
15. T. Watteyne, I. Augé-Blum, and S. Ubéda. Proposition of a hard real-time MAC protocol for wireless sensor networks. In *Proceedings of the Thirteenth IEEE International Symposium on Modeling, Analysis, and Simulation of Computer and Telecommunication Systems (MASCOTS 2005)*, pages 533–536. IEEE Computer Society, 2005.

Symbolic Semantics for the Verification of Security Properties of Mobile Petri Nets*

Fernando Rosa-Velardo and David de Frutos-Escrig

Dpto. de Sistemas Informáticos y Programación
Universidad Complutense de Madrid
{fernandorosa, defrutos}@sip.ucm.es

Abstract. We study Mobile Synchronizing Petri Nets (MSPN), that allow the description of systems composed of a collection of interacting mobile components. Unlike in other models of modular or mobile Petri Nets, we focus on security issues. For that purpose, we introduce a fresh name generation mechanism to provide special authentication tokens. These names are treated in an abstract way, which allows us to retain the decidability of some properties that hold for Place/Transition nets (P/T nets). In this paper, we are interested in checking that the desired security properties of a system still hold, even when in an arbitrary malicious environment. However, since we are dealing with security properties, we must regard that some names of the system are assumed to be secret, which restricts the set of possible environments. We develop a symbolic semantics that takes into account the behaviour of any of those environments, though in an abstract way. We establish the desired relations between the original and the symbolic semantics to conclude that the latter is correct and complete with respect to the former.

1 Introduction and Related Work

The Internet has become in the last years a computational infrastructure that is available all around the world, and of which many applications may take great advantage. Moreover, the utopia of *Ubiquitous Computing* [21] is progressively becoming a reality. The combination of both trends has been called *Global Ubiquitous Computing* [13]. The study of the resulting *engineered artifact* remains as a challenge for Computer Science. Some of the issues that arise in this context (many of them already thoroughly studied separately) are cooperation, coordination, mobility and security. We still need to develop a whole theory that allows us to design and build systems in this context. In particular, in the setting of *Global Ubiquitous Computing*, we want services to be offered globally and uniformly. Thus, we need methods to reason about our systems in the presence of an unknown, unreliable or even hostile environment, so that their safety, trustworthiness, robustness, etc., can be guaranteed even in these situations.

* Work partially supported by the Spanish projects MIDAS TIC 2003-01000, MASTER TIC 2003-07848-C02-01 and PROMESAS-CAM S-0505/TIC/0407.

S. Graf and W. Zhang (Eds.): ATVA 2006, LNCS 4218, pp. 461–476, 2006.

We think that Petri Nets offer a good starting point for the study of these issues, due to their amenable graphical representation but mainly to their solid theoretical basis. Moreover, the fact that P/T-nets are not Turing-complete makes them rather manageable, since there are many decidability results for powerful infinite-state systems, which do not hold in other Turing-complete models.

Several models for mobility based on Petri Nets have been proposed. In [1] *Mobile Petri Nets* are introduced. Token colours are tuples of place names, so that tokens at the preconditions of some transitions can specify their destination place. *Elementary Object Systems* [20] are composed of a system net and one or more object nets that move along the former like ordinary tokens. In *Nested Petri Nets* [10] the number of these net tokens, as well as the level of nestedness, is unlimited, thus obtaining multi-level nested systems. Other related models are Hypernets [3] or the Mobile Systems in [12]. In most of these formalisms the model of localities is more elaborated than the one that we consider, because they allow either movement or creation of localities.

However, the previous models do not consider security aspects, which are certainly crucial in this setting, nor any other Petri net based model for mobility, up to our knowledge. To overcome this limitation, we defined our Mobile Synchronizing Petri Nets (MSPN) [14, 15], a model consisting of a set of localized labelled coloured Petri Nets that can perform synchronizations between them and fire movement transitions. MSPN systems deal with mobility in a flat topology, so that the permission to access a location is granted by the knowledge of its name. Then, in a similar way as in [6], we represent connectivity between components, although in a dynamic way, since we also consider different locations. Apart from a colour for localities, we introduced a colour for authentication tickets and a special transition capable of producing new identifiers in a secure way. The security issues dealt with in this paper center on the management of these identifiers. Thus, the security model is mainly implemented in a similar way as in the π-calculus or the Ambient Calculus [5], by means of the generation of fresh identifiers and the restriction of synchronizations to happen in the same location, and only between components with the required permissions.

In [15] we studied the expressiveness of MSPN systems. We proved several decidability results, such as the decidability of coverability, that can be used to specify security properties such as integrity or confidentiality. However, these results were obtained when considering an MSPN system as a closed system. Whenever a system is designed as an open system which can interact somehow with an unknown environment, then it is clearly desirable to develop an alternative semantics that takes into account the existence of such an environment.

Some of the previous related models have a modular nature, as our MSPN systems. There have been several works [4, 9] to model the behaviour of open systems in the context of Petri Nets, but in them the authors have concentrated their interest in the modularity of systems, thus looking for reusable open components. In general, the compositional semantics would guarantee that we can replace any component of a system by any other having the same semantics, without altering the semantics of the whole system. Moreover, it is interesting to notice that in all these models, the notion of composition of components is completely static, in the sense that the way in which the different components of a system cooperate is fixed, which entails a static architecture and the fact that the interfaces to connect two components cannot be dynamically reused by other users, as desired in an ubiquitous system.

Instead, we take a security oriented approach, namely that of proving that a certain property holds for a system, whatever its environment is. In this way we may obtain security properties even in the presence of malicious opponents. Therefore, although we are considering component-based systems, and we are defining an open semantics to consider the behaviour of the unknown environment, the existing compositional semantics for component-based net systems are not adequate for us. This is because, whenever we want to prove some security properties of a complex system we need to globally consider the interactions between its components. For instance, as far as the intended users are not considered a part of the system, they cannot be distinguished from the malicious users and, thus, we cannot make any assumption about their expected behaviour.

In this paper we introduce a new open semantics, the *secure semantics*, that considers the behaviour of the system in every possible context. However, since we are interested in the verification of security properties, we must assume that the environment does not know any name of the system considered to be secret. Thus, every security property must be parameterized by the set of private (or public) names. Though that condition restricts the set of admissible environments, we still have a quantifier over the infinite set of admissible environments, which makes the secure semantics rather unmanageable. This is why we also present a *symbolic semantics*, which represents the environment in an abstract way, thus getting a finitary representation. Next we prove that it is correct and complete with respect to the secure semantics, so that we can use the symbolic semantics in order to prove the properties of the original one. In particular, we have proved in [17] that the coverability problem for the symbolic semantics is decidable. Therefore, any security property that can be expressed in terms of coverabilities would also be decidable.

The rest of the paper is structured as follows. Sect. 2 gives a brief overview of MSPN systems. Sect. 3 presents an example of an MSPN system. Sect. 4 defines our *secure semantics*. The *symbolic semantics* is developed in Sect. 5, as well as the relation between the secure and the symbolic semantics. Finally, conclusions and directions for further study are discussed in Sect. 6.

2 Mobile Synchronizing Petri Nets: Overview

In this section we will describe our Mobile Synchronizing Petri Nets (for more details see [14] or [15]). An MSPN $N = (P, T, F, \lambda, C)$ is a special kind of labelled coloured Petri Net [11], that is, P is a finite set of places, T is a finite set of transitions, F is a partial function that defines as its domain the set of arcs, and labels those arcs with variables taken from a set $Var = Var_{\mathcal{L}} \cup Var_{Id} \cup \{\varepsilon\}$. Each

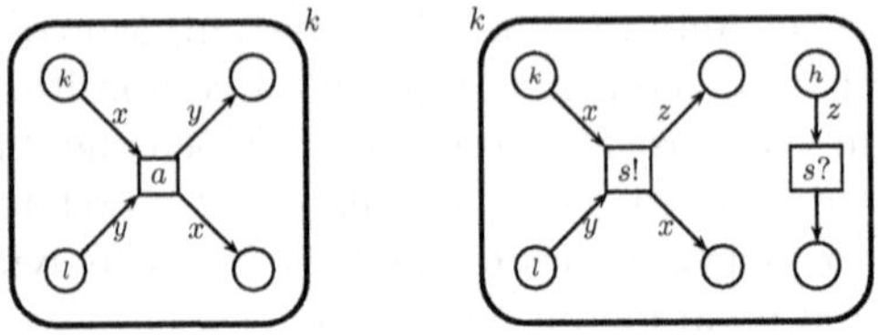

Fig. 1. Autonomous (left) and synchronizing (right) transitions

one of these three sets corresponds to one of the three different colour types that MSPN places may have: one for localities, taken from a set $\mathcal{L}$, one for identifiers, taken from a set Id, with both $\mathcal{L}$ and Id infinite, and a singleton colour type $\{\bullet\}$ for ordinary black tokens. Sometimes we will just write $\bullet$ to denote that singleton. We will use the symbol $\mathcal{T}$ to range over the set $\{\bullet, \mathcal{L}, Id\}$, *Tokens* to denote the union $\mathcal{L} \cup Id \cup \{\bullet\}$ and *CTokens* to denote the set of coloured tokens, that is, $\mathcal{L} \cup Id$. The function $C : P \to \{\bullet, \mathcal{L}, Id\}$ establishes a partition in the set of places. We will denote by $P_{\mathcal{T}}$ the subset of places of colour $\mathcal{T}$, that is, $C^{-1}(\mathcal{T})$, and we will call locality and identifier places to the elements in $P_{\mathcal{L}}$ and P_{Id}, respectively. Finally, according to $\lambda : T \to \mathcal{A} \cup Sync$, MSPN's may have two different kinds of transitions, autonomous (those with $\lambda(t) \in \mathcal{A}$) and synchronizing transitions (those with $\lambda(t) \in Sync$). The set $\mathcal{A}$ of autonomous labels has two distinguished labels *new* and *go*. The set *Sync* of synchronizing labels is the disjoint union of $S? = \{s? \mid s \in S\}$ and $S! = \{s! \mid s \in S\}$, where S is a set of service names. Intuitively, $s!$ is the offer of a service s, while $s?$ is the request of that service, although formally they are just the two symmetric sides of a synchronization.

Unlike in ordinary Coloured Petri Nets, where arbitrary expressions over some syntax can label arcs, we only allow variables to specify the flow of tokens from preconditions to postconditions. In particular, this means that only equality of identifiers can be imposed by matching, but not any other relation between them (even if using natural numbers as identifiers).

For homogeneity we are assuming in the definition that every arc (every pair (p,t) or (t,p) in the domain of F) is labelled by a variable. However, since we only need variables to distinguish between different locality tokens and identifier tokens, we introduce the special variable ε, that labels every arc that is adjacent to an ordinary black-token place. Moreover, variables from $Var_{\mathcal{L}}$ will only be used for arcs that are adjacent to locality places and those from Var_{Id} only for arcs next to an identifier place. In this way, we guarantee that the different types of tokens are never mixed.

We use $post(t)$ to denote the set of variables in arcs going from t to some place, i.e., going out of t (except for ε). Analogously, we use $pre(t)$ to denote the set of variables in arcs reaching t. We take $Var(t) = post(t) \cup pre(t)$. If t is an autonomous transition with $\lambda(t) \neq new$ then it must be the case that $post(t) \subseteq pre(t)$, so that autonomous transitions can only move or delete locality and identifier tokens, but not create them. As usual in P/T nets, we denote by $t^\bullet$ and $^\bullet t$ the set of postconditions and preconditions of t, respectively.

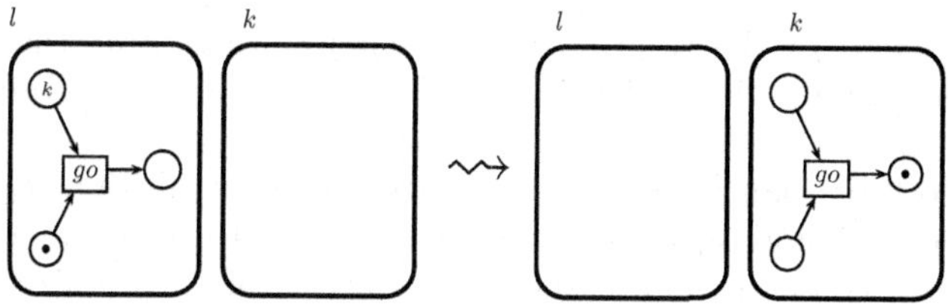

Fig. 2. Movement transitions

Then, an MSPN system $\mathcal{S}$ is just a pair $(\mathcal{N}, \mathcal{M})$, where $\mathcal{N}$ is a set of disjoint nets and $\mathcal{M}$ is the initial marking of $\mathcal{N}$. A marking of $\mathcal{N}$ is a pair (M, loc), where M is a function that maps each place to an element in $\mathcal{MS}_f(Tokens)$, that is, to a finite multiset of tokens, and $loc : \mathcal{N} \to \mathcal{L}$ maps each net to its current location, taken from the set $\mathcal{L}$. We will denote by $\uplus$ and $-$ the multiset union and the multiset difference, respectively, to distinguish them from $\cup$ and $\setminus$, the corresponding operations over sets. We will usually write $T_{\mathcal{S}}$ to denote the union of the transitions in each net of the system.

Since our nets are a particular class of coloured nets [11], their transitions fire relative to a *mode*, that chooses in an adequate way the particular tokens to be taken from the set of precondition places. Modes are defined as mappings from $Var(t)$ to $Tokens$, assigning values in $\mathcal{T}$ to variables in $Var_{\mathcal{T}}$. We will denote modes with $\sigma, \sigma', \sigma_1, \sigma_2, \ldots$

Autonomous transitions t with $\lambda(t) \notin \{new, go\}$ work as ordinary transitions in coloured nets (see Fig. 1 left). Movement transitions, those labelled by go, are autonomous transitions that change the location of the net firing it. For that purpose, every movement transition has a single distinguished locality precondition to specify the destination of the net (see Fig. 2). Name-creating transitions, those labelled by new, have exactly one identifier postcondition. They are autonomous transitions that generate a fresh identifier in its identifier postcondition.

Instead, the firing of a synchronizing transition needs the presence of a *compatible* transition in the same location, that will be fired at the same time. For a pair of synchronizing transitions t_1 and t_2 we denote by $post(t_1, t_2) = post(t_1) \cup post(t_2)$, $pre(t_1, t_2) = pre(t_1) \cup pre(t_2)$ and $Var(t_1, t_2) = post(t_1, t_2) \cup pre(t_1, t_2)$. The compatibility conditions are merely syntactical: On the one hand, their labels must be complementary, $s?$ and $s!$ for some $s \in S$; On the other hand, the pair of transitions must meet together the same constraint imposed to autonomous transitions, that is, $post(t_1, t_2) \subseteq pre(t_1, t_2)$ (see Fig. 1 right); Finally, whenever an authentication variable (a variable in $Var_{Auth} \subset Var_{Id}$) appears in a precondition arc, then it must also appear in a precondition arc of its compatible transitions; This is the way the mechanism for authentication is implemented, by forcing the matching of two identifers. Intuitively, we can see the label s of the synchronizing transition as the public information about the offer-request of that service (as its name, or even the particular protocol used). However, the secret information, that establishes a secure channel between both parties, as in π-calculus, is specified by the set of authentication tickets in authentication preconditions (those linked to the transition with variables in Var_{Auth}). These primitives are enough to capture the most widely used authentication policy in Ubiquitous Computing, namely *Transient Secure Association* [19].

In order to fire a pair of compatible synchronizing transitions t_1 and t_2 they must be co-located and separately fireable according to the ordinary firing rule, but relative to a common mode σ, so that in the case of synchronizing transitions are mappings from $Var(t_1, t_2)$ to *Tokens*.

In order to have a more compact notation we will use $u, u', u_1, u_2, \ldots$ to range both over autonomous transitions and pairs of compatible synchronizing transitions, thus writing $\mathcal{M}[u(\sigma)\rangle\mathcal{M}'$ if $\mathcal{M}'$ is the reached state after the firing of u with mode σ. We represent by $[\![\mathcal{S}]\!]$ the set of traces of $\mathcal{S}$, where a trace of length $n \geq 0$ is any sequence $\mathcal{M}_0[u_1(\sigma_1)\rangle \cdots [u_n(\sigma_n)\rangle\mathcal{M}_n$ starting from the initial marking $\mathcal{M}_0$ of $\mathcal{S}$. If tr_1 is a trace ending in a marking $\mathcal{M}_1$, tr_2 is a trace starting in $\mathcal{M}_2$ and $\mathcal{M}_1[u(\sigma)\rangle\mathcal{M}_2$, we will write $tr_1[u(\sigma)\rangle tr_2$ to denote the trace that results from the firing of all the transitions in tr_1, followed by $u(\sigma)$ and ending with those in tr_2.

3 Access Control Protocol

As a simple but illustrative example, we present a system that describes the selling of tickets and the access control mechanism for a concert at a theatre. The system is composed of three principals: a ticket office, the theatre staff and an agent that updates the theatre database with the tickets that have been sold. The ticket office and the forwarder agent are shown in Fig. 3, that represents the locality named k, and the theatre is shown in Fig. 4, that represents the locality named l. The ticket office simply generates new tickets and sells them, so that they are ready to be forwarded to the theatre. The forwarder agent (composed of two unconnected components, inside the dotted line) moves alternatively between the locations where the ticket office and the theatre are located, k and l, respectively. When it is co-located with the ticket office, it is willing to receive new valid tickets and when it is co-located with the theatre, it is willing to output those tickets. Notice that the ticket office and the forwarder agent communicate using the private shared key K_1, while the agent and the theatre use key K_2. This is formalized by assuming that the variable c is an authentication variable, that is, $c \in Var_{Auth}$, so that whenever it appears in one of the parts of a pair of compatible synchronizing transitions, then it must also appear in the other part. The theatre holds in DB all the sold tickets, those that clients may exhibit to enter the concert. The theatre has two entrances: a normal entrance, `door1`, and another one for people accompanied by a child, `door2`. Anyone entering through the latter may use a single seat for him and his child. People entering by any of the doors arrive at the same lounge, where an usher takes them to their seat.

We want to avoid the situation in which two clients are seated in the same place, if they entered through the normal entrance, or more than two, otherwise. This property (access control) can be stated in terms of coverability: Suppose some client has a ticket η and accesses through the normal door. In that case

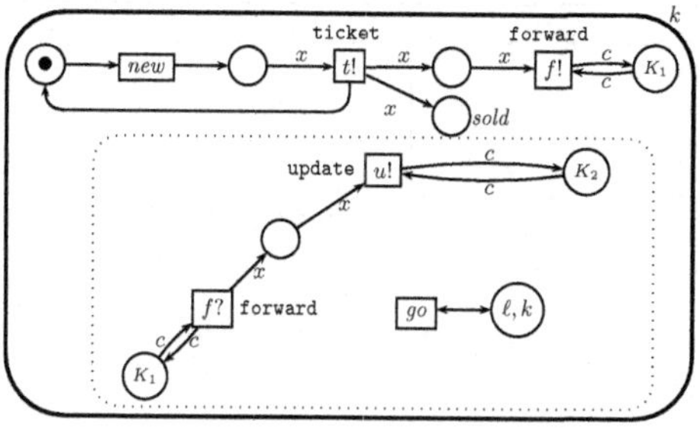

Fig. 3. Ticket office and forwarder agent

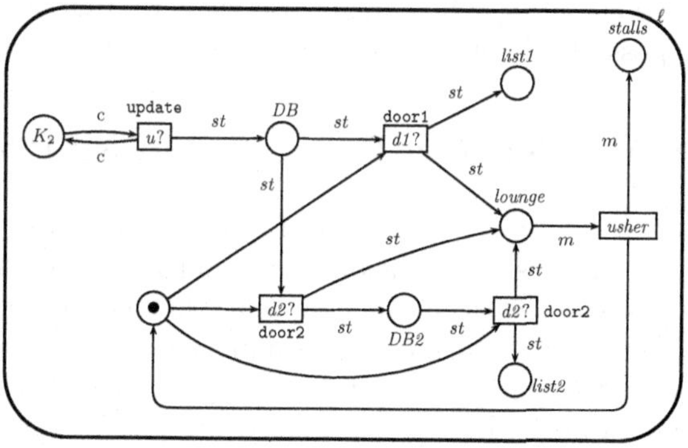

Fig. 4. Theatre

η will be annotated in the normal list, represented by the place named *list1*, so that the property is broken for that client if some marking in which η appears both in that list, and at least twice in the stalls, is reachable. Analogously, any client that enters by the other door will expect that any marking in which his ticket appears in place *list2* and more than twice in *stalls* cannot be covered. Moreover, it could be checked that any ticket exhibited by those who access the theatre was indeed one that was sold at the ticket office (integrity).

Of course, the system in isolation is trivially secure, since in the absence of clients none of the previous facts can happen (the system is blocked after the ticket office generates the first unsold ticket, except for the forwarder agent jumping between localities l and k). Thus, in order to study the security of the system, we must consider that clients are part of the environment, so that they can range from honorable parents to ruthless scalpers. All we must assume about clients is that they do not know K_1 or K_2, the private keys that the different components use to communicate, but they may know (in fact, they must know) the locations where the ticket office and the theatre reside.

We may also add to the system well behaved clients that we expect to interact with the theatre, like the one in Fig. 5, which simply goes to the ticket office, buys a ticket, moves to the theatre and uses the ticket to enter the theater. In

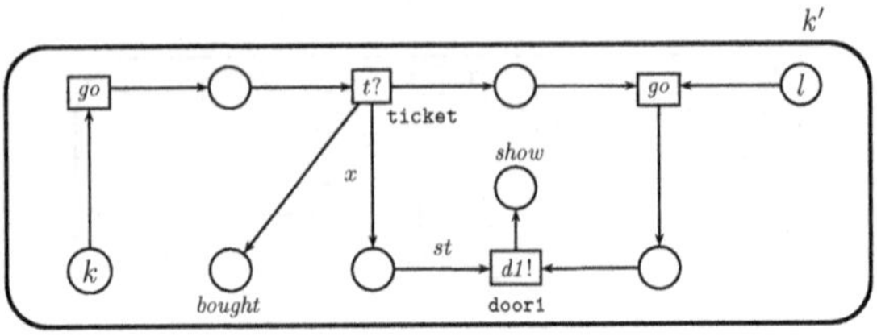

Fig. 5. Possible client

this way we may study properties that deal with these particular clients. For instance, we could be interested in checking whether it is always possible to see the show after visiting the ticket office (availability), which could be formalized as a home space property [8]. Once again, we want to guarantee this property even when other possible clients (or scalpers) are present.

4 Verification of Security Properties in MSPN Systems

We are interested in verifying properties of our systems when they are in an unknown, unreliable or possibly malicious environment. Thus, we need to define a way to merge a system with another system, that can be considered as its environment. In our setting, to merge is simply to put in parallel. Given the modular nature of our systems, the parallel composition of two MSPN systems is defined straightforwardly. In the following definition, + denotes the disjoint union of maps with disjoint domain.

Definition 1. *Let* $\mathcal{S}_1 = (\mathcal{N}_1, \mathcal{M}_{01})$ *and* $\mathcal{S}_2 = (\mathcal{N}_2, \mathcal{M}_{02})$ *be two MSPN systems with* $\mathcal{M}_{0i} = (M_i, loc_i)$ *for* $i = 1, 2$. *Denoting by* $\mathcal{M}_{01} + \mathcal{M}_{02}$ *the pair* $(M_1 + M_2, loc_1 + loc_2)$, *if* $\mathcal{N}_1$ *and* $\mathcal{N}_2$ *have disjoint sets of places and transitions then* $(\mathcal{N}_1 \cup \mathcal{N}_2, \mathcal{M}_{01} + \mathcal{M}_{02})$ *is also an MSPN system, that will be called the parallel composition of* $\mathcal{S}_1$ *and* $\mathcal{S}_2$, *denoted by* $\mathcal{S}_1 \mid \mathcal{S}_2$.

If (M_i, loc_i) is a marking of $\mathcal{S}_i$, then $(M_1 + M_2, loc_1 + loc_2)$ is a marking of $\mathcal{S}_1 \mid \mathcal{S}_2$ and, conversely, if (M, loc) is a marking of $\mathcal{S}_1 \mid \mathcal{S}_2$ then $(M|_{P_{\mathcal{N}_i}}, loc|_{\mathcal{N}_i})$ is a marking of $\mathcal{N}_i$, for $i \in \{1, 2\}$. Next we introduce an auxiliary definition, to denote the set of locality and identifier tokens appearing in some marked net.

Definition 2. *Let* $\mathcal{M} = (M, loc)$ *be a marking of an MSPN system* $\mathcal{S} = (\mathcal{N}, \mathcal{M}_0)$. *We define* $locs(\mathcal{M})$ *as the set of localities at* $\mathcal{M}$, *that is,* $locs(\mathcal{M}) = \{k \in \mathcal{L} \mid \exists p \in P_{\mathcal{L}}, k \in M(p)\} \cup loc(\mathcal{N})$. *Analogously, we define* $Ids(\mathcal{M}) = \{a \in Id \mid \exists p \in P_{Id}, a \in M(p)\}$. *We denote the union of these two sets by* $cl(\mathcal{M})$. *Moreover, we take* $locs(\mathcal{S}) = locs(\mathcal{M}_0)$, $Ids(\mathcal{S}) = Ids(\mathcal{M}_0)$, *and* $cl(\mathcal{S}) = cl(\mathcal{M}_0)$.

In the following definition we introduce our notion of admissible environment.

Definition 3. *Let* $\mathcal{S}$ *be an MSPN system and* $\Phi \subseteq CTokens$. *A* $(\Phi, \mathcal{S})$*-environment is a MSPN-system* $\mathcal{P}$ *disjoint with* $\mathcal{S}$ *such that* $cl(\mathcal{S}) \cap cl(\mathcal{P}) \subseteq \Phi$. *We denote by* $Env(\Phi, \mathcal{S})$ *the set of* $(\Phi, \mathcal{S})$*-environments.*

Next we use these environments to define an alternative semantics of MSPN systems, that will allow us to deal with open systems. Intuitively, we consider as open trace of a system, relative to Φ, any trace in the original semantics that is produced by the system when put in any environment whose initial knowledge about the system is contained in Φ. First, we give an auxiliary definition.

Definition 4. *Let tr be a trace of an MSPN system* $\mathcal{S} \mid \mathcal{P}$ *with* $\mathcal{S} = (\mathcal{N}, \mathcal{M}_0)$. *We define the projection of tr over* $\mathcal{N}$, *that we denote by* $tr|_{\mathcal{S}}$, *by induction on the length of tr, as follows:*

- $(M, loc)|_{\mathcal{S}} = (M|_{P_{\mathcal{N}}}, loc|_{\mathcal{N}})$, *with* $P_{\mathcal{N}}$ *the set of places in* $\mathcal{N}$.
- $\big(tr[u(\sigma)\rangle\mathcal{M}\big)|_{\mathcal{S}} = tr|_{\mathcal{S}}$ *if* $u \in T_{\mathcal{P}} \cup T_{\mathcal{P}} \times T_{\mathcal{P}}$.
- $\big(tr[u(\sigma)\rangle\mathcal{M}\big)|_{\mathcal{S}} = tr|_{\mathcal{S}}[u(\sigma)|_{\mathcal{S}}\rangle\mathcal{M}|_{\mathcal{S}}$ *if* $u \notin T_{\mathcal{P}} \cup T_{\mathcal{P}} \times T_{\mathcal{P}}$.

where $u(\sigma)|_{\mathcal{S}}$ *is defined as*

- $u(\sigma)|_{\mathcal{S}} = u(\sigma)$ *if* $u \in T_{\mathcal{S}} \cup T_{\mathcal{S}} \times T_{\mathcal{S}}$.
- $(t, t')(\sigma)|_{\mathcal{S}} = t(\sigma|_{Var(t)})$ *if* $t \in T_{\mathcal{S}}$ *and* $t' \in T_{\mathcal{P}}$.
- $(t, t')(\sigma)|_{\mathcal{S}} = t'(\sigma|_{Var(t')})$ *if* $t' \in T_{\mathcal{S}}$ *and* $t \in T_{\mathcal{P}}$.

Definition 5. *Let* $\mathcal{S} = (\mathcal{N}, \mathcal{M}_0)$ *be an MSPN system and* $\Phi \subseteq CTokens$. *We say that a sequence* $otr = \mathcal{M}_0[u_1(\sigma_1)\rangle\mathcal{M}_1 \ldots \mathcal{M}_{n-1}[u_n(\sigma_n)\rangle\mathcal{M}_n$ *is a* Φ*-open trace of* $\mathcal{S}$ *if there are* $\mathcal{P} \in Env(\Phi, \mathcal{S})$ *and* $tr \in [\![\mathcal{S} \mid \mathcal{P}]\!]$ *such that* $otr = tr|_{\mathcal{S}}$. *If a* Φ*-open trace ends in a marking* $\mathcal{M}$ *we say that* $\mathcal{M}$ *is* Φ*-reachable.*

Let us comment on the different concepts appearing in the definitions above. A Φ-open trace is the projection over $\mathcal{N}$ of a traces that $\mathcal{S}$ can generate in the presence of some environment, provided its initial knowledge about the system is in Φ. This fact is formalized by the condition $cl(\mathcal{P}) \cap cl(\mathcal{S}) \subseteq \Phi$, on $(\Phi, \mathcal{S})$-environments, meaning that any identifier or locality token appearing in $\mathcal{P}$, that also appears in $\mathcal{S}$, is in the set of public names Φ.

As defined above, the composition $\mathcal{S} \mid \mathcal{P}$ is an MSPN system with its ordinary trace semantics. However, we are not interested in the behaviour of these environments, but only in that of $\mathcal{S}$. For that, we take the projections of such traces over $\mathcal{N}$, removing the transitions fired autonomously by the environment and also any information about $\mathcal{P}$ in markings, modes and transitions. Once this is done, we can find as part of a trace steps like $\mathcal{M}[t(\sigma)\rangle\mathcal{M}'$, with $\lambda(t) \in Sync$, meaning that $\mathcal{S}$ has synchronized with its environment.

Though the system in Sect. 3 is (almost) blocked according to the original semantics, that is not the case at all under the secure semantics. As said before, we can assume that the only values in the system that the environment may know in its initial state are k and l. Therefore, we are interested in its behaviour as a $\{k, l\}$-open system, that is, in its $\{k, l\}$-open traces. Notice that, if we consider $\mathcal{S}$ to be the system constituted by the ticket office, the agent and the theatre, then the client in Fig. 5 can be regarded as a $(\{k, l\}, \mathcal{S})$-environment.

Once we have introduced the secure semantics, we can use it as foundation for the study of the behaviour of our systems in any valid environment. For instance, we can define the following properties in the new setting.

Definition 6. *The* Φ-reachability *problem consists on deciding, given a marking* $\mathcal{M}$ *of an MSPN system* $\mathcal{S}$*, if* $\mathcal{M}$ *is* Φ*-reachable. Analogously, the* Φ-coverability *problem consists on deciding, given a marking* $\mathcal{M}$*, if any marking covering* $\mathcal{M}$ *is* Φ*-reachable. Finally, the* Φ-home space *problem consists on deciding, given a set of markings and a* Φ*-open trace otr if there exists a* Φ*-open trace that extends otr and ends in a marking in that set.*

By using these notions we can study several interesting security properties of open systems. In particular, the properties discussed in the example in Sect. 3 can be characterized by means of $\{k, l\}$-coverability and $\{k, l\}$-home space problems. For instance, two clients entering by `door1` cannot be seated in the same place if and only if the marking containing only one token η in *list1* and two tokens η in *stalls* cannot be $\{k, l\}$-covered.

5 Symbolic Semantics of MSPN Systems

In order to make the secure semantics for MSPN systems manageable, we need a way to eliminate the quantifier in the environments that appears in its definition. For that purpose we have developed a symbolic trace semantics for MSPN systems, that takes into account in an abstract way any possible environment. The key idea to develop this semantics is to allow the firing of a synchronizing transition even if the synchronizing counterpart is not in the system, whenever it is legal according to Φ (which intuitively means that it could actually be fired in the environment), together with all other normal synchronizations. Therefore, Φ will represent the knowledge about the system accumulated by the environment along their history. Since this knowledge can change due to the interactions between the system and the environment, we must consider it as part of our markings. Therefore, we add a third component to the markings of MSPN systems, that now will have the form (M, loc, Φ), where Φ represents the knowledge that the environment has about the system. We will call those triples *symbolic markings* and we denote them by $\mathcal{M}^{\Phi}$, with $\mathcal{M} = (M, loc)$.

By "knowledge about the system" we mean the part of the set of tokens in the system that the environment knows. This knowledge comes from two different sources: The system may output some tokens that the environment does not know yet. Dually, the environment itself may give to the system a token that the system did not previously have. Such tokens become part of the system, and obviously they are already known by the environment. In order to distinguish between these two sources of knowledge we will split each Φ in Φ^{out} and Φ^{in}, so that $\Phi = (\Phi^{in}, \Phi^{out})$. We will denote by Φ^{io} the union of Φ^{out} and Φ^{in}.

The definition of the symbolic semantics is based on the notion of symbolic firing of an MSPN system. In [14] we did not need modes of synchronizing transitions, since they were never fired in isolation, but always in pairs. Now we need to define the symbolic mode of a synchronizing transition, which is simply done as expected.

Definition 7. *Let $\mathcal{S}$ be an MSPN system and $t \in T$ such that $\lambda(t) \in Sync$. A* symbolic mode *of t is any mapping $\sigma : Var(t) \to Tokens$ such that $\sigma(x) \in \mathcal{T} \Leftrightarrow x \in Var_{\mathcal{T}}$ for $\mathcal{T} \in \{\bullet, \mathcal{L}, Id\}$.*

Notice that synchronizing transitions were not syntactically restricted as autonomous transitions were, regarding the set of variables in its adjacent arcs: It can be the case that there is some variable x in an arc going out of a transition but not in an incoming arc, that is, $x \in post(t) \setminus pre(t)$. In such a case a symbolic mode for that transition can assign any value of the corresponding colour to that variable. Next we proceed with the definition of symbolic firings:

Definition 8. *Let $\mathcal{S} = (\mathcal{N}, \mathcal{M}_0)$ be an MSPN system, $\Phi = (\Phi^{in}, \Phi^{out}) \subseteq CTokens \times CTokens$ with $\Phi^{in} \cap \Phi^{out} = \emptyset$. Let us also consider $N = (P_N, T_N, F_N, \lambda_N, C_N) \in \mathcal{N}$. We define $[u(\sigma)\rangle^{\#}$ as the least relation on symbolic markings such that:*

1. *If $\mathcal{M}_1[t(\sigma)\rangle\mathcal{M}_2$ with $\lambda(t) \in \mathcal{A} \setminus \{new\}$ then $\mathcal{M}_1^{\Phi}[t(\sigma)\rangle^{\#}\mathcal{M}_2^{\Phi}$.*
2. *If $\mathcal{M}_1[t(\sigma)\rangle\mathcal{M}_2$ with $\lambda(t) = new$ and $\sigma(F(t,p)) \notin \Phi^{io}$ for all $p \in t^{\bullet} \cap C^{-1}(Id)$, then $\mathcal{M}_1^{\Phi}[t(\sigma)\rangle^{\#}\mathcal{M}_2^{\Phi}$.*
3. *If $\mathcal{M}_1[(t,t')(\sigma)\rangle\mathcal{M}_2$ with $\lambda(t) \in Sync$, then $\mathcal{M}_1^{\Phi}[(t,t')(\sigma)\rangle^{\#}\mathcal{M}_2^{\Phi}$.*
4. *Let $t \in T_N$, $\lambda(t) \in Sync$, σ a symbolic mode for t and $\mathcal{M}_1$ a marking of $\mathcal{S}$ such that $\sigma(F(p,t)) \in M_1(p)$ for all $p \in P_N$. If $loc_1(N) \in \Phi^{io}$, $\sigma(x) \in \Phi^{io}$ for every $x \in pre(t) \cap Var_{Aut}$ and $\sigma(x) \notin cl(\mathcal{M}_1) \setminus \Phi^{io}$ for every $x \in post(t) \setminus pre(t)$, then considering*
   - *$M_2(p) = \big(M_1(p) - \{\sigma(F(p,t))\}\big) \uplus \{\sigma(F(t,p))\}$ for every $p \in P$.*
   - *$\Phi_2 = \big(\Phi^{in} \cup (\sigma(post(t)) \setminus \Phi^{io}), \Phi^{out} \cup (\sigma(pre(t)) \setminus \Phi^{io})\big)$.*

   and taking $\mathcal{M}_2 = (M_2, loc_1)$ we have that $\mathcal{M}_1^{\Phi}[t(\sigma)\rangle^{\#}\mathcal{M}_2^{\Phi_2}$ is a symbolic step.

We say that a marking $\mathcal{M}^{\Phi}$ is symbolically Φ_0-reachable if there is a sequence of symbolic steps, that we will call symbolic trace, *ending in $\mathcal{M}^{\Phi}$:*

$$\mathcal{M}_0^{\Phi_0}[u_1(\sigma_1)\rangle^{\#}\mathcal{M}_1^{\Phi_1} \cdots \mathcal{M}_{n-1}^{\Phi_{n-1}}[u_n(\sigma_n)\rangle^{\#}\mathcal{M}^{\Phi}$$

Let us comment on the previous definition. Whenever the MSPN system performs a (internal) step it also performs a symbolic step, without changing the knowledge of the environment, as stated in items 1, 2 and 3. In item 2, we also say that when the system creates a new name, it must not be in Φ^{io}. This condition imposes no restriction on the set of possible firings, but only on the set of produced names: any name not in Φ^{io} could be chosen as fresh.

In 4 we recreate the other synchronizing transition needed to perform a step, even when only one of the synchronizing transitions is enabled. The environment, that intuitively fires the compatible transition, must meet a number of conditions to be able to synchronize. First, it must know the locality where the synchronization takes place, that is, $loc_1(N_i) \in \Phi^{io}$. Second, if there is any authentication arc labelled by x, then the synchronizing counterpart must know how to match the value of x, that is, it must be the case that $\sigma(x) \in \Phi^{io}$. Third, the environment cannot offer the system an identifier or a locality it does not know, so that no arc going to a postcondition can be labelled by a variable x

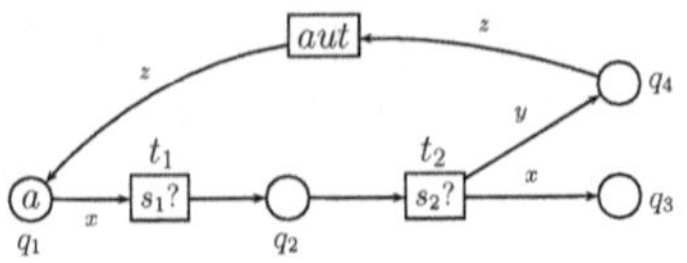

Fig. 6. Example 1

instantiated to a value known to the system but not to the environment, that is, $\sigma(x) \notin cl(\mathcal{M}) \setminus \Phi^{io}$. The marking obtained by the symbolic step is the result of firing t without its counterpart; besides, the knowledge of the environment is increased by the values in the arcs from preconditions, those that the system offers to the environment, and by the values in the arcs to postconditions, those that the environment offers to the system, that were not previously part of that knowledge.

Now let us study the relation between both semantics. In Sect. 4 we used sets $\Phi \subseteq CTokens$ to represent the knowledge of the environment. However, in the definition of the symbolic semantics in Sect. 5 we split that knowledge in two sets Φ^{in} and Φ^{out}, to distinguish the two ways in which the environment can get to know names in the system. Now, if we want to move from the symbolic frame to the open frame, all we must do is to forget that distinction, by merging both sets. Conversely, when we have $\Phi_0 \subseteq CTokens$ and we want to move to the symbolic frame we must choose a way to split that knowledge. We will denote by $split(\Phi)$ the set of pairs in which Φ can be split.

Certainly, we could get a uniform presentation of both semantics by introducing also the distinction between Φ^{in} and Φ^{out} in the definition of secure semantics or by removing that distinction in the definition of symbolic semantics. However, we have not done the former because we think that establishing that distinction at that point would be a bit ad-hoc, since at the initial state the intuition of "how a name was learnt by the environment" does not exist. And we have not done the latter either, because whenever we have indeed that distinction, it is clear that names in both sets play a different role. For instance, we can specify confidentiality properties by using the names in Φ^{out}, which does not have sense without the distinction between both sources of knowledge.

Proposition 1. *Given an MSPN system, if $\mathcal{M}^{\Phi}$ is symbolically Φ_0-reachable then $\mathcal{M}$ is Φ_0-reachable.*

The previous result states that every symbolic trace is obtained by adding the corresponding Φ components to the markings of an open trace. We illustrate its proof by means of a simple example.

Example 1. Let us consider the system $\mathcal{S}$ shown in Fig. 6, composed of a single net and with no movement transition, so that we can disregard the locality component from its markings. We will represent these markings in the form $M = (M^1, M^2, M^3, M^4)$, where $M^i = M(q_i) \in \mathcal{MS}_f(Tokens)$. Let us also consider its symbolic trace $M_0^{\Phi_0}[t_1(\sigma_1)\rangle^{\#} M_1^{\Phi_1}[t_2(\sigma_2)\rangle^{\#} M_2^{\Phi_2}$

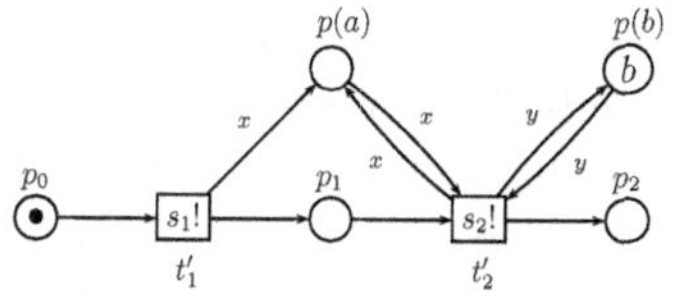

Fig. 7. $(\emptyset, \mathcal{S})$-environment $\mathcal{P}$ for trace in Example 1

where
$$M_0 = (\{a\}, \emptyset, \emptyset, \emptyset) \quad \Phi_0 = (\emptyset, \emptyset) \quad \sigma_1 = [x \to a]$$
$$M_1 = (\emptyset, \{a\}, \emptyset, \emptyset) \quad \Phi_1 = (\emptyset, \{a\}) \quad \sigma_2 = [x \to a, y \to b]$$
$$M_2 = (\emptyset, \emptyset, \{a\}, \{b\}) \quad \Phi_2 = (\{b\}, \{a\})$$

It can be checked that it is indeed a legal symbolic trace, obtained by applying rule 4 twice in the definition of symbolic firings. In the first step of the trace the environment receives the token a by synchronizing with the system on s_1, so that it gets to know a. Then, in the second firing, the environment gives a back to the system, together with a new token b, previously unknown to the system.

Given a symbolic trace, we have to construct a legal environment that would generate the corresponding $\emptyset$-open trace. Since the trace has two steps that use rule 4, the environment must have two synchronizing transitions, compatible with those in $\mathcal{S}$ and meant to be fired in a row (this is why we add p_0, p_1 and p_2 as done). Then we add to the environment two places $p(a)$ and $p(b)$, that it will use to store a and b, respectively, together with arcs that allow the environment to receive a after the first synchronization, and arcs that allow the environment to output the tokens a and b after the second synchronization. Notice that the initial marking of the environment may contain b, but not a, since it is a token of the system not in Φ_0. The result of this construction is shown in Fig. 7.

The previous result says that the symbolic semantics is correct with respect to the secure semantics. Next we state the corresponding completeness result.

Proposition 2. *Given an MSPN system, if* $\mathcal{M}$ *is* Φ_0*-reachable and* $\Phi'_0 \in split(\Phi_0)$ *then there is exactly one* Φ *such that* $\mathcal{M}^{\Phi}$ *is symbolically* Φ'_0*-reachable.*

Therefore, every Φ-open trace can be *represented* in the symbolic framework by a symbolic trace. This is true whatever the way in which we choose to split Φ, since enabledness of symbolic transitions only depends on Φ^{io}.

The two previous results prove that the symbolic semantics is in fact a *tagging* [16] of the secure semantics. A tagged semantics is a conservative extension of the original semantics with a number of tags, that capture information about the runtime history of the system. This is formalized in [16] by characterizing tagged systems as quotients of the reachability tree, by identifying those traces that capture the same information about their histories. In our case, tags are the Φ component of symbolic markings, that capture the information about the system accumulated by the environment along its execution.

Once we have established the relation between both semantics we can use the symbolic semantics for the proof of results about the secure semantics. For instance, if we prove the decidability of coverability for the symbolic semantics we immediately get the decidability of Φ-coverability. In fact, we have already done it in [17], though unfortunately we cannot show the details here for lack of space, since they are rather involved.

Proposition 3. *The coverability problem for the symbolic semantics is decidable. Therefore, the Φ-coverability problem is decidable.*

Just to give a small hint about the proof, having defined the symbolic semantics directly as a transition system between symbolic markings, we can talk about predecessors without explicitly mentioning the environment. This also generates a more compact state space so that we can apply the techniques based on well quasi-orders developed in [2]. Thus, according to Prop. 3, the security properties discussed in Sect. 3 that are expressed in terms of coverability, could be automatically verified.

6 Conclusions and Future Work

Though several models for mobility based on Petri Nets have been proposed, we think that the important issue of security has not been properly addressed yet within this framework. For that reason we introduced MSPN systems, composed of a particular class of Petri Nets with transitions that can generate fresh names to be used as security primitives and to establish security properties of the systems. In this paper we have defined an alternative semantics for MSPN systems, called *secure semantics*, that makes possible their study from a security point of view.

In order to have a manageable definition of the secure semantics, we have defined a *symbolic semantics*, that is based on an extended firing relation on markings that takes into account any possible environment in an abstract way. We have established the relation between the secure semantics and the symbolic semantics, namely that the symbolic semantics is correct and complete with respect to the secure semantics. More precisely, we have proved that every symbolic trace comes from the corresponding open trace (by erasing the Φ component) and that for every open trace there exists a symbolic trace that represents it. Since the symbolic semantics is a *tagging* of the secure semantics, we conclude that the symbolic semantics is a conservative extension of the secure one, and that this extension is also complete regarding the piece of history of our systems considered: the knowledge accumulated by the environment.

We have recently developed a prototype of a tool for the integrated design and verification of systems based in our MSPN's [18]. As supporting language for the implementation we have chosen Maude [7], that is a reflective programming language based on rewriting logic. Our prototype includes a decision procedure for the ordinary coverability problem in MSPN systems. We are currently extending our tool so that it can also deal with Φ-coverability.

In this paper we have emphasized the security properties that can be expressed in terms of coverability. However, we have seen that this is not the case for all properties, as when they imply some sort of liveness, as availability does. We plan to study which security properties can be stated in terms of usual properties in Petri Nets and whether they can be verified in our framework. Regarding the latter, we want to study whether the existing results about coverability in the well quasi-order theory can be extended to the home space property.

Besides, we plan to try to extend our results, both concerning symbolic semantics and decidability of properties, to more elaborated models where processes can replicate, locations can be created or dynamically nested, although we already know that whenever we combine too many features then decidability of coverability, in particular, is lost. This would lead us to search to what extent we can combine some of these features while preserving the decidability of the security properties of the definable systems.

References

[1] A. Asperti, and N. Busi. *Mobile Petri Nets.* Technical Report UBLCS-96-10, University of Bologna, 1996.

[2] P. Aziz Abdulla, K. Cerans, and B. Jonsson. *Algorithmic Analysis of Programs with Well Quasi-Ordered Domains.* Inf. Comput., 160(1-2):109–127, 2000.

[3] M.A. Bednarczyk, L. Bernardinello, W. Pawlowski, and L. Pomello. *Modelling Mobility with Petri Hypernets.* WADT'04. LNCS vol. 3423, Springer, 2004.

[4] P. Baldan, A. Corradini, H. Ehrig and R. Heckel. *Compositional semantics for open Petri Nets based on deterministic processes.* Mathematical Structures in Computer Science 15(1), 2005, pp. 1-35. Cambridge University Press.

[5] L. Cardelli and A. D. Gordon. Mobile ambients. In Foundations of Software Science and Computation Structures, LNCS vol. 1378, pp. 140-155. Springer, 1998.

[6] S.Christensen and N.D.Hansen. *Coloured Petri Nets Extended with Channels for Synchronous Communication.* 15th Int. Conference on Application and Theory of Petri Nets, ICATPN'94. LNCS vol. 815, pp. 159-178. Springer, 1994.

[7] M. Clavel, F. Durán, S. Eker, P. Lincoln, N. Martí-Oliet, J. Meseguer and C. Talcott. *The Maude 2.0 System.* In Proc. Rewriting Techniques and Applications, 2003. LNCS vol. 2706, pp. 76–87. Springer, 2003.

[8] C. Johnen. *Decidability of Home Space Property.* Petri Net Newsletter(29), 1988.

[9] E. Kindler. *A Compositional Partial Order Semantics for Petri Net Components.* ICATPN'94. LNCS vol. 815, pp. 159-178. Springer, 1994.

[10] I.A. Lomazova. *Nested Petri Nets; Multi-level and Recursive Systems.* Fundamenta Informaticae vol.47, pp.283-293. IOS Press, 2002.

[11] K. Jensen. *Coloured Petri Nets.Basic Concepts, Analysis Methods and Practical Use.* Volume 1,Basic Concepts. Monographs in Theor. Comp. Science. Springer,1997.

[12] C. Lakos. *A Petri Net View of Mobility.* Formal Techniques for Networked and Distributed Systems, FORTE'05. LNCS vol. 3731, pp. 174-188. Springer, 2005.

[13] R. Milner. *Theories for the Global Ubiquitous Computer.* Foundations of Software Science and Computation Structures, LNCS vol.2987, pp.5-11. Springer, 2004.

[14] F. Rosa-Velardo, O. Marroquín-Alonso and D. de Frutos-Escrig. *Mobile Synchronizing Petri Nets: a choreographic approach for coordination in Ubiquitous Systems.* In MTCoord'05. ENTCS vol.150, Issue 1. Elsevier,2006.

[15] F. Rosa-Velardo, D. de Frutos-Escrig and O. Marroquín-Alonso. *On the expressiveness of Mobile Synchronizing Petri Nets.* 3rd Int. Workshop on Security Issues in Concurrency, SecCo'05. ENTCS (to appear). `http://kimba.mat.ucm.es/~frosa`.

[16] F. Rosa-Velardo, C. Segura-Díaz and D. de Frutos-Escrig. *Tagged systems: a framework for the specification of history dependent properties.* ENTCS vol. 137(1), Elsevier, 2005.

[17] F. Rosa-Velardo, and D. Frutos-Escrig. *Deciding Coverability in Open Petri Net Systems (submitted).* `http://kimba.mat.ucm.es/~frosa`.

[18] F. Rosa-Velardo. *Coding Mobile Synchronizing Petri Nets into Rewriting Logic.* 7th International Workshop on Rule-Based Programming, RULE'06. ENTCS (to appear). `http://kimba.mat.ucm.es/~frosa`.

[19] F. Stajano. Security for Ubiquitous Computing. Wiley Series in Communications Networking & Distributed Systems. John Wiley & Sons, 2002.

[20] R. Valk. *Petri Nets as Token Objects: An Introduction to Elementary Object Nets.* App. and Theory of Petri Nets 1998, LNCS vol.1420, pp.1-25. Springer, 1998.

[21] M. Weiser. *Some Computer Science Issues in Ubiquitous Computing.* Comm. of the ACM vol.36(7), pp.74-84. ACM Press, 1993.

Sigref – A Symbolic Bisimulation Tool Box*

Ralf Wimmer[1], Marc Herbstritt[1], Holger Hermanns[2],
Kelley Strampp[1], and Bernd Becker[1]

[1] Albert-Ludwigs-University Freiburg, Germany
{wimmer,herbstri,strampp,becker}@informatik.uni-freiburg.de
[2] Saarland University, Saarbrücken, Germany
hermanns@cs.uni-sb.de

Abstract. We present a uniform signature-based approach to compute the most popular bisimulations. Our approach is implemented symbolically using BDDs, which enables the handling of very large transition systems. Signatures for the bisimulations are built up from a few generic building blocks, which naturally correspond to efficient BDD operations. Thus, the definition of an appropriate signature is the key for a rapid development of algorithms for other types of bisimulation.

We provide experimental evidence of the viability of this approach by presenting computational results for many bisimulations on real-world instances. The experiments show cases where our framework can handle state spaces efficiently that are far too large to handle for any tool that requires an explicit state space description.

1 Introduction

The infamous state space explosion problem is an omnipresent phenomenon in state-based verification. One promising approach to combat this problem is based on *bisimulation minimization*, where the state space is compressed by building the quotient under some appropriate notion of bisimulation. In the presence of internal activities and composition operators the benefits of this technique are particularly impressive [2,3,4]. The algorithmic workhorse for this minimization is a partition refinement algorithm [5,6].

Binary decision diagrams (BDDs) are another powerful approach to handle extremely large state spaces. With BDDs such state spaces can be represented symbolically in a compact way. It is well-known that only the application of symbolic methods opened the gates for model checking of large systems [7].

This paper explores the seemingly obvious idea to combine BDDs and bisimulation minimization. This idea is not new. To our knowledge, [8,9] were the first to apply BDD techniques to bisimulation minimization whereas Bouali [10] introduced the term "symbolic bisimulation minimization". Other recent work

* This work was partly supported by the German Research Council (DFG) as part of the Transregional Collaborative Research Center "Automatic Verification and Analysis of Complex Systems" (SFB/TR 14 AVACS). See www.avacs.org for more information.

S. Graf and W. Zhang (Eds.): ATVA 2006, LNCS 4218, pp. 477–492, 2006.

in the context of efficient bisimulation minimization algorithms has focussed on parallel implementations, most notably the work of Blom and Orzan [11], who introduce a parallel, signature-based, branching bisimulation minimization algorithm. A *signature* is a concise characteristic function for the bisimulation.

The basic notion of bisimulation is Milner's strong bisimulation [12], which does not abstract from internal activities. In the quest for such an abstraction, very many weak bisimulation relations have been coined in the past 20 years [12,13,14,15,16,17,18,19,20]. Van Glabbeek's seminal overview paper [21] lists 28 different variations in the spectrum between weak and branching bisimulation, and there are many more, considering for instance similar variations for safety [20], progressing [19] and orthogonal bisimulation [17]. When it comes to applying bisimulation minimization in practice, the first question is which of the many candidate bisimulations to pick. There are some canonical ones (like ordinary weak or branching bisimulation), but certain circumstances (such as maximal progress or priority [22,17]) may force one to opt for others. A second step is then to design an appropriate minimization algorithm for the particular choice.

We attack the second of the above problems by means of an efficient, fully symbolic and very flexible implementation of bisimulation minimization in the style of [5]. The flexibility of our algorithm stems from the fact that it is *parametric* in the *signature* used, i. e., by providing the appropriate signature, one can rapidly obtain a tailored, and efficient bisimulation minimization algorithm. For this purpose, signatures are built up from some generic building blocks, which naturally correspond to efficient BDD operations. We believe, that this approach exploits the full potential of a symbolic implementation. To validate this claim we provide experimental evidence with signatures for all the core bisimulations mentioned above. The results show that our approach can compete with the most efficient explicit algorithms but can handle much larger instances.

The paper is structured as follows. In Section 2 we introduce basic notations and definitions of the most important types of bisimulation. Additionally, Section 2 gives an overview of all considered bisimulations by presenting references to the original work as well as a discussion of algorithms that are different to the approach presented in this work. Then, in Section 3 we present our signature-based framework by stating the signatures for all bisimulations of interest. Section 4 describes the implementation of our signature-based approach that is implemented symbolically, i. e., by means of BDDs. Experimental results and a discussion of them are presented in Section 5. Finally, Section 6 concludes the paper and suggests topics for future work.

2 Preliminaries

Bisimulations typically define equivalent behavior of states in a discrete state space. In general, either state-based systems are used or transition-oriented systems like labelled transition systems. In this work, we focus on the latter.

Definition 1. *A* labelled transition system *(LTS) is a triple $M = (S, A, T)$ where S is a finite non-empty set of states, A is a set of actions that may* *contain the so-called non-observable action τ, and $T \subseteq S \times A \times S$ is a relation that defines labelled transitions between states.*

The usage of τ-actions depends on the application. E. g., it can serve as an abstraction mechanism to hide irrelevant actions that are internal to the system model and thus unobservable for the user. Also, in case of non-τ-actions that do not impact the property to be verified, these actions may be mapped to τ.

A bisimulation partitions the original state space into disjoint parts called *blocks* that contain those states that are equivalent regarding the applied bisimulation. It is well-known that each partition induces an equivalence relation and vice versa. Therefore, we do not distinguish between partitions and equivalence relations. We use the following notations for a partition P and an LTS $M = (S, A, T)$:

- $s \xrightarrow{a} t$ for $(s, a, t) \in T$ and $s \xrightarrow{a^*} t$ for the reflexive transitive closure of $\xrightarrow{a}$.
- $s \xrightarrow[P]{a} t$ if $s \xrightarrow{a} t$ and s and t are contained in the same block of P. Then, the transition $s \xrightarrow{a} t$ is called *inert*.
- $s \xrightarrow[P]{a^*} t$ for the reflexive transitive closure of $\xrightarrow[P]{a}$.

Bisimulations are equivalence relations on the state space of an LTS, and will be denoted in the following by $\mathfrak{B}_* \subseteq S \times S$ whereby $*$ indicates the type of the bisimulation. In the absence of τ-actions all the different notions of bisimulation considered in this work are equivalent. Otherwise, there are several ways how τ-actions can characterize the possible behavior of a state. We focus on the following bisimulations:

- Strong Bisimulation [23,13]
- Weak Bisimulation [13,14,12]
- Progressing Bisimulation [19]
- Branching Bisimulation [15]
- Orthogonal Bisimulation [17]
- Delay Bisimulation [18]
- η-Bisimulation [16]
- Safety Bisimulation [20].

Strong bisimulation treats τ-actions like any other action. It is due to Park [23] and in a different formulation already to Milner [13]. Among others, it has the important property to preserve the validity of CTL* formulae and thus all interesting system properties.

Definition 2. *$\mathfrak{B}_s$ is a* strong bisimulation *if for all $s, s', t \in S$ the following holds: If $(s,t) \in \mathfrak{B}_s$ then $s \xrightarrow{a} s'$ implies that there exists $t' \in S$ with $t \xrightarrow{a} t'$ and $(s', t') \in \mathfrak{B}_s$.*

Based on the Kanelakis/Smolka algorithm [5], a symbolic algorithm for strong bisimulation has been proposed by Bouali and de Simone [10]. Dovier et al. have suggested an improvement in the form of a preprocessing step, tailored to non-strongly connected systems [24]. Since it reduces the number of iterations needed by both Bouali/de Simone's and by our algorithm in the same way we do not consider it further. There is also a symbolic $O(n \log n)$ algorithm for strong bisimulation [25] which relies on backward pointers, which are not part of popular

BDD packages (e. g., CUDD [26]). Furthermore, the algorithm of Klarlund is designed for strong bisimulation only, and thus it is not obvious how to extend it to other kinds of bisimulation.

Weak Bisimulation was introduced by Milner (see [13,14,12]) to characterize the observable behavior of a transition system.

Definition 3. $\mathfrak{B}_w$ *is a* weak bisimulation *if for all* $s, s', t \in S$ *the following holds: If* $(s,t) \in \mathfrak{B}_w$ *then* $s \xrightarrow{a} s'$ *implies either* $a = \tau$ *and* $(s',t) \in \mathfrak{B}_w$ *or there exist* $t', t'', t''' \in S$ *with* $t \xrightarrow{\tau^*} t' \xrightarrow{a} t'' \xrightarrow{\tau^*} t'''$ *and* $(s', t''') \in \mathfrak{B}_w$.

A stronger version of weak bisimulation, called *progressing bisimulation*, was obtained by Montanari and Sassone [19] by requiring that sequences of τ-steps may be compressed but not omitted completely:

Definition 4. $\mathfrak{B}_p$ *is a* progressing bisimulation *if for all* $s, s', t \in S$ *and* $a \in A$ *the following holds: If* $(s,t) \in \mathfrak{B}_p$ *then* $s \xrightarrow{a} s'$ *implies that there exist* $t', t'', t''' \in S$ *with* $t \xrightarrow{\tau^*} t' \xrightarrow{a} t'' \xrightarrow{\tau^*} t'''$ *and* $(s', t''') \in \mathfrak{B}_p$.

Please note that in the definition of progressing bisimulation $a = \tau$ is allowed – even if it is an inert τ-step. This is the difference to weak bisimulation.

Branching bisimulation was introduced by van Glabbeek and Weijland [15] to overcome the problem of weak bisimulation that it does not preserve the branching structure. Branching bisimulation is comparable to stuttering equivalence on Kripke structures and preserves CTL* without next state quantifier.

Definition 5. $\mathfrak{B}_b$ *is a* branching bisimulation *if for all* $s, s', t \in S$ *the following holds: If* $(s,t) \in \mathfrak{B}_b$ *then* $s \xrightarrow{a} s'$ *implies either* $a = \tau$ *and* $(s',t) \in \mathfrak{B}_b$ *or there exist* $t', t'', t''' \in S$ *with* $t \xrightarrow[\mathfrak{B}_b]{\tau^*} t' \xrightarrow{a} t'' \xrightarrow[\mathfrak{B}_b]{\tau^*} t'''$ *and* $(s', t''') \in \mathfrak{B}_b$.

The fastest known *explicit* algorithm for computing the coarsest branching bisimulation of a transition system is that of Groote and Vaandrager [27].

Bergstra et al. [17] suggest a refinement of branching bisimulation called *orthogonal bisimulation.* While branching bisimulation allows sequences of τ-steps not only to be compressed but even to be omitted completely, orthogonal bisimulation does not. A state with a τ-transition cannot be orthogonally equivalent to a state without τ-transition while they may be branching equivalent.

Definition 6. $\mathfrak{B}_o$ *is an* orthogonal bisimulation *if for all* $s, s', t \in S$ *and* $a \in A$ *the following holds: If* $(s,t) \in \mathfrak{B}_o$ *then* $s \xrightarrow{a} s'$ *implies if* $a \neq \tau$ *then there is a* $t' \in S$ *with* $t \xrightarrow{a} t'$ *and* $(s',t') \in \mathfrak{B}_o$ *and if* $a = \tau$ *then there exist* $t', t'' \in S$ *with* $t \xrightarrow[\mathfrak{B}_o]{\tau^*} t' \xrightarrow{\tau} t''$ *and* $(s', t'') \in \mathfrak{B}_o$.

Delay bisimulation was introduced by Milner in 1981 [18].

Definition 7. $\mathfrak{B}_d$ *is a* delay bisimulation *if for all* $s, s', t \in S$ *the following holds: If* $(s,t) \in \mathfrak{B}_d$ *then* $s \xrightarrow{a} s'$ *implies either* $a = \tau$ *and* $(s',t) \in \mathfrak{B}_d$ *or there exist* $t', t'', t''' \in S$ *with* $t \xrightarrow{\tau^*} t' \xrightarrow{a} t'' \xrightarrow[\mathfrak{B}_d]{\tau^*} t'''$ *and* $(s', t''') \in \mathfrak{B}_d$.

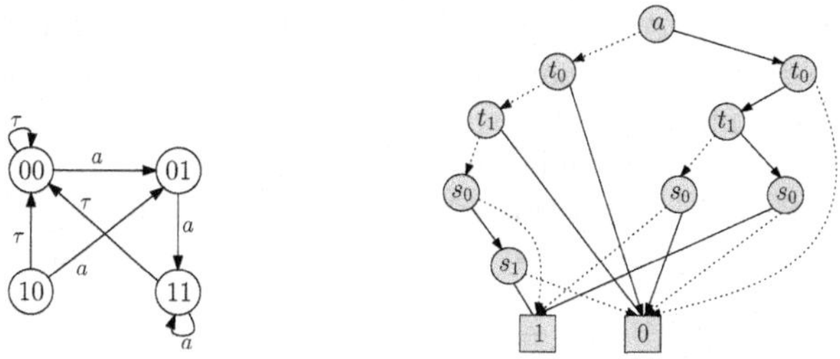

Fig. 1. An LTS and its symbolic representation

The notion of *η-bisimulation* was introduced by Baeten and van Glabbeek [16].

Definition 8. $\mathfrak{B}_\eta$ *is an* η-bisimulation *if for all* $s, s', t \in S$ *the following holds: If* $(s,t) \in \mathfrak{B}_\eta$ *then* $s \xrightarrow{a} s'$ *implies either* $a = \tau$ *and* $(s',t) \in \mathfrak{B}_d$ *or there exist* $t', t'', t''' \in S$ *with* $t \xrightarrow{\tau^*} t' \xrightarrow{a} t'' \xrightarrow{\tau^*} t'''$ *and* $(t,t') \in \mathfrak{B}_\eta$ *and* $(s',t''') \in \mathfrak{B}_\eta$.

Safety Bisimulation has been introduced by Bouajjani et al. in [20]. It preserves the reachability of actions, but not the branching structure of an LTS. It is useful when verifying safety properties where only reachability of states is of interest and not the way how they are reached.

Definition 9. $\mathfrak{B}_{\text{safe}}$ *is a* safety bisimulation *if for all* $s, s', s'', s''', t \in S$ *the following holds: If* $(s,t) \in \mathfrak{B}_{\text{safe}}$ *then* $s \xrightarrow{\tau^*} s' \xrightarrow{a} s'' \xrightarrow{\tau^*} s'''$ *and* $a \neq \tau$ *imply that there exist* $t', t'', t''' \in S$ *with* $t \xrightarrow{\tau^*} t' \xrightarrow{a} t'' \xrightarrow{\tau^*} t'''$ *and* $(s''',t''') \in \mathfrak{B}_{\text{safe}}$.

A key concept of our algorithm is the usage of binary decision diagrams (BDDs) [28] as a symbolic data structure for the representation of LTSs. BDDs are acyclic directed graphs that represent boolean functions over a predefined set of variables. They are obtained from binary decision trees by sharing subtrees as much as possible. By fixing the variable order on all paths from the root of the graph to a leaf, BDDs become a canonical representation of boolean functions. There exist efficient algorithms for the synthesis of BDDs. Since the mid-1980s, BDDs have become a standard data structure for automated analysis of large systems on the symbolic level. For a comprehensive treatment of BDDs and BDD algorithms, we refer to [29]. BDDs can be used for the representation of a finite set $M \subseteq \{0,1\}^n$ through its characteristic function $\chi_M : \{0,1\}^n \to \{0,1\}$ with $\chi_M(x) = 1$ iff $x \in M$. Fig. 1 shows an example of an LTS and the symbolic representation of its transition relation as a BDD. The states are encoded using two bits: The variables (s_1, s_0) are used for the present state and (t_1, t_0) for the next state of a transition. The variable a denotes the transition label with $a = 0$ denoting τ.

3 Signature-Based Computation of Bisimulations

In [11], Blom and Orzan have presented a distributed explicit algorithm for the computation of *branching bisimulation*. It is based on the computation of signatures of the states. A signature sig(s) can be considered as a kind of "fingerprint" of the state $s \in S$ that characterizes reachable transitions which are relevant for the bisimulation. States with different signatures are not equivalent regarding the considered bisimulation.

Starting with the initial partition $P^0 = \{S\}$ of S, we compute for $i = 0, 1, \ldots$ a new partition by putting those states into a block that have the same signature:

$$P^{i+1} = \text{sigref}(P^i) := \{\{t \in S \mid \text{sig}(s) = \text{sig}(t)\} \mid s \in S\}$$

until a fixpoint is reached, i. e., an $n \geq 0$ with $P^n = P^{n+1}$. Using the signature for branching bisimulation as given below, Blom and Orzan were able to show that this algorithm indeed computes the coarsest branching bisimulation.

We now give signatures for all eight types of bisimulations as introduced in Section 2 (see Fig. 2 for an illustration). The proofs of correctness can be established in a similar way as in [11] for branching bisimulation. Due to page limitation, these proofs are omitted, but are contained in [30]. In the following B denotes a block of the current partition P.

- *Strong Bisimulation:*
  $\text{sig}_s(s) = \{(a, B) \mid \exists s' \in B : s \xrightarrow{a} s'\}$
- *Orthogonal Bisimulation:*
  $\text{sig}_o(s) = \{(a, B) \mid (a \neq \tau \wedge \exists t \in B : s \xrightarrow{a} t) \vee$
  $(a = \tau \wedge \exists s' \in S, s'' \in B : s \xrightarrow[P]{\tau^*} s' \xrightarrow{\tau} s'')\}$
- *Branching Bisimulation:*
  $\text{sig}_b(s) = \{(a, B) \mid \exists s' \in S, s'' \in B : s \xrightarrow[P]{\tau^*} s' \xrightarrow{a} s'' \wedge (a \neq \tau \vee (s, s'') \notin P)\}$
- *η-Bisimulation:*
  $\text{sig}_\eta(s) = \{(a, B) \mid \exists s', s'' \in S, s''' \in B : s \xrightarrow{\tau^*} s' \xrightarrow{a} s'' \xrightarrow{\tau^*} s''' \wedge$
  $(s, s') \in P \wedge (a \neq \tau \vee (s, s''') \notin P)\}$
- *Delay Bisimulation:*
  $\text{sig}_d(s) = \{(a, B) \mid \exists s' \in S, s'' \in B : s \xrightarrow{\tau^*} s' \xrightarrow{a} s'' \wedge (a \neq \tau \vee (s, s'') \notin P)\}$
- *Progressing Bisimulation:*
  $\text{sig}_p(s) = \{(a, B) \mid \exists s', s'' \in S, s''' \in B : s \xrightarrow{\tau^*} s' \xrightarrow{a} s'' \xrightarrow{\tau^*} s'''\}$
- *Weak Bisimulation:*
  $\text{sig}_w(s) = \{(a, B) \mid \exists s', s'' \in S, s''' \in B : s \xrightarrow{\tau^*} s' \xrightarrow{a} s'' \xrightarrow{\tau^*} s''' \wedge$
  $(a \neq \tau \vee (s, s''') \notin P)\}$
- *Safety Bisimulation:*
  $\text{sig}_{\text{safe}}(s) = \{(a, B) \mid \exists s', s'' \in S, s''' \in B : s \xrightarrow{\tau^*} s' \xrightarrow{a} s'' \xrightarrow{\tau^*} s''' \wedge a \neq \tau\}$

4 Symbolic Computation

We will now present how this signature-based algorithm described above can be implemented symbolically. To do so, we explain in detail the BDD representation of the LTS, the symbolic computation of the signatures, the symbolic refinement, and finally the bisimulation quotient w. r. t. a given partition of the state space.

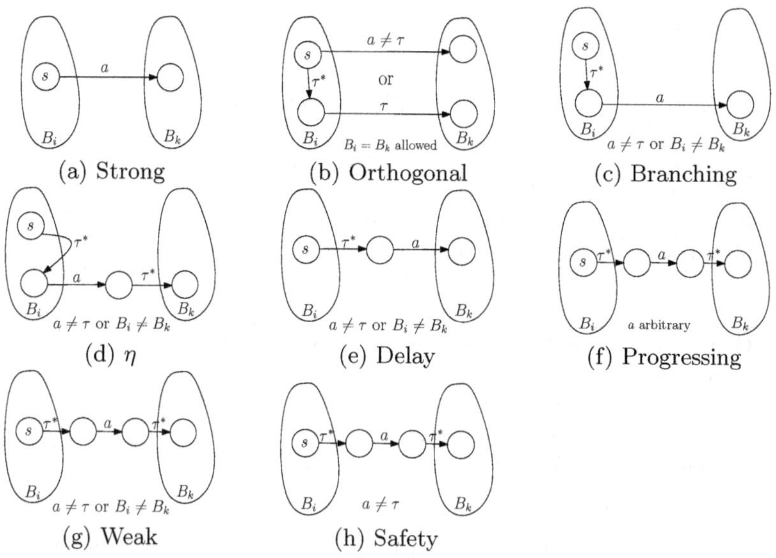

Fig. 2. Illustration of the signatures

4.1 Representation of the Data

We have to represent the following sets: the state space S of the LTS, its transition relation T, the partition P and the signatures sig. We use a binary encoding for the states (using variables s for the present state, variables t for the next state, and x as auxiliary variables) and the actions (variables a). Then, the state space is represented by a BDD $\mathcal{S}$ with $\mathcal{S}(s) = 1$ iff $s \in S$. Analogously, we have a BDD $\mathcal{T}$ for the transition relation with $\mathcal{T}(s, a, t) = 1$ iff $s \xrightarrow{a} t$. We have chosen an uncommon way for the representation of the partition P: We assigned a unique number to each block of P (encoded using variables k) and represented P by a BDD $\mathcal{P}$ with $\mathcal{P}(s, k) = 1$ iff $s \in B_k$. All other symbolic algorithms for bisimulations typically use a BDD $\mathcal{P}'(s, t)$ with $\mathcal{P}'(s, t) = 1$ iff $(s, t) \in P$. Our representation has two advantages: First, our experiments have shown that mostly $\mathcal{P}'$ is much larger than $\mathcal{P}$. Second, given $\mathcal{T}$ and $\mathcal{P}$, it is easy to compute the quotient w. r. t. P symbolically (see section 4.4). . We represent the signatures accordingly and create a BDD σ with $\sigma(s, a, k) = 1$ iff $(a, B_k) \in \text{sig}(s)$.

4.2 Computation of the Signatures

Now we describe the computation of the BDDs for the signatures of all eight kinds of bisimulation. For the computation we provide several "ingredients" which are listed in Table 1. The table contains a description of each operation and an expression for the BDD-based implementation.

Table 1. Basic operations for the signature computation

Operation	*BDD expression*
τ-transitions	$\mathcal{T}.\mathit{Cofactor}(a = \tau)$
inert τ-transitions	$\mathcal{T}.\mathit{Cofactor}(a = \tau) \land \exists k : \mathcal{P}(s, k) \land \mathcal{P}(t, k)$
non-τ- or non-inert transitions	$\mathcal{T}(s, a, t) \land \neg(\mathit{inert}_\tau(s, t) \land a \equiv \tau)$
reflexive transitive closure of $R(s, t)$	$\mathit{Closure}(R)$
concatenation of $R_1(s, t)$ and $R_2(s, t)$	$\exists x : R_1(s, x) \land R_2(x, t)$
substitute t in $R(s, t)$ by its block number	$\exists t : R(s, t) \land P(t, k)$

Algorithm 1. Signature for Branching Bisimulation

1: **procedure** SIGBRANCHING
2: $\quad \mathit{inert}(s, t) \leftarrow \mathcal{T}.\mathit{Cofactor}(a = \tau) \land \exists k : \mathcal{P}(s, k) \land \mathcal{P}(t, k)$
3: $\quad \mathit{rel}(s, t) \leftarrow \mathcal{T}(s, a, t) \land \neg(\mathit{inert}(s, t) \land a \equiv \tau)$
4: $\quad$ **return** $\exists x, t : \mathit{Closure}(\mathit{inert}(s, x)) \land \mathit{rel}(x, a, t) \land \mathcal{P}(t, k)$

There exist several symbolic algorithms for the computation of the reflexive transitive closure of a relation (e. g. [31]). We apply the iterative squaring method of [32] to compute $\xrightarrow[(P)]{\tau^*}$.

Finally we can present the algorithm for the computation of the signatures. As an example that uses all of the mentioned techniques, algorithm 1. sketches the computation of the signature for branching bisimulation.

At first, all pairs of states that are connected by an inert τ-transition are computed. In line 3 we extract all transitions that are either not inert or not labelled with τ. In the third step we put things together: the arbitrary sequence of inert τ-steps, the relevant transitions and the block numbers. The signatures for the remaining bisimulations can be computed in a similar way. Please note that everything that does not depend on the current partition, like the closure of *all* τ-steps (needed for weak, progressing, safety, η-, and delay bisimulation), can be computed as a preprocessing step.

4.3 Computation of the Refinement

We assume that we have already computed the BDD for the signatures of all states as described above. Now, we have to compute the refined partition where all states with the same signature are merged into one block.

The variable order of the BDD has to satisfy the following constraint: the s_i variables must be placed at the top of the variable order, followed by the a_j and k_l variables, i. e., $\text{level}(s_i) < \text{level}(a_j)$ and $\text{level}(s_i) < \text{level}(k_l)$ for all i, j, and l.

Then we can exploit the following observation: Let s be the encoding of a state. If we follow the path given by s in the BDD, we reach a node v. The sub-BDD at node v represents the signature of s. Furthermore, all states with the same signature as s lead to v. To get the refined partition, we have to substitute all nodes that represent the signature of a state $s \in S$ by the BDD for the encoding of a new block number k. This is sketched in algorithm 2..

Algorithm 2. Partition Refinement

procedure REFINE(signatures σ)
  if $\sigma \in$ ComputedTable **then return** ComputedTable$[\sigma]$
  $x \leftarrow topVar(\sigma)$
  if $x = s_i$ **then**
    $low \leftarrow Refine(\sigma.Cofactor(x = 0))$, $high \leftarrow Refine(\sigma.Cofactor(x = 1))$
    $result \leftarrow returnBDDnode(x, high, low)$
  else $result \leftarrow newBlockNumber()$
  ComputedTable$[\sigma] \leftarrow result$
  return $result$

The algorithm relies on a function `newBlockNumber()` that returns a BDD with exactly one path from the root node to the leaf 1. The values of the variables on that path are the binary encoding of a block number that has not been used in the current iteration. It is reset each time we call `refine`.

Furthermore, we use a dynamic programming approach to store all intermediate results in a so-called *ComputedTable*. By this, we can detect whether a node was reached before. If we reach a node already contained in the *ComputedTable*, then we return the stored result. Otherwise, if the node is labelled with a state variable s_i, the algorithm is called recursively for the two sons. If the label of the node is not a state variable, then the node is the root of a sub-BDD representing a signature. This node must be substituted with a new block number.

4.4 Computation of the Quotient LTS

After we have reached the fixpoint of the signature refinement, we have to extract the bisimulation quotient. It is defined as follows:

Definition 10. *Let $M = (S, A, T)$ be a labelled transition system. Let $P = \{B_1, \ldots, B_m\}$ be a bisimulation. Then the* quotient *of M w. r. t. P (denoted M/P) is an LTS $M/P = (S_P, A_P, T_P)$ with $S_P = \{B_1, \ldots, B_m\}$, $A_P = A$, and $(B, a, B') \in T_P$ iff there are $s \in B$ and $s' \in B'$ with $(s, a, s') \in T$.*

Let $\mathcal{P}$ be a partition (represented as BDD) with sigref$(\mathcal{P}) = \mathcal{P}$. We use the notation $[k \to s]$ to denote the renaming of the k-variables to the corresponding s-variables. To extract the bisimulation quotient w. r. t. this partition, we use the block numbers as encoding for the new states: $\mathcal{S}_P = [k \to s](\exists s : \mathcal{P}(s, k))$. Then, the transition relation can be computed as follows:

$$\mathcal{R}(s, a, t) := [k \to t](\exists t : \mathcal{T}(s, a, t) \wedge \mathcal{P}(t, k))$$
$$\mathcal{T}_P(s, a, t) := [k \to s](\exists s : \mathcal{R}(s, a, t) \wedge \mathcal{P}(s, k))$$

4.5 Improvements

During our experiments we observed that the BDD for the expression $\exists k : \mathcal{P}(s, k) \wedge \mathcal{P}(t, k)$, which is used for the computation of the inert τ-transitions, is considerably larger than the BDD for $\mathcal{P}(s,k)$. This expensive step can be avoided by computing the signatures and the refinement only *for one block at a time.* To do so, the function SIG gets an additional parameter for the states for which we have to compute the signatures. Then, a transition is inert iff the source state as well as the target state are contained in this block. We apply this technique to all bisimulations where the signature depends on the current partition (this is not the case for strong, safety, and progressing bisimulation).

The sequential refinement enables us to apply a dedicated optimization technique that we call *block forwarding*: After the refinement of one block, the current partition is updated with the result of this refinement. Hence, during the refinement of the remaining blocks this information can be used already in the same iteration. Block forwarding substantially reduces the number of iterations to the fixpoint. Both techniques result in a large speedup for almost all of our examples.

5 Experimental Results

We have implemented our approach in a tool, called SIGREF, that relies on the popular BDD-package CUDD [26]. For comparison, we also implemented the strong bisimulation algorithm presented by Bouali/de Simone in [10]. Additionally, we extended Bouali/de Simone's algorithm to weak and branching bisimulation, as it was briefly suggested in their paper. We were also able to extend Bouali/de Simone's algorithm to safety bisimulation. For comparison with bisimulation tools requiring an explicit state space representation, we use BCGMIN [33] which is part of the protocol verification toolbox CADP [34].

For the evaluation, we use examples stemming from two quite different domains: compositional process algebraic system descriptions and STATEMATE designs that are extended by failure-behavior. Regarding the meaning of the τ-action, for process algebraic descriptions τ is typically used to hide synchronization of the involved components. Our STATEMATE descriptions are designed to allow a quantitive analysis of the malfunctioning of the system, and therefore nominal non-failure-actions are exchanged by the τ-action, since only failure-actions are of interest. In [35] you will find more about our approach for quantitative analysis of STATEMATE designs.

Kanban Production System. Here, we use a process-algebraic description of a Kanban system [36] that models a production environment with four machines each having a parameterizable buffer of workpieces. From this description we generated a BDD representation of the transition system using the CASPA tool [37]. CASPA allows action-hiding, and therefore, as an example, we have hidden all internal actions that are not involved in the synchronization of the machines. This is the appropriate configuration when only inter-process communication will be analyzed.

Table 2 shows details for the generated LTSs as well as the size of the bisimulation quotient for all considered bisimulations. $|S|$ ($|T|$) denotes the number of states (transitions), respectively. For entries denoted with 'n. a.', none of the algorithms, i. e., Bouali/de Simone, BCGMIN, or SIGREF, were able to compute

Table 2. Size of the LTS for the Kanban system with different number of workpieces

p		*Original*	*Strong*	*Orthogonal*	*Branching*	η	*Delay*	*Progressing*	*Weak*	*Safety*
1	$\|S\|$	256	148	52	24	24	24	52	24	24
	$\|T\|$	904	472	111	42	42	42	111	42	42
2	$\|S\|$	63772	5725	1005	206	206	206	561	206	206
	$\|T\|$	231424	30860	3556	552	552	552	1869	552	552
3	$\|S\|$	1024240	85356	8838	872	872	872	2643	872	872
	$\|T\|$	4651520	601650	40708	2968	2968	2968	11015	2968	2968
4	$\|S\|$	16020316	778485	51805	2785	2785	2785	8964	2785	2785
	$\|T\|$	74424320	6419550	278059	10932	10932	10932	42576	10932	10932
5	$\|S\|$	16772032	5033631	n. a.	7366	7366	7366	24643	7366	7366
	$\|T\|$	133938560	46071311	n. a.	31795	31795	31795	127604	31795	31795
6	$\|S\|$	264515056	n. a.	n. a.	17010	17010	17010	58463	17010	17010
	$\|T\|$	1689124864	n. a.	n. a.	78584	78584	78584	321931	78584	78584
7	$\|S\|$	268430272	n. a.	n. a.	35456	35456	35456	124311	35456	35456
	$\|T\|$	2617982976	n. a.	n. a.	172382	172382	172382	716829	172382	172382
8	$\|S\|$	4224876912	n. a.	n. a.	68217	68217	68217	242858	68217	68217
	$\|T\|$	29070458880	n. a.	n. a.	345128	345128	345128	1451590	345128	345128

Table 3. CPU runtimes of the three tools applied to the Kanban benchmark

		1	*2*	*3*	*4*	*5*	*6*	*7*	*8*
Strong	SIGREF	0.01	2.23	93.77	1814.81	22862.70	ML	ML	ML
	bouali	0.07	152.69	13110.80	TL	TL	TL	TL	TL
	BCGMIN	0.14	1.36	99.08	2335.86	18164.83	ML	ML	ML
Orthogonal	SIGREF	0.01	6.02	388.79	16836.10	TL	TL	TL	TL
Branching	SIGREF	0.01	0.51	12.13	107.90	617.71	2685.59	15020.50	53725.40
	bouali	0.01	0.12	0.93	5.71	25.33	77.15	770.83	141591.00
	BCGMIN	0.21	0.51	10.01	193.25	559.89	ML	ML	ML
η	SIGREF	< 0.01	0.24	4.73	42.19	219.32	946.48	6636.97	22743.90
delay	SIGREF	< 0.01	0.18	3.44	33.28	183.13	806.34	4736.58	13206.90
Progressing	SIGREF	< 0.01	0.14	1.44	9.55	69.17	347.21	2400.08	5824.31
Weak	SIGREF	< 0.01	0.19	3.63	33.91	173.86	773.24	5711.58	14970.10
	bouali	< 0.01	0.11	0.89	5.49	25.05	71.83	622.29	146971.00
Safety	SIGREF	< 0.01	0.03	0.25	1.49	5.78	21.62	120.22	543.96
	bouali	0.01	0.12	0.90	5.48	27.95	71.92	709.25	140730.00

the bisimulation quotient. All bisimulations result in impressive reductions of the state space. E. g., for 8 workpieces, branching bisimulation reduces $|S|$ by a factor of nearly 62.000, and $|T|$ by a factor of about 82.000.

Table 3 gives the runtimes[1] of all three algorithms, i. e., the explicit tool BCGMIN, Bouali/de Simone's BDD algorithm, and our signature-based approach SIGREF. Please note: BCGMIN only provides strong and branching bisimulation. Typically, algorithms that use an explicit state space representation are faster than symbolic ones. Therefore, it is very interesting that SIGREF is competitive to BCGMIN for both strong and branching bisimulation. However, in contrast to BCGMIN, SIGREF is able to handle branching bisimulation for very large instances, i. e., for 5 workpieces or more. Compared to the algorithm of Bouali/ de Simone, SIGREF performs much more efficient, in particular for large instances. Except strong and orthogonal bisimulation, SIGREF is able to compute

[1] All experiments in this work were performed on an AMD Opteron 2.4 GHz CPU. We have set a time limit of 160.000 seconds and a main memory limit of 2 GB. Entries "TL" and "ML" mean that the time or memory limit was exceeded, respectively.

Table 4. Size of the STATEMATE benchmarks

Input		*Original*	*Strong*	*Orthog.*	*Branch.*	η	*Delay*	*Progress.*	*Weak*	*Safety*
etcs-1	$\lvert S\rvert$	1057	51	51	51	50	50	50	50	50
	$\lvert T\rvert$	15058	749	749	749	731	731	731	731	1172
etcs-2	$\lvert S\rvert$	428113	1312	1312	1312	1154	1214	1102	1102	1102
	$\lvert T\rvert$	16589262	48848	48848	48848	42291	45352	40540	40540	71298
etcs-3	$\lvert S\rvert$	158723041	35842	35842	35842	30173	31999	28451	28451	28451
	$\lvert T\rvert$	16658393318	3128876	3128876	3128876	2628447	2808983	2492665	2492665	4459877
bs-p	$\lvert S\rvert$	184865921	1469	1469	1177	856	951	847	847	847
	$\lvert T\rvert$	10025344274	60483	60483	42830	31970	36351	31700	31700	165312
ctrl	$\lvert S\rvert$	139623	14614	14615	9627	8077	8093	7427	7427	7427
	$\lvert T\rvert$	11867888	1033582	1033582	653303	523989	525402	482866	482866	1005666

all remaining kinds of bisimulation completely. Clearly, we have to admit that for large instances SIGREF requires a huge amount of time. However, these bisimulations cannot be computed by either BCGMIN or Bouali/de Simone's algorithm. As a summary, the results of Table 3 show that SIGREF can efficiently handle a large variety of bisimulations. Even compared to explicit state algorithms, SIGREF performs very competitive, and from an application point of view much more robust.

Failure-Enhanced STATEMATE *Descriptions.* As a second benchmark suite we analyzed LTSs that were generated from STATEMATE descriptions [38] that were extended by some failure-behavior. The first example describes a train control system stemming from the ETCS specification and models a scenario regarding the communication between trains and the Radio Block Centers (RBCs) (see [39] for details about ETCS which is part of ERTMS). The analysis tackles the problem of colliding trains on the same track. The example is scalable in the number of trains whereby we used 1, 2, and 3 trains, resulting in three benchmarks *etcs-1*, *etcs-2*, and *etcs-3*. Especially *etcs-3* samples a realistic scenario. Furthermore, we used an example, *bs-p*, from the ARP 4761 case study [40] that models a braking system from an airplane. It is about the correctness of the pilot's braking pedal and the hydraulic pressure given to the wheels of the airplane. The benchmark *ctrl* describes a redundancy controller of an industrial avionics project. A detailed description of all benchmarks can be found in [35].

Table 4 shows for each STATEMATE example the size of the LTS and of the corresponding quotient, depending on the applied bisimulation. Table 5 gives the CPU runtimes for the different algorithms. The dominant performance of SIGREF is obvious. Only the computation of branching bisimulation for the *ctrl* example shows an advantage of BCGMIN. However, SIGREF is still able to handle this example. A rough estimate of the CPU runtimes of Bouali/de Simone's algorithm shows that it performs two orders of magnitude worse than SIGREF. And for both examples *bs-p* and *ctrl*, the algorithm of Bouali/de Simone is not able to compute any of the provided bisimulations. Therefore, Table 4 again shows, but now in a much more impressive manner, that SIGREF is not only able to outperform existing approaches, but that it is applicable to a wider range of applications.

Table 5. Runtimes for the STATEMATE benchmarks

		etcs-1	*etcs-2*	*etcs-3*	*bs-p*	*ctrl*
Strong	SIGREF	0.04	8.96	958.93	21.44	106.73
	bouali	0.20	1880.16	82749.40	TL	TL
	BCGMIN	0.27	16.27	ML	ML	848.94
Orthogonal	SIGREF	0.08	49.56	16706.20	348.85	3849.29
Branching	SIGREF	0.06	49.76	20912.00	276.78	1701.22
	bouali	0.31	2594.10	98897.90	TL	TL
	BCGMIN	0.28	22.63	ML	ML	378.55
η	SIGREF	0.18	133.59	16162.10	25992.50	1124.90
Delay	SIGREF	0.08	75.63	16336.60	1328.60	1026.80
Progressing	SIGREF	0.09	43.59	2177.10	13739.50	81.03
Weak	SIGREF	0.12	99.55	13434.40	13938.40	956.00
	bouali	0.43	4340.91	113336.00	TL	TL
Safety	SIGREF	0.11	42.62	2214.39	16653.60	76.29
	bouali	0.38	4383.46	112802.00	TL	TL

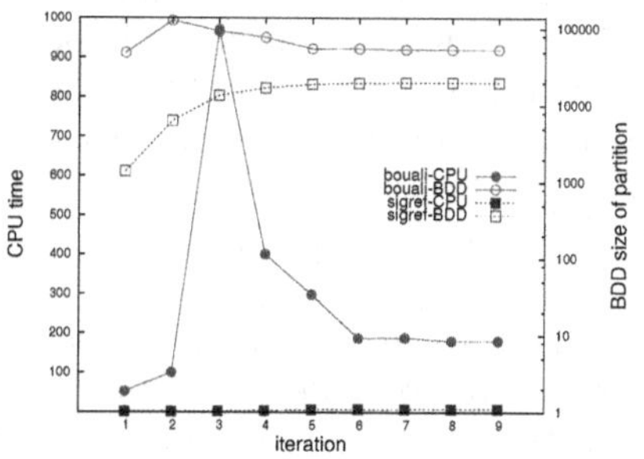

Fig. 3. Bouali/de Simone vs. SIGREF for branching bisimulation on the *etcs2* example

To get an insight why Bouali/de Simone's algorithm performs so badly, we had a detailed look at the CPU runtimes and the size of the BDDs for the representation of the partition during the iterative refinement. Figure 3 shows the corresponding data for SIGREF and the algorithm of Bouali/de Simone, respectively. The left y-axis denotes the CPU runtime and the right y-axis depicts the size of the BDD for the partition (in logarithmic scale). The x-axis corresponds to the iterations during the refinement. It it obvious that the BDD size is much more moderate for SIGREF. This directly impacts the CPU runtime. The difference between SIGREF and Bouali/de Simone's algorithm is that SIGREF relies on a predicate $\mathcal{P}(s,k)$ for storing the information that state s is contained in block k. The algorithm of Bouali/de Simone, however, uses a predicate $\mathcal{P}(s,t)$ denoting that state s and state t are contained in the same block. The advantage of SIGREF's predicate $\mathcal{P}(s,k)$ seems to be the *sharing* of the block number k, i.e., the signature refinement algorithm only needs to efficiently decide whether there are multiple states in a block k, but it is enough to *implicitly* store the information which states are in the same block. Put another way, the inherent symmetry of the predicate $\mathcal{P}'(s,t)$ of Bouali/de Simone's algorithm, i.e., $\mathcal{P}'(s,t) \Leftrightarrow \mathcal{P}'(t,s)$, is more than needed for our signature-based approach. This information overhead results in huge BDDs, which consequently leads to bad runtimes.

6 Conclusion and Future Work

In this work, we have presented a uniform and easily extendible framework for the computation of several kinds of bisimulation. We have evaluated our approach on examples from process algebra as well as from STATEMATE descriptions. Furthermore, we compared our algorithm to other state-of-the-art algorithms.

Our experiments show that in almost all cases our implementation SIGREF can handle much larger systems than other algorithms, thereby requiring less time. We found that the algorithm of Bouali/de Simone suffers from the redundant representation of partitions. On the other hand, SIGREF gains from dedicated optimizations, e. g. block forwarding. The experiments clearly show that the signature-based approach coupled with BDDs outperforms other state-of-the-art algorithms with respect to (1) the size of the system under analysis, (2) the variety of applicable models, and (3) the CPU runtimes.

As future work, we will check whether SIGREF can be extended by some input language for signatures such that new types of bisimulation can be defined without significant programming effort. Furthermore, we are investigating how the signature-based approach can be extended to compute stochastic bisimulations defined on Interactive Markov Chains (IMCs) [41].

Acknowledgments. We would like to thank the whole AVACS::S3 team for its fruitful cooperation. Especially, we'd like to thank Thomas Peikenkamp and Eckard Böde for providing the STATEMATE examples. Additionally, we are deeply grateful to Markus Siegle and Matthias Kuntz for the supply of the CASPA tool.

References

1. Wimmer, R., Herbstritt, M., Becker, B.: Minimization of Large State Spaces using Symbolic Branching Bisimulation. In: Proc. of IEEE Workshop on Design & Diagnostics of Electronic Circuits & Systems (DDECS). (2006) 9–14
2. Chehaibar, G., et al.: Specification and Verification of the PowerScale^{TM} Bus Arbitration Protocol: An Industrial Experiment with LOTOS. In: Proc. of FORTE. Volume 69. (1996) 435–450
3. Giannakopoulou, D.: Model Checking for Concurrent Software Architectures. PhD thesis, Imperial College, University of London (1999)
4. Graf, S., Steffen, B., Luttgen, G.: Compositional minimisation of finite state systems using interface specifications. Formal Asp. of Comp. **8**(5) (1996) 607–616
5. Kanellakis, P., Smolka, S.: CCS expressions, finite state processes, and three problems of equivalence. Information and Computation **86**(1) (1990) 43–68
6. Paige, R., Tarjan, R.E.: Three partition refinement algorithms. SIAM Jour. on Computing **16**(6) (1987) 973–989
7. Burch, J., et al.: Symbolic Model Checking: 10^{20} States and Beyond. Information and Computation **98**(2) (1992) 142–170
8. Bouajjani, A., Fernandez, J.C., Halbwachs, N.: Minimal model generation. In: Proc. of CAV. Volume 531 of LNCS., Springer (1991) 197–203
9. Bouajjani, A., Fernandez, J.C., Halbwachs, N., Ratel, C., Raymond, P.: Minimal state graph generation. Science of Computer Programming **18** (1992) 247–269

10. Bouali, A., de Simone, R.: Symbolic Bisimulation Minimisation. In: Proc. of CAV. Volume 663 of LNCS., Springer (1992) 96–108
11. Blom, S., Orzan, S.: Distributed Branching Bisimulation Reduction of State Spaces. ENTCS **89**(1) (2003) 990–113
12. Milner, R.: Communication and Concurrency. Prentice Hall (1989)
13. Milner, R.: A Calculus of Communicating Systems. Volume 92 of LNCS. (1980)
14. Milner, R.: Lectures on a Calculus for Communicating Systems. In: Proc. Seminar on Concurrency. Volume 197 of LNCS., Springer (1984) 197–220
15. van Glabbeek, R., Weijland, W.: Branching Time and Abstraction in Bisimulation Semantics. Journal of the ACM **43**(3) (1996) 555–600
16. Baeten, J., van Glabbeek, R.: Another Look at Abstraction in Process Algebra. In: Proc. of ICALP. Volume 267 of LNCS., Springer (1987) 84–94
17. Bergstra, J.A., Ponse, A., van der Zwaag, M.B.: Branching time and orthogonal bisimulation equivalence. Theor. Comp. Sci. **309** (2003) 313–355
18. Milner, R.: A Modal Characterization of Observable Machine-Behaviour. In: Proc. of CAAP. Volume 112 of LNCS., Springer (1981) 25–34
19. Montanari, U., Sassone, V.: Dynamic congruence vs. progressing bisimulation for CCS. Fundam. Inform. **16**(1) (1992) 171–199
20. Bouajjani, A., et al.: Safety for Branching Time Semantics. In: Proc. of ICALP. Volume 510 of LNCS., Springer (1991) 76–92
21. van Glabbeek, R.J.: The linear time – branching time spectrum II. In: Proc. of CONCUR. Volume 715 of LNCS., Springer (1993) 66–81
22. Hermanns, H., Lohrey, M.: Priority and maximal progress are completely axiomatisable. In: Proc. of CONCUR. Volume 1466 of LNCS., Springer (1998) 237–252 (Extended Abstract).
23. Park, D.: Concurrency and automata on infinite sequences. In: GI Conf. on Theor. Comp. Sci. Volume 104 of LNCS., Springer (1981) 167–183
24. Dovier, A., Gentilini, R., Piazza, C., Policriti, A.: Rank-based symbolic bisimulation (and model checking). ENTCS **67** (2002)
25. Klarlund, N.: An $n \log n$ algorithm for online BDD refinement. In: Proc. of CAV. Volume 1254 of LNCS., Springer (1997) 107–118
26. Somenzi, F.: CUDD: CU Decision Diagram Package Release 2.4.1. University of Colorado at Boulder (2005)
27. Groote, J.F., Vaandrager, F.W.: An Efficient Algorithm for Branching Bisimulation and Stuttering Equivalence. In Paterson, M., ed.: Proc. of ICALP. Volume 443 of LNCS., Springer (1990) 626–638
28. Bryant, R.: Graph-Based Algorithms for Boolean Function Manipulation. IEEE Trans. on Comp. **35**(8) (1986) 677–691
29. Wegener, I.: Branching programs and binary decision diagrams. SIAM Monographs on Discrete Mathematics and Applications. SIAM (2000)
30. Strampp, K.: Symbolische Berechnung von Bisimulationen. Diploma thesis, Albert-Ludwigs-University Freiburg, Germany (2006)
31. Matsunaga, Y., McGeer, P.C., Brayton, R.K.: On computing the transitive closure of a state transition relation. In: Proc. of DAC, ACM Press (1993) 260–265
32. Burch, J.R., et al.: Sequential circuit verification using symbolic model checking. In: Proc. of DAC, ACM Press (1990) 46–51
33. Garavel, H., Hermanns, H.: On Combining Functional Verification and Performance Evaluation using CADP. In: Proc. of FME. Volume 2391 of LNCS. (2002)
34. Fernandez, J.C., et al.: CADP: A Protocol Validation and Verification Toolbox. In: Proc. of CAV. Volume 1102 of LNCS. (1996) 437–440

35. Herbstritt, M., Wimmer, R., Peikenkamp, T., Böde, E., Adelaide, M., Johr, S., Hermanns, H., Becker, B.: Analysis of Large Safety-Critical Systems: A quantitative Approach. Reports of SFB/TR 14 AVACS 8 (2006) ISSN: 1860-9821.
36. Ciardo, G., Tilgner, M.: On the use of Kronecker operators for the solution of generalized stochastic Petri nets. Technical Report 96-35, ICASE (1996)
37. Kuntz, M., Siegle, M., Werner, E.: Symbolic Performance and Dependability Evaluation with the Tool CASPA. In: FORTE Workshops. Volume 3236 of LNCS., Springer (2004) 293–307
38. Harel, D., Politi, M.: Modelling Reactive Systems with Statecharts: The STATEMATE Approach. McGraw-Hill (1998)
39. ERTMS: Project Website (May 16, 2006) `http://ertms.uic.asso.fr/etcs.html`.
40. ARP 4761: Guidelines and Methods for Conducting the Safety Assessment Process on Civil Airborne Systems and Equipment. Aerospace Recommended Practice, Society of Automotive Engineers, Detroit, USA (1996)
41. Hermanns, H.: Interactive Markov Chains: The Quest for Quantified Quality. Volume 2428 of LNCS. Springer (2002)

Towards a Model-Checker for Counter Systems*

S. Demri[1], A. Finkel[1], V. Goranko[2], and G. van Drimmelen[2]

[1] LSV/CNRS UMR 8643 & INRIA Futurs projet SECSI & ENS Cachan
{demri, finkel}@lsv.ens-cachan.fr
[2] University of the Witwatersrand, Johannesburg
{govert, goranko}@maths.wits.ac.za

Abstract. This paper deals with model-checking of fragments and extensions of CTL* on infinite-state Presburger counter systems, where the states are vectors of integers and the transitions are determined by means of relations definable within Presburger arithmetic. We have identified a natural class of admissible counter systems (ACS) for which we show that the quantification over paths in CTL* can be simulated by quantification over tuples of natural numbers, eventually allowing translation of the whole Presburger-CTL* into Presburger arithmetic, thereby enabling effective model checking. We have provided evidence that our results are close to optimal with respect to the class of counter systems described above. Finally, we design a complete semi-algorithm to verify first-order LTL properties over trace-flattable counter systems, extending the previous underlying FAST semi-algorithm to verify reachability questions over flattable counter systems.

1 Introduction

Background. Model-checking of infinite-state systems (for a survey see [BCMS01]) is a rapidly growing area of formal verification. It has been successfully applied to real-time and hybrid systems, concurrent systems, Petri nets, asynchronous communication devices (unbounded FIFO channels), infinite and unbounded data structures (counters, queues, lists), etc. The single most important property of practical interest in infinite-state transition systems is *state reachability* which is often undecidable in structures with otherwise decidable first-order theories, such as e.g., automatic structures. Therefore, intensive research has been devoted to identifying classes of finitely presentable infinite structures with decidable reachability and related safety properties.

Transition systems defined by Presburger relations provide a large natural class of infinite-state transition systems [BFLS05], suitable for modeling in various applications such as TTP Protocol (embedded system) [BFL04] and broadcast protocols [EFM99], to quote a few examples. Important cases of such transition systems with computable reachability have been established in [Iba78, FO97, CJ98, FL02]. The method of acceleration for computing reachability has been developed in [Boi98, FL02] and completely implemented in the verification tool FAST [BFL04].

* Supported by CNRS/NRF project No 15469.

S. Graf and W. Zhang (Eds.): ATVA 2006, LNCS 4218, pp. 493–507, 2006.

Motivation. For practical (computer-aided) model-checking, an infinite-state system must be provided with an effective finitary presentation, and in particular, must admit a symbolic representation of sets of states and transitions. *Presburger arithmetic* is a particularly appropriate platform for symbolic representation of a wide variety of infinite state systems, such as *counter systems* (see [BFLP03]) where vectors of integers are subjected to linear transformations from finite control graph. These strongly extend counter automata and even very simple examples of counter systems can have notoriously difficult and unpredictable behaviour, a witness being the Syracuse problem, see e.g. [Lag85]. An important and natural class of counter systems, in which various practical cases of infinite state systems (e.g. broadcast protocols [FL02]) can be modelled, are those with a *flat* control graph, i.e, those where no control state occurs in more than one simple cycle (see [Boi98, CJ98, CC00, FL02, BFLP03, Ler03]). Strong results on verifying safety and reachability properties on flat counter systems have been obtained in [CJ98, FL02]. However, so far such properties have not been considered in the framework of any formal specification language, and thus a natural question that arises is *to identify expressive logical languages in which formal specification and verification of properties of counter systems can be conducted.*

On the other hand, most of the studies on CTL*-model checking are restricted to (unfoldings of) finite transition systems, and few decidability results for CTL*-model checking on essentially infinite state systems are known [BEM97]. Actually, most of these results are immediate consequences of stronger results about decidable modal mu-calculus, or even the whole monadic second order logic in such systems, see e.g. [Wal01]. It is therefore important *to search for larger classes of effectively generated infinite state systems [without necessarily decidable MSO], but in which natural first-order extensions of CTL* have decidable model-checking.*

Our Contribution. We address jointly both problems described above, and we obtain a nearly optimal solution of them. Our main contributions are the following:

1. We introduce a Presburger extension of CTL*, where atomic propositions range over Presburger-definable sets of configuration states; we interpret that extension over Presburger counter systems, thus proposing a very powerful specification language for them. Presburger counter systems are understood as infinite-state transition systems with states being vectors of integers (counter values) and transition relations definable in Presburger arithmetic. This class of models naturally includes Minsky machines.
2. We identify a class of Presburger counter systems, on which local model checking problem for the Presburger-CTL* is decidable. These are Presburger counter systems defined over flat control graphs with arcs labelled by Presburger formulae for which counting acceleration over every cycle in the control graph is Presburger definable.
3. We show that the decidability result described above persists in a strong extension with a class of temporal operators defined by means of CQDD (see [BH99]) in a way analogous to Wolper's Extended temporal logic [Wol83].

4. We provide evidence that our results are close to optimal wrt the class of Presburger counter systems described above, by showing that small relaxations of each of the conditions lead to undecidability.
5. We design a complete semi-algorithm to check whether a given Presburger counter system satisfies a Presburger-LTL formula extending the underlying reachability semi-algorithm used in the tool FAST [BFL04].

Related Work. On the logical side, temporal logics with Presburger constraints have been developed in [BEH95, BGP97, CC00, SS04, BDR03], some of which have quite expressive decidable fragments. However, undecidability of the reachability problem can be proved for quite restricted counter systems, see e.g. [Cor02] while at the same time very few classes of counter systems are decidable for CTL* (see e.g. [FWW97] for one-counter systems). A logical formalism closer to the one developed in this paper is presented in [BGP97] where an undecidable temporal logic with CTL-like operators and atomic formulae in Presburger arithmetic is introduced and the models are counter systems. Model checking discrete timed automata with parametric timed CTL is also shown decidable by translation into Presburger arithmetic in [BDR03].

2 Preliminaries

Flat graphs. A directed labelled graph $\mathcal{G} = \langle \Sigma, Q, E \rangle$ is a structure such that Q is a non-empty set, Σ is a non-empty finite alphabet and $E \subseteq Q \times \Sigma \times Q$. As usual, $\langle q, a, q' \rangle \in E$ is also denoted by $q \xrightarrow{a} q'$. A **cycle** in a directed labelled graph is a closed path (where the initial and final vertices coincide) with no repeating edges. A **simple cycle** is a cycle in which the only repeated vertex is the initial (and final) vertex. We define the **length of a path** $\lambda = q_0 \xrightarrow{\psi_0} q_1 \cdots \xrightarrow{\psi_{n-1}} q_n$ (each $q_i \in Q$, $\psi_i \in \Sigma$), denoted $|\lambda|$, as n. A graph is **flat** if every cycle in it is a simple cycle. Graphs with a singleton alphabet are the standard directed graphs.

Presburger arithmetic. This is the first-order theory of the structure $\langle \mathbb{N}, + \rangle$. Given a Presburger formula $\psi(x_1, \ldots, x_n)$ with free variables in $\mathbf{x} = \langle x_1, \ldots, x_n \rangle$, and $\mathbf{a} = \langle a_1, \ldots, a_n \rangle \in \mathbb{N}^n$, the truth of $\psi(x_1, \ldots, x_n)$ with respect to the interpretation $\mathbf{a}$ is denoted by $\mathbf{a} \models \psi(\mathbf{x})$. Elements of $\mathbb{N}^n$ will be usually denoted by $\mathbf{a}$, $\mathbf{b}$, $\mathbf{c}$, ... and vectors of variables will be denoted by $\mathbf{x}$, $\mathbf{y}$, $\mathbf{z}$, $\mathbf{t}$, ... (possibly decorated). A set $X \subseteq \mathbb{N}^n$ is said to be **Presburger definable** iff there is a Presburger formula $\psi(\mathbf{x})$ with free variables $\mathbf{x} = \langle x_1, \ldots, x_n \rangle$ such that $X = \{\mathbf{a} \in \mathbb{N}^n : \mathbf{a} \models \psi(\mathbf{x})\}$. A **binary relation of dimension** $n > 0$ is a relation $R \subseteq \mathbb{N}^n \times \mathbb{N}^n$; thus R is Presburger definable iff there is a Presburger formula $\psi(\mathbf{x}, \mathbf{x}')$ with free variables $\mathbf{x} = \langle x_1, \ldots, x_n \rangle$ and $\mathbf{x}' = \langle x'_1, \ldots, x'_n \rangle$ such that $R = \{\langle \mathbf{a}, \mathbf{b} \rangle \in \mathbb{N}^n \times \mathbb{N}^n : \mathbf{a}, \mathbf{b} \models \psi(\mathbf{x}, \mathbf{x}')\}$. Presburger arithmetic is known to be decidable and therefore, all the problems in the forthcoming sections that can be reduced to Presburger arithmetic are decidable.

Definition 1. *Let f be a partial function from $\mathbb{N}^n$ to $\mathbb{N}^n$ whose domain is* $\mathrm{dom}(f)$.

- *f is a **translation** if there exists $\mathbf{b} \in \mathbb{Z}^n$ such that for every $\mathbf{a} \in \mathrm{dom}(f)$ we have $f(\mathbf{a}) = \mathbf{a} + \mathbf{b}$.*
- *f is **linear** if if there exist a matrix $A \in \mathbb{N}^{n \times n}$ and $\mathbf{b} \in \mathbb{Z}^n$ such that for every $\mathbf{a} \in \mathrm{dom}(f)$ we have $f(\mathbf{a}) = A\mathbf{a} + \mathbf{b}$.*
- *f is **piecewise-linear** if there exists a finite partition of the domain $\mathrm{dom}(f) = \bigcup_{i=1}^{k} D_i$ so that the restriction on each D_i is linear.*
- *f is **Presburger definable** iff the graph of f is a Presburger definable relation.*

3 Temporal Logics for Presburger Counter Systems

In this section, we introduce a Presburger variant of standard temporal logic CTL* interpreted over Presburger transition systems.

3.1 Presburger Counter Systems

The infinite-state systems for which we investigate model checking are finitely represented by Presburger counter systems.

Definition 2. *A **Presburger counter system (PCS) of dimension** n, $\mathcal{C} = \langle \Sigma, Q, T \rangle$, is a tuple consisting of a finite set of **control states** Q, a finite set Σ composed of Presburger formulae of the form $\psi(\mathbf{x}, \mathbf{x}')$ encoding binary Presburger relations of dimension n and a set of **control transitions** $T \subseteq Q \times \Sigma \times Q$.*

- *$\mathcal{C}$ is **functional** if every element in Σ defines a partial function.*
- *a functional PCS $\mathcal{C}$, is **linear** [resp. **piecewise-linear**] if every element in Σ defines a linear [resp. piecewise-linear] function.*
- *a functional PCS $\mathcal{C}$ is a **counter automaton** if every element in Σ defines a translation.*

A PCS is therefore a labelled graph with alphabet made of specific Presburger formulae. A PCS is **flat** if its underlying control graph is flat.

Proposition 1. *It is decidable whether a given PCS is functional, linear, or a counter automaton.*

Every PCS $\mathcal{C} = \langle \Sigma, Q, T \rangle$ of dimension n naturally induces a graph $\langle S_{\mathcal{C}}, \rightarrow_{\mathcal{C}} \rangle$ (called a Presburger transition system) such that $S_{\mathcal{C}} = Q \times \mathbb{N}^n$ (set of configurations) and $\langle q, \mathbf{a} \rangle \rightarrow_{\mathcal{C}} \langle q', \mathbf{a}' \rangle$ iff there is $\langle q, \psi(\mathbf{x}, \mathbf{x}'), q' \rangle \in T$ such that $\mathbf{a}, \mathbf{a}' \models \psi(\mathbf{x}, \mathbf{x}')$. Wlog, we can assume that $S_{\mathcal{C}}$ is a subset of $\mathbb{N}^{n+1}$. Depending on the context, the configurations of $S_{\mathcal{C}}$ are indifferently written as $\mathbf{a} \in \mathbb{N}^{n+1}$ (control state encoded in the first element of $\mathbf{a}$), $\langle q, \mathbf{a} \rangle \in Q \times \mathbb{N}^n$ or as $\langle q, \mathbf{a} \rangle \in Q \times \mathbb{N}^{n+1}$ (with redundancy). A **configuration path** in $\mathcal{C}$ is an infinite path in the Presburger transition system of $\mathcal{C}$.

3.2 A Presburger Temporal Logic FOCTL*(Pr)

We now define a version of first-order CTL* that is appropriate for reasoning about Presburger transition systems of Presburger counter systems. The logic FOCTL*(Pr) differs from standard CTL* in the definition of atomic formulae. Whereas propositional variables are used in the propositional CTL*, we will use Presburger predicates, interpreted on the set of configurations, as the atomic formulae in FOCTL*(Pr). We introduce a countable set of individual variables, say VAR $= \{y, z, t \ldots\}$, for quantification over counter values. Elements of VAR are distinct from the distinguished ones in $\{x_0, x_1, \ldots, x_n\}$ that are free variables interpreted by the values of counters on configurations (the control state is encoded by x_0). In order to match the dimension of the models where such formulae will be interpreted, the Presburger predicates must have a matching number of free variables, thus giving a family of logics FOCTL*(Pr)$[n]$ parameterised by the dimension $n \geq 1$. When the dimension n is clear from the context, we just refer to FOCTL*(Pr). Atomic formulae are Presburger formulae of the form $\psi(\mathbf{x}, \mathbf{y})$ where $\mathbf{x} = x_0, x_1, \ldots, x_n$ and $\mathbf{y}$ is a vector of variables from VAR.

Formulae of FOCTL*(Pr)$[n]$ are defined as follows:

$$\varphi ::= \psi(\mathbf{x}, \mathbf{y}) \mid \neg\phi \mid \varphi \wedge \varphi \mid \mathtt{X}\varphi \mid \varphi \mathtt{U} \varphi \mid \mathtt{A}\ \varphi \mid \exists\ y\ \varphi,$$

where $y \in$ VAR. We shall freely use standard abbreviations such as the existential quantifier $\mathtt{E}$, the always operator $\mathtt{G}$ and the sometimes operator $\mathtt{F}$. The LTL fragment of FOCTL*(Pr) is made of formulae of the form either $\mathtt{E}\ \phi'$ or $\mathtt{A}\ \phi'$ where ϕ' has no path quantifiers. We define the **strict EF fragment** of FOCTL*(Pr) as the set of FOCTL*(Pr) formulae containing only the temporal operator $\mathtt{E}\ \mathtt{F}$ and no nested occurrences of $\mathtt{E}\ \mathtt{F}$.

Let π be an infinite configuration path of the system. Denote by $\pi_{\leq i}$ the initial part of π up to and including position i. Denote by π_{i+} the suffix of π starting at position i. We will give semantics of FOCTL*(Pr) over Presburger transition systems. To avoid the technical complications arising from terminating paths, we will impose the additional assumption that every configuration has some successor. This requirement can be satisfied by adding additional 'idle' states and corresponding 'idle' transitions. The satisfaction relation $\models$ is parameterized by an *environment* ρ that is a map VAR $\to \mathbb{N}$ in order to interpret the free variables from VAR that occur in formulae (we omit it when irrelevant). For a PCS $\mathcal{C} = \langle \Sigma, Q, T \rangle$ with Presburger transition system $\langle S_{\mathcal{C}}, \to_{\mathcal{C}} \rangle$, the satisfaction relation $\models$ is defined at position i of configuration path π as follows:

- $\pi, i \models_\rho \psi(\mathbf{x}, \mathbf{y})$ iff $\pi(i), \rho \models \psi(\mathbf{x}, \mathbf{y})$ in Presburger arithmetic,
- $\pi, i \models \neg\varphi$ iff $\pi, i \not\models \varphi$, $\pi, i \models \varphi \vee \varphi'$ iff $\pi, i \models \varphi$ or $\pi, i \models \varphi'$,
- $\pi, i \models \mathtt{X}\varphi$ iff $\pi, i+1 \models \varphi$,
- $\pi, i \models \varphi \mathtt{U} \varphi'$ iff there is some $j \geq i$ such that $\pi, j \models \varphi'$ and for each k, if $i \leq k < j$ then $\pi, k \models \varphi$,
- $\pi, i \models \mathtt{A}\ \varphi$ iff for every infinite configuration path π' such that $\pi'_{\leq i} = \pi_{\leq i}$ we have $\pi', i \models \varphi$,
- $\pi, i \models_\rho \exists y \varphi$ iff there is $m \in \mathbb{N}$ such that $\pi, i \models_{\rho[y \leftarrow m]} \varphi$ where $\rho[y \leftarrow m]$ is the environment obtained from ρ by only forcing y to be interpreted by m.

Apart from standard temporal properties encoded in CTL* (like liveness for instance) here are a few interesting properties that can be expressed by adding quantification over counter values:

Determinism: The graph restricted to the set of configurations reachable from the initial one is deterministic: $\mathtt{A}\ \mathtt{G} \bigwedge_{0 \leq i \leq n} \neg \exists y (\mathtt{E}\ \mathtt{X}(x_i = y) \wedge \mathtt{E}\ \mathtt{X}(x_i \neq y))$.

Boundedness: The transition graph restricted to the set of configurations reachable from the initial configuration is finite: $\exists y \mathtt{A}\ \mathtt{G} \bigwedge_{1 \leq i \leq n} x_i \leq y$.

We define below our basic problems. In the local model-checking problem considered here, we assume that all variables of the FOCTL*(Pr)[n] formula, except those in $\mathbf{x}$, are bound. We will call such formulae **semi-closed**. In that way, we do not need to specify an environment in the statement below.

1. LOCAL MODEL CHECKING: Given an PCS $\mathcal{C}$ with Presburger transition system $\langle S_{\mathcal{C}}, \rightarrow_{\mathcal{C}} \rangle$, a configuration $\langle q, \mathbf{a} \rangle \in S_{\mathcal{C}}$, and a FOCTL*(Pr)[$n$] formula ϕ, determine if for every path π such that $\pi(0) = \langle q, \mathbf{a} \rangle$, we have $\pi, 0 \models \phi$ (noted $\mathcal{C}, \langle q, \mathbf{a} \rangle \models \phi$).
2. VALIDITY CHECKING WITH AN INITIAL CONDITION: Given a PCS $\mathcal{C}$ with Presburger transition system $\langle S_{\mathcal{C}}, \rightarrow_{\mathcal{C}} \rangle$, a Presburger formula $\psi_0(\mathbf{x})$ and a FOCTL*(Pr)[n] formula ϕ, check whether for every configuration $\langle q, \mathbf{a} \rangle$ satisfying $\psi_0(\mathbf{x})$, for every configuration $\langle q', \mathbf{a}' \rangle$ reachable from $\langle q, \mathbf{a} \rangle$, we have $\mathcal{C}, \langle q', \mathbf{a}' \rangle \models \phi$.

Variants of these problems can be defined by considering subclasses of PCS or other specification languages.

4 Towards Verification of Flattable PCS

Local model checking of FOCTL*(Pr) over the whole class of PCS is known to be highly undecidable even though reachability can be decided for many classes of counter systems, see e.g. [ISD+00, CJ98, FL02, DPK03]. In the tool FAST, such a problem is solved by enumerating flattenings of some initial PCS and checking whether there is a flattening with the same reachability set. Many systems arising from applications do not have the desired flatness property, but are equivalent (in terms of the reachability relation) to flat systems. Such *flattable* systems, studied in [LS05], include e.g., reversal-bounded counter automata [Iba78]. In this section, we go one step further and propose a notion of flattening that can preserve sets of traces.

4.1 PCS with Decidable Reachability

Apart from flatness, Presburger counting acceleration property defined below is a key property to handle model-checking of PCS with a rich specification language as FOCTL*(Pr).

Definition 3. *For relation $R \subseteq \mathbb{N}^n \times \mathbb{N}^n$ we define the* **counting acceleration of** *R, as a relation $R_{\mathbf{CA}} \subseteq \mathbb{N}^n \times \mathbb{N} \times \mathbb{N}^n$ such that $\langle \mathbf{a}, i, \mathbf{b} \rangle \in R_{\mathbf{CA}}$ iff $\langle \mathbf{a}, \mathbf{b} \rangle \in R^i$. R* ***has a Presburger counting acceleration*** *if its counting acceleration is Presburger definable.*

The **cycle relation** R^λ of a cycle λ in a PCS is the composition of local transition relations of the transitions on the cycle. More formally, a cycle λ is a sequence $t_1, \ldots, t_\alpha$ of transitions of the form $t_i = q_i \xrightarrow{\psi_i} q'_i$ such that for $0 \leq i \leq \alpha - 1$, $q_{i+1} = q'_i$ and $q_1 = q'_\alpha$. We define the local relation R^{t_i} as the set of pairs $\{\langle\langle q_i, \mathbf{a}\rangle, \langle q'_i, \mathbf{a}'\rangle\rangle : \mathbf{a}, \mathbf{a}' \models \psi_i(\mathbf{x}, \mathbf{x}')\}$. The relation R^λ is then $R^{t_1} \circ \cdots \circ R^{t_\alpha}$ ($\alpha - 1$ compositions). A cycle **has the Presburger counting acceleration property** if its cycle relation has a Presburger counting acceleration.

Definition 4. *A PCS $\mathcal{C}$* ***has the Presburger counting acceleration property*** *if every cycle in the control graph of $\mathcal{C}$ has that property.*

Observe that if a PCS $\mathcal{C}$ has the Presburger counting acceleration property, we can effectively compute the Presburger formula associated to each cycle. It is sufficient to enumerate Presburger formulae $\psi(\mathbf{x}, i, \mathbf{y})$ and test whether

$$\forall \mathbf{x}, \mathbf{x}' \; (\psi(\mathbf{x}, 0, \mathbf{x}') \Leftrightarrow (\mathbf{x} = \mathbf{x}')) \wedge (\forall \, \mathbf{x}, \mathbf{x}', i \;\; \psi(\mathbf{x}, i{+}1, \mathbf{x}') \Leftrightarrow (\exists \mathbf{x}'' \; \psi(\mathbf{x}, i, \mathbf{x}'') \wedge \psi'(\mathbf{x}'', \mathbf{x}')))$$

is valid, where $\psi'(\mathbf{x}, \mathbf{y})$ is the effect of a given cycle. This is an instance of a more general result from [Ler06]. We also know that there exist counter systems of dimension 1 that do not have the Presburger counting acceleration property (for instance, consider the update $x'_1 = 2x_1$). In general, we expect that determining whether a counter system has a Presburger counting acceleration is an undecidable problem by extending similar results from [Ler06].

Flatness is another key property for PCS. For instance, every flat and linear PCS with the finite monoid property has the Presburger counting acceleration property [FL02] where a linear PCS has the finite monoid property if for every cycle λ in the system, the multiplicative monoid generated by the matrix of the linear function defining R^λ is finite (linear functions are closed under composition). Consequently, the Presburger formula defining the reachability relation in every flat and linear PCS with the finite monoid property is effectively computable. This consequence is incomparable with the main result from [CJ98]. Indeed, flatness is assumed in [CJ98] but not the finiteness of the monoid. Moreover [CJ98] and [FL02] have different and incomparable Presburger formulae labelling the transitions. For instance, transition relations in [CJ98] are not necessarily functional but they are restricted to relations on two variables. In Definition 5, the systems are more general than the ones in [CJ98] since we allow richer Presburger transition formulae.

Here we identify a large and natural class of Presburger counter systems for which model-checking of CTL* is decidable in addition to reachability.

Definition 5. *An* ***admissible Presburger counter system (ACS)*** *is a flat, functional PCS, that has the Presburger counting acceleration property.*

In particular, every flat and linear PCS with the finite monoid property is admissible. As observed in [FL02], flatness is the key property to be able to compute the reachability relation.

Proposition 2. *For every flat PCS satisfying the Presburger counting acceleration property (including ACS), one can effectively compute the reachability relation* $\rightarrow^*_{\mathcal{C}}$ *for* $\langle S_{\mathcal{C}}, \rightarrow_{\mathcal{C}} \rangle$.

The proof of Proposition 2 is based on the fact that essentially there is a finite number of types of configuration paths (see details later on) and one can effectively compute Presburger formulae associated to cycles. Definition 5 is close to optimal because relaxing any of the conditions for admissibility could easily lead to undecidability of the reachability problem, as indicated below.

Proposition 3. *The reachability problem is not decidable for all: (1) flat linear PCSs [Cor02], (2) linear PCSs with the finite monoid property (even counter automata) [Min67] and (3) flat piecewise-linear PCSs with a single control state and control transition [Min67].*

As a matter of fact, any counter automaton can be encoded as a flat piecewise-linear PCS with a single control state q_0 and control transition. Indeed, suppose that $q \xrightarrow{x:=x+1} q'$ is a transition in the counter automaton with the integer n [resp. n'] attached to q [resp. q'], then in the piecewise-linear PCS the unique transition is of the form $q_0 \xrightarrow{(x_0=n \wedge x'_0=n' \wedge x'=x+1) \vee \ldots} q_0$. There is an obvious correpondence between the transitions in the original counter automaton and the number of disjuncts in the Presburger formula labelling the unique transition.

4.2 Model-Checking for Three Main Classes of Flattable Systems

We establish in Section 5 that ACS have numerous desirable properties. For instance, FOCTL*(Pr) local model checking is decidable. However, it should not come as a surprise that the class of ACS forms a quite restricted subclass of PCS and numerous abstractions of communication protocols, concurrent systems and the like are not exactly ACS. More interestingly, many questions on specific classes of PCS can be reduced in a systematic way to reachability questions on ACS, see e.g. [FO97, CJ98, BFLP03] and a more thorough study in [LS05]. In this section, we provide the basis to understand how our results on ACS can be used to verify more general classes of PCS and under which hypotheses (see also Section 5.2). The most standard way to reduce a PCS to an ACS is via a graph homomorphism, aka a flattening [BFLS05].

Definition 6. *Let* $\mathcal{C} = \langle \Sigma, Q, T \rangle$ *and* $\mathcal{C}' = \langle \Sigma', Q', T' \rangle$ *be PCS of the same dimension and* f *be a function* $f : Q' \rightarrow Q$. $\mathcal{C}'$ *is a* f***-flattening*** *of* $\mathcal{C}$ *iff* $\mathcal{C}'$ *is flat,* $\Sigma' \subseteq \Sigma$*, for every* $\langle q, \psi(\mathbf{x}, \mathbf{x}'), q' \rangle \in T'$*, we have* $\langle f(q), \psi(\mathbf{x}, \mathbf{x}'), f(q') \rangle \in T$.

When $\mathcal{C}'$ is a f-**flattening** of $\mathcal{C}$, $\mathcal{C}$ can be viewed as an abstraction of $\mathcal{C}'$.

The tool FAST [BFL04] generates flattenings via an exhaustive search algorithm. However, verification of FOCTL*(Pr) properties of $\mathcal{C}$ by using a flattening

$\mathcal{C}'$ can only be done for those FOCTL*(Pr) properties that are preserved under such flattenings. Hence, it is important to determine which FOCTL*(Pr) properties are preserved when $\mathcal{C}$ and $\mathcal{C}'$ satisfy given relationships (see Theorem 1). The most common relationship is precisely the equality of reachability sets (leading to the notion of post*-flattening). Let $\mathcal{C} = \langle \Sigma, Q, T \rangle$ be a PCS. The reachability sets from a configuration and from a set of Presburger definable configurations are defined as follows: $\mathrm{post}^*_{\mathcal{C}}(\langle q, \mathbf{a} \rangle) \stackrel{\mathrm{def}}{=} \{\langle q', \mathbf{a}' \rangle : \langle q, \mathbf{a} \rangle \rightarrow^* \langle q', \mathbf{a}' \rangle \text{ in } S_{\mathcal{C}}\}$ and $\mathrm{post}^*_{\mathcal{C}}(q, \psi(\mathbf{x})) \stackrel{\mathrm{def}}{=} \bigcup_{\langle q, \mathbf{a} \rangle \models \psi(\mathbf{x})} \mathrm{post}^*_{\mathcal{C}}(\langle q, \mathbf{a} \rangle)$.

Definition 7. *$\langle \mathcal{C}', q' \rangle$ is a f-**post*-flattening** (post*-flattening for short) of $\langle \mathcal{C}, q \rangle$ wrt $\psi(\mathbf{x})$ iff $\mathrm{post}^*_{\mathcal{C}}(q, \psi(\mathbf{x})) = f(\mathrm{post}^*_{\mathcal{C}'}(q', \psi(\mathbf{x})))$ and $\mathcal{C}'$ is a f-flattening of $\mathcal{C}$ (f is naturally extended to states of $\langle S_{\mathcal{C}}, \rightarrow_{\mathcal{C}} \rangle$).*

Even though it is undecidable whether a PCS has a post*-flattening [BFLS05, Theorem 4.9], we can decide if a PCS is a post*-flattening of another one.

Lemma 1. *Let $\langle \mathcal{C}', q' \rangle$ be an f-flattening of $\langle \mathcal{C}, q \rangle$ such that $\mathcal{C}'$ is an ACS. It is decidable to check whether $\langle \mathcal{C}', q' \rangle$ is a post*-flattening of $\langle \mathcal{C}, q \rangle$ wrt $\psi(\mathbf{x})$.*

Let $\mathcal{C} = \langle \Sigma, Q, T \rangle$ be a PCS. A *trace* for $\langle q, \mathbf{a} \rangle$ is a (possibly infinite) sequence of the form $\langle q_0, \mathbf{a_0} \rangle \langle q_1, \mathbf{a_1} \rangle \langle q_2, \mathbf{a_2} \rangle \ldots$ such that $\langle q_0, \mathbf{a_0} \rangle = \langle q, \mathbf{a} \rangle$, and for every i, $\langle q_i, \mathbf{a_i} \rangle \rightarrow \langle q_{i+1}, \mathbf{a_{i+1}} \rangle$ in $\langle S_{\mathcal{C}}, \rightarrow_{\mathcal{C}} \rangle$. The set of traces for $\langle q, \mathbf{a} \rangle$ in $\mathcal{C}$ is denoted by $\mathrm{traces}_{\mathcal{C}}(\langle q, \mathbf{a} \rangle)$. By extension, $\mathrm{traces}_{\mathcal{C}}(q, \psi(\mathbf{x})) \stackrel{\mathrm{def}}{=} \bigcup_{\langle q, \mathbf{a} \rangle \models \psi(\mathbf{x})} \mathrm{traces}_{\mathcal{C}}(\langle q, \mathbf{a} \rangle)$.

Definition 8. *$\langle \mathcal{C}', q' \rangle$ is a f-**trace-flattening** (trace-flattening for short) of $\langle \mathcal{C}, q \rangle$ wrt $\psi(\mathbf{x})$ iff $\mathrm{traces}_{\mathcal{C}}(q, \psi(\mathbf{x})) = f(\mathrm{traces}_{\mathcal{C}'}(q', \psi(\mathbf{x})))$ and $\mathcal{C}'$ is a f-flattening of $\mathcal{C}$.*

We can decide if a PCS is a trace-flattening of another PCS as stated below.

Lemma 2. *Let $\langle \mathcal{C}', q' \rangle$ be an f-flattening of $\langle \mathcal{C}, q \rangle$ such that $\mathcal{C}'$ is an ACS. It is decidable to check whether $\langle \mathcal{C}', q' \rangle$ is a trace-flattening of $\langle \mathcal{C}, q \rangle$ wrt $\psi(\mathbf{x})$.*

Here is the more elaborate notion of flattenings but difficult to check.

Definition 9. *$\langle \mathcal{C}', q' \rangle$ is a f-**bisimulation-flattening** (bisimulation-flattening for short) of $\langle \mathcal{C}, q \rangle$ with respect to $\psi(\mathbf{x})$ iff $\mathcal{C}'$ is a f-flattening of $\mathcal{C}$ and for every $\mathbf{a}$ such that $\mathbf{a} \models \psi(\mathbf{x})$, $\langle \mathrm{post}^*_{\mathcal{C}'}(\langle q', \mathbf{a} \rangle), \rightarrow^{\mathbf{a}}_{\mathcal{C}'} \rangle$ where $\rightarrow^{\mathbf{a}}_{\mathcal{C}'}$ is the restriction of $\rightarrow_{\mathcal{C}'}$ to $\mathrm{post}^*_{\mathcal{C}}(\langle q, \mathbf{a} \rangle)$ is bisimilar to $\langle \mathrm{post}^*_{\mathcal{C}}(\langle q, \mathbf{a} \rangle), \rightarrow^{\mathbf{a}}_{\mathcal{C}} \rangle$.*

Lemma 3 below states a few easy results about flattenings and their hierarchy.

Lemma 3. *Let $\langle \mathcal{C}', q' \rangle$ be an f-flattening of $\langle \mathcal{C}, q \rangle$.*

(I) *For any $\psi(\mathbf{x})$, $f(\mathrm{post}^*_{\mathcal{C}'}(q', \psi(\mathbf{x}))) \subseteq \mathrm{post}^*_{\mathcal{C}}(q, \psi(\mathbf{x}))$.*
(II) *For any $\psi(\mathbf{x})$, $f(\mathrm{traces}_{\mathcal{C}'}(q', \psi(\mathbf{x}))) \subseteq \mathrm{traces}_{\mathcal{C}}(q, \psi(\mathbf{x}))$.*
(III) *Every bisimulation-flattening [resp. trace-flattening] is a trace-flattening [resp. post*-flattening].*

Based on standard properties of temporal logics, we provide below sufficient conditions to verify flattable PCS that are not necessarily ACS.

Theorem 1. *Let $\langle \mathcal{C}', q' \rangle$ be a post*-flattening [resp. trace-flattening, bisimulation-flattening] of the PCS $\langle \mathcal{C}, q \rangle$ wrt $\mathbf{a}$. Then, for every formula ϕ in the strict EF fragment [resp. the LTL fragment, FOCTL*(Pr)[n]], $\mathcal{C}', \langle q', \mathbf{a} \rangle \models \phi$ iff $\mathcal{C}, \langle q, \mathbf{a} \rangle \models \phi$.*

5 Model-Checking Flattable Counter Systems

Herein, we show decidability of model checking FOCTL*(Pr) over ACS and we propose a complete semi-algorithm for model checking FOLTL(Pr) formulae over trace-flattable PCS, extending what is done in [BFLS05] for post*-flattable PCS.

5.1 A FOCTL*(Pr) Decision Procedure to Verify ACS

Throughout this section, let $\mathcal{C} = \langle \Sigma, Q, T \rangle$ be ACS of dimension n. Recall that all cycles in an ACS are simple cycles.

Definition 10. *A* ***control path*** *in $\mathcal{C}$ is any infinite path in $\mathcal{C}$. A* ***path segment*** *in $\mathcal{C}$ is a single transition $t \in T$ or a cycle in $\mathcal{C}$, and so is uniformly described as a finite sequence of control states. A* ***path schema*** *in $\mathcal{C}$ is a sequence $\langle \sigma_0, \ldots, \sigma_k \rangle$ of different path segments in $\mathcal{C}$ such that: (1) for every $0 \leq i \leq k-1$, the last control state of σ_i is the first control state of σ_{i+1}, (2) any path segment occurs at most once and (3) σ_k is a cycle. Cycles in a path schema that are not the final segment are called* ***interior cycles*** *of the schema.*

From now on we fix an enumeration $\lambda_1, \ldots, \lambda_M$ of all the cycles in $\mathcal{C}$ and assume that $M > 0$. Since an ACS is flat and has a finite number of control states, the following holds:

Proposition 4. *In every ACS $\mathcal{C}$, there is a finite number of path schemas.*

The number of path schemas is generally exponential in the size of the ACS. Hereafter we fix an enumeration $\langle 1, \ldots, P \rangle$ of the path schemas of $\mathcal{C}$. A path schema with at least one interior cycle corresponds to infinitely many different control paths, since any interior cycle in the schema may be repeated an arbitrary number of times on the control path. The number of repetitions of a given cycle in a control path is called the **cycle count** of that cycle. Thus, every control path is completely characterised by its underlying path schema and the cycle counts for its interior cycles. The next definition formalises this idea.

Definition 11. *Let the ACS $\mathcal{C}$ have $M > 0$ cycles and P path schemas. A* ***cycle count vector*** *$\mathbf{c}$ is a tuple $\langle c_1, \ldots, c_M \rangle \in \mathbb{N}^M$, where c_r represents the cycle count for the cycle λ_r. A* ***control path description*** *α is a pair $\alpha = \langle p, \mathbf{c} \rangle$ where $p \in \{1, \ldots, P\}$ denotes the path schema, $\mathbf{c}$ is the cycle count vector for the control path being described, $c_i > 0$ for every interior cycle λ_i and $c_i = 0$ for any cycle λ_i in $\mathcal{C}$ which is not interior in the path schema p. Hereafter a control path description, may be written as $\langle p, c_1, \ldots, c_M \rangle$. We write α_0 for the path schema associated with control path description α.*

The following is immediate from the flatness condition on ACS.

Proposition 5. *For every control path in $\mathcal{C}$ there is a unique control path description.*

Without risk of confusion, we identify every control path with its description.

Every configuration path is uniquely described by the pair $\langle \alpha, \langle q, \mathbf{a} \rangle \rangle$ where α is its control path and $\langle q, \mathbf{a} \rangle$ is the initial configuration. Conversely, due to the functionality of $\mathcal{C}$, every such pair $\langle \alpha, \langle q, \mathbf{a} \rangle \rangle$ describes a unique path in the configuration graph starting at $\langle q, \mathbf{a} \rangle$, and progressing according to the transitions of the control path α. Note, however, that such a path may terminate and therefore not be considered as a configuration path. There exists a Presburger formula that exactly describes the configuration path associated with a control path and initial configuration as stated below.

Theorem 2. *Given the ACS $\mathcal{C}$ of dimension n with $M > 0$ cycles, one can compute a Presburger formula $PathConfig_{\mathcal{C}}(\xi, \mathbf{x}, i, \mathbf{y})$ such that for all $\alpha \in \mathbb{N}^{M+1}$, $\mathbf{a} \in \mathbb{N}^{n+1}$, $m \in \mathbb{N}$ and $\mathbf{b} \in \mathbb{N}^{n+1}$ $\alpha, \mathbf{a}, m, \mathbf{b} \models PathConfig_{\mathcal{C}}(\xi, \mathbf{x}, i, \mathbf{y})$ iff α is a valid control path description and the mth configuration of the configuration path $\langle \alpha, \mathbf{a} \rangle$ is $\mathbf{b}$.*

Now we are ready to show that model-checking FOCTL*(Pr)$[n]$ can be reduced to satisfiability in Presburger arithmetic.

Theorem 3. *Given an ACS $\mathcal{C}$ of dimension n with Presburger transition system $\langle S_{\mathcal{C}}, \rightarrow_{\mathcal{C}} \rangle$, for every FOCTL*(Pr)$[n]$ formula φ, one can compute a Presburger formula $\psi(\mathbf{x})$ such that for every $\langle q, \mathbf{a} \rangle \in S_{\mathcal{C}}$, $\langle q, \mathbf{a} \rangle \models \psi(\mathbf{x})$ iff $\mathcal{C}, \langle q, \mathbf{a} \rangle \models \varphi$.*

For a fixed ACS, the size of $\psi(\mathbf{x})$ is linear in the size of φ.

Theorem 4. *The two problems in Section 3.2 are decidable.*

Theorem 4 can be easily extended to allow past-time operators such as 'previous' $\mathtt{X}^{-1}$ and 'since' $\mathtt{S}$. By contrast, we state below an undecidability result for a fixed PCS that is almost an ACS. We present a PCS $\mathcal{C}_u$ that is obtained from an ACS by only adding a reset transition while preserving the Presburger counter acceleration property and functionality (see below).

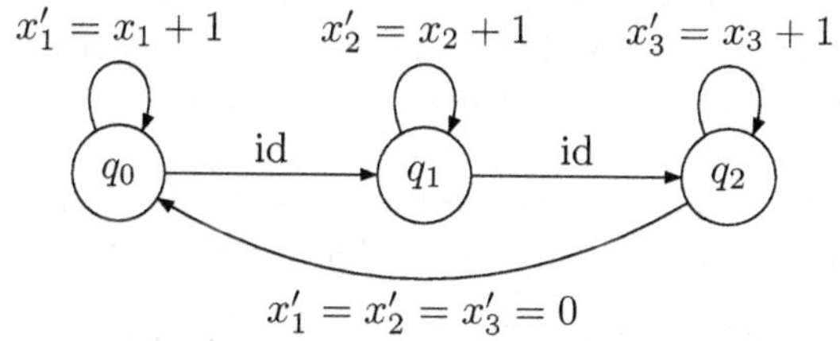

$\mathcal{C}_u$ is of dimension 4 with counters x_0, x_1, x_2 and x_3 and x_0 is the counter related to the control state. "id" denotes the identity function on the counters x_1, x_2 and x_3.

Theorem 5. *Local model-checking on $\mathcal{C}_u$ with FOLTL*(Pr)[3] is Σ_1^1-hard.*

Observe that $\mathcal{C}_u$ admits a post*-flattening with an ACS and therefore the strict EF fragment has a decidable local model-checking problem for $\mathcal{C}_u$.

5.2 Model-Checking of Trace-Flattable Counter Systems

Suppose we have a functional PCS $\mathcal{C}$ with the Presburger counting acceleration property. Typically, $\mathcal{C}$ can be a linear PCS with finite monoid. Let $\langle q, \mathbf{a} \rangle$ be a configuration for which we want to check a FOLTL(Pr) formula ϕ. We propose below the basis of a semi-algorithm `model-check` to verify whether $\mathcal{C}, \langle q, \mathbf{a} \rangle \models \phi$.

Procedure. `model-check`$(\mathcal{C}, \langle q, \mathbf{a} \rangle, \phi)$

1. $found := false$;
2. **while** not $found$ **do**
   (a) Choose fairly a flattening $\langle \mathcal{C}', q' \rangle$ of $\langle \mathcal{C}, q \rangle$;
   (b) **if** $\langle \mathcal{C}', q' \rangle$ is a trace-flattening of $\langle \mathcal{C}, q \rangle$ **then** $found := true$;
3. **return** $\mathcal{C}', \langle q', \mathbf{a} \rangle \models \phi$.

To become efficient, the semi-algorithm has to be refined in order to obtain an efficient enumeration of the flat PCS as that is done with the tool FAST. As a first step, heuristics implemented in FAST can be used, see e.g. [BFLS05]. The semi-algorithm `model-check` extends the underlying FAST algorithm [BFLS05] to trace-flattable Presburger counter systems and LTL temporal properties which paves the way to design the new generation of the tool. Using previous results shown in the paper, we can establish the following key result of the paper.

Theorem 6. *(I)* `model-check`$(\mathcal{C}, \langle q, \mathbf{a} \rangle, \phi)$ *terminates iff* $\mathcal{C}$ *has a trace-flattening wrt to* $\langle q, \mathbf{a} \rangle$. *(II) When* `model-check`$(\mathcal{C}, \langle q, \mathbf{a} \rangle, \phi)$ *terminates, it returns whether* $\mathcal{C}, \langle q, \mathbf{a} \rangle \models \phi$ *holds true.*

Proof. It is sufficient to observe the following facts:

- Checking whether $\langle \mathcal{C}', q' \rangle$ is a flattening of $\langle \mathcal{C}, q \rangle$ can be done in exponential-time.
- Checking whether $\mathcal{C}'$ is an ACS is easy since $\mathcal{C}$ has the Presburger counting acceleration property and it is functional. Hence $\mathcal{C}$ is an ACS and one can compute effectively the Presburger formulae related to cycles.
- Checking whether $\langle \mathcal{C}', q' \rangle$ is a trace-flattening of $\langle \mathcal{C}, q \rangle$ is decidable as a consequence of Lemma 2.
- Checking whether $\mathcal{C}', \langle q', \mathbf{a} \rangle \models \phi$ is decidable by Theorem 4.
- Finally, $\mathcal{C}', \langle q', \mathbf{a} \rangle \models \phi$ iff $\mathcal{C}, \langle q, \mathbf{a} \rangle \models \phi$ by Theorem 1. □

We do not know yet how to extend the above complete semi-algorithm to deal with bisimulation-flattening. Indeed, in order to have a decision procedure for the step (3) with bisimulation, we would need decidability of some kind of modal mu-calculus over ACS, which is open so far.

5.3 Decidable Extension with CQDD Patterns

We present below an extension of FOCTL*(Pr)$[n]$ for which model-checking over ACS can be also encoded into Presburger satisfiability. In a seminal paper,

Wolper extends LTL to an extended temporal logic that has the same power as Büchi automata [Wol83]. In this section, we extend the set of path formulae from FOCTL*(Pr)[n] by allowing temporal operators defined by another class of language acceptors, namely the CQDD (*constrained queue-content decision diagrams*) [BH99]. This formalism has been introduced for representing symbolically infinite sets of configurations in FIFO automata. Our use of CQDD is different and non-regular languages can be defined with CQDD. Moreover, the model-checking problem for LTL augmented with operators defined from CQDD is undecidable [Dem06] unlike the extension with regular languages [Wol83]. By contrast, we show that the model-checking problem for FOCTL*(Pr)[n] extended with CQDD-based operators is decidable over ACS. Regain of decidability is due to the flatness restriction in CQDD. Hence, we show evidence in this section that we can take advantage of flatness in models *and* in formulae. A **CQDD** is a structure $\mathcal{A} = \langle \Sigma, S, S_0, E, l, \psi(y_1, \ldots, y_m), F \rangle$ such that:

- Σ is a finite alphabet and S is a finite set of states,
- $S_0 \subseteq S$ [resp. $F \subseteq S$] is the set of initial [resp. final] states,
- $E \subseteq S \times \Sigma \times S$ is a set of transitions of cardinality m and $\langle S, E \rangle$ is flat,
- l is a bijection from E to $\{1, \ldots, m\}$ and $\psi(y_1, \ldots, y_m)$ is a Presburger formula.

An accepting run is a sequence $q_0 \xrightarrow{a_0} q_1 \xrightarrow{a_1} q_2 \ldots \xrightarrow{a_{k-1}} q_k$ such that $q_0 \in S_0$, $q_k \in F$, for every $i \in \{0, \ldots, k-1\}$, $\langle q_i, a_i, q_{i+1} \rangle \in E$, and $n_1, \ldots, n_m \models \psi(y_1, \ldots, y_m)$ in Presburger arithmetic, where each n_i is the number of occurrences of the transition $l^{-1}(i)$ in the sequence. The word $\sigma \in \Sigma^*$ is accepted by the accepting run $q_0 \xrightarrow{a_0} q_1 \xrightarrow{a_1} q_2 \ldots \xrightarrow{a_{k-1}} q_k$ whenever $\sigma = a_0 a_1 a_2 \ldots a_{k-1}$. The word σ is also said to be accepted by the automaton $\mathcal{A}$. We write $\mathrm{L}(\mathcal{A})$ to denote the set of words accepted by $\mathcal{A}$.

Let $\mathcal{A} = \langle \Sigma, S, S_0, E, l, \psi(y_1, \ldots, y_m), F \rangle$ be a CQDD with the letters from Σ linearly ordered: $a_1 < \ldots < a_k$. The extension EFOCTL*(Pr)[n] of the logic FOCTL*(Pr)[n] consists in considering formulae of the form $\mathcal{A}(\phi_1, \ldots, \phi_k)$ defined as follows: $\pi, i \models \mathcal{A}(\phi_1, \ldots, \phi_k)$ iff: either $\epsilon \in \mathrm{L}(\mathcal{A})$, or there is a finite word $a_{i_1} a_{i_2} \ldots a_{i_n} \in \mathrm{L}(\mathcal{A})$ such that for every $1 \leq j \leq n$, $\pi, i + (j-1) \models \phi_{i_j}$. For instance, in EFOCTL*(Pr)[n] we can state that there is a path and some $n \neq 0$ such that ϕ_1 holds true at the n first positions, then ϕ_2 holds true at the n next positions and then neither ϕ_1 nor ϕ_2 holds true forever. It is known that ETL is more expressive that LTL [Wol83] and this result can be lifted between FOCTL*(Pr)[n] and EFOCTL*(Pr)[n]. Theorem 3 can be extended by allowing CQDD-based operators.

Theorem 7. *Given an ACS $\mathcal{C}$ of dimension n with Presburger transition system $\langle S_{\mathcal{C}}, \rightarrow_{\mathcal{C}} \rangle$, for every EFOCTL*(Pr)[$n$] formula φ, one can compute a Presburger formula $\psi(\mathbf{x})$ such that for every $\langle q, \mathbf{a} \rangle \in S_{\mathcal{C}}$, $\langle q, \mathbf{a} \rangle \models \psi(\mathbf{x})$ iff $\mathcal{C}, \langle q, \mathbf{a} \rangle \models \varphi$.*

As a corollary, local model-checking problem for EFOCTL*(Pr)[n] over ACS is decidable.

6 Concluding Remarks

We have designed a complete semi-algorithm to verify first-order LTL properties over trace-flattable counter systems, extending the underlying semi-algorithm to verify reachability questions over post*-flattable systems in the tool FAST. We expect a smooth extension of FAST [BFLS05] to deal with trace-flattable systems. This result takes strongly advantage of the decidability of model-checking FOCTL*(Pr) over admissible counter systems, a new result we establish in the paper. Hence, we have improved the decidability boundary for model-checking ACS with CTL*-like languages. The decidability of model-checking question is open when adding fixed-point operators (Presburger mu-calculus) or monadic second-order quantification over ACS. Another direction for further work is to analyze and extend further the class of ACS. For instance, giving up the functionality assumption on transitions that do not belong to a cycle preserves decidability, while it is open whether giving up the full functionality assumption still preserves decidability in the absence of first-order quantification. Finally, we plan to verify experimentally which post*-flattable case studies [BFLS05] are indeed trace-flattable.

References

[BCMS01] O. Burkart, D. Caucal, F. Moller, and B. Steffen. Verification of infinite structures. In *Handbook of Process Algebra*, pages 545–623. Elsevier, 2001.

[BDR03] V. Bruyère, E. Dall'Olio, and J.F. Raskin. Durations, parametric model-checking in timed automata with presburger arithmetic. In *STACS'03*, volume 2607 of *LNCS*, pages 687–698. Springer, 2003.

[BEH95] A. Bouajjani, R. Echahed, and P. Habermehl. On the verification problem of nonregular properties for nonregular processes. In *LICS'95*, pages 123–133, 1995.

[BEM97] A. Bouajjani, J. Esparza, and O. Maler. Reachability analysis of pushdown automata: Application to model checking. In *CONCUR'97*, volume 1243 of *LNCS*, pages 135–150. Springer, 1997.

[BFL04] S. Bardin, A. Finkel, and J. Leroux. FASTer acceleration of counter automata in practice. In *TACAS'04*, volume 2988 of *LNCS*, pages 576–590. Springer, March 2004.

[BFLP03] S. Bardin, A. Finkel, J. Leroux, and L. Petrucci. FAST: Fast Acceleration of Symbolic Transition systems. In *CAV'03*, volume 2725 of *LNCS*, pages 118–121. Springer, 2003.

[BFLS05] S. Bardin, A. Finkel, J. Leroux, and P. Schnoebelen. Flat acceleration in symbolic model checking. In *ATVA'05*, volume 3707 of *LNCS*, pages 474–488. Springer, 2005.

[BGP97] T. Bultan, R. Gerber, and W. Pugh. Symbolic model checking of infinite state systems using Presburger arithmetic. In *CAV'97*, volume 1254 of *LNCS*, pages 400–411. Springer, 1997.

[BH99] A. Bouajjani and P. Habermehl. Symbolic reachability analysis of FIFO-channel systems with nonregular sets of configurations. *TCS*, 221(1–2):211–250, 1999.

[Boi98] B. Boigelot. *Symbolic methods for exploring infinite state spaces.* PhD thesis, Université de Liège, 1998.

[CC00] H. Comon and V. Cortier. Flatness is not a weakness. In *CSL'00*, volume 1862 of *LNCS*, pages 262–276. Springer, 2000.

[CJ98] H. Comon and Y. Jurski. Multiple counters automata, safety analysis and Presburger analysis. In *CAV'98*, volume 1427 of *LNCS*, pages 268–279. Springer, 1998.

[Cor02] V. Cortier. About the decision of reachability for register machines. *Theoretical Informatics and Applications*, 36(4):341–358, 2002.

[Dem06] S. Demri. Temporal logics. Lecture notes for MPRI, 2005/2006. `www.lsv.ens-cachan.fr/~demri/`.

[DPK03] Z. Dang, P. San Pietro, and R. Kemmerer. Presburger liveness verification of discrete timed automata. *TCS*, 299:413–438, 2003.

[EFM99] J. Esparza, A. Finkel, and R. Mayr. On the verification of broadcast protocols. In *LICS'99*, pages 352–359, 1999.

[FL02] A. Finkel and J. Leroux. How to compose Presburger accelerations: Applications to broadcast protocols. In *FST&TCS'02*, volume 2256 of *LNCS*, pages 145–156. Springer, 2002.

[FO97] L. Fribourg and H. Olsén. Proving safety properties of infinite state systems by compilation into presburger arithmetic. In *CONCUR'97*, volume 1243 of *LNCS*, pages 213–227. Springer, 1997.

[FWW97] A. Finkel, B. Willems, and P. Wolper. A direct symbolic approach to model checking pushdown systems (extended abstract). In *INFINITY'97*, volume 9 of *ENTCS*. Elsevier Science, 1997.

[Iba78] O. Ibarra. Reversal-bounded multicounter machines and their decision problems. *JACM*, 25(1):116–133, 1978.

[ISD+00] O. Ibarra, J. Su, Z. Dang, T. Bultan, and A. Kemmerer. Counter machines: Decidable properties and applications to verification problems. In *MFCS'00*, volume 1893 of *LNCS*, pages 426–435. Springer, 2000.

[Lag85] J. Lagarias. The $3x + 1$ problem and its generalizations. *The American Mathematical Monthly*, 92(1):3–23, 1985.

[Ler03] J. Leroux. *Algorithmique de la vérification des systèmes à compteurs. Approximation et accélération. Implémentation de l'outil FAST.* PhD thesis, ENS de Cachan, France, 2003.

[Ler06] J. Leroux. Regular acceleration for number decision diagrams. Technical Report 1385-06, LABRI, January 2006.

[LS05] J. Leroux and G. Sutre. Flat counter systems are everywhere! In *ATVA'05*, volume 3707 of *LNCS*, pages 489–503. Springer, 2005.

[Min67] M. Minsky. *Computation, Finite and Infinite Machines.* Prentice Hall, 1967.

[SS04] T. Schuele and K. Schneider. Global vs. local model checking: A comparison of verification techniques for infinite state systems. In *SEFM'04*, pages 67–76. IEEE, 2004.

[Wal01] I. Walukiewicz. Pushdown processes: games and model-checking. *I & C*, 164(2):234–263, 2001.

[Wol83] P. Wolper. Temporal logic can be more expressive. *I & C*, 56:72–99, 1983.

The Implementation of Mazurkiewicz Traces in POEM

Peter Niebert and Hongyang Qu

Laboratoire d'Informatique Fondamentale de Marseille, Université de Provence
{niebert, hongyang}@cmi.univ-mrs.fr

Abstract. We present the implementation of trace theory in a new model checking tool framework, POEM, that has a strong emphasis on Partial Order Methods. A tree structure is used to store trace systems, which allows sharing common prefixes among traces and therefore reduces memory cost. This structure is easy to extend to incorporate additional features. Two applications are shown in the paper: An extended structure to support a new adequate order for Local First Search, and an acceleration of event zone based state space search for timed automata.

1 Introduction

POEM (Partial Order Environment of Marseille) is a new model checking tool (framework) that has a strong emphasis on Partial Order Methods [19,7,17,10,13,18,6,14,12]. The motivation for adding POEM to the world of model checkers is the authors work on algorithms that have a common basis concerning concurrency, but which are not reflected in a single existing tool. Moreover, by allowing commonly used specification languages as input languages and allowing decent connections to analysis backends, we aim to build a platform that allows direct comparisons of different algorithms on the same model.

The formal basis of many "partial order" approaches in model checking are Mazurkiewicz traces [4]. The starting point is the notion of commutation of pairs of independent transitions which, by definition, lead to the same state independent of their order of execution. This structural property, frequently observed in asynchronous systems, can be applied to state exploration algorithms in order to remove redundant transitions or, if the search goal in question permits, even states, without changing the validity of the property. The (transitive closure of) communation of independent transitions yields a congruence relation on the free monoid of transition sequences. The congruence classes, which are called "Mazurkiewicz traces", have a natural representation as partial orders, hence the name of the domain, "*partial order methods*". Another representation close to Mazurkiewicz traces are *prime event structures* [20].

Whereas some methods (e.g. the ample set method [17], or the *sleep set method* [8]) only use Mazurkevicz traces as a theoretical justification, other algorithms actually use traces as a data structure in one form or another. This is the case in particular for the class of *Petri net unfolding algorithms* [13,6], which use event structures (an explicit graph representation of the partial orders, with sharing of

S. Graf and W. Zhang (Eds.): ATVA 2006, LNCS 4218, pp. 508–522, 2006.

common prefixes). Local First Search [2] requires explicit access to Mazurkiewicz traces and their partial orders. Other algorithms, like [12] can profit from the identification of previously visited traces for speedup, but are not compatible with the sleep set method.

Our basic motivation for the development of a library for traces was the implementation of *Local First Search*. Previously published results were based on an inefficient prototype that only allowed to estimate the reduction potential of the method, but was not competitive in run time. Like Petri net unfolding algorithms, Local First Search requires, among other operations the test of an "adequate order" relation between traces. In the literature on Petri net unfoldings, the adequate order is identified as both a theoretical difficulty and a practical concern: The run time of unfolding algorithms critically depends on the efficiency of this test.

Other aspects of the Local First Search implementation concern the extraction of partial orders from traces.

In this work, we thus present data structures and algorithms for *trace systems*, prefix closed sets of Mazurkiewicz traces, that make moderate use of memory and allow fast operations for

- Extension (computation of successor traces).
- Equality testing.
- Adequate order.

The data structure we chose is based on a simple normal form of Mazurkiewicz traces, the *lexicographically least representative*. Prefix closed sets of traces are represented in a tree like structure with sharing. Moreover, we develop an adequate order well adapted to this structure. Apart of the theoretical presentation, we also give experimental results for two application domains, our new implementation of LFS and acceleration achieved with the library for timed automata state exploration with event zones [12].

The paper is structured as follows: In Section 2, we introduce the new model checker framework, POEM. In Section 3, we introduce the formal basis of Mazurkievicz traces. In Section 4, we present our data structure and algorithms for traces. In Section 5, we show the extension of the data structure for use with LFS, in particular we give the adequate order suited for our data structure. In Section 6, we briefly report experimental results obtained for the application to timed automata state exploration with event zones. In Section 7, we give conclusions and an outlook.

2 POEM - Partial Order Environment of Marseille

The purpose of POEM is to allow the application of certain partial order oriented algorithms to a number of input languages with different sets of features, while allowing at the same time basic analysis algorithms. This gives a basic structure of POEM derived tools as "compilers", each consisting of a *frontend* (syntactic and semantic analysis), a *middle* (model transformation), and a *backend* which passes the model to the aimed analysis algorithm and allows to interpret results. For instance, "if2c" consists of a frontend for Verimag's IF2.0 [3] language, static analysis for identifying the transitions and dependency, and finally a backend generating C-code for exploration. This kind of architecture is frequently used in model checkers and originally introduced in Spin [9]. The implementation language of POEM is Objective Caml (OCaml). This choice is due to the advantages of functional programming languages for compiler writing, the efficiency of OCaml and the availability of non-functional features.

We also intend to continue the development of POEM to be a common framework for several input languages and analysis methods:

- On the specification language side, a frontend for Promela [9] is close to prototype status and a frontend for UppAal [1] is in planning. We also consider the addition of a frontend for certain Petri net formats.
- On the analysis side, state exploration as with Spin is implented, together with two partial order methods: Local First Search [2,11] for discrete systems and timed automata state exploration with event zones [12]. A backend for reduction to SAT based "bounded model checking" is in planning.

The goal driving the design of POEM is to have as much reuse of code as possible given these different front ends and backends. Reuse is essential for development effort and code quality. It is achieved in the following ways:

- Given that most of the mentioned specification languages use some kind of interleaving model of automata with shared variables and certain kinds of communication, POEM uses a common data structure as an abstract specification language (it does not have a concrete syntax) that allows relatively easy translation of specification languages into a unique meta "language".
- Since many partial order methods are based on Mazurkiewicz trace theory, static analysis and backends dealing with independence can be reused. Realized examples of such reuse include the computation of an efficient representation of independence, and the representation of Mazurkiewicz traces that is the main topic of this article.

3 Basic Trace Theory

Let Σ be an alphabet, $(\Sigma^*, \circ)$ the free monoid. We write letters $a, b, c \in \Sigma$, and words $u, v, w, \ldots \in \Sigma^*$. The concatenation of a word u and a letter a is denoted by $u \circ a$. Let $I \subseteq \Sigma \times \Sigma$ be an irreflexive and symmetric independence relation, and $D = \Sigma \times \Sigma - I$ the dual dependency relation. For two words $u, v \in \Sigma^*$, write $u \equiv_I^1 v$ if there exist words w_1, w_2 and letters a, b such that $(a, b) \in I$, $u = w_1 ab w_2$ and $v = w_1 ba w_2$, i.e. if u is obtained from v by exchanging the order of two adjacent independent letters. Let $\equiv_I$ be the reflexive and transitive closure of the relation $\equiv_I^1$. We say that u and v are *trace equivalent* [4, Chapter 2] over (Σ, I) if $u \equiv_I v$. That is, u is trace equivalent to v if u can be obtained from v by repeatedly commuting adjacent independent letters. $\equiv_I$ is a congruence with respect to concatenation and we call the quotient monoid $\Sigma / \equiv_I$ the trace monoid of (Σ, I). We write $[u] = \{v \mid u \equiv_I v\}$ for the congruence classes and for the traces. In particular, for concatenation, we obtain $[u][v] = [uv]$. We call $[u]$ a *prefix* of $[v]$ iff there exists some w such that $[uw] = [v]$. A *trace system* is a (non-empty) prefix closed set of traces.

Let $<_{alph}$ be the alphabetical order defined over Σ. For any two different letters $a, b \in \Sigma$, either $a <_{alph} b$ or $b <_{alph} a$. We also extend $<_{alph}$ for words, i.e. for two words u and v, $u <_{alph} v$ iff (1) $v = uaw$ or (2) $u = wau'$ and $v = wbv'$ and $a <_{alph} b$. Thus, $lex([u])$, a lexicographically least representive as the normal form of a trace $[u]$ is defined as follows:

$$lex([u]) \in [u] \text{ and for any word } v \in [u] \text{ with } lex([u]) \neq v, lex([u]) <_{alph} v.$$

In the rest of paper, a trace and its normal form are used interchangeably when the context allows.

For a trace u, we concider occurrences of letters such that $u = a_1 a_2 \ldots a_n$. Let $E = \{(a_1, m_1), (a_2, m_2), \ldots, (a_n, m_n)\}$ be the set of occurrences of letters in u, where m_i is the cardinality of the set $\{j | j \leq i, a_i = a_j\}$, and λ the function mapping occurrences to letters. Let $(E, \prec, \lambda)$ be a finite (Σ-labeled) partial order, where $\prec$ is the transitive closure of

$$\{\langle e_i, e_j \rangle | e_i = (a_i, m_i) \in E, e_j = (a_j, m_j) \in E, i < j, \lambda(e_i)\ D\ \lambda(e_j)\}.$$

Therefore, traces can be viewed as partial orders based on the one-to-one correspondence [4, Chapter 2]. For two occurrences $e, f \in E$, $e \prec f$ iff $\langle e, f \rangle \in \prec$. An element $e \in E$ is *maximal* if there is no $f \in E$ such that $e \prec f$.

4 The Basic Data Structure for Trace Systems

We aim to design a data structure for trace systems that minimizes memory usage. Prefix sharing is a key element to reduce the memory cost, i.e. for any two traces that have a common prefix w, only one copy of w is allowed to be allocated in memory. Therefore, it is natural to choose a tree structure to build a trace system. For the representation of partial spanning trees in search algorithms, this technique is commonly used. However, a trace with several maximal elements also has several predecessors, so a design decision has to be made on what is the predecessor of a trace: The prefix relation is by nature not a tree but a partial order. Event structure implementations as used in unfolding algorithms [6] follow the actual partial order of *events* and do not explicitely reprensent traces, which correspond to "configurations" in event structures.

Our choice here is to use the normal form introduced in Section 3 as a basis for a tree-like structure to store trace systems: Any node in a tree corresponds to a *normal form* of a trace, its lexicographically least representative, defined in Section 3. So the *root* vertex corresponds to the empty word/trace and every other node corresponds to a representative ua, i.e. is associated with an action a and has a unique predecessor (parent) corresponding to the representative u.

A node may or may not have successors (children). Even if the trace system contains a successor $[ub]$ of $[u]$, it need not contain a b-labeled successor if ub is not the lexicographically least representative of $[ub]$.

A path in a tree starting at the root, to the node associated with action a_1, then to the node a_2, until the node a_n, represents the trace $a_1a_2\ldots a_n$.

Figure 1 illustrates the tree structure. A node has three fields: "predecessor" is a pointer to its predecessor, "lastaction" is the associated action, and "children" is a pointer to a link list such that each element in the list has two fields: "first" points to a child node and "rest" points to the next element. This structure is easy to be extended to facilitate complex trace systems by adding more fields into a node. We will see in Section 5 a kind of extension.

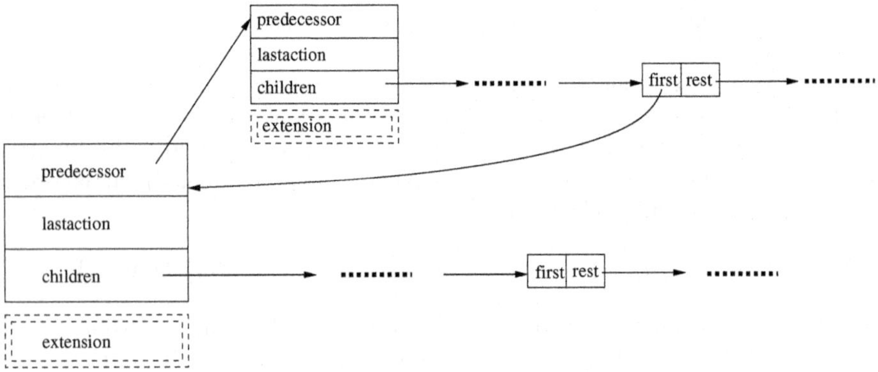

Fig. 1. The basic data structure

The following lemma and corollary show how to generate the normal form when appending an action to a trace.

Lemma 1. *Let $u = lex([u])$ be the normal form of $[u]$. Then for $a \in \Sigma$ we get $lex([ua]) = w_1aw_2$ such that $u = w_1w_2$ and for all b with $|w_2|_b > 0$ we have $a\ I\ b$.*

Proof. First note that there is a unique decomposition of $lex([ua])$ with $lex([ua]) = w_1aw_2$ with $[u] = [w_1w_2]$ and for all b with $|w_2|_b > 0$ we have $a\ I\ b$. By definition, $u \leq_{alph} w_1w_2$ and hence $ua \leq_{alph} w_1w_2a$, but on the other hand $w_1aw_2 \leq_{alph} ua$. Let $u = u_1u_2$ such that $|u_1| = |w_1|$. We obtain from the above inequalities that $u_1 \leq_{alph} w_1 \leq_{alph} u_1$, hence $u_1 = w_1$. Hence, $[u_2] = [w_2]$ and by the definition of lex, it is easy to see that $u_2 = lex([u_2])$ and $w_2 = lex([w_2])$. Hence $u_2 = w_2$. $\square$

Corollary 1. *$lex([ua])$ with $u = lex([u])$ can be generated in three steps:*

1. *Find a suffix w of u, i.e. $u = u'w$, such that for any letter in w is independent of a, and if $u' \neq \varepsilon$, i.e. $u' = u''b$, we have $\neg(a\ I\ b)$.*

2. Find a prefix w' *of* w*, i.e.* $w = w'w''$*, such that for any* c *with* $|w'|_c > 0$*,* $c <_{alph} a$*, and if* $w'' \neq \varepsilon$*, i.e.* $w'' = dv$*, we have* $a <_{alph} d$*.*
3. Insert a *after* w'*, i.e.* $lex([ua]) = u'w'aw''$*.*

Proof. It is easy to see that for any other decomposition $u = u_1u_2$ such that $a\ I\ b$ for any b in u_2, we obtain $u_1au_2 <_{alph} lex([ua])$. □

In this trace structure, a trace $t = a_1a_2 \ldots a_n$ is accessed through its last node a_n and following the predecessor pointer of each node of the trace. A trace system is generated from an initial trace t_0, which includes only the root node — a node respresenting an empty trace, by extending t_0 one action after another. Algorithm 1 describes the general steps, w.r.t. Corollary 1, to extend a trace t by an action a. In the algorithm, a stack S and three stack functions are used: $POP(S)$ gets rid of the top element of S; $TOP(S)$ accesses the top element; $PUSH(a, S)$ puts the action a onto the top of S. Note that in Algorithm 1, a variable t represents both a trace conceptually and its last node when we access the trace.

Algorithm 1. Extending a trace t by an action a using a stack S

1: $et \leftarrow t$, $pos \leftarrow 0$, $S \leftarrow$ empty
2: **while** $t \neq root$ **and** $\neg(t.lastaction\ D\ a)$ **do**
3: $\quad pos \leftarrow pos + 1$, $PUSH(t.lastaction, S)$, $t \leftarrow t.predecessor$
4: **end while**
5: **while** $pos > 0$ **and** $a < TOP(S)$ **do**
6: $\quad POP(S)$, $pos \leftarrow pos - 1$
7: **end while**
8: **for all** i such that $0 \leq i \leq pos$ **do**
9: $\quad et \leftarrow et.predecessor$
10: **end for**
11: $PATH\_SUCCESSOR(et, a)$
12: **while** S is not empty **do**
13: $\quad eptr \leftarrow TOP(S)$, $POP(S)$, $et \leftarrow PATH\_SUCCESSOR(et, eptr)$
14: **end while**
15: **return** et

The function $PATH\_SUCCESSOR$ in Algorithm 2 inserts a node with a given action into its parents's children list. The list is sorted in the ascending order on children's associated actions. When there is a node in the list that has been associated with the action already, this node is returned by the function. Otherwise, a new node is created, inserted into the list and returned.

Proposition 1. *Algorithm 1 and 2 are correct and preserve prefix sharing when appending an action* a *to a trace* t*.*

Proof. Correctness is an immediate consequence of Lemma 1 and Corollary 1 concerning the lexicographically least representative.

Let $t = uv$ where a is inserted in between u and v, such as $t \circ a = uav$. Lines (1)-(10) in Algorithm 1 returns the last node x of u, and put v in the stack.

Algorithm 2. Function $PATH\_SUCCESSOR(t : trace, a : action)$

```
1: tl ← t.children, previous ← NULL
2: while tl ≠ NULL and tl.first.lastaction < a do
3:    previous ← tl, tl ← tl.rest
4: end while
5: if tl ≠ NULL and tl.first.lastaction = a then
6:    return tl.first
7: end if
8: new_t.predecessor ← t, new_t.lastaction ← a, new_t.children ← NULL
9: new_child.rest ← tl, new_child.first = new_t
10: if previous ≠ NULL then
11:    previous.rest ← new_child
12: else
13:    t.children ← new_child
14: end if
15: return new_t
```

The proposition is proved by induction on insertion of $t' = av$, which is done by Lines (11)-(14) of Algorithm 1.

In the basis step, we check by Lines (1)-(4) of Algorithm 2 if a node y associated with a is already in the children list of x. If y exists, it is returned by Lines (5)-(7) of Algorithm 2, and therefore, there is only one copy of the prefix ua in the tree structure. Otherwise, y is created and inserted into the list, and returned by Lines (8)-(15) of Algorithm 2. In this case, ua is not a prefix of any other traces.

In the induction step, assume $w = av'$ has been inserted and prefix sharing is preserved. Let $t' = wv'$ and b the first action in v'. Similar to the basis step, insertion of b maintains prefix sharing. □

From the discussion above, we know that in the worst case, an action may be inserted at the beginning of a trace. Hence, the complexity of appending an action to a trace is $O(n)$, where n is the length of the trace.

5 Extending Trace Systems for Local First Search

Local First Search [2,14] is a partial order method to seach for *local properties*. For a property φ, a *visible* action causes the system to move from a state not satisfying φ to a state satisfying it, or vice versa. When all visible actions are pairwise dependent, such a property is a local property. In [14], it is shown that *prime traces*, i.e. traces with a single maximal element, suffice to search for local properties; in turn, to approximate all prime traces, it suffices to consider only traces with a logarithmic number of maximal elements (compared to the overall parallelism in the system); this number is called *LFS*-bound.

LFS uses a breadth-first search algorithm, which is described as follows. Consider a state in the search queue is explored with an enabled action in this state. Let t be the trace leading to the state and a the action. If the number of maximal elements of $t \circ a$ succeeds the LFS-bound, then the trace $t \circ a$ is abandoned; else, a state s reached by $t \circ a$ is generated. If s is not visited by other traces, it is put into the queue. Otherwise, let u be the trace reaching s with $u \neq t \circ a$. We need to compare u and $t \circ a$ with respect to a *total adequate order* and use the smaller trace to explore s. The adequate order implemented in POEM is presented below.

5.1 The Adequate Order for POEM

An *adequate order* [6] on $\Sigma^*/\equiv_I$ is a partial order $\sqsubseteq \subseteq (\Sigma^*/\equiv_I \times \Sigma^*/\equiv_I)$ such that the following properties are satisfied:

- $[u] \sqsubseteq [uv]$, i.e. it refines the prefix relation on traces;
- $[u] \sqsubseteq [v]$ implies $[uw] \sqsubseteq [vw]$;
- $\sqsubseteq$ is well-founded, i.e. there is no infinite strictly descending chain $[u_1] \sqsupset [u_2] \sqsupset \ldots$.

The most straight forward (partial) adequate orders are:

- The prefix relation itself, i.e. $[u] \sqsubseteq [v]$ iff there exists v_1 with $[v] = [uv_1]$.
- The length order : $[u] \sqsubseteq [v]$ iff $|u| \leq |v|$.

The first order is included in the second order. For application purposes, let us just say here that the bigger the order (in ordering more pairs), the better. The ideal case is that of total adequate orders. The first total adequate order was proposed in [6] and in the prototype used in [2] applied the order proposed in [5], which is claimed to be optimized for product systems. However, the adequate order of [6,5] are oriented towards Petri net unfoldings and evaluated on partial orders, whereas LFS deals with interleavings. Here we propose a new adequate order for interleavings, which is thus potentially better suited for use with LFS.

The order is constructed in several steps based on some total order $\leq_{alph}$ on Σ. Moreover, let $\|[u]\| = |u|$ denote the length of u, and let $\|[u]\|_a = |u|_a$ denote the number of occurrences of a in u (a property invariant under $\equiv_I$). The Parikh vector [16] $p(u)$ of u or $[u]$ is the function $p(u) : \Sigma \longrightarrow N$ such that $p(u)(a) := |u|_a$. The $\leq_{alph}$-induced lexicographical order on Parik-vectors, which was already used in [6], is defined as follows: $u <_p v$: iff

- either $|u| < |v|$
- or $|u| = |v|$ and for some $b \in \Sigma$ it holds that
  - $|u|_b > |v|_b$ and
  - for all $a \in \Sigma$ with $a <_{alph} b$ it holds that $|u|_a = |v|_a$.

If neither $u <_p v$ nor $v <_p u$ then obviously $p(u) = p(v)$.

Based on the unique representatives $lex([v])$, which is generated with respect to Lemma 1, we define $\sqsubseteq \subseteq (\Sigma^*/\equiv_I \times \Sigma^*/\equiv_I)$ as follows:
$[u] \sqsubseteq [v]$ iff

- either $u <_p v$ (Parikh order).
- or $p(u) = p(v)$ and $lex([u]) \leq_{alph} lex([v])$.

The construction of $\sqsubseteq$ follows the lines of the order in [6] except that there, the lexicographical order on the Foata normal form of traces is used rather than $lex([u]) \leq_{alph} lex([v])$. That order thus requires the computation of the Foata normal form for each comparison, which is considered the time consuming aspect.

Proposition 2. *$\sqsubseteq$ is a total adequate order.*

Proof. First observe that $<_p$ is an adequate order.

Second, observe that $\leq_{alph}$ is total on Σ^* such $lex([u]) \leq_{alph} lex([v])$ defines a total order on traces, in particular those with the same Parikh vector. Hence $\sqsubseteq$ is total. Wellfoundedness of $\sqsubseteq$ results from the fact that $<_p$ is wellfounded, that the number of traces with the same Parikh vector is finite (permutations) and that $lex([u]) \leq_{alph} lex([v])$ defines a total order on traces.

$[u] \sqsubseteq [uv]$ is also obvious since either $v = \varepsilon$ (the empty sequence, obviously $\sqsubseteq$ is reflexive) or $|u| < |uv|$.

The difficult step is to prove that $[u] \sqsubset [v]$ implies $[uw] \sqsubset [vw]$ in the case that $p(u) = p(v)$ (otherwise, the fact that $<_p$ is adequate is sufficient). It is sufficient to check that $[u] \sqsubset [v]$ implies $[ua] \sqsubset [va]$ and use induction for the general case.

So let $[u] \sqsubset [v]$, $p(u) = p(v)$ and for simplicity assume that $u = lex([u])$ and $v = lex([v])$, i.e. u and v are the lexicographically least representatives of $[u]$ and $[v]$ respectively. Let $u = wbu'$ and $v = wcv'$ with $b <_{alph} c$.

Obviously $p([ua]) = p([va])$. Let $lex([ua]) = u_1au_2$ with $u = u_1u_2$ and $lex([va]) = v_1av_2$ with $v = v_1v_2$ according to Lemma 1.

Now we have to compare the different decompositions of $v_1v_2 = wcv'$. If $|v_1| \leq |w|$ then let $u = v_1u'_2$ the according decomposition of u where $p(v_2) = p(u'_2)$ and hence $ua \equiv_I v_1au'_2$ (the importance of the same Parikh-vector here is that a commutes with all letters in u'_2) and we obtain $u_1au_2 \leq_{alph} v_1au'_2$ and we know that $u'_2 <_{alph} v_2$ hence $u_1au_2 <_{alph} v_1av_2$. If $|v_1| > |w|$ then $v_1 = wcv'_1$ and we obtain $u_1au_2 \leq_{alph} ua = wbu'a <_{alph} wcv'_1av_2 = v_1av_2$. □

Clearly, the worst case complexity of testing $[u] \sqsubseteq [v]$ is $O(\min(\min(|u|, |v|) \cdot \log|\Sigma|, |\Sigma|)$: The computation of the Parikh-vector of u means running through the word and counting the letters. For this, a letter indexed array can be used with initialisation time $O(|\Sigma|)$, increasing time $(\log|\Sigma|)$, and $|u|$ increases. If the two traces are dealt with in parallel and the length turns out to be different, we can stop. However, in POEM we decided to compute Parikh vectors incrementally by storing them (in a compressed form), as indicated in the next section.

5.2 The Extended Data Structure

For incremental computation of Parikh vectors for faster adequate order testing, the basic trace structure can be extended as follows. Figure 2 depicts the extension, where a node has three additional fields: "parikh_vector_sum" records the number of actions in the trace that is from the root to the current node, "parikh_vector" points a dynamically allocated memory to store the parikh vector. "peak_vector" is very particular to Local First Search, see [14] for details. The parikh vector has a field "length" and an array "vector". The length field records the length of the array, and each element in the array is the number of occurrences of an action in the trace. The array in the peak vector stores maximal actions in the trace.

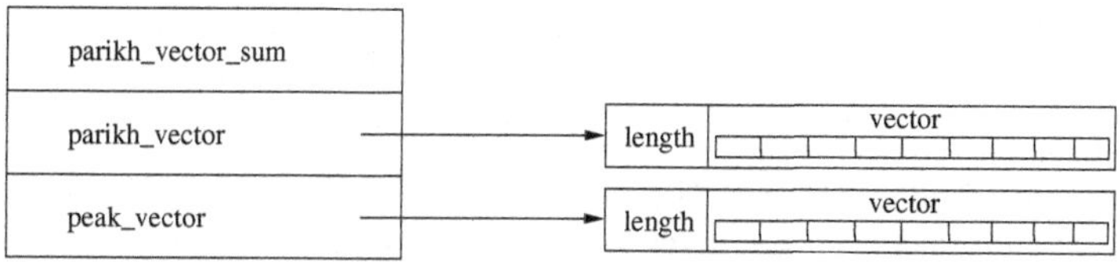

Fig. 2. The extension to the basic data structure

LFS requires to compare two traces with respect to the adequate order during state space search. In a comparison, one trace is an "old" one that has been explored, while the other is the "new" one currently being explored, i.e. it is created by appending an action to a trace. The procedure of comparison is shown in Algorithm 3 according to the definition of the adequate order:

1. Compare the length of two traces (Lines (2)-(6)). If they are equal, go to 2.
2. Compare their parikh vectors (Lines (7)-(19)). If they are still equal, go to 3.
3. Compare the lexicographical representives of these traces (Lines (20)-(30)).

The complexity of the new test now consists of two parts:

- in successor computation, increasing the "parikh_vector_sum" (logarithmic in theory, practically near constant time), updating the "parikh_vector" $O(|\Sigma|)$.
- in comparison, there are three cases:
  - The length is different, detected in constant time.
  - Otherwise, the Parikh vectors are different, detected in $O(|\Sigma|)$.
  - Otherwise, the lexicographic comparison has to be done in $O(|u|)$ in the worst case, but our data structure avoids running through the common prefix of u and v.

This means that for many cases, the comparison of the words and the successor computation is actually avoidable. The tradeoff is increased memory usage for storing Parikh vectors.

Note that a temporary trace stored in a stack is generated for $t2 \circ a$ during the comparison. If the result shows $t1 \sqsubset t2 \circ a$, the temporary trace is discarded. Otherwise, it is written into the tree structure. In this case, it is easy to know that $t1$ and $t2 \circ a$ have the same length, and therefore, the last node of $t1$ is in the search queue waiting for process. Removing this node, naming it as x, from the queue first and then appending a new node, say y, for $t2 \circ a$ to the end of queue cause difficulties on maintenance of the queue. During the implementation of LFS, we chose to reuse the space of x for y, and afterwards, remove x from the children list of the father node of x.

Also note that due to the breadth first search basis of Local First Search, Parikh vectors need to be stored only for two levels of search depth at a time. So the memory for Parikh vectors can be reused.

Algorithm 3. Compare two traces $t1$ and $t2 \circ a$ w.r.t. the adequate order

1: **Return Value:** $1 \Rightarrow [t1] > [t2 \circ a]$; $0 \Rightarrow [t1] = [t2 \circ a]$; $-1 \Rightarrow [t1] < [t2 \circ a]$
2: **if** $t1.parikh\_vector\_sum > t2.parikh\_vector\_sum + 1$ **then**
3:     return 1
4: **else if** $t1.parikh\_vector\_sum < t2.parikh\_vector\_sum + 1$ **then**
5:     return -1
6: **end if**
7: generate a new parikh vector new_pv for $t2 \circ a$
8: **for all** i such that $i \geq 0 \wedge i \leq t1.parikh\_vector.length \wedge i \leq new\_pv.length$ **do**
9:     **if** $t1.parikh\_vector.vector[i].act < new\_pv.vector[i].act$ **then**
10:         return -1
11:     **else if** $t1.parikh\_vector.vector[i].act > new\_pv.vector[i].act$ **then**
12:         return 1
13:     **end if**
14:     **if** $t1.parikh\_vector.vector[i].num < new\_pv.vector[i].num$ **then**
15:         return -1
16:     **else if** $t1.parikh\_vector.vector[i].num > new\_pv.vector[i].num$ **then**
17:         return 1
18:     **end if**
19: **end for**
20: $temp\_trace \leftarrow t2 \circ a$
21: **while** $t1.predecessor \neq temp\_trace.predecessor$ **do**
22:     $t1 \leftarrow t1.predecessor$, $temp\_trace \leftarrow temp\_trace.predecessor$
23: **end while**
24: **if** $t1.lastaction < temp\_trace.lastaction$ **then**
25:     return -1
26: **else if** $t1.lastaction > temp\_trace.lastaction$ **then**
27:     return 1
28: **else**
29:     return 0
30: **end if**

5.3   An Experiment

We use an experiment[1] to illustrate the efficiency of the implementation of the
tree structure. The experiment was performed on the famous dining philosopher
example. A philosopher pick up a fork randomly from his left side or right side
when both forks are available, but always drops down the left fork first. The
experiment were carried out in a machine with two 2.8GHz Xeon CPUs, 2GB
memory and Fedora core 4 Linux.

In the experiment, we compare the memory and the time cost for a naive state
space search without any reduction, the LFS reduction and SPIN with partial
order reductions (which are ineffective on both handed philosophers). The naive
one does not use traces, thus its memory space per state is less than that in
LFS. The LFS column uses the data structures outlined above, including parikh

---

[1] This experiment was also done in [11]. But here we consider the data from a different
angle.

vectors and peak vectors. Visibly, the memory overhead of the trace structure is not heavy; even compared with SPIN, which uses memory compression technique, it is not too much to be tolerable. Time cost shows the strength of the implementation from a different angle. As the system is getting bigger, the process time per state of LFS is closer to that of the naive search, and because SPIN uses partial order reduction, it is slower than LFS. Profiling shows that the implementation may spend up to 40% of the time in dealing with the adequate order which justifies the incremental implementation with stored parikh vectors. Given the exponential savings of the LFS method, we consider this percentage a proof of success of the approach and the data structures used.

Number of philosophers	No reduction			LFS bound			SPIN PO red		
	states	time (s)	memory (m)	states	time (s)	memory (m)	states	time (s)	memory (m)
2	13	0.01	4.1	13	0.01	4.6	13	0.00	2.6
3	51	0.01	4.1	49	0.01	4.7	51	0.00	2.6
4	193	0.01	4.1	191	0.01	4.7	193	0.01	2.6
5	723	0.01	4.1	651	0.01	4.7	723	0.02	2.6
6	2701	0.02	4.4	1937	0.02	4.8	2701	0.02	2.7
7	10083	0.05	5.4	5041	0.05	5.4	10083	0.09	3.1
8	37633	0.22	9.3	25939	0.25	8.8	37633	0.35	7.9
9	140451	1.02	25.6	70225	0.76	17.3	140451	1.59	43.8
10	524173	4.52	91.6	173031	2.13	38.1	524173	7.03	74.1
11	1956243	21.06	357.5	392701	5.28	84.9	1956243	31.03	325.1
12	7300801	106.49	1422.5	830415	12.33	183.5	7300801	127.40	1030.1
13	—	—	—	1652587	26.99	378.3	—	—	—
14	—	—	—	3121147	56.44	743.9	—	—	—
15	—	—	—	5633381	111.55	1399.0	—	—	—

Fig. 3. Results of the philosophers example

6 Application to the Event Zone Approach for Timed Automata

Event zone automata [12] are a partial order based approach to reduce one source of clock explosion, interleaving semantics. It uses vectors of event (action) occurrences, namely, event zones, instead of classical clock zones, to express clock constraints. The independence relation in event zone approach is based on reading and writing of shared variables: If for some clock x, transition a resets x and transition b has a condition on x or if both a and b reset x, then they must be dependent. Based on Mazurkiewicz trace theory and the independence relation, event zone approach successfully avoids zone splitting in a typical situation. transitions a resetting clock x and b resetting y are independent, and both enabled in a state. Executing the sequence ab and ba results two incomparable clock zones, while only one event zone: The independence relation is preserved in the symbolic automaton. We won't go into the details of the method, let us just state that it can result in dramatic savings compared to classical timed automata exploration as in UppAal when sufficient concurrency is involved.

However, computing successors and in particular checking "zone inclusion" is the most time consuming part in any timed automata exploration. Given that equivalent sequences lead to the same event zone, we can avoid this costly procedure in many cases if we do a test for a visited trace before.

This is where the data structure of this paper can help: We store the visited traces and *before computing a successor and searching for a bigger zone*, we test if we have tried a different interleaving of the same trace before. To achieve this, the trace structure in POEM supports automatic detection of equivalent traces by a minor modification of Algorithm 1 and 2: $PATH\_SUCCESSOR$ sets a flag is_old_trace if it finds out that there is a node in the children list that has been associated with the given action, and Algorithm 1 sets another flag to indicate an equivalent trace is found by checking whether each calling of $PATH\_SUCCESSOR$ sets is_old_trace.

This approach does not change the number of visited symbolic states, but the experiment indicated below shows that it can save a considerable amount of time. In order to demonstrate the effect of improvement, we made two experiments to compare the time cost before and after applying the improvement. These experiments were performed on the same machine as the one in Section 5.3.

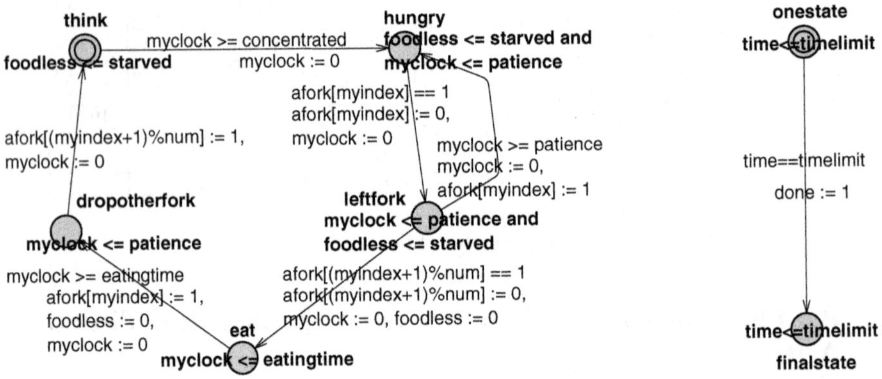

Fig. 4. The automata of a philosopher (left) and the timestopper (right)

The first experiment is a timed version of dining philosophers. There are a group of philosophers and a timestopper process, which is used to stop the execution of the system when time progresses to a limit. The automata of a philosopher and the timestopper are shown in Figure 4, respectively[2]. Figure 5 shows the results generated by POEM. The data under the title "Testing" were obtained by testing if the current trace has been seen before; the data with "No Testing" were obtained without such testing. These two methods generated exactly the same state space and we only have a switch to turn on or of the test, but the trace structure is computed in both cases. Thus only one column of memory usage is listed and we have no data for the memory overhead of the trace structure, which should be of the same order as for discrete systems in Section 5.3.

[2] Figure 4 were produced by UppAal.

Number of philosophers	Memory	Time	
		Testing	No Testing
2	16m	0.03s	0.02s
3	16m	0.05s	0.05s
4	17m	0.31s	0.52s
5	22m	5.01s	9.58s
6	72m	78.12s	173.33s
7	540m	1168.92s	2840.52s

Fig. 5. Results of the philosophers

Number of lanes	Memory	Time	
		Testing	No Testing
1	16m	0.03s	0.03s
2	16m	0.03s	0.03s
3	16m	0.03s	0.04s
4	17m	0.09s	0.12s
5	19m	1.27s	2.31s
6	36m	10.79s	22.96s
7	118m	87.46s	211.78s
8	466m	554.34	1490.43s

Fig. 6. Results of the highway

The second experiment was performed on the following example from [15]. A multi lane highway with cars on each lane and a rabbit who wants to cross. The rabbit has some freedom of going slower or faster and so do the cars. Can - with the help of the car drivers - the rabbit reach the other side of the highway alive? To model this by a network of timed automata, we choose to model the highway as a checker board of lanes and positions on lanes as indicated in the picture, cars move in the horizontal direction and the rabbit in the vertical direction. Each car and the rabbit is realised by an individual automaton. The freedom of going slower or faster is modeled by a time interval in which the rabbit can advance by one lane and an interval in which the car can advance for one unit length on a discretized highway. If a car and the rabbit are in the same field of the checker board at the same time, an accident occurs. The results are listed in Figure 6. The advantage of testing known traces in this experiment is more explicit than the first one.

7 Conclusion

We discussed the design and implementation of the trace structure in the new model checking framework POEM. On the fundamental level, we have contributed a new definition of an adequate order [6] on interleavings that shows to work very well with our implementation. While intended for Local First Search [2], it can be used by other partial order related state exploration algorithms.

We also presented the application of our data structures and algorithms to the Local First Search and the Event Zone approach to timed automata [12]. These applications show the good adaptability of the structure. The bottom line of the experiments conducted is a decent performance both in time and memory usage of a component that allows for dramatic savings in several model checking algorithms.

It is planned to release a first version of POEM in the near future so as to make our implementation available to the research community.

Acknowledgements

Thanks go to Marcos Kurban for detecting a bug in an earlier version of the definition of the adequate order and in general for his comments on the implementation.

References

1. G. Behrmann, A. David, K. G. Larsen, O. Moeller, P. Pettersson, and W. Yi. UPPAAL - present and future. In *Proc. of 40th IEEE Conference on Decision and Control*. IEEE Computer Society Press, 2001.
2. S. Bornot, R. Morin, P. Niebert, and S. Zennou. Black box unfolding with local first search. In *TACAS*, LNCS 2280, pages 386–400. Springer, 2002.
3. M. Bozga, S. Graf, and L. Mounier. If-2.0: A validation environment for component-based real-time systems. In *CAV*, LNCS 2404, pages 343–348. Springer, 2002.
4. V. Diekert and G. Rozemberg, editors. *The Book of Traces*. World Scientific Publishing Co. Pte. Ltd., 1995.
5. J. Esparza and S. Römer. An unfolding algorithm for synchronous products of transition systems. In *CONCUR*, LNCS 1664, pages 2–20. Springer, 1999.
6. J. Esparza, S. Römer, and W. Vogler. An improvement of mcmillan's unfolding algorithm. *Formal Methods in System Design*, 20(3):285–310, 2002.
7. P. Godefroid and P. Wolper. A partial approach to model checking. In *Logic in Computer Science*, pages 406–415, 1991.
8. P. Godefroid and P. Wolper. Using partial orders for the efficient verification of deadlock freedom and safety properties. *Formal Methods in System Design*, 2:149–164, 1993.
9. G. Holzmann. *The Spin Model Checker, Primer and Reference Manual*. Addison-Wesley, Reading, Massachusetts, 2003.
10. G. Holzmann and D. Peled. Partial order reduction of the state space. In *First SPIN Workshop*, Montrèal, Quebec, 1995.
11. M. E. Kurbán, P. Niebert, H. Qu, and W. Vogler. Stronger reduction criteria for local first search. Technical report, 2006. submitted to ICTAC 2006.
12. D. Lugiez, P. Niebert, and S. Zennou. A partial order semantics approach to the clock explosion problem of timed automata. *Theoretical Computer Science*, 345(1):27–59, 2005.
13. K. L. McMillan. A technique of state space search based on unfolding. *Form. Methods Syst. Des.*, 6(1):45–65, 1995.
14. P. Niebert, M. Huhn, S. Zennou, and D. Lugiez. Local first search: a new paradigm in partial order reductions. In *CONCUR*, LNCS 2154, pages 396–410. Springer, 2001.
15. P. Niebert and H. Qu. Adding invariants to event zone automata. Technical report, 2006. submitted to FORMATS 2006.
16. R. J. Parikh. On context-free languages. *Journal of the ACM*, 13(4):570–581, 1966.
17. D. Peled. All from one, one for all: on model checking using representatives. In *CAV*, pages 409–423, 1993.
18. W. Penczek and R. Kuiper. Traces and logic. In Diekert and Rozemberg [4].
19. A. Valmari. Stubborn sets for reduced state space generation. In *Applications and Theory of Petri Nets*, pages 491–515, 1989.
20. G. Winskel. Event structures. In *Advances in Petri Nets 1986, Part II*, LNCS 255, pages 325–392. Springer, 1987.

Model-Based Tool-Chain Infrastructure for Automated Analysis of Embedded Systems

Hang Su[1], Graham Hemingway[1], Kai Chen[2], and T. John Koo[3,*]

[1] Department of Electrical Engineering and Computer Science
Vanderbilt University, Nashville, TN, USA
{hang.su,graham.hemingway}@vanderbilt.edu
[2] Motorola Labs, Motorola Inc.
Schaumburg, IL, USA
kai.chen@motorola.com
[3] Departments of Electronics Engineering and Computer Science
Shantou University, Shantou, Guangdong, China
johnkoo@stu.edu.cn

Abstract. In many safety-critical applications of embedded systems, the system dynamics exhibits hybrid behaviors. To enable automatic analysis of these embedded systems, many analysis tools have been developed based on hybrid automata model. These tools are constructed by their own domain-specific modeling languages (DSMLs) but they are different in various aspects. To enable meaningful semantic interpretation of DSMLs, we propose an infrastructure for semantic anchoring that facilitates the transformational specification of DSML semantics. In the semantic anchoring infrastructure, the semantics of a DSML can be anchored to a well-defined semantic unit, which captures the operational semantics of hybrid automaton, via model transformation. The Abstract State Machine (ASM) is used as the underlying formal framework for the semantic unit. The semantics of a DSML is defined by specifying the transformation between the abstract syntax metamodel of the DSML and that of the semantic unit. The infrastructure can also enable model exchange among DSMLs while referring to the common semantic unit. Hence, hybrid automata based DSMLs can be integrated to form a meaningful tool chain by deploying this proposed infrastructure. In this paper, we demonstrate how effective the tool-chain infrastructure is by considering a practical case study involving the hybrid automata DSMLs, HyVisual and ReachLab.

1 Introduction

In many safety-critical applications of embedded systems such as avionics, automobiles and medical devices, the computational processes are strongly coupled with the physical processes and hence the system dynamics exhibit tight interaction between the discrete and continuous dynamics. However, embedded

* Corresponding author.

S. Graf and W. Zhang (Eds.): ATVA 2006, LNCS 4218, pp. 523–537, 2006.

software for these embedded systems has been produced without the necessary system models, theories, design methods, and software tools that consider the *hybrid* nature of the systems in order to provide guarantees for satisfying safety, security and reliability requirements.

Hybrid automata [10,11,12] have been successfully used as the model for the embedded systems which exhibit hybrid behaviors at the system level. Many model-based tools have been developed for the analysis of hybrid automata. An excellent survey of the model-based tools and a comparison of their capabilities can be found in [15]. However, the model-based tools are constructed using their own domain-specific modeling languages (DSMLs) which capture the modeling concepts, relationships, integrity constraints, and semantics of the application domain and allow users to program declaratively through model construction. Although these tools are designed for hybrid automata, each tool has its own DSML based on the objectives, capabilities, constraints, theoretical foundations, and computation methods considered in the tool. Therefore, the use of these DSMLs with tightly integrated analysis tool chains leads to the accumulation of design assets as models defined in a DSML. Consequently, users run a high risk of being "locked-in" to a particular tool chain and this may prevent the organization from adopting new modeling and model analysis methods. Interchange languages for hybrid systems have been proposed in [14] and [15,16] for enabling the integration of analysis tools by enabling model exchange. In [14], the interchange format syntax is defined to enable model exchange among diverse tools but these tools have significant differences in their semantics due to their objectives. In [15,16], the semantics of the interchange format is defined at an abstract level so that various concrete semantics, each capturing the model used by a different language for the specification of hybrid systems, can be refined from the abstract semantics. However, it is unclear how some relevant properties can be preserved in the refinement process.

To enable meaningful semantic interpretation of DSMLs, in our former papers [3,4,5], we proposed and demonstrated an infrastructure for semantic anchoring that facilitates the transformational specification of DSML semantics. The semantic anchoring infrastructure includes a set of well-defined "semantic units" that capture the operational semantics of basic models of computations (MOCs) [9] by using Abstract State Machines [8] as the underlying formal framework, whose language is called AsmL. The semantics of a DSML are defined by specifying the transformation between the abstract syntax metamodel of the DSML and that of the semantic unit. Leveraging our prior work with semantic units, including finite state machines and timed automata, a semantic unit for hybrid automata is developed. The semantics of the semantic unit for hybrid automata are precisely specified by using the execution definitions defined in [13]. In the semantic anchoring framework, the Generic Modeling Environment (GME) tool suite [1] is employed for defining the abstract syntax metamodels for DSMLs using the UML/OCL - based MetaGME as the metamodeling language. The semantic anchoring is defined by model transformation rules expressed in the UMT (Unified Model Transformation) language of the GReAT tool suite [2]. In

UMT, model transformations are expressed as graph transformations that can be executed (both in interpreted and compiled form) by the GReAT engine. The semantic anchoring infrastructure enables us to define the semantics of a DSML by referring to that of the semantic unit via specifying model transformation rules from the metamodel of the DSML to the Abstract Data Model of the semantic unit. The infrastructure can also enable meaningful model exchange among tools. Hence, various hybrid automata based DSMLs can be integrated to form a meaningful tool-chain by deploying this proposed infrastructure.

In this paper, we demonstrate how effective the tool-chain infrastructure is by considering a practical case study involving the hybrid automata DSMLs, HyVisual and ReachLab. HyVisual[7] is a hybrid systems modeling tool and has its own DSML called the Modeling Markup Language (MoML) while ReachLab [6] is an MIC-based analysis tool for hybrid automata and its DSML is called Hybrid System Analysis and Design Language (HADL). The rest of this paper is organized as follows. In section 2, several key concepts, such as hybrid automata, model-integrated computing, domain-specific modeling language, and semantic anchoring, are defined. In section 3, the tool-chain infrastructure for automated hybrid automata design and analysis is proposed and discussed in detail. In section 4, the effectiveness and efficiency of the proposed infrastructure is demonstrated by using the hybrid automaton for a DC-DC boost converter. And in section 5, we conclude our work.

2 Background

In the following, we will first explain model-integrated computing (MIC), metamodel transformations, and semantic anchoring, and then the definition of hybrid automata is introduced.

2.1 Definition of Hybrid Automaton

Hybrid automata belong to a special class of dynamical systems and the evolution of a hybrid automaton can be described in time by the values of a set of discrete and continuous state variables. The formal definition of hybrid automaton is given as:

Definition 1 (Hybrid Automaton[12,13]). *A hybrid automaton H is a collection $H = \langle Q, X, f, Init, D, E, G, R\rangle$, where Q is a finite set of* **discrete states***; $X \subseteq \mathbb{R}^n$ is a set of* **continuous states***; $f : Q \times X \rightarrow \mathbb{R}^n$ assigns each discrete state a* **vector field***; $Init \subseteq Q \times X$ is a set of* **initial states***; $D : Q \rightarrow P(X)$ assigns each discrete state a* **domain***; $E \subseteq Q \times Q$ is a set of* **edges***; $G : E \rightarrow P(X)$ assigns each edge with a* **guard***; $R : E \times X \rightarrow P(X)$ is a* **reset***.*

The *hybrid* state of H is referred to as $(q, x) \in Q \times X$. An acceptable evolution of the state of a hybrid automaton is called an *execution*, which could involve some combinations of continuous *flow* and discrete *jump*. The continuous flow for the continuous state is determined by the vector field and the domain while the discrete jump is determined by the associated directed graph defined by the discrete states, edges, the guard and the reset. A hybrid automaton can accept multiple executions if either there is a choice between continuous flow and discrete jump, or if a discrete jump can lead to multiple destinations. The collection of all the executions from an initial set is called (forward) reachable set. The algorithm developed in [6] can be used to compute the forward reachable set. Such reachable sets are useful for verifying the safety property of hybrid automata.

Example 1. **DC-DC Boost Converter** In [17], a DC-DC boost converter is modeled as a hybrid automaton, H. There are two discrete states, q_1 and q_2. which correspond to the configurations of the transistors. The continuous state of the system is defined as $x = [i_L \ \ v_C]^T$, and the operating region of the circuit is defined by $X = [i_{L_0}, i_{L_1}] \times [v_{C_0}, v_{C_1}]$. In each discrete state, the continuous evolution of the continuous state is governed by a differential equation where $\dot{x} = A_i x + b$ for $i = 1, 2$, in which $A_1 = \begin{bmatrix} 0 & 0 \\ 0 & -\frac{1}{RC} \end{bmatrix}$, $A_2 = \begin{bmatrix} 0 & -\frac{1}{L} \\ \frac{1}{C} & -\frac{1}{RC} \end{bmatrix}$, $b = \begin{bmatrix} \frac{v_{in}}{L} \\ 0 \end{bmatrix}$. The domains for the discrete states are defined as: $D(q_1) = [i_{L_0}, i_{L_1}] \times [v_d - \delta, v_{C_1}]$, $D(q_2) = [i_{L_0}, i_{L_1}] \times [v_{C_0}, v_d + \delta]$. There are two edges between the discrete states and the guard is defined as: $G(q_1, q_2) = \{x \in X | v_C \leq v_d - \epsilon\}$, $G(q_2, q_1) = \{x \in X | v_C \geq v_d + \epsilon\}$. The reset maps are the identity map, *i.e.* $R(q_1, q_2, x) = R(q_2, q_1, x) = x$. Given a desired voltage, v_d, this hybrid automaton keeps v_C oscillating between the range of $v_d \pm \epsilon$, and thus implements the DC-DC boost converter function.

2.2 Domain Specific Modeling Language (DSML)

The MIC approach eases the complicated task of embedded software and system design by equipping developers with DSMLs tailored to the particular constraints and assumptions of their various application domains. A well-made DSML captures the concepts, relationships, integrity constraints, and semantics of the application domain and allows users to program declaratively through model construction. Formally, a DSML can be defined as a 5-tuple.

Definition 2 (Domain Specific Modeling Language). *A DSML is a 5-tuple $L = \langle A, C, S, M_s, M_c \rangle$, where A is an* **abstract syntax**, *defining the language concepts, their relationships, and well-formedness rules available in the language; C is a* **concrete syntax**, *defining the specific notations (graphical, textual, or mixed) used to express models; S is a* **semantic domain**, *defined in some formal, mathematical framework, in terms of which the meaning of the models is explained; $M_s : A \to S$ is a* **semantic mapping**, *which relates syntactic concepts to those of the semantic domain; $M_c : C \to A$ is a* **syntactic mapping**, *which assigns syntactic constructs to elements in the abstract syntax.*

However, different tools have their own DSMLs, which exhibit different syntax as well as semantics.

2.3 Framework of Semantic Anchoring

Although DSMLs use many different modeling and model composition concepts and notations for accommodating needs of domains and user communities, semantic domains for expressing fundamental types of dynamic behaviors are more limited. Broad categories of component behaviors can be represented by behavioral abstractions, such as hybrid automata. This observation led us to propose a semantic anchoring infrastructure for defining behavioral semantics for DSMLs. The development and use of the semantic anchoring infrastructure includes the following tasks:

1. Definition of a set of modeling languages $\{L_i\}$ for capturing semantics of the basic behavioral abstractions and development of the precise specifications for all components of $L_i = \langle C_i, A_i, S_i, M_{Si}, M_{Ci} \rangle$. We use the term "semantic units" to describe these basic modeling languages.
2. Definition of the behavioral semantics of an arbitrary $L_j = \langle C_j, A_j, S_j, M_{S_j}, M_{C_j} \rangle$ DSML is accomplished by specifying the $M_{A_{ji}} : A_j \rightarrow A_i$ mapping to a predefined semantic unit L_i. The $M_{S_{ji}} : A_j \rightarrow S_i$ semantic mapping of L_j is then defined by the composition $M_{S_{ji}} = M_{Si} \circ M_{A_{ji}}$, which indicates that the semantics of L_j is anchored to the S_i semantic domain of the L_i modeling language.

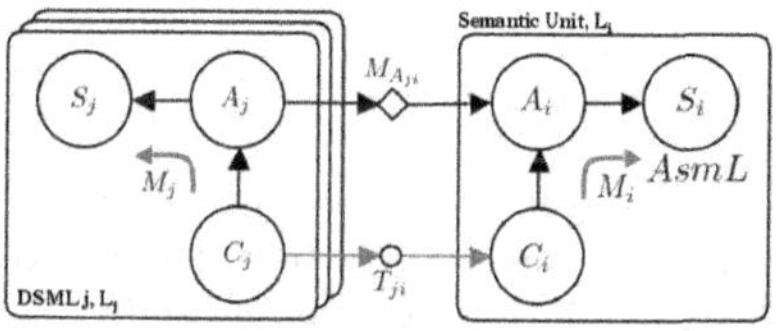

Fig. 1. Framework of Semantic Anchoring

Fig. 1 shows the framework to facilitate DSML design through semantic anchoring. It comprises (1) the ASM-based common semantic framework for specifying semantic units and (2) the MIC modeling and model transformation tool suites that support the specification of transformations between the DSML metamodels and the Abstract Data Models used in the semantic units. In the framework, $M_{A_{ji}}$ refers to the model transformation rules from A_j to A_i; T_{ji} refers to the model transformation from C_j to C_i; and M_i refers to the semantic translation in DSML$_i$, which corresponds to $M_{S_i} \circ M_{C_i}$. In particular, as we demonstrate in the next section, we use $i \in \{H\}$, where H represents the semantic unit DSML for hybrid automata, and $j \in \{V, V', R\}$, where V represents the HyVisual DSML in GME, V' represents the HyVisual MoML, and R represents ReachLab DSML (HADL). Each semantic unit must be anchored to a formal framework using a formal language. This framework must be broad enough to incorporate all three portions of the $M_S : A \rightarrow S$ definition for a DSML but flexible enough not to limit its definition or execution. There are a number of possible frameworks from which to choose.

We selected Abstract State Machine (ASM), formerly called Evolving Algebras, as a formal framework for the specification of semantic units. General forms of behavioral semantics can be encoded as (and simulated by) an abstract state machine. AsmL, developed by Microsoft Research, provides specification language simulator, test-case generation and model checking tools for ASMs. Also, previous work on the semantic units for FSM and TA both utilized ASM as the framework for formal specification. While the execution or simulation of a hybrid automata is more complex than either of these other models of computation, ASM is still a capable framework. For this reason we decided to continue using ASM. For a discussion of ASM and other possible anchoring frameworks, please refer to [3] In summary, semantic anchoring specifies DSML semantics by the operational semantics of selected semantic units (defined in AsmL) and by the transformation rules (defined in UMT). The integrated tool suite ensures that domain models defined in a DSML are simulated according to their "reference semantics" by automatically transforming them into AsmL data models using the transformation rules.

3 Tool-Chain Infrastructure

In this section, the tool-chain infrastructure for automated hybrid automata design and analysis is proposed and discussed.

3.1 Infrastructure Overview

In order to better demonstrate our semantic anchoring infrastructure, we choose HyVisual [7] and ReachLab [6] as two model-based tools that will be applied to this infrastructure. HyVisual is a typical modeling and simulation tool for hybrid automata, and ReachLab is an algorithmic analysis tool for hybrid automata. Although they are both model-based tools developed for hybrid automata, HyVisual is based on MoML language for modeling, which is XML based, while ReachLab is an MIC-based DSML. In this paper, we will show that they can be incorporated automatically by using our semantic anchoring framework.

Fig. 2 shows the semantic anchoring infrastructure that incorporates HyVisual and ReachLab. A general semantic unit (H) is presented in the center of the figure. It possesses a more general form of abstract syntax and semantics. HyVisual and ReachLab DSMLs (V and R) are inter-connected through the semantic unit. Model transformation rules between HyVisual DSML V and H, *i.e.* $M_{A_{VH}}$, and between H and R, *i.e.* $M_{A_{HR}}$, are created by using the GReAT tool, which can automatically generate model translators T_{VH} and T_{HR}. These model translators are used to transform from models in V to models in H, and then to models in R. The inter-connection of V and R via H is bi-directional, provided another set of transformation rules, $M_{A_{RH}}$ and $M_{A_{HV}}$ are created. In each DSML k ($k \in \{H, V, R\}$), a semantic translator M_k can be created to translate from C_k to S_k. For example, in H, M_H can be used to generate AsmL specification for the given hybrid automaton model, and in R, Matlab or C++ code can

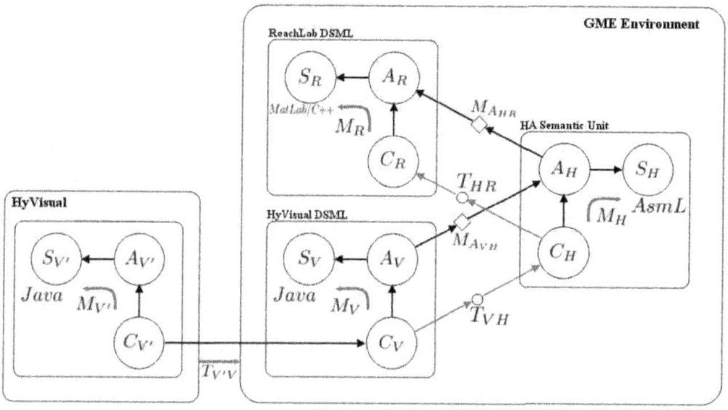

Fig. 2. Tool-chain infrastructure for hybrid automata design and analysis

be generated by different semantic translators M_R. Another translator $T_{V'V}$ in this infrastructure is used to import HyVisual, MoML models into V models. For more general cases, a set of different tools in the tool-chain can be represented as DSMLs (in the form of metamodels) in the GME environment, which are interconnected through the HA semantic unit by using model translators. In each of these DSMLs, semantic translators can be created to generate executable models. Separate translators can be used to import models from the actual format of these tools to models in their corresponding DSMLs. In the following subsections, the construction of the metamodels for HyVisual and ReachLab DSMLs, the model translators, and the semantic translators are explained in details.

3.2 Metamodeling of Semantics Units and DSMLs: A_H, A_V and A_R

In this subsection, metamodels for the DSML of the semantic unit (H), HyVisual (V), and ReachLab (R) are defined and explained.

A_H: Metamodel of HA semantic unit. Fig. 3 shows the metamodel for the HA semantic unit. This metamodel comes directly from the mathematical definition of hybrid automaton (Definition 1). In this metamodel, a *HybridAutomaton* model is composed of several *Locations* (corresponding to Q in HA definition). Each Location contains a *DomainSet* (corresponding to D) and a *VectorFieldSet* (corresponding to f), and Locations are connected through *Edges* (corresponding to E), which contain *GuardSet* (corresponding to G) and *ResetSet* (corresponding to R). An *AnalysisSet* (corresponding to X) is also defined inside the HybridAutomaton, which defines the real variables, and their domains. An attribute in each Location is used to specify whether this Location is the initial Location. In addition, a set of *Options* can be specified in a HybridAutomaton model, which are in the form of key-value pairs, to define system parameters. This metamodel is very straightforward and directly related to the mathematical definition of hybrid automata. It is also very general, so that it can be used to anchor many different tools.

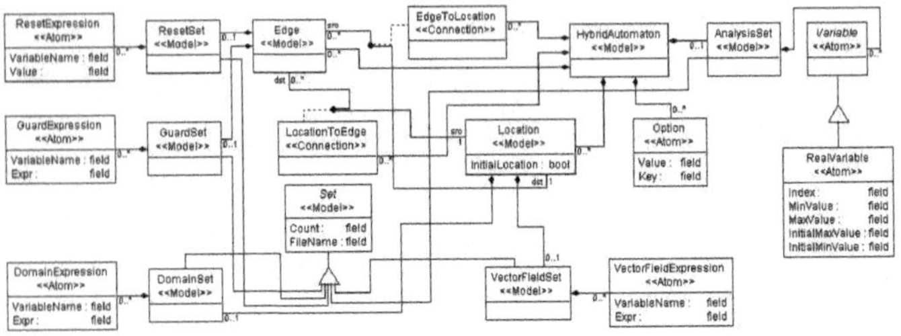

Fig. 3. A_H: Metamodel of hybrid automata semantic unit

A_V**: Metamodel of HyVisual.** Fig. 4(a) shows the metamodel for HyVisual created in the GME environment. This is a compact version of the HyVisual DSML, since it only contains the blocks necessary for modeling a hybrid automaton. In HyVisual, hybrid automata can be modeled by using Modal Models, with Refinements for continuous computation in each discrete state. This metamodel directly reflects this modeling scheme in HyVisual, and important HyVisual blocks are directly mapped to the blocks in this metamodel.

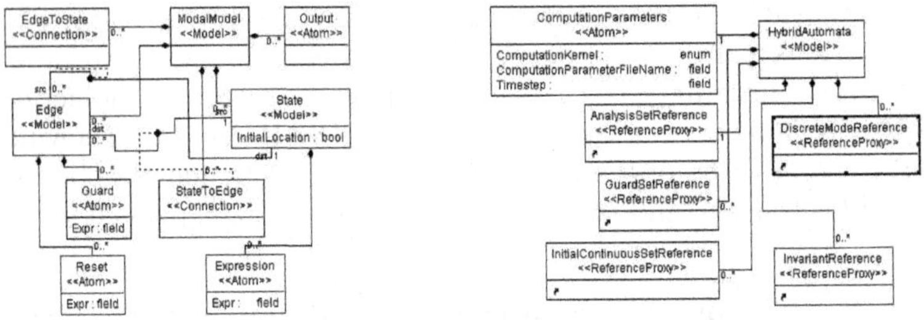

(a) (b)

Fig. 4. (a) A_V: Metamodel of HyVisual DSML; (b) A_R: Metamodel of ReachLab for HA modeling

A_R**: Metamodel of ReachLab.** In [6], we explained the language of ReachLab (HADL) in detail. ReachLab's metamodel for modeling a hybrid automaton is shown in Fig. 4(b). It is also straightforward, but different from the semantic unit metamodel, since *Invariants* (which corresponds to DomainSet in semantic unit metamodel) connects to *DiscreteModes* (which corresponds to Location in semantic unit metamodel), instead of contained inside. Also, most specifications are stored in files in ReachLab, rather than expressions as in the semantic unit metamodel. Furthermore, ReachLab uses an *InitialContinuousSet* block to indicate the initial discrete state by connecting this block directly to the corresponding DiscreteMode. Besides hybrid automata modeling, ReachLab also has a programming aspect, which allows users to design analysis algorithms for the given hybrid automaton.

3.3 Graph-Based Transformation Rules: $M_{A_{VH}}$, T_{VH} and $M_{A_{HR}}$, T_{HR}

In this subsection, model transformation rules between DSMLs of different tools and the DSML of the semantic unit are defined and explained. These transformation rules are implemented in the GReAT tool, which can automatically generate model translators.

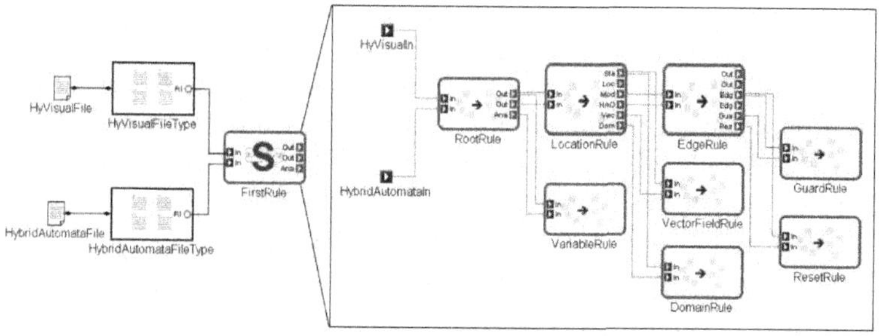

Fig. 5. T_{VH}: GReAT framework for the transformation from HyVisual DSML (A_V) to the semantic unit DSML (A_H)

GReAT takes two DSMLs, which are in form of metamodels, as source and destination DSMLs. It takes one input file, representing a model in the source DSML, and by applying transformation rules as the input model flows through these rules, an output model in the format of the destination DSML is generated automatically. Fig. 5 shows that a HyVisual model, stored in a HyVisual file, is used as the input, and by applying the "FirstRule" (which corresponds to T_{VH} transformation rules, an output model, in the format of semantic unit DSML, is generated and written to an output file.

Inside "FirstRule", detailed transformation rules are defined. Both the input and the output files are used as input to the rules, as shown in Fig. 5. By applying pattern matching and replacement of the matched blocks, each rule block makes some modifications to the output model, and creates new objects within the output model. Each rule block then passes the modified model to the next rule block, similar to an assembly line. After all the rules have been applied, the model transformation is complete. Detailed rules in "FirstRule" ($M_{A_{VH}}$) are defined as follows:

RootRule: Transform "ModalModel" in V to "HybridAutomaton" in H. Insert a new "AnalysisSet" block.

LocationRule: Transform each "State" in V to "Location" in H. Insert "VectorFieldSet" and "DomainSet" for each newly created Location block.

VariableRule: Transform each "Output" in V to "RealVariable" in H, and transform the corresponding variable domains as attributes of "RealVariable" blocks.

EdgeRule: Transform each "Edge" in V to "Edge" in H. Connect this newly created Edge to its corresponding Locations. Create new "GuardSet" and "ResetSet" for the newly created Edge block, and transform the corresponding guard and reset expressions from HyVisual model to semantic unit expressions.

VectorFieldRule: Transform the "Expression" in each "State" in V to "VectorFieldExpression" in H.

DomainRule: Since HyVisual does not have the concept of domain of each real variable, create a new "DomainExpression" block inside each newly created "DomainSet" block in H, and set the variable domain expression to "true".

GuardRule: Transform the "Guard" in each "Edge" in V to "GuardExpression" in H.

ResetRule: Transform the "Reset" in each "Edge" in V to "ResetExpression" in H.

For the transformation from the semantic unit DSML (H) to ReachLab DSML (R), rules ($M_{A_{HR}}$) can be created in a similar way. After creating the transformation rules, GReAT allows automatically generating a model translator according to these rules, which can be used to automatically translate models from the source DSML to models in the destination DSML.

3.4 Semantic Translators: M_H and M_R

The last important component in the infrastructure in Fig. 2 is the semantic translator. GME supplies a rich set of APIs that allows these semantic translators to interact with the DSML and graphical models directly via COM (Component Object Model). The key technique in constructing a semantic translator is model traversal, which traverses the entire model, and generates corresponding code. In [6], detailed traversal algorithms have been proposed for the semantic translator for ReachLab (M_R), which generates executable code for hybrid automata analysis. The semantic translator for the semantic unit (M_H) traverses the semantic unit model and records all the Locations and their relationships. Then, it generates corresponding AsmL data structures for this hybrid automaton, and inputs the hybrid automaton to the pre-defined AsmL behavioral rules, which specifies the behavioral semantics of hybrid automaton. The semantic translator for the HyVisual DSML in GME (M_V) is used to translate HyVisual models in GME into corresponding Java executable code. The development of this translator is still in progress.

3.5 Miscellaneous: $T_{V'V}$

Another translator, $T_{V'V}$, has been written to translate models in HyVisual MoML (V'), to models in V in GME. As in [18], since MoML is an XML modeling markup language, and provides a concrete syntax for the GSRC abstract syntax, this translator can be implemented as an XML schema translator, which directly converts XML files in the MoML format into the GME schema. The complete version of this translator is still under development, but a subset that can be used to translate some specific types of hybrid automata models is already finished.

4 Case Study

In this section, we will use the DC-DC boost converter introduced in Example 1 along with some parameters[1] as an example of a hybrid automaton to demonstrate how the proposed tool-chain infrastructure enables automatic analysis of hybrid automata among different tools.

The transformation flow in this case study starts from the HyVisual model of the DC-DC boost converter hybrid automaton in the MoML format. First, the MoML model is imported into the HyVisual DSML in GME. Then, it is transformed to the semantic unit model by using the model translator generated automatically with GReAT. By applying the semantic translator for the semantic unit, AsmL specification can be automatically generated. Then, the model is transformed to the ReachLab DSML by using another model translator generated by GReAT. Finally, Matlab or C++ executable code can be automatically generated by the semantic translator for ReachLab for analysis purposes. The the HyVisual model for the DC-DC boost converter is shown in Fig. 6(a). The following gives the intermediate results in the tool-chain transformation flow.

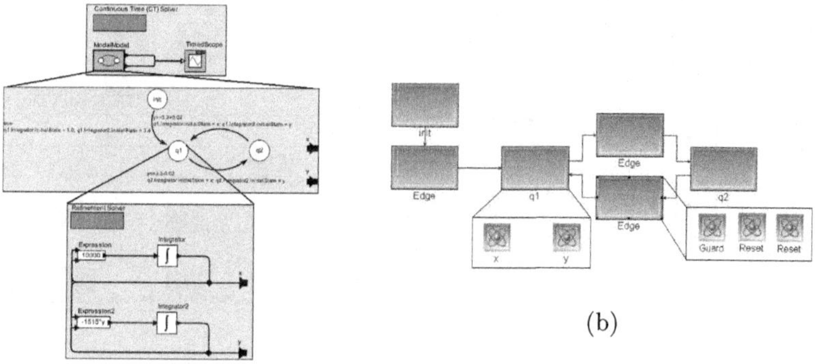

(a) (b)

Fig. 6. (a) Model of the DC-DC boost converter in HyVisual; (b) HyVisual model in the GME HyVisual DSML, translated from HyVisual model in MoML

Results for importing HyVisual model: $T_{V'V}$. After applying the XML translator ($T_{V'V}$), the HyVisual model has been imported into GME in our HyVisual DSML. The corresponding HyVisual model in GME is shown in Fig. 6(b). This translation, as explained before, is a direct XML translation based on the MoML schema and the GME HyVisual DSML schema.

Results for model transformation to the semantic unit: T_{VH}. By applying the model translator, T_{VH}, introduced in Section 3, the model in the

[1] The parameters used in this example is specified by $i_{L_0} = 1.1$, $i_{L_1} = 1.3$, $v_{C_0} = 3.25$, $v_{C_1} = 3.35$, $v_d = 3.3$, $\epsilon = 0.02$ and $\delta = 0.02$. Circuit parameters are $L = 150\ \mu H$, $C = 110\ \mu F$, $R = 6\ \Omega$ and $v_{in} = 1.5\ v$.

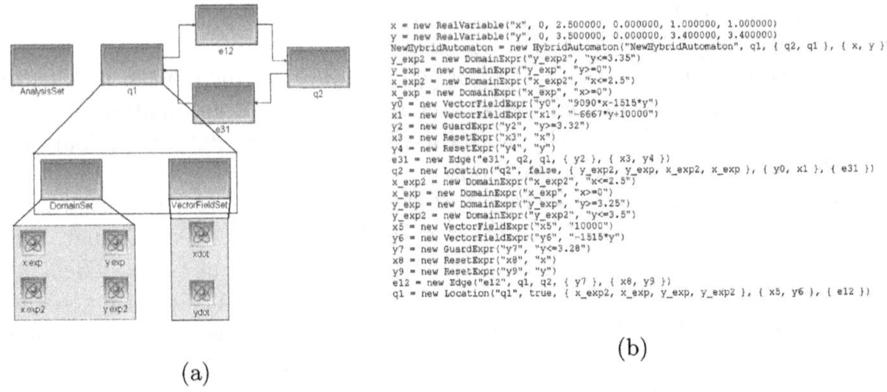

Fig. 7. (a) Semantic unit model generated from the model translation on the HyVisual DSML model; (b) AsmL specification generated from this semantic unit model by using the semantic translator M_H

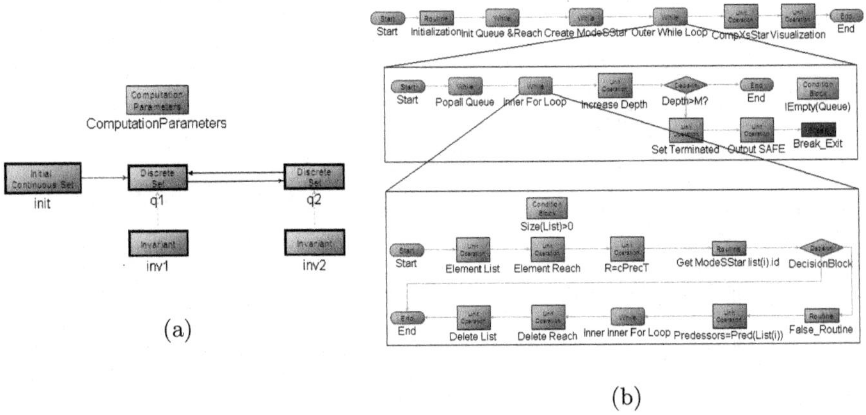

Fig. 8. (a) ReachLab model, transformed from the semantic unit model; (b) ReachLab model for the forward reachable set problem algorithm

HyVisual DSML is transformed into the semantic unit model, as shown in Fig. 7(a). This model translator is automatically generated with GReAT by using the rules $M_{A_{VH}}$.

Results for semantic translation to AsmL specification: M_H**.** Then, the semantic unit model can be translated into AsmL specification by applying the semantic translator M_H, which is also introduced in Section 3. The generated AsmL specification is shown in Fig. 7(b), which specifies the operational semantics of the hybrid automaton model. The AsmL tools [8] developed by Microsoft Research can directly simulate the behavior of the model.

Results for model transformation to ReachLab: T_{HR}**.** By applying model translator T_{HR}, the semantic unit model is transformed to ReachLab model, as shown in Fig. 8(a).

```
q1 = struct ('id', 2, 'dimensions', 2, 'f', {{ 10000; -1515*HA.g.xs(2) }}, 'inv', 'inv1');
HA.discrete_modes(length(HA.discrete_modes) + 1) = q1;
HA.edges = {};
edge__ = struct ('from', q1, 'to', q2, 'guard', guard1, 'reset', @ResetMapping_IdentityReset__);
HA.edges(length(HA.edges) + 1) = edge__;
edge__ = struct ('from', q2, 'to', q1, 'guard', guard2, 'reset', @ResetMapping_IdentityReset__);
HA.edges(length(HA.edges) + 1) = edge__;
% Initialize Qs, Qf, Xs, Xf
% Append starting discrete modes to Qs list
Qs = ndsl_append(Qs, [ ], q1);
% Append final discrete modes to Qf list
Qf = ndsl_append(Qf, [ ], q1);
Qf = ndsl_append(Qf, [ ], q2);
% Append initial continuous sets to Xs list
Xs = ndsl_append(Xs, [ ], init);
% Append final continuous sets to Xf list
Xf = ndsl_append(Xf, [ ], final);
Xf = ndsl_append(Xf, [ ], final);
m = ndsl_size(Qf, [ ]);
FinalResult = init;
% Initialize Queue=Qs
Condition = 0 < (ndsl_size(Qs, [ ]));
while Condition
    % Get Qs[0]
    temp_dm = ndsl_element(Qs, [ 0 ]);
    % Get Xs[0]
    temp_con = ndsl_element(Xs, [ 0 ]);
    % Append Qs[0] to Queue
    Queue = ndsl_append(Queue, [ ], temp_dm);
    % Append Xs[0] to Reach
    Reach = ndsl_append(Reach, [ ], temp_con);
    % Delete Xs[0]
    ndsl_delete(Xs, [ 0 ]);
    % Delete Qs[0]
    ndsl_delete(Qs, [ 0 ]);
    Condition = 0 < (ndsl_size(Qs, [ ]));
end
```

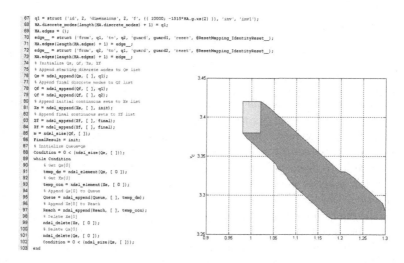

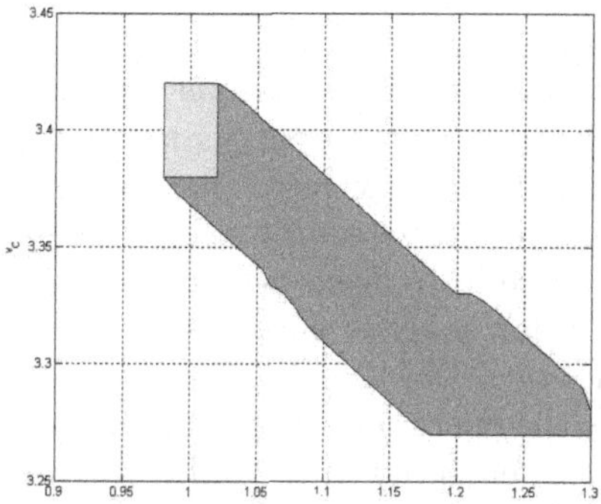

Fig. 9. A portion of the Matlab executable code generated from the semantic translator M_R and the execution result of this Matlab code

Results for semantic translation to Matlab code: M_R. The hybrid automaton model in ReachLab only represents the system aspect, which models the hybrid system. In order to perform analysis on this system, an analysis algorithm needs to be attached to the programming aspect of ReachLab. In [6], we proposed a forward reachable set algorithm, which can be used to verify the safety property of the system. In this case study, we also use this algorithm to check the safety property of the DC-DC boost converter. The corresponding analysis algorithm for the forward reachable set problem in ReachLab is given in Fig. 8(b). By applying the semantic translator M_R, this algorithm along with the hybrid automaton model in the system aspect is translated into Matlab executable code, as shown in Fig. 9.

Results for ReachLab verification. The execution result of the generated Matlab executable code is shown in Fig. 9. The dark region in the figure is the forward reachable set of the initial set $[0.98, 1.02] \times [3.38, 3.42]$ (gray box in the figure). By providing a set of bad states, and checking the intersection of the computed forward reachable set with this bad set, the system safety property can be verified. The forward reachable set correctly represents the initial climbing (dropping) and the oscillation afterwards, which means that the transformation from HyVisual to ReachLab correctly maintains the semantics of the hybrid automata.

As the entire transformation flow has been demonstrated, by applying our tool-chain infrastructure for hybrid automata analysis based on the semantic anchoring technique, the transformation from HyVisual to ReachLab is conducted automatically and correctly, and both simulation and analysis of the example hybrid automaton are performed. This case study shows the effectiveness and efficiency of the proposed tool-chain infrastructure.

5 Conclusion

Various analysis tools based on the hybrid automata model have been developed to enable automatic analysis of safety-critical embedded systems which exhibit hybrid behaviors. These tools are constructed using their own DSMLs but they are different in various aspects. The lack of formally specified semantics of DSMLs for the analysis tools and semantic mismatch between DSMLs of analysis tools may result in ambiguity in safety analysis or may produce conflicting results across different tools. We believe semantic anchoring can provide a theoretically solid yet practical solution for constructing a model-based tool-chain for analysis purposes. In the semantic anchoring infrastructure, the semantics of a DSML can be anchored to a well-defined semantic unit, which captures the operational semantics of hybrid automaton, via model transformations. The semantics of a DSML are defined by specifying the transformation between the abstract syntax metamodel of the DSML and that of the semantic unit. The infrastructure can also enable model exchange among DSMLs while referring to the common semantic unit. Hybrid automata based DSMLs can be integrated to form a meaningful tool chain by deploying this proposed infrastructure. In this paper, we demonstrate how effective the tool-chain infrastructure is by considering a practical case study involving the hybrid automata DSMLs, HyVisual and ReachLab. HyVisual is a modeling and simulation tool for hybrid automata, while ReachLab is an analysis tool for hybrid automata. The case study illustrates how rigorous modeling and analysis of the hybrid model can be automatically performed on both tools by using our semantic anchoring infrastructure.

Acknowledgments

This work is supported by the National Science Foundation Faculty Early Career Development (CAREER) Program, Award No. CNS-0448234, the National Science Foundation Information Technology Research Project, Award No. CCR-0225610, the Li Ka Shing Foundation and Shantou University.

References

1. G. Karsai, J. Sztipanovits, A. Ledeczi, and T. Bapty. Model-Integrated Development of Embedded Software. *Proceedings of the IEEE*, Vol. 91, No. 1, pp.145-164, January, 2003.
2. G. Karsai, A. Agrawal, and F. Shi. On the Use of Graph Transformations for the Formal Specification of Model Interpreters. *Journal of Universal Computer Science*, Vol. 9, Issue 11, pp. 1296-1321, November, 2003.
3. K. Chen, J. Sztipanovits, S. Neema, M. Emerson, and S. Abdelwahed. Toward A Semantic Anchoring Infrastructure For Domain-Specific Modeling Languages. *The 5th ACM International Conference on Embedded Software*, September 2005.
4. K. Chen, J. Sztipanovits, S. Abdelwahed, and E. Jackson. Semantic Anchoring With Model Transformations. *ECMDA-FA*, pp. 115-129, 2005.

5. K. Chen, J. Sztipanovits, and S. Abdelwahed. A Semantic Unit for Timed Automata Based Modeling Languages. *The 12th IEEE Real-Time and Embedded Technology and Applications Symposium*, pp. 347-360, 2006.
6. A. Dubey, X. Wu, H. Su, and T. J. Koo. Computation Platform for Automatic Analysis of Embedded Software Systems Using Model Based Approach. *Third International Symposium on Automated Technology for Verification and Analysis.* Lecture Notes in Computer Science , Vol. 3707, pp. 114-128, Springer-Verlag, Taipei, Taiwan, October 4-7, 2005.
7. A. Cataldo, C. Hylands, E. A. Lee, J. Liu, X. Liu, S. Neuendorffer, and H. Zheng. HyVisual: A Hybrid System Visual Modeler. Technical Report Technical Memorandum UCB/ERL M03/30, University of California, Berkely, 2003.
8. AsmL. `http://www.research.microsoft.com/fse/asml`.
9. E. A. Lee, and A. Sangiovanni-Vincentelli. A Framework for Comparing Models of Computation, *IEEE Transactions on Computer-Aided Design of Integrated Circuits and Systems*, 17(12):1217-1229, December 1998.
10. R. Alur, and D. L. Dill. A Theory Of Timed Automata. *Theoretical Computer Science 126*, pp. 183–235, 1994.
11. T. Henzinger. The Theory Of Hybrid Automata. *Proceedings of the 11th Annual IEEE Symposium on Logic in Computer Science*, pp. 278–292, 1996.
12. J. Lygeros. Lecture Notes on Hybrid Systems. Cambridge, 2003.
13. J. Lygeros, K. H. Johansson, S. N. Simic, J. Zhang, and S. S. Sastry. Dynamical Properties of Hybrid Automata. *IEEE Transactions on Automatic Control*, 48(1):2-17, January 2003.
14. J. Sprinkle, G. Karsai, and A. Lang. Hybrid Systems Interchange Format v.4.1.8, ISIS Technical Report, Vanderbilt University, 2004.
15. A. Pinto, A. L. Sangiovanni-Vincentelli, L. P. Carloni, and R. Passerone. Interchange Formats for Hybrid Systems: Review and Proposal. *Hybrid Systems: Computation and Control*, LNCS, volume 3414, pages 526-541, 2005.
16. A. Pinto, L. P. Carlon, R. Passerone, and A. L. Sangiovanni-Vincentelli. Interchange Formats for Hybrid Systems: Abstract Semantics. *Hybrid Systems: Computation and Control*, LNCS, volume 3927, pages 491-506, 2006.
17. M. Senesky, G. Eirea, and T. John Koo, Hybrid Modelling and Control of Power Electronic. *Hybrid Systems : Computation and Control*, Lecture Notes in Computer Science, volume 2623, pages 450-465, 2003.
18. E. A. Lee and S. Neuendorffer. MoML - A Modeling Markup Language in XML - Version 0.4. Technical report, University of California at Berkeley, March, 2000.

Author Index

Lecture Notes in Computer Science

For information about Vols. 1–4163

please contact your bookseller or Springer

Vol. 4270: H. Zha, Z. Pan, H. Thwaites, A.C. Addison, M. Forte (Eds.), Interactive Technologies and Sociotechnical Systems. XVI, 547 pages. 2006.

Vol. 4265: N. Lavrač, L. Todorovski, K.P. Jantke (Eds.), Discovery Science. XIV, 384 pages. 2006. (Sublibrary LNAI).

Vol. 4264: J.L. Balcázar, P.M. Long, F. Stephan (Eds.), Algorithmic Learning Theory. XIII, 393 pages. 2006. (Sublibrary LNAI).

Vol. 4253: B. Gabrys, R.J. Howlett, L.C. Jain (Eds.), Knowledge-Based Intelligent Information and Engineering Systems, Part III. XXXII, 1301 pages. 2006. (Sublibrary LNAI).

Vol. 4252: B. Gabrys, R.J. Howlett, L.C. Jain (Eds.), Knowledge-Based Intelligent Information and Engineering Systems, Part II. XXXIII, 1335 pages. 2006. (Sublibrary LNAI).

Vol. 4251: B. Gabrys, R.J. Howlett, L.C. Jain (Eds.), Knowledge-Based Intelligent Information and Engineering Systems, Part I. LXVI, 1297 pages. 2006. (Sublibrary LNAI).

Vol. 4249: L. Goubin, M. Matsui (Eds.), Cryptographic Hardware and Embedded Systems - CHES 2006. XII, 462 pages. 2006.

Vol. 4248: S. Staab, V. Svátek (Eds.), Engineering Knowledge in the Age of the Semantic Web. XIV, 400 pages. 2006. (Sublibrary LNAI).

Vol. 4243: T. Yakhno, E. Neuhold (Eds.), Advances in Information Systems. XIII, 420 pages. 2006.

Vol. 4241: R.R. Beichel, M. Sonka (Eds.), Computer Vision Approaches to Medical Image Analysis. XI, 262 pages. 2006.

Vol. 4239: H.Y. Youn, M. Kim, H. Morikawa (Eds.), Ubiquitous Computing Systems. XVI, 548 pages. 2006.

Vol. 4238: Y.-T. Kim, M. Takano (Eds.), Management of Convergence Networks and Services. XVIII, 605 pages. 2006.

Vol. 4236: L. Breveglieri, I. Koren, D. Naccache, J.-P. Seifert (Eds.), Fault Diagnosis and Tolerance in Cryptography. XIII, 253 pages. 2006.

Vol. 4234: I. King, J. Wang, L. Chan, D. Wang (Eds.), Neural Information Processing, Part III. XXII, 1227 pages. 2006.

Vol. 4233: I. King, J. Wang, L. Chan, D. Wang (Eds.), Neural Information Processing, Part II. XXII, 1203 pages. 2006.

Vol. 4232: I. King, J. Wang, L. Chan, D. Wang (Eds.), Neural Information Processing, Part I. XLVI, 1153 pages. 2006.

Vol. 4229: E. Najm, J.F. Pradat-Peyre, V.V. Donzeau-Gouge (Eds.), Formal Techniques for Networked and Distributed Systems - FORTE 2006. X, 486 pages. 2006.

Vol. 4228: D.E. Lightfoot, C.A. Szyperski (Eds.), Modular Programming Languages. X, 415 pages. 2006.

Vol. 4227: W. Nejdl, K. Tochtermann (Eds.), Innovative Approaches for Learning and Knowledge Sharing. XVII, 721 pages. 2006.

Vol. 4225: J.F. Martínez-Trinidad, J.A. Carrasco Ochoa, J. Kittler (Eds.), Progress in Pattern Recognition, Image Analysis and Applications. XVII, 996 pages. 2006.

Vol. 4224: E. Corchado, H. Yin, V. Botti, C. Fyfe (Eds.), Intelligent Data Engineering and Automated Learning – IDEAL 2006. XXVII, 1447 pages. 2006.

Vol. 4223: L. Wang, L. Jiao, G. Shi, X. Li, J. Liu (Eds.), Fuzzy Systems and Knowledge Discovery. XXVIII, 1335 pages. 2006. (Sublibrary LNAI).

Vol. 4222: L. Jiao, L. Wang, X. Gao, J. Liu, F. Wu (Eds.), Advances in Natural Computation, Part II. XLII, 998 pages. 2006.

Vol. 4221: L. Jiao, L. Wang, X. Gao, J. Liu, F. Wu (Eds.), Advances in Natural Computation, Part I. XLI, 992 pages. 2006.

Vol. 4219: D. Zamboni, C. Kruegel (Eds.), Recent Advances in Intrusion Detection. XII, 331 pages. 2006.

Vol. 4218: S. Graf, W. Zhang (Eds.), Automated Technology for Verification and Analysis. XIV, 540 pages. 2006.

Vol. 4217: P. Cuenca, L. Orozco-Barbosa (Eds.), Personal Wireless Communications. XV, 532 pages. 2006.

Vol. 4216: M.R. Berthold, R. Glen, I. Fischer (Eds.), Computational Life Sciences II. XIII, 269 pages. 2006. (Sublibrary LNBI).

Vol. 4213: J. Fürnkranz, T. Scheffer, M. Spiliopoulou (Eds.), Knowledge Discovery in Databases: PKDD 2006. XXII, 660 pages. 2006. (Sublibrary LNAI).

Vol. 4212: J. Fürnkranz, T. Scheffer, M. Spiliopoulou (Eds.), Machine Learning: ECML 2006. XXIII, 851 pages. 2006. (Sublibrary LNAI).

Vol. 4211: P. Vogt, Y. Sugita, E. Tuci, C. Nehaniv (Eds.), Symbol Grounding and Beyond. VIII, 237 pages. 2006. (Sublibrary LNAI).

Vol. 4210: C. Priami (Ed.), Computational Methods in Systems Biology. X, 323 pages. 2006. (Sublibrary LNBI).

Vol. 4209: F. Crestani, P. Ferragina, M. Sanderson (Eds.), String Processing and Information Retrieval. XIV, 367 pages. 2006.

Vol. 4208: M. Gerndt, D. Kranzlmüller (Eds.), High Performance Computing and Communications. XXII, 938 pages. 2006.

Vol. 4207: Z. Ésik (Ed.), Computer Science Logic. XII, 627 pages. 2006.

Vol. 4206: P. Dourish, A. Friday (Eds.), UbiComp 2006: Ubiquitous Computing. XIX, 526 pages. 2006.

Vol. 4205: G. Bourque, N. El-Mabrouk (Eds.), Comparative Genomics. X, 231 pages. 2006. (Sublibrary LNBI).

Vol. 4204: F. Benhamou (Ed.), Principles and Practice of Constraint Programming - CP 2006. XVIII, 774 pages. 2006.

Vol. 4203: F. Esposito, Z.W. Raś, D. Malerba, G. Semeraro (Eds.), Foundations of Intelligent Systems. XVIII, 767 pages. 2006. (Sublibrary LNAI).

Vol. 4202: E. Asarin, P. Bouyer (Eds.), Formal Modeling and Analysis of Timed Systems. XI, 369 pages. 2006.

Vol. 4201: Y. Sakakibara, S. Kobayashi, K. Sato, T. Nishino, E. Tomita (Eds.), Grammatical Inference: Algorithms and Applications. XII, 359 pages. 2006. (Sublibrary LNAI).

Vol. 4199: O. Nierstrasz, J. Whittle, D. Harel, G. Reggio (Eds.), Model Driven Engineering Languages and Systems. XVI, 798 pages. 2006.

Vol. 4198: O. Nasraoui, O. Zaiane, M. Spiliopoulou, B. Mobasher, B. Masand, P. Yu (Eds.), Advances in Web Minding and Web Usage Analysis. IX, 177 pages. 2006. (Sublibrary LNAI).

Vol. 4197: M. Raubal, H.J. Miller, A.U. Frank, M.F. Goodchild (Eds.), Geographic, Information Science. XIII, 419 pages. 2006.

Vol. 4196: K. Fischer, I.J. Timm, E. André, N. Zhong (Eds.), Multiagent System Technologies. X, 185 pages. 2006. (Sublibrary LNAI).

Vol. 4195: D. Gaiti, G. Pujolle, E. Al-Shaer, K. Calvert, S. Dobson, G. Leduc, O. Martikainen (Eds.), Autonomic Networking. IX, 316 pages. 2006.

Vol. 4194: V.G. Ganzha, E.W. Mayr, E.V. Vorozhtsov (Eds.), Computer Algebra in Scientific Computing. XI, 313 pages. 2006.

Vol. 4193: T.P. Runarsson, H.-G. Beyer, E. Burke, J.J. Merelo-Guervós, L. D. Whitley, X. Yao (Eds.), Parallel Problem Solving from Nature - PPSN IX. XIX, 1061 pages. 2006.

Vol. 4192: B. Mohr, J.L. Träff, J. Worringen, J. Dongarra (Eds.), Recent Advances in Parallel Virtual Machine and Message Passing Interface. XVI, 414 pages. 2006.

Vol. 4191: R. Larsen, M. Nielsen, J. Sporring (Eds.), Medical Image Computing and Computer-Assisted Intervention – MICCAI 2006, Part II. XXXVIII, 981 pages. 2006.

Vol. 4190: R. Larsen, M. Nielsen, J. Sporring (Eds.), Medical Image Computing and Computer-Assisted Intervention – MICCAI 2006, Part I. XXXVVIII, 949 pages. 2006.

Vol. 4189: D. Gollmann, J. Meier, A. Sabelfeld (Eds.), Computer Security – ESORICS 2006. XI, 548 pages. 2006.

Vol. 4188: P. Sojka, I. Kopeček, K. Pala (Eds.), Text, Speech and Dialogue. XIV, 721 pages. 2006. (Sublibrary LNAI).

Vol. 4187: J.J. Alferes, J. Bailey, W. May, U. Schwertel (Eds.), Principles and Practice of Semantic Web Reasoning. XI, 277 pages. 2006.

Vol. 4186: C. Jesshope, C. Egan (Eds.), Advances in Computer Systems Architecture. XIV, 605 pages. 2006.

Vol. 4185: R. Mizoguchi, Z. Shi, F. Giunchiglia (Eds.), The Semantic Web – ASWC 2006. XX, 778 pages. 2006.

Vol. 4184: M. Bravetti, M. Núñez, G. Zavattaro (Eds.), Web Services and Formal Methods. X, 289 pages. 2006.

Vol. 4183: J. Euzenat, J. Domingue (Eds.), Artificial Intelligence: Methodology, Systems, and Applications. XIII, 291 pages. 2006. (Sublibrary LNAI).

Vol. 4182: H.T. Ng, M.-K. Leong, M.-Y. Kan, D. Ji (Eds.), Information Retrieval Technology. XVI, 684 pages. 2006.

Vol. 4180: M. Kohlhase, OMDoc – An Open Markup Format for Mathematical Documents [version 1.2]. XIX, 428 pages. 2006. (Sublibrary LNAI).

Vol. 4179: J. Blanc-Talon, W. Philips, D. Popescu, P. Scheunders (Eds.), Advanced Concepts for Intelligent Vision Systems. XXIV, 1224 pages. 2006.

Vol. 4178: A. Corradini, H. Ehrig, U. Montanari, L. Ribeiro, G. Rozenberg (Eds.), Graph Transformations. XII, 473 pages. 2006.

Vol. 4177: R. Marín, E. Onaindía, A. Bugarín, J. Santos (Eds.), Current Topics in Artificial Intelligence. XV, 482 pages. 2006. (Sublibrary LNAI).

Vol. 4176: S.K. Katsikas, J. Lopez, M. Backes, S. Gritzalis, B. Preneel (Eds.), Information Security. XIV, 548 pages. 2006.

Vol. 4175: P. Bücher, B.M.E. Moret (Eds.), Algorithms in Bioinformatics. XII, 402 pages. 2006. (Sublibrary LNBI).

Vol. 4174: K. Franke, K.-R. Müller, B. Nickolay, R. Schäfer (Eds.), Pattern Recognition. XX, 773 pages. 2006.

Vol. 4173: S. El Yacoubi, B. Chopard, S. Bandini (Eds.), Cellular Automata. XV, 734 pages. 2006.

Vol. 4172: J. Gonzalo, C. Thanos, M. F. Verdejo, R.C. Carrasco (Eds.), Research and Advanced Technology for Digital Libraries. XVII, 569 pages. 2006.

Vol. 4169: H.L. Bodlaender, M.A. Langston (Eds.), Parameterized and Exact Computation. XI, 279 pages. 2006.

Vol. 4168: Y. Azar, T. Erlebach (Eds.), Algorithms – ESA 2006. XVIII, 843 pages. 2006.

Vol. 4167: S. Dolev (Ed.), Distributed Computing. XV, 576 pages. 2006.

Vol. 4166: J. Górski (Ed.), Computer Safety, Reliability, and Security. XIV, 440 pages. 2006.

Vol. 4165: W. Jonker, M. Petković (Eds.), Secure, Data Management. X, 185 pages. 2006.

Vol. 4164: Z. Horváth (Ed.), Central European Functional Programming School. VII, 257 pages. 2006.